PART I

Jurisdiction and Modes of Enforceability

CHAPTER 1

Sources of Admiralty Jurisdiction

As will be apparent from the Introduction, the sources of English Admiralty jurisdiction are diverse. A claimant seeking the framework must consider statute, rules of court and judicial doctrine, and must not expect to find reference from one source to another. The starting-point is the Supreme Court Act 1981,[1] but in some respects the Act simply triggers the need to define concepts used, and makes no reference at all to some elements which are inherent in the jurisdictional framework. It is, therefore, necessary both to sound a cautionary note as to the limits of the Supreme Court Act and to review the other sources to discover the framework or Admiralty jurisdiction.

The Supreme Court Act itself reflects the two often inconsistent forces of national historical development and international agreements. Conventions play an ever increasing role as a foundation for maritime legislation. More, membership of the European Union and Free Trade Association has as a consequence agreement on jurisdictional criteria which hitherto had no part to play in English law. As such criteria apply only within the European area, there are now in English law two sets of rules—one for cases connected with the Union or Association and the other for the remainder.

1. THE ADMIRALTY FRAMEWORK OF THE SUPREME COURT ACT 1981[2]

The statutory framework is founded on:

    (i) a list of claims within the jurisdiction (including the reference to jurisdiction in the past or future) (s.20);

    (ii) a specific reference to the "maritime lien" as a ground for an action *in rem* (s.21(3));

    (iii) enforcement of claims in (i) through actions *in personam* and/or actions *in rem* (ss.21–24).

1. The Act provides that the Admiralty Court is part of the Queen's Bench Division (one of three divisions) (s. 6(i)(b)), and that not surprisingly it will take Admiralty business (s. 62(2)). Appeal lies from it to the Court of Appeal and thence to the House of Lords. Subject to a power of transfer a plaintiff selects the Division of the High Court for his action (s. 64). Admiralty jurisdiction is primarily dealt with in ss. 20–24 (see Appendix 1). As to Scottish Admiralty jurisdiction see Administration of Justice Act 1956, Part V (set out in Appendix 1). As to enforceability of maritime claims through arbitration, see Chap. 7.

2. A limited Admiralty jurisdiction is conferred on some county courts, the principles following those of the High Court (see County Courts Act 1984, ss. 26–31. The monetary limits are £15,000 for a salvage claim and £5,000 for all others (s. 27(3)). Parties may confer jurisdiction without monetary limit in respect of any claim within the County Courts Act (s. 27(6) as amended by 1990 c. 41, Sch. 18).

(i) THE LIST OF CLAIMS (S.20)[3]

The detailed nature of the claims and any additions to the list through the gateway of past jurisdiction must be discovered through judicial doctrine and, possibly in the latter aspect, statutes now repealed. Although it may be expected that a statutory skeleton would need judicially created flesh it will be seen that the statutory bones are not always as connected with each other as is desirable. In particular, the reference to past jurisdiction creates problems of uncertainty and lack of uniformity of approach. Such reference requires historical reference to an age in which concepts now well established were in their infancy, in which jurisdictional quarrels with other English courts were rife and in which there was no thought of a jurisdiction based on international Conventions.[4]

(ii) THE "MARITIME LIEN" (S.21(3))[5]

The maritime lien is one half of the dual key to English Admiralty jurisdiction—the other being the action *in rem*. The maritime lien attaches to a restricted number of maritime claims as established through judicial doctrine. It is enforceable through arrest and is one of the most powerful security interests in English law. Nowhere in the Act is "maritime lien" defined either by concept or content—but the Act provides in s.21(3):

> "(3) In any case in which there is a maritime lien or other charge on any ship, aircraft or other property for the amount claimed, an action in rem may be brought in the High Court against that ship, aircraft or property."

Under this provision the action *in rem* extends to "property" but the property must be connected with the claim. Further, from the drafting of the provision as a whole it seems that the ability to rely on a maritime lien as a ground of an action *in rem* is in addition to that of the action *in rem* brought on the basis of a claim specified in s.20. But there is no clue in the statute of a relationship (if any) between those claims and the "maritime lien". In this respect as in others the Act assumes as much if not more than it provides.

(iii) ACTIONS "IN PERSONAM" AND ACTIONS "IN REM" (S.21)[6]

The Supreme Court Act 1981 provides for enforcement of each category of claim specified by the Act as within the Admiralty jurisdiction by an action *in personam* and, in respect of some, also by an action *in rem*. It also provides that a maritime lien may be enforced by an action *in rem*. However, the Act does not indicate the characteristics of either type of action, the relationship between them or, save in respect of collision actions, any prerequisites for hearing claims having a foreign element.[7] Rules relating to these

---

3. For discussion see Chap. 2.
4. That is, as enacted by statute (see further Chaps. 3 and 4). For a rather dubious approach construing a Convention in accordance with English law see *The River Rima* [1988] 2 Lloyd's Rep. 193 (H.L.)—as to which see Chap. 2.
5. The provision refers to "maritime lien or other charge". For discussion, see Chap. 2.
6. For discussion, see Chap. 9 (*in personam*), Chap. 10 (*in rem*).
7. As to which, see Chaps. 9 and 10.

matters must be sought in other statutes (particularly the Civil Jurisdiction and Judgments Acts 1982 and 1991), rules of court and judicial doctrine.

"Action in personam"

In the context of a maritime claim the action *in personam* simply describes the process for enforcing a claim which would apply in the English legal system whatever the nature of the claim. It describes an action (other than that concerned with status) aimed at a defendant, the purpose of the action being to seek a remedy against that defendant. It is not restricted to actions alleging fault of the defendant or even that any act of his necessarily is the basis of the claim. It includes (for example) the enforcement of a mortgage or a charge against the mortgagor or a purchaser of a ship as well as the more obvious enforcement of a charterparty claim against the other party to the charter.

In this context, therefore, the phrase does not describe a personal as distinct from a property claim.[8] The accurate if perhaps hardly helpful definition of an action *in personam* is simply that it is not an action *in rem*.

The Supreme Court Act 1981

The Supreme Court Act 1981, s.21(1), provides that any claim within Admiralty jurisdiction may be enforced by an action *in personam*.

"Action in rem"

The action *in rem* is the second half of the dual key to English Admiralty jurisdiction. This action is available only in the Admiralty jurisdiction. Its characteristics are complex, reflecting the current state of an unfinished development in which legislation has played a leading but not exclusive part.

The Supreme Court Act 1981

The Supreme Court Act does not state in express terms that an action *in rem* can only be brought as specified by it—but in English law its availability is restricted to those claims in relation to which the Act provides that it is available. The Act provides (in s. 21) that an action *in rem* may be brought in relation:

(a) to the claims set out in s.20(2) paras. (a)–(c) and (e)–(s);
(b) any maritime lien;
(c) any claim enforceable thereby in the future or arguably in the past.[9]

Only in relation to one claim specified in s.20(2) does the Act not provide for an action *in rem*—"damage received by a ship" (s.20(2)(d)). The action *in rem* is available for all other claims but its scope is not identical in respect of each. The Act does not define an action *in rem*. But it indicates its central theoretical feature in providing that such an action

---

8. The concepts of "*in personam*" and "*in rem*" in an Admiralty context must be distinguished from their use to differentiate between actions enforceable against an individual (*in personam*) and the world (*in rem*)—although the usage is not unconnected.

9. As to the wording of these provisions and their interpretations, see Chap. 2.

is brought "against" the ship or property in question (i.e. against a thing rather than, as with the action *in personam*, against a person).

The essential elements of the action *in rem* lie in its development over at least two centuries as the hallmark of Admiralty jurisdiction, and it is perhaps surprising that they are still not finally settled. Historically they are inextricably connected with the "maritime lien"—the other half of the dual key.

2. SOURCES OUTSIDE THE SUPREME COURT ACT 1981

It is obvious even from this brief summary that the Act provides at best a skeletal framework. The search for sources cannot be restricted to judicial development of Admiralty jurisdiction only, for the Admiralty Court is a court within the Supreme Court of Judicature. As such, it is commanded to apply principles and rules applied by other courts within that structure—it must take into account rules of common law and equity and statutory provisions. The broad framework of these rules is set out in the Supreme Court Act 1981, but the statutory framework is explicable only in a historical context.

It follows that before plunging below the surface of the Admiralty provisions of the Supreme Court Act 1981 its provisions should be put in the general framework of the court structure; and once below the surface the effect of the court structure on the rights and remedies in the maritime area should continually be borne in mind. The Supreme Court Act 1981 continues the provisions basic to the English court structure since the Judicature Acts of 1873 and 1875. It reflects earlier legislation in providing that, subject to other statutory provisions, every court in England shall continue to apply principles of equity and common law with the former taking precedence in any conflict.

ADMIRALTY, COMMON LAW AND EQUITY

English maritime law is based on Admiralty but is connected with common law and equity. Since 1873 the Admiralty Court has been part of a court structure administering the "branches" of English law called common law, equity and Admiralty and each branch is authorized to apply common law and equitable principles. These principles are at the command of the Admiralty Court as of any other Division of the High Court.[10] But the union of the courts does not mean the translation of interests from one context to another. The right or remedy must be applicable by virtue of its substance—and so classification of rights and remedies in English law has to start with reference to their common law, equitable, or Admiralty roots.

Common law and equity

Common law has its roots in custom and precedent (in rules accepted by parties as "common" to a dispute). The doctrine thereby established through Kings' courts taking over from local courts by the end of the thirteenth century contains many of the

---

10. Just as a maritime claim would attract Admiralty principles in whichever division of the High Court it is brought. As to assignment of business, see Supreme Court Act 1981, ss. 61–65, Sch. 1.

fundamental principles of English law. They are still not contained in any statute but remain common law rights, liabilities and interests.

Even when the court structure was becoming established it was recognized that the King could dispense justice where the law was defective or for some reason a party could not obtain the remedy which the law provided. At an early stage petitions for justice were referred by the King to the Chancellor and from this practice "equity" grew. As it grew so there developed a court structure (the Court of Chancery) sowing the seeds for the conflict with the common law court structure. In the seventeenth century the dispute was settled in favour of the ability of Chancery Courts to control the bringing of common law actions where this was warranted on grounds of justice.

In the nineteenth century came a radical restructuring of a court process which had burdened itself with complexity, particularly because of the twin structures of common law and equity. The Judicature Acts of 1873 and 1875 created the origins of the English courts as we know them today—one system administering both common law and equity. But the union of administration did not abolish the substantive distinctions of common law and equitable rights, liabilities and interests.

Equitable intervention in the common law

Equitable intervention took three primary forms. First, equity recognized those interests established at common law but with less formality than the common law required[11]; secondly, it created interests entirely foreign to the common law[12] and thirdly it provided equitable remedies such as the injunction and specific performance to add to the basic common law remedy of damages. The enforceability of equitable interests is less wide in scope than that of common law (or "legal") interests. A legal interest in a thing once created is enforceable against all persons claiming interests subsequently created. An equitable interest is enforceable against subsequent common law interests only if their holders take the later interest with notice of the equitable interest.[13] The principle is based on equity: interference with common law on the basis of "justice" and hence requiring notice of an equitable interest by a subsequent common law interest holder as a prerequisite for enforcing it against the later interest.

The effect of registration requirements

To some extent the rules of enforceability or "priority" are now affected by registration requirements. In some contexts (e.g. ship mortgages) priority between registered interests depends on the date of registration. An unregistered interest may run the risk of defeat by

---

11. Compare e.g. a chattel mortgage at common law requiring transfer of title to a chattel, with an equitable mortgage through deposit of documents of title.

12. As, for example, the most used, the trust in which traditionally the beneficial interest (in the beneficiary) is separated from the operating or management interest (the trustees), but modern developments have sought to use the trust as a shell for tax avoidance or financing purposes. Some interests (e.g. requitable lien) bear a superficial resemblance to common law interests but in substance are quite distinct (compare equitable with possessory lien). See Chaps. 11, 14, 15.

13. So, for example, a purchaser of a chattel subject to an equitable lien would be bound by the lien, only if he knew of the lien when he bought.

a later registered interest. The effects of registration vary according to particular applications of the principle.[14]

Admiralty

The Admiralty Court developed independently, having its own battle with common law courts over jurisdictional boundaries. During the eighteenth and early nineteenth centuries its influence and power decreased, but through statutes of 1840 and 1861 the court received a firm foundation on which it has built since. It came in from the cold into the general union of courts in 1873–75 and is now integrated into the High Court, being a branch of the Queen's Bench Division.

Admiralty had—and has—its own rights and remedies just as equity and common law. By its very nature its doctrines were applicable within an area defined by content and within that area it provided rights and remedies not available outside. The maritime lien and action *in rem* are prime examples.

Once under the umbrella of the unified court structure, common law and equitable principles became directly available in the Admiralty Court. No longer need claimants have to seek these elsewhere and no longer did jurisdictional boundaries necessarily indicate the availability of substantive rights and remedies.

So from division between common law, equity and Admiralty came connection, and from both division and connection springs the relevance of both common law and equitable doctrines. Differences between divisions of the High Court[15] do not necessarily mean the availability only of the doctrine created by the ancestor of that division. It may mean only that a claimant must go to the appropriate division or even that having started in one division the case will remain there. Conversely, connection does not necessarily mean disappearance of difference—it may mean only that all that is now obtainable is that which was obtainable before union. But after union it is all available in one place.

STATUTES, JUDICIAL CREATIVITY AND ADMIRALTY

A primary legal source in maritime law, as well as judicial development, as in all branches of English law, is statute. Statute law controls the courts and apart from directly effective or applicable provisions of the legislative framework of the European Community (or European Union)[16] cannot be questioned by the courts.

As will be obvious from the impact of common law and equity, much of English law is rooted in judicial initiative. As is to be expected there have been periods of great judicial creative activity and periods of "conservatism" when the assertion of rights depended on proof of previous recognition.

At the present stage of development judicial creativity depends largely on the predilection of the individual judge, and such as there is occurs in the context of equity.

14. As to the application of regulation requirements in Admiralty, see Chap. 17.

15. Now Chancery, Queen's Bench (including the Commercial Court and Admiralty Court) and Family (Supreme Court Act 1981, s. 5).

16. EC legislation consists of treaties between the Member States, Agreements of association and co-operation with other States, Regulations (directly applicable), Directives and Decisions—which may be directly effective.

The great age of judicial creation at common law has long gone and in most instances the existing framework could be radically changed only by statute.

The framework (if not the details) of claims and interests in the maritime area is on the whole firmly established. It will be found partly in statute and partly in judicial doctrine. To a much greater extent than other areas of English law it has been directly influenced by Civil law and on occasion courts have relied on the uniformity of maritime legal principles as between nations as part of their reasoning. It has also been greatly influenced by the focus of maritime cases in the Admiralty Court and the relatively small number of judges of that court since the eighteenth century.

English law lacks a fully comprehensive maritime code. Present day doctrine in part still reflects its origins. Court integration and statutes have had substantive effect in ironing out conflicts. However, English "maritime law" is still rooted in statute, rules of court and judicial doctrine of Admiralty, common law and equity. The consolidation of the Merchant Shipping Acts, however, goes far to provide a code of substantive rules but it is regrettable that it does not at least contain a reference to maritime issues appearing in other statutes. The critical connection between security for a claim and jurisdiction means that jurisdiction cannot be seen as a self-contained matter, and there seems no good reason why such codification as there is should not extend to all aspects of maritime law which are distinct from the rules generally applicable.

STATUTES ENACTING CONVENTIONS

Much of the recent development in maritime law has its roots in Conventions as enacted into English law. Some of these are linked to membership of the European Union or Economic Area, others having their origin in the United Nations Conference on Trade and Development (UNCTAD) or the International Maritime Organization (IMO). In the main the Conventions are concerned with substantive rules of law and on occasion these contain enforcement provisions (particularly jurisdiction). There are some which are concerned primarily and directly with enforcement.

The only Convention specifically concerned with jurisdiction over maritime claims in general is that on Arrest of Ships but an increasing number of other Conventions focused on a particular aspect of maritime law (e.g. carriage of goods and passengers) include jurisdiction provisions. So the Athens Convention 1974 (covering the carriage of passengers and luggage) has specific provisions and the Hamburg Rules 1978 include a comprehensive jurisdiction scheme. It follows that national jurisdiction rules may be subjected to these particular jurisdiction requirements insofar as these are in force and have been incorporated into national law.

Further, over the years many States have entered into bilateral and multilateral Conventions regarding jurisdiction or recognition of judgments in general. In the case of the United Kingdom, the emphasis has been on a network of bilateral Conventions providing for the mutual recognition and enforcement of judgments between the United Kingdom and another State. They are given force in English law largely through the Foreign Judgments (Reciprocal Enforcement) Act 1933. Such Conventions apply to maritime claims as to any other claims.

Of the Conventions introducing jurisdiction and judgment frameworks applicable to claims in general, the most far-reaching are the European Community Convention on

Jurisdiction and the Recognition and Enforcement of Judgments on Civil and Commercial Matters 1968 (as amended) and the parallel Convention between member States of the European Community and the European Free Trade Association 1988.

The EC Jurisdiction and Judgments Convention 1968 (as amended) (the Brussels Convention)

The Convention establishes a comprehensive jurisdiction and judgments structure in respect of "civil and commercial" matters insofar as a dispute does not fall within one of the exceptions specified within Article 1(1) of the Convention.

The Convention requires a fundamental rethinking in English law in respect of jurisdiction in cases with a foreign element and perhaps to a lesser extent recognition and enforcement of judgments. Insofar as matters fall within the scope of the Convention, jurisdiction in English law no longer can be founded simply on the presence of a person or property but on the existence of a substantive connection between the dispute and England. The recognition and enforcement of a judgment from a contracting State in England is subject only to grounds of refusal specified in the Convention.

Maritime claims fall within civil and commercial matters and are thereby covered by the Convention. Subject only to exclusion of "public law" matters and arbitration, enforcement of any maritime claim falling within the subject-matter of the Convention and raising a question of jurisdiction as against another contracting State will be governed by it. The Convention was incorporated directly into English law by the Civil Jurisdiction and Judgments Act 1982. The Act came into force on 1 January 1987.

Any State becoming a member of the European Community (now the European Union) is under an obligation to become a party to the Convention. As additional States have joined so the text has been amended by statutory instrument. The text following the accession of Portugal and Spain is set out in SI 1990 No 2591. That came into force on 1 December 1991.

The EC and EFTA Jurisdiction and Judgments Convention 1988 (the Lugano Convention)

A Convention parallel to the 1968 Convention was signed in 1988 by the States of the European Community and of the European Free Trade Association. This was enacted in the United Kingdom in the Civil Jurisdiction and Judgments Act 1991. The Act came into force on 1 May 1992.

THE CIVIL JURISDICTION AND JUDGMENTS ACTS 1982 AND 1991 AND MARITIME CLAIMS

In terms of English law the Civil Jurisdiction and Judgments Acts 1982 and 1991 are radical measures affecting English jurisdiction and recognition and enforcement of judgments. Not only did the 1982 Act incorporate the Brussels Convention into English law, it adapted it so as to allocate jurisdiction as between England, Scotland and Northern Ireland in relation to disputes connected only with the United Kingdom but not limited to one part of the United Kingdom; secondly, the Act revised and extended the statutory framework for recognition of judgments as between parts of the United Kingdom.

The Acts apply to maritime claims and in some instances introduce rules specifically geared to such claims. As a consequence the Acts must be at the forefront of the mind of those concerned in the enforcement of any maritime claim in any part of the United Kingdom or before a court of a contracting State. It should be emphasized that the relevance of this concern is not focused on plaintiffs who are connected with a contracting State. First, the jurisdiction framework is brought into play by the presence of one of a number of varied links between the dispute and the claim and, in particular, the domicile of the defendant in a contracting State or a jurisdiction agreement opting for a contracting State. Secondly, a contracting State is under an obligation to recognize a judgment of another contracting State simply because it is such a judgment. There is no further link required.

The Acts are therefore a central feature of jurisdiction and recognition and enforcement of judgments in English law. This book will consider the frameworks introduced by the Acts as they apply to the enforcement of maritime claims both as an aspect of their general application and their effect on Admiralty jurisdiction in English law.

3. CONCLUSION

The Supreme Court Act 1981 provides a starting-point for the voyage of discovery on Admiralty waters in its coverage of the general court structure and principles applicable and in the listing of Admiralty claims.[17] However, it links enforcement of maritime claims to concepts of which it provides the barest of details—the action *in personam*, action *in rem* and maritime lien. Further, it provides little guidance to available remedies to the security aspects of Admiralty claims which are their distinguishing features or to developments based on Conventions. Let us start, however, with the claims which are within Admiralty jurisdiction. The scene should then be set for examination of their jurisdictional, remedial and security aspects and a connecting link between those aspects and "liens".

---

17. It must not be forgotten that a claimant may opt for arbitration as a method of enforcement—which raises questions of the applicability of substantive and remedial rules. See Chap. 13.

CHAPTER 2

The Nature of Maritime Claims

The phrase "maritime claim" is used in the Convention Relating to the Arrest of Sea Going Ships 1952 as the general label describing all the claims in relation to which a ship may be arrested under the Convention. In English law the phrase has no technical meaning but in this work it is used to describe those claims which are within the Admiralty jurisdiction of the High Court.[1]

Admiralty jurisdiction is based on the provisions of the Supreme Court Act 1981. The jurisdictional provisions of that Act are exclusive, subject to subsequent statutory provisions either amending the Act or providing a jurisdictional foundation independent of the Act. However, as will be seen, the Supreme Court Act 1981 encompasses jurisdiction past, present and future.

Section 20(1) of the Supreme Court Act 1981 provides for four jurisdictional heads and s.20(2)–(6) elaborates on these heads. In addition, s.21(3) appears to provide or at least recognize a jurisdictional base (i.e. maritime lien) not referred to specifically in s.20. The provisions are set out in Appendix 1.

1. HEADS OF JURISDICTION—THE FRAMEWORK OF THE SUPREME COURT ACT 1981

Section 20(1)(a), (2)(4)(5)(6)

Section 20(2) of the Supreme Court Act sets out a list of categories of claims within Admiralty jurisdiction. The provisions of s.20(4)(5)(6) elaborate on three of these categories. These claims are examined later in this chapter.

Section 20(1)(b), (3)

These provisions list three categories of "proceedings" within Admiralty jurisdiction. These proceedings are dealt with later in this chapter.

---

1. Admiralty jurisdiction includes some claims in relation to aircraft (see Supreme Court Act 1981, s.20(1)(d), 20(2)(j) salvage, (k) towage and (l) pilotage) and is extended to hovercraft as if they were ships (Hovercraft Act 1968, s.1(1)(h), 2 (as amended by Supreme Court Act 1981, Sch. 5; Hovercraft (Application of Enactments) Order 1972 (S.I. 971)). As to Scotland, see fn. 257.

Section 21(3)

This provision appears in the section headed "mode of exercise of Admiralty jurisdiction". Nevertheless it recognizes "maritime lien" as a jurisdictional ground, a ground not specified in s.20—the section purporting to set out the grounds of jurisdiction. The claims attracting maritime liens will be examined later in this chapter and the concept of the maritime lien in Chapter 18.

Section 20(1)(c)

Not only has the Admiralty Court the jurisdiction substantively provided by the Supreme Court Act 1981 but through that provision "any other Admiralty jurisdiction which it had immediately before" 1 January 1982.

Section 20(1)(d)

The provision looks to the future in providing that the jurisdiction includes that of the High Court "connected with ships or aircraft" which may be assigned and directed by rules of court to the Admiralty Court.

2. APPLICATION OF THE FRAMEWORK DESPITE FOREIGN CONNECTIONS (S.20(7))

Section 20(7) of the Supreme Court Act 1981 provides:

"(7) The preceding provisions of this section apply—
    (a) in relation to all ships or aircraft, whether British or not and whether registered or not and wherever the residence or domicile of their owners may be;
    (b) in relation to all claims, wherever arising (including, in the case of cargo or wreck salvage, claims in respect of cargo or wreck found on land); and
    (c) so far as they relate to mortgages and charges, to all mortgages or charges, whether registered or not and whether legal or equitable, including mortgages and charges created under foreign law.
    Provided that nothing in this subsection shall be construed as extending the cases in which money or property is recoverable under any of the provisions of the Merchant Shipping Act 1995."

Jurisdiction

The provision prevents objection to jurisdiction based on the foreign connections specified in it. It does not *provide* positive jurisdictional rules. Such rules are to be found in other statutes, rules of court, judicial development and, to some extent, in the Supreme Court Act itself.

The applicable law

As with jurisdiction so with the law applicable to any issue. The provision is essentially negative, removing any objection based, for example, on a contention that a claim on a foreign mortgage could not fall within s.20. Whether or not a foreign law does apply to a mortgage is a question for the English conflicts process.

3. JURISDICTION BASED ON THE PAST AND THE FUTURE

Before examining the specific claims making up the Admiralty jurisdiction it is as well to deal with general jurisdiction—first looking to the past and secondly to the future.

A. LOOKING TO THE PAST

The "sweeping up" clause—"any other jurisdiction which it had immediately before the commencement of this Act" (s.20(1)(c))

The reference to jurisdiction "immediately before the commencement of" the Supreme Court Act 1981 (which came into force on 1 January 1982) means that the Administration of Justice Act 1956 is incorporated into the Act of 1981 as a secondary jurisdictional base. In particular, it would seem that any specific conferring of jurisdiction by that or any Act subsequent to that of 1956 or any jurisdiction retained by the Act of 1956 through its own sweeping up provision remains in force along with the jurisdiction specifically conferred by the Act of 1981.

It is arguable therefore that any reduction of jurisdiction by the Act of 1981 is thereby outflanked. However in *The Antonis P. Lemos*[2] Parker L.J. thought (without deciding) that the provision did not encompass actions *in rem*, as s.21 of the 1981 Act set out the claims for which an action *in rem* would lie. Against that view it may be argued that "jurisdiction" when referring to the past may well include not only the claim but the type of action by which it could be enforced. It may be preferable to restrict the backward look particularly in the light of the increasing coincidence of English and other laws through Conventions. In any event the continuation of past jurisdiction does not mean that jurisdiction presently plainly set out should be interpreted in the light of past history.

Jurisdiction conferred specifically by the Act of 1956—"damage received by a ship" (s.20(2)(e))

Under the Act of 1956 an action *in rem* would lie on the basis for a claim for "damage received by a ship". The Act of 1981 following the view expressed in *The Jade*[3] limits this ground to the foundation for an action *in personam*. But subject to the argument that only jurisdiction *in personam* is retained, may it not be argued that an action *in rem* may still be brought because it could be brought immediately prior to the Supreme Court Act 1981?

The objections advanced in the House of Lords in respect of the availability of an action *in rem* because of the nature of the claim would still apply. In expressing the view that an action *in rem* was not available Lord Diplock said that to bring it the claim must be "in connection with a ship" and in a claim based on damage received by a ship the ship would be that of the claimants. "They cannot involve the Admiralty jurisdiction by an action *in rem* against their own ship."

---

2. [1984] 1 Lloyd's Rep. 464, at p. 468. The case went to the House of Lords [1985] 1 Lloyd's Rep. 283 on a different point (see *infra*). For application of s.20(1)(c) to an action *in rem* see *The Despina G.K.* [1982] 2 Lloyd's Rep. 555 (enforcement of a foreign judgment).
3. [1976] 2 Lloyd's Rep. 1.

This argument, however, appears first to ignore an action between owner and charterer where either may wish to bring an action *in rem* against the ship as a weapon against the other, particularly in the light of the ability to bring an action *in rem* against and arrest a sister ship. Further, it may not be too far fetched to postulate an owner whose yacht is taken without permission and who wished to bring an action *in rem* against a ship owned by the wrongdoers. It is, therefore, suggested that the question of the resurrection of the action *in rem* in relation to damage received by a ship is by no means purely academic.

The sweeping up provision of the Administration of Justice Act 1956

The provision retains jurisdiction which (i) "is conferred" on the High Court by or under an Act coming into force on or after 1 November 1875 or (ii) was vested in the High Court immediately before that date.

Jurisdiction conferred by statute

In 1968 in *The Queen of the South*[4] Brandon J. suggested that this provision included jurisdiction conferred by Acts since 1875 although those Acts had been repealed. With respect it does seem that the Act of 1956 refers only to statutory jurisdiction which is extant—in contrast to any jurisdiction that "was" vested in the High Court prior to 1875. Prime examples of such statutory jurisdiction are found (a) in the Supreme Court Act 1981 itself as a successor to the Judicature Acts 1873 and 1875 conferring the powers exercisable by other divisions of the High Court on the Admiralty Court and (b) the Civil Jurisdiction and Judgments Act 1982 conferring an extended power of arrest in Admiralty proceedings.

Non-statutory jurisdiction ("that was vested" prior to 1 November 1875)

This may be relevant in two ways—first in construing a head of claim in the Act of 1981 and secondly in respect of matters not referred to in that Act.

Construction of heads of claim in Supreme Court Act 1981

Such construction may be based either on modern developments or (particularly if it should be argued that the jurisdiction is now narrower in scope that it was prior to 1875) on the sweeping up clause. In *The Zeta*[5] (decided in 1893) Lord Herschell construed the jurisdiction over "damage" in terms of jurisdiction exercised in Admiralty prior to 1840.

Jurisdiction not referred to in Supreme Court Act 1981

In *The Tubantia*[6] (decided in 1924) Sir Henry Duke relied on the "undisputed jurisdiction" of the Court of Admiralty in respect of "injurious acts on the high seas"—in

4. [1968] P. 449.
5. [1893] A.C. 468.
6. [1924] P. 78.

that case interference with salvage operations in respect of a wreck. More recently in 1982 in *The Despina G.K.*[7] Sheen J. relied specifically on the sweeping up clause in the Act of 1956 as applied by the sweeping up clause of the Supreme Court Act 1981 in deciding that a foreign judgment *in rem* can be enforced in the English Admiralty Court by an action *in rem*. Sheen J. followed the principles set out by Sir Robert Phillimore in 1879 in *The City of Mecca*[8]—those principles presumably being deemed by Sheen J. to be those applicable prior to 1 November 1875.

The power to hear claims arising out of respondentia—the charging of cargo to obtain credit to continue or start a voyage from a foreign port—is not referred to specifically in the Act. It is arguable that it is included in "bottomry"—the charging of the ship or ship and cargo for the purpose mentioned, but this can hardly fit with the provision that a claim in bottomry is exercisable against a sister ship.[9] It is also perhaps arguable that it is included through the general label of "maritime lien". If neither of these concepts may be said to include it, it was clearly within the Admiralty jurisdiction prior to 1875.[10]

Admiralty jurisdiction includes general powers inherent in the court such as the ability to prevent abuse of process. In an Admiralty context this has been held to include the ability to ensure that security demanded to prevent arrest is not excessive.[11] These examples illustrate that the statutory framework does not draw all the boundaries or spell out all the Admiralty territory within the boundaries that it does draw.

B. LOOKING TO THE FUTURE

Jurisdiction assigned to the Admiralty Court by Rules of Court (s.20(1)(d))

The Admiralty Court jurisdiction includes any jurisdiction "connected with ships or aircraft" assigned to the Queen's Bench Division by rule of court made or coming into force after 1 January 1982 *and* directed by the rules to be exercised by the Admiralty Court. The provision thus allows for the extension of jurisdiction in Admiralty by rule of court rather than by statute.[12]

4. CATEGORIES OF ENFORCEABILITY

The Supreme Court Act 1981 provides for two methods of enforcement of claims listed in it (1) *by action in rem* and (2) *by an action in personam*. The majority of claims are enforceable by *both* types of action and no claim is enforceable by an action *in rem* only.

7. [1982] 2 Lloyd's Rep. 555.
8. (1879) 5 P.D. 28; (1881) 6 P.D. 106 (reversing on the facts).
9. As to which, see Chap. 10.
10. See e.g. *The Cargo ex Sultan* (1859) Swab. 504. As to doubts about the inclusion in the sweeping up clause of *in rem* jurisdiction, see *supra*.
11. See e.g. *The Polo II* [1977] 2 Lloyd's Rep. 115. See also the power to award interest on late payments of money due (see Introduction, *supra*).
12. For current rules of court concerned with jurisdiction, as to applications under the Merchant Shipping Acts, see RSC Order 74, rule 1; as to collision actions, see RSC Order 75, rule 2(1); as to limitation and oil pollution actions, see RSC Order 75, rule 2(1)(b) and (c) and 2A. There is a general power in the Lord Chancellor to assign business to particular Divisions (Supreme Court Act 1981, s.61(3) and (5)).

CLAIMS ENFORCEABLE BY ACTION "IN REM"

Claims enforceable by action *in rem* can be divided into four categories according to the scope of their enforceability:

(i) claims attracting a maritime lien or "other charge" on the relevant property (s.21(3));

(ii) claims enforceable by an action *in rem* against the relevant property (s.21(2));

(iii) claims enforceable by an action *in rem* against the relevant ship or "sister ship" provided certain conditions in relation to liability *in personam* are met (s.21(4));

(iv) claims within the sweeping up clause if not falling within (i)–(iii) above.

As a plaintiff's enquiry will be directed essentially at the enforceability of his claim and the remedy available in respect of it, the claims will be reviewed using these categories as a base. However, it must be stressed that all the claims are enforceable *in personam*, the only importance of Admiralty jurisdiction in this context being the ability to bring the claim before the Admiralty Court as distinct from some other branch of the High Court. The expertise of that court may be valuable and in certain types of action (e.g. collision and limitation actions) Admiralty procedure essential.

Effect of establishing a limitation fund

Under the Merchant Shipping (Oil Pollution) Act 1971 and the Merchant Shipping Act 1979 (now the Merchant Shipping Act 1995) a shipowner or other person is entitled to limit liability and establish a limitation fund. The fund may become in many cases the exclusive target for claimants and other security either must or may be released. The distribution of the fund is in proportion to the claims and no lien or other right may affect it. In such cases although the claim may be by an action *in rem* the end result is fundamentally affected as to the priority of claim by the limitation of liability. (See Chapter 24).

(i) Claims attracting maritime lien or "other charge"

These claims are treated as a special category by the Supreme Court Act 1981 inasmuch as they are singled out as a group for which an action *in rem* may be brought against any ship or other property in which there is "a maritime lien or other charge".[13] The provision must be read as referring to claims which, if successful, attract a maritime lien—for the maritime lien is for the claimant to establish. However, the maritime lien if established attaches from the event on which the claim is based (see Chapter 18).

The claims so qualifying are not statutorily defined or even referred to as such. Their nature and their legal characteristics must be sought in judicial development and earlier statutory provisions. As will be seen, the claims attracting maritime liens are included in s.20 of the Supreme Court Act 1981 as claims within the Admiralty jurisdiction but simply

---

13. Supreme Court Act 1981, s.21(3). The words "or other charge" apparently add nothing of English substance and little of foreign substance—see *infra* p. 45.

as claims and not as "maritime lien" claims. They qualify both as maritime lien claims and as claims for which an action *in rem* will lie but which do not attract a maritime lien (group (iii) below).

The English list of claims accepted as attracting maritime liens is relatively short and is mainly judicial in origin.[14] It must be recalled that the category of "maritime lien" was established only in 1851 in the case of *The Bold Buccleugh*,[15] and that the characteristics of the category represent no organized creation of a concept. Rather they represent distinct causes of action linked by twin common factors:

(i) enforceability against purchasers as from the date of creation of the claim; and

(ii) priority over other creditors.

Added to these must be the availability of arrest and forced sale and the ability to use arrest as a jurisdictional ground—but note that such features are also features of statutory liens. As the ambit of the "statutory lien" is that of the action *in rem* most—but not all—maritime claims fall within it (see *infra*).

(a) Uncertainties of maritime liens

It is the connection with and the distinction from Admiralty jurisdiction which causes constant confusion in trying to draw a certain boundary line around the category of claims attracting a maritime lien. Given that not every claim enforceable by an action *in rem* attracts a maritime lien, the relatively late development of the concept of the maritime lien, and the loose judicial use of the term "lien" it is often difficult to state the effect of decided cases with any confidence. This is particularly so in relation to those decided prior to the emergence of the category of maritime liens and early authorities are, therefore, to be treated with some suspicion.

It is now accepted that maritime liens attach to claims for:

(i) salvage;

(ii) damage done by a ship;

(iii) seamen's wages;

(iv) masters' wages;

(v) masters' disbursements;

(vi) bottomry and respondentia.

All these claims, save respondentia, also appear in s.20 of the Supreme Court Act 1981 and may also (alternatively) be enforced under that provision and s.21(4). The claims listed in s.20(1) within the categories attracting a maritime lien may not always be confined to the lien claim—as, for example, damage caused by a ship or the amended category of salvage. Further, in addition to those listed in (i) to (vi) there are a number of claims in respect of which it is arguable that maritime liens are attached. These will be referred to after examining the "established" list and its relationship to the claims set out in s.20.

14. Though statutes (as judicially construed) have extended the scope of most claims. The maritime liens for masters' wages and disbursements are statutory in origin. There have been three international Conventions seeking to achieve uniformity in a list of maritime liens—1926, 1967 and 1993. The United Kingdom has not ratified any (for discussion see Chap. 18).

15. (1851) 7 Moo. P.C. 267.

(b) Foreign maritime liens

It is established that English law recognizes only those maritime liens that are equivalent to its own.[16]

(c) Maritime liens and extension of jurisdiction by statute

The question of whether principles applied in inherent or non-statutory jurisdiction of Admiralty are carried through to statutory extensions of Admiralty jurisdiction was a critical issue following the Admiralty Court Acts of 1840 and 1861. It remains relevant today in the context of later statutes.[17] A fundamental general question in relation to the extension of Admiralty jurisdiction by the Acts of 1840 and 1861 was the degree to which, if at all, the extensions of jurisdiction meant extension of maritime liens. In 1976 in *The Halcyon Skies*[18] Brandon J. summed up the eventual judicial approach:

"It was supposed for a considerable period of time after the passing of the 1840 and 1861 Acts that their effect was, in cases where they gave the court jurisdiction over new subject-matters, to create new maritime liens in respect of claims relating to them. This supposition was subsequently held to have been erroneous by the House of Lords, which decided that the statutory provisions concerned did not create new maritime liens, but only gave statutory rights of action in rem in respect of such claims. This was decided, as regards the jurisdiction in respect of necessaries conferred by s.6 of the 1840 Act, in *The Heinrich Bjorn*; and, as regards the jurisdiction in respect of masters' disbursements conferred by s.10 of the 1861 Act, in *The Sara* ... A further question arose, following the passing of the 1840 and 1861 Acts, whether in cases where those Acts had enlarged the existing jurisdiction of the court as distinct from conferring new jurisdiction, it was intended that maritime liens recognised in respect of claims under the existing jurisdiction should extend also to claims of a similar kind under the enlarged jurisdiction. This further question did not fall to be decided in *The Heinrich Bjorn* or *The Sara*."

Brandon J. went on to say that in damage and salvage cases it was now established that "the relevant maritime lien should be regarded as extending to claims under the enlarged jurisdiction". In the case before him Brandon J. held that, applying the principles on which the extensions of the salvage and damages claims were based, the maritime lien for seamen's wages accompanied the extension of wages jurisdiction. Further, and interestingly, he held that if the extension of jurisdiction and the attached maritime lien had not been achieved by the Admiralty Court Act 1861 it had been achieved by the Administration of Justice Act 1956.

(d) Established maritime liens

(i) Salvage

THE MERCHANT SHIPPING (SALVAGE AND POLLUTION) ACT 1994

Many aspects of salvage are affected by the international Convention on Salvage 1989, initially in the Merchant Shipping (Salvage and Pollution) Act 1994 and as from 1 January

16. See *The Halcyon Isle* [1981] A.C. 221; *The Acrux* [1965] P. 391. See Chap. 18. But a contractual indemnity may refer to a maritime lien of *any law* (*The Barenbels* [1984] 2 Lloyd's Rep. 388).

17. As regards, for example, maritime liens in relation to claims in respect of life and property salvage, personal injury and loss of life and claims under the Merchant Shipping (Salvage and Pollution) Act 1994, see *infra*. As to the question of extension to claims distinct in nature from those attracting maritime liens, see *infra*.

18. [1976] 1 All E.R. 856. Brandon J. referred to *The Heinrich Bjorn* (1886) 11 App. Cas. 270 and *The Sara* (1889) 14 App. Cas. 209 as authorities establishing that novel claims did not carry a maritime lien, and to *The Veritas* [1901] P. 304 as an illustration of the lien accompanying jurisdictional extension.

1996 in the Merchant Shipping Act 1995. The Convention text is annexed as a Schedule. So, for example, by the wide definition of a vessel ("any ship or craft, or any structure capable of navigation")[19] property which may be salvaged under the Convention may be more extensive than formerly. The concept of voluntariness may be of less importance and there may be a reward even if there is no success where there is a threat to the environment.

However, the Convention provides in Art. 20 that "Nothing in this Convention shall affect the salvage maritime lien under any international convention or national law" but the enforceability of the law is limited in that it cannot be enforced if satisfactory security has been provided. Read literally in regard to the establishment of a lien, no provision of the Convention will affect any principle or rule on which the maritime lien depends. If this be so, rules founded on nineteenth century authority will remain relevant for the maritime lien but not in relation to a "Convention claim". As the latter may be enforced by an action *in rem* and thereby attracts a statutory lien there will be distinct approaches according to the type of lien on which reliance is placed.[20] The 1994 and 1995 Acts are considered *infra* in relation to non-maritime lien claims.

SALVAGE APART FROM THE 1994 AND 1995 ACTS[21]

In 1824 Lord Stowell described[22] a salvor as a person who without any particular relation to a ship[23] in distress proffers useful service and gives it as a volunteer adventurer without any pre-existing covenant that connected him with the duty of employing himself for the preservation of that ship.[24] In addition to a ship,[25] subjects of salvage in a maritime context are apparel, hovercraft,[26] cargo, derelict flotsam, jetsam and lagan, freight at risk, life from ships and wreck.[27] Apart from life, the subjects of salvage also form the assets to which a maritime lien will attach.[28] Subject to agreement[29] or "engaged" services, to

19. But not to drilling units on location engaged in the exploration, exploitation or production of sea-bed resources (Art. 3). "Navigation" has been construed in English courts as "planned or ordered movement from one place to another" (*Steedman* v. *Schofield* [1992] 2 Lloyd's Rep. 163) and excluding activities on water used solely by people "messing about in boats" (*Curtis* v. *Wild* [1991] 4 All E.R. 172). See Chap. 12.

20. Lloyd's Open Form 1990 includes many of the Convention provisions (see Gaskell [1991] LMCLQ 104) but a maritime lien cannot be created by contract.

21. See as to salvage generally e.g. Kennedy's *Law of Salvage* (5th edn. 1985, Steel and Rose); Brice, *Maritime Law of Salvage* (2nd edn. 1993). As to the international Convention on Salvage 1989, see Watkins [1989] LMCLQ 416; Brice [1990] LMCLQ 32; Gaskell [1990] LMCLQ 352.

22. In *The Neptune* (1824) 1 Hag.Adm. 227, at p. 236. Salvage must be distinguished from towage. For a modern examination of that distinction, the need for "voluntary services", and the question of whether a crew could be volunteers if their employer would not, see *The Texaco Southampton* [1983] 1 Lloyd's Rep. 94 (C.A. of N.S.W.).

23. The Crown is entitled to unclaimed wreck and to derelict on the sea (which will become droits of Admiralty if no ownership is claimed). As to the limitation of salvage to ships, see *Wills* v. *Owners of Gas Float Whitton (No. 2)* [1897] A.C. 337. If things afloat on the water become droits, salvage is probably payable by the Crown (see *infra*). As to droits, see *infra*.

24. Acts done for the benefit of those providing the services do not qualify for salvage (see e.g. *Simon* v. *Taylor* [1975] 2 Lloyd's Rep. 338).

25. As to the definition of a ship, see *Wills* v. *Owners of Gas Float Whitton (No. 2)* [1897] A.C. 337; *Steedman* v. *Schofield* [1992] 2 Lloyd's Rep. 163 (jet ski not a boat or ship).

26. Hovercraft (Application of Enactments) Order 1972, Art. 8.

27. Wreck indicates that the article is cast upon a shore. (See Merchant Shipping Act 1894, s.510, defining wreck for the purpose of Part IX of the Act.)

28. As to hovercraft, see the Hovercraft Act 1968, s.2(2).

29. See e.g. *Admiralty Commissioners* v. *Valverda (Owners)* [1938] A.C. 173. Such agreements will be enforced only so far as they are consistent with equitable principles applicable to salvage (*The Crusader* [1907] P. 15).

qualify for a reward a salvor must have some degree of success.[30] Services remain engaged even if, after a request for aid is acted on, the ship is saved by another intervention (the weather or another salvor engaged instead).[31]

SALVAGE CLAIMS AND THE MARITIME LIEN

The maritime lien for salvage services is firmly established and was included in the list of claims set out in *The Bold Buccleugh* as attracting a maritime lien.[32] Until 1956 there is no hint in the development of salvage jurisdiction that the ability to bring an action *in rem* for salvage differs from the existence of a maritime lien.[33] Since 1956 the introduction of sister ship jurisdiction under certain conditions means that there is a distinction and since the enactment in 1994 of the Salvage Convention 1989 there may be substantive differences (see *infra*).

The maritime lien is founded on the benefit created by the service and, apart from life salvage, the lien attaches to the asset (ship, cargo or freight) benefited by the salvage service for the value of the claim.[34] It is independent of any salvage agreement or personal obligation.[35]

EXTENSION BEYOND THE HIGH SEAS

The lien undoubtedly extends to salvage within the body of a county as well as on the high seas.[36] However, in 1988 in *The Goring*[37] the House of Lords held that no salvage claim lay in respect of a vessel in non-tidal waters. This conclusion was based on a detailed analysis of statutory provisions from 1389 until 1956. There was, thought Lord Brandon delivering the leading judgment, no room for any "public policy" consideration—it was simply a question of whether there had been any statutory extension of an ancient defined right. Yet it was established that salvage would lie in respect of non-tidal waters enclosed by dock gates—and lie by virtue of judicial application. There could not therefore be unlimited reliance on an established statutory division between non-tidal and tidal waters. To meet the point a statutory amendment was made in the Merchant Shipping Act 1988 so to define "tidal waters" in s.546 of the Merchant Shipping Act 1894 (dealing with

30. See e.g. *The Melanie (Owners)* v. *The San Onofre (Owners)* [1925] A.C. 246. Salvors who negligently cause harm are liable for that harm (*The Tojo Maru* [1972] A.C. 242).

31. See *The Unique Mariner (No. 2)* [1979] 1 Lloyd's Rep. 37.

32. See also *The Eleanora Charlotta* (1823) 1 Hag.Adm. 156; *The Veritas* [1901] P. 304, at pp. 311, 312; *Currie* v. *M'Knight* [1897] A.C. 97, at pp. 105–106; *The Lyrma (No. 2)* [1978] 2 Lloyd's Rep. 30.

33. See *The Schiller (Cargo ex)* (1877) L.R. 2 P.D. 145, *per* Brett L.J. (dissenting—but on this point reviewing the development of the Admiralty jurisdiction in relation to life salvage). See also Brandon J. in *The Halycon Skies* [1977] Q.B. 14, at p. 30.

34. See e.g. *The Westminster* (1841) 1 W. Rob 229; *The Fusilier* (1865) 3 Moo. P.C. N.S. 51, at p. 73.

35. See e.g. *The Hestia* [1895] P. 193; *The Unique Mariner (No. 2)* [1979] 1 Lloyd's Rep. 37, at pp. 49–50. But as an agreement may extinguish or prevent a maritime lien (particularly where it provides security) and as a salvage contract will determine the rights between parties it may be as well to include a clause indicating that the agreement is not overriding the lien (as e.g. until contractual security is provided by Lloyd's Open Form 1990, Clause 5). A seaman's right in the nature of salvage cannot be renounced by agreement save by an agreement for remuneration made in connection with a ship rendering salvage services (Merchant Shipping Act 1995, s.39 replacing Merchant Shipping Act 1970, s.16).

36. Admiralty jurisdiction was extended in respect of salvage claims by the Admiralty Court Act 1840, s.6. As to the general approach to this extension in respect of established maritime liens, see *supra*. See also *The Veritas* [1901] P. 304, *The Lyrma (No. 2)* [1978] 2 Lloyd's Rep. 30.

37. [1988] A.C. 831; [1988] 1 Lloyd's Rep. 397.

salvage in coastal waters) as including the waters of any dock connected with tidal waters (see *infra*).[38]

The statutory limitation to tidal waters and the extension of such waters was continued in substance by the Merchant Shipping (Salvage and Pollution) Act 1994[39] and the Merchant Shipping Act 1995. It remains doubtful, however, whether the tidal limit can be supported otherwise than through history, once it is conceded that parts of harbours are areas where salvage will lie. Now that there are substantive differences between the maritime lien and a salvage claim there is even less justification for making the availability of the action *in rem* depend on the tide.

Foreign inland waters. As salvage is a claim unique to Admiralty the issue in *The Goring* equated the existence of the claim with Admiralty jurisdiction. A salvage claim in relation to foreign non-tidal waters could be recognized if the claim is recognized there and the existence of the claim is seen as a matter of substantive law.[40] However, if the question is treated as one of "salvage jurisdiction" the courts may well see this as a matter essentially for English law.[41] To take this view, however, would be to apply English history to matters outside its scope. The conclusion in effect depends on whether the backward look goes sideways. There is in reality little reason why the existence of a claim should not be a matter for the appropriate foreign law.

LIFE SALVAGE

In relation to salvage operations in British waters or in regard to a British vessel elsewhere started prior to 1 January 1995 there is to be a statutory right to a "reasonable amount" for the saving of life. This is to be payable in priority to all other salvage claims, but there is no reference to a maritime lien.[42] Where the ship is destroyed or the value insufficient, payment may be made by the Secretary of State out of the Mercantile Marine Fund.

In *The Fusilier*[43] the Privy Council construed the predecessor to the section[44] as simply providing "in the entire sum payable for salvage of ship and cargo a distinct reward for the preservation of human life".[45] It would seem contrary to common sense both in the light of this approach and the general public policy lying behind salvage to differentiate between life and property salvage. The statutory provisions impose liability on the owner of ship and cargo and allow the assertion of liability through proceedings *in rem*.[46] It

---

38. Sch. 5, para 3.

39. Through making a permitted reservation to the Convention in excluding it from "inland waters" where all the vessels involved are of inland navigation or there is no navigation involved (1995 Act, Sch. 11, Part II para. 2) see *infra*.

40. As to the applicable law, see Chap. 26.

41. As did the majority of the Privy Council in respect of "maritime liens" in *The Halcyon Isle* [1981] A.C. 221; [1980] 2 Lloyd's Rep. 325.

42. Merchant Shipping Act 1894, s.544. The provision is specifically brought into the Supreme Court Act 1981 (s.20(6)).

43. (1865) 3 Moo. P.C., N.S. 51.

44. Merchant Shipping Act 1854, s.458.

45. At p. 71 (meeting the point that there should be contribution without benefit to the property salved). See also *The Schiller (Cargo ex)* (1877) L.R. 2 P.D. 145 where it was held that for a claim to lie, property need only survive—it need not be salved—and that the liability of the owners of the ship or cargo is limited to the value of the property saved.

46. No reference is made to freight. As to proceedings *in rem*, see p. 64.

would be curious indeed to limit that assertion in the case of life salvage to a statutory lien and allow a maritime lien for property salvage.[47]

The specific provision as to priority in relation to other salvage claims makes the classification of the life salvage lien as a maritime lien irrelevant in that context. But it remains critical outside the narrow ambit of s.544(2)—in particular where there are claimants relying on maritime liens other than property salvage, or where property liable to a lien is sold prior to the issue of a writ by the life salvor.

The Merchant Shipping (Salvage and Pollution) Act.[48] Under the Salvage Convention 1989, Art. 16, a salvor of human life who has taken part in the services rendered is entitled to a "fair share" of the payment to the salvor. Nothing in that article affects national law. The 1894 Act provision is repealed but like provision is made by the Act for discretionary payment by the Secretary of State where the vessel is destroyed or the salvor is entitled to a less than reasonable amount under the Convention.[49]

Nothing in the Convention is to affect the "salvor's maritime lien".[50] Although the life salvor has lost any statutory priority the reasoning for the inclusion within the maritime lien remains. Because of the loss of statutory priority the classification becomes the more important. It should not be seen solely as a Convention right given its history and the express provision that the entitlement is to a share of the salvage award, rather than any independent fund.[51]

STATUTORY CLAIM FOR PROPERTY SALVAGE

(a) Prior to 1 January 1995. Section 546 of the Merchant Shipping Act 1894, as amended by the Merchant Shipping Act 1988, provides:

"(1) Where any vessel is wrecked, stranded, or in distress at any place on or near the coasts of the United Kingdom or any tidal water within the limits of the United Kingdom, and services are rendered by any person in assisting that vessel or saving the cargo or apparel of that vessel or any part thereof, and where services are rendered by any person other than a receiver in saving any wreck, there shall be payable to the salvor by the owner of the vessel, cargo, apparel, or wreck, a reasonable amount of salvage to be determined in case of dispute in manner hereinafter mentioned.[52]

(2) In this section "tidal water" means—
  (a) any waters within the ebb and flow of the tide at ordinary spring tides; or
  (b) the waters of any dock which is directly, or (by means of one or more other docks) indirectly, connected with any such waters."

47. Particularly is this so as the practice of making an enhanced award to reflect the degree of danger to human life where there are salvage services to ship and cargo rather than distinct awards seems to have survived the statute. (See *The Bosworth (No. 3)* [1962] 1 Lloyd's Rep. 483.)

48. Apart from the provisions relating to the 1992 Protocols to the 1969 and 1971 Oil Pollution Conventions the pollution provisions came into force either on 28 July 1994 or 1 October 1994 (SI 1994/1988) and the salvage provisions on 1 January 1995 (SI 1994/2971). The Supreme Court Act, s.20(2)(6), was amended to include jurisdiction as to claims based on the Convention (see *infra*). As from 1 January 1996 the 1994 Act is repealed and re-enacted in the Merchant Shipping Act 1995 Parts VI and IX with transitory texts pending the coming into force of the 1992 protocols.

49. 1995 Act, s.1; Sch. 1, Pt. II, para. 5.

50. Art. 20.

51. A conclusion supported by the provision in the Supreme Court Act 1981, s.20(6), as amended that "salvage services" in the Act includes "services rendered in saving life from a ship".

52. Brought into the Supreme Court Act 1981 specifically (see s.20(6)).

This section reproduces s.458 of the Merchant Shipping Act 1854 which in turn replaced in part s.19 of the Wrecks and Salvage Act 1846.[53] There is an overlap between the jurisdiction[54] under s.458 and that founded on the pre-statutory jurisdiction extended by the Admiralty Court Act 1840. There is no guide as to whether the statutory provision creates a maritime lien, but it would be surprising if it did not in the light of the somewhat intricate and connected statutory and non statutory framework. It certainly fits with the general proposition that geographical extensions of rights attracting maritime liens extend the liens accordingly.

Tidal waters, docks and harbours. In 1988 in *The Goring*[55] Lord Brandon saw the restriction to tidal waters as support for the exclusion of salvage in general from non-tidal waters. Prior to the defining amendment of 1988 there was difficulty caused by the exclusion of harbours from "tidal waters" by s.742 of the 1894 Act (the definition section). If applied to s.546 this means exclusion from docks—yet it was accepted that salvage could take place in docks. So far as statutory salvage is concerned the extension to dock waters is simply preserved by deeming facts to be contrary to reality.

Although "harbour" is defined in s.742 as including estuaries and navigable rivers it is not to be so construed in s.546. In *The Powstaniec Wielkopolski*[56] Sheen J. held that there could be salvage under s.546 of a ship in the River Thames although at a place which could provide shelter—the word "harbour" had to be given its natural and ordinary meaning and Gravesend Reach would not ordinarily be described as such.

(b) After 1 January 1995. Section 546 of the Merchant Shipping Act 1894 was repealed by the Salvage and Pollution Act 1994 with the consequence that the 1894 provision applies only to salvage operations started prior to 1 January 1995.[57] There is no replacement provision, property salvage now being solely a matter for the Convention as enacted or the maritime lien. The repeal removes an unnecessary complexity and the limit to tidal water, save for docks connected with such waters, applies generally by limiting the Convention to waters other than "inland waters" except where a vessel not of inland navigation is involved. Excluded from such waters are any waters within the ebb and flow of the tide and dock waters connected with "such waters".[58]

(ii) Damage by a ship[59]

The Admiralty jurisdiction based on the occurrence of "damage" is not necessarily equated with the existence of a maritime lien. In considering "damage" as the basis of a maritime lien it must be appreciated that in many decided cases the issue turned on

---

53. This provision removed a restriction to ships or sea going vessels imposed by the Admiralty Court Act 1840, s.6, on the extended salvage jurisdiction from the high seas to a body of a county conferred by that Act.

54. The outer geographical limits of the statutory jurisdiction are unclear. A place 20 miles off the coast has been held not to be within its scope (*The Fulham* [1898] P. 206; affirmed C.A. [1899] P. 251).

55. [1988] A.C. 831; [1988] 1 Lloyd's Rep. 397.

56. [1989] 1 Lloyd's Rep. 58.

57. 1994 Act, s.1(6), Sch. 2, para. 1; SI 1994/2926—as from 1 January 1996: 1995 Act Sch. 11, para. 1.

58. 1994 Act, Sch. 1, Pt. II, para. 2—as from 1 January 1996: 1995 Act, Sch. 11, Pt. II, para. 2.

59. As to assets subject to the maritime lien, see *infra* Chap. 18. The law relating to maritime liens applies to hovercraft (Hovercraft Act 1968, s.2(2) and (3)). No lien attaches to a claim for injury, loss or damage for occurrences involving nuclear matter. See Nuclear Installations Act 1965, s.14. As to liens and limitation of liability, see *supra*. See further *infra* and Chap. 6.

whether an action *in rem* would lie. The question of whether there was a maritime lien was not before the court but it would be curious to admit an arbitrary wider jurisdiction for a statutory lien in relation to subject-matter later held to attract a maritime lien. It is possible, therefore, in some contexts to use authorities dealing with the jurisdiction *in rem* as relevant to the establishment of a maritime lien.

It was the "damage lien" which was in issue in *The Bold Buccleugh*[60]—the case in which the concept of the maritime lien first emerged—and in that case it was made clear that damage caused by a ship was to be treated in the same way as a claim for salvage or for wages against the ship. In 1897 in a Scottish case, *Currie* v. *M'Knight*,[61] the House of Lords affirmed the decision in *The Bold Buccleugh* that a maritime lien attaches to a ship causing damage:

" ... it is a reasonable and salutary rule that when a ship is so carelessly navigated as to occasion injury to other vessels which are free from blame, the owners of the injured craft should have a remedy against the corpus of the offending ship, and should not be restricted to a personal claim against her owners, who may have no substantial interest in her and may be without the means of making due compensation".[62]

The lien will attach only in so far as the claim is established through proof of fault of the person in charge of the ship. However, this leaves open the question of the extent to which a maritime lien may attach to a ship in respect of which the owner is not in charge. This is a matter not so directly connected with the nature of the claim but with liability through a ship for an act for which the shipowner has no direct responsibility. To put it from the plaintiff's point of view—what is the scope of enforceability of his claim.[63]

To attract the lien it is not necessary that damage be caused to a ship. Damage to a landing stage or to goods will attract the lien,[64] but whether it extends to injury to persons or loss of life is less certain and must be considered as part of the effect of statutory extension of Admiralty jurisdiction.[65]

It is clear that the maritime lien will attach only if the ship is "the instrument of mischief", so that where the crew cut a cable of another ship and damage ensued no maritime lien was created.[66] Subject to this requirement it seems inevitable that the authorities which establish that for an action *in rem* to lie there is no requirement of physical contract[67] and that consequential damage can be the basis of a claim[68] apply to maritime liens.

---

60. (1851) 7 Moo. P.C. 267.
61. [1897] A.C. 97.
62. *Per* Lord Watson (at p. 106).
63. The lien will reflect liability for fault and the value reflect statutory limitation of liability and any contributory negligence. As to enforceability, see Chap. 18.
64. See e.g. *The Veritas* [1901] P. 304; *The Tolten* [1946] P. 135 (a foreign pier). For an example of a claim in relation to goods being treated as attracting a maritime lien, see *The Stream Fisher* [1927] P. 73.
65. See *infra*.
66. *Currie* v. *M'Knight* [1897] A.C. 97. It suffices for the exercise of "*in rem*" jurisdiction that the damage is caused by part of a ship (see *The Minerva* [1933] P. 224). In that case, the court noted the distinction between *in rem* jurisdiction and a maritime lien, but there seems little reason to draw it in this context. It does not suffice if the injury occurs in the ship (*The Theta* [1894] P. 280)—but this fact situation would fall within the Supreme Court Act 1981, s.20(2)(f) and thereby any claim would attract a statutory lien (see *infra*).
67. *The Chr Knudsen* [1932] P. 153; *The Port Victoria* [1902] P. 25; *The Dagmara* and *Ama Antxine* [1988] 1 Lloyd's Rep. 431 (allegation of dangerously approaching another vessel to drive her away from fishing grounds).
68. See e.g. *The Jade* [1976] 2 Lloyd's Rep. 1, at p. 8.

EXTENSION BEYOND THE HIGH SEAS

The Admiralty Court Act 1840, s.6 extended the jurisdiction in respect of claims for damage received by a ship from claims for damage received on the high seas to damage received within the body of a county. The Admiralty Court Act 1861 provided for jurisdiction over "any claim for damage done by any ship".[69] In several cases it was said that it could well be argued that the extension of jurisdiction in respect of some claims to events within the body of a county carried with it an extension of the maritime lien,[70] and in 1901 in *The Veritas*[71] it was held that a maritime lien attached to a claim for damage to a landing stage in the Mersey. Gorell Barnes J. pointed out that in *The Bold Buccleugh* (decided in 1851) the collision occurred in the River Humber and said in connection with the statutory extension from the high seas that "it seems to follow that it was intended that the law should be the same as to damage done by a ship elsewhere".[72] In 1979 in *The Father Thames*[73] where a collision in the River Thames was at issue no point was apparently taken on the place of act, the argument concentrating on the validity of a maritime lien attaching to demise chartered ships.

EXTENSION TO CLAIMS FOR PERSON INJURY OR LOSS OF LIFE

Personal injury. Admiralty jurisdiction prior to the Admiralty Court Acts 1840 and 1861 extended to claims for personal injuries but it appears that they were pursued by actions *in personam*.[74] Section 7 of the Admiralty Court Act 1861 provided that the court should have jurisdiction "over any claim for damage done by any ship" and in 1867 in *The Sylph*[75] and in 1869 in *The Beta*[76] it was held that an action *in rem* would lie in respect of personal injury. Both relied primarily on the statute rather than on the jurisdiction of the court prior to it. The Maritime Conventions Act 1911 provided specifically that:

"5. Any enactment which confers on any court Admiralty jurisdiction in respect of damage shall have effect as though references to such damage included references to damages for loss of life or personal injury, and accordingly proceedings in respect of such damages may be brought *in rem* or *in personam*."

The question of whether such a claim attracts a maritime lien depends upon the construction of the effect of the statutory provision in the light of the pre-existent jurisdiction. If it is seen as an extension through an elaboration of "damage" it may be argued that the maritime lien attracted to damage is extended by analogy to the statutory geographical extension. If it is seen as a novel jurisdiction it will suffer the fate of other novel claims created by statute, and be relegated to a statutory lien. Price, writing in 1940,[77] thought it probable that there was no maritime lien. Thomas,[78] writing in 1980,

---

69. Presumably without geographical restriction—although the Supreme Court of Judicature (Consolidation) Act 1925 continued to express jurisdiction in respect of damage *received* as "whether received within the body of a county or the high seas" and damage *by* a ship without qualification (see s.22(1)(a)(iii) and (iv)).

70. See *The Sara* (1889) 14 App.Cas. 209; *The Two Ellens* (1872) L.R. 4 P.C. 161, at p. 167; *The Heinrich Bjorn* (1886) 11 App.Cas. 270, at p. 282.

71. [1901] P. 304.

72. At p. 311.

73. [1979] 2 Lloyd's Rep. 364.

74. See *The Zeta* [1893] A.C. 468; *The Sylph* (1867) L.R. 2 A. & E. 24.

75. (1867) L.R. 2 A. & E. 24.

76. (1869) L.R. 2 P.C. 447.

77. *Law of Maritime Liens*, at p. 42.

78. *Maritime Liens* (Stevens), para. 220. See also Mansfield (1888) 4 L.Q.R., at pp. 388–389.

thought it "without question" that there is—relying primarily on a somewhat ambiguous illustration given by Scott L.J. in *The Tolten*[79]—a case concerned with a collision between a ship and a foreign peir.

Approaching the matter from policy, the rationale for a damage maritime lien is certainly no less applicable to personal injury than to property damage, and it would expose the law to a certain amount of ridicule to allow a maritime lien for the latter only. It has to be admitted that, adopting the accepted mode of construction of statutes extending the Admiralty jurisdiction and their relevance to maritime liens, there is an argument for denying the maritime lien to personal injury claims—for the Admiralty Court appears to have lacked jurisdiction *in rem* prior to the Admiralty Court Act 1840.

Nevertheless, it is suggested that it is open to remain true to the accepted approach and still to hold that personal injury claims attract a maritime lien.[80] The principle of "damage" caused through a tortious act was clearly accepted as the root of a maritime lien and there is every reason why a statute extending the scope of "damage" should be extending that jurisdiction rather than differentiating between different kinds of damage.[81]

Loss of life. In 1884 in *The Vera Cruz (No. 2)*,[82] the House of Lords held that a claim under the Fatal Accidents Act 1846 could not be pursued by an action *in rem* for damage done by a ship. The Act of 1846 was "legislation for the general case and not for particular injury by ships" and it "points to a common law action, points to a personal liability and a personal right to recover and is absolutely at variance with the notion of a proceeding *in rem*". It gave a new right of action entirely.

The Maritime Conventions Act 1911, s.5, provided for the incorporation of damages for loss of life in any enactment conferring on any court Admiralty jurisdiction in respect of damages. Thomas is certain that a claimant under the Fatal Accidents Act 1976 (the current successor to that of 1846) has no maritime lien as the jurisdiction is "solely statutory".[83] With respect this is to ignore the form of the statutory provision conferring the power—for it simply defines the word "damage" in other statutes.

The issue is whether the statutory jurisdiction can be seen as an extension of the jurisdiction over the claims for damage, or whether it is an "entirely new action" as was said in *The Vera Cruz*. Conversely, the reasoning of *The Vera Cruz* is not entirely destroyed by the Maritime Conventions Act 1911 for the wording of that statute does not meet the point that an action under the Fatal Accidents Act is not an action flowing from damage or loss caused by a ship. It does, however, fundamentally affect the view expressed in *The Vera Cruz* that the Fatal Accidents Act did not encompass an action in relation to a ship.

---

79. [1946] P. 135.

80. The Supreme Court Act 1981 includes a heading of claim "loss of life or personal injury" in addition to damage by a ship—this being a repetition of the Act of 1956 and a change from the Act of 1925. It presumably is intended to reflect the Arrest Convention (see Chap. 15) and should not be taken to indicate that personal injury cannot still be incorporated into "damage" for the principle of a maritime lien.

81. In *The Mary Ann* (1865) L.R. 1 A. & E. 8 (in which Dr Lushington advanced the approach to the statutes which was later affirmed in *The Sara* (1889) 14 App.Cas. 209 (although his application of the principles was overruled)) the judge gave "damage caused by a ship" as an example of extension of a maritime lien.

82. (1884) 10 App. Cas. 59, at p. 67.

83. *Maritime Liens*, op. cit., at para. 220.

It may be that to say an action under the Act is not caused by the ship is looking too narrowly at "cause". Further, it may be contended as with personal injury that the Maritime Conventions Act of 1911 was simply spelling out "damage" in the context of Admiralty jurisdiction and that in that context a damage claim has long been recognized as attracting a maritime lien.

EXTENSION TO OIL POLLUTION CLAIMS

Admiralty jurisdiction in respect of damage by a ship was extended to liability incurred under the Merchant Shipping (Oil Pollution) Act 1971[84] and any claim in respect of a liability falling on the International Oil Pollution Compensation Fund under the Merchant Shipping Act 1974.[85] It seems hardly arguable that such claims can attract maritime liens. They create a jurisdiction over claims based on a cause of damage which is entirely new—although the ultimate effect may be similar to that caused by physical damage. Furthermore, the statutory phraseology makes it clear that the "extension" is not through an extension of the concept of "damage" but through the inclusion of a claim in relation to oil pollution damage within the category of claims based on damage.

(iii) Seamen's wages[86]

The "wages" lien was included in the group of claims in *The Bold Buccleugh* as attracting a maritime lien. Before that characterization there is judicial insistence about the attachment of the wage claim to the ship "as long as a single plank" remained,[87] and to the priority of a wages lien over the claim of a mortgagee.[88] The maritime lien does not diverge from jurisdiction *in rem* in the application of a wide construction of "wages", the type of contract under which wages earned or the person earning them.[89]

In 1935 in *The British Trade*[90] it was held that a maritime lien did not coexist with Admiralty jurisdiction *in rem* where the claim arose out of a special contract on the basis that the Act of 1861, while extending Admiralty jurisdiction to wages earned under a special contract, did not thereby extend the maritime lien.[91] But in 1977 in *The Halcyon*

84. Supreme Court Act 1981, s.20(5)(a), as from 1 January 1996 amended to refer to the Merchant Shipping Act 1995 (see Sch. 13, para. 59) that Act repealing and re-enacting the 1971 Act and amendments made and to be made (see fn. 48). As to such claims, see *infra*.

85. Supreme Court Act 1981, s.20(5)(b), as from 1 January 1996 amended to refer to the Merchant Shipping Act 1995 (see Sch. 13, para. 59) that Act repealing and re-enacting the applicable provisions of the 1974 Act and amendments made and to be made (see fn. 48). As to such claims, see *infra*. It is in any event unlikely that the Fund would be the owner of the property to which any lien would attach.

86. For statutory provisions governing wages, see the Merchant Shipping Act 1970, ss.7–18 as amended by the Merchant Shipping Acts 1979, s.37(1), and 1988, s.46, and SI 1993/785 (as from 1 January 1996 all repealed and re-enacted in Merchant Shipping Act 1995 ss.30–41). As to restrictions on justification to hear claims in respect of foreign ships, see Chap. 12.

87. *The Sydney Cove* (1815) 2 Dods. 11.

88. *The Prince George* (1837) 3 Hag.Adm. 376, at p. 380.

89. As to the jurisdiction prior to 1840, see Marsden (1886) 2 L.Q.R. 357, at p. 365, and as to the probable early assumption that it amounted to a maritime lien, see p. 367.

90. [1924] P. 104.

91. A special contract was one which, because of an unusual or special term, could not be said to be the sailor's ordinary contract of employment with the master. (See e.g. *The British Trade* [1924] P. 104, at pp. 110–111.)

Skies[92] Brandon J. held that *The British Trade* was incorrectly decided. In Brandon J.'s view the judgment in the earlier case ignored the distinction long established in relation to the Admiralty Court Acts 1840 and 1861 between (i) the extension by the statute of jurisdiction in regard to claims attracting maritime liens prior to the statutes and (ii) the creation by the statutes of jurisdiction *in rem* in relation to claims not attracting such liens prior to the statutes. This analysis adopts the reasoning perhaps focused on geographical extension to the extension in relation to the contract under which the wages were earned. Such a conclusion seems only sensible. To distinguish between claims made on identical grounds because of a difference in a particular element of the claim would require strong distinction in policy. In the case of wages, as in salvage and collision, the policy is all the other way.

"WAGES"

Courts have consistently taken a liberal view of "wages".[93] In 1959 Worley L.J. in the Supreme Court of Bermuda saw the need to keep up to date and include in "wages" those additions such as "paid leave, sick leave bonuses and so on . . . which a mariner can be fairly said to have earned by his services".[94] In that case claims in respect of employees' contributions for social insurance, overtime, bonuses and food allowance, paid sick leave and pay for a period of notice for dismissal without cause were treated as claims for wages. In *The Westport (No. 4)*[95] repatriation costs[96] and union dues were allowed. In *The Halcyon Skies*[97] Brandon J. held that a maritime lien attached to claim for unpaid wages due, damages for wrongful dismissal and breach of contract by the shipowner to pay employees' contribution to funds for the benefit of seamen.[98] In so doing in effect he held that the limitation expressed in the Admiralty Court Act 1861, s.10, to wages "earned on board the ship" should be ignored as, indeed, it had been ignored in the jurisdiction exercised apart from the statute.[99] Alternatively, he held that if this was wrong the limitation had gone because of its omission from the equivalent provision of the

92. [1977] Q.B. 14; [1976] 1 Lloyd's Rep. 461.
93. The Merchant Shipping Act 1894, s.742, 1995 s.313(1), provides simply that "Wages includes emoluments"—This applies to the lien for masters' wages (Merchant Shipping Act 1970, s.18, 1995 s.41) and is a strong hint to the scope of a seaman's wages both because of the link between the master and the seaman's lien and the specific provision protecting the seaman's lien in the Merchant Shipping Act 1970, s.16, 1995 s.39. The definition has been treated as generally applicable (see e.g. *The Acrux* [1965] 1 Lloyd's Rep. 565) and certainly the judicial treatment of wages has been consistent with it. For current statutory provisions concerning wages, see fn. 86. The right to interest on late payment (1970 Act s.12; 1995 Act s.35) no doubt attracts a maritime lien.
94. *The Arosa Star* [1959] 2 Lloyd's Rep. 396, at p. 403—a phrase taken from *The British Trade* [1924] P. 104. Medical expenses or for relief and maintenance for being left behind or shipwrecked (see Merchant Shipping Act 1970, ss.26 and 62) may perhaps be equated with "sick leave" bonuses.
95. [1968] 2 Lloyd's Rep. 559.
96. See also *The Immacolata Concezione* (1884) 9 P.D. 37.
97. [1977] Q.B. 14.
98. A number of authorities were cited in which insurance and pension contributions had been declared recoverable as wages (see p. 23) but Brandon J. approached the matter afresh to discover the rationale underlying the conclusion. As to the authorities, see *The Arosa Star* [1959] 2 Lloyd's Rep. 396 (in which it was emphasized that the claim attracted a maritime lien); *The Arosa Kulm (No. 2)* [1960] 1 Lloyd's Rep. 97; *The Fairport* [1965] 2 Lloyd's Rep. 183; *The Fairport (No. 3)* [1966] 2 Lloyd's Rep. 253; *The Westport (No. 4)* [1968] 2 Lloyd's Rep. 559.
99. In *The British Trade* [1924] P. 104 the authorities were said to lead to the conclusion that a maritime lien extended to claims for damages for dismissal, i.e. beyond wages earned on board (pp. 109–110).

Administration of Justice Act 1956 (a provision repeated in its 1956 form in the Supreme Court Act 1981).[100]

In 1965 in *The Acrux*[101] Hewson J. considered payments due to an Italian corporate body carrying out governmental functions in providing social insurance to seamen employed on board ships registered in Italy. He distinguished between insurance contributions paid by employers compulsorily under statute (as these were) and contributions paid under contract. He believed that the statutory payments were not emoluments. In *The Fairport*[102] (decided some two months later) the same judge had to consider a similar type of payment made on behalf of a Greek crew on board a Panamanian ship to a Greek statutory corporation (N.A.T.). It was said that these payments involving a non Greek ship were not compulsory, but a matter of contract. Hewson J. contented himself in distinguishing *The Acrux* on the ground that the claimant there was the corporation to whom the payments should have been made while in *The Fairport* it was the crew. In 1968 in *The Westport (No. 4)*[103] it appears that it was accepted that contributions which, if the argument in *The Fairport* was correct were compulsory, were emoluments.[104] In 1981 in *The Silia*[105] there was a claim by the N.A.T. in respect of unpaid contributions in regard to the crew of a Greek-registered ship. It was apparently accepted that payment of the N.A.T. fund was wages, but it was held that no action would lie as the claimants were not the masters or crew, nor was the claim made for their benefit.[106]

The development through accepting sums in addition to "wages" in the narrow sense as within the concept so as to create a maritime lien for them was not continued so as to include severance pay. In *The Tacoma City*[107] the Court of Appeal held first that to create a maritime lien on a ship the wages must be paid for current services in that ship. Severance pay was compensation for dismissal and in the particular case was assured by the length of service in different ships. Further, not every payment under a contract of employment was wages—as for example a pension or, in the view of Dillon L.J. study leave ashore. The "welfare" payments held in the earlier cases to be "wages" all relate to current service.

It may be accepted that all payments under a contract of employment by a shipping company for service on ships would not necessarily be wages earned on ships or a particular ship. However, it is with respect too general to classify "severance pay" as such as outside a concept which includes damages for unfair dismissal and breach of contract claims. It may form part of the contract payments as a whole and, it is suggested, the critical element is the connection with a particular ship. Likewise, study leave ashore (just as sick leave) may form part of a contract of service in relation to a particular ship—to exclude this as such risks bringing back the requirement of "earned on board".

The effectiveness of the maritime lien may be affected by the change in the mode of payment of wages. Traditionally wages were paid for each voyage and on discharge. The lien arises when the wages are due. Crew agreements now may provide for monthly

---

100. Supreme Court Act 1981, s.20(2)(o).
101. [1965] 1 Lloyd's Rep. 565.
102. [1965] 2 Lloyd's Rep. 183.
103. [1968] 2 Lloyd's Rep. 559.
104. The case concerned a claim by the master for disbursements for payments made which the judge held turned on whether the payment in respect (*inter alia*) of the contributions were emoluments.
105. [1981] LMLN 36.
106. The issue was whether a caveat could be lodged in respect of the claim.
107. [1991] 1 Lloyd's Rep. 330.

payments and if so may provide for additional amounts to be paid after discharge[108] —when the ship may have left the United Kingdom.[109]

"SEAMEN"

By the Merchant Shipping Act 1995[110] reproducing the 1894 Act in turn reproducing in substance the Merchant Shipping Act 1854,[111] "seamen" includes every person except masters and pilots employed or engaged in any capacity on board any ship. On its face the definition is wide and has been construed in that way. So it includes medical practitioners,[112] pursers,[113] a steward in charge of a bar[114]—as looking at the definition, would be expected.

The Supreme Court Act 1981 follows the Administration of Justice Act 1956 in substituting "member of the crew" for "seaman", a phrase which appears narrower in scope than any person employed in any capacity on board any ship. In so far as it is more restricted the maritime lien thereby excluded is preserved either by s.21(3) or if it includes "*in rem*" jurisdiction s.20(1)(c) of the Act of 1981 through the "sweeping up" provision of the Act of 1956.[115]

(iv) Masters' wages[116]

The masters' maritime lien for wages is the creature of statutory provisions conferring (in 1844) "all the rights liens privileges and remedies belonging to any seaman or mariner",[117] and after further statutory replacements[118] (in 1995) "the same lien for his remuneration . . . as the seaman has for his wages".[119]

---

108. Merchant Shipping Act 1970 s.7 as amended by Merchant Shipping Act 1988 s.46 (after 1 January 1996 Merchant Shipping Act 1995 s.30(1)).

109. If the ship is one of a fleet there may be an action *in rem* against a "sister ship" (see *infra*)—and further the maritime lien may continue to be exercisable for a number of years (see Chapter 18).

110. Section 313(1).

111. Merchant Shipping Act 1854, s.2. Compare the equivalent statutory provisions relating to the Admiralty jurisdiction of the county courts (see *R.* v. *Judge of City of London Court and Owners of S.S. Michigan* (1890) 25 Q.B.D. 339).

112. See Merchant Shipping Act 1970, s.43; 1995, s.47; *The Prince George* (1837) 3 Hag.Adm. 376.

113. *The Prince George* (1837) 3 Hag.Adm. 376.

114. *Thompson* v. *H. and W. Nelson* [1913] 2 K.B. 523. In *R.* v. *Judge of City of London Court and Owners of S.S. Michigan* (1890) 25 Q.B.D. 339 Lord Coleridge in a *dictum* said that the definition "would undoubtedly include such a person as a stevedore".

115. i.e. s.1(1) proviso. If not "conferred" by the Supreme Court of Judicature (Consolidation) Act 1925, s.22(1)(vii) it was part of the law prior to 1875 (see Administration of Justice Act 1956, s.1)—(as to ambit of the sweeping up provision, see *supra*).

116. By the Merchant Shipping Act 1995, s.313(1), "master" includes every person (except a pilot) having command or charge of any ship and in relation to a "fishing vessel" means the skipper. As to current statutory provisions governing wages, see the Merchant Shipping Act 1995 ss.30–41.

117. Merchant Seamen Act 1844, s.16.

118. Merchant Shipping Acts 1854, s.191, and 1894, s.167(1).

119. Merchant Shipping Act 1970, s.18; 1995, s.41. There is no definition of "remuneration" which, if anything, seems wider than "wages". As to the scope of masters' wages, see *The Arina* (1886) 12 P.D. 119. The wage of masters and seamen rank *pari passu* (*The Royal Wells* [1984] 2 Lloyd's Rep. 255). The prohibition on renouncing of a seaman's lien does not apply to a master (see the positive exclusion of master from the definition of seaman introduced by Merchant Shipping Act 1970, s.100(3); Sch 3, para. 4 and now in the 1995 Act, s.313(1), and *The Wilhelm Tell* [1892] P. 337). As to renouncing of liens, see Chap. 17.

(v) Masters' disbursements

The maritime lien is statutory, originating in the Merchant Shipping Act 1889, s.1, reproduced in the Merchant Shipping Act 1894, s.167(2):

"The master of a ship ... shall so far as the case permits have the same rights liens and remedies for the recovery of disbursements or liabilities properly made or incurred by him on account of the ship as a master has for the recovery of his wages."

It thereby equated the lien ultimately with that of the seaman for his wages with the extension to "liabilities" and the qualifications of (i) "so far as the case permits" and (ii) "properly made by him". In 1892 in *The Castlegate*[120] the House of Lords held that disbursements could properly be incurred only if within the express or implied authority of the owner.[121] Lord Watson thought that the phrase "so far as the case permits" seemed to indicate that disbursements, even though properly incurred, may in certain instances not attract a lien.

The 1894 provision was replaced by the Merchant Shipping Act 1970, s.18 (as from 1 January 1996 the Merchant Shipping Act 1995, s.41), in the same section as that conferring on the master a lien for wages.

"The master of a ship shall have the same lien for his remuneration and all disbursements or liabilities properly made or incurred by him on account of the ship, as a seaman has for his wages."

The omission of the phrase "so far as the case permits" seems of no effect simply because it is difficult to appreciate what the effect of the phrase was. The direct linking of the lien to wages only accomplishes that which previous provisions accomplished indirectly, and cannot therefore be said to alter the requirement of the owner's authority—a requirement not present in the wages lien.

WHAT ARE DISBURSEMENTS OR LIABILITIES?

The meaning of the word "disbursements" in Admiralty practice is disbursements by the master for which he makes himself liable in respect of necessary things for the ship for the

"purposes of navigation, which he, as master of the ship, is there to carry out—necessary in the sense that they must be had immediately—and when the owner is not there, able to give the order, and he is not so near to the master that the master can ask for his authority, and the master is therefore obliged, necessarily, to render himself liable in order to carry out his duty as master."[122]

---

120. [1893] A.C. 38. The judgments rely partly on general principles of maritime law and partly on the construction placed on the former statutory provision (in the Admiralty Court Act 1861)—"disbursement made ... on account of the ship." As to the need for personal liability of the owner, compare *The Ripon City* [1897] P. 226. As to this requirement, see further Chap. 17.

121. The maritime lien exists whether the owner is full or part owner. (*The Feronia* (1868) L.R. 2 A. & E. 65.)

122. *The Orienta* [1895] P. 39, at p. 55 per Lord Esher M.R.). So a master who, at the shipowner's request, drew a bill of exchange on the shipowner in payment for coal could not recover—his liability was not as master but drawer of the bill. See also *The Elmville (No. 2)* [1904] P. 422. Compare *The Ripon City* [1897] P. 226 (bill drawn in pursuance of coaling contract). See also *The Fairport* (1882) 8 P.D. 48.

The provision of "liabilities" ensures the demise of the doctrine once espoused[123] that a master may claim recompense only for payments actually made. The payment made or liability incurred must be properly incurred "on account of the ship in the ordinary course of the master's employment"[124] and are linked to the concept of necessaries and bottomry. Indeed, as in a sense, the master's claim is the other side of the coin to that of the supplier of necessaries, and "disbursements" are to be understood in the same broad way as "necessaries".

The lien extends only to disbursements which a master has "a right to make on the credit of the owners of the ship" and does not extend to disbursements for which charterers are responsible.[125] There is no lien on the freight unless there is also a lien on the ship.[126] It is said by some that payment of wages can be a ground for a claim for disbursements, but it seems that this was based on the principle that a wages lien is thereby transferred.[127] As such it falls foul of the now established rule that such payment does not put the payer in the position of a wages lien holder.[128] On the other hand, it may be argued that unlike cases of payment by other than a master, it may come within the concept of disbursement.

(vi) Bottomry and respondentia

BOTTOMRY

Bottomry is a method of raising money which in 1926 was described as "out of common use at the present day and unfamiliar in current practice". Almost all textbooks now describe it as "obsolete". Yet the Supreme Court Act 1981 repeats the provision of the Administration of Justice Act 1956 in specifying that a claim arising out of bottomry is within Admiralty jurisdiction and even if the statute was silent it may fall within the "sweeping up" provision.[129]

The bottomry transaction is based on maritime risk. It provides a master or owner of a ship with a method of obtaining funds through the giving of a loan in a situation of necessity when the owner's credit will not gain such funds. "The want of personal credit, the necessity of defraying the expense of repairs and outfit to complete the voyage, the exigency occasioned by distress from wind weather and accident, the sum required—all these are circumstances which justify the execution of a bottomry bond."[130]

---

123. See e.g. *The Chieftain* (1863) B. & L. 104. But not strictly followed. See e.g. *The Elmville (No. 2)* [1904] P. 422, at p. 425; *The Fairport* (1882) 8 P.D. 48; *The Feronia* (1868) L.R. 2 A. & E. 65.
124. See *The Ripon City* [1897] P. 226, at pp. 233–234. The defence costs of a master defending himself against a false charge acting from the exercise of disciplinary duty is within the principle. *The James Seddon* (1866) 1 A. & E. 62.
125. See *The Castlegate* [1893] A.C. 38 and Chap. 3.
126. *Ibid.*
127. See *The Tagus* [1903] P. 44, at p. 54.
128. See *The Petone* [1917] P. 198.
129. As to which, see *supra*. For more recent cases in which bottomry transactions were relevant, see *The Comet* [1965] 1 Lloyd's Rep. 195; *Paschalis* v. *The Ship Tona Maria* [1975] 1 Cyp.L.R. 162.
130. *The Royal Arch* (1857) Swab. 269, at p. 275 (Dr Lushington). It was there said a bond given at a home port would not be given in necessity (see p. 277). It is the inability to rely on the owner's personal credit that supports a bottomry bond (*The Nelson* (1823) 1 Hag.Adm. 169, at p. 175); and it is evidence to show the ship's need to prosecute the voyage (see *The St. George* [1926] P. 217, at p. 226). See also *The Karnak* (1869) L.R. 2 P.C. 505.

Ship, cargo and freight may be given[131] as security for the provision of the bond, and the whole transaction is focused on the security. First, there is no personal liability on the owner,[132] and, indeed, one essential criterion for the validity of a bottomry transaction is that the owner is not seen as under any liability to repay.[133] Secondly, repayment is (and for validity of the transactions as bottomry must be) dependent on the arrival of the ship.[134] Subject to exceptions based primarily on prevention of completion of the voyage by the owner or master[135] if the ship does not arrive no repayment is due, and if it does arrive it is the ship (and cargo where appropriate) against which the lender must claim. Thirdly, the principle developed that if a master wished to enter into a bottomry bond he must make all possible efforts to contact the owner. If he did not make such effort the security was void.[136]

The security interest conferred in the bottomry transaction has been firmly distinguished from a mortgage.[137] It is said to be hypothecation to be enforced through legal process. In 1897 the interest conferred was said to be a "maritime lien" by Gorell Barnes J. in listing the claims to which such a lien attached.[138] And, prior to the creation of the concept of maritime lien in 1851, it was undoubtedly viewed as such a lien.[139] Subject to the possibility of a sister ship action the claim in Admiralty and maritime lien are one and the same.

The utility of the bottomry transaction was clearly affected by the conferring of a maritime lien on the claim for masters' disbursements and the development of a lien for necessaries. Further, and more importantly, there are fewer occasions when a master *needs* immediate funds without alternative methods of acquiring them and perhaps fewer lenders who are willing to lend on the security of the arrival of a ship.

RESPONDENTIA

Respondentia appears to be a parallel security interest to bottomry but involving only cargo.[140] The principles applicable to it seem identical to that of bottomry.[141]

131. Resort must be had to ship and freight prior to cargo where all these are made the subject of security—ship and freight being liable *pro rata* (see *The Dowthorpe* (1843) 2 W.Rob. 73, at p. 85; *The Bonaparte* (1859) 7 Not.Cas.Supp. 55. As to arrest available in relation to maritime liens, see Chap. 15.
132. See further Chap. 18.
133. But a bottomry bond may be collateral security for bills of exchange drawn on owners. If honoured, the bottomry is discharged. See *Stainbank* v. *Shepard* (1853) 13 C.B. 418, at p. 444.
134. *Stainbank* v. *Fenning* (1851) 11 C.B. 51, at pp. 87–88 (Jervis L.C.); *Stainbank* v. *Shepard* (1853) 13 C.B. 418—cases dealing with similar issues; *The Haabet* [1899] P. 295; *The James W. Elwell* [1921] P. 351.
135. See e.g. *The Dante* (1846) 2 W. Rob. 427. Prevention from sailing because of unseaworthiness is also a ground (*ibid.*).
136. See *The Royal Arch* (1857) Swab. 269, at pp. 275–276 (Dr Lushington); *The St. George* [1926] P. 217.
137. In *The Tobago* (1804) 5 C. Rob. 218 it was said not to create a property right recognizable by the Prize Court. As to the view that a lien is a proprietary interest, see Chaps. 17 and 18.
138. *The Ripon City* [1897] P. 226, at p. 242.
139. See e.g. *The Aline* (1839) 1 W. Rob. 111 (where reference is made to claims in salvage, wages, damage and bottomry); *The Janet Wilson* (1857) Swab. 261—both cases of priority. *The Dowthorpe* (1843) 2 W. Rob. 73, at p. 79.
140. See *The Atlas* (1827) 2 Hag.Adm. 48; *The Sultan (Cargo ex)* (1850) Swab. 504. It is not referred to in the Supreme Court Act 1981 but is clearly within the sweeping up provision if that provision extends to *in rem* jurisdiction (and may perhaps be implied from "bottomry").
141. See *The Sultan (Cargo ex)* (1859) Swab. 504.

(e) Statutory extensions by analogy

Although in all instances save those of masters' wages and disbursements the maritime liens have their origin in judicial doctrine, statutes have extended the scope of the liens in most categories. The intervention has not always been expressed as extending the "maritime lien", but more often than not in terms of Admiralty jurisdiction. It was for the courts to decide whether the extension of jurisdiction meant the extension of the maritime lien. Once it was clear that a right *in rem* could exist apart from a maritime lien it was also clear that any statutory extension of jurisdiction or even of remedy would not automatically carry with it a maritime lien. As has been seen, in relation to the foundation statutory framework of 1840 and 1861 where the area of jurisdiction was extended (e.g. from the high seas to "within the body of a county") it was an extension of the lien which had existed in the narrower area. Where a claim not attracting a maritime lien was brought within the Admiralty jurisdiction *in rem* it was as a statutory lien. Doubts mainly arose in the instances where claims were brought within the Admiralty jurisdiction specifically by analogy with those already attracting maritime liens.

Where, as with masters' wages and disbursements, the new claims were said to attract the same "rights liens and remedies" as one already attracting maritime lien there is no uncertainty. And even the phrase "rights and remedies" (without express reference to liens) is open to little doubt. But in some cases the analogy is restricted to means or manner of recovery—leaving a considerable doubt.

(i) Probable maritime lien by statutory analogy

RECOVERY OF FEES AND EXPENSES BY RECEIVER OF WRECK

Bearing the confusing development in a jurisdictional context in mind there seems only one additional class of claim to which in all probability a maritime lien is attached. The Merchant Shipping Act 1894 conferred on the receiver of wreck " . . . the same rights and remedies in respect of his fees and expenses as a salvor has in respect of salvage due to him".[142] Whatever the view of the maritime lien—be it right or remedy—it is difficult to argue that it is not thereby carried on from salvor to receiver.

(ii) Doubtful maritime liens by statutory analogy[143]

1. Remuneration for coastguard services in respect of wreck.
2. Compensation for damage to lands adjoining wreck.

1. REMUNERATION OF COASTGUARD IN RESPECT OF WRECK

An owner of wreck is under a statutory obligation to pay fees to coastguards who watch or protect his shipwrecked property unless the services were declined or salvage paid. The remuneration is recoverable "by the same means" as fees received by receiver.[144]

142. Merchant Shipping Act 1894, s.567(2); Merchant Shipping Act 1995, s.249(3).
143. It was suggested by Price (op. cit. *Law of Maritime Liens*, p. 2) that under the Diseases of Animals Act 1950, s.75(2) a local authority had a maritime lien in respect of expenses incurred in buying or destroying animal carcasses washed ashore. The provision ceased to have effect on the enactment of the Administration of Justice Act 1956 (see s.7(1)).
144. Merchant Shipping Act 1894, s.568(1); Merchant Shipping Act 1995, s.250(2).

It has been contended that this applies the maritime lien already applied to the receiver.[145] It is, however, not nearly so clear cut as the extension to a receiver. The difference in terminology as regards extension to receiver and further extension to coastguard is hardly meaningless. Further, a dispute procedure is provided in relation to receivers' fees and "means" therefore can carry a positive meaning apart from "rights and remedies". It therefore seems unlikely that there is a maritime lien in respect of such remuneration.

2. DAMAGE TO LANDS ADJOINING WRECK

If there is no public road a statutory right is given to pass over land adjoining wreck to render assistance to shipwrecked persons or property and to deposit articles recovered on such land.[146] Any damage sustained by an owner or occupier because of such action "shall be a charge on the vessel, cargo or articles in respect of which or by which the damage is occasioned".[147] The compensation is recoverable "in the same manner as the amount of salvage" under the 1894 or 1995 Act as applicable.[148]

It has been contended that it is "hard to resist" the conclusion that by virtue of the statutory provisions of the 1894 Act the owner or occupier has a maritime lien for the reasons that (i) a "charge" is consistent with such a lien and (ii) a maritime lien is one of the "remedies" contemplated by the Act.[149] But, with respect, first, "charge" is as consistent with a statutory as with a maritime lien[150] and indeed is connected with any statutory interest. Secondly, the phrase "in the same manner as . . . " surely refers to the procedure of recovery. Again, therefore, the existence of a maritime lien is open to doubt.

(f) Claims in respect of which a maritime lien has been suggested

(i) Necessaries.
(ii) Towage.
(iii) Pilotage.
(iv) Liability for damage done by ships to harbours, piers, etc.

(i) Necessaries

Since the latter part of the nineteenth century it has been settled in England that there is no maritime lien for necessaries.[151]

(ii) Towage

In 1889 in *Westrup* v. *Great Yarmouth Steam Co.*[152] Kay J. discussed the authorities at length and, following *dicta* of the Court of Appeal in *The Heinrich Bjorn*,[153] held that

---

145. Thomas, *Maritime Liens, op. cit.*, para. 21.
146. Merchant Shipping Act 1894, s.513(1).
147. *Ibid.*, s.513(2).
148. 1894 Act s.513(2); 1995 Act s.234(6).
149. Thomas, *Maritime Liens, op. cit.*, para. 22. See also Price, *Law of Maritime Liens, op. cit.*, p. 2.
150. Thomas finds support in a *dictum* of Hewson J. in *The St Merriel* [1963] P. 247, 254 to the effect that the provision gives to the owners "the same rights as the holder of a lien"—referring to maritime lien.
151. See *The Heinrich Bjorn* (1886) 11 App.Cas. 270.
152. (1889) 43 Ch.D. 241.
153. (1885) 10 P.D. 44; on appeal (1886) 11 App.Cas. 270.

there was no maritime lien. This decision was approved in 1923 by Hill J. when considering the question of whether an action *in rem* would lie in respect of pilotage.[154] More directly in 1919 in *Carrow Towing Co.* v. *The Ed McWilliams*[155] the Exchequer Court in Canada followed the *Westrup* case in declaring that no maritime lien exists for towage.

(iii) Pilotage

The issue was left open in the only case in England to discuss it specifically. In 1923 in *The Ambatielos and The Cephalonia*[156] Hill J. agreed that a claim by a pilot for remuneration may be brought by an action *in rem*.[157] Hill J. refused to decide whether there was a maritime lien in the absence of mortgagees of the relevant ship. He drew no analogy with towage but with seamen's wages, and the policy basis for the wages maritime lien may apply with equal force to pilotage.

Such authority as there is, therefore is in favour of a maritime lien and there is none against. Nevertheless, it may well be that the general judicial reluctance towards extensions of a powerful but unpublicized right would defeat any such contention. But it remains more uncertain than some texts would have it.[158]

(iv) Damage done by ships to harbours, piers, etc

The Harbours, Docks and Piers Clauses Act 1847, s.74, provides that:

"The owner of every vessel . . . shall be answerable to the undertaker for any damage done by such vessel . . . or by any person employed about the same, to the harbour, dock or pier, or the quays or works connected therewith . . . and the undertaker may detain any such vessel . . . until sufficient security has been given for the amount of damage done by the same."

On its wording, the section creates a possessory lien or at the most a security interest dependent initially on detention. The only argument in favour of a maritime lien must be as an extension of the judicially created "damage" maritime lien. Against that argument is the specific provision relating to detention, a provision similar to powers given in other contexts to public authorities in the enforcement of rights.

In 1874 in *The Merle*[159] Sir Robert Phillimore held that the section placed damage to a pier "in the category of damage giving a maritime lien upon the ship inflicting it". The primary issues in the case were:

  (i) whether under statutory provision, the owner of the pier succeeded to the statutory rights of the previous owner who had constructed it;
 (ii) whether there could be recovery for damage caused by inevitable accident;
(iii) whether if (i) and (ii) were answered in favour of the plaintiffs they could enforce their right by an action *in rem*.

154. In *The Ambatielos and the Cephalonia* [1923] P. 68.
155. (1919) 46 D.L.R. 506. See also *The Santa Maria* (1917) 36 D.L.R. 619.
156. [1923] P. 68.
157. Citing *The Nelson* (1805) 7 C. Rob. 227 and *The Bee* (1822) 2 Dods. 498 as early cases in which pilotage claims were heard and *The Clan Grant* (1887) 6 Asp. M.L.C. 144 as a more recent case.
158. As to the authorities, see *The Adah* (1830) 2 Hag.Adm. 326; *La Constancia* (1846) 2 W.Rob. 404; *The St. Lawrence* (1880) L.R. 5 P.D. 250; *The Servia and the Carinthia* [1898] P. 36. As to the uncertainty, see e.g. Thomas, *Maritime Liens*, p. 17, where towage and pilotage are said to have "a certain parallel".
159. (1874) 2 Asp. M.L.C. 402.

A subsidiary contention seems to have been made—that even if an action *in rem* would lie the claim did not "travel with the transfer of the property to the plaintiffs" as it did not attract a maritime lien.

The judge in effect found for the plaintiffs on the three primary questions and held that by statute the privileges of the previous owner was transferred to the present owner. He expressed his opinion that despite the lack of need to prove fault a maritime lien was attracted to the claim. Particularly was this so, he thought, because of the power of detention conferred on the pier owners by the Act.

The case is unsatisfactory in that first, the statutory provision of itself is clearly not capable of being the source of a maritime lien and, secondly, the lack of the need to prove fault distinguishes its characteristics from the established damage lien. To confer a maritime lien distinct in nature from its progenitor would surely require more specific wording—particularly as the statutory provision specifically provides the right to detain.

(g) "Or other charge"

This phrase is taken directly from the Administration of Justice Act 1956. It has been construed by Hewson J. to refer (a) in English law to "charges" which by statute are equated to maritime liens; (b) as to foreign law to "any charge on a vessel given under the law of any nation to secure claims similar to those recognized by this Court as carrying a maritime lien".[160] In other words, a charge which is attached to a claim which in substance is one recognized in English law as attracting a maritime lien. On this view the phrase adds little—but is nevertheless retained in the Act of 1981.

(ii) Claims enforceable by action in rem against the relevant property or ownership of a share in a ship

(a) Claim to ownership or possession of a ship or share in a ship (s.20(2)(a))

The jurisdiction of the Admiralty Court in disputes relating to possession has its roots in its inherent or non-statutory jurisdiction. Its power to decide questions of title was limited until the Admiralty Court Act 1840, s.4 of which conferred power to decide "all questions as to the title or ownership of any ship or vessel or the proceeds thereof remaining in the Registry arising in any cause of possession, salvage, damage, wages or bottomry . . . ". That wording was carried forward into the Supreme Court of Judicature (Consolidation) Act 1925.[161] It was replaced in the Act of 1956 by the wording of the present provision which bases the jurisdiction on claims *to* possession or ownership of a ship or ownership of a share in a ship.[162]

Any restriction to direct claims following from the change must be counterbalanced by the inclusion of the more general in the "sweeping up" provision. In that context

---

160. See, as to English law, *The St Merriel* [1963] P. 247 and *infra*; as to foreign law, *The Acrux* [1965] P. 391.

161. Supreme Court of Judicature (Consolidation) Act 1925, s.22(1)(a)(i).

162. See, for an example of exercise of jurisdiction *The Bineta* [1967] 1 W.L.R. 121, where a declaration of ownership was made in favour of a purchaser from a vendor who had exercised the right of resale following failure of another purchaser to pay the price. The declaration was necessary to allow the claimant to obtain registration in place of the first "purchaser" who had not paid the sale price.

stemming from its inherent jurisdiction the court has a power to rectify the register so as to delete an entry inconsistent with a claimant's title[163] or order delivery up of a certificate of registry of a British ship.[164] There is statutory power (i.e. discretion) to prohibit for a specific time on the application of "an interested person" any dealing in a registered ship or a registered share in a registered ship.[165] Such a power is a substantive right but "an interested person" extends only to a person with a proprietary interest[166] or at least a person having a claim against the ship which could lead to such an interest.[167] It does not include a mere personal creditor.[168]

(b) Any questions arising between co-owners of a ship as to possession, employment or earnings of the ship (s.20(2)(b), 20(4))

The court may settle any account outstanding between the parties in relation to the ship and direct the ship or share of the ship to be sold or "make any such other order as the court think fit.[169] The wording has survived from the Admiralty Court Act 1861.[170]

In *The Vanessa Ann*[171] there was a dispute between co-owners as to a charterparty. Staughton J. ordered release from arrest at the instance of one co-owner on condition that those wishing the ship to be chartered created an equitable mortgage on the ship, the ship being unregistered.[172] The judge acted on the view that arrest was a discretionary remedy but currently the judicial approach is that it is an entitlement (see Chap. 15). It may be, therefore, that the discretion in relation to co-owner claims where the issue is release from arrest is in that respect not as wide as contemplated.[173]

Foreign ownership

English law recognizes foreign ownership in the sense that actions may be brought in relation to it, and substantive questions relevant to ship ownership will be referred to the law of the state of registration of the ship. Formalities of any sale transaction may be

---

163. *Brond* v. *Broomhall* [1906] 1 K.B. 571.

164. See *The Frances* (1820) 2 Dods. 420; *The St Olaf* (1877) 2 P.D. 113. There is also clearly jurisdiction to decide a property issue in an action under another head of claim. See e.g. *The Saetta* [1993] 2 Lloyd's Rep. 268.

165. Merchant Shipping Act 1995, Sch. 1, para. 6, re-enacting Merchant Shipping (Registration etc.) Act 1993, Sch. 1, para. 6, replacing Merchant Shipping Act 1894, s.30. The power falls within Admiralty jurisdiction by virtue of s.20(3)(1), see *infra*.

166. *The Mikado* [1992] 1 Lloyd's Rep. 163. Under the 1894 Act power was not restricted to the control of unqualified persons acquiring title to British ships except by transfer even though it appears in conjunction with those powers (*ibid.* following and adopting *Beneficial Finance Corpn Ltd.* v. *Price* [1965] 1 Lloyd's Rep. 556). Although the power is now specifically restricted to registered ships there is no reason to restrict it to any particular type of dealing.

167. See *The Siben* [1994] 2 Lloyd's Rep. 420 (C.A. of Jersey)—plaintiff seeking to rescind contract of sale within provision.

168. *The Mikado* (*supra*); *The Siben* (*supra*).

169. A court may order a sale (although reluctantly) even on the application of a minority: see *The Hereward* [1895] P. 284.

170. The provision also included "ownership"—this now being unnecessary because of the generalizing of the jurisdiction to include ownership claims. As to bail in possession cases, see Chap. 15.

171. [1985] 1 Lloyd's Rep. 549. Accounts were also ordered.

172. Together with undertakings to procure a registered mortgage. As to mortgages of unregistered ships see Chap. 23.

173. Co-owners in the majority could bring an action for possession while those in the minority (as arguably in *The Vanessa Ann*) have to arrest and obtain security for their interest (an action of "restraint").

referred to the law of the place of the transaction, and any dealings in an unregistered ship should it, it is suggested, be referred to the law most closely connected with the transaction. Questions of procedure, remedies and priority should be referred to the law of the forum.[174]

(c) Any claim in respect of a mortgage of or charge on a ship or any share therein (s.20(2)(c), 20(7)(c))

Mortgage

The Supreme Court Act 1981 is in identical terms to the Administration of Justice Act 1956. The earlier Act extended the jurisdiction in regard to mortgage claims as compared to that set out in the Supreme Court of Judicature (Consolidation) Act 1925. Under the Act of 1925 jurisdiction in respect of unregistered mortgages was limited to a ship (or proceeds) under arrest of the court.[175] The jurisdiction now extends to claims in respect of any "mortgage" whether it be registered or unregistered, legal or equitable, English or foreign.[176]

"Charge"

The word "charge" does not appear before the Act of 1956, the equivalent provisions of earlier statutes referring only to mortgages.

In 1963 in *The St Merriel*[177] and in 1965 in *The Acrux*[178] Hewson J. construed the phrase to mean a charge in the nature of a mortgage. This limited construction is perhaps borne out first by the complex structure of liens ("charges" in a wide sense) created by the statute, secondly, by the reference in the equivalent Article of the Arrest Convention to "mortgage and hypothecation", and thirdly by the English concepts of the equitable charge in general and the floating charge in particular thereby providing English legal substance to the narrow interpretation.

Foreign mortgage or charges

Whatever the extent of the "charge" in the case of a foreign transaction it will be for English law to define whether it is a "mortgage" or "charge" within the statute. Only at that point will (a) jurisdiction be created under the Act[179] and (b) foreign law become

---

174. See generally Chap. 26. It may be that the court would decline to decide a question of title where there is little connection with England (see *The Jupiter (No. 2)* [1925] P. 69; *The Courageous Colocotronis* [1979] W.A.R. 19); *The Lakhta* [1992] 2 Lloyd's Rep. 269.

175. Supreme Court of Judicature (Consolidation) Act 1925, s.22(1)(a)(ix), itself extending s.3 of the Act of 1840 and incorporating s.11 of the Act of 1861.

176. As to the inherent jurisdiction to rectify the register in respect of such a claim, see *Brond* v. *Broomhall* [1906] 1 K.B. 571.

177. [1963] P. 247.

178. [1965] P. 391.

179. See the approach of Hewson J. in *The Acrux* (*supra*) in considering whether a right granted under Italian law amounted to a "maritime lien" under the Act of 1956. See further Chaps. 18 and 26.

relevant. Matters relevant to the substance of the mortgage (creation, validity, etc.) will be referred to the law of registration of the ship; matters of procedure, remedy and priority to the law of the forum.[180]

(d) Any claims for the forfeiture or condemnation of ship or goods, the restoration of ship or goods after seizure or droits of Admiralty (s.20(2)(s))

A ship

There are a number of statutory provisions relating to the condemnation and forfeiture of ships,[181] the most relevant of which today are those relevant to acts committed contrary to Customs and Excise requirements. In relation to the latter the Customs and Excise Management Act 1979 provides for proceedings either in the High Court or in a magistrates' court,[182] and s.20(2)(s) of the Supreme Court Act 1981 provides for the High Court jurisdiction to be exercised by the Admiralty Court.[183]

A ship is subject to forfeiture[184]

> (i) where the master or owner of a British ship does anything or permits anything to be done to conceal the nationality of the ship[185];
> (ii) subject to two exceptions where the master or owner of a non-British ship does anything or permits anything to be done for the purpose of causing the ship to appear to be a British ship[186];
> (iii) where property in a registered British ship or share is transmitted to a person not qualified to own it and no order of sale is granted[187];

A ship is liable to forfeiture in relation to Customs and Excise requirements if it is adapted for concealing goods,[188] used for the exporting of stores contrary to a prohibition or restriction,[189] used for shipping or carrying coastwise contrary to regulations,[190] if

---

180. See Chap. 26.

181. For an example of what presumably would now be a rarely used provision, see the Slave Trade Act 1824, s.4; A ship may be forfeited for piracy.

182. There are restrictions on the forfeiture of ships over 250 tons register (s.142). See Sch. 3. See also the Immigration Act 1971 providing under certain conditions for forfeiture of a ship used to carry illegal entrants (s.25(6)).

183. For an example of intervention *in rem* by the Commissioners of Customs and Excise, see *The Skylark* [1965] 2 Lloyd's Rep. 250.

184. As to the procedure to be adopted, see *ibid.* s.76. Forfeiture may be of the ship, tackle or furniture. It is probable that a bona fide purchaser of a ship subject to forfeiture will be protected (see *The Annandale* (1877) 2 P.D. 218). Such a limitation is hardly consistent with the right stemming from the action *in rem* (see Chaps. 10 and 19).

185. Merchant Shipping Act 1995, s.3(4), (5); Sch. 3, para. 5(4), (5). As to British ship see *ibid.*, para. 1. Illegal colours hoisted on board a British ship may be seized by an authorized officer and if seized are forfeited (*ibid.*, s.4(3), (4)).

186. *Ibid.*, Sch. 3, para. 5(1). The exceptions go to escaping capture in war and the continued display of registration marks for 14 days after ending of registration (*ibid.*, s.3(2), (3)).

187. *Ibid.* Sch. 1, para. 4(4). As to the obligation to register a British ship and exemption from that obligation, see ss.2 and 3.

188. Customs and Excise Management Act 1979, s.88.

189. *Ibid.* s.68(5).

190. *Ibid.* s.74.

cargo is jettisoned or destroyed to prevent seizure,[191] if the master is unable to account for missing cargo,[192] or is used for the carriage of any thing liable to forfeiture.[193]

Goods

Any court having Admiralty jurisdiction may declare dangerous goods, not marked as such but sent on board any vessel, forfeited together with any package or receptacle in which they are contained.[194] There are a variety of Customs and Excise provisions relating to forfeiture of goods which may in appropriate circumstances fall within s.20(2)(s).[195]

Claims for droits in Admiralty

These are perquisites of the Lord High Admiral which were transferred to the Crown in 1703 and subsequently were reserved to the Crown.[196] The proceeds are now paid into the Exchequer. They comprise:

(i) jetsam, flotsam, lagan and derelict[197] found at sea of which the owner does not appear "in due time"[198];

(ii) goods and ships taken from pirates (but apparently not property in the possession of pirates and belonging to others)[199];

(iii) royal fishes such as whale or sturgeon.[200]

The mandatory procedure provided by the Merchant Shipping Act 1894[201] for settling the title to wrecks and for their delivery to and disposal by a Receiver makes the likelihood of this aspect of High Court jurisdiction unlikely to be frequently exercised. The "wreck"

191. *Ibid.* s.89.
192. *Ibid.* s.90.
193. *Ibid.* s.141. The liability to forfeiture is absolute (subject to the restriction as to ships in s.142): *Customs and Excise Commissioners* v. *Air Canada* [1991] 2 Q.B. 446 (C.A.).
194. Merchant Shipping Act 1894, s.449(1); 1993 Act, Sch. 4 para. 11(2)(a)—as from 1 January 1996, 1995 Act, s.87(1). The power may be exercised without the owner being present at or having knowledge of the proceedings (1894 Act, s.449(2); 1993 Act, Sch. 4, para. 11(2)(1); 1995 Act, s.87(3)).
195. See Customs and Excise Management Act 1979, ss.28(2), 49, 53, 66(2), 67 and 78(4).
196. See *R.* v. *Forty Nine Casks of Brandy* (1836) Hag.Adm. 257, at pp. 280–281. They are to be distinguished from droits of the Crown which are enemy vessels or goods seized at sea, the proceeds of which are paid to the Naval Prize Fund (see e.g. *The Anichab* [1921] P. 218—a decision of the Naval Prize Tribunal).
197. "Derelict" is a ship abandoned by master and crew without any intention to return and no hope of recovery—it includes a floating and sunken ship and its cargo: *The Lusitania* [1986] Q.B. 384; [1986] 1 Lloyd's Rep. 132.
198. *R.* v. *Property Derelict* (1825) 1 Hag.Adm. 383. Due time appears to be within a year and a day (see MacLlachan, *Merchant Shipping Law*, p. 522). For an interesting view as to the rights of those finding droits on the sea to be paid as salvors, see Marsden (1899) 15 L.Q.R. 353. It is there contended that it was wrongly decided in *Wills* v. *Owners of Gas Float Whitton (No. 2)* [1897] A.C. 337 that salvage was payable only in respect of ships and their cargo.
199. *The Panda* (1842) 1 W. Rob. 423; Piracy Act 1850, s.5. One eighth of value can be claimed for restoration under this section which relates to taking by Her Majesty's ships (*ibid.*).
200. *Lord Warden of Cinque Ports* v. *R.* (1831) 2 Hag.Adm. 438, at p. 441. The whale was arrested and the case was on the issue whether the droit had been conveyed to the Lord Warden or was rightly claimed by the Crown. It was admitted that salvage would be paid to fishermen who towed the whale ashore.
201. Part IX (as amended by Merchant Shipping (Registration etc.) Act 1993, Sch. 4 (as from 1 January 1996 Merchant Shipping Act 1995 Part IX, Chapter 2). Areas in United Kingdom waters in which there are wrecks of importance or potential danger may be protected by order (Protection of Wrecks Act 1973).

over which the Receiver exercises jurisdiction is that found "in or on the shore of the sea or tidal water" and found outside the limits of the United Kingdom and brought within it.[202]

However, the right of the Crown to wreck as a droit of Admiralty is not coincidental with the jurisdiction of the Receiver. The right of the Crown is now statutorily defined as to "all unclaimed wreck found in any part of Her Majesty's dominions". Wreck found elsewhere is not a droit of Admiralty. Whether or not brought within the United Kingdom a person in possession will in the likely event of no better claim have the best proprietary right in it.[203]

(iii) Claims enforceable "in rem" against a ship or "sister ship" (s.20(2)(d)–(r)) Jurisdiction and enforceability "in rem" compared

It is essential to distinguish between (a) Admiralty jurisdiction and (b) the ability to bring an action *in rem*. Much of the discussion in regard to the latter focuses on the ability to arrest a ship which to non English eyes must create further confusion. In a number of decisions there is a tendency for the nature of the claim to be confused with the ability to enforce that claim *in rem*—to telescope the provisions of s.20(2) with those of s.21(4). In particular, the prerequisite of enforcing a claim by an action *in rem* specified in s.21(4) that "the claim arises in connection with a ship" does not *control* the jurisdictional definition of the nature of the claim in s.20(2). The meaning of the phrase as it applies to enforceability by an action *in rem* will be considered in Chapter 10.

(a) Any claim for damage received by a ship (s.20(2)(d))

The availability of the action "in rem"

This is the one ground of claim specifically set out in s.20(2) of the Supreme Court Act which is omitted from the provision of s.21 allowing enforceability by an action *in rem*. The statute thereby confirmed the view expressed by the House of Lords in 1976 in *The Jade*.[204] In that case it was said that the inclusion of this ground in the Administration of Justice Act 1956 within the category of those attracting an action *in rem* was wrong. The ship in connection with which the claim arises, said Lord Diplock, would be that of the plaintiffs who could not "invoke the Admiralty jurisdiction by an action *in rem* against their own ship".[205] Lord Diplock stressed that for an action *in rem* to lie under the statute in respect of any claim by express provision it had to be in connection with a ship. That ship must be the ship specified in the Arrest Convention as "the particular ship in respect

---

202. Merchant Shipping Act 1906, s.72 (after 1 January 1996, 1995 Act, s.236).
203. *The Lusitania* [1986] Q.B. 384; [1986] 1 Lloyd's Rep. 132.
204. [1976] 2 Lloyd's Rep. 1. In the Court of Appeal the exclusion of an action *in rem* in any circumstance was the expressed view of Scarman L.J. who based his view on the general principle that the Arrest Convention envisaged arrest of the wrongdoing ship ([1976] 1 Lloyd's Rep. 81, at p. 91 and of Sir Gordon Willmer (at p. 94)). Cairns L.J. seemed to think that the ship referred to might be a ship not belonging to the plaintiff but having some connection with the damage (p. 88).
205. *Ibid.* at p. 9.

of which the maritime claims arose"—and therefore the inclusion of this head of claim could not lead to an action *in rem*.[206]

It has been earlier argued that, if the "sweeping-up" provision of the Supreme Court Act 1981 (s.20(1)(c)) encompasses *in rem* jurisdiction, the omission of this ground from those in regard to which an action *in rem* may be brought, of itself, has no effect. There is no prohibition on bringing such action and the jurisdiction to allow it was within that of the Admiralty Court "immediately before" the Supreme Court Act 1981.

The basis of liability

The basis of claim will depend on its legal characterization, e.g. tort,[207] contract, statute or the particular claim such as salvage. The Supreme Court Act 1981 simply connects ship and damage—the criteria applicable for success must be sought in the requirements for the particular claim.

Nature of the "damage"

In *The Jade* there was a motion to stay proceedings *in rem* alleging negligent salvage. The claim itself was based on a number of the grounds set out in the Act of 1956, including "damage received by a ship". Within that claim was the:

(i) damage to a ship;
(ii) damage to cargo;
(iii) damage to personal effects of the crew;
(iv) indemnity for any pollution claim in respect of pollution caused by the washing off the deck and into the sea of drums of insecticides and consequent damage and interference with fishing.

It was "accepted as a general proposition" that "consequential loss in the form of loss during repair" would come within the paragraph. Reading the paragraph as meaning "any claim arising out of damage received" Brandon J. at first instance held that the claim for indemnity by the shipowners fell within "damage" but that the claims by the crew and cargo owners fell outside it. In his view the paragraph referred to claims by owners or other persons interested in a ship receiving damage but did not extend to others suffering in consequence of such damage.[208] The Court of Appeal agreed.[209]

206. As to the requirement see s.21(4) and Chap. 10. In earlier cases Brandon J. held that claims *in rem* by owners of boats assisting a ship by towage (*The Conoco Britannia* [1972] 2 Q.B. 543) and provision of services (*The Queen of the South* [1968] P. 449) fell within para. (h) as being in each case an agreement for the hire of a ship. No mention was made of the fact that it was the plaintiff's ships that were the ships in connection with which the claim arose (see comment by Sir Gordon Willmer in *The Jade* (C.A.) [1976] 1 Lloyd's Rep. 81, at p. 96). See also *The Span Terza* [1982] 1 Lloyd's Rep. 225; *The Daien Maru No. 18* [1986] 1 Lloyd's Rep. 387, claims in relation to plaintiff's ship chartered to defendants. See further *infra* (d) and (e).

207. As e.g. (requiring proof of negligence) damage caused through collision with another ship (*The Utopia* [1893] A.C. 492) or damage received through use of a dock (see e.g. *The Devon* (1923) 16 Asp. M.L.C. 268; *The Hoegh Silvercrest* [1962] 1 Lloyd's Rep. 9).

208. [1974] 2 Lloyd's Rep. 188, at p. 194.

209. [1976] 1 Lloyd's Rep. 81, at pp. 88, 97. Sir Gordon Willmer thought that if liability for pollution was strict it was arguable that the root would be the statute imposing it (*ibid.* at p. 97). The House of Lords did not construe "damage" in the context of damage received by a ship (because of the holding that no action *in rem* lay) but clearly admitted consequential loss in the context of "damage by a ship" (see [1976] 2 Lloyd's Rep. 1, at p. 8).

Link between damage and person or thing causing it

"Damage" in the context of the statutory jurisdiction based on damage received by a ship was not, and it seems was not prior to 1840, restricted to damage caused by a collision between ships.[210] There would be no more reason to exclude consequential damage than in the case of damage done by a ship (see *infra*).

(b) Any claim for damage done by a ship (s.20(2)(e))

It appears that this head of claim is equivalent in nature to the maritime lien for damage, save (i) for doubt that the extension of the jurisdiction may not have extended the maritime lien and (ii) any question whether statutory and judicial developments in admitting novel heads of loss, damage and injury may not have brought these heads within Admiralty claims. The maritime lien for damage was considered earlier.

Link between damage and person or thing causing it

The damage must be the direct result of something done in the course of navigation of the ship and the ship must be the "actual instrument" by which the damage was done. However there is no requirement of physical contact.

"The commonest case is that of collision, which is specifically mentioned in the convention: but physical contact between the ship and whatever object sustains the damage is not essential—a ship may negligently cause a wash by which some other vessel or some property on shore is damaged."[211]

Loss of life

It should be recalled that the reasoning which excluded claims for loss of life from jurisdiction *in rem* was the view that while damage suffered by the claimant was damage arising out of damage done by a ship it was not damage done by it.[212] If this view is still followed a claim for loss of life will not fall under this head. In *The Jade*[213] two members of the Court of Appeal seemed to read "damage received by" and "damage done by" as including "damage arising out of" so as to include consequential loss. The line distinguishing a claim for loss of life from a claim for consequential loss is thin and should be erased.

Economic loss

In *The Jade* the ability to recover for consequential loss was based on the inclusion of pecuniary loss through liability to a third party. If this be right there is no reason why economic loss should not of itself be the ground of claim.[214]

---

210. See *The Zeta* [1893] A.C. 468 disapproving *The Robert Pow* (1863) B. & L. 99.

211. *The Jade* [1976] 2 Lloyd's Rep. 1, at p. 8 (H.L.). For an example of grounding to avoid a collision, see *The Miraflores and the Abadesa* [1976] 1 A.C. 826; of running a vessel into a wall because of the negligence of another ship, *The Industrie* (1871) L.R. 3 A. & E. 303.

212. It may now be argued that such claims fall within para. (f) (*infra*)—a factor weighing against inclusion under this head.

213. [1976] 1 Lloyd's Rep. 81 at pp. 88, 97.

214. In *Caltex Oil (Australia) Pty. Ltd.* v. *The Dredge "Willemstad"* (1975–76) 136 C.L.R. 529 no damages were allowed for economic loss in an action *in rem*.

Oil pollution

Whether or not a pollution claim attracts a maritime lien the jurisdiction based on "damage done by a ship" extends to such claims[215] in respect of liability under the Merchant Shipping (Oil Pollution) Act 1971[216] in accordance with (i) the International Convention on Civil Liability for Oil Pollution Damage 1969 ("The Liability Convention") and (ii) in accordance with the International Convention on the Establishment of an International Fund for Compensation for Oil Pollution Damage 1971 (the "Fund Convention") as enacted into English law. There is therefore jurisdiction both *in personam* and *in rem*.

"THE LIABILITY CONVENTION"

The Convention was implemented in English law initially though the Merchant Shipping (Oil Pollution) Act 1971. The Convention was amended by the 1992 Protocol and once the Protocol is in force and enacted will be entitled the 1992 rather than the 1969 Convention. The Merchant Shipping (Salvage and Pollution) Act accordingly made provision for the amendment of the 1971 Act and the consolidation in the Merchant Shipping Act 1995 has transitory provisions pending the entry into force and enactment of the amendment.[217] The Protocol will come into force on 30 May 1996.

The statutory scheme of the Act is to provide for exclusive and, subject to certain narrow exceptions, strict liability of the shipowner for damage or cost caused by discharge or escape of oil from a ship constructed or adapted for carrying oil in bulk. Liability under the Act extends to damage or cost occurring within the area of the United Kingdom and, if such damage or cost occurs also, within the area of a Convention country. Relevant damage is that caused by contamination or flowing from measures reasonably taken after the discharge or escape to prevent or minimize the damage, or flowing from preventative or minimizing measures taken where there is a grave and imminent threat of such contamination. Relevant cost is that incurred by the taking of preventative or minimizing measures.[218]

The shipowner must obtain insurance or other security to cover liability. An action will lie directly against the insurer or person providing the security. The shipowner and insurer may limit liability.[219] Where liability is limited the distribution of a limitation fund is not affected by any "lien or other right in respect of any ship or property".[220] This is a like consequence to that following from or establishing a fund for global limitation. Together with the provision that liability under the Act cannot be enforced save through an action under the Act it means that the establishment of a fund not only leads to the release of any security but removes any arguable "lien" interests.[221]

"THE FUND CONVENTION"

The Convention was implemented in English law initially through the Merchant Shipping Act 1974. The Convention was amended by the Protocol of 1992 and once the Protocol

215. Supreme Court Act 1981, s.20(5) as amended by Merchant Shipping Act 1995, Sch. 13 para. 59.
216. See generally *Oil Pollution from Ships* (Ed. Abecassis, Stevens 1985).
217. See Part VII, Chapter III. The transitory provisions are set out in Sch. 4.
218. See ss.1, 1A (1995 Act, ss.153, 154).
219. Sections 4, 12 (1995 Act, ss.157, 165).
220. Section 5(7) (added by Merchant Shipping Act 1988) (1995 Act, s.158(8)).
221. As to limitation of liability generally see Chap. 24; as to liens see Chaps. 18–23.

is in force and enacted will be entitled the 1992, rather than the 1971, Convention. Provision was accordingly made in the Merchant Shipping (Salvage and Pollution) Act 1994 for amendment of the 1974 Act and the consolidation in the Merchant Shipping Act 1995 has transitory provisions pending the coming into force and enactment of the Protocol. The Protocol will come into force on 30 May 1996.

Under the Convention a Fund is established through contributions of oil importers and receivers. In accordance with the Convention the Act creates a right against the Fund of further compensation by a claimant under the 1971 Act who has failed for a reason specified in the 1974 Act to recover full compensation for damage or cost.[222] The headquarters of the Fund is presently in London and because of that the Act provides for liability under it in respect not only of damage in the United Kingdom but also in a Fund Convention country where proceedings under the Liability Convention have been brought in a non-Fund Convention country.

The Fund incurs no liability if it proves that the damage was caused by the escape of oil from a government ship not being used commercially or the claimant cannot prove the damage resulted from an occurrence involving a ship identified by him.[223] Save where the damage consists of the cost of or damage caused by preventative measures the Fund is exonerated from liability if it proves that the damage resulted from the intentional or negligent act of the person suffering it. The Fund is subject to overall limit and to allow an opportunity for that reduction any judgment against it may only be enforced with leave of the court.[224]

NUCLEAR DAMAGE

A legislative framework establishing rights and duties in respect of use of nuclear material in the United Kingdom and carriage of such materials within and outside the United Kingdom and compensation for damage or injury is established by the Nuclear Installations Act 1965. There are provisions for the imposition of an exclusive liability regime, channelling of liability, compulsory insurance and limitation of liability. However, nothing in that Act is to affect the operation of the statutes enacting Conventions relating to carriage by air, road and sea. Any payments made under the Carriage Conventions by a person other than the person liable under the 1965 Act may be a basis of claim under that Act.

In contrast to oil pollution damage, the separate category of damage caused by nuclear matters is defined by the cause of the injury or damage. It may be argued that injury by radiation is novel, but it is physical injury. Any physical injury or damage caused, for example, by an explosion is precisely the type of damage that falls within the ambit of that which, if caused by a ship, may be the basis of Admiralty jurisdiction.

There are no provisions excluding liability under the 1965 Act from Admiralty jurisdiction as such but such action cannot be brought by an action in rem.[225] No breach of duty under the 1965 Act can give rise to a lien on any ship or aircraft.

---

222. Section 4. Including expenses reasonably incurred and sacrifices reasonably made (Art. 4(6)).
223. Section 4(7), (8).
224. Section 4(12). As to limitation of liability see Chap. 24.
225. Reference is made only to Administration of Justice Act 1956 when excluding claims, but if no lien can arise it must follow that no action in rem can be brought.

(c) Any claim for loss of life or personal injury, etc. (s.20(2)(f))

"(f) any claim for loss of life or personal injury sustained in consequence of any defect in a ship or in her apparel or equipment, or in consequence of the wrongful act, neglect or default of—

  (i) the owners, charterers or persons in possession or control of a ship; or
  (ii) the master or crew of a ship, or any other person for whose wrongful acts, neglects or defaults the owners, charterers or persons in possession or control of a ship are responsible,

being an act, neglect or default in the navigation or management of the ship, in the loading, carriage or discharge of goods on, in or from the ship, or in the embarkation, carriage or disembarkation of persons on, in or from the ship; . . . ".

This head of claim reflects and elaborates on Art. 1(b) of the Convention Relating to the Arrest of Sea Going Ships 1952. Prior to the Act of 1956 such claims were not the subject of separate provision but were statutorily dealt with by providing that for the purposes of Admiralty jurisdiction "damage" included loss of life and personal injury.[226] The removing of the claim from the general provision regarding "damage" means that the restriction necessarily imposed through requirements that the ship is the instrument of mischief does not apply. So the provision covers claims for injuries suffered on board the relevant ship.[227]

Despite its separation the provision does not create a substantive right[228] any more than do any of the grounds of jurisdiction, but simply provides that any claim for loss of life or personal injury will lie in Admiralty.[229] An action relating to loss of life lies only within the terms of the Fatal Accidents Act 1976[230] or the Law Reform (Miscellaneous Provisions) Act 1934.

The provision as it appears in the Supreme Court Act 1981 is identical in substance with that of the Act of 1956 but differs from the comparable Convention provision. The Convention provides simply for "loss of life or personal injury caused by any ship or occurring in the operation of any ship". The more elaborate statutory provision requires the loss of life or personal injury to be linked to a defect in a ship, neglect or default[231] in navigation, management of the ship, loading, carriage or discharge of goods, embarkation, carriage or disembarkation of passengers.

Neither Convention nor Act is limited to loss of life and injury occurring outside the ship at which the action is aimed. Apart from this the contrast between the provisions relating to claims generally based on damage done by or received by a ship and to those for loss of life and personal injury is striking. Their relationship is far from clear. First, as

226. Supreme Court of Judicature (Consolidation) Act 1925, s.22, repealing and replacing the Maritime Conventions Act 1911, s.5. It would follow that the loss (e.g.) flowing from damages done by a ship would be recoverable even if such a claim could not fall within s.20(2)(f).

227. A ship is "equipment" for the purpose of deeming defects in it to be deemed attributable to the "negligence" of the shipowner by virtue of the Employers' Liability (Defective Equipment) Act 1969. So where a seaman who suffers injury or loss of life due to the unseaworthiness of the ship the owner is liable in negligence (*The Derbyshire* [1988] A.C. 276; [1988] 1 Lloyd's Rep. 109 (H.L.)).

228. See e.g. *The Kwasind* (1915) 84 L.J.P. 102—commenting on the Maritime Conventions Act 1911, s.5 (repealed and replaced in similar language by the Supreme Court of Judicature (Consolidation) Act 1925, s.22).

229. It was held in 1925 in *The Moliere* [1925] P. 27 that a claim for indemnity for compensation paid under statutory obligation in respect of loss of life was not within Admiralty jurisdiction.

230. As amended by the Administration of Justice Act 1982. The Act applies to foreign vessels on the high seas whether the deceased is British or foreign (*The Esso Malaysia* [1974] 2 Lloyd's Rep. 143).

231. The phrase being adopted from the Fatal Accidents Act 1976 and including breach of contractual liability under the Occupiers' Liability Act 1957 (see e.g. *The Eagle* [1977] 2 Lloyd's Rep. 70).

has been seen, "damage" includes personal injury and, it has been argued, should include "loss of life", secondly, the loss of life and injury provision quite specifically links the claims to individual liability and responsibility of the owner, charterer, a person in possession or control or any person for whose acts those persons are responsible or the master[232] or crew. Thirdly, the loss of life and injury provision specifies the context of the act—so that, for example, the act in *Currie* v. *M'Knight*[233] (cutting of the mooring rope) would not fall within the provision. As the provision is jurisdictional and does not create a substantive right it may be wondered whether the spelling out of the criteria is necessary, and whether the more succinct phraseology of the Convention might not have been clearer. Claims for injury or loss of life not within this statutory category may be construed to fall within "damage done by a ship".

(d) Any claim for loss of or damage to goods carried in a ship (s.20(2)(g))

The nature of the claim

The provision is not limited to any particular legal basis of claim and there seems no reason to restrict it.[234] In *The Tesaba*[235] salvors strove to squeeze into the provision a claim based on Lloyd's Open Form alleging failure of shipowners to use their best endeavours to ensure that cargo owners provide security before release of cargo. Sheen J. held that, giving the words of s.20(2)(g) "their ordinary and natural meaning", they did not describe the claim before him. The basis of the claim appears to have been loss to the salvors of the chance to enforce their maritime lien on the goods, but as Sheen J. said, the lien remained in being.[236] Even if, as would appear strongly arguable, the statutory provision includes loss of the right to the goods and should not be restricted to physical destruction of the goods, the lessening of the opportunity to enforce the lien can hardly amount to "loss of goods".

"The ship"

There is a tendency to confuse the nature of the claim with the ability to bring an action *in rem* to enforce it. As a result it is not always clear whether an action *in personam* lies in Admiralty. In *The Jade*[237] in the Court of Appeal, Sir Gordon Willmer thought that, looking at the statutory words "in their natural and ordinary sense", "the ship referred to in para. (g) must be the carrying ship". That is surely correct but it does not follow from the provision that the claim must be *against* that ship or any person connected with it.

In *The Jade* both the House of Lords and Court of Appeal held that a claim under para. (g) could be enforced by an action *in rem* only if the action was against the carrying ship. The basis for this reasoning lies not in the wording of para. (g) but in that of the statutory

232. As in the Merchant Shipping Acts 1894 and 1995 "master" includes every person (except a pilot) having command or charge of a ship (s.24(1)).
233. [1897] A.C. 97.
234. See (in support) the construction of "any claim" in para. (h) in *The St Elefterio* [1957] P. 179.
235. [1982] 1 Lloyd's Rep. 397. Since the Salvage and Pollution Act 1994 there is no need to attempt to apply non-salvage bases to a clearly salvage claim—the claim in the *Tesaba* is within the definition of the Act (see *infra*).
236. It may just be arguable that waiver of the lien because of the defendant's acts could amount to loss—but it does not appear that this was the case in *The Tesaba* [1982] 1 Lloyd's Rep. 397.
237. [1976] 2 Lloyd's Rep. 1.

provisions governing the bringing of the action *in rem* (i.e. s.21(4) of the Act of 1981).[238] Based on the requirement (in s.21(4)(a)) that the claim must arise "in connection with a ship" it is said that an action *in rem* will lie under s.20(2) only against the ship in connection with which the claim arose or a sister ship. If this is right in any event in most cases cargo owners will be able to use para. (e)—damage done by a ship—as a basis for a claim *in rem* unconnected with a carrying ship, and should be able to use whichever paragraph is appropriate as a foundation for a claim *in personam*.

Effect of "sweeping up" provision on the definition of "the ship"

As has been said, a jurisdictional ground in the Supreme Court Act 1981 is "any jurisdiction vested in the High Court immediately prior to the Act". It follows that the Act of 1956 and any other extant statute conferring jurisdiction must be taken into account. If this ground brings in statutory provisions now repealed[239] it becomes even more important to distinguish between the nature of the claim and any restriction imposed in its enforceability through an action *in rem*. The jurisdiction relevant to para. (g) in so far as it is exercised in relation to a non carrying ship has its root in the Administration of Justice Act 1920, s.5, and the Supreme Court of Judicature (Consolidation) Act 1925, s.22(1)(a)(xii) (which replaced the provision of the Act of 1920). Both statutes provide simply for exercise of jurisdiction *in personam* or *in rem*, and any restriction to the carrying ship having its root in the Supreme Court Act, s.21(4), has no application to jurisdiction exercised pursuant to the Acts of 1920 and 1925.

As a result, it is unclear whether an action *in personam* will lie within the Admiralty jurisdiction in relation to a claim based on para. (g) but not brought in relation to the carrying ship. As to the inability to bring an action *in rem*, unlike para. (d) the inability is based simply on a construction of the statute in the context of the Arrest Convention. The linking of the requirement in s.21(4) that a prerequisite of the action *in rem* is a claim "in connection with a ship" to the definition of the claims in s.20(2) (and hence to the ship against which an action is brought) is perhaps not as clear as asserted in *The Jade*. It would have been a simple matter to specify that link had it been intended.

"The goods"

It is provided by the Supreme Court Act 1981, s.21(4)(a), that goods include "baggage". In *The Jade* Brandon J. held that such "baggage" was restricted to passengers' or travellers' baggage only. It did not extend to the "belongings of those who are on board ship not as passengers or travellers, but as employees of the shipowners in order to man and operate" the ship.[240] As a consequence master and crew have no Admiralty action for damage to their belongings in relation to the ship on which they are employed. If this be correct it is a curious anomaly. The restrictive view is based on the decision in 1883 in *R. v. The Judge of the City of London Court*[241] which relied on the comparison as between

---

238. It was conceded before Brandon J. that the cargo owners' claim fell within para. (g) but the concession was withdrawn before the Court of Appeal. As to the meaning of "in connection with a ship", see further Chap. 4.
239. As to which, see *supra*.
240. [1974] 2 Lloyd's Rep. 188, at p. 194. No appeal was brought from this part of the decision.
241. (1883) 12 Q.B.D. 115.

"goods" and "luggage" to exclude "passenger luggage". While it may be conceded that "goods" as used in the context of a carriage claim were originally restricted to those carried under a contract of carriage of cargo, the statutory extension to "baggage" is surely capable of including belongings of all those on board.

"Loss or damage"

The claim clearly covers a claim based on physical damage but beyond that its scope is unclear. In *The Jade* it was conceded that consequential loss was included in relation to para. (e) "damage received by a ship" and the question is whether "loss or damage to goods" restricts the claim to such loss or damage or includes any claim based on such loss or damage. Without express restriction it seems unnecessarily complex to draw the boundaries of Admiralty jurisdiction according to the type of damage when more than that type can be the basis of the same action before another Division of the High Court. It is, therefore, suggested the consequential loss should be recoverable.[242]

(e) Any claim arising out of an agreement relating to the carriage of goods in a ship or to the use or hire of a ship (s.20(2)(h))

This head of claim incorporates two heads of Convention claim,[243] is identical with the wording of s.1(h) of the Act of 1956 and joins in one head two subheads of s.22(1)(a)(xii) of the Supreme Court of Judicature (Consolidation) Act 1925. Prior to 1920 the Admiralty Court's jurisdiction extended only to claims based on a bill of lading for damage to goods brought against the carrying ship.[244] Clearly, claims based on carriage of goods under para. (h) overlap with claims based on damage to goods under para. (g) but the claim under para. (h)[245] must be based on the agreement. So, a broker, not a party to the agreement, could not bring an action within the statutory provision for commission provided for by a clause of the agreement.[246] However, in 1984 it was held that subcharterers claiming in negligence against shipowners with whom they had no contract could base the claim on the statutory provision.[247]

　　In *The Jade* Brandon J. stressed that early authorities construing the statutory provision conferring jurisdiction on county courts as to agreements relating to the use or hire of a ship should be approached in their context.[248] Between 1869 and 1920 only county courts

---

242. This leaves open the question of cause and consequence. So while damages for delay or loss of profit may be recoverable, indemnity for pollution liability may not. (See *The Jade* [1976] 1 Lloyd's Rep. 81, at p. 85). Such liability, it may be argued, is hardly the result of damage to goods unless caused by the goods. To say that the provision does not include a claim for indemnity (Thomas, *Maritime Liens*, para. 183) seems too wide when basing that assertion on the exclusion of the pollution indemnity in *The Jade*.

243. Convention Relating to the Arrest of Sea Going Ships 1952, Art. 1(d) and (e) which read "(d) agreement relating to the use or hire of any ship whether by charterparty or otherwise; (e) agreement relating to the carriage of goods in any ship whether by charterparty or otherwise." For full text see Appendix 3.

244. Admiralty Court Act 1861, s.6. It was confined also to carriage into England or Wales and cases where the owners were not domiciled in England or Wales. The Administration of Justice Act 1920 enacted the provisions later appearing as s.22(1)(a)(xii) of the Supreme Court of Judicature (Consolidation) Act 1925. The County Courts Admiralty Jurisdiction Amendment Act 1869, s.2, conferred jurisdiction on a county court with Admiralty jurisdiction in relation to "any claim arising out of any agreement made in relation to the use or hire of any ship" and the early authorities on the scope of para. (g) are those construing this clause.

245. Which includes claims based on contract or tort (*The St Elefterio* [1957] P. 179, at p. 183).

246. *The Nuova Raffealina*, (1871) L.R. 3 A. & E. 483.

247. *The Antonis P. Lemos* [1985] A.C. 711; [1985] 1 Lloyd's Rep. 283 (H.L.).

248. [1974] 2 Lloyd's Rep. 188, at p. 195.

had this jurisdiction and there was a tendency to interpret it restrictively. So, for example, there was judicial disagreement as to whether claims arising out of charterparties fell within the provision.[249] In *The Jade*, in the House of Lords, Lord Diplock agreed that the provisions conferring jurisdiction on the High Court should be given "their ordinary wide meaning".[250]

Claim arising out of an agreement relating to the carriage of goods in a ship

This part of para. (h) can be read as including claims falling within para. (g), and it encompasses claims such as a claim by the shipowners which would not fall within (g). In *The Jade*, in the Court of Appeal, it was said[251] that "the ship" referred to is the carrying ship, but even if this be right (as for para. (g)) it does not of itself mean that any ship proceeded against must be that ship or that the defendants are connected with that ship.

"*Arising out of*". The head of claim simply defines the *agreement* out of which the claim must arise. It would be possible, therefore, to base a claim on para. (h) even though it did not relate directly to the carriage of goods. So, the enforcement of an arbitration award contained in that contract was held to fall within it.[252]

In 1985 in *The Antonis P. Lemos*[253] the House of Lords rejected the arguments that (i) the phrase limited the claims to those based on contract or (ii) those based on tort that were directly connected with an agreement between the parties. In respect of the first argument Lord Brandon relied on the context of the phrase in the statutory structure of Admiralty jurisdiction as a whole and the relationship between that provision and the Convention Relating to the Arrest of Sea Going Ships which it implemented. As regards the second contention Lord Brandon thought there was no such restriction in the wording and no reason to import one.[254]

"*Relating to*". In *The Sandrina*,[255] a Scottish case, the House of Lords took the opposite view of this phrase to that later taken of "arising out of", in that the House chose the narrow construction. The issue was whether an agreement to pay premiums on a policy of insurance of cargo was within the head of the claim. Lord Keith (with whom all members agreed) argued that the meaning must be wider than "for", but thought that there must be "some reasonably direct connection" with the carriage or hire. The contract of insurance did not provide such a connection.[256]

It has to be said, with respect, that the basis of that view is not apparent, refuge being taken in the principle that each case must be decided on its own facts. Lord Keith thought,

---

249. *The Alina* (1880) L.R. 5 Ex.D. 227 settles the question—in favour of inclusion of the claim. In *The Jade*, Brandon J. rejected a contention that the provision was limited to agreements similar to charterparties (see [1974] 2 Lloyd's Rep. 188, at p. 196).

250. [1976] 2 Lloyd's Rep. 1 at p. 8. See also in Court of Appeal [1976] 1 Lloyd's Rep. 81, at p. 86 (Cairns L.J.).

251. Per Sir Gordon Willmer [1976] 1 Lloyd's Rep. 81, at p. 93.

252. *The Saint Anna* [1983] 1 Lloyd's Rep. 637; *The Stella Nova* [1981] Comm. L.R. 200.

253. [1985] A.C. 711; [1985] 1 Lloyd's Rep. 283.

254. Applied in actions by cargo owners against shipowners where there is no contractual relationship: *The Hamburg Star* [1994] 1 Lloyd's Rep. 399.

255. [1985] A.C. 255; [1985] 1 Lloyd's Rep. 181.

256. Lord Wilberforce placed emphasis on the *travaux preparatoire* of the Arrest Convention. In *The Antonis P. Lemos* Lord Brandon distinguished *The Sandrina* primarily on the ground that in the Convention "arising out of" applied to all claims and the wide reading only would make sense of the phrase in that context.

however, that the reasoning of the Court of Session (Lord Wylie) in *The Aifanourios*[257] in reaching a similar decision had "much force". Lord Wylie pointed out that a wider reading would bring within the head of claim many agreements dealt with as separate heads of claim—as, for example, supply of goods and materials, liability for dock dues. Further, insurance was directed to the convenience or protection of the owner and was not essential for the operation of the ship.[258]

In 1991 in *The Maersk Nimrod*[259] *The Sandrina* and *The Aifanourios* were relied on by Phillips J. in holding that neither a c.i.f. contract for the sale of fuel oil nor the demurrage provision of it was a "contract relating to the carriage of goods". The central feature of the c.i.f. contract is not carriage and the question was whether "relating to" was to be read broadly or narrowly. Citing Lord Keith in *The Sandrina* on the need for a "sufficiently direct connection", Phillips J. thought it not of great assistance but nevertheless confirmed his conclusion. There is unfortunately no guidance as to why the undoubted connection with a contract of carriage was not sufficiently direct.

Phillips J. also held first that it was possible to sever an agreement concerned with carriage of goods and other matters so as to isolate the carriage and bring a claim on that aspect within Admiralty jurisdiction. However, the demurrage claim was an agreement relating to discharge of the cargo. In any event in relation to loading and unloading, the distinction between use of a ship and carriage of goods was, thought the judge, a fine one and he agreed with the conclusion reached on authority. Yet, even more than the supply of containers, it is difficult to see any purpose in a contract to load or unload than to support a contract of carriage of goods. If, as said in *The Sandrina*, "relating to" cannot mean only "for", a more direct connection is difficult to imagine.

The approach to both phrases is simply to assess whether the connection is sufficient for a claim "to arise out of" a contract "relating to" carriage. It seems that Lord Wylie's approach (matched by that of Lord Brandon in *The Antonis P. Lemos*), that the provisions must be construed in context, holds the key. It seems a trifle unrealistic to exclude insurance claims on the ground that they are for the convenience of the owner rather than the operation of the ship when the head of claim focuses on the contract and not the ship—but not the general restrictive approach given other provisions which would otherwise overlap.

The decision does not undermine the decision that an arbitration award may be in the category—for in that context the underlying claim was the contract of carriage.[260] Further, following the approach in *The Maersk Nimrod*, it may be possible to argue that an agreement to insure forming part of a contract or part of a contract dealing with other matters might form a sufficiently close connection. The uncertainty of Lord Keith's approach is demonstrated by his disapproval of an earlier decision of Sheen J. in *The*

---

257. [1980] 2 Lloyd's Rep. 403. The jurisdiction provisions applicable to Scotland are set out in the Administration of Justice Act 1956, s.47 (see Appendix 1) and are based more closely on the Arrest Convention than those applicable to England and Wales. The provisions equivalent to para. (h) applicable to England are s.47(2)(d) and (e) each worded identically to the Arrest Convention (as to which, see Appendix 3).

258. They also fell outside the concept of necessaries in Scotland—they also were excluded in England (*The Andre Theodore* (1904) 10 Asp. M.L.C. 94). The CMI draft revision of the Arrest Convention includes the claim (Art. 1(1)(q)).

259. [1992] 1 Q.B. 571; [1991] 1 Lloyd's Rep. 169.

260. Unlike a claim for demurrage in a charterparty where the demurrage provisions are in a c.i.f. contract: *The Maersk Nimrod*. In holding that a demurrage claim was not a carriage claim or one based on the use of a ship, Phillips J. held himself bound by *The Zeus* (1888) 13 P.D. 188, approved in *The Sandrina*.

Sonia S.[261] that a contract under which containers were leased to shipowners for carriage of goods was a contract relating to the carriage of goods. As Sheen J. said, the only purpose of the container contract was the carriage of goods—and it has to be said the context argument which may exclude insurance would, if anything, support the inclusion of the container contract.[262]

In *The Tesaba*[263] a salvor attempted to bring within the provision an action based on an alleged failure by owners of a salved ship:

    (i) not to remove the salved property without the salvor's consent; and

    (ii) (contrary to Lloyd's Open Form) to use their best endeavours to ensure that cargo owners provided security prior to releasing the cargo.

In rejecting the argument for inclusion in the paragraph, Sheen J. said: "if the ordinary businessman were to be asked "Is that an agreement relating to the carriage of goods in *Tesaba*?" the answer would undoubtedly be "No".[264]

The conclusion to be drawn is that the claim (in a wide sense) must "arise out of" (i.e. rely on) an agreement directly relating to carriage of goods,[265] it not being sufficient that the agreement is to further such carriage or, perhaps, has no purpose save in so doing. The approach seems unduly and unrealistically restrictive and should be applied only insofar as to require a less direct connection would not make sense given the other heads of jurisdiction.

Agreement relating to the use or hire of a ship

The general principles applicable to agreements relating to carriage of goods apply. The provision is to be given "an ordinary wide meaning".[266] So it has been held to include (e.g.) charterparties,[267] a management agreement entitling one party to enter into charterparties for a vessel,[268] towage contracts,[269] and salvage agreements,[270] contracts represented in bills of lading,[271] and contracts for mooring services by watermen using motor boats.[272] The agreement need not be connected with the carriage of goods and it has been said that the provision would include "any agreement which an ordinary business-man would regard as within it".[273]

---

261. [1983] 1 Lloyd's Rep. 63.

262. Containers supplied to a shipowner for use on his ships and so used are not goods supplied for the operation of a ship—a perhaps even more commercially unrealistic decision (see (i) *infra*).

263. [1982] 1 Lloyd's Rep. 397.

264. At p. 401.

265. So a claim for wrongful detention of goods carried is within the phrase: *The Gina* [1980] 1 Lloyd's Rep. 398. See also *The Samarkand* [1995] LMLN 419.

266. See *The Jade* [1976] 2 Lloyd's Rep. 1, at p. 8 (H.L.) and *supra* fn. 250. In *The Zeus* (1886) 6 Asp. M.L.C. 312 an agreement to deliver coal entered into pursuant to a charterparty between the charterers and a coal merchant was held not to be an agreement relating to the use of a ship—and there can be little argument with the conclusion.

267. *The Alina* (1880) L.R. 5 Ex. D. 227.

268. *The Stella Nova* [1981] Comm.L.R. 200.

269. *The Conoco Britannia* [1972] 2 Q.B. 543; *The Isca* (1886) 12 P.D. 34.

270. *The Jade* [1976] 2 Lloyd's Rep. 1. But see *The Tesaba* (*infra*).

271. *Pugsley & Co.* v. *Ropkins & Co.* [1892] 2 Q.B. 184—although it is not clear which branch of the provision (carriage or hire) was thought to apply.

272. *The Queen of the South* [1968] P. 449.

273. *The Jade* [1976] 1 Lloyd's Rep. 81, at p. 86 (Cairns, L.J.).

In *The Aifanourios* the claimants attempted to bring a contract to pay premiums under this sub-head as well as that of carriage of goods. And, indeed, it was perhaps in this context that they stood a greater chance. As has been said, however, the Court of Session rejected the argument on the basis that the provision, if read widely so as to include a contract of insurance, would mean that many of the other heads of jurisdiction were meaningless. It may be, however, that a contract of use or hire (e.g. a demise charterparty or an instalment sale contract) including an insurance clause provides sufficient link for the argument to succeed. This may be particularly relevant to arrangements for long term financing which will undoubtedly both be "hire" contracts and include clauses relevant to insurance.

THE NEED TO IDENTIFY "A SHIP"

In *The Lloyd Pacifico*[274] Clarke J. applied the reasoning of the House of Lords in construing the head of claim of supply of goods or materials to a ship (para. (m), see *infra*) to hold that at least for an action *in rem* to lie the contract must relate to an identifiable ship. The contract in question was for the carriage of containers containing cargoes of coffee. Matching that requirement with the approach in *The Sandrina* a claim fell within para. (h) if "the agreement has some reasonably direct connection" with the use or hire of a ship or carriage of goods on a ship—that ship being that which is named in the action. The judge accepted that the identification could be made subsequent to the contract and that part of a contract only may fall within the provision.

The conclusion may have been inevitable given the decision in *The River Rima* (see p. 68). The contract in question contemplated possible carriage both on ships owned by the defendants, the owners of the *Lloyd Pacifico*, and vessels chartered by them or engaged under a conference agreement or joint service. While, therefore, it may be that the ships actually used were not so connected with the defendants as to be the targets of an action *in rem*, that is a different question. As argued in the context of *The River Rima* it is difficult to appreciate the need to identify a particular ship for an agreement clearly providing for carriage of goods by ship to be within Admiralty jurisdiction. This would be even more so if the agreement were limited to a fleet of an owner. The case underlines the importance, however, of precise drafting of a contract providing for general carriage and the nomination of a particular vessel when implementing it. It is an approach displaying perhaps more legal technicality than those in commerce might appreciate.

Salvage agreements as to the use or hire of a ship[275]

In *The Tesaba*, as has been said, the claim was based on the breach of a salvage agreement contained in Lloyd's Open Form. Sheen J. said that the question was:

" . . . whether the plaintiffs' claim arises out of any agreement relating to the carriage of goods in *Tesaba* or to the use or hire of *Tesaba*. The plaintiffs' claim arises out of a breach by the defendants of the terms of the salvage agreement, which was an agreement to salve *Tesaba* and her cargo. It was a term of that agreement that the contractor may make reasonable use of the vessel's machinery gear equipment anchors chains stores and other appurtenances during and for the purpose of the operations free of expense. A further relevant term was cl. 5[276] quoted earlier in this judgment. Mr

274. [1995] 1 Lloyd's Rep. 54.
275. I.e. owners to use their best endeavours to ensure that cargo owners provide security (see Clause 4(d) of LOF 1990).
276. As to salvage claims as a separate category, see *infra*.

Howard submitted that it was envisaged that the ship would be used to hold the cargo until security had been given. If the ordinary businessman were to be asked 'Is that an agreement relating to the carriage of goods in *Tesaba*?', the answer would undoubtedly be 'No'.

The same emphatic answer would be given to the question 'Is that an agreement for the use or hire of *Tesaba*?'."[277]

In *The Jade* a salvage agreement in Lloyd's Open Form was held to fall within the provision on the basis that the "only possible way in which the salvors could perform their contract" was by using a tug to salve the ship in distress. The salvage agreement, therefore, related to the use of the tug. The claims in *The Jade* were by the owners of the ship and cargo salved for negligent performance of the agreement—or as Lord Diplock put it more precisely "that part of the agreement for which a ship was to be used".

In *The Tesaba* Sheen J. distinguished *The Jade* on the basis that in *The Jade* the claim fell within para. (h) on Lord Diplock's approach because the only way that the contract could be performed was by the use of the tug. In *The Tesaba* the claim was based on (i) the obligation not to release the cargo without security, and (ii) availability of the ship for the salvor to store the cargo until security was given. With respect, Sheen J.'s approach seems to confuse the nature of the claim with the nature of the agreement. If the salvage agreement is an agreement relating to the use of a ship then, on the wording of the provision surely any claim "arising out of" the agreement is within the provision.

In *The Jade* the claim was brought by an action *in rem* by the shipowners and cargo owners against the tug owners, whereas in *The Tesaba* it was sought to enforce the claim by an action *in rem* by the salvors against the shipowners. However, in both cases the action was brought against the hired or carrying ship. In *The Conoco Britannia*[278] and *The Queen of the South*[279] Brandon J. held that an action at the suit of the owner of the hired ship would lie, but in *The Jade* Sir Gordon Willmer (in the Court of Appeal) pointed out that such an action would not be said to be "in connection with" the ship in relation to which the claim arose.

The requirement of the Supreme Court Act 1981, s.21(4), as held in *The Jade*, is that an action *in rem* requires the claim to arise "in connection with a ship" and that "ship" is the ship the subject of the agreement. It follows that in *The Tesaba* the salvors could bring an action *in rem*,[280] provided the head of claim is wide enough to encompass a claim by the salvors in relation to the salved ship. It is suggested that the head of claim is not so restricted as to exclude such a claim.[281]

Claims on arbitration awards

An arbitration award may be enforceable as a judgment by leave of a judge of High Court or by an action on the award.[282] Such an action is an action *in personam*. In 1935 in *The Beldis*,[283] the Court of Appeal held that proceedings *in rem* claiming a sum payable under

277. [1982] 1 Lloyd's Rep. 397, at p. 401.
278. [1972] 2 Q.B. 543. See also *The Isca* (1886) 12 P.D. 34 (decided under the provisions of the County Courts Admiralty Jurisdiction Amendment Act 1869, s.2).
279. [1968] P. 449.
280. In *The Tesaba* [1982] 1 Lloyd's Rep. 397 the purpose of issuing the writ *in rem* appeared to obtain security as the dispute had already been submitted to arbitration—as to which see Chaps. 13 and 15.
281. The matter may be rendered less relevant by the extension in 1994 of the "salvage" head of jurisdiction (see (f) *infra*).
282. See further Chap. 13 and generally Mustill and Boyd *Commercial Arbitration* (2nd edn.) Butterworth 1989 Chap. 28.
283. [1936] P. 51.

an award made in an arbitration held pursuant to a charterparty were brought to enforce the award and did not arise out of the charterparty. The action would not, therefore, lie. However, in 1933 the Court of Appeal in *Bremer Oeltransport GmbH* v. *Drewry*[284] held, in the context of an application for leave to serve a writ *in personam* out of the jurisdiction, that an action to enforce an award was based on the contract to submit disputes to arbitration. In 1983 in *The Saint Anna*[285] Sheen J. followed the *Bremer* case rather than *The Beldis*, stressing that in an action on an award the plaintiffs had to prove the award and the agreement which was its basis. Therefore, if the contract containing the submission to arbitration was within Admiralty jurisdiction any claim on the award was also within the jurisdiction.

In *The Saint Anna* the claim was linked to Admiralty jurisdiction through the "admiralty" nature of the agreement containing the arbitration award. In 1981 in *The Stella Nova*[286] Sheen J. held that an action *in rem* would lie to enforce a claim based on an agreement to submit disputes to arbitration provided that the claim arose out of an agreement for the hire of a ship. Further, it was no obstacle that an award had been made and that a judgment *in personam* had been obtained to enforce the award. In this case the link of Admiralty jurisdiction was through the underlying basis of the claim, the failure to satisfy which led to the arbitration agreement and ultimately the award. The prerequisite for Admiralty jurisdiction was, therefore, an Admiralty root from which the claim had sprung.

(f) Salvage (s.20(2)(j))[287]

The content and ambit of this head of claim depends on whether the salvage service or act out of which the claim arises started (in the case of the service) or was done (in the case of the act) prior to 1 January 1995. On that date the Merchant Shipping (Salvage and Pollution) Act 1994 brought the Salvage Convention 1989 into English law. Admiralty jurisdiction was widened to accommodate the Convention and to rid the scope of the head of claim of some restrictions judicially imposed.[288]

1. Salvage services started or acts done before 1 January 1995 "any claim in the nature of salvage"

It is statutorily provided[289] that such claims include claims for life and property salvage under the Merchant Shipping Act 1894[290] and claims in respect of cargo and wreck found on land.[291] It has been suggested that the paragraph should be read restrictively (i.e.

284. [1933] 1 K.B. 753.
285. [1983] 1 Lloyd's Rep. 637.
286. [1981] Com. L.R. 200.
287. The substance of a salvage claim is considered in relation to claims attracting a maritime lien. See *supra*.
288. Section 1(6), Sch. 2 para. 6, substituting new text in the Supreme Court Act 1981, ss.20(2)(j), (6). Scottish and county court jurisdiction is similarly amended (Sch. 2, paras. 4, 7). The 1994 Act is repeated and consolidated with other Merchant Shipping Acts into the Merchant Shipping Act 1995 (in force on 1 January 1996).
289. Supreme Court Act 1981, s.20(6). It is also extended to aircraft (*ibid.*, ss.20(2)(j) and 20(6)).
290. As to which, see *supra*.
291. Supreme Court Act 1981, s.20(7)(b). Salvage jurisdiction is extended to hovercraft (Hovercraft Act 1968, ss.1 and 2 (as amended by the Supreme Court Act 1981, s.152(i), Sch. 5); the Hovercraft (Application of Enactments) Order 1972, Art. 8).

"confined to a salvage award arising from beneficial service") and that any matters ancillary to such a claim will fall within the "sweeping up" or some other provision.[292] With respect, such a suggestion perhaps places too great a trust in the ambit and certainty of the sweeping up provision and ignores the link between the English legislation and the Arrest Convention.[293] It is questionable whether, for example, there is any need to rely on the jurisdiction prior to 1875 for the power to consider the negligence of a salvor. The statutory phrase appears specifically to include claims falling broadly within the scope of "salvage".

The power to apportion salvage awards (statutorily provided in the Merchant Shipping Act 1894, s.556) is included either within the statutory phrase or within the sweeping up provision—being a jurisdiction that "is conferred" by a statute created since 1875.[294] As has been seen, a salvage agreement may fall within para. (h) although it may well be that claims "arising out of" such agreement would not fall within para. (j)—directed as it is to the nature of the claim itself.

In *The Jade*[295] both Brandon J. and the Court of Appeal took the view that a claim for damages against a negligent salvor fell outside para. (j). In *The Tesaba*[296] the plaintiff salvors tried to force their claim within paras. (g), (h) and (j). As has been said, the claim was against the owners of the salved ship and was based on alleged breach of the salvage agreement (i.e. Lloyd's Open Form) in failing to obtain security from the cargo owners. Sheen J. thought that the phrase "any claim in the nature of salvage" referred to a claim for a salvage reward and that both the reference in para. (j) to the Civil Aviation Act 1949 and the equivalent provision of the Arrest Convention (arising out of salvage) supported this conclusion. In *The Tesaba* Sheen J. said the claim arose out of the defendant's conduct after the completion of salvage service.

From the authorities of *The Jade* and *The Tesaba*, and indeed from the statutory wording, it appears that the head of claim is restricted to a claim in relation to salvage service, but it does not follow that the jurisdiction in relation to such a claim excludes such connected matters as apportionment or abatement or claims against the salvor. Matters connected to a claim, it is suggested, should be included in para. (j), and exclusion of claim against the salvor seems to have little in principle to support it.

Apart from the question of life and property salvage falling within the Merchant Shipping Act 1894, ss.544 and 546, there is no hint that any claim would not attract a maritime lien. The extent of the "salvage" claim and the effect of these statutory provisions have been discussed in the context of "maritime lien claims".[297]

2. Salvage services or acts done on or after 1 January 1995

Section 20(1)(j) of the Supreme Court Act provides for Admiralty jurisdiction in respect of:

292. See Thomas, *Maritime Liens*, paras. 251, 252.
293. The comparable Convention provision refers simply to "salvage" (Art. 1(c)). The sweeping up provision may not apply to *in rem* jurisdiction (see *supra*).
294. As to which, see *supra*.
295. See [1974] 2 Lloyd's Rep. 188, at p. 196; [1976] 1 Lloyd's Rep. 81, at pp. 85, 93. In the House of Lords the plaintiffs appear not to have relied on this paragraph.
296. [1982] 1 Lloyd's Rep. 397.
297. See *supra*, pp. 26–31.

"any claim—
        (i) under the Salvage Convention 1989; or
        (ii) under any contract for or in relation to salvage services."[298]

It is statutorily provided that (ii) includes any claim "arising out of" such a contract as is specified whether or not arising during the provision of services and that "salvage services" includes services rendered in saving life from a ship.[299] The provision now undoubtedly includes actions by a salvor and the type of claim for breach of contract excluded from the former provision by the decision in *The Tesaba*. As regards (ii) however it brings into play issues of construction relevant to the agreements for carriage or hire of a ship—the meaning of "arising out of" and "in relation to".

There is no reason to adopt a restricted approach to either phrase. The wide meaning given to "arising out of" in *The Antonis P. Lemos* should be adopted while the narrow view of "related to" expressed in *The Sandrina* should be confined to its own context. So there is no reason why a contract to provide equipment for salvage services should not be seen as within the phrase—unlike the claim in respect of insurance it would not render other heads of claim unnecessary.

The width of the head of claim makes it clear that it includes claims which do not attract a maritime lien—as regards both the Convention and the contract for salvage services. As discussed in the context of the salvors' maritime lien[300] the Convention provision that nothing in the Convention "shall affect" the lien may mean that there are now differences in content between a salvors' claim and the maritime lien attaching to it. If this be so, the jurisdiction over "maritime liens" in s.21(3) may take on a substantive role—but there is no doubt that the statutory jurisdiction encompasses both.

(g) Any claim in the nature of towage in respect of a ship (s.20(2)(k))[301]

The Admiralty Court Act 1840 provided that the Admiralty Court should have jurisdiction over claims "in the nature of towage".[302] In 1849 Dr Lushington "without attempting any definition which may be universally applied" described a towage service as "the employment of one vessel to expedite the voyage of another when nothing more is required than accelerating her progress".[303] In formulating the definition he was concerned to differentiate towage from salvage. Subsequent authorities have followed with that focus, there being few concerned with the jurisdictional boundary in respect of a towage claim. Again, in contrasting towage and salvage, it has been said that towage arises out of contract and it has been held that there is no jurisdiction to award a sum in

298. Or a corresponding claim in connection with an aircraft (*ibid.*). As to the extent of the claim in connection with aircraft see s.20(3)(c) as substituted by the 1994 Act, Sch. 2, para. 6(3).
299. Supreme Court Act, s.20(6), as substituted by the Merchant Shipping (Salvage and Pollution) Act 1994, Sch. 2, para. 6(3). The provisions of the Merchant Shipping Act 1894 relating to life salvage and coastal salvage (ss.544, 545, 546) cease to have effect (*ibid.* Sch. 2, para. 1(2)). As from 1 January 1996 the reference to the 1994 Act, s.1, in s.20(6)(a) becomes a reference to the Merchant Shipping Act 1995, s.224 (1995 Act, Sch. 13, para. 59(2).
300. See pp. 26–27.
301. Or aircraft while water-borne (*ibid.* s.24(1)).
302. It is uncertain whether the Admiralty Court had jurisdiction in towage prior to the Admiralty Court Act 1840, but accepting that there is no maritime lien, nothing turns on this. For an award for towage prior to 1840, see *The Isabella* (1838) 3 Hag. Adm. 427. As to possibility of such a claim attracting a maritime lien, see *supra*, pp. 43–44.
303. *The Princess Alice* (1849) 3 W. Rob. 138, at p. 140.

addition to the contract as remuneration for services rendered[304] In one of the few cases concerned with the boundary of towage it was held *The Leoborg*[305] in 1951 that escorting a ship from outside a port into a port is service in the nature of towage.

(h) Any claim in the nature of pilotage in respect of a ship (s.20(2)(l))[306]

Pilotage (i.e. the remuneration due for pilot services) did not appear as a statutory ground for Admiralty jurisdiction until the Administration of Justice Act 1956. But the Admiralty Court exercised jurisdiction *in rem* and *in personam* prior to 1840.[307]

(i) Any claim in respect of goods or materials supplied to a ship for her operation or maintenance (s.20(2)(m))[308]

This head of claim (together with (n) concerned with ship repair and dock dues) incorporates much that was covered by the age-old claim for "necessaries".[309] Although there is clearly now no requirement of "necessity"[310] the previously wide construction of that requirement makes the change of relatively little substance. It has been judicially said that the claims covered "are certainly no narrower" than necessaries and held as a consequence that the provision covers payments made by way of advance to enable goods and materials to be supplied.[311]

The provision requires a causative link between the supply of goods or materials and the operation or maintenance.[312] Clearly, the supply of material includes fuel, but in *The*

---

304. *The Hjemmet* (1880) 5 P.D. 227.

305. [1962] 2 Lloyd's Rep. 146. In *The Conoco Britannia* [1972] 2 Q.B. 543 it was argued that the provision covered a claim for indemnity under a towage contract for loss flowing from a collision between a tug supplied by the plaintiffs and the ship to which it was rendering towage service. Brandon J. decided that the claim fell within the provision concerning hire of a ship and made no finding on this point.

306. Or aircraft while water-borne (*ibid.* s.24(1)).

307. See *The Nelson* (1805) 7 C. Rob. 227; *The Bee* (1822) 2 Dods. 498; *The Eliza* (1833) 3 Hag. Adm. 87; *The General Palmer* (1828) 2 Hag. Adm. 176. As to uncertainty of a pilotage claim attracting a maritime lien, see *supra*. Harbour authorities may recover pilotage charges for provision of pilotage services "as a civil debt or in any other manner by which ship passengers and goods dues are recoverable by the authority": Pilotage Act 1987, s.10(9).

308. The equivalent Arrest Convention provision is "goods or materials wherever supplied to a ship for her operation or maintenance". (Art. 1(k)). The Australian legislation adds "services" to "goods and materials". In *The Bass Reefer* [1992] LMLN 335 the Federal Court thought there was a strong argument that a purely berthing agreement was within the meaning of "services". The draft revision of the Convention also includes "services" and supply of goods and equipment "(including containers)".

309. Jurisdiction over necessities was, with restrictions, conferred on the Admiralty Court by the Admiralty Court Act 1840, s.6, and extended by the Act of 1861, s.5. Jurisdiction over claims for ship repair, building and equipping was conferred in addition by the Act of 1861, s.4, where a ship or proceeds were under arrest. The Supreme Court of Judicature (Consolidation) Act 1925, s.22(1)(2)(i), (vii) and (x) reflected the jurisdiction as extended. In *The Queen of the South* [1968] 1 Lloyd's Rep. 182 Brandon J. suggested that the jurisdiction regarding necessaries under the latter Act was preserved through the "sweeping up" provision of the Administration of Justice Act 1956. As to this argument, see *supra*. Necessaries are connected with masters' disbursements which operated on similar principles. As to disbursements, see s.20(2)(p) of the Supreme Court Act 1981 and *infra*. As to the need for liability *in personam* of the owner for an action *in rem* to lie, see Chap. 15.

310. Old habits sometimes continue. See the claims for necessaries in *The Carmania II* [1963] 2 Lloyd's Rep. 152; *The Queen of the South* [1968] 1 Lloyd's Rep. 182.

311. *The Fairport (No. 5)* [1967] 2 Lloyd's Rep. 162—applying the reasoning applied to necessaries in *The Mogileff* [1921] P. 236.

312. Cf. *Halsbury's Laws*, 4th edn., para. 337.

Queen of the South[313] Brandon J. seemed to favour the restriction of "supply" to contracts for sale or hire in which the property or possession of the goods or materials passes to shipowners. It would be unfortunate for this head of claim to be bedevilled with concepts of the passing of property or possession. The essence is the supply and through the supply the benefit conferred. It should not be accepted without argument that the concepts of "property" and "possession" (somewhat artificial in the context of supply) create limitations on this provision.

In 1988 in *The River Rima*[314] the House of Lords construed the provision even more restrictively, holding that it applied only where the "supplied" ship is identified either in the supply contract or prior to its performance. In that case it was not enough that the contract was with a shipowner for the use of containers on a ship owned by the shipowner, with the identity of the ship being at the discretion of the shipowner. That view accords with an *in rem* approach with a particular ship as the central feature of the "necessaries" action[315]—but regrettably rather more doubtfully perhaps with commercial practice.

Goods supplied to a shipowner for use on a ship of his are surely (as Sheen J. held in this case) "supplied to a ship for her operation or maintenance". This phraseology appears in the Arrest Convention, but Lord Brandon disposed of argument based on the need to reflect that Convention by construing the Convention in accordance with English law prior to the Convention. It is at least open to question whether those drafting the Convention intended to adopt the technical characteristics of the action *in rem*.[316]

Relevance of liability in personam

Authorities on the need for or relevance of the owner's liability *in personam* as a prerequisite for an action *in rem* for necessaries are now irrelevant in so far as the framework for the bringing of such an action is set out in s.21(4).[317] Still relevant, however, to the nature of the claim are:

(i) the potential liability *in personam* required by s.21(4), and in particular the issue of liability for the acts of an agent;

(ii) the proposition that a person paying or advancing money to obtain necessaries has the priority *in rem* of the person who is paid or to whom the money is advanced[318] and

(iii) the question whether a claim where a payment is made relying on the personal security of the owner can be made *in rem* under this head.[319]

---

313. [1968] 1 Lloyd's Rep. 182, at p. 189—where it was argued that the rendering of mooring services through the provision of motor boats was a supply of materials. Brandon J. limited his comment to the context of the case before him.

314. [1988] 2 Lloyd's Rep. 193 (H.L.), applied in construing para. (i) in *The Lloyd Pacifico* [1995] 1 Lloyd's Rep. 54 (see *supra*).

315. For a similar approach in the United States see *Itel Containers Corpn* v. *Atlantrafik Express Service Ltd.*, USCA 2nd Grant, [1992] LMLN 345. For a wholly different approach based on "equitable" maritime jurisdiction in Canada, see *The Nikolay Golanov* [1994] LMLN 391. For a critique of the U.S. approach see [1994] *Tulane Journal of Maritime Law* 33, (Borchens).

316. There must be at least an argument that the identity of a particular ship goes more to the action *in rem* (i.e. s.21) than Admiralty jurisdiction—although whether an action *in personam* is within or outside that jurisdiction in a contract case may not be of the greatest importance. The argument in the text is against the need for identification of a particular ship for the supply prior to the supply itself.

317. As to the present connection of liability *in personam* and action *in rem*, see Chap. 10.

318. See Chap. 23.

319. See Chap. 10.

(j) Any claim in respect of the construction, repair or equipment of a ship or in respect of dock charges or dues (s.20(2)(n))

This head of claim reflects faithfully the Arrest Convention.[320] It includes claims formerly within "necessaries" and the comments made in respect of para. (m) apply. Independently of this head of claim a ship repairer may exercise a possessory lien and public authorities have statutory rights of detention and sale in respect of claims for dues and charges.

(k) Any claim by a master or a member of the crew of a British or non-British ship[321] for wages (including any sum allotted out of wages or adjudged by a superintendent to be due by wages) (ss.20(2)(o), and 24(2)(a))

This provision reflects Art. 1(1)(m) of the Arrest Convention—"a claim arising out of . . . wages of masters officers or crew". The Supreme Court Act, s.20(1)(b) and 20(3)(a) further provide for jurisdiction *in personam* in respect of applications under the Merchant Shipping Acts 1894–1994.[322] Provided "application" is construed to include any "claim", the recovery of money or property by master or crew now under the Merchant Shipping Act 1970 falls within Admiralty jurisdiction. (see *infra*).

Claims for wages

Jurisdiction under para. (o) is restricted to wage claims by the master or member of the crew. This jurisdiction is identical with the jurisdiction based on the maritime liens for seamen's and masters' wages with the exception that "members of the crew" may be a narrower concept than "seamen". However, subject to any restriction to *in personam* jurisdiction (as to which see *supra*), through the sweeping up provision of the Act of 1956 maintained by the Act of 1981 any jurisdiction founded on "seamen" as distinct from "members of the crew" survives. In 1981 in *The Silia*,[323] a case decided under the similar wording of the Act of 1956, Sheen J. apparently did not accept the argument that a claim by a Greek Pension Fund in respect of unpaid contributions was made "for the benefit of" the master or crew. It is not clear whether the rejection was on the facts or on the grounds that, even if it was for their benefit, it was not *by* the master and crew. It seems from the Supreme Court Act 1981 that any claim must at least be authorized by the master or crew.

Claims by a third party based on the payment of wages must presumably be founded on a head other than para. (o). In so far as the basis of the claim is a maritime lien (as it usually is) a claimant may rely directly on s.21(3) which provides jurisdiction without

320. Article 1(l). Port dues attract a maritime lien under the Conventions on Mortgages and Liens 1926, 1967 and 1993 (see Chap. 17). As to the proposed revised draft of the Convention, see Chap. 15.
321. See, for requirements of notice to the appropriate consul of arrest of a foreign ship. RSC Order 75, rule 5 (considered in Chap. 15). The Supreme Court Act provides only that ss.21–23 do not limit jurisdiction not to hear claims by masters or crew of a non-British ship (see s.24(2)(a)).
322. Supreme Court Act 1981, s.20(1)(b). See *infra*. Section 20(7) retains any limitation on the recovery of "money or property" specified in the Merchant Shipping Acts. Compare the wording of the equivalent provision of the Administration of Justice Act 1956, s.1(1)(o) of which reads:
(o) any claim by a master or member of the crew of a ship for wages and any claim by or in respect of a master or member of the crew of a ship for any money or property which, under any of the provisions of the Merchant Shipping Acts, 1894 to 1954, is recoverable as wages or in the court and in the manner in which wages may be recovered.
323. *The Silia* [1981] LMLN 36 (March).

reference to the claims listed in s.20. In so far as it may be sought to enforce the claim through an action *in rem*, without relying on the maritime lien or through an action *in personam*, the current statutory jurisdiction rests either on the acceptance of transferability of the claim or (possibly) on the sweeping up provision.

Recovery of money or property under the Merchant Shipping Act 1995[324]

CLAIMS OR APPLICATIONS

In contrast to the equivalent provisions in the Administration of Justice Act 1956[325] there is no specific reference in the jurisdictional heads of s.20(2) of the Supreme Court Act 1981 to the recovery of money or property apart from wages. However, s.20(7), which declares that the provisions apply to all ships whether British or not wherever the residence or domicile of their owners may be, specifically provides that it shall not be construed as extending the cases in which money or property is recoverable under the Merchant Shipping Act 1995 (until 31st December 1894–1994). More substantively, the Act provides (in s.20(3)) specifically for jurisdiction *in personam* in respect of "any application" under the Merchant Shipping Act 1995 (until 31st December 1894–1994).[326] As said above, a claim for money or property under those Acts if considered an "application" will be within the ambit of s.20(3).

Claims for money or property by seamen or masters are now based on the Merchant Shipping Act 1995. Claims in respect of medical expenses,[327] relief and maintenance in respect of being left behind or taken after shipment to a foreign country,[328] or property of a deceased seaman or master fall within Admiralty jurisdiction if they are "applications" within the Supreme Court Act 1981, s.20(1)(b), or are wage claims. The change in wording from the Act of 1956 while no doubt bringing the jurisdictional framework more in line with the provisions of the Merchant Shipping Act 1970, has not dispelled the jurisdictional fog. Indeed, in some respects the fog has thickened. It should not be difficult to link jurisdiction to substance more clearly than is presently done.

CLAIMS OTHER THAN APPLICATIONS

The Merchant Shipping Act 1995 also allows claims in respect of wages by the holder of an allotment note.[329]

If proceedings brought to enforce such (or any other) claim are not "applications" within the Supreme Court Act 1981, s.20(1)(b) and 20(3)(a), jurisdiction may be based through the sweeping up clause on s.1(1)(o) of the Act of 1956. But this requires provision under the Merchant Shipping Acts for recovery either as wages "or in the court or in the manner in which wages may be recovered". Save in respect of the holder of an allotment note, unlike predecessors, the Merchant Shipping Act 1970 or 1995 rarely so provides.

---

324. (Until 31 December 1995) 1894–1981 as amended by provisions in Acts in 1983, 1984, 1986, 1988, 1993 and 1994 that they be read as one with those of 1894–1981.

325. See fn. 322. Any argument as to possible restriction of jurisdiction by the Act of 1981 is met by the sweeping up provision—as to which, see *supra*.

326. Supreme Court Act 1981, s.20(1)(b) and (3)(a).

327. See s.45 (1970 Act, s.26).

328. See *ibid.* ss.73–75 (1970 Act, ss.62–64, 67).

329. *Ibid.* s.37 (1970 Act, s.14). By this provision the person to whom the wages are allotted has the right to recover in his or her own name and "the same remedies as the seaman has for the recovery of his wages".

(l) Any claim by a master, shipper, charterer or agent in respect of disbursements made on account of a ship (s.20(2)(p))

This paragraph reflects Art. 1(1)(n) of the Arrest Convention which reads:

"(n) Masters' disbursements, including disbursements made by shippers charterers or agents on behalf of a ship or her owner."

The provision first appeared in the Act of 1956 replacing in part that focusing on "necessaries" in the Supreme Court of Judicature (Consolidation) Act 1925. The concept of masters' disbursements is well established, being the basis of a maritime lien; but the provision relating to disbursements of a charterer, shipper or agent appeared only in the Act of 1956 following the terms of the Convention. Under the statutory provision expenditure must be "on account of a ship" and further in an action *in rem* on account of the ship in relation to which the action is brought. So it does not include disbursements by an insurance broker—that being seen, as is the payment of insurance premiums, as in the financial interest of the shipowners[330]—or when made in respect of a contract not identifying a ship.[331]

Masters' disbursements

Such a claim carries a maritime lien and the meaning of "disbursement" has been discussed in that context. There is no distinction between the type of claim which would attract a maritime lien and the claim which is within Admiralty jurisdiction *in personam* or *in rem*.

Charterer's, shipper's or agent's disbursements

It seems clear that the meaning of "disbursement" should remain constant whether it be by the master or other person and, therefore, include any liability incurred. It has been held that it includes any fee for services (as, for example, agent's fees).[332]

(m) Any claim arising out of an act which is or is claimed to be a general average act (s.20(2)(q))

The equivalent provision of the Arrest Convention refers simply to "any claim arising out of . . . general average".[333] The provision appeared in the English statutory jurisdictional framework for the first time in the Act of 1956. General average has been defined many times. It is based on the principle that the cost of a sacrifice of property in time of danger for the rescue of other property must be borne and shared by all those interested in the

---

330. *Bain Clarkson* v. *Owners of the Ship "Sea Friends"* [1991] 2 Lloyd's Rep. 322 (C.A.) disagreeing with a Hong Kong decision (*Clifford Chance* v. *Owners of the Vessel "Atlantic Trader"*) that legal fees came within this provision.
331. *The Lloyd Pacifico* [1995] 1 Lloyd's Rep. 54 (as to which see *supra*).
332. *The Westport (No. 3)* [1966] 1 Lloyd's Rep. 342. Agent probably includes "managing agent"—not being restricted to ship's agent (*The Cocona Energy* 1977 folio No. 174, cited in *Bain Clarkson* v. *Owners of the Ship "Sea Friends"* (*supra*)).
333. Convention Relating to the Arrest of Sea Going Ships 1952, Art. 1(1)(g). This type of claim attracts a maritime lien under the Convention on Mortgages and Liens 1926 and 1967 (as to which, see Chap. 18).

whole. A general average is statutorily defined for insurance purposes in the Marine Insurance Act 1906 as:

"where any extraordinary sacrifice or expenditure is voluntarily and reasonably made or incurred in time of peril for the purpose of preserving the property imperilled in the common adventure."[334]

This definition has been accepted as a statutory codification of the concept and an international framework for the application of the principle has been achieved in large measure through the York-Antwerp Rules.[335] The broad wording of the provision encompasses claims consequential on a general average claim. So, for example, it may be argued that it applies to a claim that a shipowner had not fulfilled his obligation to obtain security for owners of cargo lost before releasing surviving cargo or perhaps actions against insurers because of the occurrence of the act.[336]

It should be noted that a shipowner has a possessory lien on cargo for general average contributions and the duty to exercise that lien for the benefit of ship and cargo. Subject to statutory extension, the lien is possessory and, apart from any proceedings taken to enforce it against wrongful interference, is not affected or aided by para. (q).

Cargo owners, except in the unlikely event of being in possession of the cargo, cannot have a possessory lien. Any security available, therefore, stems directly from any action *in rem* available under s.20(2)(q) and s.21(4).

(n) Any claim arising out of bottomry (s.20(2)(r))

The substance of this head is identical with that which attracts a maritime lien and has been discussed in that context. In fitting this claim into the framework it must be recalled that the concept is based on lack of personal liability of the borrower. The availability of an action *in personam* or of an action *in rem* in the context of s.21(4) is, therefore, limited.[337]

CLAIMS ENFORCEABLE BY ACTION "IN PERSONAM"

Availability of action "in personam"

The Supreme Court Act 1981 provides that "an action *in personam* may be brought in the High Court in all cases within the Admiralty jurisdiction of that court."[338] The provision is subject to the limitation on the availability of collision actions arising from a collision out of inland or port waters. In these circumstances an action *in personam* may be brought in England only if the defendant has his habitual residence or place of business in England.[339] However, such a limitation is but a specific example of the general need to

---

334. Marine Insurance Act 1906, s.66(2).

335. Cf. *General Average* and *York—Antwerp Rules*, Lowndes and Rudolph 11th Edn 1990.

336. Marine insurance claims for premiums are not of themselves within Admiralty jurisdiction nor within the Arrest Convention 1952 but may fall within it if brought under any of the heads of the Supreme Court Act 1981, s.20. Cf. *supra*. The draft revision of the Arrest Convention (1995) includes such claims. See Chap. 15.

337. Presumably an action might lie *against* a bondholder or, possibly, against a borrower on some matter arising from the bond other than the liability to repay.

338. As to possible confusion between *in rem* jurisdiction and Admiralty jurisdiction see *supra*.

339. Or submission or the action arises out of the same incident in relation to which proceedings are or have been taken in the High Court. See the Supreme Court Act 1981, s.22; RSC, Order 75, rule 4.

establish jurisdiction in any action *in personam* and in particular any restriction which may flow from Conventions enacted into English law (see Chapter 3).

Claims enforceable only by action in personam

Claims included in the Supreme Court Act but excluded from its provisions for "*in rem*" enforceability are:

(i) any claim for damage received by a ship (s.20(2)(d));
(ii) applications under the Merchant Shipping Act 1995;
(iii) "collision" actions;
(iv) limitation actions;
(v) arguably, jurisdiction through the "sweeping up" clause (see *supra*).

The categories of claim

(a) Any claim for damage received by a ship

It has been argued that such a claim may arguably be enforced by an action *in rem* through the sweeping up clause, and the question of the nature of "damage" required has been considered along with claims in relation to which an action *in rem* will lie.

(b) Any application in the High Court under the Merchant Shipping Act 1995[340] (s.20(1)(b) and 20(3)(a))

There may well be an overlap with the claims specified in the Supreme Court Act 1981 and this rather vague category (as, for example, in respect of wage claims). The category as such did not appear in the Administration of Justice Act 1956 and such applications would have found their way to the Admiralty Court through rules of court or specific assignment of appropriate business to the court.[341] It was a small but welcome step in the direction of codification to find the category specifically listed as part of the basic statutory Admiralty framework, but regrettable that its wording still left its scope unclear.[342]

(c) "Collision" actions (s.20(1)(b) and 20(3)(b))

Such actions (being to enforce a claim for damage, loss of life or personal injury) stem from a collision, the carrying out or failing to carry out a manoeuvre or non-compliance with the collision regulations and are the subject of s.22 of the Act. The provision was enacted to comply with the Collision (Civil Jurisdiction) Convention 1952 and, as has

---

340. For examples of applications, see (prior to 1 January 1996) the Merchant Shipping (Registration etc.) Act 1993, Sch. 1, para. 2 (applications in connection with transfers of ships). A person with a proprietary interest in a ship may apply for an order prohibiting for a specified time any dealing in a ship (para. 2(6)) (as from 1 January 1996 Merchant Shipping Act 1995, Sch. 1, paras. 2, 6). This is a substantive right not limited to the jurisdiction of the court (such as to transmission transfer and sale of ships) to which the preceding paragraphs of the Schedule apply: *The Mikado* [1992] 1 Lloyd's Rep. 163 (construing s.30 of the Merchant Shipping Act 1894) (see *supra*). Section 55 of the Merchant Shipping Act 1894 applications under which were excluded from s.20(3)(a) was repealed by the Merchant Shipping Act 1988, Sch. 1, para. 32.
341. See RSC, Order 74, rule 1. The plaintiff selects the appropriate Division for his claims but the proceedings may be transferred (Supreme Court Act 1981, ss.64 and 65).
342. See *supra* for discussion of the applicant to claims by seamen for recovery of money or property.

been said, limits the jurisdiction of the High Court to cases with specific links with England.[343] As with applications under the Merchant Shipping Act 1995 there may be an overlap with claims listed in the Supreme Court Act 1981 (especially damage done or received by a ship). Again, the listing of collision actions in the statute is novel and welcome.[344]

(d) Limitation actions (s.20(1)(b) and 20(3)(c))

Any "actions by shipowners or other persons under the Merchant Shipping Act 1995 for the limitation of the amount of their liability in connection with a ship or other property (as to which see Chapter 24) is declared to be within Admiralty jurisdiction. Prior to statutory enactment such jurisdiction was based on rules of court.

(e) The sweeping up clause (s.20(1)(c))

The jurisdiction is arguably in both *personam* and *rem* but may extend to jurisdiction *in personam* only (see *supra*).

343. See further Chap. 9.
344. Prior to the Act the bringing of "collision actions" *as such* within Admiralty jurisdiction was based on RSC, Order 75, rule 2(1). Service of the writ *in personam* out of the jurisdiction is permitted in certain cases (see RSC, Order 75, rule 4 and Chap. 9). For the application and construction of the provision in RSC, Order 75, rule 4, see *The Aegean Captain* [1980] 1 Lloyd's Rep. 617.

PART II

Jurisdiction of English Courts and Arbitral Tribunals

CHAPTER 3

Jurisdiction Bases for Enforcement of Maritime Claims

THE SUBSTANTIVE "JURISDICTION BASE"

SERVICE OF PROCESS AND JURISDICTION BASES

Unlike many countries the English approach equated the procedure of commencement of the action with the substantive power to adjudicate on it. Traditionally, apart from submission of a defendant, the general foundation for jurisdiction in English courts was service of a writ. A writ *in personam* must be served on the defendant or by way of "substituted service", and a writ *in rem* on the maritime property in respect of which the action is brought or as otherwise provided for in the Rules of the Supreme Court. If the writ is properly served in England no further connection between the dispute and England is normally required. There are rules permitting service of a writ *in personam* out of England in certain categories of case having some substantive connection with England.

This process still remains the basic "national" English law approach but it is now much modified by the increasing application of "jurisdiction bases" (i.e. a substantive connection between England and the dispute)—largely as the result of the enactment of Conventions into English law. Where a base is required jurisdiction depends on the existence of a specified substantive connection between the case and England. The service of the writ then has a purely procedural role of commencement of the proceedings. The process (both uninfluenced and influenced by a jurisdiction base) is discussed in Chapters 9 and 10.

THE DEVELOPMENT OF JURISDICTION BASES

Limitations on "writ" jurisdiction

The assertion of jurisdiction through service of a writ has never been without limit.[1] First, limitations inherent in the process are the inability to serve a writ *in rem* abroad and the limit to specified categories or base of the ability to serve a writ *in personam* abroad.[2] The ability to serve a writ *in personam* abroad is based on substantive connections. Secondly there were (and are) restrictions even if a writ could be served abroad or even in England. So, for example, an English court will not entertain an action in respect of the title to

---

1. For jurisdiction restrictions generally, see Chap. 12.
2. See RSC, Orders 11(1), 75(4), and Chap. 9.

foreign land,[3] and there are limits to the power to order a foreigner within England to comply with its rules where compliance would be by acts outside England.[4] Thirdly, the assertion of jurisdiction has become progressively balanced by the opportunity of a defendant to seek a stay of proceedings (i.e. that jurisdiction should not be exercised) on the basis that they would more appropriately be heard elsewhere.[5]

Convention jurisdiction requirements

Apart from the necessity of substantive connection introduced through limitations on service, positive jurisdiction bases have been introduced into English law largely through the enactment of Conventions.[6] Those relevant to maritime claims are by no means each self-contained and there is, therefore, a risk of conflict of Conventions. First, there is the problem of the developing line of Conventions—as in the rules governing carriage of goods by sea. The Hague Rules 1924 were for some state parties superseded by the Hague-Visby Rules 1968 and in turn later rules for some by the Hamburg Rules 1978.

Secondly, there is potential overlap because of subject-matter. So the Hague Rules and their successors will impinge on Conventions relating to limitation of liability in respect of all claims based on a single incident. Conventions concerned with jurisdiction in general may, without express provision, clash with Conventions concerning jurisdiction on particular matters (such as collision) or substantive law Conventions having jurisdiction provisions. There is, therefore, a need to consider whether any particular Convention is expressly or impliedly subject to another.

The scope of the jurisdiction base depends on the Convention provision as enacted, but in no case does it differ domestically as between an action *in personam* and in action *in rem*.[7] All Convention bases apply to each although the mode and extent of the application will depend on the base imposed. The first jurisdictional issue in any case is therefore whether any base applies or whether jurisdiction still depends solely on the process based essentially on service of the writ or submission. As has been said, where a base is applicable the service of the writ remains relevant but only as the procedural commencement of the action. In this work consideration will first be given to the particular and general jurisdiction bases and subsequently to the rules relating to service of a writ.

Enactment or incorporation of Conventions into English law

A Convention ratified by the United Kingdom will have effect in domestic law only insofar as it is enacted either directly or indirectly by statute. That enactment may be by direct adoption of the Convention text, by enacting provisions reflecting the Convention

3. But only if title is at issue. See Civil Jurisdiction and Judgments Act 1982, s.30. The prohibition appears to extend to intellectual property (*Tyburn Productions* v. *Conan Doyle* [1991] Ch. 75).

4. *Mackinnon* v. *Donaldson Lufkin and Jenrette Securities Ltd.* [1986] 1 All E.R. 653 (order under Bankers' Books Evidence Act 1879 against a bank not a party to proceedings). *Rome* v. *Punjab National Bank, The Times,* 14 July 1988 (power to order discovery where jurisdiction challenged). As to the power (and its exercise) to order a party not to commence or continue foreign proceedings or in respect of foreign arbitrations, see Chap. 12.

5. See Chap. 12.

6. For a list of current parties to maritime Conventions see *The Ratification of Maritime Conventions*, Institute of Maritime Law, University of Southampton (Lloyd's of London Press) (looseleaf).

7. Although it was argued that an action *in rem* fell outside the Brussels Convention 1968 (see Chap. 4).

or, arguably, by incorporation through enactment of a Convention applying provisions of one not directly enacted.

Types of Convention with jurisdiction provision

Conventions enacted into English law with jurisdiction provisions are of three types —those concerned primarily with:

    (i) substantive law on a particular topic (as, for example, the Athens Convention relating to the Carriage of Passengers and their Luggage by Sea 1974);

   (ii) procedure or jurisdiction on a particular topic (as, for example, the Convention relating to the Arrest of Sea-Going Ships 1952 and the Collision (Civil Jurisdiction) Convention 1952);

  (iii) general jurisdiction structures relating to all or most commercial claims (as the European Union Convention on Jurisdiction and the Recognition and Enforcement of Judgments in Civil and Commercial Matters 1968 (as amended) (i.e. the Brussels Convention) and the treaty between the states of the European Union and the European Free Trade Association in 1988 of the same title (the Lugano Convention)).

PARTICULAR JURISDICTION BASES

1. CONVENTION TEXTS DIRECTLY ENACTED

Express jurisdiction bases relevant to maritime claims are enacted through statutory adoption of the text of (i) the Convention relating to the Carriage of Passengers and their Luggage by Sea 1974 (the Athens Convention) and (ii) the Convention relating to International Carriage of Goods by Road 1956 (the CMR Convention). It is arguable that the Hague-Visby Rules 1968 contain an implied jurisdiction provision.

(i) The Athens Convention 1974 (Merchant Shipping Act 1979, Sch. 3)

The Convention provides a liability regime for the carriage of passengers and their luggage.[8] By Article 2(1) it applies to any international carriage if:

  (a) the ship is flying the flag of or is registered in a State party to this Convention, or

  (b) the contract of carriage has been made in a State party to this Convention, or

  (c) the place of departure or destination, according to the contract of carriage, is in a State party to this Convention.

Potential conflict of Conventions is dealt with by Article 2(2):

---

8. The Convention does not modify the rights and duties under Conventions relating to limitation of liability of shipowners (i.e. global limitation) (Art. 19). As to limitation of the liability see Chap. 24. For current limitation amounts see SI 1989/1880. As to the parties see *The Ratification of Maritime Conventions* (fn. 6).

"Notwithstanding paragraph 1 of this Article, this Convention shall not apply when the carriage is subject, under any other international convention concerning the carriage of passengers or luggage by another mode of transport, to a civil liability regime under the provisions of such convention, in so far as those provisions have mandatory application to carriage by sea."[9]

The Convention is extended to journeys under the contract of carriage within the area of the United Kingdom, the Channel Islands and the Isle of Man if there is no intermediate port of call outside the area.[10]

Article 17 of the Convention provides:

"Competent jurisdiction
1. An action arising under this Convention shall, at the option of the claimant, be brought before one of the courts listed below, provided that the court is located in a State Party to this Convention:
    (a) the court of the place of permanent residence or principal place of business of the defendant, or
    (b) the court of the place of departure or that of the destination according to the contract of carriage, or
    (c) a court of the State of the domicile or permanent residence of the claimant, if the defendant has a place of business and is subject to jurisdiction in that State.
    (d) A court of the State where the contract of carriage was made, if the defendant has a place of business and is subject to jurisdiction in that State.
2. After the occurrence of the incident which has caused the damage, the parties may agree that the claim for damages shall be submitted to any jurisdiction or to arbitration."

An action under the Convention may be brought in the United Kingdom, therefore, only if one of the connections there specified exists between the case and the United Kingdom.

(ii) The CMR 1956 (Carriage of Goods by Road Act 1965, Sch.)

The Convention provides a carriage and liability regime for contracts of international carriage by road. Subject to specific exceptions relating to post, funerals and furniture removal the Convention applies to every contract for the carriage of goods by road in vehicles for reward where the place of taking over a delivery specified in the contract is in different countries one of which is a contracting State.[11] It applies to carriage by sea where part of the journey is by sea and the vehicle is not unloaded. However, where it is proved that loss, damage or delay was not caused by the road carrier but by an event which could only have occurred during the sea transport, the carrier liability is to be determined as if the contract was for carriage of goods by sea.[12]

The courts within which an action may be brought are limited. It is provided by Article 31(1):

9. Art. 2(1). The Convention does not apply to carriage subject to a Convention concerning another mode of transport to a civil liability regime mandatorily applied to carriage by sea (Art. 2(2)).
10. Carriage of Passengers and their Luggage by Sea (Domestic Carriage) Order 1987 (SI 1987/670).
11. Carriage of Goods by Road Act 1965, Sch., Art. 1. There is a prohibition against parties entering inconsistent Conventions between them save in respect of frontier traffic or transport operation entirely confined to the territory of the states (Art. 1(5)). As to the CMR see Clarke, *International Carriage of Goods by Road* (2nd edn) Sweet & Maxwell, 1991.
12. Art 2. This applies if the carrier by road is also the carrier by sea, liability being determined as if the carrier were two separate persons (Art. 10(2)).

"1. In legal proceedings arising out of carriage under this Convention, the plaintiff may bring an action in any court or tribunal of a contracting country designated by agreement between the parties and, in addition, in the courts or tribunals of a country within whose territory
- (a) the defendant is ordinarily resident, or has his principal place of business, or the branch or agency through which the contract of carriage was made, or
- (b) the place where the goods were taken over by the carrier or the place designated for delivery is situated,

and in no other courts or tribunals."[13]

(iii) The Hague-Visby Rules 1968

While there is no express jurisdiction it was held by the House of Lords in *The Morviken*[14] that the parties may not avoid the rules through agreeing on a non Hague-Visby Rules state in which the carrier may be subject to a lower limitation of liability. So in an action brought in England the rules will be applied—this does not so much found jurisdiction as removes a limit normally applicable on jurisdiction by service of writ.[15]

2. CONVENTIONS REFLECTED IN ENGLISH LAW

Relevant to maritime claims are:

- (i) the Convention Relating to the Arrest of Sea Going Ships 1952 (the Arrest Convention) enacted at least in part through (now) the Supreme Court Act 1981, s.20[16]
- (ii) the International Convention on Certain Rules Concerning Civil Jurisdiction in Matters of Collision 1952 (the Collision Jurisdiction Convention)—(the basis of Supreme Court Act 1981, s.22)
- (iii) The International Convention on Civil Liability for Oil Pollution Damage 1971 (the Oil Pollution Convention) (the Merchant Shipping (Oil Pollution) Act 1971 (as amended by the Merchant Shipping (Salvage and Pollution) Act 1994)) (as from 1 January 1996 the Merchant Shipping Act 1995 Part VI)
- (iv) The International Convention on the Establishment of an International Fund for Compensation for Oil Pollution Damage 1971 (the Fund Convention) (the Merchant Shipping Act 1974 (as amended by the Merchant Shipping (Salvage and Pollution) Act 1994)) (as from 1 January 1996 the Merchant Shipping Act 1995 Part VI)
- (v) The Rhine Navigation Convention 1868 (preserved by the Supreme Court Act 1981 s.23).

13. A judgment in proceedings within Art. 31(1) when enforceable in the contracting State in which it is given is also enforceable in other contracting States—subject only to formalities required by that state. The case may not be reopened (Art. 31(3)). As to recognition of foreign judgments see Chap. 27.
14. [1983] A.C. 565; [1983] 1 Lloyd's Rep. 1.
15. See further Chap. 12.
16. Replacing the Administration of Justice Act 1956, ss.1–8. As to jurisdiction *in rem* generally and the role of arrest in English law, see Chaps. 10, 15. As to the possible incorporation of Art. 7 through the Brussels Convention, see Chap. 12.

(i) The Arrest Convention 1952

There is set out in the Convention a list of maritime claims for which a ship may be arrested and the provision that arrest may be for no other claim. With an exception for "domestic" arrest and possible national reservations the Convention applies to any ship flying the flag of a Convention State. In addition it is provided that a ship flying the flag of a non-contracting State may be arrested in the jurisdiction of a contracting State,[17] and that "the court of the country in which the arrest is made has jurisdiction to determine the case on its merits if the domestic law of the country in which the arrest is made gives jurisdiction to such court or in six specified circumstances."[18]

The Convention provisions are not directly enacted into English law but the basis of arrest is the jurisdiction in actions *in rem* set out in the Supreme Court Act 1981. The Arrest Convention as such does not therefore provide jurisdiction bases—those remain provisions of the domestic law founded essentially on service of a writ or submission.[19] Although by the international obligation under the Arrest Convention national law should be brought in line, on the one hand the 1981 Act does not fully implement the Convention and, on the other, does not limit such implementation as there is to the ambit of the Convention. There is no difference in English law whether the parties are connected with contracting States.

(ii) The Collision (Civil Jurisdiction) Convention 1952

Articles 1, 2 and 3 provide:

"**Article 1**
(1) An action for collision occurring between seagoing vessels, or between seagoing vessels and inland navigation craft, can only be introduced:
  (a) either before the Court where the defendant has his habitual residence or a place of business;
  (b) or before the Court of the place where arrest has been effected of the defendant ship or of any other ship belonging to the defendant which can be lawfully arrested, or where arrest could have been effected and bail or other security has been furnished;
  (c) or before the Court of the place of collision when the collision has occurred within the limits of a port or in inland waters.
(2) It shall be for the plaintiff to decide in which of the Courts referred to in paragraph 1 of this article the action shall be instituted.
(3) A claimant shall not be allowed to bring a further action against the same defendant on the same facts in another jurisdiction, without discontinuing an action already instituted.

Article 2
The provisions of Article 1 shall not in any way prejudice the right of the parties to bring an action in respect of a collision before a Court they have chosen by agreement or to refer it to arbitration.

---

17. Arts. 1, 8(1)(2). A contracting State may exclude from the benefits of the Convention any government of a non-contracting State or any person whose habitual residence or principal place of business is not in a contracting State (Art. 8(3)). Nothing in the Convention affects the domestic law of a state relating to the arrest of any ship within her flag State by a person whose habitual place of residence or principal place of business is in that state (Art. 8(4)).
  18. Art. 7(1).
  19. As to the effect of "submission" in an action *in rem*, see Chaps. 9, 10.

Article 3

(1) Counterclaims arising out of the same collision can be brought before the Court having jurisdiction over the principal action in accordance with the provisions of Article 1.

(2) In the event of there being several claimants, any claimant may bring his action before the Court previously seized of an action against the same party arising out of the same collision.

(3) In the case of a collision or collisions in which two or more vessels are involved nothing in this Convention shall prevent any Court seized of an action by reason of the provisions of this Convention, from exercising jurisdiction under its national laws in further actions arising out of the same incident."

The Convention is not directly enacted but s.22 of the Supreme Court Act 1981 reflects the restrictive provisions of Art. 1 in respect of actions *in personam*.[20] There is no specific enactment of the arrest jurisdiction of Art. 1(1)(b). As with such jurisdiction under the Arrest Convention that is left to the effect of the action *in rem*. Neither the *in personam* nor the *in rem* jurisdiction is restricted to parties to the Convention.

The jurisdiction base is therefore a matter of English law. The Convention provisions are modified in that to serve a writ *in personam* out of the jurisdiction leave of the court is required. So in that context at least the court's discretion is relevant to the creation of jurisdiction.[21] The Convention jurisdiction base of arrest or security is changed in English law by the *in rem* process to service of the writ *in rem*. There is no difference in the application of the jurisdiction base as between actions connected and actions not connected to contracting States. The provisions of s.22 are not restricted to parties to the Convention.

(iii) The Oil Pollution Convention 1969 (to become the 1992 Convention on enactment of the 1992 Protocol on 30 May 1996)

The Convention (as amended) applies to pollution damage caused in the territory, territorial sea of a contracting State and the exclusive economic zone (or equivalent area) of such a State and to preventative measures wherever taken to minimize such damage.
    Article IX(1) provides:

"Where an incident has caused pollution damage in the territory . . . of one or more Contracting States[22] or preventative measures have been taken to prevent or minimise pollution damage in such a territory . . . actions for compensation may only be brought in Courts of any such Contracting State or States. Reasonable notice of any such action shall be given to the defendant."

The Convention is not directly enacted into English law.[23] However, the restriction on jurisdiction (applicable to the unamended Convention) was initially reflected in s.13(4) of the Merchant Shipping (Oil Pollution) Act 1971 and as from 1 January 1996 (as applicable both to the amended Convention and on the coming into force of the 1992 Protocol to the

---

20. See App. 1. The provision for arbitration is reflected in the rules of the Arbitration Act 1975—relating generally to stay of proceedings on the basis of an arbitration clause (see Chap. 13). As to the claims within s.22 as defined in that provision see Chaps. 9, 12.

21. See e.g. *The Aegean Captain* [1980] 1 Lloyd's Rep. 617.

22. The "territory" includes the territorial sea or other area connected to the state to which the Convention applies.

23. There is power to make the provisions of specified oil pollution Conventions part of English law once ratified by the United Kingdom: Merchant Shipping Act 1979, ss.20, 20A (as amended and inserted by the Merchant Shipping (Salvage and Pollution) Act 1994, ss.3, 4). The power has been exercised in a number of statutory orders. As from 1 January 1996 the statutory power is contained in the Merchant Shipping Act 1995, s.128.

amended Convention) s.166(2) of the Merchant Shipping Act 1995.[24] By that provision an action may be brought under the Act only if damage or preventative measures occur in "the area of the United Kingdom". If such damage or measure has occurred a court may hear a claim not only in respect of that damage or cost but any also occurring in the territory of another contracting State.[25]

(iv) The Fund Convention 1971 (to become the 1992 Convention on enactment of the 1992 Protocol)

There is no jurisdiction base as such. The Fund Convention is not directly enacted into English law but is reflected in the Merchant Shipping Act 1974 as amended by the Merchant Shipping Salvage and Pollution Act 1994 (and as from 1 January 1996 in the Merchant Shipping Act 1995 Part VI).[26] There is no prerequisite for jurisdiction as such but save for jurisdiction depending on the Fund Headquarters being in the United Kingdom an action will lie only in respect of damage (including preventative measures) in the United Kingdom.[27] The Fund Headquarters are in London and while this is so an action may be brought against the Fund in respect of pollution damage in any Fund Convention country.[28]

(v) The Rhine Navigation Convention 1868 (as amended)

The Convention is concerned, as its title implies, with navigation of the Rhine. It contains some provisions conferring jurisdiction on the Tribunal for Rhine Navigation. It is provided by s.23 of the Supreme Court Act 1981 that the High Court has no jurisdiction in such matters.[29]

3. CONVENTIONS IN FORCE TO WHICH THE UNITED KINGDOM IS NOT PARTY

Such Conventions including jurisdiction provisions are the Hamburg Rules 1978 and the Paris Convention on Third Party Liability in the Field of Nuclear Energy 1963. Care must be taken, therefore, in respect of cases within the ambit of such Conventions if litigation is contemplated in State parties thereto, or, even if litigating within the United Kingdom, if the law applicable to the dispute is arguably that of a State party to the Convention. If the Convention is applied as part of the applicable law it will dictate jurisdiction.

---

24. As amended by Merchant Shipping Act 1988, Sch. 4, Pt. I, brought into force by the Merchant Shipping (Salvage and Pollution) Act 1994, s.5.

25. *Ibid.* A similar but not so restricted territorial limitation applies to damage caused through nuclear matter, see the Nuclear Installations Act 1965, s.13. Jurisdiction under that Act may be prohibited by the relevant Minister if under a Convention that action falls to be determined by another court (s.17(1)). As to "nuclear damage" see Chap. 2.

26. Applying with adaptation amendments of the 1974 Act set out in Merchant Shipping Act 1988, Sch. 4, Pt. II (see s.5 of the 1994 Act).

27. 1974 Act, s.4(1) (as amended).

28. *Ibid.*, s.4(2).

29. See Chap. 12.

GENERALLY APPLICABLE JURISDICTION BASES

THE EUROPEAN JURISDICTION CONVENTIONS

These are contained in the Conventions on Jurisdiction and the Recognition and Enforcement of Judgments in Civil and Commercial Matters 1968 of the European Union (the "Brussels Convention") and 1988 of the European Community and European Free Trade Association (the "Lugano Convention"). The 1968 Convention is amended by accession treaties following the accession of Denmark and the United Kingdom and Ireland, Greece and, more recently, Portugal and Spain. A further accession treaty will emerge to allow Austria, Finland and Sweden to become parties. The Brussels Convention is given "the force of law" by the Civil Jurisdiction and Judgments Act 1982 and the Lugano Convention by the Civil Jurisdiction and Judgments Act 1991 amending the 1982 Act. The texts of the Conventions are set out in Schedules to the Acts.

The Brussels Convention 1968 (as amended)

The 1982 Act came into force on 1 January 1987. It was amended on the accession of Greece (SI 1989/1346) and on the accession of Spain and Portugal (SI 1990/2591). So far as the United Kingdom is concerned the current Convention text is that set out in SI 1990/2591, that text coming into force on 1 December 1991. However, subject to some judgments rendered after the date of coming into force in relation to proceedings commenced prior to that date, the Brussels Convention 1968, each Accession Convention and the Lugano Convention all apply only to proceedings in a member State started after the date of the Convention coming into force in that state.[30] Care must therefore be taken when considering Convention jurisdiction in other member States that the relevant state has ratified the latest accession treaty and hence the latest text. The Convention text of the 1982 Act is adapted by Sch. 4 to that Act (as amended by SI 1993/603) to apply to jurisdiction (and judgments) issues as between different parts of the United Kingdom.[31]

The Lugano Convention

The 1982 Act was further amended by the Civil Jurisdiction and Judgments Act 1991 to enact an almost identical Convention of 1988 between the member States and the States of the European Free Trade Association—Austria, Finland, Iceland, Norway, Sweden and Switzerland (known as the Lugano Convention). The text of that Convention is inserted into the 1982 Act as Sch. 3C. It came into force in the United Kingdom on 1 May 1992. It will apply to Austria, Finland and Sweden as new "Community" States until they become parties to the Brussels Convention—at which point they presumably will become parties to both Conventions.[32] Apart from minor differences the Brussels and Lugano Conventions differ only insofar as the European Court of Justice has jurisdiction only as regards the Brussels Convention—there being provisions in the Lugano Convention

---

30. See Art. 58 of the Brussels Convention.

31. The European Court has no jurisdiction in respect of the construction of this Schedule (*Kleinwort Benson Ltd.* v. *City of Glasgow DC* 346/93 [1995] All E.R. (E.C.) 514).

32. The same point as to the governing text as made in relation to the Brussels Convention will apply as more states accede to the Lugano Convention.

concerning uniform interpretation and also the relationship of the two Conventions (see Chap. 8).

The Conventions provide jurisdictional bases. As a consequence, as for a "particular" jurisdiction base, in relation to matters within them the function of service of a writ is procedural only. Whereas, in respect of matters outside the Convention, English law continues to see jurisdiction in such procedural terms, within the Convention the service simply implements procedurally the jurisdiction created by the Convention. The service itself cannot create jurisdiction, but within the general Convention structure fulfils the procedural role left to the national laws.

The influence of the Brussels and Lugano Conventions

The Conventions have a wide scope. Subject to any restriction in relation to non-contracting States, the Convention will apply to all proceedings in a contracting State. Depending on the nature of the proceedings, the issue and the connection (or lack of connection) between the Community and the defendant, the application is one of three differing legal regimes:

  (i) national law of the forum;
  (ii) the Convention jurisdiction rules;
  (iii) the rules of another Convention.

Because of the wide scope, parties and their advisers may no longer treat the substantive jurisdictional base as an exception in English law. A critical question which should be put in *each* case, it is suggested, is the effect of the Brussels and Lugano Conventions. The response may be simply that the pre-Convention process focused on service of the writ applies—but, apart from the relatively few matters excluded from the Conventions, it will do so because of the appropriate Convention. The inclusion of all proceedings connected solely with contracting States emphasizes that, while a principal jurisdictional base is domicile of the defendant it is by no means exclusive.

As the Lugano Convention builds on the Brussels Convention and as judicial construction to date is almost wholly of the Brussels Convention, consideration will first be given to the Brussels Convention (in Chapters 4–7). The Lugano Convention will be considered in Chapter 8 only as regards jurisdiction differences between that and the earlier Convention.

As at 1st December 1995 all member States of the European Union save Belgium and Denmark and the "new" members—Austria, Finland and Sweden—had ratified the Brussels Convention as amended on the accession of Portugal and Spain. The same member State of the Union apart from Greece and all EFTA states with the exception of Austria (i.e. Finland, Iceland, Norway, Sweden and Switzerland) had ratified the Lugano Convention.

CHAPTER 4

The Brussels Convention—Boundaries and Structure

I. THE GENERAL PATTERN

JURISDICTION AND JUDGMENTS

In providing a jurisdiction regime the contracting States arguably went beyond the obligation of the Treaty of Rome on which it is founded—focused as that is on the enforcement of judgments. However, the judgments structure of the Convention is built on its jurisdictional foundation. The basic principle is that jurisdictional enquiry is a matter for the adjudicating court, the judgment of which normally should be recognized and enforced without further enquiry. In this respect the Convention differs from the pattern of bilateral judgment conventions which make recognition or enforcement dependent on the enforcement court being satisfied that the adjudicating court had jurisdiction.

Further, the duty to recognize and enforce judgments is not limited to judgments based on Convention jurisdiction. It encompasses both judgments in proceedings outside and within the jurisdiction provisions and to an extent those within those provisions but resulting from proceedings not complying with them. The Convention necessarily imposes duties on contracting States not to exercise jurisdiction in any suit save in accordance with the Convention framework. However, the grounds of refusal to recognize or enforce judgments are specific, thereby necessarily implying that, apart from these grounds, the Convention requires recognition and enforcement of a judgment even if that judgment is obtained in proceedings brought contrary to the jurisdiction provisions. The judgment provisions are considered in Chapter 28.

CONNECTIONS WITH THE COMMUNITY

The preamble makes clear that the Convention is concerned to "strengthen the legal protection" of persons established in the Community and for this purpose "to determine the international jurisdiction" of the courts of member States, "to facilitate, recognize and introduce an expeditious procedure for the enforcement of judgments, authentic instruments and settlements". It follows that the Convention of itself has no application to any dispute wholly connected solely to one contracting State and on the other hand is not restricted to matters between parties wholly connected to contracting States.

In the context of jurisdiction a primary connection is the "domicile" of the defendant in a contracting State. Care must be taken however that such domicile is not seen as the exclusive connection factor either for the Convention to apply or, when applicable, for jurisdiction to be allocated to the state of that domicile.

INTERPRETATION OF THE CONVENTION

By virtue of the Protocol of 1971 (as amended) the primary authority for the interpretation of the Convention is the European Court of Justice. Preliminary rulings may be requested by any court specified in Article 2 of the Protocol.[1] In the United Kingdom it is by the House of Lords, any court sitting in an appellate capacity or save in the question of maintenance in the case of an appeal against a decision against enforcement of a judgment by the High Court.[2]

The original 1968 Convention, the 1971 Protocol and the Accession Conventions are drawn up in seven languages. Each text is equally authentic and in accordance with its own principles, the English court could refer to a text other than the English for clarification.[3] By section 3 of the Act the Convention must be interpreted in the light of decisions and expressions of the European Court and specific reference is made in the Act to Reports by Professor P. Schlosser and Mr P. J. Jenard on the Convention. These Reports may be taken into account in ascertaining the meaning or effect of the Convention of Protocol (s.3).[4]

There is provision for a contracting State to request an interpretative ruling from the European Court of Justice if a judgment of a court of that state conflicts in the construction of the Convention with that of the European Court or a court of another member State. Each member State and the Commission are to be given an opportunity to make submissions. A request may be made only when the judgments in respect of the proceedings giving rise to the request have become *res judicata*. The opinions rendered will not affect any judgment given (Article 4 of the 1971 Protocol).

THE ROLE OF NATIONAL LAWS

Save for specified categories of case the issue of jurisdiction in all proceedings within the ambit of the Convention where the defendant is not domiciled in a contracting State are referred to the law of the forum. On the other hand where the Convention jurisdiction regime applies the European Court has consistently held that the Convention is based primarily on Community concepts (as for example the meaning of "*lis pendens*" in respect of Articles 21, 22, in Article 5 the meaning of the "place where the harmful event occurs", in Article 20 service of a document instituting proceedings in sufficient time to arrange for a defence and the bases of exclusive jurisdiction in Article 16).

1. Compare the reference power under Article 177 of the Treaty of Rome. There must be a real question of "interpretation", and where the European Court has pronounced only if the national court wishes to see if the position is to be maintained. See generally *CILFIT Srl* v. *Ministry of Health* [1982] ECR 3415; [1983] 1 CMLR 472.

2. Protocol of 1971 Article 2—the court relevant to a maintenance question is the magistrates' court (Art. 37).

3. See *James Buchanan and Co.* v. *Babco Forwarding and Shipping (UK)* [1978] A.C. 141; [1978] 1 CMLR 1048.

4. For the text of the Reports see 1979 OJ C59 pp. 1, 66, 71. There are similar reports in relation to each Accession Convention.

However, even in the context of the Convention regime national law plays a part. The Convention specifically refers to questions of domicile or seat of a legal person to national law (Articles 52 and 53), and the court has declared that some matters are for national law (for example whether a court is "seised" of a cause of action within Article 21 and the "place of performance of a Contract" within Article 5(1)). The issues are discussed in the particular contexts.

RELATIONSHIP WITH OTHER CONVENTIONS

It is sought to fit the Convention with others with which there may be an overlap by:

(a) as regards service of documents specifically giving priority to the Hague Convention on the Service Abroad of Judicial and Extra Judicial Documents in Civil or Commercial Matters 1965 (Article 20) or any other applicable Convention on the matter (Annexed Protocol Article IV);

(b) in a specified context permitting contracting States to enter into Conventions inconsistent with the Convention in respect of recognition and enforcement of judgments (Article 59);

(c) superseding specific listed Conventions (Article 55);

(d) maintaining Conventions inconsistent with the 1968 Convention:
  (i) as to one bilateral Convention (Article 56);
  (ii) as to Conventions "on particular matters" governing jurisdiction or judgments (Article 57).

APPLICATION WITHIN THE UNITED KINGDOM

For the purposes of the 1968 Convention the United Kingdom is one state but for *intra* United Kingdom purposes it consists of three constituent parts—England and Wales, Scotland and Northern Ireland (see s. 50 of the Act). For internal United Kingdom purposes Convention jurisdiction must be geared to a part of the United Kingdom.

The Convention itself provides in certain circumstances for jurisdiction in courts of a "place" in a contracting State, that place being a place in the state in which the defendant is domiciled (as defined by national law) or the place of a thing or event. In such cases clearly jurisdiction is bestowed geographically precisely and, insofar as this has a jurisdictional connotation, within a state jurisdictionally precisely. In English law for the purposes of the Convention a person is domiciled in a particular place in the United Kingdom only if domiciled in the part of the United Kingdom where the place is and he is resident in that place. A similar provision is made for corporations—requiring the seat and registered office, central management or place of business to be in the part. In English law also a trust can be domiciled in the United Kingdom only if it is domiciled in a part (s.45).

Where the Convention confers jurisdiction simply on courts of a contracting State (as for example in Article 2, the basic jurisdiction principle of the defendant's domicile) it is necessary that that jurisdiction be allocated within the United Kingdom. This is accomplished by express provision in the Act (ss. 10, 16). It is further applied by the Act to *intra* United Kingdom disputes which, lying within one contracting State, are outside the Convention (see *infra* and Chapter 7).

APPLICATION TO OTHER UNITED KINGDOM TERRITORIES

Provisions may be made corresponding to the Convention as between the United Kingdom and the Isle of Man, the Channel Islands or any colony. Such provisions are to be made under s.39 by Order in Council. No Order in Council has yet been made.

II. THE APPLICABILITY OF THE CONVENTION

The Convention applies—

(1) when the subject-matter of the case is within it and
(2) subject to exclusion of issues connected with a non-contracting State, to any proceedings within the Convention or judgments in a contracting State in an issue not wholly connected with that state.

However the consequence of a case falling within the Convention will vary according to whether the issue is—

(i) referred to the forum, or
(ii) referred to another Convention, or
(iii) the Convention jurisdiction structure applies.

These varying consequences are discussed in Chapters 5, 6 and 12.

1. THE SUBJECT-MATTER—"CIVIL OR COMMERCIAL MATTERS"

Article 1 of the Convention provides:

"This Convention shall apply in civil and commercial matters whatever the nature of the court or tribunal. It shall not extend, in particular, to revenue, customs or administrative matters."

The Convention shall not apply to:

(1) the status or legal capacity of natural persons, rights in property arising out of a matrimonial relationship, wills and succession;
(2) bankruptcy, proceedings relating to the winding-up of insolvent companies or other legal persons, judicial arrangements, compositions and analogous proceedings;
(3) social security;
(4) arbitration.

The general definition

There is no Convention definition of the phrase "civil and commercial matters", but it has been settled by the European Court that the question of "civil and commercial matters" must be given a Convention meaning. In *LTV GmbH & Company KG* v. *Eurocontrol*[5] the Court said:

"By providing that the Convention shall apply 'whatever the nature of the Court or Tribunal' Art 1 shows that the concept 'civil and Commercial matters' cannot be interpreted solely in the light of the division of jurisdiction between the various types of courts existing in certain states. The concept in question must therefore be regarded as independent and must be interpreted by reference, first, to the objectives and scheme of the Convention and, secondly, to the general principles which stem from the corpus of the national legal systems."

The Court held that "a judgment given in an action between a public authority and a person governed by private law in which the public authority has acted in the exercise of its powers is excluded from the area of application of the Convention". In essence the boundary is drawn between private law and public law, the exclusion of the latter being underlined by the express reference to "revenue, administrative and customs matters".[6] In *State of Netherlands* v. *Ruffer*[7] the Court held that proceedings brought for redress for wreck removal by a public authority was not within the Convention. In this case the state was acting in the exercise of its public authority powers rather than as a commercial entity. It is however settled that employment issues (whether the employment is by public or private authority provided the private authority is being sued as employer) are within the Convention.[8]

The specific exclusions

The specific exclusions may cause problems of overlap. An issue of legal capacity could arise as part of a contractual dispute and enforcement of a maritime claim could involve bankruptcy. As a matter of practice it would presumably be necessary to classify a particular action by its primary characteristics to avoid differing jurisdictional rules applied to different parts of the same dispute. Of the matters excluded bankruptcy and arbitration are relevant to maritime claims:

Bankruptcy[9]

In *Gourdain* v. *Nadler*[10] the European Court of Justice held that for proceedings to be excluded on the grounds of bankruptcy "they must derive directly from the bankruptcy or winding up" and must be based on the national law relating to bankruptcy or winding up. An action by a trustee in bankruptcy to recover debts of an insolvent company arising before the bankruptcy proceeding is therefore within the Convention.[11]

---

5. 29/76 [1976] ECR 1541; [1977] 1 CMLR 88.

6. See Schlosser paras 23–29, pointing out the contrast between (a) the United Kingdom and Ireland and (b) other EC States in which the public law/private law dichotomy is well established and setting out some comparative details.

7. 814/79 [1980] ECR 3807; [1981] 3 CMLR 293.

8. See *Sanicentral* v. *Collin* 25/79 [1979] ECR 3423; [1980] 2 CMLR 164. As to its application to judgments see Chap. 28.

9. See generally Schlosser paras. 53–59.

10. 133/78 [1979] ECR 733; [1979] 3 CMLR 180.

11. See *Powell Duffryn plc* v. *Petereit* C214/89 [1992] ECR 1745; *Van Rolleghem* v. *Roth* (Trib. de Commerce, Brussels) 22 March 1979, ECD 1–1.2–B5. Compare *Maitre Pierrel* v. *Ergur* (Cour d'Appel Paris) [1993] I.L.Pr. 523 (judicial reorganization proceedings against a corporate entity).

Arbitration

The exclusion of arbitration raises particular problems. It would seem clear that the Convention does not apply to proceedings to enforce, or set aside, an award or decision incorporating an award or to any matter concerned with the conduct of arbitration proceedings.[12] However, a jurisdiction issue may well turn on the effect of an arbitration clause. Perhaps more fundamental is the question whether the Convention will apply to any issue as to the validity of an arbitration agreement, secondly whether any judgment that it will or will not apply must be recognized under the Convention, and thirdly whether a judgment in proceedings brought contrary to an arbitration clause must be enforced under the Convention.

(i) *The validity of an arbitration agreement*

In *Marc Rich and Co. AG (a Swiss Corporation)* v. *Societa Italiana Impianti PA*[13] *(an Italian Corporation)* questions were put by the English Court of Appeal to the European Court whether the arbitration exception extends—

   (a) to any litigation and judgment and, if so,
   (b) to litigation or judgment where the initial existence of an arbitration agreement is in issue.

The questions arose during the course of extended proceedings in England and Italy to pursue a claim for damages for the sale of contaminated oil. After agreeing to purchase the oil Marc Rich had telexed Impianti setting out the contract terms and for the first time providing for the application of English law and London arbitration. There was no response to that telex. Once the claim was made Marc Rich sought the appointment of an arbitrator by Impianti. Impianti asserted there was no arbitration agreement and started proceedings in Genoa for a declaration of non-liability. The issue which led to the reference to the European Court was the jurisdiction of the English court to decide the validity of the arbitration clause.

   The response of the European Court was linked directly to the precise issue making it necessary to decide the validity of the clause—the appointment of an arbitrator. The Court said that, given the existing comprehensive international arbitration Convention framework[14] it was intended to exclude from the Brussels Convention "arbitration in its entirety including proceedings brought before national Courts". "More particularly" the appointment of an arbitrator was part of the process setting arbitration in motion—it was excluded. As to validity of the arbitration clause, as the "dispute" (i.e. the appointment of the arbitrator) fell outside the Convention "the existence of a preliminary issue which the Court must resolve . . . cannot justify application of the Convention". The Court concluded that the exclusion extends "to litigation . . . concerning the appointment of an arbitrator even if the existence or validity of an arbitration agreement is a preliminary issue in that litigation". The Court did not therefore decide that the Convention did not

---

12. See Schlosser paras 64, 65; Decision of Landgericht, Hamburg, 24 April 1979, ECD 1–1.2–B12. But such a judgment may not be within the New York Convention on the Recognition and Enforcement of Foreign Arbitral Awards. See *Victrix Steamship Co. SA* v. *Salen Dry Cargo AB* (SDNY) 1987 AMC 276 at p. 279.
13. [1992] 1 Lloyd's Rep. 342.
14. i.e. in particular the New York Convention on Recognition and Enforcement of Arbitral Awards 1958 (see generally Chap. 13).

apply to the issue of validity of an arbitration clause when that matter is the sole or principal issue in the proceedings.

(ii) *Recognition of a judgment on the validity of the arbitration agreement*

In the *Marc Rich* case after the reference by the Court of Appeal but before the judgment of the European Court the Corte di Cassazione in Italy held in a reference by a lower court directly on the issue that the contract did not contain an arbitration clause. When the case returned to the Court of Appeal[15] the court thought that the judgment of the European Court was no clear authority for holding that the Italian judgment was one that by the Convention the court had to recognize and decided that the judgment should be recognized on the basis of English law.[16]

(iii) *Recognition of judgment in breach of arbitration agreement*

The most difficult question goes to the recognition of a judgment in proceedings brought contrary to the arbitration agreement. Schlosser (para. 62) simply records the arguments. It is open to a court asked to enforce the judgment to consider whether the matter is within the Convention (see Chapter 28) and the question is whether the exclusion of arbitration encompasses the question of recognition of a judgment of proceedings brought contrary to the clause. To allow the enforceability of the judgment to depend on the validity of the arbitration agreement according to forum law would necessarily mean that the enforcement court consider the agreement. This is arguably inconsistent with the principle of the simplicity of enforcement proceedings within the Convention. (See Chapter 28.)

(iv) *Consideration of the three aspects*

In 1993 in *The Heidberg*[17] the High Court had to address the three aspects of the issue. Judge Diamond Q.C. was of the view that there was little one way or the other as regards linguistic argument—it was a matter of policy. However there were "solid practical and policy reasons" for holding the validity issue as *within* the Convention. First it would mean that the decision would be binding on other contracting States. Not only would that prevent a race between different jurisdictions but also the risk that there might be conflicting judgments as to the substance of the dispute because of conflicting judgments about the validity of the clause. Thirdly, there was an obligation to recognize a judgment even if given in breach of an arbitration clause. Fourthly, there were provisions in the Convention which could arguably give jurisdiction to the courts of the place in which the arbitration was to be held and hence meet one of the objections to the inclusion of the issue within the Convention.

Judge Diamond acknowledged that the issue was difficult and that there were factors in favour of exclusion, not least that whether or not it is within the Convention will depend on whether the issue is "preliminary" or "principal". However, on balance the judge concluded that the issue was within the Convention both for the reasons of policy outlined

15. [1992] 1 Lloyd's Rep. 624.
16. i.e. because Marc Rich had participated in the proceedings that led to it and therefore submitted to the jurisdiction of the Italian court.
17. [1994] 2 Lloyd's Rep. 287 particularly pp. 296–303.

and because judgments on the issue necessarily extended to the construction of the underlying contract in which the clause appeared.

The reasons given by Judge Diamond seem, with respect, powerful and persuasive, but the principal disadvantage, the difference between exclusion and inclusion, is the accident of the way in which the issue arises. Unless that is thought to be overwhelmingly compelling inclusion would seem to further the Convention policy.

2. PROCEEDINGS TO WHICH THE CONVENTION APPLIES

Jurisdiction in one case may be both within and outside the Convention. So there may be multiple parties, some of whom are subject to the Convention[18] or it may be that the Convention will apply depending on which party is the plaintiff.[19] This is the inevitable result of a non-universal regime.

Proceedings falling outside the Convention

Proceedings are excluded from the Convention because of express provision or underlying purpose.[20]

(i) Cases having no foreign element

The preamble to the Convention refers to the "international jurisdiction" of the courts of contracting States. It is accepted that the Convention has no part to play in disputes connected only with the United Kingdom. The Convention is however adapted by United Kingdom laws to allocate jurisdiction as between the different parts of the United Kingdom.[21]

(ii) Proceedings without a defendant

The Convention is focused on the state in which a person shall be sued. If therefore the proceedings are not aimed at a "person" (i.e. a defendant) they fall outside the Convention. This was the foundation of the argument before the Court of Appeal in 1989 in *The Deichland* that an action *in rem* was not within the Convention—the argument being rejected on the basis that in that type of action there is a defendant (see Chapters 2, 10). It is conceptually possible that, for example, proceedings to establish limitation of

---

18. See e.g. *New Hampshire Insurance Co.* v. *Strabag Bau AG* [1992] 1 Lloyd's Rep. 361 (C.A.).

19. Compare *Marc Rich* v. *Impianti* (Corte di Cassazione) [1993] I.L.Pr. 402 (where Impianti sought a declaration in respect of liability to Marc Rich, the latter being domiciled in Switzerland) with the same case in the English courts in which Marc Rich was the plaintiff, Impianti being domiciled in Italy (see *supra*—arbitration).

20. *Jenard Report* (OJ 1979 C 59 p. 1 at p. 15).

21. See Chap. 7, such adaptation falling outside the jurisdiction of the European Court (*Kleinwort Benson Ltd* v. *City of Glasgow DC* 346/93 [1995] All E.R. (E.C.) 514).

liability would not involve a person being sued, but a declaration in regard to any possible claimant. It is certain however that in English law a limitation plea whether by defence, counterclaim or through a limitation action will involve a defendant (see Chapter 24).

(iii) "Multiple proceedings" as between courts of contracting and non-contracting States

By Art. 2 of the Convention, subject to other Convention provisions, a defendant domiciled in a contracting State "shall be" sued in the courts of that state. In two cases the High Court in England held that that provision was mandatory and removed the power which would otherwise exist to consider whether a forum of a non-contracting State was more appropriate.[22] In *Re Harrods (Buenos Aires) Ltd* the Court of Appeal took a different view and emphasized the underlying purpose of the Convention to create a legal system for the Community. Bingham L.J. stressed that (i) save for exceptions specifically provided in the Convention, national law would be applied to cases involving defendants not domiciled in the Community and (ii) there was no provision relating to the effect of jurisdiction agreement in favour of a non-contracting State.[23]

(iv) Proceedings to enforce judgments of non-contracting States

In *Owens Bank Ltd* v. *Bracco (No. 2)*[24] the European Court held that recognition and enforcement proceedings of a judgment of a non-contracting State are not within the Convention. This followed, said the Court, from the purpose of the Convention, the restriction of the Convention "judgment" provisions to judgments of contracting States and the lack of reference in any of the jurisdiction provisions to such proceedings.

Type of proceedings within the Convention

The Convention applies to four different types of "proceedings". It applies to proceedings brought—

    (i) to enforce a cause of action (in this work entitled "initial proceedings") (Arts. 1–20)

    (ii) in more than one state to enforce the same or a related cause of action in this work entitled ("multiple proceedings") (Arts. 21–23)

    (iii) to obtain a protective, or provisional remedy (in this work entitled "provisional proceedings") (Art. 24)

    (iv) to recognise or enforce a judgment of a contracting State.

---

22. The principle of "*forum non conveniens*". As to its role in this case outside the Convention see [1991] 4 All E.R. 348. The role of Art. 16(2)—"exclusive jurisdiction" regardless of domicile—does not seem to have been considered. It did however form part of a reference to the European Court by the House of Lords but the case was settled.

23. [1991] 4 All E.R. 334. Bingham L.J. also stressed that the Conventions abrogated by the Brussels Convention, were with one exception, all between contracting States. See Chap. 12.

24. [1994] 1 All E.R. 336. As to recognition of foreign judgments see Chap. 27.

The differing purpose of the different type of proceedings lead to distinctions as to *Convention scope*. As to initial proceedings, from a Convention point of view the national law of a contracting State may justifiably be applied to a case not having requisite connection with the Community. However, the control over multiple proceedings involving the same or a related course of action does not justify a similar restriction. In such a context the need is to prevent the risk of irreconcilable judgments as between contracting States—whether the basis of the judgment be national law or Convention provisions.[25] Wide jurisdiction provision for considering preventative measures is designed to allow for Community support of initial proceedings wherever in the Community these may be. It is to encourage (and arguably ensure) that each member States makes its interlocutory measures available in respect of proceedings in every other member State. Whether in or out of the Convention the central feature of litigation is bringing suit to enforce a claim. The need for rules governing multiple proceedings and preventative measures stems from the overall need for the undesirability of multiple proceedings and the desirability of interlocutory support for a claim. The rules relating to initial proceedings will be discussed in Chapters 5 and 6 as part of the general consideration of jurisdiction on the merits, those relating to multiple proceedings in Chapter 12 (being restriction on jurisdiction) and provisional proceedings in Chapters 14–16 (interim relief). The recognition and enforcement of judgments is considered in Chapter 28.

III. CONSIDERATION OF CONVENTION JURISDICTION BY ADJUDICATING COURT

The Convention is firmly based on the principle that jurisdiction enquiry is for the adjudicating rather than an enforcement court. The grounds on which a judgment of a Convention State may be challenged are restricted, and only in respect of insurance, consumer contracts and "exclusive" jurisdiction under Art. 16 may the jurisdiction of the court giving the judgment be considered[26] by an enforcement court. It would therefore be surprising were there no Convention duty on the adjudicating court to consider its own jurisdiction.

There must be a general duty on the adjudicating court to decline jurisdiction lacking Convention foundation once the issue is raised. On occasion the Convention goes further, imposing either an express obligation to decline jurisdiction of a court's "own motion"; or an express obligation to decline jurisdiction. Further, the Convention provides for the declining of jurisdiction where the same or a related claim has been instituted in a court of another contracting State (i.e. where there are multiple proceedings). There is a duty to stay proceedings to ensure adequate notice of them to the defendant. There are express powers of stay in respect of multi proceedings and recognition and enforcement of a judgment against which an appeal is brought.

---

25. See *Overseas Union Insurance Ltd* v. *New Hampshire Insurance* para. 14 (C 351/89) [1992] 2 All E.R. 138 at p. 160 (ECJ) and *infra*.
26. See Chaps. 5, 6.

1. DECLINING JURISDICTION

"Of the court's own motion"

Article 19 and the first paragraph of Article 20 read:

"Article 19
Where a court of a Contracting State is seised of a claim which is principally concerned with a matter over which the courts of another Contracting State have exclusive jurisdiction by virtue of Article 16, it shall declare of its own motion that it has no jurisdiction.

Article 20
Where a defendant domiciled in one Contracting State is sued in a court of another Contracting State and does not enter an appearance, the court shall declare of its own motion that it has no jurisdiction unless its jurisdiction is derived from the provisions of this Convention."

A like obligation is imposed:

    (a) (applying Article 20) on an appeal from an order for enforcement of a judgment when a party against whom enforcement is ordered does not appear (whether or not the party is domiciled in a contracting State) (Article 40).

    (b) Where there are proceedings already in process before a court in another contracting State in respect of the matter before the court (Article 21).

    (c) In respect of Article 5(1) jurisdiction asserted over a Luxembourg domiciliary who does not appear.

    (d) Where a case concerns a dispute about wages or other conditions of service between a master and crew of a sea-going ship registered in Greece, Ireland or Portugal and the relevant consular or diplomatic officer has objected (Annexed Protocol Article V(b)).

"Of its own motion"—the obligation

In the context of Article 21 Jenard (at page 41) expressed the view that the court would have to examine the possibility of pending actions "only when the circumstances are such as to lead the court to believe that this may be the case". In the negotiations preceding the Accession Convention the United Kingdom referred to the change in United Kingdom judicial practice that an obligation to decline jurisdiction "of its own motion" would cause. In the context of that comment Schlosser says of the obligations imposed by Articles 19 and 20:

"It does not necessarily follow from Articles 19 and 20 of the 1968 Convention that the courts must, of their own motion, investigate the facts relevant to deciding the question of jurisdiction, that they must for example inquire where the defendant is domiciled. The only essential factor is that uncontested assertions by the parties should not bind the court. For this reason the following rule is reconcilable with the 1968 Convention: a court may assume jurisdiction only if it is completely satisfied of all the facts on which such jurisdiction is based; if it is not so satisfied it can and must request the parties to provide the necessary evidence, in default of which the action will be dismissed as inadmissible. In such circumstances the lack of jurisdiction would be declared by the court of its own motion, and not as a result of a challenge by one of the parties. Whether a court is itself obliged to investigate the facts relevant to jurisdiction, or whether it can, or must, place the burden of proof in this respect on the party interested in the jurisdiction of the court concerned, is determined solely by national law. Indeed some of the legal systems of the original Member States, for example Germany, do not require the court itself to undertake factual investigations in a case of exclusive jurisdiction, even though lack of such jurisdiction has to be considered by the court of its own motion."[27]

Other duties to decline jurisdiction

It is mandatory to decline jurisdiction in respect of multi-exclusive jurisdictions (Article 23) and the multiple proceedings brought to enforce the same claim once it is established that a court of another contracting State was first seised (Article 21). Presumably such a duty arises if the matter is brought to the attention of the court by a party—but whether in practice there is much difference between this duty and that to decline "of its own motion" is debatable. In an English context while a court may consider itself as an umpire to judge according to that which is put before it, it would be rare that the court does not influence the issues raised—particularly where they concern jurisdiction. The duties are discussed in Chapter 12.

The power to decline jurisdiction

The power (i.e. discretion) to decline jurisdiction is conferred on a court seised of a claim "related" to another claim in respect of which a court in another contracting State is already seised (Article 22). The nature and effect of the power are discussed in Chapter 12.

2. STAY OF PROCEEDINGS

There is an express obligation by Article 20 to stay proceedings to ensure that a defendant has received notice of them or that necessary steps have been taken to that end (see *infra*). This obligation is applied to an appeal from a refusal of enforcement of a judgment in respect of the person against whom the judgment is intended to be enforced whether or not that person is domiciled in a contracting State (Article 40).

There is an express power to stay proceedings where proceedings in the same cause of action have first been instituted in a court of another contracting State until the jurisdiction of the first court is established (Article 21), where there is a related action in the court of another contracting State (Article 22), and when recognition or enforcement is sought of a judgment and an appeal is pending against the original judgment (Articles 30, 38).

It would be curious if the specification of the power to stay was to be taken as implying that it could not exist in other circumstances. This is particularly so when the jurisdiction depends on the decision of another court—as, for example, under Article 17 where jurisdiction in respect of proceedings between parties not domiciled in a contracting State may depend on the declining of jurisdiction by another court. Any power to stay under national law would be limited by the purpose of the Convention.

---

27. Para. 22 (p. 5). There is perhaps not quite the change in English law that some would assert. The Supreme Court Act 1981 s. 49(3) provides that nothing in that Act affects the power of the Court of Appeal or High Court to stay proceedings (*inter alia*) "of its own motion". In respect of English law see Chap. 8. See generally as to the overriding nature of the Convention obligation: *Duijnstee* v. *Goderbauer* 288/82 [1983] ECR 3663; [1985] 1 CMLR 220.

Procedural safeguards as jurisdictional prerequisites

Paragraphs 2 and 3 of Article 20 read:

"The court shall stay the proceedings so long as it is not shown that the defendant has been able to receive the document instituting the proceedings or an equivalent document in sufficient time to enable him to arrange for his defence, or that all necessary steps have been taken to this end.

The provisions of the foregoing paragraph shall be replaced by those of Article 15 of the Hague Convention of 15 November 1965 on the Service Abroad for Judicial and Extrajudicial Documents in Civil or Commercial Matters, if the documents instituting the proceedings or notice thereof had to be transmitted abroad in accordance with that Convention."

Article 15 of the Hague Convention reads:

"Article 15
Where a writ of summons or an equivalent document had to be transmitted abroad for the purpose of service, under the provisions of the present Convention, and the defendant has not appeared, judgment shall not be given until it is established that:
(a) the document was served by a method prescribed by the internal law of the State addressed for the service of documents in domestic actions upon persons who are within its territory, or
(b) the document was actually delivered to the defendant or to his residence by another method provided for by this Convention.
and that in either of these cases the service or the delivery was effected in sufficient time to enable the defendant to defend.
    Each contracting State shall be free to declare that the judge, notwithstanding the provisions of the first paragraph of this article, may give judgment even if no certificate of service or delivery has been received, if all the following conditions are fulfilled:
(a) the document was transmitted by one of the methods provided for in this Convention,
(b) a period of time not less than six months, considered adequate by the judge in the particular case, has elapsed since the date of the transmission of the document,
(c) no certificate of any kind has been received, even though every reasonable effort has been made to obtain it through the competent authorities of the State addressed.
Notwithstanding the provisions of the preceding paragraphs the judge may order, in case of urgency, any provisional or protective measures."

Parties to the 1968 Convention who are also parties to the Hague Convention are Belgium, Denmark, France, Federal Republic of Germany, Italy, Luxembourg, the Netherlands, Portugal and the United Kingdom.

A judgment of a contracting State may be refused recognition or enforcement "if the defendant was not duly served with the document which instituted the proceedings or with an equivalent document in sufficient time to enable him to arrange for his defence" (Arts. 27(3), 34). Matters relevant to compliance with the requirements of service are discussed in Chapter 28.

Paragraph 2 of Article 20 (and Article 40 in applying it to enforcement of judgment proceedings) makes the exercise of jurisdiction dependent on the defendant having the opportunity to prepare his defence.[28] The mandatory provision in Article 20 for stay is limited to the circumstances outlined in the first paragraph (see p. 97), i.e. where a defendant domiciled in a contracting State is sued in the court of another contracting State and does not appear. It is applied to enforcement proceedings wherever the defendant is

---

28. These obligations as other Convention obligations transcend any national procedural limitation. See *Duijnstee* v. *Lodewijk Goderbauer* 288/82 [1983] ECR 3663; [1985] 1 CMLR 220.

domiciled (Article 40). Clearly a court would have the *power* to stay in like circumstances in any case in which it has Convention jurisdiction and the defendant does not appear.

The procedural protection of Article 20 is reflected in Article 27(2) which provides that a judgment shall not be recognized:

"(2) where it was given in default of appearance, if the defendant was not duly served with the document which instituted the proceedings or with an equivalent document in sufficient time to enable him to arrange for his defence[29];"

The European Court's consideration of the substance of this important procedural protection has been in the context of Article 27(2) and will be discussed in that context in Chapter 28. Relevant to the existence and exercise of jurisdiction under the Convention is the European Court's approach that: (i) within Article 27(2) the question of whether there has been due service of the document instituting the proceedings is a matter for forum law; but (ii) whether in the circumstances this enabled the defendant to arrange for his defence is to be adjudged by Convention criteria.

---

29. The transmission of judicial and extra-judicial documents between contracting States is to be in accordance with any applicable Convention or agreement (Annexed Protocol Art. IV). See *supra* and Chap. 28.

CHAPTER 5

The Brussels Convention—Forum Law or Convention Regime?

THE BASIC DICHOTOMY

If a suit falls within the ambit of the Convention because of its subject-matter and is not excluded by the nature of the proceedings jurisdiction will be decided according to the Convention jurisdiction regime or by national law of the forum. If it is not referred to national law it will be decided either according to the Convention given precedence over the Brussels Convention (Art. 57) or the Convention jurisdiction regime.

Convention regime or national law?

The general criteria for the reference to the Convention or national law are set out in Articles 2, 4. These read:

"Article 2
Subject to the provisions of this Convention, persons domiciled in a Contracting State shall, whatever their nationality, be sued in the courts of that State.

Persons who are not nationals of the State in which they are domiciled shall be governed by the rules of jurisdiction applicable to nationals of that State.

Article 4
If the defendant is not domiciled in a Contracting State, the jurisdiction of the courts of each Contracting State shall, subject to the provisions of Article 16, be determined by the law of that State.

As against such a defendant, any person domiciled in a Contracting State may, whatever his nationality, avail himself in that State of the rules of jurisdiction there in force, and in particular those specified in the second paragraph of Article 3, in the same way as the nationals of that State."

APPLICABILITY OF NATIONAL LAW OF THE FORUM

A. WHERE DEFENDANT IS NOT DOMICILED IN A CONTRACTING STATE

Subject to specific Convention provisions, proceedings within it brought against a defendant not domiciled in a contracting State are referred by the Convention to national law. So national law applies not because the Convention does not apply but because the Convention applies it. However, once so applied save for extending national laws as to

101

jurisdiction in one respect, the Convention has no further part to play. Care must be taken however for although there is only one exception specified in Article 4 there are a number of instances in which the Convention jurisdiction regime may apply even though the defendant is not domiciled in a contracting State. To determine whether national law applies therefore it is necessary to review the applicability of the Convention regime. It is not necessarily either enough for applicability that the defendant is domiciled in a contracting State nor enough for non-applicability that he is not so domiciled.

B. EXTENSION OF SCOPE OF NATIONAL LAW RULES (ARTICLES 2, 4)

The second paragraph of Article 2 emphasizes the central Convention feature of domicile, imposing on each contracting State the duty not to treat those domiciled in the state any differently jurisdictionally than nationals of that state. The second paragraph of Article 4 builds on that in extending national law rules of so called "exorbitant" jurisdiction set out in Article 3 (and specifically outlawed as against a defendant domiciled in a contracting State) to plaintiffs domiciled in a contracting State when suing defendants not so domiciled (see Chapter 5). Article 4(2) has effect where national law differentiates in conferring jurisdiction in favour of citizens of that country (as does the French Code). The Convention changes the basis of such advantage from nationality to domicile. When matched with the ready recognition of judgments within the Community it widens the liability of defendants not domiciled in a contracting State to enforceable judgments within the Community.

The national jurisdiction rules specified in Article 3 include:

  (i) The home nationality of the plaintiff or the defendant (as in Articles 14 and 15 of the French Code. Articles 14 and 15 of the Luxembourg Code, Article 15 of the Belgian Code and Article 127 of the Netherlands Code of Civil Procedure and Article 165 of the Portuguese Code of Civil Procedure).
 (ii) The service of process on a defendant present in a contracting State (as Article 248 of the Danish Law of Civil Procedure and the Procedural Rules of the United Kingdom and Ireland).
(iii) Residence of the defendant (as in the Belgian and Danish laws) or domicile of the plaintiff (as in the Netherlands law).
(iv) The presence or seizure of property (as in the United Kingdom—particularly in Scotland—Article 23 of the Code of Civil Procedure of Germany or Article 40 of the Code of Civil Procedures of Greece).

Provisions of the Italian Code of Civil Procedure conferring wide jurisdiction and limiting the enforceability of jurisdictional agreements as against Italian nationals are also excluded.

As a counterbalance, by Article 59, save for certain proprietary, possessory or security actions, a member State may conclude a Convention with a third state so as to prohibit the recognition or enforcement of judgments when the judgment could be founded through Article 4(2) on a jurisdictional basis specified in Article 3 (see Chapter 9). Article 4(2) therefore widens the category of persons in favour of whom the national law of a contracting State may discriminate. It does not affect the jurisdiction in English law for no jurisdictional distinction is drawn between English and other plaintiffs.

C. LIMITATION ACTIONS

By Article 6a a court having jurisdiction "by virtue of this Convention" over a liability issue arising from the use or operation of a ship also has jurisdiction over claims for limitation of that liability. While, subject to other provisions, forum law controls jurisdiction over defendants not domiciled in a contracting State it seems difficult to argue that jurisdiction is "by virtue of this Convention". It is by the Convention "by virtue of forum law". Hence the jurisdiction base of Article 6a would seem to apply only when the Convention jurisdiction regime applies.

APPLICABILITY OF THE CONVENTION REGIME

1. Reference to another Convention—Article 57

The Convention either provides a jurisdiction base by its own provision or through another Convention which is applied through Article 57. Once the Convention jurisdiction regime is applicable (as distinct from a reference to national laws) the first question which arises is whether another Convention takes precedence. While if there is such a Convention its rules will apply to allocate jurisdiction rather than the allocation rule of the Brussels Convention the *applicability* of the reference to the other Convention requires the existence of a Brussels Convention jurisdiction base. It is therefore necessary first to consider applicability of the Brussels Convention regime[1] as distinct from the law of the forum.

2. Brussels Convention jurisdiction bases

As the primary rule of applicability (that the defendant is domiciled in a contracting State) applies subject to other Convention provisions the approach must be *first* to consider the criteria of applicability other than the domicile of the defendant and *secondly* the domicile of the defendant. Once the criterion of Convention applicability is identified the scene is set for the jurisdiction to be allocated (as to which see Chapter 6).

1. CRITERIA OF APPLICABILITY OTHER THAN THE DEFENDANT'S DOMICILE

In respect of initial proceedings[2] the exceptions to the general rule of applicability of the Convention regime based on the defendant's domicile in a contracting State are:

1. If the "other Convention" applies it will *ex hypothesi* apply through the national law but not necessarily to the same extent as in that law—so in the case of the United Kingdom a Convention will apply directly only as enacted, the text of the Convention may apply indirectly through Article 57. See e.g. *The Po* [1991] 2 Lloyd's Rep. 206 (as to which see *infra*).

2. Domicile is also irrelevant as regards multiple proceedings, preventative and protective measures and recognition and enforcement of judgments (see Chaps. 12, 14, 28).

  (a) matters within the "exclusive jurisdiction" provision of Article 16;

  (b) appearance by a defendant in a court of a contracting State (Article 18);

  (c) jurisdiction agreement selecting a court of a contracting State (Article 17);

  (d) the "deemed domicile" of insurers and non-consumer parties to consumer contracts (Articles 8 and 13).

A. Exclusive jurisdiction by virtue of Article 16

Article 16 reads:

"The following courts shall have exclusive jurisdiction, regardless of domicile:

 1 (a) in proceedings which have as their object rights *in rem* in, or tenancies of, immovable property, the courts of the Contracting State in which the property is situated;

  (b) however, in proceedings which have as their object tenancies of immovable property concluded for temporary private use for a maximum period of six consecutive months, the courts of the Contracting State in which the defendant is domiciled shall also have jurisdiction provided that the landlord and tenant are natural persons and are domiciled in the same Contracting State[3];

 2 In proceedings which have as their object the validity of the constitution, the nullity or the dissolution of companies or other legal persons or associations of natural or legal persons, or the decision of their organs, the courts of the Contracting State in which the company, legal person or association has its seat;

 3 In proceedings which have as their object the validity of entries in public registers, the courts of the Contracting State in which the register is kept;

 4 In proceedings concerned with the registration or validity of patents, trade marks, designs, or other similar rights required to be deposited or registered, the courts of the Contracting State in which the deposit or registration has been applied for, has taken place or is under the terms of an international convention deemed to have taken place;

 5 In proceedings concerned with the enforcement of judgments, the courts of the Contracting State in which the judgment has been or is to be enforced."

If a matter falls within this provision it is within the Convention because of that and also is within the "exclusive jurisdiction" of the state to which it is allocated. Subject to the possibility of more than one exclusive jurisdiction,[4] Article 16 therefore provides the criteria both for applicability and for allocation of jurisdiction under the Convention.

Matters within Article 16

The Article provides a potential minefield of divergency if the concepts on which the categories depend are referred to national law. It is therefore not surprising that the European Court has consistently held that the provision is based on Community concepts.[5]

(i) Immovable property (Article 16.1)

"Immovable property" is a term familiar to English lawyers only in the context of conflict of laws, and the "right *in rem*" is a phrase which in English law creates more confusion

---

 3. Inserted on the accession of Portugal and Spain. For an interpretation of the former text consistent with the amendment see *Hacker* v. *Euro Relais GmbH* 280/90 [1992] I.L.Pr. 515 (a contract for the use of a holiday home).

 4. See *infra* "Seat of a Corporation".

 5. See *Reichert* v. *Dresdner Bank* 115/88 [1990] I.L.Pr. 105.

than comfort. Nevertheless the concepts are not entirely new, nor are they impossible to apply. It should not include for example an action for specific performance or damages of a contract concerning immovable property between the parties to the contract (Cf. Schlosser, paras. 166–168).

The object of the provision is to allocate jurisdiction to the place which "is in the best position ... to have a good knowledge of the factual position" and to apply the rules of the place where the property is situated. As the provision deprives the parties of choice and is a derogation from the jurisdiction base of the defendant's domicile it is not to be given a wider interpretation than needed for its objective. So it does not include all actions relating to "rights *in rem*" nor all matters relating to tenancies. So it does not apply to an action *in personam* by a creditor to set aside a disposition in defending the creditor[6] nor where the tenancy dispute concerns the operation of a business.[7]

Any question of title to an immovable in the context of the maritime claim is likely to arise collaterally in (for example) an action involving damage to a pier or (possibly) retention of possession in a shipyard or storage of goods in a warehouse.

(ii) Corporations and associations (Article 16.2)

Through the equation of the seat of a company, legal person or association with domicile (see *infra*) this jurisdiction is based on "domicile" of the association. While the enforcement of a maritime claim would not have as its object the nullity or dissolution of a corporation or legal association it may well depend on the existence of the corporation or, even more likely, whether a decision of the board of a company was validly taken.[8] It should be recalled that bankruptcy matters fall outside the Convention (see Article 1(1)) and any action involving the winding up of a company may raise questions of construction both of Article 1 and of Article 16.[9]

The phrase "association of natural or legal persons" appears both in Article 16(2) and in Article 53 in the context of domicile (see *infra*). The contention (as with all concepts within Article 16) that the phrase should be construed in its European rather than national sense is simply underlined by its relevance in two fundamental aspects of the Convention. It would clearly be preferable to give the provision a uniform scope dependent on the nature of the association rather than a varied application turning on a domestic characterization. There is some uncertainty whether a partnership in English law is included but, as is contended in the context of domicile, there seems little reason why it should not fall within the phrase. Schlosser is of the firm opinion that the phrase does include partnership within Article 16(2) (see para. 162).

---

6. *Ibid.* A requirement of registration of judicial proceedings in respect of land does not necessarily mean exclusive jurisdiction in the state of registration (*ibid.*).

7. *Sanders* v. *Van der Putte* 73/77 [1978] 1 CMLR 331. For a similar restrictive approach see *Webb* v. *Webb* [1994] 3 All E.R. 911. See also *Rosler* v. *Rottwinkel* [1985] ECR 9; *Liebe* v. *Grobel* C292/93.

8. The phrase "decision of their organs" does not encompass abuse—rather than want or excess—of power: *Grupo Torras S.A.* v. *Sheikh Al Sabah* [1995] I.L.Pr. 667 (C.A.). As to the "object" of the proceedings, see *ibid.*; *Newtherapeutics Ltd.* v. *Katz* [1991] 2 All E.R. 151.

9. Whether this provision applies if the issue is the appropriateness of a court of a contracting State as against the court of a non-contracting State was before the European Court in *Ladenimn S.A.* v. *Intercomfinanz S.A.* 314/92 but the case was settled before hearing.

THE SEAT OF THE CORPORATION

Article 53 equates "seat" with "domicile" and refers this issue to the private international law of contracting States. As a consequence national laws may differ as a corporation may have its seat in more than one state.[10] In English law the matter is controlled by section 43 of the 1982 Act. This sets out substantive rules for the purpose of Article 16(2) thereby necessarily implying that English law will govern except insofar as the provision refers matters to foreign law.

(iii) Public registers (Article 16.3)

The scope of Article 16(3) seems uncertain.[11] In seeking the view of the European Court it should be borne in mind that jurisdiction under Article 16 should be construed restrictively for it is imposed without the consent of the parties. Whether "public register" means registers open to the public or "public" in the sense that they are governmental is not clear. Whichever it is, there is no difficulty if the clause is restricted to "validity" in the narrow sense of reflecting the interest which is registered and not the validity of that interest even if it is the registration that confers the validity.

As regards maritime claims it would include proceedings concerning the validity of entries in registers under the Companies Act 1985 and under the Merchant Shipping Act 1995. If a wider view is taken of the scope of the provision, the validity of a share transfer, a registered charge or the registration of a ship or ship mortgage could fall within this clause. On the other hand a claim based on the assertion that the failure to register meant invalidity of the interest would, unless it consequentially affected an interest on the register, not be within the clause. While it may be understandable that only the place of the register can control entries as such it does not follow that only that place resolves the validity of the interest on which the registration is based.[12]

The problem for English law is that there are numerous registration systems each having different purposes and characteristics. The provisions of Article 16(3) will make more sense the more a registered interest cannot be challenged, i.e. validity is equated with the registration. Registration of ships and mortgages does not carry that consequence in English law and it is perhaps doubtful whether the simple existence of a register should necessarily lead to exclusive jurisdiction. Particularly is this so since the transactions leading to registration may be good by laws other than the forum.

(iv) Intellectual property (Article 16.4)

In the context of maritime claims little comment is called for. It is to be noted that Article V(d) of the Annexed Protocol confers exclusive jurisdiction on the court of a contracting State in respect of the registration or validity of any European patent granted in respect of that state which is not a Community Patent. Both Article 16(4) and the Protocol go only

---

10. See *infra*.

11. Jenard comments that the provision needs little comment (p. 35). Schlosser has no comment.

12. So in adjudging priorities in a forced or judicial sale of a ship a question may arise as to the validity of foreign registration of a foreign mortgage (see e.g. *The Angel Bell* [1979] 2 Lloyd's Rep. 491). It would destroy the concept of the forced sale to vest jurisdiction of that issue in the place of registration. Cf. *Conventions Relating to Maritime Liens and Mortgages 1926, 1967 and 1993*. (See Part III.)

to registration or validity of the intellectual property and not to every interest concerning it.

(v) Judgments (Article 16.5)

The provision applies to judgments following proceedings. it does not encompass enforcement proceedings of a judgment in a non-contracting State.[13] It fits together the jurisdiction and enforcement frameworks.[14] An English court cannot exercise any power it may have under national law to enjoin a party from enforcing a judgment of a contracting State. The Convention permits resistance of enforcement only on specified grounds (see Chapter 28). However, "a party cannot make use of the jurisdiction conferred by Article 16(5) in a dispute which falls within the jurisdiction of another Contracting State under Article 2".[15]

Article 16(5) does *not* apply to an action seeking to set aside a disposition—so an action in French law to set aside a gift as a fraud on a creditor is not "enforcement".[16] Further, it has been held not to apply to an order ancillary to enforcement. In a judgment of 25 February 1974[17] the Oberlandsgericht Nurnberg dismissed an appeal against an order that a defendant (domiciled in Italy) permit the creditor (domiciled in Germany) to inspect books. It was argued that the order was contrary to Article 16(5) as being a method of enforcement of an order that the defendant produce an account of commission due in respect of sales in Germany. The court held that although the enforcement of the order was for the Italian courts, the plaintiff needed the order to get to the enforcement stage.

Such an approach is underlined by decisions of national courts that an enforcement court cannot add to any order or judgment—simply enforce it (see Chapter 28). A national court should therefore consider the limitation in the context of the territorial scope of any order it may make.

B. Appearance by a defendant (Article 18)

Article 18 reads:

"Apart from jurisdiction derived from other provisions of this Convention, a court of a Contracting State before whom a defendant enters an appearance shall have jurisdiction. This rule shall not apply where appearance was entered solely to contest the jurisdiction, or where another court has exclusive jurisdiction by virtue of Article 16."

Apart from exclusive jurisdiction under Article 16, therefore, "appearance" by a defendant in the substantive proceedings will create jurisdiction. In *Elefanten Schuh GmbH v. Pierre Jacqmain*[18] the European Court confirmed the overriding effect of appearance. The Court held that it conferred jurisdiction even if there is a jurisdiction

---

13. *Owens Bank v. Bracco* [1992] 2 All E.R. 193 (see Chap. 4).

14. See also the jurisdiction to recognize a judgment (Article 26). As to enforcement in two states see *Interpool Ltd. v. Galani* [1987] 2 All E.R. 981. Enforcement procedure applies to recognition of a judgment raised as a principal issue and when raised as an ancillary issue the court hearing the principal issue has jurisdiction (Article 26). See Chap. 28.

15. *AS Autoteile Service GmbH v. Malhe* 220/84 [1986] 3 CMLR 321 (ECJ). So there was no jurisdiction in the enforcement court to hear a claim for set off against the order when the claim sought to be set off was not within the jurisdiction of the court.

16. *Reichert v. Dresdner Bank (No. 2)* 261/90 (ECJ) 26 March 1992.

17. Case No. 9 U 167/75 ECD 1–16.5–B2.

18. 150/80 [1981] ECR 1671; [1982] 3 CMLR 1.

agreement conferring "exclusive jurisdiction" on another court under Article 17 on the basis that the actions of the parties have waived the agreement.

The provision requires the distinction—clear in principle—between challenge to the jurisdiction and submission on the merits to be reflected in procedure in each contracting State at least for the purposes of the Convention. However the Convention does not dictate national practice. It simply provides a framework within which that practice must operate.

Submission to the merits would not follow from contesting protective measures[19] nor necessarily follow from pleading a defence to the claim. It may be necessary according to national procedure that the challenge to the jurisdiction and the defence to the merits be pleaded in the alternative. In such a case submission only occurs if the defence is lodged without any indication that there is to be any contest as to jurisdiction (see *Elefanten Schuh* followed by the Court in *Rohr S.A.* v. *Ossberger*[20]). When that stage is reached is a matter for national procedure.[21]

"Appearance" in English law[22]

Under English law there will be an "appearance" (or submission) to jurisdiction on the merits through participation in the proceedings on the merits.[23] An acknowledgement of service without more is not submission nor can any undertaking to acknowledge the service of a writ be taken as submission. Furthermore, in an action *in rem*, the undertaking to acknowledge issue of the writ, the putting up of bail or the entry of a caveat against arrest will normally not be submission. Such acts do not preclude a challenge to jurisdiction.[24] Whether or not any interlocutory act amounts to appearance other than to contest the jurisdiction depends on the act—an application for discovery or for extension of time for service of the defence does not constitute appearance on the merits.[25] An act not directly connected with the court (such as the giving of a guarantee) would not without more be submission.[26]

C. Jurisdiction by agreement[27] (Article 17)

Article 17 reads:

"If the parties, one or more of whom is domiciled in a Contracting State, have agreed that a court or the courts of a Contracting State are to have jurisdiction to settle any disputes which have arisen

19. For recognition that in English law protective measure jurisdiction is not necessarily substantive jurisdiction see *The Sargasso* [1994] 2 Lloyd's Rep. 6 (C.A.).

20. 27/81 [1981] ECR 2431 [1982] 3 CMLR 29.

21. See (Germany) *Re Sublease of a Shop* (Oberlandsgericht Dusseldorf 1990) [1991] I.L.Pr. 292; *Re a Shopfitting Contract* (Oberlandsgericht Saarbrucken 1991) [1993] I.L.Pr. 393; (Ireland) *Campbell International Trading House* v. *Van Aart* [1993] I.L.Pr. 314.

22. See further Chap. 9.

23. See for an example of appearance to challenge jurisdiction *The Sydney Express* [1988] 2 Lloyd's Rep. 257.

24. See *The Anna H* [1995] 1 Lloyd's Rep. 11 (C.A.) in which dicta to that effect take a different approach to that of Clarke J. at first instance and that of Sheen J. in *The Prinsengracht* [1993] 1 Lloyd's Rep. 41—both judges giving a more positive role to the voluntary nature of joining issue through acknowledgment or obtaining release from arrest.

25. *Kurz* v. *Stella Musical Veranstaltungs GmbH* [1992] 1 All E.R. 360. It is now recognized that there may be "provisional remedy" jurisdiction without merits jurisdiction. See fn. 19.

26. *The Prinsengracht* [1993] 1 Lloyd's Rep. 41.

27. An optional alternative to the defendant's domicile by agreement is through agreement on the place of performance of a contract (see Article 5(1) and Chap. 6). Cf. *Gola Werke* (fn. 32).

or which may arise in connection with a particular legal relationship, that court or those courts shall have exclusive jurisdiction. Such an agreement conferring jurisdiction shall be either—

(a) in writing or evidenced in writing, or
(b) in a form which accords with practices which the parties have established between themselves, or
(c) in international trade or commerce, in a form which accords with a usage of which the parties are or ought to have been aware and which in such trade or commerce is widely known to, and regularly observed by, parties to contracts of the type involved in the particular trade or commerce concerned.

Where such an agreement is concluded by parties, none of whom is domiciled in a Contracting State, the courts of other Contracting States shall have no jurisdiction over their disputes unless the court or courts chosen have declined jurisdiction.

The court or courts of a Contracting State on which a trust instrument has conferred jurisdiction shall have exclusive jurisdiction in any proceedings brought against a settlor, trustee or beneficiary, if relations between these persons or their rights or obligations under the trust are involved.

Agreements or provisions of a trust instrument conferring jurisdiction shall have no legal force if they are contrary to the provisions of Articles 12 or 15, or if the courts whose jurisdiction they purport to exclude have exclusive jurisdiction by virtue of Article 16.

If an agreement conferring jurisdiction was concluded for the benefit of only one of the parties, that party shall retain the right to bring proceedings in any other court which has jurisdiction by virtue of this Convention.

In matters relating to individual contracts of employment an agreement conferring jurisdiction shall have legal force only if it is entered into after the dispute has arisen or if the employee invokes it to seise courts other than those for the defendant's domicile or those specified in Article 5(1)."

The concept of an agreement conferring jurisdiction in a Convention is a rule of Community law and that which is required to constitute it and its scope are matters for that law and not for the private international law of member States.[28] Whether or not there is agreement will be adjudged on the intention of the parties on the basis of the contents of Article 17, the sole purpose of the formal requirement being to ensure that the consensus of the parties is established (see *infra*).[29] A German court has held that the agreement may relate *only* to past or future disputes in connection with a particular contractual relationship[30]—an agreement is not valid if it relates to a general commercial arrangement.[31]

The provision does not however affect choice of law clauses—and therefore a clause going to jurisdiction and choice of law but failing to qualify under Article 17 may be valid as a choice of law clause.[32] From general principles Article 17 will apply only where there is an element connecting the dispute with more than one contracting State. It will not

---

28. See *Powell Duffryn* v. *Petereit* 214/89, 10 February 1992 (ECJ); *The Times*, 15 April 1992. But it is uncertain whether incorporation into the contract is a matter for European law. See *Custom Made Commercial Ltd.* v. *Stawa Metallbau* (Bundesgerichtshof) [1993] I.L.Pr. 490—referred to ECJ, but the Court did not find it necessary to answer this question. See [1994] I.L.Pr. 516.

29. *Iveco Fiat SpA* v. *Van Hool NV* 313/85 [1988] 1 CMLR 57 (ECJ).

30. It may however relate to contract and tort claims (*ibid.*); *Re Import of Italian Sports Cars* (fn. 34). As to third parties see *infra*.

31. *Re Missing Share Certificates* (Oberlandsgericht Munchen 1989) [1991] I.L.Pr. 298.

32. See e.g. *Allpac Holding BV* v. *Maier Am Tor* (C.A. Amsterdam) (1979) [1982] ECC 200; *Société Gola Werke Gotz KG* v. *André Barseghian* (1979) Cour d'Appel Lyon ECD 1–5.1.2–B25. As to transitional jurisdictional effect of a choice of law of part of the United Kingdom or Ireland made prior to entry into force of the Convention see Chap. 6. As to qualified application to persons domiciled in Luxembourg see *infra*; the agreement would seem to be within Art. 17 (see *infra*).

apply where two parties domiciled in a contracting State opt for the jurisdiction of that state.[33]

It will be seen that Article 17 operates differently according to the connection between parties and the Community. It applies to confer jurisdiction if one party (plaintiff or defendant) is domiciled in a contracting State or to limit jurisdiction if no party is so domiciled. Where one party is domiciled in a contracting State it imposes an obligation on the selected court to hear the case—the rule takes precedence over any national law and there is no discretion to stay the proceedings.[34]

A court selected in accordance with Article 17 has power to decline jurisdiction only if no party is domiciled in a contracting State. In such circumstances whether or not to decline is for national law and declining opens the way for Convention jurisdiction elsewhere.

An obligation to consider jurisdiction of a court's own motion is imposed if a defendant is domiciled in a contracting State and does not appear (see Chapter 4). However if a defendant does appear it will either be to contest jurisdiction, in which case the effect of any jurisdiction clause necessarily arises, or not to contest jurisdiction, in which case there will be submission by the defendant—that submission under Article 18 overriding the jurisdiction clause (see *supra*).

Subject to qualifications expressed in Article 17 and any implied by other Convention provisions (as for example appearance under Article 18), an agreement must be recognized as conferring the exclusive jurisdiction on the selected state. Once the specific formal requirements for the agreement to be recognized are met it follows that any prohibition or limitation on the ability to select a court in national law cannot operate to affect an agreement within Article 17. In *Elefanten Schuh* v. *Jacqmain*[35] the European Court held that no national law requirements of form could operate to prevent enforceability. In *Sanicentral* v. *Collin*[36] the Court held that the Belgian prohibition of contracting out of jurisdiction of an employment tribunal could not stand in the face of Article 17—indeed it would have been surprising if any other view was taken. However if another Convention is applicable through Article 57 (as to which see Chapter 6) which provides for a qualification (be it a relaxation or a restriction) on the effect of jurisdictional agreements, to that extent the provisions of the other Convention apply.

"Exclusive" jurisdiction

It has been held in English and French courts that this means exclusive of other jurisdiction bases which it may override and not that one court must be selected before an agreement will qualify. So a non-exclusive jurisdiction clause will qualify.[37] As it is so "exclusive" it matters not if a court has been earlier seised of the same action on another "non-exclusive" Convention base (such as domicile of the defendant). The exclusive provision of Article 17 takes priority over articles conferring mandatory jurisdiction on a

---

33. Nor where two parties domiciled in the forum state opt for another.
34. See e.g. *Re Import of Italian Sports Cars* (Oberlandsgericht Stuttgart 1990) [1992] I.L.Pr. 188.
35. 150/80 [1981] ECR 1671; [1982] 3 CMLR 1.
36. 25/79 [1979] ECR 3423; [1980] 2 CMLR 164.
37. *Kurz* v. *Stella* [1992] 1 All E.R. 360; *Hantorex SpA* v. *SA Digital Research* (Cour d'Appel Paris) [1993] I.L.Pr. 501 (1991). But if one jurisdiction is chosen it will be "exclusive". *IP Metal Ltd.* v. *Ruote Oz SpA* [1993] 2 Lloyd's Rep. 60 (decision affirmed [1994] 2 Lloyd's Rep. 560).

court first seised of an action.[38] An English court will, if appropriate, issue an injunction to restrain participation in the other proceeding.[39] There may however be more than one "exclusive" jurisdiction and provision is made in Article 23 of the Convention for this eventuality.

The formal requirements

As the European Court has said, the sole purpose of these requirements is to ensure that the consensus of the parties is established (*Iveco Fiat SpA* v. *Van Nool NV*).[40] The agreement must be either: (i) in writing; or (ii) evidenced in writing; or (iii) in international trade or commerce "in a form which accords with practices in that trade or commerce of which the parties are or ought to have been aware". In the 1968 Convention the requirement was that the agreement should be in writing or evidenced in writing and the requirements were strictly construed. Writing was required as evidence of consent of both parties to the jurisdiction clause itself. It was not enough for the clause to appear in general printed conditions although it could be so if those conditions confirmed a previous oral agreement or formed part of a continuous business relationship.[41]

Recognition was accorded in the Accession Treaty 1978 to practice in international trade or commerce and on the adoption of the present text in 1989 to a form according with practices established by the parties. The need to establish agreement on the clause remains and so unless there is a practice within the provision a clause on the back of a standard form contract will not of itself suffice.[42] Any practice of the parties would have to relate to the type of contract at issue. Lacking practice of the parties or of international trade or commerce there must be some indication of express consent.[43] A clause providing for jurisdiction in the carrier's place of business may suffice if carrier and shipper signify their consent, the carrier and his place of business being identified by the consent.[44]

Jurisdiction clauses in bills of lading will normally fall within the provision relating to international trade or practice. The extent to which charterparty jurisdiction clauses are incorporated into bills of lading may be more uncertain depending on any practice of

---

38. *Continental Bank NA* v. *Aeakos Compania Naviera SA* [1994] 1 Lloyd's Rep. 505 (C.A.).

39. *Ibid.*—thereby giving priority to Art. 17 over Arts. 21, 22.

40. [1988] 1 CMLR 57. For an example of the inference of consent from the required "formality" see *I.P. Metal Ltd.* v. *Ruote Oz SpA* (fn. 37). Compare *Ocarina Marine Ltd.* v. *Marcaid Stein and Co.* [1994] 2 Lloyd's Rep. 524 at p. 532.

41. See the European Court decision in *Partenreederei MS Tilly Russ* v. *Haven and Vervoerbedrijf "Nova" and Germaine Hout* 71/83 [1984] ECR 2417, [1984] 3 CMLR 499 (hereafter "The Tilly Russ Case"); *Ditta Estascis Salotti* v. *RUWA GmbH* 24/76 (1976) ECR 1831, [1977] 1 CMLR 345; *Galerier Segoura Sprl* v. *Bonakdarian* 25/76 (1976) ECR 1851, [1977] 1 CMLR 361; *Porta Leasing GmbH* v. *Prestige International SA* 784/79 1980 ECR 1517, [1981] 1 CMLR 135. See also cases cited by Schlosser fns. 45, 47; *Scan Expo* v. *Ringkøbing County* [1994] I.L.Pr. 335 (Western C.A. Denmark). A reference to trading conditions containing the clause may be sufficient *Re Yarn Sales* (Bundesgerichtshof) [1994] I.L.Pr. 180.

42. See e.g. *Luz* v. *Bertram* (Corte di Cassazione 1991) [1992] I.L.Pr. 537. Compare company articles of association, shareholders being deemed to have more detailed knowledge than parties to a commercial standard form contract: *Powell Duffryn plc* v. *Petereit* 214/89 fn. 28.

43. For application of the principle see e.g. *Perfetto* v. *Parlapiano* (Cour d'Appel Liege 1990) [1993] I.L.Pr. 190; *The Ice Express* (District Court Livorno 1987) [1990] I.L.Pr. 263—bill of lading, signed declaration expressly referring to the clause sufficient. *Jenmont-Schneider SA* v. *Ercole Marellu SpA* (Corte di Cassazione 1990) [1994] I.L.Pr. 12.

44. See e.g. *The Ice Express* (fn. 43). But see *Spedag Scheepvaart en Expeditiebedrijf BV* v. *Andria Reederei GmbH and Co. KG*, 1985 (R.B. Rotterdam) [1986] ELD 206.

which the parties could be said to have been aware. It will not be enough that in any fact situation by national law a clause would have been incorporated into the contract.[45]

Oral agreement followed by writing

In the *Tilly Russ* case[46] the European Court held that a clause in the printed conditions of a bill of lading could satisfy the requirements of written evidence if it could be regarded as a confirmation of an oral agreement. In *F. Berghoefer GmbH KG v. ASA*[47] the Court had to construe the effect of an oral jurisdiction agreement reached during a 20-year period of trading when the plaintiff had sent a letter confirming the arrangement but there had been no response. The Court said that, unlike Article I of the Annexed Protocol concerning those domiciled in Luxembourg, Article 17 "does not require written confirmation of an oral agreement to be given by the party against whom the agreement is to take effect". In the context outlined above 'it would be contrary to good faith for the party which raised no objection to dispute application of the oral agreement.[48] Where therefore there had been an oral agreement, written confirmation and no objection, the requirements of Article 17 were satisfied.

The written confirmation must be capable of referring directly to the jurisdiction clause. A printed form "confirmation of order" would not be enough.[49] In 1986 construing the unamended text the European Court followed (and extended) *Berghoefer* in *Iveco Fiat SpA v. Van Hool NV.*[50] There was a written agreement including a jurisdiction clause which by its terms had terminated but the contents of which had been implemented for some 20 years. The court held the requirement of Article 17 was satisfied:

"if in accordance with the relevant national law the parties might validly extend the initial contract without observing the requirements of writing or, if, in the opposite circumstances, one or other of the parties had confirmed that clause in writing without the other party having raised an objection to that confirmation after having renewed it."

Scope of Article 17

(i) International disputes

As the Convention is concerned with the allocation of jurisdiction as between member States it has no role in any dispute wholly connected with one state. However Article 17 should apply to a jurisdiction agreement in any claim involving any foreign element. So even if the parties are domiciled in the same state Article 17 may apply whether the court

---

45. See e.g. *I.P. Metal Ltd.* v. *Ruote Oz Spa* (fn. 37).
46. See fn. 41.
47. 221/84 [1986] 2 CMLR 13.
48. At para. 15.
49. See e.g. *Re The Written Confirmation of an Oral Contract* (Hanseatic C.A., Hamburg 1984) [1986] ECC 37 but cf. *Basso Legnami SpA* v. *The Licenses Insurance Co. and Others* (Trib. di Genova 1977) ECD 1–17.1.2.–B7—sufficient if shipper signs a notice on the bill of lading that he "expressly recognizes all the above clauses and conditions contained herein": *Re Exchange Control and a Greek Guarantor* (Bundesgerichtshof 1991) [1993] I.L.Pr. 298.
50. 313/85 [1988] 1 CMLR 57.

selected is a court of that or any other contracting State.[51] No connection between dispute and court is required save that of selection.[52]

(ii) Set off

The jurisdiction agreement will confer on the selected court the power to adjudicate not only in relation to any claim within it but also any set off connected with the legal relationship from which sprang the claim.[53] The need to rely on such consequential jurisdiction is limited by the jurisdiction conferred over counterclaims. Counterclaims arising from the same "contract or facts on which the original claim was based" are within the jurisdiction over the original claim. (See Article 6.3 and Chapter 6).

(iii) Selection of more than one court

A non-exclusive jurisdiction clause will qualify (see *supra*) as will an agreement selecting more than one state.[54] However it may be arguable that an agreement that a dispute would be referred to "courts of the United Kingdom" might not be specific enough for it does not select a court nor can national law fill the gap. On the other hand it is likely that the agreement is sufficiently certain in a Convention sense in selecting the courts of a contracting State and it would then be left to national law to make the final selection. Presumably if national law had no principle on which that could be based the agreement would be invalid.

(iv) Selection of a court of a non-contracting State

The provision does not encompass a clause conferring jurisdiction on a court of a non-contracting State. If the defendant is domiciled in a contracting State and an action is brought in that state contrary to the clause it is arguable that (subject to alternative Convention jurisdictions) *that* is the Convention jurisdiction. On the other hand there is no fundamental principle underlying the Convention of the imposition of jurisdiction in a contracting State as against jurisdiction in a non-contracting State. There is no prohibition on a plaintiff domiciled in a contracting State bringing an action in a forum outside the contracting States nor on any defendant in submitting to such jurisdiction. For the Convention to be so construed as to impose non-recognition of an agreement to litigate outside contracting States would be to exceed its purpose of allocation or jurisdiction as between contracting States (see Schlosser, para. 176).[55] If the Convention does not apply

51. See Jenard p. 38 *Anema BV* v. *Broekman Motorships BV* [1991] I.L.Pr. 285 District Court Rotterdam 1988. But see *Bassini* v. *Santor* [1986] ELD 354.
52. See e.g. *Zelger* v. *Salinitri* 56/79 [1980] ECR 89; [1980] 2 CMLR 635.
53. See *Nikolaus Meeth* v. *Glacetal* 23/78 [1978] ECR 2133; [1979] CMLR 52.
54. *Meeth* v. *Glacetal* (fn. 53)—an agreement allowing the French seller to sue in France and the German buyer in Germany. Caportorti A.G. expressed the view (i) that parties could select different courts for different disputes and (ii) selection of courts of a contracting State is sufficient—but query for the United Kingdom—see text. In a decision prior to *Meeth* a German court held that it was not sufficiently certain for parties to opt for the court of the plaintiff's domicile Oberlandsgericht Frankfurt (1978) (9 ECD 1–1211 B8). This would appear as certain as the selection in *Meeth*.
55. But see *The Atlantic Span*, 1987 ETL 40, Rechtbank van Koophandel Antwerp, 24 February 1985—Swedish jurisdiction clause held not to comply with Article 17. Compare *Re Exchange Control and a Greek Guarantor* (fn. 49).

so as to make such a clause invalid the question of whether it is to be upheld is for national law. If it is found to be invalid the Convention jurisdiction framework would apply (Schlosser, *ibid*).[56]

Waiver of the agreement

Parties may waive the agreement if the plaintiff brings an action in a court other than that selected and the defendant submits to the jurisdiction. (see *Elefanten Schuh*.) The agreement then loses its force.

Article 17 and third parties to jurisdiction agreements

In *Gerling Konzern* v. *Amministrazione del Tesoro*[57] the European Court held that a third party beneficiary of an insurance contract containing a forum clause could rely on Article 17 provided the insurer had indicated his consent in the original agreement. It was irrelevant that the third party had not satisfied the requirements of writing. The Court took into account the protective provisions of the Convention in respect of an insured (i.e. section 3—as to which see *infra*) and in particular Article 12 providing for a jurisdiction agreement allowing a "beneficiary" to bring proceedings in a court other than one specified in the Convention.[58]

This approach would not necessarily apply where the question is whether the beneficiary, insured or an injured party in a direct action against the insurer is bound by the agreement.[59] At most presumably the matter would depend on whether national law provided for such binding effect—an approach adopted by the European Court in respect of marine transport. In the *Tilly Russ* case[60] a central issue was whether the jurisdiction agreement in a bill of lading which met the formal requirements of Article 17 in respect of the carrier and the shipper would bind a third party who by national law was bound by the bill of lading. The present wording permits compliance through a form according to international trade or practice but, as with the original wording, without reference to third parties. Consistently with its approach in *Gerling Konzern*[61] the European Court held in *The Tilly Russ* that once the agreement qualified within Article 17 as between the original parties to the bill of lading it would continue to qualify as between carrier and successor to the shipper if by forum national law that successor succeeded to the shipper's rights and

---

56. As to the question of whether the court of a contracting State having Convention jurisdiction may stay proceedings in favour of a non-contracting State see Chaps. 4, 12.

57. 201/82 [1983] ECR 2503; [1984] 3 CMLR 638.

58. Compare for a similar approach the inclusion of an indemnity action under Article 6(2) (as to which see Chapter 6) within the scope of Article 17 provided the clause in the main contract is binding by national law (*Islanders Canning Corpn.* v. *Hoekstra* District Court Leeuwarden Netherlands ECD 1–17.1.1–B4) Cf. Jenard p. 27.

59. Schlosser thinks clearly not (para. 148).

60. Fn. 41.

61. Fn. 54—although it distinguished that case as being concerned with a third party beneficiary of a forum clause in an insurance contract within the Convention protective framework for such contracts, the Convention specifically contemplating insurance agreements for third party beneficiaries. It may be said that the third party in *Gerling Konzern* was bound through the Convention while in *Tilly Russ* by national law. As to insurance contract jurisdiction see Chap. 6.

obligations.[62] That aspect of the decision applies to the amended text as much as to the original.

It is unclear whether the domicile of the successor to the shipper affects the applicability of Article 17. Whether it is the first or second part of Article 17 which is relevant depends on the domicile of the parties to the agreement. It may well be that it is the original agreement which triggers the application of the appropriate part. Once triggered the provision may then operate as regards a third party only in accordance with the domicile of the third party now treating the third party as a party to the agreement.

A similar problem arises as regards the formal requirements. From the *Tilly Russ* judgment it appears that it is the original agreement which is critical. The question whether it binds the third party is a question of substitution by the national law. In other words the question is one of the validity of the transfer and rights and obligations by national law and not the validity under the Convention of the agreement as between carrier and third party.[63]

Article 17 and its limitations

(i) Exclusive jurisdiction under Article 16

An agreement cannot remove "exclusive" jurisdiction under Article 16. As the duty of a court is to declare of its own motion when such jurisdiction exists elsewhere and as a judgment delivered in proceedings contrary to Article 16 will not be recognized (see Chapter 10), such agreement has no legal force. Further, although Article 17 refers only to the invalidity of the agreement in respect of the exclusion of jurisdiction it is presumably of no effect as regards any jurisdiction selected.

(ii) Individual employment contracts

The employer is protected from the effect of a jurisdictional agreement entered into prior to a dispute.[64] Such an agreement is valid only to the extent that the employee invokes it in favour of a court other than one having jurisdiction because of the employer's domicile or under the plaintiff's option in such contracts (Art. 5.1—as to which see Chapter 6).

(iii) An agreement for the benefit of one party

By its express terms Article 17 destroys the effect of a jurisdiction agreement insofar as contracting States are concerned when the agreement is for the benefit of one party. It preserves the right of *that party* to bring an action in any contracting State having Convention jurisdiction presumably on the basis that such a clause is meant to confer an option. An agreement is not for the benefit of one party within this provision simply

---

62. So in English law it is arguable that a shipper would be bound by a jurisdiction clause in a contract between the carrier and a subcontracting carrier. See *Dresser UK Ltd.* v. *Falcongate Ltd.* [1991] 2 Lloyd's Rep. 557 (the clause there not being drafted sufficiently widely to create the obligation). As to consignees of cargo see the Carriage of Goods by Sea Act 1992.

63. For an application of this approach to formal requirements see *Basso Legnami* (fn. 49).

64. A provision added in the treaty on the accession of Portugal and Spain.

because it provides for jurisdiction in the courts of the domicile of the party. There may be many reasons why those courts were chosen.[65]

A choice in the bill of lading specifying the carrier's place of business could be construed as for the benefit of the carrier only in the context of the nature of the transaction reflected by the contract. Following the approach to the relevance of the court of the domicile of a party the "choice" would be part of the bargain reflected by the totality of the contract.

(iv) Jurisdiction through "appearance" under Article 18

In *Elefanten Schuh*[66] it was held that appearance by a defendant to a suit by a plaintiff in a court other than that selected by the agreement was voluntary submission overriding the agreement and that there was nothing in Article 17 preventing such a conclusion. Article 18 therefore applied.

Jurisdiction agreements in relation to insurance and consumer contracts

There are special regimes relating to disputes concerning insurance and consumer contracts including the effect of jurisdiction agreements (see Chapter 6). The jurisdiction framework being created specifically to protect the insured or beneficiary and the consumer, the ability to override that framework by agreement is understandably restricted. The circumstances in which they may be so overridden are set out in Articles 12, 12A (insurance) and Article 15 (consumer contracts).

Save for a concept of "deemed domicile" of insurers and consumer suppliers the insurance and consumer contract regimes are subject to Article 4 and the reference to forum law of any jurisdiction issue if the defendant is not domiciled in a contracting State (see *infra*). It follows therefore that unlike an agreement under Article 17 only, jurisdiction agreements within either regime cannot constitute a jurisdiction base unless the defendant is domiciled or deemed to be domiciled in a contracting State. Although the agreements must comply with Article 17 as well as the appropriate insurance or consumer contract requirements the effect of such agreements is therefore solely jurisdiction allocation within the Convention as distinct from applicability of the Convention whether the defendant is domiciled within or outside the contracting States. The extension of domicile is considered *infra* as part of the concept of domicile and the regimes including the scope and effect of the agreements in Chapter 6.

Persons domiciled in Luxembourg

The effect of Article 17 is qualified in the case of persons domiciled in Luxembourg by Article I of the Annexed Protocol which so far as relevant reads:

"An agreement conferring jurisdiction, within the meaning of Article 17, shall be valid with respect to a person domiciled in Luxembourg only if that person has expressly and specifically so agreed."

---

65. *Anterist* v. *Credit Lyonnais* 22/85 [1987] 1 CMLR 333 (ECJ). For an application of the provision in favour of the plaintiff's option (recourse against sureties) see *Coignet SA* v. *Banca Commerciale Italiana* [1992] I.L.Pr. 450.
66. Fn. 20.

This clause must be accepted expressly and signed—the conclusion of a contract containing such a clause is not sufficient (see *Porta Leasing GmbH* v. *Prestige International*.[67] The clause together with a qualification on the general enforceability of Article 5(1) (as to which see Chapter 6) was apparently originally inserted to protect Luxembourg domiciliaries in that contracts entered into by them tend to be international and performed in Belgium. It was said therefore that the criteria for enforcing of agreements as to non-Luxembourg jurisdiction in respect of Luxembourg domiciliaries should be more strict than for the domiciliaries in other states (see Jenard, p. 63). The provision is relevant to construction of Article 17 in that it must represent an additional requirement to that generally applicable.

D. Insurance and consumer contract regimes—"deemed domicile"

Jurisdiction in respect of matters relating to insurance and proceedings concerning consumer contracts is to be decided in accordance with rules set out in sections 3 and 4 "without prejudice to the provisions of Article 4" (Articles 7, 13).[68] So the sections take effect subject to the basic rule of reference of the question of jurisdiction to forum law where the defendant is not domiciled in a contracting State. However, the applicability of the Convention is extended from its normal scope through a concept of "deemed domicile" of insurers or suppliers under a consumer contract. So an insurer or supplier not domiciled in a contracting State is deemed to be so domiciled in respect of any dispute arising from activities of a branch, agency or other establishment in a contracting State.[69]

Save for the "deemed domicile" provision it would seem that express wording of Articles 8 and 14 (and the subjection of the insurance and consumer contract framework to Article 4) means that, apart from any issue falling within the exclusive jurisdiction of Article 16, the Convention substantive insurance and consumer contract regimes apply only to cases in which the defendant is domiciled in a contracting State. Articles 7 and 13 are also definitively worded—that (respectively) "matters relating to insurance shall be determined by this section ... " and "the 'consumer' jurisdiction shall be determined by this Section".

E. Limitation of liability (Article 6a)—the court hearing the liability action

Article 6a reads:

"Where by virtue of this Convention a court of a Contracting State has jurisdiction in actions relating to liability from the use or operation of a ship, that court, or any other court substituted for this purpose by the internal law of that State shall also have jurisdiction over claims for limitation of that liability."

A limitation claim will be within the ambit of the Convention provided it is against a defendant. It therefore may be brought in accordance with any applicable jurisdiction base. Article 6a recognizes the nature of a limitation claim by providing that in *addition*

---

67. 784/79 1980 ECR 1517; [1981] 1 CMLR 135 (ECJ); *Weber* v. *Eurocard* [1993] I.L.Pr. 55 (Luxembourg C.A.).

68. See *Brenner* v. *Reynolds* 318/93 [1994] I.L.Pr. 720.

69. Arts. 8, 13. For application of Art. 8 see e.g. *Berisford Plc* v. *New Hampshire Insurance Co.* [1990] 2 All E.R. 321.

it may be brought in the court having liability jurisdiction. The jurisdiction base of Article 6a is therefore that of the liability action—this being a sensible gateway to liability and limitation actions being heard by the same court.[70]

2. THE DOMICILE OF THE DEFENDANT IN A CONTRACTING STATE

The effect of Article 4 is subject to the Convention provisions (a) to apply the Convention regime if a defendant is domiciled in a contracting State and (b) to allocate jurisdiction to that state. Allocation is discussed in Chapter 6.

The concept of domicile

The concept of domicile is treated separately for (a) individuals and (b) corporations and associations. In both instances it is provided by the Convention that the concept is to be defined by national law. The concept of domicile is extended for the purposes of the applicability of Convention jurisdiction provisions to the two categories of case in regard to which there are special regimes—matters relating to insurance and consumer contracts.[71] A "supplier" under a consumer contract or an insurer not domiciled in a contracting State is "deemed" to be domiciled in such a state in respect of disputes arising out of the operation of a branch agency or establishment in such a state (see *supra*).

Domicile of individual[72]

By virtue of Article 52 a forum court:

(a) to determine if a party is domiciled in the forum must apply its internal law;
(b) to determine if a party is domiciled in another contracting State must apply the law of that state.

The provisions of English law spelling out criteria of domicile are set out in the Civil Jurisdiction and Judgments Act 1982 in sections 41, 44. Section 41 provides the general implementation in the United Kingdom laws of Article 52 and is expressly subject to it. Its scope is therefore restricted to the issue of whether a party is domiciled in the United Kingdom or in a state other than a contracting State. The provisions have three functions:

(i) The necessary spelling out of the Convention criteria of domicile for the purpose of ascertaining domicile in the United Kingdom;
(ii) The localization of Convention jurisdiction within the United Kingdom (i.e. England, Scotland or Northern Ireland), a step necessary when the Convention

---

70. As to consideration of the two actions as "related" and the resolution of multiple proceedings see Chap. 12.
71. As to the scope of the regimes see Chap. 6.
72. It should be stressed that an individual may be domiciled both in the UK and a contracting or a non-contracting State because first, of the different criteria which may be employed for adjudging domicile as between the contracting States and, secondly, because by English law as set out in the Act it is possible that an individual may be domiciled in the UK and another state.

confers jurisdiction on the United Kingdom as a contracting State by virtue of the defendant's domicile in a state or in a place in a contracting State;

(iii) The allocation or jurisdiction as between England, Scotland and Northern Ireland in a dispute solely connected with the United Kingdom and as such outside the Convention.

Section 44 provides for the localization within the United Kingdom of the Convention provision of "deemed domicile" of insurers and suppliers under consumer contracts by virtue of a branch agency or other establishment within the United Kingdom.

The Convention criteria are discussed in this chapter and localization and *intra* United Kingdom jurisdiction allocation in Chapter 7.

The general criteria of domicile of individuals

Domicile in the United Kingdom

An individual is domiciled in the United Kingdom if and only if

"(a) he is resident in the United Kingdom; and
(b) the nature and circumstances of his residence indicate that he has a substantial connection with the United Kingdom (s.41(2))."

The same criteria are then applied to focus the domicile in a part of the United Kingdom, i.e. in England and Wales, Scotland or Northern Ireland (section 41(3)). Domicile in a place requires domicile in the part where the place is and residence in that place (section 41(4)).

To reduce the likelihood of a connection simply not being established because of failure to satisfy the onus of proof, it is provided that present residence and past residence for three months will create a presumption of substantial connection (section 41(6)). To prevent the possibility of a person being domiciled in the United Kingdom but failing to satisfy the statutory criteria in respect of any part, a person who has no "substantial connection" with a part is domiciled in that part in which he is resident (section 41(5)).

Domicile in a state other than a contracting State

Residence and substantial connection are the criteria also applied for the purpose of deciding whether a person is domiciled in a state other than a contracting State (section 41(7)).

Domicile of corporations and associations

Article 53 of the Convention provides that the seat "of a company or other legal person or association of natural or legal persons" is to be treated as its domicile. In order to determine the seat the court of a contracting State must apply its rules of private international law. Section 42 provides in effect for English law to adjudge the issue subject to a negative veto by the law of a contracting State in respect of any decision as to a seat in that state (section 42(2)(7)). The criteria for domicile are either: (i) incorporation or formation *and* either registered office or official address (within the meaning of section 42(8)); or (ii) central management and control. From a Community viewpoint a corporation or an association may be domiciled in more than one contracting State because states may apply different criteria for domicile, and, in accordance with section 42, by English law there may be domicile both in the United Kingdom and in another state.[73]

"Corporation" includes a partnership under Scottish law and "association" means an unincorporated body of persons (section 50). Whether the provision is intended to include a partnership in English law is as uncertain as its parent Article 53. The question is relevant in English law only if the concept of association in Article 53 is to be referred to national law, but it is suggested that the interpretation of section 42 should be that partnerships are included rather than excluded, bearing the purposes of the Convention in mind.[74]

As for individuals, provision is made not only for domicile in the United Kingdom but for domicile in a part of the United Kingdom (England and Wales, Scotland or Northern Ireland) and a place in the United Kingdom. Provision is thus made for the necessary foundation for localizing Convention jurisdiction in the appropriate part, the criteria for domicile in a place for the purposes of certain Convention jurisdiction bases and the adaptation by the Act of the Convention to *intra* United Kingdom disputes (as to which see Chapter 7).

Domicile for the purposes of "exclusive" jurisdiction in company proceedings

Article 16(2) provides for exclusive jurisdiction in relation to the validity of the constitution of the nullity or dissolution of a legal person in the courts of its seat (see *supra*). Different statutory rules are provided for assessing the domicile of a corporation or association for the purposes of Article 16(2) than for other purposes.

Commentators have pointed to the anomaly of multiple exclusive jurisdictions as a rationale for the difference.[75] However the effect of section 43 is both to broaden the scope of English jurisdiction and to assert it exclusively. As a result while the possibility of multiple jurisdiction recognized by English law is decreased, the risk of multiple jurisdiction within the Community through divergence of national laws is increased.

The connections required for a seat in the United Kingdom or another contracting State are less stringent than for questions of general domicile purposes. A seat or domicile may exist under section 43 through incorporation or formation without a registered office or official address. However the possibility of an association having a seat in both the United Kingdom and another contracting State in English law is reduced (through section 43(7)(a)) by the provision that a seat in the United Kingdom by virtue of incorporation or formation means that there cannot be a seat in another contracting State.

Domicile of trusts—section 45

Contrary to the provisions in respect of individuals, associations and legal persons a trust may be domiciled in the United Kingdom only if domiciled in a part of the United

---

73. For examples of domicile because of central management and control in a contracting State of a corporation incorporated and having its registered office in a non-contracting State see *The Rewia* [1991] 2 Lloyd's Rep. 325 (C.A.); *The Deichland* [1989] 2 All E.R. 1066.

74. The same question arises as to the scope of exclusive jurisdiction under Article 16(2). See Chap. 4.

75. See e.g. Hartley, p. 37.

Kingdom. A trust is so domiciled only if the law of that part is the system with which the trust has its "closest and most real connection".

Domicile of the Crown—section 46

Subject to any Order in Council the Crown in right of the government in the United Kingdom is domiciled and has its seat in every part and place in the United Kingdom. The Crown in right of Northern Ireland has its seat and is domiciled in every place in Northern Ireland.

Summary

In deciding whether a person (other than an individual whose domicile was dependent on another) is domiciled in a contracting State therefore an English court must:

  (a) if the defendant is an individual decide whether in accordance with section 41 (and if relevant the deemed domicile provision of section 44) the defendant is domiciled in the United Kingdom;
  (b) if not so domiciled, either
    (i) whether in accordance with the law of any other contracting State the defendant is domiciled in that state, or
    (ii) whether in accordance with section 41 the defendant is domiciled in a non-contracting State.

It is suggested that in accordance with the Convention principles an English court should only go to the issue of domicile in a non-contracting State if it finds that in accordance with the principles of Article 52 the defendant is not domiciled in the United Kingdom or in a contracting State.

  In deciding whether a legal person, association or corporation is domiciled in a contracting State:

    (i) for general purposes an English court will apply section 42 of the Act and in relation to a trust section 43 of the Act;
    (ii) for the purposes of Article 16(2) an English court will apply section 43 of the Act.

An English court must decide not only whether a defendant is domiciled in the United Kingdom but also whether, if relevant, the defendant is domiciled in England so as to give jurisdiction between England, Scotland and Northern Ireland. A similar process will apply if the matter is within Article 16(2) of the 1968 Convention, for the purposes of localizing Convention jurisdiction and for *intra* United Kingdom disputes (see Chapter 7).

CHAPTER 6

The Brussels Convention—Jurisdiction Allocation in Initial Proceedings

Once the Convention jurisdiction regime is applicable by virtue of a required connection as discussed in Chapter 5 jurisdiction in initial proceedings is allocated according to one of three differing criteria in accordance with:

1. a jurisdiction Convention taking precedence over the Brussels Convention by virtue of Article 57
2. mandatory Convention allocation
3. a Convention provision conferring (in specified circumstances) an option on the plaintiff.

Where a defendant is domiciled in a contracting State the main principle is that suit should be brought there. Any provision (be it mandatory or optional) qualifying that principle is to be construed with the aims of the Convention in mind and in particular that the qualification is a derogation from the central principle.[1]

1. REFERENCE TO ANOTHER CONVENTION (ARTICLE 57)

THE SCOPE AND EFFECT OF THE REFERENCE

The Brussels Convention contains a number of provisions dealing with its relationship with other Conventions concerning jurisdiction and judgments.[2] Its relationship to the subsequent Lugano Convention is considered in Chapter 8 in the context of that Convention.

The Convention provides for the superseding of specified Conventions (Article 55); and continuing others. Where others are continued the Brussels Convention jurisdiction and judgments regime takes effect subject to the other Convention. When another Convention is given precedence it is so only to the extent of positive provisions[3] and whatever the scope of the reference it is by virtue of the Brussels Convention. That reference is subject

---

1. See e.g. *Somafer SA* v. *Saar Ferngas AG* 33/78 [1979] 1 CMLR 490; *Shearson Lehman Hutton Inc.* v. *TVB* 89/91 [1993] I.L.Pr. 199; *Handte* v. *TMCS* 26/91 [1993] I.L.Pr. 5; *Kalfelis* v. *Schroder* 189/87 [1988] ECR 5565.
2. For discussion as to Conventions on judgments see Chap. 28. In addition in one instance (Article 15 of the Hague Convention on the Service Abroad of Judicial and Extrajudicial Documents in Civil or Commerical Matters 1965) provisions of other Conventions are specifically applied by the Brussels and Lugano Conventions. See Chaps. 4, 28.
3. *The Maciej Rataj* [1995] 1 Lloyd's Rep. 302.

to Article 4, i.e. it applies only if save for the reference out the Convention regime would apply. There is no room for any reference if, by Article 4, national law applies.

(i) Conventions overridden

Article 55 specifies a list of bilateral Conventions between member States concerning jurisdiction and recognition of judgments superseded by the 1968 Convention. These Conventions continue in force in respect of matters outside the Brussels Convention (Article 56).

(ii) Conventions maintained

Articles 57 to 59 provide for the maintaining of provisions concerning jurisdiction and judgments in other Conventions despite inconsistency with the Brussels Convention.[4] Article 58 provides specifically for the continuation of a French/Swiss Bilateral Convention of 15 June 1869 on Jurisdiction and Enforcement of Judgments in Civil Matters. Articles 57 and 59[5] are of general application and importance. Article 57 provides:

"**1** This Convention shall not affect any conventions to which the Contracting States are or will be parties and which in relation to particular matters, govern jurisdiction or the recognition or enforcement of judgments.

2 With a view to its uniform interpretation, paragraph 1 shall be applied in the following manner—
  (a) this Convention shall not prevent a court of a Contracting State which is a party to a convention on a particular matter from assuming jurisdiction in accordance with that Convention, even where the defendant is domiciled in another Contracting State which is not a party to that Convention. The court hearing the action shall, in any event, apply Article 20 of this Convention:
  (b) judgments given in a Contracting State by a court in the exercise of jurisdiction provided for in a convention on a particular matter shall be recognized and enforced in the other Contracting State in accordance with this Convention.
  Where a convention on a particular matter to which both the State of origin and the State addressed are parties lays down conditions for the recognition or enforcement of judgments, those conditions shall apply. In any event, the provisions of this Convention which concern the procedure for recognition and enforcement of judgments may be applied.

3 This Convention shall not affect the application of provisions which, in relation to particular matters, govern jurisdiction or the recognition or enforcement of judgments and which are or will be contained in acts of the institutions of the European Communities or in national laws harmonized in implementation of such acts."

The scope of Article 57 is still not entirely certain.[6] It is of considerable importance in the enforcement of maritime claims in English law because of a growing tendency to include provisions relating to jurisdiction in maritime Conventions dealing with substantive matters. It gives priority only to Conventions relating to "particular matters".[7]

---

4. For lists of Conventions to which Article 57 may apply see Jenard, pp. 59–60; Schlosser, Annex 11, Fn 59. For an example of how Article 57 will apply as regards jurisdiction see Schlosser, paras. 241–245.
5. Article 59 of the 1968 Convention applies to judgments only. See Chap. 28.
6. See Schlosser, para. 239. But see also *The Maciej Rataj* (fn 3).
7. A Convention concerned generally with jurisdiction (or indeed recognition or enforcement of judgments) would not therefore be within Article 57—to be so a Convention must constitute a "special law".

The first question therefore is whether a relevant Convention "governs jurisdiction". Apart from express jurisdiction provisions it may be arguable that the mandatory application of substantive rules implies jurisdiction control.[8]

Assuming that the "other" Convention governs jurisdiction whether rules of the other Convention override, are additional to or are alternative to the Brussels Convention depends on the other Convention.[9] If the other Convention sets out exclusive rules the Brussels Convention is overridden.[10] If they are not exclusive or do not set out a complete jurisdiction framework, questions of the degree of reference to the "other Convention" necessarily arise. This is particularly so if the framework of the other Convention is permissive. The interpretative provisions underline the superiority of the other Convention in underlining that the other Convention may apply even if a defendant is domiciled in a contracting State not a party to the other Convention.

Further, given that subject to any express provisions the plaintiff's domicile is irrelevant to the application of the Brussels Convention, Article 57 will mean that a Convention to which the United Kingdom is a party will apply so that it and not the Brussels Convention will govern the jurisdiction of a case within it whether or not the state of domicile or nationality of the plaintiff was a contracting State. In addition unless the other Convention so specifies there will be no requirements that that state is a party to the other Convention.[11]

The ambit of Article 57 is that of the Convention at issue and not that of the application under national law. In *The Po*[12] the Court of Appeal held that it does not matter for the application of the other Convention that the Convention has not been enacted into English law. It was enough that the United Kingdom was a party to it, that jurisdiction was authorized by it and that jurisdiction had been created by service of a writ in accordance with English law. The court did not find it necessary to hold that the effect of Article 57 was to incorporate the other Convention into English law.[13]

RELEVANT MARITIME LAW CONVENTIONS

1. The Convention Relating to the Arrest of Sea-going Ships 1952 (the Arrest Convention).[14]

---

8. See the discussion on the Hague-Visby Rule *infra*.

9. In *State of Netherlands* v. *Ruffer* (*supra*) Warner A.G. expressed the view that if the jurisdiction rules of the "other Convention" (in that case the Ems-Dolland bilateral Convention between the Netherlands and Germany) were not exclusive the Brussels Convention could apply. However, the Ems-Dolland Convention simply conferred jurisdiction and it would seem by the most general provisions. The European Court did not consider the question as it ruled the dispute to be not within the subject matter of the Convention (see *infra*).

10. But see Schlosser (para. 240) who maintains the question was "left open". Cf. Jenard p. 60.

11. *The Po* [1991] 2 Lloyd's Rep. 206 (C.A.) (considering the Collision Civil Jurisdiction Convention 1952—as to which see *infra*). The Court also held (consistently with the interpretative provisions now in Article 57) that it mattered not that the plaintiff's state of domicile was not a party to the other Convention—although it did consider whether the state of the domicile of the defendant had made its ratification of the Collision Convention subject to reciprocity. The latter point seems relevant only if the United Kingdom recognizes that limitation on the application of the Convention so far as it is concerned.

12. See fn 11.

13. Thereby not going so far as Hobhouse J. in *The Nordglimt* [1987] 2 Lloyd's Rep. 470 who had there held that the effect of Article 57 was indirectly to incorporate the "other Convention" into English law.

14. A new Arrest Convention is under consideration.

2. The International Convention on Certain Rules Concerning Civil Jurisdiction in Matters of Collision 1952 (the Collision Jurisdiction Convention 1952).
3. The International Convention of Civil Liability for Oil Pollution Damage 1969 and the International Convention on the Establishment of an International Fund for Compensation for Oil Pollution Damage 1971 (the Oil Pollution Conventions)—insofar as the 1992 Protocols are in force in a state to be entitled to the 1992 Convention (the Protocols come into force on 30 May 1996).
4. Conventions concerning nuclear incidents and material, particularly:
    (i) the Paris Convention 1960 on Third Party Liability (as supplemented by the Brussels Convention 1963 and Additional Protocol of 1964)[15];
    (ii) the Vienna Convention on Civil Liability for Nuclear Damage 1963;
    (iii) the Convention Relating to the Liability of Operators of Nuclear Ships 1962.
5. Conventions concerning carriage of goods by sea:
    (i) The Hague Rules 1924 and Hague-Visby Rules 1968;
    (ii) The Hamburg Rules 1978;
    (iii) The Multimodal Convention 1980;
    (iv) The CMR (Carriage of Goods by Road) as relevant to carriage by sea.
6. Convention Relating to the Carriage of Passengers and Their Luggage By Sea 1974 (the Athens Convention).
7. The Convention on the Limitation of Liability for Maritime Claims 1976 (the Limitation Convention).
8. International Convention for the Unification of Certain Rules Relating to Maritime Liens and Mortgages 1926, 1967 and 1993 (the Liens and Mortgage Conventions).
9. The Rhine Navigation Convention 1868 (otherwise known as the Mannheim Convention).[16]

The problem of conflict of Conventions is increasingly met in maritime law as is shown by continuing debates in IMO and UNCTAD on alleged conflict between proposed and existing Conventions dealing with limitation of liability and multimodal transport. The obvious method of dealing with the problem is to incorporate a rule of precedence in the later Convention giving superiority to the earlier (such as Article 57). One possible but perhaps unlikely problem with this solution (as indeed with Article 57) is that if the States parties to the later Convention are not identical to the earlier Convention the consequences may be that no court has jurisdiction. Without some rule of precedence however a State party to both Conventions will face a conflict of jurisdictional rules insofar as mandatory frameworks differ.

---

15. The Paris Convention was followed by the Vienna Convention on Civil Liability for Nuclear Damage 1964 to which no contracting State is a party. The Brussels Convention Relating to Civil Liability in the Field of Maritime Carriage 1971 which came into force in 1975 exonerates those engaged in maritime transport from liability in respect of damage for which an operator of a nuclear installation is liable in accordance with (or at least to a degree as favourable as) the Paris or Vienna Conventions.
16. As amended in 1963 and Additional Protocols 1–3. There are other Conventions relating to river navigation which may arguably be relevant as (e.g.) Relating to the Moselle 1956 (Luxembourg, Germany and France) the Ems-Dolland (Germany, the Netherlands) (see fn 9 *supra*) and the Danube (1865) (as revised).

1. The Arrest Convention 1952

The Convention provides for jurisdiction over the merits of a "maritime claim" (as defined in Article 1) through arrest.[17] Article 7 provides:

"(1) The Courts of the country in which the arrest was made shall have jurisdiction to determine the case upon its merits if the domestic law of the country in which the arrest is made gives jurisdiction to such Courts, or in any of the following cases namely:

(a) if the claimant has his habitual residence or principal place of business in the country in which the arrest was made;

(b) if the claim arose in the country in which the arrest was made;

(c) if the claim concerns the voyage of the ship during which the arrest was made;

(d) if the claim arose out of a collision or in circumstances covered by Article 13 of the International Convention for the unification of certain rules of law with respect to collisions between vessels, signed at Brussels on September 23, 1910;

(e) if the claim is for salvage;

(f) if the claim is upon a mortgage or hypothecation of the ship arrested.

(2) If the Court within whose jurisdiction the ship was arrested has no jurisdiction to decide upon the merits, the bail or other security given in accordance with Article 5 to procure the release of the ship shall specifically provide that it is given as security for the satisfaction of any judgment which may eventually be pronounced by a Court having jurisdiction so to decide; and the Court or other appropriate judicial authority of the country in which the arrest is made shall fix the time within which the claimant shall bring an action before a Court having such jurisdiction.

(3) If the parties have agreed to submit the dispute to the jurisdiction of a particular Court other than that within whose jurisdiction the arrest was made or to arbitration, the Court or other appropriate judicial authority within whose jurisdiction the arrest was made may fix the time within which the claimant shall bring proceedings.

(4) If, in any of the cases mentioned in the two preceding paragraphs, the action or proceedings are not brought within the time so fixed, the defendant may apply for the release of the ship or of the bail or other security.

(5) This article shall not apply in cases covered by the provisions of the revised Rhine Navigation Convention of October 17, 1868."[18]

The Convention applies to specified maritime claims and to any vessel flying the flag of a contracting State in the jurisdiction of a contracting State, and provides that subject to reservations a ship flying the flag of a non-contracting State may be arrested for any of the maritime claims enumerated in the Convention.[19]

By Article 7 the Convention provides for mandatory jurisdiction on the merits in the country of the arrest in respect of the circumstances listed in (1)(a)–(f) and, subject to this, delegates the issue of jurisdiction to domestic law. It impliedly recognizes the validity of a jurisdiction clause (Article 7(3)) but lacking any requirement it seems that this is simply a recognition of security consequences should such an agreement be enforceable under domestic law.[20] It is uncertain therefore whether jurisdiction asserted through agreement is within the ambit of the Arrest Convention or the Brussels Convention.[21]

---

17. As to the scope of the Arrest Convention both in regard to provisional measures and merits jurisdiction see Chaps. 10, 15.

18. As to which see *infra*.

19. Arts 1, 8(1)(2). A contracting State may exclude from Convention benefits any Government of a non-contracting State or any person who at the time of the arrest does not have habitual residence or the principal place of business in a contracting State (Art. 8(3)).

20. *The Deichland* [1989] 2 All E.R. 1066 (C.A.).

21. In *Siamar* v. *Spedimex* [1990] I.L.Pr. 266 the Italian Supreme Court considered the validity of a jurisdiction agreement in accordance with the Arrest Convention in an action on the merits under that Convention.

The Arrest Convention forms an important part of the Brussels jurisdiction framework and all the present contracting States are parties to it, enabling the maintaining of jurisdiction in relation to maritime claims based on arrest of seagoing ships while removing any general jurisdiction based on seizure or arrest of property. The Convention as presently drafted requires the arrest of a ship for jurisdiction to be established. While once arrested it is provided that the ship may be released on bail or other security being given there is no jurisdiction if the ship is not arrested because of the giving of bail or such security.

2. The Collision (Civil Jurisdiction) Convention 1952

Articles 1, 2 and 3 provide:

"Article 1
   (1) An action for collision occurring between seagoing vessels, or between seagoing vessels and inland navigation craft, can only be introduced:
      (a) either before the Court where the defendant has his habitual residence or a place of business;
      (b) or before the Court of the place where arrest has been effected of the defendant ship or of any other ship belonging to the defendant which can be lawfully arrested, or where arrest could have been effected and bail or other security has been furnished;
      (c) or before the Court of the place of collision when the collision has occurred within the limits of a port or in inland waters.
   (2) It shall be for the plaintiff to decide in which of the Courts referred to in para. 1 of this article the action shall be instituted.
   (3) A claimant shall not be allowed to bring a further action against the same defendant on the same facts in another jurisdiction, without discontinuing an action already instituted.

Article 2
The provisions of Article 1 shall not in any way prejudice the right of the parties to bring an action in respect of a collision before a Court they have chosen by agreement or to refer it to arbitration.

Article 3
   (1) Counterclaims arising out of the same position can be brought before the Court having jurisdiction over the principal action in accordance with the provisions of Article 1.
   (2) In the event of there being several claimants, any claimant may bring his action before the Court previously seized of an action against the same party arising out of the same collision.
   (3) In the case of a collision or collisions in which two or more vessels are involved nothing in this Convention shall prevent any Court seized of an action by reason of the provisions of this Convention, from exercising jurisdiction under its national laws in further actions arising out of the same incident."

Of the contracting States to the Brussels Convention only the Netherlands is not a party.

The Convention applies "as regards all persons interested when all the vessels concerned in any action belong to States of the High Contracting parties" and may be made applicable to persons interested belonging to a non-contracting State (Article 8).[22] The Convention jurisdiction framework recognizes multiple claims and jurisdiction agreements. In respect of such an agreement the Convention does not specify either formal

---

22. The application to persons interested who belong to a non-contracting State may be made conditional on reciprocity (*ibid*). For application through Article 57 see *The Po* [1991] 2 Lloyd's Rep. 206 (C.A.).

requirements or any criteria for validity. Further, the effect of such an agreement under the Collision Convention is clearly permissive and whether that jurisdiction is exercised therefore remains a matter for national law.

The jurisdiction framework of the Collision Jurisdiction Convention raises the issue as to whether Article 57 incorporates it only with additional requirements stemming from the Brussels Convention or whether only that which is prescribed should be taken to be all that is necessary. It would seem more practical to take the latter view—that in respect of a Convention given priority the question of jurisdiction should be referred to that framework exclusively.[23] Otherwise even more complex issues will arise in seeking to fit part of the Brussels Convention framework into other Convention frameworks.

3. The Oil Pollution Conventions 1969 and 1971 (as amended by the 1992 Protocols and when so amended being known as the 1992 Conventions)

The Liability Convention 1969 provided a structure of substantive rules in respect of liability for oil pollution from ships creating damage to the territories of contracting States.[24] This was extended by amendment of Article II by Protocol to include the exclusive economic zone or equivalent area.[25] Jurisdiction is limited by the Convention to the state or states in which the damage or preventative measure occurs. Article IX as amended provides:

"1 Where an Incident has caused pollution damage in the territory including the territorial sea of one or more Contracting State or an area referred to in Article II, or preventive measures have been taken to prevent or minimize pollution damage in such territory including the territorial sea or area, actions for compensation may only be brought in the Courts of any such Contracting State or States. Reasonable notice of any such action shall be given to the defendant.

2 Each Contracting State shall ensure that its Courts possess the necessary jurisdiction to entertain such actions for compensation.

3 After the fund has been constituted in accordance with Article V[26] the Courts of the State in which the fund is constituted shall be exclusively competent to determine all matters relating to the apportionment and distribution of the fund."

All the present parties to the Brussels Convention are parties. Finland and Sweden are also parties.

The Fund Convention 1971 provides for the establishment of a fund to meet claims for damage in cases where the Liability Convention is inadequate and to give relief to shipowners in respect of additional financial burdens imposed by the Liability Convention.[27] As against the fund an action for compensation may only be brought in the court competent to hear the liability claim (see Article 7).

Article 7(3) provides:

23. This is not quite the same question as decided in *The Maciej Rataj* (fn 3)—that reference to a Convention applies only to the provisions of it. If there is no reference to multiple proceedings the Convention does not govern that issue (*ibid*). This approach is supported (at least in regard to a jurisdiction agreement) by a decision of a German court on the CMR. (Judgment of Landgericht Aachen of 16 January 1976 ECD 1–57–B2).
24. As to the implementation in the United Kingdom see Chap. 2.
25. An area beyond and adjacent to the territorial sea extending not more than 200 nautical miles from the baseline of the territorial sea.
26. i.e. the Limitation Fund. See Chap. 24.
27. As to the implementation in the United Kingdom see Chap. 2.

"(3) Where an action for compensation for pollution damage has been brought before a court competent under Article IX of the Liability Convention against the owner of a ship or his guarantor, such court shall have exclusive jurisdictional competence over any action against the Fund for compensation or indemnification under the provisions of Articles 4 or 5 of this Convention in respect of the same damage. However, where an action for compensation for pollution damage under the Liability Convention has been brought before a court in a State Party to the Liability Convention but not to this Convention, any action against the Fund under Article 4 or under Article 5, paragraph 1, of this Convention shall at the option of the claimant be brought either before a court of the State where the Fund has its headquarters[28] or before any court of a State Party to this Convention competent under Article IX of the Liability Convention."

Of the present parties to the Brussels Convention only Luxembourg is not a party. Finland and Sweden are parties.

A critical issue is whether the link between damage or measure and the State court having jurisdiction under the Liability and Fund Conventions replaces the 1968 Convention framework as "governing jurisdiction" or in the circumstances simply represents an additional contact requirement. In substance the prerequisite for action is that of the conventional optional jurisdiction ground applicable to tort, i.e. the place of the harmful event (see Article 5(3) and Chapter 4). It would seem therefore that this is a sufficient jurisdiction link to take the matter out of the 1968 Convention and to the extent of those aspects covered to refer the matter to the Oil Pollution Conventions. Further, the required link between territory and damage lies at the jurisdictional heart of the Oil Pollution Conventions. It is therefore suggested that the Oil Pollution Conventions do "govern jurisdiction" within the meaning of Article 57 and to the extent of their provision replace the jurisdiction regime of the 1968 Convention.

4. Conventions concerning nuclear material and ships[29]

The Paris Convention on Third Party Liability in the field of Nuclear Energy 1960 was amended by a supplementary Convention of 1963 and the Additional Protocol of 1964.[30] Of the contracting States of the Brussels Convention the following are parties to both the 1960 and 1963 Conventions: of the parties to the Brussels Convention, Belgium, Denmark, France, Germany, Italy, the Netherlands, Portugal, Spain and the United Kingdom.[31] Greece, Luxembourg and Portugal are parties to the 1960 Convention.

Damage occurring on the high seas falls within the Conventions.[32] The Paris Convention as amended restricts jurisdiction over claims primarily to the courts of the contracting State in which the nuclear incident occurred. Failing placing the incident in a contracting State, jurisdiction lies in the state in which the nuclear installation of the operator liable is placed (see Article 13).[33]

28. At present in the United Kingdom (England).
29. The Convention relating to the Liability of Operators of Nuclear Ships 1962 is not in force. It includes a provision limiting jurisdiction to the state in the territory of which damage is sustained or the state licensing the operator (Article X). The Netherlands and Portugal are parties.
30. The Vienna Convention (see fn 15) contains a jurisdiction structure and provides for recognition of judgments (Articles XI and XII).
31. Luxembourg and Portugal do not appear to be parties to the Additional Protocol.
32. See generally Street and Frame, *Law Relating to Nuclear Energy* 1966.
33. As substituted by the Additional Protocol.

5. *Conventions concerning carriage of goods by sea*

(i) The Hague Rules 1924 and Hague-Visby Rules 1968

Of the parties to the 1968 Convention: (i) Belgium, Germany, France, Ireland, Portugal and Spain remain parties to the Hague Rules 1924. (ii) Belgium, Denmark, France, Italy, Luxembourg, the Netherlands and the United Kingdom are parties to the Hague-Visby Rules. Finland and Sweden are also parties. There are no express jurisdiction provisions in the Hague or the Hague-Visby Rules. However, Article III, r. 8 provides:

> "8. Any clause, covenant, or agreement in a contract of carriage relieving the carrier or the ship from liability for loss or damage to, or in connection with, goods arising from negligence, fault, or failure in the duties and obligations provided in this article or lessening such liability otherwise than as provided in these Rules, shall be null and void and of no effect. A benefit of insurance in favour of the carrier or similar clause shall be deemed to be a clause relieving the carrier from liability."

In *The Morviken*[34] the House of Lords held that by virtue of Article 3(8) a jurisdiction and choice of law clause was invalid insofar as it could lead to the imposition of a lower limit of liability than specified in the rules.[35] To the extent to which the effect of the rule invalidates a jurisdiction clause it is clear that in English law the rules "govern jurisdiction". The question of whether the rules qualify as a Convention governing jurisdiction within Article 57 is in effect a question of whether the *Morviken* approach would be that of the European Court. If not, in English law there is a clear conflict of statutory jurisdictional frameworks.

(ii) The Hamburg Rules 1978

This Convention, intended to replace the Hague and Hague-Visby Rules, entered into force on 1 November 1992. No present contracting State of the Brussels Convention has become a party, but Austria is a party.

The Rules provide a jurisdiction regime.[36] Article 2(1) reads:

> "1. In judicial proceedings relating to carriage of goods under this Convention the plaintiff, at his option, may institute an action in a court which, according to the law of the State where the court is situated, is competent and within the jurisdiction of which is situated one of the following places:
>   (a) the principal place of business or, in the absence thereof, the habitual residence of the defendant; or
>   (b) the place where the contract was made provided that the defendant has there a place of business, branch or agency through which the contract was made; or
>   (c) the port of loading or the port of discharge; or
>   (d) any additional place designated for that purpose in the contract of carriage by sea."

Article 21(2) provides for the institution of an action in the state where the ship is arrested subject to the right of the defendant to remove it to one of the courts specified in Article 21(1) on the lodging of adequate security. It is expressly provided that no action

---

34. [1983] A.C. 565.

35. But not if as a result of the application of "global" limitations of liability based on tonnage as the Rules are subjected to such provisions by their own terms (see Article VIII). *The Benarty* [1985] Q.B. 325; [1984] 2 Lloyd's Rep. 244. Similar reasoning applies in respect of the Hague-Visby Rules and nuclear damage (Article IX). Cf. Chap. 12.

36. Article 22 provides for arbitration.

may be brought except in one of the places specified (Article 21(3)). A jurisdictional agreement made after the claim has arisen is effective (Article 21(5)).

The Rules would clearly provide a jurisdictional framework to displace that of the Brussels Convention insofar as any contracting State becomes a party. No new action may be started on the same grounds between the same parties (Article 21(4)) which reduces the likelihood of multiple claims. Questions of the degree of reference remain however (e.g. multiple defendants), raising in this context the issue of whole or partial reference of any jurisdictional issue to the "other Convention".

(iii) The Multimodal Convention 1980

This is not in force. No contracting State to the 1968 Convention is a party. The Convention has jurisdiction and arbitration provisions (Articles 26 and 27) similar to the Hamburg Rules 1978. It also provides for conflict of Conventions in maintaining in certain circumstances the mandatory jurisdictional provisions of "any other international convention" (Article 30). The effect of maintaining jurisdiction provisions will primarily be to give precedence to the other Conventions over the Multimodal Convention. Any "general" jurisdiction Convention will fall outside Article 57.

(iv) The CMR—Carriage of Goods by Road

The Convention is relevant to maritime claims in that through Article 2(1) it encompasses carriage on a ship of goods in a vehicle. Article 31(1) and (2) provides:

"1. In legal proceedings arising out of carriage under this Convention, the plaintiff may bring an action in any court or tribunal of a contracting court designated by agreement between the parties and, in addition, in the courts or tribunals of the country within whose territory:
  (a) the defendant is ordinarily resident, or has his principal place of business or the branch or agency through which the contract of carriage was made, or
  (b) the place where the goods were taken over by the carrier or the place designated for delivery is situated,
and in no other courts or tribunals.
(2) Where in respect of a claim referred to in paragraph 1 of this article an action is pending before a court or tribunal competent under the paragraph or where in respect of such a claim a judgment has been entered by such a court or tribunal no new action shall be started between the same parties on the same grounds unless the judgment of the court or tribunal before which the first action was brought is not enforceable in the country in which the fresh proceedings are brought."

Further it is provided by Article 41 that subject to the ability of carriers to agree among themselves where the carriage is by successive carriers on legal responsibility "any stipulation which would directly or indirectly derogate from the provisions of this Convention shall be null and void".

All the present parties to the Brussels Convention are parties to the CMR.

The jurisdiction framework is clearly one to which precedence is given by Article 57.[37] Insofar as jurisdiction agreements are permitted the comments made in relation to the Collision Jurisdiction Convention (see p. 128) are relevant. Again the question will arise of the degree of reference by Article 57.

---

37. Article 31 of the CMR provides a uniform set of rules as to jurisdiction (*TSM Compagnie D'Assurances Transports* v. *Geisseler Transport AG* [1993] I.L.Pr. 61 (Hoge Raad Netherlands).

National courts have recognized the superiority of the CMR over the substantive framework of the Brussels Convention through Article 57. In 1976 in *Agence Belgo-Danoise NV* v. *Rederij Hapag Lloyd AG*[38] it was held by the Rechtbank van Koophandel Antwerp that a shipowner could not rely on a jurisdiction agreement under the 1968 Convention in a combined transport bill of lading. The contract was within the CMR and by Article 31 the plaintiff had an option to sue, as in this case, in the state in which the goods were delivered (Belgium). Had the 1968 Convention applied, the jurisdiction clause would have conferred exclusive jurisdiction on the German court. Also in 1976 the Landgericht Aachen[39] upheld a jurisdiction clause in a case falling within the CMR despite its lack of enforceability under the Brussels Convention. Thirdly in *Durbeck* v. *Arco International Transport BV (1984)*[40] a Dutch District Appeal Court had regard to jurisdiction by virtue of the CMR and found the jurisdiction provisions of that Convention to be consistent with jurisdiction in the place of performance under Article 5(1) of the Brussels Convention. Strictly however surely Article 5(1) should not have been considered.

Because of Article 31(2) of the CMR a court should not be faced with any question of choice between two sets of proceedings. However, if it is, then it follows from Article 31(2) that it is the proceedings first instituted which are the relevant ones.

The CMR Convention also prohibits the requirement of security for costs from "nationals of Contracting countries resident or having their place of business in one of those countries" (Article 31(5)). The Brussels Convention has a much more limited prohibition in respect of the application for enforcement of judgments (Article 45—see Chapter 28).[41] Insofar as the security for costs provision of the CMR is a jurisdiction provision within the meaning of Article 57 of the 1968 Convention it will continue to apply. It is arguably such in that it affects the ability of plaintiffs to sue in courts other than their own.

(v) The Athens Convention on Passengers and Their Luggage 1974[42]

Article 17 provides:

"Competent jurisdiction
An action arising under this Convention shall, at the option of the claimant, be brought before one of the courts listed below, provided that the court is located in a State Party to this Convention:

    (a) the court of the place of permanent residence or principal place of business of the defendant, or

    (b) the court of the place of departure or that of the destination according to the contract of carriage, or

    (c) a court of the State of the domicile or permanent residence of the claimant, if the defendant has a place of business and is subject to jurisdiction in that State, or

    (d) a court of the State where the contract of carriage was made, if the defendant has a place of business and is subject to jurisdiction in that State.

After the occurrence of the incident which has caused the damage, the parties may agree that the claim for damages shall be submitted to any jurisdiction or to arbitration."

38. Judgment of 25 June 1976, ECD 1–57–B3.
39. Judgment of 16 January 1976, ECD 1–57–B2.
40. 1985 ECD 321.
41. As to security for costs generally as between contracting States and the application of the non-discrimination provision of the Treaty of Rome (Art. 7) see Chaps. 14, 28.
42. As to its effect in English law see Chap. 3. As to its scope and effect see Gaskell 1987 NLJ 285, 322.

The Convention came into force on 28 April 1987. Of the present contracting States to the Brussels Convention Belgium, Germany, Greece, Luxembourg, Spain and the United Kingdom are parties.

Insofar as the Athens Convention provides for the courts in which a suit may be brought it seems clear that the provision overrides the 1968 Convention: insofar as a jurisdiction agreement may confer jurisdiction the points made in relation to the CMR are relevant. As with the CMR it is doubtful if *forum non conveniens* has any role, given that the choice of jurisdiction as between the specified courts in the Athens Convention is expressly at the option of the plaintiff.

(vi) The Limitation of Liability Convention 1976[43]

The Convention is intended to replace earlier Conventions on the same topic. It came into force on 1 December 1986. It has no express jurisdiction provisions. The Brussels Convention itself provides specifically for jurisdiction in a limitation action in a court hearing a substantive claim in respect of which limitation of liability is claimed (Article 6a). It would therefore appear that the jurisdiction regime of the Brussels Convention applies without qualification to claims within the Limitation Convention.

However there are in the Limitation Convention provisions which affect jurisdiction. A limitation fund may be constituted in any State party to the Limitation Convention in which proceedings have been started in respect of claims subject to limitation, the setting up of a limitation fund being dependent on current liability proceedings. It permits limitation claims although no fund has been established but allows national laws to provide that invoking the right to limit is dependent on the setting up of a fund. Such a restriction would be on the ability to make the claim and not on the jurisdiction to hear it. It therefore lies outside the Brussels Convention.

The 1976 Convention prohibits the bringing of a second action following any claim against the fund. It provides for the mandatory release from arrest of ships when a fund has been set up. Article 13 provides:

"Bar to other actions
1 Where a limitation fund has been constituted in accordance with Article 11, any person having made a claim against the fund shall be barred from exercising any right in respect of such a claim against any other assets of a person by or on behalf of whom the fund has been constituted.
2 After a limitation fund has been constituted in accordance with Article 11, any ship or other property, belonging to a person on behalf of whom the fund has been constituted, which has been arrested or attached within the jurisdiction of a State Party for a claim which may be raised against the fund, or any security given may be released by order of the Court or other competent authority of such State. However, such release shall always be ordered if the limitation fund has been constituted:
    (a) at the port where the occurrence took place, if it took place out of port, at the first port of call thereafter; or
    (b) at the port of disembarkation in respect of claims for loss of life or personal injury; or
    (c) at the port of discharge in respect of damage to cargo; or
    (d) in the State where the arrest is made.
3 The rules of paragraphs 1 and 2 shall apply only if the claimant may bring a claim against the limitation fund before the Court administering that fund and the fund is actually available and freely transferable in respect of that claim."

43. See Chap. 24.

The provision does not select the forum. However, it indirectly controls jurisdiction insofar as jurisdiction could be based on arrest. In proceedings within the Brussels Convention based on arrest either directly through Article 5(7) (salvage of cargo or freight) or indirectly through the Arrest Convention a court of a contracting State would be obliged, where appropriate, to consider the effect of the 1976 Limitation Convention.

All matters of distribution of the limitation fund are governed by the law of the state in which the fund is constituted. Nevertheless the Limitation Convention provides no jurisdiction link between liability and limitation. It is clear that liability proceedings are governed by the Brussels Convention and, where appropriate and through Article 57, the Collision Jurisdiction Convention.

Limitation proceedings against a defendant are within the ambit of the Brussels Convention and jurisdiction is allocated by it. The power of the limitation plaintiff to bring the action in the court hearing liability proceedings is in addition to the generally applicable jurisdiction bases (see Chapter 5).

(vii) The Liens and Mortgages Conventions 1926, 1967 and 1993

The 1926 Convention is in force. Of the parties to the Brussels Convention Belgium, France, Italy, Luxembourg, Portugal and Spain are parties. Neither the 1967 nor the 1993 Conventions are in force. None of the Conventions contain express jurisdiction provisions (although Schlosser includes that of 1967 in his list of Conventions to which Article 57 is relevant). The Conventions of 1967 and 1993 however imply jurisdiction in respect of interests affected by a forced sale where the vessel is in the jurisdiction of the state where the sale is conducted.[44] Such a provision may affect jurisdiction in respect of particular claims and in particular the exclusive jurisdiction as regards entries in public registers in the state of the register.[45]

(viii) The Rhine Navigation Convention 1868

The parties to the Rhine Convention (as amended) are Belgium, France, Germany, the Netherlands, Switzerland and the United Kingdom. The Convention is concerned with the navigation of the Rhine between Basle and the open sea. It is a mixture of public and private law. It provides for the hearing of disputes on specified matters by the tribunals for Rhine navigation with an appeal.

Article 34 provides:

"The Tribunals for Rhine Navigation shall also have jurisdiction, in accordance with Article 34II(c), if the parties are bound by contract, without reference to Article 35; their jurisdiction shall not however extend to an action founded on a contract and taken against a vessel for damages caused to persons or goods on board the said vessel where liability lies with the said vessel."

Article 35 provides for allocation of jurisdiction as between the tribunals. Article 35(b) goes further, recognizing choice of jurisdiction in courts other than the tribunals. It provides:

44. There is an express obligation in contracting States to recognize the effects of a forced sale in the extinguishment of encumbrance (see Chap. 17).
45. See Chap. 5. In the 1993 Convention there are provisions for registration of ships in more than one state (see Chap. 17).

"When, in the case of Article 34II(c), the damages took place on territories of two Riparian States or when it is impossible to determine what territory the damages took place, jurisdiction shall lie with the Tribunal which is the only one before which the case is brought or is the first before which the case is brought.

When a tribunal of one of the States has decided that it has no jurisdiction in the matter, the Tribunal of the other State shall be regarded as having jurisdiction.

Article 35(c)
In a civil action, the parties may agree to take their case before a Tribunal for Rhine Navigation other than the one whose jurisdiction is provided by Articles 35 and 35b, of, if national legislation does not prohibit another jurisdiction or court."

Undoubtedly the Convention provides a jurisdiction framework which by Article 57 is to be observed rather than that of the 1968 Convention.[46]

2. MANDATORY ALLOCATION OF JURISDICTION

In a number of instances the same Convention provision applies the Convention *and* allocates jurisdiction within it. This occurs in relation to:

  (i) the "exclusive" provisions of Article 16—jurisdiction based on specified connection between the case and a contracting State
 (ii) agreements for jurisdiction in a court of a contracting State (Article 17)
(iii) appearance before a court of a contracting State (Article 18).

3. OPTIONAL ALLOCATION OF JURISDICTION

Optional allocation means that, assuming no mandatory allocation of jurisdiction, the plaintiff is given the option in specified circumstances to sue in a state other than that through the jurisdiction of which the Convention is applicable.[47] With one exception the option operates as an alternative to the defendant's domicile. The exception is the option given to a person claiming limitation of liability to bring suit in the court considering the liability claim—the option therefore being dependent on jurisdiction in a different but related matter.

The circumstances creating the option are:

  (i) claim for limitation of liability, or pre-Convention choice of law (Articles 6a, 54)
 (ii) where the defendant is domiciled in a contracting State:
      (a) suit in a state of domicile, bearing in mind there may be more than one such state
      (b) in insurance and consumer contract cases in accordance with Convention provisions (Articles 7–12a (insurance) and Articles 13–15 (consumer contracts)

---

46. See *Haeger and Schmidt GmbH* v. *Compagnie Francaise de Navigation* (C.A. of Central Commission for Navigation of the Rhine). Decision of 2 March 1977, ECD 1–57–B4. Schlosser takes the Rhine Navigation Convention to illustrate the working of Article 57 (paras 241–245).

47. As to rules governing multiple proceedings in the same or a related cause of action see Chap. 12.

(c) in a contracting State with which there is a Convention specified link with the dispute (Article 5)
(d) in suits with multi-defendant parties or counterclaims in the contracting State of one of the parties or the claim (Article 6).

(i) CLAIMS FOR LIMITATION OF LIABILITY

Article 6a reads:

"Where by virtue of this convention a court of a Contracting State has jurisdiction in actions relating to liability arising from the use or operation of a ship, that court, or any other court substituted for this purpose by the internal law of that State, shall also have jurisdiction over claims for limitation of such liability."

This provision brings within the "liability" jurisdiction of a court of a contracting State any claim for limitation of that liability. So proceedings such as in English law which a liability defendant may initiate apart from the liability proceedings may be linked jurisdictionally to those proceedings.[48] The Convention will apply to the limitation suit as to any other.[49] Article 6a simply provides an option other than the jurisdiction base which would otherwise apply directly to the limitation suit whether the Convention applies to the liability proceedings.

The taking up of the option by the liability defendant does not depend on the institution of liability proceedings but simply on the court of a contracting State in which limitation proceedings are launched having the power to adjudicate on liability.[50] While such an option clearly makes sense in that it encourages liability and limitation action in the same court, it does provide a foundation for a "pre-emptive strike" by the liability defendant. Starting limitation proceedings in one court could mean that any liability since must also be heard there.[51]

(ii) PRE-CONVENTION WRITTEN CHOICE OF LAW OF IRELAND OR PART OF THE UNITED KINGDOM

By providing for the retention of jurisdiction in the court matching the choice of law expectations of parties entering into contracts outside the ambit of the Convention, parties are protected in the application of the principle that choice of law would at least provide the basis for discretionary exercise of jurisdiction (see Chapter 26). However, it is not enough that apart from the Convention an English court would have recognized a clause as opting for English law in that the contract as a whole is in writing. The choice must be

48. If limitation proceedings have no "defendant" they will not be within the Convention (see Chap. 4).
49. So Article 6a provides an alternative to the domicile of the limitation defendant (Schlosser, para. 23).
50. Which may be through another Convention by virtue of Article 57.
51. Compare the use of declaration of no liability (see Chap. 4). The Convention Relating to Limitation of Liability 1976 has no jurisdiction provision but it appears that a limitation fund may be set up only where liability proceedings have been started. A jurisdiction provision of English law enacted to meet the jurisdictional consequences of release from arrest under the Limitation Convention cannot operate as a jurisdiction base under the Brussels Convention (as to limitation of liability see Chap. 24).

expressed in writing.[52] The retention is of the right to exercise jurisdiction and hence depends not only on choice by the plaintiff but on agreement by the court.[53]

(iii) WHERE THE DEFENDANT IS DOMICILED IN A CONTRACTING STATE

The primary principle

The general principle of suit in the defendant's domicile is underlined by the express prohibition by Article 3 on the use of particular rules of contracting States basing jurisdiction on other ("exorbitant") bases. So far as the obligation to sue in the defendant's domicile is concerned the provision is simply one of emphasis of the principle set out in Article 2, but it lays the Convention foundation for extension of the scope of some such laws in respect of defendants not domiciled in a contracting State (see Chapter 5). The primacy of the general principle is further emphasized by the established approach to the "options"—that as the provisions derogate from the principle of domicile they must be construed strictly. It must be borne in mind that the consequence of lack of option is not lack of any Convention jurisdiction, but simply that the suit must be brought in the court for which the Convention otherwise provides.

The concept of domicile

The enquiry into the applicability of the Convention through a defendant's domicile will in many cases also indicate the state of domicile of the defendant. The Convention approach to domicile is discussed in Chapter 5 in the context of applicability. Domicile for the purpose of applicability is also domicile for the purpose of jurisdictional allocation.

However, it may be clear that the defendant is domiciled in a contracting State (and therefore the Convention is applicable) but not so clear in which state he is domiciled. The criteria applied to decide applicability must then be applied further to decide the defendant's domicile and hence (subject to any exception) any jurisdiction of a contracting State based on domicile.

(a) Defendant domiciled in more than one contracting State

As indicated in Chapter 5, there is no Community concept of domicile. By Article 52 the obligation of a court to consider the law of a state other than its own arises only if the defendant is not domiciled in the forum state by the law of that state. National laws may not be at one as to the concept or any one law may provide for domicile in more than one state. In such circumstances the plaintiff would have a choice.

---

52. *New Hampshire Insurance Co.* v. *Strabag Bau AG* [1992] 1 Lloyd's Rep. 361 (C.A.). It may be that it could be implied by a written jurisdiction clause (see *ibid.*) and, if so, jurisdiction obtained even though the clause did not comply with Art. 17.
53. Leaving open therefore the plea of *forum non conveniens* (see Chap. 12).

(b) Special subject matter regimes—insurance and consumer contracts

Special mandatory regimes are set out in sections 3 and 4 for disputes in insurance and consumer contracts based on the perceived need for protection of the insured and the consumer contract concerns. They provide first for jurisdiction based on the defendant's domicile but where the defendant is the insurer or supplier for a number of plaintiffs, options differ, at least in part from those generally applicable. Secondly the regimes extend the applicability of the Convention through deeming an insurer or supplier to be domiciled in a contracting State through a branch or agency, and thirdly provide a limited ability to escape from the regimes through a jurisdiction agreement. At least where the jurisdiction selection is of a court of a contracting State, the agreement must comply with Article 17 as well as the appropriate insurance or consumer contract requirements. However not only the scope but the function of these agreements is more limited than that of Article 17. They do not of themselves provide a jurisdiction base unless the Convention already applies through the insurance and consumer contract provisions. In other words they are an alternative to those provisions—they do not create grounds of applicability of the Convention but solely jurisdiction allocation.

Insurance (section 3)

The insurance structure was amended by the Accession Convention 1978 largely to meet the needs of the United Kingdom insurance market (see Schlosser, paras 136 to 152). In particular the concern of the United Kingdom with the mandatory set of rules for the protection of the insured went to the force and frequency of jurisdiction based on agreements where the policy holder was domiciled outside the Community and secondly to the insurance of large risks particularly in shipping and aviation linking the jurisdiction with the United Kingdom.

Compromise was reached. First, an escape route is provided from the insurance framework through agreement where the policy holder is domiciled out of the Community save in cases of compulsory insurance and insurance of immovable property. Secondly, in recognizing that insurance by large undertakings does not raise the same need for protection as "consumer" insurance it was provided that as to shipping and aviation matters the parties could opt out of the insurance jurisdiction rules by agreement as to jurisdiction.

It was found impossible to define an exclusion according to the category of insurer and so a compromise was reached by providing for an opting out of the regime (i) in most types of insurance where the insurer was not domiciled in the Community and (ii) insurance concerning shipping and aviation risks.[54] The English Court of Appeal has rejected the contention that the regime as a whole applies only to domestic or private insurance—pointing to the failure of those negotiating the exclusion to reach a satisfactory exclusion definition for the commercial insurer.[55] Whether reinsurance is within the regime remains uncertain.[56]

---

54. See generally *Charman* v. *WOC Offshore BV* [1993] 2 Lloyd's Rep. 551.

55. *New Hampshire Insurance Co.* v. *Strabag Bau AG* [1992] 1 Lloyd's Rep. 362. Contrast the focus on *consumer* contracts (*infra*).

56. *Ibid.*—despite Schlosser's view (para. 151) that it did not call for the protective approach of the insurer.

The insurance regime deals with actions by and against an insurer and by or against an insured, a policy holder or a beneficiary of an insurance policy. It therefore differentiates between the person who appears on the policy and any person who may hold the benefit of the policy (see Schlosser, para. 152). Subject to this the regime adapts a number of general Convention jurisdiction bases to insurance, provides for the avoidance of the applicable insurance framework through a jurisdiction agreement and when the insurer is the defendant adds alternative bases of jurisdiction to the insurer's domicile.

The insurance section is "without prejudice" to Articles 4 and 5(5). Article 4 is concerned with defendants not domiciled in a contracting State so is not relevant in the present context. Article 5(5) provides for an extension of "domicile" in that a suit may be brought against a defendant domiciled in a contracting State in another contracting State in which the defendant, whether or not domiciled there, has a branch, agency or other establishment in that state.

Claim by insured

Article 8 reflects the basic jurisdiction rule of the Convention—where an insurer is the defendant and is domiciled in a contracting State a suit may be brought in the domicile of the insurer. The concept of domicile is extended in that an insurer who is not domiciled in a contracting State but has a "branch agency or other establishment" in a contracting State is deemed to be domiciled there in disputes arising out of the operations of the branch, agency or establishment.[57] The insurer may be sued in the state in which a branch, agency or establishment exists whether or not the defendant is domiciled in a contracting State.[58]

The multi-defendant provision (Article 6—see *infra*) applicable generally is adapted to insurance transactions. First, a co-insurer may be joined in proceedings against a leading insurer (Article 8) and, secondly, in respect of liability insurance where national law permits it a direct action is permitted against the insurer (Article 10). In the context of such direct actions jurisdiction is also conferred over the insured or policy holder if by national law they may be joined as parties.

As in the general framework a court having jurisdiction over a claim against an insurer also has jurisdiction over any counterclaim (Article 11). The most marked exception to the general jurisdictional framework is that an action against an insurer domiciled in a contracting State may be brought in any contracting State in which the policy holder (but not the insured or beneficiary) is domiciled (Article 8).

By Article 12 in specified circumstances parties may opt out of the insurance regime by an agreement on jurisdiction. Included within that provision are the marine and air risks set out in Article 12a, reflecting the compromise reached as to insurance by large undertakings. Lacking such agreement any insurance matter (marine or otherwise) falls within the regime.

Claim by insurer

Subject to a jurisdiction agreement within Article 12, a counterclaim, the joining of the policy holder or insurer in a direct action by an injured party or arguably suit in a

---

57. Article 8.
58. Articles 7, 8 (Art. 7 applying Art. 5.5 to insurance matters (as to which see *infra*)).

contracting State in which there is a branch, agency or other establishment, the insurer must sue in the defendant's domicile. The provision takes into account that the defendant may not be a policy holder but simply a beneficiary or an insured. It requires the action to be brought in the domicile of the defendant.[59]

The jurisdiction agreement

The insurance jurisdiction framework is mandatory save for jurisdiction agreements within Article 12 and complying with Article 17.[60] Articles 12 and 12a read:

"Article 12
The provisions of this Section may be departed from only by an agreement on jurisdiction:
(1) which is entered into after the dispute has arisen, or
(2) which allows the policy-holder, the insured or a beneficiary to bring proceedings in courts other than those indicated in the Section, or
(3) which is concluded between a policy-holder and an insurer, both of whom are domiciled in the same Contracting State, and which has the effect of conferring jurisdiction on the courts of that State even if the harmful event were to occur abroad, provided that such an agreement is not contrary to the law of that State, or
(4) which is concluded with a policy-holder who is not domiciled in a Contracting State, except in so far as the insurance is compulsory or relates to immovable property in a Contracting State, or
(5) which relates to a contract of insurance in so far as it covers one or more of the risks set out in Article 12a.

Article 12a
The following are the risks referred to in Article 12(5):
(1) Any loss of or damage to
    (a) sea-going ships, installations situated offshore or on the high seas, or aircraft, arising from perils which relate to their use for commercial purposes.
    (b) goods in transit other than passengers' baggage where the transit consists of or includes carriage by such ships or aircraft;
(2) Any liability, other than for bodily injury to passengers or loss of or damage to their baggage,
    (a) arising out of the use or operation of ships, installations or aircraft as referred to in point (1)(a) above in so far as the law of the Contracting State in which such aircraft are registered does not prohibit agreements on jurisdiction insurance of such risks,
    (b) for loss or damage caused by goods in transit as described in point (1)(b) above;
(3) Any financial loss connected with the use or operation of ships, installations or aircraft as referred to in point (1)(a) above, in particular loss of freight or charter-hire;
(4) Any risk or interest connected with any of those referred to in points (1) to (3) above."

Article 12(4) refers to risks and property in addition to those specified in Article 12(1)–(3). A broad approach is to be adopted (at least by English courts) to the connection required on the principle that an insurer of risks within Article 12(1)–(3) cannot be said

---

59. Article 11. The power to sue in a state in which there is a branch agency or other establishment would stem from Article 7 preserving Art. 5.5. By Art. 5.5 the power is limited to disputes arising out of the operations of the branch agency or other establishment. See *infra*.
60. See *Gerling Konzern* v. *Italian Treasury* [1983] ECR 2503; *Berisford Plc* v. *New Hampshire Insurance Co.* [1990] 1 Lloyd's Rep. 454. As pointed out in the *Berisford* case there is an express reference in Art. 17 to Art. 12. As to the relationship between Art. 12 and Art. 17 see *infra*.

to need the protection of the insurance regime simply because of inclusion of other risks. However, the risk must form a lesser part of the contract.[61]

Article 12 is narrower than Article 17 (the general "jurisdiction agreement" provision) in that the escape route from the applicable regime through agreement is specifically restricted to particular types of agreement.[62] This fits with the general protective principles on which the insurance jurisdiction is based.[63] As Schlosser says (para. 148) a jurisdiction agreement would not affect third parties and therefore direct actions by the injured party under Article 10. However, if the law permitting the action also permits a jurisdiction agreement between insurer and policy holder to apply to a direct action it would seem that the Convention would not prohibit this. This is particularly so as the basis of the direct action lies in national law.[64]

MARINE RISKS COVERED BY ARTICLE 12a[65]

Hull insurance and the insurance for the value of goods destroyed or lost are covered by Article 12a(1)(*a*), the latter including of necessity combined transport. While liability insurance is dealt with in 12a(2) Schlosser comments only that whether liability insurance in respect of repairs in the shipyard comes within "use or operation" remains to be seen. Injury to passengers and loss of or damage to their luggage are excluded, being referable to parties in need of the protective principles of the insurance regime.

The English Court of Appeal has held that only marine risks are encompassed by Article 12a. Any agreement in a policy covering marine and other risks cannot qualify. In assessing whether the risks are entirely marine, "connected risks and interests" within Article 12a(4) are to be construed widely—so long as such risks form a lesser part of the whole.[66] There may however be a valid jurisdiction clause in a policy only covering connected risks within Article 12(a)(4).[67]

RELATIONSHIP BETWEEN ARTICLES 12 AND 17

Failing agreement within Article 12a or the application of any exception specified in Article 12 the Convention insurance regime will apply. Article 17 specifically provides that no agreement contrary to Article 12 shall have any effect. Although it is uncertain whether the requirements of Article 17 apply to agreements *within* Article 12, the Convention pattern seems to encompass Article 12 agreements as included within those envisaged and defined in Article 17.

Secondly, there would seem no reason why requirements for a valid agreement which avoids jurisdictional framework specially introduced for the protection of one party should be any less strict than (or indeed different to) agreements generally recognized. On this reading the requirements of Article 12 go to elements not relevant to Article 17, i.e. such requirements are additional.

---

61. *Charman* v. *WOC Offshore BV* [1993] 2 Lloyd's Rep. 551.
62. It may be that Art. 12 is wider than Art. 17 in encompassing courts of non-contracting States—but the convention as a whole has no influence on such agreements. See Chap. 5.
63. For a list of subjects of compulsory insurance in contracting States see Schlosser, para. 138.
64. Cf. the approach to and discussion of Art. 17 as it applies to third parties (see Chap. 5).
65. See generally Schlosser paras. 141–147.
66. *Charman* v. *WOC Offshore BV* (fn 61).
67. Article 12(5).

It must be said however that the intention behind the provision inserted by the Accession Convention 1978 relating to insurance contracts with policy holders domiciled outside the Community and large shipping and aviation risks is arguably that agreements are to be valid within the Convention if valid according to forum law—without any question of the requirements of Article 17. The concern (largely of the United Kingdom) was that to impose Convention obligations as they stood prior to the Accession Convention would be to increase insurance premiums and the aim of the amendment was to allow contractual freedom (see Schlosser, para. 136). On this view the legal effect of the jurisdiction agreement would be a matter solely for forum law—if invalid the Convention would then operate. Schlosser comments specifically that jurisdiction agreements in consumer contracts are subject to Article 17 (para. 161) but makes no comment either way on insurance contracts. On the text it is difficult to justify any difference in approach.

If agreements within Articles 12 and 12a are simply Article 17 agreements with additional elements the effect is dictated by Article 17—the selected jurisdiction is mandatory and exclusive. The contention that Article 17 applies to Article 12 agreements is supported by the European Court decision in *Gerling Konzern*.[68] In this case the European Court was concerned with construing the requirements of Article 17 as they applied to an insurance contract. Had it been that Article 12 operated independently of Article 17 the point at issue would not have arisen. Further the court in finding that Article 17 did not require writing by a third party who benefited from the forum clause in an insurance contract (i.e. the insured) held that this view was supported by the Convention insurance regime.

Whatever the approach as to the connection with Article 17 it would seem that jurisdiction agreement under Article 12, just as agreements within Article 17, may be waived by appearance under Article 18.

Consumer contract jurisdiction

This jurisdiction has been generalized to consumer contracts from the original text which applied to instalment sales and loans to keep pace with Community provisions imposing consumer protection on member States. At the same time it was made clear that the protection was geared to the ultimate consumer. The protection extends only to consumers who are parties to the proceedings at issue—so where a consumer assigns his rights to a non-consumer the provisions do not apply.[69]

The regime is of restricted relevance to the enforcement of maritime claims. A critical feature is that the contract should have been concluded for a purpose "which can be regarded as outside the trade or profession" of the consumer—a Convention concept. Most maritime claims therefore fall outside the ambit of these provisions. Secondly, contracts of transport are specifically excluded and therefore fall within the general Convention. Nevertheless, they may apply for example to the sale of a yacht or supplies.

The consumer transactions within the regime are set out in Article 13:

"(1) a contract for the sale of goods on instalment credit terms, or

---

68. See fn 60.
69. *Shearson Lehman Hutton Inc* v. *TVB* 89/91 [1993] I.L.Pr. 199 (ECJ) (assignment to broker).

> (2) a contract for a loan repayable by instalments, or for any other form of credit, made to finance the sale of goods; or
> (3) any other contract for the supply of goods or a contract for the supply of services and
>> (a) in the State of the consumer's domicile the conclusion of the contract was preceded by a specific invitation addressed to him or by advertising, and
>> (b) the consumer took in that State the steps necessary for the conclusion of the contract."

Subject to the applicability of a branch, agency or other establishment, a suit against a consumer must be brought in the state of the domicile of the consumer. The consumer himself is given the option to bring suit in (i) the state of domicile of himself or (ii) of the other party or (iii) in a dispute concerning operation of a supplier in a branch agency or other establishment in the state in which the establishment is. As with an insurer a supplier who is not domiciled in a contracting State is deemed to be so domiciled in such a state in which there is a branch agency or establishment in respect of any dispute arising out of the operation of the branch agency or establishment.[70]

Jurisdiction agreements

The ability to opt out of the consumer framework through a jurisdiction agreement entered into before the dispute is limited. An agreement must (i) be entered into after the dispute or (ii) allow a consumer to bring proceedings in courts other than those specified by the consumer contracts provisions or (iii) select jurisdiction in a court of a contracting State in which at the time of the contract both the consumer and the other party to the contract were habitually resident or domiciled, the agreement being valid by the law of that state. As with insurance matters (see *supra*) unlike Article 17 the provision is apparently not restricted to jurisdiction selection of a court of a contracting State. Where the agreement does select a court of a contracting State it is clear that it was intended that it must comply with the requirements of Article 17 and the issues arising out of the relationship of Articles 15 and 17 are those discussed in the context of insurance and Articles 12 and 17 (see *supra*).

(c) Options based on connecting factor other than domicile between contracting State and dispute

"Connecting factor" options for a plaintiff where the defendant is domiciled in a contracting State and the case is not within the consumer contract or insurance regime are set out in Article 5. This reads:

"Section 2. Special Jurisdiction
Article 5
A person domiciled in a Contracting State may, in another Contracting State, be sued:
> 1 in matters relating to a contract, in the courts for the place of performance of the obligation in question; in matters relating to individual contracts of employment, this place is that where the employee habitually carries out his work, or if the employee does not habitually carry out his work in any one country, the employer may also be sued in the courts for the place where the business which engaged the employee was or is now situated;

---

70. Jurisdiction is conferred on a consumer only if the supplier is domiciled or deemed to be domiciled in a contracting State: *Brenner* v. *Reynolds* C318/93 [1995] All E.R. (E.C.) 278.

2 in matters relating to maintenance, in the courts for the place where the maintenance creditor is domiciled or habitually resident or, if the matter is ancillary to proceedings concerning the status of a person, in the court which, according to its own law, has jurisdiction to entertain those proceedings, unless that jurisdiction is based solely on the nationality of one of the parties;

3 in matters relating to tort, delict or quasi-delict, in the courts for the place where the harmful event occurred;

4 as regards a civil claim for damages or restitution which is based on an act giving rise to criminal proceedings, in the court seised of those proceedings, to the extent that that court has jurisdiction under its own law to entertain civil proceedings;

5 as regards a dispute arising out of the operations of a branch, agency or other establishment, in the courts for the place in which the branch, agency or other establishment is situated;

6 in his capacity as settlor, trustee or beneficiary of a trust created by the operation of a statute, or by a written instrument, or created orally and evidenced in writing, in the courts of the Contracting State in which the trust is domiciled;

7 as regards a dispute concerning the payment of remuneration claimed in respect of the salvage of a cargo or freight, in the court under the authority of which the cargo or freight in question

  (a) has been arrested to secure such payment, or

  (b) could have been so arrested, but bail or other security has been given;

provided that this provision shall apply only if it claimed that the defendant has an interest in the cargo or freight or had such an interest at the time of salvage."

The grounds may be categorized as:

(1) *four substantive grounds of claim* (i.e. contract, maintenance, tort and salvage—Article 5(1), (2), (3), (7);

(2) a *"place of business" ground*, i.e. carrying on operations through a branch, agency or other establishment (Article 5(5);

(3) a *"capacity" ground*—linking jurisdiction over actions brought against a party in his capacity as a party to a trust or creation of a trust to the domicile of the trust (Article 5(6));

(4) a *"linked proceedings" ground* based on the link between civil proceedings at issue and criminal proceedings from which they spring (Article 5(4)).

Not relevant to maritime claims are claims for maintenance and peripherally relevant are the provisions regarding civil claims in criminal proceedings and trusts. No comment is therefore made as to the maintenance and brief comment only as to criminal proceedings and trusts.

Each of the grounds reflects (in the European Court's view) "the existence in clearly defined situations of a particularly close connecting factor between a dispute and the court which may be called upon to hear it" (*Peters* v. *ZNAV*).[71] There are matters of construction particular to each ground and the general question arises as to the extent to which national law or European law governs these issues. The construction must be approached from the viewpoint that the grounds derogate from the primary Convention jurisdictional ground of domicile.[72] So a court having jurisdiction under one head would not thereby have

71. 34/82 [1983] ECR 987; [1984] 2 CMLR 605.

72. See e.g. *Somafer SA* v. *Saar-Ferngas AG* 33/78 [1978] ECR 2183; [1979] 1 CMLR 490; but exceptional does not mean subservient. See *Gascoigne* v. *Pyrah* [1994] I.L.Pr. 82 (C.A.); *Bank of Scotland* v. *Seitz* 1990 SLT 584 (Court of Session).

jurisdiction in regard to the same claims brought under another head. A court having jurisdiction in respect of an action in tort will not thereby have jurisdiction over the claim if based on contract.

The Court has underlined the importance in seeing the Convention as primarily concerned with Convention concepts. In relation to the interpretation of "establishment" within Article 5(5) the Court said in *Somafer*:

" . . . multiplication of the bases of jurisdiction in one and the same case is not likely to encourage legal certainty and the effectiveness of legal protection throughout the territory of the Community and therefore it is in accord with the objective of the Convention to avoid a wide and multifarious interpretation of the exceptions to the general rule of jurisdiction contained in Article 2."[73]

The approach is underlined by the comment in Article 5(3) in 1988 in *Kalfelis* v. *Schroder*[74] that it was necessary to regard the phrase "matters relating to tort delict or quasi delict" as an autonomous concept. It should be interpreted by reference principally to the system and objectives of the Convention.

The observations apply generally to the optional jurisdiction under Article 5 and particularly to jurisdiction bases within it capable of widely divergent national definitions. The approach reflects the general trend although there are exceptions. So "place of performance" within Article 5(1) is a matter for national law (see (i) below).

(1) Substantive claims

(i) Contract (Article 5(1))

Article 5(1) provides that a person domiciled in a contracting State may in another contracting State be sued in matters relating to a contract in the courts for the place of performance of the obligation in question.[75] This provision is qualified first in respect of maritime wage disputes in Denmark, Greece, Ireland or Portugal and, secondly, generally in regard to persons domiciled in Luxembourg.

MARITIME WAGE DISPUTES

Annexed Protocol Article V(b) provides:

"In proceedings involving a dispute between the master and a member of the crew of a seagoing ship registered in Denmark, in Greece, in Ireland or in Portugal, concerning remuneration or other conditions of service, a court in a Contracting State shall establish whether the diplomatic or consular officer responsible for the ship has been notified of the dispute. It shall stay the proceedings so long as he has not been notified. It shall of its own motion decline jurisdiction if the officer, having been duly notified, has exercised the powers according to him in the matter by a consular convention or in the absence of such a convention has, within the time allowed, raise any objection to the exercise of such jurisdiction."

---

73. Para. 7. See also *Peters* v. *ZNAV supra* fn 71.
74. 189/87 [1988] ECR 5565. Although the court inferred that where such proceedings are brought concurrently the entire case could be determined in the court first seised (see Chap. 12).
75. The court would have jurisdiction over a counterclaim (see Art. 6.3 and *infra*) and a Danish court has held that where there is an undisputed claim and counterclaim the claim remains the basis of jurisdiction: *Scan Expo Wortmann GmbH* v. *Ringkøbing County* [1994] I.L.Pr. 335.

PERSONS DOMICILED IN LUXEMBOURG

Annexed Protocol Article 1 provides so far as is relevant to Article 5(1):

"Any person domiciled in Luxembourg who is sued in a court of another Contracting State pursuant to Article 5(1) may refuse to submit to the jurisdiction of that court. If the defendant does not enter an appearance the court shall declare of its own motion that it has no jurisdiction."

As with the qualification on the enforceability of jurisdiction agreements by virtue of Article 17 (see Chapter 5) the clause is inserted to protect Luxembourg domiciliaries from the jurisdiction consequences of the probable place of performance of contracts in countries other than Luxembourg. It is perhaps questionable whether in the transnational context of the Convention the protection remains defensible.

AMBIT OF ARTICLE 5(1)

Subject to the two qualifications Article 5(1) raises two points for construction:

   (i) "in matters relating to contract";
   (ii) "the place of the performance of the obligation in question".

(i) "In matters relating to contract". As the phrase forms a basic jurisdictional ground, as would be expected it reflects a Convention concept. In *Peters* v. *ZNAV*[76] the European Court so held saying:

"Having regard to the objectives and the general scheme of the Convention it is important that in order to ensure as far as possible the equality and uniformity of the rights and obligations arising out of the Convention for the Contracting States and the person concerned, that concept should not be interpreted simply as referring to the national law of one or the other States concerned. It must be interpreted by reference chiefly to the system and objectives of the Convention in order to ensure that it is fully effective."[77]

The category is limited to obligations freely entered into by one party to the other. It does not include a case in which there is a remedy by national law to a purchaser not in direct contractual relation with a manufacturer. Bearing in mind the classification of such issues in most contracting States as tort or delict their inclusion could not have been foreseen in this provision.[78]

In *Effer SpA* v. *Kantner*[79] the European Court ruled that Article 5(1) may found jurisdiction "even when the existence of the contract on which the claim is based is in

---

76. Fn 71.

77. *Ibid.*, paras. 9, 10.

78. *Handte GmbH* v. *TCMS* 26/91 (ECJ) [1993] I.L.Pr. 5. An action by the beneficiary of a contract between two others (based on implied trust in English law) is to enforce the contract and therefore a matter relating to a contract: *The Gulf Grain* [1995] I.L.Pr. 600. A Scottish court has construed the wording narrowly in respect of the identical provision between England and Scotland as limited to proceedings based in contract (*Straithaird Farms Ltd.* v. *Chattaway* 1993 SLT (Sh. Ct.) 36)—applying by analogy the Scottish interpretation of Article 5(3) (as to which *infra*) but acknowledging the wider view as to 5(1) expressed by Lord Prosser in *Engdiv Ltd.* v. *Trentham Ltd.* 1990 SLT 617—interpreting a case not based directly on breach of contract as within the provision. For an example of classifying the liability of a sea carrier to a shipper as contract so as to attract this provision see *Gracechurch* v. *Assicurazioni Generato* (Corte de Cassazione, Italy) [1994] I.L.Pr. 206.

79. 38/81 [1982] ECR 825; [1984] 2 CMLR 667.

dispute between the parties". As the Court indicated, to exclude disputes going to the existence of the contract would be to allow a party to remove the jurisdictional foundation simply by pleading no contract existed.[80] To bring an action in England based on an assertion of a contract will still require the court being satisfied there was a serious question to be tried and which if right brings the matter within the provision.[81]

(ii) "The place of performance of the obligation in question." There are two issues relating to the construction of this phrase each raising the question of whether Community law applies and, if so, the Community meaning—(a) "the obligation in question"; and (b) "the place of the performance". The interpretation of each involves both Community and national law, for Community law spells out the framework within which national law may operate. The defining of the place of performance in the Convention text in respect of individual contracts of employment reflects the development by the European Court of different principles of the obligation in question as between such contracts and all other types of contract.

"The obligation in question." The concept has a Community meaning or rather meanings depending on the nature of the contract. In 1975 in *De Bloos Sprl* v. *Bouyer SA*[82] considering a contract setting up a commercial arrangement for exclusive distribution of goods, the European Court held that the "obligation in question" within Article 5(1) was the obligation that was the basis of the proceedings.[83]

It is this "obligation" which determines the place of performance in contracts other than those for employment. It is not therefore "appropriate or necessary to identify the obligation which characterizes the contract".[84] Where there was more than one obligation it is the principal obligation which controls.[85] Whether an obligation was the basis of proceedings is a matter for national law.

In *Trade Indemnity* v. *Forsakrings AB*[86] the English High Court had to consider a rather different point—the ambit of the concept of "obligation" in the context of Article 5(1). The court held that a pre-contractual duty not to misrepresent or to make disclosure were not "obligations" for the purpose of a provision for exceptional jurisdiction based on the

---

80. Whether an action claiming that no contract existed is within the provision is more doubtful for if the claim was successful the reason for jurisdiction is removed. A contractual or similar relationship may be required, restitutionary claims falling outside (see *Barclays Bank* v. *Glasgow City Council* [1994] 4 All E.R. 865 (Hirst J.)—a case concerned only with UK laws. (See Chap. 7.)

81. *Tesam Distribution Ltd.* v. *Schuh-Mode Team GmbH* [1990] I.L.Pr. 149 (C.A.); *Rank Film Distributors* v. *Lanterna Editrice Srl* [1992] I.L.Pr. 57.

82. 14/76 [1976] ECR 1497; [1977] 1 CMLR 60.

83. For application by national courts see (e.g.) *Medway Packaging Ltd* v. *Meurer GmbH* [1990] 2 Lloyd's Rep. 112 (C.A.); *Promac Sprl* v. *SA Sogeservice* [1993] I.L.Pr. 309 (Cour d'Appel Paris); *Campbell* v. *Van Aart* [1993] I.L.Pr. 314 (Irish High Court); *Societa Kretschmer* v. *Muratoir* (Corte di Cassazione) [1991] I.L.Pr. 361.

84. *Shenavai* v. *Kreischer* [1987] 3 CMLR 782, applied in *Medway* v. *Meurer* (fn 83); *Sedex* v. *Societe Vetex* [1990] I.L.Pr. 254 (Cour de Cassation). The obligation characteristic of the contract is the focal point for establishing the law applicable to the contracts under the Rome Convention Relating to the Law Applicable to Contract 1980 (as to which see Chap. 26).

85. *Shenavai* v. *Kreischer* (fn 84). The principal obligation of a tonnage to be nominated charter in the obligation to nominate and not to proceed to the loading port (*Union Transport Group Plc* v. *Continental Lines SA* [1992] 1 All E.R. 161 (H.L.).

86. [1995] 1 All E.R. 796.

place of performance. Rix J. thought that the rejection of the place where the obligation arose as the jurisdiction showed that the pre-contractual duties should not focus jurisdiction at the place of performance—pointing out that such an obligation gives no right to performance at all.

It may be said with respect that this approach means that the deliberate choice of place of performance was intended only to effect duties connected with performance. And of that there seems no suggestion either in the Convention or any commentary. The linking of the base to this kind of obligation leaves an uncomfortable feeling of reversal of the content of the base and the consequence of its application. Further it may not be entirely consistent (at least in approach) with the decision of the European Court in *Custom Made Commercial Ltd.* v. *Stawa Metallbau GmbH*.[87] In that case the court emphasized that the place of performance may have no connection with the dispute.

As with the assertion that a contractual obligation exists so with the obligation in question that to establish jurisdiction in an English court on that basis a plaintiff must show that there is a serious issue to be tried.[88]

CONTRACTS OF EMPLOYMENT. In respect of such contracts the European Court took the opposite view—that because of the need to protect the employer the "close connection" required by Article 5(1) between contract and adjudicating state was the law applicable to the contract—and that was to be determined by the obligation characterizing the contract. In employment contracts that was normally the obligation to carry out work. Such contracts created a long term relationship bringing the work into the framework of the business and are related to the place where the activities are carried on[89]—or where carried on in more than one place where the obligations are principally performed.[90] So the employee's position would be protected at that place.[91]

The Convention text relating to contracts of employment was introduced in the Treaty of Accession when Portugal and Spain became contracting States. No doubt the emphasis on the principal obligation may still be applied to identify the place of habitual work. Where there is no one place of habitual work the employer may also be sued in the place of engagement. It seems uncertain whether there may be more than one place in which work is habitually carried out.

The place of performance. In the first case referred to the European Court after the Protocol conferring interpretative jurisdiction on the Court the Court indicated that the concept was a matter for the forum conflict of law rules. In *Industrie Tessili Italiana* v. *Dunlop AG*[92] the Court indicated that it was not a Community concept. It seems as if the Court's general approach in this case has steadily been eroded in that emphasis has increasingly (and rightly it is suggested) been placed on Community concepts. However,

87. [1994] I.L.Pr. 516.
88. See *Rank Film Distributors* v. *Lanterna Editrice* (fn 81).
89. *Shenavai* v. *Kreischer* (fn 84).
90. *Mulox IBC Ltd.* v. *Geels* 125/92 [1993] I.L.Pr. 668.
91. In *Mercury Publicity Ltd* v. *Loerke* [1993] I.L.Pr. 142 the English Court of Appeal refused to apply the employment principle to an agency contract between two corporate entities—having regard both to the nature of the parties and the degree in which the agent became involved in the organizational framework of the principal.
92. 12/76 [1976] ECR 1473; [1977] 1 CMLR 26.

the decisions in the *Dunlop* case still reflect the Court's approach on the issue with which it was concerned, an approach confirmed by the Court in 1994.[93]

The reference of the place of performance to private international law has been followed and applied by many national courts.[94] Through this reference or through direct application of the Convention through Article 57, another Convention may dictate the jurisdiction through dictating either the place of performance or, for example, the place of payment which by national law is the place of performance. So the Hague Convention Relating to the Uniform Law on the International Sale of Goods 1964 provides (in Article 59) that the buyer shall pay the price at the seller's place of business or residence. This provision may dictate the place of performance for the purposes of Article 5(1).[95]

The place of performance will govern even if it has little or no connection with the dispute—it is a criterion adopted because of its certainty and allows a national court to determine its jurisdiction without considering factors going to the substance of the dispute.[96] In defining the place of performance courts tend naturally to focus on the final act required of the obligation,[97] but this is not exclusively so. Where the plaintiff seeks damages for breach of an obligation, the place of performance will normally be the place where that obligation should have been performed.[98] In *Mercury Publicity Ltd* v. *Loerke*[99] the English Court of Appeal thought the Convention difficult to apply where the obligation sued on was to make payment—although quite why this should be so is unclear. It may be that the obligation in question may differ according to which party is the plaintiff. So in respect of a contract of sale of goods it may be the place of delivery or payment depending on which party complains.[100]

Whereas in Article 5(1) a court has to decide a substantive matter in order to decide if it has jurisdiction there is always the problem of the depth of enquiry and the standard according to which the matter has to be established.[101] For an English court to have jurisdiction to decide on the law applicable to the contract and hence the place of performance (which may lead to the conclusion of no jurisdiction) the plaintiff must have a good arguable case that that place is England, i.e. that English law being the applicable law the debtor must pay in the creditor's residence or domicile. It has been held in Scottish and Irish courts that bearing in mind the derogation from the principle of domicile it is

93. *Custom Made Commercial Ltd.* v. *Stawa Metallbau GmbH* [1994] I.L.Pr. 516.

94. See e.g. *Mercury Publicity Ltd.* v. *Loerke* [1993] I.L.Pr. 142; *Bosma Meubel Impex BV* v. *Hacker Gerechsthof Leeuwarden* [1991] I.L.Pr. 384; *SCAC (Transport) (USA) Inc.* v. *Adriatica SpA di Navigazione* 1982 ECD 457.

95. The *Stawa Metallbau* case (fn. 87).

96. *Ibid.*

97. So the place of performance in a contract of carriage will normally be the port of unloading for the purpose of a claim for damage to cargo (*The AJP Pritt* [1991] I.L.Pr. 194 (Corte di Appello Genoa)); or the wrongful conduct about which the suit is brought (*Campbell* v. *Van Aart* [1993] I.L.Pr. 314 (Irish High Court)).

98. See e.g. *Bosma Meubel Impex BV* v. *Hacker Gerechsthof Leeuwarden* [1991] I.L.Pr. 384; *SCAS (Transport) (USA) Inc.* v. *Adriatica SpA di Navigazione* 1982 ECD 457.

99. [1993] I.L.Pr. 142—in the case it was arguable that the law applicable to the contract was English or German, and those laws led to opposite conclusion as to the place of the obligation to pay. As to identification under English conflicts rule of the place of performance in inter bank transactions see *Royal Bank of Scotland* v. *Cassa di Risparmia* [1991] I.L.Pr. 411.

100. See e.g. *Machinale Glasfabrieke De Maas BV* v. *Amaillerie Alsacienne SA* [1984] ECC 124 (District Court Arnhem)—place of payment. Compare *Re the M/S Koop* (Bundesgerichtshof) [1982] ECC 333—place of performance being the specified place of delivery.

101. See Chap. 9 for discussion of the problem generally in English law. See fns 81, 88 as regards assertion of a contract and obligation in question.

only a mandatory place of performance which can found jurisdiction. It is not enough that the contract may be performed.[102] However, the English Court of Appeal upheld English jurisdiction on the basis that the contract could be performed either in England or Germany.[103]

AGREEMENT BY THE PARTIES TO THE PLACE OF PERFORMANCE. The validity of any choice in the contract of the place of performance is to be adjudged according to the governing national law subject to any Convention provision. In *Zelger* v. *Salinitri*[104] the European Court was asked to decide on the jurisdictional effect (if any) on an oral agreement fixing the place of repayment of a loan which was at issue. The Court held that provided the clause is valid by the law applicable to the contract it was a valid choice of jurisdiction through the operation of Article 5(1). The requirements of Article 17 did not apply as the jurisdiction under Article 5(1) was based on a link between dispute and State. When Article 17 does apply it has the effect of setting aside the general and special rules of jurisdiction of Articles 2 and 5.

(ii) Claims in tort or delict (Article 5(3))

Article 5(3) provides that a person domiciled in a contracting State may be sued in another contracting State in matters relating to tort, delict or quasi delict in the courts of the place where the harmful event occurred. As for Article 5(1) and contract claims a central question is the extent to which the jurisdictional ground is based on Community concept or national law.

"MATTERS RELATING TO TORT, DELICT OR QUASI DELICT"

The concept of "tort delict or quasi delict" is independent of national laws and must be interpreted by reference primarily to the system and objectives of the Community. It relates to any action which seeks to establish the liability of the defendant and is not related to a matter relating to contract within Article 5(1).[105] Scottish courts have construed the identical provision as it applies between England and Scotland to mean "proceedings in delict". So a claim based against an insurer based on a statutory obligation to pay a sum awarded against the insured was outside the provision.[106]

"PLACE WHERE THE HARMFUL EVENT OCCURRED"

In *Handelswekerij Gt Bier and Stichting Rein Water* v. *Mines de Potasse d'Alsace*[107] the Court construed the phrase "place where the harmful event occurred" to confer jurisdiction on *either* the place of the act causing the damage *or* the place where the damage occurred. The Court referred to the basis of the jurisdiction grounds of Article 5—that of a close connection between issue and State. Approaching claims within Article

---

102. See *Bank of Scotland* v. *Seitz* 1990 SLT 584; [1991] I.L.Pr. 426 (Court of Session) (although also holding that payment being due under Scottish law at the creditors place of business identified the place of performance); *Hanbridge Services Ltd.* v. *Aerospace Communication Ltd.* [1993] I.L.Pr. 778 (Irish Supreme Court).

103. See *Medway Packaging Ltd.* v. *Meurer Maschinen GmbH* [1990] 2 Lloyd's Rep. 112.

104. 56/79 [1980] ECR 89; [1980] 2 CMLR 659.

105. *Kalfelis* v. *Schroder* 189/87 [1988] ECR 5565 (ECJ); *Reichert* v. *Dresdner Bank (No. 2)* 261/90 [1992] I.L.Pr. 404.

106. *Sante Fe (UK) Ltd.* v. *Gates Europe* [1991] LMLN 295; *Davenport* v. *Corinthian Motor Policies at Lloyd's* [1991] SLT 774.

107. 21/76; [1977] 1 CMLR 284. A restitutionary claim may not be within Arts. 5(3) or 5(1) (the *Barclays Bank* case fn. 80).

5(3) on that basis "it does not appear appropriate to opt for one of the two connecting factors" (i.e. of occurrence of damage or harmful event) "since each of them can depending on the circumstances be particularly helpful from the point of view of the evidence and of the conduct of proceedings. To exclude one option appears all the more undesirable in that by its comprehensive form of words Article 5(3) of the Convention covers a wide diversity of kinds of liability."[108]

Where damage is caused by an act in one state and occurs in a number of other states there is jurisdiction in the courts of each state. However, the court where the event occurred will have jurisdiction in relation to all the damage whereas the courts of the state where the damage occurred only in respect of the damage occurring in that state.[109]

There may be no foundation for Article 5(3) if the event occurs on the high seas. Any argument that it should be deemed to occur in the state of the flag of any ship involved[110] seems difficult to justify in the light of the purpose and role of this optional jurisdiction—particularly considering flags of convenience. It must always be borne in mind that the optional jurisdiction is a derogation from the principal rule of the defendant's domicile, and that lack of any option simply means that that (or any other jurisdiction base applicable) is maintained.

PLACE OF THE DAMAGE

This has now been construed by the European Court agreeing with decisions of national courts excluding the place of consequential damage.[111] In Italy the Tribunale di Monza has held that loss of business did not fall within the phrase "where the damage occurred". "Damage suffered" was not to be equated with "damage occurred"—this related to the place where the harmful circumstances came about.[112]

EVALUATION OF "HARM"

In order to decide if there is jurisdiction it may be necessary to consider if harm has occurred and therefore the standard of proof and evidence. These are matters for national law according to its conflict of laws rules provides the Convention is not thereby impaired.[113]

(iii) Remuneration for salvage (Article 5(7))

Article 5(7) provides that a person domiciled in a contracting State may be sued:

"(7) as regards a dispute concerning the payment of remuneration claimed in respect of the salvage of a cargo or freight, in the court under the authority of which the cargo or freight in question

108. Paras 17, 18. See also *Schimmel Pianoforkfabrik GmbH* v. *Hubert Bion* [1992] I.L.Pr. 199 (Cour de Cassation). It is questionable whether the phrase includes a threatened wrong. In *Geobra Brankstatten GmbH* v. *Big Spielwarenfabrik* (1977) (District Court Amsterdam) it was held that an action could not be brought at the place of damage once it had been started at the place of the event (ECD 1–5.3–B5).

109. *Shevill* v. *Presse Alliance SA* 68/93 [1995] All E.R. (E.C.) 289—a libel case concerning publication in a number of states.

110. See Kaye, *Civil Jurisdiction and Enforcement of Judgments* (1987), pp. 585 *et seq.*; Brice [1987] LMCLQ 281.

111. *Marinari* v. *Lloyds Bank* 364/93 [1995] I.L.Pr. 737. See Judgment of 3 October 1978 of (ECD 1–5.3–B9) considered in appeal proceedings (1980 ECC 263).

112. *Candy SpA* v. *Schell* (1979) ECD 1–5.3–B11.

113. *Shevill* v. *Presse Alliance SA* (fn. 109).

(a) has been arrested to secure such payment, or

(b) could have been so arrested, but bail or other security has been given;

provided that this provision shall apply only if it claimed that the defendant has an interest in the cargo or freight or had such an interest at the time of salvage."

This provision was added by the Accession Convention 1978 at the instigation of the United Kingdom delegation (see Schlosser, para. 122). Jurisdiction based on arrest of ships is preserved through Article 57 of the Convention and the Arrest Convention 1952. There was however no other saving for jurisdiction based on arrest of other property. Such jurisdiction exists in English law in relation to cargo or freight to enforce a maritime lien for salvage and may exist in respect of a maritime lien in respect of bottomry and respondentia and (at least for freight) for collision claims. It may be possible to argue that a maritime lien would lie in respect of cargo if that cargo causes damage to another ship.[114]

Whatever the scope of claims *in rem* in regard to cargo or freight, if a defendant (i.e. the person liable *in personam*) is domiciled in a contracting State jurisdiction based on arrest of cargo or freight is restricted to salvage claims within Article 5(7) unless further jurisdiction emerges from a future Convention.[115] It should be stressed that any arbitration proceedings including a suit to enforce an arbitration award (as for example under Lloyd's Open Form) will fall outside the Convention. However a judgment obtained in proceedings conducted despite an arbitration clause may be enforceable (see Chapters 3, 28).

(2) Operations of a branch, agency or other establishment (Article 5(5))

Article 5(5) provides that a person domiciled in a contracting State may be sued in another contracting State "as regards a dispute arising out of the operations of a branch, agency or other establishment, in the courts for the place in which the branch, agency or other establishment is situated". This optional jurisdiction in retained as such in the special frameworks governing insurance and consumer contract claims.[116]

The fundamental point of construction of this provision turns on the meaning of "branch, agency or other establishment". A further point arises as to whether relevant operations must have taken place in the state in which the branch, agency or establishment is situated.

"Branch agency or other establishment"—a Community concept

The European Court has held that "branch, agency or other establishment" is a Community concept.[117] In spelling out the Community meaning the Court has stressed the need for direction and control by a parent body. So for example a distributor of goods will

---

114. e.g., through the explosion of dangerous cargo or the escape of oil.

115. The International Conventions for the Unification of Certain Rules Relating to Maritime Liens and Mortgages 1926, 1967 and 1993 do not encompass cargo and only that of 1926 includes freight. None has any express jurisdictional provisions (see *supra*).

116. As well as providing a basis for domicile in a contracting State if there is no other (see *supra*).

117. *Somafer SA* v. *Saar Ferngas AG* 33/78 [1978] ECR 2183; [1979] 1 CMLR 490.

not of itself qualify,[118] nor will an independent and non-exclusive commercial agent transmitting orders without negotiating the terms of transactions.[119]

Further factors necessary to demonstrate the connection between dispute and State to provide the ground for derogation from the general jurisdictional norm of the defendant's domicile in Article 2 are:

> (i) material signs enabling the existence of the branch to be easily recognized and
> (ii) a connection between the branch and the claim against the parent body.[120]

EXTERNAL EVIDENCE OF THE EXISTENCE OF THE BRANCH

This implies a place of business "which has the appearance of permanency such as the extension of a parent body, as a management and is materially equipped to negotiate business with third parties so that the latter, although knowing that there will if necessary be a legal link with the parent body, the head office of which is abroad, do not have to deal directly with such parent body but may transact business at the place of business constituting the extension".

Such an approach is understandable bearing in mind the underlying basic principle of jurisdiction based on domicile but it may place a considerable onus (for example) on a person dealing through correspondence with a company which through its letterheads or negotiations appears to be conducting business through a branch. Today commercial business is hardly conducted through office visits and it could be argued that at the least a corporation giving the impression that a transaction is being handled by a branch should not be allowed to deny it. Such an argument was made in *Somafer* but the Court held that in that case in the light of its decision on the definition of a branch and operations it was unnecessary to deal with it. A. G. Meynas was of the view that estoppel had no place in a jurisdiction question and it would seem that the Court was impliedly taking the same view.

In favour of the view of the Court is the underlying principle in Article 2 that it is the existence of a close connecting factor which justifies the departure from jurisdiction based on domicile. It is arguable therefore that it is for the plaintiff to satisfy himself that the unit he is dealing with is a branch in substance if a jurisdiction based in that country is of importance to him in the context of the contract.

CONNECTION BETWEEN DISPUTE AND PARENT BODY

In *Somafer* the Court appeared to restrict the operation of Article 5(4) to undertakings or activities performed or engaged in the contracting State where the place of business is established. Such a restriction puts a gloss on the provision which is difficult to justify given the required connection between disputes and branch activities. However in 1995 in *Lloyd's Register of Shipping* v. *Société Campenon Bernard*[121] the Court held that such a restriction would largely nullify the extension from the courts for the place of the obligation in question. The undertaking may be performed outside the state of the ancillary establishment, possibly by another ancillary establishment.

---

118. *De Bloos Sprl* v. *Bouyer SA* 14/76 [1976] ECR 1497; [1977] 1 CMLR 60.
119. *Blankaert and Willems PVBA* v. *Trost* 139/80 [1981] ECR 819; [1982] 2 CMLR 1.
120. *Somafer* fn 117.
121. C439/93 [1995] 1 All E.R. (E.C.) 531.

(3) Suing defendant in capacity as settlor, trustee or beneficiary of a trust (Article 5(6))

It has been said by Schlosser (paras 117 and 120) that this provision is intended to apply only to trusts expressly constituted by agreement or by statute and secondly only to disputes between the parties to the trust. If this is so it seems somewhat inaptly drafted—for it does not specify intentional trusts and is focused on suits against a defendant in its capacity as settlor, trustee or beneficiary. Clearly the thought is that the domicile of the trust is a major connecting factor in regard to any proceedings concerning it and it is difficult to appreciate why this should be any the less critical however the trust comes about.

The construction may have some relevance to maritime claims because of the possibility of a "trust" imposed in favour of non-registered owners of ships and of "beneficial ownership" through, for example, a contract of sale of a ship.[122]

(4) Linked proceedings

Limitation of liability (Article 6a)

This applies generally as an alternative jurisdiction base and not simply where the defendant is domiciled in a contracting State. It is discussed *supra*.

Civil claims in criminal proceedings (Article 5(4))

Article 5(4) provides for jurisdiction in respect of damages or restitution based on an act giving rise to criminal proceedings in the court hearing those proceedings if it has such jurisdiction by its national law.[123] A judgment against a defendant a civil action in the criminal courts of another contracting State of which he is not a national for an offence which was not intentionally committed in proceedings in which the defendant having been ordered to appear fails to do so need not be recognized or enforced in other contracting States (see further Chapter 28).

(d) Multi parties or actions

Article 6 provides:

"Article 6
A person domiciled in a Contracting State may also be sued:
  1 where he is one of a number of defendants, in the courts for the place where any one of them is domiciled;
  2 as a third party in an action on a warranty or guarantee or in any other third party proceedings, in the court seised of the original proceedings, unless these were instituted solely with the object of removing him from the jurisdiction of the court which would be competent in his case;
  3 on a counterclaim arising from the same contract or facts on which the original claim was based, in the court in which the original claim is pending.

---

122. See e.g. *The Permina 3001* [1979] 1 Lloyd's Rep. 327. As to which see Chap. 10.
123. As to the scope of the provision see *Rinkau* 159/80 [1981] ECR 1; [1983] 1 CMLR 205.

4 In matters relating to a contract, if the action may be combined with an action against the
same defendant in matters relating to rights inrem in immovable property, in the court of the
Contracting State in which the property is situated."

This is qualified in respect of Germany by Article V of the Annexed Protocol. This
provides:

"The jurisdiction specified in Article 6(2)2 and Article 10 in actions on a warranty or guarantee or
in any other third party proceedings may not be resorted to in the Federal Republic of Germany. In
that State, any person domiciled in another Contracting State may be sued in the courts in pursuance
of Articles 68, 72, 73 and 74 of the code of civil procedure (*Zivilprozessordnung*) concerning third-
party notices.[124]

Other Convention jurisdiction

As with any other head of jurisdiction under the Convention multi-party jurisdiction is
subject to any other Convention maintained through Article 57 (See Chapter 5). This will
be so whether the other Convention jurisdiction is based directly on claims or is itself (as
for example the Collision Jurisdiction Convention 1952) based on third party
proceedings.

The degree of incorporation of the other Convention is critical.[125] So the Collision
Jurisdiction Convention provides for jurisdiction in the court hearing the principal claim
over counterclaims for multi-plaintiffs and also that nothing in the Convention shall
prevent any court seised of an action from exercising jurisdiction in respect of a further
action arising out of the same incident. As the Collision Jurisdiction Convention restricts
jurisdiction it is arguable that it is this provision rather than the Brussels Convention
which should control multi-party claims within both Conventions (see *supra*). If so, it
would then be national law which interpreted the meaning and scope of the Collision
Jurisdiction Convention.[126]

Co-defendants (Article 6(1))

This provision can operate only if at least one defendant is sued in the court of his
domicile. Where therefore the case is brought in a contracting State by virtue, for example,
of it being the place of the harmful event (Article 5(3)) or by virtue of a jurisdictional
agreement (Article 17) the co-defendants cannot be joined by virtue of Article 6.[127]
Although there is no express prohibition (as in Article 6(2)) the provision must not be used
to defeat the basic principle of jurisdiction based on the defendant's domicile. So a court
would not have jurisdiction in an action brought for the sole purpose of excluding one of
the defendants from the courts of his domicile.[128]

---

124. Cf. Jenard p. 27. Article V also provides that judgments given in other contracting States by virtue of
jurisdiction exercised under Article 6(2) or Article 10 are to be recognized or enforced in Germany.
125. See *The Maciej Rataj* [1995] 1 Lloyd's Rep. 302.
126. See e.g. *The Po* [1991] 2 Lloyd's Rep. 206 (C.A.).
127. See *Oving Diepeveen Sturycken NV* v. *Berlinen Franchtschiffart* [1983] ELD 361; *Société Leybold* v.
Seima (1978) ECD 1–6–B3.
128. *Kalfelis* v. *Schroder* 189/87 [1988] ECR 5563.

For the application of the article there must exist such a connection between the claims as to make it desirable to rule on them together to avoid possible irreconcilable judgments. Whether such a connection exists is a matter in each case for the national court.[129]

Third parties (Article 6(2))

Subject to the qualifications in respect of Germany set out in Article V of the Annexed Protocol[130] the existence of this jurisdiction option will bring in a third party unless it is established that the original proceedings were instituted solely to remove the third party from an otherwise competent jurisdiction. While as with Article 6(1) the prerequisite for its operation is that the defendant is domiciled in a contracting State, unlike Article 6(1) the provision is not itself dependent on a suit in the domicile of a defendant. The underlying principle is the attachment of third party proceedings to the jurisdiction applicable to the original action. This ancillary jurisdiction will however be subject to any "exclusive jurisdiction" applicable to the third party proceedings (as for example a jurisdiction agreement within Article 17).[131]

On its face the provision provides a wide exception to the Convention jurisdiction norm and optional bases. So without qualification a manufacturer or initial seller of goods may find that the court of the domicile of the vendor has jurisdiction over any claim by the purchaser because of the claim against the vendor. A consignee of a shipper may be brought into the shipper's domicile or a charterer brought into the shipowner's domicile.

However, the European Court has held that the effect of the provision is subject to national procedure. In *Kongress Agentur Hagen GmbH* v. *Zeehaghe BV*[132] the Court held that a national court could apply its own procedural law to refuse to consider an action on a guarantee in proceedings on the main claim, provided that the effectiveness of the Convention was not prejudiced. In particular it was not open to a national court to refuse jurisdiction simply on the ground that the guarantee was domiciled or resident elsewhere.

This decision has been seen as "startling" in that, it is said, it strikes at the heart of the mandatory allocation of Convention jurisdiction. In particular it may open the door to a general qualification through the doctrine of "*forum non conveniens*". The nature and application of that doctrine is discussed in Chapter 12. It is sufficient here to suggest that there is little ground for seeing the Court's approach as remarkable or for generalizing it. "Third party proceedings" is a concept for linking actions on which jurisdiction allocation depends—the purpose of the Convention is to allocate jurisdiction in claims, not to dictate the procedure by which they are brought. The boundary between substantive jurisdiction allocation and procedure continues to be a matter of degree but it seems defensible to approach the ambit of multi-party Convention jurisdiction in respect of different claims on the basis of national law rather than overriding it.

---

129. *Ibid.* For an example of a national court so holding see *Gannon* v. *Band I Steam Packet Ltd.* [1994] I.L.Pr. 405 (Irish Supreme Court). See also *Barclays Bank* v. *Glasgow City Council* [1994] 4 All E.R. 865.

130. As to which see *supra* and Jenard, p. 27.

131. See Jenard, p. 27. As to the binding effect of jurisdiction agreements on third parties see *The Tilly Russ* case (Chap. 5).

132. 365/88 [1980] 1 ECR 1845. For comment see Briggs [1991] LMCLQ 10.

Counterclaims (Article 6(3))

The jurisdiction base is directed at attaching counterclaim jurisdiction to jurisdiction over the claim. By the express terms of the provision a claim qualifies as a counterclaim only if it arises from the same contract or facts on which the original claim was based.[133] It applies, however, perhaps somewhat surprisingly only where a defendant is domiciled in a contracting State. It has therefore no application where the Convention is applicable on a different basis (or for example under Article 6 or by virtue of a jurisdiction agreement). However, "related claims" made in two jurisdictions may be heard in the court first seised (see Chapter 12).[134]

Contracts connected with rights "in rem" immovables (Article 6(4))

This provision was added by the Accession Treaty when Portugal and Spain became contracting States. It sensibly links any contract claim relating to immovables to any concurrent "property" claim against the same defendants. As with all the options in Article 6 it applies only where a defendant is domiciled in a contracting State and is therefore not to be entirely equated with the "rights *in rem*" jurisdiction in Article 16.1. Further, its ambit may be restricted as in Article 6(2) to proceedings which by national law may be "confined" to the same defendant.

---

133. It applies only where the defendant's claim would involve a separate judgment, and not to a defence classified as such by national law *Danvaern Production A/S* v. *Schuhfabrik Otterbeck GmbH* [1995] I.L.Pr. 649.
134. Claims for limitation of liability may be considered by a court having Convention jurisdiction over the liability claim (see *supra*).

CHAPTER 7

Jurisdiction as between England, Scotland and Northern Ireland

For Brussels and Lugano Convention purposes the United Kingdom is one State. However, it is made up of three constituent legal parts—England and Wales, Scotland and Northern Ireland. Because these parts have different legal systems it is domestically necessary to provide a connecting factor between a dispute and a particular part if the jurisdictional factor provided by the Conventions is a link with the United Kingdom as a whole or conversely with a "place" in the United Kingdom. In addition the United Kingdom has adapted the Brussels Convention structure to disputes having connections with two or more of the three parts. Allocation of jurisdiction within the United Kingdom has therefore three functions:

(a) For Convention purposes where jurisdiction is conferred on a "place in a Contracting State";

(b) Domestic allocation to a "part of the United Kingdom" following Convention allocation to the United Kingdom as a whole;

(c) Adaptation of the Convention framework to *intra* United Kingdom disputes.

The allocation for the purposes of (b) and (c) is accomplished largely through the same general structure provided for and set out in s.16 and Schedule 4 (as qualified by Schedule 5) of the 1982 Act. That structure applies *either* if a defendant is (or would be) domiciled in the United Kingdom *or* the proceedings are of a kind mentioned in Article 16. Only in two other types of case is it necessary to provide for allocation of Convention jurisdiction within the United Kingdom (domicile of a trust or consumer and the deemed domicile of an insurer or supplier under a consumer contract). In all other cases the relevant court can be identified directly (see *infra*).

Where the Convention jurisdiction is based on domicile there is a need to provide for domicile in a place or part of the United Kingdom. The criteria for that assessment are set out in the 1982 Act (section 41(4), (5), (6) as regards individuals and section 42(4), (5) as regards corporations or associations) and are discussed in Chapter 6.

(a) CONVENTION ALLOCATION TO A PLACE IN THE UNITED KINGDOM

Where under the Convention jurisdiction is conferred on the courts of a place in a contracting State, to confer jurisdiction on the courts of the part of the United Kingdom in which the place is will require an allocating step only where domicile is the jurisdiction base. In that case it is necessary to particularize from domicile in the United Kingdom to the appropriate part. As indicated above the applicable criteria are set out in the provisions generally providing for domicile (see Chapter 6).

(b) DOMESTIC ALLOCATION FOLLOWING CONVENTION ALLOCATION TO THE UNITED KINGDOM AS A WHOLE

This occurs in four contexts:

> (i) the general jurisdiction rule based on the defendant's domicile;
> (ii) exclusive jurisdiction under Article 16 (this being conferred on "courts of a contracting State");
> (iii) jurisdiction based on the domicile of a trust or a consumer;
> (iv) the "deemed domicile" of an insurer or supplier in insurance and consumer contract matters.

In all other cases jurisdiction is conferred by the Convention on the courts of a place, the courts in which proceedings are pending or (in the case of jurisdiction based on arrest) in cases of salvage of cargo or freight in the court under the authority of which the arrest has or could have taken place.[1] Problems may arise if a jurisdiction agreement refers to "the courts of the United Kingdom". Although such an agreement may literally comply with Article 17 it must be open to argument that the agreement is uncertain because of the differences between the parts of the United Kingdom. There is no criterion for the necessary selection within the agreement.[2] If such an agreement is not valid under Article 17 the jurisdiction will depend on the applicability of the Convention and any other jurisdiction base within it.

Jurisdiction based on the defendant's domicile or the provisions of Article 16 is allocated to the appropriate part of the United Kingdom through the general structure applying to allocation for Convention purposes and adaptation to *intra* United Kingdom disputes, by substitution of "part of the United Kingdom" for "the United Kingdom" (see *infra*). Jurisdiction based on the domicile of a trust, consumer, supplier or insurer and the deemed domicile of an insurer, consumer or supplier is allocated by two specific provisions of the 1982 Act (as amended by the 1991 Act).

DOMICILE OF TRUST, CONSUMER, SUPPLIER OR INSURER

Convention jurisdiction dependent on the domicile of a trust or consumer or the deemed domicile of a supplier or an insurer is not within the general structure based on the domicile of a defendant or the nature of the claim falling within the ambit of Article 16. However, the same needs arise as to localization within the United Kingdom. Section 10 and section 44 provide:

---

1. See Chaps. 5, 6.
2. See Chap. 5—although in *The Komninos S* [1991] 1 Lloyd's Rep. 370 the selection of British courts was construed by the Commercial Court as the English High Court.

"Allocation within UK of jurisdiction with respect to trusts and consumer contracts

10.—(1) The provisions of this section have effect for the purpose of allocating within the United Kingdom jurisdiction in certain proceedings in respect of which the 1968 Convention or the Lugano Convention confers jurisdiction on the courts of the United Kingdom generally and to which section 16 does not apply.

(2) Any proceedings which by virtue of Article 5(6) (trusts) are brought in the United Kingdom shall be brought in the courts of the part of the United Kingdom in which the trust is domiciled.

(3) Any proceedings which by virtue of the first paragraph of Article 14 (consumer contracts) are brought in the United Kingdom by a consumer on the ground that he is himself domiciled there shall be brought in the courts of the part of the United Kingdom in which he is domiciled.

Persons deemed to be domiciled in the United Kingdom for certain purposes

44.—(1) This section applies to:
- (a) proceedings within Section 3 of Title II of the 1968 Convention or Section 3 of Title II of the Lugano Convention (insurance contracts), and
- (b) proceedings within Section 4 of Title II of either of those Conventions (consumer contracts).

(2) A person who, for the purposes of proceedings to which this section applies arising out of the operations of a branch, agency or other establishment in the United Kingdom, is deemed for the purposes of the 1968 Convention or as the case may be of the Lugano Convention to be domiciled in the United Kingdom by virtue of—
- (a) Article 18, second paragraph (insurers); or
- (b) Article 13, second paragraph (suppliers of goods, services or credit to consumers),

shall for the purposes of those proceedings, be treated for the purposes of this Act as so domiciled and as domiciled in the part of the United Kingdom in which the branch, agency or establishment in question is situated."

(c) THE INTRA UNITED KINGDOM STRUCTURE

By the Act the Convention is adapted to *intra* United Kingdom disputes. The adapted structure is set out in Schedule 4 as qualified by Schedule 5.[3] The allocation of jurisdiction in respect of such disputes is based on the application of Brussels Convention principles with the United Kingdom taking the place of the Community of contracting States. A case is within the provisions if:

- (a) (subject to specified exclusions) the subject-matter of the dispute would be within the scope of a Convention; and
- (b) if a defendant is domiciled in the United Kingdom or (subject to amendments specified) the matter is one which if the Convention applied would be within Article 16 and therefore be within the exclusive jurisdiction of the appropriate contracting State.

Unless within the Conventions any case falling outside the statutory framework will therefore be subject to the jurisdictional rules of each part of the United Kingdom, the English rules being mainly based on service of process. If the defendant is not domiciled in the United Kingdom but is domiciled in another contracting State the substance of the Convention will apply; if the defendant is not domiciled in the United Kingdom nor in

3. As amended by the Civil Jurisdiction and Judgments Act 1982 (Amendment) Order 1993 (SI 1993/603). Schedule 4 is to be construed in the light of the construction of the Convention and the Schlosser and Jenard Reports are to be given "such weight as is appropriate in the circumstances". The 1993 amendment adapts the amendments made to the Convention on the accession of Portugal and Spain (as to which see Chap. 4).

another contracting State the Convention applies only to the limited extent discussed in Chapter 5, and in neither case does the *intra* United Kingdom framework apply.

The scheme is domestic

In determining any question as to the meaning or effect of the structure regard is to be had to the Brussels Convention, to any relevant principles laid down by the European Court and the Schlosser and Jenard Reports.[4] However the regime is domestic. In *Barclays Bank plc* v. *Glasgow City Council*[5] the Court of Appeal referred a question of construction of Schedule 4 to the European Court. The issue concerned two provisions directly adapted from the Convention. The question was whether a claim based on unjust enrichment, money having been paid under a contract later held to be void, fell within Article 5(1) ("matters relating to a contract") or Article 5(3) ("tort delict or quasi delict") or neither. The Schedule does not incorporate Convention provisions into United Kingdom law but takes the Convention as a model only. The United Kingdom courts are not required to apply the Convention unconditionally. Replies by the European Court cannot be advisory and given the context of the enquiry the Court had no jurisdiction.[6]

The role of rules of court

To be consistent with and implement the reformulation in the 1982 Act of *intra* United Kingdom jurisdiction rules in English law, a writ may be served out of the jurisdiction without the leave of the court in respect of a matter falling within the Civil Jurisdiction Act 1982 provided certain conditions are met (see Chapter 9). Scotland and Northern Ireland are equated to a territory of a contracting State for the purpose of these conditions.[7] There appears to be some doubt as to whether the rules permit proceedings in an Admiralty action to be brought without leave. However, as with Convention matters, in any case within Schedule 4 such leave, if required, must be a formality.

APPLICABILITY OF THE ADAPTED FRAMEWORK

Subject-matter—"civil and commercial matters"

Matters within the adapted framework

All matters within the scope of the 1968 Convention save those excluded by Schedule 5 are within the adapted allocation framework. Schedule 5 may be amended by Order in Council following a positive resolution of each House of Parliament.[8]

---

4. Section 16(3). For application of Convention concepts see e.g. (Art. 5) (England) *Sante Fe* v. *Gates* [1991] LMLN 295; *Barclays Bank plc* v. *Glasgow City Council* [1994] 4 All E.R. 865; (Scotland) *Bank of Scotland* v. *Seitz* 1990 SLT 584; *Davenport* v. *Corinthian Motor Policies* 1991 SLT 774; *Engdiv Ltd.* v. *Trentham Ltd.* 1990 SLT 617 (not cited in *Davenport*); *Strathaird Farms* v. *Chattaway* 1993 SLT (Sh. Ct.) 36; (Art. 13) *Waverley Asset Management Ltd.* v. *Saha* 1989 SLT (Sh. Ct.) 87.
5. [1994] 4 All E.R. 865.
6. *Kleinwort Benson Ltd.* v. *Glasgow City Council* C346/93 [1995] All E.R. (E.C.) 514.
7. RSC Order 11, r. 1(2).
8. Section 17. It has been statutorily amended but not as regards any matters relevant to maritime claims (see Companies Act 1989, s.200; Children Act 1989, Sch. 13; Social Security (Consequential Provisions) Act 1992, Sch. 2.

Matters excluded

The following matters possibly relevant to maritime claims are excluded by Schedule 5 as presently drafted[9]:

(i) Winding up proceedings under the Companies Act 1985. Winding up on insolvency is excluded from the Convention (see Article 1(2)): winding up a solvent company must take place at its place of incorporation and therefore it would be inappropriate to submit it to rules of allocation;

(ii) Proceedings under the Protection of Trading Interests Act 1980 for recovery of sums paid as multiple damages (as to which see Chapter 12);

(iii) Proceedings brought pursuant to a statutory provision or rule of law implementing any Convention by virtue of Article 57 of that Convention (and therefore outside the Brussels Convention) (as to which see Chapter 6);

(iv) Proceedings in Scotland in an Admiralty cause where the jurisdiction of the Court of Session or, as the case may be, of the sheriff is based on arrestment *in rem* or *ad fundandam jurisdictionem* of a ship, cargo or freight;

(v) Proceedings brought pursuant to jurisdiction conferred on a court in respect of a designated area of the Continental Shelf (Continental Shelf Act 1964, s.3).

Connecting links with the United Kingdom

The structure applies when by the Convention either the defendant is domiciled in the United Kingdom or exclusive jurisdiction is allocated to the United Kingdom by virtue of Article 16.

The general pattern of the regime

The pattern of the adapted regime is similar but not identical to that of jurisdiction allocation as between the United Kingdom and other contracting States. Subject to exceptions, a defendant must be sued in the court of the part of the United Kingdom in which he is domiciled. There are both mandatory and optional exceptions matching in part those of the Convention. So a case within the adapted Article 16 must be brought in the part specified, the appearance of a defendant will create jurisdiction and a jurisdiction agreement may (but not must) form the foundation for jurisdiction.[10] In specified circumstances a plaintiff may opt to sue a defendant in a part other than that in which he is domiciled.

Apart from the exclusion of the matters set out in Schedule 5 (see *supra*) differences between the Convention and the adapted framework in respect of initial proceedings are—

(i) the omission of special jurisdiction rules relating to insurance—thereby making it subject to the general jurisdiction regime

9. Also excluded are proceedings concerning registration or validity of patents, trade marks design or other like rights, maintenance payments to local authorities, rectification of Register of Aircraft Mortgages and such proceedings as are mentioned in section 188 of the Financial Services Act 1986.

10. There are no provisions as regards "*lis pendens*" leaving intact the *forum non conveniens* principle (see Chap. 12).

    (ii) the change of the seat of a company from an exclusive jurisdiction base to an optional alternative in respect of company proceedings

    (iii) the addition to links as grounds of optional jurisdiction alternative to the defendants domicile of (a) the place of threatened wrong and (b) the place of property in relation to property or security rights

    (iv) the change of jurisdiction agreements from a mandatory to an optional jurisdiction base.

Particular jurisdiction bases[11]

Primary basis of the domicile of the defendant in a part (Articles 2 to 4)

Articles 2 and 3 as adapted provide:

"Article 2
Subject to the provisions of this **Title**, persons domiciled in a **part of the United Kingdom** shall . . . be sued in the courts of that **part.**

Article 3
Persons domiciled in a **part of the United Kingdom** may be sued in the courts of another **part of the United Kingdom** only by virtue of the rules set out in Sections 2, **4, 5 and 6** of this Title."

Article 4 is omitted.

    The laws of the United Kingdom do not draw any jurisdictional distinction in civil and commercial matters between nationals and non-nationals. The provision of Article 2 of the Convention equating the two in respect of domiciliaries is therefore irrelevant. That part of Article 3 outlawing rules of exorbitant jurisdiction is also omitted, but the omission has no substantive effect. The jurisdiction bases are those provided by the statute—subject to the exceptional categories and the domicile of the defendant. Given the adoption of the defendant's domicile in the United Kingdom and of Article 16 as the boundaries of the framework Article 4 (apart from Article 16 referring to defendants not domiciled in a contracting State) has no relevance. It is therefore omitted.

"Exceptional category" cases—i.e. exceptions to domicile in a part of the United Kingdom as the basis of initial jurisdiction allocation (Articles 16, 17, 18)

Mandatory criteria

EXCLUSIVE JURISDICTION (ARTICLE 16)

Article 16 is applied with the exception of Article 16(4) (dealing with patents, trade marks, design and other similar rights) and that part of Article 16(2) referring to decisions of organs of a company or association.[12] Where the Convention confers jurisdiction on the "courts of a Contracting State" it is conferred on the "courts of the part of the United Kingdom".

---

11. The adapted text shows added provisions in bold type and omissions indicated by dots (see s. 16(2)).

12. As to the seat of a corporation (i.e. the domicile) for the purposes of Article 16(2) see Chap. 6. Article 5A provides an optional jurisdiction in respect of decisions of organs of a company (see *infra*). Jurisdiction in respect of patents etc. is allocated according to general principles apart from the Convention.

APPEARANCE (ARTICLE 18)

Article 18 is directly adapted by the substitution of "a court of a part of the United Kingdom" for "a court of a Contracting State".

JURISDICTION AGREEMENTS (ARTICLE 17)

Article 17 is adapted to create optional rather than exclusive jurisdiction (see *infra*).

Domicile and optional alternatives

Specific subject-matter jurisdiction (insurance and consumer contracts)

The Convention provisions relating to insurance are not included, thereby subjecting insurance matters to the basic jurisdictional framework based on the domicile of the defendant and the exceptions there listed.

The consumer contract provisions (Articles 13–15) (with the express exclusion of insurance) are adapted save that there is no requirement in relation to the general category of contract for the supply of goods or services that there was a pre-contract invitation in the consumer's domicile. As with the Convention the special jurisdiction is expressly subject to the provision for jurisdiction based on the operations of a branch agency or other establishment (Article 5(5)). In addition it is made subject to an added plaintiff's option for property claims (Article 5(8)) (as to which see *infra*).

Plaintiff's options instead of the defendant's domicile

GENERAL ALTERNATIVES (ARTICLES 5 TO 6a)

Link with dispute. Article 5 (providing categories of case in which a plaintiff may opt for a jurisdiction specified) is directly adapted to provide for suit in a part of the United Kingdom against a defendant domiciled in another part. There are two substantive amendments. First, in Article 5(3) providing for tort jurisdiction in the courts of the place where the harmful event occurred there is added the phrase "or in the case of a threatened wrong is likely to occur".[13]

Secondly, a new Article 5(8) is added providing that a person domiciled in a part of the United Kingdom may in another part of the United Kingdom be sued:

"in proceedings—
  (a) concerning a debt secured on immovable property; or
  (b) which are brought to assert, declare or determine proprietary or possessory rights, or rights of security, in or over movable property, or to obtain authority to dispose of movable property,
in the courts of the part of the United Kingdom in which the property is situated."

This reflects RSC Order 11, r. 1(1)(i) by which leave may be granted on such grounds to serve a writ out of the jurisdiction, thereby maintaining the recognition that in English law the contacts there set out provide a jurisdictional base.

A new Article 5A provides:

---

13. For a case on English/Scottish jurisdiction examining Article 5(1), (3) and 6(1) see *Barclays Bank* v. *Glasgow City Council* (fn 5 and text)—the issue (whether an unjust enrichment claim is within Article 5.1 or 5.3) will now presumably be decided by the Court of Appeal, the European Court having declined jurisdiction.

"Article 5A
Proceedings which have as their object a decision of an organ of a company or other legal person or of an association of natural or legal persons may, without prejudice to the other provisions of this Title, be brought in the courts of the part of the United Kingdom in which that company, legal person or association has its seat."

Together with the omission of the provision relating to a decision of an organ of a company from the adapted Article 16 (see *supra*) the effect is to provide for optional instead of exclusive jurisdiction based on the seat of the corporation.

Multi parties and multi claims. Article 6 (providing for multi-party optional jurisdiction) is directly adapted. However, the ground for its application—risk of irreconcilable judgments—is greatly reduced at least in terms of final judgments by the role of the House of Lords.[14]

Limitation of liability. Article 6a (providing jurisdiction on issues of limitation of liability in courts hearing liability arising from the use or operation of a ship) is directly adapted.

JURISDICTION AGREEMENTS (ARTICLE 17)

Article 17 as amended and adapted reads:

"If the parties ... have agreed that a court or the courts of a **part of the United Kingdom** are to have jurisdiction to settle any disputes which have arisen or which may arise in connection with a particular legal relationship, **and, apart from this Schedule, the agreement would be effective to confer jurisdiction under the law of that part**, that court or those courts shall have ... jurisdiction ...

The court or courts of a **part of the United Kingdom** on which a trust instrument has conferred jurisdiction shall have ... jurisdiction in any proceedings brought against a settlor, trustee or beneficiary, if relations between these persons or their rights or obligations under the trust are involved.

Agreements or provisions of a trust instrument conferring jurisdiction shall have no legal force if they are contrary to the provisions of Article ... 15, or if the courts whose jurisdiction they purport to exclude have exclusive jurisdiction by virtue of Article 16.

...

In matters relating to individual contracts of employment an agreement conferring jurisdiction shall have legal force only if it is entered into after the dispute has arisen or if the employee invokes it to seise courts other than those of the defendant's domicile or those specified in Article 5(1)."

The provision differs from the text of Article 17 in the Brussels Convention in that:

(a) By virtue of the limits on applicability of the framework the provision applies *only* if the defendant is domiciled in the United Kingdom;

(b) There are no requirements of formality and the validity of the agreement in all respects is subjected to the law of the part of the United Kingdom on which jurisdiction is conferred;

(c) The jurisdiction conferred is not "exclusive": where there are a number of possible jurisdiction bases a suit may be brought in any one applicable, raising the question of competing jurisdictions;

---

14. *Barclays Bank* v. *Glasgow City Council* [1994] 4 All E.R. 865—a case in which Article 6(1) was also held inapplicable as the various cases would not be heard and determined together.

(d) The addition of Convention requirements of jurisdiction agreements relevant to insurance and consumer contract disputes (set out in Articles 12 to 15) is relevant only insofar as the consumer contract jurisdiction is adapted.

As the provision does not confer exclusive jurisdiction there is no need for the exception in the Convention relating to an agreement for the benefit of one party. As a consequence there is little change in the national laws of each part—the sole effect of the adapted provision is to subject the validity of the jurisdiction agreement to Article 16 jurisdiction and, where appropriate, Article 15 requirements.

The "multiple proceedings" provisions (Arts. 21–23—as to which see Chapter 12) are not adapted, thereby leaving the door open for *forum non conveniens*.[15] Section 49 of the Act specifically provides that noting should prevent any court in the United Kingdom "from staying, sisting, striking out or dismissing any proceedings before it, on the ground of *forum non conveniens* or otherwise, where to do so is not inconsistent with the 1968 Convention". There is thereby preserved the jurisdiction to uphold or not a jurisdiction agreement falling within the adapted framework as against any other permitted "Convention" base.

Jurisdiction agreement in consumer contracts. Article 15 is adapted without modification and any jurisdiction agreement in a contract within the adapted Article 13 (see *supra*) must thereby comply with the additional requirements.

Procedural safeguards

The Act adapts the 1968 Convention obligation on a court to declare of its own motion in specified circumstances that it has no jurisdiction (as to which obligation see Chapter 4). The adaptation of Articles 19 and 20 (which are the foundation of this obligation) provides that a court in one part of the United Kingdom has to make such a declaration if:

(a) it is seised of a case within the exclusive jurisdiction of a court in another part; and

(b) if a defendant domiciled in another part does not appear and the jurisdiction is not derived from the Convention.

Further, a court is obliged to stay the proceedings if not satisfied that necessary steps have been taken to ensure that the defendant has received or that he has been able to receive the document instituting the process so as to enable him to prepare his defence.

---

15. For application of the principle see *Cumming* v. *Scottish Daily Record and Others, The Times*, 8 June 1995, Deahe J. acknowledging that a previous decision of his to the contrary was wrong (as to which see *Foxe* v. *Scotsman Publications Ltd.* 1994 TLR 84).

CHAPTER 8

The Lugano Convention—Divergence from the Brussels Convention

The Lugano Convention follows faithfully the pattern of the Brussels Convention.[1] It varies only in the following respects: (i) there is no central interpreting judicial authority[2]; (ii) provision is made for jurisdiction in maritime matters in respect of States not parties to the Arrest Convention for a period of three years or until they become parties to that Convention[3]; (iii) there are differences in the jurisdiction regimes relating to (a) individual employment contracts (b) rights *in rem* in immovable property[4]; (iv) there is a need to fit together the Brussels and Lugano Conventions; (v) there are distinctions in the recognition and enforcement of judgments (see Chapter 28).

The rules as to applicability, jurisdiction allocation and procedural safeguards are identical to the Brussels Convention. The pattern is therefore that, subject to Convention provisions, a defendant is to be sued in the state of his domicile and domicile is to be defined by national law. Rules of "exorbitant jurisdiction" are outlawed as between contracting States.[5] Jurisdiction bases other than the defendant's domicile are identical to the Brussels Convention.

JURISDICTION IN MARITIME CLAIMS (ARTICLE 54A)

The transitional provision in contracting States not parties to the Arrest Convention is based on a regime similar to that Convention. The list of claims and the ships which may be arrested for any claim are identical. There will be only optional jurisdiction when the defendant is domiciled in a contracting State—but extended from arrest to giving of security or bail.

INDIVIDUAL EMPLOYMENT CONTRACTS

(i) JURISDICTION AGREEMENTS (ARTICLE 17)

Such an agreement has force in relation to an individual employment contract only if entered into after the dispute has arisen. The two Conventions differ in that under the

---

1. As with the Brussels Convention there is a report which may be considered in ascertaining the meaning and effect of Convention provisions—in this instance by Mr P. Jenard and Mr G. Moller 1990 OJ C189/07.
2. There is an obligation on courts of contracting States to pay due account to decisions of courts of other contracting States when applying and interpreting the Convention (Protocol No. 2). A system of exchange of information concerning judgments under the Lugano and Brussels Convention is to be set up (*ibid.*).
3. This matches the provision of the Brussels Convention initially applicable to Denmark, Greece and Ireland. All of these are now parties to the Arrest Convention.
4. Giving the state of the defendant's domicile joint jurisdiction in specified circumstances in relation to tenancies for private use for a maximum period of six months (Art. 16(1)).
5. Article 3. Adding to Art. 3 of the Brussels Convention rules of jurisdiction in Austria, Iceland, Norway, Finland and Switzerland.

Brussels Convention a pre-dispute agreement would be valid insofar as it is invoked by the employee to sue in courts other than the defendant's domicile or place of performance. As the underlying principle of both Conventions is to protect the employee there seems no reason why the employer should not be given the same protection.

(ii) PLACE OF PERFORMANCE (ARTICLE 5(1))

The Lugano Convention provides that where an employee does not habitually carry out his work in any one country the place of performance is the place of business through which he was engaged. In the Brussels Convention it is only the employee who can take advantage of suit in those circumstances—once again a distinction difficult to appreciate.

RELATIONSHIP TO BRUSSELS CONVENTION (ARTICLE 54B)

In matters of jurisdiction the Lugano Convention is to be applied in any case in which (i) the defendant is domiciled in a contracting State not a member of the European Communities or (ii) jurisdiction is conferred on such a state as is referred to in (i) by virtue of Article 16 (by nature of the dispute) or by a jurisdiction agreement under Article 17.

Nothing in the Lugano Convention is otherwise to prejudice the Brussels Convention, but clearly if looking at the Brussels Convention alone that Convention does not apply, there will be no restriction on the application of the Lugano Convention. So where the Brussels Convention has no application because the issue involves a contracting and a non-contracting State it leaves the field open to the Lugano Convention if both states are parties to that Convention.

When the Lugano Convention is given precedence by the presence of one of the specified connecting factors this will remove the case from all aspects of the Brussels Convention. Once all parties to the Brussels Convention are also parties to the Lugano Convention[6] this should make little difference as the jurisdiction bases are common as between the Conventions. However as regards the Lugano Convention it has been indicated there is no central interpreting authority and despite obligations on courts of each contracting State to pay due account to decisions of courts of other contracting States the likelihood of development of Convention concepts must be less. Conflict of national laws are therefore more likely to be relevant to the operation of the Convention.[7]

---

6. As at 1 December 1995 Belgium, Denmark and Greece were not parties.
7. See e.g. as to *lis pendens Polly Peck International* v. *Citibank NA* [1994] I.L.Pr. 71 (see Chap. 12).

CHAPTER 9

Enforcement of Maritime Claims by an Action "in personam"

THE CLAIMS FOR WHICH AN ACTION "IN PERSONAM" IS AVAILABLE

The Supreme Court Act 1981, s.21(1) provides:

"21.—(1) Subject to section 22, an action in personam may be brought in the High Court in all cases within the Admiralty jurisdiction of that court."

Restrictions created by judicial development or statutes are based on, for example, the relative lack of English contact or power (e.g. over foreign land), immunity from suit (as in the case of a foreign government) or the lack of contact between English proceedings and the issue to be heard (e.g. collision actions). They are discussed in Chapter 12.

NATURE OF THE ACTION "IN PERSONAM" AS COMPARED TO THE ACTION "IN REM"

"Action *in personam*" as a categorization of the actions normally available to claimants pursuing a civil claim other than one based on status is rarely used in English law save in Admiralty to distinguish it from an action *in rem*.[1] The provision, therefore, simply indicates that the maritime claims specified in s.20 of the Act or any claim otherwise within the Admiralty jurisdiction may be enforced by the method which would be available were they not maritime.[2]

An "action *in personam*" is the method of enforcement of a claim by which it is sought to compel the defendant to act or cease from acting. The claim may or may not be directly enforcing some obligation directly imposed on the defendant. It could be based on the defendant's act—on the allegation that he has caused injury, damage or loss, or in cases of enforcement of proprietary interests, that a claim created through the act of another is

---

1. Examples of status claims are those based on marriage and other family relationships. The distinction between actions *in personam* and *in rem* is not to be confused with that between *rights* or *judgments in personam* and *in rem*—both of these going to the number of persons bound.
2. Although there are special procedural requirements in some Admiralty actions—see e.g. the need for the lodging of a preliminary act in collision actions. See RSC, Order 75, r. 18. Admiralty proceedings are the subject of Orders 74 and 75 although general procedural requirements also apply as appropriate.

enforceable against a defendant who had nothing to do with its creation. So, enforceability of a mortgage will lie against the mortgagor and third parties who succeed to the mortgagor's title, and a demise charterparty should be enforceable against a purchaser of a ship. On the other hand, apart from statutory provisions permitting a consignee of goods to sue, an action on a contract of carriage is enforceable only by the shipper against the carrier; but whether it is the consignee through statutory provision or the shipper who sues it may be by an action *in personam*.

So far as enforceability by an action *in personam* is concerned, it is the nature of the claim which dictates its scope, not the action which enforces it. Enforcement through an action *in personam* applies equally to claims based directly on the defendant's act (such as tort or breach of contract) and claims which may not be so based (i.e. property claims). In the Admiralty context, therefore, it is simply a label distinguishing the mode of enforcement from enforcement through an action *in rem*.

The action *in rem* (to be considered in Chapter 10) is an action connected essentially with a specified thing (in the Admiralty context ship, cargo or freight). It may be considered as lying *against* the thing or as lying against a person having an interest in the thing. However it is seen, it is focused on a thing relevant to the claim (as for example a ship carrying goods said to be damaged or a ship colliding with another). Subject to some English judicial comments to the contrary, the aim is limited to the thing and neither the person who is liable in the claim nor any other assets are subject to liability. A claim enforceable by an action *in rem* may also be enforceable concurrently by an action *in personam* (see *infra*).

Neither the action *in personam* nor the judgment obtained in such an action will of itself provide any security for the claim through any interest in the assets of the defendant. The claimant has no preferred status nor any ability to assert his claim against any person other than the defendant simply because it is an action *in personam*. Any security aspect will follow from the nature of the claim and not the legal process available to enforce it. Any judgment will be enforced against the defendant's assets through the general procedure for execution of judgments.

On the other hand, the issue of a writ *in rem* makes the plaintiff a secured creditor in respect of the thing in relation to which the writ is issued. The thing may be sold by the court and the proceeds made available for creditors *in rem*.[3]

JURISDICTION IN ACTIONS "IN PERSONAM"

Where no jurisdiction base applies jurisdiction in an action *in personam* depends on:

   (i) the service of a writ in England; or
   (ii) service out of England where necessary with leave of the court; or
   (iii) submission to the jurisdiction through express agreement or participation in the proceedings in court.

---

3. As to the availability of the preliminary remedies of arrest (action *in rem*) and *Mareva* injunction (action *in personam*) see Chaps. 15, 16.

Where no jurisdiction base applies jurisdiction will be created by the procedural step of service of the writ or by submission of the defendant. Where submission is the basis there may well need to be compliance with the procedure of service.

JURISDICTION THROUGH SERVICE OF A WRIT

The traditional general rule of English law is that jurisdiction is created either by service of the writ or other document initiating the action or by "submission" of the defendant. While, as has been seen in Chapters 4–8, considerable inroads have been made into the operation of the principle it remains where no statutory jurisdiction base applies. In those circumstances the service of the writ has the dual role of creating jurisdiction and procedurally commencing the action. Where a jurisdiction base does apply the writ and its service continues its procedural role. The relevant provisions as to the nature of the writ and service are identical whether it has a dual or simply a procedural role and are set out in rules of court.

It may be that a different construction is to be placed on the rules because of the introduction of statutory jurisdiction bases. In particular the rules cannot be continued so as to frustrate any statutory base. However, any applicable jurisdiction base will affect the availability of an action *in personam* or an action *in rem* to pursue a cause of action only insofar as the base goes to the nature of either type of action. In other words the two methods of suit will continue under English law unless limited in some way by a statutory requirement.

THE WRIT "IN PERSONAM"

Despite its jurisdictional role the writ is treated as essentially a matter of procedure. As such it is largely governed by the Rules of the Supreme Court (RSC) 1965 (as amended). Failure to comply with the rules is in the High Court an irregularity rather than rendering the process a nullity. The court has wide curative powers. However, the exercise of those powers is a matter of discretion, and it may be a matter of some commercial concern that so many issues seem to turn on simple non-compliance with requirements of the rules.

The action is begun by the issue of a writ *in personam*.[4] The writ must state concisely the nature of the claim and the remedy required.[5] It may be indorsed with or followed by a statement of claim setting out the material facts relied on. Every writ must be accompanied by a form of acknowledgment of service.[6] Unless the defendant's solicitor indorses on the writ that he accepts service of the writ on behalf of the defendant or the defendant acknowledges service (when the writ is deemed to have been served), the writ

---

4. Save where the registry is closed a writ is issued when sealed by an officer of the appropriate registry. When the register is closed a writ may be issued by the party's solicitor (Order 6, r. 7A). A concurrent writ may be issued, and this may be useful for service particularly where it may be necessary to serve a writ out of the jurisdiction (see RSC Order 6, r. 1) (see *infra*). As to the form of the writ *in personam* in Admiralty see Order 75, r. 3.

5. RSC Order 5, rr. 1 and 2; Order 6, r. 2; Order 75, r. 3.

6. Service of a writ without a form of acknowledgment of service is an irregularity which may be cured by the court under its general curative powers (*Tsai* v. *Woodworth* (1983) 127 S.J. 858; *Bondy* v. *Lloyds Bank, The Times* 13 March 1991).

must be served on the defendant in England or (when permitted by the rules of court) out of England.[7] A person may require a writ in which he is named as a defendant to be served on him.[8]

The extent to which a court will go to overcome perceived technicalities is shown by *The Golden Mariner.*[9] In that case writs were served against a number of defendants. The service on one defendant of a writ referring to another or serving a form of acknowledgment of service instead of a writ could be cured as irregularities. In each instance the plaintiff had purported to begin or take a step in the proceedings.[10] The power will not be used to avoid the requirements relating to service of a writ out of England[11] and will no doubt take into account that the requirements of the rules should normally be met.[12]

A writ *in personam* is initially valid for service on the defendant named where leave for service out is required for six months and in any other case for four months. Whether a writ is served within the period allowed may therefore depend on whether it is a writ requiring leave to serve out of the jurisdiction.[13] A writ which is not served within the appropriate period is not a nullity—it is simply not valid for service on the defendant unless the irregularity is waived by the defendant.[14] Service of a writ outside the period as an irregularity can be cured by a court.

Under the rules there may be an extension normally limited to four months, but where, despite reasonable efforts, it may not be possible to serve the writ in that period the extension may be for 12 months.[15] An application for renewal (extension) should be made during the validity of the writ and only one extension may be granted on each application. Although there are no grounds specified on where the power is to be exercised there is implied a condition that it should only be exercised "for good reason"[16] as for example an agreement that service be deferred or difficulty in finding a defendant. It remains the

7. RSC Orders 10 and 11. Service is necessary for proceedings to be valid and there is no discretion in a court (under RSC Order 2, r. 1) to dispense with good service: *Broken Hill Proprietary Co. Ltd.* v. *Theodore Xenakis* [1982] 2 Lloyd's Rep. 304. The parties may agree on a method of service outside the rules *Kenneth Allison Ltd* v. *Limehouse and Co.* [1992] A.C. 105 (H.L.). An order may be obtained for substituted service where it is impracticable for a plaintiff to effect personal service (*The Vrontados* [1982] 2 Lloyd's Rep. 241). It is not "impracticable" simply because the claim would fail unless substituted service were permitted (*Paragon Ltd.* v. *Burnell* [1991] 2 All E.R. 388). Where a defendant is in England on the date of issue of a writ and leaves prior to service, substituted service may be ordered (*Myerson* v. *Martin* [1979] 3 All E.R. 667); but otherwise substituted service may not be used to overcome legal inability to serve the writ. For an example of confusion by solicitors of the requirements of actual and substituted service, see *The Vrontados* [1982] 2 Lloyd's Rep. 241. As to service on a corporation, see *infra.* As to renewal of a writ, see *infra* and Chap. 11. As to service out of the jurisdiction, see *infra.* England means England and Wales.
8. RSC Order 12, r. 8A. Failure to comply may lead to the dismissal of the claim.
9. [1990] 2 Lloyd's Rep. 215 (C.A.) reversing Phillips J.
10. But the writ cannot be amended after the expiry of the limitation period to add defendants not named within the period—the rule being subordinate to the Limitation Act 1980 (*The Kyriaki* [1994] 1 All E.R. 401 [1993] 1 Lloyd's Rep. 137). As to the effect of the Limitation Act generally see Chap. 11.
11. i.e. England and Wales, the territorial sea (as to which see the Territorial Sea Act 1987). Jurisdiction may be conferred as to designated areas and installation under the Continental Shelf Act 1964 (s. 3) and Mineral Workings (Offshore Installation) Act 1971 (as amended by Oil and Gas (Enterprise) Act 1982).
12. As e.g. in applying to renew a writ after its validity has expired (see *infra* and Chap. 11).
13. See *infra,* Service out of the jurisdiction.
14. See *The Jay Bola* [1992] 2 Lloyd's Rep. 62 at p. 68 followed and approved in *The Nova Scotia* [1993] 1 Lloyd's Rep. 154 and *Dong Wha Enterprise Co. Ltd.* v. *Crownson Shipping Ltd.* [1995] 1 Lloyd's Rep. 113.
15. RSC Order 6, r. 8.
16. *The Myrto (No. 3)* [1987] 2 Lloyd's Rep. 1 (H.L.); Normally it will be necessary to show a good reason for failing to serve the writ. *Waddon* v. *Whitecroft Scovell Ltd.* [1988] 1 All E.R. 996 (H.L.).

duty to serve a writ promptly.[17] Only in exceptional circumstances will an application for renewal be granted as a matter of general discretion rather than as provided in the rules.[18]

Amendment of a writ

There are wide powers of amendment of a writ, leave of the court being required where the amendment is to be made after service[19] and a court may add, omit or substitute a party or add or substitute a new cause of action.[20] The power to amend is directed at "determining the real question in controversy between the parties" or correcting a defect or error.[21]

The general effect of an amendment is to amend the writ as from its issue, but there is no "relation bank" so as to resurrect a cause of action ended because of a substantive contractual or statutory time bar.[22] For the purposes of the Limitation Act 1980 and the effect of time bars within that Act an amendment relates back to the issue of the writ and, with an exception relating to personal injury, such an amendment may be permitted if the claim when brought would be time barred only if the new cause of action arises substantially out of the same facts as the old or the addition or substitution of a new party is necessary for the determination of the action.[23]

SERVICE IN ENGLAND

Individuals

Service of a writ in England may be served personally on an individual defendant or his agent or by ordinary first class post to his last known address or through a letter box at that address. Acceptance indorsed on the writ by the defendant's solicitor is deemed service.[24] Where it is served by post or through the letter box the date of service unless the contrary is shown is deemed to be the seventh day after sending as inserting in the box.[24]

17. See e.g. *The Vita* [1990] 1 Lloyd's Rep. 528.

18. *Waddon* v. *Whitecroft Scovell Ltd.* [1988] 1 All E.R. 996; *Sing* v. *Duport Foundries Ltd.* (C.A.) [1994] 2 All E.R. 889. The power to extend after expiry of validity is founded on the general power to waive rule requirements of Order 2, r. 1, or to extend the period for doing any act under Order 3, r. 5. For an almost simultaneous decision extending the period for service on application made after the period so as to cure an irregular service (and relying on Order 3, r. 5) see *The Nova Scotia* [1993] 1 Lloyd's Rep. 154.

19. Order 20, rr. 1, 5. Before service a writ may be so amended once without leave but the defendant may apply to have the amendment disallowed (Order 20, r. 4). As to amendment of pleadings see rr. 1(3)(c), 3(1), 5.

20. RSC Order 15, rr. 6–8, Order 20. An amendment may be made although a jurisdictional objection is taken under Order 12, r. 8 (*Grupo Torras SA* v. *Al Sabah* [1995] 1 Lloyd's Rep. 374).

21. See Order 20, r. 8 (referring to all documents save a judgment or order).

22. *The Jay Bola* [1992] 2 Lloyd's Rep. 62.

23. See Limitation Act 1980, s.35; RSC Order 20, r. 5. In seeking to add a new cause of action which would have been barred the plaintiff must show that it is just to allow the amendment taking into account the loss of an accrued defence—leave may be granted to add a new claim involving a small degree of additional facts: *The Casper Trader* [1992] 3 All E.R. 132 (C.A.). As to the constraints of the Limitation Act 1980 see Chap. 11. The date of the events on which the claim is based is not an essential part of a cause of action for breach of contract of carriage: *The Jangmi* [1989] 2 Lloyd's Rep. 1.

24. Order 10, r. 1(4). An affidavit must be sworn by deposing that in the deponent's belief the writ will have come to the notice of the defendant within seven days (r. 1(3)). Notice to the defendant must be shown (*Forward* v. *West Sussex C.C.* [1995] 4 All E.R. 207). Personal service is not necessary of amendment to a writ once there has been acknowledgment of service (*Grupo Torras SA* v. *Al Sabah* [1995] 1 Lloyd's Rep. 374). As to acknowledgment of service as deemed service see r. 5 and fn. 32.

The alternative method of service cannot be used to avoid the need to serve the defendant in England. Service is good if the plaintiff can show that the defendant was in England at the date of service and if not will be deemed to be on the date of return to England if it can be shown that knowledge of the writ came to the defendant on some date within the seven day period.[25]

Corporations

Service on a body incorporated in England is to be affected by personal service on the chairman, secretary of other similar officer or by postal service on its registered office.[26] A body incorporated outside Great Britain (an overseas company) has a statutory obligation to register with the Registrar of Companies and to provide the names of persons authorized to accept service of process.[27] It is sufficient for service if the writ is addressed to that person and served by post or left at the address given.[28] Service may be in no other way.[29]

If no name or address is supplied by the corporation service may be on any place of business in Great Britain.[30] Because of the wording of s.692 of the Companies Act 1985 even if the overseas company has ceased to be registered and no longer carries on such business, process may still be served on the person named in the registration.[31] This in effect extends jurisdiction based on "presence" (construed in relation to corporations as carrying on business) to former presence. The court pointed out the need to protect creditors from corporations running up debts and then leaving the country while not subjecting corporations long departed from the jurisdiction. The problem cannot be satisfactorily resolved without getting away from the equation of service of a writ and jurisdiction. It underlines the need to base jurisdiction on a substantive link.

STEPS FOLLOWING SERVICE

Failure to acknowledge service of a writ served in England within 14 days renders the defendant liable to judgment in default of acknowledgment.[32] Failure to give notice of intention to defend renders the defendant liable to judgment in default when the writ is

---

25. *Barclays Bank* v. *Hahn* [1989] 1 All E.R. 723; *India Videogran Ltd.* v. *Patel* [1991] 1 All E.R. 214.
26. RSC Order 65, rr. 1, 2.
27. Companies Act 1985, s. 695(1).
28. *Ibid.*, s. 695(2).
29. *Boocock* v. *Hilton International Co.* [1993] 4 All E.R. 19 (C.A.)—but service not complying with the requirement may in the appropriate case be treated as an irregularity and cured under RSC Order 2, r. 1 (*ibid.*). There may be service in England under foreign law if a writ may be served out of England and by the law of the place of service served in England (see *infra*).
30. RSC Order 65, r. 3.
31. *Rome* v. *Punjab National Bank (No. 2)* [1990] 1 All E.R. 58 (C.A.)—thus extending the jurisdiction from "presence" (i.e. "carrying on business") to former presence. As to the meaning of "carrying on business" see *Adams* v. *Cape Industries plc* [1991] 1 All E.R. 929 (C.A.) and authorities there discussed.
32. RSC Order 12, r. 5. A defendant may acknowledge service at any time prior to judgment, but subject to court order the time limits for delivery of defence on other acts remain as they would have been if acknowledgment had been in time (RSC Order 12, r. 6(2)). Leave of court is required for the giving of intention to defend after judgment (*ibid.*, r. 6(1)). Acknowledgment of service does not waive an irregularity (Order 12, r. 7) but if by a defendant will be deemed service if not otherwise shown (Order 10, r. 5).

indorsed for damages or detention of goods.[33] When a statement of claim has been served and the defendant has given notice of intention to defend, the plaintiff may still apply for summary judgment on the ground of lack of defence.[34]

Acknowledgment of service does not of itself constitute submission to jurisdiction[35] but a defendant wishing to dispute the jurisdiction must apply for an action to set the writ aside. To dispute the jurisdiction the defendant must give notice of intention to defend the proceedings in the acknowledgment and apply for the order within the time limited for service of a defence, the period being capable of extension.[36] The notice of intention to defend is not in these circumstances submission to the jurisdiction and if the application fails the notice ceases to have effect.[37] Lacking such an application acknowledgment may be treated as submission.[38]

THROUGH AN ACTION "IN REM"

An action *in personam* may be pursued concurrently with an action *in rem*.[39] Even if an action *in rem* only is started it was established prior to the introduction of acknowledgment of service that an "appearance" to an action *in rem* forms the basis of an action *in personam*[40] and the action continues as both *in personam* and *in rem*—sometimes termed a "hybrid action".[41] Such a consequence of appearance in an '*in rem*" action bears out the "procedural" view of the action *in rem*—that it is but a way to persuade the defendant to come to court; but its continuance with security aspects once the defendant has come to court is hardly consistent with such an approach.

The question now goes to whether any act of the defendant in proceedings *in rem* short of actual appearance in court will found an action *in personam*. Acknowledgment of

33. See RSC Order 13, r. 1. Default also applies to recovery of land. In other actions *in personam* judgment can be obtained in default of defence (as to which, see RSC Order 19).

34. RSC Order 14. As to leave to defend such an action, see RSC Order 14, rr. 3 and 4 and *European Asian Bank AG* v. *Punjab and Sind Bank (No. 2)* [1983] 1 W.L.R. 642 (C.A.). A court may decide questions of law in Order 14 proceedings rather than having arguments rehearsed again if the case is sent for trial (*ibid*). The Order was applied to Admiralty actions *in personam* from 1 July 1995. It does not apply to actions *in rem* (r.1(2)).

35. The acknowledgment is a prerequisite for the challenge to the jurisdicion and so cannot of itself be submission (see *The Anna H* [1995] 1 Lloyd's Rep. 11.

36. RSC Order 12, r. 8, Order 3, r. 5. Acceptance of service by the defendant's solicitors (see *supra*) will prevent reliance on the rule (*Manta Line Inc.* v. *Seraphim Sofianites* [1984] 1 Lloyd's Rep. 14). An application for a stay falls within the rule only if jurisdiction is disputed, see *The Messiniaki Tolmi* [1984] 1 Lloyd's Rep. 266; *The Pia Vesta* [1984] 1 Lloyd's Rep. 169. RSC Order 12 is applied to Admiralty writs *in personam* by RSC Order 75, r. 3(4). A challenge cannot be made once there is submission as, for example, consent to an interlocutory order (*Esal* v. *Pujara* [1989] 2 Lloyd's Rep. 479), but see *infra* as to distinction between interlocutory matters and merits. As to time limits generally, see Chap. 11.

37. RSC Order 12 r. 8(6). A defendant may lodge a further acknowledgment.

38. By r. 12(10) acknowledgment is to be equated with the process of "appearance" in use prior to the procedure of acknowledgment but the form of acknowledgment attached to the writ simply provides for acknowledgment of service of the writ (see *infra*).

39. Two writs must be issued (Practice Direction [1979] 2 All E.R. 155).

40. See e.g. *The Dictator* [1892] P. 304. In *The Conoco Britannia* [1972] 2 Q.B. 543 Brandon J. hinted that in his view even without appearance judgment in an action *in rem* might exceed the monetary value of the *res* and that a remedy *in personam* (an injunction) may be granted.

41. An action *in rem* does not depend for its existence on the arrest of property (see Chap. 10) and likewise release of property arrested does not change its character whether or not an action *in personam* is also in being. (As to the latter circumstance see *The Maciej Rataj* [1992] 2 Lloyd's Rep. 552.)

service of a writ *in rem* can only found jurisdiction *in personam* insofar as acknowledgment of a writ *in personam* could so operate. So acknowledgment of itself cannot be submission.[42] Nor can the filing of a praecipe for a caveat against the issue of a warrant of arrest, for it can be withdrawn and any undertakings given in it cease to have effect.[43]

However, a solicitor's indorsement of a writ *in rem* accepting service on behalf of the defendant would appear to provide the link with the defendant to found an action *in personam*. Secondly, the rules of court provide for acknowledgment of the issue of a writ *in rem* (see Chapter 10). In *The Prinsengracht*[44] it was held that such acknowledgment is submission, depending as it does on a desire to take part in the "*in rem*" proceedings. It is an act of participation in one respect more definitive than acknowledgment of service in that at the point of acknowledgment the plaintiff has not sought to establish jurisdiction through service. However this may be difficult to fit with the comments of the Court of Appeal in *The Anna H*[45] focusing on the ability of the defendant to challenge jurisdiction after the acknowledgment of service. There were therefore thought Hobhouse L.J. "problems in treating a mere acknowledgment of service or an undertaking to acknowledge issue or service as being a waiver of the right to challenge jurisdiction".[46] The question is whether acknowledgment of issue can be taken as such a waiver given its "voluntary" nature, and the risk remains of it being so held.

Bail

Even if it be said that in substance bail in an action *in rem* is given on behalf of a "defendant" it is arguable that it is no more submission than acknowledgment of service. The undertaking may be said to be no more than to be liable for whatever is adjudged but not necessarily that there is jurisdiction to adjudge. To see the giving of bail as submission *in personam* is to perpetuate the confusion between security and merits. It has the consequence that the release of a vessel arrested as security through provision of a different security cannot be obtained without submitting to jurisdiction. That is to enhance yet more the pressures on a defendant through arrest, a weapon available to the plaintiff without regard to the strength of his case or any possibility of compensation to the defendant on failure in the action.

Given the existence of merits jurisdiction based on arrest it is entirely justifiable in principle that bail in lieu of arrest should also be a jurisdiction base. But in both cases the jurisdiction depends on the validity of the arrest or bail. So the giving of bail should have no more nor less jurisdictional significance than the arrest. It is an act wholly unconnected with the issue of merits jurisdiction and it should not today be necessary to declare that it is "in protest" to prevent it being considered as submission.

---

42. *The Anna H* [1995] 1 Lloyd's Rep. 11. But if the required steps to contest the jurisdiction are not taken (see *supra*) it may be held to be submission. (See *The Lloydiana* [1983] 2 Lloyd's Rep. 313) Compare acknowledgment of the issue of the writ *in rem* (see *infra*).

43. *The Anna H* [1995] 1 Lloyd's Rep. 11. In *The Prinsengracht* [1993] 1 Lloyd's Rep. 41 the contrary view was expressed on the ground that to obtain a caveat there had to be an undertaking to acknowledge service. But as a caveat and undertaking may be withdrawn it would seem that *The Anna H* is to be preferred.

44. [1993] 1 Lloyd's Rep. 41. See also *The Anna H* [1995] 1 Lloyd's Rep. 11. As to acknowledgment of issue of a writ, see RSC Order 75, r. 3(6) and Chap. 4. As to the need for a defendant *in rem*, see Chaps. 2, 10.

45. [1995] 1 Lloyd's Rep. 11.

46. But failure to challenge the jurisdiction will in all probability be submission (see fn 42 and *infra* "submission").

The principle seems to be that any overt irrevocable action recognizing the power of the English court not only to adjudge the issue but also to control whether property be released is enough to found jurisdiction *in personam*. Even taking the principle at its most extreme, an interest in the ship is essential for a person to be a defendant *in rem*. Acknowledgment of service of a writ *in rem* by a "non defendant" *in rem* cannot create jurisdiction *in personam*.

The readiness to found jurisdiction *in personam* on a step in an "*in rem*" action shows the schizophrenic approach of English law to maritime claims. If, as is the case, a defendant cannot defend an *in rem* action without creating *in personam* jurisdiction there seems little reason to persist in the *in rem/in personam* distinction so far as initiation of proceedings is concerned. Why not adopt the civil law approach, recognize the real targets as those interested in the ship and confer a "maritime privilege" on certain claims? In other words recognize first the property or security interests as flowing directly from the claim rather than through a different "cause of action" and secondly the function of arrest as jurisdiction creating and ensuring that the property is available for enforcement of the security.

SERVICE OF A WRIT OUTSIDE ENGLAND

Service of a writ *in personam* outside England is allowed without leave if a statute permits and, in particular, in respect of claims falling within the Civil Jurisdiction and Judgments Acts 1982 (as amended by the 1991 Act),[47] i.e. within the Brussels or Lugano Convention. Service outside England is allowed with leave of the court in any other case falling within one of the categories specified in RSC Order 11 or (in respect of collision or limitation actions) RSC Order 75, rules 2 and 4 *and* in either case the plaintiff persuades the court to exercise its discretion in allowing service.[48]

RSC ORDER 11 (FOR TEXT SEE APPENDIX 2)

Service without leave

The issue of a writ to be served out of England but not requiring leave so to do is as for the writ to be served in England. Service of a writ out of England without leave is permitted where:

   (a) by enactment the High Court has jurisdiction although the defendant is not in the jurisdiction or the act giving rise to the action did not take place in England, or

---

47. RSC Order 11, r. 1(2). This rule does not apply to Admiralty proceedings (RSC Order 75, r. 4(4)) and by the rules of court leave is therefore required for "service out" in all such proceedings; and those claims for which leave is available is limited to those for which it is expressly provided by RSC Order 11 or Order 75. At least leave is mandatory but in all probability the rule is inconsistent with the jurisdiction bases and if so it follows that the period for service is four months rather than six months (see text to fn 56).

48. The power to extend the validity of a writ should not be used to circumvent the requirement of leave (*Leal v. Dunlop Bio Processes Ltd.* [1984] 2 All E.R. 207 (C.A.)—but see the cautionary note on limiting general discretion in *Boocock* v. *Hilton International Co.* [1993] 4 All E.R. 19.

(b) by the Civil Jurisdiction and Judgments Act 1982 the High Court has jurisdiction and (i) there are no pending "proceedings in the same cause of action" in the United Kingdom or a Convention State *and* (ii) the defendant is domiciled in the United Kingdom, the proceedings are within Article 16 of the Convention or jurisdiction is conferred on an English court by agreement under Article 17.

Enactments conferring jurisdiction in respect of maritime claims include those based on Conventions having jurisdiction regimes and enacted into English law. So, for example, the Athens Convention 1974 concerning the carriage of passengers and luggage provides for jurisdiction in writs linked to the carriage[49] and the Collision (Civil Jurisdiction) Convention 1952 for the courts of the defendant's habitual residence.[50]

The writ will be valid for service for a period of four months. It is not open to a plaintiff to seek leave and thereby obtain a period of validity of six months.[51]

The Civil Jurisdiction and Judgments Act 1982 (the Brussels Convention)

The ability to serve a writ without leave does not entirely coincide with Convention based jurisdiction. There are excluded:

(i) Conventions given precedence over the Brussels Convention by Article 57 of that Convention thus excluding any jurisdiction founded on a Convention not enacted into English law but ratified by the United Kingdom (see Chapter 6);

(ii) jurisdiction in a limitation action because of jurisdiction in a liability action other than based on jurisdiction agreement or where the defendant was not domiciled in the United Kingdom (e.g. appearance by the liability plaintiff or arrest under the Arrest Convention)[52];

(iii) action for interim relief by virtue of s. 25 of the Act where the conditions for service without leave are not met. So the service of a summons seeking the grant of a *Mareva* injunction in respect of proceedings in France against a defendant domiciled in Saudi Arabia required leave.[53]

Service with leave

A writ requiring leave to be served out of the jurisdiction will only be issued with leave.[54] Where the writ issued is in relation to a claim for which leave is required and such leave

---

49. See Merchant Shipping Act 1995, Sch. 6.

50. See Supreme Court Act 1981, s.22. As to these Conventions and others given priority by Art. 57 of the Brussels Convention see Chap. 6.

51. *The Reefer Creole* [1994] 1 Lloyd's Rep. 584.

52. As to which see Chap. 6.

53. *X* v. *Y* [1989] 3 All E.R. 689 (the statutory provision implementing Art. 24 of the Convention). The application for interim relief does not constitute "proceedings concerning the same cause of action": *Republic of Haiti* v. *Duvalier* [1989] 1 Lloyd's Rep. 111; [1989] 1 All E.R. 456. As to the *Mareva* injunction see Chap. 16.

54. RSC Order 6, r. 7, Order 75, r. 3(4). "Service out" may in fact be service in England if such service is not possible under English law but is under the foreign law (see e.g. *The Vrontados*, fn. 7). An application for leave to serve out must be supported by an affidavit stating the grounds, the belief there is a good cause of action and the place where the defendant probably is (see r. 11(4)). As to the standard of proof on each issue see *infra*. The time for acknowledgment of service must be specified (*ibid*).

has not been obtained the practice is to endorse the writ "not for service out of the jurisdiction". If then a need emerges for service out, the practice is to apply for such leave in relation to a concurrent writ.[55] A concurrent writ does not attract its own period of validity for service—it has the period of an original writ. However where the original writ is endorsed not for service out of the jurisdiction (and has therefore a period of validity of four months) and following a need for service out is renewed, that renewal is for a period of six months. This is so whether the leave is given before the issue of the original writ or after for the issue of the original or concurrent writ.[56] Leave may be granted *ex parte* and a defendant may seek to set aside the issue or the service.[57]

Until the decisions of the House of Lords in *The Spiliada*[58] (1986) and *Seaconsar Far East Ltd.* v. *Bank Markasi Iran*[59] (1993) there was no certain analysis of the requirements for leave. Rather there were many authorities dealing in differing ways with what seems to have been seen as a general discretionary power based on the showing that a claim fell within the Order and that the plaintiff's case was sufficient for service out.[60] The effect of the two decisions is to identify three distinct aspects and the standard of proof applicable to each. In particular the *Seaconsar* decision emphasizes the importance to the plaintiff of establishing the claim as within a "service out" category and showing that England is the most appropriate forum. That done the strength of the plaintiff's case need be no more than showing that there is a serious issue to be tried.

It was held in the *Seaconsar* case by the House of Lords that to obtain leave to serve a writ out of England in a case asserted to fall within RSC Order 11 a plaintiff must show—

(i) that there was a "good arguable case" that the claim falls within one of the specified categories of the rule[61]

(ii) that on the merits there is a serious issue to be tried

(iii) that England is the appropriate forum.[62]

Encompassed in (i) are all the elements of the particular category—so in rule 1(1)(e) (see *infra*) it must be shown to the applicable standard that there is a contract made out of the jurisdiction and a breach within the jurisdiction.

Despite past judicial comment that RSC Order 11 reflects interference with the sovereignty of other nations it would seem that its bases of jurisdiction have more substance than the traditional ground of the defendant's presence—as illustrated by the

---

55. RSC Order 6, r. 6.

56. *Dong Wha* v. *Crownson* [1995] 1 Lloyd's Rep. 113 construing RSC Order 6, r. 8—writ marked not for service out of the jurisdiction cannot be taken to be valid for six months simply because it could not be served except with leave out of the jurisdiction (*The Jay Bola* [1992] 2 Lloyd's Rep. 62; *The Nova Scotia* [1993] 1 Lloyd's Rep. 154).

57. RSC Order 12, r. 8(1). As to service see *infra*.

58. [1986] 3 All E.R. 843; [1987] 1 Lloyd's Rep. 1.

59. [1993] 4 All E.R. 456.

60. A discretion reflected in r. 1(1) and r. 4(2)—the latter providing that no leave shall be granted "unless it should be made sufficiently to appear to the court that a case is a proper one for service out of the jurisdiction under this Order".

61. Not "a probable win": *Agrafax* v. *Scottish Soc.* [1995] I.L.Pr. 753. If there is no room for further investigation into law or fact the question will be whether the case *is* on the evidence within the category, see *Hutton* v. *Mofarrij* [1989] 2 All E.R. 633—possibly weighing inconsistent evidence (see *Molnlycke* fn. 74).

62. *Seaconsar Far East Ltd.* v. *Bank Markasi Iran* [1993] 4 All E.R. 456 (H.L.). The serious issue to be tried will be shown by affidavit evidence required by r. 1(4)—deposing to facts which if proved could provide a foundation for the alleged cause of action (*ibid.*).

provisions of the Brussels Convention. They vary greatly and the likelihood of ordering service out may well depend on the nature of the claim.[63]

CATEGORIES OF CLAIM FOR SERVING OUT

The categories are set out in rule 1(1) of RSC Order 11 and rule 2(1) of Order 75. RSC Order 11, rule 1(1) reads:

"Provided that the writ does not contain any claim mentioned in Order 75, r.2(1) and is not a writ to which paragraph (2) of this rule applies, service of a writ out of the jurisdiction is permissible with the leave of the Court if in the action begun by the writ—

    (a) relief is sought against a person domiciled within the jurisdiction;

    (b) an injunction is sought ordering the defendant to do or refrain from doing anything within the jurisdiction (whether or not damages are also claimed in respect of a failure to do or the doing of that thing);

    (c) the claim is brought against a person duly served within or out of the jurisdiction and a person out of the jurisdiction is a necessary or proper party thereto;

    (d) the claim is brought to enforce, rescind, dissolve, annul or otherwise affect a contract, or to recover damages or obtain other relief in respect of the breach of a contract, being (in either case) a contract which—

        (i) was made within the jurisdiction, or

        (ii) was made by or through an agent trading or residing within the jurisdiction on behalf of a principal trading or residing out of the jurisdiction, or

        (iii) is by its terms, or by implication, governed by English law, or

        (iv) contains a term to the effect that the High Court shall have jurisdiction to hear and determine any action in respect of the contract;

    (e) the claim is brought in respect of a breach committed within the jurisdiction of a contract made within or out of the jurisdiction, and irrespective of the fact, if such be the case, that the breach was preceded or accompanied by a breach committed out of the jurisdiction that rendered impossible the performance of so much of the contract as ought to have been performed within the jurisdiction;

    (f) the claim is founded on a tort and the damage was sustained, or resulted from an act committed, within the jurisdiction;

    (g) the whole subject-matter of the action is land situate within the jurisdiction (with or without rents or profits) or the perpetuation of testimony relating to land so situate;

    (h) the claim is brought to construe, rectify, set aside or enforce an act, deed, will, contract, obligation or liability affecting land situate within the jurisdiction;

    (i) the claim is made for a debt secured on immovable property or is made to assert, declare or determine proprietary or possessory rights, or rights of security, in or over movable property, or to obtain authority to dispose of movable property, situate within the jurisdiction;

    (j) the claim is brought to execute the trusts of a written instrument being trusts that ought to be executed according to English law and of which the person to be served with the writ is a trustee, or for any relief or remedy which might be obtained in any such action;

    (k) the claim is made for the administration of the estate of a person who died domiciled within the jurisdiction or for any relief or remedy which might be obtained in any such action;

    (l) the claim is brought in a probate action within the meaning of Order 76;

    (m) the claim is brought to enforce any judgment or arbitral award;

---

63. See *The Spiliada* [1986] 3 All E.R. 843 at p. 858 per Lord Goff on likelihood or ordering service out depending on the nature of the claim.

(n) the claim is brought against a defendant not domiciled in Scotland or Northern Ireland in respect of a claim by the Commissioners of Inland Revenue for or in relation to any of the duties or taxes which have been, or are for the time being, placed under their care and management;

(o) the claim is brought under the Nuclear Installations Act 1965 or in respect of contributions under the Social Security Act 1975;

(p) the claim is made for a sum to which the Directive of the Council of the European Communities dated 15th March 1976 No. 76/308/EEC applies, and service is to be effected in a country which is a member State of the European Economic Community.

(q) the claim is made under the Drug Trafficking Offences Act 1986;

(r) the claim is made under the Financial Services Act 1986 or the Banking Act 1987;

(s) the claim is made under Part VI of the Criminal Justice Act 1988.

(t) the claim is brought for money had and received or for an account or other relief against the defendant as constructive trustee, and the defendant's alleged liability arises out of acts committed, whether by him or otherwise, within the jurisdiction.

(u) the claim is made under the Immigration (Carriers' Liability) Act 1987."

Order 75, rule 2(1) (categories excluded from Order 11, rule 1(1)) reads:

"Without prejudice to sections 61 and 62(2) of the Act, or to any other enactment or rule providing for the assignment of causes and matters to the Queen's Bench Division—

(a) every action to enforce a claim for damage, loss of life or personal injury arising out of—
  (i) a collision between ships, or
  (ii) the carrying out of or omission to carry out a manoeuvre in the case of one or more of two or more ships, or
  (iii) non-compliance, on the part of one or more of two or more ships, with the collision regulations,

(b) every limitation action, and

(c) every action to enforce a claim under section 1 of the Merchant Shipping (Oil Pollution) Act 1971 or section 4 of the Merchant Shipping Act 1974,

shall be assigned to that Division and taken by the Admiralty Court.

(2) In this rule 'collision regulations' means regulations under section 418 of the Merchant Shipping Act 1894 or section 21 of the Merchant Shipping Act 1979, or any such rules as are mentioned in subsection (1) of section 421 of the Act of 1894 or any rules made under subsection (2) of the said section 421."

RSC Order 11

The categories of claim are various going to the general legal nature of the action (as contract, tort, security on property or money had and received), types of action (as trust, probate or administration of estates), land within the jurisdiction, parties to the action, general "relief" (grant of injunction, enforcement of a judgment or arbitral award) and specific statutory causes of action. The connections with England required also vary depending on the ground, in some instances it being connection with the person on whom the writ is to be served, the place of an event leading to the claim (the contract, breach of contract or tort), the subject-matter of the claim (property), or the governing law being English (in contract or trust actions).

As with all lists of claims there are problems of construction. The list still bears the hallmarks of its historical roots, with claims or details being added as deemed appropriate. Bearing in mind the general discretion it must at least be arguable that, apart from statutory provisions, it would be preferable simply to list general connections without referring to particular causes of action, as it is for the defendant domiciled in England.

These seems no good reason to exclude a claim for breach of bailment,[64] nor, prior to the addition of para. (t), a quasi contractual claim but include one based on tort and contract (as to which see *infra*). The writ must identify the cause of action on which suit is brought. It must be set aside if not so, unless the terms of pleading were apt to cover the factual and legal basis of the claim.[65]

Some of the provisions are somewhat loosely drafted in that the jurisdiction is based on specified connections without always linking the connection to the service of the writ. In *Union International Insurance Co. Ltd.* v. *Jubilee Insurance Co. Ltd.*[66] it was held that the provision relating to an agent trading in the jurisdiction for an overseas principal ((d)(ii)) referred only to a defendant's agent. Phillips J. thought that a similar qualification had to be made in respect of rule 1(1)(a) and (c) to require the person specified to be the person served. It does seem clear that the connections are to bring a defendant not present within England within the scope of English jurisdiction because of other connections.

Chiefly relevant to maritime claims are the provisions relating to contract, tort, parties to the action and remedies. Of these it is sufficient simply to note the provisions as to tort (requiring the sustaining of damage or an act causing the damage), as to parties (the domicile of the defendant in England and the service of a writ on a person who is a "necessary or proper party" to proceedings already instituted), and enforcement of a judgment or arbitral award.

As to contract (paras. 1(d) and 1(e)) the rules focus on "a contract". In holding in 1993 in *Gulf Bank KSC* v. *Mitsubishi Ltd.*[67] that a declaration that a contract exists is within the rule Hobhouse J. expressed the view that paragraphs (d) and (e) were intended to make a comprehensive reference to contractual claims. However in 1989 in *Finnish Marine Insurance Co. Ltd.* v. *Protective National Insurance Co.*[68] it was held that seeking a declaration that there was no contract was not within the paragraph. A distinction was drawn between the assertion that a contract was discharged and that one had never been entered into at all—in the latter case there was no claim "affecting" a contract. Whether such a restriction was intended is perhaps dubious but any quasi contractual claim for return of moneys paid on the basis of a contract would now come within paragraph (t).

Seeking an injunction

By para. (1)(b) service out may be permitted if "an injunction is sought ordering the defendant to do or refrain from doing anything within the jurisdiction". In 1977 In *The Siskina*[69] it was held by the House of Lords that this ground required the existence of a legal or equitable right in England "and enforceable here by a final judgment".

According to this approach, therefore, it cannot therefore be a ground for the grant of an injunction to restrain the disposal of assets pending a claim (a "*Mareva* injunction") unless that claim is within the jurisdiction of an English court. However, by s.25 of the Civil Jurisdiction and Judgments Act 1982 (as amended by the 1991 Act) a court may order interim relief in connection with any proceedings in any matter in a court of a

---

64. See *The Agia Skepi* [1992] 2 Lloyd's Rep. 467.
65. *Excess Insurance Co. Ltd.* v. *Astra SA Insurance Co.* [1995] LMLN 396.
66. [1991] 2 Lloyd's Rep. 89.
67. [1994] 1 Lloyd's Rep. 323. Where a claim by a company against a director was not contractual or quasi contractual so the case did not fall within para. 1(d): *Newtherapeutics Ltd.* v. *Katz* [1991] 2 All E.R. 151.
68. [1989] 2 Lloyd's Rep. 99.
69. [1979] A.C. 210; [1978] 1 Lloyd's Rep. 1.

country party to the Brussels or Lugano Conventions. Paragraph 1(b) must be read in the context of that enactment so that although in some cases leave to serve will be required, that leave cannot be refused on the ground that there are no substantive proceedings before an English court. Paragraph (1)(b) is therefore available to support proceedings before an English court or proceedings before a foreign court which the English court is statutorily empowered to support.[70] Further and more broadly, any construction of *The Siskina* that, apart from statutory authority in respect of foreign proceedings, it is only in respect of English proceedings that an injunction will lie has been questioned. First, the "jurisdiction" of the English court extends to staying proceedings on grounds, for example, of an arbitration or foreign forum agreement or *forum non conveniens*. So, it is said, the criteria is the power of the English court to grant the substantive relief not whether it will in fact do so.[71] Even more generally it may be arguable that any restriction such as imposed in *The Siskina* is inconsistent with the unfettered statutory power of the courts to grant injunctions.[72]

THE MERITS

Until the House of Lords decision there was considerable uncertainty about the standard of proof and the plaintiff's task generally. A number of judges expressed concern that the issue of service out was taking on aspects of a trial of the action and the approach now adopted emphasizes more the establishment of an issue to be tried rather than the likely success of the claim.[73] Further whatever the difficulties of interpreting the concepts it is clear that in the view of the House of Lords a serious issue to be tried is a lower standard than a good arguable case.[74]

THE APPROPRIATE FORUM

In addition to showing that there is an arguable case that the claim is within Order 11 and that there is a serious issue to be tried the plaintiff must establish that England is clearly the most appropriate forum for the action. Until the decision of the House of Lords in 1986 in *The Spiliada*[75] this element of the requirement was treated as part of a general discretion to be exercised once the matter was shown within the rules. It was neither identified as akin to the issue of the plea of inappropriate forum made by a defendant seeking to

---

70. *X* v. *Y* [1989] 2 Lloyd's Rep. 561.

71. See *Channel Tunnel Group Ltd.* v. *Balfour Beatty Construction Ltd.* [1993] 1 All E.R. 664 (H.L.) per Lord Browne-Wilkinson, Lord Goff, Lord Keith.

72. *Ibid.*

73. So a cause of action may be pleaded in the alternative either as to the legal basis or the defendant there being a serious issue to be tried in respect of each. (See *The Agia Skepi* [1992] 2 Lloyd's Rep. 467; *The Ines* [1993] 2 Lloyd's Rep. 492—owners' or charterers' bills of lading.)

74. Thereby drawing a distinction between two concepts equated in the context of the Brussels Convention by Dillon L.J. in *Molnlycke AB* v. *Procter and Gamble Ltd.* [1992] 4 All E.R. 47.

75. [1987] A.C. 460; [1987] 1 Lloyd's Rep. 1.

persuade a court not to exercise an established jurisdiction, nor always separated from the question of the strength of the plaintiff's case on the merits.

In *The Spiliada* Lord Goff pointed out that whether England was clearly the most appropriate forum may well vary according to the ground on which the claim was based and further that the importance of the ground (for example a contract was governed by English law) would depend on the circumstances of the case. The factors relevant to the appropriate forum are discussed in Chapter 12. It suffices here to note that the principle is judicially neutral—that it is where the case should be tried "suitably for the interests of all the parties and the ends of justice". The difference in applying it to service to and stay of proceedings in which there is jurisdiction lies in placing the burden of proof on plaintiff or defendant. The legitimate or personal advantage of the plaintiff cannot therefore be conclusive or indeed more than a relevant factor. Other factors are, for example, damage, procedure, convenience of witnesses, limitation of time or liability, and delay in trial.

A compelling factor without contrary evidence must be the existence of an English jurisdiction agreement. An arbitration clause is not a bar to service out but where a defendant is entitled under the Arbitration Act 1975 to a stay for arbitration proceedings and intends to claim that right the order for service should not stand.[76]

The exercise of discretion in this regard is essentially for the first instance judge. An appellate court is not entitled to interfere with the exercise on simple disagreement—it must be satisfied that it was based on wrong principles.[77] And this seems to work in practice—although the extent to which courts require that it be shown that an English court is "clearly" the most appropriate may be open to some doubt. English courts have never been loath to assert the power to adjudge—even, it has to be said, where the governing law is not English. The need now simply to show a serious issue to be tried in respect of the strength of case may however shift the focus to the appropriate central element—the connection with England.

SERVICE OF THE WRIT (WITH OR WITHOUT LEAVE)[78]

There are two types of service permitted.[79] There may be (i) service by the plaintiff or his agent or (ii) where applicable, service under Convention provisions may be through a foreign government, judicial authority, British consular authority or in States parties to the Hague Convention on the Service Abroad of Judicial and Extrajudicial Document in Civil or Commercial Matters 1965, a designated Convention authority.

---

76. See *A and B* v. *C and D* [1982] 1 Lloyd's Rep. 166 (on appeal with a new scenario [1983] 2 Lloyd's Rep. 35).

77. By the rules where the application is for grant of leave to serve a writ in Scotland or Northern Ireland regard must be paid to comparative cost and convenience where there is a concurrent remedy (r. 1(3))—but this is a particular application of the general principle now accepted. An appeal from an order to serve out or refusal to permit service is not a rehearing—the critical date for consideration is the date of the order (*ISC* v. *Guerin* [1992] 2 Lloyd's Rep. 482.

78. For a summary of the regime applicable to service out of the jurisdiction without leave see Practice Direction 6 October 1989 [1989] 3 All E.R. 562.

79. RSC Order 11, rr. 5–8. The service of a writ on a foreign state is through the Central Office and the Secretary of State (r. 7).

(i) Service by the plaintiff or his agent [80]

Relevance of foreign law

No provision of the rules authorizes or requires the doing of anything contrary to the law of the country in which service is to be affected. Subject to that proviso and to any express provision the procedure for service is governed by English law as the *lex fori*. So the validity of the writ for service is for English law.[81]

PROCEDURE

Order 10 (applying to service of writs within England) applies save for the provision of service by post or through a letter box. So the writ may be served personally on an individual defendant or agent or it may be deemed to have been served by indorsement of acceptance by the defendant's solicitor or acknowledgment of service by the defendant. There is no requirement of personal service if it is served on the person in accordance with the law of the country in which service is affected. Postal service is good if permitted by an applicable Convention—the Hague Convention allowing for such service if the state of destination does not object.[82]

Service on a corporation will be valid if on the officer of the corporation as provided by Order 65, rule 3 (unless this is contrary to the law of the country in which the corporation is resident) or in a way permitted by that law (whether physically in that country or elsewhere). So in *The Vrontados*[83] it was held that service on a company incorporated in Panama would have been valid if there had been service on a director in England.

(ii) Service through governmental, judicial or consular authority[84]

The ability to use foreign governmental or judicial authorities or British consular authorities varies according to whether the state of service is a party to a Civil Procedure Convention with the United Kingdom. Unless the service is to be made in a party to the Hague Convention of 1965 service may not be through such authorities in the Republic of Ireland or any Commonwealth country or associated state or colony.

If the state is not a party to the Hague Convention but there is a Civil Procedure Convention with the United Kingdom the writ may be served through the judicial authorities or the consular authorities. Where the country in which the writ is to be served is a party to the Hague Convention of 1965 the service may be through the authority designated in the Convention or if the law of the country permits, through the judicial authorities or British consulate. If there is no Civil Procedure Convention or the Hague

---

80. RSC Order 11, r. 5(1)–(3).

81. *The Reefer Creole* [1994] 1 Lloyd's Rep. 584—service of a writ in Greece, leave not being required, must be within the four months prescribed by English law. It was not sufficient for service to be within time under Greek law. It is for the defendant to show that service is prohibited by the law of the state in which the writ is served. See e.g. *The Oinoussin Pride* [1991] 1 Lloyd's Rep. 126.

82. See *Thierry Noirhomme* v. *David Walklate* [1992] 1 Lloyd's Rep. 427.

83. [1982] 2 Lloyd's Rep. 241—but in considering whether there may be an alternative forum to England the rules of service of that forum are relevant and not the recognition of foreign law by English law. See *The Handgate* [1987] 1 Lloyd's Rep. 142.

84. RSC Order 11, r. 6. A request for service in this way is to be accompanied by a translation and made to the Central Office. It will then be transmitted to the Foreign Office (r. 6(4)–(7)). Such request must contain an undertaking to meet expenses (r. 8). An official certificate by the authority is evidence of service (r. 5(5)(6)).

Convention does not apply the service is naturally subject to the willingness of the foreign government and recognition of the local law of service through the consular authority.

RSC ORDER 75

Actions assigned to Admiralty by Order 75, rule 2, are excluded from Order 11, rule 1 (see *supra*). Service of the writ out of the jurisdiction is governed by Order 75, rule 4.

The categories of claims and the discretion to permit service out

Oil pollution claims

The discretion is expressed generally with the specific application of the provision of rule 4(2)—that no leave shall be granted unless it is made sufficiently to appear that the case is a proper one for jurisdiction under the Order. While the principles established in *Seaconsar* and *The Spiliada* in relation to Order 11 are no doubt applicable they must be applied in the context of the particular causes of action and the statutory frameworks, focusing the actions primarily on the place of damage or threat of damage (see Chapter 2).

Collision claims and limitation actions

Jurisdiction in collision claims is restricted by the Supreme Court Act, s. 22, in accordance with the Collision (Civil Jurisdiction) Convention 1952 (see Chapters 2, 12). The "service out" provisions match the collision jurisdiction *in personam* but also apply to limitation actions.[85] No writ in a collision or limitation action my be served out of England in respect of any incident not within inland waters or on a defendant not habitually resident or domiciled there unless (i) the defendant has submitted or agreed to submit to the jurisdiction or (ii) an action arising out of the same incident is or has been before the High Court. As with oil pollution claims the *Seaconsar* and *Spiliada* principles will apply in the context of the particular claims.

In 1979 in *The Aegean Captain*[86] Sheen J. rejected an argument that an application for leave to serve out of the jurisdiction should be approached as if it were made under RSC Order 11. However, although the argument based on equivalence of one Order with the other was said to focus on discretion it seems as if the issue went more to the grounds on which service could be ordered. It was argued that the ground of "arising out of the same incident" under RSC Order 75, rule 4(1)(c), should require that a defendant had been "properly served" within the jurisdiction and that the alleged defendant was a necessary and proper party to the proceedings within the meaning of Order 11, rule 1(c). Clearly, as Sheen J. said, the ground of "the same incident" is of much wider scope.[87] In the event,

---

85. RSC Order 75, r. 4(1).
86. [1980] 2 Lloyd's Rep. 617.
87. So the fact that a defendant agreed to English jurisdiction (as distinct from being served in the jurisdiction) did not prevent the service of a writ on a third party out of the jurisdiction on the basis that an action arising out of the same incident was proceeding in the High Court. In the action the plaintiff cargo owners issued a writ against the carrier and through that action sought to bring in the owner of the other ship—and succeeded.

the discretion was exercised on a ground consistent with the *Spiliada* criteria (i.e. natural forum, the need for one enquiry, the presence of assets in England, the advantages of English proceedings to the plaintiffs, the seeking of tactical advantage by the defendant).

Service of the writ

There are no provisions of Order 75 equivalent to or applying those of Order 11 relating to service. However, there is no reason for any different "service" regime to apply simply because the writ is in an Admiralty action.

SUBMISSION TO THE JURISDICTION

A. THROUGH PROCEDURAL STEPS

Submission to jurisdiction on the merits requires participation in or an express or implied agreement to participate in proceedings other than to challenge the jurisdiction.[88] Such participation may be in an action *in rem* (see *supra*). As indicated in the discussion of the procedural steps, acknowledgment of service of itself is not submission[89] but lacking any challenge to jurisdiction will probably become so, at least so far as the establishment of jurisdiction is concerned. "Acceptance" of service by a solicitor will, if authorized, be submission[90] but not necessarily so if the writ was not valid for service when served.[91] There seems a growing and welcome judicial acceptance of the distinction between interlocutory remedy jurisdiction and jurisdiction on the merits. Although each case will depend on the type of participation it seems less certain than formerly that agreement to an interlocutory remedy would necessarily be submission to the merits. That should depend on whether the court had jurisdiction to grant an interlocutory remedy apart from the merits *and* the defendant's understanding of his action.[92]

An application for a stay of proceedings is not a challenge to jurisdiction but a challenge to the exercise of jurisdiction—it may indicate there has been submission.[93] However, considering an application for a stay of substantive proceedings when there was a concurrent challenge to jurisdiction did not mean that the court assumed jurisdiction over

88. See *The Messiniaki Tolmi* [1984] 1 Lloyd's Rep. 266 (C.A.). For an example of submission of issues to the court by seeking relief in respect of arbitration see *The Paola D'Alesio* [1994] 2 Lloyd's Rep. 366.

89. Neither acknowledgment nor notice of intention to defend as such constitutes submission (Order 12, r. 8(6)(7)) and, indeed, there must be acknowledgment and notice to defend for challenge to be made to the writ (r. 8). An application for extension of time to serve a defence necessarily involves extension of time to set aside the writ and where a statement of claim was defective the application was not submission to the merits—the defendant was entitled to see the nature of the claim (*Lawson* v. *Midland Travellers Ltd.* [1993] 1 All E.R. 989).

90. *Manta Line Inc.* v. *Seraphim Sofianites* [1984] 1 Lloyd's Rep. 14. See also fn. 32.

91. *The Nova Scotia* [1993] 1 Lloyd's Rep. 154—where the writ was served out of time—in those circumstances it is a question of fact whether the irregularity was waived. This approach seems to reduce the effect of the *Manta* decision to cases where there was no ground of challenge in any event.

92. For the earlier approach see *Esal* v. *Pujara* [1989] 2 Lloyd's Rep. 479 (consent to a *Mareva* injunction)—a little hard unless it was made clear that such consent was submission to the merits jurisdiction. As to an application to strike out a claim see *Eagle Star Insurance Ltd.* v. *Yuval Insurance Ltd.* [1978] 1 Lloyd's Rep. 357.

93. See *The Messiniaki Tolmi* (fn. 88).

the substance—all that was stayed was the challenge to the jurisdiction.[94] Similarly an application for a stay under the Arbitration Act 1975 is not submission to the merits but the jurisdiction of the court to decide if it has jurisdiction.[95]

B. THROUGH SUBMISSION BEFORE THE COURT

Actual "submission" is clearly enough to establish jurisdiction *in personam*. Procedural steps may be necessary to establish required procedural contact but power to hear the case is established.[96]

REMEDIES AVAILABLE

A. ON THE MERITS

Any remedy which is part of the general rules of English law is available. There are no special maritime rules. So money judgments, injunction, specific performance, restitution, rescission and declaration of title are all applicable.[97] However, limitation of liability imposes a limit on compensation not generally applicable.[98]

B. PROVISIONAL REMEDIES—THE "MAREVA" INJUNCTION

There is no statutory link between the action *in personam* and any provisional remedy. But there is a general ability to grant interim relief. This ability is particularly employed in a pre-trial context in the *Mareva* injunction to provide some protective measure for claimants. Until the relatively recent use of this injunction English law was notoriously defective in lacking a general protective provision so as to enable a claimant to ensure that the defendant has assets available for execution of judgment. Such a defect had a great effect in the maritime area, where many defendants were either foreign based or could switch their assets out of England. The defect was underlined by the fact that many insurance funds were in England and in some cases would represent the sole assets of a defendant—or the sole assets easily available to satisfy a claim. It might now be argued that the enthusiasm to remedy the defect on occasion may have tended to the robust—with perhaps too little regard for its effect on a trading concern. Interim relief, including the *Mareva* injunction, is considered in Part III.

---

94. *Williams and Glyns Bank plc* v. *Astro Dinamico Compania SA* [1984] 1 Lloyd's Rep. 453 (H.L.).

95. *Finnish Marine Insurance Co. Ltd.* v. *Protective Insurance Ltd.* [1989] 2 Lloyd's Rep. 99; [1989] 2 All E.R. 929. Such reasoning would seem to apply only if a stay is mandatory (although it was not so restricted in the case).

96. Such procedural contact could be through acknowledgment of service of the writ (see RSC Order 15, r. 1(5)). If a defendant actually appeared to contest the merits but later refused to complete the procedural steps it is at least arguable that there would be no basis for an action (see e.g. *Broken Hill Proprietary Co. Ltd.* v. *Theodore Xenakis* [1982] 2 Lloyd's Rep. 304). The matter still depends on the extent to which procedure governs.

97. See further Chap. 25.

98. See Chap. 24.

COUNTY COURT JURISDICTION

County court jurisdiction is by district.[99] The Admiralty jurisdiction *in personam* encompasses claims identical to those listed in the Supreme Court act 1981, s.20(2)(d)–(r).[100]

The jurisdiction equivalent to the claims listed in the Supreme Court Act is limited primarily by the value of the claim. Subject to extension by agreement of the parties the general limit is £5,000 with a limit of £15,000 on salvage claims.[101] Even within these limits the courts seem not to have been greatly used but the jurisdiction should be kept in mind because of lower costs and the possibility that in a case within county court jurisdiction but fought in the High Court costs might be limited.[102]

---

99. County Courts Act 1984, s.26. It includes adjacent sea up to three miles from the shore (*ibid*). Each district now has a court for Admiralty purposes. (See Civil Courts Order 1983, SI 713/1983.)

100. County Courts Act 1984, s.27(1) as amended by Merchant Shipping (Salvage and Pollution) Act 1994, Sch. 2, para. 7, and 28(2). For procedure, see County Court Rules 1981 (as amended), Order 40.

101. County Courts Act 1984, s.27(2) and (6). Jurisdiction in regard to collision cases is limited as is that of the High Court (s.30) as to which see *supra*.

102. For specific limitation on costs in some actions, see the County Courts Act 1984, s.29. Where costs are discretionary the High Court has not been unwilling to allow costs as in a High Court action. See e.g. *The Katcher (No. 2)* [1968] 2 Lloyd's Rep. 29. But cf. (salvage) *The Golden Sands* [1975] 2 Lloyd's Rep. 166.

CHAPTER 10

Enforcement of Maritime Claims by an Action "in rem"

1. AVAILABILITY OF THE ACTION "IN REM"

Unlike the action *in personam* the action *in rem* lies only for claims within Admiralty jurisdiction, but it is not to be equated with that jurisdiction. It lies for such claims as:

   (i) are *specified* in the Supreme Court Act 1981 as being enforceable by an action *in rem* (s.21(2)–(4));
   (ii) arguably being "*in rem*" claims which fall within the "sweeping up" clause of the Supreme Court Act 1981 (s.20(1)(c));
   (iii) may be specified in statutes enacted after the Supreme Court Act 1981.

CLAIMS SPECIFIED BY THE SUPREME COURT ACT 1981

(a) Specified claims

The Supreme Court Act 1981, s.21(2) and (4) provides:

"(2) In the case of any such claim as is mentioned in section 20(2)(a), (c) or (s) or any such question as is mentioned in section 20(2)(b), an action in rem may be brought in the High Court against the ship or property in connection with which the claim or question arises.
   (4) In the case of any such claim as is mentioned in section 20(2)(e) to (r), where—
      (a) the claim arises in connection with a ship; and
      (b) the person who would be liable on the claim in an action in personam ("the relevant person") was, when the cause of action arose, the owner or charterer of, or in possession or in control of, the ship,
an action in rem may (whether or not the claim gives rise to a maritime lien on that ship) be brought in the High Court against—
      (i) that ship, if at the time when the action is brought the relevant person is either the beneficial owner of that ship as respects all the shares in it or the charterer of it under a charter by demise; or
      (ii) any other ship of which, at the time when the action is brought, the relevant person is the beneficial owner as respects all the shares in it."

The provisions do not define an "action *in rem*" any more than s.21(1) defines an action *in personam*. But in varying degrees the provisions indicate the assets (ship or property) in relation to which the action may be brought and the connection (if any) which there must be between the asset and the person liable *in personam*.[1] The claims are examined in Chapter 2.

---

1. The Act of 1981 rid the framework of the confusing concept of "invocation" of jurisdiction used in the Administration of Justice Act of 1956. "Invocation" was replaced by the more direct and simple: "an action may be brought".

(b) Maritime liens (s.21(3))

Section 21(3) provides:

"(3) In any case in which there is a maritime lien or other charge on any ship, aircraft or other property for the amount claimed, an action in rem may be brought in the High Court against that ship, aircraft or property."

Neither maritime lien nor charge are defined by the Act. Not only must the characteristics of the action *in rem* be sought elsewhere but in this instance the claims which attract such a lien. It should be emphasized that claims attracting maritime liens are all included in the claims specified in the Act as enforceable by an action *in rem*. Maritime liens are examined in Chapter 18.

(c) The "sweeping up" clause (s.20(1)(c))

Following the specification of claims within Admiralty jurisdiction the Supreme Court Act 1981, s.20(1)(c), provides that within that jurisdiction of the High Court there shall be "any other Admiralty jurisdiction which it had immediately before the commencement of this Act".

The scope of this provision was considered in Chapter 2 in the examination of "maritime claims". Even if the clause includes enforceability *in rem*, enquiry must be made in respect of the claim at issue whether an action *in rem* lies and further, any conditions (e.g. liability of a shipowner *in personam*) required for it to lie.

(d) Damage received by a ship (s.20(2)(d))

The Act does not specifically provide for an action *in rem* to enforce a claim based on "damage received by a ship", although in many cases such a claim would also fall within other headings (such as, for example, damage done by a ship). The claim based on "damage received" was included in the Administration of Justice Act 1956 in the list of those claims enforceable by an action *in rem* but, as has been said in Chapter 2, in 1976, in *The Jade*, the House of Lords intimated that it was wrongly included. The basis of that opinion was the requirement that (in common with the claims now listed in paras (e)–(r)) the claim arose "in connection with a ship". That requirement was said to refer to the ship in relation to which the action *in rem* was brought—the ship subject to arrest. It followed that claims based on "damage received by a ship" referred to the plaintiff's ship. As a plaintiff could not arrest his own ship, no action *in rem* would lie.

In examining these arguments in Chapter 2 it was contended that while the ground does not appear in the Arrest Convention:

(a) there is nothing inherently inconsistent in a claim based on damage received by a ship and an action *in rem* in relation to the damage[2];

(b) to construe the requirement of the claim being "in connection with a ship" as referring only to the ship that is the target of the claim, may be to restrict the

---

2. An owner may wish to arrest a demise chartered ship of his own or, possibly, a ship of his of which possession has been taken by a mortgagee or some other person. For an example of an owner arresting his own ship in respect of a possession claim see *The Daien Maru 18* [1986] 1 Lloyd's Rep. 387 (Singapore).

"sister ship" remedy—if an action will lie against "any other ship" if it will also lie against the ship involved in the claim;

(c) the requirement of the ship connection can be read as excluding actions *in rem* in respect of cargo and freight[3];

(d) in any event, jurisdiction "*in rem*" may arguably be maintained under the Act of 1981 through the "sweeping up" clause.[4]

2. ACTIONS "IN REM" AND SPECIFIED CATEGORIES OF CLAIM

The conditions relevant to bringing an action *in rem* vary according to whether the claim falls within (i) s.21(1)(e)–(r); (ii) s.21(1)(a), (b), (c) or (s); (iii) the sweeping up clause; or (iv) the maritime lien.

(I) ACTION "IN REM" IN RELATION TO CLAIMS WITHIN S.20(2)(e)–(r)

The action may be brought under s.21(4) against either the particular ship creating the claim or (in broad terms) a "sister ship". Although in respect of any claim any number of writs may be issued or any number of ships named in one writ, one ship only may be served with a writ or arrested in respect of one claim.[5] There are a number of prerequisites for bringing the action.

A. *Against the particular ship*

The claim must arise "in connection with a ship". The provision may be read simply as restricting the jurisdiction to "ship" claims, i.e. excluding the other "property" referred to in s.21(2) and (3).[6] Alternatively, as already discussed, it may restrict claims to the ship in relation to which claims arise. So, as in *The Jade*,[7] an owner cannot bring an action *in rem* in relation to damage received by his ship, nor, despite cases prior to *The Jade* in which such an action had been allowed,[8] a tug owner in respect of a contract of towage.[9] However, it is to be noted that in 1982 in *The Span Terza*[10] no point seems to have been taken by counsel or the court that an owner seeking to enforce an action for breach of charterparty could not bring an action *in rem* against a "sister" ship owned by the charterer.

It is arguable that a claim *in rem* based on "damage received by a ship" should not be allowed as such a ground is not provided by the Arrest Convention. However, conversely,

3. Although such jurisdiction *in rem* may arguably be founded on the sweeping up clause (see *infra* and Chap. 2).
4. Supreme Court Act 1981, s.20(1)(c)—see *infra* and Chap. 2.
5. Supreme Court Act 1981, s.21(8).
6. i.e. cargo or freight.
7. [1976] 2 Lloyd's Rep. 1.
8. *The Queen of the South* [1968] P. 449. See also *The Conoco Britannia* [1972] 2 Q.B. 543. For a criticism of the decisions, see *The Jade* [1976] 1 All E.R. 441, at p. 459 (C.A.) per Sir Gordon Willmer.
9. As e.g. *The Conoco Britannia* [1972] 1 Q.B. 543.
10. [1982] 1 Lloyd's Rep. 225.

to prohibit a claim on the ground that the statute limits the availability of the action *in rem* to claims "in connection with" the ship at which the action is aimed seems to read a restriction into the Convention not specified in the text of the Convention. In particular it may exclude the "sister ship" remedy in respect of grounds within the Convention.[11]

The person who would be liable on the claim in an action in personam[12] was *when the cause of action arose* the owner or charterer[13] or in possession or control of the ship *and when the action was brought* was either the beneficial owner of that ship as respects all the shares in it or the charterer of it under a charter by demise.

The ability to bring an action *in rem* under this provision, therefore, requires at two critical times a link between the person liable *in personam* and the ship concerned in the claim. Such a link does not appear in the provision relating to maritime liens or that relating to the claims of s.20(2)(a)–(c) and (s).

(a) Legislative history and present scope

The Supreme Court Act 1981 largely reflects the Administration of Justice Act 1956 which enacted (in part) the Arrest Convention 1952 into English law. Although the United Kingdom has ratified the Convention it still has not brought English law into line with its provisions as regards (i) the availability of arrest apart from an action on the merits in England[14]; and (ii) the link between liability *in personam* on the claim and the availability of arrest of any ship to which a claim relates. Part of the problem is that, in traditional English terms, to allow arrest necessarily implies the bringing of the action *in rem* of which arrest is an inherent part. So in both aspects of failure to enact the Arrest Convention a critical feature is the continued exclusive connection of arrest with the action on the merits.

The reform that did not succeed

The Supreme Court Bill 1981 (which was to lead to the Act) attempted to bring English law "up to the limits" provided by the Convention with the replacement of the requirement of the legislative provision requiring personal liability of persons linked with the ship. In respect of any claim now set out in s.20(2)(e)–(r) it was proposed that "being a claim which arises in connection with a ship . . . an action in rem may be brought in the High Court against that ship". Strong objection was voiced to the clause in the debate in the House of Lords by Lord Diplock acting, as he said, on behalf of various shipping

---

11. The draft revision of the Arrest Convention is based on a non-exclusive list of maritime claims (see Article 1).

12. i.e. who would be liable if the action succeeded. See *The St Elefterio* [1957] P. 179, at p. 185; *The St Merriel* [1963] 1 All E.R. 537, at p. 544. It is assumed that the relevant person has his habitual residence or place of business in England (Supreme Court Act 1981, s.21(2))—a provision designed to overcome the necessity of such a link in collision actions (see Chap. 3), but which is needed in a wider sphere in respect of actions within the Civil Jurisdiction and Judgments Act 1982 (see Chap. 4).

13. For a discussion on whether the "charterer" is confined to demise charterer, see *infra*.

14. The Civil Jurisdiction and Judgments Act 1982 (s.26) permits the retention of "property" arrested or other security given if proceedings are stayed—the arrest on security requires that an action *in rem* has been instituted. As to the lack of control of the court over the issue of the warrant of arrest, see *The Varna* [1993] 2 Lloyd's Rep. 253 and Chap. 15.

organizations. He complained that "in what is primarily a Bill to consolidate procedural matters a serious and important change in substantive law was slipping through".[15] Indeed it was. And it may be said that it was only last minute attention to the clause and its effects that prevented English law from moving towards meeting its international obligations.

Reforms that were made—extension to demise chartered ships

The scope of the action *in rem* was extended by the Supreme Court Act 1981, the action available against a ship that is demise chartered at the time the action is brought—the charterer being liable *in personam*.[16] In relation to the claims now set out in s.20(1)(e)–(r) the Administration of Justice Act 1956 linked the action *in rem* to liability *in personam* of the user (i.e. owner, charterer or in possession or control) who was or by the time of issue of writ had become the owner. An action *in rem* against the ship in respect of which the claim arose would lie only if the person liable on the claim *in personam* was the beneficial owner "as respect all the shares" in the ship when the jurisdiction was invoked.[17] In 1970 in *The Andrea Ursula*[18] Brandon J. held that demise charterers were beneficial owners within the meaning of the statutory requirement: but in 1977 in *The I Congreso del Partido*[19] Goff J. held that "beneficially owned" meant what it said, i.e. equitable ownership whether or not accompanied by legal ownership. In 1979 in *The Father Thames*[20] Sheen J. agreed that demise charterers did not qualify as beneficial owners.

The prerequisite that the person liable *in personam* should be the beneficial owner at the time that the action was brought was clearly contrary to the Arrest Convention so far as the ability to arrest was concerned. In effect, the Convention provides simply that the ship in respect of which the claim arose may be arrested, whoever is liable in respect of the claim, and there is no reference to ownership or any other link at the time the action is brought.[21]

The Supreme Court Act 1981 brings England one step closer to compliance with international obligations and the Civil Jurisdiction and Judgments Act 1982 provides a further shuffle in the same direction. And, at acceptable diplomatic pace, perhaps 25 years is a not unexpected time lag—particularly as the international obligations may move

15. H.L. Vol. 418, col. 1308 but the revised deep Convention is closer to English law. See Chap. 15.

16. Strictly the amendment means that a ship owned, chartered or in possession or control of a person liable on a claim when the cause of action arose and demise chartered by the same person at the time the action is brought may be attacked through an action *in rem*. In practice it is the ship under demise charter at both times that is the prime focus of the amendment.

17. i.e. when the writ was issued. See *The Monica S* [1968] P. 741; *The Vasso* [1984] 1 Lloyd's Rep. 235. Reliance on "invoking of jurisdiction" led to problems of interpretation (compare *The Monica S* with *The Berny* [1979] Q.B. 80) and has been sensibly replaced in the Supreme Court Act 1981 by "the bringing of an action".

18. [1973] Q.B. 265.

19. [1978] 1 All E.R. 1169. The case went to the House of Lords on a separate point of sovereign immunity ([1981] 2 All E.R. 1064).

20. [1979] 2 Lloyd's Rep. 364.

21. See Art. 3. The Convention provides that it is not to be construed as creating a right of action not arising under the law of the court having seisin of the case (Art. 9)—but there would be little point in the Convention if it did not impose an obligation to adopt its provisions. The revision draft is much closer to English law.

towards English law through adoption of a revised Arrest Convention much closer to that law (see Chapter 15).

(b) The critical "in personam" link points

"When the cause of action arose"

This refers to the happening of the event on which the claim is based (such as collision or damage to goods). The requirement is that the person who would if sued be liable *in personam*—must be the "owner, charterer or in possession or control". If, therefore, the owner would be liable *in personam* the existence of a charterparty will not affect the liability of the ship to an action *in rem* and hence arrest. Conversely, if the ship were in the possession of a person without authority of the owner this requirement would on the literal wording still be met by that person's liability *in personam*.

In 1988 in *The Evpo Agnic*[22] Lord Donaldson expressed the view that "owner" meant "registered owner" and did not in this context encompass a beneficial owner who was not a registered owner. That conclusion followed, thought Lord Donaldson, because in the statute "owners" and "beneficial owners" appeared and in the Arrest Convention "owner" is equated with "registered owner", and registered owners were a contradiction to registers of owners relied on for flag purposes.

In 1993 in *The OHM Mariana Ex Peony*[23] the Singapore Court of Appeal disagreed with the construction, holding that "beneficial owner" in this context meant the "right to sell, dispose of or alienate the ship". So where under a financing arrangement the defendants were beneficial but not registered owners they were "owners" for the purposes of the provision. And with respect this seems clearly correct—"owner" in both statute and the Arrest Convention can include beneficial owner.

In the same case Lord Donaldson also gave as his view that "charterer" meant "demise charterer" and "in possession or in control" a person in the position of a demise charterer (such as, perhaps, a salvor). This construction of demise charterer is however inconsistent with the earlier decision of the Court of Appeal in *The Span Terza*[24] reading the word as it appears. To restrict "charterer" to "demise charterer" is first to qualify a clear statutory phrase and secondly to exclude from liability *in rem* maritime property of the time or voyage charterer against whom action is brought. There seems little policy ground for this restriction (see *infra*).

It may be arguable that to attach liability of a shipowner to a ship in the possession of another without authority is going too far towards pure "*in rem*" liability, but such liability could not accrue because of the second link requirement and it would open the door to enforcement against any ship owned by the wrongdoer (see *infra*).

"When the action is brought"

This requirement greatly restricts the availability of the action *in rem* in respect of the claims to which it refers. The person who would be liable *in personam* must be either the beneficial owner as respects all the shares in the ship or the charterer by demise when

22. [1988] 2 Lloyd's Rep. 411; [1988] 3 All E.R. 810.
23. [1993] LMLN 361.
24. [1982] 1 Lloyd's Rep. 225.

the action is brought.[25] As a result, it would seem that a ship held in co-ownership will be liable to an action *in rem* only if all the co-owners would if sued be liable *in personam*.[26] The action is brought on the *issue* rather than on the *service* of the writ *in rem*.[27] As a consequence, any change in ownership after the writ is issued is irrelevant to the availability of the action *in rem*, and it follows that practical advice to plaintiffs must be to issue a writ as soon as possible.[28]

"The beneficial owner"

In the context of the equivalent provision of the Administration of Justice Act 1956 (which did not include the alternative of charterer by demise) the phrase refers "only to such ownership as is vested in a person who whether or not he is the legal owner is in any case the equitable owner".[29] The prime example of a beneficial owner is the beneficiary under a trust, but it would perhaps more often apply to an unregistered owner (e.g. having purchased but not registered). It *may* include the purchaser once a contract of sale has been entered into provided:

> (i) the vendor had no right to terminate the contract for non-payment of the price or breach of some other obligation by the purchaser; and
> (ii) the contract is capable of specific performance.[30]

THE CORPORATE OWNER—PIERCING THE VEIL?

In strict English legal theory the corporate veil provides substantive protection. No matter who the shareholders are or whether the corporate ownership is but a part of a corporate structure which in every aspect save legal theory is a whole, the corporation presents a solid legal obstacle to a plaintiff. If a ship is "owned" by a company it matters not that that company is in turn effectively owned by an individual or another company. The beneficial owner of the ship is a legal person and it is irrelevant that that "person" is itself beneficially owned by another. Clearly, such an approach is a boon to the one-ship company and encourages growth of such entities. In 1977 in *The Aventicum*[31] the issue was whether the corporate veil could be lifted so as to trace the ownership of a ship through its registered corporate owner. Slynn J. expressed some willingness to look beyond the immediate ownership. But in 1980 in *The Maritime Trader*[32] Sheen J. indicated that, in his view, it is only where the relationship between corporate "owner"

25. The connection between an action *in rem* and liability of *in personam* reflects English historical Admiralty rules rather than the Arrest Convention 1952 but in the draft revision the need for a similar link in non-maritime lien claims not based on ownership possession or mortgage is introduced (see Article 3).

26. See e.g. *The Fort Laramie* (1922) 31 C.L.R. 56.

27. See fn. 17 *supra*.

28. More than one writ may be issued and more than one ship named in one writ but only one ship may be served (see *infra*), s.21(8)). As to the renewal of writs, see *infra* and Chap. 11.

29. *The I Congreso del Partido* [1978] 1 All E.R. 1169, at p. 1201 (Goff J.).

30. See *The Permina 3001* [1979] 1 Lloyd's Rep. 327 (Singapore C.A.) and *infra*. A contract of sale specifying that ownership is transferred only on registration would also not operate to transfer any "beneficial ownership".

31. [1978] 1 Lloyd's Rep. 184.

32. [1981] 2 Lloyd's Rep. 153.

and ship is clearly a sham or amounts to fraud that any other legal person can be said to be the beneficial owner.[33] Such an approach places a heavy onus on the plaintiff.[34] However, in 1982 in *The Saudi Prince*[35] Sheen J. held that the plaintiff had satisfied the onus and that on the facts of that case would have been prepared to recognize that a transfer was a sham.

In the *Evpo Agnic*[36] the Court of Appeal maintained the effectiveness of the veil, reiterating that the possibility of lifting it depends on establishing registration as a sham. Lord Donaldson thought that a governing shareholder in a number of one-ship companies could control the use of the assets of individual companies to his advantage without any structure of holding and subsidiary companies or sham registered companies. There was a legitimate interest in running the ships as a fleet and this could be accomplished by a series of one-ship companies. The statutory provision did not permit the arrest of a ship of a sister company of the owners of a particular ship.[37]

THE EFFECT OF LONG-TERM FINANCING ARRANGEMENTS

The traditional method of ship financing through mortgage of the ship and assignment of insurance policies and charter-hire raises no question as to beneficial ownership of the ship. This clearly remains with the mortgagor borrower. But where the financing arrangement is an instalment sale or, in effect, hire purchase (with an option to buy built in) it may be argued that the "purchaser" is the beneficial owner. It seems clear that it is only if the arrangement could be enforced by specific performance that any such contention could be argued. If the vendor has the power to revoke the agreement in default of payment this is a compelling factor in the "beneficial ownership" remaining in the vendor.[38] Even where the remedy of specific performance is available it does not necessarily follow that as regards a ship (a chattel) the beneficial ownership has passed.[39] The remedy is discretionary and, further, it may be argued, the principle of transfer of equitable ownership resulting from a contract to sell has little place in the context of the code represented by the Sale of Goods Act 1979.[40]

---

33. For continued legal emphasis on the separate legal identity of companies within a group and the need to prove a sham see *Adams* v. *Cape Industries* [1991] 1 All E.R. 929 at pp. 1016–1026 (C.A.). But as accepted in *Adams* the veil is not entirely prohibitive, see e.g. (i) two cases involving RSC Order 47 (conferring the power to stay execution of a judgment or order) where the courts have expressed a willingness to look behind the corporate structure—on the basis that the discretion given by the Order is sufficiently wide for the purpose (see *Orri* v. *Moundreas* [1981] Com.L.R. 168; *Canada Enterprises Corpn Ltd.* v. *MacNab Distilleries Ltd.* [1981] Com.L.R. 167) and (ii) the scope of injunctive relief (*The Coral Rose* [1991] 1 Lloyd's Rep. 563; *The Coral Rose (No. 3)* [1991] 2 Lloyd's Rep. 374 (as to which see Chapter 16—*Mareva* injunction)).

34. Even if the somewhat wider approach of Slynn J. be followed a further hurdle for the plaintiff is whether "ownership" of the company requires ownership of 100 per cent of the shares in the company—in turn owning all the shares in the ship.

35. [1982] 2 Lloyd's Rep. 255.

36. [1988] 3 All E.R. 810; [1988] 2 Lloyd's Rep. 411.

37. Distinguishing the "spiriting away of a ship from legal owners with, however, the retention of beneficial ownership" (such as, said Lord Donaldson, had occurred in *The Saudi Prince* (*supra*)). See also for a similar approach *The Skaw Prince* [1994] LMLN 390 (Singapore High Court); *The Andres Bonifaco* [1994] LMLN 382 (Singapore High Court).

38. See *The Permina 3001* [1979] 1 Lloyd's Rep. 327.

39. See *The Despina Pontikos* [1975] E.A.R. 38 (East Africa C.A.).

40. See *Re Wait* [1927] 1 Ch. 606; *The Aliakmon* [1986] 2 All E.R. 145; [1986] 2 Lloyd's Rep. 1 (H.L.).

"THE CHARTERER BY DEMISE"

This alternative to the beneficial owner was added by the Supreme Court Act 1981. It had been judicially established that in the Administration of Justice Act 1956 beneficial ownership did not include the demise charterer.[41] But, as has been said, it was clear that in limiting the action *in rem* (and hence the ability to arrest) to a ship the beneficial owner of which was the person who would be liable *in personam*, the United Kingdom was not complying with the Arrest Convention 1952. The Convention provides for arrest without reference to the liability *in personam* of the owner.[42] As a result of amendment to the English legislation, liability of a ship to an action *in rem* (and thence arrest) where the owner is not liable may now occur where the ship is demise chartered without any reference to beneficial ownership. Such liability *may* also occur through the maritime lien provision[43] or (more unlikely) through the sweeping up clause.

B. Against a "sister" ship (i.e. a ship other than the particular ship)

For an action *in rem* to lie:

(i) the claim must arise in connection with a ship—an identical requirement to that relating to the particular ship;

(ii) the person who would be liable on the claim in an action *in personam* was *when the cause of action arose* the owner or charterer or in possession or control of the ship; *and*

when the action was brought the beneficial owner as respects all the shares in the "sister" ship.

The Arrest Convention provides in Art. 3(1) that "subject to the provisions of paragraph (4) of this Article and Article 10 a claimant may arrest the ship in respect of which the claim arose" (in Convention terms "the particular ship") or "any other ship which is owned by the person who was, at the time when the maritime claim arose, the owner of the particular ship . . . ".[44]

Article 3, para. 4 provides:

"When in the case of a charter by demise of a ship the charterer and not the registered owner is liable in respect of a maritime claim relating to that ship, the claimant may arrest such ship or any other ship in the ownership of the charterer by demise, subject to the provisions of this Convention but no other ship in the ownership of the registered owner shall be liable to arrest in respect of such maritime claims.[45]

The provisions of this paragraph shall apply to any case in which a person other than the registered owner of a ship is liable in respect of a maritime claim relating to that ship."

The construction of "beneficial owner" is identical to that discussed in relation to an action "against" the particular ship concerned in the claim. Apart from this, two questions arose in relation to the English statutory provision:

41. See *The I Congreso del Partido*, fn. 29; *The Father Thames* [1979] 2 Lloyd's Rep. 364.
42. See Art. 3(1). But the draft revised Convention does link non-maritime lien claims (other than possessory, proprietary or mortgage claims) to personal liability of the owner or bareboat charterer (see Chapter 15).
43. See *infra* and Chap. 18.
44. The provision does not apply to claims concerning ownership mortgage or dispute between co-owners (*ibid*).
45. As to the draft revision of the Convention see Chap. 15.

    (a) could an action *in rem* be brought against a "sister ship" other than one in the same ownership as the ship in respect of which the claim arose;

    (b) if so, could an action *in rem* be brought against a ship owned by any charterer (i.e. time or voyage as well as demise).

(a) May an action "in rem" be brought against a sister ship other than that in the same ownership as the ship in respect of which the claim arose?

The Administration of Justice Act 1956

Under the Act of 1956 it was clear that, as with the Convention, an action could be brought against a ship other than the ship in respect of which the claim arose if owned by the owner of the ship in respect of which the claim arose. But it was not clear whether an action could be brought against any ship owned by a charterer liable in respect of a claim.

    The suggestion of the restriction of the sister ship clause in English law to ships owned by the owner of the particular ship had its root in what can only be called a throwaway line of Lord Diplock in *The Jade*[46]—a case not at all concerned with this issue. In *The Permina 108*[47] the Court of Appeal of Singapore refused to restrict the sister ship remedy to ships in common ownership with that in respect of which the claim arose, but in *The Maritime Trader*[48] Sheen J. felt obliged to follow Lord Diplock's view. In 1981 in *The Span Terza*[49] (apparently to be approached with caution because of the hurried nature of the proceedings) the Court of Appeal felt no constraint because of Lord Diplock's dictum and approached the matter as one of construction of the Act of 1956.

    In *The Span Terza* the question was whether, in an action by shipowners against time charterers of their ship, the plaintiffs could arrest a ship owned by the time charterers. Contrary to the decision in *The Maritime Trader*, it seemed to be assumed that had the defendants been demise charterers there would be no issue—the arrest could stand. By a majority the court held that the arrest of the ship did stand (see *infra*).

The Supreme Court Act 1981

Whatever doubts there may have been because of the drafting of the Act of 1956 and Lord Diplock's statement, it seems clear that under s.21(4) of the Supreme Court Act 1981[50] an action *in rem* will lie against ships owned by "charterers" of or those in possession or control of the ship in respect of which the claim arose. Redrafting has cured the ambiguity of the language, and the only point remaining is whether "charterer" is restricted to demise charterers.

(b) If an action "in rem" may be brought in relation to a ship owned by a "charterer" does this include time or voyage charterer?

Although in *The Maritime Trader* the defendant was a time charterer the issue was decided on the basis that the Act of 1956 did not permit ships owned by defendant charterers to

46. [1976] 2 Lloyd's Rep. 1.
47. [1978] 1 Lloyd's Rep. 311.
48. [1981] 2 Lloyd's Rep. 153.
49. [1982] 1 Lloyd's Rep. 225.
50. See *supra*.

be arrested. In *The Span Terza* the majority of the Court of Appeal thought that "charterer" in the relevant provision of the Administration of Justice Act 1956 included all types of charterer. And this conclusion is strengthened in the Supreme Court Act 1981 by the specification of charter by demise in s.21(4) where that particular type of charter is meant.

The court considered Art. 3 of the Arrest Convention and, in particular, the final sentences of Art. 3(4). It appears that Donaldson L.J. (who dissented) saw that sentence as limiting the effect of Art. 3(4) to charterer by demise, presumably as a kind of emphasis.[51] The majority (Stephenson L.J. and Sir David Cairns) applied the sentence so as to adapt the rule contained in Art. 3(4) relating to demise charterers to cases within the final sentence. The majority view provides further English legal adherence to the Convention as well as accords with a policy of making ships owned by those liable on maritime claims available to claimants. It may be arguable that (as the English legislation continues to provide) a ship under time or voyage charter should not be available to a claimant who has a claim against the charterers. But if this is so it seems only sensible to make ships owned by such charterers available to arrest in the enforcement of the claim.[52]

(II) ACTION "IN REM" IN RELATION TO CLAIMS AND QUESTIONS WITHIN S.20(2)(a), (b), (c), (s)

While the provision relating to claims falling within paras (e)–(r) does not define an action *in rem* it specifies the circumstances in which it may lie. The provision in relation to claims concerning ownership, possession, forfeiture or restoration of a seized ship simply provides that an action *in rem* may be brought "against the ship or property in connection with which the claim . . . arises". It may therefore be brought against property[53] other than a ship but is restricted to *the* ship or property involved in the claim. Other characteristics, and in particular the connection, if any, between liability *in personam* and the right to bring an action *in rem* depend on judicial developments. These are considered in Chapter 2.

(III) "MARITIME LIEN OR OTHER CHARGE" (S.21(3))

The claims to which a maritime lien is attached is examined in Chapter 2. As has been said, they are well established and unlikely to be judicially extended. The claims are:

1. Bottomry and respondentia

51. In 1988 in the *Evpo Agnic* (fn. 22) the same judge in giving the judgment of the court (without reference to any case) expressed the same view—but the case turned on the meaning of "beneficial owner" in s.21(4) (see *supra*).

52. For a contrary view, see Tettenborn [1981] LMCLQ 507. It is also arguable that for some countries the Convention simply restricted "*saisie conservatoire*" and by definition therefore affected only the debtor's property. The revised draft expressly makes ships owned by demise time or voyage charterers liable to arrest in non-maritime lien claims (other than ownership or possession claims) provided that under national law there may be judicial sale of the ship (Art. 3). As to maritime lien claims see *infra*.

53. The only relevant "property" other than a ship appears to be in para. (s)—"goods" which are forfeited or condemned or subject of a claim for droits of Admiralty (cf. Chap. 2).

2. Damage done by a ship
3. Salvage
4. Seamen's and masters' wages
5. Masters' disbursements.

All such claims save respondentia fall within s.20(2)(e)–(r) and are enforceable by action *in rem* as maritime liens *or* by an action *in rem* under the framework of s.21(4). To be enforceable under s.21(4) the claim must be in connection with a ship, and against a ship, and there must be the required contact between ship and the person liable *in personam*. However, there may be an action in relation to a ship other than that directly concerned.

The action *in rem* enforcing a claim *as a maritime lien* under s.21(3) is against the "ship or other property" in which there is a maritime lien. It is clear that a claim falling within s.20 which also attracts a maritime lien may be enforced under either s.21(3) or s.21(4). However, the general restriction of arrest to "one ship for one claim" (now enshrined in respect of s.21(4) in s.21(8)) would prevent the use of both methods in enforcement of the same claim against more than one ship. There may be no action in relation to a ship not directly concerned.

The concept of maritime lien

The Supreme Court Act 1981 does not define the maritime lien. It does not specify the claims which attract it and, apart from limiting its force to the asset to which it may attach, ignores its characteristics. There is no specific indication of the "property" apart from ships to which it may attach, nor of the conditions of its attachment and there is no reference to any link with liability *in personam*. To discover the effect of s.21(3), therefore, recourse must be had to judicial definition and development. The characteristics of the maritime lien are discussed in Chapter 18.

"Or other charge"

As is said in Chapter 2, the phrase has been judicially declared to encompass only (in English law) any statutory charge equated to a maritime lien or (in foreign law) a charge amounting to an English maritime lien.[54]

(IV) THE "SWEEPING UP" CLAUSE

The clause is expressed in jurisdictional terms—and arguably incorporates without any qualification "jurisdiction" exercised by the Admiralty Court prior to the Act of 1981. If the jurisdiction encompasses "*in rem*" claims the nature of those claims and prerequisites for enforceability must be sought elsewhere than in the Act (see Chapter 2).

---

54. See *The Acrux* [1965] P. 391; *The St Merriel* [1963] P. 247.

3. JURISDICTION PREREQUISITES OTHER THAN THE SUPREME COURT ACT 1981

The statute provides *part* of the jurisdictional structure for the enforcement of maritime claims. In specifying the detailed conditions for bringing an action, (i) s.21(4) (referring to paras (e)–(r)) treats the question of enforceability through the action *in rem* as a jurisdictional question; (ii) s.21(2) and (3) (referring to paras (a)–(c) and (s) and maritime liens) omits any reference to prerequisites in bringing such an action; (iii) s.20(1)(c) (the sweeping up clause) specifies no jurisdictional or other details. No reference is made in relation to any claim to:

    (i) the link required between the dispute and England for the establishment of English jurisdiction in a case with a foreign element; and

    (ii) to the remedies available in an action *in rem*.

The prerequisite of the English link goes essentially to jurisdiction—to the ability to bring the action—and is considered in this chapter. The question of remedy is considered in Chapters 15 and 25.

LINK BETWEEN THE ISSUE AND ENGLAND REQUIRED FOR AN ACTION "IN REM" TO BE BROUGHT

The basic rule

As with the action *in personam*, no hint is given in the Supreme Court Act 1981 of the basic rule for either the establishment of substantive jurisdiction or the procedural commencement of the action *in rem*. In English law apart from statutory provisions as with the action *in personam*, substantive jurisdiction is connected with procedural commencement. Both jurisdiction and commencement depend primarily on the service of the writ *in rem* on the "defendant"—the ship or property in relation to which it is issued.[55] It does not require arrest of the ship but arrest would provide substantive jurisdiction with procedural commencement through service of writ. Unlike the writ *in personam* a writ *in rem* cannot be served out of England or its territorial waters.

The basic rule is qualified:

    (a) By statutory provisions (in practice based on Convention requirements)[56]

    (b) By the rule that service of a writ *in rem* on the ship is unnecessary where:

        (i) the defendant's solicitor accepts service on behalf of the defendant; or

        (ii) the defendant acknowledges service of the writ; or

        (iii) the defendant acknowledges issue of the writ.[57]

---

55. The rules governing issue and service of the writ *in rem* and the issue and service of the warrant of arrest are set out in RSC Order 75, "Admiralty Proceedings" (see in particular rules 3, 5, 8, 10, 11). See *infra*. As to county court jurisdiction, see *infra*.

56. As (e.g.) under the CMR Art. 36. (See Carriage of Goods by Road Act 1965, s.1 and Sch.). Under the Hamburg Rules, Art. 21, a defendant may, on providing adequate security, obtain transfer of the action in a jurisdiction based on arrest to a jurisdiction specified. See Chapter 15.

57. See RSC Order 75, rr. 3(6) and 8(2).

Such acts initiate the action *in rem* and, subject to any challenge to jurisdiction may provide the basis of submission to the jurisdiction formerly provided by appearance to create jurisdiction *in personam*.[58]

The effect of Conventions

The availability of the action *in rem* is subject to Convention jurisdiction bases just as is an action *in personam*. The action *in rem* as a national method of enforcement of a maritime claim is as such affected by Convention jurisdiction provisions restricting the courts before which a case may be brought. However, given the required Convention link (as, for example, the court of the state of embarking in the Athens Convention 1974 concerning passengers) the availability of the action as a method of suit would only be restricted if the Convention provisions went directly to the method of enforcement or essential elements of the action *in rem*. So an action under the Collision Jurisdiction Convention requires a specified connection (including arrest or security given in lieu of arrest), and so it would therefore seem service of the writ *in rem* would not of itself constitute jurisdiction if the Convention were directly enacted. Conventions and their effect are discussed in Chapter 3.

The effect of the Brussels and Lugano Conventions

The effect of the Lugano Convention is identical to that of the Brussels Convention. As said in Chapter 4 neither Convention makes any specific reference to an action *in rem*. In *The Deichland*[59] the Court of Appeal rejected the contention that the action *in rem* fell outside the Brussels Convention. For the purposes of the Conventions the person who would be liable *in personam* was "the defendant". So, apart from any other Convention jurisdiction base, the defendant charterer in that case had to be sued in the court of domicile (see Chapter 4). If the domicile was in the United Kingdom the Convention would have no relevance to suit by an action *in rem*. The Convention is concerned only with allocation of jurisdiction not in the method of its exercise.

However, as has also been seen, Convention jurisdiction may be based on elements directly relevant to the action *in rem*—arrest or security given in lieu.[60] So again, provided the Convention link is present the action *in rem* will lie. As a consequence where a dispute falls within the Brussels or Lugano Convention the action *in rem* will not lie simply through service of the writ, this not being a jurisdiction of either Convention or of a Convention applied through Article 57 (see Chapters 5, 6).

As with the action *in personam* in the face of the need to satisfy jurisdiction requirements the service of the writ loses its jurisdictional role. As with the writ *in personam* the writ *in rem* retains its procedural role in commencing proceedings, but, it also retains its function in initiating a method of suit which of itself in English law has substantive consequences. These, however, are irrelevant to the Convention jurisdiction requirements which turn entirely on assessing whether they are satisfied as they appear in the Convention (see Chapters 5, 12).

---

58. See *infra* and Chap. 9.
59. [1989] 2 Lloyd's Rep. 113; [1989] 2 All E.R. 1066.
60. Through Article 57. See *The Deichland* (fn. 59); *The Po* [1991] 2 Lloyd's Rep. 206 and Chap. 6.

Participation in the proceedings will amount to the Convention jurisdiction base of "appearance".[61] Acknowledgment of issue or service may amount to "appearance" on the same principles as applicable to an action *in personam* (as to which see Chapter 9).

4. PROCEDURE OF AN ACTION "IN REM"

COMMENCEMENT

An action *in rem* is commenced by the issue of a writ *in rem*. Where an action may be brought against a "sister ship" the writ may name one or more ships. Only one ship may, however, be served—but service on a ship liable in a claim will not be prohibited by service (in mistake) of a ship not liable.[62] If the writ is amended to delete a claim in respect of a particular ship that claim may be the subject of service of a further ship.[63] The writ is valid for service for 12 months.[64]

Renewal of the writ is subject to the same rules as for an action *in personam*—in particular that for renewal a "good reason" must be shown (see Chapter 9). As for a writ *in personam* the writ may be renewed after the expiry of a limitation period, but an explanation will be needed for the failure to serve within the period (see Chapter 11). Relevant factors in relation to the renewal of a writ *in rem* were considered in 1977 in *The Berny*[65] and in 1979 in *The Helene Roth*.[66] Even though the pronouncement of these precedes the firm establishment of "good" rather than "exceptional" reason as the criterion for extension, the relevance remains.

In 1977 in *The Berny* Brandon J. reviewed the principles of renewal of a writ when there was no question of a time bar. He said that renewal was not automatic. The plaintiff must produce a "good and sufficient cause" or issue a fresh writ. As to such a renewal of a writ *in rem* he said:

"In my opinion, when the ground for renewal is broadly that it has not been possible to effect service, a plaintiff must in order to show good and sufficient cause for renewal establish one or other of three matters as follows: (1) that none of the ships proceeded against in respect of the same claim, whether in one action or more than one action, has been, or will be, present at a place within the jurisdiction during the currency of the writ; alternatively (2) that if any of the ships has been, or will be, present at a place within the jurisdiction during the currency of the writ, the length or other circumstances of her visit to or stay at such place were not, or will not be, such as to afford reasonable opportunity for effecting service on her and arresting her; alternatively (3) that if any of the ships has been, or will be, present at a place within the jurisdiction during the currency of the writ, the value of such ship was not or will not be, great enough to provide adequate security for the claim, whereas the value of all or some or one of the other ships proceeded against would be sufficient, or anyhow more nearly sufficient, to do so."[67]

---

61. See *The Anna H* [1995] 1 Lloyd's Rep. 11 and Chap. 5.
62. Supreme Court Act 1981, s.21(8); *The Stephan J* [1985] 2 Lloyd's Rep. 344.
63. See *The Damavand* [1993] LMLN 357 (Singapore C.A.). The court also held that a plaintiff could amend the writ at any time subject to the rules of court and abuse of process and therefore was not prohibited from deleting a claim so as to remove a ship as the target for a claim.
64. RSC Order 6, r. 8(1)(a) (as amended by SI 1993/2133).
65. [1977] 2 Lloyd's Rep. 533; [1978] 1 All E.R. 1068.
66. [1980] 1 Lloyd's Rep. 477; [1980] 1 All E.R. 1078.
67. *Ibid*, at p. 103. Brandon J. thereby disapproved of previous Admiralty practice of considering renewal of a writ naming a number of ships on a ship by ship basis—it is necessary for the plaintiff to prove that none of the ships become available to him within the criteria laid down.

In 1979 in *The Helene Roth* it was argued that where, after the issue of a writ but before its service, a ship was sold, the writ should not be renewed even if the claimant satisfied the criteria set out by Brandon J. It was said that, particularly where the ship was sold after the writ had expired, it was bought with immunity from service just as if a time bar had operated and the ship had achieved immunity from suit. Sheen J. refused to accept the analogy:

"The existence of a time-bar is known to the plaintiff's advisers. They are under a duty to pursue an action diligently. If, due to their inaction, the validity of a writ expires, it is not necessarily unjust that the plaintiff should lose his right to proceed. But a change of ownership of a ship has a different quality. The sale may be carried out secretly, and it is voluntary. If it is to have the effect for which counsel contends, then the defendants are able to introduce their own time-bar without bringing it to the notice of the plaintiffs."

Sheen J. held that where the ownership had changed, the case for renewal was "overwhelming" as, unlike most actions, the claimant could not issue a fresh writ. Unless the claim attracted a maritime lien, sale of a ship subject to an action *in rem* would defeat the claim *in rem*.[68]

Service of the writ

The writ must be served within England on the property "against which the action is brought" save:

(i) in the case of freight when it is to be served on either the cargo in respect of which the freight is payable or the ship in which that cargo was carried[69];

(ii) in the case of property sold by the Marshal, when a sealed copy is filed in the registry;

(iii) where, according to the rules relevant to a writ *in personam*, it is deemed to be served (a) when the defendant's solicitor indorses on the writ that he accepts service on behalf of the defendant; (b) where the writ is not duly served but the defendant acknowledges service.[70]

Acknowledgment of issue of writ

A defendant not served may become a party by acknowledging the issue of the writ.

Acknowledgment of service of writ

As with an action *in personam* a "defendant" served with a writ may acknowledge service of it and once acknowledged may indicate that jurisdiction is contested.

---

68. Since 1 January 1982 a sale of a ship remaining under the same demise charter after issue of a writ would not defeat the claim against the demise charterer—otherwise the situation is unchanged (see Chap. 4).

69. If the suit is in relation to cargo in the custody of a person who will not permit access to it a copy of a writ should be left with that person (rule 11(2)(b)).

70. See generally RSC Order 75, rr. 8, 11. It has been held (rightly it is suggested) by the Singapore C.A. that deemed service through indorsement cannot operate to remove a plaintiff's choice of ship where a writ names numerous ships—Order 75, r. 8(2) renders service on the ship unnecessary. It does not provide that such service is deemed to have been made. See *The Fierbinti* [1994] LMLN 396. See also *The Pacific Bear* [1979] Hong Kong L.R. 125.

AMENDMENT OF THE WRIT

A writ may be amended on the same principles as a writ *in personam* including the relevance of expiry of the limitation period. The addition of a ship or property is not, it is suggested, adding a new party but it is creating either a new cause of action or a new liability in relation to which if the limitation period had expired the defendant would have an accrued defence. The amendment should not be allowed therefore, either because the claim is made outside the period or, if the claim is "related back" to the original claim, because the defendant will be deprived of a limitation defence in respect of an asset for which there could be no liability *in rem* if another action was brought.[71]

PERSONS OTHER THAN DEFENDANTS

There is a general discretion to join persons interested in a dispute to proceedings as a party or a third party. In addition in an action *in rem* a person who has an interest in property arrested or proceedings of the sale of that property in court may with the leave of the court intervene on the action. Such person thereby becomes a party.

A person whose interest in the claim is solely because of an interest in the property arising (as to the purchaser) should not acknowledge service of a writ but apply to intervene on the action.[72] In this way a clear procedural distinction is drawn between a person liable on the claim (and who would therefore be subject to *in personam* injunctions through acknowledgment) and the person whose "liability" is limited to the value of the interest in the property. There is no *in personam* jurisdiction in respect of the intervention because of the leave to intervene.[73]

DURATION OF ACTION "*IN REM*"

An action *in rem* has as its target ship, cargo or freight, although both as a matter of common sense and law there must be persons who are interested parties and who will suffer loss if the action succeeds. The "lien" created or enforced by the action *in rem* may be initially enforced through arrest, but apart from the "arrest" jurisdiction base under the Brussels or Lugano Convention the action *in rem* is not dependent initially on arrest or that such arrest continues or bail given in lieu.

The view of Sheen J. that release of a ship from arrest upon the giving of contractual security ended the action *in rem* was disapproved by the Court of Appeal in *The Maciej Rataj*.[74] Sheen J.'s view with respect ignores the double function of arrest and the difference between arrest and the action *in rem*. As the learned judge held in *The Prinsengracht*[75] a conclusion later approved by the Court of Appeal in *The Anna H*[76] as

71. See the approach in *The Kusu Island* (1989) Singapore C.A. construing the Singapore rules of court (for discussion see [1990] LMCLQ 169). As to the limitation period see Chap. 11.
72. See *The Mara* [1988] 2 Lloyd's Rep. 459.
73. For an example of the procedural distinction operating to preserve a claim see *The Soeraya Emas* (Singapore H.C.) [1992] LMLN 338.
74. [1992] 2 Lloyd's Rep. 552.
75. [1993] 1 Lloyd's Rep. 41.
76. [1995] 1 Lloyd's Rep. 11. See Chap. 15.

consistent with the Arrest Convention arrest may be permitted in addition to security where needed to establish jurisdiction. Further, without express terms a contractual security should not be taken to be more than the replacement of the property by the undertaking (while the undertaking is good). It is not to be implied that it is necessarily to replace the lien reflected by the action *in rem* or to affect any maritime lien—save not to enforce it while the contract is in existence.

5. THE INTER-RELATIONSHIP OF ACTION "IN PERSONAM" AND ACTION "IN REM"

An action *in rem* may be brought concurrently or consecutively with an action *in personam*. Even where *in personam* jurisdiction is rooted in acknowledgment of service of a writ *in rem* (as to which see Chapter 9) the two actions do not merge. They continue cumulatively. Further, the action *in rem* does not melt away through release of the ship after acknowledgment of service (see *supra*). It does not merge in a judgment *in personam*,[77] it may be brought to enforce a foreign judgment *in rem*[78] or, where an arbitration clause can be seen as part of a contract enforceable through an action *in rem*, to enforce an arbitration award.[79]

The relationship between an action *in rem* and an action *in personam* is considered in Chapter 9 in the context of the creation of jurisdiction *in personam* through acknowledgment of service of the writ or solicitor's acceptance on a defendant's behalf. However, it is only persons having an interest in the ship or other property attached in the action who can normally be defendants and who, by joining issue on the writ *in rem*, thereby submit to an action *in personam*. So an action *in personam* cannot be created through a "non defendant *in rem*" acknowledging service of the writ *in rem*. Service of the writ *in personam* or the joinder of a defendant *in personam* after creation of an action *in personam* through acknowledgment by an "*in rem* defendant" would be required.[80]

EFFECT OF THE NATURE OF THE ACTION "IN REM" ON PROCEDURE AND REMEDIES

Despite the predominant English view that an action *in rem* is but a procedural device to put pressure on the defendant shipowner to appear and defend, it has several aspects going to disprove the procedural arguments. First, it does not lie in respect of any asset, secondly (and increasingly) it is available in relation to a ship when the shipowner is not liable *in personam*, thirdly, it is arguable that available remedies are restricted to those exercisable against the ship (e.g. damages) and to the value of the ship[81] and, fourthly, it continues to

77. See e.g. *The Rena K* [1979] 1 All E.R. 397, at p. 416 and case there cited. An action *in rem* will, therefore, lie to enforce a claim within its ambit in respect of which there is an unsatisfied judgment *in personam*.
78. *The Despina GK* [1982] 2 Lloyd's Rep. 555. But only if *in rem* jurisdiction is within the sweeping up clause. See Chap. 2.
79. *The Saint Anna* [1983] 1 Lloyd's Rep. 637.
80. See generally *Caltex Oil (Australia) Pty Ltd.* v. *The dredge Willemstad* (1975–76) 136 C.L.R. 529 (High Court of Australia). A person threatened with loss through an arrest may be permitted to intervene. See *The Mardina Merchant* [1974] 3 All E.R. 749.
81. See Chaps. 2, 25.

provide security in the ship for the claim even if the defendant shipowner appears. Further, a default judgment *in personam* may be entered on proof of service whereas *in rem* proof of the case is required.[82]

The curious hybrid nature of the action *in rem* as an action "against" property but necessarily focused on a defendant is illustrated by the application to it of the "acknowledgment of service" procedure.[83] Further, a "defendant" not served may acknowledge the issue of the writ *in rem*.[84] Lacking any subsequent objection to jurisdiction acknowledgment of issue or service of a writ *in rem* will found an action *in personam*, whereas it is the service (or the deemed service) which founds an action *in rem*. A writ *in rem* cannot be served by substituted service[85] within the jurisdiction or at all outside the jurisdiction. An action for summary judgment cannot be brought by an action *in rem*,[86] and an application for judgment in default of acknowledgment of service or other procedural requirement requires proof of the case.[87]

It is arguable that the *concept* of the action *in rem* confuses provisional remedy (arrest), jurisdiction on the merits and security on the claim. However, while it continues as the centrepiece of English Admiralty law there seems little point in attempting to conceal its unique and distinct characteristics through a pretence that it has no distinct *substantive* character. Such pretence simply hides the need for the separation of the different aspects of it and, hopefully, a more logical and clearer approach to each aspect.

6. COUNTY COURT JURISDICTION

County court jurisdiction *in rem* is identical to that of the Admiralty Court in respect of those claims listed in the Supreme Court Act 1981, s.20(e)–(r).[88] As with the jurisdiction *in personam* (considered in Chapter 9) the primary limitation is the value of the claim—subject to extension by agreement of the parties the general limit is £5,000 with a limit on salvage claims of £15,000.[89]

---

82. See e.g. RSC Order 75, r. 21(7) (*in rem*); RSC Order 13, r. 7 (*in personam*).
83. RSC Order 75, r. 3.
84. RSC Order 75, r. 3(6).
85. *The Good Herald* [1987] 1 Lloyd's Rep. 236—Sheen J. holding that the availability only applied to a document requiring to be served personally, the purpose being to bring it to the notice of the defendant.
86. RSC Order 14, r. 1(2)(c). Cf. *The August 8th* [1983] 1 Lloyd's Rep. 351 (considering Rules of Supreme Court of Singapore).
87. As distinct from an action *in personam* which requires only entering of the judgment.
88. County Courts Act 1984, ss.27(1), 28(3) and (4) as amended by the Merchant Shipping (Salvage and Pollution) Act 1994, Sch. 2, para. 7. Presumably s.27(1) controls s.28(3) so that a claim in bottomry is not within the jurisdiction. As to procedure (including arrest and sale), see County Court Rules 1981, Order 40.
89. County Courts Act 1984, s.27(2) and (6). There is no limit of the value of the *res* and (unlike the Admiralty Court) the court may order sale of the property even though not under arrest (County Court Rules 1981, Order 40, rule 13). Cf. Chapter 15.

CHAPTER 11

Delay in Suit

1. EFFECT OF DELAY

The period within which an action must be brought or steps in an action taken may be imposed by statute, by rule of court or by contract.[1] It may have varying consequences dependent on the terms of the prohibition. It may destroy the foundation of any claim, ban the bringing of a claim, provide a discretion in a court to prevent suit, affect the plaintiff's task in establishing the claim or simply affect costs.

The effect of delay in court proceedings or on enforcement of a right challenged in court proceedings will depend on the rules of the legal regime of which the court is part. The effect of delay in arbitral proceedings will depend on the extent to which the applicable legal regime, first, controls such proceedings and, secondly, allows parties freedom of contract in relation to them. Insofar as the parties are free to contract for and about the conduct of arbitration and control of the effect of the contract remains with the court, the legal consequence of delay will depend on contractual remedies enforced through the courts. Delays in the arbitral process are considered in the discussion on arbitration in Chapter 13.

EXTINGUISHMENT OF RIGHT OR REMEDY?

The effect of a time bar may be to destroy the claim or merely to prevent the remedy. In English law, apart from specific exceptions,[2] a time bar affects the remedy only. Connected with this view is, first, the classification of rules of time bar as "procedural" rather than substantive, which until the Foreign Limitation Periods Act 1984 had consequences in relation to the governing law in cases with a foreign element,[3] secondly, the need to plead the defence of time bar if it is to be relied on,[4] and, thirdly, the ability to rely on barred claims by way of defence or set off. Where exceptionally a claim is

---

1. Contractual provisions should be clear, their effect being the extent to which statute permits the parties to control time limits. For construction of a contractual provision confusing arbitration and litigation see *Indian Oil Corporation* v. *Vanol* [1992] 2 Lloyd's Rep. 563 (C.A.).
2. Apart from rules having their root in Convention (e.g. the Hague-Visby Rules) the exceptions concern title to chattels and land (see Limitation Act 1980, ss.3, 17 and 25).
3. See Chap. 26.
4. See e.g. RSC Order 18, r. 8.

extinguished through passing of time it will operate whether pleaded or not unless pleading is required.[5]

AVOIDANCE OF EFFECT OF DELAY

A time bar on commencement of proceedings or renewal of writ may unless otherwise provided be relaxed by agreement between the parties[6] or be rendered of no effect through a defendant being estopped from denying that time has not run.[7] There is no reason why agreement should not extend or avoid any "time requirement" unless the statutory provision expressly prohibits it. Subject to agreement or estoppel, however, there is a general duty on parties not to delay, and a party waiting until the last moment of a permitted period for a step accepts the risk of some event occurring which prevents a timely act.[8]

2. ASPECTS OF DELAY

Delay has a number of aspects:

    (i) The effect of a foreign time bar on English proceedings;
   (ii) Notice of claim;
  (iii) Commencement of suit—issue of writ;
   (iv) Service of writ;
    (v) Want of prosecution after service of writ;
   (vi) Procedural requirements as to steps in the action;
  (vii) Assertion of remedy.

---

5. See *ibid*. The Maritime Conventions Act 1911 s.8 (as applicable to collision claims) as from 1 January 1996 contained in Merchant Shipping Act 1995, s.190, is a statute of limitation which must be pleaded (see *The Llandovery Castle* [1920] P. 119); but the passing of time under the Hague or Hague-Visby Rules extinguishes the claim and presumably the claim cannot be resurrected by failure to plead. It would appear as if the provision of the Salvage Convention 1989 (see *infra*) is procedural and therefore should be pleaded.

6. See generally RSC Order 3, r. 5 and *infra*. These may be on express agreement to extend the period of limitation (see e.g. *The Clifford Maersk* [1982] 2 Lloyd's Rep. 251) or where permitted a framework of rules alternative to that containing the time bar (see e.g. *The Strathnewton* [1983] 1 Lloyd's Rep. 219—the effect of submission to Inter Club NYPE Agreement *and* incorporation of the Hague Rules in the same charterparty).

7. See e.g. *The Ion* [1980] 2 Lloyd's Rep. 245 (letter held to be representation that there would be no reliance on time bar); *The Henrik Sif* [1982] 1 Lloyd's Rep. 456 (defendant not sued estopped from denying that he was a party to the bill of lading); *The August Leonhardt* [1984] 1 Lloyd's Rep. 322 (parties assuming that a condition on which an extension was granted would be satisfied); *The Stolt Loyalty* [1995] 1 Lloyd's Rep. 598 (C.A.) (P. & I. club acting for owners and demise charterers granting extension on behalf of "owners"—demise charterers estopped from denying extension not granted by them). For an analysis of different kinds of estoppel, see *The Henrik Sif* and *The August Leonhardt*. As to estoppel and want of prosecution see *infra*.

8. So a solicitor must take care not to leave matters to the last moment. See e.g. (service of a writ) *The Vrontados* [1982] 2 Lloyd's Rep. 241; *The Vita* [1990] 1 Lloyd's Rep. 528; *The Mouana* [1991] 2 Lloyd's Rep. 441; (issue of writ) *The Al Tabith* [1995] 2 Lloyd's Rep. 336, nor should it be assumed that settlement negotiations prevent time running for limitation purposes (see e.g. *The Mouana* (*supra*), *The "Zhi Jiang Kou"* [1991] LMLN 300 C.A. NSW). An application for stay of proceedings should be made at the outset of proceedings before costs are incurred (*Mansour* v. *Mansour, The Times*, 2 January 1989).

1. EFFECT OF FOREIGN TIME BAR

(a) *In English proceedings*

Prior to Foreign Limitation Periods Act 1984

Procedural matters are generally governed by the law of forum, and traditionally English law viewed time bars as matters of procedure. It mattered not whether the foreign law saw them as substantive, with the result that where foreign law applied substantively the risk was increased of a conclusion which neither foreign nor English law would have contemplated.[9] Even when exceptionally English law classified a time bar as substantive (as for example the Hague-Visby Rules) English law may have continued to apply if (again as with the Hague-Visby Rules) the time bar formed part of a regime which was mandatory in an English court (as to which see Chapter 26).

The Foreign Limitation Periods Act 1984

The Foreign Limitation Periods Act 1984[10] changed the classification of time bars by providing that, in effect, subject to discretionary power to disallow, any issue of limitation is to be governed by the law governing the substantive matter.[11] Further any foreign judgment based on limitation is to be treated as a judgment in the merits. The foreign law is not to apply to the extent that it would cause "undue hardship to a person who is or might be made a party to the action or proceedings".[12] "Hardship" depends on an assessment of how the foreign law affects a party. It is not a balancing exercise as between the parties.[13] "Undue" means excessive, i.e. out of proportion to any fault there may have been.[14]

The Contracts (Applicable Law) Act 1990

The view of limitation as procedure is further fundamentally affected in respect of contract issues by the Contracts (Applicable Law) Act 1990 enacting the Rome Convention on the Law Applicable to Contractual Obligations (as to which see Chapter 26). By the Convention the "various ways of extinguishing obligation, prescription and limitation of actions" are matters for the law applicable to the contract. The application of that law is subject to "mandatory" rules of the law of the forum and the non-application of any rule "manifestly incompatible" with English public policy. A time bar is very unlikely to be

9. See e.g. *National Bank of Greece and Athens SA* v. *Metliss* [1958] A.C. 509.

10. The Act applies to all proceedings (including arbitration) commenced on or after 1 October 1985 so long as the limitation period under English law had not by then expired (s.7). The application of the Act may be relevant to the discretion to give leave to serve a writ out of the jurisdiction. See *Société Commerciale de Reassurance* v. *Eras International Ltd.* [1992] 1 Lloyd's Rep. 570 (C.A.).

11. Section 1. English law continues to decide the time at which proceedings have been commenced and the Limitation Act 1980, s.35 (relating to new claims in pending proceedings) applies—as to which see *infra*.

12. Section 2. Any power to extend or interrupt the period under foreign law is to be disregarded in considering "undue hardship" (s.2(3)). It was undue hardship where a defendant assured a plaintiff that insurers were dealing with a claim for compensation for personal injury (*Jones* v. *Trollope Colls Ltd, The Times*, 26 January 1990) or an extension granted for issue of writ was good by English law but not by foreign law (see *The Komninos S* [1991] 1 Lloyd's Rep. 370).

13. *Arab Monetary Fund* v. *Hashim (No. 9)* [1993] 1 Lloyd's Rep. 543 applying *Jones* v. *Trollope Colls* (fn 12).

14. See *ibid*.

so "manifestly incompatible" and so far as contract is concerned this would appear to take over from the "hardship" provisions of the 1984 Act.

(b) Staying English proceedings

(i) Jurisdiction agreement[15]

The operation of a time bar in a particular jurisdiction may affect the enforcement of a foreign jurisdiction clause in a contract. In 1976 in *The Adolf Warski*[16] three views were canvassed—that it is

(a) a factor favouring a stay since not to uphold the jurisdiction clause would be to deprive defendants of an accrued defence;

(b) a factor against a stay since it would leave plaintiffs with no claim; and

(c) neutral because of the conflict between (a) and (b).

Brandon J. preferred (b). Two members of the Court of Appeal preferred (c), the third stating no view. The case was decided both at first instance and on appeal without the need to opt for any view.

In 1981 in *The Blue Wave*[17] Sheen J. came down firmly in favour of (b) unless the plaintiff had unreasonably or without good cause or deliberately or advisedly allowed the time limit to expire without instituting alternative proceedings. With respect, the proviso hardly goes far enough to be consistent with the upholding of jurisdiction clauses.[18] A plaintiff may simply institute proceedings in a jurisdiction other than that which he dislikes (although to which he has contracted to submit) and wait for the time limit to expire in the one which he does not prefer. In effect this is what happened in *The Adolf Warski* and the defendants in that case could not be blamed if they felt aggrieved by the court's approach. It may be however that an action would be stayed on condition or undertaking that the time bar is not raised.

(ii) Forum non conveniens[19]

The approach of Sheen J. was approved as the proper influence of a time bar in a foreign jurisdiction on a plea of a more appropriate forum. In that context is has more force—for there is no prior agreement which the plaintiff is seeking to avoid. So even if apart from the time bar it is shown that there is a more appropriate forum than England in which the action would be time barred a stay should not be ordered if the plaintiff acted reasonably in bringing suit in time in England and not unreasonably in not bringing suit in the foreign forum.[20]

---

15. As to which, see Chap. 12.
16. [1976] 2 Lloyd's Rep. 241.
17. [1982] 1 Lloyd's Rep. 151. For an application of the proviso, see *The Nedloyd Schie* [1983] HKLR 17.
18. As to which, see Chap. 12.
19. As to which, see Chap. 12.
20. See *The Spiliada* [1987] A.C. 460; [1987] 1 Lloyd's Rep. 1.

2. NOTICE OF THE CLAIM

Notice of a claim is often required by contract and, in respect of some claims, by statute. In particular, the Conventions relating to carriage of goods by sea, road and air require notice to be given on or within a short time (usually a matter of days) after delivery or receipt of the goods in respect of which the claim is made.[21] The effect of failure to give notice within the specified time varies. Under the Hague-Visby Rules (sea) and the CMR (road) the effect in regard to damage claims against the carrier is that the delivery or receipt is *prima facie* evidence that the goods were handed over in a condition complying with the contract.[22] The Athens Convention relating to carriage of passengers and luggage by sea provides likewise in relation to luggage in that failure to give notice results in a presumption that the passenger has received the luggage undamaged.[23] The consequences of failure to give notice in respect of claims and the CIM and CIV Conventions[24] (rail) and the Warsaw Convention[25] (air) are more drastic—the right of action is extinguished. Such provisions are relevant insofar as a maritime claim may also be within, or may be dragged into, a Convention format primarily aimed at transport by another mode.[26]

3. COMMENCEMENT OF SUIT—ISSUE OF WRIT

Apart from the few instances when in English law the right is destroyed through delay there are two approaches:

(1) statutory time limits on the ability to bring court proceedings; and

(2) discretionary principles.

Statutory time limits

The general pattern

The basic pattern setting out the period from the moment when a cause of action arises within which an action must be brought (i.e. a writ issued) is contained in the Limitation

---

21. The period depending on whether the damage is apparent.

22. See Carriage of Goods by Sea Act 1971, Sch. Art. III(6); Carriage of Goods by Road Act 1965, Sch. Art. 30. (As to the application of the CMR to maritime claims, see fn 34 *infra*). Whether this increases the onus or standard of proof is debatable.

23. Merchant Shipping Act 1979, Sch. 3, Art. 15 as from 1 January 1996 The Merchant Shipping Act 1995 Sch. 6, Art. 15 (no notice need be given if there is joint inspection or survey at the time of receipt (Art. 15(3)). Whether this increases the onus or standard of proof otherwise applicable is debatable.

24. CIM (International Convention concerning Carriage of Goods by Rail) 1961, Art. 46; CIV (International Convention concerning Carriage of Passengers and Luggage by Rail) 1961, Art. 46 (provision in respect of claims enacted into English law through Carriage by Railway Act 1972, s.6). See also Additional Convention (set out in Schedule to that Act) Art. 16. See now International Transport Conventions Act 1983 introducing into English law the International Carriage by Rail Convention 1980 (COTIF).

25. Carriage by Air Act 1961, Sch. Art. 46. See also Carriage by Air and Road Act 1979, Sch. 1, Art. 26 (not yet in force).

26. Combined transport creates problems not only because of the application of unimodal transport Convention to each appropriate stage and (possibly) the combined transport contract, but also in the context of delay of claims because of the difficulties of the combined transport operator complying with any notice period applicable to the unimodal transport contract—which may be shorter than that applicable to the combined transport contract (see e.g. Combidoc Clause 13).

Act 1980.[27] This was a consolidation of statutes enacted in the previous 40 years and applies to maritime claims as it does to others. However, it should be noted that it is only since 1 August 1980 that the general time bars (i.e. limitation of actions) have applied with full force to Admiralty actions.[28] Since that date the pattern applies to all Admiralty causes of action, whether arising prior to or after the date, as it does to other actions, provided no action in respect of an exempted claim had been commenced by that date.[29]

The period of limitation will depend for its commencement and duration on the particular statute governing it. The general principles of start and termination applicable to the framework of the Limitation Act 1980 have both been described as "anomalous" in that neither takes any account of the awareness of the relevant party. The period starts in the case of a contract with the creation of a present contractual obligation or, otherwise, with the occurrence of the damage, loss or injury.[30] Problems created by latent damage were dealt with by providing in the Latent Damage Act 1986 where appropriate for the period to start at the date of requirement of knowledge of the damage.[31] The period ends with the issue of the writ.

Limitation periods for particular types of claim

The Limitation Act does not apply to any action for which period of limitation is prescribed by any other statute.[32] Other statutes particularly relevant to maritime claims[33] are the Carriage of Goods by Sea Act 1971 (enacting the Hague-Visby Rules) (see *infra*), the Carriage of Goods by Road Act 1965 (enacting the CMR Convention 1956),[34] and provisions of various statutes consolidated as from 1 January 1996 in the Merchant

27. (As amended particularly by the addition of ss.14A, 14B by the Latent Damage Act 1986.) With the exception of s.35 the Limitation Act does not affect any action or arbitration commenced before 1 August 1980. As to s.35 (which deals with the institution of new claims in proceedings already commenced either by the introduction of a new cause of action, a new party or the institution of third party proceedings) the date is 1 May 1981. As to s.35, see p. 224.

28. See Limitation Amendment Act 1980, s.9. As to the meaning of the provision in the Limitation Act 1939 excluding "any cause of action within the Admiralty jurisdiction of the High Court which is enforceable *in rem*", see *The Matija Gubec* [1981] 1 Lloyd's Rep. 31.

29. *Ibid*, ss.12 and 14.

30. So a cause of action on an average bond will accrue on the liability created by the terms of the bond and not the general average act (see *The Potoi Chau* [1983] 2 Lloyd's Rep. 376).

31. The period in respect of action based on personal injury or death starts from the occurrence or the knowledge (if later than the occurrence). (Limitation Act 1980, ss.11 and 12.) As to the discretionary power to extend these periods, see *ibid*, s.33, and *infra*. The Act does not apply to contract claims (*Société Commercial de Réassurance* v. *ERAS (International Ltd.)* [1992] 3 All E.R. 82 (C.A.).) Other than an action for personal injuries an action for negligence cannot be brought after 15 years from the date of the act on what the claim is based (s.14B).

32. *Ibid*, s.39.

33. See also time limits imposed in respect of claims to wreck by Merchant Shipping Act 1894, s.521 (as from 1 January 1996 Merchant Shipping Act 1995, s.239(1)). Commencement of summary proceedings (1894 Act, s.683(1); 1995 Act, s.274(L)), order for payment of money (1894 Act, s.683(2); 1995 Act, s.275).

34. Article 2(1) of the CMR applies to a contract for road carriage involving piggy-back transport by another mode. Article 32 imposes a "period of limitation" of one year subject to extension up to three years where there is (i) wilful misconduct; or (ii) suspension of the period by written claim; or (iii) the law of the court seised of the action so provides. Barred claims cannot be pursued by way of counterclaim or set off (*ibid*). As to the scope and interpretation of these provisions, see *Worldwide Carriers Ltd.* v. *Ardtran International Ltd.* [1983] 1 Lloyd's Rep. 61; *ICI Fibres* v. *MAT Transport* [1987] 1 F.L.R. 145.

Shipping Act 1995 relating to claims based on collision,[35] salvage,[36] oil pollution,[37] and carriage of passengers and their luggage.[38]

The limitation framework

Any enquiry about time limits must, therefore, start with a search for a particular statute relevant to the claim. Lacking such a provision, the question goes to the application of the Limitation Act 1980. Of the statutes specifying limitation periods for particular types of claims the provisions of the Carriage of Goods by Sea Act 1971 and those of the 1995 Act relating to collision and salvage claims call for further comment.

(i) Statutes specifying particular limitation periods for particular types of claim

Carriage claims—Carriage of Goods by Sea Act 1971—The Hague-Visby Rules, Art. III(6)[39]

"6. Unless notice of loss or damage and the general nature of such loss or damage be given in writing to the carrier or his agent at the port of discharge before or at the time of the removal of the goods into the custody of the person entitled to delivery thereof under the contract of carriage, or, if the loss or damage be not apparent, within three days, such removal shall be prima facie evidence of the delivery by the carrier of the goods as described in the bill of lading.

The notice in writing need not be given if the state of the goods has, at the time of their receipt, been the subject of joint survey or inspection.

Subject to paragraph 6 *bis* the carrier and the ship shall in any event be discharged from all liability whatsoever in respect of the goods, unless suit is brought within one year of their delivery or of the date when they should have been delivered. This period may, however, be extended if the parties so agree after the cause of action has arisen.

In the case of any actual apprehended loss or damage the carrier and the receiver shall give all reasonable facilities to each other for inspecting and tallying the goods.

6 *bis*. An action for indemnity against a third person may be brought even after the expiration of the year provided for in the preceding paragraph if brought within the time allowed by the law of the Court seized of the case. However, the time allowed shall be not less than three months, commencing from the day when the person bringing such action for indemnity has settled the claim or has been served with process in the action against himself."[40]

---

35. Section 190 re-enacting the Maritime Conventions Act 1911, s. 8.

36. Section 224, Sch. 11 (The Salvage Convention 1989, Art. 23) re-enacting the provisions of the Merchant Shipping (Salvage and Pollution) Act 1994 which had repealed and replaced the Maritime Conventions Act 1911 as regards salvage claims based on operations starting on or after 1 January 1995.

37. Sections 162, 178—applying to claims based on the Civil Liability Convention 1969 and the Fund Convention 1971 enacted initially into English law through the Merchant Shipping (Oil Pollution) Act 1971 (as to time limits see s.9) and the Merchant Shipping Act 1974 (as to time limits see s.7)—no action "shall be entertained" by a United Kingdom court later than three years" after the claim arose and not later than six years after the occurrence by reason of which liability was incurred. As to oil pollution claims see Chap. 2.

38. The Convention provides that "any action arising out of the death or a personal injury to a passenger or for the loss of or damage to luggage shall be time barred after a period of two years" unless extended by declaration of the carrier or by agreement of the parties (Art. 16). The law of the court seised with the action governs suspension of the period—but there is an outside total limit of three years (*ibid.*). The provisions of the Convention were given the force of law in a slightly modified form as from 1 January 1981 (SI 1980/1092), and came directly into force as from 30 April 1987 (SI 1987/635).

39. Incorporation into a charterparty may apply the bar to other than "Rules" claims: *The Marinov* [1995] LMLN 418.

40. Article III 6 *bis* does not depend for its applicability on the contract under which the liability in respect of which the indemnity is claimed being under the Rules (*The Xingcheng and Andros* [1987] 2 Lloyd's Rep. 210 (P.C.) on appeal from Hong Kong). The rule does not depend on national law having specific provision (*ibid.*).

The effect of this provision is that subject to agreement or estoppel any claim[41] arising out of the carriage is extinguished and in the view of the majority of the House of Lords in *Aries Tanker Corpn* v. *Total Transport Ltd.*[42] it prevents the reliance on a claim in any way—by defence or set off. The obligation is to bring the claim in a court competent to consider it by a plaintiff competent to sue,[43] and (probably) to bring it by the method (arbitration or litigation) specified by the contract.[44] So a suit brought contrary to an arbitration clause would not be competent. If the contract provides for arbitration at the election of a party, a writ is issued within that period, but election outside the period "suit" is brought as contemplated by the rules.[45] It may be that a suit will be competent within the rule even though liability is not ultimately decided on that suit. So there may be a stay on the ground of inappropriate forum.[46] In *The Hahvelt*,[47] however, Saville J. held that a suit brought in England contrary to a Norwegian jurisdiction clause was not a "suit" within the rules. No consideration seems to have been given to any discretion not to uphold the clause.

In 1992 in *The Jay Bola*[48] Hobhouse J. held that once the time bar operates no amendment of a writ issued within time will be permitted so as to add a defendant not named as such within the one year period. Such a claim is not "related back" to the original writ[49] and there is no "useful purpose" in the amendment when no substantive cause of action exists.[50]

The difficulties facing cargo owners in identifying carriers under the Hague-Visby Rules pose a practical problem underlined by the need to act appropriately in relation to

41. There is no power to extend time under the Arbitration Act 1950 for the bar is mandatory (*The Antares* [1987] 1 Lloyd's Rep. 424) see Chap. 13.

42. [1977] 1 All E.R. 398. Lord Salmon preferred to leave for the future whether a defence was precluded—so that in the instant case if by English law charterers could deduct freight for short delivery by way of defence they could do so even if the "claim" to deduct was made after one year.

43. See *The Nordglimt* [1988] 2 All E.R. 531 considering *The Kapetan Markos* [1986] 1 Lloyd's Rep. 211 (C.A.). The suit must be against the defendant (i.e. a suit against one defendant will not open the door to a suit brought outside the period against another defendant). See *The Jay Bola* [1992] 2 Lloyd's Rep. 62; [1992] 3 All E.R. 329. Similarly a suit brought by plaintiff without title to sue will not form the foundation for an action outside by the period by a competent plaintiff: *The Leni* [1992] 2 Lloyd's Rep. 48. On the other hand errors in the detail of a pleaded case could not of themselves have the effect of rendering a suit not competent (see *The Pionier* [1995] 1 Lloyd's Rep. 223).

44. See *The Merak* [1965] 1 All E.R. 230. However, whether a suit brought in a court contrary to an exclusive jurisdiction clause will prevent time running must remain uncertain in the light of the comments in the later cases (see *infra*).

45. See *The Amazona* [1989] 2 Lloyd's Rep. 130. Even if the time bar defence had been available in the arbitration proceeding the clause providing for such an option is not itself contrary to the Hague-Visby Rules—it did not relieve liability of the carrier but provided only for a safe method of proceeding by a cargo claimant.

46. See *The Nordglimt* (*supra*)—leaving open the question of whether an action *in rem* within the period could continue the liability so that an action *in personam* after the expiry of period would not be out of time (as to the identity of these causes of action see further Chaps. 2, 11, 12).

47. [1993] 1 Lloyd's Rep. 523. Saville J. refused to hold that the proceedings in the foreign court were time barred in the absence of evidence of foreign law. The approach as to the effect of the jurisdiction clause was also taken in *The Finnrose* [1994] 1 Lloyd's Rep. 559, Rix J. holding that a suit not prosecuted in accordance with requirements of civil procedure did not prevent time running (see *infra*).

48. [1992] 2 Lloyd's Rep. 62; [1992] 3 All E.R. 329.

49. Following the acceptance by the House of Lords in *Ketteman* v. *Hansel* [1987] A.C. 189 that a claim against an added defendant did not relate back to the original issue (see *infra*).

50. The general power to amend a writ even after a limitation period under RSC Order 20, r. 5, had to be construed in the light of *Ketteman*—there being no purpose in amending because of the non relation back. Further neither the Limitation Act 1980 (providing for relation back) nor Order 20, r. 5, applies to substantive time bars (*ibid*). The decision of the Court of Appeal in *The Puerto Acevedo* [1978] 1 Lloyd's Rep. 38 appears not to have survived the 1980 Act and its limitations on adding defendants (as to which see *infra*).

the appropriate party within the limitation period. There is a danger of bringing suit against the wrong defendant. However, any representation through act, omission or word may lead to an estoppel and a defendant may then be unable to deny that he is the party to the bill of lading.[51]

"Collision" claims

The Merchant Shipping Act 1995, s.190 provides:

"(1) This section applies to any proceedings to enforce any claim or lien against a ship or her owners—
   (a) in respect of damage or loss caused by the fault of that ship to another ship, its cargo or freight or any property on board it; or
   (b) for damages for loss of life or personal injury caused by the fault of that ship to any person on board another ship.
(2) The extent of the fault is immaterial for the purposes of this section.
(3) Subject to subsections (5) and (6) below, no proceedings to which this section applies shall be brought after the period of two years from the date when—
   (a) the damage or loss was caused; or
   (b) the loss of life or injury was suffered.
(4) Subject to subsections (5) and (6) below, no proceedings under any of sections 187 to 189 to enforce any contribution in respect of any overpaid proportion of any damages for loss of life or personal injury shall be brought after the period of one year from the date of payment.
(5) Any court having jurisdiction in such proceedings may, in accordance with rules of court, extend the period allowed for bringing proceedings to such extent and on such conditions as it thinks fit.
(6) Any such court, if satisfied that there has not been during any period allowed for bringing proceedings any reasonable opportunity of arresting the defendant ship within—
   (a) the jurisdiction of the court, or
   (b) the territorial sea of the country to which the plaintiff's ship belongs or in which the plaintiff resides or has his principal place of business,
shall extend the period allowed for bringing proceedings to an extent sufficient to give a reasonable opportunity of so arresting the ship."

This section replaces the Maritime Conventions Act 1911, s.8 insofar as that section applied to claims based on the fault of another ship. Although drafted differently (and more clearly) the substance remains the same.[52] Authorities construing s.8 therefore remain relevant.

The provision applies only to claims against the vessel other than that in connection with which the damage or loss occurred, or a sister ship[53] of that vessel. Claims in respect of the carrying vessel are subject only to the general pattern of time bar rules.[54] Despite the reference to arrest in the proviso the discretion to extend applies to actions *in personam* as well as actions *in rem*.[55] For the purpose of this section "proceedings are

---

51. See *The Henrik Sif* [1982] 1 Lloyd's Rep. 456.
52. Save for subsection (6) the provision applies to Her Majesty's ships as to any other (s.192 replacing the Crown Proceedings Act 1947, s.30(1); Law Reform (Limitation of Actions) Act 1954, s.5(1) and (2) (repealed as spent). As to arrest and actions *in rem* and the Crown see Chap. 12. A jet ski is not a vessel within the Merchant Shipping Acts and a claim by a rider of a ski against the owner of a vessel for damages for personal injury after collision is not within the Maritime Conventions Act 1911 (*Steedman* v. *Schofield* [1992] 2 Lloyd's Rep. 163).
53. See *The Preveze* [1973] 1 Lloyd's Rep. 202. It applies to "fault in management" and is not restricted to navigation fault (see *The Norwhale* [1975] 1 Lloyd's Rep. 610).
54. *The Niceto de Larrinaga* [1966] P. 180.
55. *The Arraiz* (1924) 19 Ll.L.Rep. 235.

brought" by the issue of a writ.[56] As a result, a plaintiff may ensure that proceedings are brought in time even if he has no opportunity to arrest. However the statute directs an extension if there has been no opportunity to arrest.

The principles applicable to extension of time under the Act are said to be similar to those applicable generally to renewal of a writ.[57] The practice regarding the discretion to extend the time operates in the normal English framework concerning judicial discretion—that an appellate court will interfere with the exercise by a first instance judge only on proof of the application of a wrong principle.[58] Even if there has been an opportunity to arrest, a court may extend the period on the basis that there were no reasonable grounds for earlier issue of the writ.[59]

Salvage claims—The Merchant Shipping (Salvage and Pollution) Act 1994 Sch. 1 (as from 1 January 1996 the Merchant Shipping Act 1995 Sch. 11)

Article 23 of the Salvage Convention enacted by and set out in the respective schedules reads:

"1. Any action relating to payment under this Convention shall be time-barred if judicial or arbitral proceedings have not been instituted within a period of two years. The limitation period commences on the day on which the salvage operations are terminated.

2. The person against whom a claim is made at any time during the running of the limitation period extend that period by a declaration to the claimant. This period may in the like manner be further extended.

3. An action for indemnity by a person liable may be instituted even after the expiration of the limitation period provided for in the preceding paragraphs, if brought within the time allowed by the law of the State where proceedings are instituted."

This provision replaces the 1911 Act insofar as it applies to salvage claims. In contrast to the earlier Act and the provisions of the 1995 Act applicable to collision claims extension of the period is expressly by agreement. There is no power in the court to extend the period.

(ii) The general pattern—the Limitation Act 1980

Subject to periods of limitation linked to particular claims[60] there are three basic limitation periods (three, six and 12 years) each attached to differing categories of actions. Focusing on those most relevant to maritime claims,[61] the following periods apply:

56. See e.g. *The World Harmony* [1967] P. 341 (construing the 1911 Act phrase "proceedings are commenced"). As to renewal of a writ, see *infra*. As to extension in favour of claimants against a limitation fund, see *The Disperser* [1920] P. 228.

57. See *The Owenbaren* [1973] 1 Lloyd's Rep. 56—a comparison still holding good subsequent to the emphasis that the basis is "good reason" rather than "exceptional reason" (*The Myrto (No. 3)* [1987] 2 Lloyd's Rep. 1 (H.L.)—see *infra*). See *The Zirje* [1989] 1 Lloyd's Rep. 493; *The Seaspeed America* [1990] 1 Lloyd's Rep. 150. As to renewal of a writ, see *infra*. As to the exercise of the discretion, see e.g. *The Albany* [1983] 2 Lloyd's Rep. 195. Good reason is a prerequisite for discretion: *The Al Tabith* fn. 8.

58. See e.g. *The Almerck* [1965] P. 357. But see generally on appellate interference with judicial discretion: *Tsai v. Woodworth, The Times*, 30 November 1983.

59. See *The Arraiz (supra)*, fn. 55.

60. See *supra*. Actions to recover contribution between persons liable for the same damage under the provision of the Civil Liability (Contribution) Act 1978 must be brought within two years of the accrual of the right to contribution. Limitation Act 1980, s.10. Where the source of liability is a judgment or arbitration award the right accrues on the date of the giving of the judgment or arbitration (s.10(3)).

61. Most actions concerning land attract a period of 12 years (Limitation Act 1980, ss.15, 16 and 20); trust property (apart from trustees' fraud or conversion) six years (s.21). Actions for account attract the same period as that applicable to the claim which is the basis of the duty to account (s.23).

Three-year period. Actions in respect of personal injury occasioned by negligence, nuisance or breach of duty and actions under the Fatal Accidents Act 1976 by dependants of a deceased whose death was caused by a wrongful act and who would, if he had not died, have been entitled to recover damages.[62]

Six-year period. Actions in respect of tort, simple contracts (excluding some loan contracts), judgments, arbitration awards (where the arbitration agreement is not under seal), some conversions of chattels, sums recoverable under statute.[63]

Twelve-year period Actions (including actions on arbitration awards) based on a document under seal, to recover the principal sum secured by a mortgage, charge or lien, by way of foreclosure in respect of mortgaged personal property and to enforce a claim to the personal estate of a deceased.[64]

The periods are all subject to extension on the grounds of disability, fraud, concealment, acknowledgment and mistake,[65] and a court, if it thinks it equitable, may in its discretion exclude the operation of the statutory provision from a cause of action based on personal injury or death.[66] In exercising its discretion to exclude, the court is directed to have regard to the degree of prejudice imposed on either party through application or non-application of the time bar and to all the circumstances of the case including (as specified) delay and conduct of the plaintiff and defendant and disability of the plaintiff. After considerable judicial debate it was held by the House of Lords that the discretion is unfettered,[67] but if a plaintiff has issued a writ within the limitation period and fails to proceed with the action the discretion cannot operate to allow a second writ. In that instance the plaintiff is not affected by the operation of the time bar.[68]

Many of the time limits are excluded as such from any claim for specific performance, injunction or other equitable jurisdiction not to allow the action to proceed.[69] The Act does not affect the equitable jurisdiction to refuse relief on the ground of acquiescence or laches.[70]

---

62. Limitation Action 1980, ss.11, 12 and 13. The period may not start until the plaintiff has knowledge of the injury and its cause (see ss.14, 14A, the latter being inserted by the Latent Damage Act 1986). As to libel and slander see ss.4A, 32A inserted by the Administration of Justice Act 1985, s.57, action under the Consumer Protection Act 1987 see s.11A (inserted by s.6, Sch. 1 of the 1987 Act).

63. Limitation Act 1980, ss.2, 3, 5, 7, 9 and 24.

64. Limitation Act 1980, ss.8, 20 and 22. An exception in regard to ship mortgages was removed by the Limitation Amendment Act 1980, s.9(2). An action to recover interest must normally be brought within six years.

65. Limitation Act 1980, ss.28–32. The concealment may be contemporaneous with or subsequent to accrual of the cause of action: *Sheldon* v. *Outhwaite* [1995] 2 All E.R. 558 (H.L.). Written and signed acknowledgment of a claim or part payment in respect of it creates a fresh accrual of the cause of action (ss.29, 30 and 31).

66. Limitation Act 1980, s.33.

67. *Thompson* v. *Brown Construction (Ebbw Vale) Ltd.* [1981] 2 All E.R. 296.

68. *Ibid*, approving *Walkley* v. *Precision Forgings Ltd.* [1979] 2 All E.R. 548; *Chappell* v. *Cooper* [1980] 2 All E.R. 463 (C.A.). See also *Deerness* v. *John R. Keeble & Son (Brantham) Ltd.* [1983] 2 Lloyd's Rep. 260, stressing that the rule in *Walkley* did not admit of any exceptions.

69. Limitation Act 1980, s.36(1). The effect today is therefore likely to be the same as if the statute applied.

70. Limitation Act 1980, s.36(2). As to laches and its relevance to maritime claims, see *infra*.

New claims in pending actions[71]

New claims include new causes of action added or substituted, new parties added or substituted and third party proceedings. New claims made in the course of proceedings are deemed to have commenced when those proceedings commence.[72] The Limitation Act 1980 authorizes the making of rules of court allowing a party to claim relief in a new capacity in a new cause of action or a new claim after the expiry of the statutory time limit only if it is:

> (i) a counterclaim or set off by a party who has not previously made any claim in the action; or
>
> (ii) a new cause of action arising substantially out of the same facts as the existing one; or is
>
> (iii) the substitution of a party for one named by mistake or a claim in the action which "cannot be maintained by or against an existing party unless the new party is joined or substituted".[73]

By RSC Order 20 an amendment may be allowed to correct the name of a party, to substitute a new party if the mistake was genuine and did not cause reasonable doubt about the identity of the plaintiff or defendant as the case may be[74] or to recognize suit in a new capacity. The rule provides for the ability to add a new cause of action if it arises substantially out of the same facts as that in which relief has already been claimed.

By RSC Order 15 it is provided that for a party to be added or substituted after expiry of the limitation period either:

> (i) the action must be based on personal injury or death and the court exercises its statutory discretion to extend the period in respect of the new party; or
>
> (ii) the proceedings were commenced within the limitation period and "it is necessary for the determination of the action that the new party should be added or substituted".[75]

In relation to the addition or substitution of a defendant "necessary" is limited to four situations—in particular where "the new party is sued jointly with the defendant and is not also liable severally with him and failure to join the new party might render the claim

---

71. Limitation Act 1980, s.35, replacing Limitation Amendment Act, s.8, the latter of which does not appear to have come into force. Section 35 came into force on 1 May 1981 and applies to actions commenced on or after that date.

72. Limitation Act 1980, s.35(1).

73. Limitation Act 1980, s.35(3)–(7), Order 20, r. 5(5). An amendment may add a new cause of action within (ii) even if the original claim disclosed no cause of action (*Sion* v. *Hampstead Health Authority, The Times*, 10 June 1994.

74. See e.g. *The Anna L* [1994] 2 Lloyd's Rep. 374.

75. RSC Order 15, r. 6. The provisions do not affect any action commenced before that date (Limitation Act 1980, s. 40(1), Sch. 2, para. 9(2)). As to the amendment of a writ see Chap. 9.

unenforceable".[76] The rules therefore permit substitution or addition of a defendant only within precisely defined limits.[77]

The provision in the statute that any new claim is deemed to commence at the same date as the original action applies the theory of "relation back". The principle exists only through this provision. The principle is not to be implied (apart from the Limitation Act) from the general power under the rules of court to amend a writ even though the limitation period has expired.[78] In any event it cannot apply where a time bar has removed the substantive cause of action—the rule applies only to procedural time bars. Where therefore an action is subject to the Hague-Visby Rules an amendment adding a party will operate as from the date of the amendment. There can be no amendment if at that date the time limit under the rules has expired.[79]

Where the Limitation Act applies so as to relate back an amendment to the original writ the claim is time barred only if at the date of joinder the original proceedings are time barred as it is deemed to have been made at the date the original proceedings were made. On this principle any refusal to amend to add or substitute a defendant has to be on the basis that the defendant would be deprived of the right to plead the statute. In *The Kyriaki*[80] an amendment allowing service of a writ on a "new" defendant outside the limitation period of the original claim was declared bad since it was only then that the defendant was joined. The adding of a ship (or other property) to a claim is not, it is suggested, adding a new defendant. It is however, rendering the defendant liable *"in rem"* in respect of an asset to which he would not have been liable without the amendment, and therefore it would seem adding a new cause of action.[81]

Principles outside the Limitation Act

(i) Application by analogy

The time limits imposed by the Limitation Act 1980 applicable to tort, contract, enforcement of awards or judgment, statutory recovery of sums and actions on a specialty are excluded from claims for specific performance, injunctions or other equitable relief.

---

76. RSC Order 15, r. 6(6)(e). Paragraph (6) also defines "necessary" in respect of adding new parties where the cause of action is vested jointly in the new and the original, to protect an equitable interest, to allow the Attorney-General to bring relator proceedings, and to allow a company to be joined where the plaintiff is suiing on its behalf (see *ibid.* (a)–(d)) but as drafted rule 7 does not allow the substitution as plaintiff of a company which was under foreign law the "universal successor" of the company initially named (*Toprak* v. *Sale Tilney Technology plc* [1994] 3 All E.R. 483. This however ignores the power to maintain an action on transfer of interest (such as corporate restructuring): *The Choko Star* [1995] LMLN 411.

77. Due to the mandatory direction the courts will now not be able to rely on the general discretion of RSC Order 2, r. 1 (to waive time limits—see *The Kyriaki* [1993] 1 Lloyd's Rep. 137) or Order 20, rr. 5(1) and (2) (conferring power to permit amendments even after expiry of the limitation period) but may apparently still rely on rule 5(3)—the power to correct the name of a defendant (as to which, see *Evans Construction Co. Ltd.* v. *Charrington & Co. Ltd.* [1983] 1 All E.R. 310).

78. *The Jay Bola* [1992] 2 Lloyd's Rep. 62; [1992] 3 All E.R. 329 applying the reasoning of Brandon L.J. in *Liff* v. *Peasley* [1980] 1 All E.R. 623 approved by the House of Lords in *Ketteman* v. *Hansel* [1987] A.C. 189.

79. *The Jay Bola* (fn. 78).

80. [1993] 1 Lloyd's Rep. 137—approved *Welsh Development Agency* v. *Redpath Dorman Long* (C.A.), *The Times*, 4 April 1994.

81. And therefore considered under Order 20, rr. 2, 5. Such an amendment is permitted even if the original court or statement of claim does not disclose a cause of action: *Sion* v. *Hampstead Health Authority* (C.A.), *The Times*, 10 June 1994. In *The Kusu Island* [1985] IMLJ 342 the Singapore C.A. considered such an amendment under the general power to amend under the equivalent of Order 20, r. 1 (as to which see Chap. 10).

But they are applied by the courts by analogy,[82] and it is perhaps a comment on the English regard for history that they have not been brought into the limitation fold. A century of joint administration of law and equity could be thought perhaps to lead to a unity of principles applied as such and the same principles applied by analogy. But the retention of the distinction does retain the flexibility of not having to apply the time limit in regard to some of the more powerful remedies.

(ii) Delay—laches

The equitable doctrine of laches operates only where no statutory provision applied directly or by analogy.[83] It follows that whereas before the general framework applicable to limitation of actions applied to Admiralty actions (i.e. before 1 August 1980) laches formed an essential strand of the Admiralty fabric, it now takes its place as ancillary to that fabric. Insofar as claims to which the fabric now applies are concerned it is unlikely to operate. But it may continue to do so in respect of arrest as a remedy assisting the claim (see Chapter 15). More fundamentally, it may continue to affect the enforceability of a maritime lien as against third parties,[84] even though the claim on which the lien is based remains extant. The enforceability against third parties has always required "reasonable diligence" in its prosecution.[85] The delay must be inordinate or prejudicial to the defendant. Whether "*delay*" is more likely to defeat a maritime lien in a third party than a two-party context seems uncertain. In *The Alletta*[86] a 10-year delay was not sufficient to provide a defence to purchasers in the light of provision for an indemnity from the vendors.

The concept of laches seems focused more on the availability of a particular remedy (e.g. specific performance or injunction) rather than preventing a claim being brought. There are hints that more than delay and lapse of time are required for its establishment and that there is some overlap with acquiescence and estoppel. In 1974 the Privy Council saw the principle as either a waiver of the remedy or putting the defendant in a position in which it would not be reasonable if the remedy were asserted. It was said in these contexts "lapse of time and delay are most material"[87]—and it may be that sheer inactivity would be enough.[88]

4. DELAY IN SERVICE OF WRIT

The periods of the validity of a writ and general principles of renewal are discussed in respect of a writ *in personam* in Chapter 9 and in respect of a writ *in rem* in Chapter 10.

---

82. Limitation Act 1980, s. 36(1).

83. See *Re Paulings Settlement Trusts* [1963] 3 All E.R. 1.

84. As to which, see Chap. 18.

85. See *The Bold Buccleugh* (1851) 7 Moo. P.C. 267 applied in (e.g.) *The Europa* (1863) 2 Moo. N.S. 1; *The Fairport* (1882) 8 P.D. 48. See also *The Kong Magnus* [1891] P. 223; *The Alletta* [1974] 1 Lloyd's Rep. 40.

86. [1974] 1 Lloyd's Rep. 40. Compare the period of one year specified in the Convention Relating to Maritime Liens and Mortgages 1993, Art. 9 (not in force). As to the Convention see Chap. 17.

87. *Lindsay Petroleum* v. *Hurd* (1874) L.R. 5 P.C. 221, at p. 240.

88. See e.g. *Joyce* v. *Joyce* [1979] 1 All E.R. 175. Delay in pursuing an action may lead to refusal to renew a *Mareva* injunction granted in respect of the action (see *Lloyds Bowmaker Ltd.* v. *Britannia Arrow Holdings* [1988] 3 All E.R. 178).

As discussed there, by the rules of court the courts have a power to renew a writ.[89] The powers are to be exercised if the plaintiff shows "good reason" on the facts of the case. The writ may be renewed whether or not the limitation period has expired. However, where the period has expired a plaintiff must give a satisfactory explanation for the failure to apply for an extension within the period.[90]

5. DELAY IN COMPLYING WITH PROCEDURAL REQUIREMENTS

Time limits are imposed on both parties by the rules of court in respect of steps to be taken in the action—as, for example, for acknowledging service of a writ, serving of a statement of claim and defences and other pleadings.[91]

Failure to comply with a requirement of the rules as an irregularity rather than a nullity, the court having power to set aside the proceedings or allow amendments in accordance with the rules.[92] There is a general power in the court to extend time permitted and the parties may consent so to do.[93]

These general rules must be read subject to statutory provisions and to rules relating to specific requirements, particularly the expiry of any limitation periods (see *supra*).

6. WANT OF PROSECUTION OF A CLAIM

In addition to powers stemming from procedural requirements courts have an inherent power to dismiss an action because the plaintiff or his advisors do not act with reasonable dispatch.

In *Birkett* v. *James*[94] the House of Lords approved the principles according to which the inherent jurisdiction to dismiss should be exercised, earlier stated in 1968 in *Allen* v. *McAlpine*,[95] i.e.

"The power should be exercised only where the court is satisfied either (1) that the default has been intentional and contumelious, e.g., disobedience to a peremptory order of the court or conduct amounting to an abuse of the process of the court; or (2)(a) that there has been inordinate and

89. RSC Order 6, r. 8 (a renewal of writ); Order 2, r. 1 (general power to cure failure to act in time). While, in general, discretion under the specific and general power should be exercised on the same principles it is possible that the general discretion (in the interests of justice) may be exercisable when the specific amendment power ("good reason") may not (see *Boocock* v. *Hilton International Co.* [1993] 1 All E.R. 19).

90. *The Myrto (No. 3)* [1987] A.C. 597; [1987] 2 Lloyd's Rep. 1. There is no difference in criteria whether or not the court has a discretion to extend the period for original issue of the writ (as in personal injury actions): *Waddon* v. *Whitecroft Scovell Ltd.* [1988] 1 All E.R. 996 (H.L.). Legal aid delays are relevant to "good reason" and where there are matters which could constitute good reason the balance of hardship may be relevant. Hardship of itself cannot constitute good reason (*ibid.*).

91. See e.g. RSC Order 12, rr. 5, 6 and 8 (acknowledgment of service); RSC Order 18, r. 103 (pleading); RSC Order 25 (summons for directions); RSC Order 75, rr. 3 and 25 (application of rules to Admiralty actions).

92. RSC Order 2, r. 1. As to the relationship of this power, amendments to add new parties, renewal of writs, see text and fns. 77, 89. Where a statement of claim is defective an extension of time for service of defence automatically involves an extension of time for an application to set aside a writ, the defendant being entitled to see the case pleaded against him. See *Lawson* v. *Midland Travellers Ltd.* [1993] 1 All E.R. 989 and Chap. 9.

93. RSC Order 3, r. 5.

94. [1978] A.C. 297.

95. [1968] 2 Q.B. 229.

inexcusable delay on the part of the plaintiff or his lawyers, and (b) that such delay will give rise to a substantial risk that it is not possible to have a fair trial of the issues in the action or is such as is likely to cause or to have caused serious prejudice to the defendant either as between themselves and the plaintiff or between each other or between them and a third party."[96]

In *Birkett* v. *James* three further relevant factors were elaborated that:

> (i) where the limitation period has not expired when an action was dismissed for want of prosecution the plaintiff could simply issue a fresh writ[97];
> (ii) the delay of which complaint is made must relate to the time after issue of the writ although delay in issue of the writ may require greater speed after its issue than where it has been issued promptly[98];
> (iii) the possibility of the availability to the plaintiff of an action against his solicitors is not a relevant consideration.[99]

A defendant may be estopped from striking out an action as, for example, by representations that despite delay the matter would go to trial thereby causing the plaintiff to incur expense. Whether such estoppel arises is a matter of fact and weighing the effect of the defendant's actions in the context of the plaintiff's delay.[100]

The principles of *Birkett* v. *James* were in substance restated in 1992 by the Court of Appeal in *Costellow* v. *Somerset County Council*[101] following some uncertainty as to requirements where the case does not fall within the first category of intention and contumelious conduct. Whether the application is by a plaintiff for extension of time or a defendant to strike out, the same principles apply and if both summons are brought they should normally be heard together. Save in exceptional circumstances "it can rarely be appropriate" to deny a plaintiff an extension to keep the action on foot because of a procedural default causing a defendant no prejudice for which costs will not compensate.

The failure to prosecute a suit commenced within the Hague-Visby Rules may have the consequence that the suit is not "brought" within the one year period. The purpose of the provision is to bring suits promptly. A suit initiated within the year may suffice to comply with the requirement even though it is later stayed (see *supra*). Nevertheless, in *Finnrose*[102] proceedings conducted in breach of the timetable set by English civil procedure were not "brought" within the Rules. It was said that this is no different from the disqualification of a suit on the grounds of a foreign forum clause or no title to sue (as

---

96. [1978] A.C. 297, at p. 318. A counterclaim may be struck out without affecting the claim *Owen* v. *Pugh* [1995] 3 All E.R. 345.

97. In *Tolley* v. *Morris* [1979] 1 W.L.R. 592 the view was expressed that failure to comply with a peremptory order to take a necessary procedural step within a specified time in one action would be contumelious conduct sufficient to justify dismissal of a fresh action for the same cause of action as an abuse of process (at p. 603, per Lord Diplock).

98. Delay within and subsequent to the limitation period is relevant (*Trill* v. *Sacher* [1993] 1 All E.R. 961).

99. Lord Salmon thought that this factor could deserve consideration ([1978] A.C., at p. 330). When considering whether in a negligence action the primary limitation should not apply and weighing the prejudice to the parties the availability of a claim against a solicitor for the full damages is a "highly relevant consideration" (*Thompson* v. *Brown Construction* [1981] 2 All E.R. 296 (H.L.)).

100. *Roebuck* v. *Mungovin* [1994] 1 All E.R. 568 (H.L.) (overruling *County and District Properties* v. *Lyell* [1991] 1 W.L.R. 653 (C.A.) holding that as a matter of law creating of further expense prevented striking out).

101. [1993] 1 All E.R. 952. See also the guidelines set out by Neill L.J. in *Trill* v. *Sacher* [1993] 1 All E.R. 961 (a case heard earlier than *Costellow* as qualified by the decision in *Roebuck* v. *Mungovin* (fn 100).

102. [1994] 1 Lloyd's Rep. 559.

to which see *supra*). And indeed once admit a suit may not be "brought" because the exercise of jurisdiction may be challenged (see *supra*) it is a short step to apply the principle to "want of prosecution". It is, however, a step. It extends the ground of disqualification from one which was in existence at the inception of the proceedings. It reads "brought" as referring to continuing rather than instituting proceedings.

7. DELAY IN ASSERTION OF THE REMEDY

As has been said, apart from the statutory rules regarding commencement of suit, the principle of delay as a ground for barring a claim is focused on equitable remedies, in particular injunction and specific performance. In this context the principle would require timely action on the order as well as in seeking it.

JUDGMENT ON ORDER ON THE MERITS

The Limitation Amendment Act 1980 reduced the period within which an action on a judgment may be brought from 12 to six years.[103] It thereby equated the period with that within which a judgment may be executed without leave. Since leave will not be given when the right of action on a judgment is barred[104] it appears that since 1 August 1980 (the date of commencement of the Amendment Act) there is no scope for the power to grant leave to execute.[105]

PROVISIONAL REMEDIES

Delay will defeat a plaintiff's ability to obtain an interlocutory injunction just as it will a perpetual injunction and undoubtedly the availability of a *Mareva* injunction is dependent upon reasonable haste. Indeed, the need is based on call for speed.

On the other hand, wherever *in rem* proceedings remain available arrest must also remain available. The longevity of a maritime lien as such is established[106] but that of the statutory lien appears restricted because of its basis on the issue of a writ. Both are subject to the continued existence of the claim on which the particular lien is based.

---

103. See no Limitation Act 1980, s.24. Arrears of interest are recoverable within six years of the interest becoming due (s.24(2)).

104. *Laugher* v. *Donovon* [1948] 2 All E.R. 11. See also *Lamb and Sons* v. *Rider* [1948] 2 All E.R. 402. While an action will lie on a judgment establishing a debt a plaintiff must enforce it by execution if possible.

105. Conferred by RSC Order 45, r. 6.

106. See Chap. 18.

CHAPTER 12

Restrictions on Jurisdiction

The primary questions considered in this chapter are the restrictions on English court proceedings. However, a cognate issue is raised by the power of an English court to order a party not to pursue foreign proceedings. As the exercise of such a power limits the ability to sue in a desired forum it may be considered as a restriction.

A restriction on jurisdiction as discussed in this chapter reflects the prohibition on bringing suit even though there is compliance with any general or specific jurisdiction base and the service of a writ. The prohibition may go to the creation of jurisdiction in providing a further jurisdiction requirement, or it may go to the exercise of established jurisdiction. The distinction is probably of little practical significance save where the suit is at the court's discretion and weight is given to the existence of jurisdiction apart from the discretion. The rules differ according to whether the substantive regimes of the Brussels or Lugano Convention apply.

THE BRUSSELS AND LUGANO CONVENTIONS—"MULTIPLE PROCEEDINGS"

A national court must decide its own jurisdiction in accordance with the Convention. So it must decide if the subject-matter falls within the Convention (as for example whether the provision of "arbitration" excludes it—see Chapter 5). If the matter is within the Convention, is not subject to national law or another Convention and has not previously been litigated, a court in which jurisdiction is conferred prior to any other court cannot decline to hear the case. The primary purpose of the Convention is to prevent irreconcilable judgments between courts of contracting States. So there is a need to prevent relitigation of disputes decided, provide for ready recognition and enforcement of judgments[1] and allocate jurisdiction where proceedings are taken concerning the same claim or related claims in courts of different contracting States.

The need for "multiple proceedings" provisions arises first as in regard to initial proceedings there may be more than one Convention jurisdiction (as, for example, the domicile of the defendant or the place of the damage in a tort action). Secondly, the principle of prevention of irreconcilable judgments extends to judgment on any dispute whether or not the jurisdiction in each case was based on the Convention substantive

---

1. So having obtained a judgment there is an obligation to enforce that rather than seek to relitigate (*De Wolf* v. *Cox* [1977] 2 CMLR 43 and see Chap. 28).

provisions. It encompasses initial jurisdiction rules of national law—but it is to be recalled that the application of national law is itself through the Convention.

Articles 21, 22 and 23 provide:

"Article 21
Where proceedings involving the same cause of action and between the same parties are brought in the courts of different Contracting States, any court other than the court first seised shall of its own motion decline jurisdiction in favour of that court.

A court which would be required to decline jurisdiction may stay its proceedings if the jurisdiction of the other court is contested.

Article 22
Where related actions are brought in the courts of different Contracting States, any court other than the court first seised may, while the actions are pending at first instance, stay its proceedings.

A court other than the court first seised may also, on the application of one of the parties, decline jurisdiction if the law of that court permits the consolidation of related actions and the court first seised has jurisdiction over both actions.

For the purposes of this Article, actions are deemed to be related where they are so closely connected that it is expedient to hear and determine them together to avoid the risk of irreconcilable judgments resulting from separate proceedings.

Article 23
Where actions come within the exclusive jurisdiction of several courts, any court other than the court first seised shall decline jurisdiction in favour of that court."

"TO AVOID THE RISK OF IRRECONCILABLE JUDGMENTS"

The central purpose of all the "multiple proceedings" provisions is that according to which in Article 22 a national court must consider a stay—to avoid the risk of irreconcilable judgments. The purpose becomes a relevant criterion for a court only insofar as Article 21 or Article 23 are not applicable. "Irreconcilable" is not to be construed in this context in the same way as the identical phrase providing a ground for non-recognition of a judgment of a court of another state—the objectives are different. Non-recognition of a judgment requires that the decisions must have "mutually exclusive legal consequences", i.e. be necessarily inconsistent. The objective of the "multiple proceedings" provision is however to "avoid conflicting and contradictory decisions even where the separate enforcement of each of them is not precluded". In other words it is the avoidance of risk and not the necessary consequence at which provision is aimed. So proceedings in two states by different cargo owners against the same shipowner in relation to different but identical contracts of carriage in respect of different parts of the same bulk cargo were within Article 22.[2]

SCOPE OF THE "MULTIPLE PROCEEDINGS" PROVISIONS

Articles 21, 22 and "exclusive jurisdiction"

While Article 23 provides for priority as between courts each having "exclusive" jurisdiction there is no express recognition of any priority of a court having such

2. *The Maciej Rataj* [1995] 1 Lloyd's Rep. 302.

jurisdiction over another in which there is a simple jurisdiction base. In 1993 in *Continental Bank NA* v. *Aeakos Naviera SA*[3] the Court of Appeal held that where jurisdiction is said to be based on an agreement under Article 17 that court must assess the validity and effect of the clause.[4] If it is in its view effective in being "exclusive", it takes precedence over Articles 21 and 22. So the fact that the English court was second seised could not affect the jurisdiction and, more, the court had the power to issue an injunction restraining the parties from proceeding elsewhere. In the light of the agreement such conduct was a clear breach of contract and therefore vexatious and oppressive.[5] The same reasoning must apply to all "exclusive" jurisdiction bases, and is consistent with the aim of avoiding the risk of irreconcilable judgments.

As between non-exclusive jurisdictions

The provisions apply to concurrent proceedings in different contracting States[6] and probably only where proceedings become pending before different courts on different days.[7] Whether a court of a contracting State has any discretion to decline jurisdiction in favour of a non-contracting State depends first on the scope of the initial jurisdiction Convention provisions and secondly, if these provisions do not apply on national law. The Court of Appeal has held that the Conventions have no application to such an issue and national law is to apply.[8]

Subject to exclusive jurisdiction there is no distinction in Articles 21 and 22 as between Convention jurisdiction bases, and claims referred by Article 4 of the Convention to national law are therefore within the scope of the multiple proceedings provisions.[9]

Provisional measures[10]

An action for provisional measures in one state and an action on the merits in another will not without more attract these provisions.[11] The concept of *lis alibi pendens* may however be relevant to two actions for protective measures if the measures are not restricted to the state of the court ordering them or if the making of the order means that the court will hear the dispute.[12]

3. [1994] 1 Lloyd's Rep. 505. See also *IP Metal Ltd.* v. *Ruote (No. 2)* [1994] 2 Lloyd's Rep. 560.
4. In that case the jurisdiction agreement was subject to English law.
5. As to restraining of foreign proceedings see *infra*.
6. i.e. concurrent at the date of the judgment considering the issue (see *Grupo Torras* [1995] 1 Lloyd's Rep. at p. 418). So they do not apply where proceedings in one state have been concluded prior to the court in another state being seised of an action. See *Gramlesraden plc* v. *Casa De Suecia SA* [1994] 1 Lloyd's Rep. 433.
7. See *SA CNV* v. *S GmbH* [1991] I.L.Pr. 588 (Oberlandsgericht Koblenz)—it may be arguable that actions may be treated as consecutive according to the hours when lodged. As to multi defendants see *infra*. In the case at issue the court held that the question of irreconcilable judgments had to be resolved by Article 27(3)—the power not to enforce a judgment on that ground (see Chap. 28). As to multi defendants see *infra*.
8. *Re Harrods (Buenos Aires) Ltd. (No. 1)* [1991] 4 All E.R. 334; *The Po* [1991] 2 Lloyd's Rep. 206. See generally Chap. 5.
9. *Overseas Union Insurance Ltd.* v. *New Hampshire Insurance Ltd.* [1992] 1 Lloyd's Rep. 204 (ECJ).
10. As to provisional measures jurisdiction see Art. 24 of the Brussels and Lugano Conventions and Chaps. 14–16.
11. See e.g. *The Nordglimt* [1987] 2 Lloyd's Rep. 470 (Hobhouse J.); *The Sargasso* [1994] 2 Lloyd's Rep. 6 and *infra*; *Rank Film Distribution Ltd.* v. *Lanterna Editrice Svl and Another* [1992] I.L.Pr. 58 (English H.C.); *Kaptein* v. *Van Hoasten* RB The Hague (1978) ECD 1–21–B5; *Ugha Group* v. *NVBSL* (Hof van Beroep) Belgium (1979) ECD 1–22–B2.
12. See *Virgin Aviation Service Ltd.* v. *CAD Aviation Services* [1991] I.L.Pr. 79.

The power or duty to decline jurisdiction

Assuming that in any case involving Articles 21 or 22 there is no question of exclusive jurisdiction there is no power under Articles 21–23 for *the court first seised* to decline jurisdiction or stay proceedings. *The court second seised* may only refuse to decline jurisdiction:

(a) in respect of a case within Article 21 (the same cause of action) if the jurisdiction of the court first seised is contested and then only to stay proceedings until the context is decided;

(b) in respect of a case within Article 22 (related actions) while the actions are pending at first instance and either as a matter of discretion the court decides to stay the proceedings or the action may be consolidated before the court first seised.

The discretion under (b) must be exercised bearing in mind the central purpose of preventing unreconcilable judgments.

Consideration of the jurisdiction of the foreign court

A court before which it is asserted that another is seised has the jurisdiction to decide whether it is in law and in fact so seised. The law to be applied is the national law of the court said to be seised.[13] It may be that the court asked to decide the matter has a discretion whether to stay the proceedings pending a decision by the court said to be earlier seised.[14] Save where it is claimed that the court second seised has exclusive jurisdiction that court may not examine the jurisdiction of the court first seised. It would seem that where the court second seised is said to have exclusive jurisdiction it would assert it unless the court first seised also had such jurisdiction. In that event the claims would be within Article 23.

The general concept of a discretion to decline jurisdiction on the ground of inappropriateness, *forum non conveniens*, was firmly rejected by those drafting the Convention.[15] To allow it, it was thought, would simply undermine the basic principles of Convention jurisdiction allocation. A critical question therefore is the moment when a court is seised of a claim.

"Seised" of an action

In 1984 in *Zelger* v. *Salinitri*[16] the European Court rejected an argument that "seised" was a European concept. The Court said that the object of the Convention was not to unify the formalities "closely linked to the organization of judicial procedure in the various states". The question of when a court was seised fell within the area of formalities and is to be referred to the rules of each national law. However, for the purposes of the Convention a court is seised if the action is "definitively pending"—a general European concept[17]

---

13. *AGF* v. *Chiyoda* [1992] 1 Lloyd's Rep. 325 applying *Zelger* v. *Salinitri* [1984] ECR 2397 and *Dresser* v. *Falcongate* [1991] 2 Lloyd's Rep. 557 (as to which see *infra*).
14. *Ibid*—declined to stay in that case because of the delay it would cause.
15. See Schlosser, para. 181. Cf. Kay, p. 1244. But see Hartley, p. 78. As to within the UK see Chap. 7.
16. 129/83 [1984] ECR 2397; [1985] 3 CMLR 366.
17. *Zelger* v. *Salinitri* 129/83 [1984] ECR 2397.

construed by the English Court of Appeal as "decisive, conclusive, final or definitive litigational relationship between the Court and litigants".[18]

Where no steps are taken in the first proceedings, a court may take the view that no action is pending. So a Dutch court has held that the fixing of a limit of liability on application by a shipowner without appearance or lodging of security by the other party in Belgium did not lay the foundation for Article 22 let alone Article 21 in respect of the same issue being brought by the shipowner before the Dutch courts.[19]

From a domestic point of view in England a court could be said to be seised on the issue of a writ—but given the choices left open to the plaintiff whether to pursue the action and the ignorance of the defendant the matter could hardly be said to be "definitively pending". Importantly jurisdiction will depend on service.

Both in actions *in personam* and *in rem* it is now accepted that an English court is seised in the service of the writ, it not being sufficient of itself to be seised of the dispute on the merits if jurisdiction is exercised in respect of provisional measures.[20] The latter step illustrates how the courts are treading the European path of distinguishing between provisional matters and issues on the merits, thereby easing English law (at least in the context of Europe) away from the illogicality of viewing the two as necessarily interlinked.

In an action *in rem* the court may be seised on arrest of a ship where that act was the foundation of jurisdiction on the merits.[21] Where the arrest was a provisional measure only (as where the merits action is elsewhere) the court would arguably not be "seised" of the merits.[22] Although the purpose of the arrest may be irrelevant to its validity under English law it may be relevant to whether it is a provisional measure or the foundation of merits jurisdiction under the Brussels Convention or the Arrest Convention.[23]

Multi defendants

In 1994 in *Grupo Torras SA* v. *Al Sabah*[24] Mance J. had to wrestle with numerous issues relevant to Articles 21 and 22 some of which were already on their way to the European Court in *The Maciej Rataj*.[25] One issue apparently relevant to both cases but only argued in *Grupo Torras* was the date of definitive pendency in a case involving multiple defendants. Mance J. felt the only practical date was that of service on the defendant first seised. Otherwise there would be fragmentation and confusion with different courts having jurisdiction in the same related causes of action. In such actions the approach was to compare the whole and not take a defendant by defendant approach.

---

18. See *Dresser UK Ltd.* v. *Falcongate Freight Management Ltd.* [1991] 2 Lloyd's Rep. 557 (C.A.) as applied in *Grupo Torras SA* v. *Al Sabah* [1995] 1 Lloyd's Rep. 374. This refers to pendency at the moment the court is seised and requires a court of a contracting State to consider when in accordance with the law of the other state the action became definitely pending, any procedural consequence being irrelevant (*Grupo Torras SA* v. *Al Sabah* [1995] I.L.Pr. 667 C.A.).

19. *Staat der Nederlanden* v. *Partenreederei Erata* (1985) Hof The Hague 1986 ELD 207.

20. *Dresser UK Ltd.* v. *Falcongate Freight Management Ltd.* [1991] 2 Lloyd's Rep. 557 (C.A.) as qualified by *The Sargasso* [1994] 2 Lloyd's Rep. 6.

21. *The Freccia Del Nord* [1989] 1 Lloyd's Rep. 388.

22. Thus resolving the problem perceived in *The Nordglimt* [1987] 2 Lloyd's Rep. 470 but resolved through construction of Arts 21, 22 and the Arrest Convention.

23. See e.g. *The Nordglimt* [1987] 2 Lloyd's Rep. 470; *The Anna H* [1995] 1 Lloyd's Rep. 11.

24. [1995] 1 Lloyd's Rep. 374.

25. [1995] 1 Lloyd's Rep. 302.

The approach involves the concept of a defendant being treated as served although not served and being notified of proceedings without knowing of them. The subsequent decision of the European Court in *The Maciej Rataj* accepted the disadvantage of fragmentation in taking a strict view of "the same parties" in Article 21 (see *infra*). In that context Mance J. favoured the need for coincidence of parties but still took the view that the trigger for the operation of Article 21 or Article 22 in a multi-defendant case was the writ first served on a defendant. Yet there is no escape from the conclusion that at that point the defendants not served are not parties. It must surely be the responsibility of the plaintiff to ensure contemporaneous service or accept that there will be consecutive parties. So the approach of Mance J. cannot stand.[26]

The same cause of action and between the same parties (Article 21)

A court must decline jurisdiction if proceedings involving the same parties and same cause of action are in being elsewhere when proceedings are commenced before it unless the jurisdiction of the other court is contested. The matter must be considered whether or not raised by a party—the court's duty is to decline jurisdiction "of its own motion".

If the jurisdiction of the earlier court is contested the obligation to decline jurisdiction is replaced by a power to stay proceedings. The choice given by the power is between the declining of jurisdiction and staying the proceedings pending decision on the jurisdiction of the earlier court. It is not between staying or continuing the proceedings. If a court could elect not to stay the proceedings the risk remains—that there will be two judgments each unenforceable in the other state as being irreconcilable.[27]

Whether or not proceedings are based on the same cause of action is a matter for European and not national law. In *Gubisch Maschinenfabrik KA* v. *Palumbo*[28] it was held they were the same in this sense if they have the same "subject-matter". So following this criterion causes of action are the same when in respect of a collision each party sues the other[29] or as regards a sales contract the vendor sought payment and the purchaser a declaration that the contract had been revoked or rescission of the contract.[30]

In *The Maciej Rataj*[31] one issue was whether an action for damages and an action for declaration of non-liability were the "same cause of action". It was pointed out (citing *Gubisch*) that the language versions other than English distinguish between the cause of action and the object requiring that they be the same. The cause of action in this context "comprises the facts and rules of law relied on as the basis of the action" while the object is "the end of the action in view".

The court held that an action for a declaration of non-liability and an action asserting liability based on the same carriage of bulk cargo and on identical contracts had the same cause of action. Further, the two actions had the same object, the issue of liability being

26. As accepted in the C.A. [1995] I.L.Pr. 667.
27. Irreconcilability with a judgment of the recognizing court is a ground of refusal of recognition. See Article 27(3) and Chap. 28. As to declining jurisdiction see Chap. 4.
28. [1989] ECC 420.
29. See *The Linda* [1988] 1 Lloyd's Rep. 175—a view approved generally by the ECJ in *The Maciej Rataj* [1995] 1 Lloyd's Rep. 302.
30. See *Gubisch* (fn. 28) but not where two different contracts are involved (*Poomac Sprl* v. *SA Sogoservice* [1993] I.L.Pr. 309.
31. [1995] 1 Lloyd's Rep. 302 affirming the view taken by the C.A.—see [1992] 2 Lloyd's Rep. 552; see also *Charman* v. *WOC Offshore* [1993] 2 Lloyd's Rep. 551; *Re a Clothing Sales Contract* (Oberlandsgericht Munchen) [1995] I.L.Pr. 72. As to limitation and liability claims see *infra* "Related actions".

central to both. The fact that damage is sought in one but not the other "does not alter the principal object of the action" and further a declaration of non-liability disputes liability for loss. It follows that a defendant (or potential defendant) may take the initiative through a "pre-emptive strike" for a declaration of non-liability. That court would therefore be the first seised and the plaintiff will find that his claim must be adjudged in that court.

An action in personam and an action in rem

In *The Nordglimt*[32] Hobhouse J. expressed the view that until a person liable *in personam* with an interest in property which is the target of an action *in rem* chose to defend an action *in rem* the actions were not between the same parties. It was only from that moment that the action became one between the plaintiff and the person interested in the property and thereby fell within Article 21. The subsequent decision of the Court of Appeal in *The Deichland*[33] holding that for the purposes of the Convention an action *in rem* is against a "defendant" is in substance consistent with *The Nordglimt*, for there Hobhouse J. distinguished the action *in personam* and *in rem* in terms of identity rather than existence of a defendant. And, as is suggested in Chapters 2 and 4, such a view accords with common sense and the legal characteristics of the action *in rem*.

An action *in rem* may become a "hybrid" when through acknowledgment of service or otherwise a concurrent action *in personam* starts. In *The Maciej Rataj* the European Court held that the distinction between an action *in personam* and an action *in rem* was not material to the interpretation of Article 21. The identity of cause of action and parties has to be interpreted independently of "the special features of the law in force in each Contracting State". The identity did not cease when the action *in rem* had continued as a hybrid or the action had continued solely *in personam*.

The holding of the Court does not however deal with the question (faced in *The Deichland* and *The Nordglimt*) of whether an action *in personam* and an action *in rem* reflect the "same cause of action". It would seem that both have the same "object" (liability and damages), although this is accomplished by a different method. They are both based on the same facts and would only differ as to any rule of law insofar as liability in the action *in rem* was based on liability other than *in personam*. That will depend on the claim.

Apart from possible divergence as to the applicable rule of law the identity of the actions would appear to turn on whether they are "between the same parties" (see *infra*).

Between the same parties

In 1994 in *The Maciej Rataj*[34] the European Court stressed that the purpose of the provision was to preclude the non-recognition of a judgment because of irreconcilability with another between the same parties. For Article 21 to apply therefore the parties to the different proceedings must be identical. Where there is identity in the case of some parties but not others it is only in respect of the same parties in the two proceedings that Article 21 will operate. This construction would make the handling of multi-party cases

32. [1987] 2 Lloyd's Rep. 470.
33. [1989] 2 Lloyd's Rep. 113 (C.A.).
34. [1995] 1 Lloyd's Rep. 302.

somewhat difficult save that, as the Court pointed out, the actions with "new" parties will in all probability be "related actions". There must be a strong case for a stay in any court second seised where there is such common ground between actions.

Related actions (Article 22)

It is in this context that the principle of *forum non conveniens* may continue to play a part in the conferring of a power on a court other than the court first seised to stay the proceedings.[35] The power may be exercised only when both proceedings "are pending at first instance". Whether or not proceedings are pending turns on whether they are "definitively pending" and that is a matter for each national court. It may therefore be that if the date on which proceedings were instituted is contested the court second seised can only adjourn for the court first seised to decide the point.[36]

The power exists for the same purpose as the duty under Articles 21 and 22—avoiding "the risk of irreconcilable judgments" (as to which see *supra*). "Related actions" are defined accordingly.[37] There is a strong argument generally for staying the proceedings for, once the actions are related, the risk of irreconcilable (and hence) unenforceable judgments must be great.[38] If, because of the presence of additional parties, the actions do not fall within Article 21 the presence of a common party must mean the risk of irreconcilable judgments.[39] The discretion of the court second seised therefore comes into operation and that discretion must be exercised with the risk firmly in mind.[40] Further, it is possible that actions relating to identical subject-matter and defendant but brought by different plaintiffs may be "related". Where in *The Maciej Rataj* different cargo consignees of parts of the same cargo of soya bean oil brought actions against the shipowner the European Court held that Article 22 would mitigate the disadvantage of its holding that the requirement of the same parties in Article 21 meant identical parties (see *supra*). The juridical advantage of a party in a suit in the court second seised should play even less of a role than where the discretion to stay is exercised outside the Convention framework—that framework recognizing each legal system within it as equal.[41]

There is an inherent difficulty in the further power in Article 22 to decline jurisdiction if: (a) one of the parties so applies and (b) the court other than that first seised has the power to consolidate the actions and (c) the court first seised has jurisdiction over both

---

35. See e.g. of a stay *De Bloos* v. *Bouyer* ECD 1–5.1.1–B6, of refusal to stay in the exercise of the discretion, judgment of Oberlandsgericht Karlsruhe (1977) ECD 1–5.5–B8.

36. *Polly Peck International* v. *Citibank NA* [1994] I.L.Pr. 71 (English High Court) (applying the principles of the Brussels Convention to the Lugano Convention). But compare *Grupo Torras SA* v. *Al Sabah* [1995] 1 Lloyd's Rep. 374 in which Mance J. considered detailed evidence given as to Spanish law to decide when a case was definitively pending under that law. The CA approved the approach, saying that in appropriate cases it may be more ready to question conclusions other than on factual issues, but not where they depended on credibility [1995] I.L.Pr. 667.

37. So it would be difficult to envisage a related action if wholly different parties are involved. See e.g. *Société Montedison* v. *Departement de la Haute Corse* (1977) Court d'Appel Bastia ECD 1–5.3–B3; *Rohstoff Einfuhr* v. *La Continentale Nucléaire* (1977) Cour Suspencion de Justice Lux) ECD 1–22–B1 but perhaps not impossible (see *The Grupo Torras* case (fn 36)). There cannot be related actions unless the court first seised has jurisdiction over both actions *De Pina* v. *MS Birka* [1994] I.L.Pr. 694.

38. See e.g. *Virgin Aviation Services Ltd.* v. *CAD Aviation Service* [1991] I.L.Pr. 79. There can be no partial stay (*ibid*).

39. See e.g. *The Linda* [1988] 1 Lloyd's Rep. 175 (a collision case in which the parties were identical but reversed—Article 21 case and Article 22 was also considered).

40. *Ibid.*

41. See *Virgin Aviation* v. *CAD Aviation* [1991] I.L.Pr. 79; *The Times*, 2 February 1990.

actions. A national court may well be unlikely to have a power to consolidate an action brought in the court of another state.[42] In any event it appears that the power of consolidation contemplated has little to do with the hearing of the two actions—for it is even more unlikely that a court in one state could direct a court in another to hear any action "consolidated" with the one already before it.

Liability and limitation proceedings

In *Dresser UK Ltd* v. *Falcongate Freight Management Ltd*[43] the Court of Appeal accepted that limitation and liability proceedings were "related"—there was the risk of irreconcilable judgments.[44] It follows that a shipowner could therefore make "a pre-emptive strike" and then by the use of Article 22 force the liability claimant into a jurisdiction of the shipowner's choosing. It is, however, arguable that under the Limitation Convention 1976 a limitation fund may be set up only where a liability action has been commenced—where that Convention applies, a factor perhaps militating against the initiation of limitation proceedings in a jurisdiction other than that in which the fund is set up.[45]

Multiple "exclusive" jurisdiction (Article 23)

Exclusive jurisdiction is a phrase used in respect of jurisdiction: (a) imposed by Article 16 if a matter falls within it; or (b) conferred by Articles 17 and 18 through agreement or submission through appearance. Article 16 is expressly given priority over Articles 17 and 18 and it has been held that appearance under Article 18 overrides any agreement under Article 17. Article 23 must therefore be of limited scope. It will apply only where there is no priority principle—as, for example, in proceedings within Article 16 elements which lead to different jurisdiction or if an agreement under Article 17 leads to two different jurisdictions.

RESTRICTIONS ON ENGLISH PROCEEDINGS OTHER THAN UNDER THE BRUSSELS OR LUGANO CONVENTIONS

The claimant who complies with the requirements for the establishing of jurisdiction in the English Admiralty Court to hear a maritime claim may be met by objections to the exercise of that jurisdiction.[46] These possible objections are based on general principles applicable to all claims but also have consequences peculiar to the maritime area because

---

42. See e.g. *BvT* v. *General Accident* (1977) ECD 1–8–B1 (no power in Dutch court to transfer case to Belgian court).

43. [1991] 2 Lloyd's Rep. 557.

44. So, for example, a court may decline jurisdiction in liability proceedings if a court first seised of the limitation action also has jurisdiction over the liability action. The court first seised has no power to decline jurisdiction.

45. A judgment obtained in limitation proceedings would however be enforceable (see Chap. 28). Further under the Limitation Convention a state may require a fund to be established for proceedings to be brought and such a requirement may be enforceable under Art. 57 of the Brussels and Lugano Conventions. As to limitation of liability generally see Chap. 24.

46. Objections to the jurisdiction on any ground are made through application to the High Court under RSC Order 12, r. 8, which sets out the relevant procedural steps. An application for a stay is not a submission to jurisdiction and should be heard prior to a challenge to jurisdiction (*Williams & Glyn's Bank plc* v. *Astro Dinamico Compania Naviera SA* [1984] 1 Lloyd's Rep. 453 (H.L.). Cf. Chap. 9.

of the linking of provisional remedy and security aspects to jurisdiction over the merits of a claim.

The restrictions to be considered are:

1. Agreements to submit dispute to foreign forum;
2. Arbitration agreements;
3. The appropriate forum (*forum conveniens*);
4. Issue estoppel and *res judicata*;
5. State immunity (whether foreign or English);
6. Restrictions on specific claims;
7. Abuse of process.

1. FOREIGN FORUM AGREEMENTS

Many maritime contracts (in particular, bills of lading) include jurisdiction clauses; and in many cases the same clause will specify the law which is to govern the contract. To what extent will such a clause be upheld by the English courts?

The issue will usually arise:

(a) as part of a request for leave to serve a defendant out of the jurisdiction in an action *in personam* (as to which see Chapter 9);
(b) (most commonly) through a request for a stay of proceedings instituted in an English court contrary to such a clause.

Construction of the clause

The construction of a clause will be governed by the proper law of the contract as adduced apart from the Contracts (Applicable Law) Act 1990. Forum and arbitration clauses are excluded from the ambit of the Rome Convention on the Law Applicable to Contracts 1980 enacted by the 1990 Act, and it is therefore to the principles of law in being prior to that Act that reference must be made. Governing law is discussed in Chapter 26 but in the present context it should be stressed that if there is no effective choice of law in the bill of lading or other contract, the validity of the jurisdiction clause (and hence the jurisdiction) will be assessed in accordance with the law having the closest connection with the contract. In particular it should be borne in mind that English law does not recognize a "floating" choice of law substantively governing the contract—as, for example, an option as to the law given to the shipowner.[47]

The clause must not be so equivocal as to be uncertain. However given the construction of "British courts" in an international maritime contract by the Court of Appeal as the

---

47. For an example of how not to draft a clause see *The Iran Vojdan* [1984] 2 Lloyd's Rep. 380. The choice of a floating curial law for arbitration does not invalidate an arbitration clause: *The Star Texas* [1993] 2 Lloyd's Rep. 445 and see Chaps. 13, 26. For a robust striking out of a "floating" part of a jurisdiction clause see *The Frank Pais* [1986] 1 Lloyd's Rep. 529—but it would be unwise to rely on a judicial initiative to validate a clause invalid because a party seeks to retain control of the governing law.

Commercial Court and Admiralty Court[48] there may be room for evidence as to type of court that reference might have been expected to be made.

Litigation or arbitration

A persistent problem stems from the incorporation (or arguable incorporation) of charterparty terms into a bill of lading when the charterparty contains an arbitration clause. That problem is discussed in Chapter 13. Its relevance in the present context arises where the bill of lading contains a jurisdiction clause and, it may be argued, it is then more difficult to incorporate an arbitration clause particularly where it is necessary to "manipulate" a clause referring to shipowners and charterers so as to apply to charterers and shippers.

Where under the principles of incorporation the arbitration clause would be incorporated, any inconsistency with a jurisdiction clause is a matter of construction of the bill of lading and particularly the precedence given, for example, to specific provision rather than standard clauses. Provision simply for "English jurisdiction" is not necessarily inconsistent with a concurrent express reference of any dispute to arbitration—for the arbitration must itself be subject to a particular jurisdiction. Especially is this so if there is also provision for the application of the law of the place in which jurisdiction is conferred—the arbitration clause operates.[49]

Scope of the clause

The first question goes to the extent to which the parties are bound by the agreement. So a clause limited to disputes "arising under this document" (i.e. a bill of lading) does not of itself include a non-party.[50] "Provided the clause is not drafted so as to exclude them non parties to the contract may be bound under the general principles of holders of bills of lading, persons to whom the goods are delivered,[51] or bailees of the goods.[52]

Further, there may be a limitation specified by reference to the claims[53] or the kind of proceedings. In 1980 in *The Lisboa*[54] the clause read: "Any and all legal proceedings against the Carrier shall be brought before the competent court at London . . . " The *Lisboa* was arrested in Italy by cargo owners. Both cargo owners and shipowners issued writs in England and the shipowners applied for an injunction to order the cargo owners to procure the release of the ship. The Court of Appeal was prepared to consider a contention that "proceedings against the carrier" did not include proceedings against a

48. See *The Komninos S* [1991] 1 Lloyd's Rep. 370.

49. See *The Nerano* [1994] 2 Lloyd's Rep. 50 (affirmed C.A. 15 February 1995)—incorporation of charterparty terms including specifically the arbitration clause together with clause "English law and jurisdiction applies".

50. *Dresser UK Ltd.* v. *Falcongate Freight Management Ltd.* [1991] 2 Lloyd's Rep. 557. So in this as in any context of contractual dispute it may be critical as to whether the bills of lading are owners or charterers bills. See *The Rewia* [1991] 2 Lloyd's Rep. 325. A decision by a foreign court on the ambit of a jurisdiction clause creates a "classic case" of issue estoppel (*The Sennar (No. 2)* [1985] 1 Lloyd's Rep. 521) (as to issue estoppel see *infra*).

51. As under the Carriage of Goods By Sea Act 1992.

52. See e.g. the *Dresser* case (fn 50); *The K.H. Enterprise* [1994] 1 Lloyd's Rep. 593.

53. See e.g. *Trendtex Trading Corpn* v. *Crédit Suisse* [1980] 3 All E.R. 721—but, as there, may play a predominant part in the court's view as to where the claims may be heard. (Decision affirmed by H.L. [1981] 3 All E.R. 520.)

54. [1980] 2 Lloyd's Rep. 546.

ship—and, therefore, the arrest did not fall within the clause. Construction problems are inevitable but it is at least necessary to be conscious of their potential consequences, particularly in the use of standard forms.

Whether the clause is "exclusive"

A non-exclusive (i.e. a permissive) clause may have less weight than an agreement excluding all jurisdiction save that selected. English courts have construed the relevance and nature of the issue primarily in respect of English jurisdiction clauses but the principles must be identical.[55] Whether the clause is exclusive or permissive is a matter of construction—the word "exclusive" is not necessary.[56] There is nothing inherently wrong in law or practice in providing for more than one jurisdiction but if only one is specified there may be little point in so providing unless it is intended that the jurisdiction be exclusive.[57]

In deciding whether or not a clause is exclusive a distinction has been drawn between a clause by which the parties agree to submit themselves to a court and a clause having a "transitive sense" and by which the parties agree to submit disputes to a court. The former is apt to describe an intention to agree to submit while the latter imposes a contractual obligation.[58] A clause of submission followed by the reservation of an option in one party to bring suit elsewhere leads to the conclusion that the clause is "exclusive" in respect of the other party.[59]

However, it all depends on the contract. So in *Berisford* v. *New Hampshire Insurance*[60] Hobhouse J. held that a clause in an insurance contract that "this insurance is subject to English jurisdiction" was non-exclusive.[61] In that role it had a purpose in indicating to the plaintiff (who would normally be the assured) that an action could be brought in the English courts. Further it would necessarily be a strong factor in any issue of whether England was the appropriate forum—a point made even more strongly in *British Aerospace Ltd* v. *Dee Howard Co.*[62] In that case Webster J. expressed the view that in the face of an agreement for English jurisdiction the plea of *forum non conveniens* was not open to the parties. Such a view should apply to militate against English jurisdiction where

55. For an example of construction of an agreement in relation to a foreign court as non-exclusive see *The Kherson* [1992] 2 Lloyd's Rep. 261. As to non-exclusive jurisdiction clauses and the operation of the mandatory jurisdiction based on forum agreement under the Brussels and Lugano Conventions see Chap. 5.

56. *Sohio Supply Co.* v. *Gatoil* [1989] 1 Lloyd's Rep. 585.

57. *Ibid.; British Aerospace plc* v. *Dee Howard Co.* [1993] 1 Lloyd's Rep. 368 (together with English law governing contract the courts "shall have jurisdiction"). This reasoning does not apply without qualification to the Brussels or Lugano Convention for in those contexts the emphasis is on providing jurisdiction by *agreement* rather than any other jurisdiction base (see Chap. 5).

58. Compare *Cannon Screen Entertainments Ltd.* v. *Handmade Films Ltd.* 11 July 1989 (unreported) with *British Aerospace plc* v. *Dee Howard Co.* [1993] 1 Lloyd's Rep. 368 considering (*inter alia*) *Cannon*. The provision of an address for service will point to the transitive sense. See *Continental Bank NA* v. *Aeakos Compania Naviera SA* [1994] 1 Lloyd's Rep. 505 (C.A.).

59. *Continental Bank NA* v. *Aeakos* (fn. 58).

60. [1990] 1 Lloyd's Rep. 454. See also *Cannon Screen Entertainments* v. *Handmade Films Ltd.* 11 July 1989 (unreported) (Hobhouse J.).

61. Compare *Denby* v. *Hellenic Mediterranean Lines* [1994] 1 Lloyd's Rep. 320 in which it appears that (in the context of the Brussels Convention) such a clause in a well known marine insurance policy with shipowners was held "exclusive".

62. [1993] 1 Lloyd's Rep. 368.

the clause is in favour of a foreign court—but it has to be said English courts have traditionally been more ready to assert than to decline jurisdiction (see *infra*).

Limitations on agreements as a jurisdiction base

The recognition of agreement as a jurisdictional ground is subject to any requirement of a mandatory link between territory and dispute as a jurisdictional prerequisite, or the imposition of mandatory rules to the dispute. To give effect to those rules it may be held that any agreement in favour of a foreign forum is void.

In English law the imposition of jurisdiction contracts or mandatory substantive rules tends to be rooted in Conventions enacted into national law.[63] So the Collision Jurisdiction Convention 1952 requires one or more of specified links for an action *in personam*.[64] The Athens Convention Relating to the Carriage of Passengers and Their Luggage by Sea,[65] the CMR (relating to international carriage by road) but which applies in part to sea carriage,[66] the Hamburg Rules 1978[67] and the Multimodal Convention 1980[68] all specify where actions must be brought. The Athens Convention permits choice of jurisdiction after the event creating the dispute, the CMR permits actions to be brought before the courts of a contracting State by agreement, while the Hamburg Rules and the Multimodal Convention provide for actions before the courts of any state by agreement. Apart from the Athens Convention[69] jurisdictional choice is but one of a number of permissible jurisdiction grounds; and it must be arguable that in the face of an action in a permitted forum the English presumption of upholding the choice of jurisdiction by agreement (see *infra*) would not apply.

The Hague and Hague-Visby Rules

The Hague and Hague-Visby Rules contain no express jurisdiction provisions.[70] In the only reported English case on the effect of a jurisdiction clause in relation to a dispute within the English version of the Hague Rules the clause was upheld. The basis of the decision was that the law to be applied would be the same as English law.[71]

The replacement in England of the Hague Rules by the Hague-Visby Rules has changed the picture in two respects. First, the rules as enacted in England now apply by statute to many more voyages than previously and may so apply to a voyage having no connection

---

63. But not necessarily—for discussion as to whether the Carriage of Goods By Sea Act 1992 (providing for the transmission of rights and liabilities of a shipper to persons not parties to the initial contract) is mandatory in this sense see [1994] LMCLQ 280.

64. See Chap. 9.

65. Article 17.

66. The CMR is enacted into English law by the Carriage of Goods by Road Act 1965. As to specified links, see Sch. Art. 31. The Convention applies to the sea carriage of goods in vehicles (see Art. 2(1))—thereby providing an action against the road carrier for damage or loss caused in a sea leg. However, an action against the sea carrier would still lie under the Hague-Visby Rules if they apply to that leg.

67. See Art. 21.

68. See Art. 26.

69. A jurisdiction agreement is permitted only after the event creating the dispute.

70. Contrast the Hamburg Rules which (in Art. 21) specify jurisdictional provisions in a similar manner to the CMR. The Article (inserted at the urging of cargo interests) provides for a number of jurisdictions connected with the dispute at the option of the plaintiff. One such option is the jurisdiction agreed by the parties which, therefore, confers a mandatory effect on such agreements subject to exercise of the plaintiff's option.

71. See *Maharani Woollen Mills Co. v. Anchor Line* (1927) 29 Ll.L.Rep. 169.

with England. Secondly, the Carriage of Goods by Sea Act 1971 provides that the rules are to have "the force of law".

The phrase "force of law" has become the traditional method of enacting Conventions into English law where this is done by setting out the Convention provisions in a schedule to the enabling state. In particular the phrase is employed in the Carriage of Goods by Road Act 1965, s.1 (in relation to the CMR Convention); the Merchant Shipping Act 1995, s.183(1), and formerly the Merchant Shipping Act 1979, s.14 (in relation to the Athens Convention 1974); the Civil Jurisdiction and Judgments Acts 1982 and 1991 (in relation to the Brussels and Lugano Conventions); the Merchant Shipping Act 1995, s.185, and formerly the 1979 Act, s.17 (in relation to the Limitation of Liability Convention 1976); the 1995 Act, s.224, and formerly the Merchant Shipping (Salvage and Pollution) Act 1994, s.1 (in relation to the Salvage Convention 1989). On its face the phrase is not necessarily mandatory in the sense of directing an English court to apply the statute despite any choice of jurisdiction or law by a party which would evade it. It remains somewhat of a mystery why, if it was intended to be mandatory, it is not drafted in clear language so providing. A glance at s.9 of the Australian Sea Carriage of Goods Act 1924 provides a model.

"9(1) All parties to any bill of lading or document relating to the carriage of goods from any place in Australia to any place outside Australia shall be deemed to have intended to contract according to the laws in force at the place of shipment, and any stipulation or agreement to the contrary, or purporting to oust or lessen the jurisdiction of the Courts of the Commonwealth or of a State in respect of the bill of lading or document, shall be illegal, null and void, and of no effect.

(2) Any stipulation or agreement, whether made in the Commonwealth or elsewhere, purporting to oust or lessen the jurisdiction of the Courts of the Commonwealth or of a State in respect of any bill of lading or document relating to the carriage of goods from any place outside Australia to any place in Australia shall be illegal, null and void, and of no effect . . . ."

The lack of statutory clarity enabled argument and counter-argument on the issue of "force of law" to carry *The Morviken*[72] to the House of Lords in 1982. In the case, the bill of lading provided in the same clause:

    (i) for exclusive jurisdiction in the court of Amsterdam;
    (ii) choice of law and a maximum carrier's liability according to the Hague Rules (to which the Netherlands was then a party) well below that according to the Hague-Visby Rules (to which the United Kingdom was a party).

Proceedings were brought in England and it was argued by the cargo owners that because of the maximum liability less than the Hague-Visby Rules the whole clause (including the provision for jurisdiction) was invalid. It lessened the liability of the carrier and was, therefore, "null and void and of no effect" by Article III, rule 8, of the rules.

The House of Lords held that Article III, rule 8, applied not only to clauses substantively lessening the carrier's liability but to any clause which, if applied, would lessen that liability. In respect of a choice of forum clause if, when relied on, it would have that consequence "an English court is . . . commanded by the 1971 Act to treat the clause as of no effect". As a result, a choice of forum or a choice of law clause in a bill of lading to which the Hague-Visby Rules apply "by force of law" will be treated by an English

---

72. [1983] 1 Lloyd's Rep. 1.

court as void to the extent that it falls foul of Article III, rule 8, of the rules.[73] However, it will remain valid in all other respects.[74]

In 1983 in *The Benarty*[75] Sheen J. applied *The Morviken* in declaring void a clause referring all "actions under the contract of carriage" to the court of Djakarta. The basis of the declaration was that the Djakarta court would not apply the Hague-Visby Rules (as they were not incorporated into the bill of lading) but would apply a domestic statute relating to limitation of shipowner's liability. As a result, the carrier's liability would be less than the limit specified by the rules. It was argued that such a consequence was consistent with the rules, Art. VIII of which provides that the rules:

"shall not affect the rights and obligations of the carrier under any statute for the time being in force relating to the limitation of the liability of owners of sea going vessels."

Sheen J. held that a clause providing for jurisdiction in a court of a country "in which the liability of a shipowner or charterer is less than that provided by the Merchant Shipping Acts" is a clause lessening liability otherwise than as provided by the rules. Necessarily, therefore, Sheen J.'s view of Art. VIII was that in English law "statute" means English statute. The Court of Appeal disagreed, holding that as the rules were an international Convention "statute" could hardly be restricted to an English statute. Such a conclusion stems from conferring "the force of law" on the rules, as distinct from enacting an English version.

The effect in English law

(a) Stay of proceedings

In theory the presumption of upholding contracts holds full sway.[76] Yet it is difficult to trace any consistent principle through the cases. The cynic may say that the issue turns to a large extent on the identity of the jurisdiction for which the parties have opted, but even this focus (hardly a principle) is difficult to establish. Judicial concern has often been expressed at the cost in time and expense of lengthy proceedings solely directed at the place of trial. In some cases such contents may be tactical moves to further settlements[77] but whatever the motive courts are not over impressed by lengthy documentation and argument.[78]

English appellate courts take the view that the matter of upholding an agreement is one for the discretion of the trial judge. It is not enough to overrule the exercise of the

---

73. The effect of such a holding on the validity of arbitration clauses is not clear, particularly in light of the duty to recognize such clauses imposed by the Arbitration Act 1975, s.1 (see further Chap. 13). The reasoning applies to choice of law as to choice of forum, for otherwise an English court may simply have to apply the law of the source of the objection to jurisdiction. As to choice of law see Chap. 26.

74. Cf. the view of the United States Court of Appeal (2nd Circuit) in *Indussa Corpn* v. *The Ramborg* [1967] 2 Lloyd's Rep. 101, in which a clause taking a case within COGSA (US) was simply declared invalid. See also *Union Insurance* v. *SS Elikon* [1982] AMC 588 (which would allow consideration of *forum non conveniens*).

75. [1984] 2 Lloyd's Rep. 244 *reversing* [1983] 2 Lloyd's Rep. 50.

76. See e.g. *Trendtex Trading Corpn* v. *Crédit Suisse* [1980] 3 All E.R. 721, at p. 744 (per Lord Denning M.R.)—the jurisdiction clause "must be given full effect unless its enforcement would be unreasonable and unjust or that the clause was invoked for such reasons as fraud or overreaching". The United States view is similar. See *The Bremen and Another* v. *Zapata Off-shore Co.* [1972] 2 Lloyd's Rep. 315; 407 U.S. 1 (1972).

77. See the comments of Sheen J. in *The Al Battani* [1993] 2 Lloyd's Rep. 219.

78. See *The Nile Rhapsody* [1994] 1 Lloyd's Rep. 382.

discretion that the appeal court disagrees with it. It must be shown that the judge made an error in principle or that he has taken into account matters which he ought not to have done or has failed to take into account matters which he ought to have done or because of wrongful evaluation of the circumstances his decision was "plainly wrong".[79] So, in 1976, the Court of Appeal (applying these principles) upheld Brandon J. in *The Adolf Warski*[80] (refusing a stay) and *The Makefjell*[81] (granting a stay)—two decisions on very similar facts.[82]

It was Brandon J. who in 1969 formulated the factors which should be investigated to decide whether the presumption of upholding the contract is rebutted. In *The Eleftheria* he said:

"The principles established by the authorities can, I think, be summarised as follows: (1) Where plaintiffs sue in England in breach of an agreement to refer disputes to a foreign court, and the defendants apply for a stay, the English court, assuming the claim to be otherwise within its jurisdiction, is not bound to grant a stay but has a discretion whether to do so or not. (2) The discretion should be exercised by granting a stay unless strong cause for not doing so is shown. (3) The burden of proving such strong cause is on the plaintiffs. (4) In exercising its discretion the court should take into account all the circumstances of the particular case. (5) In particular, but without prejudice to (4), the following matters, where they arise, may properly be regarded: (a) In what country the evidence on the issues of fact is situated, or more readily available, and the effect of that on the relative convenience and expense of trial as between the English and foreign courts. (b) Whether the law of the foreign court applies and, if so, whether it differs from English law in any material respects. (c) With what country either party is connected, and how closely. (d) Whether the defendants genuinely desire trial in the foreign country, or are only seeking procedural advantages. (e) Whether the plaintiffs would be prejudiced by having to sue in the foreign court because they would: (i) be deprived of security for their claim; (ii) be unable to enforce any judgment obtained; (iii) be faced with a time-bar not applicable in England; or (iv) for political, racial, religious or other reasons be unlikely to get a fair trial."[83]

In *The El Amria* the same judge (as Brandon L.J.) gave the leading judgment affirming these principles subject to these qualifications. At first instance Sheen J. had expressed the view that if the matter were to be heard in Egypt the parties "would not obtain the full and thorough investigation" which they desired.[84] The Court of Appeal thought it improper for an English judge to compare the English and Egyptian system of justice and even more improper to pronounce on the respective merits.[85] Brandon L.J. (with whom Rees L.J. and

---

79. See e.g. *The Nile Rhapsody* [1994] 1 Lloyd's Rep. 382; (for a relatively rare example of Court Appeal discretion) *The El Amria* [1981] 2 Lloyd's Rep. 119. Cf. *The Abidin Daver* [1984] 1 All E.R. 470.

80. [1976] 2 Lloyd's Rep. 241—a Polish jurisdiction clause. There was a time bar question in this case but the fact was treated as neutral (see *infra*).

81. [1976] 2 Lloyd's Rep. 29—an Oslo jurisdiction clause.

82. See also the comments of the House of Lords and Court of Appeal in *Trendtex Trading Corpn* v. *Crédit Suisse* [1981] 3 All E.R. 520 (H.L.), [1980] 3 All E.R. 721, at p. 758 (C.A.).

83. [1970] P. 94, at pp. 99–100. The factors are not unlike those applicable to the appropriateness of the forum but the existence of a foreign forum agreement should make the case for a stay very much stronger. See *The Nile Rhapsody* (fn 78). For an apparent reversal of the force of the two doctrines see *The Al Battani* (fn 77).

84. Cf. *The Star of Luxor* [1981] 1 Lloyd's Rep. 139 (an Egyptian jurisdiction clause) in which Sheen J. said that *The El Amria* "was based on the special facts of the case" and that he now had the benefit of much fuller information as to the Egyptian trial procedure (p. 140).

85. But compare the somewhat more gentle "comparison" in the context of "*forum non conveniens*" made by Sir John Donaldson M.R. in *The Abidin Daver* [1984] 1 Lloyd's Rep. 339. He doubted whether Turkish courts had the "maritime experience" of the English Admiralty Court—the experience being a matter of "history and geography"—but the tone did not make the comparison less invidious (see [1984] 1 All E.R. at p. 486 (H.L.—Lord Brandon)).

Stephenson L.J. agreed) qualified this general prohibition, saying that it would be right to take into account:

(a) the availability of a remedy in an English court which is not available in the foreign court;

(b) the involvement of very great delay through foreign court procedure; and

(c) "in wholly exceptional cases" clearly established serious defects in foreign procedures.

To the extent that para. 5(d) of the principles of *The Eleftheria* might be interpreted as excluding procedural considerations it was to be qualified by (a), (b) and (c) as set out in this case.[86]

In *The Havhelt*[87] Saville J. pointed out that the deprivation of security in the foreign court (5(e)(i)) has been "somewhat overtaken" by the introduction of the statutory ability of the English court to retain security.[88] Subject to this the factors have been consistently applied[89] but there is less apparent consistency in the results of their application. Indeed, it is not easy to differentiate between *The Adolf Warski* and *The Makefjell* given that the Polish time bar in *The Adolf Warski* was put on one side. There are more than traces of suspicion that English judges have not been averse to exercising English jurisdiction, even if as a consequence they must apply foreign law. It is perhaps curious that where a jurisdiction clause is linked to a choice of law there seems little reluctance to reject the first while upholding the second.

Of the factors specifically mentioned in *The Eleftheria*, the foreign law, the time bar, and the possibility of an unfair trial call for further consideration.

The relevance of the foreign law

As Brandon J. said in *The Makefjell*: "where the decision of a dispute depends in part at least on the law of a foreign country that is a circumstance which makes it better, other things being equal, for that dispute to be decided by the Courts of that country."[90] Any such difference is a factor in favour of upholding the jurisdiction clause. It is suggested that the simple fact of choice of a law which is the law of the selected forum should be a strong factor in upholding the clause. Unless there are reasons of policy for rejecting the choice of law the matching of jurisdiction and law should not be underestimated. Reliance on easy accessibility of foreign law should perhaps be treated with caution.[91] Further, to apply the artificial rule of the presumption that foreign law is to be equated with English

---

86. The comments made it clear that procedural advantage could work both ways.

87. [1993] 1 Lloyd's Rep. 523.

88. Civil Jurisdiction and Judgments Act 1982, s.26 (as to which see Chap. 15).

89. See e.g. *Trendtex Trading Corpn* v. *Crédit Suisse* [1980] 3 All E.R. 721, at pp. 735–737, [1981] 3 All E.R. 520; *The Benarty* [1984] 2 Lloyd's Rep. 244 (C.A.), [1983] 2 Lloyd's Rep. 50; *The Al Battani* [1993] 2 Lloyd's Rep. 219; *The Nile Rhapsody* [1994] 1 Lloyd's Rep. 382; [1992] 2 Lloyd's Rep. 399 (particularly the procedural disadvantages).

90. In *The El Amria*, the Court of Appeal thought the test of "with what country is the dispute most closely concerned" (applied by Lord Denning M.R. in *The Fehmarn* [1957] 2 Lloyd's Rep. 551) too simplistic to cover all cases.

91. For reference to accessibility as a factor, see e.g. *The Adolf Warski* [1976] 1 Lloyd's Rep. 107, at p. 111; *The Atlantic Song* [1983] 2 Lloyd's Rep. 394. The unfortunate (and presumably costly) course of the proceedings in *Oppenheimer* v. *Cattermole* [1976] A.C. 249 (where the appreciation of the foreign law on which the Court of Appeal based its decision was accepted as wrong) should provide some discouragement to those ready to interpret foreign as well as English law.

law[92] is to allow a rule which may justifiably operate to prevent a court being found with "no law" to operate to prevent the application by a tribunal of its own law.

In *The Al Battani*[93] Sheen J. thought that there was no reason why as a matter of comity a jurisdiction clause should be upheld when the forum chosen would regard the clause as null and void. It still however remains a matter of contract but particularly as in that case the foreign law allowed the plaintiff an option to litigate in England there was little point in practice or principle in a stay.

The time bar

In *The Adolf Warski* bills of lading contained a Polish jurisdiction and choice of law clause. The defendants refused to waive the clause. Despite this refusal the plaintiff started an action in England and did not start an action in Poland. As a result all claims in Poland were statute barred. There are three views on the relevance of a time bar:

(1) that it operated against a stay as it would deprive the plaintiffs of any remedy;
(2) that it operated in favour of a stay as it would deprive the defendants of a defence available in the selected jurisdiction;
(3) that balancing (1) and (2) it was neutral.

Brandon J. preferred the view that it was a factor against a stay. In 1981 in *The Blue Wave*[94] Sheen J. emphatically endorsed that approach, unless the plaintiff had deliberately and advisedly allowed the time limit to expire without instituting alternative proceedings.[95] The approach favoured by Brandon J. and Sheen J. is that of the United States[96]—but it is surely unduly favourable to those who ignore jurisdiction clauses. Given that such clauses should be upheld, it is difficult to find a great deal to be said for a plaintiff who institutes proceedings in a jurisdiction of his present choice and then defends that action by the argument that it is now too late to proceed according to the jurisdiction of his earlier choice.

(b) Arrest

The effect of a jurisdiction agreement in favour of a foreign court on the power to arrest in England is considered fully in Chapter 15. It suffices here to emphasize that apart from a statutory intervention the power to arrest is dependent on the issue of a warrant, in turn dependent on the issue of a writ *in rem*; and that arguably a stay of proceedings commenced with such issue removes the basis for the arrest. The writ *in rem* is no longer

92. See e.g. *The Adolf Warski* [1976] 2 Lloyd's Rep. 241, at pp. 246 and 247.
93. Fn 89.
94. [1982] 1 Lloyd's Rep. 151.
95. In *Trendtex Trading Corpn* v. *Crédit Suisse* [1980] 3 All E.R. 721 (at p. 736) per Robert Goff (discussing a time bar) expressed a reluctance to assist an aiding a party having agreed to a jurisdiction "to escape from the procedural consequence of that choice" but in *The Spiliada* [1986] 2 All E.R. 843 the same judge (as Lord Goff) thought that in adjudging the appropriateness of the forum the plaintiff should not be shut out in this country provided the failure to commence proceedings abroad was not "unreasonable"—an approach said Lord Goff—consistent with *The Blue Wave*.
96. Declining of jurisdiction will usually be subject to waiver of any time bar. See e.g. *Vaz Borralho* v. *Keydril*, 696 F. 2d 379 (1983) (US Court of Appeals, 5th Circuit). As to the relevance to a plea of inappropriate forum see *infra*.

effective. However, even if this be analytically correct, the stay (being discretionary) may be made conditional on the provision of an equivalent security.

The inability to retain a ship under arrest pending the outcome of foreign proceedings was probably contrary to the provisions of the Arrest Convention 1952 ratified by the United Kingdom. There seemed little in principle or policy why the international obligations should not be complied with. And, more radically, it would make considerable sense for the power of arrest to be separated from the power to hear a case on its merits.

The Civil Jurisdiction and Judgments Act 1982, s. 26, goes some way towards meeting international obligations but (regrettably it is submitted) underlines the connection between arrest and "merits" jurisdiction. It provides that on the staying or dismissal of Admiralty proceedings on the basis that the dispute be submitted to another court, a court may order property arrested to "be retained as security" or order the stay or dismissal to be conditional on provision of security equivalent to the arrested property. So the principle of dependence of arrest on issue of the writ *in rem* remains[97]—but the retention under arrest is no longer dependent on the continuation of proceedings begun by the issue of the writ.

2. ARBITRATION AGREEMENTS

Such agreements are common in maritime transactions. Insofar as they are "non domestic" in character (i.e. have a relevant foreign element) English courts *must* stay proceedings commenced inconsistently with them.[98] If the arbitration clause is domestic the court has a discretion whether or not to order a stay.[99] Arbitration is discussed generally in Chapter 13 and the enforceability of awards in Chapters 25 and 27.

Arrest and arbitration clauses[100]

The principles of (i) the dependence of the power of arrest on jurisdiction in an action *in rem* and (ii) the mandatory stay of such an action created difficulties for an English court in exercising its power of arrest in the face of a non-domestic arbitration clause. In particular, the connection between arrest and writ *in rem* illustrated a policy of the inappropriateness of arrest as a security for arbitration proceedings.[101]

The "alternative security" method of avoiding the limitations on the power to retain under arrest available in the context of a jurisdictional clause (i.e. attaching of conditions to the stay of proceedings) is less obviously available where the stay is mandatory. In such circumstances a court may not attach conditions on the stay, but in 1978 in *The Rena K*[102] Brandon J. was prepared to consider attaching conditions to the release or refusing a

---

97. Proceedings leading to arrest as security for a foreign suit are not "multiple proceedings" within the Brussels or Lugano Convention obligating the release from arrest (*The Nordglimt* [1987] 2 Lloyd's Rep. 470. See Chap. 15).

98. Arbitration Act 1975, s.1. A putative English arbitration clause is a significant factor in considering the issue of the appropriate forum in the context of the service of a writ out of England. See *Oldendorff* v. *Liberia Corpn* [1995] 2 Lloyd's Rep. 64 and Chap. 9.

99. Arbitration Act 1950, s.4(1).

100. Cf. Chap. 15 (Arrest).

101. See *The Andria now renamed Vasso* [1984] 1 Lloyd's Rep. 235.

102. [1978] 1 Lloyd's Rep. 545. Cf. *The Tuyuti* [1984] 2 Lloyd's Rep. 51.

release where there was a likelihood that any arbitration award would not be met. As is argued elsewhere in this work,[103] the legal justification for this approach seemed as dubious as its commercial justification was obvious.

The Civil Jurisdiction and Judgments Act 1982, s.26, makes specific provision for the retention of property arrested or alternative security if Admiralty proceedings are stayed or dismissed, by reason of submission to arbitration. But a writ *in rem* is a prerequisite for the arrest—arbitration proceedings are still not of themselves the basis of security through arrest.

However the introduction of the provision removed any policy objection to the issue of the writ for the purpose of security in arbitration. In some part the need to attach conditions to release was removed by the later view taken by the Court of Appeal that the stay required, because of arbitration, was limited to substantive issues to be arbitrated.[104] The criteria for retaining the security remained, however, as suggested in *The Rena K* rather than the entitlement to arrest which flowed from the issue of the writ *in rem* and now flows from s.26 of the 1982 Act (see Chapter 15). There would be no need for such an indirect approach either if the power to arrest was seen in its realistic light—a provisional remedy not linked exclusively to a judicial hearing on the merits—or specific statutory provisions made for arrest in support of arbitration.

3. THE APPROPRIATE FORUM—"FORUM CONVENIENS"

An English court may refuse to exercise jurisdiction established as of right on the basis that it is an inappropriate forum. Until 1972, a defendant seeking a stay of proceedings had to prove that the continuance of the proceedings would be "vexatious and oppressive" which, it was taken to mean, indicated the plaintiff's harassment of the defendant. Simply taking advantage of English rules or causing gross inconvenience was not enough for a stay. Harassment of this kind was most easily established by the institution of duplicate proceedings by the plaintiff. Under the modern approach unless there are other factors the plaintiff may simply be required to elect in which jurisdiction the suit is to be brought—the issue of *forum non conveniens* is not reached.[105]

In 1972 in *The Atlantic Star*[106] the House of Lords moved away from the plaintiff-oriented approach which emphasized the availability of the English proceess to any plaintiff catching his defendant within the territory. In 1978 this movement was continued in *MacShannon* v. *Rockware Glass Ltd.*[107] The principles to be followed in English courts were to be gathered from the judgments in that case, but it was by no means easy to determine quite how far there had been a move from "vexatious and oppressive" towards "appropriateness" in any but a semantic sense.

---

103. Chap. 15.
104. *The Tuyuti* [1984] 2 Lloyd's Rep. 51.
105. *Australian Commercial Research and Development Ltd.* v. *ANZ Bank Ltd.* [1989] 3 All E.R. 65. Compare *Bank of Credit and Commerce (Hong Kong) Ltd.* v. *Sonali Bank* [1995] 1 Lloyd's Rep. 227—where there were many claims in respect of which apparently only in one was stay of proceedings considered on *forum non conveniens* basis and refused.
106. [1974] A.C. 436.
107. [1978] A.C. 795; [1978] 1 All E.R. 625.

In 1984, in *The Abidin Daver*[108] (a case in which foreign proceedings were in existence) the Court of Appeal (displaying a fine disregard for the developing doctrine) reverted to the view held in *The Atlantic Star* by the Court of Appeal but rejected emphatically by the House of Lords. Sir John Donaldson, referring to the expertise of the English Admiralty Court, took a similar line to that condemned so roundly by Lord Reid some 12 years previously. In the House of Lords[109] he drew a similar rebuke in the terms that he was in effect comparing English and foreign courts. The judgments in *The Abidin Daver* moved English law closer to a substantive doctrine of *forum non conveniens*.

Yet qualifications remained. First, the House of Lords in *MacShannon* made it quite clear that "balance of convenience" was not enough. Secondly, the plea for a stay could be defeated by proof that the plaintiff had a personal or juridical advantage in suing in England. Yet to allow a plaintiff to substantiate his claim to be heard on the grounds that he had a better chance to win was inconsistent with the idea of balancing one forum against another on the basis of links with the dispute. Thirdly, the question of stay remained a matter of discretion.

The uncertainties were largely set at rest in 1986 by the House of Lords (and particularly the judgment of Lord Goff) in *The Spiliada*.[110] It is that case which now forms the root of the principle. It is made clear that it applies both to discretion to permit a writ to be served out of England and the stay of proceedings in which jurisdiction is established. The principle is statutorily recognized by s. 49 of the Civil Jurisdiction and Judgments Act 1982.[111] Lord Goff stressed that the principle was not one of convenience but of appropriateness and made it clear in the application of the principle to the facts of the case it remains essentially a matter for the discretion of the trial judge. An appellate court will not interfere simply because it disagrees.[112]

Fundamental elements of the principle are that for a stay:

(a) there must be another available forum having competent jurisdiction "in which the case may be tried more suitably for the interests of the parties and the ends of justice";

(b) the defendant must show that the stay should be granted but if the court is satisfied that *prima facie* there is a more appropriate forum it is for the plaintiff to show any special circumstances why a stay should not be granted[113];

(c) the defendant must establish that the other forum is "clearly or more distinctly appropriate"—this standard recognizing that jurisdiction in England has been founded as of right[114];

(d) the court will look first to see if there are factors connecting the dispute to another forum making that the "national forum", these "connecting factors"

---

108. [1983] 3 All E.R. 46.

109. [1984] 1 All E.R. 470.

110. [1986] 3 All E.R. 843 (H.L.).

111. Providing that nothing in the Act "shall prevent" any United Kingdom court from staying or dismissing proceedings "on the ground of *forum non conveniens* where to do so is not inconsistent with" the Brussels or Lugano Conventions. It applies to cases within the Brussels Convention adapted to the UK (see Chap. 7).

112. See *The Spiliada* [1986] 3 All E.R. 843; *The Nile Rhapsody* [1994] 1 Lloyd's Rep. 382; but it may review the discretion anew if the principles have not been correctly applied. See e.g. *Du Pont* v. *Agnew* [1987] 2 Lloyd's Rep. 585; *Banco Atlantico* v. *British Bank of the Middle East* [1990] 2 Lloyd's Rep. 504.

113. As is the general principle that the evidential burden in respect of any fact rests on the party asserting it.

114. But the strength of the connection establishing it (e.g. temporary presence) being taken into account.

including matters affecting convenience, expense, place of parties' residence
or business and governing law;

(e) normally, another national forum is shown to exist (this principle encompassing the case where there is no national forum)[115];

(f) if a national forum other than in England is shown to exist, normally a stay will
be granted unless in the circumstances of the case as a whole justice required
that it be not granted.

In considering (f) relevant factors are, for example, it being shown "by cogent evidence"
that the plaintiff will not obtain justice in the other forum, and consideration of the relative
advantage and disadvantage to the parties in invoking English jurisdiction. In Lord Goff's
view a stay should not be refused simply because of such advantages as the availability
in England of higher damages, more effective discovery, power to award interest or a more
generous limitation period. However, a stay which would mean that the plaintiff would be
shut out in the foreign forum because of a time bar should not be granted if the plaintiff
did not act unreasonably in failing to commence proceedings in the foreign forum. A stay
could be granted on condition that any foreign time bar was waived. In general if a stay
is granted it would "not normally be wrong" to allow a plaintiff to keep the benefit of
security obtained in this country by commencing proceedings here.

These principles provide a framework for a balanced regime of "appropriate forum".
The curious view that a juridical advantage for the plaintiff should be a strong, if not a
conclusive, factor leading to a refusal of stay is replaced by a balancing of the relative
advantage to each party. The burden put on the defendant takes into account, without
unduly emphasizing, the establishment of jurisdiction in this country by the plaintiff,
particularly where the basis of the jurisdiction is a relatively slight connection. The role
of the appellate court remains restricted to ensuring a correct approach in principle or that
the judge was not plainly wrong in applying the principle.

The factors relevant to adjudging whether there is a natural forum are various, those
linked by Lord Goff simply being examples. In *The Spiliada* shipowners brought an action
against cargo owners in respect of damage caused by loading of a cargo of wet sulphur.
A like cargo had been loaded by the same shipper on another ship, the *Cambridgeshire*,
and an action was proceeding in England involving the same solicitors and counsel on
each side. It was held that in the circumstance of the potentially lengthy and complex
litigation the judge was entitled to treat this as the crucial point. Further relevant factors
pointing to England were English insurers and governing law.[116]

Relevant factors will vary according to the circumstances of the case but the important
categorization by *The Spiliada* is to see the appropriate forum as essentially a choice based
first on connection with the dispute (the natural forum issue).[117] Establishment that

---

115. As in a collision on the high seas.

116. *The Spiliada* was a case of service of a writ out of the jurisdiction but these elements would be as
relevant to a stay of proceedings. For consideration of the "*Cambridgeshire* factor" in respect of a foreign court
see *British Aerospace Plc* v. *Dee Howard Co*. [1993] 1 Lloyd's Rep. 368.

117. For examples of a stay based on the "natural forum" see *The Lakhta* [1992] 2 Lloyd's Rep. 269
(ownership and the right to regulate a ship, the parties being Latvia and Russia and the ship registered in St
Petersburg). See also *Cleveland Museum of Art* v. *Capricorn Art International SA* [1990] 2 Lloyd's Rep. 166.
For refusal of stay apparently on the ground of England being the natural forum see *Meadows Ltd* v. *Insurance
Corpn of Ireland* [1989] 1 Lloyd's Rep. 181, [1989] 2 Lloyd's Rep. 298 (C.A.) (all parties before English court
in one action). The *Hamburg Star* [1994] 1 Lloyd's Rep. 399 (weighing many factors).

connections to foreign courts are of more force than the English court opens the door to consideration of the nature of the proceedings and factors affecting the parties, such as delay and the level of damages.[118] A natural foreign forum will mean that factors other than "connection" will be for the plaintiff to establish as grounds for refusal of stay. Where there is no natural forum either in England or abroad the factors remain relevant but it is then for the defendant to make the case for a stay on those factors.[119]

Concurrent proceedings

Where the plaintiff has instituted proceedings in two jurisdictions (one being England) he may be asked by the court to elect in which court he may proceed. The issues are identical where there are proceedings in a foreign court by the defendant in the English proceedings and where there are no proceedings but the foreign court is said to be more appropriate.[120] The existence of the proceedings may be a relevant factor, depending for its weight on the stages reached. It does not, however, shift the burden of proof to the plaintiff in the English proceedings.[121] Nor is it sufficient that the defendant showed that the forum in which proceedings had started was *a* (as distinct from *the*) natural forum.[122]

Limitation of liability

Apart from obligations (a) to contracting States within the framework of the Limitation Convention 1976 and (b) to recognize judgments of contracting States under the Brussels and Lugano Conventions it is unlikely that an English court would simply recognize a limitation decree of another state. Limitation has traditionally been seen as a matter for the forum, particularly where the limit otherwise applicable differs.[123]

The staying of limitation actions does not seem to have been much contemplated—presumably as the forum emphasis would simply operate. In 1988 in *The Falstria*[124] a stay was refused in robust terms, first, simply on the grounds that the liability plaintiff was not necessarily the only party who would be affected by the limitation decree. Secondly, there would be no limitation action in the foreign country as the limit there exceeded the claim. So, thought Sheen J., there was no matching action or relief.

---

118. See *Banco Atlantico SA* v. *British Bank of the Middle East* [1990] 2 Lloyd's Rep. 504 (non-applicability of the non-forum governing law); *The Al Battani* [1993] 2 Lloyd's Rep. 219 (documents, witnesses, different costs and interest rules); *The Vishva Ajay* [1989] 2 Lloyd's Rep. 558 (delay and lack of availability of costs).

119. See e.g. *The Vishva Abha* [1990] 2 Lloyd's Rep. 312 (no stay—limits of liability lower abroad—no discharge of onus by defendant).

120. *The Varna (No. 2)* [1994] 2 Lloyd's Rep. 41 (applying *The Spiliada*). For cases prior to *The Spiliada* see *De Dampierre* v. *De Dampierre* [1988] A.C. 92 and (in the context of shipping) *The Abidin Daver* [1984] A.C. 398.

121. *Meadows Indemnity Co. Ltd.* v. *Insurance Corporation* [1989] 1 Lloyd's Rep. 181 applying *The Spiliada* criteria.

122. *The Varna (No. 2)* [1994] 2 Lloyd's Rep. 41—rejecting the submission that "a natural forum" was all that was required where there were foreign and English proceedings (see fn 120).

123. Although it must be arguable that enforcement of a judgment for a sum reflecting limited liability should be enforceable on general principles of recognition (as to which see Chap. 27). As to limitation of liability generally see Chap. 24.

124. [1988] 1 Lloyd's Rep. 495. The stay was also sought on the basis of the Brussels Convention, but there was no applicable ground.

While with respect the first ground seems highly relevant to a stay, the second adopts a technically narrow view of the relevance of a stay to limitation. The issue for the forum was adducing the limit of liability in relation to the claim, and this no more excludes the entire satisfaction of the claim than would the likelihood that on a stay the other party would succeed. It would mean that a stay was only to be contemplated if the plaintiff would succeed at least in part. Success of one party is not as such a relevant factor. Apart from issues of fundamental policy stemming from an agreed limitation framework, there is in truth no reason that after taking into account the common identity of the parties with the liability claim limitation should not be treated as any other action.

Limitation has been considered a relevant factor in the stay of liability actions but the justifiability for this is doubtful save again for any issue of fundamental policy. In *The Vishva Abha*[125] Sheen J. thought it would be "a grave injustice" to deprive the plaintiff of the chance to litigate in England where the limit was much higher than in the foreign court (South Africa). In 1993 in *The Hamburg Star*[126] Clarke J. tended to favour a contention before him that a higher limit in England was a legitimate juridical advantage because it was rooted in an international Convention.[127] Although there is little ground for arguing that the Limitation Convention 1976 is seen internationally as mandatory it may be justifiable to see it as reflecting principles to be upheld where there is a choice of forum.[128] It should not become the door to "juridical advantage" as a general factor.

Restraint of any foreign proceedings following refusal of stay of English proceedings

The English courts have power to order a party subject to its jurisdiction not to pursue foreign proceedings. It does not, however, follow necessarily that a refusal of stay of English proceedings will necessarily lead to such an order. The criteria are different, any order relating to foreign proceedings requiring the party seeking it to show (as under the former principles relevant to stay of English proceedings) that the continuance of the foreign proceedings would be "vexatious and oppressive" (see *infra*).

Jurisdiction agreements

In a sense these two grounds are variations on a theme. Both are essentially matters of discretion for the judge of first instance, and it may be argued that a jurisdictional agreement is but an additional factor in an overall consideration of appropriateness. Conversely, it may be said that such an agreement provides the opposite starting-point from the argument of appropriateness. An agreement should be upheld; where a stay is requested on grounds of appropriateness the onus is on the defendant to justify it.

The English law starts with the latter view but if the forum selected is equated with the natural forum the issues become similar. Yet differences in the factors elucidated in respect of each may remain. So a different attitude may be justifiably adopted in respect

125. [1990] 2 Lloyd's Rep. 312.
126. [1994] 1 Lloyd's Rep. 399.
127. On the evidence it was uncertain whether the plaintiffs would gain or lose and so the issue was neutral as a factor in a possible stay.
128. Following the general approach of *The Morviken* [1983] 1 Lloyd's Rep. 1 in prohibiting avoidance of an international framework by opting for foreign jurisdiction in law. See Chap. 26.

of limitation of liability or time bars. It has been held in the High Court that where it is contractually agreed to litigate in England (exclusively or not) it is not open to one party to raise matters foreseeable at the time of contract in support of a stay.[129] While that view may be entirely understandable it is not an approach adopted by an English court to a foreign forum clause—showing perhaps the persistence of chauvinism, or simply a desire to retain the business.

4. ISSUE ESTOPPEL AND CAUSE OF ACTION ESTOPPEL

Once there has been a judgment by an English court of an action before it, either (if successful) the cause of action becomes merged in the judgment or (if unsuccessful) the plaintiff is estopped by the judgment from relitigating it (cause of action estoppel). Where an issue (or condition) in a cause of action is resolved by judgment or a matter should have been raised in earlier proceedings the issue resolved or not raised cannot be litigated in any other action dependent upon it. Thirdly, litigation may be an abuse of process if the matter should have been raised in earlier proceedings.

A foreign judgment may lead to a cause of action estoppel, issue estoppel[130] or abuse of process in the sense that issues should have been raised in earlier proceedings. The principle of merger of judgments does not apply. The Civil Jurisdiction and Judgments Act 1982, s. 34, provides that no proceedings may be brought by a person in England on a cause of action in respect of which a judgment has been given in his favour in proceedings between the same parties or their privies. It was held in 1993 by the House of Lords in *The Indian Grace*[131] that this section does not limit jurisdiction but simply provides a defence—a defence which may be defeated by estoppel, waiver or contrary agreement.

In the case when remitted Clarke J. held that a judgment *in personam* could not operate under the section to bar an action *in rem* as at inception the two actions were not between the same parties.[132] The act of the defendant in creating jurisdiction *in personam* through acknowledgment of service could not have the effect of barring *in rem* proceedings subsequently. The intention of s. 34 was not to deprive a plaintiff of the right to proceed *in rem* where there was an unsatisfied judgment *in personam*.

Clarke J. is surely right in his approach to s. 34 in that it is not intended to change any rule dependent on the difference between actions *in personam* and action *in rem*, and that acknowledgment of service cannot of itself bring an action *in rem* within s. 34. Whether or not the action is barred under s. 34 would seem to depend essentially on the nature of the action *in rem* and whether or not there is identity of parties with an action *in personam* depends on the scope of potential defendants. It may therefore be arguable that at the date of inception the parties *may* be identical with any action *in personam* (see Chapters 25, 27).

---

129. *British Aerospace Plc* v. *Dee Howard Co.* [1993] 1 Lloyd's Rep. 368. The matter should be approached as jurisdiction having been established as of right with an agreement not to object to the jurisdiction.

130. See e.g. *The Sennar (No. 2)* [1985] 1 Lloyd's Rep. 521 (H.L.).

131. [1993] 1 Lloyd's Rep. 387.

132. *The Indian Grace (No. 2)* [1994] 2 Lloyd's Rep. 331—having held that the defendants were estopped for relying on the judgment.

5. SOVEREIGN IMMUNITY

A. Foreign governments

A claim to immunity must be decided as a preliminary issue—it is not enough to show a good arguable case for an exception to the general principle.[133]

The general framework

The long-established immunity from legal proceedings of foreign "sovereigns" can be divided into:

> (a) immunities conferred on sovereigns personally and diplomatic officials whose role is perhaps seen as an extension of that of the sovereign (diplomatic immunity)[134];
> (b) immunities of state entities from civil proceedings, concerning persons or property in which there is a state interest.

It is with the latter, as they apply to maritime claims, that this work is concerned. The rules of state immunity from civil proceedings within the United Kingdom are now to be found in the State Immunity Act 1978 which came into operation on 22 November 1978.[135]

The law prior to 22 November 1978

English law traditionally followed the theory of absolute as distinct from restricted immunity. Once it was decided that the act on which the action was based was a sovereign act the doctrine applied.[136] Unless a foreign sovereign submitted to the jurisdiction[137] English law would not allow it to be impleaded or "by its process whether the sovereign is a party to the proceedings or not seize or detain property which is his or of which he is in possession or control".[138] Insofar as the claim was aimed at assets (and, in particular, through an action *in rem*)[139] the central issue was the connection between sovereign and the asset. But once that was sufficiently established or if the action involved only personal

---

133. *Maclaine Watson* v. *Dept of Trade* [1988] 3 All E.R. 257 at p. 314 (C.A.).

134. As to diplomatic immunities, see the Diplomatic Privileges Act 1964; as to consular immunities, see the Consular Relations Act 1968.

135. The Act does not affect any immunity or privilege conferred by the Diplomatic Privileges Act 1964 or the Consular Reglations Act 1968 (s.16). It applies only to matters occurring after the date of coming into force.

136. The problem of whether an entity is part of a "sovereign" or "government" has become particularly acute with the increase in "government" bodies. So in *Trendtex Trading Corpn* v. *Central Bank of Nigeria* [1977] Q.B. 529 it was claimed that the Central Bank was a government body. The court looked at the decrees creating and governing the bank and its activities and concluded that it was not.

137. Actual submission with knowledge of the immunity is required. (See *Baccus SRL* v. *Services National del Trigo* [1957] 1 Q.B. 438). An agreement to submit is not sufficient (see *Kahan* v. *Pakistan Federation* [1951] 2 K.B. 1003).

138. *The Cristina* [1938] A.C. 485, at p. 490 (per Lord Atkin).

139. As in *The Cristina* where the issue was whether the Spanish Government, which had requisitioned all ships, had a sufficient interest for the plea. It was held that there was such an interest.

liability, the role of the sovereign was considered irrelevant—it mattered not whether the act leading to the claim was truly "governmental" or purely "commercial". This "absolute" view was replaced by the restrictive view by the House of Lords in decisions of 1975 (in respect of the action *in rem*)[140] and of 1981 (in respect of the action *in personam*).[141]

The adoption of the restrictive theory means the creation of a "boundary" problem in addition to that of the scope of a sovereign—the dividing line between governmental and trade acts. In 1981 in *The I Congreso del Partido* the difficulty posed by the division was compounded by the claim that the breach of the trading activity was a governmental act. The difficulty was reflected in the division of judicial opinion, and the criterion advanced did little more than state the two types of act:

"The conclusion which emerges is that in considering, under the 'restrictive' theory whether state immunity should be granted or not, the Court must consider the whole context in which the claim against the state is made, with a view to deciding whether the relevant act(s) upon which the claim is based, should, in that context, be considered as fairly within an area of activity, trading, or commercial, or otherwise of a private law character, in which the state has chosen to engage, or whether the relevant act(s) should be considered as having been done outside that area, and within the sphere of governmental or sovereign activity."[142]

State Immunity Act 1978

The State Immunity Act 1978[143] takes as its starting-point the general proposition that a "State is immune from the jurisdiction of the court of the United Kingdom[144] and then sets out a number of exceptions.[145] It contains particular rules for maritime claims.

A state includes a sovereign in his public capacity, a government and any department of a government, but not a "separate entity" which is "distinct from the executive organ of the State and capable of suing or being sued". Such a separate entity is immune if the relevant proceedings relate to anything done by it in the exercise of sovereign authority and if as a state it would have been immune.[146] The task of dividing government departments from separate entities remains—unhindered by any statutory aid.

There are restrictions on remedies when a state is impleaded.[147] In particular, injunctions and specific performance can be obtained only with the written consent of the state,[148] and state property not intended or being used for commercial purposes may not

---

140. *The Philippine Admiral* [1977] A.C. 373.
141. *The I Congreso del Partido* [1981] 2 Lloyd's Rep. 367.
142. *Ibid*, at p. 375.
143. The Act (*inter alia*) brought into English law the provisions of (i) the International Convention for the Unification of Certain Rules Relating to the Immunity of State Owned Ships 1926 and its Protocol; (ii) the European Convention on State Immunity 1972.
144. State Immunity Act 1978, s.1(1).
145. State Immunity Act 1978 ss.2–11.
146. State Immunity Act 1978, s.14. For disagreement as to the "sovereign" nature of acts done by a separate entity see *Kuwait Airways Corpn* v. *Iraq Airways Co. and Republic of Iraq* [1995] 2 Lloyd's Rep. 317 (H.L.).
147. State Immunity Act 1978, s.13.
148. An order for the payment of money from no specific source is not an injunction prohibited by s.13. *Soleh Bonah International* v. *Govt of Uganda and National Housing Corpn* [1993] 2 Lloyd's Rep. 208 (C.A.) (order for security). A *Mareva* injunction could not be allowed to continue in the face of an immunity claim simply on an arguable case for the plaintiff (*Company A* v. *Republic of X* [1990] 2 Lloyd's Rep. 520).

be subject to any process for the enforcement of a judgment or arbitration award or in an action *in rem* for its detention or sale.[149] Exceptions to immunity are:

Submission to jurisdiction. This can be by agreement, institution of proceedings, intervention or taking any step in proceedings. A choice of law clause is not submission and simply claiming immunity is not a step in proceedings in assessing whether there has been submission.[150]

Submission to arbitration. An arbitration clause deprives the state from any immunity claim in respect of court proceedings relating to the arbitration.[151]

Commercial transactions and contracts to be performed in the United Kingdom.[152] There is no immunity for such transactions or such contracts unless all the parties to the dispute are states or the parties have agreed to immunity.

Contracts of employment between a state and an individual made in the United Kingdom or where the work is to be performed here.[153] Parties may exclude this provision by written agreement unless the law of the United Kingdom requires the proceedings to be brought before a United Kingdom court.[154] It has limited application only where the individual is a national of the state or where the individual is neither a national of the United Kingdom nor habitually resident therein.

Death or personal injury or damage to or loss of tangible property caused by an act or omission in the United Kingdom.[155]

Interest in and possession or use of immovable property in the United Kingdom.[156]

Claims relating to patents, trademarks, designs or plant breeders' rights, copyright or business or trade names connected with the United Kingdom in a specified way.[157]

Proceedings relating to a state's membership of corporate, unincorporated body or partnership connected as specified with the United Kingdom and which has members

---

149. A current account balance to the credit of a diplomatic mission can only be garnished if it is shown that the funds are solely for commercial purposes (and a certificate by the ambassador that they were not, is conclusive—s.13(5)): *Alcom Ltd.* v. *Republic of Colombia* [1984] 2 All E.R. 6 (H.L.). There are limitations relating to the use of process relating to property of States parties to the European Convention on State Immunity 1972 where the claim is not maritime (s.13(4)).

150. State Immunity Act 1978, s.2. Claiming immunity is not a step in the proceedings for this purpose (s.2(4)). See *Kuwait Airways Corpn* v. *Iraq Airways Co.* [1994] 1 Lloyd's Rep. 276. Intervening or taking any step in ignorance of facts entitling a state to immunity is not submission for this purpose if immunity is claimed as soon as practicable (s.2(5)). Submission through waiver in an *inter partes* contract will not bind the state to waive its immunities—that required consent to the court. *Company A* v. *Republic of X* [1990] 2 Lloyd's Rep. 520.

151. State Immunity Act 1978, s.9.

152. State Immunity Act 1978, s.3. A commercial transaction means a contract for the supply of goods or services, transaction for the provision of finance and any other transaction of a "commercial industrial financial professional or other similar character entered into otherwise than in the exercise of sovereign authority" but contracts of individual employment are excluded (s.3(3)). The exception does not extend to non-commercial contracts made in the territory of the state concerned and governed by its administrative law (s.3(2)).

153. State Immunity Act 1978, s.4.

154. State Immunity Act 1978, s.4(2) and (4).

155. State Immunity Act 1978, s.5.

156. State Immunity Act 1978, s.6.

157. State Immunity Act 1978, s.7.

other than states being proceedings between the state and the body, or other members.[158]

Proceedings relating to liability for value added tax, customs or excise duty or agricultural levy or rates in respect of premises occupied for it for commercial purposes.[159]

Admiralty proceedings. See *infra*.

MARITIME CLAIMS

Maritime claims are treated as a distinct category by the Act in that they are the subject of a particular section—s.10. The effect is that the general immunity rules are bolstered in respect of maritime claims by further removal of immunities based on the commercial use of ships or other property. So, in respect of a maritime claim, a state may lose its immunity either because of a commercial transaction or because of a commercial use of a ship.

Section 10 encompasses all claims which are or would be the subject of Admiralty proceedings.[160] It applies the restrictive theory of immunity to actions *in personam* and actions *in rem* in relation to a ship or property belonging to a state, which is in its possession or control or in which it claims an interest.[161] Subject to a special rule for cargo, a state is therefore not immune if the ship or other property was, when the cause of action arose,[162] in use or intended for use for commercial purposes.[163] Where an action *in rem* is brought against cargo, immunity is lost only if both cargo and carrying ship are "commercial": where an action *in personam* is brought in respect of cargo it is enough if the carrying ship is "commercial". It is somewhat difficult to appreciate why, in relation to a claim in connection with cargo, immunity depends not on the commercial character of the cargo but of the carrying ship. The Act provides for sister ship actions and a state loses its immunity in such actions only where both ships are "commercial".[164]

An argument advanced (and accepted by some of the judges) in *The I Congreso del Partido* was that even if the relevant activity is commercial there may be immunity *still* if the act giving rise to the claim is governmental (such as statutory requirement). It seems as if this contention has only a modified place in the statutory framework in relation to maritime claims which focuses on the commercial or non-commercial use of the ship. In that context a government action must therefore have the effect of changing the use of the ship for it to create immunity in a maritime claim connected with that ship.

158. State Immunity Act 1978, s.8. Parties may agree in writing or through the constitution of the body that immunity may apply.

159. State Immunity Act 1978, s.11.

160. State Immunity Act 1978, s.10(1).

161. Procedural rules relating to service of documents and appearance set out in s.12 do not apply to actions *in rem* (s.12(7)). Arrest may play its usual role in an action *in rem* where such an action will lie (see s.13(4)).

162. The time of the issue of the writ (a critical time for the enforceability of an action *in rem* against a ship in many cases (see Chap. 10)) is therefore irrelevant.

163. State Immunity Act 1978, s.10(2) and (5). As to when an action *in rem* may lie against cargo, see Chap. 10. As to the meaning of commercial purposes, see s.3(3) (applied by s.17(1)). As to s.3(3), see fn. 152 *supra*.

164. State Immunity Act 1978, s.10(3) and (4). Cargo may presumably attract immunity under the general provisions of the statute.

The Brussels Convention Relating to State Owned Ships of 1926 equates claims in respect of the operation of such ships or cargoes carried in them to those of privately owned ships—subject to certain immunities granted to vessels employed exclusively on government and non-commercial service when the cause of action arose. In regard to states party to the Brussels Convention therefore, the State Immunity Act allows the text of the earlier Convention to control.[165] In relation to those states the rule is simply that a commercial transaction or a commercial use of a ship will remove immunity in respect of claims relevant to the transaction or ship.

B. Government of the United Kingdom

The immunity from suit of the Crown as the sovereign is rooted in history.[166] That immunity was extended from the sovereign to government, but as government increased its commercial activities so the net of immunity became at once too broad and, particularly because of the commercial nature of the activities, anomalous.

The ability to pursue a claim in contract or recover property in respect of claims other than against the sovereign in person was until 1948 available through a petition of right. This procedure was abolished by the Crown Proceedings Act 1947 and an action is now available largely as against any other defendant. General rules of Crown liability in tort (both personal and governmental) are now set out in the Crown Proceedings Act 1947.[167] The applicability of statutes to the Crown depends on the particular statute.[168]

"Crown" liability "in personam"

Apart from personal liability of the sovereign,[169] Crown liability in the sense of governmental liability is largely[170] equated to that of the private individual. However, unless otherwise provided the Merchant Shipping Acts have not applied to Her Majesty's ships (see Merchant Shipping Act 1995, s.308). Provisions applying to Her Majesty's ships are those relating to

    (i) limitation of liability in accordance with the Limitation of Liability Convention (as to which see Chapter 19);

    (ii) apportionment of liability where damage or loss is caused to a ship or ships through the fault of more than one ship;

    (iii) time limits for proceedings to enforce any claim "or lien" in respect of damage or loss caused by the fault of a ship (as to which see Chapter 11);

    (iv) salvage claims (as to which see Chapter 2);

---

165. State Immunity Act 1978, s.10(6).

166. See e.g. (in a maritime case) *The Athol* (1842) 1 W. Rob. 374.

167. As amended by Crown Proceedings (Armed Forces) Act 1987 and Merchant Shipping (Salvage and Pollution) Act 1994.

168. There is a general principle of statutory construction that, lacking express provision, the Crown is not bound by statute. Provision is usually made in modern statutes regarding the effect on the Crown—and reference must be made to each such statute to ascertain the Crown position.

169. Crown Proceedings Act 1947, s.40(1)—referring specifically to proceedings in tort.

170. Specific provisions deal with the Crown prerogative and statutory powers (s.11). For other limitations, see ss.2 and 10, s.10 being repealed by the Crown Proceedings (Armed Forces) Act 1987 subject to powers of revival.

and the provisions relating to limitation of liability of harbour, dock and canal authorities apply to the Crown.

Further provisions relating to the prevention of oil pollution, duties and offences apply to "government ships" not of Her Majesty's navy nor in the service of the navy and the civil liability for such pollution under the 1969 Liability Convention.

Further, the provisions relating to the prevention of oil pollution and offences in that regard and civil liability for oil pollution under the 1969 Liability Convention (as to which see Chapter 2) apply to "government ships" other than (in the case of prevention of oil pollution) ships of or employees for the purposes of Her Majesty's navy or (in the case of civil liability) any warship or a ship being used by the government for other than commercial purposes.[171]

Thirdly, regulations may be made for the registration under the Merchant Shipping Acts of government ships not otherwise registrable and the application of the Acts (or parts of such Acts) to them.[172]

"Crown" liability "in rem"

The Crown Proceedings Act 1947 provides in s.29(1):

"Nothing in this Act shall authorise proceedings in rem in respect of any claim against the Crown, or the arrest, detention or sale of any of Her Majesty's ships or aircraft, or of any cargo or other property belonging to the Crown, or give to any person any lien on any such ship, aircraft, cargo or other property."[173]

The Supreme Court Act 1981, s.24(2)(c), provides that nothing in the provisions conferring Admiralty jurisdiction:

"shall authorise proceedings in rem in respect of any claim against the Crown or the arrest, detention or sale of any of Her Majesty's ships or subject to section 2(3) of the Hovercraft Act 1968, Her Majesty's hovercraft, or of any cargo or any other property belonging to the Crown".[174]

The effect of such negative provisions is to require references to the rules existing prior to the statutes. The legislative approach exemplified in those statutes hardly makes for clarity in the legal rules,[175] and the failure to enact a positive framework seems as difficult to defend in this context as any other. While immunity of the Crown from suit *in rem* is well established,[176] the extent of that immunity continues to depend on pre-statute rules.

171. Merchant Shipping Act 1995, ss.149, 167, 192, 308 repealing and consolidating provisions of the Crown Proceedings Act 1947, ss.5–7, 38(2), the Prevention of Oil Pollution Act 1971, s.24, Merchant Shipping Act 1894, s.741, Merchant Shipping (Oil Pollution) Act 1971, s.14, Merchant Shipping Act 1979, Sch. 5, para. 5.

172. Merchant Shipping Act, s.308(2), repealing and re-enacting Merchant Shipping Act 1906, s.80, as amended by Merchant Shipping (Registration etc.) Act 1993, Sch. 2, para. 3. There have been numerous Orders in Council made. See e.g. Merchant Shipping (MOD Commercially Managed Ships) Order 1992, SI 1992/1293; Merchant Shipping (MOD Yachts) Order 1992, SI 1992/1294.

173. An action *in rem* instituted in the reasonable belief that the property at issue did not belong to the Crown may be permitted by the court to continue as an action *in personam* (s.29(2)). As to Arrest of Crown ships, see further Chap. 15. As to liens, see Part III. As to the effect of purchase, sale, requisition or release from requisition by a foreign government on "liens" on a ship, see Chap. 18. There is no reason why the principles should not apply to the Crown.

174. Section 2(3) of the Hovercraft Act 1968 empowers the non-application by Order in Council (*inter alia*) of the Supreme Court Act 1981, ss.20–24 and Administration of Justice Act 1956, Part V (Scottish Admiralty Jurisdiction) to hovercraft. No order has been made.

175. Compare (e.g.) the sweeping up clause of the Supreme Court Act 1981. (See Chap. 2.)

176. See e.g. *The Broadmayne* [1916] P. 64; *Young* v. *S.S. Scotia* [1903] A.C. 501 (P.C.).

The operation of the exclusion of *in rem* proceedings by the Crown Proceedings Act 1947 in regard to salvage claims is expressly only insofar as it is consistent with the Salvage Convention 1989. That Convention applies to state owned or operated non-commercial vessels only insofar as each state applies it. Likewise no Convention provision can be used as a basis for the "seizure, arrest or detention" or proceedings *in rem* against non-commercial cargo owned by the state and entitled to sovereign immunity. As a consequence the statutory prohibition on the arrest and detention is, it would seem, limited in respect of salvage operations to non-commercial Crown ships or cargo.

The "Crown" and "Crown property"

(i) The Crown

(a) The Crown Proceedings Act 1947 and Supreme Court Act 1981. Neither the Crown Proceedings Act 1947 nor the Supreme Court Act 1981 defines the Crown.[177] In the words of Lord Denning M.R. the phrase is "elastic".[178] It seems accepted that it generally includes government departments, officers, servants and agents of the Crown.[179] Departments and other bodies falling within the "Crown" for the purpose of the Crown Proceedings Act 1947 are listed by the Treasury.[180]

(b) The pre-statute framework. It would seem unlikely that the elasticity of the label "The Crown" will differ in extent whether the issue arises under positive statutory provisions or as regards an excluded "*in rem*" claim. It would seem unlikely that, subject to any specific statutory provision, the definition of the Crown (such as it is) would not be accepted as uniformly applicable.

(ii) Crown property

(a) Ships. "Her Majesty's ships", for the purpose of the negative statutory provisions of the Crown Proceedings Act 1947 and the Supreme Court Act 1981, are defined as:

" . . . ships of which the beneficial interest is vested in His Majesty or which are registered as Government ships for the purposes of the Merchant Shipping Acts 1894 to 1940, or which are for the time being demised or subdemised to or in the exclusive possession of the Crown, except that the said expression does not include any ship in which His Majesty is interested otherwise than in right of His Government in the United Kingdom unless that ship is for the time being demised or subdemised to His Majesty in right of His said Government or in the exclusive possession of His Majesty in that right . . . ".[181]

177. "Her Majesty" is defined in the Crown Proceedings Act 1947, s.7(3) dealing with liability in respect of Crown docks and harbours to "include references to any Government Department and to any officer of the Crown in his capacity as such". "Officer" is defined in the act as including "any servant of Her Majesty" including a Minister of the Crown.

178. See *Trendtex Trading Corpn* v. *Central Bank of Nigeria* [1977] 1 All E.R. 881, at p. 894.

179. The Post Office is not a servant or agent of the Crown (Post Office Act 1969, s.6(5)) but has its own immunity from liability in tort (s.29). For limitation on immunity in respect of registered inland packets, see s.30.

180. In accordance with s.17(1) of the Act. For the current list, see current *Supreme Court Practice*.

181. Crown Proceedings Act 1957, s.38(2). The phrase "Her Majesty's ships" has not been uniform in maritime legislation. See e.g. the Merchant Shipping Act 1894, s.741, 1995 Act, s.308(1)—"ships belonging to Her Majesty"; the Merchant Shipping Act 1906, s.80—"government ships" (excluding ships of "Her Majesty's Navy") applied in the Prevention of Oil Pollution Act 1971, s.24—see 1995 Act ss.149, 308(3), 313(1). Each provision must, therefore, be approached with possible distinctions of definition in mind.

Crown immunity has two connected but separate aspects. The immunity from proceedings *in rem* is straightforward in that such proceedings are not available for any claim against the Crown. But an action *in rem* may be seen as "against" the property named—usually a ship, and in addition "Crown property" may be the focus of an action not aimed at the Crown (as, for example, where the Crown has chartered a ship or has engaged in a charter of a Crown ship). Further, both the Crown Proceedings Act 1947 and the Supreme Court Act 1981 specifically prohibit the "arrest, detention or sale" of Crown property. It is, therefore, necessary both to define "Crown" and "Crown property".

It seems clear that for a ship to be considered as a Crown ship apart from the statute the Crown must exercise "dominion" and control. A demise charterparty would give that control, while a time or voyage charterparty would not.[182] Whether a requisition gave it depends on the terms of the requisition.[183] The statutory provisions of the Crown Proceedings Act and the Supreme Court Act as to Her Majesty's ships are, therefore, in line with the earlier authority, although it may be arguable that the reference to "exclusive possession" as an alternative to "demise" extends the scope of the definition.[184] Save for salvage claims whether or not the ship is used for commercial purposes appears to be irrelevant both apart from and under the statute.[185]

(b) Cargo and other property—"belonging to the Crown". There is no reason to suppose that the phrase in the Crown Proceedings Act and Supreme Court Act indicates any different connection between property and Crown than is relevant to ships—ownership by or (probably) bailment to the Crown would suffice to bring the property under the Crown umbrella.[186]

6. RESTRICTIONS ON SPECIFIC TYPES OF CLAIMS

(i) Nuclear activities

A claim arising from a breach of duty imposed by the Nuclear Installations Act 1965[187] not to cause injury or damage in connection with occurrences involving nuclear matter specified in the Act does not "give rise to any lien or other right in respect of" a ship. The provisions of the Administration of Justice Act 1956 relating to action *in rem* and maritime liens were excluded from such claims.[188] Like provisions of the Supreme Court

182. *The Bertie* (1886) 6 Asp. M.L.C. 26, in which the Crown had chartered a ship on a voyage charter—no point was taken as to immunity. Cf. *The Nile* (1875) 3 Asp. M.L.C. 11; *The Cybele* (1878) 3 P.D. 8 (cases in which there were claims for salvage by crews of ships chartered to the Crown).

183. See e.g. *The Sarpen* [1916] P. 306.

184. Cf. Thomas, *Maritime Liens, op. cit.* at pp. 80, 81. It seems doubtful, however, whether the cases can be said to hold that *despite possession* by the Crown the ship was not a Crown ship—they turn more on exclusive control.

185. See *Young* v. *S.S. Scotia* [1903] A.C. 501 (P.C.) disapproving *The Cybele* (1878) 3 P.D. 8. Contrast the immunity of foreign sovereigns and s.167(1) of the 1995 Act relating to liability for oil pollution (see *supra*).

186. Cf. State Immunity Act 1978, s.10(3) and (5) (referring to the immunity of cargo "belonging to" a foreign state)—it would be unlikely that a foreign state would be granted a wider immunity than the Crown without express provision—although the converse is perhaps not so.

187. Section 14 amended by the Merchant Shipping Act 1979, s.50(4). Nuclear claims are excluded from the Convention on Limitation of Liability for Maritime Claims 1976 (see Art. 3) (as to which see Merchant Shipping Act 1995, Part VII). As to nuclear damage as the foundation for a maritime claim see Chap. 2.

188. Nuclear Installations Act 1965, s.14. The Act provides its own liability framework (see Chap. 2).

Act 1981 do not appear to be excluded. Nevertheless, there being no right in respect of a ship, there can be no action *in rem*.

(ii) Trespass to foreign land

Such actions have long been held to be outside the jurisdiction of the English courts and in 1978 the House of Lords affirmed that the general rule extended to any action raising the issue of title, possession or simply damages.[189] But this rule did not apply in maritime law and such actions as, for example, claims in respect of damage caused by collision between a ship and a pier are subject to the general rules of actions *in rem* and *in personam*.[190]

The Civil Jurisdiction and Judgments Act 1982, s.30(1), provides that jurisdiction:

"to entertain proceedings for trespass to, or any tort affecting immovable property shall extend to cases in which the property in question is situated"

out of the part of the United Kingdom in which the court is situated

"unless the proceedings are principally concerned with a question of the title to or the right to possession of that property".

Such jurisdiction is subject to the Brussels and Lugano Conventions and special rules set out in the Act applying the Brussels Convention to *intra* United Kingdom disputes.[191]

(iii) The Rhine Navigation Convention 1868[192]

The Supreme Court Act 1981, s.23, provides:

"23. The High Court shall not have jurisdiction to determine any claim or question certified by the Secretary of State to be a claim or question which, under the Rhine Navigation Convention, falls to be determined in accordance with the provisions of that Convention; and any proceedings to enforce such a claim which are commenced in the High Court shall be set aside."

The provision is identical to that of the Administration of Justice Act 1956[193] and that provision was the cause of a sharp but swift debate in the House of Commons in 1957.[194] As was said there, and has been said a number of times, the provision is not likely to have great effect.[195] The Convention (known also as the Mannheim Convention) covers navigation in the Rhine from Basle to the open sea and provides for a system of Rhine Navigation Tribunals which have jurisdiction:

---

189. *Hesperides Hotels Ltd.* v. *Muftizade* [1978] 2 All E.R. 1168.

190. See *The Tolten* [1946] P. 135.

191. For Convention rules relating to immovable property, see (e.g.) Arts. 9, 12(4) and 16(1). For special rules see Sch. 4, Art. 16(1).

192. The authentic text is in French and is set out in British and Foreign States Papers, Vol. 59, p. 470. An unofficial translation (together with amendments of 1898, 1922 and 1923 and the provision of the Treaty of Versailles 1919 amending it are to be found in "Acts of the Rhine 1947"—a publication of the British Control Commission. The text and further amendments of 1963 are set out in Cmnd 2421/1963.

193. Even to the extent of reproducing the wrong date (see s.24(1))—it was signed on 17 October 1868. The United Kingdom became a party through the Treaty of Versailles.

194. See *Hansard*, Vol. 565, cols.717–723.

195. Partly because of undertakings not to seek the certificate of the Secretary of State in certain circumstances (see *Hansard*, Vol. 599, 5 February 1959).

"(1) in criminal matters to investigate and judge all offences to regulations regarding navigation and river police
(2) in civil matters for summary judgment in disputes concerning
    (a) the payment and amount of duties for pilotage, cranage, weighing, port and wharfage
    (b) obstructions which individuals may have caused to the use of tow-paths
    (c) damage caused by watermen or raftsmen during a voyage or in collision
    (d) complaints against owners of draught-horses employed in towing vessels up-stream for damage caused to property."[196]

(iv) Foreign ships

Wages actions

"The ancient practice was that without the express consent of the foreign consul the Court would not exercise jurisdiction" in wages claims in respect of foreign ships.[197] However, in the nineteenth century the practice was modified to require notice of any claim to be given and (lacking protest) the court heard the case.[198] If there was protest, the court would consider the protest and its grounds and exercise discretion whether to proceed.[199]

The modern framework[200] has developed in opposing directions.

    (i) under the Consular Relations Act 1968[201] Her Majesty may by Order in Council exclude or limit the jurisdiction of a United Kingdom court "to entertain proceedings relating to the remuneration or any contract of service of" the master or crew of any ship "belonging to" a state specified in the order except where a consular officer of that state has been notified and has not objected.[202] Orders have been in respect of several states—some in terms of ships registered (or the equivalent) in the appropriate state and some in terms of the ships flying the flag of the appropriate state.[203] All make the power to hear a claim within the statutory provision dependent on notification to the consul, lack of objection within two weeks of such notification and a statement to this effect included in the details of claim.[204]

    (ii) under the Rules of the Supreme Court the general requirement of notice of commencement of an action to a consul in respect of a wages action is

---

196. Article 34. The amendments in 1963 included extension of jurisdiction under 2(c) and qualifications of the first instance and the appellate jurisdictional framework. See Cmnd 2421/1963.

197. Dr. Lushington in *The Octavie* (1836) B. & L. 215, at p. 217.

198. *Ibid*. The Admiralty Rules 1859, (r. 10), required notice to be given (see also RSC Rules 1883, Order V, rule 16).

199. See e.g. *The Nina* (1867) L.R. 2 A. & E. 44 (on appeal (1867) L.R. 2 P.C. 38); *The Leon XIII* (1883) 8 P.D. 121.

200. Nothing in the Supreme Court Act 1981, ss.20–23, limits the jurisdiction to refuse to hear a claim for wages by the master or crew of a ship not being a British ship (s.24(2)(a)). As to the definition of "British ships", see the Merchant Shipping Act 1995, s.1(1).

201. Consular Relations Act 1968, s.4. There is also power to limit criminal jurisdiction (s.5).

202. It should be noted that the relevant category of claims is wider than wage claims.

203. Austria, Belgium, Bulgaria, Czechoslovakia, Denmark, Germany, Greece, Hungary, Italy, Japan, Mexico, Norway, Poland, Romania, Russian Federation, Spain, Sweden and Yugoslavia. (See SI 1970; 1903–1905; 1907–1914; 1916–1920; 1971–1846; 1976/768, 1152; 1978/275 (revoking 1970/1919).

204. Failure to comply with statutory requirements renders the proceedings a nullity (*The Andrea Ursula*, *Lloyd's List and Shipping Gazette*, 14 January 1971). The provisions with respect to Mexico allow proceedings in respect of British subjects (with some extensions) without notice (SI 1970/1911).

restricted to the issue of a warrant of arrest.[205] In this context the principles applicable to the exercise of the discretion whether to proceed (e.g. the hardship to the claimants balanced against entry into employment under a foreign law[206]) are those formerly applied in the more general discretionary area. In effect, the question is a variant of *forum conveniens.*

The requirements of notice to the consul were a central feature of the nineteenth century line of authority emphasizing the discretionary power to hear wages actions in respect of foreign ships. It seems doubtful, therefore, whether any discretionary power survives apart from that related to the statutory provisions and that generally applicable through the principle of *forum conveniens.*

Actions on contracts of service of master or crew

The provisions of the Consular Relations Act 1968 and the Orders in Council made thereunder[207] apply to actions relating to the contract of service remuneration.

Title to or possession of a foreign ship

Old authorities support restrictions on jurisdiction to hear a dispute between foreigners regarding the title to a right to possession of a foreign ship—in particular (as with wages actions) contingent upon the consent of the parties or a representative of their state or states.[208] However, it seems clear that in a modern context any such restriction is to be considered as part of a general rule of *forum non conveniens.*[209] As with wages, notice to the appropriate consul is required for the issue of a warrant of arrest of a foreign ship.[210]

(v) Trade disputes—immunity from suit in tort

The Trade Union and Labour Relations (Consolidation) Act 1992 provides:

"An act done by a person in contemplation or furtherance of a trade dispute is not actionable in tort on the ground only—
  (a) that it induces another person to break a contract or interferes or induces any other person to interfere with its performance; or
  (b) that it consists in his threatening that a contract (whether one to which he is a party or not) will be broken or its performance interfered with, or that he will induce another person to break a contract or to interfere with its performance."[211]

The provision does not restrict the jurisdiction of the court in the sense that it prohibits the hearing of a claim, but it removes jurisdiction through prevention of a claim. It thereby

---

205. RSC Order 75, r. 5(5). The notice is required only if the relevant state has a consulate in London. A copy of the notice which has been sent must be exhibited to the affidavit specifying parties and property required for every action *in rem* (see rule 5(9)(d)).
206. See e.g. *The Gobluchick* (1840) 1 W. Rob. 143; *The Octavie* (1836) B. & L. 215.
207. See *supra.*
208. See *The Jupiter (No. 2)* [1925] P. 69.
209. *Ibid.,* at pp. 74–75; *The Annett* [1919] P. 105, at pp. 114–115.
210. RSC Order 75, rule 5(5). See further note 137 *supra.*
211. Section 219(1). As to the relevance of the immunity to restitutionary claims see *Universe Tankships* v. *ITF* [1982] 2 All E.R. 67 (H.L.).

confers immunity from suit, and calls at least for a mention in the consideration of restriction on types of claim.

Trade dispute is defined in some detail. It includes a dispute as between workers and their employer relating wholly or mainly to (for example) terms and conditions of employment, engagement of employment, membership of trade unions, allocation of work, matters of discipline, facilities for trade union officials, or machinery for negotiation.[212] The immunity is excluded in respect of acts done in the course of picketing save in "lawful picketing" as defined by the Act, acts done because or partly because of non-discrimination against employment of a non-union member, that an employer has dismissed an employee in connection with unofficial action, "secondary action" beyond permitted limits, pressure to impose union recognition or inducing the taking part in industrial action unless the action is supported by ballot and the employer has been given the required notice.[213]

(vi) Insurance contracts—lack of enforceability

A similar lack of foundation of suit exists in relation to marine insurance contracts classified as "gaming and wagering" (i.e. where the insured has no insurable interest nor is likely to acquire one or where the policy is made "interest or no interest", etc). Such "contracts" are void.[214] Like the trade disputes immunity, this reflects policy and, it may be argued, both are substantive law rules. Yet they limit the availability of the relevant "claim".[215]

7. ABUSE OF PROCESS

The High Court has an inherent power to prevent abuse of its process, and the Rules of the Supreme Court now expressly provide that an action may be dismissed or stayed on this ground.[216] "Abuse of process" is an undefinable term but has been used to prevent the demand of excessive security as a condition for the release of a ship from arrest,[217] relitigation of an issue already investigated and decided if the relitigation is a collateral attack on the decision,[218] (apparently) where an action was brought to try a hypothetical case,[219] to prevent the exercise of the power to arrest in furtherance of arbitration

---

212. Section 244(1). There is provision for treating a Minister of the Crown as an employee in respect of matters referred for consideration to a joint body on which he is represented, for including of (i) a trade dispute outside the UK affecting periods in the UK and (ii) a matter which would have been a dispute if resisted (s.244(2)(3)(4) as amended by Trade Union and Employment Rights Act 1993).

213. Sections 222–226, 234A (inserted by Trade Union and Employment Rights Act 1993).

214. Marine Insurance Act 1906, s.4. See also the Marine Insurance (Gambling Policies) Act 1909.

215. As also e.g. illegality and legal incapacity. See also the grounds justifying refusal of recognition of foreign judgments (see Chap. 19).

216. R.S.C., Order 18, rule 19(1)(d). The rule also provides for dismissal of an action on the grounds that a pleading is "scandalous, frivolous or vexatious" (r. 19(1)(b)).

217. See The Moschanthy [1971] 1 Lloyd's Rep. 37.

218. See Bragg v. Oceanus Mutual Underwriting Assoc (Bermuda) Ltd. [1982] 2 Lloyd's Rep. 132 and cases there cited. In the Bragg case "relitigation" was allowed by the same defendant in different actions. See also The Indian Grace [1993] 1 Lloyd's Rep. 387, at p. 391.

219. Glasgow Navigation Co. v. Iron Ore Co. [1910] A.C. 293.

proceedings,[220] and to strike out a discontinuance of proceedings where admission of liability and interim payments has been received and foreign proceedings then instituted.[221] It is an abuse of process to issue a writ on the off-chance that grounds of claim will be discovered—but not if no action will be pursued until the chances of success are assessed.[222]

RESTRICTIONS ON FOREIGN PROCEEDINGS

As has been said earlier in this work preliminary issues face a plaintiff to a dispute having connections with more than one state as to where to sue. The choice will involve consideration not only of substantive law but also of jurisdiction, governing law and the recognition of any judgment. A defendant may react to a potential or actual suit in the light of similar considerations.

A jurisdiction or arbitration agreement is a method of ensuring so far as possible that a suit is brought in a jurisdiction acceptable to all parties, and a governing law clause that is similarly agreed. The doctrine of *forum non conveniens* enables a defendant in an English court to stop proceedings there in favour of foreign proceedings. There is a similar power in an English court to order a party with a sufficient connection with England not to pursue foreign proceedings in favour of English proceedings or arbitration.

The power to restrain, it has consistently been said, should be exercised only with caution and bearing in mind that damage for breach of contract may be an adequate remedy.[223] Unlike the approach of English courts prior to the recognition of *forum non conveniens* it seems exercised only after consideration in depth. It must be shown that the foreign proceedings are "vexatious". As in the case of stay of English proceedings an appellate court will intervene only if discretion is exercised in the wrong principles. Where proceedings are started in breach of an injunction the avoidance of the injunction by serving a notice of discontinuance may lead to a striking out of the notice.[224]

Where there is no English jurisdiction or arbitration clause the issue is not whether the English or foreign court is the appropriate forum. The grant of an injunction turns on whether the foreign proceedings are vexatious or oppressive.[225] The principles underlying stay of English and stay of foreign proceedings differ—it does not follow that because an English court takes the view that it is the appropriate forum it should "arrogate to itself" alone the power to resolve the dispute. The problem of advantages to a party in one court can be overcome by undertakings by the other party. The order is directed at a party and not a foreign court. Although most cases will involve the protection of a claim in England or the prevention of dual English and foreign proceedings, the power is not limited thereto.

220. *The Andria now renamed Vasso* [1984] A.C. 293, now see Civil Jurisdiction and Judgments Act 1982, s.26 (and Chap. 15).
221. See *Castanho* v. *Brown and Root (UK)* [1981] A.C. 557.
222. See *Barton Henderson* v. *Merritt* [1993] 1 Lloyd's Rep. 540.
223. See e.g. *Mantovani* v. *Caropelli SpA* [1980] 1 Lloyd's Rep. 375; *The Lisboa* [1980] 2 Lloyd's Rep. 546—although an English court will be ready to act if there is an English jurisdiction or arbitration clause (see *infra*). Although such an injunction is final in form it is "interlocutory" for the purposes of the Rules of Court (Ord. 29) in that there would be express or implied liberty to apply if there was a change of circumstances (*SCOR* v. *Eras Eil (No. 2)* [1995] 2 All E.R. 278).
224. *Fakih* v. *A.P. Moller Ltd.* [1994] 1 Lloyd's Rep. 103 applying the general power to strike out a discontinuance which is abuse of process (see *Castanho* v. *Brown and Root* [1981] A.C. 557).
225. See *South Carolina Insurance Co.* v. *Assurantie Maatschappij* [1986] 2 Lloyd's Rep. 317 (H.L.).

Given the meeting of the "vexatious" requirement an injunction may be granted "where it is appropriate to avoid injustice".

There has been judicial comment that the general power to grant injunctions should not be restricted through categorization of cases in which the grant is appropriate. The current state of the law in respect of restraint of participation in or pursuance of foreign proceedings has been expressed as based on showing

(i) the foreign proceedings are "vexatious and oppressive", or
(ii) the proceedings constitute an invasion of a legal or equitable right of the plaintiff, or
(iii) the proceedings amount to unconscionable conduct.[226]

There may well be a certain degree of overlap in the three principles. That set out in (i) was established in respect of foreign proceedings as a whole in rejecting that it was enough for restraint that England was the appropriate forum. The second principle is an application of that founding an application for leave to serve a writ or summons out of England where an injunction is sought. The third is a general equitable ground and emerged in the context of a plaintiff seeking to use foreign procedure in the course of English proceedings.

As to (ii), as is seen in Chapter 9, apart from cases within the Brussels and Lugano Conventions, for circumstances to fall within RSC Order 11 and hence a category for leave to serve proceedings out of England the injunction sought must be attached to the assertion of a substantive right. In this instance the principle in regard to restraint of foreign proceedings as expressed is identical to that in respect of English proceedings. However, these seems no reason why the same reasoning rejecting *forum non conveniens* should not apply. In other words the grant of the injunction would still require the proceedings to be "vexatious".

As to (iii) the generality of the ground simply maintains the generality of the discretion to grant an injunction. So in the context of the use of foreign procedure where that use stemmed from the refusal of a party to give access to documents it could not be shown that the use was unconscionable.

It will be vexatious to pursue an action in a foreign court in breach of a jurisdiction agreement to sue in an English court and which by virtue of the Brussels or Lugano Convention excludes jurisdiction of the foreign court. In so holding in *Continental Bank NA* v. *Aeakos Compania Naviera SA*[227] the Court of Appeal thought the primary factor to be the breach of contract and the loss which would be caused by persisting in it. Whether such a consequence will follow if the enforcement of the agreement is discretionary is not clear—but the foreign action remains a breach of contract. Once enforced it is arguable

---

226. See *SNI Aerospatiale* v. *Lee Kui Jak* [1987] 3 All E.R. 510 (P.C.) at p. 519 where Lord Goff reviews the jurisdiction (disagreeing with principles set out in *Castanho* v. *Brown and Root (UK) Ltd.* [1981] A.C. 557), i.e. applying the principle that prior to modern development governed *forum non conveniens*; *SCOR* v. *Eras Eil (No. 2)* [1995] 2 All E.R. 279—balancing the legitimate interests of the parties.

227. [1994] 2 Lloyd's Rep. 505. Where an injunction is sought of proceedings in a non-Convention state in respect of parties domiciled in a Convention state, any right to be sued in accordance with the Convention is not infringed (*SCOR* v. *Eras EIL (No. 2)* [1995] 2 All E.R. 278 applying *Re Harrods Ltd.* [1991] 4 All E.R. 334. As to restraint of foreign proceedings once abandoned to sue in England see *Advanced Portfolio Inc.* v. *Ainsworth, The Times*, 15 November 1995.

that an injunction should issue—distinguishing the circumstances from the "appropriate forum" because of the agreement between the parties.[228]

In 1993 in *The Angelic Grace* Rix J. granted an injunction restraining proceedings in Italy contrary to a London arbitration clause. The judge exhaustively reviewed authorities, and held that, lacking any persuasive arguments as to the ground for an Italian court not to recognize the arbitration clause there was no reason not to say that the Italian proceedings were vexatious. Approving the granting of the injunction the Court of Appeal equated the circumstances to an exclusive jurisdiction clause basing the injunction on the upholding of a contract[229] for breach of which damages would be an inadequate remedy.

The approaches in *The Aeakos* and *The Angelic Grace* cases are supported in that because of Conventions in each case the agreement enforced by the injunction would bind the courts of the foreign country as much as those of England. Further, in *The Aeakos* case the agreement (at least according to English law) was governed by English law and in *The Angelic Grace* no contention made that it was not.

In both cases the courts declined to wait for further action until the foreign court had decided its own jurisdiction. Where the clause is arguably governed by foreign law or the jurisdiction of the foreign court from its point of view is shown to be arguable, the English court may defer the matter[230]—for any injunction is necessarily some interference with the foreign jurisdiction. As was pointed out in *The Angelic Grace* a party faced with proceedings which it sought to stay in favour of other proceedings must walk the legal tightrope between ensuring that that application is made without submitting to the jurisdiction so as to render any foreign judgment enforceable in the country in which the other proceedings have been brought.[231] The consideration of an injunction will therefore take into account this dilemma as well as the likely outcome in the foreign court.[232] The English court should not feel diffident in granting the injunction provided it was sought promptly and the foreign proceedings were not too far advanced.[233]

INTERIM RELIEF PROCEEDINGS

A jurisdiction agreement may or may not apply to proceedings for interim relief. In 1980 in *The Lisboa*,[234] in interlocutory proceedings, it was held that it was arguable that proceedings against the carrier did not include proceedings against the ship; and a clause

---

228. See e.g. *Fakih* v. *A.P. Moller Ltd.* [1994] 1 Lloyd's Rep. 103—arrest contrary to guarantee and suit contrary to agreement *and* injunction—in contempt of court and order for sequestration of assets to meet any claim for damages for breach of contract.

229. [1994] 1 Lloyd's Rep. 168; [1995] 1 Lloyd's Rep. 87—applying *Continental Bank* v. *Aeakos* (see *supra*).

230. For an example of leaving the question of foreign jurisdiction to the foreign court see *The Golden Anne* [1984] 2 Lloyd's Rep. 489—a case explained in *The Angelic Grace* on the basis of the foreign court's involvement.

231. As occurred to the plaintiff in the English proceedings seeking to enforce an English arbitration clause in *Marc Rich* v. *Societa Impianti* [1992] 1 Lloyd's Rep. 624—making the error of participating in concurrent Italian proceedings (see Chaps. 5, 13).

232. It may be that an English court will simply back its own view of the effect of a jurisdiction clause, see *IP Metal Ltd.* v. *Ruote Oz SpA* [1993] 2 Lloyd's Rep. 60.

233. *The Angelic Grace* [1995] 1 Lloyd's Rep. 87 (C.A.).

234. [1980] 2 Lloyd's Rep. 546.

directed at such proceedings did not, therefore, preclude arrest of the ship.[235] In *Marazura Navegacion SA* v. *Oceanus Mutual Underwriting Assoc. (Bermuda) Ltd.*[236] Robert Goff J. doubted whether a clause submitting disputes to London arbitration covered proceedings in which interim relief was sought.

In the case of English arbitration proceedings flowing from an arbitration clause, arrest may be obtained in England only by issuing a writ *in rem* contrary to the clause, whereas in the case of an English jurisdiction clause the arrest available on issue of the writ follows from the writ issued pursuant to the clause.[237] Apart from any view that such clauses relate only to liability proceedings, the argument for prohibition of foreign proceedings for interim relief is therefore based on opposing principles depending on whether an English jurisdiction or arbitration clause is at issue. As to the jurisdiction clause, it is that security should be obtained in England and, as to the arbitration clause, that it cannot be obtained in England relying solely on the clause.

In *The Lisboa* case the court held that, assuming the jurisdiction clause covered security proceedings, an injunction would not issue, emphasizing that the shipowners were a one-ship company, that arrest provided what may be the only effective security for the cargo owners and the need to arrest where the vessel is. In the *Marazura* case Robert Goff J. held that it did not follow that because English law did not permit arrest in pursuance of arbitration proceedings, an English court should enjoin a party to English arbitration proceedings from taking advantage of a law that did. Both approaches go against the view that because liability is to be submitted to an English court so must any claim to interim relief—whether or not the clause may be said to cover such relief. The distinction between interlocutory remedies and merits in now underlined by the statutory availability of interim relief in respect of foreign proceedings.

PROTECTION OF TRADING INTERESTS ACT 1980

The Act was enacted to counter the extraterritorial effects of the anti-trust laws of the United States. It has its origins in concern about the effect of such laws on British shipping interests,[238] but is worded quite generally. It empowers the Secretary of State to prohibit compliance with any requirement or prohibition imposed through a foreign law of international trade damaging or threatening United Kingdom trading interests, and applying outside the foreign state to a person carrying on business in the United Kingdom.[239] The statute is directly relevant to the control of foreign judicial proceedings

---

235. Cf. Lord Denning's more positive view (at p. 548) that the clause *did not* affect security proceedings.

236. [1977] 1 Lloyd's Rep. 283.

237. By virtue of the Civil Jurisdiction and Judgments Act 1982, s.26, property arrested or other security may be retained on the stay of proceedings for (*inter alia*) arbitration—but there is still the need for a writ *in rem* (see Chap. 15).

238. The Act follows, extends and supersedes the Shipping Contracts and Commercial Documents Act 1964 (see s.8(5)). For the power to regulate shipping by statutory instrument see Shipping and Trading Interests (Protection) Act 1995.

239. Protection of Trading Interests Act 1980, s.1. Orders made are concerned with U.S. Re-export Control SI 1982/855, SI 1983 900 relating to US anti-trust laws as they affect certain UK airlines. 1992 No. 2449 relating to United States control of Cuban assets. SI 1988/569 relating to enforceability of judgment regarding Australian Trade Practices (see Chap. 27). As to the scope of the 1983 Order and an unsuccessful challenge to its validity see *British Airways Board* v. *Laker Airways* [1984] 3 All E.R. 39 (H.L.).

in that in the cause of national interest[240] the Secretary of State may prohibit compliance with any direction by a court to produce a commercial document not in the country of that court or to provide commercial information.[241] Failure to comply with either type of prohibition is a criminal offence.[242]

The statute is also relevant to control of foreign proceedings in rendering unenforceable foreign judgments either for multiple damages or based on any rule of law that the Secretary of State declares concerned with anti-trust matters and therefore unenforceable. The unenforceability of any judgment in the United Kingdom could be a factor in urging prohibition or participation in proceedings leading to it—particularly in the light of the strong policy expressed in the Act in regard to such proceedings. However, it must be borne in mind that the policy is directed to the effect of foreign rules of law extraterritorially and not the rules as such—and any argument in relation to participation in foreign proceedings in reliance on this policy would need to link the participation to the extraterritorial effect.

240. i.e. it infringes the jurisdiction of the United Kingdom or is otherwise prejudicial to its sovereignty, security or relations with other governments (s.2(2)). Prohibition may also be ordered if court proceedings are not the basis of the requirement or the requirement does not go to specific documents (s.2(3)).

241. Protection of Trading Interests Act 1980, s.2. Courts are also prohibited from giving effect to requests for evidence from foreign courts which otherwise could be acceded to in accordance with the Evidence (Proceedings in Other Jurisdictions) Act 1975 where the Secretary of State certifies that the request infringes on United Kingdom jurisdiction or is prejudicial to its sovereignty (s.4).

242. See s.4. The effect of the prohibition is limited to acts done in the United Kingdom in the case of non-citizens or companies not incorporated in the United Kingdom (s.3(2)).

CHAPTER 13

Arbitration

Arbitration clauses are commonplace in maritime contracts.[1] Subject to statutory limitations it is always open to parties to a dispute to agree to submit that dispute to an arbitration rather than a court either when the dispute occurs or prior to it. In English law, as is seen in Chapter 12, an arbitration agreement can form the basis for the stay of court proceedings commenced contrary to it or an injunction to restrain a party from foreign proceedings contrary to it. Such an agreement is a contract enforceable through the courts as such but with a superimposed statutory framework applicable to it through the Arbitration Acts 1950, 1975 and 1979 (as amended).[2]

ENGLISH LAW AND INTERNATIONAL AGREEMENTS

The United Kingdom is one of over 90 states to have ratified the New York Convention on the Recognition and Enforcement of Foreign Arbitral Awards 1958. This imposes on States parties the duty to stay court proceedings if a dispute exists and a valid arbitration agreement is established, and to recognize and enforce foreign arbitration awards.

The most radical and comprehensive international attempt at an agreed format for arbitrations is that contained in the UNCITRAL Model Law. This provides a model for states to adopt. Scotland is among the states to have adopted it. Although England has not adopted it, its content should be noted as an important international development.

THE UNCITRAL MODEL LAW—TRANSNATIONAL ARBITRATION

While recognizing arbitration as a valued agreed way of dispute settlement English law has been relatively slow in differentiating between private, domestic and transnational arbitrations. While advancing London as an arbitration centre, there has been a reluctance

---

1. See generally Mustill and Boyd, *Commercial Arbitration* (2nd edn) 1989; Redfern, *Law and Practice of International Commercial Arbitration* (1991). Jurisdiction may also be conferred on arbitrators by an *ad hoc* agreement (even if a contractual agreement is void) by conduct or estoppel. See e.g. *The Almare Prima* [1989] 2 Lloyd's Rep. 376; *The Amazonia* [1990] 1 Lloyd's Rep. 236; *Sim Swee Joo* v. *Shirlstar* [1994] LMLN 374.
2. To be consolidated and updated. See the draft Arbitration Bill produced by the Department of Trade and Industry and submitted for public consultation in February 1994. See also Consumer Arbitration Agreements Act 1988 (not affecting the Arbitration Act 1975).

to see international commercial arbitration in terms other than a contractual process applying English law and in regard to which courts should continue to exercise control and retain broad powers of intervention.[3]

International agreement on arbitration is taken a stage further through the UNCITRAL Model Law 1985 on international commercial arbitration. This is not a Convention but, as its name implies, provides the opportunity for states to adopt a uniform approach to matters within its scope. It has now been adopted or applied in a number of states (including Scotland) but rejected in England[4]—largely on the grounds that in English law there is a well-developed arbitral process. There is, however, the recurring danger that through non-application England will be out of step with internationally recognized principles.

The Model Law is concerned with the arbitral process as a whole—the arbitration agreement, the arbitral tribunal, the proceedings and the making of the award. It is based on the perceived distinction between international and domestic arbitrations and largely adopts the broad principles of party autonomy to opt for arbitration rather than litigation. Mandatory provisions are few and the role of courts seen as supervisory and providing assistance—rather than arbitration being a contract to be enforced within and as part of a structure of dispute resolution primarily based on litigation.

Apart from the width of party control there are fundamental differences between the approach of the Model Law and English law: (i) the conferment on the arbitral tribunal of the power to decide its own jurisdiction, including the validity of an arbitration agreement; (ii) the ability of the parties to agree to resolve the dispute not according to a particular law but *ex aequo et bono* or through the offices of an *amiable compositeur* and (iii) the prohibition on recourse to the courts save on specified grounds.

THE NEW YORK CONVENTION ON THE RECOGNITION AND ENFORCEMENT OF FOREIGN ARBITRAL AWARDS 1958

The United Kingdom ratified the New York Convention on 24 September 1975. It was enacted into national law by the Arbitration Act 1975, which came into operation on 23 December 1975. The Act carries the Convention into domestic law by providing first for a mandatory stay of court proceedings commenced contrary to a valid "non domestic" arbitration agreement[5] and, secondly, for the recognition of arbitration awards made in the territory of any other party to the Convention.[6] In both aspects the Act replaced similar

---

3. For an urging of a more "transnational" outlook see Goode 1992 8 Arb. Int. 1. The attitude of the English courts is demonstrated by their willingness to intervene in a contractual framework to order security for costs *Coppée Lavalin* v. *Ken Ren Chemicals Ltd.* [1994] 2 Lloyd's Rep. 109 (H.L.) see *infra*.

4. Report of the Department Advisory Committee on Arbitration Law, June 1989 (chaired by Lord Mustill). The Committee recommended the drafting of a new consolidating and updated statute (see fn 2). For discussion of the Model Law see (1993) 10 Arb. Int. 179 *et seq*.

5. For definition, see Stay of Proceedings *infra*.

6. The restriction to contracting States reflects the ability to make a reservation of reciprocity under Art. I(3) of the Convention and most states (including the UK) did so. Orders in Council may be made declaring the parties—and such Orders are conclusive evidence of that status (s.7(2) and (3)). As to the declaration in force, see SI 1984/1168. Such orders are not exclusive evidence, see *Government of the State of Kuwait* v. *Sir Frederick Snow & Partners* [1981] 1 Lloyd's Rep. 656, at p. 666 (Mocatta J.) (not challenged on appeal).

provisions of the Arbitration Act 1950 insofar as arbitration agreements and awards fall within the later Act.[7]

A Convention award is enforceable either by action or in the same manner as the award on an arbitration and, when enforceable, is binding for all purposes on the persons as between whom it was made. Enforcement requires production of the award and the original arbitration agreement.[8] Enforcement may be refused only on "specified" grounds (incapacity, invalidity of the agreement award or the tribunal, lack of proper notice of the proceedings or inability to put the case at the proceedings, the award deals with matters outside the scope of the agreement, the tribunal was not constituted in accordance with the agreement or law of the country of the place of arbitration or the award has not yet become binding or has been set aside by a competent authority of the country where it was made or the law applicable to it).[9]

ARBITRATION AND LITIGATION

An arbitration agreement is capable of avoiding any dispute as to the forum and method of resolution of the dispute—first only if the arbitration clause is clearly drafted and clearly agreed[10] and secondly that it is enforceable. As to the first it may be surprisingly easy to include clauses which on their face provide for both,[11] or do not express the scope of the arbitration agreement with clarity, or in particular arguably provide for arbitration in two places.[12] An arbitration agreement may be assigned.[13]

An enforceable arbitration agreement does not of itself exclude litigation—the two are not mutually exclusive. The issue of a writ while an arbitration is proceeding does not bring the arbitration to an end,[14] nor does an arbitration clause mean that any concurrent

---

7. The Act applies to awards made in states which are parties when enforcement action on the award is commenced rather than confined to the date of the award (*Government of the State of Kuwait* v. *Sir Frederick Snow & Partners* [1984] 1 Lloyd's Rep. 458 (H.L.)). The Act of 1950 enacted into domestic law the Geneva Protocol on Arbitration Clauses 1923 and the Geneva Convention on the Execution of Foreign Arbitral Awards 1927. As between the parties to the New York Convention that Convention replaced these (Art. VII). The Act applies in relation to states declared by Order in Council to be parties having made reciprocal provisions (s.35(1)).

8. Section 4 (Convention Art. IV).

9. Section 5 (Convention Art. V). It is for the person against whom the award is invoked to establish the ground relied on (*ibid.*). These grounds are exclusive and an English court should "be astute" not to apply other grounds *Rosseel NV* v. *Oriental Commercial and Shipping Co. (UK) Ltd.* [1991] 2 Lloyd's Rep. 625 (in that case rejecting an argument that enforceability required assets in the UK). But an English court has jurisdiction to stay the enforcement of an English judgment obtained to enforce the award on the same grounds as any other judgment (see RSC Order 47, r. 1). The jurisdiction would rarely be exercised (*Far Eastern Shipping Co.* v. *AKP Sovcomflot* [1995] 1 Lloyd's Rep. 520.

10. For a telling example of a basic mistake in (apparently) assuming agreement see *Marc Rich* v. *Impianti* [1992] 1 Lloyd's Rep. 624.

11. Particularly where provisions of one document are incorporated into another. See e.g. *The Nerano* (fn. 36) (English jurisdiction and arbitration not inconsistent given the supervisory jurisdiction of the English courts). *Indian Oil Corpn* v. *Vanol Inc.* [1992] 2 Lloyd's Rep. 563.

12. See e.g. *The Stena Pacifica* (whether included future disputes) [1990] 2 Lloyd's Rep. 234; *The Island Archon* [1993] 2 Lloyd's Rep. 388 (on appeal on a substantive issue [1994] 2 Lloyd's Rep. 227); *The Heidberg* [1994] 2 Lloyd's Rep. 287; *The Petr Shmidt* [1995] 1 Lloyd's Rep. 202.

13. Including on notice to arbitration proceedings started *The Jordan Nicolov* [1990] 2 Lloyd's Rep. 11; *Baytur* v. *Finagro* [1992] 1 Lloyd's Rep. 134.

14. *Lloyd* v. *Wright* [1983] 2 All E.R. 969 (C.A.).

court proceedings are in some way void. However, unless there is no remaining dispute, there is a statutory obligation on courts of member States of the New York Convention to stay court proceedings if there is a valid arbitration agreement (see *infra*). Where before the English courts there is reliance by one party on an arbitration agreement but challenge to its existence by another and an action instituted, there is inherent jurisdiction in the courts to stay the proceedings pending decision as to the validity of the agreement.[15]

The question of whether an arbitration agreement is enforceable may arise as a preliminary issue of itself or through one party initiating litigation contrary to the asserted clause. In the latter circumstances the arbitration clause is only as enforceable as the court in which the litigation is launched recognizes. If the agreement is regarded as enforceable in the state in which the arbitration is to take place but not in the state where the litigation is started, just as with multiplicity of court proceedings the party seeking arbitration may have to tread carefully in respect of the court proceedings. If it does not participate there may be judgment in default, but if there *is* participation there may be held to be submission and hence enforceability of the judgment. In any event insistence on the arbitration will mean fighting on two fronts.

In English law there are protective measures—an English court satisfied as to the validity (or not) of an arbitration clause may enjoin a party from taking proceedings or arbitrating elsewhere.[16] Even without such an injunction participation in foreign proceedings simply to contest jurisdiction will not amount to submission for the purposes of enforcing a judgment and any judgment obtained in breach of an arbitration agreement is not enforceable in England (see Chapter 27). But care must still be taken not to take any step which would result in submission to foreign proceedings.[17]

JURISDICTION TO DECIDE THE VALIDITY OF AN ARBITRATION AGREEMENT

Subject to Convention provisions this will depend on provisions of national law. So the matter will be subject to the general jurisdiction structure of English law and the emphasis on service of a writ or summons on the defendant (see Chapter 9). Where the issue arises because of an application to stay court proceedings the parties are already before the court, and, again subject to Conventions, there will be no independent jurisdiction issue.

As discussed in Chapter 5 "arbitration" falls outside the Brussels and Lugano Conventions. Where the validity of an arbitration clause arises in the context of a step in the arbitration (for example appointment of an arbitrator) the matter is outside the Convention. Where it arises as a matter of contract construction it is uncertain whether it is within or outside the Convention. If within the Convention to decide the issue there must be a Convention jurisdiction base.

---

15. See e.g. *The Gladys* [1988] 2 Lloyd's Rep. 221.
16. See e.g. *The Angelic Grace* [1995] 1 Lloyd's Rep. 87 and Chap. 12.
17. See *Marc Rich v. Impianti* [1992] 1 Lloyd's Rep. 624—a case made even more complex by the question of whether the issue of the validity of an arbitration agreement fell for jurisdiction purposes within the European Convention on Jurisdiction. (See Chap. 4).

The Hamburg Rules (Article 22) contain a detailed arbitration provision limiting the places in which it may be held.[18] Maritime Conventions containing arbitration provisions do not generally impose such limits.[19]

The law to be applied

As with other contracts, subject to mandatory rules and public policy the parties to an arbitration agreement may select the law which is to govern it substantively and procedurally—either directly or through selection of an arbitral structure (e.g. Sugar Association) which specifies the governing law.[20] A mandatory rule may be through a Convention directing that "the Convention" be applied[21] or through a particular substantive rule being of such fundamental importance to the place of arbitration that an option for another law would be void.[22] Whether there is or is not an arbitration agreement is a matter to be decided either by putative proper law (i.e. the law which would be the proper law if there was an agreement) or in some circumstances by English law, on the basis that that is to govern unless it is shown that some other law is applicable.[23]

The law governing substantive matters

Apart from selection of the applicable law and mandatory rule the provision for arbitration at a particular place will be a factor indicating that the substantive contract is to be governed by that law—but a factor that may be outweighed by other contact points in the contract.[24] When the agreement provides for an option as to the place the indication as to proper law is much less strong and will not of itself indicate a "floating" proper law. The agreement is not therefore void for lack of a governing law.[25]

It does not however necessarily follow that the same law as governs the substantive contract will govern either the arbitration agreement or individual submissions to

18. So in any contract governed by a law importing those rules the validity of any arbitration clause is dependent on compliance with the requirements. The requirements are deemed to be part of the arbitration agreement (Art. 22(5)).

19. As to the CMR 1956 (Carriage of Goods By Road) see Carriage of Goods by Road Act 1965, Sch. Arts 31 and 33. As to the application of the CMR to sea carriage, see Chap. 5. As to the Athens Convention 1974 (carriage of passengers and luggage) (enacted by the Merchant Shipping Act 1979) see Art. 17.

20. An arbitration agreement is however not within the scope of the Rome Convention on the law applicable to contractual obligation enacted in the UK by the Contracts (Applicable Law) Act 1990. But relevant to the applicable law will be the applicable law of the substantive contract—which may be subject to the Convention. As to the governing law of contracts generally see Chap. 26.

21. See e.g. the CMR Art. 33—failure to apply the Convention will invalidate the agreement—*The Tor Britannia* [1982] 1 Lloyd's Rep. 410; (regarding agreements prior to claim arising) the Hamburg Rules Art. 22(4)—any clause inconsistent with that provision is null and void (Art. 22(5)).

22. See *The Morviken* [1983] 1 Lloyd's Rep. 1 and Chap. 26.

23. See for a comprehensive discussion *The Heidberg* [1994] 2 Lloyd's Rep. 287 itself discussed in Chap. 26.

24. See the *Compagnie Tunisienne* case [1971] A.C. 572; *The Mariannina* [1983] 1 Lloyd's Rep. 12; *The Parouth* [1982] 2 Lloyd's Rep. 351 (where the arbitration clause led to a conclusion that as English law probably governed, leave could be given to serve a writ out of the jurisdiction); *The Star Texas* [1993] 2 Lloyd' Rep. 445.

25. *The Star Texas* [1993] 2 Lloyd's Rep. 445. As to the need for a governing law at the start of a contract see Chap. 26. There is no such requirement in respect of the curial law—the law governing the arbitration (*ibid.*).

arbitration under that agreement.[26] In the usual run of events the law governing the substantive contract and the arbitration agreement will be the same and that governing the individual submission will be the *lex fori*—but not always.

The law governing procedure (the curial law)

This will normally be the law of the place chosen by the parties[27]—although English law recognizes the possibility that, within the permissible limits of choice, there may be an election for the procedural laws of another country. Such an election leads to such difficulties in respect of English law that in *Union of India* v. *McDonnell Douglas Corpn*[28] Saville J. construed a contract as submission to English procedure with foreign procedure adapted insofar as not inconsistent with it.

While subject to express selection English law will govern the procedure of an arbitration in England by English arbitrators but an arbitrator is not bound to apply rules of practice applied by an English court. As with most distinctions of this nature, the concept of "rule of practice" tends to expand or decrease according to the desirability of freedom of action. So the ability to make an award in foreign currency when a court could not do so, was said to be procedural, and (it has been said) "properly described as a rule of practice".[29] But in the same case it was also said that rules of practice become so entrenched and so authoritatively pronounced as to become substantive law. As a result, once English law is applicable it is unlikely that an arbitrator can rely for any divergence from it on the classification of a remedy as a rule of practice. But in this respect he can do what a court could do.

ENFORCEABILITY OF ARBITRATION AGREEMENTS IN ENGLISH LAW

The arbitration agreements, the substantive contract and separability

It is clearly established in English law that an arbitration clause is separable from the contract to which it is relevant. Where there is an arbitration clause in a contract there are normally three sets of contractual relations: the substantive contract; the contract to submit

---

26. It may be that if by the proper law an arbitration agreement is invalid the entry into arbitration by the parties will indicate an *ad hoc* arbitration agreement governed by a different law—and even if that be invalid the parties may be bound by estoppel (itself having a governing law). See *The Amazonia* [1990] 1 Lloyd's Rep. 236.

27. I.e. the "place" of arbitration and not necessarily the physical place which may change. See *Naviera Amazonia Peruana* v. *Cie Internacional de Serguros del Peru* [1988] 1 Lloyd's Rep. 116. The curial law may differ from the place of an arbitral award see *Hiscox* v. *Outhwaite (No. 1)* [1991] 3 All E.R. 641 (H.L.).

28. [1993] 2 Lloyd's Rep. 48. Saville J. thought that in respect of an English arbitration it is not open to parties to exclude jurisdiction of the English court under the Arbitration Acts and stressed that it was not possible under English law to provide for procedures unconnected to any national law.

29. See *Tehno-Impex* v. *Gebr van Weelde Scheepvaartkantoor BV* [1981] 1 Lloyd's Rep. 587, at p. 596 (Oliver L.J.). In that case Lord Denning M.R. said that arbitrators were not bound by the "strict rules of common law courts or the statutes applicable to them" relating to the power (or lack of power) to award interest on money paid late. Oliver and Watkins L.JJ. disagreed. The issue was settled as to judicial ability as from 1 April 1983 by the conferring of power by the Administration of Justice Act 1982, s.15, Sch. 1.

future disputes to arbitration; and the individual bilateral arbitration contract arising on the assertion of claim within the general arbitration contract in contract. The substantive contract and the two arbitration contracts may be brought to an end by repudiation or frustration and consistently with the principle of separability the bringing of one to an end does not necessarily bring the others to an end.[30] While an arbitrator cannot decide on the validity of an arbitration agreement,[31] provided the agreement is wide enough in scope the principle of separability operates to confer on the arbitrator the power to decide (a) if the substantive contract is void or voidable whatever the ground asserted for the contention and (b) disputes concerning the termination of the substantive contract.[32]

As indicated earlier it is essential that any arbitration clause be clear as to scope. Further, care should be taken that there is no confusion as between different arbitration clauses, or arbitration and jurisdiction clauses.[33] There is no inconsistency between an arbitration clause in a charterparty and a jurisdiction clause in bills of lading issued under it on the charterer's orders. The parties to the dispute are different.[34] Further, it is not necessarily conclusive in an application for stay of proceedings where there is a discretion, that if the stay were granted there would be a multiplicity of proceedings in such circumstances.[35] Inconsistency may arise between the bill of lading and charterparty where terms of the charterparty are arguably incorporated into the bill of lading and there are in both, clauses relating to arbitration or jurisdiction. However, reference to jurisdiction is not necessarily inconsistent with arbitration, and an arbitration clause may be incorporated by specific reference even if this requires manipulation of the words to adapt it to the bill of lading parties.[36]

Stay of court proceedings

Recognition of the arbitration process takes the form not only of a statutory structure for arbitral proceedings but also (subject to the ability to obtain summary judgment) a stay of court proceedings brought contrary to a valid arbitration agreement.[37] Whether or not there is such an agreement is a matter for the courts and not the arbitrator. The "stay" (rather than "dismissal") of proceedings leaves it open to the court to intervene should the

---

30. See *Black Clawson International Ltd.* v. *Papierwerke Waldof-Aschaffenburg AG* [1981] 2 Lloyd's Rep. 446.

31. The power of an arbitral tribunal to decide its own jurisdiction is known to civil lawyers as Kompentenz/Kompentenz and divides the civil and common law. It is adopted by the UNCITRAL Model (Law Art. 16(1)—and is one reason for its rejection in England. The refusal to recognize the power puts a brake on arbitration unacceptable to those who support it.

32. See *Harbour Assurance Co. (UK) Ltd.* v. *Kansa General International Insurance Co. Ltd.* [1993] 1 Lloyd's Rep. 455 (C.A.); [1992] 1 Lloyd's Rep. 81 (Steyn J.).

33. See fns 11, 12 and 13.

34. See *The Vikfrost* [1980] 1 Lloyd's Rep. 560.

35. *The Jemrix* [1981] 2 Lloyd's Rep. 544.

36. See *The Nerano* C.A. (to be reported in [1996] 1 Lloyd's Rep.).

37. Where a party seeks leave to serve a writ out of the jurisdiction an English arbitration clause may indicate that the governing law of the contract is English (see e.g. *The Elli 2* [1985] 1 Lloyd's Rep. 107) but if it is clear that the defendant will elect to go for arbitration, leave would normally be refused (see *A and B and D* [1982] 1 Lloyd's Rep. 166). As to the grant of leave in respect of a counterclaim contesting the existence of an arbitration agreement to preserve the interest of both parties which depended on whether or not there was an arbitration clause see *The Gladys* [1990] 1 All E.R. 397; [1990] 1 Lloyd's Rep. 297 (H.L.).

conditions required for the stay cease to exist. Further, in the end it may be necessary to return to court to enforce the award through judgment and execution.[38]

The rules of English law relating to stay are set out in (i) the Arbitration Act 1975, s.1(1) (relating to arbitration agreements other than "domestic arbitration" agreements as defined therein) and (ii) the Arbitration Act 1950, s.4, relating to those agreements not falling within the Arbitration Act 1975.

The non-domestic agreement

The Arbitration Act 1975 enacted provisions into domestic law allowing the ratification of the New York Convention on the Recognition and Enforcement of Foreign Arbitral Awards 1958. The provisions as to stay of proceedings on the basis of a non-domestic agreement largely replaced a similar provision of the Arbitration Act 1950. The Act of 1975 imposes a mandatory duty on courts to stay proceedings in the face of a non-domestic arbitration clause.

"1(1) If any party to an arbitration agreement to which this section applies, or any person claiming through or under him, commences any legal proceedings in any court against any other party to the agreement, or any person claiming through or under him, in respect of any matter agreed to be referred, any party to the proceedings may at any time after appearance, and before delivering any pleadings or taking any other steps in the proceedings, apply to the court to stay the proceedings; and the court, unless satisfied that the arbitration agreement is null and void, inoperative or incapable of being performed or that there is not in fact any dispute between the parties with regard to the matter agreed to be referred,[39] shall make an order staying the proceedings."[40]

Only a party to the agreement who is sued may apply for a stay and it is not open to a party not sued to be joined as a party solely to obtain a stay.[41] For a stay to operate there must be an existing dispute between the parties. The plaintiff may apply for summary judgment in accordance with RSC Order 14 on the ground there is no defence and hence no dispute. On that application the court may consider any point of law which can be considered without reference to contested facts—if the plaintiff is clearly right judgment will be given, if not, then leave to defend will be given and the matter referred to arbitration.[42]

There is no "dispute" to be referred when there is admission of liability of a liquidated sum or where a sum is "indisputably due".[43] However, where a contractual time bar has operated, unless there is admission of liability and quantum the claimant must apply for extension of time. Having received it he may either pursue the arbitration or apply for summary judgment in an action.[44]

---

38. Where summary judgment is given as to liability but a stay to assess damages an interim payment may be ordered (see *Texaco Ltd.* v. *Eurogulf Shipping Co.* [1987] LMLN 194).

39. The reservation as to an existing dispute is not in the Convention.

40. So long as there is a dispute as to whether there is an arbitration agreement there is no agreement within the Act (*Willcock* v. *Pickfords* [1979] 1 Lloyd's Rep. 244). An agreement is not incapable of being performed if the claimant is unable to start proceedings due to lack of funds (*Paczy (Janos)* v. *Haendler & Natermann GmbH* [1981] 1 Lloyd's Rep. 302). Incapable of being performed refers to the agreement and not the award (*The Rena K* [1978] 1 Lloyd's Rep. 545).

41. *Etri Fans* v. *NMB (UK) Ltd.* [1987] 2 All E.R. 763.

42. *SL Sethia Liners Ltd.* v. *State Trading Corpn* [1986] 1 Lloyd's Rep. 31; [1986] 2 All E.R. 395.

43. See *The M Eregli* [1981] 2 Lloyd's Rep. 169 and authorities there cited. *Ellerine Bros (Pty) Ltd.* v. *Klinger* [1982] 2 All E.R. 737; *The Cleon* [1983] 1 Lloyd's Rep. 586 (C.A.). A "dispute" exists while one party contradicts another and it is not immediately demonstrable that there are no good grounds for disputing the claim: *Hayter* v. *Nelson Insurance Co.* [1990] 2 Lloyd's Rep. 265.

44. See *The M Eregli* [1981] 2 Lloyd's Rep. 169, at p. 175 and *infra*.

The domestic agreement

In the case of a domestic arbitration clause, a court has a discretion whether or not to stay proceedings.

"4(1) If any party to an arbitration agreement, or any person claiming through or under him, commences any legal proceedings in any court against any other party to the agreement, or any person claiming through or under him, in respect of any matter agreed to be referred, any party to those legal proceedings may at any time after appearance, and before delivering any pleadings or taking any other steps in the proceedings, apply to that court to stay the proceedings, and that court or a judge thereof, if satisfied that there is no sufficient reason why the matter should not be referred in accordance with the agreement, and that the applicant was, at the time when the proceedings were commenced, and still remains, ready and willing to do all things necessary to the proper conduct of the arbitration, may make an order staying the proceedings."

THE ENGLISH STATUTORY FRAMEWORK—THE ARBITRATION ACTS 1950 AND 1979

THE GENERAL FRAMEWORK[45]

The Arbitration Act of 1950 (as amended by later Acts) continues to govern the arbitral process, in the appointment and authority of arbitrators[46] and in provisions relating to the death or bankruptcy of a party[47]; in the conduct of proceedings[48]; provisions as to awards (including the time for making an award, the power to make interim and final awards, to correct slips and to order specific performance of contracts and as from 1 January 1992 and subject to contrary intention in the arbitration agreement dismissing a claim for delay of prosecution[49])[50]; interest on awards[51]; costs and fees.[52] It further deals with the power of the High Court to remit awards[53]; to deal with lack of impartiality of and removal of arbitrators; to set aside an award for misconduct by the arbitrator,[54] and hear any allegation of fraud by a party.[55]

---

45. The third of the statutes making up the framework is the Arbitration Act 1975 enacting the New York Convention on the Recognition and Enforcement of Foreign Arbitral Awards 1958 and considered *supra*.

46. Sections 1, 6–11. As to leave to revoke an appointment under s.1, see *Stockport Metropolitan Borough Council* v. *O'Reilly* [1983] 2 Lloyd's Rep. 70.

47. Sections 2 and 3.

48. Section 12—including the power to make an order of inspection of property (*The Vasso* [1983] 2 Lloyd's Rep. 346).

49. Arbitration Act 1979, s.5. See for an example of attaching sanctions to order of discovery *Waverley Ltd.* v. *Carnaud Metal Box Engineering Plc* [1994] 1 Lloyd's Rep. 38. As to use in preventing delay see *infra*.

50. Sections 13–17. The power to dismiss for delay is set out in s.13A inserted by the Courts and Legal Services Act 1990. the provision authorized an arbitrator after 1 January 1992 to take into account delay both after and prior to that date: *The Boucraa* [1994] 1 Lloyd's Rep. 251, [1994] 1 All E.R. 20 (H.L.).

51. i.e. treated as a judgment debt. The power to award interest on later payments of debts was conferred as from 1 April 1983 (the Administration of Justice Act 1982, s.15, Sch. 1. Prior to the Act there was no such power (*The La Pintada* [1984] 2 Lloyd's Rep. 9 (H.L.)).

52. Sections 18–20.

53. Section 22. Neither this power nor the power to set aside an award under s.23 (see fn 54) is to be used to circumvent the restrictions on judicial intervention in arbitral proceedings introduced by the Arbitration Act 1979 (see *infra*). See *Moran* v. *Lloyd's* [1983] 2 All E.R. 200. For the extent of the power since the Act of 1979, see *ibid*.

54. Sections 23–25. Misconduct extends to procedural errors (see *Moran* v. *Lloyd's* [1983] 2 All E.R. 200). As to the extent of the power since the Arbitration Act 1979, see *ibid*.

55. Section 24(2). This jurisdiction is limited by the Arbitration Act 1979, s.3(3)—see *infra*.

The Arbitration Act 1979 limited the review by the courts of arbitration awards (see *infra*). As part of the emphasis on the arbitrator's control of the arbitration it is provided in the Act that to enable a reference to continue the High Court may extend the powers of the arbitrator if there is lack of compliance with any order by the arbitrator.[56]

POWERS OF ENGLISH COURTS IN RESPECT OF ARBITRATION PROCEEDINGS

Inherent supervisory jurisdiction?

The relationship between courts and arbitrations was examined in some detail by the House of Lords in 1980 in *Bremer Vulkan Schiffbau und Maschinenfabrik* v. *South India Shipping Corpn*[57] in the context of the ability of the courts to control arbitral proceedings where there was alleged delay by one of the parties.

The House of Lords agreed that terms should be implied in the arbitration contract reflecting the statutory provisions of the Arbitration Acts. Those statutes confer powers to remove arbitrators and to set aside awards for misconduct of arbitrators or to give relief (including an injunction to restrain further proceedings) if the arbitration is not impartial. But a bare majority of the House (3–2) held that courts did not have an inherent jurisdiction to remedy or prevent injustice in the arbitration process. The control of the courts was founded on the power to enforce contracts. As to the particular issue of delay there was at that time no relevant statutory provision and any obligation to move with speed depended on the arbitration agreement (see "delay" *infra*). The majority relied heavily on the distinction between compulsory imposition of courts as instruments of resolution of disputes and the voluntary submission of parties to arbitration. The minority held that, subject to exclusion by statute, courts have a general power to enforce the right of parties to a fair arbitration.[58] It is the view of the majority that is reflected in the approach of the UNCITRAL Model Law (see *supra*).

Interim relief

By the Arbitration Act 1950 the High Court is given specific powers in relation to security for costs or[59] the amount in dispute, evidence affidavit preservation and inspection of the property in dispute, appointment of receivers and "interim injunctions"—(e.g.) securing a specific fund or enjoining a party from participating in court proceedings contrary

56. Arbitration Act 1979, s.5. See for an example of attaching sanctions to an order of discovery *Waverley Ltd.* v. *Carnaud Metal Box Engineering plc* [1994] 1 Lloyd's Rep. 38. As to the use of the power in preventing delay see *infra*.

57. [1981] 1 Lloyd's Rep. 253.

58. The minority veiw was also taken by Donaldson J. at first instance and two members of the Court of Appeal, the third not expressing an opinion. A larger measure of control over proceedings is conferred by the Arbitration Act 1979 (see *infra*).

59. Section 12(6)(a). The making of the order is discretionary—it is not sufficient that both parties are not resident in the jurisdiction. See *Coppée Lavalin* v. *Ken Ren Chemicals Ltd.* [1994] 2 Lloyd's Rep. 109. In its general discretion under the Act a court may halt the plaintiff's claim if security ordered is not produced—*The Argenpuma* [1984] 2 Lloyd's Rep. 563 (but in the *Coppée Lavalin* case Lord Mustill queried the power). Unless there is contumelious failure to comply or no reasonable chance that no future application to lift a stay would succeed, a permanent stay should not be ordered (*Petromin SA* v. *Secnav Marine Ltd.* [1995] 1 Lloyd's Rep. 603).

to the agreement.[60] As a consequence, *Mareva* injunctions may be issued in the context of arbitral proceedings and rules of court may be incorporated into the Act. Further, the courts have powers to enforce the arbitration agreement through "permanent" remedies. So an injunction may issue to prevent disclosure of documents contrary to any duty of confidence stemming from the proceedings.[61]

Jurisdictional prerequisite of connection with England?

The statutory powers of the courts under the Arbitration Act 1950 apply to arbitrations in England. The power to grant "interim relief" in respect of proceedings in a member State of the Brussels and Lugano Conventions may be extended by Order in Council to arbitration proceedings[62] but without such extension none of the powers under the Arbitration Act apply to foreign arbitrations.[63] However injunctive relief may be granted under the general discretionary power of the Supreme Court Act 1981 s.37.[64]

Where the arbitration is conducted in England under international arbitration rules providing for a framework for settling disputes an English court will assert its statutory power in respect of interim measures unless the rules prohibit the exercise of such powers. In the case of prohibition a court will probably recognize the principle of party autonomy.

In *Coppée Lavalin* v. *Ken Ren Chemicals Ltd.*[65] the House of Lords held that there was power to award security for costs in respect of an arbitration held in England under International Chamber of Commerce (ICC) Rules. Lord Mustill strongly defended the advantage of court intervention, denied that opting by the parties for ICC Rules meant non-intervention and rejected the idea that the exercise of that option meant that a court should never make an order unless absolutely necessary. Such factors went, thought Lord Mustill, to the discretion to exercise the power. In exercising that discretion the courts should bear in mind the process for which the parties had opted, in the case of the ICC rules a process as far as possible independent of the legal system of the place of arbitration and the extent to which interim measures would interfere with the arbitrator's function.

By a majority (not including Lord Mustill) the House thought an order appropriate in the case despite both parties being non-resident in England and the substantive contract out of which the dispute arose being subject to foreign law and to be performed out of England. The majority saw this as an exceptional case in that the plaintiff was insolvent and the claim funded by the Kenyan government who would not be liable for costs. The

---

60. Arbitration Act 1950, s.12(6). An arbitrator can order inspection of a ship subject to a salvage operation on behalf of cargo owners (*The Vasso* [1983] 2 Lloyd's Rep. 346). See s.12(4) and (5) as to the compelling of attendance of witnesses. The powers are linked to a reference to arbitration. They do not encompass an injunction or damages for breach of an arbitration agreement through issuing proceedings: *Sokana Industries Inc.* v. *Frere and Co. Inc.* [1994] 2 Lloyd's Rep. 57. They are "interim protection orders".

61. See e.g. *Hassneh Insurance Co.* v. *Mew* [1993] 2 Lloyd's Rep. 243; *Insurance Co.* v. *Lloyd's Syndicate* [1995] 1 Lloyd's Rep. 272. As to privilege stemming from the conduct of an arbitration between principal and agent so as to protect documents from production in the arbitration see *Leif Hoegh and Co. A/S* v. *Petrolsea Inc.* [1993] 1 Lloyd's Rep. 363.

62. Civil Jurisdiction and Judgments Act 1982, s.25(3)(c). The permitted extension is to any arbitration proceedings. As to the application to foreign proceedings see Chapters 14, 15.

63. *Channel Tunnel Group Ltd.* v. *Balfour Beatty Ltd.* [1993] 1 All E.R. 664 (H.L.).

64. *Ibid.* See further *The Lady Muriel* (1995) LMLN 413 (Hong Kong).

65. [1994] 2 All E.R. 449.

minority thought that the parties had chosen arbitration of a particular type and this was the type of interim measure which would constitute interference with that choice.

Arrest

It was held by Brandon J. in *The Golden Trader*[66] and *The Rena K*[67] that the statutory powers of the 1950 Act do not permit arrest of property as "arrest does not result from the making of any order by the court but from the party concerned causing a warrant of arrest to be issued". The issue of such a warrant depends on the issue of a writ *in rem* and this fundamental connection caused problems where a court stayed proceedings (and therefore arguably halted the effect of the writ) because of an arbitration agreement Further, in an extension of the reasoning that staying proceedings meant destroying the basis for arrest it was held in *The Cap Bon* (1967) and *The Maritime Trader* (1981) that property could not be arrested where the sole purpose of the issue of a writ *in rem* was to obtain security for arbitration proceedings.

As from 1 November 1984 arrest has been available in arbitration in the sense that a party to an arbitration agreement may issue a writ *in rem* and on those court proceedings being stayed for arbitration any property arrested may be retained in support of those proceedings. The relationship of arrest and arbitration is discussed in Chapter 15.

REVIEW OF AND APPEAL TO COURTS FROM ARBITRATION DECISIONS[68]

The Arbitration Act 1950 provided for review of arbitration awards through an application by a party to the High Court that the arbitrator state a case for the court.[69] As judicially construed, this developed into an almost unfettered right of review provided there was a point of law at issue. Paradoxically, although such review was openly available, under the Arbitration Act 1950 there was no requirement that an arbitrator state reasons for an award, and reasons were often avoided so as to remove any possibility that a court could set aside an award for an error on the face of it.[70]

Delay in the finality of arbitration awards through requests for stated cases led to judicial and commercial frustration and the right to review was severely restricted by the Arbitration Act 1979. The 1979 Act abolished the special case procedure and setting aside an award for error on the face of the record. It substituted a limited right of appeal on any question of law arising out of the award permitting even that right to be excluded in many instances.[71] The Act enables a party to obtain a reasoned award—an obvious necessity for an appeal process on points of law. Notice of the wish for such an award must generally

---

66. [1974] 1 Lloyd's Rep. 378.

67. [1978] 1 Lloyd's Rep. 545. See also *The Tuyuti* [1984] 2 Lloyd's Rep. 51. Cf. Chapter 15.

68. See generally R. Thomas, *Law and Practice Relating to Appeals from Arbitration Awards*, 1993, Lloyd's of London Press.

69. Section 21.

70. As to the setting aside of awards, see s.23.

71. Section 1(2). Subject to exclusion agreements the ability to obtain a decision of the High Court on a question of law arising in the course of reference is retained (see s.2). Compare the Arbitration Act 1950, s.21(2). An appeal on this ground to the Court of Appeal would create unacceptable delay in most cases (*The Oltenia* [1982] 2 Lloyd's Rep. 99; [1982] 3 All E.R. 244 (C.A.).

be given to the arbitrator.[72] The appeal lies only with leave of the High Court or by consent of all parties.[73] Where leave is sought, it shall not be granted unless the High Court considers that, having regard to all the circumstances, the determination of the question of law concerned could substantially affect the rights of one or more of the parties to the arbitration agreement; and the court may make any leave which it gives conditional upon the applicant complying with such conditions as it considers appropriate.[74]

An appeal lies to the Court of Appeal against refusal of the High Court to grant leave only by leave of the High Court and that leave should be granted only if the decision to grant or refuse leave called for some amplification or elucidation of existing guidelines as to the granting or refusal of leave.[75] No appeal lies to the Court of Appeal or House of Lords against a refusal of the High Court to grant leave to appeal to the Court of Appeal.[76] An appeal will lie to the Court of Appeal from a judgment of the High Court with leave of the High Court or Court of Appeal.[77] No appeal lies to the House of Lords from a refusal or grant of leave by the Court of Appeal.[78]

Intended to reduce access to the courts, the Act spawned a plethora of applications for leave to appeal which met with different judicial reactions. in 1981 in *The Nema*[79] and in 1984 in *The Antaios*[80] the House of Lords stressed that consideration of an application for leave should be approached on the basis that Parliament had intended to ensure speedy finality in arbitral awards.[81] In *The Nema* Lord Diplock, giving a judgment with which all other members of the House agreed, drew a distinction between construction of "one-off" clauses and standard terms. As to one-off clauses, he said:

"Where, as in the instant case, a question of law involved is the construction of a 'one-off' clause the application of which to the particular facts of the case is an issue in the arbitration, leave should not normally be given unless it is apparent to the Judge upon a mere perusal of the reasoned award itself without the benefit of adversarial argument, that the meaning ascribed to the clause by the arbitrator is obviously wrong: But if on such perusal it appears to the Judge that it is possible that argument might persuade him, despite first impression to the contrary, that the arbitrator might be right, he should not grant leave; the parties should be left to accept, for better or for worse, the decision of the tribunal that they had chosen to decide the matter in the first instance."

Lord Diplock continued:

72. See generally s.1(5) and (6) The reasons had to be sufficient to consider any question of law on appeal. Further reasons may be ordered but if none were given and none requested there is no power to order reasons in the absence of special reasons for lack of request: *The Niedersachsen* [1986] 1 Lloyd's Rep. 393 (C.A.).

73. As to procedure including time limits see RSC Order 73, Practice Direction: Arbitration Award: Appeal [1985] 2 All E.R. 383. Once the time limit for seeking leave has expired the award becomes final and where the parties have voluntarily allowed the time to expire by a substantive margin only in exceptional circumstances would there be an extension: *The Faith* [1993] 2 Lloyd's Rep. 408. As to the effect of delay in pursuing the application see *infra*.

74. Section 1(4). Reasons for the grant or refusal of leave should not normally be given: *The Antaios* [1984] 2 Lloyd's Rep. 235 (H.L.).

75. Arbitration Act 1979, s.1(6A) inserted by Supreme Court Act 1981, s.148. *The Antaios* [1984] 2 Lloyd's Rep. 235 (H.L.).

76. *Aden Refinery Co. Ltd.* v. *Ugland Management Co.* [1986] 2 Lloyd's Rep. 336.

77. Arbitration Act 1979, s.1(7)(a). The High Court must certify that the issue is of general public importance or for some special reason should be considered by the Court of Appeal (s.1(7)(b)). It is not open to a respondent to raise issues of law other than those certified from the High Court without obtaining leave from the High Court or C.A.: *Vitol SA* v. *Norelf Ltd.* [1995] 1 All E.R. 971 (C.A.).

78. *The Baleares* [1991] 2 Lloyd's Rep. 318; [1991] 3 All E.R. 554.

79. [1981] 2 Lloyd's Rep. 239.

80. [1984] 2 Lloyd's Rep. 235.

81. Although the parties may consent to an appeal (see Arbitration Act 1979 s.1(3)(a)).

"In deciding how to exercise his discretion whether to give leave to appeal under s.1(2) what the Judge should normally ask himself in this type of arbitration, particularly where the events relied upon are 'one-off' events, is not whether he agrees with the decision reached by the arbitrator, but: Does it appear upon perusal of the award either that the arbitrator misdirected himself in law or that his decision was such that no reasonable arbitrator could reach."[82]

He qualified this by saying that where the "one-off" event did not affect only the transaction in issue (such as the closure of the Suez Canal)

" . . . it is in the interests of legal certainty that there should be some uniformity in the decisions of arbitrators as to the effect, frustrating or otherwise, of such an event upon similar transactions, in order that other traders may be sufficiently certain where they stand as to be able to close their own transactions without recourse to arbitration."

Lord Diplock's two classes form more of a spectrum than two categories sharply divided. It has been held, first, that a strong *prima facie* case that an arbitrator is wrong is not the exclusive test; it being legitimate and proper to take into account the circumstances on which the agreement was made—which may lead to the conclusion that the arbitration decision is necessarily final.[83] Secondly, in regard to one-off events, whether or not *The Nema* test is satisfied, the court should refuse leave if the particular issue in the arbitration is minor or one of a large number of equally important issues.[84] And it will be borne in mind that the courts' powers of review "are not intended to circumvent the clear intention of the new Act which is that parties who choose to arbitrate should in the ordinary way abide by the decision of the tribunal whom they themselves have selected".[85]

Exclusion agreements

In respect of arbitrations save those specified in the Act parties may exclude by written agreement the ability to appeal to the High Court on a question of law arising out of an award, a decision on a preliminary point of law or for an order for a reasoned award.[86] The policy behind the ability to exclude was to allow exclusion in "international" "one-off"

---

82. For applications of the guidelines in "one-off cases", see *The Wenjiang* [1982] 1 Lloyd's Rep. 128; *The Nichos A* [1982] 1 Lloyd's Rep. 52; *National Rumour Compania SA* v. *Lloyd-Libra Navegacao SA* [1982] 1 Lloyd's Rep. 472. Compare *The Apex* [1982] 1 Lloyd's Rep. 476. The guidelines have been held to be inappropriate to a disciplinary arbitration (see *Moran* v. *Lloyd's* [1983] 1 Lloyd's Rep. 51 (Lloyd J.)) and in the same case the Court of Appeal issued a general warning against attempts to use powers under the Arbitration Act 1950 to remit or set aside awards to circumvent the limits placed by the Arbitration Act 1979 on the powers of a court to intervene in arbitral proceedings ([1983] 1 Lloyd's Rep. 472); *Bulk Oil (Zug) AG* v. *Sun International Ltd. and Another* [1983] 1 Lloyd's Rep. 655 in which Bingham J. held that leave to appeal should more readily be given if a question of EEC law is raised (see p. 660) (approved C.A. [1983] 2 Lloyd's Rep. 587). See also for general application of principles *The Yanxilas* [1982] 2 Lloyd's Rep. 445 (frustration as applicable to tanker voyage charters); *The Anangel Friendship* [1983] Com. L.R. 139.
83. *The Emmanuel Colocotronis (No. 1)* [1982] 1 Lloyd's Rep. 297, at p. 300.
84. *The Evimeria* [1982] 1 Lloyd's Rep. 55.
85. *The Sheba and The Shamson* [1983] 2 Lloyd's Rep. 500 (per Bingham J.). See also the comment of the House of Lords in *The Antaios* [1984] 2 Lloyd's Rep. 235.
86. It is also provided that where there is an exclusion agreement in a non-domestic arbitration the court will not exercise the jurisdiction to deal with allegations of fraud conferred by the Arbitration Act 1950, s.24(2). An exclusion agreement may be incorporated by reference (see *Arab African Energy Corpn Ltd.* v. *Olieprodukten Nederland BV* [1983] 2 Lloyd's Rep. 419; *Marine Contractor Inc.* v. *Shell Petroleum Ltd.* [1948] 2 Lloyd's Rep. 77.

arbitrations, to prohibit it in regard to domestic arbitrations[87] and international arbitrations in common usage except after the commencement of an arbitration. Exclusion agreements prior to commencement of arbitrations are prohibited in relation to:

(a) a question or claim falling within the Admiralty jurisdiction of the High Court, or

(b) a dispute arising out of a contract of insurance, or

(c) a dispute arising out of a commodity contract,

unless the award or question relates to a question expressed to be governed by a law other than the law of England and Wales.[88]

In 1984 in *The Antaios*[89] the House of Lords stressed that the guidelines were subject to adaptation but also reiterated the need for a restrictive approach as regards the construction of a standard term. Although conflicting decisions of the High Court would justify leave, in other circumstances leave required a "strong *prima facie* case" that the arbitration was wrong. It was not enough that arguably in dicta there was an indication of difference between judges as to the meaning of a term.[90] In 1988[91] Lord Donaldson expressed the understandable view that Lord Diplock's lack of sympathy for conflicting dicta as a ground should not extend to conflicting decisions either of judges or arbitrators. The emphasis on finality requires an applicant to pursue the leave application with speed. The principles generally applicable to striking out for want of prosecution based on intent, disobedience of court order or inexcusable delay and prejudice to a defendant gives way to the need for finality. It is not enough to wait for the court to provide a hearing date[92] (see *infra*).

DELAY IN ARBITRATION PROCEEDINGS

IN COMMENCEMENT OF PROCEEDINGS

The Limitation Act 1980 applies to arbitrations as it applies to actions in the High Court, and invalidates any term in an arbitration agreement providing that no cause of action is

---

87. i.e. an agreement involving neither foreign place nor foreign party (see s.3(7)).

88. The statutory provision perhaps should also specify that it is recognized in English law as being so governed. The Secretary of State may by order provide that this provision shall cease to have effect or shall not apply in relation to any arbitration award in one of the categories (s.4(3)).

89. [1984] 3 All E.R. 229. The principles apply to all types of arbitration awards with any necessary adaptation—there being a presumption of finality (see *Ipswich BC* v. *Fisons plc* [1990] 1 All E.R. 730 (C.A.)).

90. Applications for leave are heard in chambers (see RSC Order 73, r. 3). The decision should be arrived at after only brief argument (see e.g. *Ipswich BC* v. *Fisons plc* [1990] 1 All E.R. at p. 732). Any contention that any question of law does not concern a one-off clause or event and any opposing contention must be supported by affidavits (Practice Direction [1985] 2 All E.R. 383).

91. *The Ugland Obo One* [1986] 3 All E.R. 737; [1986] 2 Lloyd's Rep. 336.

92. See *Secretary of State for Environment* v. *Euston Castle Investments Ltd* [1994] 2 All E.R. 415. As to principles generally applicable to delay see *Birkett* v. *James* [1977] 2 All E.R. 801 and Chapter 11. As to the power of arbitrators in respect of want of prosecution see *infra*.

to accrue until an award is made.[93] An arbitration commences on the service of a notice requiring the appointment of an arbitrator or the submission of the dispute to an arbitrator designated in the agreement.[94]

POWER IN COURT TO EXTEND PERIODS FIXED BY ARBITRATION AGREEMENT

The Arbitration Act 1950, s.27, provides:

"27. Where the terms of an agreement to refer future disputes to arbitration provide that any claims to which the agreement applies shall be barred unless notice to appoint an arbitrator is given or an arbitrator is appointed or some other step to commence arbitration proceedings is taken within a time fixed by the agreement, and a dispute arises to which the agreement applies, the High Court, if it is of opinion that in the circumstances of the case undue hardship would otherwise be caused, and notwithstanding that the time so fixed has expired, may, on such terms, if any, as the justice of the case may require, but without prejudice to the provisions of any enactment limiting the time for the commencement of arbitration proceedings, extend the time for such period as it thinks proper."

This provision allows extension of time whenever an arbitration clause is included in a contract governed by English law[95] whether or not the arbitrator is also given power to extend time[96] unless the extension relates to commencement of proceedings and a statutory time limit would be exceeded. If, therefore, the Hague Visby Rules are incorporated into a contract with an arbitration clause the provision that the cause of action is extinguished after one year removes the power to extend the time under s.27 once the year has expired.[97] The power to extend is limited to a step to commence arbitration proceedings. It does not apply to a contractual clause extinguishing claims unless some other action is taken by a party within a specified period (as for example presenting supporting documents) or to any other time limit set in the contract.[98] Whether a requirement is a step to commence proceedings is a matter of contractual construction.[99]

In 1977 in *The Jocelyne*[100] Brandon J. summarized the guidelines laid down by the Court of Appeal in *The Pegasus*[101] relating to the exercise of discretion as to whether to grant an extension of time:

---

93. Section 34(1) and (2). Where the High Court sets aside an award or orders that an arbitration agreement shall cease to have effeect with respect to a dispute it may order that the limitation period should start with the order of the court (s.34(5)) (see e.g. *Stockport Metropolitan Borough Council* v. *O'Reilly* [1983] 2 Lloyd's Rep. 70). This Act will not apply to an arbitration for which a limitation period is set by another enactment (s.39). An action to enforce an award is treated as analogous to the enforcement of a contract and a six-year limitation period applied (see Limitation Act 1980, s.7), the time running from the breach of the implied term to perform the award (*Agromet Motoimport Ltd.* v. *Maulden Engineering Co. (Beds) Ltd.* [1985] 2 All E.R. 346.
94. See s.34(3). As to service of notice, see s.34(4). As to construction of the requirement, see *The Pendrecht* [1980] 2 Lloyd's Rep. 56.
95. See *The Castle Alpha* [1989] 2 Lloyd's Rep. 383.
96. *Comdel Commodities Ltd.* v. *Siporex Trade SA* [1990] 2 All E.R. 552 (H.L.).
97. *The Antares (Nos. 1 and 2)* [1987] 1 Lloyd's Rep. 424 (C.A.)—the Hague Visby Rules having the force of law. Where the rules are applied by contract s.27 will be applicable (see *The Virgo* [1978] 2 Lloyd's Rep. 16; [1978] 3 All E.R. 988).
98. See *The Oltenia* [1982] 2 Lloyd's Rep. 99. Cf. *The Sandalion* [1983] 1 Lloyd's Rep. 514.
99. *The Luka Botic* [1984] 2 Lloyd's Rep. 145, in which the Court of Appeal so construed the requirement in the Centrocon Arbitration Clause that the claim be in writing.
100. [1977] 2 Lloyd's Rep. 121.
101. [1967] 1 Lloyd's Rep. 303.

"(1) The words 'undue hardship' in s.27 should not be construed too narrowly.

(2) Undue hardship means excessive hardship and, where the hardship is due to the fault of the claimant, it means hardship the consequences of which are out of proportion to such a fault.

(3) In deciding whether to extend time or not, the Court should look at all the relevant circumstances of the particular case.

(4) In particular, the following matters should be considered:
   (a) the length of the delay;
   (b) the amount at stake;
   (c) whether the delay was due to the fault of the claimant or to circumstances outside his control;
   (d) if it was due to the fault of the claimant, the degree of such fault;
   (e) whether the claimant was misled by the other party;
   (f) whether the other party has been prejudiced by the delay, and, if so, the degree of such prejudice."

This summary has been approved and applied in later cases by the House of Lords and Court of Appeal.[102]

The provision must be applied with reference to the contracting parties and delay by one party in implementing the arbitral procedure may lead to refusal of extension. It has been said that the factors have to be weighed in the context of the obligations of the parties rather than that of insurance and lawyers involved.[103] However, delay caused by the solicitors (and presumably insurer) of one party will be caused by that party. The availability of an action against the solicitors may be a factor (if not of great weight) in considering whether an extension should be granted.[104]

Extension of time and summary judgment

In *The M Eregli*[105] the issue arose of the relationship of time limits expressed in an arbitration clause, s.27, and the ability of a party to mount court proceedings for summary judgment concurrently with arbitral proceedings. Kerr J. held that, when an arbitration clause contains a time limit clause, the limit can be ignored only if there is no dispute (i.e. liability and quantum is admitted). If there is a failure to comply with a time limit, extension must be sought under s.27:

"In my view, the correct position is as follows. Where there is a claim which is subject to a time limit in an arbitration clause, the claimant must operate the arbitration clause unless there is no dispute because the other party had admitted liability. If he fails to abide by the clause, then he can only recover if he succeeds in obtaining an extension of time under s.27. However, if he does, then the bar to his claim is removed, and if the claim, or part of it, is indisputably due he can either obtain a final or interim award in the arbitration, as the case may be, or summary judgment under RSC O. 14 in an action, even though the action and the arbitration are both concurrent. However, if both are concurrent, as here, and the claim is indisputably due, it is obviously far more sensible and convenient to give judgment under O. 14 then [sic] to refer the undisputed claim back to the arbitrator."[106]

102. *Comdel Commodities Ltd.* v. *Siporex Trade SA* [1990] 2 All E.R. 552 (H.L.); *The Aspen Trader* [1981] 1 Lloyd's Rep. 273; *The Ratna Vandana* [1982] 1 Lloyd's Rep. 499; *Davies (UK) Ltd.* v. *Marc Rich and Co. Ltd.* [1985] 2 Lloyd's Rep. 423 (C.A.).
103. *The Eurotrader* [1987] 1 Lloyd's Rep. 418.
104. *The Baiona* [1992] 2 Lloyd's Rep. 121; [1992] 1 All E.R. 346.
105. [1981] 2 Lloyd's Rep. 169.
106. *Ibid.*, at p. 175.

DELAY IN PROSECUTION OF PROCEEDINGS

There are rules applicable to different stages of arbitration proceedings[107] supported by general principles of control by the arbitrator and, to some extent, by the courts. Prior to the Arbitration Act 1979 the control by the arbitrator of the speed at which the proceedings were conducted once they had commenced was uncertain. By s.12(1) of the Arbitration Act 1950 (subject to contrary provision in the agreement) parties are obliged to produce relevant documents, submit to examination and "do all other things which during the proceedings" an arbitrator may require. However, there was no sanction available to the arbitrator should there be failure to comply with his directions. The High Court has power to make orders in respect of various interlocutory matters but the arbitrator was powerless. In particular, as was held in *The Bremer Vulkan*[108] by the House of Lords, an arbitrator had no power to dismiss arbitration proceedings for want of prosecution.

The Arbitration Act 1979 permits the High Court on application[109] to confer on the arbitrators the power of a judge of the High Court in respect of continuing proceedings when a party fails to comply with an order of the court or a requirement of order of court. It was apparently intended that an arbitrator can be given power to make interlocutory orders, including dismissal for want of prosecution.[110] However, there were serious limitations on the powers of court to deal with delay stemming from (i) the view that arbitration was a contractual process with mutual obligations and therefore not subject to any control as in an action through "want of prosecution" and (ii) the inherent limits of the contractual doctrines of repudiation, frustration and abandonment to control delay.[111]

As from 1 January 1992 unless there is a contrary intention expressed in the arbitration agreement an arbitrator has power to make an award dismissing a dispute if

   (a) there has been an "inordinate and inexcusable delay" on the part of the claimant in pursuing the claim and the delay
   (b) either (i) gives rise to a substantial risk that it is not possible to have a fair resolution of the claim or (ii) has caused or is likely to cause or to have caused serious prejudice to the respondent.

The delay may be either before or after 1 January.[112] The prolonged chorus of complaints about the disconformity between practices in arbitration and the High Court and the increasing importance that something be done about it show quite clearly "that the provision was intended to apply from the date it came into force. It was inconceivable that Parliament had intended that delay before that date should continue to create the risk of

---

107. See the Arbitration Act 1950, s.12, and generally in relation to arbitration proceedings RSC Order 73. A court may refuse to appoint an arbitrator because of delay: *The Frotanorte* [1995] 2 Lloyd's Rep. 254.

108. *Bremer Vulkan Shiffbau und Maschinenfabrik* v. *South India Shipping Corpn* [1981] A.C. 909 (H.L.).

109. Section 5. The application may be by the arbitrator or umpire or a party (s.5(1)) see *supra*.

110. See *The Hannah Blumenthal* [1983] 1 Lloyd's Rep. 103 (Lord Brandon). The wording of s.5 was far from satisfactory if this was the intention. Cf. Mustill and Boyd, *op. cit.* at pp. 482–485.

111. See *Bremer Vulkan Schiffbau und Maschinenfabrik* v. *South India Shipping Corpn* [1981] 1 Lloyd's Rep. 253; *The Hannah Blumenthal* [1983] 1 Lloyd's Rep. 103 and the examination by Lord Mustill in *The Boucraa* [1994] 1 All E.R. 20. This is not to say that these principles (and that of estoppel) are not of themselves applicable. For an example of abandonment see *Unisys International Services Ltd.* v. *Eastern Counties Newspapers Ltd.* [1991] 1 Lloyd's Rep. 508.

112. Arbitration Act, s.13A, inserted by Courts and Legal Services Act 1990, s.102: *The Boucraa* [1994] 1 All E.R. 20.

injustice.[113] Since the conferment of the direct power the limitations on the control disappear. Moreover, the removal of any concept of mutual obligation means delay is inexcusable if the explanation for it is not accepted by the arbitrator."[114]

THE ARBITRATION AWARD AND ITS ENFORCEMENT

ENGLISH ARBITRATION AWARDS

An award made in English arbitration proceedings is enforceable:

(i) by an action on the award, based on the implied promise of parties to an arbitration agreement to comply with the award and (possibly) the implied promise implicit in the award itself[115];

(ii) in the same manner as a court judgment or order[116] on application to and leave granted by the High Court (this being simply a mode of procedural speed). In substance it is akin to the action on the award.

As an award arises out of the arbitration agreement, if the agreement is contained in a contract within Admiralty jurisdiction it may be enforceable by an action *in rem*.[117] The issue is considered in Chapters 2, 25.

FOREIGN ARBITRATION AWARDS

Foreign arbitration awards are enforceable (a) in the same manner as English awards; (b) as a Convention award under the Arbitration Act 1975; or (c) as a "foreign award" under the Arbitration Act 1950. These methods are discussed, together with foreign judgments, in Chapter 27.

---

113. *Ibid.* at p. 33 per Lord Mustill. In exceptional circumstances a claim may be dismissed under the limitation period: *Lazenby* v. *McNicholas* [1995] 3 All E.R. 820.

114. *Ibid.* at p. 33.

115. It is argued that both elements are necessary to enforcement (Mustill and Boyd, *op. cit.* Chap. 28). A plaintiff must also at least base his case on an award "appearing to be regular and with jurisdiction" (*Kianta Osakeyhtio* v. *Britain & Overseas Trading Co. Ltd.* [1954] 1 Lloyd's Rep. 247, at pp. 250–251).

116. Arbitration Act 1950, s.26—or if within county court jurisdiction the county court (*ibid.*).

117. See *The Saint Anna* [1983] 1 Lloyd's Rep. 637. In *The Saint Anna*, Sheen J. followed *Bremer Oeltransport GmbH* v. *Drewry* [1933] 1 K.B. 753 in preference to *The Beldis* [1936] P. 51—it is submitted clearly rightly. See also *The Atlas Pride* [1994] LMLN 388 (Singapore H.C.).

PART III

Interim Relief

CHAPTER 14

Nature and Basis of Interim Relief

Interim relief is available in English courts in connection with substantive proceedings in those courts, in respect of proceedings in member States of the Brussels and Lugano Conventions, and, as regards arrest, in respect of foreign proceedings in general following the stay of English proceedings. Interim relief is relevant mainly to pre-judgment remedies but not exclusively so. Where the relief is to ensure that the interest of a party is protected if judgment is in favour of that party the point of the protection could be lost unless it continued until implementation of the judgment or order. So, for example, a *Mareva* injunction may be granted either pre or post judgment.

TYPES OF RELIEF AND PROCEDURE

In favour of the plaintiff

Interim (or interlocutory) relief is of four main kinds:

  (i) the obtaining of evidence;
  (ii) the controlling of the actions of the parties as an interim measure acting on the evidence then available;
  (iii) to ensure that the defendant has assets to meet any judgment;
  (iv) a substantive remedy provided prior to the hearing on the merits.

In favour of the defendant

A defendant may obtain interim relief (in addition to (i) and (ii) above as appropriate):

  (i) to obtain security for costs;
  (ii) an undertaking in damages should the plaintiff lose an action or the defendant suffer loss from an interlocutory order made against him which is later shown to be unfounded.

1. IN FAVOUR OF THE PLAINTIFF

The basis of the award of interim relief in the High Court is threefold—through the Supreme Court Act 1981[1] (re-enacting the Supreme Court of Judicature (Consolidation) Act 1925 which in turn re-enacted the Supreme Court of Judicature Act 1873) and the

---

1. As amended by the Administration of Justice Act 1982, s.6 (provisional damages for personal injuries).

Civil Jurisdiction and Judgments Act 1982, the Rules of the Supreme Court 1965 and the inherent jurisdiction of the court. The effect of the 1982 Act was to provide for the award in England of interim relief (save for the obtaining of evidence and arrest of property) in respect of proceedings within the Brussels or Lugano Convention in a Convention State.[2]

In English law there has long been adequate provision for interim relief ancillary to the proceedings on the merits and for weighing the factors in deciding the extent to which conduct of the parties may be controlled pending a hearing. As a general rule, where any interim relief granted may harm the defendant an undertaking in damages will be imposed as a condition of the relief. As a consequence, should the plaintiff fail in his action, the defendant would be compensated.

It has often been said, however, that English law has suffered as regards the providing of "security" in the sense of imposing restraints on the disposition of a defendant's assets. In 1890 in *Lister* v. *Stubbs*[3] it was held that there was no right in the plaintiff to obtain security for a claim simply because it was highly likely that the claim would be successful. It was to provide such security that in the early 1970s the injunction was made available. The issue of a *Mareva* injunction is an order to a defendant to an action not to dissipate assets prior to judgment. It is considered in Chapter 16.

(i) The obtaining of evidence

There are wide powers to order discovery of documents, discovery of facts (through interrogatories) attendance of witnesses and inspection, and preservation, custody, detention or photographing of property relevant to a claim. The framework of these powers is set out in the Supreme Court Act 1981[4] and in the Rules of the Supreme Court,[5] but some remain based on inherent jurisdiction.[6] The powers relating to property have been extended in recent years, particularly with respect to personal injuries and fatal accident actions. In regard to these, discovery of documents may be ordered prior to the issue of a writ and against a person not party to proceedings in existence.[7]

In 1975, in *Anton Piller KG* v. *Manufacturing Processes Ltd*[8] the Court of Appeal held that the High Court had inherent jurisdiction[9] to make an order *ex parte* that a defendant

2. Sections 24, 25(1) and (6). This power may be extended by Order in Council to other proceedings and other countries (s.25(3)). As to Scotland, see s.27. Property arrested in Admiralty proceedings in England, Wales, or Northern Ireland may be retained or other security ordered in a stay of those proceedings pending arbitration or foreign proceedings (s.26). See *infra* and Chapter 15.

3. (1890) 45 Ch. D. 1.

4. Sections 33–35.

5. See e.g. RSC Order 29 (Preservation of Property); RSC Order 31 (Discovery and Interrogatories).

6. As for example the making of orders designed to ascertain the whereabouts of property to which claim is made. (See *A* v. *C* [1980] 2 Lloyd's Rep. 200.) As to the order of disclosure of assets as a foundation for a *Mareva* injunction see Chap. 16.

7. See the Supreme Court Act 1981, ss.33–35; RSC Order 29, r. 8A. *Norwich Pharmacal Co.* v. *Customs and Excise Commissioners* [1974] A.C. 133. See also RSC Order 38 r. 13.

8. [1976] Ch. 55. As to the relationship between such an order and the privilege against self-incrimination, see the Supreme Court Act 1981, s.72. There is no such privilege in respect of offences under foreign law but the possibility is a factor in deciding whether to make an order for disclosure of assets as the foundation for a *Mareva* injunction (*Arab Monetary Fund* v. *Hashim* [1989] 3 All E.R. 461. See also *No. 2* [1990] 1 All E.R. 673)—as to which see Chapter 16.

9. The order is in effect a mandatory injunction and, therefore, it may be argued, is authorized by the Supreme Court Act 1981, s.37—but even if this is so the discretion of whether to grant an injunction in any particular case remains.

allow a plaintiff to enter premises controlled by the defendant to inspect and remove documents relevant to a case (now known as the "Anton Piller" order). It stressed that only where it was essential that the defendant be not forewarned would such an order be made and an undertaking in damages would be required.[10]

(ii) Controlling of actions of parties prior to hearing

The Supreme Court Act 1981, s.37(1), provides that: "The High Court may by order (whether interlocutory or final) grant an injunction or appoint a receiver in all cases in which it appears to the court to be just and convenient to do so."

The power to appoint a receiver is a specific type of interim relief and, except for noting its relevance to crystallization of a floating charge (see Chapter 17), calls for no further comment in a maritime context. The power to grant an interlocutory injunction provides a general method of temporary control.[11]

In considering generally whether to exercise the power to grant an interlocutory injunction an English court would have to decide first if the grant or refusal will have the practical effect of putting an end to the action in the sense that the harm done to the losing party cannot be compensated. If the granting of the injunction would have this effect the degree of likelihood of the plaintiff's success at trial is a factor in deciding whether to grant it and the court must approach the matter "on a broad principle: what can the court do in its best endeavour to avoid injustice?".[12]

If the granting of the injunction would not put an end to the case, the court must be satisfied first that there is a serious question to be tried, whether damages will be an adequate compensation and, if not, whether the defendant, if he should win, will be adequately compensated through the plaintiff's undertakings as to damages. If there is a doubt about the adequacy of damages the court must base the issue (or not) of the injunction on the balance of convenience, taking into account all relevant factors (including the status quo and any disproportionate relative strength of the case of the parties).[13] The general statutory provision is the foundation for the power to grant an injunction to prevent the defendant dissipating his assets prior to satisfaction of a judgment (see infra) and to prohibit participation in foreign proceedings (see Chapter 12).

A court may on application of "any interested person" prohibit for a time specified the dealing in any ship or any share in the ship. This is a right standing on its own in the sense

10. Where applications for such orders are unnecessary plaintiffs may have to bear the costs. *Systemica Ltd.* v. *London Computer Centre Ltd.* [1983] FSR 313.

11. For procedure see RSC Order 29. An injunction may be granted to a third party affected by or likely to become a party to the action. See *SCOR* v. *Eras Eil (No. 2)* [1995] 2 All E.R. 278 (see Chap. 12).

12. *Cayne* v. *Global Natural Resources plc* [1984] 1 All E.R. 225, applying the principle of *NWL Ltd.* v. *Woods* [1979] 3 All E.R. 614.

13. *American Cynamid* v. *Ethicon Ltd.* [1975] A.C. 396. An interlocutory injunction may be granted where the only cause of action is for a declaration: *Newport AFC* v. *F.A. of Wales Ltd.* [1995] 2 All E.R. 87. Caution is needed where the injunction sought involves a restraint on foreign proceedings (*Apple Corpn* v. *Apple Computer Inc.* [1992] RPC 70). As to restraint of foreign proceedings see Chap. 12. As to foreign arbitrations, see Chapter 13; foreign proceedings, Chaps. 9, 16. A claim to a performance guarantee may be restrained on strong evidence of fraud in the substantive transaction: *Themehelp* v. *West* [1995] 4 All E.R. 215 (C.A.). As to trade disputes see Trade Union and Labour Relations (Consolidation) Act 1992, s.221(2) and *Dimbleby and Sons Ltd.* v. *NUJ* [1984] 1 All E.R. 751 (H.L.).

that the grant is not dependent on any existing substantive claim,[14] and, it would appear, therefore does not necessarily depend on the principles applicable generally to interlocutory injunctions.[15]

(iii) Measures against dissipation of defendant's assets

Preservation of property

As part of its inherent jurisdiction the court has power to restrain a defendant to a proprietary claim from disposing of or dealing with assets where the plaintiffs are seeking to trace property acquired by the defendant. Such a power is ancillary to the proprietary claim and, unlike the power to grant a *Mareva* injunction, is based on the plaintiff's claim to an interest in the property.[16]

As mentioned in the context of the obtaining of evidence, the High Court may make an order for the preservation of property relevant to a cause of action.[17] To this extent the court has a power to "preserve" the defendant's assets for his creditors,[18] and it may be in the context of the action *in rem* that this can be achieved by judicial sale of arrested property prior to the trial of the action. A sale may be ordered to prevent the disappearance of security through continuing costs.[19]

"Mareva" injunction

In 1975 in *Nippon Yusen Kaisha* v. *Karageorgis*[20] the Court of Appeal granted *ex parte* an interim injunction restraining charterers from disposing of or removing any assets in England from England. In particular, the injunction was aimed at money in bank accounts and the court had no doubt that the predecessor to the Supreme Court Act 1981, s.37 (Supreme Court of Judicature (Consolidation) Act 1925, s.45) provided the authority. One month later the principle of this decision was challenged in the case which was to give its name to this type of injunction—*Mareva Compania Navieara SA* v. *International Bulkcarriers SA.*[21]

In 1977, in a fully argued case—*Rasu Maritima SA* v. *Perusahaan Pertambangan Minyak Dan Gas Bumi Negara (Pertamina) and Govt of Indonesia (Intervener)*—the Court of Appeal affirmed the practice. In doing so it rejected a contention that it was limited to cases in which the plaintiff was entitled to summary judgment.[22] As is well

14. As from 1 January 1996, Merchant Shipping Act 1995, Sch. 1, para. 6, re-enacting the Merchant Shipping (Registration, etc.) Act 1993, Sch. 1, para. 6, in turn re-enacting Merchant Shipping Act 1894, s.30. *The Mikado* [1992] 1 Lloyd's Rep. 163—"interested person" does refer to a person having or claiming a proprietary interest in a ship and does not include a creditor seeking execution (*ibid*—see Chap. 2).

15. See *The Myrto* [1977] 2 Lloyd's Rep. 243 (order made modified by the C.A. as to security for discharge of cargo [1978] 1 Lloyd's Rep. 11). Where the action is defended the court should examine more critically whether there is good reason for making the order. As to the power and effect of judicial sale see Chap. 25.

16. *A* v. *C* [1980] 2 Lloyd's Rep. 200; *PCW (Underwriting Agencies) Ltd.* v. *Dixon* [1983] 2 All E.R. 158 and cases cited therein (order varied by consent, see [1983] 2 All E.R. 697 (C.A.)). An order for security of costs cannot be made against a defendant (see *infra*).

17. Supreme Court Act 1981, ss.33(1), 35; RSC Order 29, rr. 2 and 7A.

18. See also RSC Order 29, r. 3, which authorizes the court to secure any specific fund at issue.

19. For an example of delay in sale causing reduction in the fund raised see *The Lyrma (No. 2)* [1978] 2 Lloyd's Rep. 30.

20. [1975] 2 Lloyd's Rep. 137.

21. [1975] 2 Lloyd's Rep. 509.

22. [1978] Q.B. 644, at pp. 661, 664, i.e. under RSC Order 14.

known, the development of the injunction since 1975 has occupied a good many pages of law reports and some controversial steps. It is not now restricted to assets or proceedings in England. It can be granted in conjunction with other modes of interim relief—in particular in addition to arrest of property[23] and it has been combined with Anton Piller orders.[24] Although the injunction is recognized in the Supreme Court Act 1981 it is "quite a different kind to any other".[25] It is considered in Chapter 16.

Arrest of ship, cargo or freight

The most direct interim relief available so as to ensure a fund against which a judgment may be enforced is through arrest of property. In this way the property arrested moves to the control of the court and out of the defendant's power.[26] In English law[27] arrest is restricted to maritime claims, requires the prior institution of an action *in rem*, and may be exercised only against ship, cargo or freight—and in many cases only against a ship. Arrest is considered in Chapter 15.

(iv) A substantive remedy prior to hearing on merits

Clearly, this will be relatively rare but there is power to take such a step. First, the Supreme Court Act 1981 provides that rules of court may be made to provide for interim payment on account of any damages, debt or other sum which may be ordered.[28] Secondly, the boundaries of the courts' interim powers are not rigid. In 1875 in *Smith* v. *Peters* it was said (in a spirit perhaps inconsistent with *Lister*) that there is "no limit to the practice of the Court with regard to interlocutory applications so far as they are necessary and reasonable applications ancillary to the due performance of its functions, namely the administration of justice at the hearing of the cause". So the question of interlocutory relief is one of the exercise rather than existence of power. In 1982 in *The Messiniaki Tolmi*[29] the Court of Appeal relied on *Smith* v. *Peters* in holding that the High Court had power to grant an order imposing an obligation on the buyer:

    (i) to sign a notice of readiness of sale of a ship, failing which it would be signed by a Master of the Supreme Court;

---

23. See *The Rena K* [1979] Q.B. 377 and *infra*.
24. See e.g. *Z Ltd.* v. *A* [1982] Q.B. 558.
25. Section 37(3). *Mercedes Benz A.G.* v. *Leiduck* [1995] 2 Lloyd's Rep. 417.
26. To prevent arrest or obtain release from arrest an owner will usually offer security to the plaintiff. Although such an arrangement is essentially contractual the High Court has inherent jurisdiction to control its amount. See Chap. 15.
27. Contrast Scottish law where (subject to the Civil Jurisdiction and Judgments Act 1982) the function of arrest of property is much broader.
28. Sections 32, 32A. See generally RSC Order 29, rr. 9 and 17. By virtue of rule 17 a court may order repayment of the sum paid and this includes interest to reflect the use of the fund: *Wardens of The Mercers of London* v. *New Hampshire Insurance Co.* [1992] 1 Lloyd's Rep. 431. The decision was appealed but no order made as the Court of Appeal allowed an appeal against the substantive ruling that the plaintiff repay the interim payment. See [1992] 3 All E.R. 57.
29. [1982] Q.B. 1248. The House of Lords affirmed the decision ([1983] 3 W.L.R. 130) on ground which rendered it unnecessary to deal with this point. For further power to make a substantive order see Torts (Interference with Goods) Act 1977, s.4—order for delivery of goods.

(ii) to instruct the relevant bank to act so that the full amount of a letter of credit in respect of this sale price be paid into the joint names of parties' solicitors pending arbitration on a claim between buyer and sellers.

The court was prepared thereby in effect to grant a decree of partial specific performance and to allow the resulting fund to await the outcome of the proceedings—thus illustrating its view of the broad power conferred on it. It was prepared, as it were, to order the creation of a state of affairs for the basis of a judgment rather than simply leaving the affairs as they were when the proceedings started.

PROCEDURE FOR OBTAINING OF INTERIM RELIEF BY PLAINTIFF

Arrest

The power of the remedy of arrest lies partly in the lack of direct judicial control over its initial operation. The warrant of arrest is obtainable (without any undertaking as to damages) once an officer of the Admiralty Registry is satisfied that the applicant's affidavit discloses the availability of an action *in rem*.[30] The warrant is executed (i.e. served) by the Admiralty Marshal.[31]

Other modes of interim relief

All types of interim relief save arrest require a court order which may initially be obtained "*ex parte*", i.e. with no representative of the party against whom it is sought being present. In many cases the effectiveness of the relief depends on its availability prior to the defendants' knowledge, but this should not lead to an over-eager readiness to grant it. An order made *ex parte* will be granted for a limited time and, once granted, it may be challenged before the court which made it.[32] The nature of *ex parte* orders is essentially provisional.

"As I have said, ex parte orders are essentially provisional in nature. They are made by the judge on the basis of evidence and submissions emanating from one side only. Despite the fact that the applicant is under a duty to make full disclosure of all relevant information in his possession, whether or not it assists his application, this is no basis for making a definitive order and every judge knows this. He expects at a later stage to be given an opportunity to review his provisional order in the light of evidence and argument adduced by the other side, and, in so doing, he is not hearing an appeal from himself and in no way feels inhibited from discharging or varying his original order."[33]

---

30. See RSC Order 75, r. 5. It was for this reason that Brandon J. held that arrest is not within the remedies made available in respect of arbitration in the Arbitration Act 1950, s.12(1), a view affirmed by the Court of Appeal in *The Tuyuti* [1984] 2 Lloyd's Rep. 51. However there was until a further change in rules in 1986, a duty of full disclosure—but since that change subject to compliance with the rules a plaintiff is entitled to issue a warrant (*The Varna* [1993] 2 Lloyd's Rep. 253 and see Chap. 15).
31. RSC Order 75, r. 10.
32. See generally RSC Orders 8, 29, 32, rr. 1–6 and *Supreme Court Practice 1985*, pp. 492–494.
33. *WEA Records Ltd* v. *Visions Channel 4 Ltd* [1983] 2 All E.R. 589, at p. 593. Once an order is executed the remedy for a defendant lies in enforceability of the damages undertaking not in setting aside the order (*ibid*).

2. IN FAVOUR OF THE DEFENDANT

Two primary methods of protecting the defendant in case the plaintiff loses his case are (i) the provision of security for costs and (ii) the requirement of an undertaking as a condition of the award of interim relief to a plaintiff or counter security.

(i) Security for costs

By the rules of court, security for the defendant's costs may be ordered to be given by a plaintiff but apart from a limited company only if the plaintiff is not ordinarily resident in the jurisdiction.[34] The discretion to make an order is wide and may be made even if there is a co-plaintiff resident within the jurisdiction. However, unless if the action fails an aliquot order for costs may be made, or the costs are unlikely to be met by plaintiffs within the jurisdiction, the discretion should not be exercised so as to make the order.[35] The purpose of the rule is to ensure that a successful defendant would have a fund within the jurisdiction available to meet costs. Although it is to prevent foreign based plaintiffs being immune from any order for costs it is not primarily to provide security against a plaintiff lacking funds.[36] An order cannot be made against a defendant.[37]

Where the plaintiff is not a limited company residence abroad is the prerequisite and that being shown or not relevant the court must then consider whether in all the circumstances of the case an order should be made. The judge should balance the interests of the parties. While the financial position of the plaintiff is not of itself a reason for making an order it is relevant to the exercise of discretion.[38] It must be considered, however, whether because of impecuniosity any order will stifle the claim.

Ease of enforcement of costs order in foreign jurisdiction where plaintiff resident abroad

It was established in the nineteenth century that because of ease of enforcement no security for costs order should be awarded against a plaintiff resident in Scotland or Northern Ireland.[39] This was not, however, extended to countries to which the Foreign Judgments (Reciprocal Enforcement) Act applies, the relative ease of enforcement not being deemed sufficiently similar.[40] It is, however, now established that the fact of ease of

34. RSC Order 23. Security for costs may be ordered against a limited company in England (Companies Act 1985, s.726). As to a limited company resident outside the jurisdiction see *DSQ Property Co. Ltd.* v. *Lotus Cars Ltd.* [1987] 1 W.L.R. 127. The criteria are much as for individuals: see *Keary* v. *Tarmac* [1995] 3 All E.R. 533 (C.A.).

35. *The Seaspeed Dora* [1988] 1 Lloyd's Rep. 36; [1987] 3 All E.R. 967 (C.A.) applied in *Corfu Navigation* v. *Mobil Shipping Co.* [1991] 2 Lloyd's Rep. 52 (emphasising the wide discretion and varying circumstances of foreign plaintiffs).

36. See *Porzelack* v. *Porzelack* [1987] 1 All E.R. 1074. Unless these are assets in the country a plaintiff one-ship company may expect to have such an order made, see *Berkeley Administration Inc.* v. *McLelland* [1990] 1 All E.R. 958 at p. 964 (Parker L.J.).

37. *CT Bowring (Insurance) Ltd.* v. *Corsi Partners Ltd.* [1994] 2 Lloyd's Rep. 567. An interlocutory application by a defendant does not make that party a plaintiff (*ibid.*).

38. *Thune* v. *London Properties Ltd.* [1990] 1 All E.R. 972 (C.A.), Bingham L.J. there examining the authorities to establish the proposition. The nationality of the defendants may be a factor—but is not of great weight (*ibid.*).

39. *Raeburn* v. *Andrews* (1874) L.R. 9 Q.B. 118.

40. See *Kohn* v. *Rinson and Stafford (Bros.) Ltd.* [1947] 2 All E.R. 839.

enforcement is generally relevant to the exercise of discretion,[41] particularly in respect of enforcement under the Brussels or Lugano Convention (see *infra*).

(ii) Requirement of undertaking or counter security

The grant of a *Mareva* injunction ordering a defendant not to dispose of assets prior to judgment will normally be made only on an undertaking by the plaintiff to indemnify the defendant should the action fail for any loss or damage caused by the injunction.[42] An arrest of property following the issue of a writ *in rem* does not carry a like contingent liability nor will a court so order.[43]

However, where property arrested is retained as security on the stay of proceedings for an action to proceed in a foreign forum or for arbitration, conditions may be imposed—including it would seem the provision of counter security should the case fail.[44] In 1992 the Court of Appeal refused to so order saying this would be a far reaching change in Admiralty procedure.[45] In a different case some two months later Saville J. did make such an order—at least until evidence of foreign law was adduced to enable the likely success of the action to be assessed.[46] While the power to order counter security is a welcome balance to the drastic powers of arrest[47] it is questionable whether it was intended to make the retention of property under arrest operate on principles so fundamentally distinct from the initial arrest.

INTERIM RELIEF IN ARBITRATION PROCEEDINGS

Arbitrators have a wide discretion to make interim awards (see Chapter 13). Further by virtue of the Arbitration Act 1950, s.12 courts have the power to award interim relief in arbitral proceedings. It has the same powers as an action for "securing the amount of dispute" and the issue of interim injunctions.[48] These powers do not encompass the arrest of property. However property arrested in an action *in rem* may be retained on the staying of proceedings because of an arbitration agreement and in such an action a warrant of arrest for property is not to be stayed or set aside simply because the proceedings concerning the substantive matter are stayed.[49]

The provisions of the Arbitration Act 1950 in respect of interlocutory matters do not extend to arbitrations held otherwise than in England and subject to a foreign law. However, English courts do have power to grant such injunctions under the general

---

41. *Thune* v. *London Properties Ltd.* (fn 38).

42. See Chap. 16. The courts power to direct an enquiry into damages on a claim based on an undertaking is discretionary and may be refused on the ground of abuse of process—the basis of the jurisdiction is that the court is being asked to release or vary the undertaking (*CT Bowring* v. *Corsi Partners Ltd.* [1994] 2 Lloyd's Rep. 567 per Millett L.J.)—but it would seem the court is being asked to enforce the undertaking.

43. See Chap. 15.

44. Civil Jurisdiction and Judgments Act 1982, s.26(2).

45. *The Bazias 3 and Bazias 4* [1993] 1 Lloyd's Rep. 101.

46. *The Havhelt* [1993] 1 Lloyd's Rep. 523.

47. As to limited availability of damages for wrongful arrest see Chap. 15.

48. *The Tuyuti* [1984] 2 Lloyd's Rep. 51. See Chap. 13.

49. Civil Jurisdiction and Judgments Act 1982, s.26. See Chap. 15.

statutory power to grant injunctions of the Supreme Court Act 1981, s.37 (as to which see *supra*).[50]

THE EFFECT OF THE BRUSSELS AND LUGANO CONVENTIONS

IN FAVOUR OF THE PLAINTIFF

Provisional measures

Provisional measures are the subject of Article 24. This reads:

"Application may be made to the courts of a Contracting State for such provision including protective measures as may be available under the law of that State even if, under this Convention, the courts of another Contracting State have jurisdiction as to the substance of the matter."

This article encompasses provisional remedies in respect of an action and a judgment.[51] It applies to measures in matters within the Convention intended to "preserve a legal or factual situation in order to safeguard rights which are the subject of a substantive legal action.[52] It reflects the distinction between provisional remedy (or interim relief) and jurisdiction on the merits more familiar traditionally perhaps to civil law rather than common law. Until recently English law has seen interim relief as essentially connected with proceedings on the merits and limited the power to grant such relief to support for proceedings in English courts. In particular arrest depends on the issue of a writ *in rem* and the *Mareva* injunction depended on the assertion of a right under English law and proceedings in an English court to enforce that right.

The underlying philosophy of the Conventions is to create a network of common jurisdiction rules and ready recognition of judgments. To support the structure interim relief must be available wherever within the network the merits are to be adjudged. The effectiveness of Article 24 depends essentially on the effectiveness of national law.[53] There is no obligation under the Article that the provisional measures provided in each member State are identical nor even that any interim relief be made available[54] for proceedings in Convention States. The obligation is to make available such relief as there is for home proceedings. Where the relief is discretionary there is no prohibition in the

---

50. *Channel Tunnel Group Ltd.* v. *Balfour Beatty Construction Ltd.* [1993] 1 All E.R. 664 (H.L.). There is power to order security of costs in exceptional cases in an international arbitration held in London under ICC Rules, and an arbitration held under rules not providing for costs did not mean that the case was not exceptional: *SA Coppée Lavalin NV* v. *Ken Ren Chemicals and Fertilisers Ltd.* [1994] 2 Lloyd's Rep. 109 (H.L.). See Chap. 13. As to the requirement of a legal or equitable right see the *Mercedes Benz* case fn. 25.

51. See *infra*. As to enforcement of judgments see Chap. 28. It has been held by the Irish High Court that measures ancillary to the enforcement of a foreign judgment must be ordered once there is an order for enforcement and jurisdiction to make the order: *Elwyn (Cottons) Ltd.* v. *Pearle Designs Ltd.* [1990] I.L.Pr. 40.

52. *Reichert* v. *Dresdner Bank (No. 2)* 261/90 [1992] I.L.Pr. 404—an action seeking to alter rather than preserve the circumstances of the case is not within Art. 24.

53. So it is the national law which determines the scope of the interim relief (see *Re an Italian Cargo of Adulterated Wine* [1991] I.L.Pr. 473 (Oberlandsgericht Koblenz); *Lowland Yachts BV* v. *Firma Dahm International* [1991] I.L.Pr. 350 (District Court The Hague)).

54. There is no prohibition on making the interim relief available when not within the Convention (e.g. prior to the Convention coming into operation): *Alltrans Inc.* v. *Interdom Holdings Ltd.* [1991] 2 All E.R. 571 (C.A.).

foreign nature of the proceedings as an element in the exercise of the discretion. A judgment awarding a provisional remedy will fall within the provisions for judgment enforcement provided it is pronounced after an *inter partes* hearing[55] and is not a purely procedural ruling made in the course of litigation.[56] It may be however that a court may be less willing to make a provisional order affecting foreign assets or acts on foreign territory when it is open to a party to obtain such an order in the foreign jurisdiction.[57] It *may* be arguable that where by national law there is a discretion in awarding interim relief it remains relevant that such an order could be more effectively made in the foreign territory. On the other hand the court hearing the substantive claim may be the more effective court to control measures ancillary to it.[58]

Effect of other Conventions (Articles 24 and 57)

By Article 57 the Brussels and Lugano Conventions do not affect any Convention relating to jurisdiction or recognition of judgments in particular matters. So, as discussed in Chapter 6 once a case is within the Conventions, other Conventions within Article 57 will apply in priority to the structure of the Brussels and Lugano Conventions. Provided that "jurisdiction" in Article 57 encompasses provisional measures it follows that an obligation on member States to apply national law in support of court proceedings in other states is subject to other Convention obligations.

So a Convention restricting the award of provisional measures or making them dependent on conditions will apply rather than the connection between home and foreign proceedings of Article 24.[59] Whether another Convention obligation not reflected in national law would increase the scope of jurisdiction seems more uncertain. Article 57 operates to create substantive jurisdiction bases in addition to those specified in the Convention but where the only Convention base is linked solely to national law it must be questionable whether the provision can indirectly enact other Convention provisions. So it must be doubtful whether the provisions of the Convention Relating to Sea Going Ships, apart from those concerning merits jurisdiction, are indirectly applied in English law.[60]

Multiple proceedings (Article 24 and Articles 21–23)

It would seem that orders for provisional measures are within the scope of Articles 21–23 in that as between such orders there is as much of a risk of irreconcilability as in substantive judgment. On the other hand it is quite clear from the Convention that a provisional measure is seen as distinct from a substantive judgment and Articles 21–23 will not apply to affect merits jurisdiction because of the granting of a provisional measure.

---

55. *Denilauler* v. *Couchet Freres* 125/79 [1981] 1 CMLR 62. See Chap. 28.
56. See *CFEM Facades SA* v. *Boris Construction Ltd.* [1992] 1 L. Pr. 561.
57. See *Derby* v. *Weldon (No. 2)* [1989] 1 All E.R. 1002 (C.A.). See Chap. 16.
58. See *CFEM Facades* case (fn 56).
59. As for example the Hague Convention concerning the service of documents in relation to interlocutory orders. See the *CFEM Facades* case (fn 56).
60. As to its operation to substantive matters see Chap. 6.

Implementation in English law

Article 24 is in substance implemented into English law by the Civil Jurisdiction and Judgments Act 1982, s.25. This applies to "interim relief" other than a warrant for the arrest of property or provision for obtaining evidence. It reads:

"(1) The High Court in England and Wales or Northern Ireland shall have power to grant interim relief where:
      (a) proceedings have been or are to be commenced in a Contracting State other than the United Kingdom or in a part of the United Kingdom other than that in which the High Court in question exercises jurisdiction; and
      (b) they are or will be proceedings whose subject-matter is within the scope of the 1968 Convention as determined by Article 1 (whether or not the Convention has effect in relation to the proceedings).
(2) On an application for any interim relief under subsection (1) the court may refuse to grant that relief if, in the opinion of the court, the fact that the court has no jurisdiction apart from this section in relation to the subject-matter of the proceedings in question makes it expedient for the court to grant it.

The power set out in section 25(1) may be extended partially or wholly by Order in Council to include the proceedings other than Convention proceedings, proceedings commenced in states other than Convention States or arbitration proceedings (s.25(3) to (5)). Section 24 extends the power to grant "interim relief" or "protective measures" pending trial or pending the determination of an appeal to a case to where:

      (a) the issue to be tried, or which is the subject of the appeal, relates to the jurisdiction of the court to entertain the proceedings; or
      (b) the proceedings involve the reference of any matter to the European Court under the 1971 Protocol.

As a consequence of these provisions an English court has the power to order, for example, a *Mareva* injunction in respect of proceedings in another contracting State. The provision is a step towards recognition that interim relief or provisional measures may have a jurisdictional life of their own. This recognition is also reflected in s.26 of the Act authorizing the retention of property arrested in an action *in rem* following the staying of proceedings for reference to arbitration or a foreign forum.[61] It serves to underline the more recent holding that the granting of a provisional measure does not necessarily imply the creation of jurisdiction over the merits.[62]

In 1994 in *Balkanbank* v. *Taher*[63] the Court of Appeal (reversing Clarke, J.) held that the bringing of proceedings under s.25 for interim relief in support of foreign actions opened the door to a counterclaim in an English court for substantive relief in the action. The procedure for seeking an injunction under s.25 is under the rules of court (Order 28, r. 7) through "an action begun by originating summons". In this context no distinction is to be drawn between the seeking of ancillary and substantive relief. Contrary to the view of Clarke J. the court viewed with equanimity the liability to substantive relief engendered by seeking ancillary relief for foreign proceedings. In the opinion of Saville L.J. interim relief often has an effect as substantively powerful as substantive relief.

---

61. See *infra* and Chap. 15.
62. See *The Sargasso* [1994] 2 Lloyd's Rep. 6 disagreeing with dicta in *Dresser* v. *Falcongate* [1991] 2 Lloyd's Rep. 557.
63. [1995] 2 All E.R. 904.

Most of the debate focused on construction of the rules of court and the ability, apart from s.25, to counterclaim substantively when ancillary relief is sought. Once that was established there was nothing in s.25 to curtail its effect. The court stressed that Balkanbank was not domiciled in a contracting State to the Brussels Convention and therefore under Art. 4 the jurisdiction was a matter for English law. It is important to stress that if the Convention rules apply it is necessary to establish a Convention jurisdiction base.

Apart from the applicability of a Convention jurisdiction base the result is as logical as it is surprising. It wholly ignores the distinction between English and foreign proceedings and uses a rule of court drafted in the context of the former to justify substantive jurisdiction under a statutory provision for supporting ancillary relief. There must be doubt that the statutory implementation of Article 24 of the Brussels Convention was ever seen as the springboard for the extention of substantive jurisdiction. The supporting relief is thereby turned into a rival jurisdiction leading possibly to inconsistent judgments. It seems a direction contrary to the separation of substantive and ancillary relief as jurisdictional bases evident in other contexts (see *supra*). It neatly reverses the traditional view that the availability of interim relief depends on substantive jurisdiction.

(i) Interim relief other than arrest or obtaining of evidence

Section 25 does not remove the procedural requirements of service of the writ or other document, but such requirements cannot qualify the Convention obligation. In English law service of a writ out of the jurisdiction is governed by RSC Order 11 and Order 75 (see Chapter 9). The terms of these Orders may not wholly match either s.25 or Article 24 but insofar as is possible they should be construed consistently with the underlying Convention obligation.[64] Where leave of the court is required, that leave should be given, any discretion applicable to non Convention cases being removed by Article 24.

(ii) Arrest in English law

Is it a provisional measure?

It is established that the purpose of the writ is irrelevant to its validity, and there is legislative provision for the retention of property arrested when the substantive proceedings are stayed because of reference to a foreign forum or arbitration.[65] Nevertheless, an arrest can only follow from the issue of a writ *in rem* and as the writ is valid only if there is jurisdiction over the substantive issue if may remain arguable that any "arrest proceedings" are not "provisional measure" proceedings. The argument is less likely to succeed as the dichotomy between "merits" and "provisional" proceedings becomes more established.

---

64. See *Haiti* v. *Duvalier* [1989] 1 All E.R. 456 (C.A.); *X* v. *Y* [1989] 2 Lloyd's Rep. 561—the latter construing the wording of rule 1(1)(b) differently simply because of the Convention context. Both cases concerned *Mareva* injunctions and are discussed in Chap. 16.

65. Civil Jurisdiction and Judgments Act 1982, s.26. For the background to and effect of this provision see Chap. 15.

Arrest in English law and the Brussels Convention

In *The Nordglimt*[66] Hobhouse J. held that concurrent *in rem* and *in personam* proceedings were not between the same parties and raised different considerations. They were therefore not within the mandatory stay imposed by Article 21 on a court second seised of the same cause of action between the same parties. The judge also pointed to different considerations under English law applicable to an action *in personam* and an action *in rem*, and, in particular, the non-merger of an action in a judgment *in personam*. To justify excluding the concurrent action *in rem* and action *in personam* from Article 21 the judge stressed the separation of arrest and merits proceedings recognized by the Convention Relating to the Arrest of Sea Going Ships 1952 and the obligation to construe Article 21 if possible consistently with the 1952 Convention.

In English law by the Civil Jurisdiction and Judgments Act 1982, s.26 provision, English courts may order the retention of property arrested when the substantive issue is stayed or dismissed because the matter is referred to arbitration or a foreign forum. While the provision still requires the issue of a writ *in rem* in order to arrest, it removes any concept of an exclusive link between arrest and English proceedings. In *The Nordglimt* it was held that s.26 was consistent with Article 21 and that the latter provision did not prevent retention of property arrested.

Matters have developed a little since *The Nordglimt* and the European Court has held that for the purposes of Article 21 the distinction between an action *in personam* and an action *in rem* is irrelevant. The question is whether the proceedings involve the same cause of action and the same parties.[67] It has to be remembered that *The Nordglimt* was one of the first English cases under the Convention. It may be now that it would be readily accepted that whatever the overlap between the two types of action insofar as a writ *in rem* is issued simply to obtain security (as it apparently was in *The Nordglimt*) it is Article 24 that is the appropriate Convention provision and hence Article 21 never enters the picture. There is surely everything to be said for approaching national law procedure realistically and consistently with the Convention concepts particularly where that law explicitly recognizes at least in part the possibility of an English arrest for foreign proceedings.

Further within the Convention the issue and service of the writ *in rem* has of itself no jurisdictional significance. Jurisdiction in an *in rem* context now depends on arrest under the Arrest Convention—and it is explicitly recognized by that Convention that arrest has the two functions of interim relief and foundation of jurisdiction on the merits. So arrest may still be permissible to create jurisdiction even though the giving of alternative security would remove any justification as a "provisional measure".[68]

While the issue of the writ remains necessary for an arrest besides implementing Convention substantive jurisdiction based on arrest, the same "double" function should be recognized. Because the same procedural act has two purposes it does not mean that the two purposes should be confused or equated—in Convention terms one is a provisional measure and the other a substantive jurisdiction base. The criteria for adjudging the

---

66. [1987] 2 Lloyd's Rep. 470.
67. *The Maciej Rataj* [1995] 1 Lloyd's Rep. 302. See Chap. 12.
68. See *The Prinsengracht* [1993] 1 Lloyd's Rep. 43; *The Anna H* [1995] 1 Lloyd's Rep. 11. Compare *The Deichland* [1989] 2 All E.R. 1066; *The Po* [1991] 2 Lloyd's Rep. 206 where arrest was asserted as the foundation of jurisdiction over the substantive claim. (See Chap. 5.)

"jurisdiction" depends on which function is applicable. That in substance is the conclusion of *The Nordglimt* in seeking to fit the English approach to the Convention structure.

Arrest and arbitration and the Brussels Convention

Arbitration is outside the Convention (Article 1). In English law interim relief available in respect of court proceedings is made applicable insofar as it is by court order in respect of arbitration (Arbitration Act 1950, s.12(f)). So a *Mareva* injunction may be granted. Although arrest is not within the general permissive provision of section 12(f)[69] if an action *in rem* is initiated by the claimant it is available within limits (see Chapter 15).

All matters concerned directly with arbitration proceedings are outside the Convention[70] and it would seem therefore that any interim relief directly ordered in support of such arbitration is excluded. However, while arrest depends on the issue of the writ *in rem* it remains arguable that the foundation is the very denial of arbitration proceedings. The basis of the retention of property under arrest was originally the possibility that the court may have a role to play should any arbitral award not be met. It may now be said however that, although somewhat indirect, the legislative authority to retain arrested property for arbitration in substance recognizes that the primary link is to arbitration rather than litigation. So once the court proceedings are stayed the issue of retention of arrested property would also be excluded from the Convention.

IN FAVOUR OF THE DEFENDANT

(i) Security for costs

Even if Article 24 may be read as encompassing security for costs it is highly unlikely that an English court would consider ordering a plaintiff in proceedings other than in England to lodge security. This type of interim relief is essentially connected with the proceedings brought and their continuation.

The effect of the Brussels and Lugano Conventions is not to increase the scope of the order for security for costs but to provide a strong factor against making an order. Although there are no express provisions for security for costs[71] the ease of enforcement of a costs order in the Convention States makes special circumstances necessary prerequisites for an order against a plaintiff resident in such a state.[72] Further any provision of national law discriminating as to the making of security of costs orders on

---

69. See *The Rena K* (fn 23)—but it may be arguable that the approach in *The Tuyuti* [1984] 2 Lloyd's Rep. 51 would bring it within s.12(f). As to the approach see Chap. 15.

70. See *Marc Rich* v. *Societa Impianti* [1992] 1 Lloyd's Rep. 342 and Chap. 4.

71. But security is prohibited in respect of enforcement of a judgment given in another contracting State on the ground that the applicant is a foreign national or not domiciled or resident in the state of enforcement (Art. 45). See Chap. 28.

72. *De Bry* v. *Fitzgerald* [1990] 1 All E.R. 560 per Dillon L.J. (at p. 566) the court approving *Porzelack* v. *Porzelack* [1987] 1 All E.R. 1074.

grounds of nationality or solely on residence abroad has been held by the European Court to be contrary to the prohibition against discrimination on nationality grounds in the Treaty of Rome.[73] In 1989 in *Berkeley Administration Inc.* v. *McLelland*[74] the Court of Appeal held the Rules of the Supreme Court conferring power to make such an order on a plaintiff resident abroad not discriminatory on the grounds of nationality. The place of residence was a prerequisite for making an order but the order depends on consideration of all the circumstances of the case, including the ease of enforcement of a costs order. It is probable that this approach is consistent with the law as declared by the European Court.

(ii) Requirement of undertaking or counter security

These measures of interim relief are by definition connected with orders made in favour of a plaintiff. Lacking any express prohibition the jurisdiction to make any "counter order" would be therefore of identical scope as the power to make the order in regard to which it provides a balance. In effect the counter order is a condition of the original order and any lack of power to provide the balance could be a factor in making the order. In the context of *Mareva* or retention of ships under arrest there is no reason for limiting the power to impose such conditions in favour of the defendant.

MEASURES AFTER JUDGMENT

As indicated earlier interim relief may need to continue until satisfaction of a judgment. Whether it may or should depends on the nature of the relief, and unless because of that nature or any express provision relief will not be limited to pre-judgment.[75] In English law arrest has been considered a pre-judgment remedy,[76] but in 1983 in the High Court of Singapore Thean J. in *The Daien Maru*[77] demonstrated the illogicality of this restriction. The illogicality as the learned judge there saw it stemmed from:

(a) the categorization of arrest as procedure and therefore the lack of any principle in any limit to its availability because of a judgment;
(b) the need to enforce a maritime lien through arrest.

If any action *in rem* is procedural there can be no merger of the power of arrest in any judgment. If arrest formed an inherent part of a maritime lien it made little sense to remove its availability by a judgment declaring the lien to exist.[78] Such arguments seem irresistible.

---

73. *Firma Mund and Fester* v. *Firma Hatrex International Transport* 398/92 [1994] 1 L. Pr. 264; *Hubbard* v. *Hamburger* 20/90 *The Times*, 16 July 1993.
74. [1990] 1 All E.R. 958.
75. *Orwell Steel* v. *Asphalt and Tarmac (UK)* [1984] 1 W.L.R. 1097, [1985] 3 All E.R. 747.
76. See *The Alletta* [1974] 1 Lloyd's Rep. 40.
77. [1986] 1 Lloyd's Rep. 387.
78. For availability through an action *in rem* to enforce a foreign judgment see *The Despina GK* [1983] Q.B. 214; [1982] 2 Lloyd's Rep. 555.

THE BRUSSELS AND LUGANO CONVENTIONS

"Protective measures" within Article 24 of the 1968 Convention include measures to enforce a judgment[79]—but not methods of execution of the judgment. The extent to which such measures are available is a matter for national law. Arrest after judgment falls outside the Arrest Convention but would be enforceable under the Brussels and Lugano Conventions directly through Article 24.

79. Protective measures are excluded from the prohibition of enforcement measures while an appeal is pending and the decision authorizing enforcement carries with it the power to proceed to such measures (Article 39).

CHAPTER 15

Arrest and Alternative Security

INTRODUCTION

THE THREE FUNCTIONS OF ARREST

Arrest is a powerful weapon. Its availability in English law is consequent only on the property being arrestable, the claim enforceable by an action *in rem* and the issue of the writ *in rem*. It does not depend on showing an arguable claim or that any judgment may not be met. There is no cross undertaking in damages and its effect on third parties is irrelevant.

The arrest of maritime property has three possible functions. First, and most obviously, it is a form of interim relief or provisional remedy—a "*saisie conservatoire*" (and in this context it should be noted that a creditor may obtain some protection through a caveat against release). Secondly, it may operate as a ground of jurisdiction over the merits. Thirdly, it is a primary method of ensuring the availability of judicial sale, itself the means of implementing the proprietary interest conferred or enforced through the action *in rem*.

The civil law approach

In civil law countries maritime and civil procedure codes aid in distinguishing between these three functions. The questions of jurisdiction and arrest will be dealt with usually in the Code of Procedure and in many cases independently of each other. Often "arrest" is relevant only as a provisional remedy and there will usually be provision for security (such as bail or guarantee) which may prevent arrest or cause the property to be released from arrest. Jurisdiction on the merits may be based on a more substantial contact between the country and the issue than the seizure of a ship temporarily there.

Security for the merits claim is based on the classification of claims as preferred claims which give priority over unsecured creditors and, in addition, may confer enforceability of the claim against purchasers from the person against whom the claim is made. These preferred claims are sometimes labelled "liens" and will be set out in the Maritime or Commercial Code.

The approach in English law

In English law arrest is a component part of the action *in rem*. It is available on the issue of the writ *in rem* and is therefore dependent initially at least on jurisdiction in the

311

substantive action. For this reason jurisdiction issues are commonly discussed in terms of the right to arrest. Its function in this context is in reality one of "security", i.e. to ensure that the asset is available for enforcement of a judgment. However, it may be that through the indirect operation of Conventions (or arguably without) arrest is itself a jurisdiction base.

ALTERNATIVE SECURITY

Arrest may be prevented or ended by the provision of alternative security through bail, payment into court, where liability may be limited through the setting up of a limitation fund, or the provision of a guarantee or undertaking. Bail or payment into court provides a fund (notional or actual) representing the ship for the claimant and proceedings continue on that basis. A limitation fund provides adequate security under the control of the court. A guarantee or undertaking, however, is contractual, and does not provide any fund for claims, but simply an agreement enforceable on the conditions specified in it. Whether or not the agreement is in addition to or replaces any lien will depend on its terms. Its replacement of arrest will not of itself affect the existence of any lien—the lien not being dependent on arrest. The "security" (both provisional as replacing arrest and on the merits claim as replacing any lien) is therefore contractual in nature.

A less effective but less costly protection than arrest may be acquired once a ship has been arrested by another through the lodging of a caveat against release from arrest. Such action will ensure that the ship is not released without an opportunity being given to the caveator to rearrest. Caveats, methods of alternative security and the effect of establishment of a limitation fund are discussed after the review of arrest.

THE INTERNATIONAL SCENE

On the international scene arrest as a provisional remedy and arrest as a jurisdiction base are matters which are the primary subjects of the Convention Relating to the Arrest of Sea Going Ships 1952, while the proprietary security aspects of maritime claims are the subjects of the Convention for the Unification of Certain Rules Relating to Maritime Liens and Mortgages 1926, 1967 and 1993. The latter Conventions refer to arrest only in the context of the nature of the claims which attract a security interest. They will be discussed in Part III.

The scene is largely governed by the International Convention Relating to the Arrest of Sea Going Ships signed at Brussels on 10 May 1952 (hereafter "the Arrest Convention").[1] This Convention which required only two ratifications to bring it into force, had been ratified by 1 June 1995 by 72 states, including the United Kingdom. It has taken on an enhanced importance through its enforcement by the Brussels and Lugano Conventions in

---

1. A draft CMI Convention to replace the 1952 Convention was agreed in 1985 and was considered in 1995 by the joint CMI/UNCTAD governmental group of experts on maritime liens, mortgages and related subjects. The suggested text is much more precise in linking arrest with the substantive remedy of judicial sale and hence liens. For a comprehensive guide to the two texts and the *travaux preparatoires* see Berlingieri, *Arrest of Ships—a Commentary on the 1952 Arrest Convention*, 1992, Lloyd's of London Press.

preference to the provisions of those Conventions. It provides for arrest as a provisional remedy in support of a maritime claim and for jurisdiction based on arrest.

Other maritime Conventions providing for jurisdiction based on arrest are the Collision (Civil Jurisdiction) Convention 1952 and the Hamburg Rules. The availability of arrest both as a provisional remedy and as a jurisdiction base is restricted by the Convention Relating to Liability for Maritime Claims 1976 on the setting up of a limitation fund.

In English law "arrest" necessarily implies the existence of a lien. This is partly a matter of terminology and party a matter of history. On the international scene the Arrest Convention refers only to the non-creation of maritime liens through any of its provisions. Liens are the subject of three Conventions of 1926, 1967 and 1993. These Conventions set out to provide a framework for the creation and priority of liens and mortgages. In their turn, they refer to arrest only as a means of enforcement of a lien and thereby reflect the civil law in separating the claim and its preference from the remedy. This carries its own defects—in particular the uncertainty of the affect of arrest on third party proprietary interests. The desirable framework calls for recognition of the connection with but distinction between the concepts and functions of arrest, jurisdiction and liens.

CONVENTION RELATING TO THE ARREST OF SEA-GOING SHIPS 1952

This Convention is concerned with arrest as (i) a provisional remedy, and (ii) a ground for jurisdiction on the merits. It defines arrest for its purposes as "the detention of a ship by judicial process to secure a maritime claim"—it "does not include the seizure of a ship in execution or satisfaction of a judgment". The Convention is limited to sea-going ships. It specifies (in Art. 1) the only claims in regard to which a ship may be arrested ("maritime claims") and (in Art. 7) the circumstances in which a court of the country in which the arrest was made has jurisdiction to adjudge the merits. It provides that subject to proof of good cause a ship may not be arrested or bail or other security given more than once in any one or more of the jurisdictions of any of the contracting States by the same claimant for the same claim (Art. 3(3)).

The Convention applies to any vessel flying the flag of a contracting State in the jurisdiction of a contracting State; and in addition provides that ships of non-contracting States may be arrested in the jurisdiction of a contracting State for any of the Convention maritime claims *and* any other claim for which arrest is permitted by the domestic law of the contracting State.[2] Finally, and importantly in the light of other Conventions, a contracting State may exclude from the effects of the Convention any person who at the time of the arrest does not habitually reside or have a principal place of business in a contracting State.[3]

The list of maritime claims is long and wide in scope. All are closely and directly connected with maritime operations.[4] For jurisdiction on the merits dependent on the Convention there must be one of a number of specified links between the claim and the

2. Article 8(1) and (2).
3. Article 8(3).
4. The list is almost identical to that set out in the Supreme Court Act 1981, s.20 (see Appendix 1). Cf. Chap. 2 for discussion of the content of the claims. The 1985 draft revision is based on a non-exclusive list.

country (e.g. habitual residence of the claimant, the place where the claims arose), the claim must concern the voyage during which the arrest was made or be a collision, salvage or mortgage claim. In addition, the Convention recognizes any circumstances in which a domestic law permits jurisdiction on the merits.[5] In particular, this means that those countries such as England, Scotland and the United States, which permit jurisdiction based on the availability of arrest, may become parties and maintain their domestic laws at international level. It follows that those countries parties to the Convention not allowing "arrest" as a jurisdictional ground must come into line to provide such jurisdiction on the basis of the specified links to fulfil their international obligations.

The Convention provides for the arrest of the ship in respect of which the claim arose or (unless a charterer is liable on the claim) another ship owned by the owner of the ship in respect of which the claim arose.[6] If the charterer and not the owner is liable in respect of the claim,[7] the offending chartered ship or any other ship owned by the charterer may be arrested. An arrested ship may be released on the lodging of adequate security and a court which lacks merits jurisdiction may demand security from the defendant prior to releasing the ship for a merits action elsewhere.[8] Nothing in the Convention is to be construed as creating a right of action which apart from the Convention would not arise under the domestic law of the court having jurisdiction nor as creating any maritime lien not existing under such law or the Convention on Maritime Mortgages and Liens if applicable.[9]

Introduction of Arrest Convention directly into English law through the Brussels and Lugano Conventions?

The relationship of the Arrest Convention to the Brussels and Lugano Conventions has been discussed in Chapter 5 in relation to substantive jurisdiction and in Chapter 14 in respect of arrest by way of security. The Brussels and Lugano Conventions and the Arrest Convention distinguish between merits and provisional measure jurisdiction. It is clearly envisaged by all these Conventions that there may be jurisdiction to award a provisional measure in one jurisdiction but jurisdiction over the substantive matter in another.

Arrest as a jurisdiction base

The effect of the primacy given to the Arrest Convention by the other two Conventions is that in respect of cases within the ambit of either of the two European Conventions arrest of a ship becomes a ground of jurisdiction on the merits. It has been held by the Court of Appeal that in the Arrest Convention the defining of arrest as "to secure a

---

5. Article 7(1). For text of Convention, see Appendix 2.
6. Article 3(1).
7. Article 3(4)—the most controversial Article. For judicial comment, see e.g. *The Span Terza* [1982] 1 Lloyd's Rep. 225; *The Permina 108* [1978] 1 Lloyd's Rep. 311. Its scope and effect is much clearer in the draft revision, being linked to the enforcement of the claim by judgment against the ship (see Article 3(3)).
8. Article 5. Prior to the enactment of the Civil Jurisdiction and Judgments Act 1982 the United Kingdom was in breach of this provision—and it is arguable to some extent will remain in breach (see text *infra*).
9. Article 9—which simply underlines the uncertainty of the effect of an arrest not linked to an enforceable substantive right.

maritime claim" does not mean that where there is alternative security an arrest to establish jurisdiction is not within that Convention.[10]

Arrest as a provisional measure

Contrary to the creation of Convention jurisdiction bases of substantive jurisdiction the Brussels and Lugano Conventions refer jurisdiction over provisional matters to national law. It is therefore arguable whether this reference or the maintaining of other Conventions by Article 57 takes precedence within the Convention, an issue which becomes relevant if a state is party to a particular Convention but has not fully implemented it into national law. So it is with the United Kingdom and the Arrest Convention.

If the Arrest Convention is given positive effect as such by Article 57 it would be possible in cases within the Brussels Convention by virtue of Article 5 of the Arrest Convention to arrest a ship in England without having any intention of litigating there. It would also mean that a ship may be arrested in circumstances other than those specified in the Supreme Court Act 1981 and in particular the link between the defendant and the ship at the date of issue of the writ *in rem* becomes irrelevant. The sole requirement would be that at the time when the maritime claim arose the defendant was owner or charterer of the ship.

The separation of arrest as a provisional measure and jurisdiction on the merits causes little difficulty, for English law has moved to a position where at least this can be achieved. By English law as for a ship to be arrested requires a writ *in rem* to be issued substantive proceedings must be instituted even if only security is sought. But a plaintiff issuing a writ *in rem* may now do so simply to obtain security and by virtue of the Civil Jurisdiction and Judgments Act, s.26, proceedings may be stayed and the ship retained under arrest. Provided a plaintiff may obtain a stay the division of security and substance may be attained—although only through divorce of the initial union. So while initial separation has still not been attained the method of suit is not now being allowed to create an artificially mandatory link between security and merits jurisdiction. England is becoming a little more integrated with the maritime world.[11]

Further, as was held in *The Nordglimt*[12] the fact that both substance and provisional measure jurisdiction depends on the writ *in rem* does not mean that if used for security the "proceedings" are within the prohibition or multiple proceedings within the Brussels Convention—that depends on the purpose of the action.

Ships which may be arrested

The divergence between the Arrest Convention and the Supreme Court Act in respect of ships which may be arrested is a more fundamental matter to the scope of arrest in English law—although it has to be said that the difference largely disappears in the revised draft

---

10. *The Anna H* [1995] 1 Lloyd's Rep. 11. See further Chap. 10.
11. For further recognition of the distinction in holding that provisional measure jurisdiction does not mean merits jurisdiction, see *The Sargasso* [1994] 2 Lloyd's Rep. 6 and Chap. 14.
12. [1987] 2 Lloyd's Rep. 470.

where the link between the ship and defendant is required both at the date of the claim arising and at the arrest. Even if it be accepted that the Arrest Convention does not become part of English law by virtue of Article 57 of the Brussels and Lugano Conventions this still leaves the argument that the Article does give positive force to the Arrest Convention. It would seem difficult to argue that the requirement under the Supreme Court Act 1981 of the link at the date of issue of the writ is procedural only and therefore even under the Brussels Convention a matter for English law. It would seem to follow that substantive jurisdiction at least may be established through arrest according to the Arrest Convention.[13]

The sole difference between the application of the Arrest Convention through the Brussels and Lugano Conventions to create a substantive jurisdiction base and to provide interim relief would seem to lie in the effect of the latter Conventions on the national law. As regards substantive jurisdiction the effect is to override national law but as regards interim relief to refer to it. It may therefore be arguable that the purpose of the two Conventions is to refer issues of interim relief entirely to national law, and while such a provision does not "affect" any other Convention it does not impose it. This is in contrast to the role of Article 57 in maintaining the jurisdiction base of another Convention which otherwise would be removed. It would not be surprising if English courts, at any rate, took this view.

THE COLLISION (CIVIL JURISDICTION) CONVENTION 1952

This Convention is enacted into English law through s.22 of the Supreme Court Act 1981. It provides a severely restrictive jurisdiction framework for collision actions (see Chapter 6). Actions must be brought before the court of the habitual residence or place of business of the defendant, the place of collision where it has occurred in a port or inland waters or the place of arrest of any bail or security provided instead of arrest.

The Convention is concerned with arrest as a substantive jurisdiction base and contains no reference to provisional measures. The Convention and its relationship to the Brussels and Lugano Conventions are matters discussed in Chapter 6.

THE HAMBURG RULES 1978

The Hamburg Rules came into force on 1 November 1992. Article 21(1), (2) and (5) of the rules provides—

"1 In judicial proceedings relating to carriage of goods under this Convention the plaintiff, at his option, may institute an action in a court which, according to the law of the State where the court

---

13. In *The Po* [1991] 2 Lloyd's Rep. 206 the Court of Appeal was content to uphold substantive jurisdiction under the Collision Jurisdiction Convention 1952 (see *infra*) on the basis that the plaintiff had complied with the Convention and English law—but that leaves the question open as to whether compliance with the Convention is, apart from procedure, enough for jurisdiction in national law.

is situated, is competent and within the jurisdiction of which is situated one of the following places:

    (a) the principal place of business or, in the absence thereof, the habitual residence of the defendant; or

    (b) the place where the contract was made provided that the defendant has there a place of business, branch or agency through which the contract was made; or

    (c) the port of loading or the port of discharge; or

    (d) any additional place designated for that purpose in the contract of carriage by sea.

2(a) Notwithstanding the preceding provisions of this article, an action may be instituted in the courts of any port or place in a Contracting State at which the carrying vessel or any other vessel of the same ownership may have been arrested in accordance with applicable rules of the law of that State and of international law. However, in such a case, at the petition of the defendant, the claimant must remove the action, at his choice, to one of the jurisdictions referred to in paragraph 1 of this article for the determination of the claim, but before such removal the defendant must furnish security sufficient to ensure payment of any judgment that may subsequently be awarded to the claimant in the action.

(b) All questions relating to the sufficiency or otherwise of the security shall be determined by the court of the port or place of the arrest.

5 Notwithstanding the provisions of the preceding paragraphs an agreement made by the parties after a claim under the contract of carriage by sea has arisen which designates the place where the claimant may institute an action is effective."

When the Hamburg Rules apply, they will govern jurisdiction. Unless an English court views its jurisdiction as mandatory, an action brought in an English court on a claim governed by a law adopting the rules may therefore be stayed because that law dictates the jurisdiction.[14] Where the ship has been arrested the action should be stayed on the application of the defendant and not in accordance with rules generally applicable to stay.[15]

The rules do not apply to or affect provisional remedies.[16] Arrest as a ground of merits jurisdiction, it appears, was a compromise reached between those countries which in their domestic laws recognize it as founding jurisdiction, and those which reject it as a foundation, maintaining that the contract of arrest between a country and an issue is minimal.

The rules also provide for arbitration.[17] They specify permitted places which, apart from the place of arrest, mirror those where a claim may be brought. Under the rules arrest has no place as a foundation for arbitration proceedings.

Finally, it should be noted that the operation of Article 21 may be modified. If a contracting party is a party to another multilateral Convention relating to jurisdictional matters, that Convention may be applied provided that the dispute in question arises between parties having their principal place of business in States members of such other Convention.[18] As a result, the Arrest Convention and the Hamburg Rules are brought more into line with each other, but some conflict remains. The Arrest Convention may be

14. No contracting State to the Brussels Convention is a party to the Hamburg Rules, and only Austria of the States parties to the Lugano Convention is a party. As a member of the European Union Austria will eventually become a party to the Brussels Convention.

15. As to the approach to a jurisdiction clause in a case which under English law would be within the Hague-Visby Rules see Chap. 26.

16. Article 21(2).

17. Article 22.

18. Article 25(2).

excluded in respect of persons neither habitually resident nor having their principal place of business in a contracting State. The Hamburg Rules permit the application of the Arrest Convention rather than their jurisdictional provisions only where *both* parties have their principal place of business in contracting States to the Arrest Convention. Both the Hamburg Rules and Convention will therefore apply to persons habitually resident, but not having their principal place of business, in States contracting parties to both Conventions.

CONVENTION ON THE CONTRACT FOR THE INTERNATIONAL CARRIAGE OF GOODS BY ROAD 1956 (THE CMR)[19]

In passing, we should take account of the CMR Convention; for Article 2 applies it to carriage by modes other than road in the case of "piggy-back" transport. It provides:

"1 Where the vehicle containing the goods is carried over part of the journey by sea, rail, inland waterways or air, and, except where the provisions of article 14 are applicable, the goods are not unloaded from the vehicle, this Convention shall nevertheless apply to the whole of the carriage. Provided that to the extent that it is proved that any loss, damage or delay in delivery of the goods which occurs during the carriage by the other means of transport was not caused by an act or omission of the carrier by road, but by some event which could only have occurred in the course of and by reason of the carriage by that other means of transport, the liability of the carrier by road shall be determined not by this Convention but in the manner in which the liability of the carrier by the other means of transport would have been determined if a contract for the carriage of the goods alone had been made by the sender with the carriage by the other means of transport in accordance with the conditions prescribed by law for the carriage of goods by that means of transport. If, however, there are no such prescribed conditions, the liability of the carrier by road shall be determined by this Convention.

2 If the carrier by road is also himself by the other means of transport, his liability shall also be determined in accordance with the provisions of paragraph 1 of this article, but as if, in his capacities as carrier by road and as carrier by the other means of transport, he were two separate persons."

The Hamburg Rules provide for the application of the CMR.[20] But there may be a conflict between the jurisdictional rules of the CMR (which do not include arrest as a ground)[21] and the Arrest Convention. The only reference in the CMR to provisional remedies is to exclude interim judgments from the obligation of member States to recognize judgments given in actions brought in accordance with the Convention.[22]

---

19. Enacted into English law by the Carriage of Goods By Road Act 1965.

20. Article 25(2) and (5). The CMR focuses on liability of the road carrier and arrest would be available in English law only in the context of "maritime" claims.

21. See Article 3(1), which provides:

"1. In legal proceedings arising out of carriage under this Convention, the plaintiff may bring an action in any court or tribunal of a contracting country designated by agreement between the parties and, in addition, in the courts or tribunals of a country within whose territory

    (a) the defendant is ordinarily resident, or has his principal place of business, or the branch or agency through which the contract of carriage was made, or

    (b) the place where the goods were taken over by the carrier or the place designated for delivery is situated,

and in no other courts or tribunals."

22. See Article 31(3)(4).

CONVENTIONS RELATING TO LIMITATION OF LIABILITY 1924, 1957 AND 1976

All these Conventions include provisions for the release from arrest of a ship after the constitution of a limitation fund. The United Kingdom is a party to the 1976 Convention.[23]

Article 13(2) of the 1976 Convention is set out *infra* in the discussion on release from arrest. It provides for mandatory release from arrest. It provides for mandatory release of any property arrested or attached if a limitation fund is constituted in the country or port where the occurrence took place or the next port of call if on the high seas, the port of disembarkation or discharge of cargo or where an arrest was made. If the fund is in any other place release is discretionary.[24]

By Article 13(3) the release provisions apply only if the claimant may bring a claim against the fund in the court administering it and only if the fund is "actually available and freely transferable in respect of that claim". In those circumstances there is no justification for any security in addition to the fund. The matter is discussed in the context of limitation of liability in Chapter 24.

SUMMARY

The international scene, therefore, is that there is a general framework to which states can adhere governing the role of arrest as a jurisdiction ground for merits actions. But only the Arrest Convention and the Convention on Limitation of Liability are concerned with arrest as a provisional measure, and only the Arrest Convention with defining the property which may be arrested.

The Brussels and Lugano Conventions have increased the direct effect of the Arrest Convention in English law. Apart however from the enactment of the various Conventions (directly or indirectly) it is to national laws that we must turn. Where a Convention is enacted into national law care must be taken to assess whether it is so enacted only in respect of other State parties or whether it has simply become part of that law.[25]

The function of arrest as a means of security in the sense that its availability of itself may provide a preferred status is nowhere dealt with on an international level. The Conventions on the Unification of Certain Rules Relating to Maritime Liens and Mortgages 1926, 1967 and 1993 deal with liens (particularly maritime liens) and rights of retention. They refer to arrest only in the context of liens and assume that such a lien carries with it the right to arrest. But they do not deal with the right to arrest as such.

Conversely the Arrest Convention deals with the right to arrest but, apart from the declaration that nothing in the Convention creates a right of action, does not provide for the consequences of the arrest on the property rights of persons interested in the property arrested. If there is no effect then once the hearing on the merits takes place the property

23. By English law the person on whose application the release is granted is deemed to submit to the jurisdiction of the English court (Merchant Shipping Act 1979, Sch. IV, Part II, para. 10 since 1 January 1996 Merchant Shipping Act 1995, Sch 8, Part II, para. 10). See further Chap. 24.

24. As to its application see Chap. 24.

25. So the principles of the Arrest Convention are made part of English law generally but when applying *as the Convention* through the Brussels Convention will apply subject to any limitation in scope in the Convention (see e.g. *The Po* [1991] 2 Lloyd's Rep. 206).

should be released. The revised draft of the Arrest Convention meets this point by limiting the right to arrest to circumstances in which there is a lien or the claim can be enforced against the ship by judicial sale (as to which see Chapter 25).

THE ARREST FRAMEWORK IN ENGLISH LAW

ARREST AND THE ACTION "IN REM"

In English law arrest is a component part of the action *in rem*. Its necessary connection with the action *in rem* seems to have led to a failure to put national law into a form which complies fully with the international obligations undertaken through ratification of the Arrest Convention. Further, it creates difficulties in implementing the distinction between provisional measures and merits jurisdiction in the Brussels and Lugano Conventions.[26]

To allow ratification of the Arrest Convention, the Administration of Justice Act 1956 consolidated and amended the internal jurisdictional rules of the Admiralty Court. The list of Admiralty proceedings which appeared in that statute and now forms part of the Supreme Court Act 1981 largely coincides with those "maritime claims" of the Arrest Convention in relation to which a ship may be arrested. But the domestic framework created to reflect the international structure mentions arrest only in the application of the principle of one arrest, one claim and, in the context of Crown ships. It creates *jurisdictional rules* for actions *in rem* and actions *in personam* modelled on the arrest rules of the Convention. And, because arrest is available once an action *in rem* will lie, the provision for the enforcement of a claim by an action *in rem* makes it an arrestable claim.

Apart from confusing the function of provisional remedy and jurisdiction on the merits, making arrest dependent on merits jurisdiction created problems when an English court declined jurisdiction. Could the court then continue or allow an arrest? These problems focused on arbitration and choice of forum clauses and the operation of the doctrine of *forum non conveniens*. They were in part cured by judicial creativity and now in great part are overcome by the Civil Jurisdiction and Judgments Act 1982, s.26, and possibly the combined operation of the Brussels, Lugano and Arrest Conventions. The continuing separation of provisional remedy and merits jurisdiction required by the Convention has been discussed earlier in the chapter. The separation at least partly recognized by s.26 of the 1982 Act is discussed after a review of the English rules concerning arrest and their effects.

ARREST AS "SECURITY"

A ship once arrested will remain arrested until release or judicial sale—usually after an order for appraisement and sale.[27] Although on the "procedural" theory of the action *in rem* the arrest is simply a means by which a defendant can be persuaded to come to court, neither appearance nor acknowledgment of the issue or service of the writ will lead to the

---

26. But for increased recognition of the distinction in English law see *The Sargasso* [1994] 2 Lloyd's Rep. 6; *The Nordglimt* [1987] 2 Lloyd's Rep. 470.
27. As to which, see Chap. 25.

ship's release. Indeed, as has been seen, arrest is a remedy providing a security for the claimant in the action on the merits not available in an action *in personam* and this, of itself, denies the theory that the difference between action *in personam* and action *in rem* is procedural only. The "security" is however simply the availability of an asset for satisfaction of a judgment. Any enforceability against third parties stems not from the arrest but from the lien either enforced or created by the action *in rem* (see Part III).

Bankruptcy or company liquidation

Arrest is a mode of establishing security for a claim and its role in the context of a bankruptcy or liquidation clearly raises potential conflicts with the rules secured and unsecured claimants in that context. The permanent "security" aspect of maritime process in which arrest plays a part is discussed in connection with the "lien" which a claim enforceable by an action *in rem* attracts.[28] Arrest in English law, when used, is simply an early step ensuring physical retention of an asset in that process. In relation to arrest as such the only relevant issue is the extent to which an arrest may be void or stayed as an interference within the bankruptcy or liquidation framework.

Bankruptcy

So long as the claim is "secured" prior to the making of a bankruptcy order, an arrest made in pursuance of that claim after such an order will not be affected. Subject to the power of a court to stay "any action, execution or legal process" when bankruptcy proceedings are pending or after an individual is adjudged bankrupt, the benefits of any "execution" against a debtor's goods issued prior to and not completed before the commencement of the bankruptcy cannot be retained as against the trustee of the bankrupt's estate.[29] There is doubt whether arrest amounts to an "execution" in this sense.[30]

Liquidation of companies

A court controls proceedings against a company commenced after winding up.[31] An arrest after such time may be stayed or declared void but if it is pursuant to a claim which has become "secured" prior to that time it is unlikely to be affected.[32]

PROPERTY LIABLE TO ARREST

Subject to the statutory "sister ship" provision in the Supreme Court Act 1981, the only property liable to arrest is the ship, cargo or freight which is the focus of the action *in*

---

28. See Chaps. 17, 18.

29. See, for the legislative framework, the Insolvency Act 1986, ss.285, 346. As to the court's exercise of discretion under s.285, see *Re Evelyn* [1894] 2 Q.B. 302; *Ex parte Coker* (1875) L.R. 10 Ch. App. 652.

30. Contrast *The Zafiro* [1960] P. 1 with *The Constellation* [1965] 2 Lloyd's Rep. 538.

31. For the legislative framework, see the Insolvency Act 1986, ss.126, 128, 130 (as compulsory winding up), ss.112, 183 (as voluntary winding up).

32. As to the exercise of the court's discretion under ss.112, 125 and 183, see *The Zafiro* [1960] P. 1; *Re Aro Co. Ltd* [1980] Ch. 196 (construing the equivalent provisions of the Companies Act 1948). As to the equation of arrest and execution in this context, see fn 30 *supra*.

rem.[33] The effect of arresting cargo is to detain the ship until discharge of cargo, and discharge is permitted only by leave of the court.[34] Cargo may be arrested in support of a claim against freight, and, it has been held, no costs will be awarded even if no freight is due provided that it is released on statement that none is due.[35] The Supreme Court Act 1981 specifically provides in s.21(8) that in respect of any claim for which a sister ship may be arrested only one ship may be arrested for each claim. But it should be stressed first that where a claim is for moneys due, for example, monthly under a charterparty, each failure to pay may be the foundation for a claim.[36] Secondly, the prohibition must be read together with s.21(4) conferring the power to bring an action *in rem* in relation to sister ships. If a ship against which such an action cannot be brought is arrested that of itself does not prohibit arrest of a ship against which an action could be brought.[37]

WARRANT OF ARREST AND WRIT "IN REM"

A plaintiff may issue a warrant of arrest after a writ *in rem* is issued.[38] It was held by the Court of Appeal in 1993 in *The Varna*[39] that an amendment to the rules in 1986 had had the effect that provided the property was within the scope of the action *in rem*, and there had been procedural compliance[40] the issue is of right. So, in contrast to common belief and authority there could be no duty of "full and frank disclosure".

The warrant takes effect when it is stamped by an officer of the registry, the function of that action being to establish compliance with procedural requirements. The warrant may be served on the ship or property at any time whether or not the writ has been served. It is valid for 12 months[41] and must be executed (served) by the Admiralty Marshal or his substitute. It will not be executed until an understaking to pay all fees and expenses of the Marshal is lodged in the Marshal's office. Although, therefore, service of the writ is required to satisfy procedural requirements and outside the Brussels and Lugano Conventions such service creates jurisdiction, arrest through execution of the warrant may nevertheless arguably also create jurisdiction even outside the Conventions where there has been no service of a writ.

---

33. As to when cargo or freight may be the focus of an action and as to what is included in the ship, see Chap. 2. As to the limitation of maritime arrest in Scotland see *The Afala* [1995] 2 Lloyd's Rep. 286.

34. As to procedure for application to discharge, see *Supreme Court Practice 1995*, Vol. 2, para. 1322.

35. *The Flora* (1886) L.R. 1 A. & E. 45.

36. See *The Permina Samudra XIV* [1978] 1 Lloyd's Rep. 315.

37. *The Stephan J* [1985] 2 Lloyd's Rep. 344. Further if a writ is amended after service and arrest of one ship to delete a claim it does not offend the single ship rule for another ship to be arrested in respect of that claim. See *The Damavand* [1993] LMLN 357 (Singapore C.A.).

38. RSC Order 75, r. 5. As to similar powers of arrest in county courts, see County Courts Act 1984, ss.28(9) and (10).

39. [1993] 2 Lloyd's Rep. 253. Prior to the amendment the issue was discretionary (*The Vasso* [1984] 1 Lloyd's Rep. 235) and such a duty existed (*ibid.*). In 1992 Sheen J. followed *The Vasso* in *The Kherson* [1992] 2 Lloyd's Rep. 261, a decision disapproved in *The Varna*.

40. I.e. subject to leave being given without an affidavit, the filing of an affidavit stating the nature of the claim and appropriate jurisdictional particulars if the claim is by virtue of s.21(4), for possession or wages or an oil pollution claim or requires notice to a consul (RSC Order 75, r. 5(4)(9)). See text at fn. 89.

41. RSC Order 75, r. 10. It is said in a note to the rule in the Supreme Court Rules that provided the writ has been served or through renewal is valid for service a further warrant may be issued—but it would seem that any purpose of so doing must be limited.

As traditionally arrest was seen essentially as part of the action *in rem* it would surely be difficult to argue that there could be an arrest without that jurisdiction. That is, however, the position to which English law may now be moving through the separation of provisional measure and substantive jurisdiction.[42] It should be recalled that in the cases when an action *in rem* may be brought against a ship other than that involved in the claim there is no restriction on the number of writs *in rem* which may be issued, but only one ship may be served with a writ or arrested in regard to any one claim.[43] Further, a writ need not be served or filed in a registry if through acknowledgment of service of a writ *in rem* by a defendant or endorsement on the writ of acceptance of service by his solicitor it would, had it been a writ *in personam*, have been deemed duly served.[44]

Whether the ship is arrested is therefore a matter for the claimant. In 1994 it was held by the Court of Appeal in Singapore that a defendant cannot remove the option of the plaintiff who has issued a number of writs or named or number of ships in one writ as to which ship to arrest by appearance.[45] In the Singapore case the action had been commenced through service on the defendant's solicitor who had entered an appearance. The court held that the power to commence an action *in rem* through endorsement on the writ by the defendant's solicitor simply had the effect of dispensing with service on the property—under the rules it did not deem service to have been made on the property. Entry of appearance then had the effect of creating jurisdiction *in personam* but could not remove the plaintiff's statutory option of arresting the particular ship concerned in the claim or a sister ship. Such reasoning is a neat and practical way of resolving the anomaly of founding *in rem* jurisdiction on service of a writ on a person when the whole purpose of the action *in rem* is to focus on property.

However, if adopted in England, the consequence is that acknowledgment of service without challenge to jurisdiction of a writ served otherwise than on the property does not found *in rem* jurisdiction—that occurs only on arrest of one ship. It therefore moves the founding of jurisdiction from the service to the arrest, an act not hitherto one of jurisdiction unless within the Brussels Convention. As the alternative would be to allow a defendant by an act under a rule of court to remove the plaintiff's option under the statute it would seem that the approach of the Singapore court should be followed.[46]

A plaintiff may proceed in an action *in rem* without arrest or with the "security" of an arrested ship, with bail lodged or payment into court in lieu or with a guarantee—usually provided by a Protection and Indemnity Club or bank. Where there is a guarantee there is no more security for the claimant than his right to the guarantee, although no doubt it is the availability of the action *in rem* that brings forth the guarantee in the first place. And the ability to arrest will be affected by the acceptance of a guarantee or undertaking strictly only by any contract to which the claimant has become a party. However, an arrest after provision of guarantee would no doubt be declared an abuse of process.[47]

---

42. The plaintiff may request service of the writ by the Marshal where a warrant of arrest has been issued (Order 75, r. 8(3)(3A)).

43. Supreme Court Act 1981, s.21(8).

44. RSC Order 75, r. 8(2), Order 10, r. 1(4)(5).

45. *The Fierbinti* [1995] LMLN 396. See also *The Pacific Bear* [1979] H.K. Rep. 125.

46. In English law the acknowledgment of service of itself would not be submission either *in personam* or *in rem* (see Chap. 10). If the "*in rem*" jurisdiction is not founded until arrest the acknowledgment even if no challenge is mounted to jurisdiction could not possibly be submission to the action *in rem*.

47. As to those alternative modes of security, see *supra*.

STAGE IN PROCEEDINGS WHEN ARREST AVAILABLE

Arrest is "provisional" in the sense it is available immediately on issue of a writ *in rem*.[48] It has been held in English law that it is not available after judgment on liability and that it cannot be used as a method of execution of a judgment of an English court.[49] However, in 1984 in the Singapore High Court it was held that it made little sense for the security provided by arrest to be terminated by a judgment in favour of the claim. While the cause of action and judgment were merged that was no reason for the loss of the right to enforce the claim through security. This seems incontestable in logic and commonsense.

Further, in 1982 in *The Despina GK*[50] Sheen J. held that an action *in rem* was available to enforce a foreign judgment *in rem* in respect of a ship still owned by the creditor at the time of arrest. No distinction was drawn in principle between English and foreign judgments.[51] With the introduction of the principle that a foreign judgment normally creates an issue estoppel[52] and the increasing direct enforceability of foreign judgments through registration, the availability of arrest to execute one but not the other would, with respect, seem to require some explanation.

Thirdly, an action *in rem*—and therefore arrest—is available indirectly to enforce an arbitration award provided that a claim on the contract containing the arbitration clause or the original cause of action is enforceable *in rem*.[53] In such contexts, in contrast to the enforcement of a judgment *in rem* the "*in rem*" characteristic is brought into play for the first time after the judgment or award. This is indicative of the two-pronged attack which can be mounted through "*in personam*" and "*in rem*" proceedings; but it remains essentially an enforcement of an award. It seems to raise identical matters of principle as an enforcement of a judgment.

Whether or not available after judgment, it appears established that arrest may take place at any time up to judgment on liability *in rem*.[54] If a ship has been arrested and released there is no reason why it should not be rearrested. Where the release is consequent on the lodging of bail the general rule is not to permit rearrest for that claim unless it would not be vexatious and oppressive.[55] If the bail later appears insufficient it

---

48. It is therefore available once a claim exists and is not dependent on likely success (see e.g. *The Gina* [1980] 1 Lloyd's Rep. 398).

49. *The Alletta* [1974] 1 Lloyd's Rep. 40. The limitation may require prejudgment bail (see *infra* p. 344). Arrest can be used to enforce a judgment by default where an undertaking to provide bail has led to caveat against arrest, the undertaking has not been fulfilled within 14 days of the service of the writ and the sum claimed does not exceed the amount of the undertaking (RSC Order 75, r. 21(1) and (2)).

50. [1982] 2 Lloyd's Rep. 555. The jurisdictional basis for the action is however arguable (see Chap. 2).

51. Reference was made to *The Alletta* (*supra*, fn 49) in which the enforcement of foreign judgments was also distinguished by a statement that they were foreign.

52. Civil Jurisdiction and Judgments Act 1982, s.34 (which came into force on 24 August 1982); *The Indian Grace* [1993] 1 Lloyd's Rep. 387 and see Chap. 27.

53. *The Saint Anna* [1983] 1 Lloyd's Rep. 637; *The Stella Nova* [1981] Com. L.R. 200—but arbitration costs would probably not be recoverable. See *The Atlas Pride* [1994] LMLN 388 (Singapore H.C.). See further Chaps. 2, 25.

54. This has been construed as final judgment on appeal. See *The Freir, The Albert* (1875) 2 Asp. M.L.C. 589; *The Miriam* (1874) 2 Asp. M.L.C. 259 and it has been suggested that after judgment it could be rearrested in respect of costs (see *The Freedom* (1871) 1 Asp. M.L.C. 136).

55. See *The Arctic Star, The Times* 5 February 1985 (C.A.)—in which the rearrest was permitted when shipowner took proceedings to restrain the use of a guarantee available when the amount of bail was initially set.

seems that the ship can be rearrested and the bail increased, presumably up to the amount which could originally have been obtained through appraisement.[56]

RESTRICTIONS ON AVAILABILITY OF ARREST

Arrest is an inherent part of the action *in rem* and it is, therefore, generally bounded by the ability to bring such an action. Restrictions on the availability of an action *in rem* are discussed in Chapter 12. It is necessary here simply to refer first to restrictions specifically imposed on the power of arrest, secondly, to problems of retaining property under arrest or enforcing alternative security when an English court declines jurisdiction *in rem* and thirdly to the effect of foreign arrest.

(a) Restrictions specifically imposed

Caveat against arrest

A person (either a defendant or in a liability action a plaintiff in a limitation action where a limitation fund has been set up under the Convention on Limitation of Liability for Maritime Claims 1976), who desires to prevent the arrest of any property may file a praecipe in the registry. The praecipe must be signed by the person or his solicitor and contain an undertaking to acknowledge the issue or service of any writ in any action begun "against the property" described in the praecipe. Save where the person is a plaintiff in a limitation action who has constituted a limitation fund in accordance with the 1976 Convention, there must also be an undertaking within three days after receiving notice that such action has begun to give bail in a sum not exceeding the amount specified in the praecipe or pay the amount into court. The plaintiff in a limitation action must state that a limitation fund has been constituted. On the filing of the praecipe a caveat is entered in the caveat book.[57]

The caveat is valid for 12 months and successive caveats may be entered.[58] It does not prevent the issue of a warrant of arrest but an arrest without good reason may lead to damages.[59] It is the duty of the person seeking the warrant to search for any caveat and where the plaintiff or his solicitor becomes aware that there is a caveat the writ *in rem* must be served on the person who obtained it.[60] Failure to comply with an undertaking in the praecipe can lead to judgment by default and committal for contempt.[61]

The caveat against arrest was rarely used in recent times but it reappeared first because of the coming into operation of the Convention on the Limitation of Maritime Claims 1976 and the right in almost all cases of the person claiming limitation to prevent arrest of property once a limitation fund is constituted. An amendment to the rules in 1990 adapted the caveat procedure to the limitation action by the person claiming limitation.

Secondly, it was used in 1994 in *The Anna H*[62] by shipowners in a case within the Brussels Convention in an attempt to prevent cargo owners obtaining jurisdiction in an

---

56. See *The Hero* (1865) B. & L. 446 and other authorities cited in *The Alletta* [1974] 1 Lloyd's Rep. 40.

57. RSC Order 75, r. 6(1)(1A)). Rule 1A (dealing with limitation actions) was added in 1990 following suggestions by Sheen J. in *The Bowbelle* [1990] 1 Lloyd's Rep. 532 consequential on the coming into force of the 1976 Convention.

58. RSC Order 75, r. 15. The caveat may be withdrawn.

59. RSC Order 75, rr. 6(2), 7. As to "wrongful arrest" generally see *infra*.

60. RSC Order 75, rr. 5(3), 8(4).

61. RSC Order 75, r. 21(1)(2).

62. [1995] 1 Lloyd's Rep. 11.

English court by arrest. It is established that arrest under the Arrest Convention is a jurisdiction base under the Brussels Convention, but as the Arrest Convention is presently worded actual arrest is needed (see Chapter 5 and *supra*). The shipowners argued that arrest under the Arrest Convention had to be to obtain security, and that because of the entry of a caveat against arrest and the undertaking to give bail there was no valid arrest under the Convention. The Court of Appeal held that arrest under the Arrest Convention was not so restricted. Even though there was security provided arrest for the purpose of establishing jurisdiction was valid. So it may be that, apart from limitation actions, the caveat will again become rarely used.

Government ships and other property

Foreign governments

The restrictions on jurisdiction over foreign sovereigns and their property are discussed in Chapter 12. It follows from the essential linking of arrest with action *in rem* that where no such action will lie no property may be arrested. Further, it is specifically provided in the State Immunity Act 1978 that the property of a state not in use or intended for use for commercial purposes cannot be arrested in an action *in rem*.[63] It is worth noting that a state may consent to the use of such process but that, as in English law arrest can only lie as a part of an action *in rem*, submission to proceedings *in rem* is required. Conversely, a provision for submission to the jurisdiction alone is not a sufficient basis for arrest to be allowed when consent is needed.[64]

Crown ships and other property

No action *in rem* lies against the Crown. Save for action in accordance with the Salvage Convention 1989, the Crown Proceedings Act 1947[65] and the Supreme Court Act 1981[66] specifically provide that nothing in those acts authorizes the arrest of any of Her Majesty's ships or any property belonging to the Crown.

Foreign ships or other property

As is said in Chapter 2 there is no limitation on Admiralty jurisdiction based simply on the foreign character of ships or other property. It follows from the connection between arrest and action *in rem* that any ship against which an action *in rem* has been instituted may be arrested. A warrant of arrest in an action *in rem* against a foreign ship "belonging to a port of a State having a consulate in London" which is an action for possession of the ship or for wages will not issue until leave of the court is obtained or notice of the action sent to the consul.[67] More generally, where by any Convention or treaty the United Kingdom has undertaken to minimize the possibility of arrest of ships of another state, no application may be made for the arrest of a ship owned by that state until notice has been sent to the appropriate consular officer. The United Kingdom and the Soviet Union entered

---

63. State Immunity Act 1978, s.13(2) and (4). See fn 68 for further restrictions on the power to arrest ships owned by the Governments of the Russian Federation.
   64. *Ibid*, s.13(3).
   65. Section 29(1) as qualified by the Merchant Shipping (Salvage and Pollution) Act 1994, Sch. 2 para 3. See for discussion Chap. 12.
   66. Section 24(2). See for discussion Chap. 12.
   67. RSC Order 75, r. 5(5).

into such an undertaking as respects such ships and cargo on board them.[68] There is no statutory reference to cargo in the rules of court but (save as regards (since 24 December 1991) the Russian Federation) there seems to be no hint of any restriction or the ability to arrest cargo owned by non-British subjects or on board foreign ships simply because of that foreign contact.

Abuse of process

A court may refuse to sustain an arrest if the arrester has abused the process of the court. Undue delay in prosecuting an action could amount to such abuse. Until an amendment to the rules of court in 1986 the issue of a warrant of arrest was discretionary. To fail to disclose the background was to fail to make "full and frank disclosure". This could lead to a refusal to sustain the arrest. A particular aspect of abuse of process was linked to the limitation on the availability for arrest to support arbitration. Arrest was not a provisional measure specified in the Arbitration Act 1950[69] as one which could be ordered by a court in arbitration proceedings. Although judicial ingenuity meant that property could be retained under arrest after a stay of proceedings the existence of arbitration proceedings was a relevant factor (see *infra*). Not to disclose that such proceedings were in being remained an abuse of process.[70]

Legislative provision in 1984 to retain property under arrest on the stay of proceedings in a foreign forum (see *infra*) removed much of, if not all, the foundation for seeing non-disclosure as an abuse of process. The 1986 amendment to the rules of court removed the general discretion as to issue of the warrant and hence *any* foundation for a requirement of full and frank disclosure[71] (see *supra*).

(b) Consequences of lack of jurisdiction on merits

As a warrant of arrest can be issued only after the issue of a writ *in rem*, the primary basis of the power to arrest is the establishment of jurisdiction on the merits in an action *in rem*.

Assertion of jurisdiction "in rem"

The issue of the writ

A writ *in rem* will be issued by an official of the Admiralty registry on presentation of the necessary supporting documents. As, once the writ is issued, a party may issue a warrant of arrest on compliance with procedural requirements, judicial control over arrest is

---

68. See Protocol to Treaty on Merchant Navigation 1977, the relevant provisions of which were brought into force in English law by the State Immunity (Merchant Shipping) (USSR) Order 1978 (SI 1978 No. 1524). The provisions of the order take precedence over the State Immunity Act 1978, s.13(4) whereby arrest will lie in respect of commercial activities. The order may apply to the member States of the Russian Federation. On 24 December 1991 those states took over responsibility for multilateral treaties under the auspices of the United Nations but see *Coreck* v. *Sevrybokholodflot* 1994 SLT 893.

69. As it was not an order of the court but a consequence of an issue by the plaintiff. See Arbitration Act 1950, s.12(f); *The Rena K* [1978] 1 Lloyd's Rep. 545; [1979] 1 All E.R. 397; *The Tuyuti* [1984] 2 Lloyd's Rep. 51.

70. See *The Vasso* [1984] 1 Lloyd's Rep. 235; [1984] 1 All E.R. 1126.

71. *The Varna* [1993] 2 Lloyd's Rep. 253.

effectively exercised on the challenge to the writ. Such a challenge may be mounted as an emergency measure, but a court may be reluctant to consider the complexities of Admiralty jurisdiction in that context.[72] In consequence, the threat of arrest is a powerful (and initially minimally controlled) weapon which may bring forth at the least a guarantee, the legal need to give which is debatable.

Ground of challenge to issue of a writ

The jurisdictional framework for actions *in rem* was examined in Chapter 10 and restrictions on jurisdictions were established in Chapter 12. The setting aside of a writ removes the basis for the arrest in the first place[73] and any power to retain property under arrest must be founded specifically on that power despite the lack of an existing writ *in rem*. Such power could go either to retention under arrest or the provision of alternative security.

Staying or dismissal of proceedings

The staying or dismissal of proceedings without dealing with the merits does not, as it were, invalidate the issue of the writ but it does (at least temporarily) terminate the jurisdiction of the court to deal with the dispute. The proceedings initiated by the issue of the writ have ended. Without statutory amendment, power to retain property arrested on the basis of the writ had to be sought in a power attached to the stay or dismissal (retention under arrest or provision of alternative security), a power not to release property arrested, or in minimizing the effect of the stay.

Problem areas—arbitration and foreign jurisdiction

Problems arising from the necessary connection between arrest and issue of the writ *in rem* arose principally in relation to the staying of proceedings by reason of arbitration agreements, foreign forum agreements,[74] or the application of *forum non conveniens*.

Of these the most difficult in terms of retention under arrest of property arrested prior to stay was the arbitration agreement. In respect of litigation in a foreign forum the stay of the English proceedings was discretionary and could be made conditional on continued provision of security. This was more doubtful in the case of arbitration where the stay was mandatory and there was no statutory power of arrest for arbitration. Judicial ingenuity found a method of so doing first through attaching the condition to the release of the property rather than the stay of proceedings[75] and secondly and more radically by

72. See e.g. *The Span Terza* [1982] 1 Lloyd's Rep. 225.

73. See e.g. the comments in *The Varna* [1993] 2 Lloyd's Rep. 253 as to the decision in *The Kherson* [1992] 2 Lloyd's Rep. 261, but the writ or the arrrest warrant may arguably not be set aside if the sole purpose is security for foreign proceedings—the English proceedings may be stayed (see *infra*).

74. As to the question of the scope of such clauses and in particular that of their reference to "security proceedings" such as arrest, see *infra* and Chap. 12.

75. See *The Rena K* [1979] Q.B. 377; [1978] 1 Lloyd's Rep. 545 (a decision commercially desirable as with respect legally doubtful—it is difficult to see any basis for discretionary imports of a condition or release when there is no authority to retain the property in the first place (i.e. the continued validity of the writ)—in effect the decision held the action *in rem* was suspended as the plaintiff may have to return to court if the award was not met).

restricting the effect of the stay to the substantive proceedings.[76] So, it was held, the mandatory stay did not remove the power to retain the property under arrest for the court's jurisdiction was not necessarily ended. However, retention required establishing that the defendant was unlikely to meet any award made for it was in that context a court was likely to come back into the picture.[77] There was therefore for the plaintiff a hurdle not present in respect of arrest as a part of the action *in rem*. There was (and is) then no requirement to show a likely defection in meeting a judgment. Many but not all the difficulties and the differences were removed on the coming into force in 1984 of s.26 of the Civil Jurisdiction and Judgments Act 1982.

The Civil Jurisdiction and Judgments Act 1982, s.26

The provision reads:

26—(1) Where in England and Wales or Northern Ireland a court stays or dismisses Admiralty proceedings on the ground that the dispute in question should be submitted to arbitration or to the determination of the courts of another part of the United Kingdom or of an overseas country, the court may, if in those proceedings property has been arrested or bail or other security has been given to prevent or obtain release from arrest—

    (a) order that the property arrested be retained as security for the satisfaction of any award or judgment which—

        (i) is given in respect of the dispute in the arbitration or legal proceedings in favour of which those proceedings are stayed or dismissed; and

        (ii) is enforceable in England and Wales or, as the case may be, in Northern Ireland; or

    (b) order that the stay or dismissal of those proceedings be conditional on the provision of equivalent security for the satisfaction of any such award or judgment.

(2) Where a court makes an order under subsection (1), it may attach such conditions to the order as it thinks fit, in particular conditions with respect to the institution or prosecution of the relevant arbitration or legal proceedings.

(3) Subject to any provision made by rules of court and to any necessary modifications, the same law and practice shall apply in relation to property retained in pursuance of an order made by a court under subsection (1) as would apply if it were held for the purposes of proceedings in that court."[78]

In part this provision met criticism that the linking of arrest to proceedings on the merits in England was contrary to the Arrest Convention. Power is conferred to retain or order alternative security on dismissal or stay or proceedings because of submission to arbitration or a non-English court. However, it is to be stressed that the power is dependent on (i) the issue of a writ *in rem* in order to bring "Admiralty proceedings"; (ii) the arrest of property or giving of bail or other security. As a consequence, a party to an arbitration or foreign forum agreement must act contrary to that agreement through the issue of a writ *in rem* in an English court *and* in all cases property must have been arrested or bail or other security been given.

---

76. *The Tuyuti* [1984] 2 Lloyd's Rep. 51—the Court of Appeal accepting the rationale of *The Rena K* as to the possibility of a return to court but retaining the foundation for arrest through limiting the effect of the stay.

77. *Ibid.*

78. In force in respect of security given after 1 November 1984 (SI 1984/1553). As to Scotland, see s.27 as amended by the Civil Jurisdiction and Judgments Act 1991, Sch. 2, para. 12.

The provision removes the need to justify retention in terms of conditional release or the limits of the stay. However, it does not confer a power directly to arrest or obtain security for arbitral or foreign proceedings,[79] or to order the provision of security if none has been given in the Admiralty proceedings prior to the stay or dismissal.[80]

The statutory power does remove the distinction between maintaining property under arrest and initially arresting it, which was seen as necessary when the power to maintain arrest was linked to the judicial stay of proceedings. That distinction applied particularly (and perhaps only) to arbitration proceedings and the lack of availability of arrest as such for those proceedings. As property could not be arrested in support of arbitration, on stay of court proceedings continuing arrest had to be justified by the risk of the award not being met and the need to return to the court.

In 1992 in *"The Bazias 3 and 4"* (vessels used as Channel ferries) the Court of Appeal rejected an argument that the statutory discretion under s.26 should be exercised to release property in any way other than applicable generally. So there would be no release unless an adequate alternative security was given—inconvenience to passengers of the shipping line and difficulty in raising the security were not sufficient reason for departing from established practice.[81] So the hurdle for the plaintiff seeking to continue arrest when proceedings are stayed of establishing that any award may not be met has been removed because of the express statutory power.

There remains room for the principles developed prior to the statutory power where there has been no arrest or security given. In *The Tuyuti* it was sought to set aside the warrant prior to service. Because of the restricted wording s.26 could not then apply, and a like case arising after the provision came into operation would necessarily attract identical principles.

THE SCOPE OF S.26

The provision is plainly directed at actions which are to be heard. If there is jurisdiction *in rem* to enforce a foreign judgment, it may be difficult to see that as falling within the basis of retention—the staying of proceedings on the ground that the dispute "should be submitted" elsewhere. On the other hand it may be said that the enforcement of the judgment has become the dispute—and if that is to be decided in the foreign court there is room for s.26 to operate.[82]

79. Compare (i) the power to grant interim relief apart from arrest conferred by the Civil Jurisdiction and Judgments Act 1982, ss.24 and 25 (see Chap. 8); (ii) the United States view in relation to arbitration (see Federal Arbitration Act 9 USC 14, 201–08, s.8); (iii) the South African Admiralty Jurisdiction Regulation Act 1983, s.5(3).

80. So a case such as *The Maritime Trader* [1981] 2 Lloyd's Rep. 153, in which a writ *in rem* had been issued but no arrest made or security given, would not be within the provision. But *The Tuyuti* principle will continue to apply. See *infra*.

81. [1993] 1 Lloyd's Rep. 101. See also *The World Star* [1986] 2 Lloyd's Rep. 274; *The Emre II* [1989] 2 Lloyd's Rep. 182, in which case Sheen J. also made an order for sale *pendente lite* because the arrest costs were consuming the security unless there was an undertaking by the defendant to pay the costs. As to arresters' costs see *infra*.

82. In *The Sylt* [1991] 1 Lloyd's Rep. 240 an attempt to use the provision to enforce a judgment of a court in Sierra Leone failed, first on the ground that proceedings should have been brought in Germany but also that the proceedings now sought to be stayed were barred as the matter had been litigated in Sierra Leone. But it is arguable that the proceedings were to enforce a judgment—and if so the question remains whether s.26 has any part to play. As to the enforcement of foreign judgments see Chaps. 27, 28.

A PLAINTIFF'S RIGHT TO STAY

For property to be arrested to support arbitration the plaintiff must issue a writ *in rem*, thereby breaching the arbitration agreement. The plaintiff having issued the writ it would be expected that it would be the defendant who seeks to stay for arbitration. However, as now seems accepted, the arbitration agreement is not normally to be construed as excluding the power to arrest, and the issue of a writ is proper despite the sole purpose being to obtain security. On that basis there should be no bar once security is obtained to the plaintiff seeking a stay of the action. If it is not so, the statutory provision leaves a plaintiff with the option of agreed arbitration without security or litigation with security, the arbitration agreement operating only at the option of the defendant.[83]

CROSS UNDERTAKING FOR DAMAGES

By virtue of s.26(2) a court may, contrary to established practice, impose a cross undertaking in damages in case the claim should fail. In the *Bazias* case the Court of Appeal refused so to do—the case was not one in which such far reaching change could be introduced. However, some two months later Saville J. felt no such hesitation at least until evidence of the applicable foreign law was adduced—ordering a vessel retained but security lodged to cover immediate losses likely to be sustained. It would seem that tradition in this regard should not be allowed to continue a somewhat one sided practice—particularly in the light of the opposite and regular imposition of a cross undertaking on a person obtaining a *Mareva* injunction.

(c) Foreign arrest

As indicated in Chapter 12 an English court may restrain a party with sufficient connection with England from participating in foreign proceedings if such participation is "vexatious and oppressive". Such power extends to arrest. In *The Lisboa*[84] the Court of Appeal refused to restrain cargo owners from arrest proceedings in Italy despite a London jurisdiction clause in the bill of lading, and emphasized that the only purpose of the arrest was to provide security for the English proceedings. Given the acceptance in English law of the principle of arrest in one state in respect of proceedings in another, an English court is unlikely to restrain a party from foreign arrest proceedings taken solely in respect of English proceedings.[85] It follows that restraint of foreign arrest for foreign proceedings would be highly unlikely.

---

83. A plaintiff may apply to stay his action in this country having also brought an action overseas (*AG* v. *Anderson, The Independent* 31 March 1988) but in *The Sylt* [1991] 1 Lloyd's Rep. 240, Sheen J. plainly disapproved of a plaintiff seeking a stay on the grounds that he ought to have brought the action elsewhere and also seeking security under s.26. Neither view touches on the point that the writ is simply linked to the obtaining of security, as to which see *The Jalamatoya* [1987] 2 Lloyd's Rep. 164 and Chap. 12.

84. [1980] 2 Lloyd's Rep. 546.

85. In 1976 in *Marazura Navegacion SA* v. *Oceanus Mutual Underwriting Assoc. (Bermuda) Ltd.* [1977] 1 Lloyd's Rep. 283 the court refused to restrain a party from arresting abroad for a London arbitration even though at that time it was throught that such arrest was not permissible under English law. A party would not normally be restrained from arrest solely for security for an English arbitration but would be from proceedings extending to the substantive issues for arbitration: *Petromin SA* v. *Secnav Marine Ltd.* [1995] 1 Lloyd's Rep. 603.

Arrest in England following a foreign arrest

The Arrest Convention prohibits more than one arrest or bail or other security in respect of the same maritime claim by the same claimant in any one or more of the contracting States.[86] So far as arrest in England is concerned, the provision is reflected in the Supreme Court Act 1981, s.21(8), and English judicial doctrine has developed in respect of the same claim, holding that without a reason affecting the value of security "double" arrests are not sustainable.[87]

ARREST PROCEDURE

The warrant of arrest[88]

An application for the issue of a warrant of arrest must be supported by an affidavit. Unless otherwise permitted by the court it must contain particulars of the applicant, the nature of the claim and the property to be arrested. If the action is against a ship under s.21(4) of the Supreme Court Act 1981 (i.e. requiring liability *in personam* of specified persons connected with the ship) the affidavit must state the name of the person *in personam*, and the relevant connections with the ship in connection with which the claim arose and against which the action is brought. It must state clearly whether or not the claim is on a "sister ship" basis. If the action is for possession of a ship or for wages, the nationality of the ship must be stated and if the action is one in relation to which notice to a consul may be required it must be stated that the notice has been sent and a copy of such notice must be attached.[89] If the claim is in respect of a liability for oil pollution under the Merchant Shipping (Oil Pollution) Act 1971 (now the Merchant Shipping Act 1995, Part VI) the facts relied on for establishing jurisdiction must be stated.[90]

   The applicant must take the required document to the registry and obtain a search in the caveat book for any caveat against arrest. On being satisfied that the affidavit complies with the procedural requirements and that the beneficial interest in the property has not since the issue of the writ changed as a result of judicial sale the party seeking the warrant is entitled to its issue.[91] The warrant is valid for 12 months and must be served (executed) on the ship or cargo against which it was issued by the Admiralty Marshal or his substitute. Where freight is to be arrested it may be served on the cargo in respect of which the freight is payable or the ship in which the cargo was carried or both.[92] A prerequisite

---

86. Article 3(3). See also Art. 7(2).
87. See *The Marinero* [1955] P. 68; *The Golaa* [1926] P. 103; *The Christiansborg* (1885) 10 P.D. 141. But compare *The Arctic Star* (fn. 55). As to the requirement to release from arrest on the establishment of a limitation fund see *infra* "Release from arrest".
88. See generally the notes to RSC Order 75, r. 5 in *Supreme Court Practice 1995*.
89. RSC Order 75, r. 5. *The Lloyd Pacifico* [1995] 1 Lloyd's Rep. 54. As to the necessity of notice to consuls, see *supra*. It is to be noted that where relevant it is the "beneficial" ownership of all the shares in the ship which must be stated.
90. As to such jurisdiction and liability see Chap. 2.
91. RSC Order 75, r. 5(2)(6). *The Varna* [1993] 2 Lloyd's Rep. 253.
92. Save for landed or transhipped cargo service of the warrant is, as for service of the writ *in rem*, by affixing the warrant for a short time on the superstructure of the relevant ship and leaving a copy. In the case of landed or transhipped cargo the warrant is to be left on the cargo or if access is not permitted the person having custody (rule 11(1)(2)).

for service is an undertaking to pay on demand all fees and expenses incurred by the Marshal in respect of the arrest and consequent care and custody.

The arrest procedure was helpfully summarized by Sheen J. in 1992 in *The Johnny Two*[93]:

"Upon issue of the warrant the Admiralty Marshal telephones the relevant officer of HM Customs and Excise and instructs him to arrest the ship. He tells the Customs Officer his requirements for ensuring the security of the arrest. That is followed up by sending a 'Note of Action' by fax confirming his instructions to arrest the ship and giving the folio number of the action, the name of the plaintiff and the name of the plaintiff's solicitors. An officer of HM then arrests the ship by attaching the Note of Action to the ship. He then carries out the Marshal's instructions for keeping the ship safely under arrest. This can be carried out within a very short space of time.

The warrant of arrest and the writ are then sent by post of HM Customs for execution and service respectively. But frequently, of course, security will have been provided and service of the writ accepted by solicitors so that the ship will have been released before these documents are received by HM Customs.

If a ship is expected to arrive at a known port a warrant of arrest should be issued. A 'Note of Action' instructing a Customs Officer to 'Arrest on arrival' will then be sent to the relevant Customs Office. The ship will then be arrested on arrival by the 'Note of Action' or by execution of the warrant if it has arrived at the Customs Office. In this way a ship may be arrested on a day when the Court Offices are closed.

Arrests in London are effected by the personal attendance of the Marshall's Officer who executes the warrant.

If a caveat against arrest is entered after a warrant is issued but before the arrest is effected, the plaintiff's solicitors will be informed. They will be asked if they still wish to arrest.

If a warrant of arrest is issued in respect of a ship when the port of arrival is not known, the warrant can be left with the Marshal with instructions, endorsed on the undertaking to pay his expenses, to arrest 'at a port to be advised during normal working hours'."

The court may have jurisdiction to order the Marshal to bring arrest to an end. When it was thought that there was discretion in the court whether or not to arrest, it was held there was a power to release where the action to which the arrest related was not being prosecuted at reasonable speed.[94] If however a court has no discretion but to issue a warrant on procedural compliance the only justification for termination is abuse of process—and undue delay may well amount to that.

During the period of arrest application may be made to the court for directions with respect to the property under arrest.[95] A ship under arrest may be sold but it remains under arrest. There can be no private sale if there is an order for sale.[96]

Admiralty Marshal's fees and expenses

Undertaking to pay

Subject to the acceptance by the Marshal of a deposit in lieu, an undertaking to pay on demand the Marshal's fees and all expenses incurred in the arrest[97] and care and custody

---

93. [1992] 2 Lloyd's Rep. 257.

94. See *The Italy II* [1987] 2 Lloyd's Rep. 162.

95. RSC Order 75, r. 12 (for example that a ship be moved). An applicant other than the Admiralty Marshal must give notice of the application to the Marshal (rule 12(3)). As to the release from arrest see *infra*.

96. See *The APJ Shalin* [1991] 2 Lloyd's Rep. 62. As to release from arrest see *infra*.

97. The expense of the necessary moving of a ship may be considered as the Marshal's expenses (*The Mardina Merchant* [1974] 3 All E.R. 749). As to expenses in relation to the discharge of cargo, see *infra*.

while under arrest are prerequisites of the execution of a warrant of arrest, service of a writ *in rem* if the plaintiff wishes the Marshal to serve it, and release from arrest.[98]

Where there is more than one arrest

In 1980 in *The Falcon*[99] The cargo owners had caused the ship to be arrested even though she was already under arrest. The ship was sold and all resulting funds applied to satisfying claims of mortgagees ranking prior to the cargo owners who then objected to being charged with a half share of the Marshal's fees and expenses. The Marshal had followed his usual practice of charging arresting parties equally. In considering the question of liability for the Admiralty Marshal's fees and expenses generally, Sheen J. set out the practice as it should be and the reason for it:

"The facts of this case demonstrate beyond doubt that justice will not necessarily be done by dividing equally between various plaintiffs the expense of maintaining the arrest of a ship. It is equally clear to me that justice may not be done by dividing those expenses in proportion to the size of the claims, even if that could be done. I can see no injustice in requiring a plaintiff who has arrested a ship to pay all the expenses of the arrest and maintenance of the arrest until the time as that plaintiff releases his arrest. If a second plaintiff arrests the ship, the expenses which the first plaintiff undertook to pay are not thereby increased. Furthermore, if a second arrest is effected, the first arrester can release his arrest and enter a caveat against release. If he takes that step then all the expenses of maintaining the arrest thereafter will fall on the second arrester.

If the first arrester maintains his arrest but a second arrester obtains an order for appraisement and sale, the Marshal will charge all expenses of custody and sale of the ship to the second arrester from the date when he lodges the commission for appraisement and sale.

In my judgment, the Marshal should adopt this practice so that each litigant will know the extent of his obligations."[100]

It should be noted that the above ruling was made in the context of a defensible arrest. If the caveat procedure[101] would suffice, a second arrester may be penalized in some way, although Sheen J.'s reasoning would apply equally to this type of case.

Arrester's expenses

An arrester is entitled to be paid the expenses of arrest and of any fund created by sale of the property arrested in priority to the payment of any claim. This includes, for example, sums paid to the Admiralty Marshal in respect of the arrest, and costs paid to repatriate the crew.[102] Sums due from the fund may be paid out prior to the arrester obtaining judgment on the claim and, indeed, even though the claim is not pursued because it becomes apparent that other claims will consume the fund.

It is not necessary for a first arrester to show that the arrest benefits the successful claimant or a second arrester. As a solicitor owes a duty to a client to arrest it is not to be

---

98. RSC Order 75, rr. 8(3), 10(3), 13(7) and 23A(2). An appeal lies to the court from any discretion or determination as to the disposal, form of undertaking or direction as to payment of expenses or release (rules 13(8) and 23A(3)).

99. [1981] 1 Lloyd's Rep. 13.

100. *Ibid*, at p. 17.

101. As to which, see *infra*.

102. See e.g. *The World Star* [1987] 1 Lloyd's Rep. 452. For a discussion of repairs for which sums may justifiably be claimed as expenditure by the Marshal see *The Ocean Blessing* [1994] LMLN 386 (Singapore High Court).

expected that this will be delayed pending enquiry into possible other claims—the claimant may decide not to pursue those claims.[103]

In *The Falcon* Sheen J. held that recovery of expense should not depend on which plaintiff obtained the order for appraisement and sale. He continued:

"I can see no justification for the view that recovery of the expenses of maintaining the arrest of a ship depends upon which plaintiff has obtained the order for appraisement and sale. In my judgment, the proceeds of sale of a ship which has been sold by order of the Court should be used first to pay the Admiralty Marshal's charges and expenses; secondly, to reimburse the plaintiff or plaintiffs who has or have incurred expense in preserving the property by arresting the ship and maintaining that arrest. Those expenses will of course include the necessary costs of that plaintiff up to the moment of that arrest. If there is only one action the plaintiff in that action must obtain judgment before he can recover the expense of arrest. If there is more that one action and if the ship is appraised and sold by an order made in a second or subsequent action, the plaintiff in the first action should make application to the Court for reimbursement of the expenses of preserving the property. The Court will so order unless he has acted in bad faith."[104]

Rights and liabilities in respect of property under or affected by arrest

Property under arrest is in the custody of the Admiralty Marshal[105] and any interference by any person[106] with that custody will be in contempt of court.[107] Such interference may vary from moving the ship (whether out of the jurisdiction or not) to removal of a warrant of arrest: intention to interfere is irrelevant but its presence or absence will be reflected in the penalty.[108] However, the prohibition extends only to active control. Rights in the ship may be created during arrest. So a ship under arrest may be sold or mortgaged, it may be arrested again and a harbour authority may exercise a statutory right of detention that does not interfere with the custody of the Marshal.[109]

The Marshal may allow activities concerning the property (e.g. movement of a ship) which will not affect the security and may apply to the court for directions.[110] Such directions may include the disposal of property not under arrest on board a ship under arrest where the ship is being affected by that property. The Marshal does not insure property under arrest and it is the responsibility of those who have interests in it to insure those interests.[111]

103. *The Rubi Sea* [1992] 1 Lloyd's Rep. 634.
104. [1981] 1 Lloyd's Rep. 13, at p. 17.
105. The Marshal has custody but not possession—all possessory rights which previously existed continue. See *The Arantzaru Mendi* [1939] A.C. 256.
106. In *The Jarlinn* [1965] 2 Lloyd's Rep. 191, Hewson J. reminded all concerned that not only ship masters but pilots and dock masters had been brought before the court for contempt. An advertisement that a ship sold by judicial sale may remain subject to encumbrances may be contempt (*The Cerro Colorado* [1993] 1 Lloyd's Rep. 58).
107. The procedure is through motion by the Admiralty Marshal for a writ of attachment to issue against the person committing the contempt or order that that person be committed to prison, and order for costs and such other orders as may be made. The court may levy a fine or simply order payment of costs.
108. See e.g. *The Jarvis Brake* [1976] 2 Lloyd's Rep. 320—attempt by owner to sell the ship after order for appraisement and sale and temporary removal of arrest document—no fine, order for costs: *The Synova* [1976] 1 Lloyd's Rep. 40—removal of arrest document by master—fine £100.
109. *The Queen of the South* [1968] P. 449. A vessel cannot remain in the custody of the Marshal and be allowed to trade out of the jurisdiction—an order to that effect is contradictory: *The Bazias 3 and The Bazias 4* [1993] 1 Lloyd's Rep. 101.
110. RSC Order 75, r. 12. This will normally include any move which may be made under the Marshal's orders or by direction of the court (see *The Mardina Merchant* [1974] 3 All E.R. 749).
111. See the practice approved in 1970 (note 75/10/3 of *Supreme Court Practice 1995*). The cost of the premium has been accepted as part of an arrester's costs (see *The Fairport* [1965] 2 Lloyd's Rep. 183, 185).

Third parties

Arrest may clearly affect the right of persons not concerned in the claim in relation to which the arrest is made. As has been said, subject to the obligation not to interfere with the Marshal's custody, interests in the ship may be created after us before the arrest.

Rights existing at or before arrest

First, the claim which is the basis of the arrest may be such that it runs against a ship even though the owner is not liable *in personam*. Secondly, a chartered ship or a ship carrying cargo may be arrested where the charterers or cargo owners have no connection with the claim. So there may be third parties with claims against the ship which claims confer interests in the ship (such as mortgagees or even charterers for breach of the charterparty).[112] Save for a plea of lack of jurisdiction there is no way in which any such interested parties can prevent an arrest.[113] Their remedies are, first, dependent on any right against any other person because of the arrest (e.g. under a charterparty where a chartered ship is removed from availability), secondly, the ability to issue a writ *in rem* on their own account and either cause a warrant of arrest to be issued or lodge a caveat against release, or, thirdly, the ability to intervene in the action which is the root of the original arrest.

Each course of action has different consequences—the issue of a writ and a second arrest could lead to unnecessary costs, the reliance on a caveat may lead to a failure to obtain the security dependent on the issue of the writ and intervention may result in a limited role in the proceedings.

Intervention in proceedings

In any proceedings brought against an owner or guarantor in respect of liability for oil pollution under the Merchant Shipping Act 1995 Part VI (re-enacting the Merchant Shipping (Oil Pollution) Act 1971) the court must grant to the International Oil Pollution Compensation Fund leave to intervene on application made *ex parte* by the Fund.[114] In any action *in rem* any person who has an "interest" in the property under arrest or proceeds of sale of such property which are in court may apply to the court for leave to intervene.[115] This is the appropriate procedure for the participation in proceedings by a purchaser of a ship after the issue of a writ. Such a person is under no liability to satisfy a claim apart from that stemming from an interest in the ship and it is therefore inappropriate to include that person in the writ.[116]

---

112. The failure to secure release of a ship under arrest may create a "lien" contrary to a contractual term prohibiting its creation. See *The Vestland* [1980] 2 Lloyd's Rep. 171 and *infra*. See also in relation to a sale guarantee *The Barenbels* [1984] 2 Lloyd's Rep. 388.

113. An arrest may be made even though the sheriff is in possession under a writ of *fieri facias* (*The James W. Elwell* [1921] P. 351).

114. RSC Order 75, r. 2A(3). (The 1995 Act came into force on 1 January 1996.) All proceedings against the fund are to be commenced in the Admiralty Registry (rule 2A(1)).

115. RSC Order 75, r. 17. The intervention is limited to the protection of the interest. See *The Lord Strathcona* [1926] A.C. 108 ([1925] P. 143) in which Hill J. held that the charterer intervenor had no *locus standi* to dispute the validity of the mortgages. Conversely, an intervenor may have to accept the role of the shipowner where he is defending the *res* (see e.g. *The Byzantion* (1922) 12 Ll.L.Rep. 9).

116. *The Mara (formerly the Mawan)* [1988] 2 Lloyd's Rep. 459. This analysis is probably unaffected by the acceptance that an action *in rem* has a "defendant" or "defendants" in person interested in the ship. See Chaps. 2, 10.

In addition, the court has inherent jurisdiction to allow a person who has no interest in the property under arrest but who suffers from the arrest to intervene. So, in *The Mardina Merchant*,[117] a harbour authority was allowed to intervene so as to enable it to apply for the moving of a ship under arrest. It may be doubted whether owners of cargo on board an arrested ship have strictly any "interest" in the property arrested to apply for leave to intervene on that basis. But clearly their interests are fundamentally affected by an arrest and they are within the broad principle applied in *The Mardina Merchant*. Certainly they have been allowed to intervene so as to obtain the discharge of the cargo.[118]

Expenses of discharge of cargo

The need to discharge the cargo of a ship arrested stems from the arrest and in contractual terms will normally be a breach of the contract of carriage. An attempt to treat the cost of discharge as analogous to the expenses of the Admiralty Marshal in the appraisement and sale of a ship failed in 1981 in *The Jogoo*.[119] Cargo owners had intervened in an action by mortgagees after arrest of the ship, the Sheen J. made an order permitting discharge of the cargo prior to judgment and for appraisement and sale. After sale, the cargo owners claimed that their discharge expenses should be a first charge on the proceeds as they should be treated as a contribution to the fund by increasing the price at which the ship could be sold. Sheen J. rejected the theory that any service to the ship after arrest meant that those who benefited from it must contribute and held as a general principle that cargo owners must bear the expenses of removal of cargo and claim against the shipowners.[120] As a result, such expenses are subject to the same priority rules as a substantive carriage claim.

"WRONGFUL" ARREST

Claimants are entitled to arrest a ship or other such property as is permitted to obtain security for the claim. It cannot be argued at the time of arrest that the arrest is improper because there is a good defence to the action.[121] Conversely, it is clear that if the arrest is in relation to a malicious claim which fails, or is of itself malicious, damages may be awarded by analogy to malicious prosecution. Damages may be awarded for an arrest made in the face of the existence of a caveat against arrest.[122]

It seems that apart from an arrest made despite the existence of a caveat, for damages to be awarded there must be either bad faith or gross negligence implying bad faith ("*mala fides*" or "*crassa negligentia*"). These criteria apply to initial arrest[123] and continuing

117. [1974] 3 All E.R. 749. See also *The World Star* [1987] 1 Lloyd's Rep. 452.
118. See e.g. *The Myrto* [1978] 1 Lloyd's Rep. 11; *(No. 2)* [1984] 2 Lloyd's Rep. 341; *The Jogoo* [1981] 1 Lloyd's Rep. 513.
119. [1981] 1 Lloyd's Rep. 513.
120. It seems irrelevant whether the order relating to the discharge is given prior to or after appraisement and sale, although the cargo owners' case in *The Jogoo* was essentially linked to the sale of the ship. For a similar approach in South Africa see *National Iranian Oil Co.* v. *Banque Paribas (Suisse)* [1993] LMLN 366.
121. See e.g. *The Gina* [1980] 1 Lloyd's Rep. 398.
122. RSC Order 75, r. 7. See *infra*.
123. *The Evangelismos* (1858) Swab. 378, approved in *The Strathnaver* (1875) 1 App. Cas. 58. A claim is dealt with at the same time as the claim on which the arrest was based. See *Astro Vencedor Compania* v. *Mabanaft GmbH* [1971] 2 Q.B. 588.

arrest.[124] In *The Borag*[125] an arrest was at the institution of managers in breach of a management contract. Damages were awarded following the normal contractual rules to compensate the owners for loss reasonably foreseeable as flowing from the breach, i.e. the arrest. Although in the case the courts referred to "wrongful arrest" the source of the wrongful characteristic lay in the breach of an agency directly related to the ship's operation. The arrest was simply the act which created the breach and is to be distinguished from damage or loss suffered simply through an arrest in support of a claim which ultimately fails.

Termination of arrest—release

Property arrested by virtue of execution of a warrant may be released only on judicial sale or by an instrument of release (called a "release")[126]—so the setting aside of a warrant of arrest is not of itself sufficient. An order for release is the appropriate remedy where an arrest is properly made but cannot be maintained (as, for example, on the stay of proceedings because of an arbitration clause).[127] Subject to the existence of a caveat against release (as to which see *infra*) and the giving of an undertaking to pay fees and expenses a release (i) must be issued on the withdrawal of the warrant prior to acknowledgment of issue or service of the writ in the action; (ii) may be issued at the instance of any party to the action if the court orders or if all other parties (except any defendant who has not acknowledged issue or service of the writ) consent.[128] When a caveat against release is in force, release will be ordered only if the property is under arrest in another action or the court orders the release.[129] Before the issue of the release the party applying for the release must give notice to the person at whose instance the caveat was entered requiring it to be withdrawn.

The usual practice is that property will be released only on the provision of sufficient security to cover the amount of the claim, interest and costs on the basis of the plaintiff's reasonably arguable best case.[130] This general rule also applies to release under statutory provisions because of a stay or dismissal of proceedings for arbitration or litigation in a foreign forum.[131] Even if there is such security, conditions may be attached[132] to the

---

124. See *The Cheshire Witch* (1864) B. & L. 362; *The Margaret Jane* (1869) L.R. 2 A. & E. 345 (arrest made "crassa negligentia"); *The Saqr Jubail* [1985] LMLN 140. As to damages for loss caused by non-release by reason of a caveat against release, see *infra*.

125. [1981] 1 Lloyd's Rep. 483.

126. RSC Order 75, r. 13(1). It should be noted that in High Court proceedings property must be under arrest for an order for appraisement and sale to be made. But see note to 75/22/2 in *Supreme Court Practice 1995* for possible qualification. Compare County Court Rules 1981, Order 40, r. 13.

127. *The Golden Elephant* [1976] 2 Lloyd's Rep. 462 (C.A. Singapore).

128. RSC Order 75, r. 13(4). The consent will usually be obtained by provision of bail or guarantee or payment into court. As to the court's role in regard to such alternative security, see *infra*.

129. RSC Order 75, r. 13(3).

130. *The Moschanthy* [1971] 1 Lloyd's Rep. 37 applied in *The Bazias 3 and Bazias 4* [1993] 1 Lloyd's Rep. 101. No release prior to trial will be ordered simply on the ground that because of other claims it was unlikely that the arrester's claim would be met: *The APJ Shalin* [1991] 2 Lloyd's Rep. 62.

131. Civil Jurisdiction and Judgments Act, s.26; *The Bazias 3 and Bazias 4* (*supra* fn. 130).

132. *The Rena K* [1979] 1 All E.R. 397; [1978] 1 Lloyd's Rep. 545; *The Tuyuti* [1984] 2 All E.R. 545; [1984] 2 Lloyd's Rep. 51 release on condition of alternative security.

release, and in the case of release without provision of security conditions would almost certainly be imposed.[133]

Limitation of liability and release from arrest

The 1957 Convention and its implementation

The Merchant Shipping (Liability of Shipowners and Others) Act 1958 gave effect in English law to the International Convention Relating to the Limitation of Liability of Owners of Sea Going Ships 1957. The Convention provided for the institution of a limitation fund in respect of claims in relation to which liability could be limited and recognition of that fund among the contracting States; and therefore provided for the release of any security given once the fund was set up. In the words of Lord Denning M.R.:

"The object is plain enough. If a ship is involved in a collision in circumstances in which the owner is entitled to limit his liability, then he should only be compelled to provide a limitation fund once and for all. If he makes it available in one country to meet all the limited claims, he should not be compelled to put up security for those claims in another country; or, if he is compelled to do so, he should be able to get the additional security released."[134]

In *The Wladyslaw Lokietek*[135] Brandon J. held that the conditions for release imposed by s.5 of the 1958 Act in giving effect to the Convention depended on (i) the discharging by a shipowner of some burden of proof that he could limit liability—it was not enough to show that he had a reasonably arguable case; and (ii) the lodging of security (by way of bail or guarantee) prior to the arrest of the ship.

In English law the Convention of 1957 has been superseded by the Convention Relating to the Limitation of Liability for Maritime Claims 1976, given the force of law by the Merchant Shipping Act 1979 and brought into force on 1 December 1986 and as from 1 January 1996 contained in the Merchant Shipping Act 1995.[136] Unlike the Act of 1958, the Acts of 1979 and 1995 enact the Convention provisions directly into English law.[137] The Convention provision relating to release from arrest is set out in Article 13(2):

"2. After a limitation fund has been constituted in accordance with Article 11, any ship or other property, belonging to a person on behalf of whom the fund has been constituted, which has been arrested or attached within the jurisdiction of a State Party for a claim which may be raised against the fund, or any security given, may be released by order of the Court or other competent authority of such State. However, such release shall always be ordered if the limitation fund has been constituted:
(a) at the port where the occurrence took place, or, if it took place out of port, at the first port of call thereafter; or
(b) at the port of disembarkation in respect of claims for loss of life or personal injury; or
(c) at the port of discharge in respect of damage to cargo; or
(d) in the State where the arrest is made."

---

133. See *The Vanessa Ann* [1985] 1 Lloyd's Rep. 549—release on execution of equitable mortgage and undertaking to enter into a statutory mortgage.
134. *The Putbus* [1969] P. 136 at p. 149.
135. [1978] 2 Lloyd's Rep. 520.
136. Replacing other legislation, including the Act of 1958.
137. Sections 17–19, Sch. 4. For discussion see Chap. 24.

In 1990 in *The Bowbelle*[138] Sheen J. held that under the 1976 Convention a shipowner could only be compelled to constitute one limitation fund and that any claim subject to limitation had to be against that fund. There was no prerequisite that the court be satisfied that limitation could be pleaded. Once the fund was established at a place specified in s.13(2) any ship arrested must be released. As a consequence of comments by Sheen J. in this case as to the need for machinery to warn would-be arresters of the existence of a fund the rules of court were amended to provide for a caveat against arrest (see *supra*).

JUDICIAL SALE

Judicial or "forced sale" is the final blunt instrument ensuring that the "security" for judgment obtained by a claimant through arrest is finally reflected in funds. The value of the security is affected by the claims of other creditors and the order of priority each claim may have in relation to the proceeds of sale. Such a sale confers on a purchaser a title free from all charges and encumbrances and any person having a claim to an interest must therefore assert that claim against the proceeds; and, indeed, must indicate the existence of a claim as soon as possible to ensure a say in the process which leads to a sale. Judicial sale will be discussed in that context.[139]

Here, it suffices to underline the essential connection between arrest and judicial sale and, in particular, that a court may not order sale unless the property is under arrest[140] and it will do so through an order for appraisement and sale granted to the Admiralty Marshal.[141] In special circumstances the court may issue a warrant to arrest and make an order for appraisement and sale at the same time. Any party (including the defendant)[142] may apply for an appraisement and sale[143] and the Marshal may apply for an order of sale. Such orders may be made prior to judgment on liability where the security of the applicant is reducing in value through the continuation of arrest[144]—this emphasizing the force of the remedy of arrest and its consequences.

SECURITY ALTERNATIVE TO ARREST

Alternative security is normally of two kinds: (i) the caveat against release from arrest, a security temporary in concept and not of itself providing the substantive protection of arrest; and (ii) bail, payment into court or guarantee, any one of which is a substitute for arrest and may be provided to prevent or obtain release from arrest.[145]

---

138. [1990] 1 Lloyd's Rep. 532; [1990] 3 All E.R. 476.
139. See Chap. 24.
140. See *The Wexford* (1883) 13 P.D. 10. As the county courts, and a High Court order for appraisement and sale see fn 126.
141. RSC Order 75, r. 23.
142. See e.g. *The Westport* [1965] 2 All E.R. 167.
143. Having undertaken to pay the Marshal's fees and expenses. See Chap. 25.
144. See *The Myrto* [1977] 2 Lloyd's Rep. 243 at pp. 259–260; *The Emre II* [1989] 2 Lloyd's Rep. 182.
145. For an example of the provision of security through a mortgage see *The Vanessa Ann* [1985] 1 Lloyd's Rep. 549.

CAVEAT AGAINST RELEASE FROM ARREST OR OF PROCEEDS OF SALE

A caveat against release of property under arrest or payment out of proceeds of sale may be entered whether or not the caveat holder has issued a writ *in rem*. Once a writ is issued by the caveat holder the caveat is unnecessary and will not prevent the release.[146] The availability of the caveat procedure means that the caveat holder is entitled to have notice of any application for release.[147] So in relation to a ship already under arrest or funds in court a claimant may ensure that the security does not disappear without his knowledge without being burdened by the costs of arrest. However, it must be noted that a claimant who is relying on a statutory lien must issue a writ *in rem* to acquire status as a preferred creditor and to ensure the enforceability of his right against purchasers of the ship. The caveat of itself is not relevant to either point but entry may be worthwhile as a first step pending investigation into the value of the asset arrested relative to the number of claims against it and assessment of the chances of recovery of any value.

A caveat against release is valid for 12 months. The time may not be extended but successive caveats may be entered.[148] The caveat remains in force even after a warrant of arrest is set aside and therefore a subsequent withdrawal of the caveat in exchange for an undertaking to pay charges is an enforceable agreement.[149] Property under arrest will not be released if a caveat against arrest is in force unless the property is under arrest in another action or the court orders.[150]

Liability in damages of caveat holder

A caveat against release of property under arrest may lead to liablitity in damages for any loss suffered by any person having an interest in the property unless the entry of that caveat was for good and sufficient reason.[151] This rule sits a little oddly in a framework a central feature of which is that loss suffered from arrest will be compensated only if the sufferer can point to more than the ultimate failure of the claim. The caveat against release make take the place of a second arrest. Yet in respect of a claim thought valid and in respect of which there is an arrest the criteria for damages are stringent—requiring fraud or gross negligence (see *supra*).

SECURITY IN SUBSTITUTION FOR ARREST

Bail, payment into court, guarantee

A claimant who has the right to arrest because of the nature of his claim has strong bargaining power. In English law arrest is largely an administrative (as distinct from a judicial) act, no undertaking in damages is required and damages for wrongful arrest are

---

146. *The Katingaki* [1976] 2 Lloyd's Rep. 372.
147. Rule 14(1).
148. RSC Order 75, r. 15.
149. *The Golden Elephant* [1976] 2 Lloyd's Rep. 462 (C.A. Singapore).
150. RSC Order 75, r. 13(3). See *supra* as to release in general.
151. RSC Order 75, r. 7.

not available in the absence of fraud or gross negligence.[152] It is not surprising, therefore, that the threat of arrest is often sufficient to bring an offer of alternative security for the claim. At least such security permits the ship to keep trading[153] or other assets than the ship to be deposited.

Bail

Bail is the substitution of personal for "asset" security. Today it is not as much used as a guarantee.[154] In English law bail is given to the court through a bail bond in which sureties (a) submit to the jurisdiction and (b) consent that if the defendant does not pay "what may be adjudged against them" in the action pending before the High Court or is agreed by settlement execution may issue against them for the sum due.[155] The defendant must serve on the plaintiff a notice of bail containing the names and addresses of "the persons who have given bail on his behalf".[156] After 24 hours (or earlier if agreed) the defendant may file the bond.[157]

It appears that by established practice bail could be given only after the defendant had "appeared" in the action or, in accordance with current procedure, acknowledged issue or service of the writ *in rem*.[158] It was permitted to give bail while reserving the right to challenge jurisdiction but the reservation had to be expressed ("bail under protest").[159] It takes the place of the ship[160] or other property and may be given initially to prevent arrest of the ship or to obtain its release.[161] The security provided cannot be ordered to exceed the value of the ship[162] but, subject to that limit, a party is entitled to "sufficient security to cover the amount of his claim with interest and costs on the basis of his reasonably best argued case".[163] It is restricted in its availability and its effect on any claim on the ship to the claim in respect of which it is lodged[164] and therefore represents the ship only in regard to that claimant. It is initially for the claimant to agree to accept an undertaking to

152. See *supra*.
153. An order maintaining arrest and permitting trading out of the jurisdiction is inherently contradictory, see *The Bazias 3 and The Bazias 4* [1993] 1 Lloyd's Rep. 101.
154. But a party can insist on bail instead of a guarantee. (*The Saudi Star* (unreported 1982). See for comment [1983] 1 LMCLQ 99.)
155. See RSC Order 75, r. 16(1). Admiralty Form 11. The form refers to "sureties" implying that there must be at least two.
156. RSC Order 75, r. 16(4).
157. *Ibid*. A corporate surety may have to make an affidavit stating the ability to pay, a non-corporate surety must make such an affidavit (rule 16(2)(3)).
158. See *The Prinsengracht* [1993] 1 Lloyd's Rep. 41 at pp. 45–46.
159. *The City of Mecca* (1879) 5 P.D. 28; *The Bulgaria* [1964] 2 Lloyd's Rep. 543. Although Clarke J. doubted that bail under protest could be given if as in *The Anna H* there was also a caveat against arrest containing as it must an undertaking to give bail (see [1994] 1 Lloyd's Rep. 287).
160. Its identification with the ship means that the bail bond is limited to the amount of the ship if the ship is worth less than the sum of the bond. See *The Staffordshire* (1872) 1 Asp. M.L.C. 365; (1872) L.R. 4 P.C. 194).
161. The entering of a caveat against arrest is dependent on an undertaking to give bail. RSC Order 75, r. 6. An undertaking to give bail continues to bind if on reliance on it a ship leaves the jurisdiction. See *The Ring* [1931] P. 58.
162. See *The Staffordshire* (1872) Asp. MLC 365; (1872) L.R. 4 P.C. 194; *The Charlotte* [1920] P. 78. In salvage cases failing agreement as to the value of ship or cargo an affidavit of value should be filed prior to release. The value stated will be binding subject to a power to rectify for a bona fide mistake. An appraisement may be requested if the arrester does not agree with the affidavit of value.
163. *The Moschanthy* [1971] 1 Lloyd's Rep. 37, at p. 44 applied in *The Bazias 3 and Bazias 4* [1993] 1 Lloyd's Rep. 101 (C.A.).
164. *The Roberta* [1928] P. 1; *The Clara* (1855) Swab. 1; *The Russland* [1924] P. 55.

give bail as sufficient security and eventually to agree to an acceptable amount. The party seeking security must not abuse his undoubted position of strength and the demanding of excessive bail may lead to a liability for costs.[165] It is for the court to be satisfied as to sufficiency and acceptability of the surety.[166]

Bail and jurisdiction

The consequence of the Brussels and Lugano Conventions that jurisdiction on the merits cannot be achieved through service of a writ but may require arrest or submission has brought the jurisdictional nature of the bond to the fore. The two issues are first whether the provision of bail prevents arrest even though the purpose of the arrest is simply to obtain jurisdiction and secondly constitutes submission to the jurisdiction.

The first issue is discussed in the context of the power to arrest (*supra*) and the second generally as relevant to jurisdiction *in personam* (Chapter 9). In the present context it is worth while stressing the difference between lodging of bail and merits jurisdiction. The giving of bail without any qualification was held to be submission to merits jurisdiction by Sheen J. in *The Prinsengracht*[167] and Clarke J. in *The Anna H*.[168] In both cases it was stressed that bail was an undertaking given to the court. In neither case was bail given under protest. In *The Anna H* in the Court of Appeal[169] the matter was dealt with only by Hobhouse L.J., and then only to state that as it was accepted that bail could be put up conditionally reserving the right to challenge jurisdiction "there are problems about treating" the provision of bail of itself as submission. It would seem, however, that whether or not bail is put up conditionally to see bail as submission on the merits is to confuse a matter of interim relief with the substantive issue.

Sheen J. was of the view that as bail could only be given following appearance it followed that bail meant submission to the jurisdiction *in personam*. Clarke J. held that having regard to the wording of notice of bail and the bail bond the defendant and sureties submitted to jurisdiction. Sheen J. thought it would be "absurd" to allow bail and also to allow the surety to rely on a plea of no jurisdiction. But with respect it is difficult to see why this should be so—particularly as it is recognized as a possibility by the process of "bail under protest". Such an approach seems to exemplify the too ready linking in English law of the provisional measure and jurisdiction on the merits. The giving of bail should be precisely as stated in the bond—a security *if* judgment is given. Nor does it seem that the notice of bail is any more than a notice indicating that bail is provided, i.e. the security given. There is equally no reason why the provision of a sum as security should mean the creation of any "merits" jurisdiction. It is perhaps in practice in the end a matter of being aware of how to avoid that creation. But, it is suggested with respect that the equation of bail with jurisdiction on the merits is fundamentally wrong.[170] There is no reason why of itself it is anything more than the arrest it prevents or ends.

---

165. See e.g. *The George Gordon* (1884) 9 P.D. 46; *The Irish Fir* (1943) 76 Ll.L.Rep. 51, at p. 54; *The Gulf Venture* [1984] 2 Lloyd's Rep. 445.

166. See *The Saudi Star* (unreported) 1982. Cf. [1983] 1 LMCLQ 99 (Matthews).

167. [1993] 1 Lloyd's Rep. 41.

168. [1994] 1 Lloyd's Rep. 287.

169. [1995] 1 Lloyd's Rep. 11.

170. Just as it is incorrect to equate the assertion by a court of jurisdiction to grant a provisional measure (e.g. a *Mareva* injunction) with assertion of jurisdiction on the merits (*The Sargasso* [1994] 2 Lloyd's Rep. 6).

Release of property arrested

If bail is agreed after arrest the claimant could then request release of the ship or other property.[171] The question of release is a matter for the court, although if adequate bail is offered the principle is that a ship should be released. At one time it was the practice not to allow bail in possession actions but these now are treated as any other. In *The Gay Toucan*[172] the claimant in a possession action for a pleasure yacht alleged that it would deteriorate if released and the defendant alleged that it would suffer damage through being broken into if held under arrest. Cairns J. ordered the release on condition of insurance on the basis that bail was as good if not better security than the yacht, that the risk of deterioration was not proved to be greater if released and that the vessel should not remain idle longer than necessary.

Rearrest

If, after judgment on liability, the bail proves to be insufficient there is no power to arrest or rearrest the ship; but it seems that this does not apply before judgment is given.[173] Even at that stage as bail represents the ship, the ship and bail provided cannot exceed the value of the ship.

A plaintiff in an action *in rem* may obtain a judgment *in personam* against a defendant who has become subject to jurisdiction *in personam* (as for example by submission) for the full amount of damages, interest, and costs. Similarly, such a judgment may be given in an action *in personam* commenced concurrently with an action *in rem*. It follows that the lodging of bail, whether or not it be the full amount, does not prevent the seizing of the ship in respect of which the bail was lodged in execution of a judgment *in personam* (whether it be for damages, interest or costs).[174]

Foreign bail in respect of English proceedings

Where a surety to an English bail bond is foreign it would seem necessary that the court be satisfied that there are assets in England to back up the undertaking.[175] As a general principle, bail lodged in a foreign jurisdiction in respect of English proceedings should be recognized to the extent that a foreign arrest is recognized. As has been seen in the discussion on foreign arrest, where a foreign jurisdiction permits such arrest an English court will probably not act in any way to order a party not to continue "the" proceedings for interim relief. So foreign bail would be similarly recognized. It would follow that an English court would not allow a further arrest (or bail) in England.[176] Where a limitation

---

171. See RSC Order 75, r. 13—release being on the basis of consent of all parties on order of the court. See *supra*.

172. [1968] 2 Lloyd's Rep. 245.

173. See *supra*. If a defendant in an action *in rem* acknowledges issue of the writ *in rem* or acknowledges service without indicating an intention to contest jurisdiction his liability is *in personam* in addition to the liability *in rem* (see Chapters 9 and 10) and the earlier provision of bail does not operate as a limitation on that liability any more than it would be limited to the ship. See *The Dictator* [1892] P. 304, at p. 332; *The Gemma* [1899] P. 285.

174. *The Gemma* [1899] P. 285; *The Joannis Vatis (No. 2)* [1992] P. 213. The seizure is through the writ of *fieri facias* (the usual method of execution available to a judgment creditor).

175. *The Saudi Star* (1982). A foreign corporation was found acceptable. It seems uncertain as to the extent to which the court insisted on proof of assets in England (see [1983] 1 LMCLQ 99).

176. See e.g. *The Arctic Star* (fn 55).

fund is constituted in a State party to the 1976 Convention on Limitation of Liability any security lodged in England must be released on the compliance with specified conditions. The matter is discussed in the context of release from arrest.[177]

English bail in respect of foreign proceedings

Such bail can be taken to the extent to which an English arrest may be maintained, i.e. in accordance with the provisions of the Civil Jurisdiction and Judgments Act 1982 when proceedings are stayed and the dispute remitted to arbitration or a foreign court.[178]

Payment into court

Payment into court is a direct alternative to the bail procedure. In involves payment into court of the amount required as security.

Guarantee or undertaking

Today a claimant is often satisfied with guarantee or a letter of undertaking to pay such amount as may be ordered by a court from a bank, insurance company or P. & I. Club, as for example:

"In consideration of your refraining from arresting the MV . . . or any other vessel in the same ownership, associated ownership or management for the purpose of founding jurisdiction and/or obtaining security in any part of the world in respect of the above mentioned claim against . . . , bareboat, charterers of the above named ship at the material time concerning damage to cargo, we the undersigned P. & I. Club, hereby guarantee to pay to your Solicitors on your behalf such sums as may be adjudged or found due to you by any competent Court or Tribunal or as may be agreed between the parties in respect of the said claim provided always that our liability hereunder shall not exceed the sum of . . . plus interest and costs, providing always in the event that the shipowners can establish before the competent Court their right to limit their liability pursuant to any applicable convention or legislation, such lesser sum as may represent the vessel's limit of liability."

In addition there should be agreement on the governing law and the forum—as regards both the undertaking and the claim, as for example:

"The owners of the above named ship agree that this undertaking and the above mentioned claims shall be subject to English law and to the exclusive jurisdiction of the English High Court."

The forum agreement is particularly necessary in a case within the scope of the Brussels or Lugano Convention. Apart from such an agreement, for jurisdiction on the merits to be created it may be necessary to arrest or establish submission (see Chapter 5).

Such arrangements are entirely contractual, no interest in the ship is created and apart from any forum or governing law agreement enforceability is primarily a matter for the parties. It has been held that the security is not in the court's control[179] but a court can control the amount of security requested under the guarantee.[180] Further, under the statutory provisions enacting the Limitation of Liability Convention a court may order the

177. See *supra*.
178. See *supra*. Presumably because of its inherent connection with arrest "bail" cannot qualify as interim relief within the Civil Jurisdiction and Judgments Act 1982, ss.24 and 25, so as to allow direct lodging in England in respect of foreign proceedings.
179. *The Alletta* [1974] 1 Lloyd's Rep. 40, at p. 50.
180. See *The Polo II* [1977] 2 Lloyd's Rep. 115; *The Moschanthy* [1971] 1 Lloyd's Rep. 37.

release of "security" (including a guarantee) given by a third party such as a P. & I. Club where a limitation fund has been constituted.[181]

It is difficult to see why a court cannot generally at least give a declaration as to a security—whether it should be retained or returned. There is little conceptually wrong and certainly everything practically sensible in a court decreeing the release of a security following a declaration that the basis of its provision is erroneous. An undertaking not honoured would no doubt at least lead to an action for breach of contract but, of itself, this may not in English law be a maritime claim.

ARREST AND DETENTION UNDER LEGISLATIVE POWERS

Arrest is essentially a remedy available as an inherent part of an action *in rem*. But it should not be forgotten that ships may be detained by numerous public authorities pursuant to legislative powers. So, for example, ships may be detained pending compliance with safety requirements, collision regulations, payment of dues for failure to carry required documents and by a receiver of wrecks.[182] Such powers are excluded from the Arrest Convention.[183]

In some instances detention may be followed by sale but the rights and power of each authority depends on the particular relevant legislation. An authority may have a claim (e.g. enforcement of port dues) which would qualify as the basis for arrest for a claim under the Supreme Court Act 1981. Where that claim and the power to detain overlap, the authority must make it clear it is acting under its statutory powers if it wishes to take advantage of any priority which the exercise of such powers would give.[184] It is not prevented from exercising the power by an earlier arrest by some other party.[185]

ARREST AND EXECUTION OF JUDGMENT

Finally, arrest as part of an action *in rem* should be distinguished from seizure as part of an execution of a judgment. The function of both types of seizure overlap.[186] However, the basis of "arrest" as independent of if not necessarily prior to judgment of an action *in rem*, is security in an action *in rem* and the more general seizure the satisfaction of a judgment.[187]

---

181. See *supra*.

182. See e.g. Merchant Shipping Act 1988, s.30A—detention of unsafe ships (inserted by Merchant Shipping (Registration etc) Act 1993 (now Merchant Shipping Act 1995, s. 95).

183. Article 2.

184. *The Charger* [1966] 1 Lloyd's Rep. 670.

185. *The Queen of the South* [1968] P. 449 applied in *The Freightline One* [1986] 1 Lloyd's Rep. 266. Port dues are payable out of proceeds of sale in respect of an arrested ship brought into port by the arrester (in this case the salvor). See *The Mari Chandris* (1942) 71 Ll.L.Rep. 225. As to the effects of a sale see *The Blitz* [1992] 2 Lloyd's Rep. 441 and Chap. 25.

186. A ship may be arrested although in possession of a sheriff as part of an execution process. (See *The James W. Elwell* [1921] P. 351.)

187. See further Chap. 25.

CHAPTER 16

The "Mareva" Injunction

NATURE AND PURPOSE

"The whole point of the *Mareva* jurisdiction is that the plaintiff proceeds by stealth so as to pre-empt any action by the defendant to remove his assets from the jurisdiction."[1] The rationale and fundamental principle is that "no court should permit a defendant to take action designed to frustrate subsequent orders of the court".[2] An added purpose and one later seen as equally important is the prevention of dissipation of assets whether within or out of England.[3] The prevention is achieved by an order directed at the defendant either prior or subsequent to an unsatisfied judgment[4] in many cases specifying a maximum value which is subject to the order. It may, however, relate to specific assets. Where there is a dispute between plaintiff and defendant as to whether an asset is owned by the defendant or a third party it depends on the circumstances whether the defendant's assertion of non-ownership is accepted, there is further enquiry or the issue is the subject of separate consideration.[5]

Despite somewhat persistent statements in the 1970s by Lord Denning M.R.[6] the injunction does not amount to an attachment of assets.[7] To this extent it is distinguishable from the arrest of a ship or other property as part of an action *in rem*. Further, its purpose

---

1. Mustill J. in *Third Chandris Shipping Corpn* v. *Unimarine SA* [1979] Q.B. 645, at p. 653. In addition to the High Court, as from 1 February 1995 a nominated senior presiding circuit judge may grant a *Mareva* in proceedings included in the Central London County Court Business List (County Court Remedies (Amendment) Regulations S.I. 1995 No. 206).

2. *Derby* v. *Weldon (No. 2)* [1989] 1 All E.R. 1002 at p. 1009 per Lord Donaldson M.R.

3. See e.g. *The Niedersachsen* [1983] 2 Lloyd's Rep. 600, at p. 617. The Supreme Court Act 1981, s.31(3), is to be construed widely so as to encompass dissipation within the jurisdiction as well as removal outside (see *Z Ltd.* v. *A* [1982] Q.B. 558). *Derby* v. *Weldon (No. 2)* (per Lord Donaldson M.R.) (*supra* fn. 2).

4. Unlike arrest it is accepted that a *Mareva* may be granted subsequent to a judgment. See *Orwell Steel Erection Ltd.* v. *Asphalt and Tarmac (UK) Ltd.* [1984] 1 W.L.R. 1097; *Mercantile Group (Europe) AG* v. *Aiyela* [1994] 1 All E.R. 110.

5. See *SCF Finance Co. Ltd.* v. *Masri* [1985] 2 All E.R. 747; *Allied Arab Bank* v. *Hajjar* (1988) *The Times*, 18 January. The issue might be tried prior to or after the main action—the criteria being that applicable to the grant of injunctions—"just and convenient".

6. See e.g. in the *Rasu Maritime SA* case [1978] Q.B. 644, at pp. 657–658 (disapproved in *Cretanor Maritime Co. Ltd.* v. *Irish Marine Management Ltd.* [1978] 1 Lloyd's Rep. 425, and *Z Ltd.* v. *A* [1982] Q.B. 558, at p. 573).

7. This follows from the concept of an injunction and was confirmed in *Cretanor Maritime Co. Ltd.* v. *Irish Marine Management Ltd.* [1978] 1 Lloyd's Rep. 425 and *The Angel Bell* [1980] 1 Lloyd's Rep. 632. See also *Bekhor & Co.* v. *Bilton* [1981] 1 Lloyd's Rep. 491 in which the court stressed that the purpose of the injunction was not to provide security for the claim; *Sanders Lead Co. Inc.* v. *Entores Metal Brokers Ltd.* [1984] 1 Lloyd's Rep. 276 (injunction not of itself a basis for becoming a party to an action concerning assets to which it relates); *Mercedes Benz A.G.* v. *Leiduck* [1995] 2 Lloyd's Rep. 417 P.C. (Lord Nicholls dissenting).

347

is not to provide security for the plaintiff's claims save insofar as it removes the risk of dissipation of the assets. The sanction for breach is contempt of court, the possible sanctions being debarring from defending the substantive action, imprisonment (for an individual), a fine or sequestration of assets. Ancillary orders (for example, of transfer) may impose on a defendant or even a third party an obligation to restore funds.

It follows that the "security" provided by the injunction is limited to the effectiveness of the injunction as against the defendant and third parties, and that the beneficiary of the injunction is in no way a secured creditor. No priority rights stem from the injunction and its scope is therefore limited by trading commitments of the defendant. It must not be used to place the defendant under undue pressure[8] and an injunction may be varied to permit use of assets for a stated purpose.

This is not to say that the injunction is ineffective. Far from it, as its effect is to render any person knowingly acting contrary to it to proceedings for contempt of court. In practice it may simply stop a business from operating. It is to say that the injunction does not create an incumbrance on the assets subject to it, although it may be argued that, its practical effect being "detention", it is within the scope of the Convention Relating to the Arrest of Sea Going Ships 1952. If that were so it is contrary to the Convention that it be used for any claim other than a maritime claim—clearly not an approach taken or likely to be taken by the English courts.[9]

ROOTS AND DEVELOPMENT

As was said in Chapter 14, the root of the injunction lies in two cases in the Court of Appeal in 1975, one of which gave its name to the injunction. Its development is a prime example of judicial creativity, although the statutory provision authorizing the granting of interlocutory injunction whenever "just and convenient" (now the Supreme Court Act 1981, s.37(1)) gives the judiciary a broad base on which to build. The *Mareva* injunction is, however, to be distinguished from the interlocutory injunction generally sought prior to a hearing. It has a precise purpose, no connection with any final relief sought and a prerequisite is that the risk of dissipation of assets must be shown. As distinct from interlocutory injunctions in general the Supreme Court Act 1981 does no more than recognize the *Mareva* injunction. In s.37(3) it is provided:

"(3) The power of the High Court under subsection (1) to grant an interlocutory injunction restraining a party to any proceedings from removing from the jurisdiction of the High Court, or otherwise dealing with, assets located within that jurisdiction shall be exercisable in cases where that party is, as well as in cases where he is not, domiciled, resident or present within that jurisdiction."

The provision assumes the power to grant and focuses on the availability against a home-based defendant, an aspect which had in effect been judicially settled prior to the statute. The essence of the *Mareva* injunction, as with the Anton Piller order to obtain evidence, is speed, and application may be made before the issue of the writ on the basis of a draft affidavit in which the plaintiff's case is to be set out. Nevertheless, such

8. See e.g. *PCW (Underwriting Agencies) Ltd.* v. *Dixon* [1983] 2 All E.R. 158 (defendant entitled to reasonable living expenses consistent with his standard of living)—order varied by consent [1983] 2 All E.R. 697.

9. The issue becomes more acute in the context of the suggested definition of arrest in the proposed draft Convention to replace that of 1952—"arrest" including "attachment or other conservatory measures".

application is within the provision of the rules of court. RSC Order 29, rule 1, provides for the application to be either by motion or summons or in cases of urgency, *ex parte*, and before the issue of the writ. Unlike the Anton Piller order, therefore, the court has no need to rely on its inherent jurisdiction as a source of power to grant. As its grant is a matter of judicial discretion the Court of Appeal will not interfere with the exercise of that discretion simply on the grounds that the court would have exercised it differently.[10]

It is not necessary however to show that the substantive proceedings would necessarily take place in an English court—the requirements are that there should be a claim under English law and that service of the writ be achieved or at least achievable. So there would be a power to grant a *Mareva* injunction where proceedings in an English court are stayed because of an arbitration or a foreign jurisdiction clause but uncertain simply because a defendant is personally subject to jurisdiction.[11]

ENGLISH AND FOREIGN ELEMENTS

Initially the *Mareva* was seen as ensuring that a foreign-based defendant in English proceedings did not move assets out of England prior to judgment. Its scope is now much wider, applying in respect of proceedings initiated in an English court to English and foreign defendants, and English and foreign assets and in respect of foreign proceedings in States party to the Brussels and Lugano Conventions to assets in England and (possibly) assets abroad.[12] But some limitations remain.

The place of the proceedings

(a) Proceedings initiated in an English court

An injunction is a remedy, the granting of which is to enforce a right. Subject to the Civil Jurisdiction and Judgments Acts 1982 and 1991 and the Arbitration Act 1950 the High Court must have jurisdiction over the claim for it to grant an injunction in regard to it. Further, as an injunction is an order against a defendant who can comply with it, it is not available as an adjunct to action *in rem*—that action relating to a ship or other property.

Jurisdiction "in personam"

Just as arrest was traditionally essentially linked to the action *in rem* so the *Mareva* injunction was initially thought to depend on the existence of a cause of action *in personam*. The cause of action had to be enforceable at the date of application for the injunction on the basis of the breach of a legal or equitable right of the plaintiff. The cause of action had to be enforceable under English law both in the sense of the recognition of

10. *The Niedersachsen* [1983] 2 Lloyd's Rep. 600. As to practice see generally Ough and Flenley, *The Mareva Injunction and Anton Piller Order* (2nd Edn) Butterworths, 1993.
11. See *Channel Tunnel Group and France Manche SA* v. *Balfour Beatty Construction* [1993] A.C. 334 (per Lord Goff); *Mercedes Benz A.G.* v. *Leiduck* fn. 7.
12. It is therefore now no longer arguable that the assertion of jurisdiction in respect of a *Mareva* injunction is assertion of jurisdiction over the substantive matter: *The Sargasso* [1994] 2 Lloyd's Rep. 6. See also Chap. 14.

the claim and the creation of jurisdiction over it. Subject to provisions of the Civil Jurisdiction and Judgment Acts 1982 and 1991 and an understanding that "jurisdiction" does not necessarily mean that the matter must be considered substantively by an English court the limitations continue.

NEED FOR ACCRUED CAUSE OF ACTION

If the right is yet to be established or has not yet arisen an injunction will not lie.[13] So it is not enough to show that an action for specific performance of a contract might lie, it must be shown that there has been a breach of the contract so that the right is immediately enforceable. Equally the injunction cannot be granted to a purchaser in respect of moneys to be paid as the purchase price of a ship where the purchaser fears that the ship will have defects.[14] The cause of action must have accrued.

INTERIM ORDERS IN ARBITRATION PROCEEDINGS

As with arrest it was arguable that where there was a stay of an action because of an arbitration agreement any power to grant interim relief was also stayed. Unlike arrest however, specific statutory powers are conferred on the courts to grant interim relief—by the Arbitration Act 1950, s.12, the courts may grant a *Mareva* injunction directly in respect of arbitration proceedings. Although this power is limited in scope to arbitrations taking place in England the staying of an action brought in England in breach of an agreement for foreign arbitration does not remove the power under the Supreme Court Act 1981 to grant interlocutory injunctions.[15] It follows that a *Mareva* injunction may be granted in such circumstances.[16]

SERVICE OUT OF THE JURISDICTION AND "MAREVA" INJUNCTION

Subject to the Civil Jurisdiction and Judgments Acts 1982 and 1991 and certain causes of action requiring specific links with the territory, jurisdiction *in personam* depends primarily on service of a writ on a defendant in England or, normally with leave of the court, out of England. In 1977 in *The Siskina*[17] the House of Lords held in establishing the need for breach of an existing right in English law that a plaintiff whose cause of action did not (apart from seeking an injunction) fall within the provisions of rules of court allowing service of a writ *in personam* out of England[18] and who could not serve the defendant in England could not obtain a *Mareva* injunction. The subrule providing for service out if in the action an injunction is sought in respect of acts within the jurisdiction

---

13. *Zucker* v. *Tyndall Holdings plc* [1993] 1 All E.R. 124. See also *Steamship Mutual Underwriting Assoc. (Bermuda) Ltd.* [1986] 2 Lloyd's Rep. 439; *Siporex Trade SA* v. *Comdel Commodities Ltd.* [1986] 2 Lloyd's Rep. 428.

14. *The Vera Cruz I* [1992] 1 Lloyd's Rep. 353; overruling *A* v. *B* [1989] 2 Lloyd's Rep. 423.

15. *Channel Tunnel Group Ltd.* v. *Balfour Beatty Construction Ltd.* [1993] A.C. 334 (H.L.)—considering that the interim relief was linked to final relief, and for that reason the injunction was refused—the relief was a matter for the agreed arbitration. See further Chap. 13.

16. The statutory power to grant interim relief in respect of foreign proceedings under the Brussels and Lugano Conventions may be extended by Order in Council to arbitration (see Chap. 14).

17. [1979] A.C. 210; [1978] 1 Lloyd's Rep. 1.

18. I.e. as to that case RSC Order 11, r. 1—"confined to originating documents which set in motion proceedings designed to ascertain substantive rights" (*Mercedes Benz A.G.* v. *Leiduck* fn. 7). See Chap. 9.

does not provide ground for service out independent of other grounds of the order. On this view there must be a cause of action entitling the applicant to service on one of those other grounds—but it is persuasively argued in a dissenting judgment in the *Mercedes Benz* case (fn 11) thus the *Mareva* "protective" jurisdiction is independent of the substantive claim.

Jurisdiction "in rem"

The more an action *in rem* is seen as an action in relation to property the less the granting of an injunction ancillary to it seems appropriate. In 1972 in *The Conoco Britannia*[19] Brandon J. held that equitable remedies *in personam* could be awarded in an action *in rem*. He saw the intention of the Judicature Acts 1873 and 1875 and their successors as not only conferring jurisdiction to deal with all legal and equitable claims in one hearing but as obligating a court to endeavour to do so.[20] As a consequence, he saw the question of granting of an injunction as one of discretion. With respect, however, to rely on such provisions ignores the distinctions between an action *in personam* and an action *in rem*. Even if an action *in rem* is seen as but a means of persuading a defendant to participate in the proceedings, until he does so the action is focused on the property in relation to which it is brought. Such a distinction is supported by the doctrine that an action *in rem* is commenced separately to an action *in personam* and does not merge with a judgment *in personam*. In 1980 in *The Stolt Filia*[21] Sheen J. held that a *Mareva* injunction could not be granted in an action *in rem* on the basis that there was no defendant against whom it could be ordered. The remedy lay in payment out of court following sale of the ship. While a person interested in the property may be a "defendant" for the purposes of the Brussels and Lugano Conventions this is so simply because of the connection with the property. That connection should not carry with it liability to a provisional remedy *in personam* any more than a substantive remedy of that kind.[22]

(b) Foreign proceedings

It followed from *The Siskina* that a *Mareva* injunction could be granted only when an English court had jurisdiction over the defendant in relation to the substantive claim.[23] Becoming a party to the Brussels Convention meant joining a general legal framework clearly contemplating the granting of provisional measures in one contracting State in support of proceedings in another contracting State. This aspect of the Convention was implemented in English law through ss.24, 25 of the Civil Jurisdiction and Judgments Act 1982 and amendments to the rules of the court, and the implementation adapted in 1991 to implement the identical provision of the Lugano Convention. The general issues

19. [1972] 2 Q.B. 543.
20. The relevant provision appears in a somewhat truncated form in the Supreme Court Act 1981, s.49. If anything, that provision is less in support of Brandon J.'s view than its predecessor in the Supreme Court of Judicature (Consolidation) Act 1925, ss.36, 37, 42 and 43.
21. [1980] LMLN 15.
22. An action *in rem* does not merge in a judgment *in personam*: *The Rena K* [1979] Q.B. 377, at p. 405; *The Stella Nova* [1981] Com. L.R. 200. Cf. Chaps. 10, 25.
23. The *Mercedes Benz* case fn 7—but see the dissenting judgment. Whether there is a need for English proceedings is uncertain but a stay will not affect the power. See *ibid.* and fn 11.

concerning the Conventions and implementation are discussed in Chapter 14. It is, therefore, sufficient here to summarize the effect on *Mareva* injunctions.

A *Mareva* may be granted in respect of Convention proceedings irrespective of the domicile of the parties. It is necessary to serve a writ in respect of the injunction on the defendant. No leave to serve is required if the defendant is domiciled in a contracting State or there is a jurisdiction agreement in respect of the proceedings or the proceedings are brought where they are by virtue of the mandatory provisions in Article 16 of either Convention. In all other cases leave is required but because of the framework of the Conventions it may be given although there is no other cause of action in England in regard to which service out may be sought.[24]

English and foreign based defendants

For some time it was uncertain whether the injunction would be granted against a defendant based in England and in one case in 1979[25] it was held that it would not be granted against a defendant resident in England. However, in 1980 it was held at first instance[26] and by the Court of Appeal[27] that there was no restriction dependent on the "base" of the defendant, the primary reason given for the extension to home-based defendants being the abolition of foreign exchange control.[28] The Supreme Court Act 1981, s.37(3), confirmed this scope of the *Mareva* jurisdiction, and there are now no doubts as to it.

English and foreign assets

The injunction is an order against the defendant, but its purpose is to prohibit removal or dissipation of assets. It follows that it has no purpose if there are no assets in regard to which it can be granted. To obtain the injunction it is belief in the existence of assets that is sufficient but the emergence of the fact that there are none will remove the basis for its grant.

Type of assets

As the *Mareva* injunction looks to the future it will extend to any type of asset whether acquired prior to or after the granting of the injunction.[29] However, an asset in which a third party has a proprietary interest which is superior to any claim of the plaintiff may be

---

24. See *Govt of Haiti* v. *Duvalier* [1989] 1 All E.R. 456; *X* v. *Y*, [1989] 3 All E.R. 689; [1989] 2 Lloyd's Rep. 561. The reasoning cannot be adapted to non-Convention cases: the *Mercedes Benz* case fn. 7.

25. *The Agrebele* [1979] 2 Lloyd's Rep. 117.

26. *Barclay-Johnson* v. *Yuill* [1980] 1 W.L.R. 1259; *MBPXL Corpn* v. *International Banking Corpn* [1975] Court of Appeal Transcript 411, cited in *Third Chandris Shipping Corpn* v. *Unimarine SA* [1979] Q.B. 645, at pp. 649–653 (per Mustill J.).

27. *Prince Abdul Rahman* v. *Abu-Taha* [1980] 2 Lloyd' Rep. 565. See also *Chartered Bank* v. *Daklouche* [1980] 1 All E.R. 205.

28. See [1980] 2 Lloyd's Rep. at p. 568.

29. See e.g. *TDK Distributors (UK) Ltd.* v. *Videochoice Ltd.* [1985] 3 All E.R. 345.

excluded.[30] In many cases an injunction may affect the rights of third parties (as, for example, a bank, a broker or shipowner). This aspect will be dealt with in considering the effect of the injunction.

The injunction is often aimed at bank accounts[31] or insurance proceeds[32] but it was held in the early days of development that it was not restricted to money.[33] It may be granted in respect of ships, it being irrelevant that a plaintiff may have arrested a ship or other property in respect of the same claim.[34] There is no restriction to assets unconnected with other assets, so that the effect of an injunction granted, for example, in respect of cargo may be to prevent the ship on which it is loaded from leaving.[35]

Place of assets

Until 1988 the prevailing view was that the *Mareva* remedy was geared to assets in England or Wales. It was a territorial remedy limited to those assets within the control of the courts. Such an approach, while understandable, reduced the efficiency of the *Mareva* as regards international activities in an era in which assets could frequently and rapidly be moved. A theory then developed that although foreign assets could be targeted, some English asset was a necessary precondition. This was followed in 1988 by recognition that this of itself made little sense.

Numerous decisions consistently recognizing the limitation to English assets culminated in 1986 in *Ashtiani* v. *Kashi*,[36] a decision of the Court of Appeal, holding that there was no obligation as a defendant to *Mareva* proceedings to disclose the existence of foreign assets as these were not subject to a *Mareva*. Later decisions of the same court leading up to *Derby* v. *Weldon (No. 2)*[37] took an opposite line, and once that line was established, applied it as a matter of precedent. In justifying the diversion in this "developing branch of the law" Lord Donaldson pointed to the unlimited statutory discretion to grant injunctions and commented that the refusal to grant was an exercise of discretion which could not provide a precedent—save as to the basic principle on which the discretion is founded—preventing frustration of court orders. While the normal practice remains that an order should be confined to assets within the jurisdiction it may cover foreign assets in a "world wide *Mareva*". Given this there is "neither rhyme nor

---

30. See e.g. *Prekookeanska Plovidba* v. *LNT Lines Spl* [1988] 3 All E.R. 897. As to transactions in relation to the assets within the scope of the injunction but unaffected by it see *infra*.

31. See e.g. *Z Ltd.* v. *A* [1982] Q.B. 558.

32. See e.g. *The Angel Bell* [1980] 1 Lloyd's Rep. 632.

33. The *Rasu Maritima* case [1978] Q.B. 644.

34. *The Rena K* [1979] Q.B. 377, [1978] 1 Lloyd's Rep. 545. It may also be used in relation to a ship released from arrest because of the restrictions on the court's jurisdiction *in rem* (*ibid*). It is irrelevant to the granting of the injunction that the ship will not be in the custody of the Admiralty Marshal (*ibid*).

35. *The Marie Leonhardt* [1981] 2 Lloyd's Rep. 458; but the damage to the shipowner (or third party) may be such as to mean the injunction would not be granted, see e.g. *The Eleftherios* [1982] 1 Lloyd's Rep. 351 (as to which see *infra*). It appears that an injunction has been granted in respect of time charterers' bunkers on the application of port agents claiming for disbursements (see [1981] LMLN 37).

36. [1986] 2 All E.R. 970. For other decisions see *Derby* v. *Weldon (No. 2)* [1989] 1 All E.R. 1002. As to disclosure in support of a *Mareva* see *infra*.

37. [1989] 1 All E.R. 1002 treating as binding *Derby* v. *Weldon (No. 1)* [1989] 1 All E.R. 469—the court in that case in effect simply taking a different approach to *Ashtiani* v. *Kashi*—"the jurisdiction is a developing one".

reason in regarding the existence of some asset within the jurisdiction" as a precondition for granting it in respect of foreign assets.[38]

It must be desirable not to allow the place of the assets however transitory to control the availability of them for any judgment in the substantive action. Implementing the desirability has to take into account in respect of foreign assets both the factual lack of control by an English court and the control of the legal system of the place where they are. From the view of the English court control is exercised through the defendant and the ultimate sanction of being debarred from defending the substantive action.[39] So the jurisdiction extends to ordering transfer of assets subject to a worldwide *Mareva* from one foreign jurisdiction to another.[40] The extent of enforceability of the order in the foreign court is a relevant but not a governing factor.[41]

From the view of the foreign court, however, the argument that the injunction is directed at the party and not the assets may carry little weight. It may be that having regard to the whole of the circumstances it is preferable to leave the parties to obtain any provisional remedy at the place of the asset—otherwise there will be a complex (and perhaps inconsistent) series of measures emanating from different source. Caution in extending the scope to assets abroad may be particularly relevant where there is easy enforceability of judgments between the relevant countries.

Where, however, the easy enforceability applies also to provisional measures (as under the Brussels and Lugano Conventions) it is arguable that the pendulum may swing again to remove some of the objections to orders by a court in one state extending to a territory of another. But the fundamental risks remain of inconsistency of judgments of the foreign and home court, and the further possibility of making orders that in respect of foreign assets may affect persons or corporations not parties to the English action or before the court. These risks increase when the *Mareva* sought is to enforce an order of a foreign court or arbitral tribunal.

In facing the risks of orders in respect of foreign assets it has been held that save in exceptional circumstances a worldwide *Mareva* would not be made when sought to enforce a judgment of a foreign court or award of a foreign tribunal.[42] Where any order in respect of foreign assets is made it should include a limiting clause:

"The terms of this order do not affect or concern anyone outside the jurisdiction of this court until it is declared enforceable or is enforced by a court in the relevant country and then it shall only affect him to the extent they have been declared enforceable or have been enforced UNLESS such person is (a) a person to whom this order is addressed or an officer of or an agent appointed by power of attorney of such a person or (b) a person who is subject to the jurisdiction of this Court and (i) has been given written notice of this order at their residence or place of business within the jurisdiction

---

38. *Ibid.* The amount at stake in the case was a sum of about £25m. An order confined to assets within the jurisdiction may lead to uncertainties as to the need to disclose other assets if there is a claim to a need to maintain trading activities.

39. See *ibid* at p. 1009.

40. *Derby v. Weldon (No. 6)* [1990] 3 All E.R. 263. The power was said to exist where the assets had been transferred initially to prevent the English court exercising jurisdiction over them or if the connection with the latter jurisdiction was the control of investments—but this seems more a matter going to the exercise of the power.

41. Just as the plea that a foreign court is the appropriate forum. For a rejection of that plea in respect of foreign bankruptcy proceedings see *Felixstowe Dock & Railway Co. and others v. United States Lines Inc.* [1988] 2 All E.R. 77, [1987] 2 Lloyd's Rep. 76.

42. *Rosseel NV v. Oriental Commercial and Shipping (UK) Ltd.* [1991] 1 All E.R. 545.

of this Court, and (ii) is able to prevent acts or omissions outside the jurisdiction of this Court which constitute or assist in a breach of the terms of this order."[43]

REQUIREMENT OF AN UNDERTAKING BY PLAINTIFF IN DAMAGES AND EXPENSES

Undertakings by the plaintiff set out in the standard forms for *Mareva* introduced on 18 July 1994[44] include complying with any order compensating the defendant for loss suffered, to issue and serve the writ in the case in the form of a draft produced to the court, to swear an affidavit in the terms of a draft produced, to serve the writ and supporting documents on the defendant, to pay reasonable costs of any person incurring them by the order and any compensation found due by the court to such a person. In a worldwide *Mareva* there are in addition undertakings that the plaintiff will not without the leave of the court—

(a) begin proceedings against the defendant in any other jurisdiction or use information obtained through the order for the purpose of proceedings in any other jurisdiction

(b) seek to enforce the order outside England and Wales or seek an order of a similar nature including an order conferring a charge or other security against the defendant or the defendant's assets.

DAMAGES

Apart from arrest a court will normally require a plaintiff to give an undertaking as to damages as a condition of awarding interim relief.[45] It will normally be required for the grant of a *Mareva* injunction. The undertaking contained in the standard form reads—

"If the court later finds that this order has caused loss to the defendant, and decides that the defendant should be compensated for that loss, the plaintiff will comply with any order the court may make."

The undertaking is to the court, and security to support the undertaking may be ordered.[46] It is an essential ingredient in any award that the injunction should not have been granted.[47] Where an injunction is discharged and it is sought to enforce the undertaking the first issue is whether or not the injunction should have been granted. It

43. See Standard Form Order for worldwide Mareva, Practice Direction of July Annex 2 [1994] 4 All E.R. 52.

44. See Practice Direction of 28 July (fn 43) Annex 2, 3 and *infra* p. 364.

45. For a useful summary of the applicable principles see *Cheltenham and Gloucester BS* v. *Ricketts* [1994] 3 All E.R. 276 at pp. 281–282 (per Neill L.J.)—the summary must be read subject to the power to adjourn the issue of whether an undertaking should be enforced (see *infra*). An undertaking will not be required where the Crown or a public authority is acting for the public at large. See e.g. *Securities and Investments Board* v. *Lloyd-Wright* [1993] 4 All E.R. 210 and authorities there cited.

46. See Practice Direction 28 July 1994 (fn 43) para. 3(2). But not if the injunction is discharged: *The Mito* [1987] 2 Lloyd's Rep. 197—the fortification is essentially a condition of the grant of injunction to which the plaintiff could agree or disqualify himself from the injunction, and to grant it after discharge is not to fortify the undertaking but to grant security for the claim to the defendant (*ibid*).

47. See *Cornhill Insurance plc* v *Barclay* [1992] LMLN 340—so a compromise of an action in respect of which the injunction was ordered precluded any assertion of the propriety of the issue of the injunction and hence any inquiry into damages (*ibid*).

appears that the Court of Appeal has retreated from a principle expressed in 1987[48] that the judge before whom the application comes should rule on whether the undertaking should be enforced and only if it is ordered that it be enforced, further order an inquiry into damages. It now appears acceptable that the judge may adjourn the whole matter leaving both issues to the inquiry. Whether an order made leaves open the question of whether the discretion to enforce depends on the terms of the order—but the discretion must be exercised at some stage.[49] It seems clearly preferable to retain flexibility but necessary that any initial order be clear as to that which is or is not left for decision.[50]

If it is ruled that the undertaking should be enforced the judge should decide whether the immediate assessment of damages is appropriate and if so direct immediate payment to the applicant.[51] If there has been a reasonable offer by the plaintiff the court may release the plaintiff from the undertaking and replace it by an undertaking to pay the amount offered. As a further option the court may direct an inquiry into the damages and it may do so without conditions or put a defendant on terms. For a defendant to be made to give security of costs for the inquiry it appears that the plaintiff would have to show that the defendant's application is or comes close to an abuse of process.[52]

The principles of the award of damages are based on breach of a notional contract that the plaintiff would not prevent the defendant from doing that which he was restrained from doing. The express principles applicable to such inquiry are not fixed beyond debate but in 1993 Waller J., after consideration of a number of authorities, held that the claimant must show that[53]:

  (i) the damage or loss would not have occurred but for the grant of the injunction;
  (ii)   (a) links between cause and consequence and
         (b) the type of loss must have been (or ought reasonably to have been) in the contemplation of the parties;
         Something which will happen in the great majority of cases should be regarded as having been in the contemplation of the parties.

It must be stressed that the root of the damage is the grant of the injunction and not the commencement of the litigation.

Such an approach may be unduly favourable to a party obtaining an injunction, for it puts the risk of unforeseen damage firmly on the (now established) "innocent party". While this may be a principle generally applicable in contractual causes of action,[54] it was the successful application for the injunction initiated by a plaintiff which created the loss.

---

48. See *Norwest Holst Civil Engineering Ltd.* v. *Polysuis Ltd.* (1987) *The Times*, 28 July (commenting on *Barclays Bank* v. *Rosenberg* [1985] LMLN 147); approved in *Cheltenham and Gloucester BS* v. *Ricketts* [1994] 3 All E.R. 276.
49. See *Zygal Dynamics plc* v. *McNulty* [1989] Court of Appeal Transcript 571, the principles discussed and followed in *Balkanbank* v. *Taher* [1995] 2 All E.R. 904.
50. See *Balkanbank* v. *Taher* (fn. 49).
51. See Practice Direction of 28 July, para. (4) [1994] 4 All E.R. 52—for discussion of the Direction as a whole see *infra*.
52. See *C.T. Bowring and Co. (Insurance) Ltd.* v. *Corsi and Partners* [1994] 2 Lloyd's Rep. 567 (C.A.). As to security of costs see Chap. 14.
53. *Tharros Shipping Co* v. *Bias Shipping Ltd.* [1994] 1 Lloyd's Rep. 577.
54. In *Cheltenham and Gloucester BS* v. *Ricketts* [1993] 4 All E.R. 276, Neill L.J. expressed the view that "it seems" that damages are to be awarded on the same basis as breach of contract (at p. 282).

The plaintiff sought "security" for a risk and it is arguable he should be responsible for any loss if that risk proves to have been non-existent.

EXPENSES

Where the injunction affects third parties, the plaintiff will be required to indemnify the third party in respect of expenses incurred.[55] However, such an undertaking will not always be accepted as a sufficient safeguard against loss caused to an innocent third party. Where the undertaking will not adequately compensate a third party, the injunction is likely to be refused.[56]

OTHER PROCEEDINGS

The undertakings in the standard form relating to a worldwide *Mareva* not without leave to begin proceedings or use information gained through the order for foreign proceedings or to enforce the order elsewhere are to prevent oppression through multiplicity of proceedings or misuse of information. Control over the proceedings is thereby retained by the English court, the sanctions being necessarily focused on the English proceedings. Whether there will be such oppression is a matter of assessment of the circumstances. It does not necessarily follow that an undertaking not to enforce the order should be accompanied by the undertaking not to mount separate proceedings.[57]

CASE TO BE MADE BY THE PLAINTIFF

The application is made *ex parte* to a Commercial court judge on the basis of a draft affidavit, or in cases of urgency an undertaking to swear and execute an affidavit. Where practicable the papers should be lodged with the judge at least two hours before the hearing. The grant of an injunction should be in the form set out in a 1994 Practice Direction[58] unless the judge considers there is a good reason for a different form. The contents of the affidavit will necessarily reflect the case to be made. There is a duty on the plaintiff to consider carefully at the *ex parte* stage all aspects of the claim and the appropriate order.

The obligation of the plaintiff on an *ex parte* application is:

(i) to show a good arguable case—"it appears likely that the plaintiff will recover judgment against the defendant"[59];

(ii) to identify assets believed to exist;

(iii) to give grounds for believing that there is a risk of dissipation of assets (and likely default) before satisfaction of the judgment or arbitral award;

(iv) to make full and frank disclosure of all material matters in his knowledge.

---

55. *Ibid. Searose Ltd.* v. *Seatrain (UK) Ltd.* [1981] 1 Lloyd's Rep. 556; *The Marie Leonhardt* [1981] 2 Lloyd's Rep. 458; *Z Ltd.* v. *A* [1982] Q.B. 558.

56. See *The Eleftherios* [1982] 1 Lloyd's Rep. 351; *The Pitsa T* [1987] 2 Lloyd's Rep. 404 and *infra*—Effect on third parties.

57. See *Re Bank of Credit and Commerce International (No. 9)* [1994] 3 All E.R. 764 (C.A.).

58. Of 28 July 1994.

59. *Z* v. *A Ltd.* [1982] Q.B. 558 at pp. 588–589.

The advice given in 1982 in *Z* v. *A Ltd.*[60] by Kerr L.J. remains relevant.

"It follows that in my view it should be accepted that at that stage it is the duty of the plaintiff and of his legal advisers to do the following:

  (i) To consider carefully whether an application for a Mareva injunction is justified, in the sense of being reasonably necessary in the particular case in order to achieve the objectives for which this procedure has been designed.

 (ii) If so, to consider very carefully what should be the extent of the injunction in order to safeguard the plaintiff's prima facie claim against a real risk of the defendant deliberately taking steps to avoid execution on a judgment which the plaintiff is likely to obtain.

(iii) On the foregoing basis, in what way and to what extent the injunction should apply to assets of the defendant within the jurisdiction.[61]

 (iv) To the extent to which the assets are known or suspected to exist, these should be identified even if their value is unknown; and if it is known or suspected that they are in the hands of third parties, in particular banks, everything should be done to define their location to the greatest possible extent. Thus, to take the example of bank accounts, the plaintiff should make every effort to try to indicate (a) which bank or banks hold the accounts in questions, (b) at which branches, and (c) if possible, under what numbers.

  (v) The plaintiff should consider how soon and in what manner the defendant can be served as expeditiously as possible, both with the writ (if this has not already been served) and the injunction if it is granted, and he should generally give an undertaking about service on the defendant as part of the order. Further, the plaintiff should consider on what third parties it is meanwhile intended, and reasonably necessary, to serve a copy of the injunction.

 (vi) All the foregoing matters should be fully and frankly dealt with in an affidavit supporting the ex parte application or, if it is urgent, in a draft affidavit coupled with an undertaking to swear and file this forthwith."

The grant of the injunction remains discretionary (i.e. whether its grant is "just and convenient") and even if these requirements are apparently satisfied an injunction may be refused if the plaintiff declines or is unable to give an undertaking as to damages or provide supporting security (see *supra*) or on balance the risk of dissipation is exceeded by the harm the injunction would do to the defendant[62] or to third parties (see *infra*).

On granting of the injunction *ex parte* a return date will be set for reconsideration, the opportunity being thereby provided for a hearing *inter partes* and re-examination of the various aspects of the grounds of grant and circumstances since the grant. Among such circumstances relevant to continuation of the injunction are delay in issuing substantive proceedings[63] or pursuing the action,[64] or change in any material circumstances which if existing at the date of application would have to have been disclosed.[65] If the injunction granted *ex parte* is discharged because, for example, of failure to make disclosure the court may simply discharge the injunction, (apparently) continue the injunction leaving the defendant to damages after the trial, discharge the injunction and grant a further injunction. To confine a defendant to damages for non-disclosure will leave the defendant

60. [1982] Q.B. 558, at p. 585. For an example of rejection because of failure to show sufficient prospects of success, see *The Tatiangela* [1980] 2 Lloyd's Rep. 193. It was in 1977 in the *Rasu Maritima* case [1978] Q.B. 644 that the move was made to "the arguable case" rather than attaching the injunction to entitlement to a summary judgment.

61. Adapted now as necessary to any application for a worldwide *Mareva*.

62. See e.g. *Polly Peck International plc* v. *Asil Nadir* [1992] 2 Lloyd's Rep. 238 (balancing the type of cause of action against the harm); *The Pitsa T* [1987] 2 Lloyd's Rep. 404 (balancing the financial loss of third party shipowners and the plaintiffs).

63. *Siporex Trade SA* v. *Comdel Commodities Ltd.* [1986] 2 Lloyd's Rep. 428.

64. *Lloyd's Bowmaker Ltd.* v. *Britannia Arrow Holdings plc* [1988] 1 W.L.R. 1337.

65. See *Commercial Bank of the Near East plc* v. *ABC and D* [1989] 2 Lloyd's Rep. 319.

with a possibly quite inadequate remedy. Which option is taken will depend on weighing all the factors relevant at the *inter parte* stage.[66]

RISK OF DISSIPATION OF ASSETS AND LIKELY DEFAULT

The injunction will be granted only if the risk of the disappearance of the asset is evident to the court. So, in *Etablissement Esefka International Anstalt* v. *Central Bank of Nigeria*,[67] the Court of Appeal refused to sanction an injunction because no such risk had been established. In *Barclay Johnson* v. *Yuill*[68] Sir Robert Megarry V.C. stressed not only the need for proof of risk but that of likely default, while pointing out that danger of default may be inferred from the risk itself. In *Z Ltd* v. *A* Kerr L.J. expressed the view that the granting of *Mareva* injunctions as a matter of course to give the plaintiff security for any judgment where there was no real danger of dissipation of assets was an abuse of power.[69] In *The Niedersachsen*[70] the Court of Appeal stressed that the test for the exercise of the *Mareva* jurisdiction was whether a refusal of the injunction "would involve a real risk that a judgment or award in favour of the plaintiff would remain unsatisfied".

Permitted use of assets

As the purpose of the injunction is simply to make assets available for any judgment which may be obtained, it cannot be allowed to confer priority on the person obtaining it over other creditors, and it should not be used so as to force other creditors to proceed to judgment "with consequent loss of credit and commercial standing"[71] as regards the person against whom the injunction is granted.

There are usual provisions for the payment of trade debts and living expenses falling due after the injunction resulting from carrying on business and living in the normal way. In particular, assets within the scope of the injunction may be used to honour rights of set off and banking facilities granted prior to the injunction so as to meet accrued debts and to "carry on business in the ordinary way".[72] Payment of legal costs connected with the substantive dispute is not "dissipation".[73] The question of permitting the use of assets to allow a defendant to carry on his life and his business and to defend against the claim is a matter of balance between oppression bringing cessation of trading and the risk of an unsatisfied judgment. It often arises in the context of variation, where the defendant seeks amendment of a widely drafted order—but the variation is necessarily based on principles applicable initially.

---

66. See e.g. *The Bowmaker case* (fn 64); *Ali Fahd Shoboksha Group* v. *Moneim* (1989) *The Times*, 8 March.

67. [1979] 1 Lloyd's Rep. 445. See also *Third Chandris Shipping Corpn* v. *Unimarine SA* [1979] Q.B. 645, at pp. 671–672 (per Lawton L.J.); *Z Ltd.* v. *A* [1982] Q.B. 558, at p. 571 (per Kerr L.J.).

68. [1980] 1 W.L.R. 1259.

69. [1982] Q.B. 558, at p. 585.

70. [1983] 2 Lloyd's Rep. 600.

71. *The Angel Bell* [1981] Q.B. 65; [1979] 2 Lloyd's Rep. 491.

72. See *The Angel Bell* (fn 71); *KS/AS Admiral Shipping* v. *Portlink Ferries* [1984] 2 Lloyd's Rep. 166; *Avant Petroleum Inc.* v. *Gatoil Overseas Inc.* [1986] 2 Lloyd's Rep. 236; *Derby* v. *Weldon (No. 2)* [1989] 1 All E.R. 1002.

73. *Cala Cristal SA* v. *Emran Al-Borno* (1994) *The Times*, 6 May; [1994] LMLN 383. Ferris J. refused to become a taxing body for the amount of costs, being concerned only with evidence of extravagances or ulterior purposes.

There is no inflexible requirement that a defendant seeking a limitation so as to pay debts must satisfy the court that no other assets are available,[74] although the obligation to make full disclosure cannot be avoided through the application being made by the creditor.[75] Further, a bank seeking to be allowed to exercise rights of set off in connection with facilities granted to the defendant before being notified of the injunction is not obliged to disclose the state of the defendant's account or state whether the defendant has other assets. To do so would be to go against the policy of the *Mareva* injunction through interference with contractual rights between a third party and the defendant.[76]

At the heart of any plea to permit the use of funds which increases the risk of an unsatisfied judgment lies good faith, the existence of other assets and the establishment of the need for the funds to be used.[77] In 1990 in *The Coral Rose* the Court of Appeal refused to vary an injunction to allow a wholly owned subsidiary corporation (Avalon) to repay a debt due to the "owning" corporation (Marc Rich and Co. AG). Marc Rich had provided funds for Avalon to purchase a ship. The substantive action was by the vendor of the ship for asserted breach of contract of sale by Avalon. In refusing the variation the Court of Appeal looked behind (as distinct from "piercing") the corporate veil[78]—it should do so thought Neill L.J. when considering the scope of injunctive relief. All the circumstances of the case and the debt should be taken into account. It was not, thought Staughton L.J., a case of carrying on business in the normal way but a desire to use assets caught by the injunction "merely to evade its underlying purpose". Even if there was no such purpose it was proper to consider the nature of the debt—in this case the repayment of loan capital which would normally not have been demanded by Marc Rich until Avalon could pay.

ANCILLARY ORDERS IN AID OF THE INJUNCTION

The High Court has power to make all ancillary orders "as appear to the court to be just and convenient to ensure that the exercise of the *Mareva* jurisdiction is effective to achieve its purpose". It may order discovery and interrogatories, and delivery up of chattels.[79] The

74. *Campbell Mussels* v. *Thompson* (1984) Law. Soc. Gaz. 2140 "correcting", *A and B* v. *C (No. 2)* [1981] 1 Lloyd's Rep. 559. In *The Angel Bell* the only asset of the defendants was the insurance proceeds, the subject of the injunction.

75. *A* v. *B, X intervening* [1983] 2 Lloyd's Rep. 532.

76. *The Theotokos* [1983] 2 Lloyd's Rep. 204. The court recognized the rights of a bank in respect of pre-existing rights of set-off (see *infra*) and rights of an intervenor party to an agreement specifically relating to assets caught by a *Mareva* injunction.

77. In the *Cala* case (fn 73) Ferris J. warned against the setting up of a series of "mini trials" as to assets through the requirement of full disclosure of assets in order to decide if payment could be made.

78. As a different division of the court did in *The Coral Rose (No. 3)* [1991] 2 Lloyd's Rep. 374 in refusing the payment of legal fees—being satisfied that Marc Rich would make funds available.

79. *Bekhor & Co.* v. *Bilton* [1981] Q.B. 923 (C.A.); *Z Ltd* v. *A* [1982] Q.B. 558, at pp. 577–578 (Lord Denning M.R.). It seems that all three members of the court in *Bekhor* though that the power was implicit in the statutory jurisdiction to grant injunctions, and that it did not stem from the Rules of the Supreme Court (Orders 24 and 26) dealing with such orders in "matters in question in the action" (which would not be relevant to a *Mareva* injunction). Whether the High Court has inherent power apart from the statutory jurisdiction remains uncertain as the members of the court took differing views. See also *CBS UK Ltd* v. *Lambert* [1982] 3 All E.R. 237. In a Chambers judgment in July 1988 a sale of decaying assets subject to a *Mareva* was ordered pursuant to RSC Order 29, r. 4—sale of perishable property (LMLN 229).

order must be to support the grant of the *Mareva* and not some other order,[80] and should not be used to overcome the obligations on a plaintiff to establish grounds for the granting of the injunction. An order for discovery is no longer necessary once opposition to the injunction is abandoned.[81] The court may appoint a receiver of foreign assets in support of a *Mareva*.[82] To prevent a breach of the injunction or aid in its enforcement the court may also order transfer of the assets from one account to another[83] or even to one country from another.[84] A defendant may be restrained by injunction from leaving the country.[85]

The most common of ancillary orders is that of disclosure of assets and if a *Mareva* is granted only in respect of English assets any order of disclosure will, it would seem, be restricted to those assets. However, independently of any *Mareva* once there is a judgment or arbitral award there may be an order for disclosure of assets within and outside the jurisdiction—so a post judgment or post award order may include a *Mareva* restricted to assets within the jurisdiction and a disclosure order in respect of worldwide assets.[86] An order of disclosure may be made against a third party who has "become mixed up" in arrangements to defeat the injunction.[87]

Any order for disclosure may be made subject to an undertaking that the information divulged may be used only in respect of the action which the *Mareva* supported.[88] Quite how effective such an undertaking is must be open to question—in particular whether it is realistic to limit the use to which such information is put once it is gained.

EFFECT OF THE INJUNCTION

IN RELATION TO THE DEFENDANT

As has been stressed, the injunction is directed at the defendant and is an order *in personam*. It is not an attachment of the assets to which it relates; nor does the obtaining of it provide a ground for addition of the person who obtains it as a party to the action. An act in breach will render the defendant liable for contempt of court, with the

---

80. *Bekhor & Co* v. *Bilton* [1981] Q.B. 923, at p. 942 (Ackner L.J.), p. 948 (Griffiths L.J.). In *Bekhor & Co* v. *Bilton* the majority held that Parker J. had purported to order discovery in aid of a *Mareva* injunction but had done so rather to establish whether there had been non-compliance with an order made by the judge and had, therefore, no jurisdiction to achieve his aims by the order made.

81. See *Bank of Crete SA* v. *Koskotas* [1991] 2 Lloyd's Rep. 587 (C.A.).

82. See *Derby* v. *Weldon (No. 2)* [1989] 1 All E.R. 1002.

83. *Bank Mellat* v. *Kazmi* [1989] 1 All E.R. 925 (C.A.).

84. *Derby* v. *Weldon (No. 6)* [1990] 2 All E.R. 263.

85. *Bayer AG* v. *Winter* [1986] 1 All E.R. 733 (C.A.)—exercise of general statutory discretion. But given the technical conditions of issuing a writ "*ne exeat regno*" it is unlikely that that writ would be used in support of a *Mareva*—it is restricted to support in "prosecution of an action" and requires action to be one for which the defendant was formerly liable to arrest at law and that the claim is equitable. See *Allied Arab Bank Ltd.* v. *Hajjar* [1987] 3 All E.R. 739.

86. *Gidrxslme Shipping* v. *Tantomar-Transportes* [1994] 2 Lloyd's Rep. 392; [1994] 4 All E.R. 507.

87. *Mercantile Group (Europe) AG* v. *Aiyela* [1994] 1 All E.R. 110—a post-judgment *Mareva*, but applicable to pre-judgment *Mareva* subject to the rule preventing discovery against a person who would later be compelled to give the information (*ibid*).

88. See e.g. *Gidrxslme Shipping* v. *Tantomar-Transportes* (fn 86); *Arab Monetary Fund* v. *Hashim (No. 2)* [1990] 1 All E.R. 673. See generally as to non-disclosure *Omar* v. *Omar* [1995] 3 All E.R. 571.

consequential sanctions of being barred from defending the substantive action, of a fine in the case of an individual, imprisonment and sequestration or seizure of assets.[89]

IN RELATION TO THIRD PARTIES

A major problem in relation to the granting of *Mareva* injunctions is that they are often granted in respect of assets owned by the defendant but in the possession or under the control of others. These parties may be of two distinct types. First, the asset may be in the hands of another who holds it (loosely speaking) either on behalf of or as due to the defendant. So a bank or an insurance broker may have funds due to the defendant. Secondly, a third party may have control of the defendant's assets as part of a contract with the defendant under which he is to deal with them in some way. So a shipowner may have the defendant's cargo on board his ship.

It is clear that, whatever the relationship with the defendant, a third party who knowingly acts contrary to an injunction directed at the defendant is liable to a finding of contempt of court. The injunction, therefore, imposes a considerable burden on those who have little connection with the dispute and no responsibility for its existence. in *Z Ltd* v. *A* and *The Theotokos*[90] the court was concerned particularly with the problem of banks where the bank was not a defendant. In *Z Ltd* v. *A* the Court of Appeal stressed the need for precise drafting of the order so that a bank could identify the assets subject to the order and would know the extent of its obligations. The order should not encompass assets in respect of which the bank had obligations to others unless clearly stated. In *The Theotokos* Lloyd J. held that set-off rights pursuant to contractual relationships predating notification of the injunction are not affected by the injunction.

The "knowledge" required for breach

In *Z Ltd* v. *A* Eveleigh L.J. examined in some detail the basis of the liability of third parties for contempt of court—it being a knowing interference "with the administration of justice by causing the order of the court to be thwarted". A prerequisite for liability, said Eveleigh L.J. was knowledge in the third party that "what he is doing is a breach of the terms of that injunction". In the case of a corporation it is necessary to show that an employee has knowingly acted in breach—liability would not necessarily follow if a breach occurred through an act of one employee who did not know of the order although another did, nor unless the bank was indifferent "to such a degree that was contumacious" should carelessness or recklessness lead to liability. However a bank may be in contempt through the failure of officers to carry out the necessary internal steps and ensure such internal communication as was necessary to comply with the injunction—where the failure was due to intent to flout the order or a high degree of negligence.[91]

---

89. See generally *Z Ltd.* v. *A* [1982] Q.B. 558; *Derby* v. *Weldon (No. 2)* [1989] 1 All E.R. 1002; *Z Bank* v. *Di* [1994] 1 Lloyd's Rep. 656.
90. [1983] 2 Lloyd's Rep. 204.
91. *Z Bank* v. *Di* [1994] 1 Lloyd's Rep. 656—sequestration of assets ordered.

Limitation on restrictions of action of third party by injunction

In *Z Ltd* v. *A* the Court of Appeal agreed that the freezing of a defendant's bank account did not affect obligations undertaken prior to the making of the order—such as letters of credit, bills of exchange,[92] to honour transactions backed by credit cards.[93] And, as has been said, the court stressed the need to specify any assets in regard to which the bank had obligations to others. In *The Theotoks*[94] Lloyd J. in effect applied this principle to set-off arrangements.

Effect of injunction on third party as grounds for refusal to grant

Where an injunction imposes a burden on a third party in the sense that an obligation is imposed or action is required, an indemnity for expenses may meet any reasonable claim based on inconvenience. Where, however, it would seriously affect the carrying on of business by a third party the balance must tilt against the granting of the injunction. In 1982 in *The Eleftherios*[95] the Court of Appeal had some harsh words to say in respect of the granting of a *Mareva* injunction restraining the removal from the jurisdiction of cargo loaded on board the ship named. The ship was on voyage charter and the evidence was that if she did not sail on the day the case was heard she would be delayed a week with consequence not only on trade but on the crew's private arrangements. Kerr L.J. contrasted this type of case—where the granting of the injunction would interfere with a contract between the defendant and the third party—with that where assets of the defendant are held incidentally to the general business of the third party.[96] In the former case, the rights of the third party must always prevail and a plaintiff cannot "merely to secure a benefit for himself coerce the third party into a serious risk of litigation or arbitration with the defendant". The plaintiff could not obtain the advantage of the order at the expense of the third party's business rights simply by proffering an indemnity. The other two members of the court expressed similar sentiments. The case provides a salutary balance to the enthusiasm for a remedy which in some cases may be too easily obtained in the light of its potentially drastic consequences.[97]

THE FORM OF THE ORDER—THE "MAXIMUM SUM" APPROACH

In 1982 in *Z Ltd* v. *A*[98] the normal practice of making a maximum sum order (whereby the defendant's assets are frozen up to a maximum amount) was approved. However, in cases where a bank account is a target, it was accepted that such an order was unworkable so

---

92. Although the proceeds paid into the defendant's account subject to the order will be affected by the order.

93. But it may be prudent to withdraw credit facilities once the order is known (per Kerr L.J. at p. 592). See for liability when no action was taken by a bank *Z Bank* v. *Di* (fn 89).

94. [1983] 2 Lloyd's Rep. 204. See now standard form [1994] 4 All E.R. 52.

95. [1982] 1 Lloyd's Rep. 351.

96. In *The Theotokos* Lloyd J. applied the principle of *The Eleftherios* to contractual arrangements between a bank and the defendant on the basis that contractual rights must prevail over the plaintiff's desire for security. See also *Sanders Lead Co. Inc.* v. *Entores Metal Brokers Ltd.* [1984] 1 Lloyd's Rep. 276.

97. In *The Pitsa T* [1987] 2 Lloyd's Rep. 404 Hirst J. applied *The Eleftherios* in weighing the potential loss of the shipowner and plaintiff voyage charterers suing time charterers, the time charter having expired.

98. [1982] Q.B. 558.

far as the bank was concerned as it would not know of other assets the defendant had. It was suggested, therefore, that the order should make different provisions in relation to his assets generally and those known to be in the hands of third parties. So, in relation to a particular bank account, the injunction should prohibit dealing in it except to the extent it exceeded the general maximum.[99] In *The Theotokos*[100] Lloyd J. elaborated on this guidance in advising that a *Mareva* injunction intended to be served on banks should contain a proviso indicating that it did not affect the exercise of any rights of set-off in respect of facilities granted to the defendant prior to the date of the injunction.[101] He stressed that by far "the greatest burden of policing *Mareva* injunctions falls on banks".

THE STANDARD FORMS 1994

Standard forms to be used, unless the judge hearing the application considers there is a good reason not to, are set out in a Practice Direction of 28 July 1994.[102] There is one form for prohibiting disposal of assets worldwide and another for prohibition of disposal within England and Wales. The forms are comprehensive and reflect the principles outlined in this chapter. There is a warning that disobedience may lead to imprisonment (in the case of an individual), a fine or seizure of assets. The form prohibits disposal of assets up to a maximum value with mention if appropriate of particular assets, and provides for exceptions to the order (living and legal expenses and dealing in the ordinary course of business). In a worldwide *Mareva* there is the clause limiting the effect on third parties, set out *supra*.

There is a direction that the defendant must not avoid the injunction through others. It is stated that no third party notified of the order must knowingly assist in breach, but that banks are exempt as regards right of set off. A bank is under no obligation to enquire as to the application of any money withdrawn by a defendant if the withdrawal appears to be permitted by the order. The order may be varied. In addition the form contains the undertakings by the plaintiff discussed earlier in this chapter.

COMPARISON OF ARREST AND "MAREVA" INJUNCTION AS PROVISIONAL REMEDIES—A SUMMARY

(i) Arrest lies only as part of an action *in rem* and is available only as ancillary to an action within the jurisdiction of the English court; a *Mareva* injunction is a remedy *in personam*, and, apart from the Civil Jurisdiction and Judgments Act 1982, ss.24 and 25, is available only as ancillary to an action *in personam* when the defendant is within the jurisdiction of the English courts.

(ii) Arrest is available in support of arbitral proceedings only indirectly after issue of a writ *in rem*; a *Mareva* injunction is available directly in arbitral proceedings.

---

99. *Ibid*, at p. 589 (Lord Denning M.R., Kerr L.J.). It seems as if Lord Denning was more ready to accept the propriety of an order referring to all the defendant's assets (*ibid*).
100. [1983] 2 Lloyd's Rep. 204.
101. It would perhaps be preferable to refer to the date (and time) of notification of the injunction.
102. [1994] 4 All E.R. 52.

(iii) Only one ship (and/or one ship's cargo or appropriate freight) may be arrested for each claim: a *Mareva* injunction has no restriction as to the number of assets save the amount of the claim.

(iv) The use of an asset under arrest for any purpose is inconsistent with custody of the Marshal; the use of assets subject to a *Mareva* injunction will be permitted contrary to the injunction to allow for the carrying on of business or personal life.

(v) Arrest initially depends on the issue of a warrant by a registry official to which an applicant is entitled in compliance with procedural requirements; a *Mareva* injunction depends on the exercise of judicial discretion.

(vi) Arrest is available *ex parte* simply on assertion of claim *in rem* through issue of writ *in rem*; a *Mareva* injunction *ex parte* requires establishment of a good arguable case and of the risk of the defendant failing to satisfy a judgment or award.

(vii) Save for the possible application of the Civil Jurisdiction and Judgments Act 1982, s.26, no security or undertaking is required from the plaintiff on arrest; the granting of a *Mareva* injunction will normally require an undertaking in damages.

(viii) Arrested ship, cargo or freight is in the custody of the Admiralty Marshal; a *Mareva* injunction does not affect custody or possession.

(ix) An arrest follows an issue of a writ *in rem* which creates a preferred claim and enables the claim to be asserted against purchasers; the *Mareva* injunction creates no proprietary interest in any asset.

(x) Third parties may intervene in an action *in rem* and may protect their interests by a caveat; there seems less right to intervene in proceedings for a *Mareva* injunction except through substantive process started on that party's behalf.

(xi) In arrest, a solicitor's undertaking in respect of the Admiralty Marshal's expenses and costs is required; in a *Mareva* injunction expenses and costs may depend on the plaintiff's undertaking.

(xii) The effect on third parties of arrest (as, for example, arrest of a ship on owners of cargo shipped in it) is irrelevant to the grant of the warrant of arrest; the effect on third parties of a *Mareva* injunction may be a critical factor in the discretion to grant the injunction.

(xiii) Procedural distinctions reflecting the well developed remedy of arrest include the need for an affidavit to be filed (in *Mareva* proceedings an undertaking to file may be sufficient), proceedings to be started (in relation to *Mareva* injunctions again an undertaking to start may suffice), and the need for the court office to be open (*Mareva* injunctions depend on the availability of a judge).

(xiv) Whether arrest will lie after an English or foreign judgment is doubtful; a *Mareva* injunction may be granted to aid execution of a judgment.

(xv) Arrest may serve the function both of "security" for the claim and a jurisdiction ground for the substantive action—apart from possible arguments as to submission the grant of a *Mareva* injunction does not found any substantive jurisdiction.

(xvi) It would seem that a court may be more ready to pierce the corporate veil in the context of a *Mareva* than arrest.

(xvii) Arrest is available only for property within England; the *Mareva* may relate to property within or outside England.

(xviii) That a "defendant in an action *in rem* is irrelevant to arrest; in regard to *Mareva* the defendant must be amenable to jurisdiction *in personam*.

(xvix) A stay of substantive proceedings does not mean that arrest is not available or that there is no power to grant a *Mareva*.

(xx) Apart from (xvix) above there is no power to arrest for foreign proceedings; whether, given jurisdiction over the defendant ((xviii) above), there is power to grant a *Mareva* is uncertain.[103]

---

103. For a review of the availability of provisional measures in numerous jurisdictions in respect of foreign assets, see *Attacking Foreign Assets*, ed. Campbell, Lloyd's of London Press, 1992.

PART IV

Security on the Merits—
The Lien Concept

We come now to the "security" aspect of maritime claims in the sense that such claims attract an interest in an asset, enabling the claimant to enforce the claim against that asset in priority to at least the ordinary claim for damages. Inextricably connected with that aspect is the overused and ill-defined term "lien". Each maritime claim listed in the Supreme Court Act 1981 if enforced by an action *in rem* is said to attract a lien and, in a more general sense, liens are attached to claims outside those there listed. Further, maritime claims may attract differing kinds of lien—based on maritime concepts and adapted from the general legal framework. The first task therefore is to give meaning to the word "lien" and to contrast it with other similar, but distinct, legal concepts.

CHAPTER 17

Nature and Development of Liens

1. THE NATURE OF A "LIEN"—OR WHAT'S IN A WORD?

The legal idea of a "lien" as giving some benefit to the claimant over and above a simple legal claim for a remedy against a particular defendant is common to both civil and common law. Its application is not. The label "lien" serves often to conceal the varieties of benefit which flow from it as between and within different legal systems.

For the most part, liens are not registrable and, therefore, those who may seek to acquire interests in assets have no means of checking for the prior existence of a lien save enquiry from the seller, mortgagor or other creditor—not always a method of certain reliability. Further, the transferability of liens is a matter of some doubt. They are therefore interests of prime importance and of no inconsiderable uncertainty.

The primary purpose of a "lien" is to confer a proprietary interest in an asset as security for a judgment or a claim, the claim itself being based on one of a number of substantive and recognized legal relationships. As a proprietary interest, the "lien" is enforceable against third parties. As such, it has characteristics in common with a "mortgage" and a "charge" and (particularly as regards the "charge") is sometimes not distinguished from them. At the very least, loose terminology tends to confusion and at the worst creates it.

LIEN AND MORTGAGE

Just as in English land law so in sea law the lien must be compared to the mortgage. It is said in the context of land that the distinction lies in its root—mortgage rooted in intention and lien in implication of law. But in the context of chattels, a lien can be and often is, rooted in contract. It is said in the context of chattels that the distinction is based on the vesting of ownership.[1] In a mortgage it vests in the mortgagee, in a lien it remains in the lienor. But a mortgage of chattels may be created by giving the mortgagee simply a right of seizure or by a transfer only of "equitable ownership" which leaves the legal title in the mortgagor.

It is suggested that the distinction between mortgage and lien cannot be seen in the method of creation or in the presence or absence of intention. The mortgage and lien are distinct in purpose and largely in nature. The mortgage is a well-established method of financing a venture. It arises only on the intentional acts of the mortgagor and mortgagee

---

1. See Megarry's *Manual of The Law of Real Property* (1993). Pledge is akin to a possessory lien insofar as possession is at its heart but it is said the pledgee has a "special property" in the chattel. See Bridge, *Personal Property Law*, 1993 at p. 138. See further *infra*.

and rights flow from the transaction. Once into the mortgage framework the rights *and* remedies follow as a necessary consequence.

It is not so with the developed lien. The common characteristic of all liens is the purpose of providing security for a claim based on a legal transaction or situation which is *not* described by the word *"lien"*. So, a seaman to whom wages are due has a lien—*to enforce his contractual right.* The lien is built on a right having its root not in a "lien transaction" but in something which has a legal character of its own. A "mortgage" describes the transaction and its remedies (it now envelops its contractual root); a lien describes only how a right is to be enforced. It does not describe the right. Indeed, in Admiralty, a mortgage is also a statutory lien.

LIEN AND CHARGE

The word "charge" (at least in English law) is used even more loosely than "lien". In some contexts (usually land) it means any encumbrance on a title. In its narrower meaning it carries the meaning of security for a debt or other obligation and in this sense it overlaps with both the lien and the mortgage. The idea of "charge" in some instances has been developed along the lines of the development of the mortgage to create an independent legal concept. But in other contexts similar to the lien it remains simply a general description of a method of enforceability of a claim based on specified substantive grounds (such as, for example, a breach of contract). And, more, a lien has been described as resulting in a charge, indicating that a charge may be regarded as a security interest encompassing the lien.

Certainly the lien is seen by many as usually indicating a security interest arising by operation of law imposed on certain relationships such as is the unpaid vendor's lien. But just as certainly (particularly in maritime law) liens may be created by contract and in that respect may be identical to a charge. Whether or not it is will depend on the nature of the lien created.[2]

The floating charge

A floating charge is one taken on corporate assets leaving the company free to deal with the assets in the ordinary course of business. The charge "floats over" the assets until, in accordance with the contract creating it, an event occurs (such as the appointment of a receiver) which causes it to crystallize and become a charge on specific assets.

Initially a lien was envisaged as a security interest in a tangible asset but the courts have construed "lien" clauses in contracts in accordance with their purpose. There is little evidence that a court would take the view that a contract to create a "lien" would be non-effective because it was aimed at a security interest which apart from the contract the law did not categorize as such. So in *The Annangel Glory*[3] Saville J. construed a clause in a charterparty declaring that an owner had a lien on all sub freights for any amounts due to

2. See e.g. *The Lancaster* [1980] 2 Lloyd's Rep. 497. In *The Ugland Trailer* [1985] 2 Lloyd's Rep. 372 Nourse J. distinguished between the equitable lien created by operation of law and a lien (a charge) created by contract—but thought the distinction one of terminology only. See generally Chaps. 21, 22.

3. [1988] 1 Lloyd's Rep. 45. See also *The Lancaster* [1980] 2 Lloyd's Rep. 497, a "lien" in favour of a time charterer against an owner being construed as the right to retain use of the ship similar to a possessory lien. See Chap. 22.

create as from the contract a floating security consisting of a right to be exercised if sums became due. Such an approach simply underlines that in English law "lien" of itself has little meaning save that of a security interest recognized by the law—perhaps other than a mortgage.

2. THE DEVELOPMENT OF LIENS IN ENGLISH LAW

In English law the types of lien are maritime, possessory, statutory and equitable. Of these all but the "maritime" exist both within and outside Admiralty.

A. COMMON LAW, EQUITY AND STATUTE

These liens are applicable in Admiralty as they are elsewhere. They therefore apply in respect of all maritime claims.

The possessory lien

The possessory lien as a concept is rooted in judicial creativity in the common law and was well established at the beginning of the nineteenth century. It was based on the enforceability of a claim through retention of chattels in which the person against whom the claim was to be made had an interest. In many systems such a right is encompassed in a "right of retention" without applying the label "lien". In English law the right of retention is the possessory lien. It is both a remedy in that it is a method of asserting a claim based on grounds entirely independent of the "lien" (e.g. debt), and it creates a "right" in that it may translate a claim enforceable only against the other party into an interest enforceable against a third party (creditors or purchasers). Parties may create it by contract and, subject to contract, it is implied into certain transactions. It is discussed in Chapter 20.

The equitable lien

Being a creature of equity the enforceability of the equitable lien against third parties is limited. As with other equitable interests, it is enforceable against the creator and those who acquire interests subsequently to it and, if the interest acquired is "legal", have notice of it.[4] On the surface it appears to be an example of an equitable recognition of a common law concept. Its affinity with the right of retention is, first, that it may be implied into a relationship or created by contract. As is usual, courts of equity were more ready than at common law to imply (or impose) a "lien" because of fairness or conduct. As a consequence, the equitable right remains more flexible today. Secondly, its effect follows that of the common law in that it translates a claim into a proprietary security interest enforceable against third parties (other creditors or purchasers), but in this instance only with the limitation based on notice. But it differs fundamentally from the common law "possessory lien" in that it does not depend on the retention—or acquisition—of possession. It is discussed in Chapter 21.

---

4. Registration (as to which, see *infra*), statutory provisions and conduct of the parties affect this principle. See generally Chaps. 1 and 23.

The statutory lien

Liens may be created by statute. Their characteristics are those specified in the statute. A prime example is the right of retention conferred on the unpaid seller of goods by the Sale of Goods Act 1979.[5] Such a provision may be the basis for an argument that it operates not only to create a lien but in that context to exclude all other liens.

B. ADMIRALTY

Applicability of liens of common law, equity and statute

The liens established outside Admiralty apply within it. So a clause in a charterparty may create an equitable lien. In addition to the application of common law possessory liens (for example, to the ship repairer) Admiralty itself applied the lien to maritime relationships as, for example, in creating the salvor's possessory lien.

Admiralty liens—the maritime lien and statutory lien

The concept of the lien has developed to a greater extent than elsewhere through the *maritime lien* and the action *in rem* or *statutory lien*. The maritime lien is discussed in Chapter 18 and the statutory lien in Chapter 19.

The development of the lien in the maritime sphere has been part of a pattern drawn not only by statute, common law and equity but through the application of civil law principles by the Court of Admiralty. The jurisdiction of the Admiral's Court and its successors is as important to the development of maritime law as is that of the Chancellor to the development of general principles through equity. The conflict between the common law courts and the Court of Admiralty in the seventeenth century has been well documented even if its results are not entirely agreed.[6] It is sufficient here to note that through the Court of Admiralty came principles not applicable outside that court and that the conflict itself may have been the root of the development of the liens unique to maritime law.

3. WHICH LIEN AND WHEN?

Liens and other interests may, therefore, be created by contract[7] or may follow from the creation of a particular relationship. The four types of lien vary as to the scope and methods of enforceability. It is therefore important to identify not only the various types of liens recognized by a legal system but to appreciate the extent to which the creation of

---

5. Sections 41 and 43. As to the effect of sale by a seller who has exercised his lien, see s. 48.

6. See Wiswall, "The Development of Admiralty Jurisdiction and Practice since 1800", CUP 1970. See also Ryan (1968) 7 Western Ontario L.R. 173.

7. As to the difficulties which may be caused to established financing arrangements, see the comments of Roskill L.J. in *The Panglobal Friendship* [1978] 1 Lloyd's Rep. 368, at p. 371.

a lien is (a) by operation of the law and (b) is permitted to be by contract. The "maritime lien" and "statutory lien" follow by operation of law from a relationship or claim. A number of maritime liens are contractually based (as, for example, seaman's wages) but will follow from the contract unless waived. The possessory and equitable lien may either follow from a relationship recognized as founding the lien or be created by contract.

It is sometimes a difficult matter of construction as to which interest has been created[8] and if a lien it may be uncertain as to which type of lien has been created. A contract giving a party simply a "lien" may be construed as either conferring a possessory lien such as the lien for freight normally given in a bill of lading to a shipowner over cargo or an equitable lien.[9] A possessory lien will start only on the obtaining of possession and the equitable lien on the event specified as creating it.[10] So it is essential in respect of an equitable lien to identify whether an agreement contemplating future security is a contract to create a lien on an event occurring or the immediate creation of a lien to come into effect on an event occurring. Issues arising from imprecise contractual terms (particularly in standard form charterparties or bills of lading) are discussed in Chapter 22.

The effect of a lien created by contract or its exercise on any other interest created by the same or another contract will depend on the contract. The exercise by an owner against a charterer of a possessory lien on cargo will not render the vessel off hire,[11] but the claiming of possession of cargo by a salvor may be either as a bailee or as a lienee, with consequential effect on the parties' rights.[12]

ONE LIEN OR MORE?

It will not always follow that only one lien exists. So a claim may qualify for both a statutory lien in Admiralty and a maritime lien, and a claimant may rely on that which is most beneficial to him. On the other hand it is essential to appreciate that events may lead either to the creation of more than one lien or the supervention of one by another. Where an interest is established as flowing from a relationship and the contract creating the relationship provides for another interest which, by its nature, supervenes, it may be that in the event of the express interest failing no claim be made that the implied one survives. So the equitable lien which attaches in favour of an unpaid vendor may be prevented from arising by the stipulation for a legal charge.[13] Contractual provision of security may

---

8. A deposit of documents may create an equitable mortgage or simply be a pledge of the documents. See Bridge *op. cit.* at p. 139. As to the effect of delivery of a bill of lading, sea waybill or ship's delivery order to a consignee to whom the rights in the contract are transferred, see Carriage of Goods By Sea Act 1992 (as to which see 1993 LCMLQ 436).

9. Or possibly an equitable charge, fixed or floating. See e.g. *The Panglobal Friendship* [1978] 1 Lloyd's Rep. 368; *The Annangel Glory* [1988] 1 Lloyd's Rep. 45. On the particular point of that case (the construction of NYPE Clause 18—1993 Clause 23) see *The Lancaster* [1980] 2 Lloyd's Rep. 497 and Chap. 21.

10. However, the contractual right to the lien may be good against not only the other party to the contract but also an assignee of the contract in much the same way as a set-off good against the assignor may be good against the assignee. See *George Barker (Transport) Ltd* v. *Eynon* [1974] 1 Lloyd's Rep. 65 and Chap. 22.

11. *Lyle Shipping* v. *Cardiff Corpn* [1900] 2 Q.B. 638, nor affect an otherwise valid notice of readiness, see *Gill and Duffus SA* v. *Ronda Futures* [1994] 2 Lloyd's Rep. 67.

12. See *The Winson* [1982] A.C. 939, [1982] 1 Lloyd's Rep. 117.

13. See e.g. *Burston Finance* v. *Speirway* [1974] 1 W.L.R. 1648.

operate as a waiver or suspension of a lien, or a prohibition of its exercise unless the security proved non-effective.[14]

PRIORITIES

Priorities between liens and between liens and other interests will be discussed in Chapter 23. In this general introduction it is sufficient to emphasize that not all liens have an identical scope of enforceability and that the critical question for a claimant is often not whether a lien has been created but whether it confers priority over other claimants. Priority depends on particular rules, the distinction between legal and equitable interests and the effect of registrability and registration.

4. FOREIGN LIENS

Foreign law plays a large role in the maritime area. As in all areas involving cases with a foreign element, an essential issue is the law which governs the creation and enforceability of the lien. Secondly, reference to a foreign law raises the question of recognition of foreign liens by the forum. These questions will be discussed in Chapter 26.

There have been three attempts at the creation of an international framework in respect of some of the rules relevant to maritime liens and mortgages. These attempts resulted in the International Conventions for the Unification of Certain Rules Relating to Maritime Liens and Mortgages 1926 and 1967 and the International Convention on Maritime Liens and Mortgages 1993. Neither of the Conventions of 1926 or 1967 has been a conspicuous success. The 1993 Convention was agreed by 65 states on 6 May 1993 and it was then said by the Secretary General of the International Maritime Organization that conditions for attracting a large number of ratifications could not be better. Certainly there is much to be said for uniformity in the area. However, little seems to have changed either in content or atmosphere since 1967. It is to be hoped that there will be greater national efforts than those to date. The Conventions are discussed in Chapter 18.

5. LIENS AND THE REGISTRATION OF INTERESTS

Registration of interests can perform one of three functions: first, simple publicity—to ensure notice; secondly, provision of priority over subsequent interests, non-registration rendering a registrable interest liable to defeat; and thirdly, priority over both prior and subsequent non-registered interests.

Registration plays a limited part in English maritime law. It is provided in respect of ownership and mortgage of some but not all ships and even in these fields its particular functions have not been precisely worked out. It is also relevant through the application in a maritime context of principles of other areas, in particular, registration provisions relating to company shares and charges. The effect of non-registration varies at least in degree, in that non-registration of a transfer of company shares simply affects its priority

14. See Chap. 18.

over other non-registered interests while non-registration of a charge by a company renders it void against the liquidator and any creditor.

6. INSOLVENCY AND LIENS

Insolvency of a company or bankruptcy of an individual has its effect on liens insofar as there may be restraint of proceedings, adjustment of transactions, avoidance of dispositions of property and possessory liens, and power to dispose of an asset so as to remove any security interest in it.

1. COMPANIES

Winding up or liquidation

A company which is insolvent or threatening to become insolvent may be wound up (or liquidated). Winding up may be voluntary or by order of the court[15] and marks the end of the company. Once a winding up petition is made to a court, it has power to restrain proceedings against the company.[16]

In a winding up by a court any disposition of company property or transfer of shares is void unless the court otherwise orders. There are powers to "adjust" some prior transactions within specified periods prior to the commencement of the winding up—where preference has been shown, extortionate credit transfers, transfers at undervalue and avoidance of certain floating charges.[17] Possessory liens on books and documents (save documents of title held as such) are unenforceable to the extent that possession may be denied.[18] Further, any attachment, sequestration, distress or execution put in force against the company after the commencement of the winding up is void.[19] After the winding up order the court may give leave to proceed against the company.[20]

Administration orders

An administration order may be made by a court in relation to a company heading for or having arrived at insolvency with the object of restoring it to profitability and preventing it being wound up. Under the order an administrator will be appointed to manage the company.[21] The achievement of the purpose is unlikely to succeed if all outstanding

---

15. Insolvency Act 1986, s. 73. A voluntary winding up application may be made to a court for the exercise of powers available on a winding up by a court (s.112).

16. *Ibid*, s. 126. A secured creditor would normally be allowed to proceed. See *Re Aro Co. Ltd.* [1980] 1 All E.R. 1067 and Chap. 18.

17. *Ibid*, ss.127, 238–247.

18. *Ibid*, s.246.

19. *Ibid*, s.128. This provision is to be read subject to the power to stay proceedings (s.126) and to permit proceedings against the company once a winding up order is made (s.130(2)). See *Re Exhill Coal Mining Co.* (1864) 4 De G.J. and Sm. 377. As to arrest and winding up see Chap. 10.

20. Section 130(2).

21. An alternative and a possibly preceding attempt to avoid winding up is the appointment of an "administrative receiver" by or on behalf of debenture holders secured by a floating charge (*ibid*, s.29(2)). Such a receiver must vacate office on the making of an administration order (s.11(1)(b)).

claims are made and so a balance has to be struck between creditors rights and company survival.[22]

So for a converse reason to the winding up of a company many of the court's powers to contest claims are applicable on the making of an administration order. Once a petition for an administrative order is presented, save with the leave of the court no steps may be taken to enforce any security over the company's property and "no other proceedings or no execution or other legal process" may be commenced or continued.[23] Once an order is made the prohibition continues with the qualification that there may be enforcement or legal process with the consent of the administrator. The administrator may dispose of company property subject to a floating charge and by court order any other security as if it were not so subject.[24] A condition of a court order must be that the proceeds of the disposal are to be applied discharging the sums secured by the security.[25]

2. INDIVIDUALS—BANKRUPTCY

Similar to the provision in relation to a company any time when bankruptcy proceedings are pending or an individual has been adjudged bankrupt a court may stay "any action execution or other legal process against the property or person" of the debtor or bankrupt.[26] After the making of a bankruptcy order no unsecured creditor may have any remedy in respect of the debt against the property or person of the bankrupt and may commence proceedings only with the leave of the court.[27] It is further provided that no creditor who prior to the bankruptcy order has issued execution against the goods or land of the bankrupt or attached a debt can retain the benefit against the trustee of the estate or the official receiver unless the execution or attachment was complete before the making of the order.[28]

7. MARITIME LIENS, STATUTORY LIENS IN ADMIRALTY AND THE ACTION "IN REM"

A certain number of claims are foundations for the "maritime lien" and the security interest thereby created enforceable by an action *in rem*, and certain other specified claims form the basis for the bringing of an action *in rem* without qualifying as maritime liens. The bringing of the action *in rem* confers on the claimant a security interest in the property

---

22. These provisions of the Insolvency Act should be construed with the underlying purpose in mind (see *British Airport plc* v. *Powdrill* [1990] 2 All E.R. 493).
23. Section 11(3)(c)(d). Security is "any mortgage charge lien or other security" (s.248).
24. Section 15(1)–(3).
25. Section 15(4)(5). Where the disposal does not yield a sum which would be gained in the open market the deficiency must be made up in discharging the sum owed (*ibid*).
26. Section 285(1)(2). There is no reason to think that the former practice of not staying proceedings by a secured creditor (see *Re Evelyn* [1894] 2 Q.B. 302) has changed.
27. Section 285(3)(4).
28. Section 346(1), the provision being subject to the court's power under s.285 to stay the proceedings.

of which it is the target similar in nature to but not equivalent in priority or arguably scope of enforceability to a maritime lien. In some instances (ownership, possession and mortgage) the interest enforced by the action *in rem* is proprietary. In the majority the claim or interest is of itself not proprietary (e.g. carriage of goods) but the issue of the writ *in rem* makes it so. In both contexts a proprietary interest exists.

To call the proprietary interests *created* by the writ *in rem*, where apart from the writ no such interest existed, anything but "*liens*" would be to ignore the similarity as regards security and enforceability characteristics which they have in common with other proprietary interests. To call them simply "statutory liens" is to put them into a rag-bag of different liens so called only because they are founded on statutes. It would be to ignore the paramount importance in maritime law of their common characteristics. They are a legal category and should be recognized as such. In this work they are entitled "statutory liens in Admiralty".

Whether claims which by their nature are enforceable as proprietary interests (owner-ship, possession and mortgage) are also accurately described as "statutory liens in Admiralty" depends on whether the action *in rem* brings to them a security interest not already attached to the claim. The categorization as liens or not is important in defining the characteristics of the claim (see Chapter 23).

Because of the essential connection with the action *in rem* any enquiry into the characteristics of maritime liens and statutory liens in Admiralty involves enquiry into the nature and scope of the action *in rem*. The characteristics of the maritime and statutory lien cannot be defined apart from the nature and scope of the action *in rem*. While, however, the scope of the action *in rem* may indicate the scope of a maritime or statutory lien, focus on the action *in rem* instead of the lien would be misleading.

The action in rem and action in personam

It may be that historically the action *in rem* was but a means to persuade a defendant to participate *in personam*, and arrest and judicial disposal of property an additional method of persuasion. In modern times while the connection with *in rem* to *in personam* jurisdiction is maintained, the primary element of enforceability by an action *in rem* is the resulting lien. The lien (maritime or statutory) is a substantive interest enforced or created by the issue of a writ *in rem* and, if necessary, arrest and judicial sale.

Focus on the action *in rem* has led to confusion in English law between provisional measure (arrest), jurisdiction to consider a claim (through the action *in rem*), the interest being enforced (lien) and enforcement (judicial sale). As has been seen, international connections are leading to the destruction of the mandatory and somewhat narrow link between provisional measure and English substantive proceedings. Similarly neither historical development nor failure internationally to link arrest and lien should now conceal the realization that the fundamental justification for arrest and the action *in rem* itself is the enforcement of the lien. It is the liens which have to be justified in terms of policy. The acceptance of the lien as lying at the heart of many unique Admiralty concepts means that the action *in rem* is seen as what it now is—a method of enforcing specified proprietary interests in relation to an asset—by definition against others having interests in that asset. It is therefore not as a cause of action as a means to *in personam* jurisdiction that the enquiry into the nature and scope of the action *in rem* must be approached but to identify the scope of the lien itself or even as simply a separate cause of action.

1. THE CATEGORIES OF CLAIM ENFORCEABLE BY ACTION *"IN REM"*

The action *in rem* for claims to which maritime liens did not attach came on the scene in 1840 and 1861 at about the same time as the "maritime lien" became recognized as a general concept with a number of applications. It may have once been arguable that the sole differences between the maritime and statutory liens lay in the time of their creation and in priority. If this was so the action *in rem* operated in an identical way whatever claim or whichever category of liens it was relevant in enforcing.

2. THE SUPREME COURT ACT 1981[29] AND THE ACTION *"IN REM"*

The claims enforceable by an action *in rem* are now set out in the Supreme Court Act 1981. Under that Act and its predecessors the action *in rem* is linked to maritime claims in four distinct categories.

First, in s.21(3) the Act provides for the enforcement of maritime liens by an action *in rem*. Secondly, in s.21(2) the Act simply provides for enforceability of the claims listed in s.20(2)(a)–(c) and (s) through an action *in rem* against the ship or property involved. Thirdly, through the "sweeping up" clause (s.20(1)(c)) it arguably retains such jurisdiction *in rem* as existed prior to 1 November 1875. Finally, in s.21(4) the Act specifies the conditions of liability *in personam* required for an action *in rem* to lie in enforcing the claims listed in s.20(1)(e)–(r).

(i) Claims based on maritime lien (s.21(3))

The critical questions are, first, the characteristics of the maritime lien and, secondly, the scope of the action *in rem*. Only by enquiry into the historical development of these two matters can s.21(3) of the Supreme Court Act 1981 be given meaning.

(ii) Claims based on s.20(2)(a)–(c), (s)

These claims relate to ownership, possession, mortgage and the collection of claims based on forfeiture or condemnation of a ship or goods and droits of Admiralty. They are, therefore, not the most common of claims but, certainly as regards the first three, not unimportant. As with the maritime lien, the statute provides simply that the claims are enforceable by an action *in rem*, leaving the characteristics and scope to be unearthed through historical reference. So, again, it requires enquiry to give meaning to the statutory provision.

(iii) Claims within the sweeping up clause (s.20(1)(c))

If *in rem* jurisdiction is maintained the enquiry is purely historical and amounts to a voyage of discovery on nineteenth century seas. It is relevant to liens in Admiralty insofar as Admiralty jurisdiction *in rem* prior to 1 November 1875 exceeded that now expressed in the Supreme Court Act 1981.

---

29. For relevant text, see Appendix 1.

(iv) Claims based on s.20(2)(e)–(r)

Liability *in rem* depends on liability *in personam* as specified in s.21(4). The prerequisites for the creation of the "lien" flowing from the use of the action *in rem* are, therefore, matters of statutory construction. The historical nature of the action *in rem* is irrelevant.

It will be seen therefore that only in respect of (iv) are the characteristics of the action *in rem* specified by the statute. In (ii) and (if the jurisdiction exists) in (iii) the "action *in rem*" may define the claim but the scope of the action *in rem* is not defined. In (i) (maritime liens) neither the interest nor its method of enforceability are defined. It is therefore essential to any discussion of maritime and statutory liens in Admiralty that the nature and role of the action *in rem* is examined.

3. REMAINING UNCERTAINTIES OF THE ACTION "*IN REM*"

Lacking statutory specification the characteristics of the maritime lien and the action *in rem* must be gathered from judicial development and, to some extent, rules of procedure such as RSC Order 75. There is one aspect which remains unsettled and which reflects on nature and scope of the maritime lien and, insofar as it is not defined by statute, the statutory lien, i.e. the extent to which *in personam* liability is required for liability *in rem*—in particular the extent to which the action is enforceable against property the owner of which is not liable *in personam*.[30]

This issue will be discussed in succeeding chapters in relation to particular claims but common to each is the origin of the action *in rem*. Historians continue to argue vehemently about the origin and judges continue to use their views of it as reasons for adjudging the present consequences and characteristics of the action. The contest focuses essentially on the basic principle—is it procedural or based on personification of the ship?

4. LIEN AND ACTION "*IN REM*"

As the action *in rem* is the mode of enforceability of the maritime lien and the foundation for the statutory lien it follows that the nature and scope of the lien are dependent on the nature and scope of the action *in rem*. It is, however, important to stress that the labels of "procedure" and "personification" are descriptions rather than any foundation for a conclusion—and modern reality may dictate that neither label can fully describe the action as it now is.

(i) Historical development of the action in rem

Procedure

One school of thought (followed in part by English courts) maintains that the action *in rem* was procedural in origin. Its purpose was to persuade a defendant to appear and one

---

30. Other unsettled aspects go to *in personam* aspects of an *in rem* claim—the liability in an action *in rem* of a person in excess of the value of the property or to *in personam* remedies. These issues do not as such affect the lien save insofar as such liabilities if they exist blur the boundaries between the concepts of *in rem* and *in personam* liability.

powerful weapon was the seizure of his assets. The view is exemplified by the judgment in 1892 in *The Dictator*[31] in which Jeune J. held that shipowners were liable for the full salvage award once they had appeared in an action *in rem* even though bail of less value had been accepted. The judge made it clear that the basis of liability was liability for the full amount found due, rather than any principle based on the ability of claim up to the full value of the ship if the bail lodged was less than that value.[32]

The judgment started from the proposition that in the eighteenth century courts of common law, in considering limitations on Admiralty jurisdiction through prohibition on proceedings, distinguished between actions based on jurisdiction over a *res* and jurisdiction over individuals. Secondly, said Jeune J., Admiralty did not regard the action *in rem* as a "special form of action" but looked upon arrest of personal property as a means of obtaining bail for satisfaction of a judgment. The distinction between "*in rem*" and "*in personam*" turned on whether goods or person was arrested. Thirdly, arrest of the person had become obsolete by the end of the eighteenth century and, finally, the limitation that the property arrested was that in regard to which a claim was made, became established "as the idea of a pre-existing maritime lien developed". As a result, said Jeune J., arrest became the distinctive feature of the action *in rem*. In supporting this approach, it has been said the maritime lien is "a later outgrowth from the practice of arrest."[33]

This historical doctrine is supported by Marsden[34] and Roscoe[35] who both stressed that in early Admiralty practice actions would be started by arrest of the debtor or of his goods. In 1935 in *The Beldis*[36] the Court of Appeal rejected a contention that arrest was not restricted to the property in connection with the claim, primarily on the ground that such restriction was clearly accepted by 1851 (in *The Bold Buccleugh*).[37] The court accepted the accounts of Marsden and Roscoe and emphasized that in all probability arrest was a procedure to provide security (as Marsden said) and provided a jurisdictional ground in the struggle between Admiralty and common law courts. Roscoe had argued that the prohibitions issued by common law courts in respect of actions against individuals encouraged the development of proceedings "*in rem*", with which the common law courts had nothing to do.

Personification

The personification school (followed in the United States and Canada) looks on the action *in rem* as an action against the "*res*" (usually the ship) as the defendant. It follows that the action is independent of any action against the owner and that it is based on a substantive claim against the thing.

Price[38] and Hebert[39] see the availability of an action *in rem* independent of a maritime lien as a consequence of the procedural view. But this is so only if the action *in rem* itself is seen as procedural and substantive effects limited to the maritime lien. In effect, it is an

31. [1892] P. 64, 304.
32. As to the ability to rearrest a ship after the lodging of bail, see Chap. 15.
33. Mansfield (1888) 4 L.Q.R. 385.
34. See "Select Pleas in Court of Admiralty", Seldon Soc. p. xxi.
35. *Admiralty Practice* (3rd edn) at p. 27, citing Clark's *Praxis*.
36. [1936] P. 51.
37. (1851) 7 Moo. P.C. 267.
38. *Law of Maritime Liens* (1936) at p. 12.
39. See 4 Tulane Law Review 380 (1929–30) at p. 388.

argument which depends for its validity on the assumption that once the "action *in rem*" spread outside the "maritime lien" it somehow changed its character. It therefore begs the question of procedure or substance through an assumption that a change in character flowed from a wider scope. But, in reality, the question of the nature of the action remains.

There are eighteenth century (and earlier) cases stressing the liability of the ship as distinct from the owners.[40] So the maritime lien may not simply have developed from the weapon of arrest used to get at the defendant but may have been attached to substantive rights which in *The Bold Buccleugh* were brought together into a legal group. On this view the lien is not the consequence of arrest but rather the continued acceptance of a substantive right enforced by arrest and sale. In a sense, the arrest is procedural but it is so because it is attached to a substantive right.

A third view—hypothec and deodand

Holmes J. attempted to trace the origins of the liens insofar as they were contractual to the Roman law of hypothec and insofar as they were tortious (i.e. collision) to a responsibility of the thing for the harm analogous to the old English idea of deodand. Under this theory the "thing" doing the harm is delivered up. The historical evidence to support this third view is even more slight than that supporting its opponents. But, by the middle of the nineteenth century, the language of the hypothec was being used to describe the lien in maritime law[41] and to distinguish it from the possessory lien of common law.

The three views are of relevance today not only because, according to their protagonists, they reflect the development of the action *in rem*, but because each view has certain consequences as to enforceability and liability flowing from it. In particular they are relevant to the issue of whether the whole edifice of action *in rem* arrest and lien is simply a matter of procedure or whether the action *in rem* and arrest are, with judicial sale, methods of enforcement of either a maritime or statutory lien.

(ii) Current factors of substance and procedure

Substance

Where the role of the action *in rem* is to enforce a maritime lien it is difficult to see how it is being used except to implement a substantive interest. The lien exists as from the event creating it and, as with any other interest, is enforced by the appropriate cause of action. Where the action lies to enforce a claim to which no maritime lien attaches the now accepted primary characteristics of the action *in rem* are that:

> (i) it translates the claimant into a secured creditor in relation to the property involved—but only in relation to that property or a "sister ship";

---

40. See *Johnson* v. *Shippin* (1704) 1 Salk. 35 (necessaries); *Clay* v. *Sudgrave* (1700) 1 Salk. 33; *Wells* v. *Osman* (1704) 2 Ld. Ray. 1044 (seaman's wages); *The Two Friends* (1799) 1 C. Rob. 271 (salvage); *Menetone* v. *Gibbons* (1789) 3 T.R. 267, 270 (bottomry); *Greenway and Barkers Case* (1577) Godb. 260; 3 Black Book of Admiralty 103, 243, 245, 261–263; *Corser* v. *Husely* Comb. 135 (1688); Roscoe, *op. cit.* note 118, at pp. 213 and 214.

41. See *The Young Mechanic* (1845) 30 Fed. Cas. 873; *The Nestor* (1831) 18 Fed. Cas. 9; *The Bold Buccleugh* (1851) 7 Moo. P.C. 267. In *The Nestor* Story J. cited Lord Tenterden, the author of *Abbott's Merchant Ships*.

(ii) the interest created is enforceable against purchasers of the property involved;

(iii) the interest created is extinguished if the property is destroyed.

Further, the restriction to arrest of the property involved in the claim in the case of the maritime lien and the action *in rem* in respect of ownership, possession and mortgage claims gives that property an exclusive importance in regard to the claim. The security available is that property and nothing else. In the face of such substantive consequences it is difficult to argue that the action is procedural only. But to view the action *in rem* itself as creating substantive rights is not necessarily to subscribe to the "personification" approach.

Procedure

Elements arguably in favour of the "procedural view" are

(i) the statutory extension of the "property" liable to an action *in rem* to sister ships in that the focus is on the defendant and not the ship;

(ii) the rule that on acknowledgment of issue of a writ *in rem* or service without contesting jurisdiction the action becomes one *in personam* as well as one *in rem*[42];

(iii) the practice blessed by RSC Orders 10 and 75, by which an action *in rem* can be based on acknowledgment of service by a defendant or endorsement of a writ by his solicitor, the action continuing as both an action *in rem* and *in personam*[43];

(iv) that after 1883 the writ *in rem* is addressed to the owners and this, it may be said, illustrates that whatever it was prior to that date it is now a proceeding *in personam* against the owner and not the ship;

(v) the view taken in 1989 in *The Deichland*[44] that for the purposes of the Brussels and Lugano Conventions an action *in rem* is a suit against a defendant rather than the property in regard to which the action is brought.

(iii) The views, the flaws in them and liens

None of the factors in support of the procedural view alter the essential substantive elements of the lien created or enforced by the action *in rem*. Apart from the extension of the property liable to the lien the factors are simply a recognition that behind all property there are persons interested in it. The extension of property liable serves only to widen the scope of the assets subject to the substantive interest. The critical factor is that the lien reflects a proprietary interest in the appropriate assets.

42. This was established in relation to the then procedural framework of appearance by the defendant by *The Dictator* [1892] P. 64, 304 disagreeing with two decisions of Dr Lushington in *The Hope* (1840) 1 W. Rob. 154 and *The Kalamazoo* (1851) 15 Jur. 885.

43. See Chaps. 9, 10. The further the move from seizure of ship and the nearer to service on or acknowledgment of service by the defendant the more difficult it is to categorize the action as against the ship. Wiswall, *op. cit.* in 7 (at p. 192 *et seq.*) contends that the view that the action starts with issue of the writ rather than arrest of the ship removed a linchpin of the true action *in rem* and may cause difficulty as regards enforcement of default judgments in such actions.

44. [1989] 2 All E.R. 1066 (C.A.). See Chaps. 4, 5.

The procedural view taken in its pure form in effect equates the action *in rem* with the availability of arrest or seizure of assets prior to judgment. If it is a mode of procedure to persuade a defendant to appear so as to make him a target, it must follow that no substantive consequences follow from it. First, therefore, there should be no restriction as to the assets of the defendant that could be seized as security. Secondly, logically the action should not affect third parties and once the defendant appeared the security should be released. If its role was simply persuasive and the defendant was persuaded to defend, the action *in rem* would be spent and the action would continue as an action *in personam*. If the defendant did not acknowledge service or if even after acknowledgment the property was retained as "security" it should be no more an asset available for enforcement of the judgment than any other.

But none of these factors applies so as to affect the substantive interest of the lien. There *is* a restriction as to the assets available and there are rights created against third parties by the maritime lien or issue of the writ *in rem*. Further, liability in the action depends on the existence of the property and is probably limited to its value.

In 1907 in *The Burns*[45] the Court of Appeal stressed that the action *in rem* was not a variant of an action *in personam*. The issue was whether the Public Authorities Protection Act 1893 (which imposed a six-month limitation period for "actions or proceedings against any person" in relation to acts done under a public duty) applied to an action *in rem*. The court followed *The Longford*[46]—a decision of the Court of Appeal delivered in 1889 under an earlier Act, and it also dealt with the contention that the change in the nature of address of the writ and the effect of appearance of the defendant meant that both actions *in personam* and actions *in rem* were against persons. The court agreed that owners are directly concerned in an action *in rem* but, as Fletcher Moulton L.J. said, the question of whether in addition it is to be transposed into an action *in personam* is for the defendants. They must choose (in terms of the former procedure) to appear or not to appear. Further, as regards the form, it was clear that "the writ was intended to apply to the old-established Admiralty action *in rem* and not intended to have the effect of creating a new type of action of altering the nature of the action".

The connection between the action *in personam* and action *in rem* has come to the fore in the context of the Brussels and Lugano Conventions. The matters there at issue are first whether for the purposes of the Conventions in the action *in rem* a "defendant" is sued and secondly, if so, whether concurrent actions *in personam* and *in rem* are the same or related causes of action. As to the first in *The Deichland*[47] the Court of Appeal took a realistic and international view in holding that the action *in rem* is against a defendant. As to the second, the European Court has held that the distinction is irrelevant to the question of the identity or relation between the causes of action. That depends on the identity of the parties, the cause and object of the action. Just as the national law distinction is irrelevant to the Convention so the Convention is irrelevant to the connection between lien and actions *in rem*. It is incontrovertible that whatever the identity or similarities between the action *in personam* and action *in rem*,[48] one essential characteristic of the action *in rem* is that it is based on or creates a lien. In other words the Convention has no relevance to the substantive interest to which the action *in rem* is connected.

45. [1907] P. 137.
46. (1889) 14 P.D. 34.
47. [1989] 2 All E.R. 1066.
48. As to which see e.g. *The Nordglimt* [1987] 2 Lloyd's Rep. 470 and Chap. 12.

It may be arguable that today the action *in rem* is "procedural" in the sense that it is a method of pursuing a cause of action which has different consequences to the action *in personam*. And so it is—but this does not mean that the consequence of the action *in rem* is also procedural—the unique character of the action *in rem* is that the issue of the writ creates the lien. Once that is recognized the action then performs identical functions to its role when implementing a maritime lien. The critical factor is to recognize the liens for the substantive interests that they are.

The personification view takes the ship as the defendant.[49] It would follow that the claim is limited to the ship, that the claimant has an interest in the ship assertible in bankruptcy proceedings, and that transfer of ownership or the fault of the shipowner is irrelevant. To be logical, any limit to the availability of the action must come from factors affecting the claimant (e.g. delay) or the ship (e.g. destruction). Conversely, it depends on the existence of the ship and must be confined to the ship involved. The one accepted characteristic which renders this view unacceptable today is the statutory provision allowing the action to be brought in relation to sister ships. But, as regards maritime liens and actions based on claims outside the sister ship provisions, it remains arguable.

However as has been said, it is accepted in English law that once a defendant has acknowledged issue of a writ *in rem* or service of the writ and does not contest jurisdiction the action proceeds as an action *in personam* as well as an action *in rem*. In a sense this denies pure personification, for acknowledgment in an action *in rem* should not logically be taken to have anything to do with an action *in personam*. More fundamentally, the view is destroyed by common sense in that in the end those who have interests in the ship (especially the owners) suffer through any enforcement of claims against the ship. Particularly is this so when the ship is liable to forced sale.

Neither the procedural nor the personification view can today be seen as defining or describing the action *in rem* in English law. As is usual in common law development, theory has given way to a kind of subjective pragmatism. The judicial use of historical antecedents has tended to be selective so as to support a particular answer to a particular question. And the reference to the "procedural" or "personification" approach tends to conceal matters of policy to which the debate may today be seen as relevant—the need for liability *in personam*, the linking of the amount recoverable to the value of the property at which the action is aimed, and the availability of remedies *in personam*. The resolution of the diverse issues does not lie in what is an artificial generalization of the action *in rem* as procedural or based on personification of the ship.

Of the three relevant policy matters only the need for *in personam* liability is directly relevant to the nature and scope of the lien created or enforced by the action *in rem*. The limitations on recovery and remedies go to the identification of the action *in rem* with the lien. However if it were accepted that in an action *in rem* there could be recovery above the value of the *res* or a remedy *in personam* this would simply mean that the action *in rem* was not solely linked to the lien—that it was a type of course of action with a number of consequences. The lien is not affected by acceptance or rejection of the limitations. The need for liability *in personam* will be discussed in the context of the particular liens (Chapters 18 and 19) and the amount recoverable and the kind of remedy in the context of remedies (Chapter 25).

---

49. For a review of the personification view, see 77 Harvard L.R. 1122 (1964).

Finally as has been indicated, concentration on the dichotomy of procedure and personification conceals the substantive nature of the maritime lien and the statutory lien in Admiralty. The substantive characteristics flowing from the availability of the action *in rem* were referred to earlier in this Chapter. It is important to acknowledge these characteristics without becoming enmeshed in any debate concerning any untenable concept of personification. The failure to define with certainty the nature of the action *in rem* has led to uncertainty as to its enforceability and hence that of the liens of which it is an inherent part. Further, it has led to the English view that in English proceedings any question of whether a claim attracts a maritime lien is for English law a matter of procedure. Whether or not the issue should be referred to English law should however be based on a consideration of the policy relating to liens in Admiralty and not on an artificial characterization of the nature of those liens. The question is discussed in Chapters 18 and 26.

CHAPTER 18

Maritime Liens

1. CLAIMS TO WHICH A MARITIME LIEN MAY ATTACH

The claims are:

1. Bottomry and respondentia.
2. Damage caused by a ship.
3. Salvage.
4. Seamen's wages.
5. Master's wages and disbursements.

The nature of these claims was discussed in Chapter 2. It was there stressed that these claims also attract statutory liens in Admiralty in that an action *in rem* may be brought in accordance with the Supreme Court Act 1981, s.21(4). The claimant, therefore, may plead both maritime and statutory lien. As only one writ *in rem* may be served on one ship for one claim[1] the basis of the claim must be in the alternative. There would seem to be no obstacle, however, to the service of a writ *in rem* on cargo in respect of the same claim in respect of a maritime lien and another on a ship in respect of a statutory lien.[2]

2. CONSEQUENCES OF ATTRACTING A MARITIME LIEN

Some consequences are uniform to all the claims a maritime lien, and, indeed, as was said in Chapter 17 it is only uniform legal consequences which create a legal category. But some consequences are not uniform and the variations remain uncertain. First, let us summarize the consequences which are accepted as flowing from the maritime lien:

(i) the lien confers a right and a remedy in addition to any available against a defendant liable "*in personam*" ("liability *in personam*" meaning simply liability of the defendant for the claim);

(ii) the lien is enforceable through an action *in rem* and inherent in that action

---

1. For discussion of other claims to which a maritime lien (or its equivalent) may be attracted also, see Chap. 2. See also for general discussion Thomas, *Maritime Liens*, 1980, *British Shipping Laws*, Vol. 14.
2. See Supreme Court Act 1981, s.21(8). In appropriate cases a maritime lien may lie in respect of ship, cargo and freight. But its availability in respect of freight depends on its availability against the ship earning the freight (see *infra*).

> (a) the ship, cargo or freight subject to it is liable to arrest prior to hearing on the merits;
>
> (b) jurisdiction on the merits is founded on service of a writ *in rem*, arrest or permitted substitute[3];
>
> (iii) the lien arises on the event creating it (such as a collision or wages becoming payable)[4];
>
> (iv) in respect of the ship, cargo or freight the target for the action, the "lien" is enforceable against other creditors (whether secured or unsecured) and, subject to existing possessory liens, takes priority over all other creditors whether the claims of those creditors arose before or after the creation of the lien;
>
> (v) once created, the "lien" is enforceable even though the ship be sold whether or not the purchaser has notice of it;
>
> (vi) where the person liable *in personam* is a charterer of the ship in respect of which a lien arises in certain circumstances the "lien" may be enforced against the ship (see *infra*);
>
> (vii) it is uncertain whether, as the enforcement is through the action *in rem*,
>
> (a) damages can be recovered in excess of the value of the ship or fund;
>
> (b) remedies *in personam* (e.g. injunction) are available;
>
> (viii) apart from bottomry bonds, whether a maritime lien can be transferred is unclear: it is accepted that a bottomry bond may be transferred;
>
> (ix) property arrested as part of an action *in rem* in the High Court enforcing the lien is subject to judicial (or "forced") sale and the proceeds are then available to a lien holder and other claimants *in rem*;
>
> (x) judicial sale as a step in enforcement of the lien extinguishes it and transfers the "lien" to the proceeds;
>
> (xi) the lien is extinguished by the destruction of the ship, cargo or freight to which it attaches;
>
> (xii): the lien may be extinguished by laches, waiver or satisfaction of the debt and, possibly, by lodging of bail, or provision of a guarantee and the claims attracting the lien may be extinguished by rules relating to effluxion of time.[5]

It should be recalled that in English law maritime liens are "secret" interests. There is no provision for their registration. Despite the usual indemnity clause in sale contracts, purchasers and other creditors run the risk of the ship or cargo being burdened by such liens.[6]

Not only secrecy but uncertainty remains about maritime liens, and the uncertainties are not decreased by legislative inaction. Nothing is to be found in statutes about their characteristics save that they may be enforced by an action *in rem*. Much of the uncertainty is due primarily to a combination of lack of statutory provision, together with

3. See Chaps. 2 and 10.
4. As to difficulties which may be caused in wages claims because of the introduction of payment after discharge see Chap. 2.
5. See *infra* as to discussion on extinction (and in particular the effect of state immunity). It has been held that property may not be arrested after judgment on liability (see Chap. 15) but such a rule is suspect as the lien (maritime or statutory) is not terminated by the judgment (see text *infra*).
6. Such an indemnity may be construed as providing protection against any incumbrance under any law. See *The Barenbels* [1984] 2 Lloyd's Rep. 388.

an inability to point accurately at historical roots. This inability tends to encourage in particular cases a selection of historical development according to the practical and conceptual conclusion thought preferable.

3. THE NATURE OF THE MARITIME LIEN

I. THE MARITIME LIEN AND THE ACTION "IN REM"

The action *in rem* lies at the heart of Admiralty practice and has been discussed in Chapters 2 and 10. It is the means of enforcing maritime liens and it is largely equated with statutory liens in Admiralty. Indeed, many would prefer the description of the latter to be simply "actions *in rem*". But this would be to confuse them with maritime liens also enforceable by actions *in rem* and to ignore the substantive proprietary characteristics conferred by the availability of the action *in rem*. Statutory liens in Admiralty are discussed in Chapter 19.

To summarize the nature of the action *in rem* in English law—it is confined to Admiralty and is available only in enforcing maritime and statutory liens in Admiralty. Its distinguishing features are:

  (i) its availability concurrently or consecutively with an action *in personam*;
 (ii) the availability of arrest of an asset relevant to the action (i.e. a ship, "sister ship", cargo or freight) or of a fund in lieu as "security" for the claim;
(iii) the establishing of jurisdiction through service of the writ normally on or arrest of the relevant ship or cargo;
(iv) the availability of judicial sale and the transfer of the "security" to the proceeds of sale.

The action *in rem* is essentially historically linked with the maritime lien. Statutory liens in Admiralty appear at their earliest in the Admiralty Court Act 1840 and possibly not until the Admiralty Court Act 1861. It is unclear whether prior to these enactments proceedings *in rem* were limited to claims now recognized as attracting maritime liens. The early role of the action *in rem* is shrouded in some mystery, that mystery having practical consequences today in the uncertainties over enforceability and remedies referred to in Chapter 17.

II. THE "MARITIME LIEN" AS A LEGAL CATEGORY OF CLAIMS

The category of "maritime lien" in English law originated in 1851 in *The Bold Buccleugh*.[7] Its subsequent development required a distinction between such claims and other types of claim in respect of which statute provided for proceedings *in rem*. *The Bold Buccleugh* has been described as a case "not where the maritime lien was born but rather where it was unveiled and placed in full view". However, the case seems rather more creative, exemplifying the generalization from specific cases which is a stage in the classic development process of the common law. In English law *The Bold Buccleugh* is to maritime liens what *Donoghue* v. *Stevenson* is to negligence.

7. (1851) 7 Moo. P.C. 267.

It is subsequent development that puts *The Bold Buccleugh* in its place as the originating authority on maritime liens as the category now is. However, in the case itself, the judgment not only classified a claim for collision damage with claims for wages, salvage and bottomry as attracting an action *in rem*,[8] but stated that "in all cases where a proceeding *in rem* is the proper course there a maritime lien exists ... "[9] As such an equation was clearly erroneous by 1885 it has cast some doubt on *The Bold Buccleugh* as an unquestioned authority.

At the time of "The Bold Buccleugh"—in 1851

It is uncertain whether, prior to 1840, the Admiralty Court allowed proceedings *in rem* in regard to any claim apart from the wages, salvage and bottomry claims specified in *The Bold Buccleugh* as attracting maritime liens.[10] Price suggests that claims for pilotage, towage on the high seas and necessaries supplied on the high seas may have attracted such liens. And certainly there are some general judicial dicta in support.[11]

Whether or not there was such jurisdiction, the Admiralty Court Act 1840 conferred a power to hear claims in addition to those then within Admiralty jurisdiction.[12] Section 6 provided:

"VI. And be it enacted. That the High Court of Admiralty shall have Jurisdiction to decide all Claims and Demands whatsoever in the Nature of Salvage for Services rendered to or Damage received by any Ship or Sea-going Vessel, or in the Nature of Towage, or for Necessaries supplied to any Foreign Ship or Sea-going Vessel, and to enforce the Payment thereof, whether such Ship or Vessel may have been within the Body of a County, or upon the High Seas, at the Time when the Services were rendered or Damage received, or Necessaries furnished, in respect of which such Claim is made."

If this provision means that proceedings *in rem* could be brought in relation to salvage, damage, towage and necessaries and if the equation drawn in *The Bold Buccleugh* was correct, in 1851 claims for towage and necessaries under the statute attracted maritime liens. At the date of hearing of *The Bold Buccleugh* it may well have been thought that towage did attract a maritime line.[13] As to necessaries, Dr Lushington seems at that time to have been in the middle of a change of direction from his view expressed in 1841[14] that no maritime lien was conferred by the statute to this later view (in 1854) that it did,[15] and his still later view (in 1864) that it did not.[16]

8. See e.g. (bottomry) *Menetone* v. *Gibbons* (1789) 3 T.R. 267; (seamen's wages) *The Neptune* (1824) 1 Hag. Adm. 227. This was extended by statute masters' wages and disbursements (the Merchant Shipping Acts 1854 and 1889) and see 7 & 8 Vict. c. 112, s.16; (salvage) *The Two Friends* (1799) 1 C. Rob. 271.

9. (1851) 7 Moo. P.C. 267, at p. 284.

10. It seems certain tht there was a jurisdiction *in personam* (see e.g. *The Elton* [1891] P. 265 and authorities there cited; *R* v. *Judge of City of London Court* [1892] 1 Q.B. 273, at p. 294).

11. See e.g. Lord Fitzgerald, Lord Bramwell in *The Heinrich Bjorn* (1886) 11 App.Cas. 270, 278. But contrast Lord Watson in the same case (at p. 286).

12. The number of claims within Admiralty jurisdiction was increased again by the Admiralty Court Act 1861.

13. See *The La Constancia* (1846) 4 Not.Cas. 512; Mansfield (1888) 4 L.Q.R. at p. 381.

14. *The Alexander Larsen* (1841) W. Rob. 288.

15. *The Ella A. Clarke* (1863) B. & L. 32.

16. *The Pacific* (1864) B. & L. 243; *The Troubadour* (1866) L.R. 1 A. & E. 302, affirmed by the Court of Appeal and Privy Council in *The Two Ellens* (1871) L.R. 3 A. & E. 345, (1872) L.R. 4 P.C. 161 and the Court of Appeal and House of Lords in *The Heinrich Bjorn* (1885) 10 P.D. 44; (1886) 11 App.Cas. 270. It has been suggested that prior to 1840 there were claims enforceable by proceedings *in rem* but not attracting a "*lien*"—but this is by no means settled.

The later rejection of the view that proceedings *in rem* led necessarily to a maritime lien did not affect the decision in *The Bold Buccleugh* that a claim for collision damage fell within the same category as salvage, wages and bottomry, nor the conclusion that these claims made up the category of "maritime lien". Subsequent developments confirmed the boundaries of that category and the creation of the category of statutory liens in Admiralty (discussed in Chapter 19).

III. THE MODERN MARITIME LIEN AND STATUTORY LIEN IN ADMIRALTY COMPARED

The two types of lien now overlap in that all claims which attract a maritime lien are included in the list of claims set out in s.20 of the Supreme Court Act 1981 as being claims enforceable by an action *in rem*. The maritime lien is more powerful than the statutory lien in that:

    (a) a maritime lien arises on the event creating it (whereas a statutory lien arises only on the issue of a writ *in rem*);

    (b) (following from (a)) a maritime lien is enforceable against purchasers as from its creation (whereas a statutory lien is so enforceable only from the issue of a writ);

    (c) In some circumstances a maritime lien is enforceable against a chartered ship even when the charterer and not the owner is liable *in personam* (whereas in relation to most claims a statutory lien would only be so if at the time of the issue of the writ the charterer has become owner or has become or remained demise charterer by the date of the issue of the writ)[17];

    (d) Save for possessory liens existing at the time of the creation of a maritime lien, a maritime lien takes priority over other liens and encumbrances whenever created, such as mortgage, possessory liens and statutory liens (whereas a statutory lien is subject to maritime liens, whenever created and mortgages and possessory liens certainly when created prior to the statutory lien).[18]

The statutory lien is more powerful than the maritime lien in that it may be enforced against a "sister ship". The maritime lien is confined to the ship involved in the claim[19] and it has been suggested that the sale of a sister ship would not extinguish any "maritime liens" adhering to a ship involved in the claim.[20]

IV. THE MARITIME LIEN—PROCEDURE OR SUBSTANCE?

A maritime lien is attached to the asset which it affects from the event causing it to arise. Despite this fundamental element of the lien, it was held by the Privy Council in 1980 in

17. The enforceability of claims *in rem* in respect of ownership, possession, mortgage and forfeiture claims is not clear. See Chap. 19.

18. And subject to Admiralty Marshal's costs, costs of arrest, and some statutory rights of harbour and other like authorities. See generally Chap. 23.

19. A claim attracting a maritime lien is enforceable against a sister ship as a statutory lien. See *The Leoborg (No. 2)* [1964] 1 Lloyd's Rep. 380.

20. See Wiswall, *op. cit.*, p. 171. As to statutory liens, see Chap. 19.

The Halcyon Isle[21] that the maritime lien is procedural and remedial rather than substantive. The classification is of critical importance in cases of claims adjudged by one law to be maritime liens and by another to be of lesser force. According to English law the issue of whether a claim attracts a maritime lien will be resolved by the law of the forum and a primary ground for that conclusion is the application of the general choice of law rule that matters of procedure are referred to the law of the forum.[22] Whether a maritime lien is regarded as conferring a substantive right or is merely a procedure for asserting a claim is, therefore, of fundamental importance.

"The Bold Buccleugh"

The English root of the view that the maritime lien is procedural is a description of the lien by Jervis C.J. in *The Bold Buccleugh*: "The claim or privilege travels with the thing into whosoever's possession it may come. It is inchoate from the moment the claim or privilege attaches and when carried into effect by legal process by a proceeding *in rem*, relates back to the period when it first attached."[23]

In *The Bold Buccleugh* the Privy Council was concerned to assert the liability of a vessel in a proceeding *in rem* after sale to a bona fide purchaser, the sale being prior to the institution of proceedings. The judgment is directed both to asserting a lien for collision damage on a like basis to the lien for salvage and recovery of wages and the effect of such liens as against purchasers. The primary argument of Jervis C.J. aimed first to distinguish the maritime lien from the common law possessory lien in that the maritime lien does not depend on possession; secondly, to distinguish the lien from the process of "foreign attachment" by which goods of a foreign debtor could be seized; and, thirdly, to establish that the lien was not merely a device to compel the appearance of the defendant.

The aim of the judgment is, therefore, to contrast the "substantive" nature of the maritime lien with the procedural nature of "foreign attachment". Yet subsequent authorities have either ignored the decision entirely in drawing an analogy between a lien and attachment or used the "inchoate" nature of the right as a basis for the conclusion that it is procedural.

In arriving at his description, Jervis C.J. drew first on the label conferred by Story J. in the United States case of *The Nestor*[24]—"the inchoate right"—and, secondly, on Lord Tenterden's description in *Abbott on Shipping*, i.e. "claim or privilege on a thing to be carried into effect by legal process".[25] In *The Nestor* Lord Tenterden was quoted in more detail. It appears that his "privilege" was an express contract of hypothecation[26] by a master of a ship—to be contrasted with the transfer of property of the ship. Story J. then adapted Lord Tenterden's description of the effect of the express hypothecation to the effect of the "tacit hypothecation" resulting from a "lien by the maritime law".

So, in *The Bold Buccleugh*, Jervis C.J. was concerned to assert the very converse of that which his words have since been used to support. He sought to distinguish the maritime

---

21. [1981] A.C. 221.
22. See Chap. 26.
23. (1851) 7 Moo. P.C. 267, at pp. 284–285.
24. (1831) 18 Fed. Cas. 9.
25. See *Abbott on Merchant Ships and Seamen* (5th edn) (1827) p. 122 (where Lord Tenterden is discussing the transaction of respondentia).
26. And not as Lord Diplock said in *The Halcyon Isle* a reference to French law (see [1981] A.C. 221, at p. 232).

lien (substantive) from foreign attachment (procedural). And clearly both Story J. and Lord Tenterden were using substantive analogies in their various approaches. It is suggested that the views of all these are consistent with the description of the maritime lien in the United States case of *The Young Mechanic*.[27] Curtis J. said that a maritime lien is "not merely a privilege to resort to a particular form of action to recover a debt . . . It is an appropriation made by the law of a particular thing as security for the debt or claim; the law creating an incumbrance thereon and vesting in the creditor what we term a special property in the thing which subsists from the moment when the debt or claim arises and accompanies the thing into the hands of a purchaser".

Modern views of "The Bold Buccleugh"

In *The Halcyon Isle* Lord Diplock (delivering the majority judgment) said that a maritime lien was unlike a mortgage in that it created "no immediate right of property". The lien was "devoid" of any legal consequences unless and until carried into effect by a proceeding *in rem*, but once carried into effect "the charge dates back to the time that the claim on which it is founded arose". Thereby, said Lord Diplock, the lien can be pursued "as it were proleptically in a proceeding *in rem* against the ship[28] at a time when it no longer belongs to the shipowner who was personally liable to satisfy the claim in respect of which the lien arose". With respect, the statement of the *effect* of the dating back cannot establish the validity of what can only be called (with some admiration) a tortuous explanation of a development, the roots of which seem to have borne a surprising fruit. The lien may be enforceable in this way either because it is "proprietary" from its creation *or* because of its relation back.

Secondly, is it not semantic to draw a distinction between an "inchoate" right depending for its substance on the taking of legal proceedings and a right of substance which, if necessary, has to be enforced by legal proceeding? The enforcement of the mortgage (contrasted by Lord Diplock with a lien) depends no less on the ability of the mortgagee to enforce it against his security. If a court does not recognize the proprietary nature of the security the mortgagee cannot enforce it, just as if a court does not recognize the right to enforce the lien there is no lien. In this context, whether proceedings can be brought and whether a claim exists is simply to put the same issue in different ways.

Is the maritime lien any more "inchoate" than any other substantive right? Prior to the proceedings *in rem* it is as much an encumbrance on the vessel as is a charge on a fund or an equitable lien on land or on a fund. In the case of the charge or equitable lien the failure to assert the claim within the applicable time limit leads to the loss of the right to claim: as regards a maritime lien it is no different. There is in effect no distinction between saying that (i) the lien is inchoate until legal process but the process relates back to the

---

27. (1845) 30 Fed. Cas. 873. Accepted in 1888 as accurate with the substitute of "right" for "special property". See Mansfield (1888) 4 L.Q.R. 379, at p. 381. Compare *The Tobago* (1804) 5 C. Rob. 218 in which the right of a bottomry bond holder was held not to bind the English captor of a French vessel—it being a right of action and not of property. Such a holding however, is an exception in the particular circumstances to the binding effect of a maritime lien on third parties and was used in *The Maria Glaeser* [1914] P. 218 (at p. 230) as authority establishing that a mortgage "*ex hypothesi*" would suffer from a similar lack of enforceability of the interest.

28. See [1981] A.C. 221, at p. 235. Lord Diplock did not cite that part of the judgment of *The Bold Buccleugh* which indicates that the right was substantive. See *infra*.

moment of creation or (ii) a lien exists from that moment but may be lost if not enforced. It is in effect a conclusion sought to be given the force of a reason.

In 1981 in *The Silia* it was argued that if bunkers were part of a ship for the purposes of making the proceeds of sale available to claimants who issue writs *in rem*, "a maritime lien would attach to the bunkers whenever the circumstances gave rise to such a lien". In reply, Sheen J. said:

"That argument imports a logical nicety which is inappropriate to the nature of a maritime lien. The inchoate right which attaches to a ship in favour of the lienor (e.g. the owner of another ship damaged in collision) is not perfected until the moment of arrest. A ship which is damaged in collision is frequently repaired before there is an opportunity to arrest her. She is then more valuable than when the lien attached. On the other hand she may have had to engage salvage tugs to enable her to reach port. The salvors would have a lien taking priority over the lien for collision damage. The claimant with a maritime lien takes the vessel as he finds her at the moment when he is able to exercise his lien."[29]

With respect, it is unfortunate that the phrase "inchoate right" was cited on the way to the incontestable conclusion that it is the vessel as it is at the moment of arrest which is the asset to which the lien attaches.[30] This conclusion has its own logic for it fits with the need of the existence of the asset for the lien to come into existence and to continue to exist. It simply reflects the concept of the creation of an encumbrance on an asset, the asset to be defined on the taking of further action.

Even if it be accepted that the taking of this further action is a necessary step in the concept of a maritime lien, it does not follow that prior to that step the lien is but a shadow. It is an actual encumbrance although its content or value could be defined as conditional on arrest or obtaining security in lieu.[31] It is to be noted that, as Sheen J. said, it is the arrest which operates to define the asset just as it is the obtaining of security which defines the value. The bringing of proceedings is but one step towards this.

It is therefore suggested that the persistent emphasis on the "inchoate" character of a maritime lien is misleading. It is no more of a shadow than (for example) a maritime mortgage. It is suggested that the contrast between maritime and statutory lien as to time of creation reflects a real difference and the reality of the nature of the maritime lien. So the maritime lien exists in substance from the event creating it and the statutory lien from the issue of the writ.

4. ASSETS SUBJECT TO A MARITIME LIEN

The Supreme Court Act 1981 provides that an action *in rem* will lie in any case in which there is a maritime lien or other charge on "any ship, aircraft or other property". What may be the object of a maritime lien is to be found in judicial development of the definition of a "ship" and "other property".[32]

29. [1981] 2 Lloyd's Rep. 534, at p. 537.

30. But this goes only to the identification of the asset because of its existence. So, for example, if part of the ship was sold it would remain subject to the lien.

31. Compare the creation of an "equitable lien" by contract even though the content of the right is not then fixed (see Chap. 22).

32. Section 21(4). Aircraft fall outside the scope of this work. The use of the wide phrase "other property" means that there is no need to refer to the "sweeping up" jurisdiction to investigate any question of a wider jurisdiction that specified by the Act (as to which and as to "other charge", see Chap. 2).

I. A SHIP

Things that go upon the water

There seems no reason to doubt that when the Supreme Court Act 1981 recognizes the ability to bring an action *in rem* "in any case in which there is a maritime lien . . . on any ship . . . " it is on any "ship" now recognized as such.[33] The Supreme Court Act 1981 defines a ship as including "any description of vessel used in navigation", a definition reflected in the Merchant Shipping Act 1995.[34] Hovercraft are included in the definition for most purposes. By the Hovercraft Act 1968 the law relating to maritime liens is specifically applied to hovercraft and property connected with hovercraft, whether the hovercraft is on land or at sea.[35] Under the more restricted definition of the Merchant Shipping Act 1894, s.742 ("every description of vessel used in navigation not propelled by oars"), a hopper barge[36] and a dumb barge[37] have been held to be vessels used in navigation; a floating landing stage,[38] a floating beacon[39] and a jet ski[40] have been held to fall outside the definition. Whether an oil rig is included will depend on the extent to which any particular rig can be said to be "used in navigation".[41]

A ship, its parts and things on board

The question of the asset to which the maritime lien attaches as from the creation of the cause of action creating it must be distinguished from that of the assets available to the claimant through arrest. The lien appears to attach to the ship in the narrower sense of its hull, machinery and other fixed parts.[42] In 1981 in *The Silia*[43] Sheen J. held that the assets

33. Once a ship qualifies as such the lien may continue to attach to a part even if it could not longer be used in navigation ("to the last plank") (see *The Neptune* (1824) 1 Hag. Adm. 227) but there will surely come a time when the whole has disappeared and each part becomes in itself a whole. Where a ship sinks it seems preferable to regard the lien as continuing rather than "suspended" until refloated (as to which see *The Cargo Ex Schiller* (1877) 2 P.D. 145).

34. 1981 Act, s.24(1). 1995 Act, s.313(1). See also the International Convention on Salvage 1989, Art. 1(6), enacted by the Merchant Shipping (Salvage and Pollution) Act 1994 and now by the Merchant Shipping Act 1995—any "structure" capable of navigation excluding some platforms and offshore drilling vessels on location (Art. 3)—but nothing in the Convention "shall affect the salvors maritime lien" (Art. 20). As to the Convention and liens see further *infra* and Chap. 2.

35. Hovercraft Act 1968, s.2(2). The law relating to maritime liens may be excluded by Order in Council (s.2(3)). No order has been made. It has been held that a ship does not include a sea plane (see *Polpen Shipping Co.* v. *Commercial Union Assurance Co. Ltd* [1943] K.B. 161) but as a maritime lien is available against aircraft such exclusion is unimportant in this context.

36. See e.g. *The Mac* (1882) 7 P.D. 126.

37. See e.g. *The Harlow* [1922] P. 175; *The Champion* [1934] P. 1.

38. *The Craighall* [1910] P. 207.

39. *The Gas Float Whitton (No. 2)* [1897] A.C. 337.

40. *Steedman* v. *Schofield* [1992] 2 Lloyd's Rep. 163—neither a "vessel" nor "used in navigation".

41. The Secretary of State may provide that "a thing designed and adapted for use at sea" may be treated as a ship for the purpose of any provision of the Merchant Shipping Acts or the Prevention of Oil Pollution Act 1971 (Merchant Shipping Act 1979, s.41) or any instrument made by virtue of any of those Acts. No provision was made for the purposes of the Administration of Justice Act 1956, Part 1, and the Supreme Court Act 1981 does not advert to it. See now Merchant Shipping Act 1995, s.311. For a detailed but inconclusive discussion of the problem of definition of ships, see Summerskill, *Oil Rigs: Law and Insurance* (1979), Chap. 2.

42. A question of "accession" could arise if machinery not owned by the shipowners is attached to the ship. As to accession generally, see Bridge, *Personal Property Law, op. cit.* at pp. 82, 83.

43. [1981] 2 Lloyd's Rep. 534.

available for arrest by the claimant *in rem* include "all property aboard the ship other than that which is owned by someone other than the owner of the ship".[44]

The distinction between the assets to which the lien attaches and the assets available to enforce the lien may be said in part to reflect the schizophrenic nature of the maritime lien. The value of the security is not ascertained until it is enforced through arrest, but the security is created as an interest on the event on which the relevant claim is based.

However, also in part, it follows from the essential link between the lien and the asset as it exists at any particular time. So if, while under arrest, a ship is destroyed the lien would be extinguished. The difference between the ship and "connected" assets appears to be that no lien attaches to the assets but that those in being at the critical point of implementation of arrest are available for enforcement—provided, presumably, they still exist at the point of judicial sale. There is a certain inconsistency about the ability to fasten on to assets not subject to the lien in order to enforce it. If the ship is damaged after the security is created but before enforced it is understandable that the value is the damaged ship and if the ship is repaired it is understandable that the value is its enhanced value. But it by no means follows that items identifiable apart from the ship are available for the enforcement of the lien.

In *The Silia* it was argued that bunkers (although owned by the shipowners) were not part of the ship for the purposes of arrest and subsequent sale, and that where the oil had been sold, its proceeds ought to be kept in a separate fund and made available to any creditor who with a judgment *in personam* could attach it through a charging order.[45] It was argued that if the bunkers were to be treated as part of the ship for the purpose of being a source of the fund available to those who had claims *in rem* it must mean that they were subject to a maritime lien. Sheen J. held that the proceeds of the sale of bunkers formed part of the fund (as did all property on board other than that not owned by the shipowner) available only to those who had issued writs *in rem*. He based his decision on:

(a) the proposition that there was no reason why property of the shipowner on board a ship should not be available to pay the shipowner's creditors;
(b) a claimant with a maritime lien takes the vessel as he finds her when he exercises the lien;
(c) it may be impossible for a claimant *in rem* to obtain a judgment *in personam* —and thereby get at the funds;
(d) if bunkers were not part of the ship on every ship sale there would always be funds in court not available to the claimants *in rem*.

However, with respect, ground (a) proves too much—for it can then be extended to the shipowner's personal effects—if he had on board a valuable necklace would this be available "*in rem*"? Ground (b) simply asserts the principle that was challenged. Ground (d) simply sets out the consequence of holding otherwise than was held. Finally, ground (c) follows from the jurisdictional rules relating to "*in personam*" claims which presumably are based on policy relevant to those claims—and it is perhaps hardly convincing to argue that a claim is not *in personam* because it will attract the rules of such claims.

44. [1981] 2 Lloyd's Rep. 534, at p. 537. It has been held that the value of repairs done after arrest is not subject to the lien (*St Olaf* (1869) L.R. 2 A. & E. 360).
45. As to which, see Chap. 17.

In the end, is it not simply a matter of policy in making available property to which the lien has not attached in order to satisfy it? Nothing will conceal the anomaly of enforcement on assets to which the lien was not initially attached, which seems simply to flow from historical practice. It seems now as well established as it is anomalous. The availability of bunkers and other property on the ship for enforcement of the lien or claim is subject to any limitation of the security to the ship itself. So a mortgagee may be limited to enforcing his security as such to the ship, leaving any fund arising from the sale of bunkers to a different set of priorities.[46] Where the bunkers are not owned by the shipowner defendant they are not party of any "*in rem*" fund—a neat reversal of true "*in rem*" liability.[47] Such limitations demonstrate the curious extension of "lien liability" from one asset to another in common ownership without any real analysis of why this should be so.[48] If the asset is not part of a ship nor so connected as to be an "appurtenance" it is difficult to see why it should come into the "*in rem*" reckoning.

The ship's apparel and salvage claims

It is understandable that the maritime lien for salvage should attach to all property linked to a ship that was salved. In respect of salvage services started before 1 January 1995 "apparel" is specifically referred to (though not defined) in the Merchant Shipping Act 1894, ss.544 and 546, providing for (i) life salvage; and (ii) property salvage near the coasts of the United Kingdom. It clearly refers to property closely connected with a ship such as its equipment, furniture and boats. The property is not only available for enforceability of the lien—the lien attaches to it.

In respect of salvage services started on or after 1 January 1995 the 1894 Act provisions are repealed and there is no equivalent reference in the replacement legislation—the Merchant Shipping (Salvage and Pollution) Act 1994. That statute does not affect the salvor's maritime lien[49] and whether a connected asset is a part of a ship for the purpose of the lien depends on the general principles discussed above.

II. OTHER PROPERTY

It must be stressed, first, that a lien attaches to property other than the ship not as a consequence of its connection with the ship but because independently it is subject to the lien. It follows that cargo is liable only if the lien attaches to the cargo.

"Other property" in the context of a maritime lien is primarily cargo and freight but in the case of salvage claims extends to wreck and anything remaining from the ship or cargo.[50] A maritime lien for freight is "consequential upon" and is absolutely dependent on the existence of a maritime lien on the ship earning the freight.[51] Subject to the

---

46. See *The Eurostar* [1993] 1 Lloyd's Rep. 106. Where a charter ends the property in bunkers owned by the charterer passes to the owner. As to the effect of a retention of title clause in favour of the suppliers of the bunkers see *The Saetta* [1993] 2 Lloyd's Rep. 268; [1994] 1 All E.R. 851.

47. *Ibid.*

48. Presumably bunkers owned by a charterer would be available for an *in rem* claim where the charterer is liable—even if the ship to which the liability attaches is not owned by the charterer.

49. The statute enacts the Salvage Convention 1989 and it is provided by Article 20 that the maritime lien is not affected (see *infra* and Chap. 2). It is repealed and re-enacted by the Merchant Shipping Act 1995.

50. Presumably as still retaining the character of the ship and cargo.

51. *The Castlegate* [1893] A.C. 38.

limitation in respect of freight, the lien attaches severally to all assets liable to it[52] in respect of the amounts chargeable thereto.

(a) Freight

Subject to the need for a maritime lien on the carrying ship, such a lien may attach to freight being earned and due at the time the lien is created[53] in respect of all claims. A maritime lien against freight may be asserted through the service of a writ *in rem* or a warrant of arrest (or both) on the cargo or the ship.[54] The person entitled to the freight is entitled to give bail.[55]

Various principles have been established in relation to cases involving particular types of claim but there is no reason to suppose that they are limited to those claims. The freight liable to the maritime lien is that which is due at the moment the lien arises as distinct from the time of arrest[56]—a principle contrary to that adopted in defining "liable property" for the purposes of enforcing a lien on a ship. The liability extends to freight payable under a subcharter[57] or payable to a charterer.[58] The latter principle illustrates the essential nature of a claim *in rem*, for the lien on freight depends not on entitlement to the freight but on the existence of a lien against the ship. Once that is established the lien against the freight due accompanies it.[59]

The lien is terminated by the payment of freight to the shipowner. There is, therefore, no lien on advance freight paid.[60]

(b) Cargo

Cargo[61] is susceptible to a maritime lien in respect of claims based on bottomry and respondentia and salvage.[62] If improperly detained, the owner is entitled to damages.[63]

---

52. See e.g. *The Dowthorpe* (1843) 2 W. Rob. 73.

53. *The Orpheus* (1871) L.R. 3 A. & E. 308 (where freight due on a homeward voyage was liable when the event occurred on the outward voyage). In bottomry the freight liable is that carried on the voyage which is the maritime risk (*The Staffordshire* (1872) L.R. 4 P.C. 194). The freight due under charter is attachable (see *The Salacia* (1862) Lush. 545).

54. RSC Order 75, rr. 8(1) and 10(5). Where property has been sold by the Marshal the writ is not to be served on it but a sealed copy must be filed in the registry (rule 8(1))—and clearly the property could not be arrested. As to the limitation on the requirement of service on the property because of deemed personal service, see Chap. 10.

55. *The Ringdove* (1858) Swab. 310. Only when the cargo is arrested will freight be ordered to be paid into court as a condition of release.

56. *The Roecliff* (damage) (1869) L.R. 2 A. & E. 363.

57. *The Andalina* (wages) (1886) L.R. 12 P.D. 1.

58. See *The Castlegate* (disbursements) [1893] A.C. 38.

59. *The Kaleten* (1914) 30 T.L.R. 572.

60. See e.g. *The Castlegate* (fn. 58).

61. Cargo does not include personal effects of master, crew and passengers (*The Willem III* (1871) L.R. 3 A. & E. 487, 490) but it probably includes cargo in tow (*The Gas Float Whitton (No. 2)* [1897] A.C. 337, at p. 345).

62. Cargo does not attract the lien in a damage claim but may be arrested to compel payment into court of freight due to the shipowner. See *The Leo* (1862) Lush. 444. The extension of the law of maritime liens to hovercraft is limited to "hovercraft and property connected with hovercraft"—the Hovercraft Act 1968, s.2(2).

63. See *The Victor* (1860) Lush. 72 (where it was said that there was no right to retention of the cargo).

Bottomry and respondentia

Despite its contractual root, in bottomry when ship, cargo and freight are charged, cargo may only be used to enforce the lien when ship and freight are exhausted and a lien on freight will be implied in a lien on ship and cargo.[64] Cargo may be charged only after shipment, for only then may a master deal with it.[65] In respondentia the cargo *is* the security.

Salvage

In addition to cargo as such, a maritime lien for salvage attaches to flotsam and jetsam and lagan, derelict and wreck. Flotsam, jetsam and lagan[66] all relate to cargo lost from a ship which has sunk, derelict is a ship or cargo abandoned without hope of recovery and with no intention in those abandoning of returning to it,[67] and wreck seems a term which encompasses anything remaining of ship, equipment or cargo.[68]

"Property" within the compass of the International Convention on Salvage 1989 is defined as "any property not permanently and intentionally attached to the shore line" (Article 1(c)). The Convention specifically provides in Article 20 that nothing in it shall affect the salvor's maritime lien and there is nothing in the Merchant Shipping (Salvage and Pollution) Act 1994 (now the Merchant Shipping Act 1995) enacting the Convention referring to the maritime lien. Although an action *in rem* will lie in respect of any claim in the nature of salvage under the Convention or under any contract in relation to salvage services it would appear that at the widest the maritime lien will attach only to property connected with the ship. The extent remains arguable.

5. ENFORCEABILITY OF MARITIME LIENS

PROCEDURE OR PERSONIFICATION

In Chapter 17 the debate between procedural and personification theories of maritime liens was put into the context of enforceability and remedies. The practical consequences of adopting one or the other view is that the theory, representing a generalization of characteristics of a maritime lien, becomes a basis for drawing a conclusion. As the enforceability of a maritime lien appears to differ in some respects depending on the claim to which it is attached it is misleading to link one or the other theory to the "maritime lien" as a category. Further, and more fundamentally, neither theory can claim to apply

64. See *The Dowthorpe* (1843) 2 W. Rob. 73.

65. *The Jonathan Goodhue* (1858) Swab. 355.

66. Flotsam is goods floating on the sea after sinking, jetsam is goods cast into the sea prior to the sinking but where the ship still sinks and lagan is goods which would be jetsam except that because of their weight they would sink and are prevented from doing so by a buoy (*Constables case* (1610) 5 Co. Rep. 106a).

67. See *The Lusitania* [1986] 1 All E.R. 1011; [1986] 1 Lloyd's Rep. 132. Once abandoned, and there being no intention to return, the thing becomes a derelict and change of mind has no effect (*The Sarah Bell* (1864) 4 Not. Cas. 144). Abandonment because of force does not create a derelict (*Bradley* v. *Newsom* [1919] A.C. 16).

68. For the purposes of the Merchant Shipping Act 1894, Part IX, (now the Merchant Shipping Act 1995) wreck "includes jetsam flotsam lagan and derelict found in or on the shores of the sea or any tidal water" (1894 Act, s.510(1); 1995 Act, s.255); "derelict" in this provision includes a sunken vessel abandoned without hope of recovery (*The Lusitania* [1986] 1 All E.R. 1011; [1986] 1 Lloyd's Rep. 132).

fully in respect of all claims. It is necessary to examine each aspect of enforceability in regard to each claim.

DIFFERENT ASPECTS OF ENFORCEABILITY

To say that a maritime lien is enforceable against an asset simply conceals the obvious—that it is enforceable against those who have interests in that asset, at least up to the value of that asset. There are, however, four different aspects in respect of enforceability of claims to which a maritime lien is attached:

    (i) enforceability *in personam* against a person connected with the asset and who is liable *in personam*;

    (ii) enforceability against other creditors;

    (iii) enforceability against a purchaser of the asset, once the lien has become attached;

    (iv) enforceability against an asset when the owner of the asset at the time the lien is attached is not liable on the claim *in personam*.

(i) Enforceability of the claim "in personam"

Such method of enforceability operates independently of the maritime lien. While liability *in personam* may be a prerequisite for the enforceability of the lien, the lien has no relevance to the enforceability *in personam* as such. Enforceability of a maritime claim by an action *in personam* is discussed in Chapter 9.

(ii) Enforceability against other creditors

This is a matter of priority, i.e. rivalry between claims valid in and of themselves. A maritime lien holder is a secured creditor and, save for a claim based on an earlier possessory lien, has the highest priority among secured creditors. The matter is discussed in Chapter 23.

(iii) Enforceability against purchasers

It is clear that a maritime lien is enforceable against a purchaser of the asset whether or not the purchaser has notice of the lien or claim to which it attaches. It will be recalled that the maritime lien attaches once the event creating it occurs (i.e. the cause of action arises) and, therefore, subsequent sale will not affect enforceability.[69] A term in the contract of sale that warrants that property is sold free from maritime liens is effective only as a contractual undertaking sounding in indemnity or damages (or presumably repudiation in appropriate cases). Following basic principles, it cannot affect a lien held by a person not a party to the contract.

---

69. See *The Bold Buccleugh* (1851) 7 Moo. P.C. 267.

(iv) Enforceability against asset when the present owner is not liable "in personam"

The issue is somewhat reduced in importance by the provision in the Supreme Court Act 1981 that claims within s.20(2)(e)–(r) are enforceable against a demise chartered ship provided the demise charterer would if sued be liable *in personam*.[70] However, it remains relevant as, first, a claimant may wish to rely on the maritime lien as distinct from the statutory lien for priority purposes and, secondly, the question of liability in respect of ships in the possession of or used by other than the owner or a demise charterer remains. The approach is not necessarily identical in respect of (a) every context in which the issue arises; (b) all the claims to which a maritime lien attaches.

(a) The differing contexts in which the lack of personal liability of the shipowner arises

The most common circumstances raising the questions of lack of personal liability is the chartered ship, and particularly the ship on demise charter. But there are other circumstances, and the question of whether the owner should suffer through a lien attaching to the ship need not receive the same answer in each context. There seem to be three primary categories of case which may pose the issue:

  (i) involving government ships;
  (ii) where the owner has by agreement relinquished control of the ship (as by charter);
  (iii) where the owner has involuntarily lost control of the ship (as by requisition, through illegal use or imposition of compulsory pilotage).

(i) Government ships

The immunity from suit of foreign states and the United Kingdom Government in relation to the property in which it has an interest is discussed in Chapter 12. The immunity is specifically conferred on property as well as persons and, therefore, there is no question as to whether a personal immunity prevents action in relation to the property. However, there is uncertainty as to the extent to which or in relation to which claims a maritime lien may attach to a ship after requisition has ended for events occurring while it was requisitioned. In one case, concerned with a damage lien, it was held that it would not lie, but in another that a salvage lien would lie.[71]

(ii) Transfer of control by agreement

An argument in favour of enforcing a maritime lien against a chartered ship is that agreements made by the owner that transfer control not affect the claimant's security. Although demise charterers are often described as temporary owners, this seems largely irrelevant to the point at issue in that the argument is about the risk of the actual owner. It is much more that the creation of temporary ownership by the owner cannot relieve him

---

70. As to conditions of liability, see Chap. 2.
71. Compare *The Tervaete* [1922] P. 259 with *The Meandros* [1925] P. 61. See *infra*.

of the risk that the ship may be made subject to a maritime lien.[72] It may then be argued on the one hand that no agreement between owner and charterer should affect a lien, or on the other that an agreement of which the claimant has or should have notice may limit his claim. Such a limitation need not be general. It has no relevance to claims for damage and, it may be argued, should play no part in salvage or wages claims on policy grounds. It may have a role to play in claims based on masters' disbursements, particularly today when there is almost always an ability to contact the owner.

(iii) Involuntary transfer

The relevance of personal liability in respect of requisitioned ships and ships taken without consent remains a matter of general application. Compulsory pilotage is no longer a general issue as the Pilotage Act 1987 provides that the fact that pilotage is compulsory does not affect the liability of the owner or master for any loss or damage caused by the ship or by the manner in which it is navigated.[73]

However, the issue of lack of personal liability in the owner may still arise in respect of compulsory pilotage if the pilot is not the employee of the owner but an independent contractor[74] and secondly if the event creating the claim arises in territorial waters of a country still recognizing the defence of compulsory pilotage.[75] In the latter case it may be that there would be no liability because of the application of the foreign law.[76]

(b) A general principle of shipowner's liability?

As was discussed in Chapter 17, whether personal liability of a shipowner is required for a maritime lien to exist has been seen on occasion as a contest between the theories of "procedure" and "personification". However, it is a matter of policy. The maritime lien has developed differently in different circumstances, and it is unhelpful to subsume particular issues under the general labels of procedure and personification. First, it is hardly arguable that a maritime lien remains mere procedure in the light of its diverse substantive characteristics. Secondly, to "personify" the ship is to conceal the balancing factors relevant to fastening liability on a shipowner not liable in an action *in personam* for a claim attracting a maritime lien. To enforce a lien against purchasers and to make its holder a secured creditor indicates that it is more than procedure: but this is far from indicating of itself that the lien should necessarily be enforced against the owner at the time the cause of action arises where the owner is not personally liable on the claim.

In discussing the necessity of personal liability of the shipowner, courts tend to take a distinction between (i) bottomry and wages claims and (ii) the remainder of the claims attracting maritime liens. Such generalization may have followed from the categorization of the "maritime lien" in *The Bold Buccleugh*, but it should be recalled that the issue in

---

72. Where a ship is demise chartered to a government and its use creates immunity from suit the argument may be reversed—for the risk accompanying the charter cannot *ex hypothesi* be that a maritime lien would be created.

73. Section 16 replacing the Pilotage Act 1983, s.35 (a provision equating compulsory to non-compulsory pilotage—re-enacting the Pilotage Act 1913, s.15(1).

74. As where supplied by a pilotage authority. See *The Cavendish* [1993] 2 Lloyd's Rep. 292.

75. Perhaps an unlikely event given the wide application of the Convention for the Unification of certain rules of Law regarding Collision 1910—and the imposition of liability by that Convention.

76. As to which see Chap. 26.

that case was enforceability of the lien against *purchasers*. And it was within that context that collision damage was equated with bottomry, seamen's wages and salvage.

The concept of the owner's authority

In *The Castlegate*[77] Lord Watson founded the limitation of the lien for masters' disbursements to those authorized by the owner on "the general principle of maritime law" that "every proceeding *in rem* is in substance a proceeding against the owner of the ship". He added that the only exception to that rule was the lien for masters' and seamen's wages—basing the exception on legislative provisions.[78] He specifically denied that collision damage was a further exception. In *The Ripon City*[79] Gorell Barnes J. added bottomry to seamen's wages as an exception. He rationalized the general principle of the maritime lien as being "a subtraction from the absolute property of the owner in the thing". It follows that the conferring of the lien must "in some way have been derived from the owner either directly or through the acts of persons deriving their authority from the owner".[80]

Gorell Barnes J. based his reasoning on the view that apart from bottomry and wages in action *in rem* must have a connection with the owner, i.e. he did not see the ship as a defendant. But he placed the risk of a lien firmly on the owner who may choose to hand over control of a ship to another, saying that arrangements of the owner should not deprive the claimant of security. He compared the liability of a mortgagee who may be subjected to liens arising after the mortgagee and created by the mortgagor—a comparison sometimes lost sight of through a curious separation of issues of ownership from issues of encumbrances.

In 1980 in *The Father Thames*[81] (dealing with collision damage) Sheen J. stressed the role of charterers as "owners *pro hac vice*", but, with respect, it is rather the placing of them in that position by the owner that is the critical point. It seems artificial to base the enforceability of a lien on the characterization of those in control as temporary owners when the effect of the enforceability will fall primarily on the actual owner. Such an approach accepts the principle of personal liability but changes its effect by ignoring its focal point—the "owner". And it denies that any importance should be attached to the choice that the owner has in retaining or handing over control.[82]

Liability of the shipowner rather than the ship as a general principle

On the authorities and the general approach in English law it seems that the general basis of a maritime lien lies in the connection with the owner rather than the ship. And this is entirely sensible as *that* is its effect. In effect the action is "against" the owner (or other

---

77. [1893] A.C. 38.
78. See now the Merchant Shipping Act 1995, ss.39, 41 and Chap. 2.
79. [1897] P. 226.
80. *Ibid.*, at p. 242.
81. [1979] 2 Lloyd's Rep. 364.
82. It would be further arguable that no distinction should be drawn between voluntary and involuntary transfer. As to this, see *The Ticonderoga* (1857) Swab. 215.

persons interested).[83] It is limited in its target and effect to the asset in which the lien exists—but provides in respect of that asset the right of a preferred creditor.

That description applies whether or not the lien itself is limited by connection with the owner, but in most cases a lien will not arise in circumstances where the owner had neither control of the ship nor choice in the selection of the person having control. There is no inconsistency in distinguishing between an action *in rem* and an action *in personam* and at the same time limiting the action *in rem* by a principle linked to the owner. The requirement of connection with the owner reinforces the conclusion that a lien cannot attach to a government ship immune from a suit. Even if the action *in rem* is directed at the ship it would indirectly implead the "sovereign" as the owner.[84] Secondly, if the rationalization of *The Ripon City* is accepted, if there is a general principle it is that of the necessity for the shipowner's liability *in personam* modified by voluntary transfer of control and presumed authority.

The principle of the need for shipowners' liability applies to the liens for damage and masters' disbursements and by its statement of general application (though lacking specific authority) to salvage: wages and bottomry are admitted to lie outside it. *Within* the area of operation of the principle, whether a lien will lie in respect of a requisitioned ship or in respect of acts outside the *authorized* operation of a ship (such as intentional damage), may depend on whether the emphasis is placed on the temporary ownership, voluntary transfer of control or presumed authority. It is a question of where the balance is to be struck between a claimant who is in no position to know the circumstances of ownership and control and an owner who has either not surrendered his control voluntarily or cannot be taken to have authorized a particular act. On the authorities as they stand, it seems likely that *voluntary* transfer of control would be seen as the focal point with presumed authority as the additional guiding principle.

(c) The different claims and the development of the need for the shipowner's liability

Damage

It is in regard to damage cases that the necessity for personal liability of the owner has been most stressed. In 1842 in *The Druid*[85] Dr Lushington said that "the liability of the ship and responsibility of the owners are convertible terms". In 1880 in *The Parlement Belge*[86] it was held that no lien for collision damage could arise as regards a government ship owned by a foreign government, for the ship "cannot be made the means of compensation if those in charge of her were not the servants of the then owner". In 1888 in *The Tasmania*[87] it was held that a maritime lien would not arise where "the injury was done by the act of someone navigating the ship not deriving his authority from the owner". In 1893 in *The Utopia*[88] the Privy Council held that the argument that "the ship

---

83. And, it is suggested, it is not necessary for this conclusion that persons interested will if they choose to defend the action render themselves liable *in personam*. See the approach adopted by the Court of Appeal in *The Deichland* [1989] 2 All E.R. 1066; [1989] 2 Lloyd's Rep. 213 and generally Chap. 10.
84. See *The Tervaete* [1922] P. 259.
85. (1842) 2 W. Rob. 391.
86. (1880) 5 P.D. 197.
87. (1888) 13 P.D. 110.
88. [1893] A.C. 492.

may be held liable though there be no liability in the owners" was "contrary to principles of maritime law now well recognized". The Privy Council approved of a passage taken from *The Parlement Belge* which a few months prior to *The Utopia* had been approved by the House of Lords in *The Castlegate*.[89] In 1922 in *The Tervaete*[90] it was said that a collision lien must have its roots in the personal liability of the owner or person for this purpose in the position of an owner. Therefore it could not arise in respect of a state-owned ship. In 1923 in *The Sylvan Arrow*[91] it was held that where a ship had been requisitioned and later returned to its owner no lien arose in regard to damage suffered while requisitioned as the handing over was not voluntary. In 1979 in *The Father Thames*[92] Sheen J. relied on the principles of "deemed authority"[93] and "owners *pro hac vice*"[94] and followed (if a trifle erratically) through the cases to hold that a maritime lien for collision damage attached to a ship under demise charter. Drawing an analogy with enforceability against purchasers, the learned judge said:

"In my judgment a similar situation arises when a vessel is on demise charter, because the demise charterers are regarded as the temporary owners of the ship, or her owners for this occasion (pro hac vice). The fact that a ship is on demise charter is unlikely to become known to the injured party until after the ship has been arrested. No injustice will have been done to the owners of the ship by the arrest of their property because (a) the demise charterers will have to put up bail if they want the ship released from arrest, and (b) the owners will have protected themselves by an indemnity clause in the charter-party".[95]

The principle is, therefore, clear.

Master's disbursements

The decision in *The Castlegate* established that a master has a lien for only such disbursements as are authorized by the owner. In *The Ripon City* Gorell Barnes J. held that there was a presumption that when an owner hands over possession and control of a ship it must be presumed he gives authority to "subject the vessel to claims in respect of which maritime liens may attach to her arising out of matters occurring in the ordinary course of her use or employment".[96] The principle of personal liability of the owner therefore underlies the lien for disbursements.

Salvage

None of the authorities relevant to the issue of the availability of a maritime lien in relation to an owner not liable *in personam* are concerned with a salvage lien. Statements of general principle include it. But in 1925 *The Meandros*,[97] concerning a salvage claim in relation to a requisitioned ship, Lord Merrivale made the points, first, that requisition had not removed the ownership of the ship but simply the possession and control, and,

89. [1893] A.C. 38.
90. [1922] P. 259.
91. [1923] P. 14. But see *The Meandros* [1925] P. 61 (salvage)—see *infra*.
92. [1979] 2 Lloyd's Rep. 364.
93. See e.g. *The Ripon City* [1897] P. 226.
94. See e.g. *The Tervaete* [1922] P. 259; *Baumwoll Manufactur v. Furness* [1893] A.C. 8, at p. 16.
95. [1979] 2 Lloyd's Rep. 364, at p. 368.
96. [1897] P. 226, at p. 244.
97. [1925] P. 61.

secondly, that the owners had benefited from the services. Lord Merrivale distinguished the case before him from *The Tervaete*[98] in which it was held that no lien attached for damages caused by a requisitioned ship. In the case before him, he said the acts relied on were those of the salvor and not those of the crew of the requisitioned ship in relation to which no action would lie.

However, the question is surely not the basis of the liability but the liability itself. Clearly, no action *in personam* would lie against the government whatever its basis, and the question in each case was whether the sovereign immunity which prohibits such an action operates to prevent the creation of a maritime lien. Two points stressed by Lord Merrivale form more substantive distinctions between the two types of claim than that on which he relied. First, in *The Tervaete*, the ship was owned by a foreign government at the time of the event creating the lien and had been later sold to the defendants to the action, whereas in *The Meandros*, at the equivalent time, the ship was owned by the defendants to the action and was under requisition by the foreign government.[99] Secondly, in *The Meandros*, the defendants benefited from the services whereas in *The Tervaete* they simply suffered from the acts of government servants.

The basis of the decision in *The Tervaete* was that it was impossible to create a maritime lien as regards a ship owned by a government[100] immune from suit for:

(i) it would implead the government even if an action *in rem* is against a ship; and

(ii) a maritime lien is a right to take proceedings and, therefore, would not stand with the prohibition on the taking of proceedings against a sovereign.

The latter ground was relevant to *The Meandros* and would have defeated the salvor on the basis of *The Ripon City* that a lien required personal liability of the owner or the voluntary surrender of control to the person liable *in personam*. Lord Merrivale made no attempt to fit *The Meandros* into or distinguish it from any rule applicable generally. The justification as an exception to the requirement of personal liability is that of the benefit conferred on the owner, although in the case it was not advanced as anything more than a general reason for upholding the lien. *The Meandros* is an unsatisfactory decision but it *is* an authority dependent on the view that the owner's liability *in personam* is irrelevant to a maritime lien. And it is possible to justify this in salvage because of the benefit to the owner. In the state of the authorities this can be little more than a possible argument.

Wages

In 1892 in *The Castlegate*[101] Lord Watson stated as a general principle that a "proper maritime lien must have its root" in the personal liability of the shipowner. The one exception in his view was that of wages of master and crew. It appears from early cases that a claim for seamen's wages lay "against the ship"[102] and this view was followed in

98. [1922] P. 259.
99. See also *The Sylvan Arrow* [1923] P. 14 where the ship was requisitioned from the owner. On an interlocutory issue the right to proceed against the ship was linked to the owner's responsibility for some person on board.
100. As to ships demise chartered *to* a government see fn. 72.
101. [1893] A.C. 38, 52.
102. See *Wells* v. *Osman* (1704) 2 Ld. Ray. 1044; *Clay* v. *Sudgrave* (1700) 1 Salk 33.

the nineteenth century.[103] There is, therefore, nothing to contradict Lord Watson and a good deal to support him.

Lord Watson's dictum, apparently approved in *The Ripon City*, was based on legislative recognition of "the rule that the lien attached to ships independently of any personal obligation of the owner". This presumably referred to the change in wording between the Merchant Seamen Act 1844, s.16, and the Merchant Shipping Act 1854, s.191. Both provisions extended to masters the rights of seamen to recover wages but the words in the earlier Act (of 1844) limiting the claim to one "from the owner of any ship" were omitted in the Act of 1854. The Admiralty Court Act 1861 made no reference to the owner and by s.10 conferred jurisdiction over seamen's or masters' claims for wages "earned by him on board the ship".[104]

Lord Watson based the exception of wage claims from the general rule on "obvious considerations of public policy"—as indeed exist. And the policy, it can be argued, outweighs the imposition on an owner of a sanction in respect of claims over which he has no control—unlike damage and disbursements claims.

Bottomry

The classic description of a bottomry transaction is that "the advance is made upon the credit of the ship, not upon the credit of the owner, and the owner is never personally responsible".[105] But a prerequisite for the validity of a bottomry bond is either that the master must have received authority from the ship or cargo owner or that it was impractical to contact the owner.[106] The question remains whether in any case a charterer may be treated as the owner for the purpose of giving notice by the master in order to create the lien. It seems clear that this could arise in the case of a demise charter only where, by adapting the reasoning in damage lien cases, the demise charterer is treated as temporary owner. It would be logical for the master to contact the demise charterer to whom he is responsible; and the arguments advanced in damage lien cases as to the owner permitting the creation of a lien through transfer of control would apply equally, if not with greater force, to bottomry.[107]

6. TRANSFERABILITY OF MARITIME LIENS

It is curious that, apart from the lien attaching to a bottomry claim, the question whether maritime liens are transferable is uncertain. There are few rules either statutory or judicial specifically related to maritime liens. In most contexts the issue turns on applicability of general rules relating to the transferability of rights and interests. Transferability is voluntary or involuntary.

103. See e.g. *The Edwin* (1864) B. & L. 281; *The Ferret* (1883) 8 App. Cas. 329.
104. See now the Supreme Court Act 1981, s.20(2)(o). The limitation to wages earned on board did not appear in the Administration of Justice Act 1956 (see s.1(1)(o)) and had apparently not been strictly applied before that Act (see *The Halcyon Skies* [1977] Q.B. 14).
105. *Stainbank* v. *Shepard* (1853) 13 C.B. 418.
106. *Stainbank* v. *Fenning* (1851) 11 C.B. 51, 89; *The Oriental* (1851) 7 Moo. P.C. 398; *The Bonapart* (1853) 8 Moo. P.C. 459.
107. But see e.g. *The Panama* (1870) L.R. 3 P.C. 199.

I. VOLUNTARY TRANSFER

Voluntary transfer has three different aspects: (i) assignment (ii) subrogation and (iii) payment of another's claims.

(i) Assignment

Bottomry bonds

It is established that a maritime lien attached to a bottomry bond is assignable.[108] The commercial nature of the bottomry bond resulting from a security transaction distinguishes it from the other claims attracting liens.

Maritime liens apart from bottomry bonds

(a) General principles of assignability

As a general rule, in English law a proprietary interest is presumptively assignable; but it does not *necessarily* follow that because an interest is proprietary in the sense of enforceability against a third party that it is assignable. Different policy questions are raised. It has been suggested in Chapter 17 that a maritime lien is proprietary in nature, although, as was said, it has consistently been argued by others that it is procedural and remedial.

Whether it is seen as proprietary or remedial it is likely that it would be seen, for assignment purposes, as a "chose in action"—for the lien is essentially a method of assuring that a claim is met. It is not an interest, the enjoyment of which lies in its continuing use—such as a charterparty.[109] Clearly, a maritime lien is more than a bare right of litigation. It may be seen as conferring on the claim to which it attaches a substantive quality so that the claim becomes more than such a right. In *Trendtex Trading Corporation* v. *Crédit Suisse* Lord Roskill summarized the rules relating to assignability. "The court should look at the totality of the transaction . . . If the assignment is of a property right or interest and the cause of action is ancillary to that right or interest or if the assignee had a genuine commercial interest in taking the assignment and in enforcing it for his own benefit"[110] the assignment of a chose in action is valid. It was emphasized in a later case[111] that this principle does not mean that the assignee may not make a profit, nor that the general interest has to be that of a party to a transaction or a creditor.

The question in each assignment must, therefore, be whether the assignee has either a property interest (as distinct from a personal right) or a genuine commercial interest. A maritime lien is, it is suggested, a property right but it may well be argued that *it* is incidental to the claim and not vice versa. In a sense it provides a contrast to the right to sue for damages for breach of contract (i.e. a claim) which, it may be argued, is identical to the right based on the contract itself. So it is the nature of the claim which should

---

108. See e.g. *The Rebecca* (1804) 5 C. Rob. 102, at p. 104; *The Petone* [1917] P. 198. There is no suggestion that it is negotiable, only that it is assignable.

109. Even a charterparty has been held to be a "chose in action". See *Mangles* v. *Dixon* (1852) 3 H.L. Cas. 702, at p. 726.

110. [1981] 3 All E.R. 520, at p. 531. In this context "property right" appears to be contrasted with a right essentially personal in character such as the right to damags for personal injury.

111. *Brownton Ltd.* v. *Edward Moore Inbucon Ltd.* [1985] 3 All E.R. 499 (C.A.).

govern its assignability and the maritime lien of itself, it is suggested, does not supply the necessary "property" interest.

If this is right it would lead to the conclusion already established that a bottomry bond is assignable, that a claim for disbursements and (less likely) for salvage services may be assignable if supplied pursuant to a contract, and that wages and damage claims are non-assignable. The general principles of assignability are always subject to public policy exceptions and to extensions on the "genuine commercial interest" ground. So presumably (for example) a salvage claim, it may be contended, is assignable to a person who had a commercial interest in a ship burdened by the claim.

Even if a claim is assignable it does not necessarily carry the maritime lien with it. It may be said a lien was created to benefit a particular category of claimants only. It could be argued that assignment destroys the privilege, but in answer to that there is no reason to deprive a claimant of the value to him of a secured right if he decides to assign it in lieu of enforcing it. It is only where the right reflected in the claim itself is non-assignable on general principles that a maritime lien should not be assignable. Even if a claim is non-assignable the fruits of a claim (such as damages) may remain assignable.[112]

(b) Maritime lien principles of assignability

The general principles relating to assignability of rights of action have been developing with an ever increasing liberality since the nineteenth century but there has been no discussion of contractual assignability in a maritime lien context.[113] It may well be, therefore, that in the face of the development of general principles in favour of assignability it would require a strong policy ground for them not to be applied to the maritime lien. It is suggested that, insofar as the claim to which the lien is attached are assignable, policy is in favour of assignability of the lien on the basis that it is for the holder of the lien to decide how best to take advantage of it. It must be admitted, however, that the courts have insisted that the voluntary payment of wages will give the wages lien to the person paying only where the payment is with judicial consent. It should be noted, however, that the general principles of assignability would require that the assignee had a genuine commercial interest.

In 1867 in The Wasp[114] Dr Lushington held that an assignment of a shipbuilding claim prior to arrest of the ship included the "inchoate" right to proceed in rem which would accrue after arrest. It would certainly follow that if an assignment of a claim included a right of action in rem which had not accrued, such an assignment would carry with it a maritime lien which is created from the time of the event creating it. The case at least points in the direction of assignability at a time when the law took a more limited view of assignability in general than it now does.

Another point, though less direct, may be seen in enforcement of legal arrangements whereby, when suppliers of necessaries had a limited claim in rem, supplies would be provided for a ship under contract with the master. Such a contract would take place within a framework set up by the shipowner, such as a forward contract for supply of coals from a coal supplier in a particular port. The coals would be supplied against the master's

112. See Glegg v. Bromley [1912] 3 K.B. 474.
113. In The Petone [1917] P. 198, a case concerned with the voluntary payment of wages, Hill J. specifically said that he did not consider the result of contractual assignment (see p. 208).
114. (1867) L.R. 1 A. & E. 367.

draft, which meant that he had made a disbursement for which he could claim a maritime lien. Without more, this is simply ensuring that commercial arrangements are fitted into a legal pattern providing maximum security for suppliers. Provided the master was acting as a party to the supply and in the course of his employment, the root of the supply arrangement is irrelevant.[115]

In *The Ripon City*[116] the master agreed with the suppliers that they should enforce his lien through an action in his name and apply the proceeds to meet his liability to them. This agreement was not challenged by the owners and Gorell Barnes J. said that he was "not required to express an opinion on this matter". But he did hold that a settlement between the plaintiff master and the defendant owner was void as against the suppliers because the owner had knowledge of the agreement between the master and the supplier in regard to the enforceability of the lien. It certainly seems that this was an assignment of the master's claim in all but name. Such an assignment would clearly fit within the general principle of assignability suggested above.[117]

RESTRICTIONS ON ASSIGNMENT OF WAGES

Any assignment of wages by a seaman employed on board a ship registered in the United Kingdom before they accrue does not bind the seaman and payment to him after such an assignment is valid.[118] Further, a seaman cannot renounce by agreement his right to and lien for his wages,[119] or (subject to any agreement made in relation to a ship employed on salvage services)[120] any rights in the nature of salvage.[121] These prohibitions appear to extend to assignment.[122]

(ii) Subrogation

An insurer who, under his contract of insurance, indemnifies an insured for loss or damage is entitled to the rights and remedies of the insured in respect of that loss or damage. The Marine Insurance Act 1906 provides that a marine insurer is "subrogated to all the rights and remedies of the assured in and in respect of" the subject matter insured.[123] The subrogation is coextensive with the indemnity paid as in the general law of insurance.[124] A maritime lien, however viewed, must fall within the "rights and remedies" specified in the Act.

115. Compare *The Ripon City* [1897] P. 226 and *The Castlegate* [1893] A.C. 38 with *The Orienta* [1894] P. 271.
116. [1897] P. 226.
117. As to assignability under the Liens and Mortgages Conventions of 1926, 1967 and 1993, see *infra*.
118. Merchant Shipping Act 1995, s.34(1)(c), re-enacting statutory provisions originally enacted in 1844.
119. *Ibid*, s.39.
120. The provision simply renders such an agreement valid but enforceability remains under the control of the Admiralty Court and depends on the agreement being equitable. See *The Ganges* (1869) L.R. 2 A. & E. 370.
121. The provision does not prohibit agreements for the apportionment of salvage which if equitable will be enforced. See *The Wilhelm Tell* [1892] P. 337. Under the Salvage Convention 1989 as enacted into English law apportionment between persons in the service of the salving vessel is to be determined by the law of the flag of the vessel, or if not carried out from a vessel the law governing the contract between the salvor and his servants (Article 15). See Merchant Shipping Act 1995, Part IX, Chapter I.
122. *The Rosario* (1866) 2 P.D. 41.
123. Section 79.
124. *Yorkshire Insurance* v. *Nisbet Shipping Co. Ltd.* [1962] 2 Q.B. 330. As to the Convention on Maritime Liens and Mortgages 1993 see *infra*.

(iii) Voluntary payment of claims[125]

Most of the discussion on transferability of maritime liens has occurred in the context of payment of wages by other creditors. It is now firmly established (a) that such payment of itself does not operate as a transfer of the lien[126] but that (b) such payment may be authorized by the court and in that event the payer is entitled to the lien attached to the claim.[127] The practice of granting judicial approval for the payment has long been followed,[128] and there seems no reason why the principle should not apply to all maritime liens.[129]

II. INVOLUNTARY TRANSFER

(i) Bankruptcy and death

On bankruptcy all interests in the bankrupt's assets (with some exceptions relating to personal earnings and chattels) and rights of action, apart from those which are "purely personal", are vested in the trustee for bankruptcy.[130] On death, all causes of action "subsisting against or vested in" the deceased survive against or for the estate.[131]

(ii) Statutory right to contribution

Under the Maritime Conventions Act 1911, s.2, liability of shipowners for loss of life or personal injury on board a ship caused by the carrying or another ship is joint and several. If damages are recovered from one vessel which exceed the proportion reflecting the relative fault of that vessel there is a right of contribution from any other at fault. The Act specifically provides (in s.3(2)) that the plaintiff in such an action has "the same rights and powers as the person entitled to sue for damages in the first instance".[132] This would appear to attach a maritime lien to the contribution action.

---

125. This is not subrogation—which is a consequence of a contract of indemnity and not of simple payment.

126. See *The Petone* [1917] P. 198 in which Hill J. reviewed the authorities; *The Cornelia Henrietta* (1866) L.R. 1 A. & E. 51. The doctrine that payment without judicial approval entitled the assignee to the lien has support—see e.g. *The St Lawrence* (1880) L.R. 5 P.D. 250; *The Tagus* [1903] P. 44—but the need for such approval seems now to be accepted, at least in England. The Scottish view is less clear. See *Clark* v. *Bowring* 1908 S.C. 1168; *Clydesdale Bank* v. *Walker and Bain* 1926 S.C. 72; *Inter Islands Exporters Ltd.* v. *Bernia S.S. Ltd.* 1960 S.L.T. 21.

127. *The Cornelia Henrietta* (*supra*); *The James W. Elwell* [1921] P. 351, at p. 357.

128. See *The Leoborg (No. 2)* [1964] 1 Lloyd's Rep. 380; *The Berostar* [1970] 2 Lloyd's Rep. 402; *The Vasilia* [1972] 1 Lloyd's Rep. 51.

129. It may be arguable that in regard to claims which are assignable voluntary payment should be treated as an assignment—but there remains a distinction between payment and agreement to assign.

130. See generally Insolvency Act 1986, s.283. As to exclusion of personal actions, see *Beckham* v. *Drake* (1849) 2 H.L. Cas. 579. Rights against an insurer of third party liability on incurring a liability are transferred to the third party (Third Party (Rights Against Insurers) Act 1930). For discussion, see Mance [1995] LMCLQ 34.

131. Law Reform (Miscellaneous Provisions) Act 1934, s.1(1) as amended by Administration of Justice Act 1982, s.4.

132. Compare the Civil Liability (Contributions) Act 1978, s.1(1)—any person liable "may recover contribution from any other person liable".

7. EXTINCTION OF MARITIME LIENS

Apart from satisfaction of the claim to which the lien is attached there are nine primary bases on which a lien might be destroyed. In some contexts (for example, the stay of proceedings or giving of contractual guarantee) it is arguable that the circumstances affecting the lien are not necessarily permanent. So although while they exist they do affect the lien they should not be deemed to extinguish it. It is suggested that unless there is clear waiver (implied or express) the lien should continue while it may be enforced. Any action or event qualifying the claimant's right should be construed in the light of that right—and where appropriate seen as preventing the enforcement of the lien rather than destroying it.[133]

I. IMMUNITY FROM SUIT

Foreign states

The general question of sovereign immunity is discussed in Chapter 12. It is clear that ships' cargo and other property belonging to a foreign state and not in or intended to be for commercial use are immune from arrest and the action *in rem*. It follows that once a ship is transferred into the ownership of a foreign state for non-commercial use no lien can be enforced. A lien created prior to the acquisition of ownership or some other interest by the foreign government may therefore be destroyed by that acquisition.

In *The Tervaete*, Bankes L.J. indicated that on acquisition of ownership by a foreign government an existing maritime lien may lie dormant until transfer out of the hands of the government. In principle, there is no reason why an existing maritime lien should be *destroyed* simply by acquisition by a foreign government of the property to which it is attached—particularly in the case of the requisition.[134] This is the more so since immunity now extends only to non-commercial use. Any argument based on affecting the value of property of a foreign government has little force in that the government acquired the property with the lien attached. Whether the maritime lien is seen as a substantive interest (as is argued in this work) or a right to take proceedings, sovereign immunity is immunity from proceedings and does not destroy the right on which those proceedings are based.

The United Kingdom Government

Identical reasoning applies to ships and other property immune from suit and arrest because of the interest of the Government of the United Kingdom.

II. DELAY OF SUIT

This is discussed in Chapter 11.

---

133. It is suggested with respect that the focus on prevention of enforcement is preferable to any concept of suspension and revival (see approach in *The Birchglen* (fn. 150)).

134. And even more so if the ship is demised chartered to a government. There may be destruction through delay—even though the delay is caused by acquisition of an interest by a sovereign.

III. EFFECT OF STAY OF PROCEEDINGS

The effect of the existence of a maritime lien to stay of proceedings because of an arbitration or a foreign jurisdiction clause or on the grounds of *forum non conveniens* turns on any consequential inability of a claimant to get at the property in England to which his lien would attach. The general question of stay is discussed in Chapter 12.

Effect on maritime lien attached to property the target for the action

The effect of stay or dismissal of the proceedings before an English court on the existence of a maritime lien depends on whether the lien is essentially the right to bring such proceedings or is a substantive interest in the property. If the lien is viewed as procedural and, as Lord Diplock argued in *The Halcyon Isle*,[135] dependent on the bringing of proceedings *in rem* in an English court, it is difficult to escape the conclusion that inability to bring those proceedings does affect the substance of the right. The effect of a dismissal of proceedings[136] is in effect the converse of the issue in *The Halcyon Isle*—which was the recognition of a claim as a maritime lien if recognized as such by a foreign law. But it is but two sides of a coin and the critical issue is whether the maritime lien is seen as a security interest of substance. If so, its existence depends on the law linked to it as a matter of substance and not upon the bringing or ability to bring proceedings on the claim. As Brandon J. said in *The Rena K*[137]: "The choice of forum for the determination of the merits of a dispute is one thing. The right to security in respect of maritime claims under the Admiralty law of this country is another."[138]

Arbitration, foreign jurisdiction clause or forum non conveniens stay

The Civil Jurisdiction and Judgments Act 1982, s.26, confers power on a court to retain property arrested in proceedings later stayed or dismissed because of submission to arbitration or to a foreign court or on grounds of *forum conveniens* or to attach a condition to such stay that equivalent security be lodged. (See Chapter 15.)

Effect on maritime lien attached to property retained

It is specifically provided by s.26(3) that subject to any rule of court or "necessary modifications" "the same law and practice" applies to property so retained as would apply if held for purposes of proceedings in court. The effect of that phrase as regards a maritime lien is uncertain. It would seem to indicate that having obtained a foreign judgment a plaintiff could enforce that judgment in relation to the asset as if the judgment were by an English court in the proceedings initially brought there. Such a provision would be an inroad into the principles underlying the predominant view in English law of the maritime

---

135. [1981] A.C. 221.

136. If the proceedings are stayed, as distinct from dismissed, the stay may be removed and if a stay be seen as "suspending" a lien it would presumably return with the proceedings.

137. [1979] Q.B. 377, at p. 404.

138. A distinction supported by the recognition of foreign arrest and normal prohibition of a concurrent English arrest by the claimant. See *The Christiansborg* (1885) 10 P.D. 141; *The Arctic Star* (1985) *The Times* 5 February. As to the need for maritime liens enforced in England to be "English", see Chaps. 2 and 26. Compare the ability to enforce a foreign judgment *in rem*. (See Chap. 27.) As to arrest generally see Chap. 15.

lien being a jurisdictional and procedural matter. It would mean the separation of the question of any lien from that of the claim, and the governing of the lien issue by English law simply because the asset is in England. But there is no compelling reason why the substantive security interest created by the claim must be adjudged by the law of the place where the asset physically is—that is to allow the implementation of the interest to control the interest itself.[139]

Equivalent security

The rules relevant to alternative security[140] should apply to any security given. So bail should be treated as the ship and any guarantee as a contractual undertaking.

IV. LODGING OF BAIL OR PROVISION OF OTHER SECURITY

(a) Bail

The role of bail and, in particular, its relation to arrest is discussed in Chapter 15. Bail takes the place of the property as the asset subject to attachment for the claim to the extent that it reflects the value of that asset[141] but it seems unclear whether, for the claimant, the bail is truly a substitute security.

If bail is not taken to the full value of the property,[142] as the property (usually a ship) may be rearrested up to the amount of judgment on liability, a lien should remain to the extent of any difference between the amount of bail and value of the property. It is possible to argue that the claimant having accepted bail as a substitute should not be able to return to the ship—but bail should be seen as the amount to be lodged to obtain release rather than necessarily a replacement for the ship for the purposes of the lien.

In at least one case, however, it was held that a claimant accepting insufficient bail could not claim payment in respect of the amount not covered by the bail in priority to other claimants *in rem*. But if the bail turns out to be defective as, for example, where a surety becomes insolvent, the claimant should not be able to return to the property for security in lieu of the bail. It would be illogical to view bail as a replacement of the property in respect of which it is given and then to allow recourse to that property if the bail is defective. In that case it is as if the bail was destroyed.

Limitation of liability—limitation action

Under the Convention Relating to the Limitation of Liability for Maritime Claims 1976 (as enacted by the Merchant Shipping Act 1979 and now the Merchant Shipping Act 1995) a ship is to be released once a fund is established in a contracting State as specified in the Convention. The release must operate at least to prevent the enforcement of any lien in respect of that claim up to the amount of the "alternative security" provided. Given that

---

139. As to issues of governing law, see Chap. 26.
140. See Chap. 15.
141. It would appear that any termination of the lien would depend on the lodging of bail rather than the actual release—for it would be the consequence of the loss of the lien which would be the reason for the release, not vice versa.
142. i.e. at the moment of original arrest. See *The Flora* (1886) L.R. 1 A. & E. 45 and *supra*.

the fund reflects the amount recoverable, unless for some reason the fund is not effective or liability not limited the lien will be extinguished on satisfaction of the claim. Liens are irrelevant to the distribution of such a fund.[143]

(b) Payment into court

On occasion, payment into court has been accepted as a security to prevent arrest or to obtain the release of property.[144] No provision is made in the Supreme Court Rules for this role for such a payment but its availability seems to be as established as its use is rare.[145] Release of property from arrest will depend on the consent of the arresting party or an order of the court. If the property is released it would seem that the consequences applicable to release after lodging of bail will apply.

(c) Security by way of guarantee or undertaking

As is said in Chapter 15, this is a contractual agreement to pay. It is not paid into court although the court in its inherent jurisdiction can prevent the demanding of excessive security.[146] The effect of the acceptance of security of this kind on a maritime lien is less certain than that of bail, not only because of its relative novelty but more because of its contractual nature. It is clear that no English court would permit the claimant to rearrest of the property or even issue another writ *in rem* while the undertaking remains in force.[147] However, if for any reason it was not fulfilled, it may be argued rather more forcefully than with respect to bail that the power to arrest is revived. A contractual understanding is surely a basis for preventing or releasing from arrest[148] and at the least an undertaking not to enforce the lien. But the lien would seem to remain until at least judgment on liability.[149]

The uncertainty of whether a maritime lien continues despite an undertaking may well affect the practicality of sale of a ship. In the Canadian case of *The Birchglen*[150] shipowners failed to obtain a declaration that a lien had been extinguished by a guarantee.

---

143. See generally Chap. 24.

144. See e.g. *The Bramarand* (1968) Unreported (Fo. 265); *The Monaco Philomel* (1968) Unreported (Fo. 414) (cited in *Admiralty Practice* (*British Shipping Laws*, Vol. 1), McGuffie, 34d Cumulative Supp. 1975, para. 340).

145. See *Supreme Court Practice 1995*—Notes to RSC Order 75, r. 13. As to procedure of payment into court and payment out, see RSC Order 75, r. 24, which applies appropriate provisions of Order 22. As to apportionment to different salving ships see *The Talamba* [1965] 2 All E.R. 775.

146. See e.g. *The Moschanthy* [1971] 1 Lloyd's Rep. 37; *The Polo II* [1977] 2 Lloyd's Rep. 115.

147. See e.g. *The Christiansborg* (1885) 10 PD 141, at pp. 155–156. See also the requirement that release be ordered upon the establishing of a limitation fund; Merchant Shipping Act 1995, Sch. 7, Art. 13(2) and *supra*.

148. Property under arrest must be released through a court order but, as for bail, it would seem the loss of lien is dependent on the undertaking or in limitation action the provision of the fund rather than the release (see fn. 141, *supra*).

149. By the Merchant Shipping Act 1894, s.554, a salvor could agree to abandon his lien in return for an agreement to abide by the decision of the High Court and the giving of security. As the agreement binds the ship, cargo and freight it takes on proprietary characteristics but its precise effect is unclear. It does not appear to add anything to general principles of waiver. The provision is repealed 1 May 1994 by the Merchant Shipping (Registration etc.) Act 1993, Sch. 5. Property detained by a receiver of wreck for salvage and released upon provision of satisfactory security under the Merchant Shipping Act 1894, s.552 (now the Merchant Shipping Act 1995, s.226(3)), cannot be rearrested and any lien appears terminated (see *The Lady Katherine Barham* (1861) Lush 404).

150. [1990] 3 F.C. 301.

The court accepted that it was premature to make that order, there necessarily being no certainty that the undertaking would be enforceable and the lien being known to all.

V. BANKRUPTCY AND LIQUIDATION

The question is whether a maritime lien attracted to a claim is affected by the bankruptcy of an individual or the winding up of a company the owner of the property to which the lien is attached. As a maritime lien holder is a secured creditor in respect of the property to which the lien is attached, it should follow that the security remains. However, problems have occurred because of the separate development of bankruptcy and liquidation proceedings and maritime liens.

Bankruptcy

By virtue of being a secured creditor, the holder of a maritime lien created prior to a bankruptcy order is protected against its effect.[151]

Winding up or liquidation

Winding up may be voluntary or compulsory. The effect of winding up on liens generally is discussed in Chapter 17. In both types of liquidation the court has power to control proceedings against the company. The effect of the provisions of the Insolvency Act 1986 is as summed up in *Re Aro Co. Ltd*[152] in relation to equivalent provisions of the Companies Act 1948.

"A winding up order has been made, proceedings are automatically stayed but the court may on application by the creditor allow them to be continued: while on a voluntary winding up or where a petition has been presented but not adjudicated on, there is no automatic stay but the court may on application by the interested party restrain proceedings."[153]

Normally a secured creditor will be allowed to proceed and, indeed, in *Re Aro Co. Ltd* the Court of Appeal held that "leave will automatically be given" to the holder of a maritime lien.

VI. AGREEMENT, WAIVER AND ESTOPPEL

The maritime lien attached to a claim depends for its existence on the continued existence of the claim.[154] Subject to statutory restrictions[155] any claim to which a maritime lien attaches may be waived or the claimant estopped for asserting it through the application

---

151. Insolvency Act 1986, s.285(3)(4). A court has power to stay actions after presentation of the bankruptcy petition (s.285(1)(2)) but in practice will not restrain an action by a secured creditor (*Re Evelyn* [1894] 2 Q.B. 302). As to the effect of bankruptcy proceedings on arrest see Chap. 10.
152. [1980] 1 All E.R. 1067. As to the effect of a winding up on arrest see Chap. 10.
153. *Ibid*, at p. 1071.
154. So, a bottomry bond given as a collateral security for a bill of exchange will be discharged on payment of the bill. See e.g. *Stainbank v. Shepard* (1853) 13 C.B. 418.
155. As to restrictions on assignment and waiver, see *supra*.

of general principles.[156] As a consequence, the lien would fall with the claim. There seems no reason in principle why (again subject to statutory restrictions) a claimant should not be permitted to renounce his lien[157] or, even more likely by his action, held to be estopped from asserting it.[158] The acceptance of payment, compensation or security in lieu of a lien, if it be held to be freely done, could amount to waiver[159] and the voluntary postponement of a claim might of itself affect its enforcement against third parties arriving on the scene after the postponement and not knowing of the claim.

There is a statutory prohibition on a salvor enforcing his maritime lien "when satisfactory security for his claim including interest and costs has been duly tendered or provided".[160] As the prohibition appears in the Salvage Convention 1989 and the Convention also provides that nothing in it is to affect the maritime lien,[161] the lien continues in being until extinguished in accordance with general principles.

VII. DESTRUCTION OF THE PROPERTY

Subject to judicial sale, a maritime lien is essentially and exclusively linked to the property to which it is attached. If that is destroyed the lien is extinguished.[162]

VIII. JUDGMENT ON LIABILITY

The rule that the power to arrest terminates on an English judgment on liability sits ill with the undoubted continuation of a maritime lien until judicial sale or payment of the moneys for which it reflects a security interest. As arrest is inherent in an action *in rem* it must follow that an action *in rem* will not lie. A maritime lien not enforceable by an action *in rem* is a strange creature indeed. It seems, therefore, that any limitation on arrest not coincidental with a lien (be it maritime or statutory) is suspect.[163]

IX. JUDICIAL SALE

The effect of judicial sale is discussed in Chapter 25. Suffice it to say here that it extinguishes not only the lien which led to the arrest and sale but all other liens attached to the property.[164] The liens are transferred to the fund created by the proceeds.

156. See *The William Money* (1827) 2 Hag. Adm. 136. Cf. *The Simlah* (1851) 18 L.T. (O.S.) 35; *The Goulandris* [1927] P. 182 (security under Lloyd's Open Form). If the claim is paid but the moneys left in the hands of the payer the lien does not remain in existence—the claim is paid and the claimant has decided how to deal with that paid (see *The Rainbow* (1885) 5 Asp. M.L.C. 479). However, it must be paid not simply postponed (see *The Simlah* (1851) 18 L.T. (O.S.) 35)).
157. See *The Royal Arch* (1857) Swab. 269. For the effect of undue delay, see Chap. 11 *supra*.
158. See e.g. *The Leon Blum* [1915] P. 290; *The Goulandris* [1927] P. 182 (but in this case the agreement provided for security).
159. The agreement may amount to suspension or to extinguishment (see *The Goulandris* (*supra*)) or may go only to claims *in personam* against the owner or charterer (see *The Chieftain* (1863) B. & L. 104, 212).
160. Merchant Shipping Act 1995, Sch. 11, Art. 20.2. (See also Lloyd's Open Form 1990.)
161. *Ibid*, Art. 20.1.
162. Unless construed as an equitable floating charge all types of lien are linked to the property in an identical way to the maritime lien. Compare the effect of the equitable doctrine of tracing. See generally Chap. 17.
163. See Chap. 15.
164. The English rule applies to sales by English and foreign courts. From time to time courts express concern (rightly) about hints that a foreign law will not recognize a clear title. See e.g. *The Cerro Colorado* [1993] 1 Lloyd's Rep. 58.

8. THE INTERNATIONAL FRAMEWORK RELATING TO MARITIME LIENS

There have been three international attempts to create a uniform framework, the first two not meeting with great success. The International Convention for the Unification of Certain Rules Relating to Maritime Liens and Mortgages 1926 had, by 4 January 1995 been ratified by 28 states. The Convention of the same name of 1967, intended to replace that of 1926, has been ratified by four states and the domestic legislation of a number who have not ratified is consistent with its provisions.[165] Many of the more powerful maritime nations such as Japan, the United Kingdom and the United States have not ratified either Convention. A third attempt has resulted in the acceptance on 6 May 1993 by delegates of 65 states of the International Convention on Maritime Liens and Mortgages 1993. The Convention is to come into force six months after the consent of five states, and in respect of each consenting state three months after the expression of such consent.[166]

The continued lack of success in attracting more support seems to reflect distinctions between national laws going more to the nature of the claims to which the lien is attached than the characteristics conferred by a "lien". Insofar as difficulty in reaching agreement stems from the priority on maritime liens over mortgages—the conflict between the operating and financial interests—it is questionable whether national maritime interests are best served by the reluctance to concede that the international list might not entirely match the domestic list. This is indicated by the lack of consensus on conflict of laws principles governing the creation and operation of maritime liens—with the consequences that a lien may be attached and may be lost as a ship sails from one country to another.

The Conventions are limited in scope—justifiably given the difficulties of obtaining agreement. As regards mortgages they encompass only provisions for registration, priority, transfer of ownership and rules relating to forced sale. As regards liens the Conventions provide for maritime liens and recognize liens under national law.[167] Uncertainty remains as to the effect of the enforcement or lapse of one type of lien on the other.

Further the provision for lapse of any lien by arrest within a specified and short period emphasizes the prime method of enforcement of the liens.[168] However, it would have been

---

165. Contracting parties to the 1926 Convention can opt not to apply its rules in favour of nationals of non-contracting States (Art. 14). The 1967 Convention (subject to any restrictions specified in it) applies to ships of contracting and non-contracting States (Art. 12). Neither Convention creates rights against state vessels in non-commercial service (1926) Art. 15, (1967) Art. 12. In the 1967 Convention it is specified that parties may reserve the right to apply the Convention relating to limitation of shipowner's liability (Art. 14). The 1926 Convention provides that payment of claims shall not exceed sums due under limitation rules (Art. 7).

166. States may consent to the Convention through signature subject to and followed by ratification approval or acceptance signature above or accession (Art. 18). There are no provisions for substantive reservations. Subject to any restrictions specified in the Convention it applies to ships registered in contracting States and ships registered in a non-contracting State if within the jurisdiction of a non-contracting State (Art. 13(1)). The Convention creates no rights against vessels owned or operated by a state and used only on government non-commercial services (Art. 13(2)). It does not affect any national law or international Convention concerning limitation of liability (Art. 15).

167. The Salvage Convention 1989 provides that nothing in it shall affect the salvors maritime lien—but also prohibits enforcement if alternative adequate security is tendered or given (Art. 20).

168. There remains uncertainty in respect of the extinguishment in national law following sale to a bona fide purchaser—for in that context there is no reference to effect of arrest—yet just as in other contexts arrest surely would amount to enforcement of the lien (see p. 425).

preferable to refer to the implementation of liens as such rather than simply the prevention of lapse. The relationship of arrest and lien would thereby be clarified,[169] for as the 1967 and 1993 Conventions stand it appears that a claimant must arrest the ship to ensure enforcement of the lien—the acceptance of bail or guarantee in lieu would therefore mean that on the expiry of the period the lien would lapse. Conversely there are no provisions as to extinguishment through consent, waiver or acceptance of other security.[170]

The latest Liens and Mortgages Convention reflects the continuing need for agreement, but, despite expressions of favourable conditions for a large number of ratifications, differs as regards liens little in substance from its predecessors. Identical factors operate in favour and against success, but with a growing incredulity at the inability of states to get together on the highly technical, rather narrow but critical aspect of maritime property interests and financing of the industry. Changes would be required in English law, but hardly of great substance in the nature of claims. A radical and welcome change would be the limited period for enforcement of liens, certainty of priorities and uniformity in the basic framework. Issues as to the governing law would be rendered redundant as to Convention liens and a uniform framework provided for mortgages. The adoption would not affect the distribution of a limitation fund.[171]

I. THE CONVENTION OF 1926

Mortgages

The Convention provides for the recognition of such mortgages "hypothecations and other similar charges" as are created and registered in accordance with the law of the contracting state to which the vessel belongs, and for their ranking in priority immediately after the claims attracting a maritime lien.[172]

Maritime liens

The Convention recognizes five categories of claims attracting maritime liens: law costs, light, harbour, tonnage and pilotage dues and taxes; claims arising out of the contract of engagement of the masters and crew; salvage and general average claims; collision, personal injury and cargo damage claims and masters' disbursements.[173] The Convention does not apply to vessels of war or government ships on public service.[174] A maritime lien

169. The draft of the revised Arrest Convention cures the uncertainty of the present Arrest Convention because the lack of link between arrest and the power under national law to order judicial sale. The uncertainty of the Mortgages and Liens Convention goes to the opposite point of the dependence of the existence of a lien on arrest.

170. Compare the provision of the Convention Salvage 1989 that a salvor may not enforce the maritime line if satisfactory security is provided (Art. 20(2)).

171. The Convention does not affect the application of any Convention or limitation of liability or national legislation giving effect to such a Convention (Art. 15). In English law it is provided that distribution of the limitation fund is not to take account of any lien. See Merchant Shipping Act 1995 Sched. 7, Part II, para. 9 and Chap. 24.

172. Article 1. There is no definition of mortgage or charge. The Convention of 1967 omits "other similar charges".

173. Article 2. The English translation makes no distinction between pilotage and other dues but the French translation refers to "Frais de pilotage" as distinct from (e.g.) "droits de tonnage".

174. Article 15.

may attach to a ship, freight or a ship's accessories as defined in the Convention.[175] A claim to which limitation of liability rules apply will not exceed the sum due under those rules.[176]

A maritime lien within the Convention is enforceable against a ship "into whatever hands it may pass" and against a chartered ship[177]: it ranks above mortgage and any other liens recognized by national laws, and an order of priority is provided as between claims attracting maritime liens.[178] Apart from masters' disbursements the liens are extinguished after one year—the lien in relation to disbursements lasts only six months.[179] National law may provide for other grounds of extinction (where judicial sale is such a ground publicity being required); may extend the periods where arrest has not been possible in the claimant's state[180]; and may require formalities for loans raised on security of the ship or for the sale of cargo.[181]

Other liens

National laws may recognize claims other than those listed in the Convention as attracting liens but not so as to modify Convention priorities.[182]

II.THE CONVENTION OF 1967[183]

Principal changes from the Convention of 1926

The Convention follows a like pattern to that of 1926 but amends and clarifies it. In particular the ambit of the Convention is increased by provisions as to deregistration and re-registration of a vessel to ensure the protection of mortgagees. The most important substantive amendments are:

(1) Save for forced sale in relation to mortgages the imposition of an obligation on each contracting State not to deregister a vessel without the consent of holders of registered mortgages and hypotheques or to register a vessel which has been registered in another such state without a certificate of deregistration;

(2) as to the claims attracting maritime liens
   (i) omission of masters' disbursement claims;
  (ii) widening of "collision claims";
 (iii) exclusion of claims involving nuclear activities;

175. Articles 2, 4 and 10.
176. Article 7. But cf. the Convention provisions relating to limitation of liability whereby a limitation fund must be distributed without regard to liens see fn. 171.
177. Articles 8, 13.
178. Articles 3 and 5.
179. Article 9.
180. *Ibid.*
181. Article 11.
182. Article 3.
183. The Convention comes into force three months after the fifth ratification (Art. 19). By 31 December 1995 it had been ratified by Denmark, Sweden and Norway and acceded to by Syria and Morocco but this does not seem to bring the Convention into force. Compare the wide definition of "consent" in the 1993 Convention. Finland has denounced the Convention of 1926 but has not ratified the Convention of 1967. Despite the Convention provisions the four Scandinavian countries have introduced its provisions into their domestic law.

     (iv) substitution of provision for law costs in the context of judicial sale instead of by a maritime lien;

(3) restriction of Convention maritime liens to sea-going vessels;

(4) permitting national law to give priority over mortgages to shipbuilders and ship repairers' right of retention;

(5) provision for assignment of liens;

(6) more detailed provision concerning judicial sale and distribution of proceeds;

(7) provision of an option to a party to apply the Convention Relating to the Limitation of Liability of Owners of Sea Going Ships 1957.

The pattern of the Convention

Mortgage and hypotheques

The Convention provides for the recognition of mortgages created and registered in accordance with the law of the state where the ship is registered, for requirements of the register, including priority *inter se*, for the law to govern the creation, priority and enforceability, and for the need of holders of mortgages and hypotheques to agree to deregistration of a ship.[184]

Maritime liens

The Convention provides for five categories of claims attracting maritime liens: (i) wages; (ii) dues; (iii) claims in respect of loss of life or personal injury; (iv) claims in tort in respect of property damage occurring in direct connection with the operation of the vessel; (v) salvage, wreck removal and general average claims. Excluded are claims based on nuclear activities.[185] The Convention does not apply to ships in which a state has an interest and which is appropriated to public non-commercial service.[186] The lien attaches to a ship only but is enforceable despite any change of ownership and may attach to a chartered ship, or a ship operated by a person other than the owner, whether the person liable for the claim is the owner or operator.[187]

    Maritime liens are given priority over mortgages and any other liens created by a state and rules are specified relating to the priority of maritime liens *inter se*.[188] A maritime lien is extinguished after one year unless there is an earlier arrest and subsequent forced sale. Time does not run while a lienor is legally prevented from arresting a ship.[189] Publicity is required prior to a forced sale[190] and it is provided that on such sale "all liens and other encumbrances of whatsoever nature" save a charterparty or contract of hire of a ship shall

---

184. Articles 1, 2 and 3. Article 3(2) provies a general prohibition on registration without judicial sale or a certificate of deregistration.

185. Article 4.

186. Article 12(2).

187. Articles 4(1) and 7.

188. Article 5.

189. Article 8.

190. Article 10.

cease to attach to the ship.[191] The proceeds are to be distributed in accordance with the Convention priority provisions.[192]

Other liens

Contracting States may grant other liens or rights of retention. Apart from liens attached to shipbuilding and ship repairing claims, such liens rank in priority lower than Convention maritime liens and registered mortgages and cannot affect their enforceability. A national law may give priority to possessory liens attached to shipbuilding or ship repairing claims over that of mortgage, but such liens are extinguished upon loss of possession by the holder of the lien.[193] A forced sale will transfer a lien given such priority from the ship to the proceeds of sale.[194]

III. THE CONVENTION OF 1993

The Convention follows the pattern of its predecessors.[195] The principal changes from the Convention of 1967 are:

- (1) as to registration—
  - (i) provision where a vessel is temporarily registered in a state
  - (ii) more detailed provisions concerning change of ownership and registration.
- (2) as to the claims attracting maritime liens—
  - (i) the exclusion of wreck removal and general average contributions
  - (ii) the exclusion of damage in connection with carriage of oil or other hazardous substances for which compensation is payable under another Convention or statutory regime
  - (iii) change in the definition of tortious claims arising out of physical loss or damage
  - (iv) some change in priorities as between Convention maritime liens
  - (v) provision for extinguishment of national law liens by expiry of time without enforcement
  - (vi) exclusion of compensation payable under an insurance contract from effect of subrogation of a claim attracting a maritime lien
  - (vii) yet more detailed provisions concerning forced sale and no exception in respect of charterparties ceasing to attach to the vessel
  - (viii) making the Convention subject to any Convention providing for limitation of liability.

---

191. Article 11(1). The exception of the charterparty was included to avoid penalizing a mortgagee who normally will have taken assignment of charter hire as additional security; but it could create problems in the light of the use of long term charterparties instead of sale as a means of ship financing. Given the exemption a demise charterparty may cause a lien to arise which survives a sale. All mortgages and hypotheques not assumed by the purchaser with the consent of the holders also cease to attach to the ship (*ibid*).
192. Article 11(2).
193. Article 6.
194. As to forced sale, see Chap. 25.
195. For a comprehensive review and comparison with the 1967 Convention see Berlingieri [1995] LMCLQ 57.

The pattern of the Convention

Registration of vessels

The Convention applies to all sea going vessels save state-owned vessels on government service (i) which are registered in a State party or (ii) registered elsewhere but within the jurisdiction of a State party.[196] It is directly concerned with mortgages, hypotheques, "registrable charges of the same nature", maritime liens and rights of retention.

As with the 1967 Convention, the ambit of the 1993 Convention extends beyond mortgages and liens in the sense that it sets out rules for change of registration following change of ownership. There may be no deregistration without (i) deletion of registered mortgages, hypotheques and charges or (ii) written consent of the holders of the interests or (iii) where by national law deregistration is mandatory or transfer otherwise than by voluntary sale, notice to such holders and the expiry of a period of not less than three months. A vessel may not be re-registered without a certificate of deregistration.[197]

Where a vessel is permitted temporarily to fly the flag of another state the matters referred by the Convention to the state of registration are referred to the state or registration immediately prior to the temporary registration. There must be cross references in the registers of each state, and the temporary registration is dependent on satisfaction of registered mortgage or written consent of their holders. On production of a certificate of deregistration following forced sale, on request of the purchaser the vessel's right to fly the temporary flag must be revoked.[198]

Registered mortgages hypotheques and "registrable charges"[199]

As with its predecessors the Convention's role is restricted to provision for recognition, enforcement and priority of such interests registered in accordance with the law of the state of the vessel's registration. There is recognition only where the register is open to public inspection and contains details of the interest, its creation and the holder. Matters of priority and effect on third parties are for the law of the state of registration, matters of enforcement for the law of the state of enforcement. Holders of registered interests are entitled to notice of pending deregistration because of non-voluntary sale and of any forced sale. They are protected by the prohibition on deregistration without deletion, consent or, where appropriate, notice.[200] The interests will cease on forced sale.[201]

"Maritime liens and right of retention"

The Convention provides for five groups of maritime lien which take priority over all other interests including mortgages and for the recognition of other liens created by national laws.[202] A right of retention may be created by national law in favour of

---

196. Article 13. Unregistered vessels therefore fall outside it.
197. Article 3.
198. Article 16.
199. The Convention provisions are concerned only with registered charges—"registrable" therefore simply excludes the non-registrable but of itself confers no benefit.
200. Articles 1–3.
201. Article 12(1).
202. Articles 4, 5.

shipbuilders and ship repairers, the satisfaction of the right on forced sale ranking only after Convention maritime liens.[203]

Save for claims arising from the radioactive properties of nuclear fuel or radioactive waste and carriage of hazardous or noxious substances "Convention" maritime liens attach to claims against the "owner, demise charterer, manager or operator of the vessel" in the following groups—

(a) wages of the master, officers and other "members of the vessel's complement" in respect of employment on the vessel including repatriation costs and social security contributions

(b) for loss of life or personal injury occurring whether on land or on water in direct connection with the operation of the vessel

(c) "reward for the salvage of the vessel"

(d) port, canal and other waterway dues and pilotage dues

(e) tortious claims arising out of physical loss or injury caused by the operation of the vessel "other than loss of or damage to cargo, containers and passengers' effects carried on the vessel".

The liens follow the vessel[204]

Save for any provision in national law for payment of removal of a sunken or stranded vessel or forced sale the lien takes priority over every other claim. Priorities between those liens in (a)–(e) are in the order listed save that salvage takes precedence over all other liens attached prior to it. Claims within each paragraph rank *pari passu* and salvage claims as between themselves in inverse order to the date of the salvage operation giving rise to the claim.[205]

The satisfaction in judicial sale of a claim arising out of a right of retention ranks after Convention liens.[206] The assignment or subrogation of a claim secured by a lien entails the assignment or subrogation to such a lien but claimants with maritime liens are not to be subrogated to compensation payable to an owner under another insurance contract.[207]

Convention liens are extinguished by forced sale or after one year unless the vessel has been arrested or seized, thus leading to forced sale.[208] Notice of forced sale must be given to the authority in charge of the register of the state of registration, the registered owner, holders of registered mortgages, hypotheques or charges not issued to bearers and to such holders of "bearer" charges if claimants have given notice of the claims to the authority conducting the sale.[209]

Forced sale will extinguish all registered mortages save those continued by consent and all liens and "other encumbrances of whatever nature" provided that the sale is conducted in the state where the vessel is and in accordance with the law of that state. The funds are paid out to meet seizure and sale costs, the claims recognized under the Convention and

203. Articles 7, 12(4).
204. Article 8.
205. Article 5.
206. Article 12(4).
207. Article 10—the proviso, it is said ensuring that the insurance compensation remains available to the mortgagee.
208. Articles 9, 12.
209. Article 11.

any residue to the owner. The proceeds are to be made available and freely transferable. On request by a purchaser a certificate as to the interest free sale must be provided and on production of such a certificate the vessel is to be deregistered or registered as appropriate.[210]

Other liens

National law liens follow the vessel. Assignment and subrogation are as for Convention liens. They rank after Convention liens, rights of retention and registered mortgages. They are extinguished after a period of six months unless arrest or seizure takes place within that period and leads to a forced sale or after 60 days following registration of a bona fide purchaser whichever period expires first.[211]

---

210. Article 12. Unlike the Convention of 1967 there is no exception for charterparties.
211. Article 6.

CHAPTER 19

Statutory Liens in Admiralty

THE ACTION "IN REM" AND STATUTORY LIENS IN ADMIRALTY

The claims enforceable by action *in rem* are those listed or referred to in the Supreme Court Act 1981, s.20. They are discussed in Chapter 2. As said in Chapter 17, the label "statutory liens" when used in an Admiralty context is used as equivalent to "statutory rights *in rem*", and to some the latter is the more accurate description of the right. The present legislative framework provides for three categories of claim which, apart from the maritime lien, attract the action *in rem* and a fourth category which arguably does so. These are claims based on:

    (i) s.20(2)(e)–(r)[1];
   (ii) s.20(2)(a)(b)(c) and (s);
  (iii) future jurisdiction (s.20(1)(d)); and
  (iv) (arguably) the sweeping up clause (s.20(1)(c)).

It will be suggested that it is only in respect of (i) that the label "statutory lien" precisely applies. The legislative development of and judicial comments on the nature of the action *in rem* have helped to confuse its substantive and procedural security aspects. These should be disentangled.

1. NATURE OF THE "STATUTORY LIEN"

I. ORIGINS AND EARLY DEVELOPMENT

The statutory lien in Admiralty followed recognition of the concept of "maritime lien". Statutory liens in Admiralty originate in the Admiralty Court Acts 1840 and 1861, both of which provided that the High Court of Admiralty "shall have jurisdiction" over a number of claims. The Act of 1861, s.35, further specifically provided that the jurisdiction conferred by that Act "may be exercised either by proceedings *in rem* or by proceedings *in personam*". The statutory liens in Admiralty are based and depend on the availability of the action *in rem*.

---

1. As amended by the Merchant Shipping (Salvage and Pollution) Act 1994, Sch. 2, para. 6 (s.20(2)(j)) (applicable to salvage services started on or after 1 January 1995).

Admiralty Court Acts 1840 and 1861 and maritime liens

The two statutes were judicially construed to mean that unless a maritime lien existed in relation to the claim prior to the statute or was expressly conferred by the statute, the rights conferred were simply to enforce a claim by Admiralty proceedings and in particular by proceedings *in rem*.[2] As a result, the limited effect these and later statutes had as regards maritime liens was to include within claims for attracting a maritime lien (a) damage or salvage arising within the body of a county,[3] (b) wages claims on special contracts,[4] (c) (possibly) claims for life salvage and property damage under statutory provisions,[5] and (d) (possibly) claims for personal injury and loss of life.[6] Apart from these claims the provisions in the Acts that the Admiralty Court "shall have jurisdiction . . . " meant just that.

Statutory extensions of the action "in rem" between 1861 and 1925

The availability of the action *in rem* in Admiralty was increased through enlarging Admiralty jurisdiction in the Maritime Conventions Act 1911 (maritime personal injury or wrongful death); the Merchant Shipping (Stevedores and Trimmers) Act 1911 (claims by such persons); and the Administration of Justice Act 1920 (in relation to foreign shipowner defendants, charterparties, carriage of goods and torts in respect of goods carried). The Supreme Court of Judicature (Consolidation) Act 1925 further extended the scope of proceedings *in rem* by removing territorial restrictions from claims for necessaries and salvage and towage.

II. THE SUPREME COURT ACT 1981—THE PRESENT FRAMEWORK FOR THE ACTION "IN REM"

The Administration of Justice Act 1956 greatly extended the territorial jurisdiction, added to the number of claims for which proceedings *in rem* will lie and formed the foundation for the present framework set out in the Supreme Court Act 1981 (as amended). That (discussed in Chapter 2) clearly distinguishes the exercise of the Admiralty jurisdiction through (a) an action *in personam*, (b) a maritime lien and (c) an action *in rem* apart from a maritime lien.[7]

As to the framework of the 1981 Act:

---

2. See e.g. *The Heinrich Bjorn* (1866) 11 App. Cas. 270; *The Mary Ann* (1865) L.R. 1 A. & E. 8; *The Sara* (1889) 14 App. Cas. 209; *Currie v. M'Knight* [1897] A.C. 97; *The Halcyon Skies* [1977] Q.B. 14.

3. Admiralty Court Act 1840, s.6; 1861, s.7.

4. See *The Halcyon Skies* [1977] Q.B. 14 (jurisdiction extended by the Admiralty Court Act 1861, s.10).

5. See the Admiralty Court Act 1861, s.9 and Chap. 2. These provisions "cease to have effect" from 1 January 1995 (Merchant Shipping (Salvage and Pollution) Act 1994, Sch. 2, para. 1(2)). As to life salvage see Chaps. 2, 18.

6. See Chap. 2. It was held that the jurisdictional provisions relating to masters' disbursements (Admiralty Court Act 1861, s.10) did not confer a maritime lien (*The Sara* (1889), s.1). As to the continued operation of prior statutory provisions defining the ambit of claims see *infra* and Chap 1.

7. The distinction is blurred by the statutory linking of "other charge" to maritime lien as a basis for an action *in rem*. The phrase has been construed to a mean such charge as is in English law statutorily equated with a maritime lien or under foreign law is similar to an English maritime lien. *The Acrux* [1965] P. 391; *The St Merriel* [1963] P. 247 and Chap. 2.

(a) statutory provisions have settled a dispute once relevant whether Admiralty jurisdiction includes claims attracting proceedings *in rem* which are neither statutorily based nor maritime liens. At most, these claims related to pilotage, towage and necessaries[8] and all are included in the claims now statutorily set out;

(b) the statute creates two categories of specific heads of claims which whether or not they attract a maritime lien attract the action *in rem*—those specified in s.20(2)(a)(b)(c) and (s) and those specified in s.20(2)(e)–(r)[9];

(c) the claims attracting maritime liens are included in the list of heads of claims for which an action *in rem* may be brought. It is clear that a claimant whose claim attracts a maritime lien may base his claim on the provision relating to maritime lien (s.21(3)) and also, when the claim is within the provision, on that relating to the action *in rem* apart from the maritime lien (s.21(4))[10];

(d) there are catch-all provisions including jurisdiction (other than the claims specified) allocated after the coming into force of the Act or (arguably) exercised immediately prior to the Act. These provisions do not specify any particular claims.

III. "THE STATUTORY LIEN IN ADMIRALTY"—IS IT TO BE EQUATED WITH THE ACTION "IN REM"?

Some take the view that all claims apart from maritime liens enforceable by an action *in rem* should be lumped together simply as "actions *in rem*".[11] But this fails (a) to indicate the substantive proprietary and priority characteristics conferred by the action on those claims to which it is attached, and (b) to distinguish between the two statutory categories of claim referred to in II(b) above.

(a) The action "in rem"—substance and procedure

In Chapter 18 it was suggested that a maritime lien confers a right of substance rather than procedure. Much of the supporting reasoning applies to the bringing of action *in rem* in respect of an otherwise non-proprietary claim. In *The Heinrich Bjorn*, delivering the judgment of the Court of Appeal, Fry L.J. drew a distinction between a maritime lien and the right to the exercise of Admiralty jurisdiction. He contrasted arrest as a means of giving effect to a pre-existent lien (the maritime lien) and arrest as "one of several alternative modes of procedure". In the first case, he said, the proceeding related back to the first moment the lien attached: in the second it did not. And further, he added, arrest to enforce a maritime lien can only be of the ship involved, but the lien does travel with

---

8. Necessaries are not specifically referred to but seem to be covered by s.20(2)(m) and (n).

9. As to s.20(2)(j) see fn 1.

10. Although only one ship will ultimately be available for enforcement of the claim (s.21(8)). See generally Chaps. 10, 15.

11. It is an easy step from such a description to "statutory rights *in rem*" (see e.g. Price, *op. cit.*, at p. 92). But so to label the availability of an action *in rem* is to generalize still further in that there may well be rights *in rem* apart from actions *in rem* (e.g. any common law property right). And it unnecessarily introduces an overused and uncertain concept (see for example, of confusion through the use of "*in rem*" in more than one sense, *The Angel Bell* [1979] 2 Lloyd's Rep. 491). As to the use of right *in rem* in the Brussels and Lugano Conventions see Article 16 and Chap. 5.

the ship: arrest in other contexts could be of other assets of the defendant but is available only against the property of the person liable *in personam*.[12]

However, it is now clear that almost all claims not being maritime liens attracting an action *in rem* will be effective against a purchaser[13] and that arrest can only be of the ship involved[14] or (within the parameters of the Supreme Court Act 1981, s.21(4)), a sister ship. Further, the "relation back" of the maritime lien goes to the moment of creation of the "lien" rather than any unique enforceability against purchasers, and the issue of a writ *in rem* means that (whether the claim attracts a maritime lien or not) the claimant becomes a secured creditor.[15] The distinction, therefore, is not between a "maritime lien" in the sense of a substantive right[16] *and* a right to benefit from proceedings (a procedural right) but between rights of substance. Whether all claims attracting an action *in rem* should be classified together as having identical characteristics is a question to be debated; but, with enforcement against third parties and the holder having the status of secured creditor, the basic right can hardly be described as simply "one of several alternative modes of procedure". It is proprietary.

This is not to say that the action *in rem* as such is not also a method of procedure. It is the means of asserting an interest—that interest being a maritime lien, a statutory lien or a proprietary right itself. The error is to equate the statutory lien with the method of enforcement—an error, particularly liable to occur when the lien is created by the issue of the writ *in rem*. In that context the same act creates the interest as initiates the enforcement process.

Further, the proprietary interest created by the lien does not mean that the cause of action being enforced by a writ *in rem* is any different to that enforced by a writ *in personam* simply because of the method of enforcement.[17] The basis of the claim is identical, the distinctions stemming from the interest (the lien) recognized by English law as enforceable (or available to be created), *its* method of enforceability and any difference in the identity of the parties.[18]

(b) The nature of the claims attracting the action "in rem"

To the extent to which a claim enforceable by an action *in rem* asserts a proprietary interest, the action *in rem* may be said to be primarily procedural. However, the majority of claims assertible by an action *in rem* have no proprietary characteristic in themselves. It is the availability of the action *in rem* which transposes a claim against the person liable *in personam* in the narrow sense of direct responsibility for the act of which complaint is

12. (1885) 10 P.D. 44, at p. 54.

13. *The Monica S* [1968] P. 741. But it is not clear that, for example, an equitable mortgagee would be able to enforce his claim against a bona fide purchaser or whether forfeiture can operate against a bona fide purchaser (see Chaps. 2 and 23).

14. *The Beldis* [1936] P. 51; Supreme Court Act 1981, s.21(8) (as to claims within s.20(2)(e)–(r)).

15. *Re Aro Co. Ltd.* [1980] Ch. 196. Because of the historical distinctions drawn between maritime and statutory liens the same cause of action may relate to a maritime lien or a statutory lien. So a salvage claim under the 1989 Convention will only attract a maritime lien if it does so in accordance with principles established outside that Convention. As to categorization of the claims see generally Chap. 2.

16. See Chap. 18 for argument that a maritime lien is a substantive right.

17. So in respect of the Brussels and Lugano Conventions concurrent actions *in personam* and *rem* will involve the same cause of action insofar as they are between the same parties (*The Maciej Rataj* [1995] 1 Lloyd's Rep. 302 (ECJ)).

18. See e.g. *The Varna (No. 2)* [1994] 2 Lloyd's Rep. 41.

made to a claim enforceable against third parties.[19] On the other hand, claims in respect of ownership and mortgage (and possibly possession) are "proprietary", quite apart from the availability of the action *in rem* in the sense that enforceability of the interest the basis of the claim is *not* restricted to the person creating the relationship. The differing nature of these claims and their characteristics are acknowledged in the priority context, for enforceability against purchasers is treated separately to enforceability against creditors, and mortgage is given a priority ranking of its own.[20]

More generally it is arguable that ownership and possession claims not involving claims otherwise within Admiralty jurisdiction raise questions different in kind to other claims attracting actions *in rem*. So a question of title may raise different policy issues in its enforceability against other claimants than a creditor's claim. Finally, claims based on forfeiture or condemnation of a ship or goods carried in a ship, restoration of a ship or goods after seizure or for droits of Admiralty seem to involve considerations apart from liability in a purely civil suit. They focus on public aspects of Admiralty jurisdiction far removed from the majority of claims in respect of which the jurisdiction exists.

(i) Claims in s.20(2)(e)–(r)—the proprietary role of the action "in rem"

As to those claims falling within s.20(2)(e)–(r), i.e. (claims not generally proprietary)[21] the Act specifies the characteristics of the right in setting out the framework for bringing the action *in rem*. The substantive interest created by the availability of the action *in rem* is, therefore, made clear by the rules governing the bringing of it. These rules were discussed in Chapter 2. It is clear that the claims within s.20(2)(e)–(r) have common proprietary characteristics flowing from attracting the action *in rem* in respect of the property at which the action is aimed (preferred creditor status, enforceability against purchasers and, in the case of demise charters, owners at the time of creation of the claim). These characteristics are sufficiently distinct from those attaching to claims not attracting the action *in rem* to justify a grouping to indicate that substantive proprietary nature. It is therefore appropriate that they should be labelled "statutory liens in Admiralty".

(ii) Claims in s.20(2)(a)(b)(c) and (s)—the procedural role of the action "in rem"

In contrast to the provisions relating to s.20(2)(e)–(r) the Act does not specify the framework for bringing the action *in rem* in respect of claims included in s.20(2)(a)(b)(c) and (s). In relation to claims based on ownership, possession, mortgage, forfeiture, condemnation or droits in Admiralty the Act provides simply that proceedings *in rem* against the ship involved will lie. It therefore makes enforceability depend on, first, the nature of the action *in rem* of itself and, secondly, the nature of the claim. Further, apart from mortgage claims, there is little if any guidance in judicial decisions as to the priority of these claims as against others or as between themselves. Conversely, as to mortgages, it is certain that they have a higher priority than other claims attracting an action *in rem* but not qualifying as maritime liens.

---

19. i.e. other creditors and purchasers and where the demise charterer is liable *in personam*, the present owner.

20. See Chap. 23.

21. But not exclusively non-proprietary, e.g. a claim to enforce a demise charterparty would be within s.20(2)(h), a bottomry claim is the subject of s.20(2)(r) and a salvage claim of s.20(2)(j).

The common characteristics between the group of claims set out in s.20(2)(e)–(r) and those set out in s.20(2)(a)(b)(c) and (s) is the availability of the action *in rem*. But in regard to the latter first, the action is available in some cases against property other than a ship; secondly, the action is available only against the property in question and not against any "sister" property; thirdly, any required link between liability *in personam* and the relevant property is left to be gathered from the nature of the action *in rem* itself; finally, at least one claim—mortgage—is given a distinct priority. It seems, therefore, that the availability of the action *in rem* for claims in s.20(2)(e)–(r) has undeniable substantive consequences, but that in its availability in relation to claims within s.20(2)(a)(b) and (c) it fulfils much more of a procedural role.

In the case of mortgage claims its primary role seems to be to provide arrest and the availability of judicial sale to enforce a claim by nature proprietary and having a high priority.

A *claim for ownership or possession* will depend in substance on the legal foundation for the claim, and, again, its scope of enforceability will depend on the claim rather than the availability of the action *in rem*. Further, the relevance of the judicial sale as a remedy is somewhat peripheral to such claims—a claimant will be primarily seeking a declaration of ownership or acquisition of possession through a specific order, and taking advantage of the arrest process to ensure that the ship is available when the order is made.[22]

Claims based on forfeiture, condemnation or droits of Admiralty are of a completely different order to all other claims for which the action *in rem* is available and, once again, enforceability will primarily depend on the nature of the claim.

In these groups, therefore, the twin primary characteristics of the action *in rem* (the preferred creditor status and enforceability against purchasers) established in relation to claims in s.20(1)(e)–(r) are of doubtful application except as characteristics of the claims themselves.

(iii) Claims within s.20(1)(c)—past jurisdiction

It is arguable that on the statutory wording this head of jurisdiction applies only to actions *in personam*—the 1981 Act, it is said, specifying that the *in rem* jurisdiction is exclusively there set out.[23] However, as indicated in Chapter 2 it all depends on which provision of the Act takes precedence—that conferring *in rem* jurisdiction or the sweeping up clause. Given the presence of the provision, there seems just as strong an argument for inclusion of "*in rem*" jurisdiction in the latter given its presence and the importance of such jurisdiction to Admiralty claims.

Assuming the inclusion of "*in rem*" jurisdiction within the clause the claims are those which attracted the action *in rem* prior to 1 November 1875. Their proprietary characteristics depend, therefore, on first, the nature of the claim and, secondly, the effect of the action *in rem*, both of which questions must be the subject of enquiry in each particular case. In the *Despina GK* Sheen J. based the ability to issue a writ *in rem* in respect of a foreign judgment on this ground. He held specifically that the beneficiary of a foreign judgment *in rem* did not have a maritime lien but that:

22. Although claims as between co-owner may be for accounts or damages. See e.g. *The Vanessa Ann* [1985] 1 Lloyd's Rep. 549.
23. See *The Antonis P. Lemos* [1984] 1 Lloyd's Rep. 464 (C.A.).

"A judgment creditor who has obtained a final judgment against a shipowner by proceeding in rem in a foreign Admiralty Court can bring an action in rem in this Court against that ship to enforce the decree of the foreign Court if that is necessary to complete the execution of that judgment, provided that the ship is the property of the judgment debtor at the time when she is arrested."[24]

In this case the claim itself (action on a judgment) is not proprietary. The approach of the learned judge meant that the "action *in rem*" was equated (almost) with the action *in rem* as specified in s.21(4) of the Supreme Court Act. It is not clear why the property must remain in the judgment debtor until arrest rather than the issue of *in rem* proceedings. Such a requirement adds one more complication in differentiating between the characteristics of the action *in rem* depending on the claim to which it attaches; and it emphasizes that each claim in this category must be scrutinized to discover its own characteristics.

IV. SUMMARY

(i) The need for precise analysis

Legislative development of maritime claims has ignored the distinction between the provision of (i) a positive security interest created through the availability of an action *in rem*; and (ii) a method of enforcement of a security interest already held or that created by the issue of the writ *in rem* through the action *in rem* and hence the availability of arrest and (consequently) judicial sale. Judicial comment has largely been restricted to an overall classification of maritime and statutory liens as "procedural" or "substantive". But this, with respect, simply confuses the interest the basis of the claim with the method of enforcement.

In effect, the over-generalized and rather bland labels of substance and procedure tend to conceal the hard analysis required to link claim and action *in rem* and to conclude whether there is any "lien" characteristic. Even if a claim (such as ownership or mortgage) is proprietary, the availability of judicial sale (through arrest) may add another proprietary dimension. But the extent to which it does confer a proprietary characteristic needs examination in the context of each claim and each characteristic. So, for example, the effect of the availability of an action *in rem* (if any) on enforceability and priority of the claim to enforce an equitable mortgage or a claim for possession between demise and sub-demise charterer remains uncertain. The link between nature of claim and effect of the availability of the action *in rem* has never been examined, but the place of the action *in rem* in the Brussels and Lugano Convention has required more precise analysis than has perhaps traditionally been given.[25]

(ii) The need for legislative clarification

(a) Priority

It is suggested that the legislative aim must be to ensure that the availability of an action *in rem* carries common characteristics whatever the claim, and that apart from any clearly indicated exceptions it is the action *in rem* (and not the claim) which rules enforceability and priority *in rem*. The presently established exceptions are the maritime lien and the

24. [1982] 2 Lloyd's Rep. 555, at p. 559.
25. See Chap. 5.

mortgage. In both cases it is internationally recognized that of themselves they form priority categories and have "*in rem*" enforceability characteristics of their own. Uncertainty exists as to the unregistered ship mortgage recognized in English law but not universally. Because of the lack of international recognition it is arguable that it should be treated as having no more powerful priority or enforceability than a statutory lien. The issue is discussed in Chapter 23.

(b) Enforceability against third parties

The uncertainty of the scope of the action *in rem* in relation to claims for which it is provided but not defined[26] goes to enforceability against third parties. First, it would appear that historically it was available only in relation to property, the owners of which are liable *in personam*[27]—it would take statutory provisions to render a ship liable if personal liability lay with, for example, a charterer. However, as the court controls the imposition of judicial sale it is arguable that an action *in rem* could be brought in relation to a possession dispute between a charterer by demise and a subcharterer by demise. So long as the aim is the availability of a ship for an order of restoration of possession such an action would not offend against basic principles. However, any action resulting in liability being attached to a ship so as to affect the owner's interest would be contrary to principle.

It is suggested that, subject to limitations on the use of judicial sale in such a case, the enforceability of any action *in rem* against purchasers should be placed on an identical footing with that applicable to claims under s.20(2)(e)–(r), i.e. that once a writ is issued it is good against purchasers. Save for a mortgage claim (for which there are established special rules) the priority *in rem* of all claims *in rem* not being maritime liens is and should be equal.[28]

While the action *in rem* governs enforceability and priority *in rem* it is the claim which governs enforceability and priority *in personam*. However, *in personam* liability will not affect *in rem* liability (except insofar as the latter depends on it) in respect of the "*in rem*" fund (i.e. the "*res*" or the proceeds of its sale).

2. CREATION OF THE LIEN

The statutory lien is created on the issue of the writ. As from that time, therefore, the claimant is a secured creditor and can enforce his right against purchasers and subject to other creditors. The modern authorities supporting these propositions were concerned with claims now falling within the Supreme Court Act, s.21(4). However, there is no reason why in this aspect there should be any distinction between that category of claim and that making up s.21(2) or, subject to any rule applicable to a particular claim, any claims enforceable "*in rem*" within s.20(1)(c) and (d).

The claims under s.21(4) may be enforced by an action *in rem* provided there are specified links between the person liable *in personam* and the ship against which proceedings are taken. The claims under s.21(2) and probably any claim enforceable "*in*

---

26. i.e. claims within ss.21(2), 20(1)(c) and 20(1)(d).
27. See *Shell Oil Co.* v. *The Ship Lastrigoni* [1974–75] 131 C.L.R. 1 (H.C. of Australia).
28. See Chap. 23.

rem" under s.20(1)(c) may be enforced by an action *in rem* against the relevant property without the need for such conditions. Any difference between the two categories is, therefore, limited to the conditions required for the bringing of the action and the assets subject to the lien. There is no reason for any distinction as to creation.

3. ASSETS SUBJECT TO THE LIEN

I. CLAIMS UNDER S.21(4)

The statutory lien under s.21(4) is exercisable against the ship involved or a "sister ship" within s.21(4)(b). The ambit of the "sister ship" clause was discussed in Chapter 10. By statutory wording, cargo and freight are excluded as assets to which the lien may attach. Yet claims in relation to salvage include life and property salvage under any contract relating to salvage service and in the nature of salvage generally. The amendments by the Merchant Shipping (Salvage and Pollution) Act 1994 have extended the scope of the salvage action *in rem* in respect of ships without necessarily increasing the scope of the maritime lien. Insofar as cargo is liable *in rem* otherwise than through a maritime lien it can only be by virtue of jurisdiction which the Admiralty Court had immediately prior to the Supreme Court Act 1981.[29] Likewise, the extension of Admiralty jurisdiction in damage claims to personal injury and loss of life presumably rendered freight liable to the lien. Again, if either claim does not attract a maritime lien it is to the jurisdiction prior to the Act that a claimant must look for any lien against freight.[30] And it is arguable that no "*in rem*" jurisdiction is preserved by the 1981 Act.

In both *The Silia*[31] and *The Eurostar*[32] Sheen J. held that bunkers owned by the shipowner were an asset subject to the *in rem* liability of the ship—apparently on the ground that they were property on the ship of the owner of the ship. Unless, however, they were to be considered part of the ship or the express phraseology limiting the ambit of s.21(4) is ignored it is difficult to see how any liability can attach in respect of claims brought under that provision.

II. CLAIMS UNDER S.21(2) OR S.20(1)(C)

The lien is limited to the property relevant to the claim, thereby encompassing cargo and freight. By s.20 claims for forfeiture and condemnation and droits of Admiralty extend to goods but claims in relation to ownership, possession and mortgage are limited by the statutory wording to ships. So the point made in relation to bunkers in the context of claims under s.21(4) applies.[33]

29. Through an application of s.20(1)(c), as to which see *supra*.
30. No such question can arise in regard to wages (see *The Halcyon Skies* [1977] Q.B. 14) or masters' wages or disbursements, Admiralty jurisdiction *in rem* being co-extensive with maritime liens. See generally Chap. 2.
31. [1981] 2 Lloyd's Rep. 534.
32. [1993] 1 Lloyd's Rep. 106.
33. The point was not taken in either case.

4. TRANSFERABILITY

Identical considerations apply as apply to maritime liens. These considerations are discussed in Chapter 18.

5. TERMINATION

In addition to the factors relevant to the termination of a maritime lien, as the validity of the lien depends on the issue of a writ *in rem* its existence depends on either:

    (i) the continued validity of the writ or, at least, the proceedings consequent on its issue, or

    (ii) the establishment of the claim through a conclusion of the proceedings in the plaintiff's favour.

The need for continuing proceedings does not mean that if proceedings properly commenced are stayed and property arrested is maintained under arrest that the "lien" is extinguished. It is provided by s.26 of the Civil Jurisdiction and Judgments Act 1982 that the same "law and practice" applies as if the property is held for proceedings in the English court.[34] Further, for the lien to be effective, as for the maritime lien it must continue to exist in the property until a claim is satisfied.

6. THE LEGAL CONSEQUENCES OF ATTRACTING THE ACTION "IN REM"—A SUMMARY

The legal effect of a claim attracting the action *in rem* is that:

    (i) The action *in rem* confers a right and a remedy in addition to any available against the defendant "*in personam*" (i.e. by reason of the defendant's responsibility for acts the basis of the claim).

    (ii) Inherent in the action *in rem*

        (a) the ship, cargo or freight subject to it is liable to arrest prior to the hearing on the merits;

        (b) jurisdiction on the merits is founded outside the Brussels and Lugano Conventions on service of a writ *in rem*, on the property in the registry or on a defendant or his solicitor pursuant to RSC Order 75, rule 8(1), (2) and RSC Order 10, rule 1(4) and (5), or it is suggested, arrest without such service; or within either of the Conventions establishment of a Convention jurisdiction base *and* probably compliance with the "*in rem*" service rules procedurally to satisfy English law.

    (iii) If a lien is created it arises on the bringing of the action *in rem* (i.e. the issue of the writ).

---

34. So it would appear that in an English court, English law would continue to govern enforceability against the security. See further Chap. 25.

(iv) The enforceability of the lien against property other than the ship and against persons other than the shipowner liable *in personam* depends on the nature of the claim.

(a) *If the claim is within (s.20(2)(e)–(r)*[35] *it would appear that the lien*:

(1) (unless within s.20(1)(c)) will not attach to cargo or freight, the rules for jurisdiction based on s.20(1)(c) depending on the rules applicable to each claim;

(2) will attach to a ship relevant to the claim provided that the person liable *in personam*[36] was at the time the cause of action arose the owner, charterer or in possession or control at the time of the act the basis of the claim *and* is at the issue of the writ either owner or demise charterer;

(3) will attach to the ship relevant to the claim and is enforceable against a purchaser as it is enforceable against the owner;

(4) will be enforceable against a ship other than that relevant to the claim if, on the issue of the writ, that ship is owned by the person who was owner, charterer or in possession or control of the relevant ship at the time the action arose and that person is liable *in personam*;

(5) is enforceable against unsecured creditors (whenever the creditor's claim arises) but (apart from any personal liability because of representations made), is subject to (i) mortgages arising before the issue of the writ, (ii) maritime liens whenever created, (iii) possessory liens created before the issue of the writ.[37]

It is clear that the effect of the action *in rem* on these claims confers on them common proprietary characteristics: for want of a better phrase they are "statutory liens in Admiralty".

(b) *If the claim is within s.20(2)(a)(b)(c) or (s)* (i.e. relates to ownership, possession, or mortgage of a ship or forfeiture or condemnation of a ship or goods or droits of Admiralty) or is *within s.20(1)(c)(d)* (i.e. past or future *in rem* jurisdiction having its roots outside the Act)

(1) ship, cargo or freight as relevant to the claim may be arrested; but

(2) the enforceability by virtue of the action *in rem* against persons not liable *in personam*, purchasers and other creditors is uncertain.

(v) Any lien created is extinguished on destruction of the ship or other property.

(vi) A ship or other property arrested as part of an action *in rem* enforcing the lien is subject to judicial sale and the proceeds available to the claimants *in rem*.

(vii) It is uncertain whether, as the enforcement is through the action *in rem*,

(a) recovery of damages can be in excess of the value of the ship, property or fund;

---

35. For an argument that a claim within s.20(2)(d) (damage received by a ship) can found an action *in rem* and hence a statutory lien on the same basis, see Chap. 2.

36. i.e. would if sued successfully be liable *in personam*. See *The St Merriel* [1963] P. 247; *The St Elefterio* [1957] P. 179, at p. 185. And see s.21(7).

37. And possibly whenever created. As to priorities between statutory liens, see Chap. 23.

(b) remedies *in personam* (e.g. injunction) are available.[38]

(viii) Judicial sale as a step in enforcement of any lien extinguishes the lien and transfers it to the proceeds.

(ix) Any lien may be extinguished by laches, waiver or satisfaction and possibly the lodging of bail to the extent to which the bail reflects the value of the ship or other property.

(x) The claims attracting the lien may be extinguished by rules relating to effluxion of time, or the withdrawal or nullity of proceedings, and hence the lien would also be extinguished.

38. See Chaps. 2 and 10.

CHAPTER 20

Possessory Liens

NATURE OF A POSSESSORY LIEN

The doyen of the lien in a general domestic context of English law is the most restricted. It is a common law right conferring by contract, usage or statute a right of retention of a chattel already in the lien holder's possession.[1] Such a right of retention is a common feature of many legal systems.[2]

Whether possession has been acquired prior to the purported exercise of a lien is a matter of fact—so whether a ship is in the possession of repairers or repairs are undertaken simply as a matter of contract depends on the circumstances.[3] There is no ability to acquire possession to create the lien and no right to enforce the right through action unless the possession is wrongly terminated[4] or is surrendered to allow judicial sale in an action *in rem*. There is no right of self help to ensure that possession is not lost—such as by removing equipment from a ship.[5] It is arguable that an excessive claim which is due prevents creation of the lien.[6]

While a possessory lien may be created by contract, there is not infrequently a critical issue of contractual construction as to the type of "lien" created. Simply to use the word "lien" invokes uncertainty and may be construed as not only not creating a "lien" based on possession but as a floating charge fastening on a particular asset only on a specified event. The issues of construction are discussed in Chapter 22.

ASSETS SUBJECT TO THE LIEN

As a general policy, the lien extends only to chattels retained in possession. Unless provided by contract or statute, the lien does not extend to any charge for or expenses in

1. The possession must be rightfully acquired and, apart from surrender for a particular limited purpose (e.g. deposit), be continuous. Because of the requirement of rightful acquisition possession transferred by a person who has no right to do so cannot found a lien. But a person obliged to receive goods (such as a common carrier) is not affected by the defect in transfer unless he knows of it (see e.g. *Johnson* v. *Hill* (1822) 3 Stark. 172).

2. Rights of retention are recognized as international maritime concepts in the Conventions for the Unification of Certain Rules Relating to Maritime Liens and Mortgages 1967 (Art. 6) and 1993 (Art. 7). Whether or not a right of retention is conferred by a contract will be a matter for the law governing the contract (see e.g. *Re Leyland Daf* [1993] B.C.C. 426) or the property right (see Chap. 26).

3. See *The Gregos* [1985] 2 Lloyd's Rep. 347.

4. i.e. there is no right of sale (see e.g. *Mulliner* v. *Florence* (1878) 3 Q.B.D. 484). But such a right may be provided by contract or statute. See e.g. the Sale of Goods Act 1979, ss.39 and 48; the Torts (Interference with Goods) Act 1977, ss.12 and 13 (as amended by SI 1991/724).

5. *The Gregos* (fn. 3).

6. *Ibid.* But it is arguable that its effect is limited to the lien for the amount demanded—not any lien if the amount is amended. Until it is amended however the lien claimant would be wrongfully retaining the goods.

keeping the chattel.[7] However, the lien may extend to expenditure before any demand for possession necessary for the preservation of a chattel from deterioration and thus benefiting the owner.[8]

The common law possessory lien based on usage and the power to create a possessory lien by contract apply in the maritime as in any other context. In addition there are liens dependent on particular commercial relationships. First, let us consider common law principles.

A. COMMON LAW POSSESSORY LIENS (APPLYING TO BUT NOT CREATED PRIMARILY IN MARITIME LAW)

The common law divides the right of retention into (a) *general* and (b) *particular* liens. A general lien gives a claimant the right to retain any chattel of the person against whom the claim is made until the claim is met, there being no necessary connection between claim and chattel. A particular lien is a right to retain a chattel until all claims made in respect of it are met.

1. GENERALLY APPLICABLE PRINCIPLES

(i) Commencement of the lien

The possessory lien depends understandably enough on possession.[9] A court cannot declare that the lien may continue even though possession ceases.[10] The lien will normally fasten on to the chattel at the time when the claim arises. So a lien dependent on work done will generally not arise until that work is done. However, it has been held that for priority purposes a lien in favour of a shiprepairer arises at the moment the ship goes to the yard.[11]

A contractual right to a possessory lien

A contract providing for a possessory lien creates a contractual right arising at the moment of contract. So, as a matter of priority of contractual rights, the right to the lien incorporated in a trading contract entered into before the appointment of a receiver will take priority over rights consequent on that appointment even though possession is gained

7. *Somes* v. *British Empire Shipping Co.* (1860) 8 H.L. Cas. 338; *The Katingaki* [1976] 2 Lloyd's Rep. 372. It was said in the latter case that there is no possessory lien for damages for breach of contract of repair but this must be read as referring to a lien unconnected with or incidental to the repair.

8. See *The Winson* [1982] A.C. 939, at p. 963 (H.L.).

9. Possession requires control, and, for example, simply leaving men on board a ship will not necessarily give that control. See *The Scio* (1867) L.R. 1 A. & E. 353. See also *The Gregos* [1985] 2 Lloyd's Rep. 347. But arrest or the exercise of a statutory power of sale may not affect the lien. So a court would be bound to hold the proceeds of a ship sold by judicial sale subject to any rights that a possessory lien holder had in it. (See *The Tergeste* [1903] P. 26; *The Ally* [1952] 2 Lloyd's Rep. 427.) For an extension of the concept of the possessory lien to a contracting party not having possession, see *The Lancaster* [1980] 2 Lloyd's Rep. 497 and Chap. 22.

10. See *The Ally* [1952] 2 Lloyd's Rep. 427.

11. See *The Tergeste* [1903] P. 26.

after it.[12] However, the lien itself could be created only on the retention of possession pursuant to the lien.[13]

(ii) Enforceability of the lien

At its least a possessory lien means the inability of the creator of the lien to get his hands on the asset. Apart from this, insofar as rules of enforceability against creditors or purchasers can be identified, they have been worked out in relation to the categories of "general" or "particular" liens or attached to a specific type of lien. While, therefore, it is arguable that such rules apply generally, their roots cannot be ignored.

(a) Against creditors or liquidator

It seems that a possessory lien created by a company would not be a registrable charge within the Companies Act 1985 (see Chapter 22) but that it is within the Companies Act 1989 intended to replace the earlier provisions (see Chapter 22). If so and it is not registered it is void as against a liquidator or any creditors. Its enforceability may be affected by the making of an administration order under the Insolvency Act 1986 (see *infra*).

The passive ability to retain possession is exercisable against unsecured creditors whether the interests are created prior to or after the lien. Its enforceability against secured creditors presents complex questions of priority (see Chapters 17, 23).

(b) Against third parties other than creditors

Successors in title

The effect of a possessory lien against third parties other than creditors is uncertain but it should be enforceable against successors in title to the party subject to the lien.[14] If it is not good against successors its ability is greatly restricted and it is surprising that there remains any doubt.[15] The question is further considered in Chapter 23.

Present owners

In some cases, a possessory lien may be enforceable against an owner of a chattel to which the lien has attached because of the act of some other person such as a bailee or an agent.[16] However, enforceability against parties whose interests were established prior to the creation of the lien raises considerable problems for investors and owners. The basis of such enforceability must lie in the overriding need of all interested in a chattel in

---

12. *George Barker (Transport) Ltd.* v. *Eynon* [1974] 1 All E.R. 900. The issue concerned the binding effect of obligations of an assignor on an assignee.

13. See e.g. the judgment of Stamp L.J. in *George Barker (Transport) Ltd.* v. *Eynon* (fn. 12) (at p. 909) distinguishing the issue from that of "priority" and the approach in *The Lancaster* [1980] 2 Lloyd's Rep. 497, at p. 503 (concerning an equitable lien).

14. See e.g. *Jowitt* v. *Union Cold Storage Co.* [1913] 3 K.B. 1 (warehouseman); *The Ally* (*supra*) (shiprepairer).

15. But see *Crossley Vaines Personal Property* (5th edn) p. 139 (referring to warehousemen).

16. See *Chellaram & Sons (London) Ltd.* v. *Butlers Warehousing & Distribution Ltd.* [1978] 2 Lloyd's Rep. 412.

maintaining it,[17] or in implied authority to the creator of the lien to encumber a chattel with the lien.[18] It carries serious consequences for the financier whose security is clearly affected, and it may be that different enforceability rules should apply to different liens much as they do in respect of the liens peculiar to maritime law. The general question will be considered in Chapter 23 in the context of priorities, but particular rules relating to possessory liens are referred to in the present chapter.

Enforcement of the lien

The lien is enforced by denying possession to the person against whom it is claimed, that denial being on the basis of the lien. It will be a matter of construction whether the retention of possession is on the basis of another legal relationship or the lien. So a bailee may be claiming possession by reason of the bailment or by virtue of an asserted lien arising from the failure of the owner to meet the terms of the bailment. Where a possessory lien is created by contract, the event creating the basis for the lien will either be specified by the contract or simply flow from adaptation of the common law lien.

(c) The effect of insolvency

Company insolvency

A possessory lien held over company assets may be affected by the making of an administration order in regard to the winding up of a company. It is expressly provided that save for a lien on documents giving title to property no lien or right to retain possession of any books, papers or other records of the company is enforceable insofar as it would deny possession once an administration order is made, a company goes into liquidation or a provisional liquidator is appointed.[19]

Further, it has been held that a possessory lien is a "security" which requires the consent of an administrator or leave of the court to enforce once an administration order is made and there is a claim by the administrator. Enforcement for this purpose is simply the assertion of the lien against the owner seeking possession, but it is open to the administrator or court refusing consent or leave to impose terms and maintain the right or, save for the surrendering of possession, provide alternative security.[20] Concern was expressed by members of the court at the practical consequences of the decision and it was emphasized that the obligation to seek leave arose only when steps were taken to enforce the lien *and* there was a claim by the administrator. Further it was said that a lien holder would not be taking such steps if there was a retention (or detention) while proceedings

---

17. This is the reason for the priority, for example, of subsequent salvage liens over earlier liens (see *infra*).

18. This is sometimes advanced as the reason for the priority of later maritime liens over earlier mortgages (see *infra*). A bailee may create a lien against an owner if the giving of the possession upon which the lien is based is reasonably incidental to the use for which the chattel is bailed (see e.g. *Tappenden* v. *Artus* [1964] 2 Q.B. 185).

19. Insolvency Act 1986, s.246. As to an administration order see Chap. 17.

20. *Bristol Airport plc* v. *Powdrill* [1990] 2 All E.R. 493—a statutory right of detention (as to which see *infra*). But the assertion of a possessory lien is not the commencing or taking of "proceedings" nor the levying of distress which are also acts requiring consent or leave. "Proceedings" are legal proceedings—distress indicates seizure and detention, not merely detention (*ibid*).

were brought to obtain leave. That, it was thought, would meet the problem of immediate loss of security.

It would appear, however, that apart from any lien on books or company records a possessory lien of itself would not be affected by a winding up order whether the lien is asserted before or after the order. On the surface at any rate it does not fall within an "attachment" rendered void by the order or a "procceding" which after the order is made may be pursued only by the leave of the court.[21]

Individual insolvency

The assertion of a possessory lien is arguably within the proceeding, that which may by statute be restrained—"action, execution or other legal process". Even if it is within that phrase the holder of the lien is certainly a "secured creditor" and hence free to "enforce" the security.[22]

(iii) Termination of the lien

(a) Loss of possession

Save where the possession has been fraudulently obtained to defeat the lien, the lien ceases on loss of possession.[23] As a general rule possession regained after being surrendered otherwise than by reason of fraud will not resurrect the lien. But in an early case it was held that an insurance broker's lien on a policy did revive on possession being regained.[24]

(b) Taking of action inconsistent with a possessory lien

A general lien will be lost through assertion of a particular lien,[25] or the giving of credit terms or the taking of security for payment at a future date.[26] Any lien may be waived by contract or conduct. It will be a matter of construction as to whether waiver has occurred.[27]

In 1983 in *A* v. *B*[28] it was held that solicitors who arrested a ship of clients to enforce a claim for costs (and thereby discharged themselves) did not waive their possessory lien on the client's papers. Some two months after the arrest the solicitors entered a default judgment against the clients. Leggatt J. held that the arrest was "part of a process of enforcement and is to be distinguished from such contractual arrangements as a solicitor might in the ordinary course make for the provision of his client of a security that can properly be regarded and given in substitution for the lien". With respect, arrest is no more

---

21. Insolvency Act 1986, ss.126, 128, 130(2). The powers of the court to stay proceedings apply to a voluntary winding up (s.112).

22. Although the phraseology may not encompass the passive right of the possessory lien. See Insolvency Act 1986, s.285. For discussion see Chap. 17.

23. Where there is judicial sale the lien holder's rights are transferred to the proceeds and subjected to priority rules. See *infra* and *The Tergeste* [1903] P. 26.

24. *Levy* v. *Barnard* (1818) 8 Taunt. 149.

25. See e.g. *Morley* v. *Hay* (1829) 7 L.J.K.B. (O.S.) 104. As to general and particular liens, see *infra*.

26. See also *Burston Finance* v. *Speirway* [1974] 1 W.L.R. 1648. See also fn. 78 *infra*.

27. See e.g. (re broker's lien) *Fisher* v. *Smith* (1878) 4 App. Cas. 1.

28. [1984] 1 All E.R. 265, at p. 272.

a process of enforcement than the possessory lien itself. It is a method of ensuring that an asset in which there is a security right is available for the exercise of that right. However, it is dubious whether as a method of security inherently available in an action on the merits it should be thought inconsistent with a different type of security on different assets rooted in a distinct principle.[29]

(c) Tender of amount due[30]

The lien will be extinguished on tender or payment of the amount due.

2. GENERAL LIENS

A general lien may be created by usage, contract or statute.

(a) By usage

Claims to which a general lien may attach

General liens have been established "by usage" in favour of bankers, factors, insurance brokers[31] (by City of London custom), stockbrokers and solicitors.[32] There are examples of such liens being upheld for other trades, the most relevant to maritime law being packers and wharfingers.[33] It appears that wharfingers would have to rely on local usage. There is no general lien by usage in favour of warehousekeepers.[34]

Enforceability of the lien

The enforceability of such liens against third parties has not been worked out satisfactorily. Such liens fall within the general principles of enforceability in respect of unsecured creditors and (probably) successors in title to the owner.[35] It has been said that no general

---

29. In *The Winson* [1982] A.C. 939, at p. 962 it was said that the question whether the security provisions of Lloyd's Open Form were inconsistent with a salvor's possessory lien "raises difficult and hitherto undecided questions of law". The salvor is specifically providing for contractual security and arguably thereby exclusively doing so. See now LOF 1990 Clauses 4, 5—there is certainly an agreement not to enforce the lien if adequate security is provided.

30. It has been held that the lien will continue despite the debt for which it has been created becoming statute barred (*Spears* v. *Hartley* (1800) 3 Esp. 81)—but this must depend on whether the time bar goes to right or remedy—and whether the lien is considered a remedy (see Chap. 1).

31. See *infra* as to the importance of this lien in maritime law.

32. A solicitor's lien is not enforceable against a third party who would be entitled to production against the client (see *Re Aveling Barford* [1988] 3 All E.R. 1019). Normally a solicitor must hand over papers on which he has a lien to a person other than the debtor if they are required for an action provided suitable undertakings are given; he does not thereby lose his lien (see *Hughes* v. *Hughes* [1958] P. 221). However, it is a matter of balancing the hardship to be suffered and a court may refuse to order that the papers be handed over. See *A* v. *B* [1984] 1 All E.R. 265. The lien cannot prevent production of documents by solicitors of a company following an order obtained by a receiver of the company under the Insolvency Act 1986 s.236, the receiver being treated as a third party (*Re Aveling Barford Ltd.*, *supra*). As to waiver of the lien, see fn. 27 and text. As to the solicitor's lien under the Solicitors Act 1974, see Chaps. 17, 23.

33. Others being calico printers and dyers.

34. *Chellaram & Sons (London) Ltd.* v. *Butlers Warehousing & Distribution Ltd.* [1978] 2 Lloyd's Rep. 412 (C.A.).

35. But it is said in at least one instance there must be notice—a concept alien to the common law (see *Jowitt* v. *Union Cold Storage Co.* [1913] 3 K.B. 1).

lien created by usage by a non-owner is enforceable against the owner[36] but this may not be universally applied.[37] Enforceability against secured creditors *in personam* and *in rem* will be considered in Chapter 23 in the context of priorities.

(b) By contract

A contract can create a general lien. It can provide for the assets to which the lien is to attach, for the claims for which it is to exist and for its enforceability against third parties. Whether a contractual provision creates a general or particular lien is a matter of construction. A contractual term simply creating "a general lien" without more will import the general uncertainty as to its enforceability against present owners, and any term ought therefore to include specific provision for enforceability of the lien against the holder of a prior interest. In *Chellaram* v. *Butlers Warehousing and Distribution Ltd.*[38] a general lien was created by a contract between a corporation "consolidating" goods into containers and an air transport undertaking. It was held that this lien could be enforced against the owner of the goods in respect of a claim against the undertaking, provided it was shown that the owner knew that the goods would be handled by the "consolidating" company on the contractual terms (including the lien) under which it acted in regard to the transport undertaking.[39]

(c) By statute

Statute may create a general lien as it may create any other interest. Lacking statutory definition of characteristics it will import such general characteristics discussed above as are established as making up such a lien.

3. PARTICULAR LIENS

A particular lien may be created by usage, contract or statute.

(a) By usage

Claims to which a particular lien attaches

Unlike the general lien, particular liens at common law have not been recognized with respect to specified trades and professions. They are based more broadly on acts done in a context which, it has been held, entitled those who have done the acts to security. They are recognized

---

36. See *US Steel Products Co.* v. *G. W. Rly. Co.* [1916] 1 A.C. 189, 195–196.

37. An insurance broker may be able to assert his general lien on a policy created by a non-owner against an owner. However, a broker who knows or should reasonably know that the instructing person is not the assured has no general lien on the policy for the balance of the account with the giver of the instructions (*Cahill* v. *Dawson* (1857) 3 C.B. (N.S.) 106); and a broker who makes this discovery during the course of dealings has no such lien in respect of debts accruing after it (*Near East Relief* v. *King, Chasseur & Co.* [1930] 2 K.B. 40 (see *infra*).

38. [1978] 2 Lloyd's Rep. 412.

39. The court followed *Cassils and Sassoon* v. *Holdenwood Bleaching Co. Ltd.* (1914) 84 L.J.K.B. 834, a case concerning the bleaching of calico on the instructions of printers not expressly authorized by the owners to act as they did.

(i) in favour of those who have no choice in accepting chattels for services (such as the common carrier);

(ii) for work done on a chattel in pursuance of a contract;

(iii) in favour of an agent for work done for his principal; and

(iv) (it would seem) as a lien on goods by a co-owner in respect of expenses to be met in relation to those goods by other co-owners.

(i) Obligation to accept goods

This applies to common carriers and innkeepers.[40] It has little relevance in the maritime area even as regards carriers. A common carrier is a person who holds himself out as a carrier of goods for hire and does not reserve the right to deal only with those whom he chooses—"he will carry for hire so long as he has room the goods of all persons indifferently who send goods to be carried".[41] This rarely applies to sea carriers. Apart from Acts of God or the Queen's enemies, inherent vice or fault of the consignor, a common carrier is responsible for the loss of or damage to the goods. Because of his inability to refuse to act as a carrier[42] he is given a lien on the goods carried for the payment of the hire. It has been held that in general a private carrier has no such lien,[43] but, conversely, it is well established that a shipowner has a possessory lien for freight and contributions to general average (see infra).

(ii) Work done on a chattel

The work must be done in pursuance of a contract. There is no lien for work done without instruction,[44] and at common law there is no lien for storage or salvage. Of particular relevance in the maritime area is the possessory lien of a person who does work on a ship—the shiprepairer or shipbuilder.

THE SHIPREPAIRER/SHIPBUILDER

This is simply an application of the common law possessory lien conferred for work on a chattel, and there is no distinction for this purpose, for example, between repair of a ship or a car. Following general principles the shiprepairer has a lien in respect of the cost of materials supplied and work done, together with any incidental costs or expenses. But, unless provided by contract, the lien does not extend to damages for breach of contract nor to any charge for keeping the ship.[45]

(iii) Agent's lien

An agent has a particular lien on goods of his principal in respect of all claims against his principal arising out of his employment, save where it would be inconsistent with the

40. The innkeeper's lien does not now extend to motor vehicles or live animals (the Hotel Proprietors Act 1956, s.2).

41. *Nugent* v. *Smith* (1875) 1 C.P.D. 19, at p. 27; decision reversed (1876) 1 C.P.D. 423.

42. *Ibid* (1876) 1 C.P.D. 423, at p. 433.

43. *Electric Supply Stores* v. *Gaywood* [1909] 100 L.T. 855.

44. But there may be restitution for a benefit conferred under the misapprehension that it was being done on a chattel owned by the person doing the work. *Greenwood* v. *Bennett* [1973] Q.B. 195.

45. *The Katingaki* [1976] 2 Lloyd's Rep. 372.

contract of employment.[46] Except as regards negotiable instruments and money, the lien is enforceable against third parties only to the extent that the principal has such a lien.

(iv) Co-owner's lien

In 1824 in *Holderness* v. *Shackels*[47] it was recognized that a co-owner of cargo has a possessory lien on the cargo for disbursements of the ship to be met by other co-owners—and that this was an application of the common law lien.

Enforceability of the lien

The general area of uncertainty about the extent of enforceability against third parties applies to the particular as to the general lien. Particular liens are certainly enforceable against unsecured creditors and probably successors in title to the person subject to the lien.[48] Enforceability against secured creditors *in personam* and *in rem* will be considered in Chapter 23 in the general context of priorities.

The rules relating to enforceability against owners where the possession creating the lien is surrendered to the claimant by a non-owner seem clearer than for general liens. A common carrier can assert his lien against an owner of goods.[49] A person asserting a lien for work done can assert it if the giving of possession to him was with the express authority of the owner or that authority could be implied from the owner's dealings.[50] Given that authority, any agreement between hirer (or bailee) and owner that the former cannot create a lien is ineffective so far as a lien holder without notice of the prohibition is concerned.[51]

(b) By contract

The creation of a particular lien by contract raises the same issues as the creation of a general lien by contract. Any contractual creation of a "lien", simply by the use of the term, it may be argued, adapts the rules discussed under "usage". It would follow that for enforceability against an owner it is enough if surrender of possession to the lien holder by a hirer can be seen as fitting with the nature of the transaction between owner and hirer. Actual knowledge by the owner of the terms of the arrangement under which possession is given up is not necessary.

(c) By statute

Statute may create a particular lien. So, for example, under the Sale of Goods Act 1979 an unpaid vendor of goods has a right of retention of those goods.[52] He is also given a right of resale.

---

46. See (e.g.) *Foxcraft* v. *Wood* (1828) 4 Russ. 487. Later authorities deal primarily with the question of general lien but seem to assume the existence of a particular lien. See e.g. *Brandao* v. *Barnett* (1846) 3 C.B. 519; *Bock* v. *Gorrissen* (1861) 30 L.J. Ch. 39; *Re Bowes* (1886) 33 Ch. D. 586.
47. (1824) 8 B. & C. 612.
48. See *The Ally* [1952] 2 Lloyd's Rep. 427.
49. *Skinner* v. *Upshaw* (1702) 2 Ld. Ray. 752.
50. See e.g. *Tappenden* v. *Artus* [1964] 2 Q.B. 185.
51. See *Bowmaker Ltd.* v. *Wycombe Motors Ltd.* [1946] K.B. 505.
52. See ss.39 and 48. The lien originated at common law—see e.g. *Swan* v. *Barber* (1879) 5 Ex. D. 130.

B. MARITIME POSSESSORY LIENS

MARITIME AND OTHER POSSESSORY LIENS

It should be stressed again that all the liens established at common law are applicable, where appropriate, in the maritime area. So most general liens and the particular lien for work done are relevant—particularly that of the shiprepairer, shipbuilder and co-owner (see *supra*). Their principles do not depend on any particular maritime application but there is a danger that that application is considered apart from the basic common law framework of which it is part.[53] Any study of liens in maritime law must be in the context of the general national law as well as the sometimes unique characteristics of maritime law.

Under general common law principles a possessory lien may be created by contract and is commonly created in charterparties in favour of the shipowner for demurrage and for all monies due under the charter. Whether it is so created and whether or not any other security interest is created is a matter of construction and is discussed in Chapter 22.

CLAIMS TO WHICH MARITIME POSSESSORY LIENS ATTACH BY USAGE

Maritime possessory liens based on common law principles either of relationship or work done are:

(i) shipowner's claim for freight—lien on cargo;
(ii) shipowners' claim for general average contributions—lien on cargo;
(iii) salvor's claim—lien on ship and cargo;
(iv) (until 5 November 1993) warehouseman's claim for charges under the Merchant Shipping Act 1894—lien on landed cargo;
(v) broker's claims for premiums, charges and balance of account under the Marine Insurance Act 1906—lien on policies;
(vi) harbour authorities under statutes governing such authorities—lien on (or right of detention of) ship.

It will be seen that apart from the broker's lien all are particular liens—and, unlike the common law variety, are focused on specific commercial relationships.

ENFORCEABILITY, ENFORCEMENT AND TERMINATION

Enforceability insofar as it can be generalized is based on that of the common law particular possessory lien. Apart from specific provisions the liens would appear enforceable against successors in title and all unsecured creditors. Priority in relation to *in personam* and *in rem* secured creditors will be examined in Chapter 23. The general

---

53. So, for example, there appear to be differences in the commencement of the lien for work done between shiprepairers and others (see supra fn 11) and differences between enforceability of a broker's lien against the assured and other general liens against owners where a non-owner has dealt with the lien claimant (see text *infra*).

principles of enforcement and termination apply—enforcement through denial of possession and termination through loss of possession, action inconsistent with the lien and
tender of the amount due (see *supra*). Insofar as enforceability against an owner who did
not create the lien goes, it seems clear that the possessory liens based on salvage and
general average are enforceable, even if the act creating them was done without the
express authority of the owners.[54]

Enforcement of the lien

The lien is enforced by retaining possession of the cargo, ship or policy and denying that
possession to the owner on the owner's demand—in the case of cargo normally refusing
to discharge it until freight is paid. Following general principles the denial of possession
must be based on the lien and not on any other legal relationship—as for example a
bailment of the goods.[55] The lien on cargo is enforceable only when the freight is
payable—and that depends on the contract.[56] So if under a charterparty freight in any part
of the cargo is not payable until discharge of all, there can be no lien unless after the
"discharge" the cargo remains in the possession of the owner—as where it is discharged
into a barge.[57]

THE INDIVIDUAL LIENS

(i) The shipowner's lien on cargo for freight

The lien attaches for freight payable contemporaneously with delivery of cargo. It attaches
to all goods consigned in the same ship on the same voyage to the same consignee. It is
a well established lien but curiously often treated quite apart from other liens in maritime
matters. However, the cargo lien is part of the "lien" framework in maritime law and in
particular it raises priority problems with any other lien which may attach to the cargo. It
is also frequently the subject of a contract, and where this is so it will be a matter of
construction as to the extent to which the contract defines the ambit of the lien—it may
create an interest in substitution for the common law lien or simply provide the framework
for its operation.

Continued existence after delivery of possession to warehouse

Statutory provisions in force until 5 November 1993 (see *infra*) permitted the continuation
of the lien in certain circumstances after the goods have been landed. By the Merchant
Shipping Act 1894, s.493, a shipowner may land goods imported into the United Kingdom
if the cargo owner fails to take delivery within the time specified in the bill of lading,

---

54. See *Hingston* v. *Wendt* (1876) 1 Q.B.D. 367.
55. *The Winson* [1982] A.C. 939. The retention of possession of a bill of lading by a seller may be construed
as the exercise of a possessory lien over the document pending payment or the retention of the right of disposal
of the goods. See e.g. Bridge, *op. cit.* at p. 65.
56. The payment of freight and delivery of cargo being concurrent obligations at common law.
57. See *The Fort Kipp* [1985] 2 Lloyd's Rep. 168.

charterparty or other agreement or, lacking such specification, within 72 hours.[58] The shipowner is obliged to place them on a wharf or in a warehouse on or in which such goods are usually placed. If a wharf or warehouse is specified in the document of carriage the goods must be placed there.[59]

In succeeding provisions (ss.494–496) the Act provides for the continuation of the shipowner's lien where goods are landed and placed in the custody of a wharfinger or warehouseman. It is uncertain whether these provisions are limited to the landing of goods under s.493, i.e. when the cargo owner is at fault in not taking delivery.[60] But whether or not this is so, to maintain the lien the shipowner must give notice that the goods are to remain subject to the lien. If notice is given[61] the goods must be retained until the lien is satisfied and, if they are not, the wharfinger or warehouseman is responsible for loss to the shipowner.[62]

Termination

Following general principles, the shipowner's lien is lost on surrender of possession save that to a wharf or warehouse on which its continuation is based. It will be lost if goods are surrendered to a salvor.[63]

The lien on landed goods may be discharged (i) by the production of and delivery to the warehouseman of a receipt of payment of the amount due or a release of freight; or (ii) deposit by the cargo owner of the amount due.[64] In the latter case, there are rules covering retention and payment out of the deposit if the amount admitted due does not match that claimed.[65]

Sale of landed goods

Unlike the shipowner's possessory lien from which the statutory extension springs, the goods may be sold to secure payment for the amount due.[66] Notice is required of the sale but failure to observe the notice requirements does not affect the title of a bona fide purchaser. The proceeds of sale must be applied first to Customs dues, expenses of sale and charges of wharfinger or warehouseman before payment of the amount due.[67]

The lien provisions for landed goods were repealed by the Statute Law (Repeals) Act 1993 (Sch. 1, Part XV, Group 6). It is perhaps not the preferable way of repeal of

58. Section 493(1). An owner in default for not taking delivery may take delivery of the goods if ready to do so any time before landing (s.493(3)). A shipowner landing goods under this section when the owner is ready to take delivery may be liable for the owner's expenses (s.493(4) and (5)).

59. Section 493(2).

60. See *Dennis and Sons* v. *Cork Steamship Co. Ltd.* [1913] 2 K.B. 393.

61. A sum in excess of the amount due inserted in the notice to the warehouseman amounts to wrongful detention of the goods. See *The Energie* (1875) L.R. 6 P.C. 306, at p. 316.

62. Section 494. The section provides for a lien for freight "and other charges". This has been held to include demurrage where the shipowner has a lien for this. See *A/S Helsingors Sö & Handelscompagnie* v. *Walton* (1921) 9 Ll.L.Rep. 105.

63. *The Winson* [1982] A.C. 939.

64. Section 495.

65. Section 496.

66. Section 497. The time provided for discharge of the lien is 90 days or less if the goods are perishable. The goods must be sold if the shipowner requires it.

67. Section 498. The wharfinger or warehouseman has the right to rent and at the expense of the owner of the goods to do all necessary acts and a lien for the rent and expenses (s.499). See text *infra*.

provisions contained in a statute approaching a "code" of maritime law rights and conferring proprietary rights on a particular occupation.

(ii) Shipowner's lien for average contributions

(a) General average

The shipowner has a lien on cargo for general average contributions. Further—subject to contract—a shipowner has a duty to exercise the lien in favour of those entitled to claim contribution.[68] If the cargo is released against security the security requested must be reasonable.[69]

(b) Particular average

The lien may be exercised in relation to expenditure caused by the saving of articles owned by a number of owners or one owner only. The reasoning underlying the general average lien applies to cases where action is taken in respect of less than the whole.[70] The lien extends in favour of an agent.[71]

(iii) The salvor's lien

While there is no lien for salvage in general at common law, common law will recognize a possessory lien of a salvor in Admiralty.[72] There is little authority, presumably because of the maritime lien conferred on salvors. Once Admiralty and common law jurisdictions ceased to be in opposition to each other the inherently more powerful lien took over. It is uncertain to what extent, if at all, the Lloyd's Open Form has, by providing for security inconsistent with a possessory lien, superseded that lien in respect of salvage.[73]

Agent's lien

A ship's agent who has expended money and done work in discharging cargo to save property at risk but without any express authority from the owner has a lien on the cargo for his expenses on an analogy with salvage and general average.[74]

(iv) Warehouseman's lien for wharf or warehouse charges

Under Statutory provisions in force until 5 November 1993 where goods have been landed by a shipowner under his power so to act where the cargo owner has failed to take

68. See e.g. *Huth & Co.* v. *Lamport* (1886) 16 Q.B.D. 735.
69. See *Strang Steel & Co.* v. *Scott* (1889) 14 App. Cas. 601—where the lien is expressed to be that of each cargo owner whose cargo has been jettisoned but exercisable only by the master who has possession (see p. 606).
70. See *Hingston* v. *Wendt* (1876) 1 Q.B.D. 367.
71. *Ibid.*
72. *Hartford* v. *Jones* (1698) 1 Ld. Ray. 393 recognized in e.g. *The Fulham* [1899] P. 251 (C.A.); *Hingston* v. *Wendt* (1876) 1 Q.B.D. 367, at p. 373.
73. See fn 29 *supra*.
74. *Hingston* v. *Wendt* (1876) 1 Q.B.D. 367. As to agent's lien in general, see text *supra*.

delivery, a wharfinger or a warehouseman has a lien on the goods for rent and expenses.[75]

(v) The broker's lien

The Marine Insurance Act 1906, s.53(2) provides:

"Unless otherwise agreed, the broker has, as against the assured, a lien upon the policy for the amount of the premium and his charges in respect of effecting the policy; and, where he has dealt with the person who employs him as a principal, he has also a lien on the policy in respect of any balance on any insurance account which may be due to him from such person, unless when the debt was incurred he had reason to believe that such person was only an agent."

By the provision, therefore, a broker may have a "general" lien in respect of his insurance account on a policy against an assured where he deals with a principal, and, in any event, a particular lien in respect of expenses connected with the policy. If the lien is treated as a true possessory lien it is restricted to retention of the policy[76] and would not extend to the proceeds.

The broker's lien may cause problems in ship financing for it interposes a right between a ship financier's endeavour to secure security through insurance policies in respect of a ship and the funds representing that security. The broker's undertaking intended to protect a financier through imposing obligations on the broker to hold the benefit of the policies for the financier will normally make any such obligation subject to the lien on the particular policies. If the undertaking amounts to a contract[77] this will replace the lien imposed by statute and confine the lien on a policy to premiums unpaid on that policy.[78]

Enforceability

The broker's lien originates at common law, and on general principles is, therefore, enforceable against all, provided possession is retained. It has been held that the broker's general lien is not enforceable in relation to policies affected by an agent for debts owed by that agent—"he cannot pledge the property of (a) principal to another with whom he is dealing for his own private debt".[79] However, if the broker reasonably believes that he is dealing with a principal the lien will be upheld.[80] The enforceability of the liens created by statute will, naturally, be affected by any relevant provision of the statute.

---

75. Merchant Shipping Act 1894, s.499. The lien is distinct from the shipowner's lien on landed goods conferred by s.494—*The Energie* (1875) L.R. 6 P.C. 306. As to priorities, see Chap. 23. As with the shipowner's lien under s.494 the provision was repealed by the Statute Law (Repeals) Act 1993. See text *supra*.

76. See *West of England and S. Wales District Bank* v. *Batchelor* (1882) 46 L.T. 132 (solicitor's lien). The possession of the policy under a lien makes the brokers agents of the assured to collect claims. See *Xenos* v. *Wickham* (1863) 14 C.B. (N.S.) 435; *Hine Bros* v. *The Steamship Syndicate Ltd.* (1895) 72 L.T. 79.

77. See, for a holding that a particular undertaking did not amount to a contract, *Fairfield Shipbuilders & Engineering Co. Ltd.* v. *Gardner, Mountain & Co. Ltd.* (1911) 104 L.T. 288.

78. See *Fairfield Shipbuilders & Engineering Co. Ltd.* v. *Gardner, Mountain & Co. Ltd.* (1911) 104 L.T. 288. A financier may be able to control the amount of the lien through his own contract with the broker. And a broker allowing credit to the assured in respect of unpaid premiums must run the risk that he will destroy a possessory lien through action inconsistent with the lien (see text *supra*).

79. See *Maunns* v. *Henderson* (1801) 1 East 335, at p. 337.

80. *Cahill* v. *Dawson* (1857) 3 C.B. (N.S.) 106; *Westwood* v. *Bell* (1815) 4 Camp. 349. Discovery that a principal is an agent means that any general lien extends only to the moment of discovery. *Near East Relief* v. *King, Chasseur & Co.* [1930] 2 K.B. 40.

(vi) Harbour and other public authorities

Statutory rights of detention

Such rights are conferred on port and harbour authorities to enforce payment of dues,[81] safety provisions,[82] oil pollution measures[83] and payment of removal of wreck.[84] The power to detain is often accompanied by the ability to sell as a final measure of enforcement and to this extent the right resembles an active lien rather than the possessory passive lien.[85]

Need to detain

The authority must detain if reliance is to be placed on the statutory power. In *The Charger*[86] the harbour authority sought to recover dock dues but did not detain the ship. It was held that in a priority conflict such a claim could not rank higher than a claim for necessaries—that being the head of claim under which the claimant had to bring the case if statutory powers had not been used.[87]

The power of sale

In *The Ousel*[88] it was held that a harbour authority could exercise its statutory right to sell even if the ship had been arrested, and that the sale would confer a title free from encumbrances. Any lien claim would be transferred to the proceeds. In 1968 in *The Queen of the South*[89] Brandon J. examined the nature of the statutory right of detention and concluded that it was a statutory possessory lien, despite the ability to seize and despite the added power to sell. He likened this power to the mortgagee's power of sale, but also held that the authority could seize a ship under arrest. The sale was ordered in the best interests of all the claimants.

In 1985 in *The Freightline One*[90] Sheen J. held that no order of the court was required to preserve a statutory right of detention in favour of the Port of London Authority as against other claims. An order granting leave to intervene did preserve the right to be paid, and the consent to an order of sale *pendente lite* had been on the basis that the authority would not suffer financially. There would, however, have to be clear words for the right to detain and sale to be exercisable after judicial sale.

81. See e.g. the Harbours, Docks and Piers Clauses Act 1847, ss.44 and 47; the Merchant Shipping Act 1894, ss.650 and 651 (light dues) (as from 1 January 1996 the Merchant Shipping Act 1995, ss.208, 209) and special Acts relating to different ports.

82. See e.g. Merchant Shipping Act 1988 s.30A (as from 1 January 1996 Merchant Shipping Act 1995, s.95(1)); Merchant Shipping (Load Lines) Act 1967, s.3(4) (as from 1 January 1996 Merchant Shipping Act 1995, Sch. 3, para. 3(3)).

83. Prevention of Oil Pollution Act 1971, s.20 (from 1 January 1996 Merchant Shipping Act 1995, s.146).

84. See the Merchant Shipping Act 1894, ss.530 and 531 (from 1 January 1996 Merchant Shipping Act 1995, ss.252, 253).

85. Compare the right to remove a vessel under the Harbours, Docks and Piers Clauses Act 1847, s.56. After removal the control and possession reverts to the owner (see *The Clupea* [1982] LMLN 62 (Court of Session)).

86. [1966] 1 Lloyd's Rep. 670.

87. See also Chap. 23.

88. [1957] 1 Lloyd's Rep. 151.

89. [1968] P. 449.

90. [1986] 1 Lloyd's Rep. 266.

From these two authorities it would appear that although an authority must assert its claim through possession, it may do so through seizure and, once seized, it may sell under its statutory powers or may ask the court to sell. In either case the purchaser will obtain a title free from other claims, and those other claims will be transferred to the proceeds, and it appears as if the authority will have priority over liens and other claims against the proceeds.[91] In *The Freightline One* Sheen J., applying *The Queen of the South*, directed that charges due to the Port of London Authority be paid out of a fund raised by sale of a ship *pendente lite*. The payment was to be made as part of the arrest and sale expenses and in priority to pilotage and mortgagee claimants. In 1993 in *The Blitz*[92] Sheen J. held that on sale by a harbour authority the purchaser obtained a title free from encumbrances including a registered mortgage. The risk of non-payment should fall on the unwise lender rather than the authority or an innocent purchaser.[93] There was no obligation on either party to the sale to investigate the mortgage register.

The effect of company insolvency

The implementation of the statutory right may be affected by the making of a company administration order by a court under the Insolvency Act 1986. To achieve the purpose of the order (to make the company a going concern) one effect is to make the enforcement of any "security" over the company's property subject to the consent of the administrator or leave of the court. In 1990 in *Bristol Airport plc* v. *Powdrill* the Court of Appeal[94] held a statutory right of detention of an aircraft under the Civil Aviation Act 1982 was "a lien or other security" requiring leave to enforce. It was held that a possessory lien was within the statutory provision and that the exercise of the right to retain was "enforcement" of the right. The statutory right of detention was not critically different, the detention of the aircraft enforcing (and not merely creating) the right. Responding to the objection that it was impractical to make the holder of a possessory lien apply for leave it was pointed out that the administrator could consent and the administrator or the court impose terms. Further, a lien holder retaining the chattel while seeking leave would not be in contempt of court.

---

91. See Chap. 23.
92. [1992] 2 Lloyd's Rep. 441.
93. Following the approach of Eve J. in *Manchester Ship Canal Co.* v. *Horlock* [1914] 1 Ch. 453. Sheen J. pointed out that otherwise an owner could defeat a harbour authority's claim by mortgaging the ship.
94. [1990] 2 All E.R. 493. As to liens and insolvency see Chap. 17.

CHAPTER 21

Equitable Liens

1. THE SUBSTANCE OF THE LIEN

An equitable "lien" is no more than a right to go against an asset for a claim. It creates an equitable interest in the asset and, therefore, security for the claim. It may initially be construed as a floating charge focused on a number of assets fastening on a particular asset (i.e. crystallizing) on a specified event. It is similar to the common law lien in that it may be created by contract or recognized as stemming from a legal relationship. It is distinct from the common law lien in that:

    (i) it may be created by conduct;
    (ii) it is not dependent on possession;
    (iii) following from (ii) it may be enforced through action and eventually through sale of assets on execution of a judgment;
    (iv) its scope of enforceability is dependent on its equitable character, i.e. (a) it is enforceable between the parties and against all third parties acquiring interests subsequently except a person giving value for an interest in the asset recognized at common law without notice of the lien,[1] (b) it can be enforced through tracing the asset in which the lien exists into funds or other assets which have been substituted for it.

In construing an "equitable lien" created by contract on occasion as a floating charge the courts have both moved it further away from the traditional common law lien focusing on a particular asset and made the concept even more imprecise.[2]

EQUITABLE LIEN AND EQUITABLE CHARGE

A charge is simply an interest in an asset held as security for a claim—usually a monetary claim. As an expressly created interest, it is to be contrasted with a mortgage insofar as a mortgage implies transfer of the mortgagor's interest with a right of redemption. A charge simply creates an interest in the asset commensurate with the claim in relation to

---

1. The courts are reluctant to impart any suggestion of "constructive" notice (such as applies (e.g.) in land law) into commercial law. See e.g. *Port Line* v. *Ben Line Steamers Ltd.* [1958] 2 Q.B. 146. As to "notice" of charge registered under the Companies Act 1985 as amended by the Companies Act 1989 see Chap. 23.
2. For an early rejection of a contention that equity could extend the notion of the possessory lien see *Gladstone* v. *Birley* (1817) 2 Mer. 401. For construction of contractually based "liens" see Chap. 22.

which the charge exists. Apart from land, in English law it is an equitable concept. In terms of enforceability it does not differ from an equitable mortgage.

"Equitable lien" is synonymous with "equitable charge" in respect of an expressly created security interest, but "lien" is perhaps more frequently used than "charge" to describe security interests imposed by law as, for example, on the basis of conduct. As the description "equitable charge" may be used, even in this context, there is little difference in substance between the two concepts.[3]

The floating charge

The floating charge is an equitable charge which is on all or part of a company's assets. It does not "crystallize" on any particular asset until a specified event occurs and the company is therefore free to continue to deal in and with the assets until that event. As an equitable charge which is directly relevant to the priority of "liens" as against other interests the construction by the court of contractual "liens" in charterparties as floating charges bring it directly into the "lien" area.

The contractual floating charge created as such will usually include clauses attempting to prevent the creation by the company of later fixed charges having priority over it—a "negative pledge" clause. Further, although crystallization necessarily follows from enforcement, a clause may be included providing for automatic crystallization[4] either on an occasion specified in the charge or on notice to the company. The registrability of such charges and their particulars under the Companies Act 1985 and their priority is discussed in Chapter 23.

RESERVATION OF TITLE CLAUSE

In a contract of sale a seller may attempt both to transfer the title to allow the buyer to deal with that which is sold and to reserve the beneficial title should the buyer default. It is not possible to have it both ways and any right in the buyer to the beneficial title may result in the seller's right being classified as an equitable charge—i.e. a security interest instead of the beneficial title (see Chapter 23).

2. THE EQUITABLE LIEN IN ADMIRALTY

An equitable lien or equitable charge may be created in relation to ship, cargo or freight in the same way as it may be in relation to chattels or choses in action generally. A claim based on an equitable charge or lien on a ship is within Admiralty jurisdiction as being a claim "in respect of a mortgage or a charge or a ship or share therein". It may be enforced by an action in personam or an action in rem against the ship.[5] There is no provision for

---

3. Both a charging order made under the Charging Orders Act 1979 in favour of a judgment creditor and a writ of *fieri facias* (in execution of a judgment) take effect as an equitable charge. A floating charge over company assets is an equitable charge. See *infra*.
4. Such a clause is valid, the event of crystallization being a contractual matter. *Re Brightlife Ltd.* [1986] 3 All E.R. 673.
5. Supreme Court Act 1981, s.20(2)(c), s.20(7)(c), s.21(2). Cf. Chaps. 2, 10.

a claim in Admiralty jurisdiction based on an equitable lien on cargo or freight (unless it can be argued that such jurisdiction follows from jurisdiction in relation to a ship).

3. CREATION OF THE LIEN

I. BY CONTRACT

The ability freely to create a lien by contract means that at will parties can create security interests enforceable against third parties.[6] Whether a contractual "lien" clause creates an equitable lien is a matter of construction and the issue as it affects charterparties and bills of lading is the subject of Chapter 22. If construed as an equitable lien its enforceability as a lien may be affected by registration requirements of either the Bills of Sale Acts 1878 and 1882, or more likely in maritime matters, the Companies Act 1985 as amended when in force by the Companies Act 1989.

Bills of Sale Acts 1878 and 1882

An instrument creating or evidencing an equitable lien created by contract by an individual (i.e. other than a company) is within the framework of the Bills of Sale Acts 1878 and 1882.[7] Security transactions fall within the Bills of Sale Act 1882 but many maritime documents are excluded from the operations of the Acts.[8]

Companies Act 1985[9]

An equitable lien created by a company is a charge within the Companies Act 1985, s.396, and if within the terms of the section will require registration[10] for enforceability against a liquidator or other creditors. Such charges include a charge on a ship or share in a ship, a charge on calls made but not paid, a charge on book debts and any charge created or evidenced by an instrument which, if executed by an individual, would require registration as a bill of sale.[11] The provisions are to be replaced by a more comprehensive framework on the coming into force of the appropriate provisions of the Companies Act 1989.[12]

---

6. A lien or other charge created by a public company on its own shares is void except for a charge (i) for any amount payable in respect of them or (ii) arising in the ordinary course of business of a money-lending company, or (iii) in existence prior to a statutory registration period (the Companies Act 1985, s.150). As to the need for registration of charges, see Chap. 23.

7. As to the framework, see the Bills of Sale Act 1878, s.4 (adopted by the Bills of Sale Act 1882, s.3 and Chaps. 17 and 23.

8. Including assignments and transfers of ships, bills of lading, warehousekeeper's certificates and any documents used in the ordinary course of business or proof of possession or control of goods or documents of title thereto. See Chap. 23.

9. Part XII ("Registration of Charges") will be replaced by new provisions when the appropriate part of the Companies Act 1989 is brought into force.

10. I.e. delivery of particulars of the charge for registration. There is provision in the amendments enacted by the Companies Act 1989 for late delivery of the particulars (added s.400).

11. See the Companies Act 1985, s.396. A "floating charge" is also within the provision. As to further scope of the provision, see Chap. 23.

12. See generally Chap. 23. Non-registration will also render the charge void against an administrator appointed to restore a potentially or actually insolvent company to solvency (as to which see Chap. 17).

Shipowner's lien on subfreight

A lien on subfreights (often found in a charterparty)[13] is, it has been held, an equitable
assignment by a charterer of the future right to receive freight. This constitutes an
equitable floating charge on a book debt. Hence it is registrable under the Companies Act
1985, and if not registered will be void against a liquidator or creditor.[14] However, its
express removal by the Companies Act 1989 from the category of book debt will on the
coming into force of those provisions render the lien non-registrable.[15]

II. ARISING FROM THE RELATIONSHIP OF THE PARTIES[16]

Vendor's lien for unpaid purchase money

This is primarily relevant to the sale of land and arises on the contract, counterbalancing
the purchaser's equitable interest. But, as with the purchaser's interest, it may be
applicable to the sale of chattels (including a ship) if equity would decree specific
performance of the sale of the chattel.[17] Its scope may be limited in that, unless
specifically provided otherwise, a transaction within the Sale of Goods Act 1979 may
create only the rights (including the liens)[18] specified in that Act.[19] If, however, the Act
does not provide an exclusive framework the equitable lien would have a role to play
alongside or consecutive to the possessory lien conferred on the vendor by the Act.

III. ARISING FROM A COURSE OF CONDUCT

No equitable lien is created simply by expenditure on another's land, chattel, or
intangible,[20] but if such expenditure is made in reliance on a representation a lien based
on estoppel may arise. In a string of modern cases working out the role of estoppel in
regard to the occupation and improvement of land, courts have claimed through the
principle of "proprietary estoppel" a freedom to impose the remedy which is seen to fit
the particular circumstances. So it could be transfer of title,[21] occupation for a specified
period,[22] or a lien for any amount spent.[23] The Court of Appeal, while conceding that
proprietary estoppel exists in regard to land and could extend to forms of property other
than land (such as goods), has held that it should not be extended further.[24] Even accepting

---

13. As to the contractual scope and nature of the "lien" see Chap. 22 and as to priorities generally see
Chap. 23.
14. See *The Ugland Trailer* [1985] 2 Lloyd's Rep. 372; *The Annangel Glory* [1988] 1 Lloyd's Rep. 45. See
further Chap. 23.
15. See generally Chap. 23.
16. An equitable lien is created in favour of a partner over partnership assets, a trustee over trust property for
expenditure, and beneficiaries over land purchased with trust moneys.
17. See e.g. *Langen* v. *Bell* [1972] 1 All E.R. 296 (shares).
18. See s.41.
19. See e.g. *Re Wait* [1927] 1 Ch. 606; *The Aliakmon* [1986] 2 All E.R. 145, at p. 151 (Lord Brandon).
20. As a consequence there is no lien for salvage outside the maritime concept.
21. *Pascoe* v. *Turner* [1979] 1 W.L.R. 131.
22. See e.g. *Inwards* v. *Baker* (life interest) [1965] 2 Q.B. 29; *Matharu* v. *Matharu, The Times*, 13 May
1994.
23. See e.g. *Chalmers* v. *Pardoe* [1963] 3 All E.R. 552; *Wayling* v. *Jones* [1993] EGCS 153.
24. *Western Fish Products* v. *Pentworth D.C.* [1981] 2 All E.R. 204, at p. 218.

such a limitation, an equitable lien could be created in relation to a ship or cargo. While therefore, the principle appears most frequently in the context of land it *may* be applicable commercially[25] and, therefore, to maritime transactions.

4. ENFORCEABILITY OF THE LIEN

I. AGAINST THIRD PARTIES

Once created, an equitable lien protects the claim to which it attaches by enabling the claimant to assert an equitable interest in a particular asset. It does not give any right to pre-trial attachment but it confers enforceability against all interests created subsequently if acquired with notice of it and against any equitable interest acquired subsequently whether with or without notice. To that extent it gives priority against purchasers and other creditors. But it is not enforceable against those who hold interests created prior in time to the "lien". In particular, an owner cannot be made subject to a lien created by an agent, bailee or charterer except on grounds of express or implied authority.

The requirement of registration of interests has in some fields affected the general equitable rule that purchasers without notice take free of an equitable interest. Registration provides the "notice" and where it is available failure to register an interest may render the interest void as against later purchasers. In English law registration is relevant to liens other than in land only under the Bills of Sale Acts 1878 and 1882 or the Companies Act 1985[26] and as regards other registrable interests vying for priority with a lien.[27]

II. TRACING INTO OTHER ASSETS

Through the beneficial interest created by it the equitable lien provides a foundation for tracing in equity.[28] Tracing is available in relation to assets substituted for that in which the lien existed by any party against whom the lien is enforceable. It is a remedy which overcomes the problem inherent in the concept of "lien" of continued existence of a thing to which the security interest is attached[29]; but it does not increase the scope of enforceability (i.e. the number of persons against which it can be enforced). The assets into which the lien may be traced must be seen as representing the original asset but equity will allow tracing into a bank account or other fund to which money paid for the asset has been credited. However, insurance moneys do not represent the asset in respect of which they are paid and a claimant cannot trace an interest held in that asset through to the moneys.[30]

25. See *Moorgate Mercantile Co. Ltd.* v. *Twitchings* [1976] Q.B. 225 (reversed [1977] A.C. 870) and, it is arguable, the Sale of Goods Act 1979, s.21.
26. See *supra* and Chap. 23.
27. Such as a requirement of registration of a mortgage (as to which, see Chap. 23).
28. For general principles, see *Re Diplock* [1948] Ch. 465 (C.A.) (affd. [1951] A.C. 251). The court will assist through ancillary orders in discovering the whereabouts of the assets (see *A* v. *C* [1980] 2 Lloyd's Rep. 200).
29. With the exception of the fund created through judicial sale in an action *in rem*. As with every other lien if the asset to which it is attached is destroyed or incorporated into another the lien is extinguished (see *Borden (UK)* v. *Scottish Timber Products* [1981] Ch. 25) but tracing also requires the existence of an asset—an overdrawn bank account will not suffice (*Bishopgate Finance* v. *Homan, The Times*, 14 July 1994).
30. See *The Lancaster* [1980] 2 Lloyd's Rep. 497.

5. TRANSFERABILITY

Ex hypothesi the transfer of an equitable lien would depend on the transfer of the claim
to which it is attached. Given such a transfer, as an equitable interest an equitable lien is
in principle transferable generally. However, in developing proprietary interests dependent
on estoppel, the courts have on occasion created non-transferable interests; and where the
basis of a lien is reliance on a representation it may be that such lien would be limited to
the person relying. Such a restriction has been imposed in respect of social relationship
issues. It may have less appeal in a commercial context.

6. TERMINATION

The equitable lien would fall with the claim to which it is attached, and to that extent is
subject to statutory limitation of action provisions. It is also subject to the equitable
principle of laches—delay will destroy the lien. And, naturally, it is subject to the general
principles of waiver and loss by consent.

CHAPTER 22

Creating a Lien by Contract

While some maritime liens and statutory liens are founded on contract they are consequences imposed by the law on the contract. The parties have no freedom to create either type of lien by a contract other than that which by law exists in the lien.[1] On the other hand under English law possessory and equitable liens may be created by contract in respect of any type of transaction. Subject to estoppel or statutory provision[2] a lien may not be created by contract in respect of any asset in which a contracting party has no interest to support the lien.

The basic concept of "lien" is at common law the assertion of an interest in an asset under the lien holder's control as security for a claim. But, as has been seen, the meaning is now far wider and encompasses interests of varying nature and effect. The maritime lien is an early example of movement away from "control" or possession, followed by the statutory lien in Admiralty. Approaching from a different startpoint a "lien" may include in equity a security interest in an intangible, including a floating charge on a company's assets.

A major problem with many contracts, including standard form bills of lading and charterparties is that provision is simply made for a "lien". There is therefore a preliminary and fundamental matter of construction. The uncertainty through the use of the undefined "lien" is underlined by the use of "lien" in one context in a standard form charterparty to refer to a relationship similar to a possessory lien, i.e. not a lien but something like it.[3]

1. THE LIEN CLAUSE—GENERAL CONSIDERATIONS

COMMON CLAUSES

Lien clauses appear in many standard form and other charterparties and bills of lading. Their effect may vary according to whether the lien is solely a creation of contract or is

---

1. So the express provision of a salvor's maritime lien in LOF 1990 Clause 5 can only operate (if at all) to counter any argument that the lien was waived by the agreement. Further the practice of a provision for a maritime lien for bunker suppliers cannot create such a lien and is but an illustration of the uncertainty created by misuse of the term "lien". (As to the practice see *The Saetta* [1994] 1 All E.R. 851 at p. 868.)

2. As e.g. Sale of Goods Act 1979, ss.24, 25—s.25 providing for transfer of an interest to buyer in possession after sale "without notice of any lien or other right of the original seller".

3. Uncertainty is not restricted to contract. In *The Saetta* (fn 1) Clarke J. commented that the meaning of "lien" in s.25 of the Sale of Goods Act 1979 was not clear. As to that Act and equitable interests see Chap. 21.

the application of a lien created by operation of law. Clauses commonly provide for a lien on cargo for freight, dead freight and demurrage and other expenses[4] or any amounts due under this charter.[5] In respect of dead freight, demurrage expenses in general and amounts due under the charter this will create whatever interest is specified by and through the contract. Provided that it is to be construed as a possessory lien, the lien for freight will, it would seem, take the place of the lien for freight due which would exist because of the legal relationship. It may be, however, that the scope of the "lien" or the event creating it will indicate that it is either not that lien in all its aspects or is another type of security interest entirely. So the extension of the lien to cargo delivered into the possession of another[6] cannot be a possessory lien and can take effect only insofar as whatever interest is created is enforceable against the person to whom the cargo is delivered. The only possible interest is the equitable lien. Further, the lien on cargo for freight will involve consideration of the difference, if any, between "hire" and "freight". A lien on freight involves the same issue and in addition consideration of the type of lien in an intangible (see *infra*).

Whether the lien is exercised or, if so, is properly exercised will be a matter of construction of the contract—so a lien exercisable on completion of discharge might defeat itself unless after discharge the cargo remains in the possession of the owner.[7] Refusal to continue a voyage may or may not of itself be exercise of a lien on cargo, depending on the legal basis of the act and its effect on other contractual obligations. It is a matter of construction how the exercise of a lien affects other contractual rights. So the exercise of a lien on cargo for non-payment of freight or demurrage does not prevent demurrage accruing.[8]

The right to implement the lien may be qualified by the provision for alternative security.[9] In a charterparty the provisions of the lien may be accompanied by a declaration of continued or cessation of liability of the charterers (in the latter instance a "cesser" clause—see *infra*).

MULTI-LIEN CLAUSES

A clause may create not only liens in respect of various obligations but more than one type of lien.

The New York Produce Exchange Charterparty

Clause 23 of the New York Produce Exchange (NYPE) time charterparty 1993 provides:

4. See e.g. Conbill Clause 4, Shell Bill of Lading Clause 11, Gencon Clause 8 (see *infra*), Multiform 1982 Clause 24, Asbatankvoy Clause 21, Nuvoy 86 Clause 42, Hevycon Clause 18.
5. See e.g. NYPE Clause 18 (now also including hire as well as freight), Baltime Clause 18 (*infra*). For discussion of those matters which are the charterer's responsibility see *The Cebu (No. 2)* [1990] 2 Lloyd's Rep. 316 and *infra*.
6. See e.g. Asbatankvoy Clause 21. See also for the construction of "lien" and "encumbrance" in Saleform, *The Barenbels* [1984] 2 Lloyd's Rep. 388.
7. See e.g. *The Fort Kipp* [1985] 2 All E.R. 168.
8. See *Lyle Shipping* v. *Cardiff Corpn* [1900] 2 Q.B. 638; *The Boral Gas* [1988] 1 Lloyd's Rep. 342.
9. See e.g. Nuvoy 84, Clause 42.

"The Owners shall have a lien upon all cargoes, and all sub-freights and/or sub hire for any amounts due under this Charter Party, including general average contributions, and the Charterers to have a lien on the Vessel for all monies paid in advance and not earned, and any overpaid hire or excess deposit to be returned at once.

The Charterers will not directly or indirectly suffer, nor permit to be continued, any lien or encumbrance, which might have priority over the title and interest of the owners in the vessel. The Charterers undertake that during the period of this Charter Party they will not procure any supplies or necessaries or services including any port expenses and bunkers on the credit of the Owners or in the Owner's time."

This clause replaces Clause 18 of the earlier edition of the charterparty. It differs in (a) providing expressly for a lien on sub-hire; (b) adding the undertaking not to procure supplies or necessaries; and (c) in the obligation not to suffer a lien to be created, replacing a reference to agents with the reference to "directly or indirectly".

The addition of sub-hire avoids the problem of whether "freight" includes "hire" (see *infra*). The undertaking not to procure supplies on the credit of the owners operates contractually to impose a specific obligation. So far as the possible creation of liens is concerned it at most adds only an obligation not to create *any* lien (and not only one which might have priority over the owner's lien). Whether any implied prohibition is effective turns on the same factors as are relevant to the express prohibition (see *infra*). Apart from these two matters the uncertainties relevant to liens endemic in the earlier version of the standard remain.

The clause appears to provide for four types of lien, namely:

   (i) owners' lien on cargo;
   (ii) owners' lien on subfreights and/or sub-hire;
   (iii) charterers' lien on ship;
   (iv) the lien which the charterer is obliged not to "suffer directly or indirectly nor permit to be continued."[10]

"Lien" is not used consistently in these clauses.[11] The owner's lien on cargo is probably the traditional possessory lien, but as it appears in a time charter and the charterer is not granted possession of the ship the charterer's lien on the ship cannot be a possessory lien.[12] Similarly insofar as the right to receive freight is a chose in action, a lien on freight cannot be a possessory lien—and arguably is not accurately described as a lien. Finally, the "lien" which a charterer must not suffer to remain attached to the ship arguably refers to any type of lien. It is difficult to defend the loose use of the lien concept as exemplified in these standard form charterparties. On occasion commercial sense necessitates legal risk but it is hard to appreciate the commercial sense of lack of clarity of right or obligation.

The Baltime Charterparty

Clause 18 of the Baltime Uniform Time Charter reads:

---

10. See also e.g. Barecon A, Clause 15.
11. See *The Lancaster* [1980] 2 Lloyd's Rep. 497.
12. As also in a voyage charterparty.

"18. Lien
The Owners to have a lien upon all cargoes and sub-freights belonging to the Time-Charterers and any Bill of Lading freight for all claims under this Charter, and the Charterers to have a lien on the Vessel for all moneys paid in advance and not earned."[13]

The clause (a) limits the owners' lien on cargoes and subfreights to such cargoes or subfreights as belong to the time charterers, and (b) specifically refers to bill of lading freight and (c) provides for a charterer's lien on the ship. In *The Nanfri*[14] Lord Russell said bill of lading freight added nothing to subfreights—"the lien operates as an equitable charge on what is due from the shippers to the charterers".[15] As the clause stands it covers sub-hire only if "freight" includes hire.

The Gencon Charterparty

The Gencon Charterparty as revised in 1994 provides in Clause 8:

"The Owners shall have a lien on the cargo and on all sub freights payable in respect of the cargo for freight, dead freight, demurrage claims for damages and for all other amounts due under this Charter Party including costs of recovering the same."

While the clause specifies the grounds for the lien attaching to a greater extent than the NYPE in Baltime clauses, as with the Baltime it does not refer to hire.

THE LIEN CLAUSE IN CONTEXT

Whatever the degree of clarity construction arguments are perhaps unavoidable. In 1979 in *The Nanfri* it was emphasized in the House of Lords that the lien clause in a charterparty must be read in conjunction with other clauses and, in particular, with the purpose of the charterparty. So, in a time charterparty, the clause "cannot be read as interfering with the time charterer's primary right to use the ship and to direct the master as to its use". It cannot be used as a basis for arguing that the master cannot sign prepaid bills of lading on the ground that this would deprive the owners of their lien on subfreights. It gives the owners "a lien on such freights or subfreights as in the event come to be payable and which in fact are payable".[16]

Given that the lien clause has to be construed as part of the whole it is instructive to examine the liens referred to in the charterparties cited and set these in a general context.

2. THE LIENS CREATED

I. OWNER'S LIEN ON CARGO

(a) Nature of lien

It seems clear that in a time or voyage charterparty or bill of lading this is a contractual creation of a possessory lien. In the case of a demise charter it is difficult to escape the

13. Also Barecon A, Clause 15.
14. [1979] A.C. 757.
15. But see the dispute as to whether "freight" included "hire" (*infra*).
16. [1979] A.C. 757, at p. 777 (Lord Wilberforce).

conclusion that as the charterer is in possession, it would be an equitable lien. It would not be a lien akin to a possessory lien (as held in the case of a time charterer's lien on the chartered ship) as the owner would have no power to prevent delivery and it is only as an equitable lien that such a clause makes sense in the context of a demised charterparty.

(b) The cargo

In a charterparty such as NYPE or Gencon does the contract purport to create a lien over cargo not owned by the charterer? In *The Aegnoussiotis*[17] Donaldson J. held that the then applicable NYPE clause imposed on the charterer an obligation to procure a contractual lien over cargo not owned by them and, failing this, that cargo owners have a cause of action against the owners if the owners assert the lien. In *The Agios Georgis*[18] Mocatta J. held to the contrary on the simple but persuasive reasoning that a contractual lien cannot be imposed on a third party. In *The Cebu (No. 1)*[19]—concerned with the lien on freight—Lloyd J. preferred the view that "all cargoes" meant what it said in support of his view that all "subfreights" included those not due to the head charterer.

It seems clear that apart from estoppel, a lien clause cannot create a lien over assets in which the contracting party has no interest. So the charterparty clause cannot create a lien over cargo not owned by the charterers and the owners of which are not parties to any arrangement conferring a lien in favour of the shipowners.[20] The question is simply whether the clause must be read down to fit the impossibility or read as obligating the charterers to create such an arrangement. Lloyd J.'s view must be approached with some caution as in the context of freight the "lien" will operate successfully because of a contractual basis—the charterers agreed to assign freight due directly to them or to which they were entitled as assignees. The question regarding freight would be similar to that of cargo as it was posed in *The Aegnoussiotis* and *The Agios Georgis* if there was *no* lien clause in the sub-sub-charter.

It is suggested, with respect, that Mocatta J.'s view is to be preferred. The approach of Donaldson J. would impose on third parties at least the burden of a lawsuit. To suggest that A, by contract with B, can create an interest over C's goods although C may challenge that interest seems a curious exception not only to the doctrine of privity underlying the rule relating to carriage of goods but also to fundamental property principles. It may also be considered unjust. This is supported by Mustill J.'s approach in *The Miramar*. Mustill J. thought it clear that to be useful such a clause must be intended to create rights against third parties, it being only in a minority of cases that the cargo would belong to the charterer throughout the transit. As "a clause in the charter cannot do this directly ... it must, therefore, have been intended that the clause would operate by way of incorporation into the bill of lading".[21] The most general form of incorporating words would produce this result.

17. [1977] 1 Lloyd's Rep. 268.
18. [1978] 2 Lloyd's Rep. 192.
19. [1983] 1 Lloyd's Rep. 302.
20. A bill of lading clause purporting to create a lien on all goods received from a shipper may raise similar issues. See e.g. Nedlloyd Bill of Lading, Clause 14.
21. [1983] 2 Lloyd's Rep. 319, at p. 324—holding also there was no personal liability of the bill of lading holder through incorporation of the charterparty—this being the issue affirmed on appeal [1984] 2 Lloyd's Rep. 129 (H.L.). See also *The Chrysovolandou Dyo* [1981] 1 Lloyd's Rep. 159. It may be arguable that even where there is no incorporation, a lien clause in the charterparty would impose on a charterer an obligation to enforce any lien clause in a bill of lading.

The creation of a lien over a shipper's goods through a charterparty to which he is not a party could be defended only on the basis that the shipper takes the risk of such a lien for the policy reason that otherwise the owner will not know which goods are susceptible to the lien. In the end it is a matter of the balancing of commercial factors—and it seems difficult to defend a proposition that a shipper must take the risk of submitting his cargo to a lien to which he does not consent and of which he has no knowledge. It is to favour a carrier too greatly to allow him to pass on the contractual risk taken with the charterer to a shipper with whom he has no contract.

II. OWNER'S LIEN ON SUBFREIGHTS OR SUB-HIRE

(a) Nature of the lien

"The lien operates on an equitable charge on what is due from the shippers to the charterers and in order to be effective requires an ability to intercept the subfreight (by notice of claim) before it is paid by shipper to charterer."[22] In effect it is an equitable assignment of the right to receive the freight and its enforceability against the shippers will therefore depend on notice to them.[23]

Arguments seeking to limit the meaning of the clause to circumstances where the owner is acting as agent for the charterer or to matters within the lienor's control (or when freight is due) have been roundly rejected.[24] The purpose of the clause, it is said, is to confer on the owners security for amounts falling due under the charter, a right to be exercised by owners in their own right.

The right conferred by the contract is to assign future subfreight by way of security when and if there is default by the assignor of the contractual obligation secured. It is not simply an agreement to create a charge on the coming into being of specified conditions. It is

"an agreement by the charterers to assign (i.e. to transfer) to the owner by way of floating security the right to payment of sub freight falling due under contracts to be made by the charterers in respect of the vessel the subject of the head charter."[25]

It has to be said that, as argued early in this century, the description of such a right as a "lien" was as much misleading as accurate.[26] In fact the label identifies the right not at all. While it is appreciated that the meaning of the clause has only been reached after much judicial deliberation it remains surprising that a right of such complexity continues to be expressed with such concealing simplicity.

22. *The Nanfri* [1979] A.C. 757, at p. 781 (Lord Russell). See also *The Ugland Trailer* [1985] 2 Lloyd's Rep. 372. It is too late to exercise the lien after payment to the charterer (*ibid.*).
23. *The Cebu (No. 1)* [1983] 1 Lloyd's Rep. 302; *The Ugland Trailer* [1985] 2 Lloyd's Rep. 372; *The Annangel Glory* [1988] 1 Lloyd's Rep. 45; *The Cebu (No. 2)* [1990] 2 Lloyd's Rep. 316. An equitable assignment for security is not to be distinguished from an equitable charge (see *The Annangel Glory*). Notice to the shipper is a prerequisite of entitlement to the subfreights as between shipper and assignee (i.e. shipowner) but as between the shipowner and charterer it is such a prerequisite only of a statutory assignment (see the Law of Property Act 1925, s.136(1)). Even without such notice it may be an equitable asssignment and notice going to priority between assignees (as to which see *The Attika Hope* [1988] 1 Lloyd's Rep. 439 and Chap. 23).
24. See *The Ugland Trailer* [1985] 2 Lloyd's Rep. 372 commenting on a dictum in *The Cebu (No. 1)* 1 Lloyd's Rep. 302 arguably hinting to the contrary.
25. See *The Annangel Glory* [1988] 1 Lloyd's Rep. 45.
26. See *Taggert Beaton and Co.* v. *James Fisher and Sons* [1903] 1 K.B. 391.

The content of the right

It is established that the "lien" extends only to unpaid freight. It is terminated when the freight is paid and there is no right to follow the funds into the charterer's hands or those of third parties.

(b) Does "freight" include charterparty hire?

In *The Cebu (No. 1)*[27] Lloyd J. held that, while in some contexts it made sense to distinguish freight from hire, in the context of the lien clause "freight" included "hire", but in *The Cebu (No. 2)*[28] Steyn J. held that at the date of entry into the charter before him (1979) there was a well established commercial restriction of "freight" to that payable under a bill of lading and voyage charterparty. "Freight" in a contract had to be construed with the accepted usage in mind at the date of entering into the contract and it therefore did not include that payable under a time charterparty. Even if the meaning had been ambiguous account should be taken of its effect on third parties (i.e. the party on which lay the obligation to pay). In contrast to voyage charters moneys due under time charters were not easily identifiable as the periodic payments reflected a balance of credits (such as ballast or bunkers) and debits (e.g. off hire). Further the sub-charterers may face a dilemma in knowing that if hire was not paid promptly the ship may be withdrawn yet being unsure to which party it should be paid—"only a clear lien clause should be enforceable against the third party".

In *The Cebu (No. 1)* Lloyd J. had expressed the view that there was little commercial sense in making the security depend on the type of charter under which a trip was made. Steyn J. clearly took the view that the construction in accordance with commercial practice also made commercial sense—particularly from the view of the sub-charterer. What is clear is that not only should any lien clause be clear but that it is to be expected that commercial terms will be construed as normally used. So the wording of commercial bargains must reflect any change in that use. In this respect the amendment of the NYPE clause is to be welcomed.

(c) Are "sub-subfreights" and "sub-subcharter hire" included?

This turns on the entitlement (or not) of the owner (or head charterer) to payments due *to* the charterer with which there is a direct contractual relationship. While where the security is "freight" the relevance of the issue will depend on the ambit of that term, the matter becomes relevant either if the decision in *The Cebu (No. 1)* is to be preferred or, as in the amended NYPE form, the clause includes hire.

In *The Cebu (No. 1)*, having held that freight included hire, Lloyd J. held that the clause included sub-sub-charter hire due to sub-charterers on the basis that the clause was an equitable assignment of all "freight" due to the charterers either directly or through a sub-charter including a like clause. In so doing, Lloyd J. approved the view that in its reference to "cargo" the clause included cargo not owned by the charterer. While the issues are similar as regards the ambit of the security the operation of the two clauses seems directly

27. [1983] 1 Lloyd's Rep. 302.
28. [1990] 2 Lloyd's Rep. 316.

contrary—the "lien" on freight or hire works because of the contractual claim, the lien on cargo cannot work directly because of a lack of such a claim.

III. CHARTERER'S LIEN ON SHIP

Nature of the lien

In the context of a time or voyage charter the charterer is not in possession and, therefore, the lien cannot be a possessory lien. In 1980 in *The Lancaster*[29] it was argued that in respect of a time charter the lien was an equitable lien (or charge) in the true sense that it gave the charterers the right to enforce it against rival claimants to the ship and, in that case, to insurance moneys representing the ship. Robert Goff J. held that the "lien", although it was not a possessory lien, had similar effect. It conferred "on time charterers the right to postpone delivery of the ship to the owners" and nothing more.[30] In the case of a demise charter it follows that the lien is a "true" possessory lien.

IV. LIEN NOT TO BE SUFFERED OR PERMITTED TO CONTINUE

The express prohibition in the NYPE clause is against any "lien or encumbrance incurred" by the charteres which might have priority over the interest of the owners. The clause is clearly intended to catch *any* interest which would take priority over that of the owner. In 1980 in *The Vestland*[31] it was held that the clause was aimed at a lien or encumbrance which the charterers or their agents have caused to be incurred; and that an arrest of a ship due to the charterers' act was a "lien" within the meaning of the phrase. The arrest gave the arrester a "statutory lien" which carried the right of a secured creditor.[32] While, with respect, it is not the arrest which creates the lien but the issue of the writ *in rem* which precedes the arrest, the reasoning is equally applicable.

3. CHARTERER'S LIABILITY DEPENDENT ON EXERCISE OF OWNER'S LIEN—THE "CESSER CLAUSE"

By terms of the charterparty a charterer may be liable only to the extent to which the owner has been unable to exercise the lien conferred by the charterparty.[33] In such a case, an owner cannot claim against the charterers if he (the owner) fails to exercise his lien, but

29. [1980] 2 Lloyd's Rep. 497. In *The Panglobal Friendship* [1978] 1 Lloyd's Rep. 368 Lord Denning had suggested that the lien may be an equitable charge—but as the case was settled there was no authoritative pronouncement.

30. [1980] 2 Lloyd's Rep. 497, at pp. 501. 502. The exercise of the lien means that the ship is effectively redelivered for the purposes of the hire clause. Robert Goff J. went on to hold that if it was an equitable lien: (i) it gave no right to trace into insurance proceeds as these did not "represent" the ship; (ii) if there was a right to trace there were no grounds for tracing; (iii) if there was a lien and a right to trace the charterers' lien came into existence only on the event creating it and was, therefore, subject to prior assignment of the moneys. As to the priorities, see Chap. 23.

31. [1980] 2 Lloyd's Rep. 171.

32. As to statutory lien, see Chap. 19.

33. See e.g. Nuvoy 84, Clause 42—charterers continuing responsibility but "Owners shall take all reasonable steps to obtain satisfaction of their claim by exercising the lien".

if the owner can show that the right of lien was "either legally or practically[34] an ineffective right the failure to attempt to exercise it will not debar his claim".[35]

4. THE NEED FOR REGISTRATION

A "charge" created by a company of a type specified by the Companies Act 1985 must be registered to be valid against a liquidator or other creditors. Where the charge is created by contract[36] and falls within the ambit of the provision it will arguably be registrable whatever its nature.[37]

5. THE GOVERNING LAW[38]

It is clear that subject to any overriding forum interest the law of the place where the assets are when the lien is exercised must control the exercise of the lien and arguably its existence as a proprietary interest. The validity and construction of the lien clause as a contractual provision, on the other hand, may be seen as issues for the law governing the contract.

---

34. e.g. the absence of storage facilities coupled with the loss of berth facilities (see *The Tropwave* [1981] 2 Lloyd's Rep. 159) or where cargo is consigned to a foreign government which would not allow the lien to be exercised. *The Sinoe* [1972] 1 Lloyd's Rep. 201 (C.A.).
35. *The Tropwave* [1981] 2 Lloyd's Rep. 159, following *The Sinoe* [1972] 1 Lloyd's Rep. 201 (C.A.).
36. And not by operation of law.
37. See Chap. 23.
38. See generally Chap. 26.

CHAPTER 23

Priorities

I. THE GENERAL PROBLEMS OF PRIORITY

Priority of claims implies that there is competition between interests which (i) are not only enforceable against the person creating them but are based on an interest in the asset itself,[1] and (ii) when regarded individually are valid and enforceable through the asset, i.e. they are "proprietary".[2] Priority becomes important when the total amount of all valid proprietary claims exceeds the total value of assets available to meet them.

The question of priorities in maritime law is usually taken to mean priority between holders of maritime security interests in relation to a fund in court representing the *res* against which an action *in rem* has been brought. However, priority is of wider scope, and encompasses not only maritime security priority but also:

    (i) other (non-security) proprietary interests of purchasers, charterers and others between themselves and between those and security interests; and

    (ii) other security interests not maritime in origin which apply to assets in which maritime security interests exist.

It is, therefore, misleading to discuss priorities in maritime law as if priority is a matter involving only the weighing of maritime security interests. As a first step, the priority scene should be set, and in setting it it is important to bear in mind the fundamental distinction between "actions *in personam*" and "actions *in rem*". Priorities outside the maritime area are between proprietary claims enforced through actions *in personam*. "Actions *in rem*" are restricted to maritime claims but as regards such claims actions *in personam* and actions *in rem* may be brought in relation to the same asset. There must, therefore, be enquiry into both the *in personam* and *in rem* priority frameworks *and* their relationship to each other.

---

1. Holders of "personal" (as distinct from "proprietary") claims have no interests enforceable against third parties and are unsecured creditors in bankruptcy sharing equally among themselves. A contractual benefit may be assigned and statutory provision may be made for transfer of the burden or transfer of the contract (as in respect of lawful holders of a bill of lading made by the Carriage of Goods by Sea Act 1992). A *Mareva* injunction confers no priority (see Chapter 16). The phrase *in personam* is confusing in that it may indicate that a claim is personal only, i.e. is non-proprietary in the sense that it lies only against the person undertaking the obligation (as e.g. a contractual claim); but in the maritime context an action *in personam* simply indicates that the action not being *in rem* is being enforced as any other claim, and whether it is proprietary or not depends on the nature of the claim (see *infra*).

2. A preliminary question is to identify the interest created. So an attempt to reserve "title" may be construed as a lien with differing consequences to those intended. See e.g. *Re Bond Worth Ltd.* [1980] Ch. 228. Compare *Clough Mill Ltd. v. Martin* [1984] 3 All E.R. 982. See also fn 16.

II. PRINCIPLES OF PRIORITY IN ENGLISH LAW

1. THE BASIC PRINCIPLES OF "IN PERSONAM" PRIORITY

The basic *in personam* priority principles in English law generally between proprietary interests are:

  (i) first in time prevails; and
  (ii) no person can transfer more than he has (*nemo dat quod non habet*).

However, considerable inroads are made into the operation of the principles by the rule limiting the enforceability of equitable interests and other modifications.

Legal and equitable interests

The priority framework in respect of claims *in personam* is based on the fundamental distinction of enforceability between legal and equitable interests. It will be recalled that

  (i) a "legal interest" (i.e. rooted in the common law) is enforceable (subject to registration requirements) against all subsequently created interests; and
  (ii) an "equitable interest" (i.e. rooted in equity) is enforceable (subject to registration requirements) against any subsequently created interest except a legal interest acquired without notice of the earlier equitable interest.

Equitable interests fall into three broad categories:

  (a) those interests (such as the trust) created anew through exercise of equitable jurisdiction over the years;
  (b) contracts to create common law interests (e.g. contract of sale) capable of specific performance or title or interests that would have qualified as a common law interest but for lack of a required formality (e.g. a deed or perhaps registration), a prime example being the equitable mortgage;
  (c) informally created interests based on common law concepts but which have developed a life of their own (e.g. equitable lien or equitable charge).

Other modifications

Other important modifications on the priority principle of first in time are:

  (a) the introduction of registration of interests as a criterion of priority[3];
  (b) allowing conduct (such as fraud or a representation) to affect the priority rules;
  (c) the introduction of specific statutory rules.[4]

---

3. As e.g. the Companies Act 1985, Part XII; the Bills of Sale Acts 1878 and 1882. The Merchant Shipping (Registration etc.) Act 1993 as from 1 January 1996 repealed and re-enacted in the Merchant Shipping Act 1995, Parts I and II and Sch. 1 (see *infra*).
4. See e.g. the Sale of Goods Act 1979, ss.24, 25 and 47; the Factors Act 1889, ss.8, 9 and 10 (purchasers in good faith defeating earlier interests) (see *infra*).

Maritime claims "in personam"

All maritime claims may be enforced by an action *in personam* either solely or where enforceable by action *in rem* together with an action *in rem*. Whether a claim enforced *in personam* attracts any preference over unsecured creditors depends on the rules applicable to claims in general. If the interest on which the claim is based is enforceable against a third party and, *therefore*, proprietary, it will confer a right in that asset not only against that third party but also against a liquidator or trustee in bankruptcy.[5] Maritime claims based on ownership, mortgage, charge, lien, whether legal or equitable, or demise charterparty, provide the basis for such enforceability. Priority as between these interests and any other brought within the proprietary area through judicial construction[6] is governed by the general principles of *in personam* priority.

2. THE ADMIRALTY RULES OF PRIORITY "IN REM"

An action *in rem* is focused on a *res* which may be ship, cargo, freight, or a fund representing the asset against which the action is taken.[7] A number of general principles operate:

(i) statutory rights of detention of public authorities[8] and claims stemming from such rights are treated as having a priority over claims by individuals;

(ii) subject to (i)

  (a) Admiralty Marshal's costs and expenses,[9] and

  (b) the arrester's costs in the creation of the fund (in that order)

are prior charges on any fund representing the *res*[10];

---

5. Subject to any statutory restriction—as, for example, when a registrable interest is not registered.

6. As (possibly) proprietary estoppel.

7. And, as from the coming into force of the Merchant Shipping (Salvage and Pollution) Act 1994, s.1(6) and Sch. 2 in relation to salvage claims under the Salvage Convention 1989 any property "non permanently and intentionally attached to the shoreline" (Art. 1(c)). See now Merchant Shipping Act 1995, s.224, Sch. 11.

8. *The Charger* [1966] 1 Lloyd's Rep. 670; *The Blitz* [1992] 2 Lloyd's Rep. 441. As to the question of whether the priority is assertable against a fund resulting from the sale, see *The Queen of the South* [1968] P. 449; *The Freightline One* [1986] 1 Lloyd's Rep. 266 and *infra*. But see *The Sea Spray* [1907] P. 133 which considered priority.

9. Whether a due payment is an expense of the Marshal or a claimant is liable is a matter of construction of responsibility. So wharfage charges will only form part of the expenses if they are increased directly as part of the Marshal's duties arising out of custody of the ship—see *The Nagasaki Spirit* (Singapore H.C.) [1994] LMLN 386 and authorities there considered. Costs of discharging cargo are not part of the Marshal's expenses and have to be borne by the cargo owner—*The Jogoo* [1981] 1 Lloyd's Rep. 513. Classification fees are recoverable from the proceeds of sale if the ship is sold as a classified ship and benefit obtained thereby (*The Honshu Gloria* [1986] 2 Lloyd's Rep. 63).

10. See *The Falcon* [1977] 2 Lloyd's Rep. 243; *The World Star* [1987] 1 Lloyd's Rep. 452; *The Rubi Sea* [1992] 1 Lloyd's Rep. 634. As to the ambit of such costs see Chap. 15. The arrester's right is not dependent on the priority ranking of the arrester's claim (*The Immacolate Concezione* (1883) 9 P.D. 37). See generally *The Conet* [1965] 1 Lloyd's Rep. 195; *The Zigurds* [1932] P. 113; *The Leoborg (No. 2)* [1964] 1 Lloyd's Rep. 380, and Chap. 15.

      (iii) the courts retain an overall discretion exercised on equitable grounds[11] in assessing priorities[12] though precedent has established a strong *prima facie* framework. In exercising that discretion, courts will take into account the conduct of the claimant, such as the acceptance of a personal liability or inequitable conduct.[13]

      (iv) subject to (i)–(iii), priority between claims made through an action *in rem* depends first on classification into one of the "priority" categories and secondly on rules of (or perhaps simply decisions as to) priority within each category.

"In rem" priority categories

The priority categories of claims *in rem* are maritime liens, possessory liens, mortgages and statutory liens. The mortgage claim (itself a statutory lien for enforceability purposes) is thereby given special priority status.

    A central feature of enforceability *in rem* is that the very bringing of the action *in rem* confers preference on the claimant and confers a proprietary interest in the sense that the claim is enforceable against third parties. Further, the ability to arrest the thing attached and to request that it is to be judicially sold means *ex hypothesi* that the remedy affects every other claimant. Should the court order sale, all interests will be transferred to the proceeds.[14] The detailed pattern of *in rem* priority is discussed later in this chapter.

"In personam" priority principles in the "in rem" framework

On occasion *in personam* priority principles have been adopted as *in rem* priority principles. Further, as regards *in rem* priority the force of the legal and equitable dichotomy remains uncertain. The issues will be considered in the context of each claim.

3. PRIORITY BETWEEN "IN REM" AND "IN PERSONAM" CLAIMS

The relationship of the *in rem* and *in personam* priority pattern is not entirely clear. The lack of clarity is particularly marked, first, when the *in personam* principle of enforceability against third parties comes up against the *in rem* principle of clear title conferred by judicial sale and, secondly, in the scope of enforceability of the action *in rem*. The

---

11. Such as the availability of an alternative remedy (see *The Linda Flor* (1857) Swab. 309; *The Elin* (1882) 8 P.D. 39). "Marshalling", or arranging of funds to the benefit of all has been applied in Admiralty. See *The Constancia* (1846) 2 W. Rob. 460. As to marshalling, see *infra* fn. 58.

12. See *The Mons* [1932] P. 109; *The Leoborg (No. 2)* [1964] 1 Lloyd's Rep. 380. Agreement as to priority will remove a priority issue (see e.g. *The Zigurds* [1932] P. 113, where for some unreported reason a demurrage claim was given high priority). For Canadian authorities accepting equitable considerations as relevant to priority see e.g. *The Galaxias* [1989] IEC 386; *The Hull No. 1 and Hull No. 2* [1991] LMLN 310; *The Alexandros G Tsavlivis* [1993] LMLN 369.

13. E.g (re personal liability) a master's wages claim may be subordinated to a claim for goods supplied where the master takes on personal liability for the latter (*The Jenny Lind* (1872) L.R. 3 A. & E. 529; *The Eva* [1921] P. 454); e.g. (as to conduct) a mortgagee allowing necessaries to be supplied on credit of an insolvent shipowner (*The Pickaninny* [1960] 1 Lloyd's Rep. 544).

14. However, bail or a guarantee lodged in lieu of arrest is available only to the claimant—and provides no fund available *in rem*.

issues will be discussed after examining the *in personam* and *in rem* priorities in English law.

III. THE PRIORITY STRUCTURE OF ENGLISH LAW

Priority affects every proprietary interest but is usually discussed in the context of creditors or security interests. However, the priority of those interests is relevant not only as against like interests but against ownership and user proprietary interests such as demise charterparties. Priority will, therefore, be discussed in relation to (i) title or ownership; (ii) use for a specified period of time; and (iii) security interests.

1. TITLE (OR OWNERSHIP)

"In personam" priority—the basic rules

The structure is a straight adaptation of the general principles of *in personam* priority, i.e. first in time modified by exceptions based on the legal/equitable dichotomy and other rules.

(i) Equitable interests

(a) Creation of beneficial title through a trust

A beneficial title may be created through imposition of a trust in which the management of an asset or fund is separated from the benefit. So a ship may be registered in the name of one person but the beneficial owner may be another.[15] While the trust is not a common commercial maritime transaction it may be that an asset or fund the subject of such a transaction is held under a trust. A dealing by the trustee may create a priority question between beneficial owner and creditor.

RESERVATION OF TITLE

In English law it is possible to reserve a beneficial title in goods sold. However, any right in the buyer to terminate it on any use of the goods in manufacturing others will lead to a conclusion that the right retained is not beneficial title or even that no interest has been reserved.[16] Further where an interest has been reserved it may be construed not as title but as an equitable charge or other interest subject to the rules (including the need to register) applicable to such an interest.[17]

---

15. Equitable interests (and beneficial title) are specifically recognized by the Merchant Shipping Act 1995 (see *infra*—Registration) and the Supreme Court Act 1981. As to the relevance of beneficial ownership to the availability of an action *in rem* see Chap. 10.

16. Compare *Borden (UK) Ltd.* v. *Scottish Timber Products Ltd.* [1981] Ch. 25; *Re Bond Worth Ltd.* [1980] Ch. 228; *Romalpa Case* [1976] 1 All E.R. 552. It is a question of construction whether any proprietary interest is transferred to the proceeds of sale. *Hendy Lennox Ltd.* v. *Puttick Ltd.* [1984] 2 All E.R. 152. See generally McCormack, *Reservation of Title*, Sweet & Maxwell, 1990.

17. See e.g. *Re Bond Worth Ltd.* [1980] Ch. 228; *Clough Mill Ltd.* v. *Martin* [1984] 1 All E.R. 721.

(b) Contract of sale—transfer of equitable title

It is questionable whether, in a transaction for the sale of goods, an "equitable" (i.e. beneficial) title can pass as, it is argued, the Sale of Goods Act 1979, by providing a statutory framework of rules for the transfer of title, excludes the operation of equity.[18] If it be possible for a purchaser to have an equitable title prior to title under the Act, it cannot be created unless there is a clear entitlement to specific performance of the contract without any obstacle because of conditions or rights in the vendor.[19]

(ii) Other modifications of "first in time"

(a) Registration provisions

The provision of registration necessarily raises the question of its effect on title. Registration may have a variety of roles. So (a) it may create a new "registered interest" superior to the legal interest; (b) replace the legal interest with the registered interest; (c) create a new priority scheme; (d) provide a method of giving notice; (e) provide simply a process of recording interests created. Each registration framework must be analysed to assess its effect.

Generally, in English law, registration has little relevance to the transfer of title in goods or choses in action. However, the Bills of Sale Act 1878 and the Merchant Shipping Act 1995 (replacing provisions of the Merchant Shipping Acts 1894 and 1988) do provide registration frameworks.[20]

(i) THE BILLS OF SALE ACT 1878[21]

The only generally applicable requirements imposed by the Bills of Sale Act 1878 are on documents recording a sale on which title passes but possession does not. The aim of the legislation was to enforce publicity of transactions not reflected by the facts as they appeared to be. As many of the documents commonly used in maritime transactions are excluded from the scope of the Act, the Act is of limited importance in the maritime area.

---

18. See *Re Wait* [1927] 1 Ch. 606 per Atkin L.J.; *The Aliakmon* [1978] 2 Lloyd's Rep. 499 (H.L.) per Lord Brandon. As regards ships this reasoning may be affected by the procedure for the sale of a ship. See *infra*. The rules of the 1979 Act as to the passing of property are amended by the Sale of Goods (Amendment) Act 1995 in respect of goods brought as part of a bulk stock—because of the nature of the sale it is difficult in these instances to conceive of any equitable title prior to the passing of the legal title.

19. See fn 38.

20. The 1995 Act repealed and re-enacted (as from 1 January 1996) the Merchant Shipping (Registration etc.) Act 1993. Other specific registration requirements include the provision of the Companies Act 1985 providing for the registration of shares. An unregistered transfer for consideration will make the transferee beneficial owner and an unregistered gift of shares may do so (see e.g. *Re Rose* [1952] Ch. 499). A transferee of shares for consideration will be bound by a beneficial unregistered interest only if he receives notice of it prior to the time at which he is entitled to registration. As to the question generally and the method of protection open to the beneficial owner, see Gower, *Principles of Modern Company Law*, 5th edn, 1992, at pp. 400–402. Other registration provisions apply to patents, designs and trademarks.

21. The Bills of Sale Act 1882 provides a registration framework for documents creating security interests (see *infra*). As to both statutes, see generally *Crossley Vaines on Personal Property* (5th edn) (1973) Chapter 33; Bridge, *Personal Property Law* Blackstone Press, 1993, at pp. 149–151.

Documents falling outside the Act include (i) transfer of ships; (ii) transfer of goods in the ordinary course of business; (iii) bills of sale of goods in foreign territories or at sea; (iv) bills of lading, warehousekeepers' certificates and any other documents used in the ordinary course of business or documents of title thereto.[22]

A bill of sale within the Act must be registered within seven days of its execution, attested by a solicitor and specify the consideration given for it. If the bill does not comply with the requirements of registration, form and attestation, it is void against creditors and the trustee in bankruptcy in respect of such chattels the subject of the bill of sale as remain in the possession of the grantor at the time of execution of process or filing of the bankruptcy petition. In the case of bills of sale relating to the same chattel priority depends on the order of registration.[23]

(ii) MERCHANT SHIPPING ACT 1995

The Merchant Shipping Act 1894, s.3, provided for the registration of British ships exceeding a specified net register tonnage, the Merchant Shipping Act 1983 for the registration of small ships, and the Merchant Shipping Act 1988 for registration of fishing vessels. These provisions were consolidated in the Merchant Shipping (Registration etc.) Act 1993 and now form Part II of the Merchant Shipping Act 1995. Regulations made under the 1993 Act continue in force.[24] Under that Act there is created a register of British ships divided into four parts—Part I, all qualifying ships save those encompassed by Part II (fishing vessels) or Part IV (ships registered in a country other than the United Kingdom and demise chartered to British charterers) or registered in Part III (small ships).[25] The qualifications for registration, set out in the regulations in respect of each part of the register, are based on a connection between the owner or a majority of owners (individual or corporate) or (in the case of Part IV) the demise charterer and the United Kingdom or a member State through citizenship or incorporation or a European Economic Interest Grouping.[26]

The registration scheme is based essentially on entitlement to the benefits of recognition as a "British ship" and for the ship to be recognized as "belonging" to the United Kingdom. A ship may be detained until a declaration is made as to the country to which the ship belongs.

22. See Vaines op. cit., at p. 453.
23. Bills of Sale Act 1878, ss.8 and 10.
24. Merchant Shipping (Registration of Ships) Regulations 1993 (SI 1993/3138) remaining in force as subordinate legislation after repeal and re-enactment (see Interpretation Act 1968, s.17(2)(b)). As to statutory rights of detention see infra. The regulations do not apply to government ships exempt from the Merchant Shipping Acts but registrable under the Merchant Shipping Act 1906 (reg. 10)—the 1906 Act is applied to ships demise chartered to the government by Merchant Shipping Act 1988, s.47. Orders in Council have been made providing for registration under the 1906 Act. The authority for registration provisions of such ships is after 1 January 1996, the Merchant Shipping Act 1995, ss.308, 309.
25. "Small ships" must be less than 24 metres in length other than fishing or submersible vessels (regs 1, 88). The fishing vessels register is divided according to whether the provisions relating to transfer by bill of sale and registered mortgage apply (reg. 3). The difference appears to lie in the evidence required for registration. As to registered mortgages see infra.
26. See regs 7–13. As to interest grouping see SI 1989/638. For further connections required for and dispensation regarding fishing vessels see regs 14, 15. Save for specified exemptions a registrable fishing vessel or one wholly owned by qualified persons not registered under the 1993 Act or abroad and fishing for profit is liable to forfeiture (1995) Act, s.15(1). As to excluded fishing vessels see reg. 17.

The registration provisions. There are public law and private law provisions. In the public law context registration is a prerequisite for all ships to be British ships save small ships other than fishing vessels. These may qualify as British ships even if unregistered provided they are not registered elsewhere and they have the required British connection through their owners. The private law provisions set out rules for the holding and transfer of interests in ships. They do not apply to ships registered as demise chartered to British charterers, any matter within the ambit of the provisions being determined by reference to the law of the country of original registration.[27] Provisions relating to transfer by bill of sale and those relating to registered mortgages do not apply to small ships registered on the small ships part of the register or fishing vessels with "simple" rather than "full" registration.[28]

The private law provisions are focused not on "British ships" but on registered ships and "registered owners". Subject to any entry on the register the registered owner has power "absolutely to dispose" of the ship provided the disposal is made in accordance with the Act,[29] and there are provisions specifically referring to the transfer or mortgage of a registered ship.[30]

The general power of transfer has not, it seems, been construed as overriding non-registrable interests created by operation of law—in particular maritime liens or statutory liens in Admiralty. Further the power

"does not imply that interests arising under contract or other equitable interests cannot subsist in relation to a ship or a share in a ship and such interests may be enforced by or against owners and mortgagees of ships in respect of their interest in the ship or share in the same manner as in respect of any other personal property."[31]

Under the Act a transfer of "a registered ship" or share, save for registered small ships and fishing vessels with "simple" registration, is by bill of sale which may then be registered, and a mortgage by statutory form which may then be registered.[32] The provision regarding equitable interests applies to any ship.

The principles underlying registrations are unchanged from the repealed legislation. However, there may be "provisional registration" for ships intended to be registered on Part I or II which are outside the British Isles and for fishing vessels simple or full registration (i.e. as registration for other ships). It would seem that provisional registration is to have the same effect as registration.[33]

No ship may be registered in more than one Part.[34] The register is based on the concept of property in a ship being divided into 64 shares and subject to specified exceptions up to 64 persons may be registered as owners. There is no joint registered ownership of shares in a ship but up to five persons may be registered as joint owners of a ship.[35] No trust may be entered in the register but equitable interests may be created and enforced as

27. 1995 Act, s.17(7).
28. Regs. 3, 91.
29. 1995 Act, Sch. 1, para. 1(1).
30. 1995 Act, Sch. 1, paras 2–13.
31. *Ibid*, para. 1(2).
32. *Ibid*, Sch. 1, paras 1(2), 7(2).
33. See regs 3, 64–70 the provisional registration may be for three months or until the ship's arrival in the UK.
34. Reg. 5.
35. Reg. 2.

in any other personal property.[36] So a ship may be beneficially owned so that the registered owner or owners holds it on trust for the beneficial owner.[37] It is not clear whether in this context an agreement to sell a ship could result in the creation of a beneficial interest in the purchaser.[38]

A registered ship or share in it is transferred by a bill of sale[39] and the new owner is entitled to be registered on application and compliance with requirements for registration.[40] However, it is established that the title is transferred on the execution of the bill of sale.[41] The bill of sale, which apart from small ships and exempted fishing vessels is the mandatory method of transfer, is not a bill of sale within the Bills of Sale Acts 1878 and 1882. There are detailed provisions for the registration of mortgages (see *infra*).

Private law consequences from public law benefits. Although the 1995 Act (reflecting the 1993 Act) separates the public and private law provisions, as a consolidating Act there has been no attempt to clarify the private law role of registration. As the system is based on entitlement to the benefits of "British ships" the failure to register has no other consequence than the exclusion from those benefits and any of the statutory private law powers relating to British ships. So the owner of an unregistered ship does not have the statutory power of disposition, of granting registered mortgages and the priority given by registration. However, non-registration does not mean either the invalidity of title or the inability to create any interests in the ship.

That the private law provisions are seen as flowing from the qualification for public law benefits is underlined by the non-application of the private law provisions to certain categories of registered ships. As a whole they do not apply to ships registered on the basis of being demise chartered to British charterers,[42] and the provisions relating to transfer by bill of sale or the creation of registered mortgages do not apply to the "simple registration" of fishing vessels or small ships registered on the small ships part of the register.[43]

Priorities. It is clear that as between registered interests priority goes to the first registered interest[44] but despite the age of the registration provisions[45] there certainty ends. A prime problem is that there is no provision as to the effect of registration or its

---

36. *Ibid.*, para. 1(2), reg. 6; *Behnke* v. *Bede Shipping Co.* [1927] 1 K.B. 649. A purchaser seeking specific performance would have to show that damages were not an adequate remedy. See *The Stena Nautica (No. 2)* [1982] 2 Lloyd's Rep. 336.

37. See definition of "beneficial owner" in reg. 1.

38. See *The Permina Samudra XIV* [1978] 1 Lloyd's Rep. 315; *The Despina Pontikos* [1975] E.A.R. 38.

39. 1995 Act, Sch. 1, para. 2(1)—the provisions do not apply to small ships or exempted fishing vessels, see *infra*. The requirement of bill of sale applies only to registered ships. See *Union Bank of London* v. *Lenanton* (1878) 3 C.P.D. 243. The sale of a ship not within this provision is, therefore, outside this Act and the Bills of Sale Act 1878. See *Gapp* v. *Bond* (1887) 19 Q.B.D. 200.

40. *Ibid.*, para. 2(2)–(4)—including the retention of a British connection. There are provisions for registration on transmission of title other than by transfer and sale by a court or forfeiture if transmission would result in loss of a British connection (paras. 3–5).

41. See e.g. *Stapleton* v. *Hayman* (1864) 2 H. & C. 918; *The Two Ellens* (1871) L.R. 3 A. & E. 345.

42. 1995 Act, s.17(7).

43. SI 1993/3188, regs 3, 91.

44. The title of a bona fide purchaser who has registered cannot be attacked on the grounds of the fraud practised by his vendor. *The Horlock* (1877) 2 P.D. 243.

45. See Act for registering of British vessels 1825 (6 Geo. IV, c. 110) the provisions of which were repealed in 1833 (3 and 4 Wm. IV, c. 54) and led to the Merchant Shipping Act 1854 which in turn led to the Merchant Shipping Act 1894 and now through the Merchant Shipping (Registration etc.) Act 1993 to the Merchant Shipping Act 1995, Part II.

availability on the creation of legal or equitable unregistered interests or as to the rules of priority as between unregistered interests. Although there seems to have been little litigation the case of *The Shizelle*[46] in 1992 illustrates the problems that remain—and, it has to be said, could be resolved without too much difficulty. Unfortunately, while upholding the non-statutory interest framework in respect of unregistered interests in a non-registered but registrable ship the decision in *The Shizelle* may have further complicated the matter through a distinction between such a ship and a registered ship.

Registrability, registration, legal and equitable interests. It seems that following from the statutory power of disposal unregistered interests in a registered ship are seen as equitable and subject to any registered interest.[47] Such a conclusion is solely an inference from the provisions as a whole for the statutory power to dispose subject only to interests on the register does not necessarily mean that legal unregistered interests cannot exist—only that unregistered interests are overridden. Further, the provision as to equitable interests could be read as maintaining the rule that it is lack of notice rather than registration which limits their enforceability.

Given the inferred view of the result of registration it is irrelevant to the priority between an unregistered interest and a registered interest whether the unregistered interest is seen as legal or equitable. However, as between unregistered interests the classification may be critical.

In *The Shizelle* it was held by Mr Adrian Hamilton Q.C. that there was nothing in the provisions of the 1894 Act (identical in substance to the 1993 Act) which could "possibly be construed as altering the common law position" in relation to a mortgage of an unregistered but registrable small ship. So the mortgage would be legal or equitable depending on the law apart from the Act. Further, concluded the learned judge, under the Act the power to dispose of an interest according to the Act meant that in respect of a registered ship there could be no legal unregistered charge. But, with respect, this does not follow—for just as the legal title to the ship is transferred by bill of sale so the mortgage is created by completion of the statutory form. The issue remains as to whether construing the registration provisions as a whole the interest then created is legal or equitable.

Even if there can be no legal unregistered interest in a registered ship this leaves the question of whether unregistered ships are to be treated differently in respect of proprietary interests depending on the statutory role of registration in qualifying as a "British ship". The analysis in *The Shizelle* was focused specifically on a ship in regard to which there was no obligation to register to qualify as a British ship and a contrast drawn with the registered ship. There is little indication in the judgment of whether for the purpose of creating proprietary interests a distinction was seen to exist between unregistered ships according to whether registration is a prerequisite to qualify as a British ship. It may be said that the very concentration on the one type of unregistered ship is some hint that the distinction was thought relevant. However, it is difficult to see any relevance of an element going to nationality to the creation of proprietary interests, particularly as in respect of neither category is registration obligatory in order to create such interests. The title is transferred by bill of sale.

---

46. [1992] 2 Lloyd's Rep. 445.
47. See fn 95.

Statutory powers of owners of small ships and fishing vessels. It is arguable that the registration of small ships as such and the simple registration of fishing vessels have no effect on the creation of proprietary interests in such ships. However, in contrast to demise chartered ships the private law provisions are not excluded as a whole but solely those provisions relating to transfer by bill of sale and registered mortgages. It is arguable therefore that the power of a registered owner "absolutely to dispose" of the ship together with the express maintaining of equitable interests apply. If that is so, if the power is to mean anything it must carry priority consequences—i.e. the power to override an unregistered title. It must be borne in mind however that while the title of such ships may be registered there is no provision for registered mortgages. Further the exclusion of the bill of sale provisions creates yet more uncertainty as to the role of registration in the transfer of title.

The need for clarification. Registration seems clearly in the public interest both from a private and public law standpoint. There is no reason why this should not be reflected in its role, matching policy with simplicity and creating a comprehensive framework of registrable, registered and unregistered interests. Until that kind of coherence and simplicity is enacted there is no basis for distinguishing the interests available in any unregistered ship. It is to be hoped that consolidating the past is not seen as a basis for freezing the future.

(b) Statutory provisions relating to priority of title. Sale of Goods Act 1979 and Factors Act 1889

Both ship and cargo are "goods" within the Sale of Goods Act 1979 and the Factors Act 1889. Interests are, therefore, subject to the priority principles enshrined in those statutes modifying the basic rule that first in time prevails. These provisions are based either on the conduct of the owner or on the appearance of title given to a potential purchaser. So, an owner by his conduct in holding out another as having authority to sell, may be precluded from denying the transfer of the title[48]; a mercantile agent in possession of goods with the consent of the owner has power to transfer the owner's title[49]; a seller or buyer in possession after sale may, under certain circumstances, transfer the title or an interest not at that time in him; and a seller with a voidable title may transfer a good title.[50]

"In rem" priority

An ownership claim (whether as registered, legal or beneficial owner) can be enforced through an action *in rem*. The basis of the claim is a title defined in accordance with the *in personam* priority rules (i.e. registered, legal or equitable). However, the title thus established will be subject in an *in rem* claim to the *in rem* priority framework. For this

---

48. See e.g. Sale of Goods Act 1979, s.21, but see *Moorgate Mercantile Co. Ltd.* v. *Twitchings* [1977] A.C. 870.
49. Factors Act 1889, s.2.
50. Sale of Goods Act 1979, ss.23–25; see also the Factors Act 1889, ss.8 and 9.

purpose an ownership claim seems to be no higher than a statutory lien. Whether it will rank equally with other such liens on an *in rem* priority basis is unclear.

2. USE FOR A SPECIFIED PERIOD OF TIME

(i) Charterparty

"In personam" priority

Subject to the effect of registration of ships and enforceability against prior mortgages, first in time is the governing principle. Insofar as a charterparty creates a proprietary interest (as, it is submitted, does a demise charterparty) it is enforceable against third parties who interfere with it and all subsequent charterparties, mortgagees and purchasers.[51] Further, any charterparty may be enforced by an injunction against a subsequent and inconsistent charterparty.[52]

A charterparty is enforceable against a mortgage created prior to it where the mortgagor is in possession unless the mortgagee can establish that the granting of it initially affected his security. A mortgagee is taken to authorize the operation of the mortgaged ship—an authorization which without qualification would include the granting of charterparties.[53]

"In rem" priority

Priority *in rem* of a charterer's claim in relation to the ship or fund will depend primarily on the classification of the claim as a maritime or statutory lien and on the priority rules applicable thereto. However, it would seem that a mortgage which, according to the *in personam* rules, would be subject to a charterparty should not be given priority over a charterparty simply through automatic operation of the *in rem* framework. In such a case the link between the two interests should be sufficient to qualify the normal *in rem* priority rules.[54]

The effect of registration

There are no provisions for registration of charterparties save that ships demise chartered to British charterers may be registered until the end of the charter. Where a ship is so registered the private law matters for which the 1995 Act provides are to be determined by reference to the law of the country of original registration.[55]

Charterparties of registered ships other than those registered because of the charterparty are unregistered interests. In accordance with the principles discussed in the context of ownership insofar as they are proprietary interests they will therefore be equitable rather than legal. A charterparty of an unregistered ship will be enforceable according to the principles discussed in the context of ownership.

51. *Port Line Ltd.* v. *Ben Line Steamers Ltd.* [1958] 2 Q.B. 146. Cf. *The Celtic King* [1894] P. 175.
52. See e.g. *The Oakworth* [1975] 1 Lloyd's Rep. 586. See also Chap. 14.
53. See e.g. *The Fanchon* (1880) 5 P.D. 173. Compare *Law Guarantee and Trust Soc.* v. *Russian Bank for Foreign Trade* [1905] 1 K.B. 815.
54. See *The Heather Bell* [1901] P. 143; *The Blanche* (1887) 6 Asp. M.L.C. 272.
55. S.17(7); the 1993 Act, s. 7(7).

(ii) Lease or bailment of goods

"In personam" priority

First in time prevails subject to conduct and any statutory modification. A "lessee" or bailee has the right to sue third parties who interfere with the interest[56] and presumably can enforce the interest against subsequent purchasers.

"In rem" priority

Any claim *in rem* must be assessed according to the statutory provisions of the Supreme Court Act 1981. Priority in relation to the assets depends on the priority category of the claim (i.e. maritime or statutory lien) and not on the nature of the claim itself.

The effect of registration

Bailment as such is affected by registration only insofar as the transaction may fall within the provisions of the Bills of Sale Acts or the Companies Acts (see *infra*).

3. SECURITY INTERESTS

The number and characteristics of security interests are discussed in Chapter 17 in examining the nature and development of liens. Security interests in English law are mortgage, charge, pledge and lien. As indicated there is considerable uncertainty over definitions and distinction between the interests, due in no small part to the overuse of the labels of "charge" and "lien".

There may be a legal or equitable mortgage or a legal or equitable lien. The charge is essentially an equitable concept and the pledge a legal concept. Of the "active" security interests (i.e. those apart from the possessory lien) only the pledge requires transfer of possession. Indeed, all the other interests assume that normally possession will be retained by the grantor of the interest. Conversely, it is only in regard to the mortgage that transfer of ownership is contemplated, but a mortgage *may* be entered into without such transfer. In particular, save as may be necessary for making the ship available as a security, a statutory ship mortgage does not involve transfer of ownership.[57]

At the extremes the mortgage and the pledge are fairly well recognizable. Both are transactions expressly entered into and both have well defined characteristics. However, as said in Chapter 17 the charge and the lien are ill defined. The labels describe consequences of transactions rather than prerequisites of creation. Unless specified by statute no formality is required but simply a definitive indication that an interest in an asset is granted as security for a benefit. On occasion "charge" and "lien" are used to describe any security interest however informally created, apart from the mortgage and pledge. On other occasions they describe a particular interest around which rules have grown (as, for example, the floating charge or the maritime lien).

56. *The Winkfield* [1902] P. 42 but cannot recover damages from a defendant if the bailor has already done so, the bailor having to account to the bailee for such damages as reflected the bailee's interest (*O'Sullivan* v. *Williams* [1992] 3 All E.R. 385). See generally Bridge, *op. cit.* at pp. 50–52.

57. See the 1995 Act, Sch. 1, para. 10. Possession is the root of the possessory lien.

A. General principles

"In personam" priority

Where a particular interest (e.g. a mortgage) has developed, *in personam* priority rules have formed around it. Otherwise the priority rules of all security interests are based on the general framework of first in time qualified by conduct, the dichotomy between legal and equitable interests and statutory modifications (particularly concerning registration).[58] A "floating charge" (if not made conditional) created by a company is created on the contract[59] but has priority only when it crystallizes, i.e. becomes a fixed charge on a particular aspect. Only on that event is the company prevented from dealing with the assets (see *infra*).

Registration provisions

Security interests in general are subject to two registration frameworks—those provided by (i) the Bills of Sale Acts 1878; and (ii) the Companies Act 1985, Part XII. Ship mortgages are also subject to the registration provisions of the Merchant Shipping Act 1995, which will be discussed in the context of mortgages.

THE BILLS OF SALE ACTS 1878 AND 1882

The Bills of Sale Act 1878 is relevant to the transfer of title of a chattel, and the Bills of Sale Act 1882, building on the earlier Act, to the creation of a security interest in a chattel. Both Acts have as their primary purpose to publicize interests created when the grantor retains possession, his interest thereby appearing to be less encumbered than it is.

As is said in the discussion of the Act of 1878 the context of ownership, the Acts have limited application in the maritime area. Bills of sale in the sense of documents granting a security interest not within the Acts, include[60] (i) transfers or assignments of ships; (ii) charges registrable under the Companies Act; (iii) a pledge; (iv) a common law lien; (v) transfers of goods in the ordinary course of business of any trade or calling; (vi) bills of sale of goods in foreign parts or at sea; (vii) bills of lading, warehousekeepers' certificates and any other document used in the ordinary course of business as proof of the possession of goods; (viii) (in certain circumstances) instruments creating security in imported goods.[61] As the Acts are focused on documents, a security interest created orally does not fall within them.

Where it applies, the Act requires registration of the document creating the interest. If not registered the bill (and hence the interest) is void as between the parties and as against third parties in respect of the chattels comprised in it. If not made in the form prescribed by the Act it is absolutely void.[62] Further, a bill is void as against third parties if the

---

58. Through "marshalling" a creditor may be directed to enforce his right against one of two funds available if by so doing another creditor may be paid. Priorities are not affected. See generally Snell, *Principles of Equity* (1990) pp. 421–422.

59. See *The Annangel Glory* [1988] 1 Lloyd's Rep. 45 and Chap. 22.

60. Bills of Sale Act 1878, s.4; 1890, s.1.

61. This does not cover a document creating a general charge on all future goods (*Slavenburg Case* [1980] 1 All E.R. 955—see *infra*).

62. Act of 1882, ss.8 and 9.

chattels are not accurately described and in respect of any chattels of which the grantor was not the owner at the time of execution.[63]

THE COMPANIES ACT 1985

The provisions of the Companies Act 1948 for registration of charges created by a company are reflected in the Part XII of the Companies Act 1985. These are to be repealed and replaced by provisions of the Companies Act 1989, but these are not yet in force and will apply only from the date of coming into force. It is relevant therefore to summarize the framework of the 1985 Act. There is little difference in substance between the 1948 and 1985 Act, and earlier authorities continue to be relevant.

A charge (whether fixed or floating) of any category specified in the Act created by an English company in any of its assets will be void as against the liquidator and creditors[64] unless particulars are delivered to or received by the registrar within 21 days of creation of the charge.[65] The invalidity does not affect the obligation to repay the money secured. When a charge becomes void the money becomes repayable.[66] Charges (including mortgages) requiring registration include:

  (a) a charge for the purpose of securing debentures;
  (b) a charge on uncalled share capital;
  (c) a charge created or evidenced by a document which, if made by an individual, would require registration as a bill of sale;
  (d) a charge on land;
  (e) a charge on book debts;
  (f) a floating charge on the undertaking or property of the company;
  (g) a charge on calls made but not paid;
  (h) a charge on a ship or aircraft or any share in a ship;
  (j) a charge on goodwill, patents, trade mark and copyright and licences thereunder and trademarks.

In 1985 it was held in *The Ugland Trailer*[67] that a shipowner's lien on subfreights was a "book debt" requiring to be registered as such. In 1988 in *The Annangel Glory*[68] it was held that such a lien was a floating charge and was registrable under that head, and, further, there was no prerequisite for such a charge that the property (i.e. the debt) must exist. The charge was created by the agreement to be implemented when the debt arose—it was a present charge on future property. It therefore had to be registered within 21 days of the contract.

---

63. Act of 1882, ss.4 and 5.
64. Section 395(1).
65. Such requirement is in addition to the registration provisions of the Merchant Shipping Act 1995 (as to which, see *infra*). Where a company acquires an asset subject to a charge it is under an obligation to register but there is no consequence of invalidity if it fails to do so (s.97). The charge is valid on particulars being delivered to the Registrar (*Slavenburg Case* [1980] 1 All E.R. 955). The obligations appear to extend to English and foreign assets of English companies but such scope may be open to a choice of law argument. As to overseas companies, see *infra*.
66. Section 395(2).
67. [1985] 2 Lloyd's Rep. 372.
68. [1988] 1 Lloyd's Rep. 45. See further Chap. 22.

The obligation to register is limited to charges "created by" a company. While, therefore, any "charge" within the categories specified[69] is within the Act charges imposed by law are not. So a vendor's lien for unpaid purchase money,[70] a possessory lien[71] or (it has been held) a charging order obtained by a judgment creditor[72] are not registrable. It would seem to follow that neither a maritime lien nor a statutory lien in Admiralty is registrable but an equitable lien or even a possessory lien created by contract may well be. By creating a charge a company may be held to abandon a charge imposed by law.

A "charge" must be distinguished from reservation of title—where title is reserved there is no interest in the potential purchaser out of which a charge may be created. It will however be a matter of construction and circumstances as to whether title has not passed or has passed with the purchaser creating a charge in the vendor's favour.[73]

The provisions apply to companies registered in England and (by s.409) extend to companies incorporated outside Great Britain which have established a place of business in England and have assets in England on which charges are created. In *NV Slavenburg's Bank* v. *Intercontinental National Resources Ltd.*[74] Lloyd J. held that the provision applied to overseas companies whether or not registered in England and that a liquidator appointed in a foreign liquidation similar to an English winding up could rely on it. As the provision applies to floating charges it was not restricted to a charge on assets existing when it was made. It was irrelevant that the company had ceased to have an English place of business prior to the liquidation.

Considerable concern was voiced over the application to overseas companies not registered in England for it may be difficult to discover if a company has or had a place of business in England or when it has assets here. So the obligation to lodge particulars will be imposed if a ship owned by a company is within English territorial waters when a floating charge is created or, indeed, when a ship comes into those waters after the charge is created.

THE COMPANIES ACT 1989

English and overseas companies.[75] The whole of Part XII of the Companies Act 1985 will be replaced by a more comprehensive structure when the appropriate provisions of the 1989 Act (ss.92–107) are brought into force providing replacement sections in the 1985 Act. Subject to limitations concerning registration of subsequent charges, agreement and third party rights, on insolvency proceedings starting subsequent to the charge a charge requiring registration[76] will be void against (i) an administrator or liquidator of the company and (ii) any person who for value acquires an interest in the property subsequent

---

69. A pledge is not within the provision (*Wrightson* v. *Macarthur and Hutchinsons Ltd.* [1921] 2 K.B. 807).

70. See e.g. *Capital Finance Co. Ltd.* v. *Stokes* [1969] Ch. 261; *London and Chesham* v. *Lapaglene* [1971] Ch. 499.

71. *Brunton* v. *Electrical Engineering Corporation* [1892] 1 Ch. 434.

72. *Re Overseas Aviation Engineering (GB) Ltd.* [1963] Ch. 24.

73. *Clough Mill Ltd.* v. *Martin* [1984] 3 All E.R. 982 and see *supra*.

74. [1980] 1 All E.R. 955.

75. There is a separate register for companies registered in Scotland. As to unregistered companies see Companies Act 1989, s.106. As to overseas companies see *infra*.

76. A charge created by a company or on property acquired by a company (s.398(1)). The date for assessment of registrability is the date of creation or acquisition (s.396(3))—as to that date see s.414.

to the charge unless particulars of the charge are delivered for registration within 21 days after the date of creation of the charge.[77] Where a charge becomes void the whole of the sum secured is payable.[78] A "charge" is widely defined as "any form of security interest (fixed or floating) over property other than an interest arising by operation of law".[79] Property includes future property and it is immaterial where it is situated.[80]

The provisions apply to companies registered in Great Britain and are applied to unregistered companies.[81] There are new provisions relating to companies registered overseas,[82] these being applicable only to a company which has delivered documents of registration and has not subsequently given notice that it has ceased to have an established place of business in Great Britain.[83] Registrable charges are those registrable in respect of companies registered in Great Britain and apply only to property situated in Great Britain.[84] The obligation to register and consequences of not so doing are of the same nature as for companies registered in Great Britain.

Charges requiring registration[85] are:

(a) a charge on land other than a charge for rent;
(b) "a charge on goods or interest in goods other than a charge under which the chargee is entitled to possession either of the goods or of a document of title to them"[86];
(c) a charge on intangible movable property of any of goodwill, intellectual property, book debts and uncalled share capital of the company or calls not made;
(d) a charge for securing an issue of debentures;
(e) a floating charge on the whole or part of the company's property.

This list is qualified by exclusion of specified charges on assets which would or arguably would fall within one or more of the categories.[87] A shipowner's lien for subfreight is "not to be treated" as a charge on "book debts" or as a "floating charge."[88]

The void consequence of an unregistered charge is now qualified. To render a charge void against a subsequent charge at least some of the particulars of the later charge

---

77. Section 399(1). The company has a duty to deliver the particulars but they may be delivered by a person other than the company (s.398). The charge is void to the extent that particulars delivered do not disclose rights which should be disclosed (s.402) and against an administrator, liquidator or purchaser for value if a memorandum is given wrongly recording the ending of a charge (s.403). There are qualifying provisions in respect of late delivery, delivery of further particulars (ss.400, 401).

78. Section 407(1)—even if the sum secured is also subject to other security (*ibid*).

79. Section 395(2). Regulations may make further provision (s.413).

80. Sections 395(2)(3), 703A.

81. See ss.92, 106 of the 1989 Act.

82. Section 105 of the 1989 Act, Sch. 15 (inserting provisions into Part XXIII of the Companies Act 1985).

83. Thereby reversing *Slavenburg's* case in the holding that the provision applied to any overseas company having established a place of business in this country.

84. A ship is situated in Great Britain only if registered the (s.703L). Future property is situated there unless it cannot after coming into existence or being acquired be situated there (s.703L(2)).

85. Section 396(1).

86. "Goods" means tangible movable property and a charge is not excluded because the chargee may take possession on some event or default (s.396(2)(b)(c)).

87. Section 396(2).

88. Section 396(2)(9)—thereby reversing the effect of *The Ugland Trailer* (fn 67) and *The Annangel Glory* (fn 68).

inconsistent with the earlier charge must be delivered for registration.[89] The acquisition of a later interest may be made subject to the unregistered charge and the charge is not affected when insolvency proceedings or acquisition of interest takes place after the company has disposed of the whole of its interest in the property.[90] The chargee may dispose of property freed from any interest arising from a charge becoming void. However in that case, the proceeds are held by the chargee on trust to discharge prior incumbrances, costs, the sum secured by the charge and incumbrances ranking *pari passu* with the charge, and subsequent incumbrances in that order—with payment of the residue to a person authorized to receive proceeds of sale of the property.[91]

Notice of crystallization of floating charge. Regulations made under the Act may require notice to be given of the occurrence of any event affecting the security under a floating charge and the taking of such action in exercise of powers conferred by a fixed or floating charge.[92] It may be provided that failure to give such notice leads to liability to a fine and that any crystallization shall be ineffective until the notice is delivered.

"In rem" priority

The priority depends, first, on the classification of the claim—as to whether it is a maritime lien, a possessory lien, a mortgage or a statutory lien other than a mortgage; and, secondly, on the principles (such as overall judicial discretion modifying the *in rem* priority category ladder). Priority will be discussed in relation to each claim.

B. Priority and each security interest

The interests are mortgage, charge, pledge and lien.

1. Mortgage

(i) Mortgage of ships

(A) REGISTRABILITY OF MORTGAGE

A mortgage of a registered ship may be registered under Part II of the Merchant Shipping Act 1995 and the Merchant Shipping (Registration of Ships) Regulations 1993. Any mortgage of a ship by a company also requires registration as a charge under the Companies Act 1985, Part XII for the mortgage to be enforceable against a liquidator or other creditors (see *supra*). The Bills of Sale Acts 1878 and 1882 do not apply to ship mortgages.

---

89. Section 404.
90. Section 405.
91. Section 406. Prior incumbrances include any to the extent that the charge is void against them (s.406(3)).
92. Section 410. Such a provision will require notification of provision for automatic crystallization (see Chap. 22). Particulars may also be required to be delivered of any "negative pledge"—a term in a floating charge prohibiting the company from creating a security interest to take priority to the charge (s.415(2)(a)).

A registered ship. Save for a small ship registered as such and a fishing vessel registered by simple registration[93] a British ship which is registered may be mortgaged by registered mortgage under the Merchant Shipping Act 1995. Any registered ship may be mortgaged by unregistered mortgage.[94] Although it remains arguable that a legal mortgage may be created otherwise than by registration, it seems that an unregistered mortgage of a registered ship will be treated as an equitable mortgage.[95]

An unregistered ship. It was held in *The Shizelle*[96] that a mortgage of a small ship which was a British ship although unregistered would be legal or equitable depending on the law apart from the statutory provisions.[97] The argument that the Merchant Shipping Acts constituted a code for the creation of mortgages of British ships was rejected and in that context it was held that the statutory power to create equitable interests could not be read to mean that a mortgage of an unregistered ship which would otherwise be legal was converted into an equitable interest. As discussed earlier there is the suggestion in the judgment of a distinction between ships which could only qualify as British ships through registration and ships which may be British ships although not registered.

However the only ground for distinguishing between unregistered ships in relation to the mortgage provisions is that the Act constitutes a code of available private law interests for unregistered ships which to be "British" must be registered, but not for ships which are British though unregistered. Such a conclusion can only be an implication from the provision that a registered ship may be mortgaged in statutory form and the maintaining of equitable interests. As has been argued in the context of ownership any emphasis on British ships in respect of the private law provisions is to ignore the focus of the Acts on entitlement to registration and thereby the obtaining of benefits rather than any obligation to register. Registration not being mandatory, there is nothing in the Acts to justify drawing a different conclusion as regards the mortgage framework as between unregistered British ships. In other words if *The Shizelle* is correct, it is correct in respect of all unregistered ships.

Just as the maintaining of equitable interests in registered ships does not mean that equivalent interests in unregistered ships are equitable, so the power to create a registered mortgage of a registered ship does not mean that, until registered, the interest is equitable. Indeed the existence of the statutory power does not necessarily mean that an unregistered mortgage of a registered ship is equitable any more than it overrides the maritime lien. It is all a matter of assessing the effect of registrability of the ship or mortgage and the statutory provisions as a whole on interests which could otherwise be created. While as has been said it appears that the statutory mortgage will be construed as in effect in substitution for the legal mortgage it does not follow that the mortgage of an unregistered ship is equitable. So to construe it means the imposition prior to registration of a

---

93. See Merchant Shipping (Registration of Ships) Regulations 1993, reg. 3 (fishing vessels), 91 (small ships).

94. 1995 Act, s.16(1), Sch. 1, paras 1, 7.

95. See *Black* v. *Williams* [1895] 1 Ch. 408; *Burgis* v. *Constantine* [1908] 2 K.B. 484. In *The Shizelle* it was said that this followed from the statutory power of disposition subject only to registered interests—but this is not necessarily so as between unregistered interests (see *supra*). In *The Halcyon Isle* [1981] A.C. 221 Lord Diplock stated somewhat cryptically that all mortgages other than British registered took effect according to their dates of creation.

96. [1992] 2 Lloyd's Rep. 445.

97. Which, it may be argued, is contrary in principle to Lord Diplock's view in *The Halcyon Isle* that as between each other non-registered mortgages take effect according to their date of creation.

framework following from registration of a ship even though such registration is not mandatory for the creation of title in and hence mortgage of the ship.

A power of an owner of a ship which would qualify as a British ship though unregistered to create legal interests may have a bearing on whether to construe the Acts as a code for the interests of private law. Such a power plays down the private law importance of registration and may fail to encourage exercising the right to become a "British ship". Further, if the Acts had no effect on unregistered ships there would seem little point in the provision relating to equitable interests encompassing all ships. Despite this to hold that there can be no legal interest in an unregistered ship would require the provision that a mortgage may be created in a registered ship in statutory form to be read with the provision relating to equitable interests as prohibiting any but equitable mortgages in unregistered ships. Given that the owner of an unregistered ship may dispose of it, such a creative (or destructive) construction is difficult to maintain. The decision in *The Shizelle* seems therefore correct but applies generally to unregistered ships.

It follows that there being no obligation to register a ship qualifying as a British ship, mortgages in an unregistered ship are unaffected by the Merchant Shipping Acts. Priorities therefore depend on general principles—subject to conduct, whether the mortgage is legal or equitable, notice of a prior equitable mortgage by a subsequent legal mortgagee and as between equitable mortgagees the order of creation. The recognition of legal interests in unregistered ships but not registered ships means a change in the enforceability of rights as between holders of unregistered interests having nothing to do with the cause of the change (the registration).

There seems no reason why, if necessary subject to liens, registration should not be made the focal point of private law provisions of transfer and mortgage. Just as the registered charges provisions of the Companies Act 1989 are applied to unregistered companies there is nothing to prevent a system of registered interests in a ship which has not been registered as a British ship. At the least the public and private aspects of registration should be related to each other and the role of registration in each context clarified. It is regrettable that quite unnecessarily complexities are being repeated through more and more consolidations.

(B) EFFECT ON "IN PERSONAM" PRIORITY

In registered ships. By the 1995 Act the priority as between registered mortgages is to be determined by the order of registration—"and not by reference to any other matter".[98] However, where the mortgages are by a company the registration requirements of the Companies Act 1985 will also apply (as to which see *supra*).

A registered mortgage will take priority over an unregistered mortgage whether the latter is entered into before or after the registered mortgage, notice being irrelevant.[99] A registered mortgage will be subject to any legal interest other than a mortgage created in the ship prior to the registration of the mortgage[100] subject to the creation of charter-

---

98. 1995 Act, Sch. 1, para. 8. Notice is therefore irrelevant. An intending mortgage may obtain priority by notification of a priority notice (Sch. 2, para. 8(2); Merchant Shipping (Registration of Ships) Regulations 1993, reg. 59).

99. See *Black* v. *Williams* [1895] 1 Ch. 408. But see *Lombard North Central Ltd.* v. *Lord Advocate* 1983 S.L.T. 361 (lack of good faith leading to loss of priority).

100. Subject to any priority of any agreement to create the registered mortgage over any legal interest created after it.

parties and, the purchaser from a harbour authority exercising its statutory right to sell for unpaid dues.[101] It has been said that where the harbour authority may sell ships of any nationality neither the authority nor the purchaser can be expected to investigate the register and, more, if a mortgage were to take priority an owner could mortgage it and deprive the harbour authority of its remedy. The priority is between rights of different statutory sources and to the extent that the purchaser does not take subject to a registered mortgage, the rights of the harbour authorities qualify the provisions of the 1995 Act conferring the power of the registered owner to dispose of a ship.[102] The registered mortgage will take priority over any equitable interest created prior to or after it.

Priority between unregistered mortgages and between such a mortgage and any other interest will follow the priority rules applicable to equitable interests.[103] The basic rule is, therefore, first in time qualified by (i) to the extent that any unregistered interest may be a legal interest (see *supra*) the limitation applicable to equitable interests of being subject to a later legal interest acquired without notice of the equitable interest; and (ii) the postponement of priority because of conduct or other equitable reason.[104]

In unregistered ships. The only private law provision of the Merchant Shipping Acts relating to interests in unregistered ships is the recognition that equitable interests may still be created. If it be right that there is nothing in the Merchant Shipping Acts to prevent or control the creation of legal interests, the creation and priority of mortgages are subject to general common law and equitable rules.

(C) FOREIGN MORTGAGES

Under English conflicts rules the validity of a foreign mortgage will be referred to the law of the state of registration of the ship. Its priority will be referred to the law of the forum. As a result, foreign mortgages should be slotted into the priority ladder on the same basis as English mortgages.[105]

Except where there is direct reference to the law of another country the statutory provisions relating to registered mortgages are concerned only with mortgages registered in the United Kingdom. In assessing priority between the United Kingdom and a foreign registered mortgage, therefore, the statute has no direct application. There is little doubt however that the statutory rules would (and should) be applied by analogy.

In 1992 in *The Betty Ott*[106] the New Zealand Court of Appeal reached the startling and narrow conclusion on provisions similar to those of English law that foreign registration was irrelevant to priority under New Zealand law. As apart from the registration the interest was an equitable charge it was subject to an earlier unregistered charge. The conclusion followed from a simple and blunt application of the law of the forum but, as

---

101. *The Blitz* [1992] 2 Lloyd's Rep. 441. It is not clear whether the purchaser registered the title—but this would appear irrelevant to the principle of giving priority to the statutory sale powers over those of the registered owner.
102. 1995 Act, Sch. 1, para. 1(1).
103. i.e. the general principles of equitable interests are maintained (1995 Act, Sch. 1, para. 1(2).
104. See e.g. *Burgis* v. *Constantine* [1908] 2 K.B. 484.
105. See further Chap. 26.
106. [1992] 1 NZLR 655.

pointed out in a strong critique of the decision,[107] its consequences for ship financing are extreme. Such an approach means either that registration operates to preserve and govern priority only in respect of the state of registration so, if permitted, a mortgagee must register wherever possible. *The Betty Ott* in effect applied provisions of forum law clearly geared to ships connected with the forum so as to have a contrary effect on ships not so connected. The approach looks at the language of a statute without considering its scope, its purpose or its maritime context. Its effect in New Zealand has been corrected by legislation[108] and its principle should not be followed.

The Merchant Shipping Act 1995 provides that in respect of ships registered to British charterers "any matter or question" corresponding to the private law provisions of the Act is to be determined by reference to the law of the country of original registration. The provision underlines the effect of the statutory provisions as concerned with interests under United Kingdom laws.[109] The reference to the equivalent governing law of the state of "substantive" registration has no effect on the application of the conflicts rules as to priority between interests under different laws simply because the matters referred are not relevant to that issue (see *supra*).

(D) "IN REM" PRIORITY

In *in rem* terms a mortgage of a ship is a statutory lien but is given a special priority status. The priority will be discussed in the context of liens.

(ii) Mortgage of cargo[110]

"IN PERSONAM" PRIORITY

Mortgage of cargo would be a chattel mortgage, its priority depending on whether it was legal or equitable.[111] Such a transaction does not appear in the Supreme Court Act 1981 as being within Admiralty jurisdiction.[112] One method of creation of a security interest over cargo is the deposit of a bill of lading. Whether such a transaction amounts to a mortgage, lien or pledge is a matter of construction.[113]

"IN REM" PRIORITY

As the transaction is not within Admiralty jurisdiction it cannot be enforced by an action *in rem*.

107. Myburgh [1992] LMCLQ 155.
108. It is resolved by statutory application of the law of registration (Ship Registration Act 1992, s.70). For comment on the wider implications see Myburgh [1993] LMCLQ 444.
109. Section 17(7) re-enacting the Merchant Shipping (Registration etc.) Act 1993, s.7(7).
110. Respondentia—(a security interest in cargo only) is equivalent to bottomry where a ship is the subject of security. As with bottomry it is subject to its own rules. See Chap. 2.
111. This assumes the validity of the mortgage which *may* require registration under the Bills of Sale Act 1882. See *supra*.
112. But naturally can be pursued in the appropriate Division of the High Court subject to jurisdictional prerequisites.
113. See *Sewell* v. *Burdick* (1884) 10 App. Cas. 74. As to the separation of the rights and liabilities of bills of lading holders from the passing of property see the Carriage of Goods By Sea Act 1992.

(iii) Mortgage of freight or charterparty hire or insurance moneys

"IN PERSONAM" PRIORITY

Creation. The right to receive freight, charterparty hire or insurance moneys is a chose in action capable of legal or equitable mortgage by assignment.[114] A legal mortgage must comply with statutory requirements of writing under the hand of the assignor. It requires assignment of the whole of the freight due and notice to the person from whom the money is due.[115] There can be only one legal mortgage as the entire title to the freight is assigned.

An equitable mortgage requires no form but does require consideration. It may take the form of a charge or a contract to create a legal mortgage. Notice to the debtor is not a prerequisite[116] but is relevant to priority.

Enforceability. A legal mortgage is enforceable against all subsequent interests. An equitable mortgage may be defeated by a legal mortgage or other legal interest, the holder of which acquires the legal interest without notice of the equitable mortgage. Priority between equitable mortgagees of the same freight is according to the date of notice given to the person who is to pay it.[117] Failing such notice, it is according to the date of the assignment. Whether the assignment is legal or equitable the debtor may plead against the assignee all the defences that were available to him as against the assignor at the date of notice of the assignment to him.

ADMIRALTY JURISDICTION

It is arguable that "mortgage" of freight (including charterparty hire) through an equitable assignment of the right to receive it is not only within Admiralty jurisdiction but may be enforced by an action *in personam* or an action *in rem*.[118] Where the issue is between assignee and debtor it is simply a claim for freight and it could hardly be argued that in adjudicating on that the court could not if necessary pronounce on the validity of the assignment. As no insurance claim falls within Admiralty jurisdiction it is difficult to see how a mortgage of insurance moneys could do so.

"IN REM" PRIORITY

Insofar as a "mortgage" of freight or charterparty hire may be enforced *in rem* it is a statutory lien and will be considered in the context of liens.

---

114. In modern terminology freight may not include time charterparty hire (see Chap. 22). Assignment for consideration of a "future" chose in action (i.e. a right to receive moneys when due) may create an interest in the chose when the money is due or a "charge" on the entering into the contract to be implemented when the money is due (see *The Annangel Glory* [1988] 1 Lloyd's Rep. 45). A bare cause of action as distinct from a "property interest" cannot be assigned. As to the distinction, see *Trendtex Trading Corpn* v. *Crédit Suisse* [1982] A.C. 679; *Brownton Ltd.* v. *Edward Moore Inbucon Ltd.* [1985] 3 All E.R. 499 (C.A.).

115. Law of Property Act 1925, s.136(1).

116. See e.g. *Gardner* v. *Lachlan* (1838) 4 Myl. & Cr. 129.

117. *The Zigurds* [1934] A.C. 209; *The Annangel Glory* [1988] 1 Lloyd's Rep. 45 (priority of "equitable liens"). This applies the central feature of a priority rule applicable to the mortgage of equitable interests under trusts known as the rule in *Dearle* v. *Hall* (1823) 3 Russ. 1.

118. *The Zigurds* (*supra*). As to enforcement procedure see *Three Rivers D.C.* v. *Bank of England* [1995] 4 All E.R. 312.

(iv) Bottomry and/or respondentia

In these security transactions, the lender took the risk of a successful voyage and personal liability could be incurred only in respect of obligations ancillary to the loan and security. Priority questions, regarding security for the loan, could, therefore, arise only in respect of claims *in rem* and in this respect both bottomry and respondentia attract a maritime lien or, assuming personal liability can arise, a statutory lien.[119]

2. Charges

Equitable charge—nature

The rules are as for mortgage—in modern usage "charge" tends to encompass all types of security interest, and particularly in respect of goods no distinction seems to be drawn between mortgage and charge.[120]

CHARGING ORDERS

A charging order made under the Charging Orders Act 1979 has the effect of an equitable charge.[121] Such an order may be made to aid in the enforcement of a judgment debt requiring the payment of a sum of money in land, securities specified in the Act, or funds in court.

"Mareva" injunction

A *Mareva* injunction creates no charge and, therefore, in relation to such an injunction no question of priority can arise.[122] (See Chapter 16.)

"In personam" priority—the structure

The priority of equitable charges not classified as other interests depends on the normal priority rules based on interests at common law and in equity, as amended by any applicable registration framework, or modified by conduct. When registration is required the consequences of non-registration depend on the Bills of Sale Acts or the Companies Act 1985, Part XII (see *supra*).

Floating charge

A floating charge is an equitable charge on assets and, while floating, allows trading in those assets. At the moment of enforceability it crystallizes as a fixed charge on the assets held at that moment on the floating charge. Floating charges are usually created by limited companies[123] and in England will crystallize on the winding up of the company, the

---

119. Supreme Court Act 1981, s.20(2)(r). Only bottomry is expressly mentioned. See Chap. 2.
120. See the Law of Property Act 1925, s.136(1).
121. Section 3(4). See further Chaps. 21, 25.
122. *The Cretan Harmony* [1978] 3 All E.R. 164; *The Angel Bell* [1980] 1 Lloyd's Rep. 632; *Mercedes Benz AG* v. *Leiduck* [1995] Lloyd's Rep. 417 (P.C.); but note that in *Z Ltd.* v. *A* [1982] Q.B. 558 Lord Denning M.R. was maintaining his view that the issue of the injunction was a kind of attachment.
123. I.e. by issue of debentures. In theory it appears that they may be created by individuals but they would be difficult to register as required under the Bills of Sale Acts.

company ceasing to carry on business on the appointment of an administrative receiver or on an occurrence specified in the debenture ("automatic crystallization"). Subject to any prohibition on creating later charges the priority of the charge would attach at that moment—for only then is the company prevented from dealing in the asset.[124] Where there is a prohibition on the creation of later charges (a "negative pledge"), priority will depend on whether the later charge is legal or equitable. If it is legal it will depend on notice of the prohibition and if equitable on general priority principles—any circumstances indicating that the company had power to deal in the assets.[125] When the appropriate provisions of the Companies Act 1989 come into force any such prohibition may have to be registered.

"In rem" priority

In the Supreme Court Act 1981 a "charge" is linked to the mortgage in s.20(2) and to the maritime lien in s.21(2) (see Chapter 2). Of these, the charge linked to the maritime lien has been in essence equated with that lien. It is, therefore, arguable only in respect of that linked to mortgage that a charge as such is an *in rem* concept. At most, such a charge is a statutory lien though it may receive the preferential *in rem* priority of the mortgage. The matter will be considered in the context of liens.

3. Pledge

"In personam" priority

In the context of maritime law a pledge of goods themselves is not of great significance but it should be noted that a pledge is relevant only to corporeal movables. It requires and depends on the transfer of possession and does not need registration under either the Bills of Sale Acts or the Companies Acts 1985, 1989 (see *supra*). A pledge may be created through instruction to a warehousekeeper to hold goods lodged with him for the order of the pledgee.[126] Of more immediate relevance is that a bill of lading may be pledged by endorsement and delivery.[127] The pledgee may then take delivery of the goods.[128]

PRIORITY AS AGAINST OTHER INTERESTS

As a basic rule, the pledgee's interest depends for its validity on the title of the pledgor. However, as with the acquisition of ownership, a pledgee acquiring an interest bona fide from one whose title is subject to rescission for fraud will not be subject to attack based on fraud. Further, a pledgee may receive an interest good against a vendor from a

---

124. See *supra*. As to preferential creditors taking priority over floating charges on company insolvency see Gower, *op. cit.* at pp. 420–422.

125. As to "negative pledge" see *supra*. As to priority see *Brunton* v. *Electrical Engineering Corpn* [1892] 1 Ch. 434 (a legal interest—a possessory lien) and generally Gower, *op. cit.* at pp. 415, 416.

126. As to which, see Chap. 20.

127. See *Sewell* v. *Burdick* (1884) 10 App. Cas. 74.

128. As to the effect of the Carriage of Goods By Sea Act 1992 on the liabilities as if a party to the contract see Reynolds [1993] LMCLQ 436 at p. 443.

purchaser in possession or good against a purchaser from a vendor in possession, or from a mercantile agent good against the principal.[129]

Priority issues between pledgees will be rare but normally the rule is that first in time prevails subject to any conduct by a pledgee misrepresenting the pledgor's power to deal with the goods.

"In rem" priority

A pledge may not be enforced *in rem*.

4. Liens

1. *"In personam" priority*

(A) "STATUTORY" LIENS

The enforceability and priority of a lien created by statute depends entirely on the statute. Unless the context indicates to the contrary, it is probable that the lien will simply be an adaptation of the common law possessory lien.[130] Its priority will depend either on its own rules or on those of the appropriate lien which the statute is applying.

Solicitor's statutory lien.[131] A charging order may be made by a court under the Solicitors Act 1974 for a solicitor's costs on any property preserved or recovered through his efforts.[132] It is enforceable against any transfer operating to defeat it, save any conveyance to a bona fide purchaser for value without notice.[133] The making of the charging order is discretionary and will normally be declared subject to any prior subsisting equity.[134] Naturally, it takes priority to the client's interest in the property made subject to the charge.[135]

(B) THE POSSESSORY LIEN

(a) As against interests other than a possessory lien. The lien is "enforceable" (i.e. the right of retention may be asserted) against any interest subsequently acquired. It may be enforced against legal interests created earlier generally only if the holder of that interest may be said to have permitted a transaction on which the lien depends. So a mortgagee

---

129. Factors Act 1889, ss.2, 8 and 9; the Sale of Goods Act 1979, ss.24 and 25 (1893, s.25). A pledged bill of lading may be handed back to the borrower to allow him to sell the goods, but probably in exchange for a trust receipt undertaking to hold the proceeds in trust for the lender. The borrower will then be in possession as the lender's agent.

130. See e.g. the unpaid seller's lien under the Sale of Goods Act 1979 (s.41) (*infra*); the broker's lien under the Marine Insurance Act 1906 (s.53(2)). Compare the charge which a solicitor may claim under the Solicitors Act 1974, s.73.

131. A solicitor has (i) a common law general possessory lien for costs in relation to clients' property; and (ii) an equitable lien on any fund recovered by him. The statutory "lien" reflects a claim to the "equitable interference of a court to have a judgment held as security for the solicitor's debt" (see *Fairfold Properties Ltd. v. Exmouth Dock Co. Ltd. (No. 2)* [1992] 4 All E.R. 289).

132. "Property" includes property of any kind—including a consent order for the assessment of damage (*ibid*) and a costs order where the costs had not been taxed (*Fairfold Properties Case* fn 131).

133. Solicitors Act 1974, s.73 (formerly in the Solicitors Act 1860, s.28; 1932, s.69; 1957, s.72).

134. See *The Paris* [1896] P. 77.

135. The basis of the client's claim to the property is irrelevant (*The Jeff Davis* (1867) L.R. 2 A. & E. 1; *The Heinrich* (1872) L.R. 3 A. & E. 505; *The Paris* [1896] P. 77; *The Marie Gartz (No. 2)* [1920] P. 460).

of a ship may be taken to agree to a possessory lien either arising out of a charterparty[136] or imposed by a law in a situation arising out of the operation of the charterparty (as on the repair of the ship).[137]

On general principles it should be enforceable against an equitable interest created earlier if the holder has no notice of the earlier interest.[138] If created by a company (i.e. through a contract) a possessory lien may be within the Companies Act 1985 requiring delivery of particulars for full enforceability.[139] It would seem to be within the definition of the "security interest" within the replacement registration provisions of the Companies Act 1989 (see *supra*). It would not seem affected by the registration scheme of the Merchant Shipping Act 1995.

Rights of unpaid seller of goods. The unpaid seller's rights under the Sale of Goods Act 1979 include, but are not restricted to, a possessory lien.[140] The right of stoppage in transit confers a right to resume possession of goods while in transit when the buyer becomes insolvent, and exercise of that right creates a priority issue just as much, if not more, than a possessory lien. It is defeated if there is a sale of the goods by transfer of a document of title to a person taking it in good faith and for valuable consideration and it is subject to any security interest created by such a transfer. Apart from these exceptions, however, the right of stoppage is not affected by any sale or disposition that the buyer makes unless the seller consents.[141] It is, however, subject to the shipowner's lien for freight.[142]

Statutory rights of detention and sale.[143] The statutory rights of port authorities to detain ships are statutory possessory liens but with a power of sale attached. An authority selling by virtue of the power of sale will confer a title free from encumbrances including any registered mortgage.[144]

(b) As between possessory liens. Such a conflict would be unusual as, *ex hypothesi*, the lien depends on possession. It is only if a possession is surrendered by fraud or if it were held that a redelivery was for a specific purpose[145] that any such priority question would arise. First in time would prevail.

---

136. See *Williams* v. *Allsup* (1861) 10 C.B. (N.S). 417; *The Scio* (1967) L.R. 1 A. & E. 353. Where there is authority, an agreement between owner and mortgagee that the owner would not create a lien would not affect the lien holder unless he had notice of the agreement (see e.g. *Bowmaker Ltd.* v. *Wycombe Motors Ltd.* [1946] K.B. 505).

137. It is questionable whether, apart from common carriers bound to provide services, a lien imposed by law in a situation not authorized by the owner (e.g. repairs of a ship wrongfully taken) would be good against the owner (see *Electric Supply Stores* v. *Gaywood* (1909) 100 L.T. 855). But it is arguable that policy should give priority to the repairer.

138. It will take priority over an earlier floating charge and, if acquired without notice of any "negative pledge" not to create any later charges having priority, over any interest created by that pledge (see *supra*).

139. Such a lien implied by law does not require such registration but if conferred by contract will do so if it amounts to a "charge"—it is arguable that it does not amount to a charge if it cannot be enforced by sale (see Chap. 17).

140. See s.48.

141. *Ibid*, s.47.

142. *Booth Steamship Co. Ltd.* v. *Cargo Fleet Iron Ltd.* [1916] 2 K.B. 570.

143. As to which, see Chap. 20.

144. *The Blitz* [1992] 2 Lloyd's Rep. 441.

145. See e.g. *Albermarle Supply Co. Ltd.* v. *Hind & Co.* [1928] 1 K.B. 307—but on numerous occasions courts have refused to allow ships to be moved without affecting the possessory lien (see e.g. *The Ally* [1952] 2 Lloyd's Rep. 427 following *The Gaupen* (1925) 22 Ll.L.Rep. 57). But the criteria is control of possession—and within that control use may be permitted (see *The Tergeste* [1903] P. 26).

(C) THE EQUITABLE LIEN

As with the equitable charge and equitable interests generally, the equitable lien is subject to the general priority framework of first in time subject to conduct, statute (including registration provisions) and the possibility of defeat by a later legal interest acquired without notice of the lien. Priorities between equitable liens are governed by the general priority framework of first in time subject to the modifications of conduct and statute.

(D) THE "MAREVA" INJUNCTION

Despite the view of Lord Denning that the issue of a *Mareva* injunction was akin to attachment of assets,[146] it is established that it remains a remedy *in personam* directed at the owner of the assets.[147] It creates no proprietary interest in the assets and, therefore, does not confer any right of priority *in personam* or *in rem* over any other unsecured creditor or against a purchaser.[148]

2. *"In rem" priority*

Subject to Admiralty Marshal's and arrester's costs[149] and statutory rights of detention of harbour authorities[150] the *in rem* priority categories are (i) maritime liens; (ii) possessory liens; and (iii) statutory liens in Admiralty. In *in rem* terms mortgages are statutory liens but are considered as of themselves forming a priority category.[151] Priority issues go to (a) priority of claims in each priority category as against claims in other categories; (b) priority of claims within each category; (c) the relationship between the *in rem* and *in personam* priority schemes.

(a) Priority between the categories of liens

A fairly definitive priority ladder has been built but uncertainties persist, particularly in respect of the relevance of the order of creation of interests and the effect of conduct.

(i) Maritime liens. It is established that maritime liens have priority over mortgages and statutory liens,[152] no matter in which order the claims arise. However, it appears that though a maritime lien has priority over a possessory lien created subsequently to it,[153] it will be subject to a possessory lien created prior to it.[154] On the grounds of waiver if

---

146. See *Z Ltd.* v. *A* [1982] Q.B. 558.
147. See *The Cretan Harmony* [1978] 1 Lloyd's Rep. 425; *The Angel Bell* [1980] 1 Lloyd's Rep. 632; *K/S A/S Admiral Shipping* v. *Portlink Ferries Ltd.* [1984] 2 Lloyd's Rep. 166.
148. *Ibid.* See *Mercedes Benz AG* v. *Leiduck* [1995] 2 Lloyd's Rep. 417 and Chap. 16.
149. As to which see Chap. 15.
150. As to which see Chap. 20.
151. As to distinctions as to attracting statutory liens between claims enforceable by an action *in rem*, see *infra*. Presumably charges are in the same priority category as mortgages. See *infra*.
152. Insofar as mortgage and statutory liens may exist in cargo and freight the priority of maritime liens would seem to apply as it applies to ships.
153. A contention that a subsequent possessory lien could be given priority on the basis of preservation of the *res* was rejected in *The Russland* [1924] P. 55.
154. See *The Tergeste* [1903] P. 26; *The Gustaf* (1862) Lush 506; *The Immacolata Concezione* (1883) 9 P.D. 37. As to the time of creation of the possessory lien, see *The Tergeste* (*supra*) and Chap. 20.

nothing else, the precedence of a maritime lien would be subject to any interest created with the authority of the maritime lien holder.[155]

(ii) Possessory liens. The lien is applied in Admiralty in its common law application and also has its maritime application in, for example, the lien for general average or freight. The lien has been fully incorporated into "priorities" *in rem* with little difference from the priority accorded *in personam*. As a result, the person asserting a possessory lien cannot object to the arrest of a ship or other arrest by the Admiralty Marshal,[156] but subject only to claims for the Marshal's expenses and arrester's costs the priority will be recognized[157] as regards interests created subsequent to its creation. So a maritime lien, mortgage and a statutory lien created subsequently to the possessory lien will be subject to it.

A possessory lien is subject to a maritime lien created prior to it, and there seems to be no reason why its *in rem* priority based on possession should differ from its *in personam* priority. If so, apart from any argument based on authority to create, it will be subject to any statutory lien (mortgage or other) created prior to it.

(iii) Statutory liens in Admiralty.[158] For the purpose of priority rules mortgages are put into a special category and priority between mortgages and other statutory liens in Admiralty treated as a matter of priority between categories. It is suggested that charges should be equated with mortgages.

Mortgage and charges

(i) Registered mortgage. It is not clear that registration of a mortgage has any effect on the priority as against an interest other than the registrable interest of a purchaser or mortgagee. It would indeed be odd if the act of registration of itself gave priority over interests which could not be protected by registration or at least an interest the purpose of which could not be accomplished by a registered interest.[159] On the other hand the failure to register could justifiably mean loss of priority (see *infra*).

As a matter of general principle a mortgage claim is subject to a maritime lien whether it arises before or after the mortgage, but takes priority over any statutory lien arising subsequent to the mortgage being created.[160] Priority between a statutory lien other than a mortgage and a subsequent mortgage is unclear and perhaps became a realistic possibility only on the ruling that a statutory lien is created on the issue of the writ *in rem* rather than on arrest.[161] Within the *in rem* framework a mortgage is a statutory lien and should be accorded priority as such, except insofar as it can be demonstrated that its nature

155. See further Chap. 18—Termination of Maritime Liens.
156. *The Harmonie* (1841) 1 W. Rob. 178; *The Nordstjernen* (1857) Swab. 260.
157. So there is no need to intervene in the action of others. Each claimant should make its own claim. See *The Athenic* (1932) 42 Ll.L.Rep. 7.
158. As to the definition and scope, see Chap. 19.
159. As, for example, the use of an equitable charge instead of a registered mortgage.
160. *The Two Ellens* (1871) L.R. 3 A. & E. 345; see also (e.g.) *The Leoborg (No. 2)* [1964] 1 Lloyd's Rep. 380. In *The Halcyon Skies* [1977] Q.B. 14 and *The Halcyon Isle* [1981] A.C. 221 the critical issue was whether the claimant opposed to the mortgagee had a maritime or statutory lien. If it was the former, it took priority and if the latter the mortgage had priority. As to cargo and freight, see fn 152.
161. In *The Halcyon Isle* (*supra*) the mortgage remained unregistered for over 12 months and the repairs which later led to a statutory lien took place within that period—although the writ was issued after registration.

creates grounds for an exception. While long-term financing interests are recognized in conferring priority over interests created subsequently it does not follow that the lender should be able to assert his security so as to destroy security interests already created.

(ii) Unregistered mortgage. The Supreme Court Act 1981 provides for the enforcement by action *in rem* of a legal or equitable mortgage and makes no distinction as to enforceability between registered and unregistered mortgages.[162] So all types may be enforced by an action *in rem*.

If an unregistered mortgage is *an equitable mortgage* and the *in personam* limitations apply a purchaser would not be bound by it unless he knew of it. Presumably, the ability to enforce the equitable mortgage *in rem* would be remedial and limited accordingly. However, as in the *in rem* framework, a purchaser is subject to claims which outside the *in rem* area have no proprietary force (as, for example, a claim for cargo damage) it would be curious if a claim which did have such proprietary force was treated as less powerful in that it is binding only on notice.

In 1922 in *The Byzantion*[163] Hill J. intimated that the lack of registration of a mortgage may have priority consequences in any conflict with other statutory liens. However, it could be argued that if a legal unregistered mortgage is recognized it is because of the limited role given to registration.[164] Further, notice is largely irrelevant to the security aspects of statutory liens and even if the unregistered mortgage is equitable it may be that as against liens the priority of the *mortgage* as such be recognized. On the other hand, it is "registered" mortgages which are recognized internationally and the failure to register should perhaps be penalized—at least so as to make the claimant (whether a legal or equitable mortgagee) share *pari passu* with other claimants having statutory liens.

(iii) Equitable charge and equitable lien. An equitable charge is included within the *in rem* framework by virtue of the Supreme Court Act 1981, s.21(2)(c) and 21(7)(c). The priority conferred on an equitable mortgage should also be conferred on an equitable charge insofar as these are treated as like concepts. An equitable lien expressly created by contract is in substance the same as an equitable charge and its priority should be treated accordingly. The equitable lien imposed by law rather than agreement should, it is suggested, also carry the same priority ratings, as from a policy point of view English law sees an imposed lien as justified without express provision. It is indeed arguable that the equitable charge or equitable lien should have a claim to higher priority than an equitable mortgage where there is a registration scheme of which the mortgagee may take advantage.

Statutory liens other than mortgage or charge claims

For *in rem* priority purposes, apart from mortgages and charges, all claims enforced through actions *in rem* should be treated as equal in force. Whether or not the claim is proprietary in *in personam* terms, it is suggested that the priority *in rem* focuses on the action *in rem*.

The priority of claims attracting statutory liens as against maritime liens, possessory liens and mortgages is set out in the consideration of those interests. A statutory lien is

---

162. See s.20(7).
163. (1922) 12 Ll.L.Rep. 9, at p. 12.
164. See *The Shizelle* [1992] 2 Lloyd's Rep. 445 and *supra*.

subject to maritime liens whenever created and to registered mortgages and possessory liens created prior to the creation of the statutory lien. The priority between a statutory lien and (i) a subsequent registered mortgage, and (ii) an unregistered mortgage (legal or equitable) whenever created is not clear. The availability of registration provides justification for the priority given to a later registered mortgage over an earlier unregistered mortgage but it is at least arguable that the act of registration should not confer priority over an earlier non-registrable lien. In other words unless non-registration was to operate against the holder of a registrable interest the "*in rem*" rules of priority (statutory liens being of equal priority) should prevail. The alternative is to accept that enforcement through the action *in rem* does not lead to *in rem* priorities, and that, apart from any factor depending on registrability it is the common law/equity *in personam* rules that apply.

(b) Priority within each category of lien

A. MARITIME LIENS[165]

General principles. In developing a priority framework some general principles have emerged—but cannot be said to have developed into rules. General principles on which the framework is founded are the following:

(a) the person who preserves the *res* for the benefit of all claimants has a prior claim to other claimants[166]—so that the claim based on an event latest in time which "has the result of preserving the interest of the holder of another existing lien"[167] will be given priority.[168]

(b) reasons of public policy in:

    (i) interests of masters and seamen (the wages lien)[169];

    (ii) encouragement of salvage (the salvage lien)[170];

    (iii) safe navigation and recompense for loss suffered through failure to carry it out (the damage lien).[171]

(c) a distinction between liens resulting from:

    (i) arrangements consciously entered into; and

    (ii) events occurring outside such arrangements.

    Where the basis of the lien is an arrangement entered into the claimant may be said to have joined the adventure, to have acquired a "voluntary lien", or

---

165. A claim which, if brought against a particular ship, would be a maritime lien must be treated as a statutory lien if brought against a sister ship (see the Supreme Court Act 1981, s.21 and *The Leoborg (No. 2)* [1964] 1 Lloyd's Rep. 380).

166. See e.g. *The Mons* [1932] P. 109; *The Lyrma (No. 2)* [1978] 2 LLoyd's Rep. 30; *The Veritas* [1901] P. 304; *The Inna* [1938] P. 148. The principle of inverse order of attachment must, it seems, be viewed in the context of preservation and not simply as governing of itself. (See *The Lyrma (No. 2)* [1978] 2 Lloyd's Rep. 30, at p. 34).

167. *The Lyrma (No. 2)* [1978] 2 Lloyd's Rep. 30—but the later event *must* preserve the lien—a characteristic held in this case not to apply in the case of wages earned after salvage. See also *The Gustaf* (1862) Lush. 506.

168. There seems little room for "first in time", a basic priority principle outside actions *in rem*.

169. So they were given priority over bottomry bonds (see e.g. *The Hope* (1873) 1 Asp. M.L.C. 563) which could also rest on the "joint adventure" approach—but not (e.g.) over salvage (see *The Lyrma (No. 2)* [1978] 2 Lloyd's Rep. 30).

170. See e.g. *The Inna* [1938] P. 148.

171. See e.g. *The Veritas* [1901] P. 304.

become the holder of a lien based on contract (*ex contractu*). Where the claimant has in no sense joined in any project, the action is based on an "involuntary lien" or a lien *ex delicto*, and for these reasons (being in essence variants on a theme) should have priority. The only "involuntary lien" is the damage lien.[172]

(d) an adaptation of the principle applicable to priorities between categories—the conduct of the lien holder.[173]

The particular liens

(i) **The damage lien.** *(a) As against other maritime liens.* The public policy basis of the damage lien of the need to ensure safe navigation gives it high priority. It is outweighed only by a lien arising subsequently to it and preserving the *res*. A damage lien, therefore, has priority over all prior liens but is subject to a subsequent salvage lien,[174] a bottomry lien insofar as it preserves the *res*[175] and (possibly) a wages lien.[176]

(b) As between damage liens. Damage liens rank equally and the claims are dealt with *pari passu*.[177]

(ii) **The salvage lien.** *(a) As against other maritime liens.* " . . . the salvage service concerned has preserved the property to which the earlier liens have attached".[178] It follows that a salvage lien has priority over all prior liens. As to subsequent liens, it appears to be subject only to a later damage lien[179] and any other lien which preserves the *res*.[180]

(b) As between salvage liens. The "inverse order of attachment" rule holds full sway—the later takes priority over the earlier. The rule is based firmly in this context on the principle of preservation of the *res*.[181]

(ii) **Wages lien.** *(a) As against other maritime liens.* As regards other liens, seamen's and masters' wages are not distinguished. The policy of protection of the seaman provides a foundation for giving a wages claim a high priority supported on appropriate occasions by subordinating a master's claim for wages or disbursements to the seaman's claim if the

---

172. For a rejection of the contention that a salvage lien was not *ex contractu*, see *The Veritas* [1901] P. 304, at p. 314.

173. See e.g. *The Daring* (1868) L.R. 2 A. & E. 260. Priority of the decree was at one time said to be a factor pointing to priority but the modern decree reserves priorities and the order is now of no priority relevance. Delay may affect priority. (see generally *The Stream Fisher* [1927] P. 73).

174. See *The Elin* (1882) 8 P.D. 39; *The Inna* [1938] P. 148.

175. See *The Aline* (1839) 1 W. Ro. 111.

176. See *The Elin* (1882) 8 P.D. 39; *The Linda Flor* (1857) Swab. 309; *The Chimera* (1852) 11 L.T. 113.

177. *The Stream Fisher* [1927] P. 73.

178. *The Lyrma (No. 2)* [1978] 2 Lloyd's Rep. 30, at p. 33 (Brandon J.).

179. See *supra*.

180. As to the general requirement of preservation, see *The Lyrma (No. 2)* [1978] 2 Lloyd's Rep. 30, at p. 34 (holding later wages to be subject to earlier salvage) and doubting *The Hope* (1873) 1 Asp. M.L.C. 563 in applying the inverse order of attachment mechanically to a later wage and earlier bottomry claim.

181. See e.g. *The Lyrma (No. 2)* [1978] 2 Lloyd's Rep. 30 at p. 34. Where there is a salvage service with a common object the claims under it rank *pari passu*. (See *The Russland* [1924] P. 55, at p. 60). The priority given to life salvage by the Merchant Shipping Act 1894, s.544, was removed by the Merchant Shipping (Salvage and Pollution) Act 1944. As to life salvage see the Salvage Convention, Art. 16, and Merchant Shipping Act 1995, Sch. 11, Part II, para. 5. As to the salvage lien see Chap. 18.

master undertakes a personal liability for payment of wages. On the other hand, wages liens are not treated as necessarily having the highest priority, the policy supporting damage and salvage liens outweighing that of the wages lien.

A wages claim is subject to a damage or salvage lien occurring subsequent to the earning of the wages and, unless the earning of the wages can be seen as preserving the *res*, even when the claim is based on wages earned after the damage lien is created.[182] A wages claim has been held to have priority over a bottomry bond entered into both before and after the earning of wages on the same voyage.[183] If today it were to become a question other than academic as against a bottomry bond, a wages lien would be displaced only by considerations of personal liability on the bond[184] or preservation of the *res*.

(b) Between wages liens. Until 1984 a seamen's wages lien seems to have priority over a masters' wages lien while the wages of seamen and wages of masters as between themselves rank *pari passu*.[185] However, in *The Royal Wells*,[186] Sheen J. thought the rule outmoded and unjust. Master and crew are all employees of the shipowner and their claims are to be ranked *pari passu*. It may be that wages earned at different times may have a different priority if separated by a claim for salvage.[187]

(iv) Disbursements lien. *(a) As against other maritime liens.* A master's disbursement lien appears to be treated as a master's lien for wages.[188]

(b) Between disbursements liens. Whether the claimant is the same or there are different claimants, disbursements liens rank "on precisely the same footing as his claim for wages"[189]—the claims rank *pari passu*.

(v) Bottomry.[190] *(a) As against other maritime liens.* It appears that bottomry bonds were subject to

    (a) a wages claim arising from the same voyage[191] if the wages are earned prior to the bond[192] and probably if earned after the bond[193]

---

182. *The Lyrma (No. 2)* [1978] 2 Lloyd's Rep. 30; *The Elin* (1882) 8 P.D. 39.

183. See *The William Safford* (1860) Lush. 69; *The Union* (1860) Lush. 128; *The Madonna D. Idra* (1811) 1 Dods. 37; *The Sydney Cove* (1815) 2 Dods. 11. In *The Hope* (1873) 1 Asp. M.L.C. 563, where wages were earned both prior to and after a bottomry bond, the rule of inverse order of attachment seems to have been mechanically applied—and later criticized (see fn 180). As to a previous voyage, see *The Mary Ann* (1845) 9 Jur. 94.

184. See *The Salacia* (1862) Lush. 545; *The Jenny Lind* (1872) L.R. 3 A. & E. 529; *The Edward Oliver* (1867) L.R. 1 A. & E. 379.

185. See *The Mons* [1932] P. 109.

186. [1984] 2 Lloyd's Rep. 255. For authorities for the earlier proposition, see *The Salacia* (1862) Lush 545; *The Athena* (1921) 8 Ll.L.Rep. 482; *The Mons* [1932] P. 109.

187. i.e. where the later wage earnings can be said to preserve the *res*. See *supra*.

188. See *The Mons* [1932] P. 109. But will it rank *pari passu* with seamen's wages? (See fn 186.)

189. *The Mons* [1932] P. 109, at p. 111.

190. Respondentia appears to follow the rules of bottomry.

191. A wages claim from a previous voyage may be subordinated to a bond. See *The Mary Ann* (1845) 9 Jur. 94; *The Hope* (1873) 1 Asp. M.L.C. 563.

192. See *The Union* (1860) Lush. 128.

193. *The William Safford* (1860) Lush. 69; *The Hope* (1873) 1 Asp. M.L.C. 563 (but in *The Lyrma (No. 2)* [1978] 2 Lloyd's Rep. 30, Brandon J. doubted the principle except insofar as the wage earning preserved the *res*). A master who binds himself personally on the bond will lose his priority over it—*The Salacia* (1862) Lush. 545.

(b) a damage lien save insofar as a later bond increased the value of the *res*.[194]

However, in opposition to a salvage lien, a bottomry bond has been treated much as an equal and priority has operated on the principle of inverse order of attachment.[195] If bottomry bonds were to be re-established as security interests of importance priority should depend on the analysis of their function in relation to other liens. Priority in relation to salvage should surely depend on the respective roles in the preservation of the *res*.

(b) Between bottomry bonds. The last in time ranks first.[196]

B. STATUTORY LIENS

For purposes of priority between statutory liens, the liens must be classified into three categories: (i) mortgages and charges (given a priority category of themselves); (ii) ownership (raising distinct questions of policy going to the nature of the action *in rem*); and (iii) the remainder.

1. Mortgage or charge. *(i) Mortgage of ships.* In English law there are registered and unregistered ship mortgages. As ship mortgages are treated in an *in rem* action as a *distinct* priority category, there is no reason why the *in rem* priority rules *within* that category should be different to those applicable to a claim *in personam*. There may, however, be reasons why as against other statutory liens the important factor is the mortgage rather than its legal or equitable character.

The priority of registered mortgages depends by statute on the date of registration, it being irrelevant whether they are enforced by action *in rem* or action *in personam*. The recognition of the legal unregistered mortgage in *The Shizelle*[197] flows from the restricted role of the statutory registration scheme. In that case the holders of a mortgage in an unregistered (but registrable) ship sought to enforce it by action *in rem* against a later bona fide purchaser without notice. An application to strike out the action failed, it being held that the common law principles applied and that priority was dependent on whether the mortgage was legal or equitable.

No point was taken as to any difference between "*in personam*" or "*in rem*" priority. On the facts of the case the issue of the writ *in rem* could create no "lien" enforceable against the purchaser, and the "*in rem*" process was therefore seen solely as enforcing a proprietary interest defined according to "*in personam*" principles, as modified by statutory registration provisions. It may be, however, that subject to statutory registration provisions where a proprietary interest is *created* by the *in rem* process it is the "*in rem*" or statutory lien categorization that should prevail. Further in may be that registration provisions will have to be construed with "*in rem*" principles in mind (see *infra*).

---

194. *The Aline* (1839) 1 W. Rob. 111.
195. See *The Selina* (1842) 2 Not. Cas. 18.
196. *Cargo ex Galam* (1863) 2 Moo. P.C., N.S. 216; *The Priscilla* (1859) Lush. 1. Bonds forming part of the same dealing rank *pari passu* (see *The Exeter* (1799) 1 C. Rob. 173).
197. [1992] 2 Lloyd's Rep. 445.

(ii) Mortgage of cargo. An action *in rem* will not lie to enforce a mortgage of cargo.[198]

(iii) Mortgage of freight or charterparty hire. Only if an action *in rem* will lie against cargo or freight will any question of "lien" priority arise. The Supreme Court Act 1981 provides specifically for an action *in rem* against property other than a ship only in regard to maritime liens and forfeiture. Any ability otherwise to bring an action *in rem* would have to be, therefore, rooted in the sweeping up clause and thereby through the Administration of Justice Act 1956 to the general Admiralty jurisdiction prior to 1 November 1875.[199]

THE RIGHT OF AN ASSIGNEE OF FREIGHT. In 1933 in *The Zigurds*[200] Langton J. held that a claim enforceable *in rem* could be so enforced by an assignee of that claim. Although the decision was reversed by both the Court of Appeal and House of Lords[201] it was on the application of priority principles rather than on whether an action *in rem* would lie.

On the assumption that an *in rem* claim will lie, the priority principles adopted in *The Zigurds* between two assignees of the same claim are those applicable in an action *in personam*—i.e. as between two equitable assignees priority goes to the first to give notice to the debtor,[202] and if neither have given notice it is the first in time. On this approach as with mortgage, on the issue of priority between assignees the rules generally applicable *in rem* would give way to the *in personam* approach. The principle must however be subject to any priority as between the claims themselves.

(iv) Equitable charge and equitable lien. An equitable charge and equitable lien should be treated for priority purposes at least as equivalent to an equitable mortgage. Such interests may have a claim to higher priority where registration is available to the mortgagee. However, having regard to the balance between long term financing and other security interests the priority of the charge or lien should not be equated with the registered mortgage.

2. Ownership claims.[203] Through the availability of an action *in rem* claims of ownership or co-ownership may be said technically to be statutory liens. But, as has been argued, the action *in rem* differs in its function in relation to an ownership or mortgage claim from that in relation to claims which without the action *in rem* would not be proprietary. To date, unlike mortgages, ownership claims have not been seen as falling into a unique *in rem* priority category. Unless such a category is created on policy grounds the priority of an *in rem* claim based on ownership must, it is suggested, be ranked with other claims of the same category, i.e. statutory liens. If, apart from statutory registration provisions, an ownership claim were to be ranked higher than other statutory liens it could fundamentally affect the *in rem* concept, a primary element of which is security *against* an owner. It is

198. It may be argued that this illustrates a gap in the Admiralty framework—for it means that different priority principles may apply to competing interests (e.g. maritime lien and mortgage *in personam* principles). See *infra.*

199. As to the applicability of this clause to actions "*in rem*" see Chap. 2.

200. [1932] P. 113. See also *The Eskbridge* [1931] P. 51 apparently recognizing a claim *in rem* against cargo for freight. The provisions on which the admission was based are now repealed (as to the effect of this, see Chap. 2).

201. See [1933] P. 87 (C.A.); [1934] A.C. 209 (H.L.).

202. For an application of which see *The Attika Hope* [1988] 1 Lloyd's Rep. 439.

203. Claims to possession would fall in this category only insofar as it was alleged that the possession was the *root* of ownership (as through limitation of actions).

suggested that, subject to priority conferred by statute on registered ownership, in the *in rem* priority framework an ownership claim is enforceable and takes priority as a statutory lien. It does not appear that registration under the Merchant Shipping Act 1995 or its predecessors will affect maritime liens or statutory liens in Admiralty.

Beneficial ownership. Although there is no specific reference in The Supreme Court Act 1981, s.20, to beneficial ownership the concept is recognized in the statutory provisions for registration[204] and, indeed, in regard to defendants, in the Supreme Court Act, s.21(1) and (4). It would seem inconceivable that an equitable mortgagee or chargee could enforce a claim through an action *in rem* but an equitable owner could not.

Given the ability to enforce the claim through an action *in rem*, equitable ownership would have a lower priority than other statutory liens only through importation of the *in personam* principle of notice. However, it is urged that certainly as regards other claims not based on a proprietary interest *in personam* enforcement through an action *in rem* as a statutory lien should carry the priority of that lien. The legal and equitable distinction thought too fundamental to be obliterated by the *in rem* framework may (with some difficulty) be retained as between claims in respect of which the *in rem* process is primarily a method of enforceability rather than conferring of a lien.

3. Statutory liens in Admiralty other than those based on ownership, mortgage or charge. *(i) As between different liens.* Statutory liens seem to be ranked equal—the claims sharing *pari passu*. There is no clear judicial statement to this effect but such authorities as are reported all treat differing claims as having identical ranking.[205]

(ii) As between liens of the same class. All the authority is focused on claims for necessaries, stating clearly that such claims rank *pari passu*.[206] In the light of the general application of the principle of *pari passu* as between different statutory liens there is no reason why the principle should not apply generally as between liens of the same class.

IV. PRIORITY RELATIONSHIP BETWEEN ACTIONS "IN REM" AND "IN PERSONAM" PROPRIETARY INTERESTS

Although English law has long supported the cumulative effect and often concurrent availability of actions *in personam* and actions *in rem* it has not addressed itself to the relationship of interests enforceable by those actions. The concept of the action *in rem* means that:

    (i) the provisional remedy of arrest is available;

    (ii) specified claimants are given preferred creditor status in relation to a particular asset or its substitute;

---

204. See The Merchant Shipping Act 1995 and Merchant Shipping (Registration of Ships) Regulations 1993 (SI 1993/3138)—as to which see *supra*.

205. See (e.g.) *The Leoborg (No. 2)* [1964] 1 Lloyd's Rep. 380 (wages—as claimed against sister ships treated as statutory lien—and goods supplied); *The Charger* [1966] 3 All E.R. 117 (dock dues, goods supplied).

206. *The Rene* (1922) 12 Ll.L.Rep. 202; *The Africano* [1894] P. 141; *The Zigurds* [1932] P. 113; *The Stream Fisher* [1927] P. 73.

(iii) there has developed an "*in rem*" priority scheme with its own relative values, encompassing proprietary interests created by the action *in rem* and those enforceable as such by an action *in personam* but enforced by an action *in rem*.

(iv) a sale of the asset by the court wipes off all such claims which could have been made in relation to the asset prior to the sale and transfers them to the proceeds.[207]

However, the same asset may be subject to proprietary interests *in personam* with "*in personam*" priorities, such claims in regard to that asset being affected in "*in personam*" terms by a sale by the court only when the asset is sold in execution of the claim. Such a sale does not have the effect of conferring the clear title of the judicial sale as part of an action *in rem*.[208] No doubt historical jurisdictional conflicts between common law, equity and Admiralty have led in this context as in others to a legacy of separate but connected frameworks. It is surely time for a statutory attempt at incorporation.

Apart from statutory priority rules applying to both actions *in personam*[209] and actions *in rem* the first requirement in integration of the *in personam* and *in rem* priority ladders is the identification of the function of the action *in rem* in respect of the particular claim. Where claims involve any claim which but for the action *in rem* would not be proprietary (as for example a carriage claim) there seems no alternative to applying *in rem* priorities and enforcement through judicial sale. Where the case concerns solely proprietary interests enforceable as such by action *in personam* (as for example ownership and mortgage), as is shown by *The Shizelle*,[210] it is arguable that it is the *in personam* priorities which control. If that is so the function of the action *in rem* is simply to provide for the provision of arrest and judicial sale.

As is also illustrated by *The Shizelle* it is unclear how the statutory scheme of registration of and mortgages in ships fit with rights created by and through the action *in rem* and in particular maritime liens and statutory liens in Admiralty. As indicated earlier there is a need for the role of registration to be made clear.

1. OWNERSHIP

The action *in rem* and its characteristics of the preferred claim, enforceability against purchasers and the judicial sale is *ex hypothesi* an exception to the general *in personam* priority framework. In particular, according to *in personam* rules with few exceptions,[211] subject to proprietary interests created in a ship before he acquired it or created *by* him, a shipowner has an interest enforceable against all the world. Through actions *in rem* a shipowner is liable to attack through a far greater number of antecedent interests and some interests created subsequently, even though he was not responsible for their creation. As

207. See e.g. *The Acrux* [1962] 1 Lloyd's Rep. 405; *The Igor* [1956] 2 Lloyd's Rep. 271; *The Cerro Colorado* [1993] 1 Lloyd's Rep. 58.
208. See Chap. 25.
209. As statutory registration provisions (as to which see *supra*) and statutory rights of detention and sale (as to which see *infra*).
210. [1992] 2 Lloyd's Rep. 445. See *supra*.
211. As e.g. a seller or buyer in possession under the Sale of Goods act 1979, ss. 24, 25.

part of the enforceability of these interests his ship may be sold and his interest reduced to a claim of low priority on the resulting fund.

Given the *in rem* framework it is difficult to argue as a matter of general principle that ownership rules applicable *in personam* have any place within the *in rem* framework, save as they may be adapted in that framework. An ownership claim through an action *in personam* should be subject to all *in rem* claims.

On the other hand the function of the action *in rem* in an ownership claim is arguably simply to enforce an interest recognized *in personam* as proprietary and therefore subject to "*in personam*" rules. The *in personam* proprietary characteristics may well control (see *supra*).

2. MORTGAGE, CHARGE AND LIEN

Claims based on mortgage or charge are integrated into the *in rem* framework. An equitable lien would seem enforceable by an action *in rem* under the general label of an equitable charge. As with ownership a mortgage or charge enforced through an action *in personam* should be subject to all *in rem* claims, but when sought to be enforced by an action *in rem* is arguably governed by the *in personam* proprietary characteristics.

3. INTERESTS CREATED BY STATUTE

The effect of an interest created by statute depends on an initial construction of the statute as to whether it amounts to a novel concept or simply an adaptation of a concept already recognized (such as a possessory lien). Insofar as the statute creates a "novel" interest its relationship to the *in rem* framework requires examination in the context of its provisions.[212]

Statutory rights of port authorities to detention and sale of ships

It is established that the statutory rights of port authorities to detain and sell a ship "is not within the ambit of priorities" which operate in the case of judicial sale on the residue of the proceeds once they are paid into court.[213] Although the authority may have a lien for its claim the entitlement to prior payment depends not on the assertion of that lien but on the exercise of statutory rights.[214]

The statutory right of detention is a statutory possessory lien in the sense that it is what it says but its differing priority rank makes it confusing to use that label. It is not settled in English law whether the statutory right is transferred to the proceeds of sale if a ship is sold by the Admiralty Marshal,[215] but, if not, it appears that the right persists despite

---

212. As (e.g.) an unpaid seller's lien under the Sale of Goods Act 1979 (see fn 140 *supra*).

213. *The Charger* [1966] 3 All E.R. 117; *The Blitz* [1992] 2 Lloyd's Rep. 441 (not subject to registered mortgage) see *supra*. It seems as if a port authority may insist on its power of sale and its enforceability of its right in this way (*ibid*).

214. *The Charger* [1966] 3 All E.R. 117. Standing by may lead to a holding that the statutory rights have been waived. See *The Acrux* [1962] 1 Lloyd's Rep. 405.

215. *The Sierra Nevada* (1932) 42 Ll.L.Rep. 309.

such a sale. In *The Queen of the South*[216] and later in *The Freightline One*[217] it was held that, with the consent of the authority, the claim could be (and was) transferred to the proceeds to be paid prior to other claims out of the fund. The difficulties in treating statutory rights of detention and sale as rights only against the ship have therefore been resolved so as to permit their enforceability—but that resolution is but an illustration of the need to fit together the *in rem* process and other claims.

Solicitor's lien under the Solicitors Act 1974[218]

The lien has been held to be subject to an existing maritime lien[219] and to take priority over necessaries supplied after the institution of the original suit.[220] However, the authorities seem to follow no principle but simply a balancing of claims in particular circumstances. It should be recalled that the "security interest" of the lienee is created only on the making of a charging order and that the security interest of a statutory lien in Admiralty is created only on the issue of the writ *in rem*. The authorities seem to look at the institution of the original suit, (where appropriate) the time of supply of necessaries and the arrest of the ship all as relevant factors. However, in principle, it would seem that if order of creation of the interest is to govern, it is order of creation of the security interest. Further, it *may* be arguable that a maritime lien is of such force that it should be given priority whether created before or after the solicitor's lien.

Limitation funds

There may be a number of claimants against a limitation fund established pursuant to the Convention on the Limitation of Liability for Maritime Claims 1976 as initially enacted by the Merchant Shipping Act 1979 and as from 1 January 1996 by the Merchant Shipping Act 1995. In distributing the fund it is statutorily provided that no lien in respect of any ship or property affects the proportions.[221] The fund is distributed *pari passu* in proportion to the claims.

4. THE EXECUTION CREDITOR

The delivery of a writ of *fieri facias* to the sheriff makes a judgment creditor a preferred creditor.[222] In *The James W. Elwell*[223] an execution creditor procured a writ of *fieri facias*

---

216. [1968] P. 449. See also *The Spermina* (1923) 17 Ll.L.Rep. 52 at p. 53.
217. [1986] 1 Lloyd's Rep. 266.
218. See *supra*.
219. *The Livietta* (1883) 8 P.D. 209. It takes priority over the client's lien whatever type of lien it is. (See *The Heinrich* (1872) L.R. 3 A. & E. 505).
220. *The Heinrich* (1872) L.R. 3 A. & E. 505.
221. Merchant Shipping Act 1995, Sch. 7, Part II, para. 9. A like provision introduced in legislation now repealed overruled a decision of the House of Lords (*The Countess* [1923] A.C. 345) which gave priority to a claimant with a possessory lien. As to limitation of liability generally see Chap. 24.
222. See Chap. 25.
223. [1921] P. 351. See also *The Ile de Ceylan* [1922] P. 256.

prior to the issue of various writs *in rem* for claims for necessaries, wages advanced and by the master for wages. Pursuant to the writ of *fieri facias* the sheriff took possession of the ship and tried to sell it. Because of the claims against it he failed and the judge ordered a sale by the Marshal which, as Hill J. said, gave a "title free from all liens".

Hill J. first gave priority to the master for wages earned prior to and after the issue of the writ of execution. He said that the creditor could seize only what the debtor has. He treated the execution creditors in the same way as necessaries claimants whose claims are made subject to any claim for wages earned after arrest, saying that with the consent of the court the execution creditors could have paid off the master.

However, Hill J. gave priority to the execution creditors over the claims for necessaries which, as he said, only became secured claims *after* the claim of the judgment creditors had become secured. In this respect, he refused to apply the *in rem* rule of *pari passu* applicable to statutory liens but applied the *in personam* rule of first in time. As a result, the judgment creditors were able to obtain execution of their judgment from the proceeds of sale representing the ship, and in priority to statutory liens created *after* the creation of their security. In principle, therefore, the execution creditors will take subject to any statutory liens created by an issue of a writ *in rem* prior to the issue of the writ of *fieri facias*, but in priority to such liens created subsequent to the issue.

A charging order

Such an order takes effect as an equitable charge. In 1981 in *The Silia*[224] the ship (including fuel) was sold in an action *in rem*. After the sale, judgment creditors of the shipowners obtained a charging order nisi on the proceeds of the sale of the fuel oil contending that the oil was not part of the ship and, therefore, was available to them as secured creditors *in personam*. Sheen J. held that the oil was part of the ship and that, therefore, the oil proceeds were part of the fund available only to judgment creditors *in rem*. The plaintiffs' claim was within Admiralty jurisdiction but they had not issued a writ *in rem*.

It does not seem to have argued that even if within "*in rem*" jurisdiction the funds are as available to secured creditors *in personam* as *in rem*. Yet do they not represent assets of the shipowner and, if a creditor has a security interest in those assets, by what rule is he excluded simply because there are creditors *in rem*? The assumption implied in such a view is that there is no problem of priority between *in personam* and *in rem* creditors (at least in respect of proceeds of sale) as only the *in rem* creditors have a claim. As the claimant in *The Silia* could have enforced the claim *in rem* this approach is to be supported in that case.

However, if the approach is applied to judgment creditors who cannot enforce their claims *in rem* proprietary interests are enforceable in relation to the ship only to the extent of any funds remaining after the *in rem* claims are satisfied. Such an approach would be inconsistent with the approach to issues under the Solicitors Act 1974 and to the decision in *The James W. Elwell*. The priority relationship between *in personam* proprietary interests and *in rem* claims requires examination.

---

224. [1981] 2 Lloyd's Rep. 534.

5. EFFECT OF JUDICIAL SALE IN ACTION "IN REM"

It is suggested that subject to statutory provisions[225] no proprietary interest *in personam* can survive the judicial sale in an action *in rem*. Insofar as such an interest is enforceable *in rem* the claimant should be made so to claim so as to qualify to share alongside other claimants *in rem*. Insofar as a proprietary interest cannot be enforced *in rem* the policy behind judicial sale is clear and compelling enough to transfer such a claim to the proceeds of sale.

6. SUMMARY

The function of the action *in rem* may vary according to whether the right enforced is, in *"in personam"*, proprietary. It may be that *"in personam"* proprietary rights enforced *in rem* retain their *in personam* proprietary characteristics. But that should not affect the enforceability against them of interests which become proprietary through the action *in rem*. Further, any proprietary claim enforceable as such only *in rem* but not so enforced should be subject to all claims *in rem*. The priority of a proprietary interest enforceable only *in personam* and a claim *in rem* must depend on the view taken of relative policies behind each claim. Attempts to work these out in particular cases can be seen in *The James P. Elwell* and cases concerned with solicitor's statutory lien. Much as with the adaptation of *in personam* rules within the *in rem* framework, it calls for a priority evaluation to be consciously taken in the context of fitting together the two schemes and the consequences of preferring one to the other. As part of the general preference of the *in rem* scheme as against the *in personam* scheme subject to statutory provisions, a judicial sale in *in rem* proceedings should clear the title of all interests.

V. ATTEMPTS AT INTERNATIONAL FRAMEWORKS—MORTGAGES AND LIENS

The Conventions on Liens and Mortgages of 1926, 1967 and 1993, reflecting attempts to create a framework for recognition of and priority between maritime liens and mortgages, are discussed in Chapter 17. It suffices here to refer to that discussion and to stress that the achievement of at least some common ground would seem well worth the occasional domestic deletion or addition of a lien or two on the part of the maritime nations.

---

225. As, for example, statutory rights of detention of public authorities (as to which see *supra*).

PART V

Remedies

CHAPTER 24

Limitation of Liability

THE GENERAL PRINCIPLE

Limitation of liability is an accepted concept generally in the use of corporate personality to limit individual liability. In shipping it has long been accepted that in addition a shipowner or operator may directly limit liability for compensation for damage, loss or injury caused through his acts.[1] In English law such limitation now applies to all claims arising from one incident or occurrence ("global" limitation) save where because of the risk of claims for huge compensation (for example, oil pollution or nuclear damage) a special scheme has been created. Within the global regime there is a second level of limitation in respect of carriage of goods and passengers based on an amount per package or number of passengers.

The justification for all types of limitation is the need to encourage investment in trade and insurability of risk. The balancing factor for claimants for the limit on compensation is the lessening of the possibility of non-recovery. To an extent this is achieved through insurance itself, and the spreading of the cost of compensation. However, unless a compensation fund made up from contributions of interested parties is set up the basic question of "who pays?" remains. The setting up of such a fund depends on the ability to identify the interested parties and international agreement as to its criteria. Further, it cannot entirely remove the need to establish that a particular claim falls within the scheme (i.e. that damage or loss was caused as alleged).

The ability to limit does not therefore *necessarily* affect the principles of liability. Apart from oil pollution and nuclear damage claims, limitation of liability operates through a limit on compensation not linked to any principle of liability without fault or without any regard to the conduct of the limitation claimant. The claiming of limitation is also not exclusively linked to the provision of any security for the claim. However, the setting up of a "limitation fund" and the claiming of global limitation may relieve the person claiming limitation from provision of further security and also channel claims against him to the fund.

Although the limitation framework does not normally include mandatory security for a claim, in maritime law there are compensating factors favouring a liability claimant. So until other security is lodged the claimant will in most cases have or be able to create a "lien" on the ship involved in the incident and prior to judgment be able to arrest the ship to ensure that it is available for enforcement of the claim through the lien.

---

1. For early English statutes see Responsibility of Shipowners Act 1733; Merchant Shipping Act 1854. For a robust defence of limitation of liability as a principle see Steel [1995] LMCLQ 71.

Limitation of liability—as any defence—is only as good as the legal system within which it operates and the recognition of the defence in any other system where a claim may be brought. A declaration of limitation may therefore be of value only in the state in which it is obtained. More, a limitation fund may only be effective not only where it is recognized but where claims against other assets are excluded.

Limitation is therefore a principle ripe for international agreement. Such agreement has been reached to a greater or lesser extent through Conventions both as regards global limitation and in relation to particular claims. The effectiveness of such a Convention depends not only on the number of parties to it but the will of those parties to make the provisions mandatory in each national law. In order so to do there must be a prohibition on opting out of a jurisdiction or law which does not recognize or enforce the Convention. Limitation of liability in English law now largely reflects Conventions to which the United Kingdom is a party.

THE LINK BETWEEN LIABILITY AND LIMITATION PROCEEDINGS

The connection between limitation and liability issues is obvious. However, there is no necessary dependence if limitation is seen purely as concern with the limit on compensation assuming that liability is established. The view of the English courts seems to have been that where limitation may be pleaded as a defence or counterclaim (i.e. where there is only one liability claimant) then it would be expected that the claim be made as part of the liability proceedings. Otherwise it may be argued that any finding in either proceedings on liability including the amount was *res judicata* in respect of the other proceedings. However, so far as global limitation is concerned, it has long been possible to obtain a decree binding all claimants. Where this was sought it was seen as requiring as a prerequisite an admission or a finding of liability. So a limitation decree of this kind may be sought in a "limitation action" and this could take place (and might have to take place) after judgment on liability.

The more limitation is seen as dependent on the establishing of liability the more the likelihood of identical issues arising in both types of proceedings. This in turn not only poses the question in any case whether limitation should have been raised in liability proceedings but, where the proceedings are separate, whether the findings in one are binding in the other. In *The Wladyslaw Lokietek*[2] Brandon J. took the view that a right of recovery declared in liability proceedings was not "*res judicata*" in respect of limitation proceedings. Whether in English law this means that, lacking admission of liability, the whole question of liability remains open to argument despite a finding on liability seems unclear. For the general proposition Brandon J. relied on *C. A. Van Eijk and Zoon-Somerville*[3]—a case concerned only with challenge in limitation proceedings to the value of the ship assessed in liability proceedings. The value of the ship, it may be argued, lies at the heart of limitation proceedings affecting the amount available for all claimants—but, it may also be argued, so does the liability of the shipowner to each claimant.

2. [1978] 2 Lloyd's Rep. 520.
3. [1906] A.C. 489.

While, therefore, in limitation proceedings an English court may approach a claim unsullied by any finding in liability proceedings it is clear a court has the power to decide liability in limitation proceedings. The power is emphasized by the ability conferred by statute to enjoin claimants from taking other proceedings.[4] In Canada, the Federal Court of Appeal has stressed that such a power to stay should not be used to prevent a claimant establishing liability if the shipowner does not admit it, particularly if the claimant challenges the shipowner's right to limit.[5]

Under the Convention on Limitation of Liability for Maritime Claims 1976 the connection between liability and limitation is lessened in that the right to limit and obtain release of security following constitution of a limitation fund does not require the establishing either of liability or that no factor is present preventing limitation (see *infra*). Nevertheless, where liability is not admitted potential overlap remains[6] and where liability and limitation proceedings are taken in different states the questions arise of the view taken to a party in one or the other seeking tactically to litigate both issues in the one place. So far as English law is concerned, apart from the Brussels and Lugano Conventions this is a matter for the court's discretion if a party seeks either to stay proceedings already started or leave to serve a writ outside the jurisdiction.

The limitation procedure and amounts of the law of a country asserted by a liability defendant as more appropriate for the hearing of a liability claim is a relevant element in any discretion as to whether the liability proceedings should be stayed. In *The Vishva Abha*[7] Sheen J. regarded lesser maximum compensation in South Africa as a factor working against a stay of English liability proceedings. That is to favour the interest of the liability claimant, but probably justifiably because of the policy of the English law founded on the 1976 Limitation of Liability Convention (see *infra*). Were the limits in the foreign country to be higher, whether this would be in favour of or against a stay of liability proceedings depends on whether the home policy frowns on or favours imposed higher limits. Where a case is within either the Brussels or Lugano Convention as the liability and limitation proceedings are related the court in which proceedings are lodged second in time must decide whether to order a stay (see *infra*).

INTERNATIONAL LIMITATION FRAMEWORKS

GLOBAL LIMITATION

Global limitation operates in relation to specified types of claim, the liability for which is a matter for national law. The liability principles may be based on other Conventions (as for example carriage claims) or may depend directly on national law. In English law, save in the case of conduct entitling a liability claimant to break the limit (see *infra*), liability of an owner, charterer, manager or operator of a British ship is specifically excluded in respect of:

4. Merchant Shipping Act 1995, Sch. 7, Part II, para. 8(2).
5. See *Nishen Kisen Kaishan Ltd.* v. *Canadian National Railway Co.* [1982] 1 F.C. 530. For imposition of conditions on a stay as a balancing act see *The Sea Cap XII* [1995] LMLN 415 (F.C.).
6. See e.g. *Dresser* v. *Falcongate Ltd.* [1991] 2 Lloyd's Rep. 557 at p. 563—treating as self evident that liability and limitation proceedings are "related action" within the EC Jurisdiction Convention 1968 (see *infra*).
7. [1990] 2 Lloyd's Rep. 312.

(a) property on board lost or damaged by reason of fire on board the ship
(b) gold, silver watches, jewels or precious stones lost or damaged by reason of
theft, robbery or other dishonest conduct and their nature in value not declared
by the owner or shipper to the owner or master in the bill of lading or in
writing.

Liability for such damage or loss is likewise excluded (a) of a master or member of the
crew or servant of the owner where the damage or loss arises from anything done or
omitted by that person in that capacity and (b) any person of whom the master, crew
member or the servant and who is not himself excluded from liability under the
provision.[8]

The development of an effective international limitation framework is bedevilled as
ever by the problem of the overlapping of consecutive Conventions caused by the
appreciation of the need for change or that general rules are not appropriate for particular
claims as they emerge. The most recent Convention seeking to provide a general
limitation for all claims arising from a single incident, save those excepted, is the
Convention on Limitation for Liability for Maritime Claims 1976. Excepted claims
include claims within the limitation schemes of the Convention on Civil Liability for Oil
Pollution Damage 1969 and those within limitation of liability Conventions or national
provisions relating to nuclear damage.[9] As of 5 December 1994 26 states (including the
United Kingdom) are parties to the 1976 Convention.

The 1976 Convention was intended to replace the International Convention Relating to
the Limitation of Liability of Owners of Sea Going Ships 1957 in turn intended to replace
the International Convention for the Unification of Certain Rules Relating to the
Limitation of Liability of Owners of Sea Going Ships 1924. But not all States parties to
earlier Conventions become (or at least immediately become parties to later Conventions).
Hence the very achievement of some international agreement tends at least initially to
create a conflict between laws.

LIMITATION FOR PARTICULAR CLAIMS IN ADDITION TO "GLOBAL" LIMITATION

Claims for damage to or loss of cargo or injury or death of passengers are subject to
further limitation within the global limitation.

Carriage Conventions

The Conventions relating to carriage of goods provide for principles of liability and
impose limitation of liability on the basis of limit per package.[10] By the Athens
Convention Relating to the Carriage of Passengers and their Luggage 1974 principles of
liability for the death or personal injury to passengers are established and compensation

8. Merchant Shipping Act 1995, s.186.
9. See *infra*. Negotiations continue for a Convention relating to Noxious and Hazardous Substances by Sea.
As to the Convention and its effect see generally *Limitation of Shipowners Liability—the New Law*, ed. Gaskell,
Sweet & Maxwell, 1986.
10. See The Hague-Visby Rules, Art. 6; Hamburg Rules, Art. 5 (in force but United Kingdom not a party).
The limits may be increased by agreement.

limited to a sum per carriage.[11] These Conventions all provide that the limitation provisions do not affect the rights and duties under any Convention relating to limitation of liability in respect of sea going ships (i.e. global limitation).[12]

Of the particular Conventions the Hague-Visby Rules concerning carriage of goods by sea and the Athens Convention concerning the carriage of passengers and luggage by sea are part of English law. The Hague-Visby Rules reflect the stage of development in an international agreement on liability for loss of or damage to cargo carried by sea. An earlier stage is reflected by the Hague Rules to which the United Kingdom was a party until it became a party to the Hague-Visby Rules and a later stage by the Hamburg Rules to which the United Kingdom is not a party. Both these Conventions, however, are in force in a number of states.

Mortgages and liens Conventions

The International Conventions for the Unification of Certain Rules Relating to Maritime Liens and Mortgages 1926, 1967 and 1993 each refer to limitation of liability. The Convention of 1926 (Art. 7) provides simply that no sum apportioned to a creditor may exceed the sum due under limitation of liability rules. The Convention of 1967 (Art. 14(2)) provides any party may reserve the right to apply the 1957 Limitation Convention. Article 15 of the 1993 Convention reads that nothing in the Convention "shall affect the application of any international convention providing for limitation of liability or of national legislation giving effect thereto".

The Morgage and Lien Conventions are relevant to the 1976 Limitation Convention insofar as they create or recognize liens based on claims subject to limitation and provide for priority between them. Limitation of liability necessarily imposes a limitation on the amount secured by a lien and the establishment of the fund in essence provides an alternative security to that which the lien would arguably attach. However, the provision in the 1976 Convention, Article 12(1), that subject to the Convention priority provisions . . . "the fund shall be distributed among the claimants in proportion to their established claims against the fund" is clearly inconsistent with the priority rules set out in the Lien and Mortgage Conventions. The overriding effect of the 1976 Convention is reflected in English law through the statutory provision that "no lien or other right in respect of any ship or property shall affect the proportion in which . . . the fund is distributed among several claimants".[13] None of the Mortgage and Lien Conventions is ratified by the United Kingdom.

Other relevant Conventions

Conventions relevant to provisions of the Limitation of Liability Convention concerning jurisdiction to hear limitation claims are the (European) Brussels and Lugano Conventions

11. Article 7. The limit may be raised by national law. As to the raising of limits see SI 1987/855 as amended by SI 1989/1800.

12. Hague-Visby Rules, Art. VIII. So a jurisdiction clause opting for a state in which the global limitation limits are lower than the particular carriage of goods limits is valid—the rules providing an exception (*The Benarty* [1984] 2 Lloyd's Rep. 244). As to general prohibition on opting out through jurisdiction and choice of law clauses see *infra*.

13. Merchant Shipping Act 1995, Sch. 7, Part II. para. 9 (re-enacting Merchant Shipping Act 1979, Sch. 4, Part II, para. 9).

on Jurisdiction and Recognition and Enforcement of Judgments in Civil and Commercial Matters. Other Conventions dealing with more particular matters but relevant to limitation are the Collision (Civil Jurisdiction) Convention 1952 and, insofar as the possibility of release of security is concerned upon the establishment of a limitation fund, the Convention relating to the Arrest of Sea Going Ships 1952. These Conventions are either reflected in or part of English law and are discussed generally in the context of their primary purposes. They are considered later in this chapter as regards jurisdiction and security in respect of limitation claims.

LIMITATION OF LIABILITY IN ENGLISH LAW

THE GENERAL PATTERN

Claims subject to limitation

Save where liability itself is excluded or the appropriate Convention qualified, claims subject to limitation are:

    (i) those within the 1976 Convention relating to global limitation currently incorporated into English law[14]

    (ii) those relating to particular claims in respect of (a) oil pollution (b) carriage of goods and passengers

    (iii) those relating to nuclear damage

    (iv) those against pilots, harbour authorities and those supplying pilotage services under the Pilotage Act 1987

    (v) those against harbour authorities and dock owners in respect of damage to ships and cargoes.

Claiming limitation

Limitation claimed as against the particular liability claimant may always be pleaded as part of the defence or counterclaim.[15] Apart from jurisdictional issues where there may be foreign liability or other limitation proceedings there is no reason why limitation should not be the subject of an action for declaration. Thirdly, limitation of liability may be claimed through a limitation action in respect of all loss or damage arising from one incident or occurrence and hence against numerous potential claimants concurrently. This type of limitation is geared to claims against categories of persons concerned with ships (e.g. shipowners and operators, pilots, and harbours and docks authorities) or exceptionally with a particular type of claim (i.e. oil pollution claims). The procedure (in a varying degree of detail or certainty) is set out in statute and rules of court.

    The jurisdiction of English courts in relation to limitation claims, the law which governs them and the recognition of any foreign decree or settlement in English law, was

---

14. As to exclusion of liability of an owner of a British ship for property damaged or lost through fire or valuable articles lost through dishonest conduct see Merchant Shipping Act 1995, s.186 and fn 8.

15. See RSC Order 18, r. 22. As an example of limitation as a counterclaim see *The Radiant* [1958] 2 Lloyd's Rep. 596.

traditionally approached on the basis that the issue was essentially procedural or remedial. It was therefore seen as a matter solely for English courts and English law. A claimant entitled to a limitation decree under an English statute was not deprived of such a decree because of foreign proceedings, foreign connection, foreign judgment or foreign payments. At most any payment made abroad would be taken into account on the basis on which such a claim could be made in English law.[16]

This almost exclusive forum based approach has been qualified by:

(i) Conventions on Limitation of Liability 1957 and 1976 and the attempts at provision of a limitation fund in one state, with the focus of claims where the fund is established.

(ii) Convention provisions as to jurisdiction and recognition of judgments over claims in relation to which limitation may be claimed—in particular the Brussels and Lugano Conventions on jurisdiction between European States, Conventions concerning claims for oil pollution and rules relating to nuclear damage.

(iii) Consideration of the connection between liability and limitation when deciding whether to exercise jurisdiction (or possibly assessing the governing law) in one or the other type of proceedings.

Where limitation is pleaded in a liability action there are no distinct issues of jurisdiction, applicable law or recognition of judgments. Issues of this kind unique to limitation arise in the context of the limitation action—the claim by the liability defendant to limit. It is particularly this type of action that is the subject of this chapter, through the consideration of claims in regard to which such an action may be brought. These are claims (1) within the Merchant Shipping Act 1995, Part VII ("global limitation") (repealing and re-enacting the Merchant Shipping Act 1979), (2) made in oil pollution claims under the Merchant Shipping Act 1995, Part VI (repealing and re-enacting the Merchant Shipping (Oil Pollution) Act 1971 and the Merchant Shipping Act 1974), (3) under the Pilotage Act 1987 and (4) by docks and canal owners, harbour and conservancy authorities.

1. GLOBAL LIMITATION

The limiting of liability in respect of all claims arising from a single incident has long been recognized by many states. Some follow the system of removing personal liability from the shipowner with the ship and freight the target of the claims. Others, notably the United States, allow the shipowner to avoid liability by abandoning the ship (or what is left of it) to the claimant. The United Kingdom approach (also that adopted in the 1976 and 1957 Limitation Conventions) was to fix an amount per ton of the ship and create from that a fund to be distributed in proportion to the claims.

The United Kingdom is a party to the Convention for Liability for Maritime Claims 1976. Insofar as the parties to the 1976 Convention are concerned that Convention

---

16. *The Giacinto Motta* [1977] 2 Lloyd's Rep. 221 and cases there discussed. See *infra*.

abrogates earlier Conventions. The 1976 Convention came into force in the United Kingdom on 1 December 1986.

The United Kingdom was a party to the 1957 Convention which was incorporated into English law through the Merchant Shipping (Liability of Shipowners and Others) Act 1958. Difficulties were almost invited by incorporation in that manner without the direct application of the Convention text. More fundamentally the framework of the Convention was soon seen as defective, permitting claimants to break the limits too easily while setting compensation amounts too low. Dissatisfaction with the Convention played its part in the creation of separate frameworks for oil pollution claims.[17] Further, the construction of the Convention provision that no other security could be held once security was provided by limitation fund was largely defeated in English law because of an unduly restrictive judicial construction of the English statute.[18]

The 1976 Convention is directly enacted into English law, the text forming Part I of Schedule 4 to the Merchant Shipping Act 1979, with Part II adding English law provisions "having effect in connection with the Convention". The Convention adopts as the basis of limitation the tonnage of the ship in respect of which the claim is made, the tonnage being measured in accordance with the International Convention on Tonnage Measurements of Ships 1969.[19] As from 1 January 1996 the text and accompanying provisions are set out in Schedule 7 of the Merchant Shipping Act 1995. As a consequence, subject to any argument as to the applicable law the Convention will be applied in any proceedings in an English court to any limitation matter within the scope of the Convention.

The 1976 Convention

The Convention provides a framework for limitation of liability[20] of shipowners, ship operators and salvors in respect of the aggregate of all claims arising on a distinct occasion and for the setting up by the persons claiming limitation of a limitation fund.[21] Invoking limitation is not an admission of liability.[22] Once a fund is constituted in a State party having a Convention connection with the claim, other assets held as security *must* be released by the court of any State party, and, if the fund is constituted elsewhere *may* be ordered to be released.[23] Any person making a claim against the fund is barred from "exercising any right in respect of such claim against any other asset" of the person setting up the fund.[24]

---

17. Through the International Conventions on Civil Liability for Oil Pollution Damage 1969; International Convention on the Establishment of an International Fund for Compensation for Oil Pollution Damage 1971. These Conventions were radically amended in 1992. The Conventions were initially enacted into English law through the Merchant Shipping (Oil Pollution) Act 1971 and the Merchant Shipping Act 1974 both as amended by the Merchant Shipping Act 1988. As from 1 January 1996 they are enacted through the Merchant Shipping Act 1995, Part VI. See Chaps. 2, 4.

18. See e.g. *The Wladyslaw Lokietek* [1978] 2 Lloyd's Rep. 520 (fn. 2).

19. Article 6(5). Incorporated into United Kingdom laws by the Merchant Shipping (Tonnage) Regulations SI 1982/841 amended by SI 1988/1910.

20. Articles 1, 9. The Convention does not apply to air cushion vehicles or floating platforms constructed for exploiting the sea bed or subsoil (Art. 15(5)). The Convention is not to be applied to ships engaged in drilling when there is higher limit of liability for such ships (Art. 15(4)).

21. Articles 9, 11.

22. Article 1(7).

23. Article 13(2).

24. Article 13(1).

Applicability of the Convention[25]

The Convention applies to claims within it once a person within the Convention entitled to limit liability seeks before the court of a State party to limit liability or procure the release of a ship or other security in respect of a claim within the Convention. A State party may limit the ambit of the Convention in a number of ways. First, it may exclude from the Convention (a) any person not having his habitual residence in a State party; (b) any ship not flying the flag of a State party. Secondly, it may provide its own system of limitation for (a) ships intended for navigation on inland waterways; (b) ships of less than 300 tons; (c) ships engaged in drilling[26]; (d) claims in which only its own nationals are involved and (e) it may reserve the right to exclude claims in respect of wreck removal.[27]

Courts in which limitation may be claimed

There is no provision expressly specifying any connection between forum and dispute as a prerequisite for claiming limitation. A limitation fund may be constituted in accordance with Article 11 with "the court or other competent authority in any State Party in which legal proceedings are instituted in respect of claims subject to limitation". Limitation may be claimed without constituting a fund but a State party may provide that limitation may be invoked only if a fund has been constituted (Article 10). In that event therefore a limitation claim may be made only where a liability action has been brought so preventing a pre-emptive jurisdictional strike by the limitation claimant. As the Convention makes no jurisdictional provision it is arguable that a national law may impose its own restrictions. Conversely it may be argued that as the Convention specifically gives one restrictive option (to require a fund) it impliedly permits the bringing of a limitation action in any court.

It has been contended[28] that the requirement of liability proceedings is to be applied "by analogy" where there is no prerequisite of a fund. It would then follow that limitation cannot be claimed save where liability proceedings are brought. However, with respect, this construction changes an express Convention optional jurisdictional requirement (constitution of a fund) into a mandatory one. That seems contrary to the Convention.

It has further been contended that the arrest of a vessel amounts to the institution of legal proceedings for the purpose of jurisdiction over limitation claims. This contention is based on the argument that arrest is a preliminary step for the enforcement of a claim and if the vessel is not released the claim may be enforced on the vessel. However, a vessel may be arrested solely for security with proceedings taken elsewhere. If such arrest is seen as the institution of proceedings it provides the shipowner with the power to constitute a fund in a jurisdiction solely invoked for security. At the least it poses a problem of multiple proceedings.

There are no Convention provisions in respect of multiple proceedings and in this context there is little doubt that the Convention role is restricted to its emphasis on one fund and jurisdiction in respect of the state in which it is constituted. It is then a matter

25. See generally Art. 15.
26. When a higher limit is adopted or the state has become a party to a Convention regulating the system of liability in respect of such ships (Art. 15(4)).
27. Article 18(1).
28. Berlingieri [1993] LMCLQ 433.

for that court to consider whether to stay limitation proceedings on the ground of limitation or liability proceedings elsewhere (as to which see *infra*). In this context it is important to consider the power of a limitation claimant to establish a jurisdiction by starting first—and then dragging in the liability claimant.

Persons entitled to limit liability[29]

By the Convention liability may be limited in respect of claims within the Convention by

(a) a shipowner—this including owner, charterer, manager or operator of a seagoing ship
(b) a salvor—this being defined as a person rendering services in direct connection with salvage services, and
(c) an insurer of liability for claims subject to limitation.

The liability of a shipowner includes liability in an action brought against the vessel itself. Limitation may also be claimed by any person for whose act, neglect or default the shipowner or salvor is responsible.

Claims within the Convention[30]

Subject to exceptions and conduct (see *infra*) the claims are set out in Article 2.1 and 2.2. Article 2.1 provides:

"Subject to Articles 3 and 4 the following claims, whatever the basis of liability may be, shall be subject to limitation of liability:

(a) claims in respect of loss of life or personal injury or loss of or damage to property (including damage to harbour works, basins and waterways and aids to navigation), occurring on board or in direct connexion with the operation of the ship or with salvage operations, and consequential loss resulting therefrom;
(b) claims in respect of loss resulting from delay in the carriage by sea of cargo, passengers or their luggage;
(c) claims in respect of other loss resulting from infringement of rights other than contractual rights, occurring in direct connexion with the operation of the ship or salvage operations;
(d) claims in respect of the raising, removal, destruction or the rendering harmless of a ship which is sunk, wrecked, stranded or abandoned, including anything that is or has been on board such ship;
(e) claims in respect of the removal, destruction or the rendering harmless of the cargo of the ship;
(f) claims of a person other than the person liable in respect of measures taken in order to avert or minimize loss for which the person liable may limit his liability in accordance with this Convention, and further loss caused by such measures."[31]

Article 2.2 provides:

---

29. Article 1.
30. Article 2.
31. Claims under (d) are not subject to limitation to the extent they relate to remuneration under a contract with the person liable (*ibid.*) and claims under (d) and (e) may be excluded (Art. 18(1)). The UK has made (d) dependent on the establishment of a fund to compensate harbour authorities for the reduction of amounts recoverable (see *infra*).

"Claims set out in paragraph 1 shall be subject to limitation of liability even if brought by way of recourse *or* for indemnity under a contract or otherwise. However, claims set out under paragraph 1(d), (e) and (f) shall not be subject to limitation of liability to the extent that they relate to remuneration under a contract with the person liable."

Claims excepted by Article 3 are:

(a) claims for salvage or contribution in general average;
(b) claims for oil pollution damage within the meaning of the International Convention on Civil Liability for Oil Pollution Damage, dated November 29 1969 or of any amendment or Protocol thereto which is in force;
(c) claims subject to any international Convention or national legislation governing or prohibiting limitation of liability for nuclear damage;
(d) claims against the shipowner of a nuclear ship for nuclear damage;
(e) claims by servants of the shipowner or salvor whose duties are connected with the ship or the salvage operations, including claims of their heirs, dependants or other persons entitled to make such claims, if under the law governing the contract of service between the shipowner or salvor and such servants the shipowner or salvor is not entitled to limit his liability in respect of such claims, or if he is by such law only permitted to limit his liability to an amount greater than that provided for in Article 6.

In regard to the exclusion under (e) in English law the Convention is excluded from liability for loss of life, personal injury or property of a person "on board the ship in question or employed in connection with that ship or with the salvage operation in question" if he was on board or employed under a contract of service governed by the law of any part of the United Kingdom. It has been pointed out that this may be construed to exclude a wider category of persons than provided for by the Convention—the Convention focus on "servants of the shipowner or salvor" being replaced by persons "on board the ship or employed in connection with the ship or salvage operation".[32]

"Breaking the limits" (Article 4)

It is provided in Article 4 that a person may not limit his liability "if it proved that the loss resulted from his personal act or omission, committed with the intent to cause such loss or recklessly and with knowledge that such loss would result".

This reflects a critical change of approach to the breaking of the limits under the 1957 Convention. Under that Convention the test was that the damage was due to the "actual fault or privity" of the person seeking to limit. The more stringent criteria now adopted is coupled with a change in burden of proof. Formerly it was for the shipowner to show lack of actual fault or privity. Now it is for the liability claimant to show at least the knowledge by the person claiming limitation that loss would result. The difficulty of establishing that there is no limit is increased when the defendant is a company. It must then be shown that acts of the person responsible for the damage are the acts of the company—this depending on where the person is in the company hierarchy. It seems accepted that the limits will normally be unbreakable—a trade off for the higher limits

32. Gaskell in *The New Law* (fn. 9) at p. 57. As to Art. 6 see *infra*—"the limitation amounts".

established in the 1976 Convention. The higher limits have, however, now met the fate of those which they replaced—they are out of date.[33]

The limitation amounts[34]

The amounts are calculated by special drawing rights as defined by the International Monetary Funds.[35] They are converted into the currency of the state in which limitation is sought according to the value of the currency at the date the limitation fund is constituted. In respect of loss of life and personal injury the amounts are—

    (i) 333,000 Units of Account for a ship with a tonnage not exceeding 500 tons;

    (ii) for a ship with a tonnage in excess thereof, the following amount in addition to that mentioned in (i):

        for each ton from 501 to 3,000 tons, 500 Units of Account;

        for each ton from 3,001 to 30,000 tons, 333 Units of Account;

        for each ton from 30,001 to 70,000 tons, 250 Units of Account; and

        for each ton in excess of 70,000 tons, 167 Units of Account,

In respect of other claims the amounts are—

    (i) 167,000 Units of Account for a ship with a tonnage not exceeding 500 tons;

    (ii) for a ship with a tonnage in excess thereof the following amount in addition to that mentioned in (i):

        for each ton from 501 to 30,000 tons, 167 Units of Account;

        for each ton from 30,001 to 70,000 tons, 125 Units of Account; and

        for each ton in excess of 70,000 tons, 83 Units of Account.

The limits of liability for a salvor operating without a ship are calculated according to a tonnage of 1,500 tons.

Where the amount calculated on the personal injury basis is insufficient to meet the claims in full the amount calculated for other claims is available to meet the unpaid balance. The unpaid balance then ranks rateably for all claims, including, with one exception,[36] personal injury and other claims made against the non-personal injury balance.

The Limitation Fund[37]

Subject to Convention provisions relating to the constitution and distribution of the fund and its effect on other actions and security, rules in respect of the fund and connected procedure are governed by the law of the State party in which the fund is established.[38]

---

33. There is provision for revision of the limits through a Conference convened by IMO at the request of not less than one fourth of the States parties.

34. Articles 6, 7.

35. There is provision in monetary units measured in gold for states not members of the International Monetary Fund (Art. 8(2)).

36. A State party may provide that claims in respect of damage to harbour works, basins, waterways and aids to navigation may take priority over claims other than for loss of life or personal injury (Art. 6(3)). As to the United Kingdom see *infra*.

37. Articles 11–14.

38. Article 14.

A person alleged to be liable may constitute a limitation fund in a State party "in which legal proceedings are instituted in respect of claims subject to limitation".[39] The fund is to be of such amount as is set out in the Convention as the limits applicable to the claims made together with interest from the date of the occurrence giving rise to the liability until the date of constitution of the fund. The fund is constituted either by depositing the sum or producing a guarantee acceptable under national legislation of the state where the fund is constituted and considered to be adequate by the court or other competent authority.

Consequences of establishing a fund

Provided a claimant may bring a claim against a fund and the fund is actually available and freely transferable in respect of that claim, any claims so brought will bar the exercise of any right in respect of such a claim against any other asset of the person setting up the fund.[40]

Effect on liability jurisdiction—release of security[41]

Any ship or other property arrested or attached within a State party in respect of a claim lying against the fund must be released if the fund is actually available and freely transferable in respect of the claim and was constituted—

  (a) at the port where the occurrence took place or if it took place out of port at the first port of call thereafter
  (b) at the port of disembarkation in respect of claims for loss of life or personal injury, or
  (c) at the port of discharge in respect of damage to cargo, or
  (d) in the state where an arrest was made.

If arrested or attached in any other State party the ship or property *may* be released. It is for national law to prevent any effect of the release of security on the jurisdiction to consider the liability or limitation claim.

Application of the 1976 Convention in United Kingdom laws

The text of the Convention is applied directly (i.e. has "the force of law") with accompanying provisions specifying the national options taken by the United Kingdom and where necessary translating Convention into national law.[42] The Convention applies to occurrences taking place on or after 1 December 1986.[43]

---

39. See *supra*. Any suggestion that "proceedings" refers to limitation claims seems contrary to the wording linking the proceedings to claims subject to limitation.

40. Article 13(1).

41. Article 13(2).

42. 1979 Act, s.17; 1995 Act, s.185(1). As to the exclusion of liability of owners of British ships for property loss or damage caused by fire or loss of or damage to precious articles through deceitful conduct see s.18 and *supra*. 1979 Act s.18; 1995 Act, s.186.

43. 1979 Act. s.17(4); SI 1986/1052. The Convention itself does not contain any provision limiting its application to acts subsequent to coming into force and State parties have not all made express statutory provisions. However the tendency is understandably to construe it in that way. See (e.g.) (Australia) *The Lorna Doon* [1993] LMLN 367; (Greece) Court of First Instance Piraeus, No. 2505/1991; (France) Cour d' Appel d'Aix en Provence, 9 June.

The national law options under the Convention and the adaptation of Convention provisions into national law are set out in the 1979 and 1995 Acts.[44] The Convention is applied to any ship whether seagoing or not, a ship including any structure (whether completed or in the course of completion) launched and intended for use in navigation as a ship, and to ships under 300 tons with lower limitation amounts. There is no provision making the setting up of a limitation fund a prerequisite for claiming limitation. Where security is released because of the constitution of a limitation fund, the applicant seeking release is deemed to have submitted to the jurisdiction of the English courts.

In respect of wreck removal the Convention is applied only where a fund has been established by order of the Secretary of State to compensate harbour authorities for reduction of amounts recoverable under the Act. Claims excepted from the Convention in respect of oil pollution damage, nuclear damage are specified in terms of English law. It is further specified that the exclusion of salvage claims encompasses a claim for special compensation in respect of damage or threatened damage to the environment.[45]

"Limitation actions"

Prior to 1 December 1986

Prior to 1 December 1986 it was statutorily provided that where "several claims were made or apprehended" the person liable could apply for the determination of the amount of liability and the court could distribute the amount rateably among the defendants.[46] The action was *in personam* and instituted by writ (see *infra*) and the establishment of jurisdiction was as any other action—subject to satisfying any substantive jurisdiction base through service of the writ.

Unless a decree restricted to named defendants was sought, compliance with the procedural steps in the proceedings or service of documents and publicity led to a limitation decree binding against the world. Secondly, even if there was only one claimant it was probably open to a person liable to seek a declaration of limitation. It was judicially suggested that the setting up of the limitation fund under the 1957 Convention as applied in the United Kingdom could found an action for the declaration of the rights flowing from the fund being set up.[47] As a finding or admission of liability was seen as a necessary prerequisite for the finding on limitation the only restriction on claiming after judgment on liability was arguably that that judgment was *res judicata* in respect of the amount of that liability.

From 1 December 1986

The 1976 Convention enacted initially through the 1979 Act differs markedly from its predecessors both as to the Convention provisions and in the United Kingdom because of

---

44. 1979 Act, s.35(2), Sch. 4, Part II; 1995 Act, s.185(4), Sch. 7, Part II, implements Art. 3(e) of the Convention (see *supra*).

45. 1979 Act Sch. 4, Part II, para. 4 as amended by the Merchant Shipping (Salvage and Pollution) Act 1994 Sch. 2, para. 5; 1995 Act, Sch. 7, Part II, para. 4.

46. Merchant Shipping Act 1894, s.504—a provision limited to cases in which there were several claimants (see *The Penelope II* [1980] 2 Lloyd's Rep. 17).

47. Per Brandon L.J. in *The Penelope II* (fn 6) requiring "special circumstances" so as to remove the operation of "the principle"; *The Mekhanik Egrafor (No. 2)* [1988] 1 Lloyd's Rep. 33.

the direct application of the Convention text. First, the claims subject to limitation differed in their categorization.[48] Secondly, the limits will apply unless a claimant proves intention to cause damage or a reckless act with knowledge that damage would probably result. It is not therefore for the shipowner to establish his claim to limit but for the liability claimant to establish (on narrow grounds) that the limits do not apply.

Thirdly, the Convention provisions directly applied means that, although a limitation fund is not a prerequisite for claiming limitation, the fund may be constituted prior to any liability decision. It then follows that any claim made against the fund bars the claimant from an action against any other assets of the defendant and, if the fund is constituted in a Convention country with a specified connection with the claim, no other security may be taken or retained (see *supra*).

The aim of these provisions is to create one fund as a target and to break any link between providing that fund and proof of liability. The purpose is therefore to ensure that where any right to limit is asserted any liability claim should be brought in relation to any fund constituted to support that assertion.

Although there have been fundamental changes in the international framework there is little change to the provisions of enforcement within the United Kingdom. The methods of claiming limitation remain identical and the establishment of a fund is not a prerequisite for invoking limitation. Unless the plaintiff is content with a restricted decree the effect of a limitation decree remains as before—against the world.

The rules of court provide, as before the 1979 Act, for a limitation action. The action is defined simply as: "An action by shipowners or other persons under the Merchant Shipping Act 1979 for a limitation of the amount of their liability in connection with a ship or other property."[49]

Although there is no indication in that definition that a limitation action would not encompass a case in which there was one defendant, the rule providing for service of the writ in the action is arguably drafted on that premise. The constitution and distribution of the limitation fund is governed by Order 75, rule 37A. It is there provided that the fund may be constituted by "by paying into court" the amount to which it is claimed that the liability is limited together with interest from the date of payment into court.[50] Notice must be given "to every defendant".

There has been a change in the rules of court to implement the Convention provision in relation to the release of security upon the constitution of the funds. Under the construction of the 1957 Convention by the English courts the release of other security was dependent upon the limitation claimant satisfying the court of the entitlement to limit. There was no provision in the rules, therefore, for any procedure indicating to liability claimants that a fund had been established. Following the 1979 Act and the link between the right to limit and the claim to do so, the person setting up the fund may warn liability claimants of its existence by the entry of a caveat against arrest in the caveat book.[51]

---

48. See e.g. *The New Law, op. cit.* Chapter II (Brice). Despite some change of wording the Convention did not remove the right of shipowners to limit liability for claims by cargo owners for stevedoring and transhipment costs following a fire and consequent salvage (*The Breydon Merchant* [1992] 1 Lloyd's Rep. 373).

49. RSC Order 75.

50. With the concurrence of the Treasury the Secretary of State may prescribe the rate of interest (Merchant Shipping Act 1979, Sch. 4, para. 8(1)).

51. Order 75, r. 6A—following the suggestions of Sheen J. in *The Bowbelle* [1990] 1 Lloyd's Rep. 532. *The Bowbelle* demonstrates the applicability of the Convention in the United Kingdom even if the circumstances are entirely domestic.

A second consequential change (but not in the rules) is the liability to costs. As has been said, prior to the 1979 Act it was for the shipowner to establish entitlement of limitation and it was held that the shipowner was therefore liable to pay the costs for making good his claim. Since under the 1979 Act it is now for the liability claimant to show non-entitlement to limitation, once the claim has been shown to be subject to limitation the costs of any investigation follow the event. Once the limitation claimant shows that the claim is within the Act the costs will fall on the liability claimant.[52]

The procedure

The limitation action must be brought in the Admiralty Court. It is an action *in personam*.[53] The person seeking relief must be named as the plaintiff and at least one of the liability claimants against him must be named as a defendant. Other defendants may be described generally. The writ must be served on one of the named defendants.[54] The writ may be served in England in accordance with general principles of service of writs *in personam* and out of the jurisdiction in accordance with the rules applicable to collision actions.[55]

A named defendant may acknowledge the issue or service of the writ. Within seven days of such acknowledgment or if there is no acknowledgment within seven days of the time limit for acknowledgment the plaintiff must take out a summons returnable before the registrar asking for a decree limiting liability or, in default of a decree, directions as to further proceedings in the action. The summons and affidavit in support must be served on any defendant who has acknowledged issue or service.[56]

On the hearing of the summons the decree will be made if it appears to the registrar that it is not disputed that the plaintiff has a right to limit. If there is a dispute directions will be given as to the trial of the action (dealing with such matters as pleadings, discovery and summons for directions). If the plaintiff succeeds at trial a decree will issue.[57]

Where a plaintiff seeks a decree good against the world the decree must be advertised as directed in the decree with a time limit of not less than two months from the date of advertisement for claims to be filed against the limitation plaintiff. The decree may be set aside by a person who was not named as a defendant or who has not acknowledged issue of the writ or been served with it. A summons to set aside the decree must be taken out within the period for filing claims. At the hearing of the summons the decree may be set aside if it appears that there is a claim against the plaintiff and sufficient *prima facie* grounds for the contention that the plaintiff is not entitled to the decree.

The Limitation Fund

The plaintiff may constitute a limitation fund by paying into court the amount of the liability as limited and interest at the set rate running from the date of the incident to the

---

52. *The Capitan San Luis* [1993] 2 Lloyd's Rep. 573.

53. Supreme Court Act 1981, s.20(3)(c); Order 75, r. 2. The writ must be in a specified form (rule 3(3)).

54. Order 75, r. 37. A name may be a firm name and a liability claimant describing himself as the owner or as bearing some other relation to the property may be so described in the limitation writ (rule 37(5)).

55. Order 75, rr. 2, 4(1). See Chap. 9 and *infra*.

56. Order 75, r. 38(1)–(4). The summons must be served at least seven days before the hearing on any defendant who has acknowledged issue or service of the writ.

57. Order 75, r. 38(5)–(9). Any person ceasing to dispute liability must file a notice to that effect in the registry (rule 35(8)).

payment in. Subject to the opportunity to file claims or to set aside the decree limits in the funds may be distributed on the making of the decree. Subject to statutory qualifications the fund is distributed to claimants rateably according to the claim,[58] no lien or other rights in respect of the ship or property affecting the proportions (see *supra*).

Discretion in establishing or exercising jurisdiction

The traditional view is that a limitation decree is a matter for the English court. Until the 1957 Convention the existence of a foreign fund appears to have been ignored and the sole recognition of foreign limitation proceedings or settlement was to take payments made into account when distributing the funds. The 1957 Convention appears to have had little effect on this partly because of the restrictive construction by the English courts of the prerequisites for the release of other security once a fund was constituted. On the other hand the 1976 Convention may well be the instrument for linking liability and limitation proceedings and giving scope for discretion in the establishing or the exercise of any jurisdiction in respect of each type of claim. Apart from the need to comply with substantive jurisdiction bases such discretion is relevant to the giving of leave to serve a writ out of England and to the consideration of stay of English proceedings because of a foreign jurisdiction agreement or on the grounds of *forum non conveniens*.

1. Service of writ out of the jurisdiction

Prior to the 1979 Act

As English law has traditionally seen limitation as a matter essentially for the forum in which it is sought, apart from any statutory provision therefore, leave may well be obtained to serve a limitation writ out of England. As a limitation action falls within Order 75 of the rules of court, it is excluded from Order 11, rule 1(1). Further, as is pointed out in the general discussion of jurisdiction in actions *in personam* it is specifically provided that Order 11, rule 1(2), providing for service out without leave, shall not apply to a writ by which any Admiralty action is begun. This exclusion rather curiously seems to have survived the radical change in the content of rule 1(2) following the implementation of the European Conventions on Jurisdiction. As a consequence, leave of the court is required for service of a writ in an "Admiralty action" out of England but where there is jurisdiction under a statute (as to which see *infra*) such leave must be granted (see Chapter 9).

Whatever the definition of "Admiralty action" it certainly includes a limitation action and a limitation action is subject to the prerequisites of connection that apply to a collision action for service out of the jurisdiction. So under Order 75, rule 4, a writ may be served out of the country only if—

(a) the defendant has his habitual residence or a place of business within England and Wales, or

(b) the cause of action arose within inland waters of England and Wales within the limits of a port of England and Wales, or

---

58. Order 75, rr. 39, 40. The claim to set aside must be supported by an affidavit showing that the defendant has a "bona fide claim" against the plaintiff and sufficient *prima facie* ground for the contention that the plaintiff is not entitled to the relief given by the decree (rule 40(2)). The plaintiff may choose to seek a decree only in respect of defendants named in the decree (rule 39(1)).

    (c) an action arising out of the same incident or series of incidents is proceeding in the High Court or has been heard and determined in the court, or

    (d) the defendant has submitted or agreed to submit to the jurisdiction of the High Court.

Such prerequisites reflect the distinction between liability and limitation which flows through English decisions but do not entirely fit with the traditional right of the limitation claimant to select the jurisdiction for litigation.

THE DISCRETION OF THE COURT IN GRANTING LEAVE

Despite some suggestion that the discretion as between Order 75 and Order 11 is not identical it would seem that the principles and the factors set out in *The Spiliada*[59] are those which would be relevant as regards any Admiralty action. In the case of the limitation action the very fact of initiating the proceedings in England would carry great weight given the predominantly forum approach to limitation issues. On the other hand previously instituted limitation proceedings in a foreign court by another claimant in liability proceedings in respect of the same incident would be a factor against service. It may be that the institution of liability proceedings in a foreign court would also militate against service but there is no principle in English law that liability and limitation proceedings should be in the same court.[60]

In *The Volvox Hollandia*[61] a liability claimant sought to make the shipowner defendant litigate limitation in England. The action was based on damage said to have been caused in dredging operations undertaken pursuant to contracts containing English jurisdiction and law clauses. After the damage the Dutch shipowners initiated limitation proceedings in Rotterdam and there constituted a limitation fund. After the start of these proceedings the liability action was brought in London. The writs claimed damages and a declaration that the shipowners were not entitled to limit their liability. The issues were whether there was jurisdiction to make such a declaration and if there was such jurisdiction should leave be granted to serve the writ in Holland given that a limitation action had already been started there. The Court of Appeal was divided on both points.

The court agreed that there was jurisdiction to grant a negative declaration but that that jurisdiction should not be exercised where no proceedings had been brought against the person seeking the declaration. A majority thought that the limitation proceedings in Holland provided compliance with this requirement and emphasized that such proceedings were essentially similar to English limitation actions.

Staughton J. in the court below had granted leave to serve out. The majority of the court reversed him. Kerr L.J. and Nicholls L.J. thought that the first instance judge had overemphasized the importance of the liability and limitation actions being tried in the same court, Nicholls L.J. stressing that "a shipowner is at liberty to choose his domicile court as the forum to set up his limitation fund and establish his right to limit". Kerr L.J. underlined the need for caution in respect of negative declarations because of the encouragement to forum shopping.

---

59. [1987] A.C. 460; [1987] 1 Lloyd's Rep. 1.

60. See e.g. the comments of Kerr L.J. in *The Volvox Hollandia* (reported as *Saipen SpA* v. *Dredging VO2 BV and Geosite Surveys Ltd.*) [1989] ECC 16 para. 36 per Kerr L.J.

61. See fn 60.

Dillon L.J. disagreed, thinking it important to have all the disputes decided in the one court. He appeared, however, to accept that the effectiveness of any English judgment depended on the Dutch view of it and he accepted that where there were multiple liability claimants the shipowner must be able to select the forum. As the case before the court was in reality a one claimant case limitation could be considered in the liability proceedings.

The majority, therefore, placed great weight on the right of a shipowner to limit and the power to choose where to limit, Dillon L.J. and Staughton J. looking more to the link between limitation and liability.

Effect of the 1979 Act

Under the Merchant Shipping Act 1979 (as from 1 January 1996 the Merchant Shipping Act 1995) the link between liability and limitation proceedings has lessened in the sense that a finding of liability is not a prerequisite for limitation claims, there is little chance of limits being broken and no obligation on the person claiming limitation to establish the right to claim it. On the other hand the link between the proceedings has been strengthened in that the limitation fund is the focus of a limitation claim, only one fund need be established and it may be constituted only where liability proceedings have been brought. If that be correct and Holland a party to the Limitation Convention on the facts of *The Volvox Hollandia* there could be no fund constituted there for there had been no liability proceedings instituted. There would therefore be strong grounds for service out of a writ designed to bring limitation proceedings to the liability jurisdiction. The matter is further discussed *infra* in the context of *forum non conveniens*.

2. Stay of proceedings

Relevant to the staying of proceedings after jurisdiction is established is first any statutory rule relevant to the jurisdiction considered mandatory under English law, secondly apart from any mandatory provision the English interest in the proceedings, thirdly on whether the parties have agreed to go elsewhere, and fourthly, lacking any jurisdiction agreement, whether there is a more appropriate forum (*forum non conveniens*).

(a) *The 1976 Convention, jurisdiction agreements and forum interest*

It is possible to envisage a jurisdiction agreement relating solely to limitation proceedings entered into after the events creating the liability to be limited. It is more likely that any jurisdiction agreement affecting limitation proceedings would relate directly to liability proceedings—either in the case of a collision action entered into after the event creating liability[62] or as part of a contract of carriage, liability under which is subject to the 1976 Convention limitation rules.

The 1976 Convention directly affects reliance on a jurisdiction agreement only insofar as it provides uniform limitation rules for contracting States. It could, therefore, be argued that on general principle, any clause opting for a jurisdiction in a contracting State other than the forum be upheld on the basis of enforcement of contract or, conversely, that there

---

62. As provided for in liability proceedings by the Collision (Civil Jurisdiction) Convention 1952, Art. 2—enacted into English law by the Supreme Court Act 1981, s.22(5).

is no reason to uphold it as the law will be the same. The approach will depend on the force given to jurisdiction clauses by the national law.

In the light of the enactment of the text of the 1976 Convention into English law (as distinct from the method of implementing the 1957 Convention) it may be thought arguable that it would be contrary to policy to allow evasion through choice of jurisdiction of a non-contracting State. The purpose of the Convention, it may be said, is to create a uniform system.[63] At the International Conference leading to the 1976 Convention, Liberia proposed the insertion of a clause that would avoid any contractual provision depriving a person of the benefits of the Convention.[64] The proposal received little support, there being some feeling that to prevent waiver of the Convention provisions would be to favour shipowners to an unacceptable degree.

Such evidence as there is, therefore, points against any international Convention mandatory principle, although a national law may create its own. The validity of a jurisdiction agreement having the consequence of application of a different limit or limitation process would be affected only in that event. Even if such an agreement is valid it may that a contracting State would not uphold such an agreement if the selected jurisdiction imposed a lower limit of liability. So an English court may hold that forum interest is sufficiently strong to outweigh the upholding of such an agreement.

(b) *Forum non conveniens*

As pointed out in *The Spiliada*[65] this is simply the other side of the coin to the service of the writ out of the jurisdiction. Apart from any Convention provisions excluding its operation the possible application of *forum non conveniens* to limitation proceedings is twofold—a stay of limitation proceedings either because of such proceedings elsewhere or because of liability proceedings elsewhere. In addition the varying national approaches to limitation may be a factor in a stay of liability proceedings.[66]

Prior to the 1976 Convention the traditional English view that limitation is a matter for the forum made any stay unlikely in either context. A similar situation to that of *The Volvox Hollandia* was posed a little earlier in 1988 in *The Falstria*[67] in that the liability claimants were seeking to make the limitation claimants litigate in the court hearing the liability claims. In this case, however, the liability action was in the foreign court and the limitation claim in the English court. The liability claimants sought a stay of the limitation action—the underlying reason being that at the material time the limitation amounts were higher in Denmark. The case was decided on the basis that there was more than one potential liability claimant and Sheen J. robustly rejected the stay application. The judge held that there was no jurisdiction to stay such an action and, it would seem, that if there was, it would have been unjust in his view to stay a limitation action in which there may be English as well as foreign claimants.

That view is at one with the majority in *The Volvox Hollandia* but the distinction drawn in both cases between single and multiple liability claimants is not as stark as it is made

---

63. And hence mandatory as the Hague-Visby Rules were held to be in *The Morviken* [1983] 1 Lloyd's Rep. 1.

64. Conference Proceedings, pp. 142, 247.

65. [1987] A.C. 460; [1987] 1 Lloyd's Rep. 1.

66. See *The Vishva Abha* [1990] 2 Lloyd's Rep. 312; *Aldington Shipping* v. *Bradstock Shipping* [1988] 1 Lloyd's Rep. 475; *Adhiguna Meranti* [1988] 1 Lloyd's Rep. 384 (overruled [1994] 3 All E.R. 749).

67. [1988] 1 Lloyd's Rep. 495.

to appear. It is with respect to put the matter back to front to hold that a stay should not be granted because it was only through an English decree that the shipowner could effectively limit against all claimants. The effectiveness in reality depends on focusing the liability action on the place of the limitation fund or, at the least, recognition of such a fund by any court before which a liability action is brought.

The existence of multiple claimants is a relevant factor in considering the exercise of jurisdiction in the limitation action but no more than a factor. The view that the place of the limitation proceedings is a matter for the shipowner seems to depend on an insistence on a forum decree. In *The Falstria* Sheen J. took the view that the purpose of limitation action in England was to obtain a limitation decree in relation to claims in the United Kingdom and that could only be declared by a court in the United Kingdom. The only concession to foreign proceedings is the recognition of payments made in pursuance of foreign decrees or settlements—provided this recognition is limited to the principles of payment applied by the English court.[68]

The view that the place of limitation proceedings is a matter for the shipowner seems to put an undue insistence on a forum decree—even where there are multiple claimants. So long as that attitude is prevalent it puts limitation actions into a class of their own in which the whole focus is on English jurisdiction and English law. On this view limitation will be a factor in considering a stay of proceedings only in respect of liability. This seems to be of dubious defensibility particularly in the light of the 1976 Convention.

EFFECT OF THE 1976 LIMITATION CONVENTION

The consequence of the 1976 Convention seems as between contracting States clearly to be the removal of any foundation for undue forum emphasis. There are common limitation principles and once a fund is established a focus of claim is on that fund.[69] There is no Convention provision dealing with multiple proceedings.[70] However, if the Convention intention is to focus on the fund there are strong reasons for staying or preventing any limitation proceedings brought in a contracting State other than that in which the fund is established. If, as appears so, the fund could be constituted only if liability proceedings had been commenced this would support not only a stay of limitation proceedings but any liability proceedings also commenced in another contracting State.[71]

The effect of the 1976 Convention as between contracting States on cases such as *The Falstria* or *The Volvox Hollandia* depends initially on whether the Convention is seen as limiting the establishment of the fund to a country in which liability proceedings are brought.[72] If so, the emphasis on the right and desirability of the shipowner choosing his own jurisdiction for limitation in each case no longer has force. In *The Falstria* there would have been no limitation proceedings in England and in *The Volvox Hollandia* there

---

68. See *The Crathie* [1897] P. 178; *The Kronprinz Olav* [1921] P. 52, (1920) 5 Ll.L.Rep. 203; *The Giacinto Motta* [1977] 2 Lloyd's Rep. 221.

69. See e.g. *The Bowbelle* [1990] 1 Lloyd's Rep. 532. Once the fund is constituted other security must or may be released (see *supra*).

70. An attempt by the United States delegation to introduce such a provision at the Conference considering the Convention met with little support (Conference Proceedings, pp. 325–326).

71. The constitution of more than one fund will call for a *Spiliada* type consideration of the factors relevant to any stay of proceedings in one state (see *supra*).

72. As to whether arrest of a vessel of itself may constitute the bringing of liability proceedings see *supra*.

may have been a case for service out if England was the sole liability forum. There seems no case for forcing a liability claimant into a Convention limitation jurisdiction unless the Convention permits the establishment of a fund when no liability proceedings are brought. The simple starting of limitation proceedings should not be a ground for dragging in the liability plaintiff—it is the constitution of a limitation fund which provides the necessary focal point.

The Convention has no effect on *forum non conveniens* as between an English court and a court of a non-contracting State. However, there must be doubt as to the desirability of continuing any philosophy of absolute forum dominance. The circumstances would seem to call more for a *Spiliada* type of balancing approach.

3. Effect of the Brussels and Lugano Conventions on jurisdiction (as amended)

The Conventions apply to limitation proceedings as to any other, provided that in national law such proceedings are against a defendant. The general jurisdiction bases therefore apply (see Chapters 5, 6). As is seen in Chapter 6 there is a jurisdiction base addressed specifically to limitation proceedings in that it is provided by Article 6a that the court having power to hear the liability action has power to consider any limitation claims.

A serious consequence of the limitation provision is that, subject to any limitation on jurisdiction through the need under the 1976 Limitation Convention for liability proceedings to have been commenced, it authorizes a pre-emptive strike by the person claiming limitation. Because the limitation action is "related" to a liability action (ignoring for the moment any effect of the Limitation Convention) it may then be that the only jurisdiction for both types of action is that of the limitation action (see *infra*).

A subsidiary effect of the 1976 Convention may be, because of the release of property from arrest on the constitution of a limitation fund, to remove reliance on arrest or equivalent security as a basis of liability proceedings within the Brussels of Lugano Conventions.[73] The provision in English law that, where security is released because of the constitution of a limitation fund, the applicant seeking release is deemed to have submitted to the English jurisdiction will not of itself constitute a European Convention jurisdictional base. If the case fell within the substantive provisions of either Convention the question of jurisdiction would then be a matter for the rules of that Convention.

(a) *The service of the writ out of England*

The apparent retention of the need for leave to serve a writ out of the jurisdiction and the prerequisites for the consideration of such leave cannot remain as jurisdictional provisions. At most they reflect procedural requirements but insofar as they conflict with the EC Convention they can have no force. Whether the duration of the writ for service is four or six months depends on whether the requirement of leave is seen as realistic. It would seem difficult to contend that it has any function save automatic procedure given the entitlement to serve (see Chapter 9).

---

73. Through Art. 57, the Arrest Convention 1952 or the Collision Jurisdiction Convention 1952 (as to which see Chap. 5).

(b) *Staying proceedings*

As between courts of States parties it is recognized in English courts that liability and limitation proceedings are "related actions" within Article 22.[74] The court second seised has therefore a discretion to stay the proceedings, whether they be liability or limitation. The court first seised has no such discretion and the court second seised may then be faced with staying liability proceedings because of previously instituted limitation proceedings. It follows that, considering the Conventions alone, the liability defendant may have some control over the place of liability jurisdiction in the sense of being able to initiate proceedings in the jurisdiction of his choice. This could have the consequence that the court first seised would have no power to stay a limitation action even though no limitation fund had been established—despite the fact that it was only in the court second seised that a fund could be constituted through liability proceedings having been initiated there. Where the court second seised has a discretion there normally would be a stay but much lower limitation limits or the setting up of a limitation fund could work against such a stay—particularly if no fund had been constituted in the other court.

The law applicable to limitation issues

The general question of applicable law is the subject of Chapter 26. Limitation poses issues particular to it because of forum dominance. In the light of ever increasing Convention influences and the interrelation between liability and limitation proceedings reference is made to those issues in this chapter.

Apart from Conventions English courts have traditionally viewed all aspects of limitation as an issue for English law—or more generally the law of the forum.[75] The refusal to recognize any rules but the English probably stems from seeing limitation as a matter of procedure or remedy. There is the added factor that principles of limitation vary fundamentally. Further, and importantly, global limitation may apply to multiple liability claims governed by different laws—although the problems thereby caused would not necessarily be relevant to a recognition of foreign decrees (as to which see *infra*). Where there is only one claimant or where all liability claims are subject to the same law arguably limitation should be referred to that law.[76]

Limitation is not however viewed universally as wholly for the forum. A distinction may be drawn between the right to limit (a substantive right) and the amount recoverable (a procedural matter). In the United States *liability* in respect of an event occurring in territorial waters would presumptively be referred to the law of the state in which the waters are.[77] In respect of the amount recoverable the United States Limitation of Liability Act is applied to all limitation proceedings within the United States.

Consistent with the conflicts rule, subject to the limit under the United States Act, insofar as a foreign limitation of liability statute attaches to the right rather than simply limits the sum recoverable as damages the United States courts will apply that statute. So the ability of a time charterer to limit liability or a restriction on a right so that a sum

74. See *Dresser* v. *Falcongate* [1991] 2 Lloyd's Rep. 557.
75. See e.g. *The Giancinto Motta* [1977] 2 Lloyd's Rep. 221; *The Falstria* [1988] 1 Lloyd's Rep. 495.
76. The law of the flag is a further possibility—marred however by the possibility of a flag of convenience and complication of two flags where a vessel is demise chartered (see Chap. 26).
77. For a discussion of the US approach as compared to the approach in Canadian, English and French law see Tetley [1992] 23 JMLC 588.

recoverable is less in amount than recoverable under United States law may be referred to foreign law.[78]

The fundamental requirements in respect of governing law are for an effective international limitation scheme, the constitution of one limitation fund (and one only) to focus all claims on that fund, and to adopt common criteria for assessing limitation and fixing the limits. Even lacking agreement on criteria and accepting that the law of the forum has the strong claim there is much to be said for also accepting that paying no regard to concurrent foreign proceedings with the same aim is neither inevitable nor always desirable. This is, however, as much a matter of jurisdiction as of governing law.

In 1992 in *The Sylt* the Dutch Supreme Court refused to apply the 1976 Convention where under Dutch conflicts rules the right to limit was governed by the law of a non-contracting State. Such an approach has been justifiably criticized as contrary to the purposes of the Convention.[79] Under English law there is little danger of the issue arising because of the reference of all limitation issues to English law. Even if foreign law was considered as relevant to such issues, lacking express choice of law or jurisdiction, foreign law will surely have no part to play in English proceedings where the Convention reflects an international framework and is given the force of law.

From the *travaux préparatoires* it appears highly arguable that no intention can be implied from the Convention that its structure is intended to be mandatory (*see supra*). However, it may be made so by national law and in English law giving it the "force of law" is at the least an indication that in the light of the approach of the House of Lords in *The Morviken*[80] the Convention rule as enacted in English law may be considered as mandatory. Whether or not the Convention is mandatory, because of the forum interest it is highly unlikely that the Convention would not be applied to a limitation action starting in England in accordance with its provisions or where action is taken for the release of security following limitation proceedings in another contracting State.

This approach is qualified in two ways. First, the Convention does not provide a wholly uniform set of rules for matters within it. In some instances it permits national law options and in others refers issues to national law. In particular, subject to the Convention provisions, rules relating to the constitution and distribution of a limitation fund are governed by the law of the state in which the fund is constituted.[81] Secondly and more generally, as indicated in the discussion on jurisdiction within the Convention framework, there is considerable ground for moving away from the exclusive forum focus of the English courts. At the heart of the Convention lies a single limitation fund and once that is constituted in accordance with the Convention all liability in limitation proceedings should be focused on it. By this token forum law will continue to govern but attention will be concentrated not on the right to limit in England but the right to limit once, with the constitution of a fund as a security. There is no reason why such a principle should not operate whether or not the fund is in a Convention state—always subject to non-reference to a foreign jurisdiction or law because of disapproval of criteria or limits.

---

78. See e.g. *The M/4 Swibon* [1985] AMC 722; *The Arctic Explorer* [1984] AMC 2413.
79. Berlingieri [1993] LMCLQ 433.
80. [1983] A.C. 565; [1983] 1 Lloyd's Rep. 1.
81. Art. 14 (see *supra*). The right against a fund of an insurer or other person who has paid a claim is specifically limited to the extent to which subrogation is permitted under national law (Art. 12(3)).

Recognition of foreign limitation decrees

The general question of recognition of foreign judgments is the subject of Chapters 27 and 28. Reference is made here to issues particular to limitation decrees. Apart from the 1976 Convention and the Brussels and Lugano Conventions recognition seems confined to taking account in distributing the fund of payments due or made.

In *The Wladyslaw Lokietek*[82] Brandon J. clearly thought that in many countries and in most cases a plaintiff would have to prove his claim in the country in which the fund against which he was claiming was established. It would help the plaintiff not at all to have established his claim elsewhere. The most in English law that recognition of any foreign act or declaration in respect of limitation achieves for a party is credit for payments made. Even in this respect the person liable must establish that the payment reflects liability under that law. So in *The Giacinto Motta*[83] following a collision shipowners had settled a claim by cargo owners made in the United States on the basis of a liability under that law leading to a payment of double the amount recoverable in English law. They were held entitled to have taken into account in distribution of a fund in England only such sum as the cargo owners could have claimed against the fund, and that was the sum which was recoverable under English law.

Save for the reference to future compulsion to pay compensation the 1976 Convention contains no provision relating to the recognition of judgments. At the International Conference, Australia sought to introduce a comprehensive clause imposing a duty to recognize a judgment "in respect of a claim enforceable under this Convention"[84] given in courts of the state of the defendant's residence or place of business or in courts to the jurisdiction of which the defendant submitted.[85] It received minimal support, primarily on the basis that there were Conventions concerned with the enforcement of judgments and there was some indication that under such Conventions liability judgments would be recognized.

There seems no reason why the general principles of *res judicata* and issue estoppel should not apply in respect of any issue of limitation just as of liability—particularly if litigated within the framework of the 1976 Convention. If this be right, foreign limitation decrees should be recognized as enforceable judgments subject to the general defences.

The Brussels and Lugano Conventions

Any decree pronounced in a court of a contracting State is a judgment to be recognized in all other such states. Only an extreme version of "public policy" could provide a ground for non-recognition on the ground that it was a limitation matter and as between contracting States of the 1976 Convention there should be little room even for that.[86]

---

82. [1978] 2 Lloyd's Rep. 520.
83. [1977] 2 Lloyd's Rep. 221.
84. For the text see Conference Proceedings, pp. 93–96.
85. Later amended (see Conference Proceedings, p. 192) to provide that "if necessary" a contracting State should ensure that a judgment given in another contracting State should be enforceable against a limitation fund in the first state.
86. Although there is an implied preference for limitation proceedings to be in the state in which the limitation fund is constituted there remains the availability of claiming without consulting a fund. As to the recognition of judgments under the Convention and the role of "public policy" see Chap. 28.

2. OIL POLLUTION CLAIMS

A shipowner and (where sued directly) a person providing a security for any claim (the insurer) may limit liability for oil pollution claims made in accordance with the International Convention on Civil Liability for Oil Pollution Damage 1969 initially enacted into English law by the Merchant Shipping (Oil Pollution) Act 1971 (as from 1 January 1996 the Merchant Shipping Act 1995, Part VI, Chapter III).[87] An owner or insurer who has or is alleged to have incurred a liability under that Act may apply to the court for limitation. After a liability finding payment into court may be directed, such payment providing a limitation fund.

Under the Merchant Shipping Act 1974 (as from 1 January 1996 the Merchant Shipping Act 1995, Part VI, Chapter IV)[88] where a claimant cannot obtain full compensation the Oil Compensation Fund is liable for further compensation for such claims, and that liability is itself limited to an amount specified by statute or statutory instrument. In this context the Fund becomes the limitation fund.

(a) *Claiming limitation*

There is no reason why, where in the perhaps unlikely event of there being only one claimant, limitation may not be claimed by the liability defendant through defence, counterclaim or action for a declaration. However, where there are multiple claimants limitation may be claimed as for global limitation through a limitation action under Rules of Supreme Court Order 75.

The limitation action

The 1995 Act provides (in s.158) in terms identical with s.5 of the 1971 Act:

"(1) Where the owner of a ship has or is alleged to have incurred a liability under section 153 he may apply to the court for the limitation of that liability to an amount determined in accordance with section 157.

(2) If on such an application the court finds that the applicant has incurred such a liability and is entitled to limit it, the court shall, after determining the limit of the liability and directing payment into court of the amount of that limit,—

    (a) determine the amounts that would, apart from the limit, be due in respect of the liability to the several persons making claims in the proceedings; and

    (b) direct the distribution of the amount paid into court (or, as the case may be, so much of it as does not exceed the liability) among those persons in proportion to their claims, subject to the following provisions of this section.

(7) The court may, if it thinks fit, postpone the distribution of such part of the amount to be distributed as it deems appropriate having regard to any claims that may later be established before a court of any country outside the United Kingdom.

---

87. The 1969 Convention becomes the 1992 Convention on the coming into force of 1992 Protocols on 30 May 1996. The 1995 Act contains transitory provisions pending the amendment.

88. The 1971 Convention becomes the 1992 Convention on the coming into force of 1992 Protocols on 30 May 1996. The 1995 Act contains transitory provisions pending the amendment.

(8) No lien or other right in respect of any ship or other property shall affect the proportions in which any amount is distributed in accordance with subsection (2)(b) of this section."

The limits may be broken against the owner on much the same narrow grounds as for global limitation, i.e. where the liability claimant proves that the discharge escape or contamination threat resulted from anything done or omitted to be done either with the intent to cause the damage or cost or recklessly and in the knowledge that any such damage or cost would result.[89] In a direct action against the insurer the limits may not be broken.[90]

Under the Convention as reflected in the Act actions are to be brought in a State party where the damage occurs subject only to the possibility of damage occurring in more than one such state. As limitation may be claimed in respect of liability incurred or alleged to have incurred under the Act it must follow that a limitation action may be brought in England only where the liability includes liability for damage or cost in the United Kingdom. A limitation action under Part VI of the 1995 Act is governed by the same jurisdictional and procedural rules as for that under Part VII[91] (see *supra*).

Stay of proceedings

As the Convention framework seeks to concentrate claims in respect of damage or cost in a State party in the courts of that party the scope for declining jurisdiction in respect of Convention countries is restricted. However, as recoverable damage or cost extends to other Convention countries there is in that context the implied possibility of a more appropriate forum within the Convention—including the agreement of the parties on one forum. Further, as under the Act the establishment of a limitation fund in another Convention country is to be recognized it would seem that both or either liability and limitation proceedings may be the subject of an application for stay. Declining jurisdiction in respect of a non-Convention country would mean in effect not applying the liability or limitation scheme reflected in the 1971 Act. That is hardly likely.

THE "LIMITATION FUND" AND THE CONSEQUENCES OF CONSTITUTING SUCH A FUND

On any application for limitation a court must first find liability, and then direct payment into court of the amount of the limit. So unlike a limitation action under Part VII ("global limitation") the court is under an obligation to find liability before considering limitation and to direct that a "fund" be constituted. Once the fund is established

    (i) the court "shall order" the release of any other security
    (ii) no judgment or decree for any claim shall be enforced save as to costs
    (iii) the making of the payment relieves from liability any other person who is liable for the damage or cost and is entitled to limit his liability in respect of the ship.[92]

---

89. Merchant Shipping (Oil Pollution) Act 1971 (as amended) s.4(3); Merchant Shipping Act 1995, s.157(3).
90. *Ibid.*, s.12(3); 1995 Act, s.165(3).
91. A claim must be brought within such time as the court directs (1971 Act, s.5(3); 1995 Act s.158(4)).
92. 1971 Act, ss.6(1), 7; 1995 Act, ss.159, 160.

LIMITATION FUNDS OUTSIDE THE UNITED KINGDOM

Where a person is liable under both the laws of the United Kingdom and the law of another Convention country for the same damage or cost, any limitation fund established in that other country will have the same consequence in the United Kingdom as one established there.[93] As a result any security must be released and any judgment resulting from any action in the United Kingdom not enforced.

The applicable law

There is little doubt that the statutory principles are mandatory. It follows that any agreement as to applicable law will have no effect. The laws of Convention countries apply insofar as a limitation fund established there is to be recognized as a basis for release of security and the channelling of liability to the person liable under Part VI of the 1995 Act where there is concurrent liability and power to limit.

Recognition of foreign judgment

A judgment of a court of a Convention country to enforce a claim in respect of liability on corresponding grounds to the Act is to be recognized under the general principles of the Foreign Judgments (Reciprocal Enforcement) Act 1933.[94] Such recognition will resolve any issue of liability including limitation.

Global limitation and oil pollution limitation compared

There are therefore a number of differences between the oil pollution and global limitation schemes. That relating to oil pollution retains many of the characteristics of the global limitation scheme as it was prior to the Limitation of Liability Convention 1976 and the Merchant Shipping Act 1979. So there is an interaction between liability and limitation issues and the establishment of the fund is through court direction. On the other hand the release of other security is mandatory in respect of an oil pollution claim while only mandatory in certain circumstances where global limitation is claimed.

Further, any judgment of a Convention court "to enforce a claim" within the ambit of Part VI of the 1995 Act is to be recognized and enforced in the United Kingdom. While, therefore, limitation may be pleaded if the judgment simply goes to liability it is difficult to argue that any judgment as to the amount for which a defendant is liable is not also to be recognized or enforced.

(b) *Limited liability of the International Fund for Compensation for Oil Pollution*

The International Fund is liable only if the claimant for damage or cost has been unable to recover full compensation against the person liable, one of the narrow exclusions does not apply and the reason for the failure to recover is one specified in the 1995 Act.[95] One

---

93. 1979 Act, s.8; 1995 Act, s.169.
94. 1979 Act, s.13(3); 1995 Act, s.166(4).
95. See Chap. 2. Apart from the cost of and damage caused by preventative measures the Fund may be exonerated from liability if it proves that the pollution damage resulted from an act or omission of the claimant against it intending to cause or negligently causing the damage (s.4(8)–(9A)); 1995 Act, ss.175(8)(10).

such reason is that the damage or cost exceeds the limited liability of the person liable. The liability of the Fund is in turn limited in respect of any incident to an amount calculated in accordance with the Fund Convention as set out in Schedule 5 to the Merchant Shipping Act 1995.[96]

Proceedings may be taken against the Fund directly under the Merchant Shipping Act 1995. Notice of any claim against a defendant asserted to be liable may be given to the Fund and the Fund may be granted leave to intervene in any action against that defendant (whether notice is given or not) (see Chapter 9). So the Fund is provided with an opportunity to raise limitation in proceedings concerning it.

Limitation is enforced through the requirement that a court must notify the Fund of any judgment against it and that no such judgment is to be enforced without leave of the court. Such leave is not to be given unless and until the court is notified by the Fund of any reduction in the amount for which the Fund is liable. The judgment is then enforceable only for the reduced amount.[97]

Jurisdiction, applicable law and recognition of judgments

As limitation by the Fund is implemented through leave to enforce a liability judgment against it, there is no separate limitation action or limitation decree. Issues of jurisdiction applicable law and recognition of judgments are therefore those applicable in the context of the liability claim and are considered in Chapter 26.

(c) *Effect of the Brussels and Lugano Conventions*

As indicated in Chapter 5 these Conventions will affect oil pollution claims only insofar as matters relating to jurisdiction and judgments are not covered by the Oil Pollution Conventions.

3. THE PILOTAGE ACT 1987

The liability of an authorized pilot, the harbour authority or the person supplying pilotage services (the agent) and employing a pilot for loss or damage caused upon any one distinct occasion by an act or omission by a pilot employed by it may be limited. The liability of the pilot is not to exceed £1,000 together with the cost of pilotage charge and that of the authority and the agent £1,000 multiplied by the number of authorized pilots employed by the authority or agent respectively at the date the loss or damage occurs.[98]

In any action against the authority or agent the limit may be broken only by the type of personal act or omission which would be grounds for breaking the limit in respect of global limitation claimed under the Merchant Shipping Act 1995, Part VII, i.e. "personal

---

96. Section 176. Merchant Shipping Act 1974, s.4A, Sch. 1. The provisions may be amended by statutory order to give effect to any Convention amendment (s.4A(5)).
97. Merchant Shipping Act 1974, s.4A(3); 1995 Act, s.176(3).
98. Pilotage Act 1987, s.22(1)–(3).

act or omission committed with the intent to cause such loss or recklessly and with knowledge that such loss would probably result".[99]

Nothing in the limitation provision relating to harbour authorities or agent "shall affect any liability that may be limited" or "is excluded" under Part VII of the 1995 Act. This somewhat curious wording presumably means that the power to limit under the Pilotage Act does not affect the power to limit under the 1995 Act. As a consequence, as with carriage claims, limitation works within the global limitation scheme and not in substitution for it.

Claiming limitation

As in other contexts of limited liability there is no reason why limitation may not be pleaded as a defence or be the basis of an action for a declaration. In addition s.22(6) of the Pilotage Act 1987 provides:

"Where any proceedings are taken against any person ('the defendant') for any act or omission in respect of which liability is limited as provided by this section and other claims are or appear likely to be made in respect of the same act or omission, the court in which the proceedings are taken may—

    (a) determine the amount of the liability;
    (b) upon payment by the defendant of that amount into court, distribute that amount rateably amongst the claimants;
    (c) stay, or in Scotland sist, any proceedings pending in any other court in relation to the same matter;
    (d) proceed in such manner and subject to such requirements as the court thinks just—
        (i) as to making interested persons parties to the proceedings;
        (ii) as to the exclusion of any claimants whose claims are not made within a certain time;
        (iii) as to requiring security from the defendant;
        (iv) as to payment of any costs."

The right to claim limitation is therefore restricted to liability proceedings. The court is given broad powers in those proceedings as to procedure, discretion as to security and ensuring that all interested persons are before the court. While this is a limitation right to be exercised in relation to a specific type of claim (as with the plea of limitation in a carriage claim) it covers all liability arising out of a distinct occasion (as with oil pollution claims).

There is express power to stay other proceedings but no power to reopen the distribution once made. However, the discretion in respect of the proceedings is wide enough to ensure the defensibility of any distribution through a notice to potential claimants and general procedural control.

Jurisdiction, applicable law and recognition of judgments

A court may consider limitation only in liability proceedings. There are, therefore, no issues going solely to limitation, jurisdiction, applicable law or recognition of judgments.

---

99. See s.22(3)(4).

4. DOCK AND CANAL OWNERS, HARBOUR AND CONSERVANCY AUTHORITIES

Subject to the criteria for breaking limits under the Merchant Shipping Act 1995, Part VII, the liability of dock and canal owners, harbour and conservancy authorities is limited in respect of loss or damage caused to a vessel or anything on board arising upon one distinct occasion.[100] The limit is ascertained by applying to the ship the calculation of the 1976 Convention applying to claims other than loss of life *or* personal injury as applied in the United Kingdom (see *supra*). The provisions relating to constitution and distribution of the Limitation Fund in the 1976 Convention and the statutory provisions relevant thereto having effect in connection with the Convention apply. So no lien can affect the distribution (see *supra*).

Limitation may be claimed as a defence, counterclaim or by declaration. The applicability of the Limitation Fund provisions of the 1976 Convention necessarily equates limitation proceedings with those of global limitation. The limitation action will therefore lie under RSC Order 75 with the same procedure as for global limitation. The issues of jurisdiction, governing law and recognition of judgments are identical to those of global limitation.

---

100. Merchant Shipping Act 1995, s.191 re-enacting the Merchant Shipping (Liability of Shipowners and Others) Act 1900, s.2, as amended by Merchant Shipping Act 1979, s.19, Sch. 5, Part 1. Where the defendant is a dock owner the entitlement to limit depends not on the capacity in which the work is done but on the fact that it is done in the dock (*The Ruapehu* (1927) 27 Ll.L.Rep. 385 (H.L.))—and that means where the damage is caused (*Mason* v. *Uxbridge Boat Centre* [1980] 2 Lloyd's Rep. 592). For discussion see *The New Law, op. cit.* at pp. 57–60 (Gaskell). The power to limit liability applies to damage or loss resulting from directions by a harbour master to control dangerous vessels under the Dangerous Vessels Act 1985 (see s.2 as amended by the Merchant Shipping Act 1995, Sch. 13, para. 74).

CHAPTER 25

Remedies in Actions on the Merits

FINALITY OF LITIGATION—THE EFFECT OF A JUDGMENT OR ARBITRATION AWARD

A critical feature of many legal systems is the prohibition of relitigation of a cause of action or issue upon which judgment has been pronounced in a case in which the person seeking relitigation was a party. In English law the principle is implemented generally through *res judicata* but appears on occasion as cause of action, issue estoppel or simply abuse of process. Essentially connected with it is the concept of merger of a cause of action into a judgment so that the judgment becomes the sole source of the remedy. There may well be a critical distinction between merger and estoppel in that merger destroys the cause of action while estoppel can be countered by a contrary estoppel. So the party relying on issue or cause of action estoppel may itself be estopped by conduct from that reliance—as for example where the parties have agreed that the action should have limited effect on any further action.[1]

The focus of any prohibition on relitigation and of merger into judgment is the issue on which judgment has been given and the parties bound by it. Connected to this essential requirement is the question of the extent to which either principle applies when a cause of action may be pursued in different ways with different consequences. This raises the question of the nature of and relationship between an action *in personam* and an action *in rem*.

It is established that a cause of action *in personam* or *in rem* merges into the equivalent judgment, but that a judgment in one is no bar to an action in the other. The recent need to analyse the action *in personam* and *in rem* in the context of the Brussels Convention (see Chapters 2, 4) has led to a focus on reality rather than technicality. In truth it would seem impossible not to agree with the underlying philosophy of the decision of the European Court in *The Maciej Rataj*[2] that the difference between the two is anything more than alternative routes to achieve the same end. However, the parties are not necessarily the same, and, even if they are, the differences in the scope and nature of remedies attached to each justify the conclusion that there is no merger of both in a judgment in one. Further, as Clarke J. held in 1994 in *The Indian Grace (No. 2)*[3] issue and cause of action

---

1. *The Indian Grace* [1993] A.C. 410; [1993] 1 All E.R. 998 (see Chapter 27). An issue estoppel may arise when there has been no argument on the merits if a case has been put followed by submission to an order—the issue could have been litigated. See *SCF Finance Co. Ltd.* v. *Masri (No. 3)* [1987] 1 All E.R. 194.

2. [1995] 1 Lloyd's Rep. 302.

3. [1994] 2 Lloyd's Rep. 331.

estoppel will play their part in any attempt to relitigate just as in two actions *in personam* or *in rem*.

As has been held in a number of cases it may be that the parties to an action *in rem* are not identical to an action *in personam*, for any person having an interest in the property that is the target of the action *in rem* is a potential party. But the fact that a person may suffer loss as the result of the action does not necessarily make that person a party and whether the parties are the same an action *in personam* will depend on the identity of the actual parties. It will be on the common identity that the relevance of any issue estoppel or cause of action estoppel will depend. It *may* be that the presence of different parties in one cause of action makes the principles non-applicable.

It follows that where a judgment has been obtained *in personam* or *rem* no party to the cause of action can relitigate it by the same route. However a plaintiff may obtain a judgment in an action *in personam* or *in rem* and then pursue the alternative route —subject always to issue estoppel or a plea of abuse of process. It seems that by adapting the principles applicable to judgments to arbitration awards the original cause of action *in personam* is merged in the award but a cause of action *in rem* is not merged.[4] As a consequence an award or judgment on an award will not prevent further suit *in rem* in respect of any unsatisfied part of the claim.[5] It appears that an action *in rem* may be brought on the award if it will lie on the original claim.[6]

REMEDIES GENERALLY AND IN ADMIRALTY

Remedies and grounds

There are two primary aspects relating to the remedy:

1. the remedy awarded by a court or arbitral tribunal; and
2. the enforcement of the judgment.

1. THE REMEDY AWARDED

The general pattern

Jurisdiction over remedies

Once the court exercises jurisdiction on the merits it has jurisdiction in respect of any applicable remedy. Whether, however, any order is made to do or refrain from doing an act outside England will depend on the nature of the remedy and connections between England and the elements of the dispute—particularly the defendant. Normally the enforcement of a judgment on the merits out of England will require recognition and enforcement through the courts of the state of enforcement. However, where a defendant is within the jurisdiction of the English court there is power to make an order in relation to acts outside England. Whether or not the power is exercised is a matter for discretion bearing in mind "the self-imposed limitation" that "a state should refrain from demanding

4. See *The Rena K* [1979] 1 All E.R. 397 at p. 416; *The Stella Nova* [1981] Com.L.R. 200.
5. *The Stella Nova* (fn 4).
6. *The Saint Anna* [1983] 1 Lloyd's Rep. 637.

obedience to its sovereign authority in respect of their conduct outside the jurisdiction", the intervention in another state through any order to act or not to act in that state and whether or not any order is directly enforceable.[7]

The question of remedies directed at acts outside England has usually arisen in the context of interim relief but the principle there asserted would seem not to be restricted to such relief.[8] Further there is power to prohibit a party from participating in initiating or continuing foreign proceedings and thereby ensuring in the appropriate case that it is the remedy in English proceedings which in English eyes at least is that which is to be enforced. The power is to be exercised with due regard to the powers of the foreign court, and the plaintiff is required to show that the proceedings are vexatious or frivolous. A strong factor in so showing would be an English jurisdiction or arbitration clause. Where such a clause confers exclusive jurisdiction (as under the Brussels Convention) the case is unanswerable, and where the court concludes there is a valid arbitration clause the case is very strong. The award of the injunction is always open to the argument that it is for the foreign court to determine its own jurisdiction and that an English court considering a foreign jurisdiction clause would itself exercise discretion. It is a matter of assessing the arguability of the case that the foreign court may take a different view.[9]

As is discussed in Chapters 27 and 28 an English court will enforce a foreign judgment in accordance with established criteria. Any remedy awarded must, however, be recognized in English law.[10]

Remedies in actions "in personam"

The types of remedy and modes of enforcement in actions *in personam* in Admiralty are with some exceptions simply adaptations of those types and modes available generally. The Supreme Court Act 1981 encompasses in a general provision (s.49) the section of the Supreme Court of Judicature (Consolidiation) Act 1925 (s.43) enacting that all remedies are available in all divisions of the Supreme Court.

Some types of claims are recognized only in Admiralty and it follows that the appropriate remedy is peculiar to Admiralty.[11] So, in a salvage claim, the salvage award and, in general average contribution claim, the contribution ordered find no direct counterpart in other commercial claims. However, in essence, the orders are for money payments based on a particular claim, and the peculiarity of Admiralty goes to the claim rather than the remedy.

Remedies in actions "in rem"

It is in respect of the Admiralty action *in rem* that rules peculiar to Admiralty primarily apply. It may be argued that just as with salvage and general average the claim and not the remedy is peculiar to Admiralty so in the context of the action *in rem* it is procedure and

7. See e.g. the discussion in *Mackinnon* v. *Donaldson Lufkin Corpn* [1986] 1 All E.R. 653; *Derby* v. *Weldon (No. 2)* [1989] 1 All E.R. 1002.
8. As to interim relief in litigation see Chaps. 14–16, in arbitration proceedings see Chap. 13.
9. See e.g. *The Continental Bank* v. *Aeakos Compania Naviera* [1994] 1 Lloyd's Rep. 505; *The Angelic Grace* [1995] 1 Lloyd's Rep. 87. Such a stay is not interim relief—see *Sakana* v. *Freyre* [1994] 1 Lloyd's Rep. 57.
10. See *Phrantzes* v. *Argenti* [1960] 2 Q.B. 19.
11. So the principle of limitation of liability in respect of maritime claims attracts principles of its own, see Chap. 24. The *remedy*, however, is, in the end, an order for payment of money as compensation for loss.

not the remedy which is unique. In 1972 in *The Conoco Britannia*[12] Brandon J. intimated that, in his view, the statutory provisions empowering each branch of the High Court to consider the remedies available in every branch meant that in an action *in rem*, first, an equitable remedy could be awarded and, secondly, that it was arguable that a money judgment exceeding the value of the *res* could be awarded.

Such an approach necessarily implies that the power to award remedies overrides any distinction in concept between actions *in personam* and actions *in rem* (as to which see *infra*). Whether or not remedies *in personam* are available in actions *in rem* the action *in rem* carries with it its own unique remedy—the judicial sale. The ability to bring an action *in rem* creates the ability to arrest the property (usually a ship) in respect of which the action is brought. Once under arrest, the claimant may ask that the property be sold and, subject to priority questions, the proceeds made available for claimants *in rem*—i.e. all those who issue writs *in rem* prior to the distribution of the fund.

Types of remedies

Actions "in personam"

A major division, when considering the enforceability of judgments and awards, is that between money judgments and orders focusing on acts other than payment of money.

(i) Payment of money

GROUNDS OF THE REMEDY

The category of "money judgments" should not be allowed to conceal distinctions between grounds of money judgments—compensation for loss, proprietary relief, repayment of debt, reward for services rendered. A liquidated sum of money may be due because of agreed compensation, because the action is to enforce a debt as the result of proprietary relief or the consequence of particular statutory provisions. An unliquidated sum of money may be due not only as compensation for loss but as a reward for services rendered or as a contribution to a loss suffered directly by others. Apart from any application of unjust enrichment the award for services rendered is not developed in English law except for salvage in maritime law, and the principle of contribution towards loss applies generally only in respect of those jointly liable for loss. In maritime law, however, it applies so as to enforce contribution from those who have not suffered loss to those who have—a sacrifice of some for all (general average). Any distinction between maritime and other claims lies in their substantive basis rather than in the remedies available. Once decide on liability and the remedy follows.

JUDGMENTS IN FOREIGN CURRENCY

After some judicial skirmishing it was established in 1975 by the House of Lords that English courts may give judgments in foreign currency.[13] In 1973 the courts had recognized that arbitrators sitting in England had power to make awards in foreign currency.[14] In establishing that judgments could be given in foreign currency the House of

---

12. [1972] 2 Q.B. 543.
13. *Miliangos v. George Frank (Textiles) Ltd.* [1976] A.C. 443.
14. *Jugoslavenska Oceanska Plovidba v. Castle Investment Co. Inc.* [1974] Q.B. 292 (C.A.).

Lords also held that, if there was need to enforce the judgment, the amount awarded should be converted into sterling at the date of leave to levy execution or enforce an award.[15] Judgment should be given in the currency in which the loss was sustained, i.e. that currency in which a plaintiff normally conducts business or (failing the establishment of such a currency) that in which the loss immediately arose.[16]

INTEREST ON DEBTS AND DAMAGES

Prior to the union of the court structure in 1875 the power to award interest varied as between courts of common law, equity and Admiralty. By the Judgments Act 1838 decrees and orders of courts of equity were made to have the effect of judgments at common law. Every judgment debt was to carry interest at a statutory rate from the date of judgment, this being applied to arbitration (Arbitration Act 1950, s. 20). The rate is amended by statutory instrument under the Administration of Justice Act 1970, s. 44 (see SI 1993/564). By the Private International Law (Miscellaneous Provisions) Act 1995, s. 1 the 1970 Act is amended to provide that the rate of interest where a judgment is expressed in foreign currency is to be that declared by the court or arbitration.

The provision in the Law Reform (Miscellaneous Provisions) Act 1934 conferring the power to order the payment of interest between cause of action and judgment[17] failed to take account of late payments of money due prior to the judgment and made no reference to arbitration. However, the Administration of Justice Act 1982[18] provided for power to award interest on late payments, adding s. 35A to the Supreme Court Act 1981:

"(1) Subject to rules of court, in proceedings (whenever instituted) before the High Court for the recovery of a debt or damages there may be included in any sum for which judgment is given simple interest, at such rate as the court thinks fit or as rules of court may provide, on all or any part of the debt or damages in respect of which judgment is given, or payment is made before judgment, for all or any part of the period between the date when the cause of action arose and—
(a) in the case of any sum paid before judgment, the date of the payment; and
(b) in the case for which judgment is given, the date of the judgment."

Further, where the debt is paid in full after proceedings are instituted but before judgment, the court may order interest to be paid in respect of the period between the date

---

15. *Miliangos* v. *George Frank (Textiles) Ltd.* [1976] A.C. 443. See Practice Direction [1976] 1 W.L.R. 83. Where a company goes into liquidation the conversion date in respect of foreign currency creditors is the starting of the winding up (*Re Lines Bros Ltd.* [1983] Ch. 1), disagreeing with the suggestion in *Miliangos* that it is the date of admission of the claim.

16. *The Despina R* [1979] A.C. 685. As to agreed rate of exchange, see *The Agenor* [1984] LMLN 130. Where there is a claim and counterclaim the liability is finalized on settlement of the amounts owing and that is the date for any necessary conversion. See *The Transoceanica Francesca* [1987] 2 Lloyd's Rep. 15.

17. Interest may be awarded on the order to make interim payments and if there is repayment that interest may be ordered to be repaid and further interest to be paid for the use of money without legal right. See *Mercer Co. of the City of London* v. *New Hampshire Insurance Co.* [1992] 1 Lloyd's Rep. 431 (this judgment being later rendered of no effect as the Court of Appeal set aside the judgment on which repayment depended—see [1992] 3 All E.R. 57). In exercising its power to backdate costs in favour of a successful appellant the Court of Appeal should normally select the date of the first instance judgments but may select a date which would fairly take account of fluctuating interest rates (*Kuwait Airways Corp.* v. *Iraqi Airways Co. (No. 2)* [1995] 1 All E.R. 790). The 1995 Act provision comes into force on an appointed date.

18. Section 15, Sch. 1, Part 1. In respect of damages for personal injuries or death exceeding £200 interest shall be included unless the court finds special reasons why it should not be (s.35A(2)). Interest may not be so awarded for any period while interest is already running (s.35A(3)). As to the prior rule, see *The La Pintada* [1984] 2 Lloyd's Rep. 9.

of the debt arising and the date of payment.[19] Subject to contrary provision, arbitration agreements are deemed to contain a provision allowing arbitrators to award simple interest on any sum awarded or on any payment made prior to the award.[20]

(ii) Orders other than for the payment of money

PROPRIETARY RELIEF

Such relief is claimed on the basis of entitlement—that the defendant has or claims the use or control of an asset which the plaintiff claims as owner or holder of a lesser proprietary interest. It may be that as a remedy the plaintiff is *entitled* only to damages as compensation. In some cases, however, the claim is essentially to funds on the basis of ownership and in others, delivery up of a tangible asset which would be difficult to resist—such as, for example, where a shipowner claims possession from a charterer after the ending of the charter.

Tracing. The legal and equitable remedy of "tracing" permits a plaintiff to follow a proprietary interest he claims in an asset through to other assets (including money) substituted for it.[21] Care must be taken to distinguish between the right to follow the interest in the hands of the person originally having it and the right to follow it as against others. Tracing is essentially a remedy to overcome loss of identity—whether it can be used against parties other than the "original" defendant depends on whether the claim enables it to be enforced against a third party (i.e. is proprietary).

ENFORCEMENT OF CONTRACTS AND OTHER ACTS

Specific performance is available as a discretionary remedy and has been used to enforce a contract for the sale of a ship.[22] It must be recalled that ships and other chattels are "goods" under the Sale of Goods Act 1979, and, it may be argued, that the availability of the remedy does not mean that the claimant is a "beneficial owner"—as it would in the case of land.[23] Mandatory injunctions may be granted to enforce other acts, but not to compel performance of a time charter.[24]

TERMINATION OF CONTRACTS—RESCISSION AND RECOGNITION OF REPUDIATION

A party to a contract is entitled to rescind a contract on the basis of an element external to the contract rendering it voidable (as, for example, fraud or other misrepresentation or, in some instances, mistake). The effect is to place the parties in the position they were in prior to the contract and a court order may be required to accomplish this. A party to a

---

19. Section 35A(3).

20. Arbitration Act 1950, s.19A (inserted by Administration of Justice Act 1982, s.15, Sch. 1, Part IV).

21. See e.g. *Romalpa Case* [1976] 2 All E.R. 552; *Borden (UK) Ltd.* v. *Scottish Timber Products* [1981] Ch. 25 and Chap. 21. As to tracing as an ancillary remedy to a *Mareva* injunction, see Chap. 16.

22. See e.g. *Behnke* v. *Bede Shipping Co.* [1927] 1 K.B. 649; *The Stena Nautica (No. 2)* [1982] 2 Lloyd's Rep. 336. A contract may be rectified to reflect the parties' intention. See e.g. for an application of the principle to a charterparty *The Nai Genova* and *Nai Superba* [1984] 1 Lloyd's Rep. 353; *The Rhodian River* [1984] 1 Lloyd's Rep. 373.

23. The remedy is made available by the Sale of Goods Act 1979, s.52. As to the consideration of "equitable ownership" in such a context, see *The Permina 3001* [1979] 1 Lloyd's Rep. 327. A purchaser must show that damages are not adequate—*The Stena Nautica (No. 2)* [1982] 2 Lloyd's Rep. 336.

24. Compare *The Iran Bohonar* [1983] 2 Lloyd's Rep. 620 with *The Scaptrade* [1983] 2 All E.R. 763.

contract is entitled to treat the contract as "repudiated" if the other party is so in breach that the contract is deemed terminated. Such a breach may arise because of breach of a specific term stating that breach will have that effect or because it goes to the root of the contract. The effect is to relieve the innocent party (or in some cases both parties) from future obligation.[25] There is no court order required in the exercise of this remedy, issues before the court turning simply on whether treating the contract as repudiated was justified.

ENFORCEMENT OF ARBITRAL AGREEMENTS AND AWARDS

An arbitration agreement will, if non-domestic, mean a mandatory stay of proceedings in England contrary to it. If the agreement is domestic, the court has discretion to order a stay.[26] It will, however, be for a court to decide on the validity of the agreement should that be challenged.

An arbitral award may be enforced by an action *in personam* on the award (i.e. the contract to comply with the award) or under the Arbitration Act 1950, s.26.[27] The two differ only in the means, there being no need under the Arbitration Act for an action on the award. In both there is a need to establish the arbitration agreement and the award. A court may remit or set aside an award.[28]

(iii) Prohibition or restraint of acts—injunctions

As is seen in Chapter 14, the interlocutory injunction has become a much used remedy in respect of maritime claims. The injunction is available in its interlocutory or final form both as a substantive remedy and as an aid to execution of a judgment.

(iv) Compensatory orders

Many judgments and orders are compensatory—compensating the claimant for loss or damage. In the main these will be money judgments.

(v) Declaratory orders

A court may make a binding declaration of right.[29]

---

25. See *Photo Production Ltd.* v. *Securicor Transport Ltd.* [1980] A.C. 827. As to the right to choose whether to treat the contract as at an end and claim damages, or seek to enforce it, see *The Alaskan Trader* [1984] 1 All E.R. 129 (shipowners' no legitimate interest in keeping a charterparty in existence). The obligation accrued by the date of acceptance of repudiation remains. See *The Blankenstein* [1983] 3 All E.R. 510 (the deposit due in contract of sale of a ship).

26. See Chap. 13.

27. As to the procedure see RSC Order 73. An application may be made *ex parte* but the court may direct a summons (rule 10). Such a summons may be served out of England by leave of the court (rule 7). The award itself is confidential unless it was reasonably necessary to disclose it to establish legal rights against a third party: *Hassneh Insurance* v. *Mew* [1993] 2 Lloyd's Rep. 243; *Insurance Co.* v. *Lloyd's Syndicate* [1994] LMLN 392.

28. See Arbitration Act 1950, s.23, RSC Order 73.

29. See RSC Orders 15 and 16. It will not however use this power to decide hypothetical or future disputes: *Re Barnato* [1949] Ch. 258. As to the use of and limitations on declarations of right when the parties have nominated a body other than the courts to resolve disputes see *Mercury Communications Ltd.* v. *DG of Telecommunications, The Times*, 10 February 1995 (H.L.).

Actions "in rem"

Ex hypothesi an action *in rem* relates to a thing—a thing which may be a chattel or security lodged in its stead. Where it is a chattel it is available for all claims *in rem* and the issue of priority is necessarily raised. Where bail is lodged with the court or security is provided on the basis of a contractual arrangement between plaintiff and defendant there is no question of priority—there is simply a sum of money available to satisfy the claim. Where security other than a *res* is provided, the "thing" remains the defendant's asset and is, therefore, also liable in an action *in personam*—and the question of priority of claim again becomes relevant. And it must be recalled that in many cases actions *in personam* or *in rem* are concurrent proceedings in relation to the same claim.

Apart from priority the primary remedial questions relevant to an action *in rem* are (i) the availability of the judicial sale; and (ii) the restriction (if any) on remedies *in personam*.

Judicial sale

(A) GENERAL POWERS

In any action a court has power to order the sale of property (the subject of a claim) which is perishable, likely to deteriorate or in relation to which there is good reason for sale.[30] Such a sale of itself would be subject to encumbrances existing prior to the sale.

(B) PROPERTY UNDER ARREST

The Admiralty Court may order the appraisement and sale of property[31] under arrest[32] on the motion of a party to the action or the Admiralty Marshal.[33] An order for sale may have added to it an order specifying the period after which priorities will be determined and publication of the details of sale and the opportunity to lodge claims within the period.[34] An order may be made at the hearing of the action or under the general power of sale, pending suit.[35]

A sale pending suit is normally ordered on the grounds that retention of the property will cause the plaintiff's security to diminish if for no other reason than the mounting costs of arrest. It is unusual that such an order is made in a defended case where alternative

30. RSC Order 29, r. 4.
31. The sale of a ship includes all property on board other than that owned by someone other than the shipowner (*The Silia*) [1981] 2 Lloyd's Rep. 534). As to bunkers see *The Eurosun and the Eurostar* [1993] 1 Lloyd's Rep. 106; *The Saetta* [1993] 2 Lloyd's Rep. 268. For jurisdiction as to proceedings, cf. the Supreme Court Act 1981, s.21(6) and Chap. 2.
32. RSC Order 75, r. 23. A sale under this rule is confined to property that must be under arrest but it would seem that sale under RSC Order 29, r. 4 is available in all Admiralty actions and, indeed, the power to order sale pending suit stems from RSC Order 29, r. 4. (See *The Myrto* [1977] 2 Lloyd's Rep. 243, at pp. 259–261.) In any event, a court may order the discharge and sale of cargo not under arrest where a ship in which the cargo is loaded is under arrest and an order for sale is made in respect of it. (See *The Myrto* [1978] 1 Lloyd's Rep. 11, at p. 13.) Compare County Court Rules, Order 40.
33. Such an application is within the Marshal's general power to make applications in respect of property under arrest (RSC Order 75, r. 12). Arrest cannot it seems be used to enforce an English judgment *in rem* but may arguably be used to enforce a foreign judgment *in rem*. (See Chap. 15.)
34. RSC Order 75, r. 22. The period may be extended by application (*ibid*).
35. The order may be directed to lie in the office until crew still aboard her have left. (See e.g. *The Vasilia* [1972] 1 Lloyd's Rep. 51; *The Fairport* [1965] 2 Lloyd's Rep. 183 or, pending repairs, see e.g. *The Sullivar* [1965] 2 Lloyd's Rep. 350.)

security will be provided, but it may be made where it would be unreasonable to keep property (particularly a ship) under arrest for a long period.[36] However, where (i) the plaintiff would be in no better position except that arrest costs would cease; and (ii) a sale after release would bring a greater price, the ship may be released from arrest rather than sold.[37]

Notice of motion must be served on any person who has obtained judgment against the ship and all caveators. Upon an order being made, the party obtaining it[38] must file a praecipe in the form specified in the rules of court regarding a commission for the appraisement and sale.[39] The commission will be issued to the Admiralty Marshal ordering the property to be sold "for the highest price that can be obtained" but not for less than the appraised value except with leave of the court. The commission will be executed only on an acceptable undertaking by the party requesting the sale to pay all fees and expenses. Once a commission is issued it is contempt of court for the owner to attempt to sell the ship.[40] To allow such a course would make the Marshal's task impossible.[41]

The Marshal may sell the property in a foreign currency. The proceeds, whether in a foreign currency or in sterling, will be paid into court and will be invested only on application.[42] The effect of a sale of property under arrest in an action *in rem* is to give a title free of encumbrances to the purchaser.[43] The practicality of such an order depends on mutual recognition between states.[44]

Remedies "in personam"

Since the decision in *The Dictator* in 1982 the English rule is clear in that participation in the proceedings of any kind will mean that henceforth the action is one of *personam* as well as *rem* (see Chapter 9). As a consequence all remedies *in personam* and *in rem* are available.

If in an action *in rem* no person appears as a defendant the weight of English authority supports the proposition that there can be no liability attaching to him as a person. The liability is limited to the thing.[45] In 1907, in *The Burns*,[46] the Court of Appeal emphasized the distinction between actions *in personam* and *in rem* and that "no personal liability can

---

36. See *The Myrto* [1977] 2 Lloyd's Rep. 243, at pp. 259–261 where Brandon J. considered the principle of sale *pendente lite*. On appeal, his decision on this point was upheld ([1978] 1 Lloyd's Rep. 11).

37. See *The Marco Reefer* [1981] LMLN 50.

38. For an example of a defendant owner requesting the order, see *The Westport* [1965] 1 Lloyd's Rep. 547.

39. RSC Order 75, r. 23(1). In *The Halcyon the Great (No. 2)* [1975] 1 Lloyd's Rep. 525, Brandon J. ordered a re-offering of a ship on the undertaking of parties opposing a sale below the appraised value to indemnifying the court against any loss following from non-acceptance of the highest bid then available.

40. *The Jarvis Brake* [1976] 2 Lloyd's Rep. 320.

41. *Ibid.* But an arrest and subsequent order for appraisement and sale does not affect the terms of a charterparty in relation to the ship. So if by those terms a ship is redelivered by charterer to owner and the owner takes over and pays for fuel on board the title to the fuel passes to the owner despite the order (*The Span Terza (No. 2)* [1982] 2 Lloyd's Rep. 72 reversed on a construction point [1984] 1 Lloyd's Rep. 199 (H.L.)).

42. *The Halcyon the Great (No. 2)* [1975] 1 Lloyd's Rep. 525. Practice Direction [1982] 2 W.L.R. 660.

43. See e.g. *The Acrux* [1962] 1 Lloyd's Rep. 405; *The Cerro Colorado* [1993] 1 Lloyd's Rep. 58. It may be contempt of court to place an advertisement stating that despite any sale the ship will remain encumbered (*ibid*). Compare the sale under the writ of *fieri farias* (see *supra*).

44. See *The Acrux* (fn 43); *The Ship Galaxias* [1989] LMLN 240 (Fed. Ct. Canada).

45. Although there are "defendants" in actions *in rem*. See Chaps. 2, 10.

46. [1907] P 137. See further Chap. 10.

be established" against owners who do not appear. It follows that the remedies are limited in kind and amount to the *res*.

However, in 1972 in *The Conoco Britannia*,[47] Brandon J. suggested that if the issue of liability for an action greater than the value of the thing arose a court would have to look carefully "at the form of judgments in Admiralty actions *in rem* in the High Court and the relevance and applicability of the present rules of the Supreme Court relating to money judgments". He suggested that perhaps the provisions of the Supreme Court of Judicature (Consolidation) Act 1925 and the Administration of Justice Act 1956 would lead to the disappearance of any distinction between "what can be done when a defendant appears and what can be done when he does not appear". However, with respect, neither practice as to forms of judgment nor statutory provisions relating to money judgments can overturn the clear distinction between actions *in rem* and actions *in personam*.

(A) DAMAGES

Even granting the procedural approach, there is no basis for the award of damages against a defendant against whom there is no action brought. To move to such a position is to move to an acceptance that seizure of assets gives jurisdiction generally over a defendant. And that, surely, is contrary to accepted English jurisdictional principles.

(B) EQUITABLE REMEDIES

In *The Conoco Britannia*, Brandon J. held that a claim for specific performance could be made in an action *in rem*, and that any question of whether it should be made against a "defendant" who has not appeared was a matter of discretion and not jurisdiction. The view was based on statutory provisions conferring the power to consider all claims (legal or equitable) in one proceeding. But, with respect, this assumes the validity of the argument that there is no difference between an action *in personam* and an action *in rem*—the question at issue. It is the same question as that raised in the context of damages.

The principle that equitable remedies *in personam* require jurisdiction *in personam* was applied in 1973 in the Canadian Federal Court in *Antares Shipping Corpn* v. *The ship "Capricorn"*[48] and in 1980 by Sheen J. in the High Court in *The Stolt Filia*.[49] So long as jurisdiction *in personam* is not based on seizure or presence of property it is difficult to see how liability *in personam* can follow from an action *in rem* only.

2. ENFORCEMENT OF JUDGMENTS OF ENGLISH COURTS

A judgment for the payment of money or delivery of goods will order the defendant to pay or render up the goods. Interest runs in respect of a judgment debt from the moment of judgment or damages assessed. A judgment for an order other than the payment of money will simply order that an act be done or be not done.

---

47. [1972] 2 Q.B. 543. See further Chap. 10.
48. [1973] F.C. 955, Pratt J. The case went on appeal but this issue was not raised.
49. [1980] LMLN 15.

Judgment for money payment

A judgment for the payment of money may be enforced through one of the following:

(i) A *writ of fieri facias* authorizes the sheriff to seize and sell the debtor's goods to satisfy the judgment, although the execution of this may be stayed.[50] The effect of such a sale of property by a sheriff in execution of a judgment does not provide a purchaser with any better title than that held by the debtor. A purchaser with notice of the issue of the writ will take subject to any claim reflected in it once the writ is delivered to the sheriff.[51]

(ii) Through *garnishee proceedings* the court may order any person in the jurisdiction indebted to the judgment debtor to pay the judgment creditor. The service of a garnishee order nisi attaches the funds and an order absolute operates an order to pay. Included in that which may be attached is a deposit account in a bank or other deposit-taking institution or any withdrawable share account.[52]

(iii) *An order for foreclosure or sale.* A mortgage may be enforced by an order for foreclosure, for sale or appointment of a receiver. An equitable charge may be enforced by an order for sale or appointment of a receiver.

(iv) A *charging order*[53] on a judgment debtor's interest in land, securities or funds in court will create an equitable charge enforceable against a trustee in bankruptcy or liquidator of a company—such charge not being a direct method of enforceability but providing security for the claim. An order will be enforced by the remedy applicable to an equitable charge, i.e. by obtaining an order for sale.

(v) *Appointment of a receiver by way of equitable execution.*[54] As a method of execution the appointment of a receiver is seen as available lacking any other method. It amounts to a charge over personal property but only if the receiver is directed to pay the money to or hold it for the execution creditor.[55]

(vi) *An order for sequestration of property or committal of or fine imposed on the defendant for contempt of court* may result from failure to comply with an order of the court.[56]

(vii) Proceedings may be taken in *bankruptcy* or *winding up* of a company.

---

50. See RSC Order 45, r. 1. The execution of the writ may be stayed (see RSC Order 47, r. 5). In granting a stay under this rule the court has declared its powers to pierce the corporate veil and to probe into real control of companies. *Orri* v. *Moundreas* [1981] Com.L.R. 168; *Canada Enterprises Corpn Ltd.* v. *MacNab Distilleries Ltd.* [1981] Com.L.R. 167.

51. Supreme Court Act 1981, s. 138. Notice of an issued but unexecuted warrant of execution in the hands of a county court registrar results in a similarly lower priority of a purchaser (*ibid*). As to the effect of withdrawal of a sheriff because of an erroneous court order—no loss of priority—see *Bankers Trust* v. *Galadari* [1986] 3 All E.R. 794 (C.A.).

52. RSC Order 49. See *Choice Investments Ltd.* v. *Jeromninon* [1981] 1 All E.R. 225. Seamen's wages may not generally be attached. (See the Merchant Shipping Act 1995, s. 34(1) (see Chap. 18). As to that which may be attached, see extension of procedure through the Supreme Court Act 1981, s.40, as amended by the Administration of Justice Act 1982, s.53. For construction of Order 49 generally see *SCF Finance Co. Ltd.* v. *Masri* [1987] 1 All E.R. 194.

53. See Charging Orders Act 1979; RSC Order 50.

54. See the Supreme Court Act 1981, s.37(1); RSC Order 51.

55. See e.g. *Re Potts* [1893] 1 Q.B. 648; *Re Pearce* [1919] 1 K.B. 354. As to appointing a receiver in respect of foreign assets see *Derby* v. *Weldon (No. 2)* [1989] 1 All E.R. 1002.

56. See RSC Order 45, r. 5; RSC Order 52.

(viii) A *Mareva injunction* may be granted to ensure the non-dissipation of assets pending execution of a judgment,[57] with the sanctions set out in (vi) for failure to comply with the injunction.

Judgment other than for money payment

A judgment for an order other than the payment of money may be enforced:

(a) through a writ of delivery up of goods or money or where the order is to deliver within a specified time and delivery is not made, a writ of sequestration or order of committal[58];

(b) in the case of an order to do or refrain from doing an act through a writ of sequestration or order of committal.[59]

---

57. See *Orwell Steel Erections* v. *Asphalt and Tarmac (UK) Ltd.* [1985] 3 All E.R. 747. As there is a power to grant such an injunction as incidental to and dependent on the enforcement of a substantive right it may be granted in respect of a judgment debt owed by another (*Mercantile Group AG* v. *Aiyela* [1994] 1 All E.R. 110).

58. RSC Order 45, rr. 4 and 13. As to procedure relating to the issue of the writ, see RSC Order 46.

59. RSC Order 45, r. 5.

PART VI

Foreign Law

CHAPTER 26

Application of Foreign Law

I. THE ENGLISH APPROACH

The presence of a foreign element of any kind in any disputes raises the possibility that a foreign rule may be used by an English court to resolve that dispute. To decide which of a number of potentially applicable rules applies, English law adopts what might be labelled an automatic pigeon-hole approach. It groups claims into categories (i.e. it "classifies" a claim) and attaches to these categories choice of law rules. As a safety valve to prevent a domestic explosion through an unacceptable result by this automatic process it provides for rejection of the rule because of "public policy".

The conflicts process of English law is largely judge made, and it is relatively rare to find a choice of law rule in a statute. However, a statutory dispositive provision may be construed as "mandatory" in that it is to apply to every case within it whether or not according to the process it would be the governing law. More fundamentally there may be statutes providing for choice of law in respect of particular matters. Of these, three are "choice of law" statutes—the Foreign Limitation Periods Act 1984, the Contracts (Applicable Law) Act 1990 and the Private International Law (Miscellaneous Provisions) Act 1995.

The 1984 Act was intended to bring English law more in line with other systems in recognizing that rules as to limitation of time applicable to a claim should be those of the law governing the claim rather than (as a matter of procedure) the forum. The Contracts (Applicable Law) Act 1990 implemented in English and Scottish law the Rome Convention 1980 on the law applicable to contractual obligations.[1] The Act provides rules for deciding the law applicable to contracts within its scope including provision for the mandatory dispositive rule (see Contract *infra*). By the Private International Law (Miscellaneous Provisions) Act 1995 rules are provided for the law applicable to substantive issues characterized as tort or, for Scottish law, delict (see Tort *infra*). There is no doubt that, unless qualified, where statutory rules provide for choice of law these are mandatory in the sense that parties cannot contract out of them.

1. THE THREE STAGE PROCESS

1. Subject to statutory provisions as to choice of law the process consists of three stages. The relevant issue before the court is classified as either "procedure" or substance.

---

1. Including the Brussels Protocols 1988 on the interpretation of the Convention by the European Court (not yet in force) and as amended by the Luxembourg Convention 1984 (on the accession of Greece). The Act is to be amended by SI 1994/1900 on UK ratification of the Convention bringing into its ambit the Funchal Convention 1992 (on the accession of Portugal and Spain). As to the Convention and its effect see generally Plender, *The European Contracts Convention*, Sweet & Maxwell, 1991; Kaye, *The New Private International Law of Contract of the European Community* (Dartmouth), 1993.

If classified as procedure the issue is referred to forum law: if substantive, as falling into one of a number of categories based on legal concepts (such as contract, tort or property).[2]

2. Each category has attached to it "selection rules" which automatically apply—leading to the rule which will apply to the disposal of the issue (the dispositive rule). So, for example, any question relating to the validity and effect of a transfer of a tangible thing is referred to the law of the place where the property was at the time the issue arose and a contractual issue to the "proper law of the contract". Where a statute creates a cause of action but does not contain its own choice of law provision[3] it may classified within an established substantive category such as tort or simply as a statutory claim *sui generis*. So a claim under the Fatal Accidents Act 1976 could be viewed as statutory or (if it is based on the defendants' negligence) tortious.[4] A wages claim within the Supreme Court Act 1981, s.20(2)(o), could be regarded as a statutory claim having its own choice of law rules or a claim in contract, its resolution depending on the property law of the contract.

3. In appropriate cases there will be consideration of "public policy"—does it nullify the selection process of stages 1 and 2? Public policy flits as a ghost throughout the choice of law process. On occasion, it seems to have been used fairly unashamedly to "classify" as issue so as to provide the basis for selection of the desired dispositive rule; but its primary manifestation is an escape route from an unpalatable result reached through the application of stages 1 and 2. If the application of the dispositive rule selected by the process produces a domestically unacceptable result it seems as if the result will be replaced by the application of English law.

The operation of English "public policy" on foreign legislation

English courts will not enforce foreign revenue laws,[5] foreign penal laws[6] or laws repugnant to public policy.[7] Non-penal laws providing for expropriation of assets will be

---

2. This being recognised as regards tort by the Private International Law (Miscellaneous Provisions) Act 1995 (s. 9(2)).

3. For provisions dealing with choice of law in respect of particular matters, see e.g. the Unfair Contract Terms Act 1977, s.27; the Employment Protection (Consolidation) Act 1978, s.153(3); the Civil Jurisdiction and Judgments Act 1982, s.26(3) (property retained pending foreign court's judgment); The Merchant Shipping Act 1995, s.17(7) (law governing ownership and mortgages of ships registered in UK because of demise charters). See also Civil Liability (Contribution) Act 1978, s.1(5); Merchant Shipping Act 1995, Sch. 7—the Limitation Convention 1976, Article 14 (as to which see Chap. 24). As to insurance within the E.U. see p. 583.

4. See e.g. *Koop* v. *Bebb* (1957) 84 C.L.R. 629 (High Ct. of Australia).

5. See e.g. *Government of India* v. *Taylor* [1955] A.C. 491; *Brokaw* v. *Seatrain UK Ltd.* [1971] 2 Q.B. 476.

6. I.e. a law imposing a penalty by a state as distinct (e.g.) from a "penalty" in a contract. It is for the English court to determine if a law is "penal" in this context. See *Attorney General of New Zealand* v. *Ortiz and Others* [1982] 2 Lloyd's Rep. 224. A further category of unenforceable foreign laws is said to be "public laws" but the existence and content of this group is debatable. See e.g. *Attorney General of New Zealand* v. *Ortiz (supra)*. Compare Staughton J. (at first instance) [1982] 1 Lloyd's Rep. 173, at pp. 185–187; Lord Denning, M.R. (in C.A.) [1982] 2 Lloyd's Rep. 224, at pp. 231–233. See also Private International Law (Miscellaneous Provisions) Act 1995, s.14(3), referring to "penal revenue or other public law".

7. A concept as impossible to define in this context as any other, but it does not extend to foreign laws simply inconsistent with English law—it is focused on laws contrary to fundamental concepts or national interest. See also the exception to governing law principles of the Rome Convention of "*ordre public*" (Art. 16)—as to which see *infra*.

recognized insofar as they affect assets in the relevant foreign territory at the date of seizure.[8]

2. LIMITATIONS ON THE SELECTION PROCESS

(a) The scope of the dispositive rule

Substantive limitation

Clearly, it is only if the rule by its own terms applies to an issue that it comes into contention as a potentially governing rule; but it must be stressed that its scope is a matter of domestic law of which it is part as distinct from its application as a result of the choice of law process. So the Hague-Visby Rules apply by virtue of Art. X:

"Article X
The provisions of these Rules shall apply to every bill of lading relating to the carriage of goods between ports in two different States if:
   (a) the bill of lading is issued in a contracting State, or
   (b) the carriage is from a port in a contracting State, or
   (c) the contract contained in or evidenced by the bill of lading provides that these Rules or legislation of any State giving effect to them are to govern the contract,
whatever may be the nationality of the ship, the carrier, the shipper, the consignee, or any other interested person."

It is only if the case is within Art. X or any statutory provision applying the rules[9] that the question arises whether the provisions apply as part of the law governing the issue.[10] So in *The Komninos S*[11] the contractual application of English law to a contract of carriage of goods by sea did not include the rules—for the case fell outside the ambit of the rules as applied by the rules themselves and the Act applying them. If the case is within the ambit of the rules whether or not they apply depends on the conflicts process of the forum.

Statutory provisions—is a connecting link required?

Provided a matter falls within the material scope of a statutory provision the question arises of the connection (if any) required between the matter and England for the provision to operate. Traditionally where there was no indication the general presumptive limitations

---

8. See *William and Humbert Ltd.* v. *W. and H. Trade Marks (Jersey) Ltd.* [1986] 1 All E.R. 129 (H.L.) and authorities there considered. A discriminatory law (e.g. based on racial grounds) may not be recognized. See *Oppenheimer* v. *Cattermole and Co.* [1975] 1 All E.R. 538 (H.L.). As to positive provisions for non-recognition or enforcement see Protection of Trading Interests Act 1980; Shipping and Trading Interests Act 1995.

9. As ss.1(3)(6)(a) of the Carriage of Goods by Sea Act 1971.

10. See also International Regulations for Preventing Collisions at Sea 1972 which apply to "all vessels upon the high seas and in all waters connected therewith navigable by seagoing vessels" (rule 1(a)) (see SI 1989/1798). The conflicts rule may require the applicability of the English regulations applying the rules as part of the governing laws or as a mandatory rule (see *infra*). The scope of any Convention in any country depends on the national enacting provisions. For a case turning on the construction of the Carriage of Goods by Sea Act 1971, s.1(3) (enacting the Hague-Visby Rules) see *Mayhew Foods Ltd.* v. *Overseas Containers Ltd.* [1984] 1 Lloyd's Rep. 317.

11. [1991] 1 Lloyd's Rep. 370. The bill was not issued in a contracting State, the carriage was not from a contracting State and, it was held, simply opting for "British law" did not of itself mean that the legislation giving effect to the rules should apply to the contract.

were to acts within the territory of the United Kingdom and (possibly) to British subjects wherever they may be. The limitations to the territory is a recognition of practicality and recognition of other legal systems, but in today's world it is unlikely that the reach of English civil legislation would be seen to extend generally to British citizens when in other states. In 1974 in *The Esso Malaysia*[12] Brandon J. considered the application of the Fatal Accidents Act 1976 to a claim based on the death of a foreign seaman resulting from a collision between two foreign ships on the high seas. Brandon J. drew a distinction between statutes[13] (i) creating new rules of conduct and (ii) removing exceptions to common law liabilities or attaching new liabilities to the violation of existing rules of conduct. The territorial limitation, in the judge's view, attached only to category (i). Such a dichotomy makes sense only if it accepted that the common law rules being amended themselves apply extraterritorially. And, it may be asked, wherein lies the rationale between common law and statutes in respect of territorial application.

Despite any presumption relating to extra-territoriality the scope of the statute will depend on the nature of the statute and the response to the enquiry as to persons and events intended by Parliament to be within the provisions. It is in essence an enquiry as to the need for a connecting link and if seen as requiring such a link, identifying it. Apart from express provision identification of the link depends on the policy of the statute.[14] So it may be held that the connecting link is a relevant event in England (as arbitration in England in respect of the power under the Arbitration Act 1950 to grant interim relief[15] or in respect of carriage at least departure or arrival in the United Kingdom[16]), or that the statute applies only if English law is the governing law[17] or that it applies in English proceedings whatever the governing law (the mandatory dispositive rule).

(b) The mandatory dispositive rule

Until 1982 (apart from the general application of public policy) English law had rarely consciously considered the question of whether a rule "overrode" the conflicts process.[18] However, in 1965, in a maritime context, the construction of "maritime liens" in the statutory jurisdiction framework was construed in *The Acrux*[19] to mean English maritime

---

12. [1974] 2 Lloyd's Rep. 143; [1974] 2 All E.R. 705.

13. Adopting Dicey and Morris, *Conflict of Laws*, 9th edn p. 352, see now 12th edn (general discussion of statutes) pp. 16–17.

14. See the discussion in *Re Paramount Airways Ltd.* [1992] 3 All E.R. 1—holding that "any person" in the Insolvency Act 1986, s.238 (in the context of reversal of transactions for under value) included a person abroad having a connection with England. Compare the approach of the New Zealand C.A. to a statutory provision relating to the priority of registered ship mortgages in *The Betty Ott* [1992] 1 NZLR 655 (as to which see Chap. 23).

15. See *Channel Tunnel Group* v. *Balfour Beatty Construction* [1993] 1 Lloyd's Rep. 291, [1993] 1 All E.R. 664 (H.L.) (and the principles discussed by Staughton L.J. in the Court of Appeal [1992] 2 Lloyd's Rep. 7).

16. So the power to legislate in respect of "carriage by air" is limited to carriage within the UK or carriage having departure or destination in the UK—it could not apply to carriage within a foreign state (*Holmes* v. *Bangladesh Biman Corpn* [1985] 1 All E.R. 852 H.L.)).

17. See e.g. *The Acrux* [1965] P. 391 (maritime lien); *The Betty Ott* (New Zealand) fn 14.

18. In tort until the introduction of statutory reform through the 1995 Act the general selection principles impose actionability under English and foreign law—thereby mandatorily applying English law to every case as *part* of the conflicts process. (See generally Tort, *infra*.)

19. [1965] P. 391. Compare e.g. *Sayers* v. *International Drilling Co. NV* [1971] 2 Lloyd's Rep. 105; *The Rosso* [1982] 2 Lloyd's Rep. 120, in which the Court of Appeal ignored the question of whether a relevant statutory provision was mandatory.

liens. In 1982 in *The Morviken*[20] the House of Lords held that the statutory provision prohibiting derogation from the Hague-Visby Rules could not be avoided by choice of law. The concept of the mandatory rule attains statutory recognition through the Private International Law (Miscellaneous Provisions) Act 1995 (see *infra* "Tort") and the Contracts (Applicable Law) Act 1990 in which basic references of substantive contractual issues are to the law selected by the parties or where there is no selection, the law of the country most closely connected to the contract. These however are subject to (i) forum mandatory rules,[21] and (ii) despite choice the rule of another country if that rule cannot be derogated from by choice and all other relevant elements point to that country.[22] Forum mandatory rules are those which apply irrespective of choice of law, foreign mandatory rules are those which cannot be derogated from by contract.

(c) Foreign law deemed to be English law

Foreign law must be proved as a matter of fact. If it is not proved (or pleaded) it is deemed to be identical with English law. Parties may, therefore, control the application of foreign law.

3. CHOICE OF LAW AND JURISDICTION

(a) Discretionary jurisdiction—relevance of governing law

In most contexts questions of governing law arise only after jurisdiction has been established. However, jurisdiction may depend on governing law. First, where there is an express and enforceable choice by contract the law selected may impose a jurisdiction framework (as, for example, through the Hamburg Rules[23] and Athens Convention on Carriage of Passengers and their Luggage[24]). Secondly, where leave of the English court is required to create jurisdiction through service of a writ out of England the exercise of discretion to grant leave may depend on a contract being governed by English law.[25] Thirdly, a jurisdiction or arbitration agreement will depend for its validity either on that agreement as such or the law governing the substantive contract.[26]

It may be arguable that in deciding whether to *exercise* jurisdiction courts should pay more attention than they presently do to the question of which law they will have to

---

20. [1983] A.C. 565. See also *The Benarty* [1984] 2 Lloyd's Rep. 244 (C.A.). The prohibition of evasion through a jurisdiction clause in favour of a member State of the European Union or EFTA country is now subject to the mandatory recognition of jurisdiction clauses under the Brussels and Lugano Conventions (see Chap. 5).

21. Sch. Art. 7(2). Art. 7(1) (providing for the discretionary application of the mandatory rules of a country of close connection) is not enacted into English law.

22. Sch. Art. 3(3)—the choice is "not to prejudice" the application of these rules. See *infra* "Contract".

23. See Art. 21.

24. See Art. 17.

25. RSC Order 11, r. 1(1)(d)(iii). Although this rule applies only outside the Brussels and Lugano Conventions whether or not English law is arguably the governing law will, it would seem, depend on the Rome Convention if the matter is within it. See *Bank of Baroda* v. *Vysya Bank Ltd.* [1994] 2 Lloyd's Rep. 87. For discussion of the point see Morse [1994] LMCLQ 560.

26. Neither type of agreement is within the Rome Convention (Contracts (Applicable Law) Act 1990, Sch. Art. 1(2)(d)). See *infra*.

apply.[27] So where jurisdiction depends on the existence of a transaction (such as a contract) or a right (such as a maritime lien) it may be preferable to refer that question to a law other than the forum (i.e. the putative proper law). It has however been said that such a matter of an English court's "procedural competence" should be determined by an English rule.[28]

However, the Rome Convention 1980 now provides that the existence and validity of a contract or a term is, with one qualification, to be adjudged by the law applicable if it were valid.[29] So, provided the contract (or term) falls within it, there will remain no question of an English court applying the *lex fori* to decide on its jurisdiction if that jurisdiction depends on the existence of the contract.[30] But the provision does not meet the issue of the applicable law depending on which of a number of terms is valid. Further, the Convention does not encompass arbitration or jurisdiction agreements and the validity of such an agreement clause may be critical to the identification of the proper law. The English courts have applied the principle now in the Convention in considering whether to grant leave to serve a writ out of the jurisdiction—at least where it was an English arbitration clause.[31] On the other hand where the issue was whether a contract incorporated an arbitration clause, and there were two possible such clauses (with different consequences) the law of the forum (English law) was applied.[32] This is but another example of the limitations of a principle of choice based on a particular factor (i.e. here, the putative proper law) and there is more than one such factor. The issue does not, however, differ whether or not jurisdiction is at stake (see *infra*) and the view in essence that the only practical course is to apply the *lex fori* is difficult to contest.

(b) Statutory claims

A claim based on a statute may be restricted either by the statutory provision or judicial construction to a claim valid in English law. Jurisdiction and choice of law thereby merge. So, for example, the restriction of maritime liens recognized in English courts to English maritime liens may be seen as a jurisdictional or choice of law rule.[33]

4. MARITIME CLAIMS AND THE ENGLISH CHOICE OF LAW PROCESS

The problem of the high seas

Any choice of law rule linking a dispute to a legal system on the basis of locality or territoriality must be modified as regards events occurring at a place not within the

27. This is said to be relevant in deciding whether to uphold a foreign jurisdiction clause but on occasions English courts refuse to uphold such clauses without considering the task they impose on themselves of applying foreign law (see Chap. 12). For an example of the rejection of the argument that the appropriate forum was the country the law of which governed the issue, see *The Traugutt* [1985] 1 Lloyd's Rep. 76.
28. See e.g. *Mackender v. Feldia AG* [1966] 2 Lloyd's Rep. 449, [1966] 2 All E.R. 847.
29. Article 8(1)—an alternative is the law of country of habitual residence of a party where it is not reasonable to determine the effect of the conduct under the law specified (Art. 8(2)).
30. As under RSC Order 11, r. 1(1)(d)(iii).
31. *The Parouth* [1982] 2 Lloyd's Rep. 351; *The Atlantic Emperor (No. 1)* [1989] 1 Lloyd's Rep. 554; *Oldendurff v. Liberia Corpn* [1995] 2 Lloyd's Rep. 64.
32. *The Heidberg* [1994] 2 Lloyd's Rep. 287—it not being shown any other law should apply and rejecting the contention that the matter should be considered as if there was *no* arbitration clause.
33. Compare the approach in *The Acrux* [1965] P. 391 with *The Halcyon Isle* [1981] A.C. 221. See further Chap. 18.

territory of any legal system. The need for such modification may be minimized in maritime law by treating ships as territory and limiting the area of uncertainty to events occurring otherwise than on board a ship.[34]

Classification of maritime claims

The preliminary classification of procedure/substance applies to maritime claims as to other claims. In regard to substance, maritime claims as listed in the Supreme Court Act 1981, s. 20, can be classified for the purpose of choice of law selection rules into the established categories on which selection is based, i.e. contractual, tortious, proprietary, restitution (or based on unjust enrichment), and statutory.[35] To be consistent with the general approach, the classification should be based on the issue raised by a particular claim and not the categories of claim listed in the Act. So, for example, (i) s. 20(2)(d) in specifying "any claim arising out of any agreement relating to the carriage of goods in a ship or to use or hire of a ship"encompasses claims in contract and tort; (ii) claims in the nature of salvage may be contractual or based on unjust enrichment; and (iii) mortgage claims may be proprietary or contractual.[36]

Statutory claims—Admiralty jurisdiction and choice of law

Alternatively, a statutory maritime claim may be construed as raising a statutory issue and having its own choice of law provision. So an application under the Merchant Shipping Acts or an oil pollution claim may be so regarded. Apart from mortgage claims (in regard to which statute provides for the power to hear such claims based on foreign law[37]) and any other statutory provision[38] the question of whether a claim based on foreign law will lie depends on statutory construction. So far as actions in personam are concerned there is no reason why the general choice of law process should not apply. If this is correct any claim falling within Admiralty jurisdiction will be adjudged by the rule selected by the classification and selection rule process—subject only to forum mandatory rule and public policy.

As regards actions in rem, whether an action based on foreign law will lie turns entirely on the construction of ss.20 and 21 of the Supreme Court Act 1981. Where foreign law has been applied it appears to be approached rather as a matter of jurisdiction (i.e. whether to admit the foreign law claim) than applicable law (i.e. a conscious assessment of the law to govern the validity of the claim). English courts have admitted claims, the characterization of which under foreign law matches those of similar claims in English law within the in rem jurisdiction. So foreign law has been consulted to ascertain the rights of seamen.[39] In particular, a payment of social security contributions under foreign law has been admitted as a wage claim just as such a contribution under English law would be

34. As to which, see infra "Tort".

35. As to a discussion of these categories, see infra.

36. Further, a provision (such as, for example, that concerned with limitation of liability) could be construed as procedural and therefore entirely for forum law. As to the limitation of liability and conflicts see further Chap. 24.

37. Supreme Court Act, s.20(7)(c). The provision extends to mortgage "or charge". See Chaps. 2 and 17.

38. As e.g. The Merchant Shipping Act 1995, s.17(7) referring issues of transfer and mortgage of foreign registered ships registered in the UK as chartered to a British charterer.

39. See The Fairport [1965] 2 Lloyd's Rep. 183.

admitted.[40] Further, on occasion, courts have suggested that the question of whether a claim fell within necessaries could be referred to foreign law.[41]

On the other hand, in 1965 in *The Acrux*,[42] Hewson J. held that as regards s.21(3)—which provides for the availability of an action *in rem* to enforce a "maritime lien or other charge"—"maritime lien" meant an English maritime lien and that "other charge" was restricted to a foreign claim having the characteristics of one of those attracting an English maritime lien. In respect of a maritime lien, the judge thereby reached the same conclusion as later reached by the Privy Council in *The Halcyon Isle*[43]—that in English law maritime liens are in substance English maritime liens.

It does not, however, necessarily follow from limiting maritime liens to English maritime liens that the ability to bring an action *in rem* is similarly limited. Because of the differing legal consequences of maritime liens and actions *in rem*, different issues of policy are involved. Further, the issue in *The Acrux* went to the type of claim attracting a maritime lien while the issue in respect of the ability to bring an action *in rem* is restricted to whether claims within the statutory concept (e.g. of disbursements) can be admitted because of characteristics identical with those recognized in English domestic law as falling within the category. In this sense the analogy is more accurately with a mortgage, in which respect English law, having defined "mortgage", recognizes foreign rights satisfying the definition.

Lacking specific statutory limitation, it is suggested that any statutory heads of claim should be taken to encompass foreign claims falling within the concept reflected by the head. There is no doubt, however, that a foreign claim not falling within any head would not be admitted as the basis of an action in an English court. There is no "gate" in the statute through which it could go.

II. ALTERNATIVE APPROACHES TO SELECTION BY CLASSIFICATION QUALIFIED BY PUBLIC POLICY

The "classification" approach has been strongly critized in the United States where in many jurisdictions the applicable law is that with which the issue has either the "most significant relationship" or the law having the greatest "governmental interest". The two approaches are sometimes distinguishable in theory but often overlap in application. Unlike the "classification" approach these approaches are openly based on an assessment of dispositive rules which might govern the dispute, and on occasion an evaluation of the rules in the context of elements assessed as relevant to the issue (including the contacts between issue and the various rules).[44]

The selected dispositive rule is reached on assessment of its claim to resolve the dispute. So, in applying "the most significant relationship" test a court must decide which

---

40. See e.g. *The Arosa Kulm (No. 2)* [1960] 1 Lloyd's Rep. 97; *The Arosa Star* [1959] 2 Lloyd's Rep. 396.

41. See *The Arzpeta* (1921) 15 Asp. M.L.C. 426; *The Andre Theodore* (1904) 10 Asp. M.L.C. 94 (insurance premiums).

42. [1965] P. 391.

43. [1981] A.C. 221. See also *Comoco v. M/V El Centro Americano* [1984] AMC 1434.

44. For an English sceptical approach see *Macmillan Inc. v. Bishopgate Investment Trust plc (No. 3)* [1995] 3 All E.R. 747.

legal system because of its contacts and the purpose of its relevant rule, is "most significantly" connected with the dispute. In applying "governmental interest" criteria a court would assess the interest in each state connected with the dispute in adjudging it.

In the United States the application of these criteria is commonplace in some states but their application in Admiralty matters is uncertain. In England the criterion of the significant legal relationship is reflected at least to some extent in the reference of contractual issues both within and outside the Rome Convention to the law having the closest connection. In tort, the criteria made a brief appearance in the House of Lords in 1979 in *Boys* v. *Chaplin*[45] (a case involving a collision between vehicles). Despite relatively few subsequent reported cases it is established that the significant legal relationship may exceptionally be accepted as the selection basis, a development continued in the Private International Law (Miscellaneous Provisions) Act 1995 (see *infra*). There is no evidence of any influence in regard to other issues.

III. THE CATEGORIES AND THEIR SELECTION RULES

1. SUBSTANCE OR PROCEDURE

In English law procedural issues[46] are referred to the law of the forum. Such a choice of law rule is common to many legal systems. It makes complete sense insofar as "procedure" refers to the steps in proceedings to enforce the claim and formal requirements for bringing a claim. It may be, however, that the purpose of a legal rule may be achieved either through procedure or substantive provision—liability may be made to depend either on "liability" in substance or on the availability of a remedy. So, for example, there may be no liability unless others are sued (substantive) or there may be no implementation of liability unless others are sued (procedure). On the classification will depend whether the rule is such as to attract the law applicable to the substantive issues or is governed by the law of the forum.[47] While the classification gives control for the scope of each law to the legal system of which it is part such a distinction of itself is perhaps more technical than real—the query should go to control over liability, whether by lack of foundation for the remedy or remedy. The consequences of classification of a right inherently substantive as procedural were emphasized by the approach of the majority of the Privy Council in *The Halcyon Isle*[48] that a maritime lien is essentially a matter either of procedure or jurisdiction (see *infra*).

Further, in English eyes "procedure" is not restricted to steps leading to or in proceedings and (at least arguably) encompasses questions of (a) time bars; (b) priorities; (c) remedies; and (d) evidence—all of which undeniably have substantive connotations. While it is arguable that these are matters which may be for the forum such allocation should not be on the artificial basis that they are "procedural".

---

45. [1971] A.C. 356.
46. To some it is the "rule" which is classified as procedural or substantive but the rule can only be reached on the basis of its application to the issue. It is, therefore, essential to formulate the issue precisely.
47. See e.g. *Johnson Matthey and Wallace Ltd.* v. *Ahmad Alloush* [1985] N.L.J. 1012 (C.A.).
48. [1981] A.C. 221; [1980] 2 Lloyd's Rep. 325.

(a) Time bars

Until the Foreign Limitation Periods Act 1984[49] English law viewed the issue of time within which any action must be brought to enforce a claim as procedural. By that Act save for matters to be determined by the law of England and of some other countries limitation questions arising in English proceedings are referred to the law governing the substantive matter in dispute.[50] The exception as to public policy is to be to the causing of "undue hardship" to a party or a person who might be made a party.[51] The Act applies to proceedings and arbitrations commenced after 1 October 1985 and to limitation periods that had not by then expired. The issue of whether a right exists is on any view substantive and therefore the termination of a right after a period of time is rightly seen as a matter of substance. Any issue of destruction of the claim is substantive and is for the law governing the action.[52]

Since the coming into force of the Contracts (Applicable Law) Act 1990 (i.e. 1 April 1991) the escape route from foreign law limitation periods may not be open in respect of contracts. The Rome Convention enacted by the statute provides that the law applicable to a contract shall apply to "the various ways of extinguishing obligations and presumptions and limitation of actions" (Article 16).

(b) Priorities

The general rule is said to be that priority is a matter for the law of the forum. This "rule" assumes that questions of the substance or nature of a right (which should be a matter for the law governing its creation) and priority of the right as against other rights are distinct issues. But, on the contrary, priority may be dictated by the nature. So, under United States law, there are a considerable number of maritime liens which as between them are subject to a priority framework geared to the classification of the liens. In English law there are a restricted number of maritime liens with a priority framework geared to the relationship of the varying types of lien. To distinguish nature and priority is to draw a distinction inherently inconsistent with the whole framework of which the two aspects are part.[53]

Following that argument, the role of the forum as such in any matter of priority can be questioned when the governing law of all relevant transactions is the same or where there are differing laws each leading to the same result. It is only where there is a conflict because of differences in the laws governing the competing transactions that the forum

---

49. As to Scotland see Prescription and Limitation (Scotland) Act 1973, s.23A.

50. See s.1. The scope of the exception (which refers to tortious issues) is affected by the Private International Law (Miscellaneous Provisions) Act 1995 removing the "double actionability" choice of law rule (see *infra*). Any foreign extension or interruption because of absence from the country is to be disregarded (1984 Act, s.2(3)). The English law principles of acquiescence and other grounds of refusal of equitable belief may be applied, but where the case turns on like foregin law principles the court "shall have regard" to those principles (s.4(3)).

51. Section 2(1)(2) i.e. "excessive hardship" or hardship more than the circumstances warranted (*Jones* v. *Trollope Colls Cementation Overseas Ltd.* (1990) 26 January, *The Times*). Such hardship may be caused by the application of a governing law not realized by the parties to be such (see *The Komninos S* [1991] 1 Lloyd's Rep. 370). An argument that a foreign law disapplied on hardship grounds could then, if substantive, apply as a consequence of the conflicts process was rejected. See also (applying these decisions) *Arab Monetary Fund* v. *Hashim* [1993] 1 Lloyd's Rep. 543.

52. See e.g. *Huber* v. *Steiner* (1835) 2 Bing N.C. 202; *Harris* v. *Quine* (1869) L.R. 4 Q.B. 653.

53. See further p. 605.

may be said to have an umpire's role simply because it is the forum. Otherwise, it is artificial to refer the connected issues of priority and substance to different laws.

The role of the law of the forum

The rule that priorities are for the forum seems firmly established only as regards claims between creditors in bankruptcy, winding up of companies, administration of estates[54] and *in rem* creditors in Admiralty.[55] Policy arguments provide strong reasons for priorities as between interests in land to be "referred to the law" of the place of the land.[56] Proprietary aspects of assignments of choses in action (as, for example, freight or hire under a bill of lading or charterparty) fall within Article 12 of the Rome Convention. This includes provision for the mutual obligations of assignee and debtor and the conditions under which the assignment can be invoked against the debtor. The mutual obligations are referred to the law governing the contract between assignor and assignee and the other matters to "the law governing the right to which the assignment relates" (see *infra*). It would seem that any question of priority between assignor and assignee and between assignee and assignee falls within one or other parts of the provision.[57]

Maritime claims

It is in the area of maritime claims *in rem* that the distinction between the nature and priority of a right is most frequently debated. The authorities are unclear and unsatisfactory but, it is possible to argue that the distinctions between substance (or nature) and priority and the choice of law consequences have been judicially maintained. The decision of the Privy Council in 1980 in *The Halcyon Isle*[58] widens the scope of the law of the forum through rejection of the concept of the maritime lien as substantive (as to which seen *infra*).

Prior to *The Halcyon Isle* the preferred doctrine was that an English court, faced with a claimant relying on a right, the nature of which was governed by foreign law, should identify the characteristics of the right according to that law.[59] The court should then fit those characteristics into the English domestic hierarchy. If the foreign right had by its governing law the characteristics (for example) of a maritime lien it should be so labelled. Any question of priority would then be referred to English law. As has been said, the problem with this neat theory is that its application takes no account of the rationale of the forum system of priority.

The argument that priority is a matter of substance leads to the contention that the role of the forum as forum is one of umpire as between competing priorities of differing laws. However, in that context it is arguable that for the forum's intervention to stop at priority between claims, the nature of which is referred to another legal system, makes as little

---

54. *Pardo* v. *Bingham* (1868) L.R. 6 Eq. 485; *Ex parte Melbourn* (1870) L.R. 6 Ch. App. 64; *Re Kloebe* (1884) 28 Ch. D. 175.
55. *The Halcyon Isle* [1981] A.C. 221. See *infra*.
56. See e.g. *Norton* v. *Florence Land Co.* (1877) 7 Ch. D. 332.
57. Apart from the provision it was arguable that that law governed priority—the authorities are unsatisfactory but support can be extracted from *Kelly* v. *Selwyn* [1905] 2 Ch. 117 and *Le Feuvre* v. *Sullivan* (1855) 10 Moo. P.C. 1 in order to overcome dicta in *Republica de Guatemala* v. *Nunez* [1927] 1 K.B. 669.
58. [1981] A.C. 221.
59. See e.g. *The Colorado* [1923] P. 102; *The Zigurds* [1932] P. 113. Compare *The Tagus* [1903] P. 44.

sense as to impose its priority rules on a situation wholly governed otherwise by another more closely connected law. A proprietary hierarchy simply cannot be split into matters of creation and matters or priority. So, for example, in English law an essential element of the concept of equitable interests is their priority as against interests at common law. (See p. 605.)

It is suggested that a priority issue necessarily poses a proprietary issue and the whole should be considered a matter of substance, the law of the forum having a claim to govern it only as an arbiter. In that role it is justifiably imposed, always accepting that jurisdiction is based on some substantial connection with the dispute and that no other one law has a greater claim as being more closely connected with it.

(c) Remedies

It seems clear that only the type of remedy recognized in English law is available[60] but such restriction has little importance in respect of maritime claims based on common commercial considerations. It is questionable, however, where the concept of "remedy" begins and ends. As regards damages, subject to statutory provisions matters of quantification are for the forum but matters of remoteness arguably are substantive and to be referred to whatever law governs the primary issue.[61] Similarly, "heads of damage" (i.e. the damage or injury which may be the basis of an award) are matters of substance.[62]

(d) Limitation of liability

It is arguable that the right to limit is substantive and the amount recoverable procedural or remedial. However, in English proceedings limitation of liability has traditionally been seen as a matter for the forum. The only concession has been to recognize that a payment made out of England will be taken into account in repsect of the amount due—but only on the basis of English law. The more the Convention on the Limitation of Liability for Maritime Claims 1976 is applied the less the need for a uniform approach on conflicts rules.[63] The emphasis on forum law, however, does little to assist in resolving difficulties inherent in the insistence of states on applying their own domestic principles to a topic the existence of which is widely recognized. The principles relevant to limitation of liability and their modern relevance (including the applicable law) are discussed in the context of the topic in Chapter 24.

---

60. See *Phrantzes* v. *Argenti* [1960] 2 Q.B. 19.

61. *Mackinnon* v. *Iberia Shipping Co. Ltd.* 1955 S.C. 20; *Coupland* v. *Arabian Gulf Petroleum Co* [1983] 2 All E.R. 434; [1983] 3 All E.R. 226 (C.A.); *D'Almeida Araujo Lda.* v. *Becker & Co.* [1953] 2 Q.B. 329 (contract) (but see the Contracts (Applicable Law) Act 1990, Sch. 1, Art. 10(1)(c)). Under the Rome Convention assessment of damages is seen as substantive but made subject to the "procedural law" of the member States (Art. 10(1)(c)—see *infra*).

62. *Boys* v. *Chaplin* [1971] A.C. 356—it must be said that it is difficult to extract a common principle from this unfortunate case and that two members of the House viewed *all* questions of damage in that case as matters of quantification. See Private International Law (Miscellaneous Provisions) Act 1995 focusing on "the issues".

63. Although the existence of a number of Conventions with the earlier superseded by the later may add to the problem of conflict because of the difference in parties and the importance given by states to laws based on Conventions.

(e) Evidence

Subject to statute, admissibility and proof are matters for the law of the forum[64] but the question of which facts are in issue[65] and the interpretation of any document is clearly a matter of substance for the law governing the issue to which it is relevant. By general principle presumption of law is arguably substantive,[66] while it is clear that the question of burden of proof is for the forum.[67]

By the Contracts (Applicable Law) Act 1990 the law governing the contract applies "to the extent it contains in the law of contract rules which raise presumptions of law or determine the burden of proof".[68] It appears therefore that for this provision to operate not only must the matter be contractual but the rule be a "contractual" rule or presumption. It remains arguable that general rules of burden and presumption are outside the Act.

2. CHOICE OF LAW FOR SUBSTANTIVE ISSUES

The choice of law framework is based on the connection of selection rules to legal "categories" reflecting in large measure domestic concepts. So established choice of law categories in English law are (a) contract; (b) tort; and (c) property; (d) restitution or "unjust enrichment". Of necessity, a choice of law question raised by a statutory claim will be subject to the selection rule relevant to the issue posed. As has been said, that issue may be *sui generis* or may be classified as falling within one of the established categories. "Statutory claims" must therefore be considered as a category—though without any implication of a selection rule common to the category.

These categories are applied to maritime claims but two types of claim not forming part of the general law (general average and salvage) require further consideration. Each has aspects of contract and unjust enrichment.

Classification of an issue into a category is therefore fundamental to the present English choice of law process. Classification should be a matter for English law and, once classified, the claim referred to the law attached to that category. The view on classification of the law to which the matter should be referred is irrelevant, for the issue is being referred to it for disposition, not for an answer as to how *it* would regard the issue for its choice of law process. So it is irrelevant whether the "proper (or applicable) law"

---

64. *Leroux* v. *Brown* (1852) 12 C.B. 801; *Brown* v. *Thornton* (1837) 6 Ad. & E. 185. The Crown has power to make Orders in Council providing that copies of entries in foreign public registers shall be admissible in English proceedings (Evidence (Foreign, Dominion and Colonial Documents) Act 1933, as amended by Oath and Evidence (Overseas Authorities and Countries) Act 1963, s.5).

65. See *The Gaetano and Maria* (1882) 7 P.D. 137—where Italian law was the governing law and under which a bottomry bond was valid. The requirement of English law (the law of the forum) of the need of the master to communicate with the owner was not relevant.

66. See Dicey and Morris, op. cit., 12th edn, p. 180. As to the Rome Convention see *infra*. It seems unclear whether apart from the Convention the question of ability to sue and liability to be sued in a particular action is substantive or procedural. As to the relevance of the question to the application of the Carriage of Goods By Sea Act 1992 to bills of lading governed by foreign law see Toh [1994] LMCLQ 280.

67. See e.g. *The Roberta* (1937) 58 Ll.L.Rep. 159. But see Dicey and Morris, *op. cit.* p. 179.

68. Article 14(1). Modes of proof may be according to those recognized by the law of the forum or of any country by the law of which under the Convention the contract is formally valid (Art. 14(2)).

of a contractual issue itself regards it as *"contractual"*—the question is how it would dispose of the *issue*.[69]

A case may concern issues falling into more than one category, e.g. contract and a tort. It is essential to "classify" each issue and analyse it in the context of the dispute as a whole. If one issue is paramount it is arguable that all issues should be referred to the law governing it, but whether that be considered or not it is necessary clearly to define the role each issue plays in the dispute. In *Sayers* v. *International Drilling Co. NV*[70] the plaintiff (an Englishman) was injured on an oil rig off the Nigerian coast while employed by a Dutch oil company. His action against his employer was based on negligence of his fellow employees. The employment contract excluded any liability for injury save as provided in a compensation scheme by the company. Such a clause was void in English law but valid in Dutch law. The majority of the Court of Appeal approached the question of liability as one of contract—and in choice of law terms of which law was to govern the validity of the contract. However, the action was based on tort and the role of the contract, if any, was to provide a defence. Therefore, the question as to the proper law of the contract should have been regarded more accurately as a preliminary issue leading to the question whether such a contract, if valid, provided a defence in the law (or laws) applicable to the tortious claim.

(a) Contract

The conflicts framework differs at least in approach depending on whether the contract falls within the scope of the Rome Convention on the Law Applicable to Contractual Obligations 1980 as enacted into English law by the Contracts (Applicable Law) Act 1990. By Article 2 any law specified by the Convention applies whether or not it is the law of a contracting State, and it is therefore irrelevant for its application in English law whether the dispute has any connection with a contracting State. So far as cases are within it the Convention as enacted reflects English law. Further by s.2(3) of the Act the Convention is expressly applied in the case of conflicts between the laws of different parts of the United Kingdom.

Although most substantive maritime contracts entered into on or after April 1 1991 are within the Convention jurisdiction and arbitration agreements are excluded, and there are other issues falling outside it. The pre Act law remains relevant therefore both generally in respect of contracts entered into before the specified date and excluded matters after the date. Whether a contract is within or outside the Convention when seeking the law governing a contract or a contractual issue the necessary first step is to identify the contract or issue. Where there are a number of arguably interlinked contracts it is essential

---

69. If the law to which the matter is referred is allowed to reclassify (e.g. from substance to procedure or contract to tort) it may create a reference back to the law of the forum, and undermines the foundation for the reference. For an example of reclassification see *Re Cohn* [1945] 1 Ch. 5. The Private International Law (Miscellaneous Provisions) Act 1995 provides that "the characterisation for the purposes of private international law of issues arising in a claim as issues relating to tort or delict is a matter for courts of the forum" (s.9(2)).

70. [1971] 3 All E.R. 163; see also *Coupland* v. *Arabian Gulf Petroleum Co.* [1983] 3 All E.R. 226 and *infra*. Compare *Brodin* v. *Seljan* 1973 S.C. 213 (a contract of employment governed by Norwegian law could not effect tortious liability under Scottish statute where all events took place in Scotland and Scotland was the forum).

to decide on the connections between them (if any) for an analysis of the governing law or laws.[71]

The law apart from the 1990 Act

The proper law of the contract

The basic general principle is that, subject to statutory provisions and public policy, issues will be referred to the "proper law" of the contract—a concept which under the 1990 Act becomes the "law applicable to the contract". The "proper law" is that which the parties have selected (expressly or by implication),[72] or, if no selection has been made, that law with which the transaction has its closest and most real connection.[73] It follows that there can be no "floating proper law"—it cannot be determined by an event occurring after the contract was entered into,[74] such as the selection of a venue for general average adjustment[75] or the hearing of a dispute in a jurisdiction at a place at the option of one of the parties.[76] However the option to arbitrate in different places is not the adoption of a floating proper law—the provision of an optional place of arbitration is unlikely to imply a choice of law.[77]

The ambit of the proper law

It is by no means clearly established through authority, however, that the law governing each and every issue is the same. Where there is no selection by the parties there may still be argument as to whether a particular "category" such as, for example, performance, should be identified as raising issues distinct from any general question of right or obligation[78] or enforceability. The tendency is to refer all matters to *the* proper

---

71. So a substantive commercial transaction is to be distinguished from a documentary credit or performance bond (*Attock Cement Co. Ltd.* v. *Romanian Bank for Foreign Trade* [1989] 1 Lloyd's Rep. 572) but there may be such a connection as to mean the proper law of one contract controls the others. See e.g. *Turkiye Is Bankasi SA* v. *Bank of China* [1993] 1 Lloyd's Rep. 132 (guarantees); *The Njegos* [1936] P. 90 (bill of lading and charterparty); *Bank of Baroda* v. *Vysya Bank* [1994] 2 Lloyd's Rep. 87 (contracts relevant to letters of credit); *Wahda Bank* v. *Arab Bank plc* [1994] 2 Lloyd's Rep. 411 (counter guarantees and performance bonds).

72. See e.g. *Vita Food Products Inc.* v. *Unus Shipping Co. Ltd.* [1939] A.C. 277. As to limitations on choice, see *infra*. Choice may be implied but care must be taken not to overemphasize one factor. The use of the English language is not necessarily the choice of English law as it used for many maritime standard forms. See e.g. *The Al Wahab* [1983] 2 All E.R. 884 (H.L.); *The Armar* [1980] 2 Lloyd's Rep. 450.

73. See e.g. *Compagnie d'Armement Maritime SA* v. *Compagnie Tunisienne de Navigation SA* [1971] A.C. 572. There is no presumption in favour of any particular connection (*Coast Lines Ltd.* v. *Hudig & Veder Chartering NV* [1972] 1 Q.B. 34).

74. See *The Armar* [1981] 1 All E.R. 498, and *infra*.

75. *The Armar* [1981] 1 All E.R. 498.

76. *The Tenacia* [1982] LMLN 55; *The Iran Vojdan* [1984] 2 Lloyd's Rep. 380.

77. *The Star Texas* [1993] 2 Lloyd's Rep. 445 (C.A.). Further there is no requirement that the law governing the arbitration proceedings has to be fixed at the date of the arbitration agreement (*ibid.*).

78. Such as, for example, liability under a charterparty (*The Tunisienne Case* (*supra* fn. 73)); entitlement to sell cargo (*The Industrie* [1894] P. 58); whether loss of goods due to "perils" excepted by the bill of lading (*Chartered Mercantile Bank of India* v. *Netherlands India Navigation Co.* (1883) 10 Q.B. 521); liability under a bill for short delivery (see *The Assunzione* [1954] P. 150); claim under an average bond (*The Armar* [1981] 1 All E.R. 498); international organisation constitution (*Westland* v. *Arab Organisation* [1995] 2 All E.R. 387).

law—matters of formation, illegality and formality arguably may involve other laws. Renvoi is not applicable to contract.[79]

MATTERS OF FORMATION—AGREEMENT, FORMALITY, CAPACITY

There is little authority specifically on any of these matters, and such as there is may arguably be dismissed as outdated. In respect of formality, it is sufficient to comply with the law of the place of contracting and, as to capacity, it may be sufficient to comply with the law of domicile. Lacking convincing authority it would seem to require strong argument to sever any particular category from the general modern rule of the "proper law". However, in any given circumstance (as, for example, regards formality) it may be possible to contend that the expectation of the parties or one party is a factor strongly pointing to an application of a "proper law" to that aspect which would not necessarily be the "proper law" applicable to other aspects.

The "putative proper law". An unresolved question is whether the issue of agreement (i.e. whether there *is* a contract) is a matter for the *lex fori* or the putative proper law.[80] The trend of authority[81] and international agreement[82] tends to the proper law of the contract as the governing law at least in the sense that it is sufficient for validity to comply with that law.[83]

If it is the putative proper law the reference could either be to the proper law if the contract was valid or to the proper law "objectively" ascertained—which, presumably, means ignoring any question of validity. The "objective" approach is perhaps more logical in theory but may result in a contract being valid by one law only to be invalid by the law which *then* becomes the proper law. Is the contract then to be declared invalid or treated as valid despite the view of the law applicable to it?

The argument for the *lex fori* is that there is no route to the proper law until it is established that there is a contract and that it is for the forum to decide the basis of the reference. To refer the validity to the proper law is to beg the question—particularly if the terms of the contract at issue are relevant to ascertainment of the proper law (such as a jurisdiction, arbitration or choice of law clause).

It seems preferable to accept that if the putative proper law is to be the appropriate law to resolve any issue of agreement is that which would apply if agreement were established. However, this cannot work if there is more than one potentially putative proper law depending on the content of the agreement (as, for example, where there are two

---

79. See *Re United Railways of Havana and Regla Warehouses Ltd.* [1960] Ch. 52, at pp. 96–97, 115 (C.A.); *The Al Wahab* [1983] 2 All E.R. 884. For a suggestion that an English court applying English law as the proper law may refer matters to a foreign law *through* the proper law, see *The Armar* [1981] 1 All E.R. 498, at p. 505. Renvoi is excluded by the Rome Convention (Art. 15).

80. See e.g. Dicey and Morris, *op. cit.*, at p. 1228 (distinguishing between existence and validity of consent).

81. As to offer and acceptance, see *Albeko Schuhmaschinen* v. *Kamborian Shoe Machine Co. Ltd.* (1961) 111 L.J. 519; as to consideration, see *Re Bonacina* [1912] 2 Ch. 394; as to parties, see *The El Amria and El Minia* [1982] 2 Lloyd's Rep. 28. As to the service out of a writ based on an asserted contract see *The Parouth* [1982] 2 Lloyd's Rep. 351. See generally the discussion in *The Heidberg* [1994] 2 Lloyd's Rep. 287. For an application of the *lex fori* in such circumstances see *Mackender* v. *Feldia AG* [1966] 2 Lloyd's Rep. 449.

82. See the Rome Convention on the Law Applicable to Contractual Obligations (1980), Arts 8 and 9 (discussed *infra*).

83. Compare Art. 11 giving a limited capacity role to the law of the place of contracting or where the issue is whether a contract has been created, the putative proper law.

arbitration clauses at issue). In that case there is little alternative to the law of the forum—if only on the ground there is no law with a greater claim.[84]

ILLEGALITY

It seems accepted that a contract illegal by its proper law or, England being the forum, by English law is unenforceable in England.[85] Further, it is arguable that a contract illegal according to the law of the place of performance will not be enforced; but, it is also said that such lack of enforceability is restricted to cases where the proper law would declare the contract unenforceable.[86]

THE PRIMACY OF THE PARTIES' CHOICE AND ITS LIMITATIONS ON THE PARTIES' CHOICE

In the traditionally accepted leading case establishing the supremacy of the parties' choice—the *Vita Foods* case[87]—it was said that the choice must be "bona fide and legal". Such a limitation can be stretched or restricted almost at will and in a sense obviously begs the question. Essentially, the limitations will be of two kinds:

   (i) prohibition from evasion of a forum mandatory rule[88]; and
   (ii) refusal to recognize the choice as to do so will lead to the application of a rule or the reaching of a conclusion contrary to English public policy.

(i) The forum mandatory rule. The principle was applied by the House of Lords in *The Morviken*[89] to the Hague-Visby Rules as enacted by the Carriage of Goods by Sea Act 1971. The obligation specified in the rules (Art. III, rule 8) not to derogate from the liability of the carrier or the ship cannot be avoided by selection of a law which would not apply the rules.

Parties may apply the Hague-Visby Rules as enacted in England to a contract not within the boundary provisions of the rules (e.g. to a charterparty). If in the contract they *also* opt for a law other than English law, any application of "English" rules to the dispute by an English court can only rest on *selection* by the parties of the mandatory rules despite the choice of law. In such an instance, the application of the English rules is one of the construction of the contract rather than imposition by statute. The effect may be simply to incorporate the English version of the rules into a contract governed by a foreign law.[90]

The choice of English law to govern a contract of carriage will only of itself necessarily make the rules applicable if they are applied to the contract mandatorily by that law. If it is a charterparty to which the rules are applied only by the contract it is a question of

---

84. As was decided in *The Heidberg* [1994] 2 Lloyd's Rep. 287.

85. A contract illegal by English law and that law being the proper law is voidable by an English court. It is irrelevant that it is lawful where performed. *The Evia Luck* [1992] 1 Lloyd's Rep. 115 (H.L.).

86. In *Ralli Bros* v. *Compania Naviera Sota y Aznar* [1920] 2 K.B. 287 a shipowner's actions to recover freight of a value of the difference between the contract price and the price allowed as "legal" at the place of discharge failed—but in this case the contract was governed by English law.

87. [1939] A.C. 277.

88. As to arguable application of a Scottish statute to override a contractual defence to a tort see *Brodin* v. *Seljan* 1973 S.C. 213. Compare *Sayers* v. *International Drilling Co. NV* [1971] 3 All E.R. 163.

89. [1983] 1 Lloyd's Rep. 1.

90. See *The Happy Pioneer* [1983] HKLR 43. The forum mandatory rule is to be distinguished in principle from the application of a forum rule as a result of the choice of law process.

construction whether they are applied. In 1990 in *The Komninos S*[91] it was held that a choice simply of "British law" did not apply the rules. Concern has been expressed at the consequence of non-application of rules of either English law (as applied to the contract) or Greek law (the other possible proper law) which would have applied. However the decision seems correct. Unlike some circumstances where neither of two identical domestic rules applied because of the reference of different issues to the two laws, in this context the apparent gap is the need *in English law* to specify a particular aspect of that law for it to operate.

(ii) Public policy. Public policy is as impossible to define in this context as any other and represents the "fail safe" mechanism of the English choice of law process. To some, particularly in the United States public policy should play a primary selective role but, certainly in relation to the proper law, it should be construed as referring to fundamental principles at the heart of the English system.[92]

Where there is no selection—"closest and most real connection"

This concept has been expressed in terms of intention—i.e. the law that reasonable businessmen would have intended to govern if they had thought about it.[93] It is, however, preferable to move away from inferred intention and to assess the connections objectively. Certainly that is the approach in recent cases.[94]

   The major criticism of the English approach is that it amounts to a numerical totting up of contacts with the verdicts going to the majority. With the rejection of any presumption there is certainly a danger that in despair a court will base its conclusions on quantity rather than weigh the contacts in the context of the transaction.[95] In *Coast Lines* v. *Hudig and Veder*[96] Megaw L.J. emphasized that the focal point was the transaction and not the contract which formed the first part of the transaction. As a consequence, he concluded that as the relevant transaction to the issue of the case was a charterparty of an English ship dealing with activities of that ship the proper law was English. This approach is to be preferred rather than an approach which concentrates on particular aspects of the contract itself or simply "weighs" without indicating the relevance of that which is put in the scale.[97]

Jurisdiction or arbitration agreement

SELECTION OF LAW AND JURISDICTION

A clause selecting a place of jurisdiction (or arbitration) *and* law will operate as a selection of both. Further, English courts will not shrink from rejecting the choice of a foreign court

---

91. [1991] 1 Lloyd's Rep. 370.

92. See e.g. *Loucks* v. *Standard Oil Co*. 224 N.Y. 99, at p. 111 (1918).

93. See e.g. *The Assunzione* [1954] P. 150 (Willmer J.).

94. See e.g. *Compagnie d'Armement Maritime SA* v. *Compagnie Tunisienne de Navigation SA* [1971] A.C. 572, in which the distinction between inferred intention and objective assessment is clearly drawn.

95. It has been suggested that there may be a presumption towards a law which regards the contract as valid in opposition to one that regards it as invalid. (See e.g. *Coast Lines Ltd*. v. *Hudig & Veder Chartering NV* [1972] 2 Q.B. 34.) But see *The Rosso* [1982] 2 Lloyd's Rep. 120. As to the law to govern validity see *supra*.

96. [1972] 1 Q.B. 34.

97. Compare the Convention focus on "characteristic performance".

while upholding the choice of law.[98] An inference of choice of law may be drawn from an arbitration or jurisdiction clause[99] but the validity of the clause depends on the law applicable to the contract.

VALIDITY OF THE CLAUSE

An arbitration or jurisdiction agreement raises issues of formation, rights and obligations and performance identical to a contract on a substantive matter. Such agreements are, however, often part of a contract on a substantive matter. An arbitration clause is separable from the substantive contract (see Chapter 13). However, it would be unusual for the validity of the arbitration or jurisdiction agreement forming part of or attached to the substantive contract to be different from that contract (see *infra*).

As indicated earlier whether an arbitration, jurisdiction or choice of law agreement is valid is part of establishing the foundation for ascertaining the proper law of the substantive contract. It was held by the Court of Appeal in *The Parouth*[100] that whether arguably there is a contract governed by English law so as to justify service of a writ out of the jurisdiction is a matter for the putative proper law of the contract—and that in identifying that law an arbitration clause should be taken into account. In 1981 in *The Atlantic Emperor* the Court of Appeal was of the view that if *The Parouth* was right the approach applied to a case in which the issue was confined to the validity of the clause rather than the contract as a whole.

Where the substantive contract is within the 1990 Act such an approach would mean a reference to the law which would be applicable under the Convention to the contract if the clause was valid and the issue was the law applicable to the substantive contract. However, if the issue is the validity of the arbitration or jurisdiction clause this would fall outside the Convention. If the law applicable to the substantive contract depends at least in part on the validity of the arbitration or jurisdiction clause this, it would seem, would have to be decided as a preliminary point so as to identify the factor relevant to the selection of the applicable law under the Convention.

The reference to the putative proper law will not work however where the clause itself refers to more than one law nor where the issue is which of two or more clauses are part of the contract. So in *The Heidberg*[101] after an exhaustive examination of the authorities Judge Diamond Q.C. applied English law as the *lex fori* to decide whether either of two arbitration clauses were incorporated into a bill of lading—no other law had been shown to have a greater claim. The alternative was to apply the proper law of the bill of lading ignoring either clause but as the learned judge pointed out that is to assume what is at issue—for the arbitration clause is a valid factor in deciding the proper law. The conclusion therefore seems as practical as it is justifiable—particularly given that reference to foreign laws is in the end a matter of how much control over an issue is to

---

98. See e.g. *The Adolf Warski* [1976] 2 Lloyd's Rep. 241; *The El Amria* [1981] 2 Lloyd's Rep. 119. For standard bill of lading form, see e.g. Visconbill, Clause 20.
99. An option of an arbitration place would give no indication of the proper law and it cannot be argued that it is provision of a floating applicable law (*The Star Texas* [1993] 2 Lloyd's Rep. 445).
100. [1982] 2 Lloyd's Rep. 351.
101. [1994] 2 Lloyd's Rep. 287.

be surrendered by the forum. The basis for that surrender (or transfer) must in practice be for the forum.

THE CONTENT OF ARBITRATION AND JURISDICTION CLAUSES

(a) **Arbitration clause.** In 1981 in *Black Clawson International Ltd* v. *Papierwerke Waldhof-Aschaffenburg AG (No. 2)*[102] Mustill J. pointed out that in relation to a contract containing an arbitration clause there are four relevant systems of law:

> (i) the law governing the substantive agreement to submit future disputes to arbitration;
> (ii) the law governing the agreement to arbitrate;
> (iii) the law governing the contract to refer a particular matter to arbitration;
> (iv) the law governing the arbitral proceedings.

On the distinction between the differing laws, Mustill J. said:

"If this analysis proves correct, so that the individual contract to refer has a life which is independent of, though springing from, the original agreement to arbitrate future disputes, it must follow that at least in theory the two sets of contractual relations may be governed by different laws. It may be objected that this piles up the proper laws absurdly high: we already have the substantive proper law, and the lex fori; to these we must now add the proper law of the continuous agreement and the proper law of the individual contract to refer. In practice, this objection is unlikely ever to arise. In the great majority of the cases the same law governs all aspects of the matter. Where the laws diverge at all, one will find in most instances that the law governing the continuous agreement is the same as the substantive law of the contract in which it is embodied and that the law of the reference is the same as the lex fori."

However, it was clear, he said, that the individual contract to refer the matter to arbitration and the original arbitration agreement could be governed by different laws.

(i) The law governing the substantive agreement. The selection of an English arbitration is a "strong indication" of a selection of English law as the law governing the substantive agreement. The clause must be construed with the rest of the contract but it will require strong contrary evidence to displace the conclusion that choice of place of arbitration is not also choice of law.[103] However where the arbitration provides for "a dual situs" (i.e. one of two places) the indication that both laws are to apply is "much less strong". No inference can be drawn as to the proper law simply from the provision as to the place of the arbitration.[104]

(ii) The law governing the agreement to arbitrate. While this may be subject to a law different to that governing the substantive agreement[105] it is likely to be the same.

(iii) The law governing the agreement to arbitrate a particular dispute. In most cases where this differs from the law governing the substantive contract it will be identical with that governing the proceedings—but it is all a matter of construction. There may, however, be an ad hoc agreement superseding the continuing agreement, particularly where the

---

102. [1981] 2 Lloyd's Rep. 446.
103. *Compagnie d'Armement Maritime SA* v. *Compagnie Tunisienne de Navigation SA* [1971] A.C. 572.
104. *The Star Texas* [1993] 2 Lloyd's Rep. 445.
105. In *Black Clawson* (fn 102) Mustill J. thought the two agreements may be subject to differing laws.

continuing agreement is void. The ad hoc agreement may be subject to a different law to the continuing agreement.[106]

(iv) The law governing the proceedings. This need not be apparent at the time of the agreement—there can be a floating curial law[107] and will normally be the law of the place of proceedings but a different selection could be upheld[108]—although this amounts to allowing choice of procedure, contrary to the normal rule that procedure is for the forum. It may well be that a court will strain to construe such an agreement as being a selection of the place of arbitration with the incorporation of consistent provisions of the other law.[109]

(b) Jurisdiction clause. The relationship between the proper law and a jurisdiction clause may be analysed in the same way as the proper law and an arbitration clause. While a jurisdiction clause is strong evidence of the proper law of the contract of which it is part, it is not of conclusive effect[110]; and it is arguable, as with an arbitration clause, that the clause itself is subject to the proper law to be gathered from the contract as a whole. Arguably the clause *may* be governed by its own proper law.

Where a party takes proceedings pursuant to a jurisdiction clause, unlike an arbitration clause there is not likely to be a separate agreement to submit a particular matter apart from the clause in the contract. Proceedings taken under a jurisdiction clause will be governed by the law of the forum.

The Contracts (Applicable Law) Act 1990

The law applicable to a contract entered into on or after 1 April 1991 (if within the Convention) is to be identified in accordance with the criteria of the Rome Convention on the Law Applicable to Contractual Obligations 1980 (as amended) as enacted in the 1990 Act.[111] If the issue falls outside the Convention it will remain subject to the criteria in operation prior to the Act. The Convention adopts as its basic principles those in force in English law (though with different terminology)—the choice of the parties and, lacking choice, the law of the country most closely connected with the contract.

In addition to special protective provisions in respect of consumers and employees the Convention differs from the common law in adopting, where there is no choice of law by the parties, the "characteristic performance" of the contract as the focal point for identifying the governing law and rebuttable presumptions of the applicable law as the law of the place of residence or of the party undertaking that performance. As with the common law renvoi is excluded.

106. See *The Amazonia* [1990] 1 Lloyd's Rep. 236.
107. *The Star Texas* [1993] 2 Lloyd's Rep. 445.
108. See e.g. *James Miller & Partners Ltd.* v. *Whitworth St. Estates (Manchester) Ltd.* [1970] A.C. 583.
109. See *Union of India* v. *McDonnell Douglas Corpn* [1993] 2 Lloyd's Rep. 48—choice of English law in respect of an arbitration in England matched with Indian law provisions in respect of the internal content of the arbitration inconsistent with English law.
110. See *Dunbee Ltd.* v. *Gilman & Co. (Australia) Pty.* [1968] 2 Lloyd's Rep. 394 (N.S.W.).
111. The Convention is amended by the Luxembourg Convention 1984 (on the accession of Greece) and the Funchal Convention 1992 (on the accession of Portugal and Spain). The Luxembourg Convention forms Schedule 2 of the Act and the Funchal Convention when ratified by the UK will be enacted through SI 1994/1900. As to the application of Convention principle to jurisdiction issues under RSC Order 11 see fn 25. The report of Giuliano and Lagarde, OCJ 31 October 1990, may be considered in interpreting the Convention.

Special mandatory protection is accorded to consumers under certain consumer contracts[112] and individual employment contracts. The effect of a choice of law by the parties is qualified.[113] If there is no choice (a) in specified circumstances the consumer contract is governed by the law of the country of the consumer's habitual domicile; (b) an individual employment contract is governed by the law of the place of habitual work or if there is no such law that of the place of business through which the employee was engaged.[114]

Apart from provisions relating to the application of mandatory rules of foreign law, rather than the law applicable to the contract and issues of nullity, the Convention is given the force of law and applies whether or not the law applicable is the law of a contracting State.[115] It is subject to the interpretation of national courts and, when the appropriate Protocols are in force, the European Court of Justice.[116]

Matters excluded from the Convention

Article 1 provides:

"1. The rules of this Convention shall apply to contractual obligations in any situation involving a choice between the laws of different countries.
2. They shall not apply to:
   (a) questions involving the status or legal capacity of natural persons, without prejudice to Article 11;
   (b) contractual obligations relating to:
       — wills and succession,
       — rights in property arising out of a matrimonial relationship,
       — rights and duties arising out of a family relationship, parentage, marriage or affinity, including maintenance obligations in respect of children who are not legitimate;
   (c) obligations arising under bills of exchange, cheques and promissory notes and other negotiable instruments to the extent that the obligations under such other negotiable instruments arise out of their negotiable character;
   (d) arbitration agreements and agreements on the choice of court;
   (e) questions governed by the law of companies and other bodies corporate or unincorporated such as the creation, by registration or otherwise, legal capacity, internal organisation or winding up of companies and other bodies corporate or unincorporate and the personal liability of officers and members as such for the obligations of the company or body;
   (f) the question whether an agent is able to bind a principal, or an organ to bind a company or body corporate or unincorporate, to a third party;
   (g) the constitution of trusts and the relationship between settlors, trustees and beneficiaries;
   (h) evidence and procedure, without prejudice to Article 14.

---

112. Article 5. A consumer contract is the supply of goods or services or provision of credit for that purpose to a person for a purpose outside his trade or profession (Art. 5(1)). The protection does not extend to contracts of carriage nor, apart from contracts for travel and accommodation, to contracts for services in a country other than that of the consumer's habitual residence (Art. 5(4)(5)).

113. Articles 5(2), 6(1).

114. Articles 5(3), 6(2).

115. See s.2(1)(2) Art. 2 It applies to conflicts between the parts of the UK as well as between the UK and other countries (s.2(3)).

116. See the Brussels 1st Protocol 1988 (Sch. 3 of the Act). The jurisdiction of the European Court will probably not be accepted on any extension outside the Union. As of 1 December 1995 the Protocol providing for interpretation by the European Court is not yet in force as the 2nd Protocol is not in force (see Art. 6).

3. The rules of this Convention do not apply to contracts of insurance which cover risks situated in the territories of the Member States of the European Economic Community. In order to determine whether a risk is situated in these territories the court shall apply its internal law.

4. The preceding paragraph does not apply to contracts of re-insurance."[117]

Matters within the Convention

Save for the exceptions specified the Convention applies to "contractual obligations" in any situation involving a choice between the laws of different countries (Article 1). The Convention is concerned solely with purely contractual issues save for assignment of choses in action and subrogation. Apart from arbitration and jurisdiction and within 1(3) insurance agreements few matters directly relevant to maritime contracts will fall outside the 1990 Act. Problems of classification (whether a matter is contractual or falls into some other category such as tort or property) will remain.

Many of the exclusions relate to matters which, although they may involve contract, may be seen as essentially within another legal category—such as, for example, legal capacity, company law trusts and negotiable instruments. It is for this general reason that the consequences of nullity of a contract are excluded—in English law they are seen as matters of restitution. Conversely where excluded matters are seen as contractual the common law principles will apply. So the pre Act contract rules will apply to contracts of arbitration or jurisdiction, capacity to enter a contract, whether an agent can bind a principal and such other contract issues as may arise in any of the excluded matters. Bills of lading would be excluded only if classified by the forum (either by the *lex fori* or law applied) as negotiable instruments—not simply as creating a transferable obligation.

The Convention rules

Subject to provisions relating to mandatory provisions of national laws, *ordre public* and protection of consumers and employees and some specific qualifications the Convention law applicable to the contract will be (a) if demonstrated with reasonable certainty the law chosen by the parties or (b) if there is no choice the law of the country with which the contract is most closely connected (Articles 3, 4—see *infra*).

ASPECTS OF THE CONTRACTS SUBJECT TO APPLICABLE LAW

It applies specifically to material and formal validity (with alternative applicable laws), interpretation, performance (with qualification), consequence of breach and extinction and limitation of claims, and rules of presumption or burden of proof and (not enacted in the United Kingdom) the consequences of the nullity of a contract. In relation to "the manner of performance and the steps to be taken in the event of defective performance" "regard is to be had to the law of the country of performance".

---

117. Article 11 (referred to in 2(a)) imposes a limitation on a plea of incapacity to contract and Article 14 (referred to in 2(h)) burden of proof. "Internal law" within the UK for the purposes of 1(3) is set out in the Insurance Companies Act 1982, s.94B, Sch. 3A (inserted by SI 1990/1333 and amended by 1993/174 and 2519, 1994/1696) and the Friendly Societies Act 1992, s.101, Sch. 20 (amended by SI 1993/2579)—providing rules for the determining of applicable law.

THE LAWS TO BE APPLIED IN ADDITION TO OR SUBSTITUTION FOR THE LAW
GENERALLY APPLICABLE

The existence and material validity of any choice is to be determined by the law applicable
if it were valid but if it is not reasonable to use that law, to adjudge the conduct of a party,
that party may rely on the law of his habitual residence (Article 8).[118] The formal validity
of a contract is to be governed (subject to consumer contracts and some contracts relating
to immovables) by the law applicable if it were valid or, depending on whether parties are
in the same or different countries when concluding the contract, the law of the country in
which it is concluded or the country in which either of the parties is (Article
9(1)(5)(6)).

An act intended to have legal effect in respect of an existing or contemplated contract
is formally valid if it satisfies the law governing the contract or the law of the country
where it was done (Article 9(4)). Where a contract is concluded by parties in the same
country incapacity by a different law may be raised only if the other party was aware or
negligently unaware of it.

It is difficult to see how regard is to be had in relation to the manner of performance and
steps to be taken in the event of defective performance unless that law is to be applied at
least in the sense that nothing inconsistent with that law should be permitted. More,
despite the relative vagueness of the phrase in comparison with other provisions it would
seem to confer a discretion on a court to consider if the law of the place is more relevant
than the generally applicable law to the matters specified. It makes it easier to apply the
law of the place of performance as the law governing a severable part of the contract.

Third party rights. The mutual obligations of assignor and assignee under a voluntary
assignment of a right against a debtor is governed by the law applicable to the contract
between the assignor and assignee. "The law governing the right to which the assignment
relates" determines its "assignability, the relationship between the assignee and the
debtor, the conditions under which the assignment can be invoked against the debtor and
any question whether the debtor's obligations have been discharged" (Article 12).

Subrogation. The law governing a third person's duty to satisfy the creditor of a debtor
or the satisfaction of a claim by one of a number liable determines whether the person
paying is entitled to exercise against the debtor the rights of the person satisfied has under
the law governing the relationship of creditor and debtor.[119]

"Mandatory rules"

The effect of a mandatory rule is to override the general selection principles of choice and
close connection. Whether a rule is "mandatory" must be a matter initially for the
enacting country. Where it is a rule of a state other than the forum, the courts of the forum
will have to decide whether in its national role the rule is "mandatory". The Convention
provides for the application of mandatory rules—

---

118. Applied to a jurisdiction issue in *Oldendorff* v. *Liberia Corpn* [1995] 2 Lloyd's Rep. 64, the onus of
showing its applicability being on the party relying on it. This provision may prevent problems where there is
more than one potential proper law (see *supra*).
119. Article 13(1), (2).

(i) in the sense of law which cannot be derogated from by contract and "all the other elements relevant to the situation at the time of the choice" are connected with the country having the mandatory rule (Article 3.3)

(ii) of the forum "in a situation where they are mandatory irrespective of the law otherwise applicable to the contract" (Article 7.2)

(iii) of a country other than that of the law otherwise applicable if that country has a close connection and the rules would be there applied whatever the law applicable to the contract[120] (Article 7.1).

The United Kingdom has enacted (i) and (ii) but not (iii). In none of these contexts is there a Convention obligation to apply the mandatory rule. As to (i) to apply the "mandatory rule" the choice of the parties "shall not prejudice" the application of the mandatory rule, in (ii) "nothing in the Convention" restricts the application of such a rule and in (iii) "effect may be given" to the rule in the light of its nature and purpose and the consequences of its application. There is little doubt that (in (ii)) a forum would apply its own mandatory rule (as, for example, the House of Lords did in *The Morviken*[121] in applying the Carriage of Goods By Sea Act 1971). Application of a foreign mandatory rule under (ii) is discretionary taking into account the factors expressed and under (i) appears to be at the general discretion of the forum court.

The Convention creates no change in English law in respect of the concept and application of forum mandatory rules save the general principle is expressed. On the other hand while the foreign mandatory rule applicable under Article 3(3) could in theory have been applied prior to the Convention as a limitation on choice based on "public policy", this would have been highly unlikely, the concept of such policy being almost exclusively policy of forum law.[122]

"Ordre public" (Article 16)

The application of a rule of the law of any country may be refused "only if such application is manifestly incompatible with the public policy ('*ordre public*') of the forum". This simply applies the established negative limitation on the general selection principles. It is expressed in narrow and strict language. As with the domestic "public policy" reservation there is no provision for any further consequential enquiry into any other appropriate foreign law.

THE CHOICE OF THE PARTIES (ARTICLE 3)

The existence and validity of the choice is governed by the Convention rules relating to material and formal validity (see *supra*). The choice must be express or demonstrated with reasonable certainty. It may go to the whole or a part only of the contract. The choice may subject the contract to a law other than that earlier governing it whatever the basis on which that law governed the contract.

It is certainly arguable that as the parties may "at any time" agree to a change, the change may be part of the initial agreement. This does not seem to authorize a floating

---

120. As e.g. The Hamburg Rules where enacted.
121. [1983] 1 Lloyd's Rep. 1.
122. See the *Vita Foods* case [1939] A.C. 277.

choice but the ability to contract for a change in the selection, for example, at the carrier's option.[123]

Subject to the exceptions considered above, where there is no choice within Article 3 the law applicable to the contract is that of the country with which it is most closely connected. Subject to specified exceptions and another country appearing more closely connected the general presumption is that the law most closely connected is, if the characteristic performance can be determined, that of the country in which the party who is "to effect the performance which is characteristic of the contract" has his habitual residence or if a corporation its central administration. As an exception to the general rule a severable part of the contract which has a close connection with another country may be governed by the law of that country (Article 4(1)(5)).

Exceptions to the general presumption

These are:

   (i) if the contract is entered into in the course of the trade or business of the party effecting the characteristic performance, the country most closely connected is presumed to be that of the principal place of business *or* where the performance is to be effected in a place of business elsewhere, the country in which that place is situated (Article 4(2));

  (ii) to the extent the subject of the contract is a right in or to use immovable property the country presumed most closely connected is that in which the property is situated (Article 4(3));

 (iii) in respect of a contract for the carriage of goods[124] the general presumption has no application—the only presumption which operates to identify the law most closely concerned is that of the law of a country (a) in which when the contract is concluded the carrier has its principal place of business *and* (b) which is either the place of loading or discharge or the principal place of business of the consignee (Article 4(4)).

The general and exceptional presumptions are to be disregarded if it appears from the circumstances as a whole the contract is more closely connected with another country (Article 4(5)). Where this occurs or the characteristic performance cannot be determined the assessment of the "connection" is therefore at large.

    While the selection of the governing law is according to a criterion identical to that of English law prior to the Act the method of selection is different. As indicated earlier, under English law outside the Convention the weighing of various and unspecified types of connecting factors had some of the appearance of a lottery depending on the importance given by any particular court to any particular link. The approach was in direct contrast to that of selection by single factors as, for example, the place of the contract or the place

---

123. Compare the common law prohibition on the floating law (see *supra*). Presumably any change would bind the consignee of a bill of lading who claims under the contract (see the Carriage of Goods By Sea Act 1992, s.3(1)—being "subject to the same liabilities under that contract as if he had been a party to that contract").

124. Including single voyage charterparties and other contracts the main purpose of which is carriage of goods.

of business of the parties. The Convention adopts a middle line—and, it may be said, a more satisfactory approach than either of the extremes. It provides a startpoint but allows for that to be overridden.

While it may be argued that in the end there is little difference between the English and Convention approach the distinctions in approach give focus to the enquiry. First, there is introduced the concept of "characteristic performance", secondly the approach by rebuttable presumption, thirdly the importance given as a presumptive principle to the residence or place of business of the party undertaking the critical obligation under the contract, and fourthly the presumptions applicable to contracts relating to immovable property and carriage of goods.

Performance characteristic of the contract

The focus on this concept resolves the preliminary question of whether that which is to be linked to a law is the contract as a whole or the particular issue before the court. There may be difficulties in ascertaining the performance but it is concept which makes sense in that it focuses selection on the heart of the contract. There is recognition that it may not be discoverable, but if it is it provides the focal point lacking in the law outside the Convention.

The concept is new to English law. It is said in the Report on the Convention that such performance will not normally be that of a party providing monetary worth for some act (service or provision of goods). However this does not necessarily resolve the identification of the central obligation of contracts solely concerned with the provisions of funds or credit. These must be analysed to identify the focus of the contract.

The rebuttable presumptions. Again it may be argued that because the presumptions are not to apply if it appears that the contract is more closely connected to another country little has changed. But, as with the characteristic performance, the presumptions provide a startpoint for enquiry. It will require positive evidence of connection to prevent their application and they prevent the type of case arising where it is difficult to evaluate numerous connections pointing in different directions. They reflect the emphasis on residence of the party on whom the critical obligation falls—much as the Brussels and Lugano Conventons adopt the domicile of the defendant as the generally applicable rule of jurisdiction.

The Convention approach is well illustrated by the decision of Mance J. in 1994 in *The Bank of Baroda* v. *The Vysya Bank Ltd.*[125] In the context of a writ sought to be served out of the jurisdiction the issue was the law applicable to a contract between the bank issuing a letter of credit and the bank confirming the credit. It involved the consideration of the presumption of Article 4(2) (place of residence, business or incorporation) and the justifiability of applying Article 4(5) because the circumstances as a whole pointed elsewhere. Also relevant to the law applicable to the contract between the banks were the contracts between the beneficiary and each bank. The learned judge agreed with the general principle that the place of residence of Article 4(2) would easily be rebutted where the place of performance was elsewhere. Mance J. held that the performance characteristic

---

125. [1994] 2 Lloyd's Rep. 87. For comment see Morse [1994] LMCLQ 560. As to the applicability of the Convention in a jurisdiction context see fn 118.

of the contract between the banks was the confirmation and the honouring of the obligation of the issuing bank to the beneficiary, rather than the obligation of the issuing bank to reimburse the confirming bank—the latter was consequential on the character of the contract. By Article 4(2) of the Convention on the facts the presumption therefore was that of English law and the ground established for service of the writ out of the jurisdiction.

Mance J. also dealt with the law applicable to the contracts between the banks and the beneficiary, pointing out that it would be impracticable and uncommercial if contracts relating to the same credit were subjected to different laws. The contract between beneficiary and confirming bank was clearly subject to English law (whether by Art. 4(2) or Art. 4(5)) but by Article 4(2) of the Convention the contract between beneficiary and issuing bank was subject to the law of India (the place of incorporation of the issuing bank). However the escape route from the presumptions (Art. 4(5)) was applied to select English law (the law of the place of payment). And this, it was held, would be so whether the credit was confirmed or not. The law of the place of performance was the appropriate law to apply. While this conclusion is clearly right in respect of letters of credit, the place of performance should not be thought always to apply—it will depend on the issue.

(b) Tort

As in other areas, questions of procedure are referred to the forum. The traditional English choice of law rules relating to substantive issues in tort were (to some extent) hardly defensible in a legal system which admits a choice of law process. First, foreign law became relevant only to a tort committed outside England. Secondly, until recently even if the tort is committed out of England, English law largely controlled. As regards the latter there were some judicial inroads and legislative reform of 1995 has rid the approach of this application of English law as such rather than because of its connection with the dispute. The forms of the governing law is now on the place of injury or damage or a country having a significant connection with the issue (see p. 591).

(i) Torts committed in England

Apart from the 1995 Act English law applies[126]—but whether on the same or a different basis as the rule applicable to tort on foreign territory seems uncertain (see *infra*).

(ii) Torts committed on the high seas

(a) Acts occurring on board one ship

There seems to be no English authority, but on principle the relevant foreign law is the law of the country of registration of the ship. It follows that so far as the relevant choice of law

---

126. See e.g. *Szalatray-Stacho* v. *Fink* [1947] 1 K.B. 1; *Metall und Rostoff* v. *Donaldson Lufkin Inc* [1989] 3 All E.R. 14. Whether a defence in a contract governed by foreign law would be recognized depends on whether the tort rule is seen as mandatory (see e.g. *Brodin* v. *Seljan* 1973 S.C. 213).

framework is concerned the situation does not differ to that in which a tort is committed on land,[127] the ship being foreign territory.

(b) More than one ship involved

It is established that the "general maritime law" (i.e. English law) applies.[128] While the fact that a tort is committed at a place not within any country gives the circumstances a particular character, it is difficult to defend the automatic application of English law. Wrapping English law in general maritime clothes perhaps illustrates that its application as English law could be attacked, but it does nothing to conceal the body.

(iii) Torts committed on foreign land or waters—prior to 1969[129]

Prior to 1969 and the decision of the House of Lords in *Boys* v. *Chaplin*[130] there was no doubt that to succeed in England in an action based on a tort committed in another country in regard to substantive issues a plaintiff had to overcome two hurdles. Proof was required that:

   (i) the act would have been actionable if committed in England; and
   (ii) the act was not justifiable (or actionable) according to the law of the place where the tort was committed.

The rule reflects a primitive view of the role of English law in a case involving a foreign element. Instead of searching for a "governing law" this choice of law rule refers to foreign law only as a preliminary hurdle for a plaintiff. As a result, a plaintiff must satisfy the criteria of *two* legal systems and English law would not recognize a tortious liability "in respect of an act which according to its own principles imposes no liability on the person from whom damages are claimed".[131]

This approach comes close to denial of a process aimed at selection of a governing law dependent on close connection with an issue. The traditional rule in the United States was to refer the question to the law of the place of the act. Such a rule at least recognizes the "reference" role of a choice of law process, but has its own defects. Apart from the difficulty of selecting *a place*, the place may be entirely coincidental or at the least have little contact with the issue.

Since 1963 courts in the United States have moved towards an approach similar in some respects to that adopted in England to contractual issues—"the centre of gravity" approach. According to the original judicial expression of this approach reference is to be

127. For a Canadian application, see *Canadian National S.S. Co.* v. *Watson* [1959] 1 D.L.R. 273.
128. See e.g. *The Leon* (1881) 6 P.D. 148; *Chartered Mercantile Bank of India* v. *Netherlands India Steam Navigation Co.* (1883) 10 Q.B.D. 521. The proposed statutory reform will not affect this rule (see *infra*).
129. I.e. on land or within territorial waters. As to territorial waters, see *The Halley* (1868) L.R. 2 P.C. 193; *The Arum* [1921] P. 12; *The Wazirstan* [1953] 2 Lloyd's Rep. 361, but see also *Sayers* v. *International Drilling Co. NV* [1971] 3 All E.R. 163 in which, however, the predominant view was that it was a case in contract. For an example of a collision between a ship and a foreign pier, see *The Tolten* [1946] P. 135. The rule that English courts lacked jurisdiction to hear actions in regard to foreign land does not apply to maritime claims (*ibid.*), and is greatly modified by the Civil Jurisdiction and Judgments Act 1982, s.30. (See Chap. 12.)
130. [1971] A.C. 356.
131. *The Halley* (1868) L.R. 2 P.C. 193—stemming from a collision in Belgian waters which raised the defence of compulsory pilotage—a defence in English law but not in Belgian law. The vessels were Belgian and Norwegian. As to the effect of a contractual defence and the relevant choice of law process, see *supra*.

made "to the law of the jurisdiction which because of its relationship or contact with the occurrence or the parties has the greatest concern with the specific issue raised in the litigation".[132]

Somewhat similar, but less precise in its criteria, was an English suggestion in 1949 that the English rule should give way to the "proper law of the tort", i.e. an adaptation of the rule in contract by reference to law of the place "with the most significant relationship to the occurrence and the parties". In *Boys* v. *Chaplin*, however, the House of Lords failed to take the opportunity to move away from the traditional "double-barrelled" rule. Worse, each member of the House followed his own track with the result that tradition was maintained primarily through lack of any positive move away from it.

Boys v. Chaplin and its consequences

Following *Boys* v. *Chaplin*, in considering an action based on an act done abroad, The English court would:

(i) continue to refer all "procedural" matters to English law as the law of the forum (matters of quantification of damage being a "procedural" matter for this purpose)[133];

(ii) require the plaintiff to prove that civil liability would ensue under the law of the place of the act;

(iii) require the plaintiff to prove that the act would have been actionable in English law.

However, in the case, Lord Hodson applied the most significant relationship test. Lord Wilberforce, having approved the application of (ii) and (iii) above as a general rule, stated that it should be considered whether the general rule should always apply to particular issues. He expressed the qualification only in terms of the application of the relevant foreign rule (i.e. (ii) above). He suggested that in considering the qualification it was necessary "to identify the policy of the rule, to enquire to what situation with what contacts it was intended to apply; whether or not to apply it in the circumstances of the instant case would serve any interest which the rule was devised to meet".[134]

The exception created by Lord Wilberforce was recognized by text book writers[135] and in 1983 by Hodgson J.[136] It was not until 1991 however, that in *Johnson* v. *Coventry Churchill International Ltd*[137] the availability was judicially applied and it was given approval by the Privy Council in 1993 in a Hong Kong case—*Red Sea Insurance Co. Ltd*

132. *Babcock* v. *Jackson* 240 N.Y.S. 2d 743 (1963); [1963] 2 Lloyd's Rep. 286, 289 (an action in New York arising out of a vehicle collision in Ontario). Such a formula, taken on its own, is not limited to tort. The approach may have been varied in 1967 in *Reich* v. *Purcell* 432 P. 2d 727 (1967) through assessment of state interests.

133. Lord Guest and Lord Donovan included the question of the head of damage (in this case "pain and suffering") as procedure. See [1971] A.C. 356, at pp. 382, 383.) As to time bars, see *supra*.

134. [1971] A.C. 356, at p. 391—on rejection apparently applying only English law.

135. See e.g. Morris, *Conflict of Laws* (McLean), 4th edn, 1993, p. 288; Dicey and Morris, 12th edn, 1993, p. 1480; Cheshire and North, 12th edn, 1992, Chap. 20.

136. *Coupland* v. *Arabian Gulf Petroleum* [1983] 2 All E.R. 434, at p. 446. The traditional rule was applied without argument by the Court of Appeal, see [1983] 3 All E.R. 226. Hodgson J. stressed that the question of quantification of damages was for the forum in any event.

137. [1992] 3 All E.R. 14 (J. W. Kay Q.C.).

v. *Bouygues SA*.[138] In the *Johnson* case it was applied to an action by an English employee against an English employer for injury suffered during work in Germany. The matter was not actionable in Germany but English law was applied on the basis that the country with the most significant relationship to the occurrence was England, the result gave certainty and protection to English employees in such circumstances and the defendants, having taken out insurance, were not likely to be taken unaware by the application of English law.

In the *Red Sea Insurance* case the issue was whether insurers could counterclaim in Hong Kong against contractors in respect of alleged negligence in Saudi Arabia. The contractors were part of a consortium claiming against the insurers (incorporated in Hong Kong) under a policy indemnifying the consortium for loss or damage in respect of damage occurring in building constructed in Saudi Arabia. The insurers sought to claim that if they were liable on the policy they were entitled by subrogation to recover against the negligent contractors for breach of duty of care to other members of the consortium. Under Hong Kong law the insurers could not sue the contractors directly for tort but Saudi Arabia law provided for such liability.

The Privy Council affirmed the general "double actionability" rule but applied "the most significant relationship" to exclude the *lex fori*—and held that it could apply to the whole claim (and not merely one issue as in *Boys* v. *Chaplin*) if all or virtually all the significant factors pointed to the law of the place of the occurrence. In this case such factors all pointed to Saudi Arabia.

There seems little doubt that English law in this respect was on the familiar route of judicial step by step reform (as for example occurred in the acceptance of *forum non conveniens* as a doctrine). One of the problems of this type of self-imposed judicial limitation is that the cost of reform is laid at the door of litigants—and each step creates the uncertainty of the next step. But that is not to deny an unqualified welcome to the move away not only from double actionability but, at last, from English law as always controlling. And so, to legislation.

Statutory reform

The judicial development is to find its way into and itself be developed by statute through the Private International Law (Miscellaneous Provisions) Act 1995. In respect of acts or omissions occurring after a date to be appointed the rules of common law requiring double actionability and as an exception allowing "the law of a single country" to be applied are abolished. In their place is put the following:

"11.—(1) The general rule is that the applicable law is the law of the country in which the events constituting the tort or delict in question occur.

(2) Where significant elements of those events occur in different countries, the applicable law under the general rule is to be taken as being—

    (a) for a cause of action in respect of personal injury caused to an individual or death resulting from personal injury, the law of the country where the individual was when he sustained the injury;

    (b) for a cause of action in respect of damage to property, the law of the country where the property was when it was damaged; and

    (c) in any other case, the law of the country in which the most significant element or elements of those events occurred.

138. [1994] 3 All E.R. 749 (Lord Slynn giving the judgment of the Board).

(3) In this section 'personal injury' includes disease or any impairment of physical or mental condition.

12.—(1) If it appears, in all the circumstances, from a comparison of—

(a) the significance of the factors which connect a tort or delict with the country whose law would be the applicable law under the general rule; and

(b) the significance of any factors connecting the tort of delict with another country,

that it is substantially more appropriate for the applicable law to be the law of the other country, the general rule is displaced and the applicable law is the law of that other country.

(2) The factors that may be taken into account as connecting a tort or delict with a country for the purposes of this section include, in particular, factors relating to the parties, to any of the events which constitute the tort or delict in question or to any of the circumstances or consequences of those events."[139]

The substitution of the rules of sections 11, 12 for the double actionability rule is to apply to events occurring in the forum as it applies to events in another country. However the introduction of sections 11, 12 is limited to the abolition double actionability and any exception.[139]

Whether the provisions apply to a tort committed in England depends therefore on the basis of the pre-statute rule that English law was solely applicable. About that there must be considerable doubt, it being said that that rule had no application to a tort committed in England (see fn. 126). Further, the new approach does not apply to torts at sea involving more than one ship—an exception difficult to justify.

The forum mandatory rule

Apart from the statutory reform and apart from the application of the most significant relationship exception English law applies to all tort actions before English courts. It is specified in the Private International Law Act that the reform is without prejudice to any mandatory rule (s.14(4)).

The context of the applicable English law

English law (particularly statute) does not necessarily apply to acts outside England as it does to acts within England.

Torts on the high seas involving more than one ship

Even after the 1995 Act in proceedings before English courts English law alone applies to all torts occurring on the high seas involving more than one ship. The only issue as to the applicability of a statutory provision of such torts is therefore whether, considering the purposes of the provision, it applies to the tortious act (i.e. is within the boundary rule). So, for example, in *The Esso Malaysia*[140] the court had to decide whether the Fatal Accidents Act applied to a collision on the high seas.

---

139. By s.14(2) it is expressly specified that change applies only where the common law rules also specified would have applied. The change is not to affect any rule of law except as abolished, and in particular is not to authorize any question of procedure to be determined otherwise than by the *lex fori* or affect the non-application of foreign law because of public policy or that it consists of a penal, revenue or other public law as would not be enforceable under formal law.

140. [1974] 2 Lloyd's Rep. 143; [1975] Q.B. 198.

Torts in foreign territory or on board a foreign ship

Where a tort occurs on foreign land or waters or on board a foreign ship the applicability of an English legislative provision will first depend on whether the circumstances fall within the provision (i.e. the boundary rule). Assuming that the provision by its terms is applicable the second issue is whether it is mandatory. If not it will apply, apart from the 1995 Act as part of the applicable English law[141] and under the 1995 Act only if according to its criteria English law is applicable.

English statutory implementation of maritime international provisions

The exclusive applicability of English statutory frameworks reflecting international Conventions outside English territorial waters has tended to be assumed[142]—probably because of the relevance of English law to all issues of tortious liability. Given that the statute by its terms applies, it forms part of English law applying to the high seas where more than one ship is involved. Whether it applies to the high seas where only one ship is involved or to foreign waters is, as was said above, a matter of construction. In this context applicability may be supported if the statute is based on an international Convention.

Included in the statutory provision of international rules relating to tortious liability are:

    (i) the rule as to division of loss where more than one ship is to blame for a collision enshrined initially in the Maritime Conventions Act 1911[143];

    (ii) the statutory limitation of liability framework (if not procedural) (see Chapter 24);

    (iii) the Collision Regulations.[144]

The International Collision Regulations apply to "all vessels upon the high seas and in all waters connected therewith navigable by seagoing vessels". They are applied by statutory instrument to United Kingdom vessels wherever they may be and to other vessels within the territorial waters of the United Kingdom.[145] Within the ambit of the Order the first question is whether the regulations constitute a mandatory rule, for if the English

---

141. The foreign law should apply whether or not the acts take place only on one ship and whether the ship is British or not. See *Mackinnon* v. *The Iberia Shipping Co.* 1955 S.C. 20 (Sc.). But cf. *Sayers* v. *International Drilling Co.* [1971] 3 All E.R. 163 in which the Court of Appeal treated the foreign law as irrelevant. It *may* be that foreign law should be excluded.

142. So Sturt, *The Collision Regulations* (3rd edn, para. 1.15) ignores both choice of law process and the mandatory rule in declaring that "within the territorial jurisdiction of a foreign State the application of the rule would be subject to the relevant municipal law of that State". The Regulations as enacted by SI 1989/1798 (as amended by SI 1991/1638) apply to UK vessels wherever they may be and to other vessels within the UK or territorial waters of the UK (reg. 2). They have been extended under the power conferred by Merchant Shipping Act 1979, s.47 to Bermuda, Falkland Islands, Montserrat, St Helena and Turks and Caicos Islands (SI 1989/2400 as amended by SI 1993/1786). There is a power to apply to ships other than those of the United Kingdom the provisions of an international agreement involving safety (Merchant Shipping Act 1979, s.21(2)) and provisions of the Merchant Shipping Acts generally (Merchant Shipping (Registration etc) Act 1993, Sch. 4, para. 4(5)) (as from 1 January 1996 Merchant Shipping Act 1995, s.307).

143. Section 1 (after 1 January 1996, Merchant Shipping Act 1995, ss.187, 188).

144. Currently enacted into English law by the Merchant Shipping (Distress Signals and Prevention of Collision) Regulations 1989, SI 1989/1798 amended by SI 1991/1638 made under the Merchant Shipping Act 1979, ss.21, 22 (after 1 January 1996 Merchant Shipping Act 1995, ss.85, 86).

145. See fn. 142.

regulations are not mandatory there is no reason why the general conflicts approach should not apply.

In 1973 *The Esso Brussels*[146] the Court of Appeal held that the Collision Regulations applied within Belgian territorial waters only through Belgian law—apparently on the basis that the law of the place of the collision governed the issue. However, there are many cases in which the regulations have been applied simply on the basis that the collision occurred in waters connected with the high seas and therefore within the boundary rules of the regulations.[147] Neither in *The Esso Brussels* nor in the cases applying the regulations directly did the court approach the question on the basis of the accepted choice of law framework for tortious issues; and in no case did the court refer to the imposition of the regulations through a mandatory legislative provision. Apart from the 1995 Act—

(i) the regulations themselves and the statutes under which they are made set out the limitations of their application[148] (the boundary rules);

(ii) by general choice of law rules civil liability stemming from an event in foreign waters depends on actionability under foreign law *and* (assuming that it had occurred in England) English law;

(iii) where an English mandatory rule is applied to foreign waters or a foreign ship on the high seas it is arguable that it excludes foreign law. If so, in *The Esso Brussels* it was wrong to hold that the Collision Regulations applied only through Belgian law.[149]

Under the 1995 Act in relation to the governing law of tortious matters the issue of the applicability remains but in a different form. In relation to a ship of a foreign country not within the regulations the first question is, as before, whether the English regulations are mandatory—if not and the act occurred in foreign territorial waters the foreign law applies unless displaced because of significant facts pointing elsewhere.

(c)   Restitution or unjust enrichment

The nature of claims within the "category"

In English law restitution—once known more artificially as "*quasi contract*" and perhaps more accurately unjust enrichment—tended at one time to be more a label of desperation than a term of definition. Under it would be found claims which do not spring from tort or contract. The use of "unjust enrichment" at least describes the ground of claim whereas

146. [1973] 2 Lloyd's Rep. 73. For an example of a US court applying foreign law to a collision in foreign waters, see *Ishikazi Kisen Co. Ltd.* v. *US* (18–975) AMC 287 (US Ct. of Appeals).

147. *The Toluca* [1981] 2 Lloyd's Rep. 548; *The Maritime Harmony* [1982] 2 Lloyd's Rep. 400; *The Savina* [1975] 2 Lloyd's Rep. 141; *The Troll River* [1974] 2 Lloyd's Rep. 181; *The Francesco Nullo* [1973] 1 Lloyd's Rep. 72; *The Bovenkerk* [1973] 1 Lloyd's Rep. 63; *The Adolf Leonhardt* [1973] 2 Lloyd's Rep. 318; *The Ore Chief* [1974] 2 Lloyd's Rep. 427; *The Martin Fierro* [1974] 2 Lloyd's Rep. 203; *The Sabine* [1974] 1 Lloyd's Rep. 465; *The Oldekerk* [1974] 1 Lloyd's Rep. 95; *The Boleslaw Chrobry* [1974] 2 Lloyd's Rep. 308. Cf. SI 1989/1798.

148. By the Collision Regulations and Distress Signals Order 1977 (SI 1977/682) and the Safety (Collision Regulations and Distress Signals) Regulations 1979 (SI 1979/1659) the Regulations were extended to vessels of specified foreign countries whether within British jurisdiction or not. These provisions were revoked by SI 1983/708, in turn revoked by SI 1989/1798.

149. This argument assumes that the relevance of the Collision Regulations in assessing civil liability is a matter of substance. If it is a matter of procedure, burden of proof, or evidence it is a matter for the forum and the English regulation would again apply.

"restitution" may indicate too narrowly a claim for restoration of some interest lost. "Quasi contract" indicates nothing at all.

As might be expected from its general development pattern, in English law the claims which may fall within "unjust enrichment" or restitution have developed piecemeal. So recovery of money paid by mistake or fraud (including tracing into the hands of their parties), the consequences of the invalidity of a contract, or illegality or duress on the validity of contracts, the right to contribution between wrongdoers, the relief from unreasonable bargains and in maritime law payment for salvage services have tended to develop as heads of claim, distinct in nature rather than as application of any general principle. However "restitutionary claims" now seem recognized as having a common theme.[150]

There is therefore a growing tendency to recognize "restitutionary" claims as a category—although the boundaries are still to be worked out. As with other domestic categories it then becomes a basis for the selection of governing law. Such claims are almost by definition "non-contractual", and a restitutionary claim based on invalidity of a contract has been held not to be a claim "relating to a contract" for the purposes of jurisdiction under the Brussels Convention.[151] The concept is being given shape with the recognition that the basis of the claim is unjust enrichment at the expense of the plaintiff and that change of position is a good defence.[152] There remains, however in each case whether the restitutionary claim creates a proprietary interest or is simply a claim *in personam*[153]—a matter directly relevant to identifying the governing law. Further, the relationship between tort, contract and restitution remains open to debate.[154] Any uncertainty as to the boundary of the category must be reflected in its application as a foundation for identifying the governing law. So classification remains as the first and fundamental step.

The governing law

The identification of rules for assessing the governing law in relation to unjust enrichment in general remains speculative.[155] Dicey and Morris suggest that it is the proper law which is the focus—if the claim arises out of a contract, the proper law of the contract and in any other circumstances (save that involving an immovable) the law of the country where the enrichment occurs.[156] This has been judicially applied through the general principle that the proper law of any restitutionary claim is the country in which the receipt takes

---

150. See generally Goff and Jones, *Law of Restitution*, 4th edn, 1993; Birks, *Restitution—The Future*, Federation Press, 1992; Jones, *Restitution in Public and Private Law*, Sweet and Maxwell, 1991, and the advent of the *Restitution Law Review* 1993. The consequences of nullity of contract are excluded from UK enactment of the Rome Convention as a matter of restitution (see *supra*).

151. *Barclays Bank* v. *Glasgow City Council* [1994] 4 All E.R. 865.

152. See *Lipkin Gorman* v. *Karpnale Ltd.* [1992] 4 All E.R. 512 (H.L.); Birks, "English Recognition of Unjust Enrichment"[1991] LMCLQ 473.

153. See *Napier* v. *Hunter* [1993] 1 All E.R. 385 and e.g. Key [1994] LMCLQ 421 and authorities there cited.

154. For an example of the limitations on the role of restitution see *The Trident Beauty* [1994] 1 Lloyd's Rep. 365 (H.L.)—a charterer cannot recover from an assignee of receivables including hire or charter monies paid in advance and not earned. For discussion see Barker [1994] LMCLQ 305.

155. See e.g. Goff and Jones, *Law of Restitution*, 1st edn, at p. 506. In the second edition the authors omitted the subject of conflict of laws, having, they said, little to add to Dicey and Morris. In the 4th edn it is dealt with (at pp. 730–731) in the context of tort.

156. 12th edn, rule 201.

place.[157] Whether, however, this should be taken necessarily to be the governing law is perhaps open to the same type of objection as a single factor rule applying to contract. The place of performance does not have the same dominant force as for a commercial credit, for the place of receipt may be as transitory as the payment of funds. The substance of the enrichment may have a quite different focus and it is certainly arguable that in many cases it will have more of the character of property than tort or even contract.

Whether or not a restitutionary claim is based in domestic law on a proprietary interest such as a trust, where it is an assertion of entitlement to restoration it is arguable that its "property" element should control. That, it is suggested, should lead to the law of the place of that which is claimed rather than the place of the enrichment. Even if the unjust enrichment is not so much "restitution" of a claim as a claim to a benefit (as, for example, for salvage) and is seen simply as a claim *in personam* the law of the place of the unjust enrichment seems to have less to offer than an analogy to a contract claim. There seems no reason not to apply the proper law approach—if desirable, qualified by presumptions.

Maritime claims—general average and salvage

Dicey and Morris suggest that, as regards general average and salvage, maritime law has worked out its own rules of governing law, and as regards general average has adopted an international structure in the York-Antwerp Rules, thereby avoiding conflicts problems. It is true that bills of lading and charterparties almost invariably incorporate the York-Antwerp Rules (a new text having been agreed in 1994) but it does not follow that no issues remain as to the governing law as respects general average. And it certainly is not the case that salvage claims are somehow immune from problems of identifying the law which governs them.

Either contract or unjust enrichment may form a basis for claims in salvage and general average. There is a readiness in courts to intervene on the grounds of "injustice" in salvage agreements where the agreements are regarded as unconscionable.[158]

General average[159]

A general average claim may be based on contract—either as part of the contract of carriage or based on an average bond—or on unjust enrichment.

(i) CONTRACTUAL

Contract of carriage and adjustment of average. The proper law of (or within the Rome Convention the "law applicable" to) a charterparty, bill of lading or other contract of carriage will apply to resolve the validity of a general average clause. However, apart from the Rome Convention, it is not necessarily (or perhaps even presumptively) the case that

---

157. *El Ajou* v. *Dollar Land Holdings plc* [1993] 3 All E.R. 717; *Chase Manhattan Bank* v. *Israel British Bank* [1979] 3 All E.R. 1025. In both cases the court thought it unnecessary to enquire if the basis of claim was procedural or substantive—in the *Chase Manhattan* case as the right existed in foreign and English law however classified and in the *El Ajou* case as English law was the law of the place of receipt and law of the forum.

158. See e.g. *The Port Caledonia and the Anna* [1903] P. 184; *Akerblom* v. *Price Potter Walker & Co.* (1881) 7 Q.B.D 129, 132–133 (per Brett C.J.). The Salvage Convention 1989 provides for annulment or modification if the terms are inequitable (Art. 7).

159. See generally Lowndes and Rudolph, *General Average and the York Antwerp Rules*, 11th edn, 1990.

the law which will govern the adjustment of average is that governing the contract.[160] A specific choice of law to govern the adjustment[161] will be recognized as with any other express choice. Lacking that, it appeared accepted that the governing law was the law of the port of destination.[162] Where there is a reference to the York-Antwerp Rules this will be recognized but when, as usual, the reference is coupled with adjustment at the port of destination it will follow that the rules as interpreted at that place will apply.

Prior to the Rome Convention it was held that a contract must have a proper law from and at its inception and therefore a clause providing (e.g.) a carrier with an option to select a law would not operate to postpone the selection of a law but would itself be subject to the proper law ascertained from the contract as a whole. A general average clause may give the carrier an option as to port or place of adjustment,[163] and the question is whether the proper law of the contract would allow the option to operate.

Under the Rome Convention the parties choice remains the primary ground of selection of the governing law. Lacking choice the law of the port of destination may govern the adjustment even if the law generally applicable to the contract as a whole be some other law. The adjustment arguably is a severable part of the contract, although hardly severable from the provisions of general average. Even if not severable it may be referred to the law of the place of performance as going to the manner of performance (see *supra*).

Average bond. On general principles the governing law is the law having the closest and most real connection. Apart from the Rome Convention an express selection of the place of adjustment would be a strong—but not apparently a conclusive—indication of its proper law.[164] Under the Convention for the reasons suggested in respect of the adjustment of average it is arguable that the law of the place would govern the bond.

In 1980 in *The Armar*[165] the Court of Appeal held that a decision as to the place of adjustment reached after the entry into an average bond could not dictate the proper law of the bond. The bond as a contract had to have a proper law from its inception. Such a decision goes only to the rejection of the dependence of the proper law of a *contract* relating to average (as distinct from the law governing the adjustment) on a subsequent selection of the place of adjustment. It is arguable that, unlike the need for a proper law applicable to a contract because of the possibility of disputes at any time, there is no such need in relation to adjustment. The proper law of the adjustment applies only to the adjustment and there is, therefore, no reason not to recognize selection by the parties—or postponement of its ascertainment.[166] Under the Rome Convention parties may change the law applicable to the contract by subsequent selection (see *supra*) but the specification of

160. See *ibid* G38–G53.
161. As, for example, Gencon 1994 cl. 12 and to be stated in NYPE 1993 cl. 25.
162. See *Simonds* v. *White* (1824) 2 B. & C. 805; *Lloyd* v. *Guibert* (1865) L.R. 1 Q.B. 115; *Wavertree Sailing Ship Co.* v. *Love* [1897] A.C. 373. The port may be where a voyage is broken by agreement or necessity (see *Hill* v. *Wilson* (1879) 4 C.P.D. 329).
163. See *The Armar* [1980] 2 Lloyd's Rep. 450.
164. *The Armar* (*supra*) at p. 454. It should be noted that the issue in this case was whether the contract was governed by English law so as to allow service of writ out of the jurisdiction under RSC Order 11, rule 1(1)(f)(iii) and therefore that no question arose as to whether different issues were governed by different laws (Megaw J.).
165. [1980] 2 Lloyd's Rep. 450.
166. Just as there is no reason not to permit postponement of decision as to the place of arbitration—the only effect is to neutralize that factor as relevant to the law governing the substantive contract. See *The Star Texas* [1993] 2 Lloyd's Rep. 445 and *supra*.

the place of adjustment would not of itself be a selection of the law applicable to the bond.

(ii) UNJUST ENRICHMENT

It may be argued that even when raised in a contractual context an average claim is based on the obligation to contribute to the general sacrifice. Whatever its basis in a contract context, an average obligation can arise where there is no contract on which it can possibly be based—as where it exists between cargo owners. It would appear clear that the same rule applies as for average claims arising out of contract—that adjustment is referred to the law of the place of destination.

Salvage

(i) CONTRACT

Where salvage services are rendered pursuant to contract the governing law is ascertained as any other contract. Lloyd's Standard Form of Salvage Agreement contains a specific choice of English law.[167]

(ii) UNJUST ENRICHMENT

Where salvage services are rendered without agreement the basis for recovery is the conferment of benefit and therefore enrichment which would be unjust without payment. As regards salvage services started on or after 1 January 1995 the principles are enshrined in the Salvage Convention 1989 which is given the force of law in the United Kingdom by the Merchant Shipping (Salvage and Pollution) Act 1994. The Convention applies whenever relevant judicial or arbitral proceedings are bought in a State party.[168] While it sets out the criteria of and conditions for an award the apportionment as between persons in the service of each salving vessel is to be determined by the law of the flag of the vessel.[169]

As regards salvage prior to 1 January 1995 the law of the flag is applied to a dispute as to apportionment between persons in the service of a foreign vessel.[170] Apart from that there is no evidence that the law applied would be other than English law.

(d) Proprietary issues

General approach

A substantive proprietary claim in relation to a tangible movable or immovable is governed by the law of the place of the thing, and in relation to an intangible the law of residence of the "debtor". A proprietary claim may involve either or both of two distinct issues:

---

167. See LOF 1990 cl. 1(d).
168. Article 1.
169. Article 15(2). If there is no vessel involved the matter is to be governed by the law of the contract between salvor and his servants (*ibid*).
170. Maritime Conventions Act 1911, s.7.

    (i) the assertion of an interest against a defendant who is not a party to its creation (i.e. against a third party) where (a) the claim is against a defendant who has no interest in the relevant asset (as where he has inflicted damage) or (b) the defendant has a competing interest (e.g. ownership or a similar interest to the claimant);

    (ii) the enforcement of a claim on the basis of the transfer of a proprietary interest which may create two competing interests within (i) (see p. 605).

Some claims will clearly have proprietary *and* other aspects. So, the ability of a cargo owner to sue for damage to the cargo carried prior to his acquisition of ownership of the cargo,[171] or a time charterer for loss caused through damage to the ship, poses issues which can be seen as either property or tort or both. The enforcement of a security by a mortgagee against a mortgagor or a purchaser of a ship in respect of the sale could be seen as contract or property.

The difficulty of classification underlines the artificiality of using domestic concepts (some not at all clear) as a basis for the selection of a governing law and the constant need to focus on the issue before the court. There is, therefore, a preliminary question of construction. Once the issue is classified as a property issue the choice of law process requires the identification of the "asset" in which the interest is held (e.g. a ship, goods or a debt) as tangible (and if tangible movable or immovable) or intangible. The base for the application of the choice of law process is then established.

The philosophy behind the choice of law framework is not difficult to appreciate. "Title" is essentially connected with the thing in relation to which it is claimed and is fully enforceable only where the thing is. This applies with most force to immovables and, until the coming into force of s.30 of the Civil Jurisdiction and Judgments Act 1982, on 24 August 1982, English courts adopted the general principle, save for maritime claims,[172] that they would not even adjudicate on matters involving any question of title to foreign immovables.[173] The general focus on the place of the thing applies with less logic to movables or intangibles, for the place at a critical time may have little to do with the parties, the dispute, or the ability to enforce the claim, particularly where it is for damages. The Rome Convention applies the law governing the contract to matters connected with an assignment of contractual rights, including assignability and enforceability against the debtor.[174]

Proprietary maritime claims

Such claims concern aspects of:

    (a) ownership, mortgages, liens and chartering of ships (ship claims);

    (b) ownership, mortgages and liens of cargo (cargo claims);

171. As to which see now Carriage of Goods By Sea Act 1992—a statutory transfer of contractual rights. It is uncertain whether the Act will be seen as mandatory or whether, there being no express provision, it applies only to contracts in relation to which the applicable law is English. There is no enactment of a Convention to lead to the former and there seems little in principle to suppose a mandatory approach. See Toh [1994] LMCLQ 280.

172. See *The Tolten* [1946] P. 135.

173. The jurisdiction is now excluded only where the proceedings are principally connected with title or the right to possession.

174. Article 12(2). As to subrogation see Article 13 (and *supra*).

(c) ownership, mortgages and liens (where applicable) of freight or charter or insurance moneys (money claims).

(i) Assertion of a proprietary interest

(a) SHIP CLAIMS

It is likely that questions of ownership and mortgage of ships would be referred to the law of the flag, on the principle that a ship reflects the territory of the flag. In 1979 in *The Angel Bell*[175] Donaldson J. equated ships to land for the purpose of deciding on the law to govern a mortgage and applied the law of the flag. The reasoning applies with as much if not greater force to ownership. Even apart from the reasoning (and on the basis that a ship was "a floating piece of the nation whose flag it wears") it scarcely makes sense to refer questions of the validity and effect of proprietary transactions to the law of the place of a ship at the time of the transaction. It is commercially unrealistic to follow the approach applicable generally and link a transfer or creation of an interest to a *situs* when the transaction is between parties whose physical contact with the ship is probably minimal and the very purpose of the ship is that it continuously changes its *situs*. Further, the normal maritime framework for ownership and mortgage is built on registration under the law of the flag and it would be contrary to the principle of uniformity to adapt a different reference point.

Even if the general rule of reference of proprietary questions to the *situs* applies to ships, there are specific statutory rules applicable to registered ships. The Merchant Shipping (Registration etc.) Act 1993[176] (as from 1 January 1996 repealed and re-enacted by the Merchant Shipping Act 1995, Part I) provides a code for governing the transfer of a title to a registered ship (which must be a British ship) or a share therein and the creation or transfer of a registered mortgage in such a ship or share.[177] It specifies those qualified to own British ships and the effect of transfer or transmission on death, marriage or bankruptcy to unqualified persons. Such provisions are not exclusive in the sense that a proprietary interest may be created in ways other than provided by statute.[178] It is, however, unlikely that a transaction creating rights under foreign law in a British ship or even more so a registered British ship would be recognized if contrary to the law of the applicable part of the United Kingdom.[179]

Mortgage and sale contracts. Contractual issues are governed by the law applicable to such contracts but the creation of proprietary interests by virtue of the contract, it is suggested, should be referred to the law governing the validity of such interests. However, in considering the validity of a mortgage claim against a third party in *The Angel Bell*, Donaldson J. held that a contract to create a mortgage governed by English law created an equitable mortgage as that was the result in English law. With respect, this confuses

---

175. [1979] 2 Lloyd's Rep. 491.
176. And The Merchant Shipping (Registration of Ships) Regulations 1993 made under the Act.
177. See Chap. 23.
178. *Ibid.*
179. In *Union Bank* v. *Lenanton* (1878) C.P.D. 243 no question of foreign law seems to have been contemplated in respect of a ship sold by British owners to Turkish buyers, the issue being whether title could pass by bill of sale in a ship which in English law was unregistered (and unregistrable).

contractual and property questions. While the English "classification" approach may be open to criticism, while it is there it should be followed.

Liens.[180] In English law it seems that the question of whether a lien attaches to a claim is a matter for the law of the forum—primarily on the basis that the question is procedural.[181] This argument formed at least one ground of the decision of the Privy Council in *The Halcyon Isle*[182] concerning maritime liens. If it applies to maritime liens, even more so will it apply to statutory liens in Admiralty. It is arguable that even accepting these as procedural an equitable lien and a possessory lien are substantive in that neither depends on legal proceedings for its existence.

It has already been contended (i) in Chapters 17, 18 that the question of whether a lien attaches is substantive; (ii) earlier in this chapter that it makes little sense to separate matters of priority from the characteristics of proprietary interests unless such interests are governed by separate laws. However, the present English law in respect of maritime liens and hence statutory liens in Admiralty hinges on the decision in *The Halcyon Isle*. Possessory liens and equitable liens could be governed by the law of the place of the asset[183]—or treated as procedural and be brought within the principle of *The Halcyon Isle*. Whatever its scope the decision calls for comment.

The decision of "The Halcyon Isle". In this case the High Court in Singapore was faced with claims against a fund resulting from the sale of a ship by a mortgagee and a shiprepairer. The ship was a British ship registered in London and the mortgage was also registered in London. The repair was carried out in New York. There were insufficient funds to meet both claims. According to the law of the United States the shiprepairer has a maritime lien which would take priority to the mortgage. According to the law of Singapore (which was identical with English law) the shiprepairer had a statutory lien and the mortgagee's claim took priority over it. The Court of Appeal in Singapore had followed a decision of the Supreme Court of Canada (*The Ioannis Daskalelis*[184]) in holding that the question of whether a claim attracted a maritime lien was for the law of the place where it was created (the *lex loci contractus*) whereas the question of priority was for Singapore (the law of the forum). By a majority of 3–2 the Privy Council took the contrary view, holding that:

" . . . the English authorities on close examination support the principle that, in the application of English rules of conflict of laws, maritime claims are classified as giving rise to maritime liens which are enforceable in actions in rem in English courts where *and only where* the events on which

---

180. The question of whether a lien created by foreign law and recognized in English law is relevant only if the claim can be brought in an English court—i.e. if the court has jurisdiction. As regards maritime claims, therefore, the claim must comply with the Supreme Court Act 1981, ss.20 and 21. As to the availability of claims under foreign law under these provisions, see *supra* and Chap. 2.

181. Compare a US approach of assessing which law should apply on the basis of connecting factors between state and the issue where the rival interests are a contractually created lien and that of a non-party to the contract (see *Arochem* v. *Wilomi* 962 F. 2d 496 (1992)).

182. [1981] A.C. 221.

183. In relation to contractual liens a third possibility is the proper law of any contract creating such a lien and this seems sometimes to have been confused with the law of the place of creation of the lien (see *The Halcyon Isle* [1981] A.C. 221, at p. 230). Such a possibility confuses contract and property.

184. The Federal Court of Appeal in Canada approved and followed *The Ioannis Daskalelis* in *Marlex Petroleum* v. *The Ship "Har Rai"* (1984) 4 D.L.R. (4th) 739. See also *The Galaxias* 1989 1 Can. Fed. 386. After some uncertainty the approach in *The Halcyon Isle* was approved in South Africa (*The Andrico Unity* 1989 (4) S.A. 325 (A)). See generally Staniland [1989] LMCLQ 174; [1990] LMCLQ 491.

the claim is founded would have given rise to a maritime lien in English law, if those events had occurred within the territorial jurisdiction of the English court".[185]

Previous authorities are by no means certain in their direction but in *The Halcyon Isle* the minority roundly declared that "the balance of authorities, the comity of nations, private international law and natural justice" all supported its view that in English law the matter of whether a maritime lien based on contracts exists is for the *lex loci contractus*.

The effect of the decision. If the decision is followed by English courts it settles for English law the issue of the law governing the creation of maritime liens. It obviates and removes the necessity for the kind of examination of previous authority that judges and text writers hitherto traditionally undertook on the question. Substantively, first, the superiority of English law in English courts on this matter avoids problems posed by reference to the law of the place of the thing or the act when the root of the maritime lien is tortious, a problem accentuated if the event causing the lien to arise occurs on the high seas. Secondly, it appears that the issue of creation is one for the law of the forum only. It is not necessary to show that a maritime lien exists under any other law. Thirdly, it resolves the problem of separation of issues of nature and priority. Both are referred to the law of the forum.

However, because of reference to forum law a ship will attract and shed maritime liens as she journeys around the world. Such a selection rule encourages forum shopping. There is much to be said for a uniform Convention on liens but pending the acceptance of the 1993 Convention by a reasonable number of states the view of the majority in *The Halcyon Isle* may not be thought consistent with a common international view. The majority did use present confusion of national policies in support of its own nationalist approach, and it may be that continued national emphasis will bring international agreement out of desperation.

Rationale of the decision. It is suggested that as much because of its reasoning as its conclusion the decision is unsatisfactory. The majority relied on the arguments that questions of the existence of a maritime lien were (i) jurisdictional and (ii) procedural or remedial. The minority founded its opinion on the classification of a maritime lien as a "right of property". The decision therefore reflects the dependence of the English approach on classification of issues into choice of law "categories". A primary danger is that classification is a first step away from reality.

(i) JURISDICTION. The argument relied on by the majority that the proprietary characteristics of a maritime lien (in its enforceability against purchasers and the question of its creation) are matters of jurisdiction seems to confuse an issue of whether a right (a matter of substance) exists with whether a court can adjudicate on whether it can exist (a matter of jurisdiction). Even if an English court is directed by a mandatory statutory rule that only those claims attracting maritime liens in English domestic law *can* be recognized in English proceedings as attracting such liens this is a matter of choice of law and not jurisdiction.[186] At the least, it leads to lack of clarity to confuse the nature of rights with the power to decide on their existence.

---

185. [1981] A.C. 221, at pp. 238–239.
186. The "jurisdictional" approach is encouraged by the statutory framework of Admiralty jurisdiction in that it provides that an action *in rem* will lie to enforce a maritime lien (see Chapter 2). (Compare *The Acrux* [1965] P. 391 with *The Halcyon Isle* [1981] A.C. 221.)

(ii) PROCEDURE OR REMEDY. It has been argued in this work that a "lien" is a proprietary concept and that a maritime lien is part of that concept (see Chapter 18). It simply destroys any meaning of the term "procedure" to apply it to describe characteristics of enforceability and priority.

The issue in the case. Under United States law, priority (in English law terms) was conferred on the shiprepairer through the conferring of a maritime lien on the claim. Therefore, it may be argued, the issue is not priority but the nature of the right. Whether the claim is one focusing on nature or priority depends simply on the national approach—but in substance the issue was priority between two preferred claims. The issue, therefore, was a straight fight between a shiprepairer and a mortgagee with different views as to their priority being taken by the relevant legal systems. This was lost in the classification or labelling process adopted.

The desirable approach. As has been argued, there is much to be said for referring priority matters to the law governing the validity and enforceability of the competing interests where only one law is relevant to all such interests. Where more than one law is relevant (as where the question of creation is referred to more than one law) forum law has a claim as umpire.

Clearly where the issue is priority between interests in chattels or intangibles the controlling law will be that of the place of the thing or debtor and the scenario for the intervention of forum law may occur not infrequently. However, there is an internationally accepted link between a ship and the country of her flag and the registration framework relevant to ownership and mortgages reflecting that link. It is strongly arguable that, lacking uniform substantive rules introduced through a Convention, all issues of property in a ship should be referred to the law of the flag.[187] Such a rule would avoid the comings and goings of rights involved in any reference to the law of the forum, avoid the difficulties of reference to "place" in relation to acts occurring on the high seas and provide the maximum amount of certainty for those proposing to create interests in the ship.

Chartering of ships. English law draws a distinction between demise charters on the one hand and time and voyage charters on the other. It has concluded that as possession and control of the ship is not transferred under a time or voyage charter the charterer has no proprietary interest. It follows that such a charterer cannot enforce the charter against a purchaser of the ship,[188] nor can he recover damages for loss suffered as a result of damage to the ship.[189] It is by no means certain that such a distinction would be universally recognized[190] and it is, therefore, relevant to decide which law should apply to decide the proprietary consequences of a charterparty.

Insofar as a charterer's claim depends on a proprietary interest in the ship, the question should be referred to the law of the flag. The very presence of a proprietary issue means that a party unconnected with the original transaction is involved and it will often mean that a matter of priority between claimants is at issue. It would be preferable to refer the question of all proprietary consequences of transactions to the same law, unless there are

187. See e.g. *The Epimenidis* [1986] LMLN 186 (Court of Appeal Ghent).
188. See *Port Line Ltd.* v. *Ben Line Steamers Ltd.* [1958] 12 Q.B. 146. As to prior mortgages cf. Chap. 23.
189. See e.g. *The World Harmony* [1967] P. 341.
190. See e.g. *The Struma* [1978] AMC 2146.

strong reasons to select a particular law for a particular transaction. In the case of charterparties, the only reason displacing the law of the flag would seem to be the expectation of the parties that the proper law of the contract should govern its contractual and proprietary characteristics. Insofar as the issue concerns those parties, the factor is of predominant importance but insofar as either party is vying with a third party it is less so. When the question is the effect of one transaction on another, it seems desirable and logical to refer the question of the effect of each to the same law and that that law should be the law of the flag.

(b) CARGO CLAIMS AND (c) MONEY CLAIMS

The factors of the flag, registration and the inherent element of continuous movement relevant to ships do not apply to cargo or freight, charter or insurance moneys. There is no reason why the general choice of law framework should not apply.

(ii) Transfer of a proprietary interest

Clearly, the issue of acquisition of a proprietary interest overlaps with its assertion, for its validity may depend on the validity of a transfer. Such a transfer may be a voluntary transfer during the life or on the death of the owner, a contract between owner and potential purchaser, assignment[191] or bankruptcy[192] or (in the case of tangibles) user, or the imposition of a lien by the legal system. It cannot be said that the general rules governing the question of the governing law to these questions are clearly established. It must suffice to draw attention to the contenders.

The validity of the transfer *inter vivos* of an interest in a tangible movable (formalities and validity) is governed by the law of its *situs*. The assignment of a contractual right is by the Rome Convention governed by the law applicable to the contract between assignor and assignee (see *supra*). Apart from the Convention the transfer of an intangible thing (such as a debt) will be referred either to the law of its *situs* (the residence of the debtor) or to the proper law of the assignment with formal validity being governed by the law of the place of the assignment. As has been said, apart from the Rome Convention, priorities generally are taken to be governed by the law of the forum. Succession to intangibles or tangible immovables is governed by the law of the deceased's domicile.

Apart from succession, therefore, little distinction is drawn for choice of law purposes between issues of assertion and transfer of a proprietary interest. It may be that different national laws will apply to different issues for the focus of the enquiry may differ according to whether acquisition or assertion forms the point of enquiry. As the Rome Convention indicates the choice of law process within the Convention in respect of choses in action would seem to be identical.

---

191. Assignment on marriage is not treated here as its relevance to commercial maritime claims must be peripheral. However, it should not be ignored as a root of ownership. Where there is a marriage contract its validity will be referred to its proper law; where there is no contract the effect of marriage on movable assets seems to depend on the domicile of the parties but the rules are imprecise and unclear. Cf. Dicey and Morris, 12th edn, Chapter 28.

192. Questions in bankruptcy include the effect of an English adjudication on assets situated out of the jurisdiction, the effect of a foreign adjudication, the ability to prove foreign debts and the effect of discharge in England or a foreign country. Cf. Dicey and Morris, 12th edn, Chapter 31. As to winding up of companies and choice of law, see *ibid.*, Chapter 30.

Assertion, transfer and priority

Whether a transfer (or purported transfer) of an interest can affect that interest may be seen as an assertion of ownership, transfer of ownership or priority. So the nature of the equitable interest and the power of a bona fide purchaser from a non-owner to defeat the interest of an owner involve all three proprietary aspects. Priority cannot be distinguished from the substantive ownership issue.

It would seem that in this regard there is no call for initial forum intervention but that the governing law should be that applicable either to the creation and validity of interest or the transfer on which the transferee relies.[193] The problem with the latter solution is that if there is more than such transfer and more than one such law. The reference to the law of validity (as under the Rome Convention) would remove the need for the forum to act as umpire.

SUMMARY

In many cases, a maritime claim will involve a foreign element. Selection of the law to govern the issue is, therefore, a necessary preliminary step in its resolution. To some extent in the maritime area Conventions have introduced a measure of uniformity but realization that there is a question of the governing law is a commercial necessity. The availability of choice of law by parties and its limitations should be considered on entry into any contract and the choice of law through choice of forum appreciated in initiating legal proceedings. Finally, undue emphasis by English courts on English law will simply lead to forum shopping—both home and away—as well as the global uncertainty which is brought through any nationalistic approach.

In addition, in basing the selection system on classification of legal issues, English law runs a serious risk of selection of a law on a base removed from the problem at issue. The decision in *The Halcyon Isle* seems as prime example of concealment of reality through abstruse legal labels. If English law is to govern, let it be seen that the choice is geared to the issue before the court in its commercial context (in that case the mortgagee as against the shiprepairer) rather than artificial legal categories (such as priority and substance).

---

193. As applied in *Macmillan Inc.* v. *Bishopgate Investment Trust plc (No 3)* [1995] 3 All E.R. 747.

CHAPTER 27

Enforcement of Foreign Judgments and Arbitral Awards outside the Brussels and Lugano Conventions

I. FOREIGN JUDGMENTS[1]

APPLICATION OF MERGER AND ISSUE ESTOPPEL

In English law an action *in personam* merges into a judgment of an English court on the action and an action *in rem* into the judgment on that action. As a result the basis of any further action by a party is the judgment. Like principles are those of issue or cause of action estoppel, "issue estoppel" being in essence a variant of cause of action estoppel. In regard to cause of action estoppel a party is estopped from asserting that a cause of action exists (or does not exist) when the question has been judicially determined. Through "issue estoppel" that general doctrine is applied to a particular issue common to consecutive proceedings.

The probable difference between merger and estoppel lies in the conclusive effect of merger (the cause of action simply is determined) and the possible counterplea by a party to a claim of estoppel. So the other party may establish that the party relying on the cause of action or issue estoppel is himself estopped by conduct from that reliance (see Chapter 26).

In English law prior to 24 August 1982 the cause of action of a claim did not merge in a foreign judgment, and it followed that a claimant having a foreign judgment could bring an action in England either on the original claim or the judgment. However, cause of action and issue estoppel were applied. The Civil Jurisdiction and Judgments Act 1982, s.34, which came into operation 24 August 1982, provides:

"34. No proceedings may be brought by a person in England and Wales or Northern Ireland on a cause of action in respect of which a judgment has been given in his favour in proceedings between the same parties, or their privies, in a court in another part of the United Kingdom or in a court of an overseas country, unless that judgment is not enforceable or entitled to recognition in England and Wales or, as the case may be, in Northern Ireland."[2]

This provision either applied the principle of merger to foreign judgment or simply recognized estoppel as applicable. In *The Indian Grace*[3] the House of Lords, assuming that estoppel could not be pleaded where merger operates, held that the effect of this

---

1. i.e. judgments given in courts outside England and Wales.
2. The scope of s.34 is not restricted to proceedings in which a plaintiff is a party from the start or where the proceedings are exclusively civil—it contemplates foreign proceedings in which plaintiff and defendant have participated to adjudge a dispute—so an intervenor may be bound or a party where proceedings include civil and criminal elements (*Black* v. *Yates* [1991] 1 Lloyd's Rep. 181).
3. [1993] A.C. 410; [1993] 1 Lloyd's Rep. 387.

provision was to allow for a plea of issue estoppel rather than merger. The phrase "no proceedings shall be brought", it was held, simply creates a defence to any proceedings subject to a counter assertion rather than destroying the cause of action. The case was remitted to the Admiralty Court for the plea to be adjudged on the evidence.

On remittal Clarke J. held that for the purpose of s.34, although actions *in rem* and *personam* if based on the same facts were founded on the same cause of action, they were between different parties. However that did not mean that estoppel had no application and the defendants were estopped from relying on a judgment in a court in Cochin, India (a judgment in an action *in personam*) as a defence in proceedings later brought in England (an action *in rem*).[4] As estoppel could be pleaded prior to the statutory provision its effect seems purely declaratory.

In taking the view he did of the relationship of the action *in personam* and the action *in rem* Clarke J. followed decisions of the English courts dealing with the effect of Articles 20 and 21 of the Brussels Convention concerned with concurrent actions and requiring construction of the "same cause of action and between the same parties".[5] Since the decision in the *Indian Grace* the European Court has held in *The Maciej Rataj*[6] that the national difference between the two types of action does not mean that the cause of action is different but that the requirement of "the same parties" in the Convention has the effect that it is only in relation to parties common to both actions that the cause of action is considered the same. Adopting that approach to s.34 would mean that the factor which brought it into operation is a common party and not, as seems as expressed in the decisions of English courts, a difference in the abstract concepts of the action *in personam* and action *in rem*. In other words the action *in personam* and action *in rem* do not by their nature involve different parties—it all depends on whether a party to the one is also party to the other.

Clarke J. was much persuaded to his view because the effect of holding that s.34 did apply would have been to remove from a plaintiff the ability to bring an action *in rem* following an unsatisfied judgment *in personam*—and to read s.34 in that way would have *created* a difference between judgments of English and foreign courts. But as held in the European context whether it can generally be said that an action *in personam* and an action *in rem* is *never* between the same parties seems dubious. It is certainly the same as regards parties to both actions and, further, it could be that at the date of cause of action all parties were the same. So it could depend on the evidence.

The purpose of the provisions of the European Convention in preventing concurrent actions is fundamentally different to that of s.34—preventing consecutive actions. As to the first, the parties are still litigating but as to the second the question is whether there can be further litigation in circumstances where it may have been impossible under national procedure to mount an action *in personam* and an action *in rem*. It may be therefore that cause of action estoppel could operate to prevent an uncalled for use of a *second* type of action having litigated the first. The feeling remains however that while the approaches of Clarke J. and the House of Lords are based on sound common and commercial sense, it is difficult on the words of the statute to exclude from its ambit consecutive actions *in*

4. [1994] 2 Lloyd's Rep. 331. See Chaps. 10, 12.
5. See e.g. *The Nordglimt* [1987] 2 Lloyd's Rep. 470.
6. [1995] 1 Lloyd's Rep. 302.

personam and *in rem* simply because of their nature. In truth it seems probable that not only the differences between *in personam* and *in rem* but those between estoppel and merger were never in the minds of those creating the provision. The sole motive was to rid English law of an anomaly in the application of merger. Its effect, as it turns out, is to leave the law as it was, and whether or not the matter is within the ambit of that provision is irrelevant to the application of cause of action or issue estoppel, and to the non-operation of merger to foreign judgments.

COMPETING FOREIGN JUDGMENTS

The general rule is that subject to estoppel by conduct of two judgments, each of which is enforceable in England, it is the first in time which takes priority. The rule therefore mirrors that of the enforcement of any foreign judgment in that the party seeking to enforce may be estopped, for example, because of representations made as to the effect of either judgment.[7]

RECOGNITION AND ENFORCEMENT

Following the general principle of *res judicata* a foreign judgment may be "recognized" or "enforced" by English courts without any requirement that under English law the result of the case would be identical.[8] A judgment declaring a status or title or dismissing a claim may require no more than recognition, while a judgment awarding damages will require positive enforcement. Recognition and enforcement are based on a mixture of statutory provision and rules of Admiralty and common law, and a fundamental distinction must be drawn between judgments within and outside the scope of the Brussels or Lugano Conventions. Judgments within those Conventions are discussed in Chapter 28. The framework in existence prior to the Conventions will continue to apply as amended by the Civil Jurisdiction and Judgments Act 1982 to judgments not within them. They are the subject of this chapter.

A distinction is drawn between other United Kingdom courts and courts outside the United Kingdom. A judgment of a court of another part of the United Kingdom may be recognized or enforced only by registration in accordance with a statutory structure applicable only to such judgments. Enforcement of a judgment of a court outside the United Kingdom may be through action or registration in accordance with statutory rules.

---

7. See *Showlag* v. *Mansour* [1994] 2 All E.R. 129 (Privy Council sitting on appeal from Jersey considering English and Egyptian judgments). In the case the focus of conduct was on the obtaining of the second judgment but the principle must apply generally.

8. But the same principle will prohibit reliance on a foreign judgment subsequent to settlement of the claim in an English action in which the issues on which the foreign judgment was given could have been raised. See *E.D. and F. Man (Sugar) Ltd.* v. *Hariyanto (No. 2)* [1989] 2 Lloyd's Rep. 192 (the principle being that a party should raise all issues in the initial proceedings applying in respect of a foreign judgment). See also fn 41.

Judgments of other United Kingdom courts

Prior to the Civil Jurisdiction and Judgments Act 1982 the structure was that of the Judgment Extension Act 1868[9] and the Inferior Courts Judgments Extension Act 1882 and at least so far as England is concerned, the common law. The statutory provisions were restricted to money judgments. There is now statutory provision for money and non-money judgments through the domestic adaptation of the Brussels Convention. The rules are contained in s.18 and Schedules 6 and 7 of the 1982 Act—Schedule 6 providing for money judgments and Schedule 7 for non-money judgments. Subject to specific exclusions[10] a judgment of a court in civil proceedings given in one part of the United Kingdom may be recognized or enforced by an "interested party" in another part on registration of a certified copy of the judgment. No distinction is drawn between actions *in personam* and actions *in rem* or judgments *in personam* and *in rem*.

(a) Recognition

The Civil Jurisdiction and Judgments Act 1982 provides for *"enforcement"*. The principles of *"recognition"*, which by its nature requires no positive act, are changed from those in existence prior to the Act only in one particular, though a fundamental one. Prior to the Act English courts would recognize foreign judgments (including those in Scotland and Northern Ireland) only if the foreign court had jurisdiction.

Section 19(1) of the Act provides that, with specified exceptions, no judgment of a court within the enforcement framework shall be refused recognition solely on the ground that under the private international law rules of the enforcement court the adjudicating court lacked jurisdiction.[11] The provision thereby removes the principal criterion for recognition of judgments under the common law and in effect adapts the Brussels Convention principle of placing jurisdiction enquiry in the adjudicating court. Excluded are an award of a tribunal enforceable without court order, and an arbitration award enforceable where it was given in the same manner as a judgment given by a court of law (see *infra*).

(b) Enforcement

Under the 1982 Act apart from arbitration awards enforceable in the same manner as a judgment the rules provide the *exclusive* method by which a judgment within its scope may be recognized or enforced. Judgment is defined broadly. It includes a judgment or order given by a court of law in the United Kingdom or entered in the High Court or county court in England or Northern Ireland and a tribunal or arbitration award enforceable without court order. Excluded from the provisions is a judgment on a judgment, i.e. a judgment of a court outside the United Kingdom which is to be enforced as such by virtue of the Civil Jurisdiction and Judgments Act 1982, Administration of Justice Act 1920 or the Foreign Judgments (Reciprocal Enforcement) Act 1933. Excluded also is a judgment which is "a provisional (including protective) measure other than an

9. And the Inferior Courts Judgments Extension Act 1882.

10. Including within the exclusions any part of any judgment concerning the legal capacity of an individual or a provisional measure other than an order for interim payment (s.18(5)(b)(d), and foreign judgments registered for enforcement (s.18(7)).

11. The exceptions relate to Scottish decrees regarding the recovery of rent charges and penalties and English orders having the effect of a judgment relating to fines and forfeiture of recognizance for contempt of court.

order for the making of an interim payment"—thus differing from the 1968 Convention.

General effect of registration

Registration gives the judgment "for the purpose of its enforcement . . . the same force and effect" as if the judgment had originally been given by the registering court and (if relevant) entered.[12]

COSTS, EXPENSES AND INTEREST

Reasonable costs and expenses in relation to registration are recoverable. Provision is made for the recovery of interest including interest on the costs or expenses (Schedule 6, paras 7, 8, Schedule 7, para. 7).

Money provisions of judgments (Schedule 6)

The rules leave little room for refusal of enforcement providing the simple procedure is followed. The provisions apply to any money provisions in a judgment within the Act. The enforcement process is through:

(a) a certificate granted on application by an interested party made to the designated officer of the adjudicating court[13]; and

(b) registration of that certificate within six months of its issue through application made to the proper officer of the registering court.

A court for this purpose is in relation to England and Wales and Northern Ireland the High Court and in relation to Scotland the Court of Session.

The certificate may not be issued unless, under the law of the part of the United Kingdom in which the judgment was given, the time for appeal against the judgment has expired or an appeal having been brought has been disposed of, secondly, the enforcement of the judgment is not suspended, and thirdly its time for enforcement has not expired.

Provided none of these grounds for refusal of issue exist a certificate shall be issued.[14]

STAYING OF ENFORCEMENT PROCEEDINGS (SCHEDULE 6, PARA. 9)

Proceedings for enforcement of the certificate may be stayed if the court is satisfied that the person against whom it is sought to enforce the certificate intends to apply for a remedy which could result in the setting aside or quashing of the judgment sought to be enforced. It must also be satisfied that the applicant is entitled so to apply.

---

12. Schedule 6 (money provisions), para. 6; Schedule 7 (non-money provisions), para. 6. Both paragraphs expressly provide that enforcement proceedings may be taken as if the judgment had been given by the registering court.

13. As to the supporting affidavit setting out the details of the judgment see RSC Order 71, r. 37.

14. Schedule 6, para. 5.

SETTING ASIDE OF REGISTRATION (SCHEDULE 6, PARA. 10)

Where a certificate has been registered the registration must be set aside if it was contrary to Schedule 6 and may be set aside if the court is satisfied that the matter on which the judgment was given had previously been the subject of a judgment by another court having jurisdiction in the matter.

Non-money provisions (Schedule 7)[15]

In the case of non-money provisions the basis is a certified copy of the judgment.[16] The enforcement provisions are similar to those applicable to enforcement of money provisions. Grounds of refusal to issue go solely to the possibility of an appeal and are as for the enforcement of money provisions (see *supra*). Provided none of the grounds exist a certified copy of the judgment as a whole must be issued and a certificate stating that the conditions going to the possibility of an appeal are satisfied.

THE REGISTRATION PROCESS

The registration process provides greater opportunity for challenge than that applicable to money provisions. It does not depend (as in the case of money provisions) simply on the production of a certificate. The application for registration must be made to the High Court and may be refused if compliance with a non-money provision contained in the judgment would involve a breach of the law of the part of the United Kingdom in which it is sought to enforce the judgment.

In England the application may be made *ex parte*; the court hearing the dispute has power to direct the issue of a summons—so as to make the proceedings *inter partes*.[17] As with the rules applicable to money provisions, registration proceedings may be stayed if other proceedings are to be taken to set aside or quash the judgment sought to be enforced. The effect of registration and incorporation of reasonable expenses and interest is as for money provisions.

As with judgments within the Convention the order giving leave to register must contain notification that execution will not issue until after the determination of any appeal or expiry of period for appeal.[18] Notice of registration must be served on the person against whom the judgment is to be enforced. The notice must set out the judgment, the name and address for service of the person who made the application and notification of the right and period available for appeal. Leave is not required for service of the notice out of the jurisdiction and (as for a writ) acknowledgment of service by the defendant or acceptance by his solicitor may be deemed to be service.[19] The power and the obligation to set aside registration of a judgment are identical to those in respect of money provisions. No distinction is drawn between judgments in actions *in personam* and judgments in actions *in rem*.

---

15. Cf. RSC Order 71, r. 38.
16. As to the procedure and supporting affidavit see Order 71, r. 38(6) applying r. 37(3).
17. Order 71, r. 38(1).
18. Order 71, r. 38(3) applying r. 30.
19. Order 71, r. 38(3) applying r. 32.

Judgments of courts other than of the United Kingdom

Judgments may be enforced through one of the two methods available—

- (i) without registration by an action on the foreign judgment; or
- (ii) if a judgment *in personam* directing the payment of a sum of money, through registration and enforced as a judgment of an English court.[20]

(i) Recognition and enforcement without registration

Judgments "in personam" and "in rem"

A judgment *in rem* must be distinguished from an action *in rem*. In this context a judgment *in rem* is a judgment which binds the world and therefore any person having an interest in or claim on the thing in relation to which the judgment is given. Such judgments are those connected with status such as marriage, adoption and the like.[21] A judgment in an action *in rem* will bind any person having an interest in the *res* to the extent of that interest. Further, it will have the consequence that on judicial sale of the *res* the purchaser will obtain a title good against the world. To that extent it is akin to a judgment *in rem*.

Judgments in actions "in rem"

The only judgment *in rem* directly relevant to maritime claims is that resulting from an action *in rem*.[22] Given that the action is limited to the *res*, where the court giving the judgment has control of the *res* in relation to which the action is brought, the only forum for enforcement is the controlling court. However, the question may arise of recognition of that judgment, particularly as a judicial sale, when completed, confers a title on a purchaser clear of liens and mortgages.

Further, in an English court, an action *in rem* may be instituted without arrest, or there may be no compliance with a contractual undertaking or retention under arrest after stay of proceedings. Actions *in rem* in foreign countries may likewise contemplate a judgment in relation to a ship or other asset not then within the court's power. In such cases an English court may be asked to enforce a judgment conferring a title on a purchaser of an asset within the jurisdiction of the English court.

WHEN IS A JUDGMENT "IN REM"?

In recognizing and enforcing a judgment an English court will first decide if the judgment was *in rem*. An English court will have regard to the nature of the foreign proceedings and decide whether in English terms they were aimed at a thing or a person in the sense of the English dichotomy of action *in rem* and action *in personam*.[23]

20. Under the Civil Jurisdiction and Judgments Act 1982, Sch. 4 replacing for the purposes of the Brussels and Lugano Convention the Judgments Extension Act 1868 (concerning United Kingdom judgments); the Administration of Justice Act 1920 (concerning Commonwealth judgments); the Foreign Judgments (Reciprocal Enforcement) Act 1933 (concerning foreign and Commonwealth judgments). Each statute specifies conditions of enforceability. The most important of the statutory frameworks is that set out in the Act of 1933, the principles of which have been extended to judgments of courts of countries parties to various Conventions enacted into English law (see p. 618).

21. See *Salvesen* v. *Admin. of Austrian Property* [1927] A.C. 641, at p. 662.

22. A judgment in prize proceedings vests the property immediately as against the whole world.

23. Compare *Castrique* v. *Imrie* (1870) L.R. 4 H.L. 414 with *The City of Mecca* (1881) 6 P.D. 106.

Apart from the effect of judicial sale the application of "judgment *in rem*" to Admiralty actions is probably erroneous. It stems from an undue emphasis on the method of assertion of proprietary interests in ships, cargo and freight to the detriment of the interests themselves. So if a foreign judgment of any kind may be enforced by an action *in rem* there is no reason in principle why that method should not be available in respect of any judgment declaring an interest which in English law would be the consequence of an action *in rem*. But a judgment declaring a lien to exist is no more a judgment *in rem* than is a judgment recognizing a proprietary interest in any asset.

The only true "*in rem*" aspect of a maritime law judgment is the "clear title" conferred by judicial sale. A judgment or order conferring title by judicial sale is the only aspect of a judgment in a maritime case which has the character of "good against the world". The use of the action *in rem* to assert that title fits with the ability to assert ownership claims in such a way.

The enforcement of a foreign judicial sale will simply be through the recognition of the effect of that sale. That was the course followed in at least one modern case, but there is uncertainty about the jurisdiction to accomplish this by an action *in rem*. Undoubtedly it would lie in the nineteenth century and in 1982 in the *Despina GK*[24] Sheen J. relied on the "sweeping up" clause in the Supreme Court Act for the foundation for jurisdiction. It has been doubted however whether the jurisdiction maintained by the Act in respect of pre Act jurisdiction includes "*in rem*".[25] Without that base there is no power to enforce a foreign judgment "*in rem*" save by use of remedies available in respect of "*in personam*" judgments. It would seem, given the finding of ownership by the foreign court, that the primary disadvantage would go to interim relief—to the inability to arrest the *res*, a disadvantage modified by the availability of the *Mareva* injunction.

Prerequisites for and defences to recognition and enforcement

Prerequisites for and the defences against recognition and enforcement are usually discussed in the context of actions *in personam* leading to judgments *in personam*; but they seem equally applicable to actions *in personam* leading to judgments *in rem* and actions *in rem* leading either to judgments *in rem* or arguably judgments *in personam*. The prerequisites of recognition and enforcement are that:

(i) the foreign court had jurisdiction to hear the claim as recognized by English conflicts rules and probably by its own internal rules[26];

(ii) the judgment is final and conclusive by the law of the state in which it was given;

(iii) the judgment must not be for tax or a penalty[27];

---

24. [1982] 1 Lloyd's Rep. 553.

25. See *The Antonis P. Lemos* [1984] 1 Lloyd's Rep. 464 (C.A.)—see Chap. 2. A complicated attempt to use the power to maintain maritime property under arrest pending a judgment in foreign proceedings following a stay of English proceedings although the judgment had already been given failed in *The Sylt* [1991] 1 Lloyd's Rep. 240.

26. See *Pemberton* v. *Hughes* [1899] 1 Ch. 781; *Papadopoulos* v. *Papadopoulos* [1930] P. 55. Distinguish, however, a defect in the jurisdiction from an error in procedure which is no bar. It is for the person seeking to enforce the judgment to establish the competence of the court (*Adams* v. *Cape Industries Inc.* [1991] 1 All E.R. 929 at p. 1031).

27. This is a requirement stated in respect of claim *in personam* (see e.g. *Govt. of India* v. *Taylor* [1955] A.C. 491), but there is no reason in this respect to distinguish between a judgment *in personam* and a judgment *in rem*.

(iv) If *in personam* the judgment must be for a fixed sum.[28]

The defendant has a limited number of defences available—that the judgment

(i) was obtained by fraud—it not being necessary as it would be in seeking to set aside an English judgment that there must be fresh evidence, the merits being subject to being reopened[29];

(ii) is contrary to English public policy[30];

(iii) is contrary to English natural justice[31];

(iv) was given in proceedings brought contrary to an agreement that the dispute would be settled otherwise than by proceedings in the courts of that country, the agreement was valid and there was no submission to jurisdiction.[32]

It follows from general principles that an English court will not enquire into whether or require that the claims on which such a judgment is based are recognized in English law. So, in enforcing a foreign judgment as distinct from any attempt to obtain an English judgment, foreign liens will be recognized.[33] It is only with respect to the requirement of foreign court jurisdiction that there is any distinction in substance between the perequisites for and defences against enforcement of judgments in actions *in personam* and actions *in rem*.

FOREIGN COURT JURISDICTION

Judgments "in personam". A foreign court will be recognized as having jurisdiction if the defendant either:

(a) (being an individual) was present or (being a corporation) was resident or present in the state of the court; or

(b) submitted to the jurisdiction of the court.

Presence. The temporary presence of an individual is enough.[34] A corporation is likely to be "present" within the meaning of the requirement only if for more than a minimal period of time either it had maintained at its own expense a fixed place of business from which it had carried on its own business through servants or agents, or a representative had

28. Following upon the basis of enforcement—an obligation stemming from the judgment. See e.g. *Sadler* v. *Robins* (1808) 1 Camp. 253. As a consequence a decree (e.g.) of specific performance is not enforceable.

29. See *Owens Bank Ltd.* v. *Bracco* [1992] 2 All E.R. 193 (H.L.); *Vadala* v. *Lawes* (1890) 25 Q.B.D. 310, at pp. 316, 317; *Syal* v. *Heyward* [1948] 2 K.B. 443.

30. i.e. against some fundamental English view. See e.g. *Re Macartney* [1921] 1 Ch. 522, at p. 527. As to policy reflected in Protection of Trading Interests Act 1980, see *infra*.

31. See *Jacobson* v. *Frachon* (1927) 138 L.T. 386 (ability to present case). The concept is however not restricted to requirements of due notice and ability to put a case. So in *Adams* (fn 26) the Court of Appeal held a judgment unenforceable where a judge of a Texas court left it to plaintiffs' counsel to divide up a global sum awarded among the various plaintiffs without assessing the liability of the defendants to each plaintiff—the defendants having no notice of this approach.

32. Civil Jurisdiction and Judgments Act 1982, s.32. See *infra*.

33. See *Minna Craig Steamship Co.* v. *Chartered Mercantile Bank of India* [1897] 1 Q.B. 55 (affirmed *ibid.*, p. 460)—this authority would not seem affected by *The Halcyon Isle* (as to which see Chap. 26) as there has always been a clear distinction between enforceability of a foreign claim and of a foreign judgment.

34. *Adams* v. *Cape Industries Inc.* [1991] 1 All E.R. 929 following the English rule of jurisdiction and holding against the hitherto favoured view. An earlier case which could be cited in favour of presence as a ground (*Carrick* v. *Hancock* (1895) 12 T.L.R. 59) could also be based on submission. The carrying on of business is not sufficient to establish the "residence" of an individual. See *Blohn* v. *Desser* [1962] 2 Q.B. 116, at p. 123.

carried on the corporation business from a fixed place of business. Whether a representative had so acted depends on the function and the nature of relationship between the representative and the corporation—particularly the degree of control and authority. The fact that a representative never made contracts for the corporation would point strongly against presence.[35]

Submission. Submission may be through the bringing of an action or counterclaim, the voluntary entry into the proceedings on the merits or a jurisdiction agreement. The Civil Jurisdiction and Judgments Act 1982, s.33, provides that an appearance limited to contesting the jurisdiction, applying for the dispute to be submitted to arbitration or the courts of another country or to protect or obtain the release of property seized or threatened with seizure is not submission.[36] But a defendant must take care not to participate in the proceedings particularly by lodging pleadings going to the merits.[37] Although it remains arguable that participation in proceedings regarding an interlocutory remedy (other than seeking release of property seized) could be submission, it would now seem likely that an English court would accept the distinction between such a remedy and the merits. Even consent to such a remedy may not of itself amount to consent to proceedings on the merits.[38]

JUDGMENTS IN PROCEEDINGS BROUGHT CONTRARY TO AGREEMENT

The Civil Jurisdiction and Judgments Act 1982, s.32 provides:

"32.—(1) Subject to the following provisions of this section, a judgment given by a court of an overseas country in any proceedings shall not be recognised or enforced in the United Kingdom if—

(a) the bringing of those proceedings in that court was contrary to an agreement under which the dispute in question was to be settled otherwise than by proceedings in the courts of that country; and

(b) those proceedings were not brought in that court by, or with the agreement of, the person against whom the judgment was given; and

(c) that person did not counterclaim in the proceedings or otherwise submit to the jurisdiction of that court.

(2) Subsection (1) does not apply where the agreement referred to in paragraph (a) of that subsection was illegal, void or unenforceable or was incapable of being performed for reasons not attributable to the fault of the party bringing the proceedings in which the judgment was given.

(3) In determining whether a judgment given by a court of an overseas country should be recognised or enforced in the United Kingdom, a court in the United Kingdom shall not be bound by any decision of the overseas court relating to any of the matters mentioned in subsection (1) or (2)".[39]

---

35. *Adams* v. *Cape Industries Inc.* [1991] 1 All E.R. 929 applying *Littauer Glove Corpn* v. *F.W. Millington Ltd.* (1928) 44 T.L.R. 746. In *Adams* the court refused to lift the corporate veil where there was nothing illegal in the corporate structure so as to treat the presence of the representative as the presence of the corporation.

36. This provision which came into force on 24 August 1982 applies to England and N. Ireland. Judgments given by courts required to be recognized or enforced by the Brussels or Lugano Conventions (see *supra*) are excluded (s.33(2) as amended by Civil Jurisdiction and Judgments Act 1991, Sch. 2, para. 15).

37. *Marc Rich* v. *Societa Italiana Impianti PA (The Atlantic Emperor No. 2)* [1992] 1 Lloyd's Rep. 624.

38. See discussion of submission to English jurisdiction Chap. 9.

39. The provisions of s.32 apply to all judgments coming before an English court on or after 24 August 1982 regardless of when the foreign judgment was given, save for those judgments specifically excluded by Sch. 13, Part II, para. 8(i). See *Tracomin SA* v. *Sudan Oil Seeds (No. 1)* [1983] 3 All E.R. 137.

By subsection (4) as amended it is provided that nothing in subsection (1) shall affect the recognition or enforcement of judgments within the Brussels or Lugano Conventions or judgments to which the Foreign Judgments (Reciprocal Enforcement) Act 1933 is applied by specified statutes (mainly enacting Conventions into English law).[40]

It follows that, subject to other statutory provisions, a judgment in proceedings brought contrary to a jurisdiction or arbitration clause not illegal, void or unenforceable will not be recognized or enforced in England unless the defendant consented to the action being brought there, submitted to the jurisdiction or counterclaimed. In assessing whether there has been submission s.33 of the 1982 Act will apply (see *supra*).

Recognition and enforcement

RECOGNITION

Provided that the foreign court had jurisdiction, the prerequisites to all the requirements listed above are satisfied and none of the defences listed above apply, a foreign judgment will be recognized or enforced as an English judgment.[41] In addition, a satisfied foreign judgment on the merits will be a good defence to an action on it in England.[42] However, the cause of action is not merged with the judgment—further proceedings being prohibited by the operation of issue estoppel (see *supra*).

ENFORCEMENT

Provided the foreign court had jurisdiction, the prerequisites above are satisfied, and none of the defences above apply, a foreign court judgment may be enforced by action upon it.

Judgments "in rem". Whether the issue concerns a physical *res*[43] jurisdiction depends on the simple test of whether the foreign court had physical control of the *res* at the time of judgment.[44]

Recognition and enforcement of judgments "in rem"

RECOGNITION

Provided the foreign court had jurisdiction, the prerequisites listed above are satisfied, and none of the defences listed apply a judgement *in rem* will be recognized. It follows that

---

40. See fn 59.

41. So apart from fraud a defendant cannot prevent recognition or enforcement through a plea that defences were not raised when they could have been raised—the matter will be *res judicata*. See *Israel Bank* v. *Hadjapateras* [1983] 2 All E.R. 129.

42. See *Barber* v. *Lamb* (1860) 8 C.B. (N.S.) 95. But not if based on a time bar. (See *Harris* v. *Quine* (1869) L.R. 4 Q.B. 653). But see the Foreign Limitation Periods Act 1984, s.3.

43. For status judgments the jurisdictional requirements are those appropriate to status actions according to English conflicts of law rules. As to recognition of a foreign court judgment as to immovables (which may be *in rem*), see *Re Trepca Mines* [1960] 1 W.L.R. 1273, at p. 1277.

44. See *Castrique* v. *Imrie* (1870) L.R. 4 H.L. 414. The precise date of the requirement of control is loosely stated but it surely must be at the time of the judgment if *the judgment* purports to create a right *in rem* or the action so creating it is consequent on the judgment (e.g. sale).

the sale of a ship effected as the result of such a judgment will be recognized and that the purchaser's title will be free of encumbrances.[45]

ENFORCEMENT

Insofar as the foreign judgment *in rem* imposes any consequence which may be enforced by an action *in personam* there is no reason why, subject to compliance with the prerequisites, it should not be so enforced by an English court. Subject to jurisdiction requirements and where the subject matter falls within the Admiralty jurisdiction, an English court will enforce a judgment *in rem* through an action *in rem*.[46]

(ii) Recognition and enforcement through registration

Courts of specified Commonwealth countries

The Administration of Justice Act 1920[47] provides a discretionary framework for the enforcement of judgments given in actions *in personam* under which money is payable, by courts of Commonwealth countries to which the Act has been extended.[48] An English court may, if it thinks it just and convenient to enforce such a judgment, on application order a judgment to be registered.[49] Once registered, the judgment is of the same force and effect as a judgment of the registering court.

Registration requires jurisdiction of the foreign court on the same criteria as for enforcement by action to enforce the judgment directly and the defences open to a defendant are akin to those available in an action on the judgment.[50]

Courts of specified countries

FOREIGN JUDGMENTS (RECIPROCAL ENFORCEMENT) ACT 1933[51]

The Act applies to any judgment *in personam* by which a sum of money is payable[52] given by a court[53] of a country to which Part 1 of the Act has been extended. It was originally

45. Similarly, an English court will recognize the title acquired by a purchaser through a sale in the course of administration on death or bankruptcy.

46. *The Despina GK* [1982] 2 Lloyd's Rep. 555, following *The City of Mecca* (1879) 5 P.D. 28 (at first instance). See Chap. 10 for comment on the distinction between enforcement of foreign and English judgments by an action *in rem* and *supra* as to jurisdictional uncertainty.

47. As amended in a minor way by the Civil Jurisdiction and Judgments Act 1982, s.35(2)—(amending ss.10 and 14).

48. Administration of Justice Act 1920, ss.12, 13 and 14. The basis of the scheme is reciprocity of enforcement and the machinery of enforcement set out in RSC Order 71. For a list of countries to which the Act has been extended, see RSC Order 71, rule 1. *Supreme Court Practice 1995*, Note 71/1/3. A judgment creditor may bring an action on the judgment (see *supra*) instead of using the registration procedure—but this may lead to deprivation of costs (see s.9(5)).

49. An application must be supported by an affidavit exhibiting a certified copy of the judgment and deposing to its enforceability.

50. See s.9(2). See e.g. *Owens Bank* v. *Bracco* [1992] 2 All E.R. 193 (H.L.).

51. As amended in scope by the Civil Jurisdiction and Judgments Act 1982, s.35(1), Sch. 10, which substitutes text for s.1(1) and (2) and (10) and inserts ss.2A and 10A.

52. Not being by way of taxes, fine or other penalty, s.1(2). A sum representing exemplary damages has been held not to be a penalty (see *SA Consortium General Textiles* v. *Sun and Sand Agencies Ltd.* [1978] Q.B. 279) but for a provision limiting enforcement of a judgment for multiple damages see the Protection of Trading Interests Act 1980 (*infra* fn. 64).

53. The Civil Jurisdiction and Judgments Act extends the provisions of the Act of 1933 to courts other than "superior" courts and to arbitration awards enforceable as judgments (see s.35(2), Sch. 10).

intended to replace the Administration of Justice Act 1920 and apply to both non-Commonwealth and Commonwealth courts; but the two systems continue in being.[54]

The Act follows the pattern of the Administration of Justice Act 1920[55] and that applicable to actions to enforce the judgment directly. Registration must be set aside if the foreign court had no jurisdiction or on proof of one of the defences to direct enforcement of a judgment already noted.[56] Registration may be set aside if, prior to the foreign judgment, the issue had been the subject of an earlier judgment.[57] A judgment on the merits will be recognized as a defence.[58]

STATUTES ADAPTING THE FOREIGN JUDGMENTS (RECIPROCAL ENFORCEMENT) ACT 1933

A number of statutes enacting into English law Conventions requiring the recognition of foreign judgments apply the statutory framework of the Act of 1933 to comply with the obligation.[59] Where a foreign country provides for the enforcement of judgments given in the United Kingdom to recover amounts paid under foreign judgments for multiple damages in excess of compensation, the Act of 1933 may be extended to that country to allow enforcement in the United Kingdom of like judgments of courts of that country.[60]

Restrictions on enforcement of foreign judgments

PROTECTION OF TRADE

Following concern at the extraterritorial application of the anti-trust laws of the United States, legislative action was taken in the United Kingdom to protect trading interests. The Protection of Trading Interests Act 1980 encompasses protection through government direction (backed by criminal sanctions):

(a) not to comply with overseas measures regarding extraterritorial action, or with extraterritorial orders for production of commercial documents or information;

(b) limiting the power of taking evidence in English courts on behalf of foreign courts; and

(c) restriction on the enforcement of foreign judgments.

54. Extension is allowed only if there is substantial reciprocity. The Act has been extended to specified foreign countries and a number of Commonwealth countries. See *Supreme Court Practice*, paras. 71/1/5 and 71/1/6.

55. The machinery for enforcement is, as with the 1920 Act, set out in RSC Order 71.

56. Section 4(1)(a). The Protection of Trading Interests Act 1980, s.5(1), specifically provides that no judgment prohibited from enforcement under that Act may be registered.

57. Section 4(1)(b).

58. Since the Foreign Limitation Periods Act 1984 came into force (i.e. as from 1 October 1985) a determination based on a time bar is a judgment on the merits (s.3).

59. See e.g. the Merchant Shipping (Oil Pollution) Act 1971, s.13(3) (1995 Act, s. 166(4)); The Merchant Shipping Act 1974, s.6(4) (1995 Act, s.177(4)); the Nuclear Installations Act 1965, s.17(4); the Carriage of Goods by Road Act 1965, s.4; Carriage of Passengers by Road Act 1974, s.5; the International Transport Conventions Act 1983, s.6. As to the effect of an action brought contrary to an agreement not to bring it in a foreign jurisdiction, see s.4(3)(b) of the Act of 1933 which continues to apply to such judgments registered before 24 August 1982 (Civil Jurisdiction and Judgments Act, s.32(4), Sch. 13, para. 8(2)).

60. Protection of Trading Interests Act 1980, s.7, as amended by the Civil Jurisdiction and Judgments Act 1982, s.38. As to the general effect of the Act of 1980, see *infra*.

The statute is wide in scope. Insofar as the enforcement of foreign judgments is concerned, it prohibits the enforcement of:

(i) a judgment[61] based on a rule of law concerned with competition or regulation of agreements specified by the Secretary of State[62]; or

(ii) a judgment[63] for multiple damages.[64]

The prohibition seems consistent with the framework of enforcement between European Union and EFTA member States countries in that it reflects English public policy and therefore falls within the exception to the obligation to enforce judgments within the Brussels and Lugano Conventions.[65]

JUDGMENTS AGAINST STATES

(a) Against "the United Kingdom" in overseas countries. Without statutory intervention a foreign judgment given against the United Kingdom Government may be enforced (and presumably recognized) according to the rules making up the structure

(i) for enforcement of judgments generally; and

(ii) of domestic actions against the Crown.

The State Immunity Act 1978 provides positively for conclusive recognition in any court in the United Kingdom of final judgments in proceedings in courts of countries parties to the European Convention on State Immunity 1972, provided that the United Kingdom was not entitled to immunity by virtue of provisions corresponding to those applicable to overseas states by virtue of the Act.[66] A court "need not give effect" to the judgment if to do so would be manifestly contrary to public policy; if any party to proceedings lacked opportunity to present his case; there was no service of process in and no submission to jurisdiction by the United Kingdom; duplicate proceedings instituted first are pending in the United Kingdom or another contracting State; the judgment is inconsistent with another given in the United Kingdom or another contracting State; the foreign court either would not have had jurisdiction according to English rules or it applied a law other than that indicated by "the United Kingdom rules of private international law", and would have reached a different conclusion by that route.[67]

---

61. Given before or after enactment of the provision.

62. Section 5(1), (2) and (4), i.e. anti-trust matters. Including a claim for contribution in respect of damages awarded by such a judgment (s.5(2)(c)). The specification is through statutory instrument (s.5(5)). An order has been made specifying s.81(1A) of the Trade Practices Act of Australia (SI 1988/569).

63. Given before or after enactment of the provision.

64. Section 5(1) and (2), i.e. a judgment arrived at by multiplying a sum assessed as compensation (s.5(3))—aimed primarily at the treble damages possible under the Clayton Act in the United States in respect of anti-trust actions. Such prohibition may be seen as an extension of the rule that an English court will not enforce a penalty but it is far from clear whether multiple damages would be considered as such. The prohibition includes a claim for contribution to such damages (s.5(2)(c)). There are provisions for recovery of any sums paid in excess of the compensation element (s.6).

65. See Chap. 28.

66. State Immunity Act 1978, s.18.

67. *Ibid.*, s.19. The reference to private international rules of the United Kingdom ignores any difference between Scottish and English rules.

(b) Against states other than the United Kingdom. A judgment given by foreign courts against a foreign state[68] will be recognized and enforced in the United Kingdom provided, first, it would have been so recognized and enforced if the defendant had been other than a state and, secondly, the foreign court would have had jurisdiction in accordance with rules corresponding to the State Immunity Act 1978.[69]

II. ARBITRAL AWARDS

AS BETWEEN PARTS OF THE UNITED KINGDOM

An arbitral award enforceable in the same manner as a judgment is within the definition of a judgment for the purposes of recognition and enforcement within the United Kingdom. As such it may (but unlike a judgment not must) be enforced by registration.[70]

AWARDS MADE OUTSIDE THE UNITED KINGDOM

There are two international Convention frameworks providing for the enforcement and recognition of arbitral awards in general and which apply to maritime as to other arbitrations:

(i) under the Protocol of Arbitral Clauses 1923 and the Convention for the Execution of Foreign Arbitral Awards 1927 (enacted into English law by the Arbitration Act 1950, Part II); and

(ii) under the New York Convention on the Recognition and Enforcement of Foreign Arbitral Awards 1958 (enacted into English law by the Arbitration Act 1975).[71]

(a) *Without registration*

(i) An award may be enforced under the Arbitration Act 1950, Part II (i.e. under the procedure of the Convention of 1927). A foreign award within the Convention framework is enforceable in England either by action under the Act, by action at common law or with leave of the High Court.[72] To fall within the Act an award must be made under an

68. Civil Jurisdiction and Judgments Act 1982, s.31. A state includes a government, a government department, the sovereign or Head of State in the public capacity, judgments against entities distinct from government but exercising the sovereign authority of the State (s.3(2)).

69. Judgments required to be recognized or enforced because of statutory enactments of specified Conventions are excluded from this provision (see s.31(3)). The rules of the 1978 Act are set out in ss.2–11 (see Chap. 12).

70. Civil Jurisdiction and Judgments Act 1982, s.18(1)(2)(e)(8), Sch. 6. Unlike judgments there is no provision prohibiting refusal of recognition or enforcement because of lack of jurisdiction under the rules of private international law in which the award was made (s.19(1)).

71. There is also (i) the European Convention on International Commercial Arbitration 1961, to which there are 19 parties but which the United Kingdom has not ratified; and (ii) the Inter-American Convention on International Commercial Arbitration 1975. See also Arbitration (International Disputes) Act 1966 enacting Convention provisions for the settlement of international investment disputes.

72. Arbitration Act 1950, ss.36(1) and 40(a). And without proceeding to a foreign judgment (see, for the principle, *Union Nationale des Cooperatives Agricoles* v. *Catterall* [1959] 2 Q.B. 44). For the application of domestic procedure to a foreign award, see *Dalmia Cement* v. *National Bank of Pakistan* [1975] Q.B. 9.

arbitration agreement governed by a law other than English law, made between persons, "subject to the jurisdiction"[73] of different States parties to the Convention and in a territory of a contracting State.[74] Requirements of enforceability are—much as for enforcement without the aid of statute—validity of the agreement by its proper law, and of the award by the law governing the proceedings and finality of judgment. In addition, the award must be in respect of a matter which could be referred to arbitration in English law, and not contrary to English public policy.[75]

(ii) An award may be enforced under the Arbitration Act 1975, i.e. under the procedure of the Convention of 1958. This replaces the Act of 1950 in respect of contracting States to the Convention of 1958. An award may be enforced by action or by leave of the High Court under the Arbitration Act 1950.[76] An award within this Act is one "made in pursuance of an arbitration agreement in the territory of a State other than the United Kingdom which is a party to the New York Convention."[77]

An award is enforceable on the production of a certified copy (and, translation, where appropriate) subject to requirements of public policy, fitness of the matter for arbitration or to establishment of one or specified grounds of defence by the defendant (incapacity of a party to the agreement; invalidity; lack of notice of proceedings or inability to present the case; inappropriate matters dealt with by the award; improper composition of the tribunal; award not binding on the parties). Even if the defendant establishes such a defence a court *may* enforce an award.[78] Where the enforcement court is also the curial court it may exercise the power of both courts. If appropriate as the curial court it may set aside or suspend the award.[79]

(b) Through registration

A further route of enforcement is by registration under the Administration of Justice Act 1920[80] or Foreign Judgments (Reciprocal Enforcement) Act 1933.[81] The provision of the Act of 1933 that no proceedings for the enforcement of the judgment within the Act may

---

73. i.e. reside *and* carry on business in two different states, the contract containing the arbitration submission having resulted from such businesss (*Brazendale & Co. Ltd.* v. *Saint Freres SA* [1970] 2 Lloyd's Rep. 34).

74. The states must be declared by Order in Council to be parties to the Convention of 1927. The current Order is the Arbitration (Foreign Awards) Order 1984 (SI 1984/1168).

75. See the Arbitration Act 1950, s.37(1).

76. Arbitration Act 1975, ss.3 and 6. As to enforcement of English arbitral awards (the procedure adapted to foreign awards) see Chap. 25. A court should not normally refuse leave to serve out of the jurisdiction to enforce an award (as to which see RSC Order 73, r. 7) when the grounds for enforcement are established. See *Rosseel NV* v. *Oriental Shipping Ltd.* [1991] 2 Lloyd's Rep. 625.

77. Arbitration Act 1975, s.7(1), i.e. in a State which has become a party to the Convention by the date on which proceedings to enforce the award are started. See *Govt. of the State of Kuwait* v. *Sir Frederick Snow & Partners* [1984] 1 Lloyd's Rep. 458 (H.L.). The award is "made" where it is perfected (i.e. usually signed) (*Hiscox* v. *Outhwaite (No. 1)* [1991] 3 All E.R. 641 (H.L.)).

78. Arbitration Act 1975, ss.4 and 5.

79. *Hiscox* v. *Outhwaite* (fn 77).

80. An arbitration award enforceable by the law of the place where made in the same manner as a judgment of a court of that place is included within "judgment" for the purposes of the Act (s.12(1)). As to enforcement provisions of that Act, see *supra*.

81. See s.10A (inserted by Civil Jurisdiction and Judgments Act 1982, Sch. 10) to the same effect as s.12(1) of the Act of 1920 (as to which see fn 80). The Act had been extended in 1956 to arbitral awards made in countries to which the Act of 1920 applied and to which it later applied (Administration of Justice Act 1956, s.51(1)—repealed by the Act of 1982). The Act is specifically applied to arbitrations under the CMR (Carriage of Goods by Road Act 1965, s.7).

be taken except though the Act does not apply to arbitral awards.[82] The Act is thereby extended to such awards in a manner consistent with the availability of enforcement under the Arbitration Act 1950 and the Arbitration Act 1975.

82. See s.10A. Where a 1958 Convention award is converted into a judgment the enforcement of the judgment may be stayed as any other judgment (see RSC Order 47, r. 1) but it will rarely be appropriate to order a stay (*Far Eastern Shipping Co.* v. *Sovcomflot* [1995] 1 Lloyd's Rep. 520).

CHAPTER 28

Judgments and Settlements within the Brussels or Lugano Convention

I. THE GENERAL PATTERN

The relationship of the Brussels and Lugano Conventions is discussed in Chapter 8. The Brussels Convention, as amended, provides for the recognition and enforcement as between the 12 member States of the European Union who were members prior to the accession of Austria, Finland and Sweden of court judgments, authentic instruments and settlements. The Lugano Convention applies as between the member States of the European Union and those of the European Free Trade Area who are parties to the Convention. Until Finland and Sweden accede to the Brussels Convention they will remain parties to and be governed by the Lugano Convention.[1]

JUDGMENTS

Apart from the necessary provisions for the relationship between the Conventions and two additional grounds of refusal the "judgments" structure of the Brussels and Lugano Conventions is identical. The structures apply to any judgment within the scope of the Convention given by a court or tribunal of a contracting State. The underlying principles are that (i) save for specified exceptions jurisdictional enquiry is for the adjudicating court and (ii) subject to specific and limited exceptions once a judgment is given on a civil and commercial matter by a court of a contracting State it is to be recognized and enforced in each contracting State.

Grounds of non-recognition or non-enforcement common to both Conventions are that the judgment is within the Convention provisions in insurance and consumer contract cases only, lack of jurisdiction of the adjudicating court; the judgment was in proceedings based on an exorbitant jurisdiction and listed grounds of refusal concerning the nature of the judgment or the proceedings leading to it. There are powers to stay enforcement or recognition proceedings pending appeals from the judgment at issue. Under no circumstances may a judgment be reviewed as to its substance.

Under the Lugano Convention there are two further grounds relating only to non-Community enforcement, one going to the lack of Convention jurisdiction in the proceedings leading to the judgment and the other, more generally, requiring in specified

---

1. As of 1 December 1995 Austria, Belgium, Denmark and Greece had not ratified the Lugano Convention.

circumstances the judgment to be recognized or enforced according to the law of the state addressed. These grounds are considered in detail later in this chapter.

Accompanying these specific Convention grounds is a principle akin to issue estoppel—that a judgment creditor should, once he has a judgment, seek to enforce that judgment and not attempt to bring a further action on the same claim.[2] A judgment is however enforceable even if not *"res judicata"* in the court issuing it—the sole criterion is its enforceability by that court.[3]

The "freedom of movement" of judgments means that security for costs in proceedings is more difficult to obtain[4] and that any discrimination between orders for security for costs in a member State in relation to proceedings in that state and in other member States is contrary to the Treaty of Rome. In the view of the European Court the territory of the contracting parties "may be regarded as constituting a single entity"—"the condition for the enforcement of judgments and the risks connected with the difficulties to which it leads are the same in all the member States".[5]

THE LINK BETWEEN RECOGNITION AND ENFORCEMENT

Enforcement is *ex hypothesi* the focal point of enforcement proceedings but recognition may be sought as the primary issue or as incidental to the outcome of other proceedings. Recognition or enforcement may be sought by "any interested party". Save that a judgment may not be enforced because of non-enforceability in the country of the adjudicating court, grounds for non-recognition or non-enforcement are identical whatever the context of the issue.[6]

"AUTHENTIC INSTRUMENTS" AND COURT SETTLEMENTS[7]

Articles 50 and 51 provide for the enforcement of settlements and authentic instruments and adapt the judgments process to settlements. The "authentic instrument" is not known to English law but in some legal systems (including that of Scotland) a specified type of instrument once registered may be enforced as if it were a judgment.[8]

An authentic instrument or settlement enforceable drawn up, registered and enforceable in one state is to have an order for its enforcement issued in another on application made in accordance with the procedure for enforcing judgments. However the sole ground for non-enforcement is that it is contrary to the public policy of the enforcement state. An authentic instrument or settlement is *not* a judgment unless given as such by a court and it is not open to a defendant to rely on an instrument or settlement as an irreconcilable

---

2. *De Wolf* v. *Cox BV* 42/76 [1976] ECR 1759; [1977] 2 CMLR 43.

3. *Van Dalfsen* v. *Van Loon* 183/90 [1992] I.L.Pr. 5.

4. See Chap. 14. As to security in enforcement and recognition proceedings see *infra*.

5. *Firma Mund and Fester* v. *Firma Hatrex* 398/92 [1994] I.L.Pr. 264.

6. See Articles 27, 28 (non-recognition) applied to non-enforcement by Article 34. As to the need for enforceability in the state of origin see Article 31.

7. The Civil Jurisdiction and Judgments Act 1982 (as amended) is applied to these matters by SI 1993/604.

8. For an example of the enforcement of such an instrument (a land charge under German law) see *Deutsche Genossenschaftsbank* v. *Brasserie du Pecheur* 148/84 [1986] 2 CMLR 496 (ECJ).

judgment.[9] It is therefore essential for full and conclusive effect that in any settlement of an action the terms be incorporated in a court order.

II. JUDGMENTS WITHIN THE CONVENTION

"CIVIL OR COMMERCIAL MATTERS"

As with jurisdiction, whether a judgment concerns a civil or commercial matter is a Community concept. It remains for the recognition or enforcement court to decide whether the judgment falls within this category whether or not the adjudicating court has also made a finding.[10] The enforcement court is not bound by any decision on the issue of the adjudicating court but following Articles 29 and 34(3) in no case will there be any review of the substance of the judgment (see *infra*).

CONNECTION WITH A MEMBER STATE

The primary connecting factors of the substantive jurisdiction and judgment structures are different—in jurisdiction it is the domicile of the defendant, in judgments the judgment of a court of a contracting State. Further, unlike jurisdiction there are no exceptions to the basic rule of applicability, in that the Convention does not purport to concern itself with a judgment of a non-contracting State.

TYPES OF JUDGMENTS

"Judgment" includes "any judgment given by a court or tribunal of a Contracting State whatever the judgment may be called, including a decree, order, decision or writ of execution as well as the determination of costs or expenses by an officer of the court" (Article 25).[11]

Judgments in action "in rem"

It is clear from the judgment of the European Court in *The Maciej Rataj*[12] and the Court of Appeal in *The Deichland*[13] that for the purposes of the Convention the action *in rem* is

---

9. *Solo Kleinmotoren GmbH* v. *Boch* 414/92 [1994] I.L.Pr. 457. The equation of authentic instruments and settlements to judgments by SI 1993/604 for enforceability purposes in the United Kingdom must be read subject to this decision.

10. *LTV GmbH and Co. KG* v. *Eurocontrol* 29/1976 [ECR] 1541; [1977] 1 CMLR 88. *Gourdain* v. *Nadler* 133/78 [1979] ECR 733; [1979] 3 CMLR 180. The civil parts of a judgment of a criminal court constitute a "civil matter": *Sonntag* v. *Waidmann* 172/91 21 April 1993 (ECJ).

11. The question of costs cannot be reargued in an enforcement court. See *Re the Enforcement of a Foreign Costs Order* (1984) Oberlandsgericht Frankfurt [1986] ECC 481. As to the distinction between settlements and judgments see *supra*.

12. [1995] 1 Lloyd's Rep. 302.

13. [1989] 2 All E.R. 1066.

as such simply a matter of national procedure. The distinction may have relevance in Convention terms in identifying the parties to an action but it poses no difficulty in respect of recognition or enforcement. The judgment will be enforced "against" such defendants as have either appeared or, having received notice, failed to appear. The procedure for service of a writ *in rem* may however be relevant to recognition or enforcement in deciding on whether and by which document a defendant is informed of proceedings (see *infra*).

"Ex parte" orders

The definition of judgment is wide, including both interim relief and final judgment,[14] but must be read in the context of the Convention as a whole. It is only judgments in proceedings in which the defendant had the opportunity to put his case which are to be enforced or recognized. This is demonstrated by the provision that a judgment may be challenged on the ground that the defendant has not had that opportunity (see *infra*). It follows, therefore, that although a default judgment qualifies for enforcement provided notice has been given, an order obtained *ex parte* does not.[15] While therefore an order for arrest of a ship or an injunction is within the Convention, recognition or enforcement is an obligation only if the order is made after the defendant has been given the opportunity to oppose the making of the order.

Ancillary or procedural orders

Orders for costs are expressly included in the Convention framework by Article 25 but the Convention structure does not provide for interest on judgments. According to Schlosser ancillary orders going to the production of evidence at a trial or conduct of a trial are not included for the reasons, first, that the member States (with the exception of Ireland) are parties to the Hague Conventions of 1965 and 1970 on the service abroad of judicial documents and the taking of evidence abroad. Secondly, says Schlosser, the parties would be unable to comply with any order in respect of the conduct of foreign proceedings without the co-operation of the foreign court.[16] Article 43 recognizes the enforcement of judgments for periodic payments by way of a penalty—a provision aimed apparently at least in part at judgments ordering such payments because of delay in payment of money due.[17]

---

14. The limiting of "judgment" to a final determination permanently dispositive of substantive rights (the holding by Ognall J. in *Virgin Aviation Services Ltd.* v. *CAD Services* [1991] I.L.Pr. 448) is consistent with the argument that "procedural" orders are not judgments (see *infra*)—but distinguish protective or provisional measures (under Article 24) (arrest or *Mareva*) affecting substantive rights.

15. *Denilauler* v. *SNC Freres* 125/79 [1980] ECR 1553; [1981] 1 CMLR 62. Enforceability of such a judgment cannot result from an opportunity to have the judgment set aside nor is the exclusion limited to orders intended to be enforced without service (see *EMI Records* v. *Modern Music* [1992] 1 All E.R. 616).

16. For discussion as to the ambit of the Convention in respect of procedural orders see Schlosser, paras. 184–187. See also *supra* fn. 14.

17. And payment of penalty for breach of an order. See *S. C. Johnson* v. *Mobilar Export Import GmbH* [1984] ECC 360, District Court Rotterdam—enforcement requires the amount of the penalty to be finally determined by the court in which the judgment was delivered: *Medicale Equipex SA* v. *Farmitalia Erba* Cour d'Appel Versailles [1990] I.L.Pr. 192.

Procedure or substance—who controls?

The Schlosser report reads—

"191. The effects of a court decision are not altogether uniform under the legal system obtaining in the Member States of the Community. A judgment delivered in one State as a decision on a procedural issue may, in another State, be treated as a decision on an issue of substance. The same type of judgment may be of varying scope and effect in different countries. In France, a judgment against the principal debtor is also effective against the surety, whereas in the Netherlands and Germany it is not.

The Working Party did not consider it to be its task to find a general solution to the problems arising from these differences in the national legal systems."

Although there will be difficulties on the borderline, as Schlosser indicates, it seems clear that a procedural order in the course of a trial is not a "judgment" within the Convention in that the process is aimed at determination of substantive rights—although including provisional or protective measures such as seizure or maintaining a status quo. But apart from such orders it should not be open to an enforcement court to take its own view that a judgment is procedural. An enforceable judgment must have in principle the same effect in the enforcement state as in the state in which it was issued.[18]

The difficulties which will be created by any other approach are demonstrated by Schlosser's assertion of the effect of a judgment declining jurisdiction:

"Judgments dismissing an action as unfounded must be recognized. If a German court declares that it has no jurisdiction, an English court cannot disclaim its own jurisdiction on the ground that the German court was in fact competent. Clearly, however, German decisions on procedural matters are not binding, as to the substance, in England. An English court may at any time allow (or, for substantive reasons, disallow) an action, if proceedings are started in England after such a decision has been given by a German court" (para. 191).

However it would destroy the Convention framework to invent boundary rules for recognition just as much as it would to allow reallocation through *forum non conveniens*. Even more is this likely to be so if generalized labels (such as procedure and substance) are used which find no place in the Convention itself. Further, whatever boundary is fixed it cannot be left to national laws to fix it for to do so would undermine the whole concept of the Convention obligation of recognition or enforcement. In truth the issue is an aspect of the scope of a judgment and the obligation to recognize or enforce a judgment which may not exist under the national law of the enforcement court.[19]

Judgments on judgments

What of a judgment recognizing or enforcing another judgment? So far as judgments given in proceedings mounted in a contracting State are concerned there is no point in seeking such an order. On the other hand, to require enforcement of an order of a court of a contracting State enforcing a judgment of a court of a non-contracting State would have meant using the Convention framework to enforce judgments of non-contracting States.

In *Owens Bank* v. *Bracco*[20] the European Court held that the Convention had no application to judgments of non-contracting States. The court stressed that the provisions

18. See e.g. *Hoffman* v. *Kreig* 145/86 [1990] I.L.Pr. 4 (ECJ).
19. As e.g. where an order affects assets or third parties in the territory of the enforcement court.
20. [1992] 2 All E.R. 193.

for enforcement had to be read in the context of the definition of judgment in Article 25, and that the conferring of exclusive jurisdiction on an enforcement state in respect of enforcement of judgments had also to be read in conjunction with that article.[21] Furthermore the Court held that no distinction could be drawn for the purpose of assessing the application of the Convention between an order for enforcement and an issue arising in enforcement proceedings. So Articles 21 and 22 of the Convention concerning concurrent proceedings had no application when enforcement proceedings were first taken in Italy in respect of a judgment of a court of a non-contracting State and then (concurrently) in England.[22]

Judgments within other Conventions given precedence

Articles 55–59 deal with the relationship of the Brussels and Lugano Conventions to other Conventions concerning jurisdiction or judgments. By Article 55 and 56, certain listed Conventions are specifically superseded insofar as either Convention applies. Article 58 of the Brussels Convention preserves the rights of Swiss nationals in a bilateral French-Swiss Jurisdiction and Judgment Convention of 1869. Article 59 of both Conventions provides expressly that a contracting State may assume an obligation not to recognize or enforce judgments against a party not domiciled in a contracting State based only on "exorbitant jurisdiction" grounds. Such an obligation is a ground of non-recognition or non-enforcement (see *infra*).

Article 57 preserves the provisions which "govern the recognition or enforcement of judgments" in Conventions on particular matters. The recognition and enforcement of judgments falling within the Brussels or Lugano Convention and another Convention is therefore first a matter for the application of the other Convention. Article 57 of the Brussels Convention continues with a view to the uniform interpretation of the "other Convention" rule (the text in the Lugano Convention being identical in substance):

"judgments given in a Contracting State by a court in the exercise of jurisdiction provided for in a convention on a particular matter shall be recognised and enforced in the other Contracting States in accordance with this Convention.

Where a convention on a particular matter to which both the State of origin and the State addressed are parties lays down conditions for the recognition or enforcement of judgments, those conditions shall apply. In any event, the provisions of this Convention which concern the procedures for recgonition and enforcement of judgments may be applied."[23]

As a consequence a judgment falling within Article 57 is to be recognized and enforced as if it was within the Brussels Convention subject only to the application of conditions of the other Convention if the countries of both issuing and enforcement court are parties

---

21. But a Contracting State obliged by its law to recognize the judgment of a non-contracting State is not also obliged to recognize an inconsistent later judgment of a contracting State (Article 27(5) see *infra*).

22. The "issue" in the proceedings arose because in both England and Italy the defendants pleaded that the judgment (of a court in St Vincent) had been obtained by fraud.

23. Inserted into Article 57 by Art. 25(2)(b) of the San Sebastian Convention 1989. The form of Art. 57 of the Lugano Convention differs slightly but the content is identical save for the provision of a ground for non-recognition or enforcement of a judgment when the enforcement or recognizing state is *not* a party to such a Convention (see *infra*).

to the other Convention. That the procedural provisions of the Brussels Convention "may be applied" presumably simply emphasizes their availability if a national law wishes to adopt them.

Many of the Conventions specified by Article 55 of each of the Brussels and Lugano Conventions as being superseded are concerned with the general provision of mutual recognition and enforcement of judgments. Even if a Convention of this type is not specified it is difficult to see how it would qualify for continuation through the two Conventions. To do this through Article 57 a Convention must relate to a particular matter and "particular" cannot include the general question of recognition and enforcement of judgments which is at the very heart of the Brussels and Lugano Conventions.

Maritime Conventions within Article 57

Some Conventions relating to particular matters in maritime law which have jurisdiction provisions and which are discussed in Chapter 6 also have "recognition and enforcement" provisions. The following contain recognition and enforcement provisions.

The CMR

Article 31(3) and (4) provides:

"3. When a judgment entered by a court or tribunal of a contracting country in any such action as is referred to in paragraph 1 of this article has become enforceable in that country, it shall also become enforceable in each of the other contracting States, as soon as the formalities required in the country concerned have been complied with. The formalities shall not permit the merits of the case to be re-opened.

4. The provisions of paragraph 3 of this article shall apply to judgments after trial, judgments by default and settlements confirmed by an order of the court, but shall not apply to interim judgments or to awards of damages, in addition to costs against a plaintiff who wholly or partly fails in his action."

Judgments otherwise within the Brussels Convention will be governed by this provision only insofar as the judgment falls within Article 31(4) of the CMR. If it does and if both states are parties, however it is arguable that once formalities are complete in the issuing state the judgment is enforceable in the enforcement state. The defences of the Brussels Convention would seem to have no application. It would not seem possible to argue consistently with the purpose of Article 57 that the lack of provision for any defences means that once enforceable under the CMR the case moves back as it were to the Brussels Convention. Unlike the omission of a particular aspect such as concurrent proceedings the provision of enforceability without any defence is as "positive" a condition as provision for a defence.[24] However, it may be arguable that the use of "formalities" in conjunction with the national law and prohibition on reopening of the

---

24. There is no room thereby for the approach to Art. 57 in *The Maciej Rataj* [1995] 1 Lloyd's Rep. 302 that there is only a move out of the Brussels Convention insofar as there are provisions relating to the particular issue in the other Convnetion—so lack of provisions dealing with concurrent actions meant *in that respect* the Brussels Convention applied. In the case of the *CMR* there is a provision for recognition and enforcement.

merits could be the foundation for the applicability of national law defences such as fraud and natural justice.

The Oil Pollution Conventions 1969 and 1971[25]

The Liability Convention (1969) provides in Article X:

"1. Any judgment given by a Court with jurisdiction in accordance with Article IX which is enforceable in the State of origin where it is no longer subject to ordinary forms of review, shall be recognized in any Contracting State, except:

  (a) where the judgment was obtained by fraud; or
  (b) where the defendant was not given reasonable notice and a fair opportunity to present his case.

2. A judgment recognized under paragraph 1 of this Article shall be enforceable in each Contracting State as soon as the formalities required in that State have been complied with. The formalities shall not permit the merits of the case to be re-opened."

Article 8 of the Fund Convention of 1971 provides similarly.

As with jurisdictional matters it is suggested that these provisions establish a code (however basic) for recognition and enforcement. As a consequence it is to the Liability and Fund Conventions that attention must be directed for any limitation on or conditions of recognition and enforcement.

The Maritime Liens and Mortgage Conventions 1926, 1967 and 1993

It is arguable that a duty to recognize and enforce any judgment in respect of liens, mortgages and other security interests in a ship is implied from the frameworks of these Conventions, particularly as regards judicial sale. The Convention of 1967 (Article 11) refers specifically to the effect of a forced sale in freeing the ship from (with specified exceptions) encumbrances. The Convention of 1993 (Article 12) provides that apart from those assumed by a purchaser with consent all registered mortgages, liens and encumbrances cease to attach to the vessel.

Conventions on liability in respect of nuclear incidents

The Paris Convention 1960 (as amended) (Art. 13) and the Vienna Convention 1964 (Art. XII) provide for the enforcement of judgments in sufficient detail, it would seem, to remove the issue from the Brussels and Lugano Conventions.

III. THE JURISDICTION OF THE RECOGNIZING OR ENFORCING COURT

Subject to the question of recognition arising incidentally the court in which a judgment has been or will be enforced has exclusive jurisdiction in respect of proceedings concerned with the enforcement of judgments (Articles 16 (5), 26). It is for the enforcement court to

---

25. To become the Conventions of 1993 once the London Protocols are in force (see Chap. 5).

be satisfied that the matter is within the Convention having regard to its nature and subject matter (i.e. is concerned with a civil and commercial matter), that recognition or enforcement is not governed by a Convention under Article 57 and that where it is sought to enforce a judgment the judgment is enforceable in the state of origin.

Once so satisfied and in the case of enforcement there is compliance with the procedure (see *infra*) the judgment must be recognized or enforced as appropriate unless there is a Convention ground for refusal or there are grounds for a stay of proceedings. The grounds of refusal go in a very limited number of cases to the jurisdiction of the adjudicating court, and generally to public policy, default of appearance in the adjudicating court, irreconcilability of judgments, or a preliminary question of status. Under no circumstance is the judgment to be reviewed as to substance. Recognition or enforcement proceedings may be stayed in specified circumstances pending an appeal against the judgment at issue.

IV. GROUNDS OF NON-RECOGNITION OR NON-ENFORCEMENT

RELEVANCE OF JURISDICTION OF ADJUDICATING COURT

Under both the Brussels and Lugano Conventions a judgment may not be recognized or enforced on a ground going to the jurisdiction of the court of the contracting State of origin *only* if:

(i) the case is within the structure applicable to insurance or consumer contracts (Sections 3 and 4) and there was no Convention jurisdiction; or

(ii) the case is within the "exclusive jurisdiction" category of Article 16 and there was no Convention jurisdiction;

(iii) the case is within a Convention imposing an obligation of non-recognition in accordance with Article 59.

An additional ground going to the jurisdiction of the adjudicating court appears in the Lugano Convention (Articles 28, 54B(3)). Recognition or enforcement may be refused if:

(i) the ground of jurisdiction of the proceedings on which the judgment was based differs from "that resulting from" the Convention, *and*

(ii) recognition or enforcement is sought against a party domiciled in a contracting State which is a *non-Community* State, *and*

(iii) the judgment would not be recognized or enforced by any rule of law in the state addressed.

This is an exception to the idea of a Convention recognition and enforcement code without reference to the ground of jurisdiction on which the judgment is based. The national law of the state addressed (not necessarily that of the defendant's domicile) becomes a critical factor if the judgment is not based on Convention jurisdiction ground—and depending on that law there may be an enquiry into the jurisdiction of the adjudicating court. As the qualification for its operation is the defendant's domicile in a non-Community State the provision would seem to have no operation in relation to defendants domiciled in Austria, Finland or Sweden even prior to those states becoming parties to the Brussels Convention.

Unless therefore the case falls within one of the categories listed, refusal cannot be based on the ground that the proceedings in which the judgment was given were without jurisdiction.[26] Even in regard to these categories the enforcement court is bound by findings of fact in which the adjudicating court based its jurisdiction. In no other type of case may a judgment not be recognized or enforced on the ground that it is given in proceedings without Convention jurisdiction. The ground of "public policy" forming a ground of non-recognition or enforcement may not be applied to jurisdiction rules.

Judgments based on the extended "exorbitant" jurisdiction set out in Article 3 (Article 59)

Article 4 provides that specified rules of national law of "exorbitant jurisdiction" outlawed by Article 3 in respect of defendants domiciled in a contracting State may be relied on in respect of a defendant not domiciled in a contracting State by a plaintiff domiciled in a contracting State, whatever his nationality, in the same way as nationals of that state. So, in this respect rules of jurisdiction dependent on connections too slight to be Convention jurisdiction bases are extended by the Convention (see Chapter 4).

To meet concern expressed by countries outside the Community (in particular the United States), subject to limitations, the Conventions permit a contracting State to enter into a Convention with a non-contracting State imposing an obligation not to recognize a judgment in proceedings the jurisdiction of which can be based only on the grounds set out in Article 3.

Article 59 provides:

"This Convention shall not prevent a Contracting State from assuming, in a convention on the recognition and enforcement of judgments, an obligation towards a third State not to recognise judgments given in other Contracting States against defendants domiciled or habitually resident in the third State where, in cases provided for in Article 4, the judgment could only be founded on a ground of jurisdiction specified in the second paragraph of Article 3.

However, a Contracting State may not assume an obligation towards a third State not to recognise a judgment given in another Contracting State by a court basing its jurisdiction on the presence within that State of property belonging to the defendant, or the seizure by the plaintiff of property situated there:
1. if the action is brought to assert or declare proprietary or possessory rights in that property, seeks to obtain authority to dispose of it, or arises from another issue relating to such property, or
2. if the property constitutes the security for a debt which is the subject-matter of the action."

---

26. See e.g. *Re an English Judgment* [1993] I.L.Pr. 653. So the enforcement court cannot consider whether the adjudicating court should have declined jurisdiction of its own motion under Article 20 (see *Société Launay v. Deyglat* (Cour d'Appel Orleans) (1979) ECD 1–28–B2. See also *Genel Maklyati SA v. Compagnie Générale Maritime SA* (1982) 1983 ECD 144. The prerequisite that jurisdiction under Article 5(1) requires specific assent by a Luxembourg domiciliary (Article I of the Annexed Protocol) held not to provide a ground of refusal: *Weinor v. Sarl Wirion Mod'enfants* (1975) Cour Superieure de Justice Lux. ECD 1–28–B1. As to possible refusal of enforcement because of the scope of the judgment or its effect in the state of the enforcement court see *supra*.

To give express Convention force to Article 59 it is provided by Article 28 that a judgment to which such an obligation attached is not to be recognized.[27]

2. GROUNDS OTHER THAN JURISDICTION OF THE ADJUDICATING COURT

Article 27 (as applied to enforcement by Article 34) provides that a judgment shall not be recognized:

"1. if such recognition is contrary to public policy in the State in which recognition is sought;
2. where it was given in default of appearance, if the defendant was not duly served with the document which instituted the proceedings or with an equivalent document in sufficient time to enable him to arrange for his defence;
3. if the judgment is irreconcilable with a judgment given in a dispute between the same parties in the State in which recognition is sought;
4. if the court of the State in which the judgment was given, in order to arrive at its judgment, has decided a preliminary question concerning the status or legal capacity of natural persons, rights in property arising out of matrimonial relationship, wills or succession in a way that conflicts with a rule of the private international law of the State in which the recognition is sought, unless the same result would have been reached by the application of the rules of private international law of that State;
5. if the judgment is irreconcilable with an earlier judgment given in a non-Contracting State involving the same cause of action and between the same parties, provided that this latter judgment fulfils the conditions necessary for its recognition in the State addressed."

An additional ground in the Lugano Convention (Articles 28, 57(4)) is where:

(i) the recognizing or enforcement state is *not* a party to any relevant Convention within Article 57 *and*
(ii) the defendant is domiciled in the recognizing or enforcement state *and*
(iii) the judgment may not be recognized or enforced under any rules of law of that state.

In effect this means that save where the governing Convention is applicable through Article 57 no judgment may be enforced or recognized in a state in which the defendant is domiciled unless the law of that state permits it. As a consequence, therefore, the Convention grounds are *additional* to instead of in substitution for the national laws—an approach wholly contrary to that of the Brussels Convention.

Grounds common to Brussels and Lugano Conventions

(i) Public policy (Article 27(1))

Article 27(1) reads that "a judgment shall not be recognised if such a judgment is contrary to public policy in the State in which recognition is sought". Clearly if this were to be

---

27. The United Kingdom has provided that an obligation within Article 59 is assumed in relation to specified courts of Canada (SI 1987/468 as amended—for amendments see SI 1992/1731) and to specified courts of Australia on the coming into force of a Convention for the reciprocal recognition and enforcement of judgments 1990 (SI 1994/1901)—commencement 1 September 1994.

interpreted broadly it could destroy the Convention structure and just as clearly the intention is that it should be confined to the "fundamental principles" at the heart of the legal system of the recognition and enforcement court. This has been described by the German Federal Supreme Court as "so strongly contrary to the basic considerations behind the German rules and concepts of justice and . . . unacceptable in a domestic situation",[28] while a French court has emphasized the need to assess the matter in the light of the international public policy of the enforcing court.[29]

One obvious ground for consideration is the obtaining of a judgment by fraud. Of this Schlosser says (para. 192):

"The 1968 Convention does not state in terms whether recognition may be refused pursuant to Article 27(1) on the ground that the judgment has been obtained by fraud. Not even in the legal systems of the original Contracting States to the 1968 Convention is it expressly stated that fraud in obtaining a judgment constitutes a ground for refusing recognition. Such conduct is, however, generally considered as an instance for applying the doctrine of public policy. The legal situation in the United Kingdom and Ireland is different inasmuch as fraud constitutes a special ground for refusing recognition in addition to the principle of public policy. In the conventions on enforcement which the United Kingdom concluded with Community States, a middle course was adopted by expressly referring to fraudulent conduct, but treating it as a special case of public policy.

As a result there is no doubt that to obtain a judgment by fraud can in principle constitute an offence against the public policy of the State addressed. However, the legal system of all Member States provide special means of redress by which it can be contended, even after the expiry of the normal period for an appeal, that the judgment was the result of a fraud (see paragraph 197, et seq). A court in the State addressed must always, therefore, ask itself, whether a breach of its public policy still exists in view of the fact that proceedings for redress can be, or could have been lodged in the courts of the State of origin, against the judgment allegedly obtained by fraud."

If fraud is alleged and there are means of redress in the issuing court there would be no breach of English public policy in recognizing the judgment.[30] Where the foreign Convention court has ruled on the matters now asserted, an English court will not review them—the "fraud" ground had to be read subject to the prohibition on review of substance.

Apart from fraud any ground of "public policy" requires particular justification and is applicable only in exceptional cases.[31] The other express grounds of refusal of Article 27 cannot form grounds of "public policy". Refusal must be justified on the appropriate ground (as, for example, irreconcilable judgments).[32] Subject to any estoppel operating against the person relying on the judgment "the English court should not normally

---

28. *Re Foreign Exchange Rates* [1994] I.L.Pr. 703. See also *Interdesco SA* v. *Nullifire Ltd.* (Phillips J.) [1992] 1 Lloyd's Rep. 180 (see *infra*—fraud).

29. *Maitre de Grandpu* v. *Ifafood SA* (Cour d'Appel Paris) [1993] I.L.Pr. 657. In considering whether the regularity of the proceedings satisfied this criterion the court throught the procedure of the issuing court to be irrelevant. See also *Polypetrol* v. *Société Générale Routière* (French Cour de Cassation) [1993] I.L.Pr. 107—contrary to such policy if no reasoning.

30. *Interdesco SA* v. *Nullifire Ltd.* [1992] 1 Lloyd's Rep. 180; approved by Court of Appeal in *Société d'Informatique Service* v. *Ampersand Software BV* 432/93 [1995] All E.R. (E.C.) 783. As to similar views in other countries see e.g. *Soc. Sectom* v. *Soc. Fremo* (Cass. Civ. Italy) (1981) 1982 ECD 230. See also on the general question of the ability to raise a defence which would have been raised before the adjudicating court, *Re Enforcement of a French Sequestration Order* (1977) (Bundesgerichthof) [1979] ECC 321.

31. *Hoffman* v. *Kreig* 145/86 [1990] I.L.Pr. 4.

32. *Ibid.*—but there may be connected grounds such as the procedural irregularity.

entertain a challenge to a Convention judgment on grounds of public policy where it would not permit a challenge to an English judgment.[33]

(ii) The defendant's opportunity to put his case (Article 27(2))

Article 27(2) reads that a judgment shall not be recognized "where it was given in default of appearance, if a defendant was not duly served with the document which instituted the proceedings or with an equivalent document in sufficient time to enable him to arrange for his defence."[34]

Connection with like jurisdiction requirement

By Article 20, subject to the Hague Convention on Service of Documents Abroad 1965, a court before which a case is brought against a defendant not domiciled in that state must stay the proceedings so long as it is not shown that (i) the defendant has been able to receive the document instituting the proceedings or an equivalent document in sufficient time to enable him to arrange for his defence or (ii) all necessary steps have been taken to this end. Where the document instituting the proceedings or notice "has to be transmitted abroad" according to the Hague Convention the obligation of service as set out in that Convention applies (as to which see Chapter 4). The issue in any recognition or enforcement proceedings of a judgment obtained in the absence of a defendant is whether the adjudicating court having had the opportunity and duty to consider the validity of service, an enforcement court can also consider it.

In *Pendy Plastic Products* v. *Pluspunkt Handelsgesellschaft Mbh*[35] the European Court held that the question of compliance of service is also within the jurisdiction of the enforcement court. After viewing the terms of Article 27(2) and Article 20 of the Convention the Court said:

" . . . although they do not seek to harmonise the different systems of service abroad of legal documents which are in force in the Member States the provisions of the Brussels Convention are designed to ensure that the defendants rights are effectively protected. For that reason jurisdiction to determine whether the document introducing the proceeding was properly served was conferred both on the court of the original State and on the court of the State in which enforcement is sought. Thus, in accordance with the objective of Article 27 of the Convention, the court of the State in which enforcement is sought must examine the question posed by paragraph (2) of that Article, notwithstanding the decision given by the court of original State on the basis of the second and third paragraphs of Article 20. That examination is subject only to a limitation set by Article 34(3) to the Convention to the effect that the foreign judgment may under no circumstances be reviewed as to its substance."[36]

---

33. *Interdesco SA* v. *Nullifire Ltd.* (fn 30). As to the general principle as defining "public policy" see *supra* text to fns 28, 29.

34. Article 27(2) does not require consideration by the enforcement court of its own motion. See *Wagner* v. *Tettweiler* Cour de Cassation France [1985] ECC 258. In the case of a person prosecuted for an offence in a contracting State other than his domicile he may be ordered by the court to appear. If he does not do so any judgment in "the civil action" need not be recognized or enforced unless the person concerned has the opportunity of arranging for his defence (Annexed Protocol Art. II).

35. 228/81 [1983] 1 CMLR 665.

36. Para. 13, Article 29 prohibits the review of the substance of a judgment in recognition proceedings or (as applied by Art. 34) in enforcement proceedings.

The Court therefore concluded that the matter of compliance with Article 27(2) was within the jurisdiction of the enforcement court.

The requirements of Article 27(2)

Article 27(2) requires: (i) that the defendant has been "duly served" with the appropriate document; *and* (ii) that that service be in sufficient time to enable the defence to be arranged. The first requirement

"entails a decision based on the legislation of the State in which judgment was given and on the conventions binding on that State in regard to service whilst the second, concerning the time necessary to enable the defendant to arrange for his defence, implies appraisals of a factual nature. A decision concerning the first of those conditions made in the State in which the judgment was given accordingly does not release the court in the State in which enforcement is sought from its duty to examine the second condition, even if that decision was made in the context of separate adversary proceedings."[37]

"DULY SERVED"

The requirements must be read together with Article IV of the Annexed Protocol that "judicial and extra judicial documents drawn up in one Contracting State shall be transmitted in accordance with the procedures laid down in the Conventions and agreements concluded between the Contracting States".[38] The Convention most relevant to such service is the Hague Convention on the Service Abroad of Judicial and Extra Judicial Documents 1965. By that Convention a central authority of the state addressed must be designated to effect service (Article 1), but if the state of destination does not object service may be by post from the state of origin.[39] Further, the Convention does not affect other methods of transmission permitted by the state of destination.[40] In *Thierry Noirhomme* v. *David Walklate*[41] it was held that the effect of Article IV of the Protocol was not to make service provisions actually specified (i.e. "laid down") in other Conventions mandatory but simply to allow service in accordance with such Conventions. As service by national law was permitted by the Hague Convention it was good service for the purpose of Article 4 of the Protocol and Article 17(2).

If there is a decision by the adjudicating court that there was proper service in that state in accordance with that law it may be difficult for the enforcement court to go behind it. However, it may be open to the enforcement court to consider the matter if service is on the defendant in a state other than that of the adjudicating court and is governed by a Convention. Even more so would this apply if between the countries the "service" was

37. *Klomps* v. *Michel* 166/80 [1981] ECR 1593; [1982] 2 CMLR 773, para. 15. See also *Isabelle Lancray SA* v. *Peters and Sicket* C 305/88, [1991] I.L.Pr. 99 (ECJ) (any defence in service being curable by that law); *Noirhomme* v. *Walklate* [1992] 1 Lloyd's Rep. 427.
38. Unless a state objects by declaration the documents may be sent by the public authorities in the judgment state to the authorities in the enforcement state who are competent to forward it to the party—and the forwarding is to be in accordance with the receiving state recorded by a certificate and sent to the state of origin.
39. See Article 10—Germany has apparently objected. See *Re an English Judgment* [1993] I.L.Pr. 653 (Oberlandsgericht Hamm).
40. Article 19.
41. [1992] 1 Lloyd's Rep. 427. The court rejected a further argument that non-compliance with *Article 15 of the Hague Convention* (incorporated into Article 20 of the Brussels Convention—see Chap. 4) requiring specified methods of service where the defendant has not appeared could be a ground of non-recognition—such grounds are limited to those specified in Articles 27, 28. In any event in the case, it was held, there had been compliance.

on the defendant in the territory of the enforcement court and a Convention governs both the adjudicating and the enforcement court. In *Thierry Noirhomme* v. *David Walklate*[42] no point was taken as to the power of the English court (as the enforcement court) to enquire into service in England of Belgian proceedings in the context of the provisions of the Hague Convention on the Service of Documents Abroad 1965.[43]

SUFFICIENT TIME FOR PREPARATION OF DEFENCE

The second requirement of Article 27(2) qualifies the effect of national law rules of service. It is irrelevant for the application of the provision that the defendant resides within the territory of the adjudicating court. In so holding in *Debaecker* v. *Bouwman*[44] the European Court said that the provision takes account of the fact that certain contracting States make provision for:

" . . . the fictitious service of process where the defendant has no known place of residence. The effects that are deemed to follow from such fictitious service vary and the probability of the defendant's actually being informed of service, so as to give him sufficient time to prepare his defence, may vary considerably, depending on the type of fictitious service provided for in each legal system."

The Court concluded:

"For that reason Article 27(2) must be interpreted as being intended to protect the right of a defendant to defend himself when recognition of a judgment given in default in another Contracting State is sought, even if the rules on service laid down in that Contracting State were complied with."[45]

THE SCOPE FOR ENQUIRY BY THE ENFORCEMENT COURT

In reviewing the area open to investigation to the enforcement court in considering this question, the European Court said in *Klomps* v. *Michel*:

" . . . having regard to the exceptional nature of the grounds for refusing enforcement and to the fact that the laws of the Contracting States on the service of court documents like the international conventions on this subject have as their objective the safeguarding of interests of the defendants, the court in which enforcement is sought is ordinarily justified in considering that, following due service, the defendant is able to take steps to defend his interest as soon as the document has been served on him at his habitual residence or elsewhere. As a general rule that court in which enforcement is sought may accordingly confine its examination to ascertaining whether the period reckoned from the date on which service was duly effected allowed the defendant sufficient time to arrange for his defence. Nevertheless the court must consider whether, in a particular case, there are exceptional circumstances which warrant the conclusion that although service was duly effected it was however inadequate for the purposes of enabling the defendant to take steps to arrange for his defence and accordingly could not cause the time stipulated by Article 27(2) to begin to run."[46]

The Court continued:

---

42. [1992] 1 Lloyd's Rep. 427.
43. As to which see *supra*. See also the enquiry by German courts into service of Belgian proceedings in *Re a Belgian Default Judgment* [1992] I.L.Pr. 528.
44. 49/84 [1986] 2 CMLR 400.
45. Para. 12.
46. 166/80 [1981] ECR 1593; [1982] 2 CMLR 773. Para. 19.

"In considering whether it is confronted with such a case the court in which enforcement is sought may take account of all the circumstances of the case in point, including the means employed for effecting service, the relations between the plaintiff and the defendant or the nature of the steps which had to be taken in order to prevent judgment from being given in default. If, for example, the dispute concerns commercial relations and if the document which instituted the proceedings was served at an address at which the defendant carries on his business activities the mere fact that the defendant was absent at the time of service should not normally prevent him from arranging his defence, above all if the action necessary to avoid a judgment in default may be taken informally and even by a representative."[47]

It is open to the enforcement court to hold that there was inadequate service although at the time service was effected it appeared to be adequate. In considering whether there were exceptional circumstances showing that due service was inadequate a court is not restricted to circumstances which were apparent at the time service was effected. In *Debaecker* v. *Bouwman* the European Court said:

"If the circumstances to be taken into account were confined to those which were known at the time of service, there would be a danger of interpreting the requirement of service in sufficient time in such a restrictive and formalistic manner that it would in fact coincide with the requirement of due service, thus negating one of the safeguards laid down by the Convention for the protection of the defendant."

The Court concluded:

"Accordingly in order to ascertain whether the requirement of service in sufficient time was fulfilled—that requirement being laid down precisely in order to ensure that the defendants rights are effectively protected—regard must be had to facts which although occurring after service was effected, may nonetheless have had the effect that service did not in fact enable the defendant to arrange for his defence."[48]

THE RELEVANCE OF THE DEFENDANT'S CONDUCT OR ACTS

The defendant cannot rely on lack of adequate service if he has appeared, or at least where he was informed of the details of the proceedings and given a chance to make a defence.[49] However, in *Debaecker* the Court rejected an argument that if the reason for non-receipt of service was due to the defendant's act this removed *any* obligation on the plaintiff to do any more to ensure service, even if he subsequently discovered an address at which service could be effected. The Court held that as the purpose of Article 27(2) was to enable a defendant "to defend himself effectively":

" . . . the defendant's behaviour cannot automatically rule out the possibility of taking into account exceptional circumstances which warrant the conclusion that service was not effected in sufficient time. Instead, such behaviour may be assessed by the court in which enforcement is sought, as one

---

47. *Ibid, para.* 20.

48. It was held by the Oberlandsgericht Hamm in an order of 10 September 1979 that notice of proceedings from a source other than the document instituting the proceedings was not sufficient to satisfy Article 27(2) (ECD 1–27.2–B11). Delivery of a hearing date was held to be insufficient notice in *Trans Atlantica SpA* v. *Vertom Shipping* 1984 ELD 393 (Italy).

49. See *Volker Sonntag* v. *Hans Waidmann* C 172/91 21 April 1993 (ECJ)—there was appearance where a defendant appeared through French counsel (Cour de Cassation) to a criminal charge but did not respond to civil proceedings grafted on to the criminal charge—although they were dealt with orally in the presence of counsel.

of the matters in the light of which it determines whether service was effected in sufficient time. It will therefore be for that court to assess, in a case such as the present, to what extent the defendant's behaviour is capable of outweighing the fact that the plaintiff was apprised after service of the defendant's new address."[50]

In 1992 in *Minalmet GmbH* v. *Brandeis Ltd*[51] the European Court held unenforceable an English default judgment where proceedings were "served" on the defendant through a note in a letter box indicating that the formal documents were at the police station and the matter did not come to the notice of the defendant in time for preparation of the defence. It was no ground for enforcement that the defendant knew of the judgment in time to set it aside in England. That was not a remedy equivalent to defence before judgment.

THE DOCUMENT INSTITUTING THE PROCEEDINGS

A question may arise as to the "document which instituted the proceedings" where the recognition process does not distinguish clearly between the notice that recognition is sought and authority for such recognition.[52] In *Klomps* v. *Michel*[53] the Court had to consider the application of Article 27(2) to the German legal process. By that process the recognition (or enforcement) process consisted of two stages at each of which the defendant could lodge an objection. First an order for payment was served. If no objection was received the court issued an enforcement order to which the defendant could also object. Either objection changed the proceedings hitherto summary into adversary proceedings but the enforcement order once issued would remain provisionally in force despite any objection to it. The Court examined the purpose of the orders for payment and enforcement in the light of Article 27(2) saying:

"Article 27, point 2 is intended to ensure that a judgment is not recognised or enforced under the Convention if the defendant has not had an opportunity of defending himself before the court first seised. It follows that a measure, such as the order for payment in German law, service of which on the defendant enables the plaintiff, where no objection to the order is made, to obtain a decision which is enforceable under the Convention, must be duly served on the defendant in sufficient time to enable him to arrange for his defence and accordingly that such a measure must be understood as being covered by the words of the document which instituted the proceedings in Article 27, point 2. On the other hand a decision, such as the enforcement order in German law, which is issued following service of an order for payment and which is in itself enforceable under the Convention, is not covered by those words even although the lodging of an objection against the enforcement

---

50. Para. 32. See also *Re an English Judgment* [1993] I.L.Pr. 653 Oberlandsgericht Hamm—sending by post and not returned no evidence of receipt. In a judgment delivered before *Debaecker* the Tribunal de Grande Instance Paris held that a judgment would not be unenforceable under Article 27(2) where a defendant heard of the proceedings only after the hearing date but took no action prior to delivery of the judgment three months later (*Rosco BV* v. *Fraisgel* [1986] ECC 175). This does not seem inconsistent with the principle of *Debaecker* but the detailed facts require consideration. Also see *Re a Belgian Default Judgment* (German Federal Supreme Court) [1992] I.L.Pr. 528—deemed service on only known address when it is believed to be the address through the defendant's conduct.

51. [1993] I.L.Pr. 132.

52. It is only the document instituting the proceedings that is relevant in calculating the time available to prepare a defence. See *Société Biomécanique Integue Fabrique National de Heutal SA* [1993] I.L.Pr. 227. The document must contain particulars of the claim: *Polypetrol* v. *Société Générale Routière* [1993] I.L.Pr. 107 (French Cour de Cassation).

53. Fn 46.

order, like the objection to the order for payment, transforms the procedure into adversary proceedings."

The relevant time for ensuring that there was an opportunity for preparation of a defence within Article 27(2) was therefore that between service of the order for payment and liability to a judgment in default enforceable under the Convention.

(iii) Irreconcilability of judgments (Article 27(3), 27(5))

The central principles of the 1968 Convention are the allocation of jurisdiction and the ready enforcement of the judgment resulting from the proceedings. These principles are qualified by the option to bring proceedings in different jurisdictions. In turn the risk of concurrent actions is balanced by the rules requiring or permitting jurisdiction to be declined if an action is already in being elsewhere.[54] There remains however the possibility of two judgments in actions involving identical or similar issues either first, as between Convention states because a court acts contrary to Convention rules or the rules are construed differently by national courts, or secondly, because of a judgment in a non-contracting State.

The question of irreconcilability with the judgment of another contracting State is not addressed directly. Indeed it would be difficult to justify refusal on the basis simply that another judgment existed on the same point which itself should be recognized or enforced. However, to obtain enforcement at least, any judgment of a contracting State would need a judgment of the court in the state in the enforcement was sought. And a ground of refusal is therefore understandably irreconcilability with an earlier judgment in a dispute between the same parties in the recognition state.[55] So, much as the question of concurrent jurisdiction is resolved by "first in time", enforcement of irreconcilable judgments appears met in the same way.

"Irreconcilable"

To be irreconcilable in the context of refusal to recognize, the two judgments must have "mutually exclusive legal consequences".[56] The phrase "risk of irreconcilable judgments" in the definition of "related actions" for jurisdiction purposes does not import the same stringency. The objects of the two provisions differ, that of judgments being to derogate from the obligation to recognize judgments and that of a jurisdiction to focus on one court and thereby improve "consideration of the exercise of judicial functions in the Community"—the phrase in that context meaning simply the risk of conflicting judgments.[57]

---

54. And by the principle that a second action on a claim should not be allowed once a judgment is obtained (see *supra*).

55. It was intended also to cover judgments resulting from proceedings in other states. See Jenard, p. 45—although it is there said that irreconcilability with a judgment of another state entitled to recognition is within Article 27(3). This seems outside the scope of its wording—and the uncertainties created were the cause of adding Art. 27(5) in 1978. See Schlosser, para. 205.

56. See *Hoffman* v. *Kreig* [1987] ECR 645.

57. *The Maciej Rataj* C 406/92 [1995] 1 Lloyd's Rep. 302. As to "related actions" see Chap. 12.

(A) JUDGMENT OF A COURT OF THE ENFORCEMENT STATE (ARTICLE 27(3))

Such a ground simply recognizes a realistic ground of national public policy.[58] It is noticeable that while non-recognition requires identity of the parties it does not require identity of cause of action. Unlike the provisions relating to non-contracting States (see *infra*) there is no requirement that the judgment of the court of the enforcement State be earlier to that which it is sought to enforce.

(B) JUDGMENT OF A COURT OF A NON-CONTRACTING STATE (ARTICLE 27(5))

Article 27(5) differs from Article 27(3) referring to judgments of the enforcement state in that it requires:

    (a) identity of cause of action and parties
    (b) the irreconcilable judgment be an earlier judgment.

Subject to these requirements a judgment of a non-contracting State entitled to recognition in the enforcement state is equated with a judgment of that state as a ground of non-recognition of a judgment of a court in a contracting State. There would be little to support a structure which simply asserts a right of recognition of judgments rendered by courts within it despite earlier judgments relating to the same cause of action by courts outside it particularly when a contracting State may be faced with a clash of obligation.[59]

(iv) Preliminary status questions (Article 27(4))

This ground is of limited if any relevance to maritime claims. It is sufficient to stress that the matters listed in Article 27(4) are outside the Convention by virtue of Article 1(1)—the ground simply ensures that the obligation to recognize judgments on matters within the Convention does not mean overriding specified choice of law rules of the enforcement state which in that state's view affect the recognition of judgments in that state.

V. THE RECOGNITION AND ENFORCEMENT PROCESS

RECOGNITION AS AN INCIDENTAL ISSUE

Where recognition is the primary issue the process is as for enforcement (see *infra*). Where recognition is incidental to a dispute being adjudicated, understandably the jurisdiction to resolve the recognition issue is that of the court hearing the dispute.[60] That court may stay the proceedings if in any contracting State other than the United Kingdom or Ireland an "ordinary appeal" has been brought against the judgment. In the case of a judgment given in a court of the United Kingdom or Ireland there may be a stay of the

---

58. Although it was specifically referred to as such it was thought it would lead to too wide an application to make it part of public policy. See Jenard, p. 45.
59. See Schlosser, para. 205.
60. Article 26.

proceedings in which the recognition is sought if enforcement of the judgment is suspended in the state of origin.[61]

A judgment of a contracting State must be recognized in other contracting States without "any special procedure being required", and where recognition is the primary issue the procedure is as for enforcement.[62]

THE ENFORCEMENT PROCESS

Where enforcement is the issue the Convention is concerned with authorization rather than enforcement or execution. This is left to national law. In the words of the European Court:

"The Convention merely regulates the procedure for obtaining an order for the enforcement of foreign enforceable instruments and does not deal with execution itself, which continues to be governed by the domestic law of the court in which execution is sought, so that interested third parties may contest execution by means of the procedures available to them under the law of the State in which execution is levied."[63]

Unlike incidental recognition, enforcement of a recognition decision necessarily requires an initiating act. However, to fulfil the Convention aim of few requirements for enforcement there is a "very simple enforcement procedure whilst giving the party against whom enforcement is sought an opportunity to lodge an appeal".[64] The process consists of an *ex parte* application for a declaration of enforcement with provision for appeal against authorization or refusal of enforcement. At the appeal stage the process becomes adversarial and a further but limited right of appeal is granted from any decision at the first level appeal stage.[65]

Except in the United Kingdom enforcement will follow the issue of an order of enforcement on the application of the interested party. In the United Kingdom enforcement follows from registration for enforcement in that part of the United Kingdom (i.e. England and Wales, Scotland or Northern Ireland) in which enforcement is sought (Article 31).

Subject to specific Convention procedural requirements on matters such as notice of the decision to enforce or documentary evidence of the judgment sought to be enforced, procedural details are necessarily left to national laws.[66] Such details must be in

---

61. Article 30—an equivalent provision applies to recognition as a primary issue or enforcement (Art. 38—see *infra*).

62. Article 26.

63. *Deutsche Genossenschaftsbank* v. *Brasserie du Pecheur* 148/84 [1986] 2 CMLR 496, para. 18. The "order for enforcement" is now a declaration of enforceability. See *infra* Article 31. Article 43, providing for the enforcement of periodic payments by way of penalty, is geared to the system of enforcing orders in the legal systems of the original member States of the EEC. As Schlosser says, courts in the UK will have to use the domestic system to enforce a registered judgment (para. 212). The Convention does not refer to the date of conversion of currency of a judgment—this should therefore be regarded as a matter of execution for the enforcement court.

64. See *Brennero SAS* v. *Wendel GmbH* 258/83 [1986] 1 CMLR 59 approved by the Court again in *Capelloni* v. *Pelkmans* 119/84 [1986] 1 CMLR 388.

65. This process also applies to any proceedings in which a recognition decision is sought (see *supra*). For a review of the differing approaches in the contracting States and the steps taken to "adjust" the Convention to meet the approaches of Denmark, Ireland and the UK see Schlosser, paras 206–224.

66. Article 33.

accordance with the Convention and its principles. In England the details of national law applicable are contained in the Civil Jurisdiction and Judgments Acts 1982 and 1991 and in an amended rule of the Supreme Court concerned with recognition or enforcement of judgments generally, i.e. RSC, Order 71.

The ex parte application (Articles 31 to 33, 46, 47)

Article 31 provides:

"A judgment given in a Contracting State and enforceable in that State shall be enforced in another Contracting State when, on the application of any interested party, it has been declared enforceable there.[67]
    However, in the United Kingdom, such a judgment shall be enforced in England and Wales, or Scotland, or in Northern Ireland when, on the application of any interested party, it has been registered for enforcement in that part of the United Kingdom.

The Convention specifies the courts in each contracting State to which the application must be made (Article 32). Where local jurisdiction is relevant within a state because of the judicial structure the jurisdiction is dependent on the place of domicile of the defendant within the state or if the defendant is not domiciled in the state in which enforcement is sought, the place of enforcement (Article 32).

Article 33 provides that procedure is for the national law. However the Convention requires that the applicant give an address for service within the jurisdiction or if state law does not require such an address appoint a representative *ad litem* (Article 33). Further, although the law of the enforcing court governs the *procedure* for furnishing an address for service, if that law provides no time for service the Convention requires that "the formality must be observed no later than the date on which the decision authorising enforcement is served".[68]

Similarly although any sanction for not providing such an address is governed by the law of the state in which enforcement is sought the aims of the Convention must be respected. Therefore "the sanction provided for may neither cast doubt on the validity of the enforcement order nor in any way prejudice the rights of the party against whom enforcement is sought".[69]

Security for costs

An applicant cannot be required to lodge any "security bond or deposit solely on the ground that he is not domiciled or habitually resident in the jurisdiction of the enforcement court"[70] (Article 45). Any national law provision for security for costs must accord with the fundamental Community prohibition on discrimination because of nationality. There may be a covert discrimination on this ground if such security is made available more

---

67. Changed by the Accession Treaty on the accession of Spain and Portugal (1989) from "the order for an enforcement has been issued there".
68. *Carron* v. *Federal Republic of Germany* 198/85 [1987] 1 CMLR 838 (ECJ) para. 14.
69. *Ibid.*
70. As to security for costs on appeal against the authorization of enforcement see Art. 38 and *infra*.

easily in respect of enforcement of judgments of other Community States than the state in which enforcement is sought.[71]

Documentary support required

Subject to a dispensing power an application must be supported by four types of documents. Articles 46 and 47 provide:

"Article 46
A party seeking recognition or applying for enforcement of a judgment shall produce:
  1. a copy of the judgment which satisfies the conditions necessary to establish its authenticity;
  2. in the case of a judgment given in default, the original or a certified true copy of the document which establishes that the party in default was served with the document instituting the proceedings or with an equivalent document.

Article 47
A party applying for enforcement shall also produce:
  1. documents which establish that, according to the law of the State in which it has been given, the judgment is enforceable and has been served;
  2. where appropriate, a document showing that the applicant is in receipt of legal aid in the State in which the judgment was given."

A court may specify the time for the production of the documents or their equivalents and, if required, a certified translation. If it considers it has sufficient information before it a court may dispense with the document relating to the service of the instituting document in default proceedings and the document relating to legal aid (Article 48). No legalization or similar formality is to be required of the documents to be produced or any document appointing a representative *ad litem* (Article 49).

Stay of recognition or enforcement proceedings pending appeal in state of origin

Articles 30 and 38 provide:

"Article 30
A court of a Contracting State in which recognition is sought of a judgment given in another Contracting State may stay the proceedings if an ordinary appeal against the judgment has been lodged.
    A court of a Contracting State in which recognition is sought of a judgment given in Ireland or the United Kingdom may stay the proceedings if enforcement is suspended in the State in which the judgment was given by reason of an appeal.

Article 38
The court with which the appeal under the first paragraph of Article 37 is lodged may, on the application of the appellant, stay the proceedings if an ordinary appeal has been lodged against the judgment in the State in which that judgment was given or if the time for such an appeal has not yet expired; in the latter case, the court may specify the time within which such an appeal is to be lodged.

71. See *Firma Mund* v. *Firma Hatrex* 398/92 [1994] I.L.Pr. 264 (ECJ). As to the provisions in English law as to security for costs generally see RSC Order 23, r. 1; *Berkeley Administration* v. *McLelland* [1990] 1 All E.R. 958. In *Berkeley* it was held that *Order 23* was not overtly or covertly discriminating and there seems sufficient distinction between it and the national rule at issue in *Mund* for that view to be upheld. See Chap. 14.

Where the judgment was given in Ireland or the United Kingdom, any form of appeal available in the State in which it was given shall be treated as an ordinary appeal for the purposes of the first paragraph.

The court may also make enforcement conditional on the provision of such security as it shall determine."

Scope of the provisions

Because of the equation of any application for a recognition decision with enforcement *Article 30* applies only to proceedings in which an incidental question of recognition is raised. In terms of an application for a recognition decision or enforcement declaration the power to stay applies to the first stage appeal from an authorization for enforcement, i.e. the first adversarial stage.[72] There is no equivalent power expressed in respect of an appeal against refusal of enforcement.

Subject to provisions applicable to the United Kingdom and Ireland the power to stay is dependent on the lodging of (or in the case of Article 38 the power to lodge) an "ordinary appeal". In neither case does the power to stay necessarily preclude an examination as to whether the judgment as it stands meets Convention requirements for recognition or enforcement.[73]

Is the provision for stay "free standing"?

There remains some uncertainty as to whether the provision for stay under Article 38 is "free standing" or is linked exclusively to the grounds for refusal of recognition or enforcement under Article 27 or 28. It would seem odd if the enforcement court could only grant a stay on the basis of an appeal against the judgment at issue if the ground of the appeal was one of the grounds of non-enforcement. Surely the more sensible view is that power is conferred to suspend enforcement pending the maintaining of the judgment. Despite the focus of the Convention on simple enforcement without delay[74] the "free standing" view seems much the preferable.

The provisions for stay or security were analysed in detail in 1989 by Judge Diamond Q.C. in *Petereit* v. *Babcock International Holdings Ltd.*[75] The conclusion reached was that there is an unfettered discretion to stay, that *prima facie* a judgment is enforceable if there is no Convention ground of refusal and that the purpose of Articles 30 and 38 is to ensure that a defendant's appeal against the judgment which succeeds is not deprived of effect because of unconditional enforcement. The court should decide in any particular case if this purpose is best met by a stay (whether with or without terms), or enforcement on security, bearing in mind that the difference of ordering a stay and enforcement on security is the beneficiary of the funds until the appeal against the judgment is decided.

In substance the provision authorizes the reserving of judgment or giving of security because of a reasonable doubt that the outcome of the case resulting in the judgment—that does not conflict with the prohibition or review of substance[76] nor has any necessary link

---

72. By definition of a judgment enforceable in another state a judgment is within Art. 38 only if enforceable despite the possibility of appeal. As to the courts specified in Art. 37 see *infra*.

73. See Jenard, p. 46.

74. See *Société d' Informatique Service Realisation Organisation* v. *Ampersand Software BV* 432/93 [1995] All E.R. (E.C.) 783.

75. [1990] 2 All E.R. 135.

76. See *Medicale Equipex SA* v. *Farmitalia Erba Srl* (Cour d'Appel Versailles) [1990] I.L.Pr. 192.

with the grounds of refusal. If the free standing view be right it would seem that the power is limited only by Convention principles[77] and further that the omission of a reference to a stay in an appeal against refusal does not mean that national law could not provide one.[78] If the provision is linked to Articles 27 and 28 it is difficult to argue that there is any wider power of stay.

The "ordinary appeal"

This concept has no domestic significance in the United Kingdom or Ireland but has direct relevance when a court in either of those countries is the enforcement court. In *Industrial Diamond Supplies* v. *Riva*[79] (dealing with the power to stay) the European Court held that, particularly in the circumstances of different national law meanings, the concept had a European rather than a national meaning. An "ordinary appeal" in Convention terms is one which is part of the procedural development of a case which a party might reasonably expect. This would include an appeal available on the decision and for a limited time after the decision.[80] An appeal dependent on events unforeseeable at the date of the original judgment or upon actions taken by persons extraneous to the judgment would not be an "ordinary appeal". A review procedure which may be instituted at any time after judgment is not an ordinary appeal.[81]

Schlosser records that no satisfactory way was found to fit this concept directly to the legal systems of the United Kingdom and Ireland:

"The Working Party therefore made prolonged efforts to work out an equivalent for the United Kingdom and Ireland of the Continental distinction between ordinary and extraordinary appeals, but reached no satisfactory result. This failure was due in particular to the fact that the term 'appeal' is so many-sided and cannot be regarded, like similar terms in Continental law, as a basis for 'ordinary appeals'. The Working Party therefore noted that the legal consequences resulting from the distinction drawn in Articles 30 and 38 between ordinary and extraordinary appeals do not have to be applied rigidly, but merely confer a discretion on the court. Accordingly, in the interests of practicality and clarity, a broad definition of appeal seemed justified in connection with judgments of Irish and United Kingdom courts. Continental courts will have to use their discretion in such a way that an equal balance in the application of Articles 30 and 38 in all Contracting States will be preserved. To this effect they will have to make only cautious use of their discretionary power to stay proceedings, if the appeal is one which is available in Ireland or the United Kingdom only against special defects in a judgment or which may still be lodged after a long period. A further argument in favour of this pragmatic solution was that, in accordance with Article 38, a judgment is in any event no longer enforceable if it was subject to appeal in the State of origin and the appellate court suspended execution or granted a temporary stay of execution."

---

77. See the view taken in *Thierry Noirhomme* v. *David Walklate* [1992] 1 Lloyd's Rep. 427 relying on the 1982 Act, s.4(3), equating the jurisdiction in respect of a registered judgment with an English judgment, the jurisdiction to stay being based on RSC Order 47, r. 1(1).

78. In considering a stay under Art. 38 an enforcement court may only take into account arguments which an applicant could not have made before the adjudicating court (*Van Dalfsen* v. *Van Loon* 183/90 [1992] I.L.Pr. 5)—a limitation which would have to be adopted by national laws.

79. 43/77 [1977] ECR 2175; [1978] 1 CMLR 349. See for discussion of the ordinary appeal in detail Schlosser, para. 195.

80. See for application to an appeal in cassation *SA Continental Pharma* v. *SA Labaz* (Brussels) (1978) ECD 1–38–B3, the reasoning being that the appeal had to be lodged within a particular time and could result in variation of the decision.

81. See (considering the French "*recours en revision*") *Interdesco* v. *Nullifire Ltd.* [1992] 1 Lloyd's Rep. 180.

The decision on the application for enforcement (or in the United Kingdom, registration)

The decision must be made without delay (Article 34) and in accordance with the procedures of the state must be brought to the notice of the applicant without delay (Article 35). The party against whom enforcement is sought is not entitled at this stage to make any submission.[82]

VI. APPEALS AGAINST RECOGNITION DECISION OR ENFORCEMENT DECLARATION

1. PROTECTIVE MEASURES DURING PERIOD FOR APPEAL

Article 39 reads:

"During the time specified for an appeal pursuant to Article 36 and until any such appeal has been determined, no measures of enforcement may be taken other than protective measures taken against the property of the party against whom enforcement is sought.

The decision authorising enforcement shall carry with it the power to proceed to any such protective measures."

Article 39 is somewhat unclear as to the ability of an applicant to take advantage of protective measures without further order.[83] The procedure relating to protective measures depends on national law but only insofar as the laws are consistent with the Convention.

In 1986 in *Capelloni* v. *Pelkmans*[84] the European Court held that:

(i) Article 39 authorizes the taking of protective measures once the order for enforcement was made; there was no role for any further decision whether prior to or confirmatory of such measures.

(ii) Whether national law procedures are compatible with this principle is a matter to be decided in respect of each specific procedure at issue.

(iii) A national law procedure may not impose a time limit for the exercise of provisional measures inconsistent with the period permitted by the Convention, i.e. during the time for appealing and until any appeal made is determined.

2. APPEAL FROM AUTHORIZATION OF ENFORCEMENT (OR LEAVE TO REGISTER)

The appeal from authorization of enforcement is governed by Articles 36–39. It is only at the appellate stage that the enforcement process becomes adversarial. If enforcement is authorized an appeal against the decision may be made to a national court as specified in

---

82. It was not intended that the "debtor" should normally have notice of the application (Schlosser, para. 219).

83. The provision is apparently based on French law under which enforcement may be an administrative act over which the court has no control (Schlosser, para. 221).

84. 119/84 [1986] 1 CMLR 388.

Article 37. The appeal must be lodged "in accordance with the rules governing procedure in contentious matters" in the enforcement state. If the defendant is domiciled in the state of the court making the order the appeal must be lodged within one month of service of the order: otherwise it must be lodged within two months of service of the order on the defendant "in person or at his residence"[85] (Articles 36 and 37).

Article 36 provides for an appeal by "the party against whom enforcement is sought". In *Deutsche Genossenschaftsbank* v. *Brasserie du Pecheur*[86] the European Court held that it is not open to third parties to appeal against an enforcement order even if permitted to do so by national law. The reason given was that the Convention judgment's framework was intended to "simplify procedures in the State in which enforcement is sought". To that end, said the Court, the Convention enforcement procedure "constitutes an autonomous and complete system including the matter of appeals".

The European Court pointed out that the Convention is not concerned with execution and that a third party entitled under domestic law to intervene could protect its interest at that stage. However, it may well be by national law that challenge to execution may be made only if there has been challenge to the order—in which case the domestic provisions would be overridden. The Court's approach is logical in distinguishing between those parties bound by the order and those affected by it, but whether the distinction drawn between enforcement and execution processes is more than procedural may be doubtful. However, the more procedural it is, the easier member States can adapt their procedures to meet the Convention.

In contrast to an appeal against the refusal of an enforcement declaration (see *infra*) there is no Convention requirement that the respondent be summoned to appear. It is arguable that the Convention obligation on a court to ensure that a defendant has adequate notice so as to prepare his case is not applicable to the plaintiff when an appeal is lodged against a judgment in his favour. Yet it may be thought, as the appellate proceedings are the first stage adversarial proceedings, there should be some obligation to serve the respondent.

Enforcement made conditional on provision of security

The first stage appeal court has power to make enforcement conditional on the provision of such security as it determined[87] (Art. 38). The purpose of the provision is to protect the defendant's interest once a plaintiff is able to take enforcement measures other than protective measures. No such measures could be taken when an appeal was brought until the appeal was determined but at *that point* enforcement measures could be taken. The wording of Article 38 therefore reflects its purpose and a court may not order security until it delivers the judgment on appeal.[88] The order of security is an alternative to the stay of enforcement proceedings and whether the defendant's interest is most fairly protected by conditional enforcement or a stay must be decided in the circumstances of each case.[89]

---

85. No extension of time may be granted on account of distance (Article 36).

86. [1986] 2 CMLR 496.

87. For an example of a refusal to order security because of an undertaking that if as the result of a review procedure the judgment was amended there would be repayment see *Interdesco* v. *Nullifire Ltd*. [1992] 1 Lloyd's Rep. 180.

88. *Brennero* v. *Wendel* 258/83 [1986] 2 CMLR 59.

89. See *Petereit* v. *Babcock International Holdings Ltd*. [1990] 2 All E.R. 135 and *supra*—stay of enforcement proceedings.

3. APPEAL FROM A REFUSAL OF ENFORCEMENT

Appeals against refusal of enforcement are governed by Articles 40 and 41. If the application for enforcement is refused the applicant may appeal to a court specified in Article 40.[90] The court specified is not in all contracting States identical with that to which an appeal from an order for enforcement lies.

The defendant's opportunity to put his case

In an appeal against a refusal to authorize enforcement the person against whom enforcement is sought must be summoned to appear before the appellate court. If there is no appearance the procedural safeguards for a defendant as to jurisdiction generally apply. Proceedings must be stayed unless it is established that the defendant either had adequate notice so as to prepare a defence or that the necessary steps had been taken to provide such notice (Articles 20, 40).[91] The requirement mirrors the ground (Article 27(2)) on which recognition or enforcement of a judgment may be refused (as to which see *supra*). In enforcement and recognition proceedings the requirement applies whether or not the defendant is domiciled in a contracting State—an understandable difference from the basic jurisdictional rule as the domicile of the defendant is irrelevant to recognition and enforcement of judgments.

In *Firma P* v. *Firma K*[92] the Court stressed the distinction between the *ex parte* initial enforcement process and the adversarial appellate proceedings in the context of the need to give adequate notice to a defendant of an appeal against refusal of enforcement. In that case an application for enforcement before a German court of a judgment of a Dutch court against a Saudi defendant was dismissed for lack of the required documentary evidence. On appeal the plaintiff produced supplementary documents and the enforcement court asked of the European Court:

"Is the appellate court required to hear the party against whom enforcement is sought under the first sentence of Article 40(2) of the Convention on Jurisdiction and the Enforcement of Judgments in Civil and Commercial Matters if (a) the application for an enforcement order was dismissed simply because documents were not produced at the appropriate time and (b) the enforcement order is applied for in a State which is not the State of residence of the party against whom enforcement is sought, so that the latter person will normally be able to establish against which asset (in the present case: a claim against a bank) enforcement is to take place in that State and thus be in a position to dispose of that asset before execution is levied?"

The Court held that there was no exception to the rule that, given a defendant has no right to be heard at the initial application for enforcement, "on appeal he must be given a hearing". The reason for the dismissal of the application and the domicile of the defendant were irrelevant to this requirement.

Where the Convention is silent national law remains in control—particularly where the silence as to one topic is to be contrasted with provisions on the same topic in another context, as for example the lack of detailed provisions as to the process on further appeal (see *infra*). However, the operation of national law will be controlled by fundamental

---

90. No time limit is fixed by the Convention for appealing but national law may provide such a limit (cf. Jenard, p. 53).
91. For discussion of the obligation see *supra*.
92. 178/83 [1985] 2 CMLR 271.

Convention principles. It would seem that the adversarial nature of appellate proceedings is one such principle and national law procedures should comply with it.

4. FURTHER APPEAL

One further appeal lies from the decision on appeal from the initial order or refusal, but only in limited circumstances specified in Articles 37 and 41 respectively. It follows from the exclusion of third parties from the first stage appeal that any further appeal is similarly limited.[93] The circumstances of such an appeal vary according to the nature of the national legal system of each contracting State. In the United Kingdom the appeal must be on a point of law. In most of the original contracting States it is an appeal in cassation.[94] Such an appeal lies only in respect of the decision by the first stage appellate court in respect of enforcement of the judgment. There is no appeal from any ancillary order made by that court (such as stay or refusal of stay of proceedings or provision of security).[95] There can be no reliance on national law procedure inconsistent with the limitations of the Convention—the enforcement procedure is "an autonomous and complete system independent of the legal systems of the contracting States".[96]

There are no Convention procedural provisions applicable to the second stage appeal in particular relating to notice of the proceedings, the stay of proceedings or security for enforcement. The Convention power to stay proceedings pending an appeal from the adjudicating court is specifically confined to the first level.

Following Convention principles proceedings at the second stage, the appeal should remain adversarial, ensuring each party has the opportunity to put his case. Within such a Convention principle national laws remain free to control procedures, for the non-inclusion of specific provisions in the Convention does not mean that national laws cannot include them.

---

93. *Volker Sonntag* v. *Hans Waidmann* 172/91 21 April 1993 ECJ.
94. See generally Jenard, pp. 51–52, Schlosser, para. 217.
95. *Van Dalfsen* v. *Van Loon* 183/90 [1992] I.L.Pr. 5; the *Ampersand* case (fn. 96).
96. *Société d'Informatique Service Realisation Organisation* v. *Ampersand Software BV* 432/93 [1995] All E.R. (E.C.) 783.

APPENDIX 1

Statutes

ADMINISTRATION OF JUSTICE ACT 1956, SS. 45–50 (AS AMENDED)

(4 & 5 Eliz. 2, c. 46)

Jurisdiction in relation to collisions, etc.

45.—(1) Subject to the provisions of this Part of this Act, any court having Admiralty jurisdiction shall have jurisdiction to entertain, as against any defender, an action to which this section applies if, but only if,—

(a) the defender has his habitual residence or a place of business in the area for which the court acts, or

(b) the cause of action arose in the area for which the court acts and either within inland waters or within the limits of a port, or

(c) an action arising out of the same incident or series of incidents is proceeding in the court or has been heard and determined by the court, or

(d) the defender has prorogated the jurisdiction of the court, or

(e) a ship in which the defender owns one or more shares has been arrested (whether ad fundandam jurisdictionem or on the dependence of the action) within the area for which the court acts.

(2) Where an action to which this section applies is raised in a court having jurisdiction by virtue only of one or more of the provisions of the preceding subsection other than paragraph (d) thereof, and it appears to the court that cognate proceedings are depending in a competent court outside Scotland, the first mentioned court shall sist the action if so moved by any party thereto, and shall not recall the sist until satisfied that the cognate proceedings have been discontinued or have otherwise come to an end:

Provided that nothing in this subsection shall prevent the first mentioned court from entertaining any application as to diligence in the action.

In this subsection "cognate proceedings", in relation to any action, means proceedings instituted, before the granting of warrant for service in the action, by the pursuer in the action against any other party to the action, being proceedings in respect of the same incident or series of incidents as those with which the action is concerned.

(3) This section applies to actions for payment of reparation arising out of one or more of the following incidents, that is to say—

(a) any collision between ships, or

(b) the carrying out of, or the ommission to carry out, a manoeuvre in the case of one or more of two or more ships, or

(c) the non-compliance, on the part of one or more of two or more ships, with the collision regulations.

(4) In this section—

"inland waters" includes any part of the sea adjacent to the coast of the United Kingdom certified by the Secretary of State to be waters falling by international law to be treated as within the territorial sovereignty of Her Majesty apart from the operation of that law in relation to territorial waters;

"port" means any port, harbour, river, estuary, haven, dock, canal or other place so long as a person or body of persons is empowered by or under an Act or charter to make changes in respect of ships entering it or using the facilities therein, and "limits of a port" means the limits thereof as fixed by or under the Act in question or, as the case may be, by the relevant charter or custom;

"charges" means any charges with the exception of light dues, local light dues and any other charges in respect of lighthouses, bouys or beacons and of charges in respect of pilotage.

(5) For the avoidance of doubt it is hereby declared that any reference in this section to an action for payment of reparation does not include a reference to an action to make good a lien.

(6) Section six of the Sheriff Courts (Scotland) Act, 1907 (as amended by any subsequent enactment), shall cease to have effect in relation to actions to which this section applies.

Exclusion of jurisdiction in cases falling within Rhine Convention

46. No court shall have jurisdiction to determine any claim or question certified by the Secretary of State to be a claim or question which, under the Rhine Navigation Convention, falls to be determined in accordance with the provisions thereof.

In this section "the Rhine Navigation Convention" means the Convention of the seventh of October, eighteen hundred and sixty-eight, as revised by any subsequent Convention.

Arrest of ships on the dependence of an action or in rem*

47.—(1) Subject to the provisions of this section and section fifty of this Act, no warrant issued after the commencement of this Part of this Act for the arrest of property on the dependence of an action or in rem shall have effect as authority for the detention of a ship unless the conclusion in respect of which it is issued is appropriate for the enforcement of a claim to which this section applies, and, in the case of a warrant to arrest on the dependence of an action, unless either—

(a) the ship is the ship with which the action is concerned, or
(b) all the shares in the ship are owned by the defender against whom that conclusion is directed.

(2) This section applies to any claim arising out of one or more of the following, that is to say—

(a) damage done or received by any ship;
(b) loss of life or personal injury sustained in consequence of any defect in a ship or in her apparel or equipment, or of the wrongful act, neglect or default of the owners, charterers or persons in possession or control of a ship or of the master or crew thereof or of any other person for whose wrongful acts, neglects or defaults the owners, charterers or persons in possession or control of a ship are responsible, being an act, neglect or default in the navigation or management of the ship, in the loading, unloading or discharge of goods on, in or from the ship or in the embarkation, carriage or disembarkation of persons on, in or from the ship;
(c) the Salvage Convention 1989;
(ca) any contract for or in relation to salvage services;
(d) any agreement relating to the use or hire of any ship whether by charterparty or otherwise;
(e) any agreement relating to the carriage of goods in any ship whether by charterparty or otherwise;

* Proceedings excluded from Civil Jurisdiction and Judgments Act 1982, Part III (see Sch. 9, para. 6).

    (f) loss of, or damage to, goods carried in any ship;
    (g) general average;
    (h) any bottomry bond;
    (i) towage;
    (j) pilotage;
    (k) the supply of goods or materials to a ship for her operation or maintenance;
    (l) the construction, repair or equipment of any ship;
   (m) liability for dock charges or dues;
    (n) liability for payment of wages ... of a master or member of the crew of a ship;
    (o) master's disbursements, including disbursements made by shippers, charterers or agents on behalf of a ship or her owner;
    (p) any dispute as to the ownership or right to possession of any ship or as to the ownership of any share in the ship;
    (q) any dispute between co-owners of any ship as to the ownership, possession, employment or earnings of that ship;
    (r) the mortgage or hypothecation of any ship or any share in a ship;
    (s) any forfeiture or condemnation of any ship, or of goods which are being, or have been, carried, or have been attempted to be carried, in any ship, or for the restoration of a ship or any such goods after seizure.

  (3) In any proceedings having a conclusion appropriate for the enforcement of any claim such as is mentioned in paragraphs (q) to (s) of the last preceding subsection a warrant may be issued—

    (a) if the conclusion is a pecuniary conclusion, for the arrest of a ship on the dependence of the action; or
    (b) in any other case (whether or not the claimant is entitled to a lien over the ship), for the arrest of the ship in rem;

but there shall not be issued in respect of any such conclusion as aforesaid (whether pecuniary or otherwise) a warrant to arrest, either in rem or on the dependence of the action, any ship other than the ship to which the conclusion relates.

  (4) Subject to the preceding subsection, nothing in this section shall be taken to authorise—

    (a) the use of an arrestment on the dependence of an action otherwise than in respect of a pecuniary conclusion, or
    (b) the use of an arrestment in rem otherwise than in respect of a conclusion appropriate for the making good of a lien.

  (5) A warrant for the arrest of a ship in rem issued by virtue of paragraph (b) of subsection (3) of this section in a case where the person in whose favour it is issued is not entitled to a lien over the ship shall have effect as authority for the detention of the ship as security for the implementation of the decree of the court so far as it affects that ship;

Provided that the court may, on the application of any person having an interest, recall the arrestment if satisfied that sufficient bail or other security for such implementation has been found.

  (6) Nothing in this section shall authorise the arrest, whether on the dependence of an action or in rem, of a ship while it is on passage.

  (7) Nothing in this section shall authorise the arrest, whether on the dependence of an action or in rem, of a ship in respect of any claim against the Crown, or the arrest, detention or sale of any of Her Majesty's ships or Her Majesty's aircraft.

In this subsection "Her Majesty's ships" and "Her Majesty's aircraft" have the meanings assigned to them by subsection (2) of section thirty-eight of the Crown Proceedings Act, 1947.

  (8) In—

    (a) paragraph (c) of subsection (2) above, the "Salvage Convention, 1989" means the International Convention on Salvage 1989 as it has effect under section 224 of the Merchant Shipping Act 1995;
    (b) paragraph (ca) of that subsection, the reference to salvage services includes services rendered in saving life from a ship and the reference to any claim arising out of any

contract for or in relation to salvage services includes any claim arising out of such a contract whether or not arising during the provision of such services,

and the claims mentioned in subsections (2)(c) and (ca) shall be construed as including claims available by virtue of section 87 of the Civil Aviation Act 1982."

Interpretation of Part V

48. In this Part of this Act, unless the context otherwise requires,—

(a) references to an action, a pursuer and a defender include respectively references to a counter-claim, the person making a counter-claim and the person against whom a counter-claim is made;

(b) any reference to a conclusion includes a reference to a crave, and "pecuniary conclusion" does not include a conclusion for expenses;

(c) any reference to a warrant to arrest property includes a reference to letters of arrestment and to a precept of arrestment;

(d) any reference to a lien includes a reference to any hypothec or charge;

(e) ...

(f) the following expressions have the meanings hereby assigned to them respectively, that is to say—

"collision regulations" means safety regulations under section 85 of the Merchant Shipping Act 1995;

"goods" includes baggage;

"master" has the same meaning as in the Merchant Shipping Act, 1995, and accordingly includes every person (except a pilot) having command or charge of a ship;

"ship" includes any description of vessel used in navigation not propelled by oars;

"towage" and "pilotage" in relation to an aircraft, mean towage and pilotage while the aircraft is waterborne.

Repeals

49.—(1) Section one hundred and sixty-five of the Merchant Shipping Act, 1894 (which imposes restrictions on proceedings for the recovery of wages or seamen and apprentices) shall cease to have effect and is hereby repealed.

(2) So much of subsection (2) of section seventy-five of the Disease of Animals Act, 1950, as enables a local authority to recover expenses incurred in burying or destroying carcases in the same manner as salvage is recoverable, shall cease to have affect; and accordingly the words in the said subsection (2) from "and the local authority" to the end of the subsection are hereby repealed. (Repealed c. 22 1981 Sch. 6.)

Application and commencement of Part V

50.—(1) This Part of this Act shall apply to Scotland only.

(2) This Part of this Act shall come into operation on such day as the Secretary of State may appoint by order made by statutory instrument.

(3 Nothing in this Part of this Act shall affect any action in respect of which warrant for service has been granted before the commencement of this Part of this Act.

ARBITRATION ACT 1975

(1975 c. 3)

An Act to give effect to the New York Convention on the Recognition and Enforcement of Foreign Arbitral Awards.

Effect of arbitration agreement on court proceedings

Staying court proceedings where party proves arbitration agreement

1.—(1) If any party to an arbitration agreement to which this section applies, or any person claiming through or under him, commences any legal proceedings in any court against any other party to the agreement, or any person claiming through or under him, in respect of any matter agreed to be referred, any party to the proceedings may at any time after appearance, and before delivering any pleadings, or taking any other steps in the proceedings, apply to the court to stay the proceedings; and the court, unless satisfied that the arbitration agreement is null and void, inoperative or incapable of being performed or that there is not in fact any dispute between the parties with regard to the matter agreed to be referred, shall make an order staying the proceedings.

(2) This section applies to any arbitration agreement which is not a domestic arbitration agreement; and neither section 4(1) of the Arbitration Act 1950 nor section 4 of the Arbitration Act (Northern Ireland) 1937 shall apply to an arbitration agreement to which this section applies.

(3) In the application of this section to Scotland, for the references to staying proceedings there shall be substituted references to sisting proceedings.

(4) In this section "domestic arbitration agreement" means an arbitration agreement which does not provide, expressly or by implication, for arbitration in a State other than the United Kingdom and to which neither—

(a) an individual who is a national of, or habitually resident in, any State other than the United Kingdom; nor
(b) a body corporate which is incorporated in, or whose central management and control is exercised in, any State other than the United Kingdom;

is a party at the time the proceedings are commenced.

Enforcement of Convention awards

Replacement of former provisions

2. Sections 3 to 6 of this Act shall have effect with respect to the enforcement of Convention awards; and where a Convention award would, but for this section, be also a foreign award within the meaning of Part II of the Arbitration Act 1950, that Part shall not apply to it.

Effect of Convention awards

3.—(1) A Convention award shall, subject to the following provisions of this Act, be enforceable—

(a) in England and Wales, either by action or in the same manner as the award of an arbitrator is enforceable by virtue of section 26 of the Arbitration Act 1950;
(b) in Scotland, either by action or, in a case where the arbitration agreement contains consent to the registration of the award in the Books of Council and Session for execution and the award is so registered, by summary diligence;
(c) in Northern Ireland, either by action or in the same manner as the award of an arbitrator is enforceable by virtue of section 16 of the Arbitration Act (Northern Ireland) 1937.

(2) Any Convention award which would be enforceable under this Act shall be treated as binding for all purposes on the persons as between whom it was made, and may accordingly be relied on by any of those persons by way of defence, set off or otherwise in any legal proceedings in the United Kingdom; and any reference in this Act to enforcing a Convention award shall be construed as including references to relying on such an award.

Evidence

4. The party seeking to enforce a Convention award must produce—

(a) the duly authenticated original award or a duly certified copy of it; and
(b) the original arbitration agreement or a duly certified copy of it; and
(c) where the award or agreement is in a foreign language, a translation of it certified by an official or sworn translator or by a diplomatic or consular agent.

Refusal of enforcement

5.—(1) Enforcement of a Convention award shall not be refused except in the cases mentioned in this section.

(2) Enforcement of a Convention award may be refused if the person against whom it is invoked proves—

(a) that a party to the arbitration agreement was (under the law applicable to him) under some incapacity; or
(b) that the arbitration agreement was not valid under the law to which the parties subjected it or, failing any indication thereon, under the law of the country where the award was made; or
(c) that he was not given proper notice of the appointment of the arbitrator or of the arbitration proceedings or was otherwise unable to present his case; or
(d) (subject to subsection (4) of this section) that the award deals with a difference not contemplated by or not falling within the terms of the submission to arbitration or contains decisions on matters beyond the scope of the submission to arbitration; or
(e) that the composition of the arbitral authority or the arbitral procedure was not in accordance with the agreement of the parties or, failing such agreement, with the law of the country where the arbitration took place; or
(f) that the award has not yet become binding on the parties, or has been set aside or suspended by a competent authority of the country in which, or under the law of which, it was made.

(3) Enforcement of a Convention award may also be refused if the award is in respect of a matter which is not capable of settlement by arbitration, or if it would be contrary to public policy to enforce the award.

(4) A Convention award which contains decisions on matters not submitted to arbitration may be enforced to the extent that it contains decisions on matters submitted to arbitration which can be separated from those on matters not so submitted.

(5) Where an application for the setting aside or suspension of a Convention award has been made to such a competent authority as is mentioned in subsection (2)(f) of this section, the court before which enforcement of the award is sought may, if it thinks fit, adjourn the proceedings and may, on the application of the party seeking to enforce the award, order the other party to give security.

Saving

6. Nothing in this Act shall prejudice any right to enforce or rely on an award otherwise than under this Act or Part II of the Arbitration Act 1950.

General

Interpretation

7.—(1) In this Act—

"arbitration agreement" means an agreement in writing (including an agreement contained in an exchange of letters or telegrams) to submit to arbitration present or future differences capable of settlement by arbitration;

"Convention award" means an award made in pursuance of an arbitration agreement in the territory of a State, other than the United Kingdom, which is a party to the New York Convention; and

"the New York Convention" means the Convention on the Recognition and Enforcement of Foreign Arbitral Awards adopted by the United Nations Conference on International Commercial Arbitration on 10th June 1958.

(2) If Her Majesty by Order in Council declares that any State specified in the Order is a party to the New York Convention the Order shall, while in force, be conclusive evidence that that State is a party to that Convention.

(3) An Order in Council under this section may be varied or revoked by a subsequent Order in Council.

SUPREME COURT ACT 1981, SS. 20–24 (AS AMENDED)

(1981 c. 54)

Admiralty jurisdiction

Admiralty jurisdiction of High Court

20.—(1) The Admiralty jurisdiction of the High Court shall be as follows, that is to say—

  (a) jurisdiction to hear and determine any of the questions and claims mentioned in subsection (2);

  (b) jurisdiction in relation to any of the proceedings mentioned in subsection (3);

  (c) any other Admiralty jurisdiction which it had immediately before the commencement of this Act; and

  (d) any jurisdiction connected with ships or aircraft which is vested in the High Court apart from this section and is for the time being by rules of court made or coming into force after the commencement of this Act assigned to the Queen's Bench Division and directed by the rules to be exercised by the Admiralty Court.

(2) The questions and claims referred to in subsection (1)(a) are—

  (a) any claim to the possession or ownership of a ship or to the ownership of any share therein;

  (b) any question arising between the co-owners of a ship as to possession, employment or earnings of that ship;

  (c) any claim in respect of a mortgage of or charge on a ship or any share therein;

  (d) any claim for damage received by a ship;

  (e) any claim for damage done by a ship;

  (f) any claim for loss of life or personal injury sustained in consequence of any defect in a ship or in her apparel or equipment, or in consequence of the wrongful act, neglect or default of—

      (i) the owners, charterers or persons in possession or control of a ship; or

      (ii) the master or crew of a ship, or any other person for whose wrongful acts, neglects or defaults the owners, charterers or persons in possession or control of a ship are responsible,

      being an act, neglect or default in the navigation or management of the ship, in the loading, carriage or discharge of goods on, in or from the ship, or in the embarkation, carriage or disembarkation of persons on, in or from the ship;

  (g) any claim for loss of or damage to goods carried in a ship;

  (h) any claim arising out of any agreement relating to the carriage of goods in a ship or to the use or hire of a ship;

    (j) any claim—

          (i) under the Salvage Convention 1989;
          (ii) under any contract for or in relation to salvage services; or
          (iii) in the nature of salvage not falling within (i) or (ii) above;

    or any corresponding claim in connection with an aircraft;

    (k) any claim in the nature of towage in respect of a ship or an aircraft;
    (l) any claim in the nature of pilotage in respect of a ship or an aircraft;
    (m) any claim in respect of goods or materials supplied to a ship for her operation or maintenance;
    (n) any claim in respect of the construction, repair or equipment of a ship or in respect of dock charges or dues;
    (o) any claim by a master or member of the crew of a ship for wages (including any sum allotted out of wages or adjudged by a superintendent to be due by way of wages),
    (p) any claim by a master, shipper, charterer or agent in respect of disbursements made on account of a ship;
    (q) any claim arising out of an act which is or is claimed to be a general average act;
    (r) any claim arising out of bottomry;
    (s) any claim for the forfeiture or condemnation of a ship or of goods which are being or have been carried, or have been attempted to be carried, in a ship, or for the restoration of a ship or any such goods after seizure, or for droits of Admiralty.

(3) The proceedings referred to in subsection (1)(b) are—

    (a) any application to the High Court under the Merchant Shipping Act 1995;
    (b) any action to enforce a claim for damage, loss of life or personal injury arising out of—

          (i) a collision between ships; or
          (ii) the carrying out of or omission to carry out a manoeuvre in the case of one or more of two or more ships; or
          (iii) non-compliance, on the part of one or more of two or more ships, with the collision regulations;

    (c) any action by shipowners or other persons under the Merchant Shipping Act 1995 for the limitation of the amount of their liability in connection with a ship or other property.

(4) The jurisdiction of the High Court under subsection (2)(b) includes power to settle any account outstanding and unsettled between the parties in relation to the ship, and to direct that the ship, or any share thereof, shall be sold, and to make such other order as the court thinks fit.

(5) Subsection (2)(e) extends to—

    (a) any claim in respect of a liability incurred under Chapter III of Part VI of the Merchant Shipping Act 1995;
    (b) any claim in respect of a liability falling on the International Oil Pollution Compensation Fund or on the International Oil Pollution Compensation Fund 1984 under Chapter VI of Part VI of the Merchant Shipping Act 1995.

(6) In subsection (2)(j)—

    (a) the "Salvage Convention 1989" means the International Convention on Salvage, 1989 as it has effect under section 224 of the Merchant Shipping Act 1995;
    (b) the reference to salvage services includes services rendered in saving life from a ship and the reference to any claim under any contract for or in relation to salvage services includes any claim arising out of such a contract whether or not arising during the provision of the services;
    (c) the reference to a corresponding claim in connection with an aircraft is a reference to any claim corresponding to any claim mentioned in sub-paragraph (i) or (ii) of paragraph (j) which is available under section 87 of the Civil Aviation Act 1982.

(7) The preceding provisions of this section apply—

(a) in relation to all ships or aircraft, whether British or not and whether registered or not and wherever the residence or domicile of their owners may be;

(b) in relation to all claims, wherever arising (including, in the case of cargo or wreck salvage, claims in respect of cargo or wreck found on land); and

(c) so far as they relate to mortgages and charges, to all mortgages or charges, whether registered or not and whether legal or equitable, including mortgages and charges created under foreign law:

Provided that nothing in this subsection shall be construed as extending the cases in which money or property is recoverable under any of the provisions of the Merchant Shipping Act 1995.

Mode of exercise of Admiralty jurisdiction

21.—(1) Subject to section 22, an action in personam may be brought in the High Court in all cases within the Admiralty jurisdiction of that court.

(2) In the case of any such claim as is mentioned in section 20(2)(a)(c) or (s) or any such question as is mentioned in section 20(2)(b), an action in rem may be brought in the High Court against the ship or property in connection with which the claim or question arises.

(3) In any case in which there is maritime lien or other charge on any ship, aircraft or other property for the amount claimed, an action in rem may be brought in the High Court against that ship, aircraft or property.

(4) In the case of any such claim as is mentioned in section 20(2)(e) to (r), where—

(a) the claim arises in connection with a ship; and

(b) the person who would be liable on the claim in an action in personam ("the relevant person") was, when the cause of action arose, the owner or charterer of, or in possession or in control of, the ship,

an action in rem may (whether or not the claim gives rise to a maritime lien on that ship) be brought in the High Court against—

(i) that ship, if at the time when the action is brought the relevant person is either the beneficial owner of that ship as respects all the shares in it or the charterer of it under a charter by demise; or

(ii) any other ship of which, at the time when the action is brought, the relevant person is the beneficial owner as respects all the shares in it.

(5) In the case of a claim in the nature of towage or pilotage in respect of an aircraft, an action in rem may be brought in the High Court against that aircraft if, at the time when the action is brought, it is beneficially owned by the person who would be liable on the claim in an action in personam.

(6) Where, in the exercise of its Admiralty jurisdiction, the High Court orders any ship, aircraft or other property to be sold, the court shall have jurisdiction to hear and determine any question arising as to the title to the proceeds of sale.

(7) In determining for the purposes of subsections (4) and (5) whether a person would be liable on a claim in an action in personam it shall be assumed that he has his habitual residence or a place of business within England or Wales.

(8) Where, as regards any such claim as is mentioned in section 20(2)(e) to (r), a ship has been served with a writ or arrested in an action in rem brought to enforce that claim, no other ship may be served with a writ or arrested in that or any other action in rem brought to enforce that claim; but this subsection does not prevent the issue, in respect of any one such claim, of a writ naming more than one ship or of two or more writs each naming a different ship.

Restrictions on entertainment of actions in personam in collision and other similar cases

22.—(1) This section applies to any claim for damage, loss of life or personal injury arising out of—

(a) a collision between ships; or

(b) the carrying out of, or omission to carry out, a manoeuvre in the case of one or more of two or more ships; or

(c) non-compliance, on the part of one or more of two or more ships, with the collision regulations.

(2) The High Court shall not entertain any action in personam to enforce a claim to which this section applies unless—

(a) the defendant has his habitual residence or a place of business within England or Wales; or

(b) the cause of action arose within inland waters of England or Wales or within the limits of a port of England or Wales; or

(c) an action arising out of the same incident or series of incidents is proceeding in the court or has been heard and determined in the court.

In this subsection—

"inland waters" includes any part of the sea adjacent to the coast of the United Kingdom certified by the Secretary of State to be waters falling by international law to be treated as within the territorial sovereignty of Her Majesty apart from the operation of that law in relation to territorial waters;

"port" means any port, harbour, river, estuary, haven, dock, canal or other place so long as a person or body of persons is empowered by or under an Act to make charges in respect of ships entering it or using the facilities therein, and "limits of a port" means the limits thereof as fixed by or under the Act in question or, as the case may be, by the relevant charter or custom;

"charges" means any charges with the exception of light dues, local light dues and any other charges in respect of lighthouses, bouys or beacons and of charges in respect of pilotage.

(3) The High Court shall not entertain any action in personam to enforce a claim to which this section applies until any proceedings previously brought by the plaintiff in any court outside England and Wales against the same defendant in respect of the same incident or series of incidents have been discontinued or otherwise come to an end.

(4) Subsections (2) and (3) shall apply to counterclaims (except counterclaims in proceedings arising out of the same incident or series of incidents) as they apply to actions, the references to the plaintiff and the defendant being for this purpose read as references to the plaintiff on the counterclaim and the defendant to the counterclaim respectively.

(5) Subsections (2) and (3) shall not apply to any action or counterclaim if the defendant thereto submits or has agreed to submit to the jurisdiction of the court.

(6) Subject to the provisions of subsection (3), the High Court shall have jurisdiction to entertain an action in personam to enforce a claim to which this section applies whenever any of the conditions specified in subsection (2)(a) to (c) is satisfied, and the rules of court relating to the service of process outside the jurisdiction shall make such provision as may appear to the rule-making authority to be appropriate having regard to the provisions of this subsection.

(7) Nothing in this section shall prevent an action which is brought in accordance with the provisions of this section in the High Court being transferred, in accordance with the enactments in that behalf, to some other court.

(8) For the avoidance of doubt it is hereby declared that this section applies in relation to the jurisdiction of the High Court not being Admiralty jurisdiction, as well as in relation to its Admiralty jurisdiction.

High Court not to have jurisdiction in cases within Rhine Convention

23. The High Court shall not have jurisdiction to determine any claim or question certified by the Secretary of State to be a claim or question which, under the Rhine Navigation Convention, falls to be determined in accordance with the provisions of that Convention; and any proceedings to enforce such a claim which are commenced in the High Court shall be set aside.

Supplementary provisions as to Admiralty jurisdiction

24.—(1) In sections 20 to 23 and this section, unless the context otherwise requires—

"collision regulations" means safety regulations under section 85 of the Merchant Shipping Act 1995.

"goods" includes baggage;

"master" has the same meaning as in the Merchant Shipping Act 1995, and accordingly includes every person (except a pilot) having command or charge of a ship;

"the Rhine Navigation Convention" means the Convention of the 7th October 1868 as revised by any subsequent Convention;

"ship" includes any description of vessel used in navigation and (except in the definition of "port" in section 22(2) and in subsection (2)(c) of this section) includes, subject to section 2(3) of the Hovercraft Act 1968, a hovercraft;

"towage" and "pilotage", in relation to an aircraft, mean towage and pilotage while the aircraft is water-borne.

(2) Nothing in sections 20 to 23 shall—

(a) be construed as limiting the jurisdiction of the High Court to refuse to entertain an action for wages by the master or a member of the crew of a ship, not being a British ship;

(b) affect the provisions of section 226 of the Merchant Shipping Act 1995 (power of a receiver of wreck to detain a ship in respect of a salvage claim); or

(c) authorise proceedings in rem in respect of any claim against the Crown, or the arrest, detention or sale of any of Her Majesty's ships or Her Majesty's aircraft, or, subject to section 2(3) of the Hovercraft Act 1968, Her Majesty's hovercraft, or of any cargo or other property belonging to the Crown.

(3) In this section—

"Her Majesty's ships" and "Her Majesty's aircraft" have the meanings given by section 38(2) of the Crown Proceedings Act 1947;

"Her Majesty's hovercraft" means hovercraft belonging to the Crown in right of Her Majesty's Government in the United Kingdom or Her Majesty's Government in Northern Ireland.

CIVIL JURISDICTION AND JUDGMENTS ACT 1982

(1982 c. 27)

PART I. IMPLEMENTATION OF THE CONVENTIONS

Main implementing provisions

Interpretation of references to the Conventions and Contracting States

1.—(1) In this Act—

"the 1968 Convention" means the Convention on jurisdiction and the enforcement of judgments in civil and commercial matters (including the Protocol annexed to that Convention), signed at Brussels on 27th September 1968;

"the 1971 Protocol" means the Protocol on the interpretation of the 1968 Convention by the European Court, signed at Luxembourg on 3rd June 1971;

"the Accession Convention" means the Convention on the accession to the 1968 Convention and the 1971 Protocol of Denmark, the Republic of Ireland and the United Kingdom, signed at Luxembourg on 9th October 1978;

"the 1982 Accession Convention" means the Convention on the accession of the Hellenic Republic to the 1968 Convention and the 1971 Protocol, with the adjustments made to them by the Accession Convention, signed at Luxembourg on 25th October 1982;

"the 1989 Accession Convention" means the Convention on the accession of the Kingdom of Spain and the Portuguese Republic to the 1968 Convention and the 1971 Protocol, with the adjustments made to them by the Accession Convention and the 1982 Accession Convention, signed at Donostia—San Sebastián on 26th May 1989;

"the Brussels Conventions" means the 1968 Convention, the 1971 Protocol, the Accession Convention, the 1982 Accession Convention and the 1989 Accession Convention;

"the Lugano Convention" means the Convention on jurisdiction and the enforcement of judgments in civil and commercial matters (including the Protocols annexed to that Convention) opened for signature at Lugano on 16th September 1988 and signed by the United Kingdom on 18th September 1989.

(2) In this Act, unless the context otherwise requires—

(a) references to, or to any provision of, the 1968 Convention or the 1971 Protocol are references to that Convention, Protocol or provision as amended by the Accession Convention, the 1982 Accession Convention and the 1989 Accession Convention; and;

(b) any reference in any provision to a numbered Article without more is a reference—

(i) to the Article so numbered of the 1968 Convention, in so far as the provision applies in relation to that Convention, and

(ii) to the Article so numbered of the Lugano Convention, in so far as the provision applies in relation to that Convention,

and any reference to a sub-division of a numbered Article shall be construed accordingly.

(3) In this Act—

"Contracting State" without more, in any provision means—

(a) in the application of the provision in relation to Brussels Conventions, a Brussels Contracting State; and

(b) in the application of the provision in relation to the Lugano Convention, a Lugano Contracting State;

"Brussels Contracting State" means—

(a) one of the original parties to the 1968 Convention (Belgium, the Federal Republic of Germany, France, Italy, Luxembourg and The Netherlands); or

(b) one of the parties acceding to that Convention under the Accession Convention (Denmark, the Republic of Ireland and the United Kingdom), or under the 1982 Accession Convention (the Hellenic Republic), or under the 1989 Accession Convention (Spain and Portugal),

being a State in respect of which the Accession Convention has entered into force in accordance with Article 39 of that Convention, or being a State in respect of which the 1982 Accession Convention has entered into force in accordance with Article 15 of that Convention, or being a State in respect of which the 1989 Accession Convention has entered into force in accordance with Article 32 of that Convention, as the case might be.

"Lugano Contracting State" means one of the original parties to the Lugano Convention, that is to say—

Austria, Belgium, Denmark, Finland, France, the Federal Republic of Germany, the Hellenic Republic, Iceland, the Republic of Ireland, Italy, Luxembourg, the Netherlands, Norway, Portugal, Spain, Sweden, Switzerland and the United Kingdom.

being a State in relation to which that Convention has taken effect in accordance with paragraph 3 or 4 of Article 61.

The Brussels Conventions to have the force of law

2.—(1) The Brussels Conventions shall have the force of law in the United Kingdom and judicial notice shall be taken of them.

(2) For convenience of reference there are set out in Schedules 1, 2, 3, 3A and 3B respectively the English texts of—

(a) the 1968 Convention as amended by Titles II and III of the Accession Convention, by Titles II and III of the 1982 Accession Convention and by Titles II and III of, and Annex I(d) to, the 1989 Accession Convention;

(b) the 1971 Protocol as amended by Title IV of the Accession Convention, by Title IV of the 1982 Accession Convention and by Title IV of the 1989 Accession Convention;

(c) Titles V and VI of the Accession Convention (transitional and final provisions) as amended by Title V of the 1989 Accession Convention;

(d) Titles V and VI of the 1982 Accession Convention (transitional and final provisions); and

(e) Titles VI and VII of the 1989 Accession Convention (transitional and final provisions),

being texts prepared from the authentic English texts referred to in Articles 37 and 41 of the Accession Convention, in Article 17 of the 1982 Accession Convention and in Article 34 of the 1989 Accession Convention.

Interpretation of the Brussels Conventions

3.—(1) Any questions as to the meaning or effect of any provision of the [Brussels Conventions] shall, if not referred to the European Court in accordance with the 1971 Protocol, be determined in accordance with the principles laid down by and any relevant decision of the European Court.

(2) Judicial notice shall be taken of any decision of, or expression or opinion by, the European Court on any such question.

(3) Without prejudice to the generality of subsection (1), the following reports (which are reproduced in the Official Journal of the Communities), namely—

(a) the reports by Mr P. Jenard on the 1968 Convention and the 1971 Protocol; and

(b) the report by Professor Peter Schlosser on the Accession Convention; and

(c) the report by Professor Demetrios I. Evrigenis and Professor K. D. Kerameus on the 1982 Accession Convention; and

(d) the report by Mr Martinho de Almeida Cruz, Mr Manuel Desantes Real and Mr P. Jenard on the 1989 Accession Convention,

may be considered in ascertaining the meaning or effect of any provision of the [Brussels Conventions] and shall be given such weight as is appropriate in the circumstances.

The Lugano Convention to have the force of law

3A.—(1) The Lugano Convention shall have the force of law in the United Kingdom, and judicial notice shall be taken of it.

(2) For convenience of reference there is set out in Schedule 3C the English text of the Lugano Convention.

Interpretation of the Lugano Convention

3B.—(1) In determining any question as to the meaning or effect of a provision of the Lugano Convention, a court in the United Kingdom shall, in accordance with Protocol No. 2 to that Convention, take account of any principles laid down in any relevant decision delivered by a court of any other Lugano Contracting State concerning provisions of the Convention.

(2) Without prejudice to any practice of the courts as to the matters which may be considered apart from this section, the report on the Lugano Convention by Mr P. Jenard and Mr G. Möller (which is reproduced in the Official Journal of the Communities of 28th July 1990) may be

considered in ascertaining the meaning or effect of any provision of the Convention and shall be given such weight as is appropriate in the circumstances.

Supplementary provisions as to recognition and enforcement of judgments

Enforcement of judgments other than maintenance orders

4.—(1) A judgment, other than a maintenance order, which is the subject of an application under Article 31 of the 1968 Convention or of the Lugano Convention for its enforcement in any part of the United Kingdom shall, to the extent that its enforcement is authorised by the appropriate court, be registered in the prescribed manner in that court.

In this subsection "the appropriate court" means the court to which the application is made in pursuance of Article 32 (that is to say, the High Court or the Court of Session).

(2) Where a judgment is registered under this section, the reasonable costs or expenses of and incidental to its registration shall be recoverable as if they were sums recoverable under the judgment.

(3) A judgment registered under this section shall, for the purposes of its enforcement, be of the same force and effect, the registering court shall have in relation to its enforcement the same powers, and proceedings for or with respect to its enforcement may be taken, as if the judgment had been originally given by the registering court and had (where relevant) been entered.

(4) Subsection (3) is subject to Article 39 (restriction on enforcement where appeal pending or time for appeal unexpired), to section 7 and to any provision made by rules of court as to the manner in which and conditions subject to which a judgment registered under this section may be enforced.

5. . . .

Appeals under Article 37, second paragraph and Article 41

6.—(1) The single further appeal on a point of law referred to in Article 37, in the 1968 Convention and in the Lugano Convention, second paragraph and Article 41 in relation to the recognition or enforcement of a judgment other than a maintenance order lies—

    (a) in England and Wales or Northern Ireland, to the Court of Appeal or to the House of Lords in accordance with Part II of the Administration of Justice Act 1969 (appeals direct from the High Court to the House of Lords);

    (b) In Scotland, to the Inner House of the Court of Session.

(2) Paragraph (a) of subsection (1) has effect notwithstanding section 15(2) of the Administration of Justice Act 1969 (exclusion of direct appeal to the House of Lords in cases where no appeal to that House lies from a decision of the Court of Appeal).

(3) The single further appeal on a point of law referred to in each of those Conventions in Article 37, second paragraph and Article 41 in relation to the recognition or enforcement of a maintenance order lies—

    (a) in England and Wales, to the High Court by way of case stated in accordance with section 11 of the Magistrates' Court Act 1980;

    (b) In Scotland, to the Inner House of the Court of Session;

    (c) in Northern Ireland, to the Court of Appeal.

Interest on registered judgments

7.—(1) Subject to subsection (4), where in connection with an application for registration of a judgment under section 4 or 5 the applicant shows—

    (a) that the judgment provides for the payment of a sum of money; and

    (b) that in accordance with the law of the Contracting State in which the judgment was given interest on that sum is recoverable under the judgment from a particular date or time, the rate of interest and the date or time from which it is so recoverable shall be registered with the judgment and, subject to any provision made under subsection (2), the debt resulting, apart from section 4(2), from the registration of the judgment shall carry interest in accordance with the registered particulars.

(2) Provision may be made by rules of court as to the manner in which and the periods by reference to which any interest payable by virtue of subsection (1) is to be calculated and paid, including provision for such interest to cease to accrue as from a prescribed date.

(3) Costs or expenses recoverable by virtue of section 4(2) shall carry interest as if they were the subject of an order for the payment of costs or expenses made by the registering court on the date of registration.

(4) Interest on arrears of sums payable under a maintenance order registered under section 5 in a magistrates' court in England and Wales or Northern Ireland shall not be recoverable in that court, but without prejudice to the operation in relation to any such order or section 2A of the Maintenance Orders Acts 1958 or section 11A of the Maintenance and Affiliation Orders Act (Northern Ireland) 1966 (which enable interest to be recovered if the order is re-registered for enforcement in the High Court).

(5) Except as mentioned in subsection (4), debts under judgments registered under section 4 or 5 shall carry interest only as provided by this section.

8. ...

Other supplementary provisions

Provisions supplementary to Title VII of 1968 Convention

9.—(1) The provisions of Title VII of the 1968 Convention and, apart from Article 54B, of Title VII of the Lugano Convention (relationship between the Convention in question and other conventions to which Contracting States are or may become parties) shall have effect in relation to—

    (a) any statutory provision, whenever passed or made, implementing any such other convention in the United Kingdom; and

    (b) any rule so far as it has the effect of so implementing any such other convention,

as they have effect in relation to that other convention itself.

(1A) Any question arising as to whether it is the Lugano Convention or any of the Brussels Conventions which applies in the circumstances of a particular case falls to be determined in accordance with the provisions of Article 54B of the Lugano Convention.

(2) Her Majesty may by Order in Council declare a provision of a convention entered into by the United Kingdom to be a provision whereby the United Kingdom assumed an obligation of a kind provided for in Article 59 (which allows a Contracting State to agree with a third State to withhold recognition in certain cases from a judgment given by a court in another Contracting State which took jurisdiction on one of the grounds mentioned in the second paragraph of Article 3).

Allocation within UK of jurisdiction with respect to trusts and consumer contracts

10.—(1) The provisions of this section have effect for the purpose of allocating within the United Kingdom jurisdiction in certain proceedings in respect of which the 1968 Convention or the Lugano Convention confers jurisdiction on the courts of the United Kingdom generally and to which section 16 does not apply.

(2) Any proceedings which by virtue of Article 5(6) (trusts) are brought in the United Kingdom shall be brought in the courts of the part of the United Kingdom in which the trust is domiciled.

(3) Any proceedings which by virtue of the first paragraph of Article 14 (consumer contracts) are brought in the United Kingdom by a consumer on the ground that he is himself domiciled there shall be brought in the courts of the part of the United Kingdom in which he is domiciled.

Proof and admissibility of certain judgments and related documents

   11.—(1) For the purposes of the 1968 Convention and the Lugano Convention—

   (a) a document, duly authenticated, which purports to be a copy of a judgment given by a court of a Contracting State other than the United Kingdom shall without further proof be deemed to be a true copy, unless the contrary is shown; and

   (b) the original or a copy of any such document as is mentioned in Article 46(2) or 47 (supporting documents to be produced by a party seeking recognition or enforcement of a judgment) shall be evidence, and in Scotland sufficient evidence, of any matter to which it relates.

   (2) A document purporting to be a copy of a judgment given by any such court as is mentioned in subsection (1)(a) is duly authenticated for the purposes of this section if it purports—

   (a) to bear the seal of that court; or

   (b) to be certified by any person in his capacity as a judge or officer of that court to be a true copy of a judgment given by that court.

   (3) Nothing in this section shall prejudice the admission in evidence of any document which is admissible apart from this section.

Provision for issue of copies of, and certificates in connection with, UK judgments

   12. Rules of court may make provision for enabling any interested party wishing to secure under the 1968 Convention or the Lugano Convention the recognition or enforcement in another Contracting State of a judgment given by a court in the United Kingdom to obtain, subject to any conditions specified in the rules—

   (a) a copy of the judgment; and

   (b) a certificate giving particulars relating to the judgment and the proceedings in which it was given.

Modifications to cover authentic instruments and court settlements

   13.—(1) Her Majesty may by Order in Council provide that—

   (a) any provision of this Act relating to the recognition or enforcement in the United Kingdom or elsewhere of judgments to which the 1968 Convention or the Lugano Convention applies; and

   (b) any other statutory provision, whenever passed or made, so relating,

shall apply, with such modifications as may be specified in the Order, in relation to documents and settlements within Title IV of the 1968 Convention or, as the case may be, Title IV of the Lugano Convention (authentic instruments and court settlements enforceable in the same manner as judgments) as if they were judgments to which the Convention in question applies.

   (2) An Order in Council under this section may make different provision in relation to different descriptions of documents and settlements.

   (3) Any Order in Council under this section shall be subject to annulment in pursuance of a resolution of either House of Parliament.

Modifications consequential on revision of the Conventions

   14.—(1) If at any time it appears to Her Majesty in Council that Her Majesty's Government in the United Kingdom have agreed to a revision of the Lugano Convention or any of the Brussels Conventions, including in particular any revision connected with the accession to the Lugano Convention or the 1968 Convention of one or more further states, Her Majesty may by Order in Council make such modifications of this Act or any other statutory provision, whenever passed or made, as Her Majesty considers appropriate in consequence of the revision.

(2) An Order in Council under this section shall not be made unless a draft of the Order has been laid before Parliament and approved by a resolution of each House of Parliament.

(3) In this section "revision" means an omission from, addition to or alteration of any of the Conventions and includes replacement of any of the Conventions to any extent by another convention, protocol or other description of international agreement.

Interpretation of Part I and consequential amendments

15.—(1) In this Part, unless the context otherwise requires—

"judgment" has the meaning given by Article 25;
"maintenance order" means a maintenance judgment within the meaning of the 1968 Convention or as the case may be, the Lugano Convention;
"payer", in relation to a maintenance order, means the person liable to make the payments for which the order provides;
"prescribed" means prescribed by rules of court.

(2) References in this Part to a judgment registered under section 4 or 5 include, to the extent of its registration, references to a judgment so registered to a limited extent only.

(3) Anything authorised or required by the 1968 Convention the Lugano Convention or this Part to be done by, to or before a particular magistrates' court may be done by, to or before any magistrates' court acting for the same petty sessions area (or, in Northern Ireland, petty sessions district) as that court.

PART II. JURISDICTION, AND RECOGNITION AND ENFORCEMENT OF JUDGMENTS, WITHIN UNITED KINGDOM

Allocation within UK of jurisdiction in certain civil proceedings

16.—(1) The provisions set out in Schedule 4 (which contains a modified version of Title II of the 1968 Convention) shall have effect for determining, for each part of the United Kingdom, whether the courts of law of that part, or any particular court of law in that part, have or has jurisdiction in proceedings where—

(a) the subject-matter of the proceedings is within the scope of the 1968 Convention as determined by Article 1 (whether or not that or any other Convention has effect in relation to the proceedings); and
(b) the defendant or defender is domiciled in the United Kingdom or the proceedings are of a kind mentioned in Article 16 of the 1968 Convention (exclusive jurisdiction regardless of domicile).

(2) In Schedule 4 modifications of Title II of the 1968 Convention are indicated as follows—

(a) modifications by way of omission are indicated by dots; and
(b) within each Article words resulting from modifications by way of addition or substitution are printed in heavy type.

(3) In determining any question as to the meaning or effect of any provision contained in Schedule 4—

(a) regard shall be had to any relevant principles laid down by the European Court in connection with Title II of the 1968 Convention and to any relevant decision of that court as to the meaning or effect of any provision of that Title; and
(b) without prejudice to the generality of paragraph (a), the reports mentioned in section 3(3) may be considered and shall, so far as relevant, be given such weight as is appropriate in the circumstances.

(4) The provisions of this section and Schedule 4 shall have effect subject to the 1968 Convention and the Lugano Convention and to the provisions of section 17.

(5) In section 15(1)(a) of the Maintenance Order Act 1950 (domestic proceedings in which initial process may be served in another part of the United Kingdom), after sub-paragraph (v) there shall be added—

"(vi) Article 5(2) of Schedule 4 to the Civil Jurisdiction and Judgments Act 1982; or".

Exclusion of certain proceedings from Schedule 4

17.—(1) Schedule 4 shall not apply to proceedings of any description listed in Schedule 5 or to proceedings in Scotland under any enactment which confers jurisdiction on a Scottish court in respect of a specific subject-matter on specific grounds.

(2) Her Majesty may by Order in Council—

(a) add to the list in Schedule 5 any description of proceedings in any part of the United Kingdom; and

(b) remove from that list any description of proceedings in any part of the United Kingdom (whether included in the list as originally enacted or added by virtue of this subsection).

(3) An Order in Council under subsection (2)—

(a) may make different provisions for different descriptions of proceedings, for the same description of proceedings in different courts or for different parts of the United Kingdom; and

(b) may contain such transitional and other incidental provisions as appear to Her Majesty to be appropriate.

(4) An Order in Council under subsection (2) shall not be made unless a draft of the Order has been laid before Parliament and approved by a resolution of each House of Parliament.

Enforcement of UK judgments in other parts of UK

18.—(1) In relation to any judgment to which this section applies—

(a) Schedule 6 shall have effect for the purpose of enabling any money provisions contained in the judgment to be enforced in a part of the United Kingdom other than the part in which the judgment was given; and

(b) Schedule 7 shall have effect for the purpose of enabling any non-money provisions so contained to be so enforced.

(2) In this section "judgment" means any of the following (references to the giving of a judgment being construed accordingly)—

(a) any judgment or order (by whatever name called) given or made by a court of law in the United Kingdom;

(b) any judgment or order not within paragraph (a) which has been entered in England and Wales or Northern Ireland in the High Court or a county court;

(c) any document which in Scotland has been registered for execution in the Books of Council and Session or in the sheriff court books kept for any sheriffdom;

(d) any award or order made by a tribunal in any part of the United Kingdom which is enforceable in that part without an order of a court of law;

(e) an arbitration award which has become enforceable in the part of the United Kingdom in which it was given in the same manner as a judgment given by a court of law in that part;

and, subject to the following provisions of this section, the section applies to all such judgments.

(3) Subject to subsection (4), this section does not apply to—

(a) a judgment given in proceedings in a magistrates' court in England and Wales or Northern Ireland;

  (b) a judgment given in proceedings other than civil proceedings;
(ba) a judgment given in the exercise of jurisdiction in relation to insolvency within the meaning of section 426 of the Insolvency Act 1986
  (c) a judgment given in proceedings relating to—

      (i) (repealed Insolvency Act 1985 Schedule 10)
      (ii) (repealed *ibid.*)
      (iii) the obtaining of title or administer the estate of a deceased person.

(4) This section applies, whatever the nature of the proceedings in which it is made, to—

  (a) a decree issued under section 13 of the Court of Exchequer (Scotland) Act 1856 (recovery of certain rentcharges and penalties by process of the Court of Session);
  (b) an order which is enforceable in the same manner as a judgment of the High Court in England and Wales by virtue of section 16 of the Contempt of Court Act 1981 or section 140 of the Supreme Court Act 1981 (which relate to fines for contempt of court and forfeiture of recognisances).

(4A) This section does not apply as respects—

  (a) the enforcement in Scotland of orders made by the High Court or a county court in England and Wales under or for the purposes of Part VI of the Criminal Justice Act 1988 or the Drug Trafficking Act 1994 (confiscation of the proceeds of certain offences or of drug trafficking); or
  (b) the enforcement in England and Wales of orders made by the Court of Session under or for the purposes of Part I of the Criminal Justice (Scotland) Act 1987 (confiscation of the proceeds of drug trafficking).

(5) This section does not apply to so much of any judgment as—

  (a) is an order to which section 16 of the Maintenance Orders Act 1950 applies (and is therefore an order for whose enforcement in another part of the United Kingdom provision is made by Part II of that Act);
  (b) concerns the status or legal capacity of an individual;
  (c) relates to the management of the affairs of a person not capable of managing his own affairs;
  (d) is a provisional (including protective) measure other than an order for the making of an interim payment;

and except whether otherwise stated references to a judgment to which this section applies are to such a judgment exclusive of any such provisions.

(6) The following are within subsection (5)(b), but without prejudice to the generality of that provision—

  (a) a decree of judicial separation or of separation;
  (b) any order which is a Part I order for the purposes of the Family Law Act 1986.

(7) This section does not apply to a judgment of a court outside the United Kingdom which falls to be treated for the purposes of its enforcement as a judgment of a court of law in the United Kingdom by virtue of registration under Part II of the Administration of Justice Act 1920, Part I of the Foreign Judgments (Reciprocal Enforcement) Act 1933, Part I of the Maintenance Orders (Reciprocal Enforcement) Act 1972 or section 4 or 5 of this Act.

(8) A judgment to which this section applies, other than a judgment within paragraph (e) of subsection (2), shall not be enforced in another part of the United Kingdom except by way of registration under Schedule 6 or 7.

Recognition of UK judgments in other parts of UK

19.—(1) A judgment to which this section applies given in one part of the United Kingdom shall not be refused recognition in another part of the United Kingdom solely on the ground that, in relation to that judgment, the court which gave it was not a court of competent jurisdiction according to the rules of private internal law in force in that other part.

(2) Subject to subsection (3), this section applies to any judgment to which section 18 applies.

(3) This section does not apply to—

> (a) the documents mentioned in paragraph (c) of the definition of "judgment" in section 18(2);
> (b) the awards and orders mentioned in paragraphs (d) and (e) of that definition;
> (c) the decrees and orders referred to in section 18(4).

PART III. JURISDICTION IN SCOTLAND

. . .

PART IV. MISCELLANEOUS PROVISIONS

Provisions relating to jurisdiction

Interim relief and protective measures in cases of doubtful jurisdiction

24.—(1) Any power of a court in England and Wales or Northern Ireland to grant interim relief pending trial or pending the determination of an appeal shall extend to a case where—

> (a) the issue to be tried, or which is the subject of the appeal, relates to the jurisdiction of the court to entertain the proceedings; or
> (b) the proceedings involve the reference to any matter to the European Court under the 1971 Protocol.

(2) Any power of a court in Scotland to grant protective measures pending the decision of any hearing shall apply to a case where—

> (a) the subsection of the proceedings includes a question as to the jurisdiction of the court to entertain them; or
> (b) the proceedings involve the reference of a matter to the European Court under the 1971 Protocol.

(3) Subsections (1) and (2) shall not be construed as restricting any power to grant interim relief or protective measures which a court may have apart from this section.

Interim relief in England and Wales and Northern Ireland in the absence of substantive proceedings

25.—(1) The High Court in England and Wales or Northern Ireland shall have power to grant interim relief where—

> (a) proceedings have been or are to be commenced in a Brussels or Lugano Contracting State other than the United Kingdom or in a part of the United Kingdom other than that in which the High Court in question exercises jurisdiction; and
> (b) they are or will be proceedings whose subject-matter is within the scope of the 1968 Convention as determined by Article 1 (whether or not that or any other Convention has effect in relation to the proceedings).

(2) On an application for any interim relief under subsection (1) the court may refuse to grant that relief if, in the opinion of the court, the fact that the court has no jurisdiction apart from this section in relation to the subject-matter of the proceedings in question makes it inexpedient for the court to grant it.

(3) Her Majesty may by Order in Council extend the power to grant interim relief conferred by subsection (1) so as to make it exercisable in relation to proceedings of any of the following descriptions, namely—

(a) proceedings commenced or to be commenced otherwise than in a Brussels or Lugano Contracting State;

(b) proceedings whose subject-matter is not within the scope of the 1968 Convention as determined by Article 1;

(c) arbitration proceedings.

(4) An Order in Council under subsection (3)—

(a) may confer power to grant only specified descriptions of interim relief;

(b) may make different provision for different classes of proceedings, for proceedings pending in different countries or courts outside the United Kingdom or in different parts of the United Kingdom, and for other different circumstances; and

(c) may impose conditions or restrictions on the exercise of any power conferred by the Order.

(5) An Order in Council under subsection (3) which confers power to grant interim relief in relation to arbitration proceedings may provide for the repeal of any provision of section 12(6) of the Arbitration Act 1950 or section 21(1) of the Arbitration Act (Northern Ireland) 1937 to the extent that it is superseded by the provisions of the Order.

(6) Any Order in Council under subsection (3) shall be subject to annulment in pursuance of a resolution of either House of Parliament.

(7) In this section "interim relief", in relation to the High Court in England and Wales or Northern Ireland, means interim relief of any kind which that court has power to grant in proceedings relating to matters which its jurisdiction, other than—

(a) a warrant for the arrest of property; or

(b) provision for obtaining evidence.

Security in Admiralty proceedings in England and Wales or Northern Ireland in case of stay, &c

26.—(1) Where in England and Wales or Northern Ireland a court stays or dismisses Admiralty proceedings on the ground that the dispute in question should be submitted to arbitration or to the determination of the courts of another part of the United Kingdom or of an overseas country, the court may if in those proceedings property has been arrested or bail or other security has been given to prevent or obtain release from arrest—

(a) order that the property arrested be retained as security for the satisfaction of any award or judgment which—

(i) is given in respect of the dispute in the arbitration or legal proceedings in favour of which those proceedings are stayed or dismissed; and

(ii) is enforceable in England and Wales or, as the case may be, in Northern Ireland; or

(b) order that the stay or dismissal of those proceedings be conditional on the provision of equivalent security for the satisfaction of any such award or judgment.

(2) Where a court makes an order under subsection (1), it may attach such conditions to the order as it thinks fit, in particular conditions with respect to the institution or prosecution of the relevant arbitration or legal proceedings.

(3) Subject to any provisions made by rules of court and to any necessary modifications, the same law and practice shall apply in relation to property retained in pursuance of an order made by a court under subsection (1) as would apply if it were held for the purposes of proceedings in that court.

Provisional and protective measures in Scotland in the absence of substantive proceedings

27.—(1) The Court of Session may, in any case to which this subsection applies—

(a) subject to subsection (2)(c), grant a warrant for the arrestment of any assets situated in Scotland;

(b) subject to subsection (2)(c), grant a warrant of inhibition over any property situated in Scotland; and

(c) grant interim interdict.

(2) Subsection (1) applies to any case in which

(a) proceedings have been commenced but not concluded, or, in relation to paragraph (c) of that subsection, are to be commenced, in another Brussels, or Lugano Contracting State or in England and Wales or Northern Ireland;

(b) the subject matter of the proceedings is within the scope of the 1968 Convention as determined by Article 1; and

(c) in relation to paragraphs (a) and (b) of subsection (1), such a warrant could competently have been granted in equivalent proceedings before a Scottish court;

but it shall not be necessary, in determining whether proceedings have been commenced for the purpose of paragraph (a) of this subsection, to show that any document has been served on or notice given to the defender.

(3) Her Majesty may by Order in Council confer on the Court of Session power to do anything mentioned in subsection (1) or in section 28 in relation to proceedings of any of the following descriptions, namely—

(a) proceedings commenced otherwise than in a Brussels, or Lugano Contracting State;

(b) proceedings whose subject-matter is not within the scope of the 1968 Convention as determined by Article 1;

(c) arbitration proceedings;

(d) in relation to subsection (1)(c) or section 28, proceedings which are to be commenced otherwise than in a Brussels or Lugano Contracting State.

(4) An Order in Council under subsection (3)—

(a) may confer power to do only certain of the things mentioned in subsection (1) or in section 28;

(b) may make different provision for different classes of proceedings, for proceedings pending in different countries or courts outside the United Kingdom or in different parts of the United Kingdom, and for other different circumstances; and

(c) may impose conditions or restrictions on the exercise of any power conferred by the Order.

(5) Any Order in Council under subsection (3) shall be subject to annulment in pursuance of a resolution of either House of Parliament.

Application of s. 1 of Administration of Justice (Scotland) Act 1972

28. When any proceedings have been brought, or are likely to be brought, in another Brussels, or Lugano Contracting State or in England and Wales or Northern Ireland in respect of any matter which is within the scope of the 1968 Convention as determined by Article 1, the Court of Session shall have the like power to make an order under section 1 of the Administration of Justice (Scotland) Act 1972 as amended by the Law Reform (Misc. Provisions) Scotland Act 1985 as if the proceedings in question had been brought, or were likely to be brought, in that court.

Service of county court process outside Northern Ireland

29. The County Court Rules Committee established by Article 46 of the County Courts (Northern Ireland) Order 1980 may make county court rules with respect to the service of process outside Northern Ireland and the conditions subject to which process may be so served; and accordingly in Article 48 of that Order (powers of Rules Committee), after paragraph (e) there shall be added—

"(f) the service of process outside Northern Ireland, and the conditions subject to which process may be so served.".

Proceedings in England and Wales or Northern Ireland for torts to immovable property

30.—(1) The jurisdiction of any court in England and Wales or Northern Ireland to entertain proceedings for trespass to, or any other tort affecting, immovable property shall extend to cases in which the property in question is situated outside that part of the United Kingdom unless the proceedings are principally concerned with a question of the title to, or the right to possession of, that property.

(2) Subsection (1) has effect subject to the 1968 Convention and the Lugano Convention and to the provisions set out in Schedule 4.

Provisions relating to recognition and enforcement of judgments

Overseas judgments given against states, etc

31.—(1) A judgment given by a court of an overseas country against a state other than the United Kingdom or the state to which that court belongs shall be recognised and enforced in the United Kingdom if, and only if—

    (a) it would be so recognised and enforced if it had not been given against a state; and

    (b) that court would have had jurisdiction in the matter if it had applied rules corresponding to those applicable to such matters in the United Kingdom in accordance with sections 2 to 11 of the State Immunity Act 1978.

(2) References in subsection (1) to a judgment given against a state include references to judgments of any of the following descriptions given in relation to a state—

    (a) judgments against the government, or a department of the government, of the state but not (except as mentioned in paragraph (c)) judgments against an entity which is distinct from the executive organs of government;

    (b) judgments against the sovereign or head of state in his public capacity;

    (c) judgments against any such separate entity as is mentioned in paragraph (a) given in proceedings relating to anything done by it in the exercise of the sovereign authority of the state.

(3) Nothing in subsection (1) shall affect the recognition or enforcement in the United Kingdom of a judgment to which Part I of the Foreign Judgments (Reciprocal Enforcement) Act 1933 applies by virtue of section 4 of the Carriage of Goods by Road Act 1965, section 17(4) of the Nuclear Installations Act 1965, s. 166(4) of the Merchant Shipping Act 1995, section 6 of the International Transport Conventions Act 1983 or section 5 of the Carriage of Passengers by Road Act 1974.

(4) Sections 12, 13 and 14(3) and (4) of the State Immunity Act 1978 (service of process and procedural privileges) shall apply to proceedings for the recognition or enforcement in the United Kingdom of a judgment given by a court of an overseas country (whether or not that judgment is within subsection (1) of this section) as they apply to other proceedings.

(5) In this section "state", in the case of a federal state, includes any of its constituent territories.

Overseas judgments given in breach of agreement for settlement of disputes

32.—(1) Subject to the following provisions of this section, a judgment given by a court of an overseas country in any proceedings shall not be recognised or enforced in the United Kingdom if—

    (a) the bringing of those proceedings in that court was contrary to an agreement under which the dispute in question was to be settled otherwise than by proceedings in the courts of that country; and

    (b) those proceedings were not brought in that court by, or with the agreement of, the person against whom the judgment was given; and

    (c) that person did not counterclaim in the proceedings or otherwise submit to the jurisdiction of that court.

(2) Subsection (1) does not apply where the agreement referred to in paragraph (a) of that subsection was illegal, void or unenforceable or was incapable of being performed for reasons not attributable to the fault of the party bringing the proceedings in which the judgment was given.

(3) In determining whether a judgment given by a court of an overseas country should be recognised or enforced in the United Kingdom, a court in the United Kingdom shall not be bound by any decision of the overseas court relating to any of the matters mentioned in subsection (1) or (2).

(4) Nothing in subsection (1) shall affect the recognition or enforcement in the United Kingdom of—

    (a) a judgment which is required to be recognised or enforced there under the 1968 Convention or the Lugano Convention;

    (b) a judgment to which Part I of the Foreign Judgments (Reciprocal Enforcement) Act 1933 applies by virtue of section 4 of the Carriage of Goods by Road Act 1965, section 17(4) of the Nuclear Installations Act 1965, section 6 of the International Transport Corporation Act 1983, section 5 of the Carriage of Passengers by Road Act 1974 or section 177(4) of the Merchant Shipping Act 1995.

Certain steps not to amount to submission to jurisdiction of overseas court

33.—(1) For the purposes of determining whether a judgment given by a court of an overseas country should be recognised or enforced in England and Wales or Northern Ireland, the person against whom the judgment was given shall not be treated, as having submitted to the jurisdiction of the court by reason only of the fact that he appeared (conditionally or otherwise) in the proceedings for all or any one or more of the following purposes, namely—

    (a) to contest the jurisdiction of the court;

    (b) to ask the court to dismiss or stay the proceedings on the ground that the dispute in question should be submitted to arbitration or to the determination of the courts of another country;

    (c) to protect, or obtain the release of property seized or threatened with seizure in the proceedings.

(2) Nothing in this section shall affect the recognition or enforcement in England and Wales or Northern Ireland of a judgment which is required to be recognised or enforced there under the 1968 Convention or the Lugano Convention.

Certain judgments a bar to further proceedings on the same cause of action

34. No proceedings may be brought by a person in England and Wales or Northern Ireland on a cause of action in respect of which a judgment has been given in his favour in proceedings between the same parties, or their privies, in a court in another part of the United Kingdom or in a court of an overseas country, unless that judgment is not enforceable or entitled to recognition in England or Wales or, as the case may be, in Northern Ireland.

Minor amendments relating to overseas judgments

35.—(1) The Foreign Judgments (Reciprocal Enforcement) Act 1933 shall have effect with the amendments specified in Schedule 10, being amendments whose main purpose is to enable Part I of that Act to be applied to judgments of courts other than superior courts, to judgments providing for interim payments and to certain arbitration awards.

(2) For section 10 of the Administration of Justice Act 1920 (issue of certificates of judgments obtained in the United Kingdom) there shall be substituted—

    "10.—(1) Where—

        (a) a judgment has been obtained in the High Court in England or Northern Ireland, or in the Court of Session in Scotland, against any person; and

(b) the judgment creditor wishes to secure the enforcement of the judgment in a part of Her Majesty's dominions outside the United Kingdom to which this Part of this Act extends,

the court shall, on an application made by the judgment creditor, issue to him a certified copy of the judgment.

(2) The reference in the preceding subsection to Her Majesty's dominions shall be construed as if that subsection had come into force in its present form at the commencement of this Act.".

(3) In section 14 of the Administration of Justice Act 1920 (extent of Part II of that Act), after subsection (2) there shall be inserted—

"(3) Her Majesty may by Order in Council under this section consolidate any Orders in Council under this section which are in force when the consolidating Order is made.".

36. ...

37. ...

Overseas judgments counteracting an award of multiple damages

38.—(1) Section 7 of the Protection of Trading Interests Act 1980 (which enables provision to be made by Order in Council for the enforcement in the United Kingdom on a reciprocal basis of overseas judgments directed to counteracting a judgment for multiple damages given in a third country) shall be amended as follows.

(2) In subsection (1) for "judgments given under any provision of the law of that country corresponding to that section" there shall be substituted "judgments of any description specified in the Order which are given under any provision of the law of that country relating to the recovery of sums paid or obtained pursuant to a judgment for multiple damages within the meaning of section 5(3) above, whether or not that provision corresponds to section 6 above".

(3) After subsection (1) that shall be inserted—

"(1A) Such an Order in Council may, as respects judgments to which it relates—

(a) make different provisions for different descriptions of judgment; and
(b) impose conditions or restrictions on the enforcement of judgments of any description.".

Jurisdiction, and recognition and enforcement of judgments, as between
United Kingdom and certain territories

Application of provisions corresponding to 1968 Convention in relation to certain territories

39.—(1) Her Majesty may by Order in Council make provision corresponding to the provision made by the 1968 Convention as between the Contracting States to that Convention, with such modifications as appear to Her Majesty to be appropriate, for regulating, as between the United Kingdom and any of the territories mentioned in subsection (2), the jurisdiction of courts and the recognition and enforcement of judgments.

(2) The territories referred to in subsection (1) are—

(a) the Isle of Man;
(b) any of the Channel Islands;
(c) any colony

(3) An Order in Council under this section may contain such supplementary and incidental provisions as appear to Her Majesty to be necessary or expedient, including in particular provisions corresponding to or applying any of the provisions of Part I with such modifications as may be specified in the Order.

(4) Any Order in Council under this section shall be subject to annulment in pursuance of a resolution of either House of Parliament.

PART V. SUPPLEMENTARY AND GENERAL PROVISIONS

Domicile

Domicile of individuals

41.—(1) Subject to Article 52 (which contains provisions for determining whether a party is domiciled in a Contracting State), the following provisions of this section determine, for the purposes of the 1968 Convention, the Lugano Conventions and this Act, whether an individual is domiciled in the United Kingdom or in a particular part of, or place in, the United Kingdom or in a state other than a Contracting State.

(2) An individual is domiciled in the United Kingdom if and only if—

(a) he is resident in the United Kingdom; and
(b) the nature and circumstances of his residence indicate that he has a substantial connection with the United Kingdom.

(3) Subject to subsection (5), an individual is domiciled in a particular part of the United Kingdom if and only if—

(a) he is resident in that part; and
(b) the nature and circumstances of his residence indicate that he has a substantial connection with that part.

(4) An individual is domiciled in a particular place in the United Kingdom if and only if he—

(a) is domiciled in the part of the United Kingdom in which the place is situated; and
(b) is resident in that place.

(5) An individual who is domiciled in the United Kingdom but in whose case the requirements of subsection (3)(b) are not satisfied to any particular part of the United Kingdom shall be treated as domiciled in the part of the United Kingdom in which he is resident.

(6) In the case of an individual who—

(a) is resident in the United Kingdom, or in a particular part of the United Kingdom; and
(b) has been so resident for the last three months or more,

the requirements of subsection (2)(b) or, as the case may be, subsection (3)(b) shall be presumed to be fulfilled unless the contrary is proved.

(7) An individual is domiciled in a state other than a Contracting State if and only if—

(a) he is resident in that state; and
(b) the nature and circumstances of his residence indicate that he has a substantial connection with that state.

Domicile and seat of corporation or association

42.—(1) For the purpose of this Act the seat of a corporation or association (as determined by this section) shall be treated as its domicile.

(2) The following provisions of this section determine where a corporation or association has its seat—

(a) for the purpose of Article 53 (which for the purposes of the 1968 Convention or, as the case may be, the Lugano Convention equates the domicile of such a body with its seat); and

(b) for the purposes of this Act other than the provisions mentioned in section 43(1)(b) and (c).

(3) A corporation or association has its seat in the United Kingdom if and only if—

(a) it was incorporated or formed under law of a part of the United Kingdom and has its registered office or some other official address in the United Kingdom; or
(b) its central management and control is exercised in the United Kingdom.

(4) A corporation or association has its seat in a particular part of the United Kingdom if and only if it has its seat in the United Kingdom and—

(a) it has its registered office or some other official address in that part; or
(b) its central management and control is exercised in that part; or
(c) it has a place of business in that part.

(5) A corporation or association has its seat in a particular place in the United Kingdom if and only if it has its seat in the part of the United Kingdom in which that place is situated and—

(a) it has its registered office or some other official address in that place; or
(b) its central management and control is exercised in that place; or
(c) it has a place of business in that place.

(6) Subject to subsection (7), a corporation or association has its seat in a state other than the United Kingdom if and only if—

(a) it was incorporated or formed under the law of that state and has its registered office or some other official address there; or
(b) its central management and control is exercised in that state.

(7) A corporation or association shall not be regarded as having its seat in a Contracting State other than the United Kingdom if it is shown that the courts of that state would not regard it as having its seat there.

(8) In this section—

"business' includes any activity carried on by a corporation or association, and "place of business" shall be construed accordingly;
"official address", in relation to a corporation or association, means an address which it is required by law to register, notify or maintain for the purpose of receiving notices or other communications.

Seat of corporation or association for purposes of Article 16(2) and related provisions

43.—(1) The following provisions of this section determine where a corporation or association has it seat for the purposes of—

(a) Article 16(2) of the 1968 Convention or of the Lugano Convention (which confers exclusive jurisdiction over proceedings relating to the formation or dissolution of such bodies, or to the decisions of their organs);
(b) Articles 5A and 16(2) in Schedule 4; and
(c) Rules 2(12) and 4(1)(b) in Schedule 8;

(2) A corporation or association has its seat in the United Kingdom if and only if—

(a) it was incorporated or formed under the law of a part of the United Kingdom; or
(b) its central management and control is exercised in the United Kingdom.

(3) A corporation or association has its seat in a particular part of the United Kingdom if and only if it has its seat in the United Kingdom and—

(a) subject to subsection (5), it was incorporated or formed under the law of that part; or

(b) being incorporated or formed under the law of a state other than the United Kingdom, its central management and control is exercised in that part.

(4) A corporation or association has its seat in a particular place in Scotland if and only if it has its seat in Scotland and—

(a) it has its registered office or some other official address in that place; or
(b) it has no registered office or other official address in Scotland, but its central management and control is exercised in that place.

(5) A corporation or association incorporated or formed under—

(a) an enactment forming part of the law of more than one part of the United Kingdom; or
(b) an instrument having effect in the domestic law or more than one part of the United Kingdom.

shall, if it has a registered office, be taken to have its seat in the part of the United Kingdom in which that office is situated, and not in any other part of the United Kingdom.

(6) Subject to subsection (7), a corporation or association has its seat in a Contracting State other than the United Kingdom if and only if—

(a) it was incorporated or formed under the law of that state; or
(b) its central management and control is exercised in that state.

(7) A corporation or association shall not be regarded as having its seat in a Contracting State other than the United Kingdom if—

(a) it has its seat in the United Kingdom by virtue of subsection (2)(a); or
(b) it is shown that the courts of that other state would not regard it for the purposes of Article 16(2) as having its seat there.

(8) In this section "official address" has the same meaning as in section 42.

Persons deemed to be domiciled in the United Kingdom for certain purposes

44.—(1) This section applies to—

(a) proceedings within Section 3 of Title II of the 1968 Convention or Section 3 of Title II of the Lugano Convention (insurance contracts), and
(b) proceedings within Section 4 of Title II of either of those Conventions (consumer contracts).

(2) A person who, for the purposes of proceedings to which this section applies arising out of the operations of a breach, agency or other establishment in the United Kingdom, is deemed for the purposes of the 1968 Convention or, as the case may be, the Lugano Convention to be domiciled in the United Kingdom by virtue of—

(a) Article 8, section paragraph (insurers), or
(b) Article 13, second paragraph (suppliers of goods, services or credit to consumers),

shall, for the purposes of those proceedings, be treated for the purposes of this Act as so domiciled and as domiciled in the part of the United Kingdom in which the branch, agency or establishment in question is situated.

Domicile of trusts

45.—(1) The following provisions of this section determine, for the purposes of the 1968 Convention the Lugano Convention and this Act, where a trust is domiciled.

(2) A trust is domiciled in the United Kingdom if and only if it is by virtue of subsection (3) domiciled in a part of the United Kingdom.

(3) A trust is domiciled in a part of the United Kingdom if and only if the system of law of that part is the system of law with which the trust has its closest and most real connection.

Domicile and seat of the Crown

46.—(1) For the purposes of this Act the seat of the Crown (as determined by this section) shall be treated as its domicile.

(2) The following provisions of this section determine where the Crown has its seat—

   (a) for the purposes of the 1968 Convention and the Lugano Convention (in each of which Article 53 equates the domicile of a legal person with its seat); and
   (b) for the purposes of this Act.

(3) Subject to the provisions of any Order in Council for the time being in force under subsection (4)—

   (a) the Crown in right of Her Majesty's government in the United Kingdom has its seat in every part of, and every place in, the United Kingdom; and
   (b) the Crown in right of Her Majesty's government in Northern Ireland has its seat in, and every place in, Northern Ireland.

(4) Her Majesty may by Order in Council provide that, in the case of proceedings of any specified description against the Crown in right of Her Majesty's government in the United Kingdom, the Crown shall be treated for the purposes of the 1968 Convention the Lugano Convention and this Act as having its seat in, and in every place in, a specified part of the United Kingdom and not in any other part of the United Kingdom.

(5) An Order in Council under subsection (4) may frame a description of proceedings in any way, and in particular may do so by reference to the government department or officer of the Crown against which or against whom they fall to be instituted.

(6) Any Order in Council made under this section shall be subject to annulment in pursuance of a resolution of either House of Parliament.

(7) Nothing in this section applies to the Crown otherwise than in right of Her Majesty's government in the United Kingdom or Her Majesty's government in Northern Ireland.

Other supplementary provisions

Modifications occasioned by decisions of European Court as to the meaning or effect of the Brussels Conventions

47.—(1) Her Majesty may by Order in Council—

   (a) make such provision as Her Majesty considers appropriate for the purpose of bringing the law of any part of the United Kingdom into accord with the Brussels Conventions as affected by any principle laid down by the European Court in connection with the Brussels Conventions or by any decision of that court as to the meaning or effect of any provision of the Brussels Conventions; or
   (b) make such modifications of Schedule 4 or Schedule 8, or of any other statutory provision affected by any provision of either of those Schedules, as Her Majesty considers appropriate in view of any principle with Title II of the 1968 Convention or of any decision of that court as to the meaning or effect of any provision of that Title.

(2) The provision which may be made by virtue of paragraph (a) of subsection (1) includes such modifications of this Act or any other statutory provision, whenever passed or made, as Her Majesty considers appropriate for the purpose mentioned in that paragraph.

(3) The modifications which may be made by virtue of paragraph (b) of subsection (1) include modifications designed to produce divergence between any provision of Schedule 4 or Schedule 8

and a corresponding provision of Title II of the 1968 Convention as affected by any such principle as is mentioned in that paragraph.

(4) An Order in Council under this section shall not be made unless a draft of the Order has been laid before Parliament and approved by a resolution of each House of Parliament.

Matters for which rules of court may provide

48.—(1) Rules of court may make provision for regulating the procedure to be followed in any court in connection with any provision of this Act the Lugano Convention or the Brussels Convention.

(2) Rules of Court may make provision as to the manner in which and to conditions subject to which a certificate or judgment registered in any court under any provision of this Act may be enforced, including provision for enabling the court or, in Northern Ireland, the Enforcement of Judgments Office, subject to any conditions specified in the rules, to give directions about such matters.

(3) Without prejudice to the generality of subsections (1) and (2), the power to make rules of court for magistrates' courts, and in Northern Ireland the power to make Judgment Enforcement Rules, shall include power to make such provision as the rule-making authority considers necessary or expedient for the purposes of the provisions of the Lugano Convention, the Brussels Conventions and this Act relating to maintenance proceedings and the recognition and enforcement of maintenance orders, and shall in particular include power to make provision as to any of the following matters—

(a) authorising the service in another Contracting State of process issued by or for the purposes of a magistrates' court and the service and execution in England and Wales or Northern Ireland of process issued in another Contracting State;

(b) requesting courts in other parts of the United Kingdom or in other Contracting States to take evidence there for the purposes of proceedings in England and Wales or Northern Ireland;

(c) the taking of evidence in England and Wales or Northern Ireland in response to similar requests received from such courts;

(d) the circumstances in which and the conditions subject to which any powers conferred under paragraphs (a) to (c) are to be exercised;

(e) the admission in evidence, subject to such conditions as may be prescribed in the rules, of statements contained in documents purporting to be made or authenticated by a court in another part of the United Kingdom or in another Contracting State, or by a judge or official of such a court, which purport—

(i) to set out or summarise evidence given in proceedings in that court or to be documents received in evidence in such proceedings or copies of such documents; or

(ii) to set out or summarise evidence taken for the purposes of proceedings in England and Wales or Northern Ireland, whether or not in response to any such request as is mentioned in paragraph (b); or

(iii) to record information relating to the payments made under an order of that court;

(f) the circumstances and manner in which a magistrates' court may or must vary or revoke a maintenance order registered in that court, cancel the registration of, or refrain from enforcing, such an order to transmit such an order for enforcement in another part of the United Kingdom;

(g) the cases and manner in which courts in other parts of the United Kingdom or in other Contracting States are to be informed of orders made, or other things done, by or for the purposes of a magistrates' court;

(h) the circumstances and manner in which a magistrates' court may communicate for other purposes with such courts;

(i) the giving of notice of such matters as may be prescribed in the rules to such persons as may be so prescribed and the manner in which such notice is to be given.

(4) Nothing in this section shall be taken as derogating from the generality of any power to make rules of court conferred by any other enactment.

Savings for powers to stay, sist, strike out or dismiss proceedings

49. Nothing in this Act shall prevent any court in the United Kingdom from staying, sisting, striking out or dismissing any proceedings before it, on the ground of *forum non conveniens* or otherwise, where to do so is not inconsistent with the 1968 Convention or as the case may be the Lugano Convention.

General

Interpretation: general

50. In this Act, unless the context otherwise requires—

"the Accession Convention", "the 1982 Accession Convention" and "the 1989 Accession
   Convention" have the meaning given by section 1(1);
"Article" and reference to sub-divisions of numbered Articles are to be construed in
   accordance with section 1(2)(b);
"association" means an unincorporated body of persons;
"Contracting State" has the meaning given by section 1(3);
"the 1968 Convention" has the meaning given by section 1(1), and references to that
   Convention and to provisions of it are to be construed in accordance with section 1(2)(a);
   . . .
"Brussels Contracting State" has the meaning given by section 1(3);
"the Brussels Conventions" has the meaning given by section 1(1);
"Lugano Contracting State" has the meaning given by section 1(3);
"the Lugano Convention" has the meaning given by section 1(1);
"corporation" means a body corporate, and includes a partnership subsisting under the law of
   Scotland.
"court" without more, includes a tribunal;
"court of law", in relation to the United Kingdom, means any of the following courts,
   namely—

   (a) the House of Lords,
   (b) in England and Wales or Northern Ireland, the Court of Appeal, the High Court, the
      Crown Court, a county court and a magistrates' court,
   (c) in Scotland, the Court of Session and a sheriff court;

"the Crown" is to be construed in accordance with section 51(2);
"enactment" includes an enactment comprised in Northern Ireland legislation;
"judgment" subject to sections 15(1) and 18(2) and to paragraph 1 of Schedules 6 and 7, means
   any judgment or order (by whatever name called) given or made by a court, in any civil
   proceedings;
"magistrates court", in relation to Northern Ireland, means a court of summary jurisdiction;
"modifications" includes additions, omissions and alterations;
"overseas country" means any country or territory outside the United Kingdom;
"part of the United Kingdom" means England and Wales, Scotland or Northern Ireland;
"the 1971 Protocol" has the meaning given by section 1(1), references to that Protocol and to
   provisions of it are to be construed in accordance with section 1(2)(a);
"rules of court", in relation to any court, means rules, orders or regulations made by the
   authority having power to make rules, orders or regulations regulating the procedure of that
   court, and includes—

   (a) in Scotland, Acts of Sederunt;
   (b) in Northern Ireland, Judgment Enforcement Rules;

"statutory provision" means any provisions contained in the Act, or in any Northern Ireland legislation, or in—

    (a) subordinate legislation (as defined in section 12(1) of the Interpretation Act 1978); or
    (b) any instrument of a legislative character made under any Northern Ireland legislation;

"tribunal"—

    (a) means a tribunal of any description other than a court of law;
    (b) in relation to an overseas country, includes, as regards matters relating to maintenance within the meaning of the 1968 Convention, any authority having power to give, enforce, vary or revoke a maintenance order.

Application to Crown

51.—(1) This Act binds the Crown.

(2) In this section and elsewhere in this Act references to the Crown do not include references to Her Majesty in Her private capacity or to Her Majesty in right of Her Duchy of Lancaster or to the Duke of Cornwall.

Extent

52.—(1) This Act extends to Northern Ireland.

(2) Without prejudice to the power conferred by section 29, Her Majesty may by Order in Council direct that all or any of the provisions of this Act apart from that section shall extend, subject to such modifications as may be specified in the Order, to any of the following territories, that is to say—

    (a) the Isle of Man;
    (b) any of the Channel Islands;
    (c) any colony;

Commencement, transitional provisions and savings

53.—(1) This Act shall come into force in accordance with the provisions of Part I of Schedule 13.

(2) The transitional provisions and savings contained in Part II of that Schedule shall have effect in relation to the commencement of the provisions of this Act mentioned in that Part.

Repeals

54. The enactments mentioned in Schedule 14 are hereby repealed to the extent specified in the third column of that Schedule.

Short title

55. This Act may be cited as the Civil Jurisdiction and Judgments Act 1982.

SCHEDULE 1 (S. 2(2)). TEXT OF 1968 CONVENTION, AS AMENDED

CONVENTION ON JURISDICTION AND THE ENFORCEMENT OF JUDGMENTS IN CIVIL AND COMMERCIAL MATTERS

PREAMBLE

THE HIGH CONTRACTING PARTIES TO THE TREATY ESTABLISHING THE EUROPEAN ECONOMIC COMMUNITY,

Desiring to implement the provisions of Article 220 of that Treaty by virtue of which they undertook to secure the simplification of formalities governing the reciprocal recognition and enforcement of judgments of courts or tribunals;

Anxious to strengthen in the Community the legal protection of persons therein established;

Considering that it is necessary for this purpose to determine the international jurisdiction of their courts, to facilitate recognition and to introduce an expeditious procedure for securing the enforcement of judgments, authentic instruments and court settlements;

Have decided to conclude this Convention and to this end have designed as their Plenipotentiaries;

(*Designations of Plenipotentiaries of the original six Contracting States*)

WHO, meeting within the Council, having exchanged their Full Powers, found in good and due form.

HAVE AGREED AS FOLLOWS:

TITLE 1. SCOPE

Article 1

This Convention shall apply in civil and commercial matters whatever the nature of the court or tribunal. It shall not extend, in particular, to revenue, customs or administrative matters.

The Convention shall not apply to—

1. The status or legal capacity of natural persons, rights in property arising out of a matrimonial relationship, wills and succession.
2. Bankruptcy, proceedings relating to the winding-up of insolvent companies or other legal persons, judicial arrangements, compositions and analogous proceedings.
3. Social security.
4. Arbitration.

TITLE II JURISDICTION

Section 1. General provisions

Article 2

Subject to the provisions of this Convention, persons domiciled in a Contracting State shall, whatever their nationality, be sued in the courts of that State.

Persons who are not nationals of the State in which they are domiciled shall be governed by the rules of jurisdiction applicable to nationals of that State.

Article 3

Persons domiciled in a Contracting State may be sued in the courts of another Contracting State only by virtue of the rules set out in Sections 2 to 6 of this Title.

In particular the following provisions shall not be applicable as against them—

— in Belgium: Article 15 of the civil code (Code civil—Burgerlijk Wetboek) and Article 638 of the judicial code (Code judiciaire—Gerechtelijk Wetboek),
— in Denmark: Article 246(2) and (3) of the law on civil procedure (Lov om rettens pleje),
— in the Federal Republic of Germany: Article 23 of the code of civil procedure (Zivilprozeβordnung),
— in Greece, Article 40 of the code of civil procedure (Κωδικας Πολιτικης Δικουομίας),
— in France: Articles 14 and 15 of the civil code (Code civil),
— in Ireland: the rules which enable jurisdiction to be founded on the document instituting the proceedings having been served on the defendant during his temporary presence in Ireland,

— in Italy: Articles 2 and 4, nos 1 and 2 of the code of civil procedure (Codice di procedura civile),
— in Luxembourg: Articles 14 and 15 of the civil code (Code civil),
— in the Netherlands: Articles 126(3) and 127 of the code of civil procedure (Wetboek van Burgerlijke Rechtsvordering),
— in Portugal: Article 65(1)(c), Article 65(2) and Article 65A(c) of the code of civil procedure (Código de Processo Civil) and Article 11 of the code of labour procedure (Código de Processo de Trabalho),
— in the United Kingdom: the rules which enable jurisdiction to be founded on:

  (a) the document instituting the proceedings having been served on the defendant during his temporary presence in the United Kingdom; or
  (b) the presence within the United Kingdom of property belonging to the defendant; or
  (c) the seizure by the plaintiff of property situated in the United Kingdom.

Article 4

If the defendant is not domiciled in a Contracting State, the jurisdiction of the courts of each Contracting State shall, subject to the provisions of Article 16, be determined by the law of that State.

As against such a defendant, any person domiciled in a Contracting State may, whatever his nationality, avail himself in that State of the rules of jurisdiction there in force, and in particular those specified in the second paragraph of Article 3, in the same way as the nationals of that State.

Section 2. Special jurisdiction

Article 5

A person domiciled in a Contracting State may, in another Contracting State, be sued—

  1. In matters relating to a contract, in the courts for the place of performance of the obligation in question; in matters relating to individual contracts of employment, this place is that where the employee habitually carried out his work, or if the employee does not habitually carry out his work in any one country, the employer may also be sued in the courts for the place where the business which engaged the employee was or is now situated.
  2. In matters relating to maintenance, in the courts for the place where the maintenance creditor is domiciled or habitually resident or, if the matter is ancillary to proceedings concerning the status of a person, in the court which, according to its own law, has jurisdiction to entertain those proceedings, unless that jurisdiction is based solely on the nationality of one of the parties.
  3. In matters relating to tort, delict or quasi-delict, in the courts for the place where the harmful event occurred.
  4. As regards a civil claim for damages or restitution which is based on an act giving rise to criminal proceedings, in the court seised of those proceedings, to the extent that that court has jurisdiction under its own law to entertain civil proceedings.
  5. As regards a dispute arising out of the operations of a branch, agency or other establishment, in the courts for the place in which the branch, agency or other establishment is situated.
  6. As settlor, trustee or beneficiary of a trust created by the operation of a statute, or by a written instrument, or created orally and evidenced in writing, in the courts of the Contracting State in which the trust is domiciled.
  7. As regards a dispute concerning the payment of remuneration claimed in respect of the salvage of a cargo or freight, in the court under the authority of which the cargo or freight in question—

  (a) has been arrested to secure such payment, or
  (b) could have been so arrested, but bail or other security has been given;

provided that this provision shall apply only if it is claimed that the defendant has an interest in the cargo or freight or had such an interest at the time of salvage.

Article 6

A person domiciled in a Contracting State may also be sued—

1. Where he is one of a number of defendants, in the courts for the place where any one of them is domiciled.
2. As a third party in an action on a warranty or guarantee or in any other third party proceedings, in the court seised of the original proceedings, unless these were instituted solely with the object of removing him from the jurisdiction of the court which would be competent in his case.
3. On a counter-claim arising from the same contract or facts on which the original claim was based, in the court in which the original claim is pending.
4. In matters relating to a contract, if the action may be combined with an action against the same defendant in matters relating to rights *in rem* in immovable property, in the court of the Contracting State in which the property is situated.

Article 6a

Where by virtue of this Convention a court of a Contracting State has jurisdiction in actions relating to liability from the use or operation of a ship, that court, or any other court substituted for this purpose by the internal law of that State, shall also have jurisdiction over claims for limitation of such liability.

Section 3. Jurisdiction in matters relating to insurance

Article 7

In matters relating to insurance, jurisdiction shall be determined by this Section, without prejudice to the provisions of Articles 4 and 5 point 5.

Article 8

An insurer domiciled in a Contracting State may be sued—

1. in the courts of the State where he is domiciled, or
2. in another Contracting State, in the courts for the place where the policy-holder is domiciled, or
3. if he is a co-insurer, in the courts of a Contracting State in which proceedings are brought against the leading insurer.

An insurer who is not domiciled in a Contracting State but has a branch, agency or other establishment in one of the Contracting States shall, in disputes arising out of the operations of the branch, agency or establishment, be deemed to be domiciled in that State.

Article 9

In respect of liability insurance or insurance of immovable property, the insurer may in addition be sued in the courts for the place where the harmful event occurred. The same applies if movable and immovable property are covered by the same insurance policy and both are adversely affected by the same contingency.

Article 10

In respect of liability insurance, the insurer may also, if the law of the court permits it, be joined in proceedings which the injured party had brought against the insured.

The provisions of Articles 7, 8 and 9 shall apply to actions brought by the injured party directly against the insurer, where such direct actions are permitted.

If the law governing such direct actions provides that the policy-holder or the insured may be joined as a party to the action, the same court shall have jurisdiction over them.

Article 11

Without prejudice to the provisions of the third paragraph of Article 10, an insurer may bring proceedings only in the courts of the Contracting State in which the defendant is domiciled, irrespective of whether he is the policy-holder, the insured or a beneficiary.

The provisions of this Section shall not affect the right to bring a counterclaim in the court in which, in accordance with this Section, the original claim is pending.

Article 12

The provisions of this Section may be departed from only by an agreement on jurisdiction—

1. which is entered into after the dispute has arisen, or
2. which allows the policy-holder, the insured or a beneficiary to bring proceedings in courts other than those indicated in this Section, or
3. which is concluded between a policy-holder and an insurer, both of whom are domiciled in the same Contracting State, and which has the effect of conferring jurisdiction on the courts of that State even if the harmful event were to occur abroad, provided that such an agreement is not contrary to the law of that State, or
4. which is concluded with a policy-holder who is not domiciled in a Contracting State, except in so far as the insurance is compulsory or relates to immovable property in a Contracting State, or
5. which relates to a contract of insurance in so far as it covers one or more of the risks set out in Article 12a.

Article 12a

The following are the risks referred to in point 5 of Article 12—

1. Any loss of or damage to—

   (a) sea-going ships, installations situated offshore or on the high seas, or aircraft, arising from perils which relate to their use for commercial purposes;
   (b) goods in transit other than passengers' baggage where the transit consists of or includes carriage by such ships or aircraft.

2. Any liability, other than for bodily injury to passengers or loss of or damage to their baggage—

   (a) arising out of the use or operation of ships, installations or aircraft as referred to in point 1(a) above in so far as the law of the Contracting State in which such aircraft are registered does not prohibit agreements on jurisdiction regarding insurance of such risks;
   (b) for loss or damage caused by goods in transit as described in point 1(b) above.

3. Any financial loss connected with the use or operation of ships, installations or aircraft as referred to in point 1(a) above, in particular loss of freight or charter-hire.
4. Any risk or interest connected with any of those referred to in points 1 to 3 above.

Section 4. Jurisdiction over consumer contracts

Article 13

In proceedings concerning a contract concluded by a person for a purpose which can be regarded as being outside his trade or profession, hereinafter called "the consumer", jurisdiction shall be determined by this Section, without prejudice to the provisions of Article 4 and point 5 of Article 5, if it is—

1. a contract for the sale of goods on instalment credit terms, or
2. a contract for a loan repayable by instalments, or for any other form of credit, made to finance the sale of goods, or
3. any other contract for the supply of goods or a contract for the supply of services, and

  (a) in the State of the consumer's domicile the conclusion of the contract was preceded by a specific invitation addressed to him or by advertising; and
  (b) the consumer took in that State the steps necessary for the conclusion of the contract.

Where a consumer enters into a contract with a party who is not domiciled in a Contracting State but has a branch, agency or other establishment in one of the Contracting States, that party shall, in disputes arising out of the operations of the branch, agency or establishment, be deemed to be domiciled in that State.

This Section shall not apply to contracts of transport.

Article 14

A consumer may bring proceedings against the other party to a contract either in the courts of the Contracting State in which that party is domiciled or in the courts of the Contracting State in which he is himself domiciled.

Proceedings may be brought against a consumer by the other party to the contract only in the courts of the Contracting State in which the consumer is domiciled.

These provisions shall not affect the right to bring a counter-claim in the court in which, in accordance with this Section, the original claim is pending.

Article 15

The provisions of this Section may be departed from only by an agreement—

1. which is entered into after the dispute has arisen, or
2. which allows the consumer to bring proceedings in court other than those indicated in this Section, or
3. which is entered into by the consumer and the other party to the contract, both of whom are at the time of conclusion of the contract domiciled or habitually resident in the same Contracting State, and which confers jurisdiction on the courts of that State, provided that such an agreement is not contrary to the law of that State.

Section 5. Exclusive jurisdiction

Article 16

The following courts shall have exclusive jurisdiction, regardless of domicile:

1. (a) in proceedings which have as their object rights *in rem* in immovable property or tenancies of immovable property, the courts of the Contracting State in which the property is situated;
   (a) however, in proceedings which have as their object tenancies of immovable property concluded for temporary private use for a maximum period of six consecutive months, the courts of the Contracting State in which the defendant is domiciled shall also have jurisdiction, provided that the landlord and the tenant are natural persons and are domiciled in the same Contracting State.

2. In proceedings which have as their object the validity of the constitution, the nullity or the dissolution of companies or other legal persons or associations of natural or legal persons,

or the decisions of their organs, the courts of the Contracting State in which the company, legal person or association has its seat.

3. In proceedings which have as their object the validity of entries in public registers, the courts of the Contracting State in which the register is kept.

4. In proceedings concerned with the registration or validity of patents, trade marks, designs, or other similar rights required to be deposited or registered, the courts of the Contracting State in which the deposit or registration has been applied for, has taken place or is under the terms of an international convention deemed to have taken place.

5. In proceedings concerned with the enforcement of judgments, the courts of the Contracting State in which the judgment has been or is to be enforced.

Section 6. Prorogation of jurisdiction

Article 17

If the parties, one or more of whom is domiciled in a Contracting State, have agreed that a court or the courts of a Contracting State are to have jurisdiction to settle any disputes which have arisen or which may arise in connection with a particular legal relationship, that court or those courts shall have exclusive jurisdiction. Such an agreement conferring jurisdiction shall be either—

(a) in writing or evidenced in writing, or
(b) in a form which accords with practices which the parties have established between themselves, or
(c) in international trade or commerce, in a form which accords with a usage of which the parties are or ought to have been aware and which in such trade or commerce is widely known to, and regularly observed by, parties to contracts or the type involved in the particular trade or commerce concerned.

Where such an agreement is concluded by parties, none of whom is domiciled in a Contracting State, the courts of other Contracting States shall have no jurisdiction over their disputes unless the court or courts chosen have declined jurisdiction.

The court or courts of a Contracting State on which a trust instrument has conferred jurisdiction shall have exclusive jurisdiction in any proceedings brought against a settlor, trustee or beneficiary, if relations between these persons or their rights or obligations under the trust are involved.

Agreements or provisions of a trust instrument conferring jurisdiction shall have no legal force if they are contrary to the provisions of Articles 12 or 15, or if the courts whose jurisdiction they purport to exclude have exclusive jurisdiction by virtue of Article 16.

If an agreement conferring jurisdiction was concluded for the benefit of only one of the parties, that party shall retain the right to bring proceedings in any other court which has jurisdiction by virtue of this Convention.

In matters relating to individual contracting of employment an agreement conferring jurisdiction shall have legal force only if it is entered into after the dispute has arisen or if the employee invokes it to seise courts other than those for the defendant's domicile or those specified in Article 5(1).

Article 18

Apart from jurisdiction derived from other provisions of this Convention, a court of a Contracting State before whom a defendant enters an appearance shall have jurisdiction. This rule shall not apply where appearance was entered solely to contest the jurisdiction, or where another court has exclusive jurisdiction by virtue of Article 16.

Section 7. Examination as to jurisdiction and admissibility

Article 19

Where a court of a Contracting State is seised of a claim which is principally concerned with a matter over which the courts of another Contracting State have exclusive jurisdiction by virtue of Article 16, it shall declare of its own motion that it has no jurisdiction.

Article 20

Where a defendant domiciled in one Contracting State is sued in a court of another Contracting State and does not enter an appearance, the court shall declare of its own motion that it has no jurisdiction unless its jurisdiction is derived from the provisions of the Convention.

The court shall stay the proceedings so long as it is not shown that the defendant has been able to receive the document instituting the proceedings or an equivalent document in sufficient time to enable him to arrange for his defence, or that all necessary steps have been taken to this end.

The provisions of the foregoing paragraph shall be replaced by those of Article 15 of the Hague Convention of 15th November 1965 on the service abroad of judicial and extrajudicial documents in civil or commercial matters, if the document instituting the proceedings or notice thereof had to be transmitted abroad in accordance with that Convention.

Section 8. Lis pendens—related actions

Article 21

Where proceedings involving the same cause of action and between the same parties are brought in the courts of different Contracting States, any court other than the court first seised shall of its own motion stay its proceedings until such time as the jurisdiction of the court first seised is established.

Where the jurisdiction of the court first seised is established, any court other than the court first seised shall decline jurisdiction in favour of that court.

Article 22

Where related actions are brought in the courts of different Contracting States, any court other than the court first seised may, while the actions are pending at first instance, stay its proceedings.

A court other than the court first seised may also, on the application of one of the parties, decline jurisdiction if the law of that court permits the consolidation of related actions and the court first seised has jurisdiction over both actions.

For the purposes of this Article, actions are deemed to be related where they are so closely connected that it is expedient to hear and determine them together to avoid the risk of irreconcilable judgments resulting from separate proceedings.

Article 23

Where actions come within the exclusive jurisdiction of several courts, any court other than the court first seised shall decline jurisdiction in favour of that court.

Section 9. Provisional, including protective, measures

Article 24

Application may be made to the courts of a Contracting State for such provisional, including protective, measures as may be available under the law of that State, even if, under this Convention, the courts of another Contracting State have jurisdiction as to the substance of the matter.

TITLE III. RECOGNITION AND ENFORCEMENT

Article 25

For the purposes of this Convention, "judgment" means any judgment given by a court or tribunal of a Contracting State, whatever the judgment may be called, including a decree, order, decision or writ of execution, as well as the determination of costs or expenses by an officer of the court.

Section 1. Recognition

Article 26

A judgment given in a Contracting State shall be recognised in the other Contracting States without any special procedure being required.

Any interested party who raises the recognition of a judgment as the principal issue in a dispute may, in accordance with the procedures provided for in Sections 2 and 3 of this title, apply for a decision that the judgment be recognized.

If the outcome of proceedings in a court of a Contracting State depends on the determination of an incidental question of recognition that court shall have jurisdiction over that question.

Article 27

A judgment shall not be recognized—

1. If such recognition is contrary to public policy in the State in which recognition is sought.
2. Where it was given in default of appearance, if the defendant was not duly served with the document which instituted the proceedings or with an equivalent document in sufficient time to enable him to arrange for his defence.
3. If the judgment is irreconcilable with a judgment given in a dispute between the same parties in the State in which recognition is sought.
4. If the court of the State of origin, in order to arrive at its judgment, has decided a preliminary question concerning the status or legal capacity or natural persons, rights in property arising out of a matrimonial relationship, wills or succession in a way that conflicts with a rule of the private international law of the State in which the recognition is sought, unless the same result would have been reached by the application of the rules of private international law of that State.
5. If the judgment is irreconcilable with an earlier judgment given in a non-contracting State involving the same cause of action and between the same parties, provided that this latter judgment fulfills the conditions necessary for its recognition in the state addressed.

Article 28

Moreover, a judgment shall not be recognized if it conflicts with the provisions of Sections 3, 4 or 5 of Title II, or in a case provided for in Article 59.

In its examination of the grounds of jurisdiction referred to in the foregoing paragraph, the court or authority applied to shall be bound by the findings of fact on which the court of the State of origin based its jurisdiction.

Subject to the provisions of the first paragraph, the jurisdiction of the court of the State of origin may not be reviewed; the test of public policy referred to in point 1 of Article 27 may not be applied to the rules relating to jurisdiction.

Article 29

Under no circumstances may a foreign judgment be reviewed as to its substance.

Article 30

A court of a Contracting State in which recognition is sought of a judgment given in another Contracting State may stay the proceedings if an ordinary appeal against the judgment has been lodged.

A court of a Contracting State in which recognition is sought of a judgment given in Ireland or the United Kingdom may stay the proceedings if enforcement is suspended in the State of origin, by reason of an appeal.

Section 2. Enforcement

Article 31

A judgment given in a Contracting State and enforceable in that State shall be enforced in another Contracting State when, on the application of any interested party, it has been declared enforceable there.

However, in the United Kingdom, such a judgment shall be enforced in England and Wales, in Scotland, or in Northern Ireland when, on the application of any interested party, it has been registered for enforcement in that part of the United Kingdom.

Article 32

1. The application shall be submitted—

— in Belgium, to the tribunal de première instance or rechtbank van eerste aanleg,
— in Denmark, to the byret,
— in the Federal Republic of Germany, to the presiding judge of a chamber of the Landgericht,
— in Greece, to the Μονομελές Πρωτοδικείο,
— in Spain, to the Juzgado de Primera Instancia,
— in France, to the presiding judge of the tribunal de grande instance,
— in Ireland, to the High Court,
— in Italy, to the corte d'appello,
— in Luxembourg, to the presiding judge of the tribunal d'arrondissement,
— in the Netherlands, to the presiding judge of the arrondissementsrechtbank,
— in Portugal, to the Tribunal Jucicial de Círculo,
— in the United Kingdom—

    (a) in England and Wales, to the High Court of Justice, or in the case of maintenance judgment to the Magistrates' Court on transmission by the Secretary of State;
    (b) in Scotland, to the Court of Session, or in the case of a maintenance judgment to the Sheriff Court on transmission by the Secretary of State;
    (c) in Northern Ireland, to the High Court of Justice, or in the case of a maintenance judgment to the Magistrates' Court on transmission by the Secretary of State.

2. The jurisdiction of local courts shall be determined by reference to the place of domicile of the party against whom enforcement is sought. If he is not domiciled in the State in which enforcement is sought it shall be determined by reference to the place of enforcement.

Article 33

The procedure for making the application shall be governed by the law of the State in which enforcement is sought.

The applicant must give an address for service of process within the area of jurisdiction of the court applied to. However, if the law of the State in which enforcement is sought does not provide for the furnishing of such an address, the applicant shall appoint a representative *ad litem*.

The documents referred to in Articles 46 and 47 shall be attached to the application.

Article 34

The court applied to shall give its decision without delay; the party against whom enforcement is sought shall not at this stage of the proceedings be entitled to make any submissions on the application.

The application may be refused only for one of the reasons specified in Articles 27 and 28.

Under no circumstances may the foreign judgment be reviewed as to its substance.

Article 35

The appropriate officer of the court shall without delay bring the decision given on the application to the notice of the applicant in accordance with the procedure laid down by the law of the State in which enforcement is sought.

Article 36

If enforcement is authorized, the party against whom enforcement is sought may appeal against the decision within one month of service thereof.

If that party is domiciled in a Contracting State other than that in which the decision authorizing enforcement was given, the time for appealing shall be two months and shall run from the date of service, either on him in person or at his residence. No extension of time may be granted on account of distance.

Article 37

1. An appeal against the decision authorizing enforcement shall be lodged in accordance with the rules governing procedure in contentious matters—

  — in Belgium, with the tribunal de première instance or rechtbank van eerste aanleg,
  — in Denmark, with the landsret,
  — in the Federal Republic of Germany, with the Oberlandesgericht,
  — in Greece, with the Εφετείο,
  — in Spain, with the Audiencia Provincial,
  — in France, with the cour d'appel,
  — in Ireland, with the High Court,
  — in Italy, with the corte d'appello,
  — in Luxembourg, with the Cour supérieure de justice sitting as a court of civil appeal,
  — in the Netherlands, with the arrondissementsrechtbank,
  — in Portugal, with the Tribunal de Relação,
  — in the United Kingdom—

    (a) in England and Wales, with the High Court of Justice, or in the case of a maintenance judgment with the Magistrates' Court;
    (b) in Scotland, with the Court of Session, or in the case of a maintenance judgment with the Sheriff Court;
    (c) in Northern Ireland, with the High Court of Justice, or in the case of a maintenance judgment with the Magistrates' Court.

2. The judgment given on the appeal may be contested only—

  — in Belgium, Greece, Spain, France, Italy, Luxembourg and in the Netherlands, by an appeal in cassation,
  — in Denmark, by an appeal to the højesteret, with the leave of the Minister of Justice,
  — in the Federal Republic of Germany, by a Rechtsbeschwerde,
  — in Ireland, by an appeal on a point of law to the Supreme Court,
  — in Portugal, by an appeal on a point of law,
  — in the United Kingdom, by a single further appeal on a point of law.

Article 38

The court with which the appeal under Article 37(1) is lodged may, on the application of the appellant, stay the proceedings if an ordinary appeal has been lodged against the judgment in the State of origin or if the time for such an appeal has not yet expired; in the latter case, the court may specify the time within which such an appeal is to be lodged.

Where the judgment was given in Ireland or the United Kingdom, any form of appeal available in the State of origin shall be treated as an ordinary appeal for the purposes of the first paragraph.

The court may also make enforcement conditional on the provision of such security as it shall determine.

Article 39

During the time specified for an appeal pursuant to Article 36 and until any such appeal has been determined, no measures of enforcement may be taken other than protective measures taken against the property of the party against whom enforcement is sought.

The decision authorizing enforcement shall carry with it the power to proceed to any such protective measures.

Article 40

1. If the application for enforcement is refused, the applicant may appeal—

— in Belgium, to the cour d'appel or hof van berop,
— in Denmark, to the landsret,
— in the Federal Republic of Germany, to the Oberlandesgericht,
— in Greece, to the Εφετείο,
— in Spain, to the Audiencia Provincial,
— in France, to the cour d'appel,
— in Ireland, to the High Court,
— in Italy, to the corte d'appello,
— in Luxembourg, to the Cour supérieure de justice sitting as a court of civil appeal,
— in the Netherlands, to the gerechtshof,
— in Portugal, to the Tribunal da Relação,
— in the United Kingdom—

　(a) in England and Wales, to the High Court of Justice, or in the case of a maintenance judgment to the Magistrates' Court;
　(b) in Scotland, to the Court of Session, or in the case of a maintenance judgment to the Sheriff Court;
　(c) in Northern Ireland, to the High Court of Justice, or in the case of a maintenance judgment to the Magistrates' Court.

2. The party against whom enforcement is sought shall be summoned to appear before the appellate court. If he fails to appear, the provisions of the second and third paragraphs of Article 20 shall apply even where he is not domiciled in any of the Contracting States.

Article 41

A judgment given on appeal provided for in Article 40 may be contested only—

— in Belgium, Greece, Spain, France, Italy, Luxembourg and in the Netherlands, by an appeal in cassation,
— in Denmark, by an appeal to the højesteret, with the leave of the Minister of Justice,
— in the Federal Republic of Germany, by a Rechtsbeschwerde,
— in Ireland, by an appeal on a point of law to the Supreme Court,
— in Portugal, by an appeal on a point of law,
— in the United Kingdom, by a single further appeal on a point of law.

Article 42

Where a foreign judgment has been given in respect of several matters and enforcement cannot be authorized for all of them, the court shall authorize enforcement for one or more of them.

An applicant may request partial enforcement of a judgment.

Article 43

A foreign judgment which orders a periodic payment by way of a penalty shall be enforceable in the State in which enforcement is sought only if the amount of the payment has been finally determined by the courts of the State of origin.

Article 44

An applicant who, in the State of origin has benefited from complete or partial legal aid or exemption from costs or expenses, shall be entitled in the procedures provided for in Articles 32 to 35, to benefit from the most favourable legal aid or the most extensive exemption from costs or expenses provided for by the law of the State addressed.

However, an applicant who requests the enforcement of a decision given by an administrative authority in Denmark in respect of a maintenance order may, in the State addressed, claim the benefits referred to in the first paragraph if he presents a statement from the Danish Ministry of Justice to the effect that he fulfils the economic requirements to qualify for the grant of complete or partial legal aid or exemption from costs or expenses.

Article 45

No security, bond or deposit, however described, shall be required or a party who in one Contracting State applies for enforcement of a judgment given in another Contracting State on the ground that he is a foreign national or that he is not domiciled or resident in the State in which enforcement is sought.

Section 3. Common provisions

Article 46

A party seeking recognition or applying for enforcement of a judgment shall produce—

1. a copy of the judgment which satisfies the conditions necessary to establish its authenticity;
2. in the case of a judgment given in default, the original or a certified true copy of the document which establishes that the party in default was served with the document instituting the proceedings or with an equivalent document.

Article 47

A party applying for enforcement shall also produce—

1. documents which establish that, according to the law of the State of origin the judgment is enforceable and has been served;
2. where appropriate, a document showing that the applicant is in receipt of legal aid in the State of origin.

Article 48

If the documents specified in point 2 of Articles 46 and 47 are not produced, the court may specify a time for their production, accept equivalent documents or, if it considers that it has sufficient information before it, dispense with their production.

If the court so requires, a translation of the documents shall be produced; the translation shall be certified by a person qualified to do so in one of the Contracting States.

Article 49

No legalization or other similar formality shall be required in respect of the documents referred to in Articles 46 or 47 or the second paragraph of Article 48, or in respect of a document appointing a representative *ad litem*.

TITLE IV. AUTHENTIC INSTRUMENTS AND COURT SETTLEMENTS

Article 50

A document which has been formally drawn up or registered as an authentic instrument and is enforceable in one Contracting State shall, in another Contracting State, be declared enforceable there, on application made in accordance with the procedures provided for in Article 31 *et seq*. The application may be refused only if enforcement of the instrument is contrary to public policy in the State addressed.

The instrument produced must satisfy the conditions necessary to establish its authenticity in the State of origin.

The provisions of Section 3 of Title III shall apply as appropriate.

Article 51

A settlement which has been approved by a court in the course of proceedings and is enforceable in the State in which it was concluded shall be enforceable in the State addressed under the same conditions as authentic instruments.

TITLE V. GENERAL PROVISIONS

Article 52

In order to determine whether a party is domiciled in the Contracting State whose courts are seised of a matter, the Court shall apply its internal law.

If a party is not domiciled in the State whose courts are seised of the matter, then, in order to determine whether the party is domiciled in another Contracting State, the court shall apply the law of that State.

Article 53

For the purposes of this Convention, the seat of a company or other legal person or association of natural or legal persons shall be treated as its domicile. However, in order to determine that seat, the court shall apply its rules of private international law.

In order to determine whether a trust is domiciled in the Contracting State whose courts are seised of the matter, the court shall apply its rules of private international law.

TITLE VI. TRANSITIONAL PROVISIONS

Article 54

The provisions of the Convention shall apply only to legal proceedings instituted and to documents formally drawn up or registered as authentic instruments after its entry into force in the State of origin and, where recognition or enforcement of a judgment or authentic instruments is sought, in the State addressed.

However, judgments given after the date of entry into force of this Convention between the State of origin and the State addressed in proceedings instituted before that date shall be recognized and enforced in accordance with the provisions of Title III if jurisdiction was founded upon rules which accorded with those provided for either in Title II of this Convention or in a convention concluded between the State of origin and the State addressed which was in force when the proceedings were instituted.

If the parties to a dispute concerning a contract had agreed in writing before 1st June 1988 for Ireland or before 1st January 1987 for the United Kingdom that the contract was to be governed by the law of Ireland or of a part of the United Kingdom, the courts of Ireland or of that part of the United Kingdom shall retain the right to exercise jurisdiction in the dispute.

Article 54a

For a period of three years from 1st November 1986 for Denmark and from 1st June 1988 for Ireland, jurisdiction in maritime matters shall be determined in these States not only in accordance with the provisions of Title II, but also in accordance with the provisions of paragraphs 1 to 6 following. However, upon the entry into force of the International Convention relating to the arrest of sea-going ships, signed at Brussels on 10th May 1952, for one of these States, these provisions shall cease to have effect for that State.

1. A person who is domiciled in a Contracting State may be sued in the Courts of one of the States mentioned above in respect of a maritime claim if the ship to which the claim relates or any other ship owned by him has been arrested by judicial process with the territory of the latter State to secure the claim, or could have been so arrested there but bail or other security has been given, and either—

(a) the claimant is domiciled in the latter State, or
(b) the claim arose in the latter State, or
(c) the claim concerns the voyage during which the arrest was made or could have been made, or
(d) the claim arises out of a collision or out of damage caused by a ship to another ship or to goods or persons on board either ship, either by the execution or non-execution of a manoeuvre or by the non-observance of regulations, or
(e) the claim is for salvage, or
(f) the claim is in respect of a mortgage or hypothecation of the ship arrested.

2. A claimant may arrest either the particular ship to which the maritime claim relates, or any other ship which is owned by the person who was, at the time when the maritime claim arose, the owner of the particular ship. However, only the particular ship to which the maritime claim relates may be arrested in respect of the maritime claims set out in (5)(o), (p) or (q) of this Article.

3. Ships shall be deemed to be in the same ownership when all the shares therein are owned by the same person or persons.

4. When in the case of a charter by demise of a ship the charterer alone is liable in respect of a maritime claim relating to that ship, the claimant may arrest that ship or any other ship owned by the charterer, but no other ship owned by the owner may be arrested in respect of such claim. The same shall apply to any case in which a person other than the owner of a ship is liable in respect of a maritime claim relating to that ship.

5. The expression "maritime claim" means a claim arising out of one or more of the following—

(a) damage caused by any ship either in collision or otherwise;
(b) loss of life or personal injury caused by any ship or occurring in connection with the operation on any ship;
(c) salvage;
(d) agreement relating to the use of hire of any ship whether by charterparty or otherwise;
(e) agreement relating to the carriage of goods in any ship whether by charterparty or otherwise;
(f) loss of or damage to goods including baggage carried in any ship;
(g) general average;
(h) bottomry;
(i) towage;
(j) pilotage;
(k) goods or materials wherever supplied to a ship for her operation or maintenance;
(l) construction, repair or equipment of any ship or dock charges and dues;
(m) wages of master, officers or crew;
(n) master's disbursements, including disbursements made by shippers, charterers or agents on behalf of a ship or her owner;
(o) dispute as to the title to or ownership of any ship;
(p) disputes between co-owners of any ship as to the ownership, possession, employment or earnings of that ship;

(q) the mortgage or hypothecation of any ship.

6. In Denmark, the expression "arrest" shall be deemed as regards the maritime claims referred to in 5(o) and (p) of this Article, to include a "forbud", where that is the only procedure allowed in respect of such a claim under Articles 646 to 653 of the law on civil procedure (lov om rettens pleje).

TITLE VII. RELATIONSHIP TO OTHER CONVENTIONS

Article 55

Subject to the provisions of the second subparagraph of Article 54, and of Article 56, this Convention shall, for the States which are parties to it, supersede the following conventions concluded between two or more of them—

- the Convention between Belgium and France on jurisdiction and the validity and enforcement of judgments, arbitration awards and authentic instruments, signed at Paris on 8th July 1899,
- the Convention between Belgium and the Netherlands on jurisdiction, bankruptcy, and the validity and enforcement of judgments, arbitration awards and authentic instruments, signed at Brussels on 28th March 1925,
- the Convention between France and Italy on the enforcement of judgments in civil and commercial matters, signed at Rome on 3rd June 1930,
- the Convention between the United Kingdom and the French Republic providing for the reciprocal enforcement of judgments in civil and commercial matters, with Protocol, signed at Paris on 18th January 1934,
- the Convention between the United Kingdom and the Kingdom of Belgium providing for the reciprocal enforcement of judgments in civil and commercial matters, with Protocol, signed at Brussels on 2nd May 1934,
- the Convention between Germany and Italy on the recognition and enforcement of judgments in civil and commercial matters, signed at Rome on 9th March 1936,
- the Convention between the Federal Republic of Germany and the Kingdom of Belgium on the mutual recognition and enforcement of judgments, arbitration awards and authentic instruments in civil and commercial matters, signed at Bonn on 30th June 1958,
- the Convention between the Kingdom of the Netherlands and the Italian Republic on the recognition and enforcement of judgments in civil and commercial matters, signed at Rome on 17th April 1959,
- the Convention between the United Kingdom and the Federal Republic of Germany for the reciprocal recognition and enforcement of judgments in civil and commercial matters, signed at Bonn on 14th July 1960,
- the Convention between the Kingdom of Greece and the Federal Republic of Germany for the reciprocal recognition and enforcement of judgments, settlements and authentic instruments in civil and commercial matters, signed in Athens on 4th November 1961,
- the Convention between the Kingdom of Belgium and the Italian Republic on the recognition and enforcement of judgments and other enforceable instruments in civil and commercial matters, signed at Rome on 6th April 1962,
- the Convention between the Kingdom of the Netherlands and the Federal Republic of Germany on the mutual recognition and enforcement of judgments and other enforceable instruments in civil and commercial matters, signed at The Hague on 30th August 1962,
- the Convention between the United Kingdom and the Republic of Italy for the reciprocal recognition and enforcement of judgments in civil and commercial matters, signed at Rome on 7th February 1964, with amending Protocol signed at Rome on 14th July 1970,
- the Convention between the United Kingdom of the Netherlands providing for the reciprocal recognition and enforcement of judgments in civil matters, signed at The Hague on 17th November 1967,
- the Convention between Spain and France on the recognition and enforcement of judgment arbitration awards in civil and commercial matters, signed at Paris on 28th May 1969,

— the Convention between Spain and Italy regarding legal aid and the recognition and enforcement of judgments in civil and commercial matters, signed at Madrid on 22nd May 1973,

— the Convention between Spain and the Federal Republic of Germany on the recognition and enforcement of judgments, settlements and enforceable authentic instruments in civil and commercial matters, signed at Bonn on 14th November 1983,

and, in so far as it is in force—

— the Treaty between Belgium, the Netherlands and Luxembourg on jurisdiction, bankruptcy, and the validity and enforcement of judgments, arbitration awards and authentic instruments, signed at Brussels on 24th November 1961.

Article 56

The Treaty and the conventions referred to in Article 55 shall continue to have effect in relation to matters to which this Convention does not apply.

They shall continue to have effect in respect of judgments given and documents formally drawn up or registered as authentic instruments before the entry into force of this Convention.

Article 57

1. This Convention shall not affect any conventions to which the Contracting States are or will be parties and which in relation to particular matters, govern jurisdiction or the recognition or enforcement of judgments.

2. With a view to its uniform interpretation, paragraph 1 shall be applied in the following manner—

(a) this Convention shall not prevent a court of a Contracting State which is a party to a convention on a particular matter from assuming jurisdiction in accordance with that Convention, even where the defendant is domiciled in another Contracting State which is not a party to that Convention. The court hearing the action shall, in any event, apply Article 20 of this Convention;

(b) judgments given in a Contracting State by a court in the exercise of jurisdiction provided for in a convention on a particular matter shall be recognized and enforced in the other Contracting State in accordance with this Convention.

Where a convention on a particular matter to which both the State of origin and the State addressed are parties lays down conditions for the recognition or enforcement of judgments, those conditions shall apply. In any event, the provisions of this Convention which concern the procedure for recognition and enforcement of judgments may be applied.

3. This Convention shall not affect the application of provisions which, in relation to particular matters, govern jurisdiction or the recognition or enforcement of judgments and which are or will be contained in acts of the institutions of the European Communities or in national laws harmonized in implementation of such acts.

Article 58

Until such time as the Convention on jurisdiction and the enforcement of judgments in civil and commercial matters, signed at Lugano on 16th September 1988, takes effect with regard to France and the Swiss Confederation, this Convention shall not affect the rights granted to Swiss nationals by the Convention between France and the Swiss Confederation on jurisdiction and enforcement of judgments in civil matters, signed in Paris on 15th June 1869.

Article 59

This Convention shall not prevent a Contracting State from assuming, in a convention on the recognition and enforcement of judgments, an obligation towards a third State not to recognize judgments given in other Contracting States against defendants domiciled or habitually resident in the third State where, in cases provided for in Article 4, the judgment could only be founded on a ground of jurisdiction specified in the second paragraph of Article 3.

However, a Contracting State may not assume an obligation towards a third State not to recognize a judgment given in another Contracting State by a court basing its jurisdiction on the purchase within that State of property belonging to the defendant, or the seizure by the plaintiff of property situated there—

1. if the action is brought to assert or declare proprietary or possessory rights in that property, seeks to obtain authority to dispose of it, or arises from another issue relating to such property, or
2. if the property constitutes the security for a debt which is the subject-matter of the action.

TITLE VIII. FINAL PROVISIONS

Article 60

[Deleted]

Article 61

This Convention shall be ratified by the signatory States. The instruments of ratification shall be deposited with the Secretary-General of the Council of the European Communities.

Article 62

This Convention shall enter into force on the first day of the third month following the deposit of the instrument of ratification by the last signatory State to take this step.

Article 63

The Contracting States recognize that any State which becomes a member of the European Economic Community shall be required to accept this Convention as a basis for the negotiations between the Contracting States and that State necessary to ensure the implementation of the last paragraph of Article 220 of the Treaty establishing the European Economic Community.

The necessary adjustments may be the subject of a special convention between the Contracting States of the one part and the new Member States of the other part.

Article 64

The Secretary-General of the Council of the European Communities shall notify the signatory States of—

(a) the deposit of each instrument of ratification;
(b) the date of entry into force of this Convention;
(c) [Deleted]
(d) any declaration received pursuant to Article IV of the Protocol;
(e) any communication made pursuant to Article VI of the Protocol.

Article 65

The Protocol annexed to this Convention by common accord of the Contracting States shall form an integral part thereof.

Article 66

This Convention is concluded for an unlimited period.

Article 67

Any Contracting State may request the revision of this Convention. In this event, a revision conference shall be convened by the President of the Council of the European Communities.

Article 68

This Convention, drawn up in a single original in the Dutch, French, German and Italian languages, all four texts being equally authentic, shall be deposited in the archives of the Secretariat of the Council of the European Communities. The Secretary-General shall transmit a certified copy to the Government of each signatory State.

(Signatures of Plenipotentiaries of the original six Contracting States)

ANNEXED PROTOCOL

The High Contracting Parties have agreed upon the following provisions, which shall be annexed to the Convention.

Article I

Any person domiciled in Luxembourg who is sued in a court of another Contracting State pursuant to Article 5(1) may refuse to submit to the jurisdiction of that court. If the defendant does not enter an appearance the court shall declare of its own motion that it has no jurisdiction.

An agreement conferring jurisdiction, within the meaning of Article 17, shall be valid with respect to a person domiciled in Luxembourg only if that person has expressly and specifically so agreed.

Article II

Without prejudice to any more favourable provisions of national laws, persons domiciled in a Contracting State who are being prosecuted in the criminal courts of another Contracting State of which they are not nationals for an offence which was not intentionally committed may be defended by persons qualified to do so, even if they do not appear in person.

However, the court seised of the matter may order appearance in person; in the case of failure to appear, a judgment given in the civil action without the person concerned having have the opportunity to arrange for his defence need not be recognized or enforced in the other Contracting States.

Article III

In proceedings for the issue of an order for enforcement, no charge, duty or fee calculated by reference to the value of the matter in issue may be levied in the State in which enforcement is sought.

Article IV

Judicial and extrajudicial documents drawn up in one Contracting State which have to be served on persons in another Contracting State shall be transmitted in accordance with the procedures laid down in the conventions and agreements concluded between the Contracting States.

Unless the State in which service is to take place objects by declaration to the Secretary-General of the Council of the European Communities, such documents may also be sent by the appropriate public officers of the State in which the document has been drawn up directly to the appropriate public officers of the State in which the addressee is to be found. In this case the officer of the State of origin shall send a copy of the document to the officer of the State applied to who is competent to forward it to the addressee. The document shall be forwarded in the manner specified by the law of the State applied to. The forwarding shall be recorded by a certificate sent directly to the officer of the State of origin.

Article V

The jurisdiction specified in Articles 6(2) and 10 in actions on a warranty or guarantee or in any other third party proceedings may not be resorted to in the Federal Republic of Germany. In that State, any person domiciled in another Contracting State may be sued in the courts in pursuance of Articles 68, 72, 73 and 74 of the code of civil procedure (*Zivilprozeßordnung*) concerning third-party notices.

Judgments given in the other Contracting States by virtue of point 2 of Article 6 or Article 10 shall be recognized and enforced in the Federal Republic of Germany in accordance with Title III. Any effects which judgments given in that State may have on third parties by application of Articles 68, 72, 73 and 74 of the code of civil procedure (*Zivilprozeßordnung*) shall also be recognized in the other Contracting States.

Article Va

In matters relating to maintenance, the expression "court" includes the Danish administrative authorities.

Article Vb

In proceedings involving a dispute between the master and a member of the crew of a sea-going ship registered in Denmark, in Greece, in Ireland or in Portugal, concerning remuneration or other conditions of service, a court in a Contracting State shall establish whether the diplomatic or consular officer responsible for the ship has been notified of the dispute. It shall stay the proceedings so long as he has not been notified. It shall of its own motion decline jurisdiction if the officer, having been duly notified, has exercised the powers accorded to him in the matter by a consular convention, or in the absence of such a convention has, within the time allowed, raised any objection to the exercise of such jurisdiction.

Article Vc

Articles 52 and 53 of this Convention shall, when applied by Article 69(5) of the Convention for the European patent for the common market, signed at Luxembourg on 15th December 1975, to the provisions relating to "residence" in the English text of the Convention, operate as if "residence" in that text were the same as "domicile" in Articles 52 and 53.

Article Vd

Without prejudice to the jurisdiction of the European Patent Office under the Convention on the grant of European patents, signed at Munich on 5th October 1973, the courts of each Contracting State shall have exclusive jurisdiction, regardless of domicile, in proceedings concerned with the registration or validity of any European patent granted for that State which is not a Community patent by virtue of the provisions of Article 86 of the Convention for the European patent for the common market, signed at Luxembourg on 15th December 1975.

Article VI

The Contracting States shall communicate to the Secretary-General of the Council of the European Communities the text of any provisions of their laws which amend either those articles of their laws mentioned in the Convention or the lists of courts specified in Section 2 of Title III of the Convention.

(Signatures of Plenipotentiaries of the original six Contracting States)

SCHEDULE 3B (S. 2(2)). TEXT OF TITLES VI AND VII OF 1989 ACCESSION CONVENTION

TITLE VI

Transitional provisions

Article 29

1. The 1968 Convention and the 1971 Protocol, as amended by the 1978 Convention, the 1982 Convention and this Convention, shall apply only to legal proceedings instituted and to authentic instruments formally drawn up or registered after the entry into force of this Convention in the State of origin and, where recognition or enforcement of a judgment or authentic instrument is sought, in the State addressed.

2. However, judgments given after the date of entry into force of this Convention between the State of origin and the State addressed in proceedings instituted before that date shall be recognized and enforced in accordance with the provisions of Title III of the 1968 Convention, as amended by the 1978 Convention, the 1982 Convention and this Convention, if jurisdiction was founded upon rules which accorded with the provisions of Title II of the 1968 Convention, as amended, or with the provisions of a convention which was in force between the State of origin and the State addressed when the proceedings were instituted.

SCHEDULE 3C (S. 1(3) OF THE 1991 ACT). THE LUGANO CONVENTION (EXTRACTS)

TITLE II

Section 2. Special jurisdiction

Article 5

A person domiciled in a Contracting state may, in another Contracting State, be sued:

   1. in matters relating to a contract in the courts for the place of performance of the obligation in question; in matters relating to individual contracts of employment, this place is that where the employee habitually carries out his work, or if the employee does not habitually carry out his work in any one country, this place shall be the place of business through which he was engaged;

Section 5. Exclusive jurisdiction

Article 16

The following courts shall have exclusive jurisdiction, regardless of domicile:

   1. (a) in proceedings which have as their object rights *in rem* in immovable property or tenancies of immovable property, the courts of the Contracting State in which the property is situated;
      (b) however, in proceedings which have as their object tenancies of immovable property concluded for temporary private use for a maximum period of six consecutive months,

the courts of the Contracting State in which the defendant is domiciled shall also have jurisdiction, provided that the tenant is a natural person and neither party is domiciled in the Contracting State in which the property is situated;

Article 17

5. In matters relating to individual contracts of employment an agreement conferring jurisdiction shall have legal force only if it is entered into after the dispute has arisen.

TITLE III. RECOGNITION AND ENFORCEMENT

Section 1. Recognition

Article 28

Moreover, a judgment shall not be recognised if it conflicts with the provisions of Section 3, 4 or 5 of Title II or in a case provided for in Article 59.

A judgment may furthermore be refused recognition in any case provided for in Article 54B(3) or 57(4).

In its examination of the grounds of jurisdiction referred to in the foregoing paragraphs, the court or authority applied to shall be bound by the findings of fact on which the court of the State of origin based its jurisdiction.

Subject to the provisions of the first and second paragraphs, the jurisdiction of the court of the State of origin may not be reviewed; the test of public policy referred to in Article 27(1) may not be applied to the rules relating to jurisdiction.

TITLE VI. TRANSITIONAL PROVISIONS

Article 54

The provisions of this Convention shall apply only to legal proceedings instituted and to documents formally drawn up or registered as authentic instruments after its entry into force in the State of origin and, where recognition or enforcement of a judgment or authentic instrument is sought, in the State addressed.

However, judgments given after the date of entry into force of this Convention between the State of origin and the State addressed in proceedings instituted before that date shall be recognised and enforced in accordance with the provisions of Title III if jurisdiction was founded upon rules which accord with those provided for either in Title II of this Convention or in a convention concluded between the State of origin and the State addressed which was in force when the proceedings were instituted.

If the parties to a dispute concerning a contract had agreed in writing before the entry into force of this Convention that the contract was to be governed by the law of Ireland or of a part of the United Kingdom, the courts of Ireland or of that part of the United Kingdom shall retain the right to exercise jurisdiction in the dispute.

Article 54A

For a period of three years from the entry into force of this Convention for Denmark, Greece, Ireland, Iceland, Norway, Finland and Sweden, respectively, jurisdiction in maritime matters shall be determined in these States not only in accordance with the provisions of Title II, but also in accordance with the provisions of paragraphs 1 to 7 following. However, upon the entry into force of the International Convention relating to the arrest of sea-going ships, signed at Brussels on 10 May 1952, for one of these States, these provisions shall cease to have effect for that State.

1. A person who is domiciled in a Contracting State may be sued in the courts of one of the States mentioned above in respect of a maritime claim if the ship to which the claim relates or any other ship owned by him has been arrested by judicial process within the territory of the latter State to secure the claim, or could have been so arrested there but bail or other security has been given, and either:

    (a) the claimant is domiciled in the latter State; or
    (b) the claim arose in the latter State; or
    (c) the claim concerns the voyage during which the arrest was made or could have been made; or
    (d) the claim arises out of a collision or out of damage caused by a ship to another ship or to goods or persons on board either ship, either by the execution or non-execution of a manoeuvre or by the non-observance of regulations; or
    (e) the claim is for salvage; or
    (f) the claim is in respect of a mortgage or hypothecation of a ship arrested.

2. A claimant may arrest either the particular ship to which the maritime claim relates, or any other ship which is owned by the person who was, at the time when the maritime claim arose, the owner of the particular ship. However, only the particular ship to which the maritime claim relates may be arrested in respect of the maritime claims set out in 5(o), (p) or (q) of this Article.

3. Ships shall be deemed to be in the same ownership when all the shares therein are owned by the same person or persons.

4. When in the case of a charter by demise of a ship the charterer alone is liable in respect of a maritime claim relating to that ship, the claimant may arrest that ship or any other ship owned by the charterer, but no other ship owned by the owner may be arrested in respect of such claim. The same shall apply to any case in which a person other than the owner of a ship is liable in respect of a maritime claim relating to that ship.

5. The expression "maritime claim" means a claim arising out of one or more of the following:

    (a) damage caused by any ship either in collision or otherwise;
    (b) loss of life or personal injury caused by any ship or occurring in connection with the operation of any ship;
    (c) salvage;
    (d) agreement relating to the use or hire of any ship whether by charterparty or otherwise;
    (e) agreement relating to the carriage of goods in any ship whether by charterparty or otherwise;
    (f) loss of or damage to goods including baggage carried in any ship;
    (g) general average;
    (h) bottomry;
    (i) towage;
    (j) pilotage;
    (k) goods or materials wherever supplied to a ship for her operation or maintenance;
    (l) construction, repair or equipment of any ship or dock charges and dues;
    (m) wages of masters, officers or crew;
    (n) master's disbursements, including disbursements made by shippers, charterers or agents on behalf of a ship or her owner;
    (o) dispute as to the title to or ownership of any ship;
    (p) disputes between co-owners of any ship as to the ownership, possession, employment or earnings of that ship;
    (q) the mortgage or hypothecation of any ship.

6. In Denmark, the expression "arrest" shall be deemed, as regards the maritime claims referred to in 5.(o) and (p) of this Article, to include a "forbud", where that is the only procedure allowed in respect of such a claim under Articles 646 to 653 of the law on civil procedure (lov om rettens pleje).

7. In Iceland, the expression "arrest" shall be deemed, as regards the maritime claims referred to in 5.(o) and (p) of this Article, to include a "lögbann", where that is the only procedure allowed in

respect of such a claim under Chapter III of the law on arrest and injunction (lög um kyrrsetningu og lögbann).

TITLE VII. RELATIONSHIP TO THE BRUSSELS CONVENTION AND TO OTHER CONVENTIONS

Article 54B

1. This Convention shall not prejudice the application by the Member States of the European Communities of the Convention on Jurisdiction and the Enforcement of Judgments in Civil and Commercial Matters, signed at Brussels on 27 September 1968 and of the Protocol on interpretation of that Convention by the Court of Justice, signed at Luxembourg on 3 June 1971, as amended by the Conventions of Accession to the said Convention and the said Protocol by the States acceding to the European Communities, all of these Conventions and the Protocol being hereinafter referred to as the "Brussels Convention".

2. However, this Convention shall in any event be applied:

    (a) in matters of jurisdiction, where the defendant is domiciled in the territory of a Contracting State which is not a member of the European Communities, or where Article 16 or 17 of this Convention confers a jurisdiction on the courts of such a Contracting State;

    (b) in relation to a *lis pendens* or to related actions as provided for in Articles 21 and 22, when proceedings are instituted in a Contracting State which is not a member of the European Communities and in a Contracting State which is a member of the European Communities;

    (c) in matters of recognition and enforcement, where either the State of origin or the State addressed is not a member of the European Communities.

3. In addition to the grounds provided for in Title III recognition or enforcement may be refused if the ground of jurisdiction on which the judgment has been based differs from that resulting from this Convention and recognition or enforcement is sought against a party who is domiciled in a Contracting State which is not a member of the European Communities, unless the judgment may otherwise be recognised or enforced under any rule of law in the State addressed.

Article 55

Subject to the provisions of the second paragraph of Article 54 and of Article 56, this Convention shall, for the States which are parties to it, supersede the following conventions concluded between two or more of them:

— the Convention between the Swiss Confederation and France on jurisdiction and enforcement of judgments in civil matters, signed at Paris on 15 June 1869,

— the Treaty between the Swiss Confederation and Spain on the mutual enforcement of judgments in civil or commercial matters, signed at Madrid on 19 November 1896,

— the Convention between the Swiss Confederation and the German Reich on the recognition and enforcement of judgments and arbitration awards, signed at Berne on 2 November 1929,

— the Convention between Denmark, Finland, Iceland, Norway and Sweden on the recognition and enforcement of judgments, signed at Copenhagen on 16 March 1932,

— the Convention between the Swiss Confederation and Italy on the recognition and enforcement of judgments, signed at Rome on 3 January 1933,

— the Convention between Sweden and the Swiss Confederation on the recognition and enforcement of judgments and arbitral awards, signed at Stockholm on 15 January 1936,

— the Convention between the Kingdom of Belgium and Austria on the reciprocal recognition and enforcement of judgments and authentic instruments relating to maintenance obligations, signed at Vienna on 25 October 1957,

— the Convention between the Swiss Confederation and Belgium on the recognition and enforcement of judgments and arbitration awards, signed at Berne on 29 April 1959,

— the Convention between the Federal Republic of Germany and Austria on the reciprocal recognition and enforcement of judgments, settlements and authentic instruments in civil and commercial matters, signed at Vienna on 6 June 1959,

— the Convention between the Kingdom of Belgium and Austria on the reciprocal recognition and enforcement of judgments, arbitral awards and authentic instruments in civil and commercial matters, signed at Vienna on 16 June 1959,

— the Convention between Austria and the Swiss Confederation on the recognition and enforcement of judgments, signed at Berne on 16 December 1960,

— the Convention between Norway and the United Kingdom providing for the reciprocal recognition and enforcement of judgments in civil matters, signed at London on 12 June 1961,

— the Convention between the United Kingdom and Austria providing for the reciprocal recognition and enforcement of judgments in civil and commercial matters, signed at Vienna on 14 July 1961, with amending Protocol signed at London on 6 March 1970,

— the Convention between the Kingdom of the Netherlands and Austria on the reciprocal recognition and enforcement of judgments and authentic instruments in civil and commercial matters, signed at The Hague on 6 February 1963,

— the Convention between France and Austria on the recognition and enforcement of judgments and authentic instruments in civil and commercial matters, signed at Vienna on 15 July 1966,

— the Convention between Luxembourg and Austria on the recognition and enforcement of judgments and authentic instruments in civil and commercial matters, signed at Luxembourg on 29 July 1971,

— the Convention between Italy and Austria on the recognition and enforcement of judgments in civil and commercial matters, of judicial settlements and of authentic instruments, signed at Rome on 16 November 1971,

— the Convention between Norway and the Federal Republic of Germany on the recognition and enforcement of judgments and enforceable documents, in civil and commercial matters, signed at Oslo on 17 June 1977,

— the Convention between Denmark, Finland, Iceland, Norway and Sweden on the recognition and enforcement of judgments in civil matters, signed at Copenhagen on 11 October 1977,

— the Convention between Austria and Sweden on the recognition and enforcement of judgments in civil matters, signed at Stockholm on 16 September 1982,

— the Convention between Austria and Spain on the recognition and enforcement of judgments, settlements and enforceable authentic instruments in civil and commercial matters, signed at Vienna on 17 February 1984,

— the Convention between Norway and Austria on the recognition and enforcement of judgments in civil matters, signed at Vienna on 21 May 1984, and

— the Convention between Finland and Austria on the recognition and enforcement of judgments in civil matters, signed at Vienna on 17 November 1986.

Article 56

The Treaty and the conventions referred to in Article 55 shall continue to have effect in relation to matters to which this Convention does not apply.

They shall continue to have effect in respect of judgments given and documents formally drawn up or registered as authentic instruments before the entry into force of this Convention.

Article 57

1. This Convention shall not affect any conventions to which the Contracting States are or will be parties and which, in relation to particular matters, govern jurisdiction or the recognition or enforcement of judgments.

2. This Convention shall not prevent a court of a Contracting State which is party to a convention referred to in the first paragraph from assuming jurisdiction in accordance with that convention,

even where the defendant is domiciled in a Contracting State which is not a party to that convention. The court hearing the action shall, in any event, apply Article 20 of this Convention.

3. Judgments given in a Contracting State by a court in the exercise of jurisdiction provided for in a convention referred to in the first paragraph shall be recognised and enforced in the other Contracting States in accordance with Title III of this Convention.

4. In addition to the grounds provided for in Title III, recognition or enforcement may be refused if the State addressed is not a contracting party to a convention referred to in the first paragraph and the person against whom recognition or enforcement is sought is domiciled in that State, unless the judgment may otherwise be recognised or enforced under any rule of law in the State addressed.

5. Where a convention referred to in the first paragraph to which both the State of origin and the State addressed are parties lays down conditions for the recognition or enforcement of judgments, those conditions shall apply. In any event, the provisions of this Convention which concern the procedures for recognition and enforcement of judgments may be applied.

Article 58

[None]

Article 59

This Convention shall not prevent a Contracting State from assuming, in a convention on the recognition and enforcement of judgments, an obligation towards a third State not to recognise judgments given in other Contracting States against defendants domiciled or habitually resident in the third State where, in cases provided for in Article 4, the judgment could only be founded on a ground of jurisdiction specified in the second paragraph of Article 3.

However, a Contracting State may not assume an obligation towards a third State not to recognise a judgment given in another Contracting State by a court basing its jurisdiction on the presence within that State of property belonging to the defendant, or the seizure by the plaintiff of property situated there:

1. if the action is brought to assert or declare proprietary or possessory rights in that property, seeks to obtain authority to dispose of it, or arises from another issue relating to such property, or
2. if the property constitutes the security for a debt which is the subject-matter of the action.

TITLE VIII. FINAL PROVISIONS

Article 60

The following may be parties to this Convention:
   (a) States which, at the time of the opening of this Convention for signature, are members of the European Communities or of the European Free Trade Association;
   (b) States which, after the opening of this Convention for signature, become members of the European Communities or of the European Free Trade Association;
   (c) States invited to accede in accordance with Article 62(1)(b).

Article 62

1. After entering into force this Convention shall be open to accession by:
   (a) the States referred to in Article 60(b);
   (b) other States which have been invited to accede upon a request made by one of the Contracting States to the depositary State. The depositary State shall invite the State concerned to accede only if, after having communicated the contents of the communications that this State intends to make in accordance with Article 63, it has obtained the unanimous agreement of the signatory States and the Contracting States referred to in Article 60(a) and (b).

2. If an acceding State wishes to furnish details for the purposes of Protocol No. 1, negotiations shall be entered into to that end. A negotiating conference shall be convened by the Swiss Federal Council.

3. In respect of an acceding State, the Convention shall take effect on the first day of the third month following the deposit of its instrument of accession.

4. However, in respect of an acceding State referred to in paragraph 1(a) or (b), the Convention shall take effect only in relations between the acceding State and the Contracting States which have not made any objections to the accession before the first day of the third month following the deposit of the instrument of accession.

Article 63

Each acceding State shall, when depositing its instrument of accession, communicate the information required for the application of Articles 3, 32, 37, 40, 41 and 55 of this Convention and furnish if need be, the details prescribed during the negotiations for the purposes of Protocol No. 1.

PROTOCOL NO. 1

ON CERTAIN QUESTIONS OF JURISDICTION, PROCEDURE AND ENFORCEMENT

The High Contracting Parties have agreed upon the following provisions, which shall be annexed to the Convention:

Article I

Any person domiciled in Luxembourg who is sued in a court of another Contracting State pursuant to Article 5(1) may refuse to submit to the jurisdiction of that court. If the defendant does not enter an appearance the court shall declare of its own motion that it has no jurisdiction.

An agreement conferring jurisdiction, within the meaning of Article 17, shall be valid with respect to a person domiciled in Luxembourg only if that person has expressly and specifically so agreed.

Article Ia

1. Switzerland reserves the right to declare, at the time of depositing its instrument of ratification, that a judgment given in another Contracting State shall be neither recognised nor enforced in Switzerland if the following conditions are met:

   (a) the jurisdiction of the court which has given the judgment is based only on Article 5(1) of this Convention; and
   (b) the defendant was domiciled in Switzerland at the time of the introduction of the proceedings; for the purposes of this Article, a company or other legal person is considered to be domiciled in Switzerland if it has its registered seat and the effective centre of activities in Switzerland; and
   (c) the defendant raises an objection to the recognition or enforcement of the judgment in Switzerland, provided that he has not waived the benefit of the declaration foreseen under this paragraph.

2. This reservation shall not apply to the extent that at the time recognition or enforcement is sought a derogation has been granted from Article 59 of the Swiss Federal Constitution. The Swiss Government shall communicate such derogations to the signatory States and the acceding States.

3. This reservation shall cease to have effect on 31 December 1999. It may be withdrawn at any time.

Article Ib

Any Contracting State may, by declaration made at the time of signing or of deposit of its instrument of ratification or of accession, reserve the right, notwithstanding the provisions of Article 28, not to recognise and enforce judgments given in the other Contracting States if the jurisdiction of the court of the State of origin is based, pursuant to Article 16(1)(b), exclusively on the domicile of the defendant in the State of origin, and the property is situated in the territory of the State which entered the reservation.

Article II

Without prejudice to any more favourable provisions of national laws, persons domiciled in a Contracting State who are being prosecuted in the criminal courts of another Contracting State of which they are not nationals for an offence which was not intentionally committed may be defended by persons qualified to do so, even if they do not appear in person.

However, the court seised of the matter may order appearance in person; in the case of failure to appear, a judgment given in the civil action without the person concerned having had the opportunity to arrange for his defence need not be recognised or enforced in the other Contracting States.

Article III

In proceedings for the issue of an order for enforcement, no charge, duty or fee calculated by reference to the value of the matter in issue may be levied in the State in which enforcement is sought.

Article IV

Judicial and extrajudicial documents drawn up in one Contracting State which have to be served on persons in another Contracting State shall be transmitted in accordance with the procedures laid down in the conventions and agreements concluded between the Contracting States.

Unless the State in which service is to take place objects by declaration to the Swiss Federal Council, such documents may also be sent by the appropriate public officers of the State in which the document has been drawn up directly to the appropriate public officers of the State in which the addressee is to be found. In this case the officer of the State of origin shall send a copy of the document to the officer of the State applied to who is competent to forward it to the addressee. The document shall be forwarded in the manner specified by the law of the State applied to. The forwarding shall be recorded by a certificate sent directly to the officer of the State of origin.

Article V

The jurisdiction specified in Articles 6(2) and 10 in actions on a warranty or guarantee or in any other third party proceedings may not be resorted to in the Federal Republic of Germany, in Spain, in Austria and in Switzerland. Any person domiciled in another Contracting State may be sued in the courts:

— of the Federal Republic of Germany, pursuant to Articles 68, 72, 73 and 74 of the code of civil procedure (Zivilprozeβordnung) concerning third-party notices,
— of Spain, pursuant to Article 1482 of the civil code,
— of Austria, pursuant to Article 21 of the code of civil procedure (Zivilprozeβordnung) concerning third-party notices,
— of Switzerland, pursuant to the appropriate provisions concerning third-party notices of the cantonal codes of civil procedure.

Judgments given in the other Contracting States by virtue of Article 6(2) or Article 10 shall be recognised and enforced in the Federal Republic of Germany, in Spain, in Austria and in Switzerland in accordance with Title III. Any effects which judgments given in these States may have on third parties by application of the provisions in the preceding paragraph shall also be recognised in other Contracting States.

Article Va

In matters relating to maintenance, the expression 'court' includes the Danish, Icelandic and Norwegian administrative authorities.

In civil and commercial matters, the expression 'court' includes the Finnish ulosotonhaltija/ överexekutor.

Article Vb

In proceedings involving a dispute between the master and a member of the crew of a sea-going ship registered in Denmark, in Greece, in Ireland, in Iceland, in Norway, in Portugal or in Sweden concerning remuneration or other conditions of service, a court in a Contracting State shall establish whether the diplomatic or consular officer responsible for the ship has been notified of the dispute. It shall stay the proceedings so long as he has not been notified. It shall of its own motion decline jurisdiction if the officer, having been duly notified, has exercised the powers accorded to him in the matter by a consular convention, or in the absence of such a convention has, within the time allowed, raised any objection to the exercise of such jurisdiction.

Article Vc

[None]

Article Vd

Without prejudice to the jurisdiction of the European Patent Office under the Convention on the grant of European patents, signed at Munich on 5 October 1973, the courts of each Contracting State shall have exclusive jurisdiction, regardless of domicile, in proceedings concerned with the registration or validity of any European patent granted for that State which is not a Community patent by virtue of the provision of Article 86 of the Convention for the European patent for the common market, signed at Luxembourg on 15 December 1975.

Article VI

The Contracting States shall communicate to the Swiss Federal Council the text of any provisions of their laws which amend either those provisions of their laws mentioned in the Convention or the lists of courts specified in Section 2 of Title III.

PROTOCOL NO. 2

ON THE UNIFORM INTERPRETATION OF THE CONVENTION

Preamble

The High Contracting Parties,

Having regard to Article 65 of this Convention,

Considering the substantial link between this Convention and the Brussels Convention,

Considering that the Court of Justice of the European Communities by virtue of the Protocol of 3 June 1971 has jurisdiction to give rulings on the interpretation of the provisions of the Brussels Convention,

Being aware of the rulings delivered by the Court of Justice of the European Communities on the interpretation of the Brussels Convention up to the time of signature of this Convention,

Considering that the negotiations which led to the conclusion of the Convention were based on the Brussels Convention in the light of these rulings,

Desiring to prevent, in full deference to the independence of the courts, divergent interpretations and to arrive at as uniform an interpretation as possible of the provisions of the Convention, and of these provisions and those of the Brussels Convention which are substantially reproduced in this Convention,

Have agreed as follows:

Article 1

The courts of each Contracting State shall, when applying and interpreting the provisions of the Convention, pay due account to the principles laid down by any relevant decision delivered by courts of the other Contracting States concerning provisions of this Convention.

Article 2

1. The Contracting Parties agree to set up a system of exchange of information concerning judgments delivered pursuant to this Convention as well as relevant judgments under the Brussels Convention. This system shall comprise:

— transmission to a central body by the competent authorities of judgments delivered by courts of last instance and the Court of Justice of the European Communities as well as judgments of particular importance which have become final and have been delivered pursuant to this Convention or the Brussels Convention,
— classification of these judgments by the central body including, as far as necessary, the drawing-up and publication of translations and abstracts,
— communication by the central body of the relevant documents to the competent national authorities of all signatories and acceding States to the Convention and to the Commission of the European Communities.

2. The central body is the Registrar of the Court of Justice of the European Communities.

Article 3

1. A Standing Committee shall be set up for the purposes of this Protocol.
2. The Committee shall be composed of representatives appointed by each signatory and acceding State.
3. The European Communities (Commission, Court of Justice and General Secretariat of the Council) and the European Free Trade Association may attend the meetings as observers.

Article 4

1. At the request of a Contracting Party, the depository of the Convention shall convene meetings of the Committee for the purpose of exchanging views on the functioning of the Convention and in particular on:

— the development of the case-law as communicated under the first paragraph first indent of Article 2,
— the application of Article 57 of the Convention.

2. The Committee, in the light of these exchanges, may also examine the appropriateness of starting on particular topics a revision of the Convention and make recommendations.

PROTOCOL NO. 3

ON THE APPLICATION OF ARTICLE 57

The High Contracting Parties have agreed as follows:

1. For the purposes of the Convention, provisions which, in relation to particular matters, govern jurisdiction or the recognition or enforcement of judgments and which are, or will

be, contained in acts of the institutions of the European Communities shall be treated in the same way as the conventions referred to in paragraph 1 of Article 57.

2. If one Contracting State is of the opinion that a provision contained in an act of the institutions of the European Communities is incompatible with the Convention, the Contracting States shall promptly consider amending the Convention pursuant to Article 66, without prejudice to the procedure established by Protocol No. 2.

CONTRACTS (APPLICABLE LAW) ACT 1990

(1990 c. 36)

An Act to make provision as to the law applicable to contractual obligations in the case of conflict of laws.   [26th July 1990]

Meaning of "the Conventions"*

1. In this Act—

 (a) "the Rome Convention" means the Convention on the law applicable to contractual obligations opened for signature in Rome on 19th June 1980 and signed by the United Kingdom on 7th December 1981;

 (b) "the Luxembourg Convention" means the Convention on the accession of the Hellenic Republic to the Rome Convention signed by the United Kingdom in Luxembourg on 10th April 1984; and

 (c) "the Brussels Protocol" means the first Protocol on the interpretation of the Rome Convention by the European Court signed by the United Kingdom in Brussels on 19th December 1988;

and the Rome Convention, the Luxembourg Convention and the Brussels Protocol are together referred to as "the Conventions".

Conventions to have force of law

2.—(1) Subject to subsections (2) and (3) below, the Conventions shall not have the force of law in the United Kingdom.

(2) Articles 7(1) and 10(1)(e) of the Rome Convention shall not have the force of law in the United Kingdom.

(3) Notwithstanding Article 19(2) of the Rome Convention, the Conventions shall apply in the case of conflicts between the laws of different parts of the United Kingdom.

(4) For ease of reference there are set out in Schedules 1, 2 and 3 to this Act respectively the English texts of—

 (a) the Rome Convention;

 (b) the Luxembourg Convention; and

 (c) the Brussels Protocol;

(1A) The internal law for the purposes of Article 1(3) of the Rome Convention is whichever of the following are applicable, namely—

 (a) the provisions of Schedule 3A to the Insurance Companies Act 1982 (law applicable to certain contracts of insurance with insurance companies), and

---

* On 18 May 1992 the Funchal Convention was signed on the accession of Portugal and Spain to the Rome Convention. It will be implemented through amendment to the 1990 Act on its entry into force in respect of the United Kingdom (see S.I. 1994 No. 1900).

(b) the provisions of Schedule 20 to the Friendly Societies Act 1992 as applied by subsections (1)(a) and (2)(a) of section 101 of that Act (law applicable to certain contracts of insurance with friendly societies).

Interpretation of Conventions

3.—(1) Any question as to the meaning or effect of any provision of the Conventions shall, if not referred to the European Court in accordance with the Brussels Protocol, be determined in accordance with the principles laid down by, and any relevant decision of, the European Court.

(2) Judicial notice shall be taken of any decision of, or expression of opinion by, the European Court on any such question.

(3) Without prejudice to any practice of the courts as to the matters which may be considered apart from this subsection—

(a) the report on the Rome Convention by Professor Mario Giuliano and Professor Paul Lagarde which is reproduced in the Official Journal of the Communities of 31st October 1980 may be considered in ascertaining the meaning or effect of any provision of that Convention; and

(b) any report on the Brussels Protocol which is reproduced in the Official Journal of the Communities may be considered in ascertaining the meaning or effect of any provision of that Protocol.

Revision of Conventions etc.

4.—(1) If at any time it appears to Her Majesty in Council that Her Majesty's Government in the United Kingdom—

(a) have agreed to a revision of any of the Conventions (including, in particular, any revision connected with the accession to the Rome Convention of any state); or

(b) have given notification in accordance with Article 22(3) of the Rome Convention that either or both of the provisions mentioned in section 2(2) above shall have the force of law in the United Kingdom,

Her Majesty may by Order in Council make sure consequential modifications of this Act or any other statutory provision, whenever passed or made, as Her Majesty considers appropriate.

(2) An Order in Council under subsection (1) above shall not be made unless a draft of the Order has been laid before Parliament and approved by a resolution of each House.

(3) In subsection (1) above—

"modifications" includes additions, omissions and alterations;

"revision" means an omission from, addition to or alteration of any of the Conventions and includes replacement of any of the Conventions to any extent by another convention, protocol or other description of international agreement; and

"statutory provision" means any provision contained in an Act, or in any Northern Ireland legislation, or in—

(a) subordinate legislation (as defined in section 21(1) of the Interpretation Act 1978); or

(b) any instrument of a legislative character made under any Northern Ireland legislation.

Consequential amendments

5. The enactments specified in Schedule 4 to this Act shall have effect subject to the amendments specified in that Schedule.

Application to Crown

6. This Act binds the Crown.

44744

Commencement

7. This Act shall come into force on such day as the Lord Chancellor and the Lord Advocate may by order made by statutory instrument appoint; and different days may be appointed for different provisions or different purposes.

Extent

8.—(1) This Act extends to Northern Ireland.

(2) Her Majesty may by Order in Council direct that all or any of the provisions of this Act shall extend to any of the following territories, namely—

(a) the Isle of Man;
(b) any of the Channel Islands;
(c) Gibraltar;
(d) the Sovereign Base Areas of Akrotiri and Dhekelia (that is to say, the areas mentioned in section 2(1) of the Cyprus Act 1960).

(3) An Order in Council under subsection (2) above may modify this Act in its application to any of the territories mentioned in that subsection and may contain such supplementary provisions as Her Majesty considers appropriate; and in this subsection "modify" shall be construed in accordance with section 4 above.

Short title

9. This Act may be cited as the Contracts (Applicable Law) Act 1990.

SCHEDULE 1. THE ROME CONVENTION

The High Contracting Parties to the Treaty establishing the European Economic Community,
Anxious to continue in the field of private international law the work of unification of law which has already been done within the Community, in particular in the field of jurisdiction and enforcement of judgments,
Wishing to establish uniform rules concerning the law applicable to contractual obligations,
Have agreed as follows:

TITLE I. SCOPE OF THE CONVENTION

Article 1. Scope of the Convention

1. The rules of this Convention shall apply to contractual obligations in any situation involving a choice between the laws of different countries.
2. They shall not apply to:

(a) questions involving the status or legal capacity of natural persons, without prejudice to Article 11;
(b) contractual obligations relating to:

— wills and succession,
— rights in property arising out of a matrimonial relationship,
— rights and duties arising out of a family relationship, parentage, marriage or affinity, including maintenance obligations in respect of children who are not legitimate;

(c) obligations arising under bills of exchange, cheques and promissory notes and other negotiable instruments to the extent that the obligations under such other negotiable instruments arise out of their negotiable character;
(d) arbitration agreements and agreements on the choice of court;

(e) questions governed by the law of companies and other bodies corporate or unincorporate such as the creation, by registration or otherwise, legal capacity, internal organisation or winding up of companies and other bodies corporate or unincorporate and the personal liability of officers and members as such for the obligations of the company or body,

(f) the question whether an agent is able to bind a principal, or an organ to bind a company or body corporate or unincorporate, to a third party;

(g) the constitution of trusts and the relationship between settlers, trustees and beneficiaries;

(h) evidence and procedure, without prejudice to Article 14.

3. The rules of this Convention do not apply to contracts of insurance which cover risks situated in the territories of the Member States of the European Economic Community. In order to determine whether a risk is situated in these territories the court shall apply its internal law.

4. The preceding paragraph does not apply to contracts of re-insurance.

Article 2. Application of law of non-contracting States

Any law specified by this Convention shall be applied whether or not it is the law of a Contracting State.

TITLE II. UNIFORM RULES

Article 3. Freedom of choice

1. A contract shall be governed by the law chosen by the parties. The choice must be express or demonstrated with reasonable certainty by the terms of the contract or the circumstances of the case. By their choice the parties can select the law applicable to the whole or a part only of the contract.

2. The parties may at any time agree to subject the contract to a law other than that which previously governed it, whether as a result of an earlier choice under this Article or of other provisions of this Convention. Any variation by the parties of the law to be applied made after the conclusion of the contract shall not prejudice its formal validity under Article 9 or adversely affect the rights of third parties.

3. The fact that the parties have chosen a foreign law, whether or not accompanied by the choice of a foreign tribunal, shall not, where all the other elements relevant to the situation at the time of the choice are connected with one country only, prejudice the application of rules of the law of that country which cannot be derogated from by contract, hereinafter called "mandatory rules".

4. The existence and validity of the consent of the parties as to the choice of the applicable law shall be determined in accordance with the provisions of Articles 8, 9 and 11.

Article 4. Applicable law in the absence of choice

1. To the extent that the law applicable to the contract has not been chosen in accordance with Article 3, the contract shall be governed by the law of the country with which it is most closely connected. Nevertheless, a severable part of the contract which has a closer connection with another country may by way of exception be governed by the law of that other country.

2. Subject to the provisions of paragraph 5 of this Article, it shall be presumed that the contract is most closely connected with the country where the party who is to effect the performance which is characteristic of the contract has, at the time of conclusion of the contract, his habitual residence, or, in the case of a body corporate or unincorporate, its central administration. However, if the contract is entered into in the course of that party's trade or profession, that country shall be the country in which the principal place of business is situated or, where under the terms of the contract the performance is to be effected through a place of business other than the principal place of business, the country in which that other place of business is situated.

3. Notwithstanding the provisions of paragraph 2 of this Article, to the extent that the subject matter of the contract is a right in immovable property or a right to use immovable property it shall

be presumed that the contract is most closely connected with the country where the immovable property is situated.

4. A contract for the carriage of goods shall not be subject to the presumption in paragraph 2. In such a contract if the country in which, at the time the contract is concluded, the carrier has his principal place of business is also the country in which the place of loading or the place of discharge or the principal place of business of the consignor is situated. It shall be presumed that the contract is most closely connected with that country. In applying this paragraph single voyage charter-parties and other contracts the main purpose of which is the carriage of goods shall be treated as contracts for the carriage of goods.

5. Paragraph 2 shall not apply if the characteristic performance cannot be determined, and the presumptions in paragraphs 2, 3 and 4 shall be disregarded if it appears from the circumstances as a whole that the contract is more closely connected with another country.

Article 5. Certain consumer contracts

1. This Article applies to a contract the object of which is the supply of goods or services to a person ("the consumer") for a purpose which can be regarded as being outside his trade or profession, or a contract for the provision of credit for that object.

2. Notwithstanding the provisions of Article 3, a choice of law made by the parties shall not have the result of depriving the consumer of the protection afforded to him by the mandatory rules of the law of the country in which he has his habitual residence:

— if in that country the conclusion of the contract was preceded by a specific invitation addressed to him or by advertising, and he had taken in that country all the steps necessary on his part for the conclusion of the contract, or
— if the other party or his agent received the consumer's order in that country, or
— if the contract is for the sale of goods and the consumer travelled from that country to another country and there gave his order, provided that the consumer's journey was arranged by the seller for the purpose of inducing the consumer to buy.

3. Notwithstanding the provisions of Article 4, a contract to which this Article applies shall, in the absence of choice in accordance with Article 3, be governed by the law of the country in which the consumer has his habitual residence if it is entered into in the circumstances described in paragraph 2 of this Article.

4. This Article shall not apply to:

(a) a contract of carriage;
(b) a contract for the supply of services where the services are to be supplied to the consumer exclusively in a country other than that in which he has his habitual residence.

5. Notwithstanding the provisions of paragraph 4, this Article shall apply to a contract which, for an inclusive price, provides for a combination of travel and accommodation.

Article 6. Individual employment contracts

1. Notwithstanding the provisions of Article 3, in a contract of employment a choice of law made by the parties shall not have the result of depriving the employee of the protection afforded to him by the mandatory rules of the law which would be applicable under paragraph 2 in the absence of choice.

2. Notwithstanding the provisions of Article 4, a contract of employment shall, in the absence of choice in accordance with Article 3, be governed:

(a) by the law of the country in which the employee habitually carries out his work in performance of the contract, even if he is temporarily employed in another country; or
(b) if the employee does not habitually carry out his work in any one country, by the law of the country in which the place of business through which he was engaged is situated;

unless it appears from the circumstances as a whole that the contract is more closely connected with another country, in which case the contract shall be governed by the law of that country.

Article 7. Mandatory rules

1. When applying under this Convention the law of a country, effect may be given to the mandatory rules of the law of another country with which the situation has a close connection, if and in so far as, under the law of the latter country, those rules must be applied whatever the law applicable to the contract. In considering whether to give effect to these mandatory rules, regard shall be had to their nature and purpose and to the consequences of their application or non-application.

2. Nothing in this Convention shall restrict the application of the rules of the law of the forum in a situation where they are mandatory irrespective of the law otherwise applicable to the contract.

Article 8. Material validity

1. The existence and validity of a contract, or of any term of a contract, shall be determined by the law which would govern it under this Convention if the contract or term were valid.

2. Nevertheless a party may rely upon the law of the country in which he has his habitual residence to establish that he did not consent if it appears from the circumstances that it would not be reasonable to determine the effect of his conduct in accordance with the law specified in the preceding paragraph.

Article 9. Formal validity

1. A contract concluded between persons who are in the same country is formally valid if it satisfies the formal requirements of the law which govern it under this Convention or of the law of the country where it is concluded.

2. A contract concluded between persons who are in different countries is formally valid if it satisfies the formal requirements of the law which governs it under this Convention or of the law of one of those countries.

3. Where a contract is concluded by an agent, the country in which the agent acts is the relevant country for the purposes of paragraphs 1 and 2.

4. An act intended to have legal effect relating to an existing or contemplated contract is formally valid if it satisfies the formal requirements of the law which under this Convention governs or would govern the contract or of the law of the country where the act was done.

5. The provisions of the preceding paragraphs shall not apply to a contract to which Article 5 applies, concluded in the circumstances described in paragraph 2 of Article 5. The formal validity of such a contract is governed by the law of the country in which the consumer has his habitual residence.

6. Notwithstanding paragraphs 1 to 4 of this Article, a contract the subject matter of which is a right in immovable property or a right to use immovable property shall be subject to the mandatory requirements of form of the law of the country where the property is situated if by that law those requirements are imposed irrespective of the country where the contract is concluded and irrespective of the law governing the contract.

Article 10. Scope of the applicable law

1. The law applicable to a contract by virtue of Articles 3 to 6 and 12 of this Convention shall govern in particular:

   (a) interpretation;
   (b) performance;
   (c) within the limits of the powers conferred on the court by its procedural law, the consequences of breach, including the assessment of damages in so far as it is governed by rules of law;
   (d) the various ways of extinguishing obligations, and prescription and limitation of actions;
   (e) the consequences of nullity of the contract.

2. In relation to the manner of performance and the steps to be taken in the event of defective performance regard shall be had to the law of the country in which performance takes place.

Article 11. Incapacity

In a contract concluded between persons who are in the same country, a natural person who would have capacity under the law of that country may invoke his incapacity resulting from another law only if the other party to the contract was aware of his incapacity at the time of the conclusion of the contract or was not aware thereof as a result of negligence.

Article 12. Voluntary assignment

1. The mutual obligations of assignor and assignee under a voluntary assignment of a right against another person ("the debtor") shall be governed by the law which under this Convention applies to the contract between the assignor and assignee.
2. The law governing the right to which the assignment relates shall determine its assignability, the relationship between the assignee and the debtor, the conditions under which the assignment can be invoked against the debtor and any question whether the debtor's obligations have been discharged.

Article 13. Subrogation

1. Where a person ("the creditor") has a contractual claim upon another ("the debtor"), and a third person has a duty to satisfy the creditor, or has in fact satisfied the creditor in discharge of that duty, the law which governs the third person's duty to satisfy the creditor shall determine whether the third person is entitled to exercise against the debtor the rights which the creditor had against the debtor under the law governing their relationship and, if so, whether he may do so in full or only to a limited extent.
2. The same rule applies where several persons are subject to the same contractual claim and one of them has satisfied the creditor.

Article 14. Burden of proof, etc.

1. The law governing the contract under this Convention applies to the extent that it contains, in the law of contract, rules which raise presumptions of law or determine the burden of proof.
2. A contract or an act intended to have legal effect may be proved by any mode of proof recognised by the law of the forum or by any of the laws referred to in Article 9 under which that contract or act is formally valid, provided that such mode of proof can be administered by the forum.

Article 15. Exclusion of renvoi

The application of the law of any country specified by this Convention means the application of the rules of law in force in that country other than its rules of private international law.

Article 16. "Ordre public"

The application of a rule of the law of any country specified by this Convention may be refused only if such application is manifestly incompatible with the public policy ("ordre public") of the forum.

Article 17. No retrospective effect

This Convention shall apply in a Contracting State to contracts made after the date on which this Convention has entered into force with respect to that State.

Article 18. Uniform interpretation

In the interpretation and application of the preceding uniform rules, regard shall be had to their international character and to the desirability of achieving uniformity in their interpretation and application.

Article 19. States with more than one legal system

1. Where a State comprises several territorial units each of which has its own rules of law in respect of contractual obligations, each territorial unit shall be considered as a country for the purposes of identifying the law applicable under this Convention.

2. A State within which different territorial units have their own rules of law in respect of contractual obligations shall not be bound to apply this Convention to conflicts solely between the laws of such units.

Article 20. Precedence of Community law

This Convention shall not affect the application of provisions which, in relation to particular matters, lay down choice of law rules relating to contractual obligations and which are or will be contained in acts of the institutions of the European Communities or in national laws harmonised in implementation of such acts.

Article 21. Relationship with other conventions

This Convention shall not prejudice the application of international conventions to which a Contracting State is, or becomes, a party.

Article 22. Reservations

1. Any Contracting State may, at the time of signature, ratification, acceptance or approval, reserve the right not to apply:

(a) the provisions of Article 7(1);
(b) the provisions of Article 10(1)(e).

2. Any Contracting State may also, when notifying an extension of the Convention in accordance with Article 27(2), make one or more of these reservations, with its effect limited to all or some of the territories mentioned in the extension.

3. Any Contracting State may at any time withdraw a reservation which it has made; the reservation shall cease to have effect on the first day of the third calendar month after notification of the withdrawal.

TITLE III. FINAL PROVISIONS

Article 23

1. If, after the date on which this Convention has entered into force for a Contracting State, that State wishes to adopt any new choice of law rule in regard to any particular category of contract within the scope of this Convention, it shall communicate its intention to the other signatory States through the Secretary-General of the Council of the European Communities.

2. Any signatory State may, within six months from the date of the communication made to the Secretary-General, request him to arrange consultations between signatory States in order to reach agreement.

3. If no signatory State has requested consultations within this period or if within two years following the communications made to the Secretary-General no agreement is reached in the course of consultations, the Contracting State concerned may amend its law in the manner indicated. The measures taken by that State shall be brought to the knowledge of the other signatory States through the Secretary-General of the Council of the European Communities.

Article 24

1. If, after the date on which this Convention has entered into force with respect to a Contracting State, that State wishes to become a party to a multilateral convention whose principal aim or one of whose principal aims is to lay down rules of private international law concerning any of the matters governed by this Convention, the procedure set out in Article 23 shall apply. However, the period of two years, referred to in paragraph 3 of that Article, shall be reduced to one year.

2. The procedure referred to in the preceding paragraph need not be followed if a Contracting State or one of the European Communities is already a party to the multilateral convention, or if its object is to revise a convention to which the State concerned is already a party, or if it is a convention concluded within the framework of the Treaties establishing the European Communities.

Article 25

If a Contracting State considers that the unification achieved by this Convention is prejudiced by the conclusion of agreements not covered by Article 24(1), that State may request the Secretary-General of the Council of the European Communities to arrange consultations between the signatory States of this Convention.

Article 26

Any Contracting State may request the revision of this Convention. In this event a revision conference shall be convened by the President of the Council of the European Communities.

Article 27

1. This Convention shall apply to the European territories of the Contracting States, including Greenland, and to the entire territory of the French Republic.

2. Notwithstanding paragraph 1:

    (a) this Convention shall not apply to the Faroe Islands, unless the Kingdom of Denmark makes a declaration to the contrary;

    (b) this Convention shall not apply to any European territory situated outside the United Kingdom for the international relations of which the United Kingdom is responsible, unless the United Kingdom makes a declaration to the contrary in respect of any such territory;

    (c) this Convention shall apply to the Netherlands Antilles, if the Kingdom of the Netherlands makes a declaration to that effect.

3. Such declarations may be made at any time by notifying the Secretary-General of the Council of the European Communities.

4. Proceedings brought in the United Kingdom on appeal from courts in one of the territories referred to in paragraph 2(b) shall be deemed to be proceedings taking place in those courts.

Article 28

1. This Convention shall be open from 19 June 1980 for signature by the States party to the Treaty establishing the European Economic Community.

2. This Convention shall be subject to ratification, acceptance or approval by the signatory States. The instruments of ratification, acceptance or approval shall be deposited with the Secretary-General of the Council of the European Communities.

Article 29

1. This Convention shall enter into force on the first day of the third month following the deposit of the seventh instrument of ratification, acceptance or approval.

2. This Convention shall enter into force for each signatory State ratifying, accepting or approving at a later date on the first day of the third month following the deposit of its instrument of ratification, acceptance or approval.

Article 30

1. This Convention shall remain in force for 10 years from the date of its entry into force in accordance with Article 29(1), even for States for which it enters into force at a later date.

2. If there has been no denunciation it shall be renewed tacitly every five years.

3. A Contracting State which wished to denounce shall, not less than six months before the expiration of the period of 10 or five years, as the case may be, give notice to the Secretary-General of the Council of the European Communities. Denunciation may be limited to any territory to which the Convention has been extended by a declaration under Article 27(2).

4. The denunciation shall have effect only in relation to the State which has notified it. The Convention will remain in force as between all other Contracting States.

Article 31

The Secretary-General of the Council of the European Communities shall notify the States party to the Treaty establishing the European Economic Community of:

    (a) the signatures;
    (b) the deposit of each instrument of ratification, acceptance or approval;
    (c) the date of entry into force of this Convention;
    (d) communications made in pursuance of Articles 23, 24, 25, 26, 27 and 30;
    (e) the reservations and withdrawals of reservations referred to in Article 22.

Article 32

The Protocol annexed to this Convention shall form an integral part thereof.

Article 33

This Convention, drawn up in a single original in the Danish, Dutch, English, French, German, Irish and Italian languages, these texts being equally authentic, shall be deposited in the archives of the Secretariat of the Council of the European Communities. The Secretary-General shall transmit a certified copy thereof to the Government of each signatory State.

PROTOCOL

The High Contracting Parties have agreed upon the following provision which shall be annexed to the Convention:

Notwithstanding the provisions of the Convention, Denmark may retain the rules contained in Søloven (Statute on Maritime Law) paragraph 169 concerning the applicable law in matters relating to carriage of goods by sea and may revise these rules without following the procedure prescribed in Article 23 of the Convention.

SCHEDULE 2. THE LUXEMBOURG CONVENTION

The High Contracting Parties to the Treaty establishing the European Economic Community.

Considering that the Hellenic Republic, in becoming a Member of the Community, undertook to accede to the Convention on the law applicable to contractual obligations, opened for signature in Rome on 19 June 1980,

Have decided to conclude this Convention, and to this end have designated as their plenipotentiaries:

(Designation of plenipotentiaries)

Who, meeting within the Council, have exchanged their full powers, found in good and due form,

Have agreed as follows:

Article 1

The Hellenic Republic hereby accedes to the Conventions on the law applicable to contractual obligations, opened for signature in Rome on 19 June 1980.

Article 2

The Secretary-General of the Council of the European Communities shall transmit a certified copy of the Convention on the law applicable to contractual obligations in the Danish, Dutch, English, French, German, Irish and Italian languages to the Government of the Hellenic Republic.

The text of the Convention on the law applicable to contractual obligations in the Greek language is annexed hereto. The text in the Greek language shall be authentic under the same conditions as the other texts of the Convention on the law applicable to contractual obligations.

Article 3

This Convention shall be ratified by the Signatory States. The instruments of ratification shall be deposited with the Secretary-General of the Council of the European Communities.

Article 4

This Convention shall enter into force, as between the States which have ratified it, on the first day of the third month following the deposit of the last instrument of ratification by the Hellenic Republic and seven States which have ratified the Convention on the law applicable to contractual obligations.

This Convention shall enter into force for each Contracting State which subsequently ratifies it on the first day of the third month following the deposit of its instrument of ratification.

Article 5

The Secretary-General of the Council of the European Communities shall notify the Signatory States of:

(a) the deposit of each instrument of ratification;
(b) the dates of entry into force of this Convention for the Contracting States.

Article 6

This Convention, drawn up in a single original in the Danish, Dutch, English, French, German, Greek, Irish and Italian languages, all eight texts being equally authentic, shall be deposited in the archives of the General Secretariat of the Council of the European Communities. The Secretary-General shall transmit a certified copy to the Government of each Signatory State.

SCHEDULE 3. THE BRUSSELS PROTOCOL

The High Contracting Parties to the Treaty establishing the European Economic Community,

Having regard to the Joint Declaration annexed to the Convention on the law applicable to contractual obligations, opened for signature in Rome on 19 June 1980,

Have decided to conclude a Protocol conferring jurisdiction on the Court of Justice of the European Communities to interpret that Convention, and to this end have designated as their Plenipotentiaries:

(Designation of plenipotentiaries)

Who, meeting within the Council of the European Communities, having exchanged their full powers, found in good and due form,

Have agreed as follows:

Article 1

The Court of Justice of the European Communities shall have jurisdiction to give rulings on the interpretation of—

    (a) the Convention on the law applicable to contractual obligations, opened for signature in Rome on 19 June 1980, hereinafter referred to as "the Rome Convention";

    (b) the Convention on accession to the Rome Convention by the States which have become Members of the European Communities since the date on which it was opened for signature;

    (c) this Protocol.

Article 2

Any of the courts referred to below may request the Court of Justice to give a preliminary ruling on a question raised in a case pending before it and concerning interpretation of the provisions contained in the instruments referred to in Article 1 if that court considers that a decision on the question is necessary to enable it to give judgment:

    (a) —in Belgium:

        —la Cour de cassation (het Hof van Cassatie) and le Conseil d'Etat (de Raad van State),

        —in Denmark:

        Højesteret,

        —in the Federal Republic of Germany:

        die obersten Gerichtschöfe Bundes,

        —in Greece:

        τα αυῶτατα Αιχαστήφια,

        —in Spain:

        et Tribunal Supremo,

        —in France

        la Cour de cassation and le Conseil d'Etat,

        —in Ireland:

        the Supreme Court,

        —in Italy:

        la Corte suprema di cassazione and il consiglio di Stato,

        —in Luxembourg;

        la Cour Supérieure de Justice, when sitting as Cour de cassation,

        —in the Netherlands:

        de Hoge Raad,

        —in Portugal:

        o Supremo Tribunal de Justiça and o Supremo Tribunal Administrativo,

        —in the United Kingdom:

        the House of Lords and other courts from which no further appeal is possible;

    (b) the courts of the Contracting States when acting as appeal courts.

Article 3

1. The competent authority of a Contracting State may request the Court of Justice to give a ruling on a question of interpretation of the provisions contained in the instruments referred to in Article 1 if judgments given by courts of that State conflict with the interpretation given either by

the Court of Justice or in a judgment of one of the courts of another Contracting State referred to in Article 2. The provisions of this paragraph shall apply only to judgments which have become *res judicata*.

2. The interpretation given by the Court of Justice in response to such a request shall not affect the judgments which gave rise to the request for interpretation.

3. The Procurators-General of the Supreme Courts of Appeal of the Contracting States, or any other authority designated by a Contracting State, shall be entitled to request the Court of Justice for a ruling on interpretation in accordance with paragraph 1.

4. The Registrar of the Court of Justice shall give notice of the request to the Contracting States, to the Commission and to the Council of the European Communities; they shall then be entitled within two months of the notification to submit statements of case or written observations to the Court.

5. No fees shall be levied or any costs or expenses awarded in respect of the proceedings provided for in this Article.

Article 4

1. Except where this Protocol otherwise provides, the provisions of the Treaty establishing the European Economic Community and those of the Protocol on the Statute of the Court of Justice annexed thereto, which are applicable when the Court is requested to give a preliminary ruling, shall also apply to any proceedings for the interpretation of the instruments referred to in Article 1.

2. The Rules of Procedure of the Court of Justice shall, if necessary, be adjusted and supplemented in accordance with Article 188 of the Treaty establishing the European Economic Community.

Article 5

This Protocol shall be subject to ratification by the Signatory States. The instruments of ratification shall be deposited with the Secretary-General of the Council of the European Communities.

Article 6

1. To enter into force, this Protocol must be ratified by seven States in respect of which the Rome Convention is in force. This Protocol shall enter into force on the first day of the third month following the deposit of the instrument of ratification by the last such State to take this step. If, however, the Second Protocol conferring on the Court of Justice of the European Communities certain powers to interpret the Convention on the law applicable to contractual obligations, opened for signature in Rome on 19 June 1980, concluded in Brussels on 19 December 1988, enters into force on a later date, this Protocol shall enter into force on the date of entry into force of the Second Protocol.

2. Any ratification subsequent to the entry into force of this Protocol shall take effect on the first day of the third month following the deposit of the instrument of ratification provided that the ratification, acceptance or approval of the Rome Convention by the State in question has become effective.

Article 7

The Secretary-General of the Council of the European Communities shall notify the Signatory States of:

(a) the deposit of each instrument of ratification;
(b) the date of entry into force of this Protocol;
(c) any designation communicated pursuant to Article 3(3);
(d) any communication made pursuant to Article 8.

Article 8

The Contracting States shall communicate to the Secretary-General of the Council of the European Communities the texts of any provisions of their laws which necessitate an amendment to the list of courts in Article 2(a).

Article 9

This Protocol shall have effect for as long as the Rome Convention remains in force under the conditions laid down in Article 30 of that Convention.

Article 10

Any Contracting State may request the revision of this Protocol. In this event, a revision conference shall be convened by the President of the Council of the European Communities.

Article 11

This Protocol, drawn up in a single original in the Danish, Dutch, English, French, German, Irish, Italian, Portuguese and Spanish languages, all 10 texts being equally authentic, shall be deposited in the archives of the General Secretariat of the Council of the European Communities. The Secretary-General shall transmit a certified copy to the Government of each Signatory State.

APPENDIX 2

Rules of the Supreme Court

ORDER 2

EFFECT OF NON-COMPLIANCE

Non-compliance with rules (O. 2, r. 1)

1.—(1) Where, in beginning or purporting to begin any proceedings or at any stage in the course of or in connection with any proceedings, there has, by reason of any thing done or left undone, been a failure to comply with the requirements of these rules, whether in respect of time, place, manner, form or content or in any other respect, the failure shall be treated as an irregularity and shall not nullify the proceedings, any step taken in the proceedings, or any document, judgment or order therein.

(2) Subject to paragraph (3) the Court may, on the ground that there has been such a failure as is mentioned in paragraph (1) and on such terms as to costs or otherwise as it thinks just, set aside either wholly or in part the proceedings in which the failure occurred, any step taken in those proceedings or any document, judgment or order therein or exercise its powers under these rules to allow such amendments (if any) to be made and to make such order (if any) dealing with the proceedings generally as it thinks fit.

(3) The Court shall not wholly set aside any proceedings or the writ or other originating process by which they were begun on the ground that the proceedings were required by any of these rules to be begun by an originating process other than the one employed.

ORDER 6

Duration and renewal of writ (O. 6, r. 8)

8.—(1) For the purposes of service, a writ (other than a concurrent writ) is valid in the first instance—

  (a) if an Admiralty writ *in rem*, for 12 months;
  (b) where leave to serve the writ out of the jurisdiction is required under Order 11 or Order 75, Rule 4 for 6 months,
  (c) in any other case, for 4 months

beginning with the date of its issue.

(1A) A concurrent writ is valid in the first instance for the period of validity of the original writ which is unexpired at the date of issue of the concurrent writ.

(2) Subject to paragraph (2A), where a writ has not been served on a defendant, the Court may by order extend the validity of the writ from time to time for such period, not exceeding 4 months at any one time, beginning with the day next following that on which it would otherwise expire, as may be specified in the order, if an application for extension is made to the Court before that day or such later day (if any) as the Court may allow.

(2A) Where the Court is satisfied on an application under paragraph (2) that, despite the making of all reasonable efforts, it may not be possible to serve the writ within 4 months, the Court may, if it thinks fit, extend the validity of the writ for such period, not exceeding 12 months, as the Court may specify.

(3) Before a writ, the validity of which has been extended under this rule, is served, it must be marked with an official stamp showing the period for which the validity of the writ has been so extended.

(4) Where the validity of a writ is extended by order made under this Rule, the order shall operate in relation to any other writ (whether original or concurrent) issued in the same action which has not been served so as to extend the validity of that other writ until the expiration of the period specified in the order.

ORDER 10

SERVICE OF ORIGINATING PROCESS: GENERAL PROVISIONS

General provisions (O. 10, r. 1)

1.—(1) A writ must be served personally on each defendant by the plaintiff or his agent.

(2) A writ for service on a defendant within the jurisdiction may, instead of being served personally on him, be served—

    (a) by sending a copy of the writ by ordinary first-class post to the defendant at his usual or last known address, or

    (b) if there is a letter box for that address, by inserting through the letter box a copy of the writ enclosed in a sealed envelope addressed to the defendant.

    In sub-paragraph (a) "first-class post" means first-class post which has been pre-paid or in respect of which prepayment is not required.

(3) Where a writ is served in accordance with paragraph (2)—

    (a) the date of service shall, unless the contrary is shown, be deemed to be the seventh day (ignoring Order 3, rule 2(5)) after the date on which the copy was sent to or, as the case may be, inserted through the letter box for the address in question;

    (b) any affidavit proving due service of the writ must contain a statement to the effect that—

        (i) in the opinion of the deponent (or, if the deponent is the plaintiff's solicitor or an employee of that solicitor, in the opinion of the plaintiff) the copy of the writ, if sent to, or, as the case may be, inserted through the letter box for, the address in question, will have come to the knowledge of the defendant within seven days thereafter; and

        (ii) in the case of service by post, the copy of the writ has not been returned to the plaintiff through the post undelivered to the addressee.

(4) Where a defendant's solicitor indorses on the writ a statement that he accepts service of the writ on behalf of that defendant, the writ shall be deemed to have been duly served on that defendant and to have been so served on the date on which the indorsement was made.

(5) Subject to Order 12, rule 7, where a writ is not duly served on a defendant but he acknowledges service of it, the writ shall be deemed, unless the contrary is shown, to have been duly served on him and to have been so served on the date on which he acknowledges service.

(6) Every copy of a writ for service on a defendant shall be sealed with the seal of the office of the Supreme Court out of which the writ was issued and shall be accompanied by a form of acknowledgment of service in Form No. 14 in Appendix A in which the title of the action and its number have been entered.

(7) This rule shall have effect subject to the provisions of any Act and these rules and in particular to any enactment which provides for the manner in which documents may be served on bodies corporate.

Service of writ in pursuance of contract (O. 10, r. 3)

3.—(1) Where—

   (a) a contract contains a term to the effect that the High Court shall have jurisdiction to hear and determine any action in respect of a contract or, apart from any such term, the High Court has jurisdiction to hear and determine any such action, and
   (b) the contract provides that, in the event of any action in respect of the contract being begun, the process by which it is begun may be served on the defendant, or on such other person on his behalf as may be specified in the contract, in such manner, or at such place (whether within or out of the jurisdiction) as may be so specified,

then, if an action in respect of the contract is begun in the High Court and the writ by which it is begun is served in accordance with the contract, the writ shall, subject to paragraph (2) be deemed to have been duly served on the defendant.

(2) A writ which is served out of the jurisdiction in accordance with a contract shall not be deemed to have been duly served on the defendant by virtue of para. (1) unless leave to serve the writ out of the jurisdiction has been granted under Order 11, rule 1(1) or service of the writ is permitted without leave under Order 11, rule 1(2).

(3) Where a contract contains an agreement conferring jurisdiction to which Article 17 of Schedule 1, 3c or 4 to the Civil Jurisdiction and Judgments Act 1982 applies and the writ is served under Order 11, rule 1(2) the writ shall be deemed to have been duly served on the defendant.

ORDER 11

SERVICE OF PROCESS, ETC., OUT OF THE JURISDICTION

Principal cases in which service of writ out of jurisdiction is permissible (O. 11, r. 1)

1.—(1) Provided that the writ does not contain any claim mentioned in Order 75, r. 2(1) and is not a writ to which paragraph (2) of this rule applies, service of a writ out of the jurisdiction is permissible with the leave of the Court if in the action begun by the writ—

   (a) relief is sought against a person domiciled within the jurisdiction;
   (b) an injunction is sought ordering the defendant to do or refrain from doing anything within the jurisdiction (whether or not damages are also claimed in respect of a failure to do or the doing of that thing);
   (c) the claim is brought against a person duly served within or out of the jurisdiction and a person out of the jurisdiction is a necessary or proper party thereto;
   (d) the claim is brought to enforce, rescind, dissolve, annul or otherwise affect a contract, or to recover damages or obtain other relief in respect of the breach of a contract, being (in either case) a contract which—
      (i) was made within the jurisdiction, or
      (ii) was made by or through an agent trading or residing within the jurisdiction on behalf of a principal trading or residing out of the jurisdiction, or
      (iii) is by its terms, or by implication, governed by English law, or
      (iv) contains a term to the effect that the High Court shall have jurisdiction to hear and determine any action in respect of the contract;
   (e) the claim is brought in respect of a breach committed within the jurisdiction of a contract made within or out of the jurisdiction, and irrespective of the fact, if such be the case, that the breach was preceded or accompanied by a breach committed out of the jurisdiction that rendered impossible the performance of so much of the contract as ought to have been performed within the jurisdiction;
   (f) the claim is founded on a tort and the damage was sustained, or resulted from an act committed, within the jurisdiction;
   (g) the whole subject-matter of the action is land situate within the jurisdiction (with or without rents or profits) or the perpetuation of testimony relating to land so situate;

    (h) the claim is brought to construe, rectify, set aside or enforce an act, deed, will, contract, obligation or liability affecting land situate within the jurisdiction;

    (i) the claim is made for a debt secured on immovable property or is made to assert, declare or determine proprietary or possessory rights, or rights of security, in or over movable property, or to obtain authority to dispose of movable property, situate within the jurisdiction;

    (j) the claim is brought to execute the trusts of a written instrument being trusts that ought to be executed according to English law and of which the person to be served with the writ is a trustee, or for any relief or remedy which might be obtained in any such action;

    (k) the claim is made for the administration of the estate of a person who died domiciled within the jurisdiction or for any relief or remedy which might be obtained in any such action;

    (l) the claim is brought in a probate action within the meaning of Order 76;

    (m) the claim is brought to enforce any judgment or arbitral award;

    (n) the claim is brought against a defendant not domiciled in Scotland or Northern Ireland in respect of a claim by the Commissioners of Inland Revenue for or in relation to any of the duties or taxes which have been, or are for the time being, placed under their care and management;

    (o) the claim is brought under the Nuclear Installations Act 1965 or in respect of contributions under the Social Security Act 1975;

    (p) the claim is made for a sum to which the Directive of the Council of the European Communities dated 15th March 1976 No. 76/308/EEC applies, and service is to be effected in a country which is a member State of the European Economic Community.

    (q) the claim is made under the Drug Trafficking Offences Act 1986;

    (r) the claim is made under the Financial Services Act 1986 or the Banking Act 1987;

    (s) the claim is made under Part VI of the Criminal Justice Act 1988.

    (t) the claim is brought for money had and received or for an account or other relief against the defendant as constructive trustee, and the defendant's alleged liability arises out of acts committed, whether by him or otherwise, within the jurisdiction.

    (u) the claim is made under the Immigration (Carriers' Liability) Act 1987.

(2) Service of a writ out of the jurisdiction is permissible without the leave of the Court provided that each claim made by the writ is either—

    (a) a claim which by virtue of the Civil Jurisdiction and Judgments Act 1982 the Court has power to hear and determine, made in the proceedings to which the following conditions apply—

        (i) no proceedings between the parties concerning the same cause of action are pending in the courts of any other part of the United Kingdom or of any other Convention territory, and

        (ii) either—

        the defendant is domiciled in any part of the United Kingdom or in any other Convention territory, or

        the proceedings begun by the writ are proceedings to which Article 16 of Schedule 1, 3c or 4 refers, or the defendant is a party to an agreement conferring jurisdiction to which Article 17 of Schedule 1, 3C or 4 to that Act applies,

    or

    (b) a claim which by virtue of any other enactment the High Court has power to hear and determine notwithstanding that the person against whom the claim is made is not within the jurisdiction of the Court or that the wrongful act, neglect or default giving rise to the claim did not take place within its jurisdiction.

(3) Where a writ is to be served out of the jurisdiction under paragraph (2), the time to be inserted in the writ within which the defendant served therewith must acknowledge service shall be—

    (a) 21 days where the writ is to be served out of the jurisdiction under paragraph (2)(a) in Scotland, Northern Ireland or in the European territory of another Contracting State, or

(b) 31 days where the writ is to be served under paragraph (2)(a) in any other territory of a Contracting State, or

(c) limited in accordance with the practice adopted under r. 4(4) where the writ is to be served under paragraph (2)(a) in a country not referred to in sub-paragraphs (a) or (b) or under paragraph (2)(b).

(4) For the purposes of this rule, and of r. 9 of this Order, domicile is to be determined in accordance with the provisions of sections 41 to 46 of the Civil Jurisdictions and Judgments Act 1982 and "Convention territory" means the territory or territories of any Contracting State, as defined by s. 1(3) of that Act, to which, as defined in s. 1(1) of that Act, the Brussels or the Lugano Convention apply.

Application for, and grant of, leave to serve writ out of jurisdiction (O. 11, r. 4)

4.—(1) An application for the grant of leave under rule 1(1) must be supported by an affidavit stating—

(a) the grounds on which the application is made,

(b) that in the deponent's belief the plaintiff has a good cause of action,

(c) in what place or country the defendant is, or probably may be found, and

(d) where the application is made under rule 1(1)(c), the grounds for the deponent's belief that there is between the plaintiff and the person on whom a writ has been served a real issue which the plaintiff may reasonably ask the Court to try.

(2) No such leave shall be granted unless it shall be made sufficiently to appear to the Court that the case is a proper one for service out of the jurisdiction under this Order.

(3) Where the application is for the grant of leave under rule 1 to serve a writ in Scotland or Northern Ireland, if it appears to the Court that there may be a concurrent remedy there, the Court, in deciding whether to grant leave shall have regard to the comparative cost and convenience of proceeding there or in England, and (where that is relevant) to the powers and jurisdiction of the sheriff court in Scotland or the county courts or courts of summary jurisdiction in Northern Ireland.

(4) An order granting under rule 1 leave to serve a writ, out of the jurisdiction must limit a time within which the defendant to be served must acknowledge service.

Service of writ abroad: general (O. 11, r. 5)

5.—(1) Subject to the following provisions of this rule, Order 10, rule 1(1), (4), (5) and (6) and Order 65, rule 4, shall apply in relation to the service of a writ, notwithstanding that the writ is to be served out of the jurisdiction, save that the accompanying form of acknowledgment of service shall be modified in such manner as may be appropriate.

(2) Nothing in this rule or in any order or direction of the Court made by virtue of it shall authorise or require the doing of anything in a country in which service is to be effected which is contrary to the law of that country.

(3) A writ which is to be served out of the jurisdiction—

(a) need not be served personally on the person required to be served so long as it is served on him in accordance with the law of the country in which service is effected; and

(b) need not be served by the plaintiff or his agent if it is served by a method provided for by rule 6 or rule 7.

(4) [*Deleted by R.S.C. (Amendment No. 2) 1979 (S.I. 1979 No. 402).*]

(5) An official certificate stating that a writ as regards which rule 6 has been complied with has been served on a person personally, or in accordance with the law of the country in which service was effected, on a specified date, being a certificate—

(a) by a British consular authority in that country, or

(b) by the government or judicial authorities of that country, or

(c) by any other authority designated in respect of that country under the Hague Convention,

shall be evidence of the facts so stated.

(6) An official certificate by the Secretary of State stating that a writ has been duly served on a specified date in accordance with a request made under rule 7 shall be evidence of that fact.

(7) A document purporting to be such a certificate as is mentioned in paragraph (5) or (6) shall, until the contrary is proved, be deemed to be such a certificate.

(8) In this rule and rule 6 "the Hague Convention" means the Convention on the service abroad of judicial and extra-judicial documents in civil or commercial matters signed at the Hague on November 15, 1965.

ORDER 12

ACKNOWLEDGMENT OF SERVICE OF WRIT OR ORIGINATING SUMMONS

Dispute as to jurisdiction (O. 12, r. 8)

8.—(1) A defendant who wishes to dispute the jurisdiction of the court in the proceedings by reason of any such irregularity as is mentioned in rule 7 or on any other ground shall give notice of intention to defend the proceedings and shall, within the time limited for service of a defence, apply to the Court for—

(a) an order setting aside the writ or service of the writ on him, or

(b) an order declaring that the writ has not been duly served on him, or

(c) the discharge of any order giving leave to serve the writ on him out of the jurisdiction, or

(d) the discharge of any order extending the validity of the writ for the purpose of service, or

(e) the protection or release of any property of the defendant seized or threatened with seizure in the proceedings, or

(f) the discharge of any order made to prevent any dealing with any property of the defendant, or

(g) a declaration that in the circumstances of the case the court has no jurisdiction over the defendant in respect of the subject matter of the claim or the relief or remedy sought in the action, or

(h) such other relief as may be appropriate.

(2) *[Revoked by R.S.C. (Amendment No. 2) 1983 (S.I. 1983 No. 1181)].*

(3) An application under paragraph (1) must be made—

(a) in an Admiralty action *in rem*, by motion;

(b) in any other action in the Queen's Bench Division, by summons;

(c) in any other action, by summons or motion,

and the notice of motion or summons must state the grounds of the application.

(4) An application under paragraph (1) must be supported by an affidavit verifying the facts on which the application is based and a copy of the affidavit must be served with the notice of motion or summons by which the application is made.

(5) Upon hearing an application under paragraph (1) the Court, if it does not dispose of the matter in dispute, may give such directions for its disposal as may be appropriate, including directions for the trial thereof as a preliminary issue.

(6) A defendant who makes an application under paragraph (1) shall not be treated as having submitted to the jurisdiction of the Court by reason of his having given notice of intention to defend the action; and if the Court makes no order on the application or dismisses it, the notice shall cease to have effect, but the defendant may, subject to rule 6(1), lodge a further acknowledgment of

service within 14 days or such other period as the Court may direct and in that case paragraph (7) shall apply as if the defendant had not made any such application.

(7) Except where the defendant makes an application in accordance with paragraph (1) the acknowledgment by a defendant of service of a writ shall, unless the acknowledgment is withdrawn by leave of the Court under Order 21, rule 1, be treated as a submission by the defendant to the jurisdiction of the Court in the proceedings.

ORDER 75*

ADMIRALTY PROCEEDINGS

Application and interpretation (O. 75, r. 1)

1.—(1) This Order applies to Admiralty causes and matters, and the other provisions of these rules apply to those causes and matters subject to the provisions of this Order.

(2) In this Order—

"action in rem" means an Admiralty action in rem;

"caveat against arrest" means a caveat entered in the caveat book under rule 6;

"caveat against release and payment" means a caveat entered in the caveat book under rule 14;

"caveat book" means the book kept in the registry in which caveats issued under this Order are entered;

"limitation action" means an action by shipowners or other persons under the Merchant Shipping Act 1979 for the limitation of the amount of their liability in connection with a ship or other property;

"marshal" means the Admiralty marshal;

"registry" (except where the context otherwise requires) means the Admiralty and Commercial Registry;

"ship" includes any description of vessel used in navigation.

Certain actions to be assigned to Admiralty (O. 75, r. 2)

2.—(1) Without prejudice to sections 61 and 62(2) of the Act, or to any other enactment or rule providing for the assignment of causes and matters to the Queen's Bench Division.

(a) every action to enforce a claim for damage, loss of life or personal injury arising out of—

    (i) a collision between ships, or

    (ii) the carrying out of or omission to carry out a manoeuvre in the case of one or more of two or more ships, or

    (iii) non-compliance, on the part of one or more of two or more ships, with the collision regulations.

(b) every limitation action, and

(c) every action to enforce a claim under section 1 of the Merchant Shipping (Oil Pollution) Act 1971 or section 4 of the Merchant Shipping Act 1974,

shall be assigned to that Division and taken by the Admiralty Court.

(2) In this rule "collision regulations" means regulations under section 418 of the Merchant Shipping Act 1894 or section 21 of the Merchant Shipping Act 1979, or any such rules as are mentioned in subsection (1) of section 421 of the Act of 1894 or any rules made under subsection (2) of the said section 421.

---

* The extracts from the Order apply as they appear until 31 December 1995. As from 1 January 1996 references to the various Merchant Shipping Acts are to be read as references to the provisions of the Merchant Shipping Act 1995 repealing and re-enacting them.

Proceedings against, or concerning, the International Oil Pollution Compensation Fund (O. 75, r. 2A)

2A.—(1) All proceedings against the International Oil Pollution Compensation Fund (in this rule referred to as "the Fund") under section 4 of the Merchant Shipping Act 1974 shall be commenced in the registry.

(2) For the purposes of section 6(2) of the Merchant Shipping Act 1974, any party to proceedings brought against an owner or guarantor in respect of liability under section 1 of the Merchant Shipping (Oil Pollution) Act 1971 may give notice to the Fund of such proceedings by serving a notice in writing on the Fund together with a copy of the writ and copies of the pleadings (if any) served in the action.

(3) The Court shall, on the application made ex parte by the Fund, grant leave to the Fund to intervene in any proceedings to which the preceding paragraph applies, whether notice of such proceedings has been served on the Fund or not, and paragraphs (3) and (4) of rule 17 shall apply to such an application.

(4) Where judgment is given against the fund in any proceedings under section 4 of the Merchant Shipping Act 1974, the registrar shall cause a stamped copy of the judgment to be sent by post to the Fund.

(5) The Fund shall notify the registrar of the matters set out in section 4(12)(b) of the Merchant Shipping Act 1974 by a notice in writing, sent by post to, or delivered at, the registry.

Issue of writ and acknowledgment of service (O. 75, r. 3)

3.—(1) An action in rem must be begun by writ; and the writ must be in Form No. 1 in Appendix B.

(2) The writ by which an Admiralty action in personam is begun must be in Form No. 1 in Appendix A with the following modifications:

    (a) in the heading after the word "Division" there shall be inserted the words "Admiralty Court";

    (b) where the writ is issued out of the registry, for the references to the number of the action and to the Central Office there shall be substituted references to the folio number and to the Admiralty and Commercial registry respectively.

(3) The writ by which a limitation action is begun must be in Form No. 2 in Appendix B.

(4) Subject to the following paragraphs, Order 6, rule 7, shall apply in relation to a writ by which an Admiralty action is begun, and Order 12 shall apply in relation to such an action, as if for references therein to the Central Office there were substituted references to the registry.

(5) An acknowledgment of service in an action in rem or a limitation action shall be in Form No. 2B in Appendix B.

(6) A defendant to an action in rem in which the writ has not been served, or a defendant to a limitation action who has not been served with the writ, may, if he desires to take part in the proceedings, acknowledge the issue of the writ by handing in at, or sending to, the appropriate office an acknowledgment of issue in the same form as an acknowledgment of service but with the substitution for the references therein to service of references to issue of the writ.

(7) These rules shall apply, with the necessary modifications, in relation to an acknowledgment of issue or service in Form No. 2B in Appendix B as they apply in relation to an acknowledgment of service in Form No. 14 in Appendix A which contains a statement to the effect that the defendant intends to contest the proceedings to which the acknowledgment relates.

Service of writ out of jurisdiction (O. 75, r. 4)

4.—(1) Subject to the following provisions of this rule, service out of the jurisdictions of a writ, containing any such claim as is mentioned in rule 2(1)(a) or (b) is permissible with the leave of the Court if, but only if—

    (a) the defendant has his habitual residence or a place of business within England and Wales, or

(b) the cause of action arose within inland waters of England and Wales or within the limits of a port of England and Wales, or

(c) an action arising out of the same incident or series of incidents is proceeding in the High Court or has been heard and determined in the High Court, or

(d) the defendant has submitted or agreed to submit to the jurisdiction of the High Court.

(1A) Service out of the jurisdiction of a writ in an action containing any such claim as is mentioned in r. 2(1)(c) is permissible with the leave of the Court.

(2) Order 11, rule 3 and rule 4(1), (2) and (4) shall apply in relation to an application for the grant of leave under this rule as they apply in relation to an application for the grant of leave under rule 1 or 2 of that Order.

(3) Paragraphs (1) and (1A) shall not apply to an action in rem.

(4) The proviso to rule 7(1) of Order 6 and Order 11, rule 1(2) shall not apply to a writ by which any Admiralty action is begun.

Warrant of arrest (O. 75, r. 5)

5.—(1) In an action in rem the plaintiff or defendant, as the case may be, may after the issue of the writ in the action and subject to the provisions of this rule issue a warrant in Form No. 3 in Appendix B for the arrest of the property against which the action or any counterclaim in the action is brought.

(2) Where an action in rem in proceeding in a district registry, a warrant of arrest in the action may be issued out of that registry but, except as aforesaid, a warrant of arrest shall not be issued out of a district registry.

(3) Before a warrant to arrest any property is issued the party intending to issue it must procure a search to be made in the caveat book for the purpose of ascertaining whether there is a caveat against arrest in force with respect to that property and, if the warrant is to issue out of a district registry, the registrar of that registry shall procure a search to be made in the said book for that purpose.

(4) A warrant of arrest shall not be issued until the party intending to issue the same has filed an affidavit made by him or his agent containing the particulars required by paragraph (9); however, the Court may, if it thinks fit, give leave to issue the warrant notwithstanding that the affidavit does not contain all those particulars.

(5) Except with the leave of the Court or where notice has been given under paragraph (7) a warrant of arrest shall not be issued in an action in rem against a foreign ship belonging to a port of a State having a consulate in London, being an action for possession of the ship or for wages, until notice that the action has been begun has been sent to the consul.

(6) A warrant of arrest may not be issued as of right in the case of property whose beneficial ownership has, since the issue of the writ, changed as a result of a sale or disposal by any court exercising Admiralty jurisdiction.

(7) Where, by any convention or treaty, the United Kingdom has undertaken to minimise the possibility of arrest of ships of another State, no warrant of arrest shall be issued against a ship owned by that State until notice in Form No. 15 in Appendix B has been served on a consular officer at the consular office of that State in London or the port at which it is intended to cause the ship to be arrested.

(8) Issue of a warrant of arrest takes place upon its being sealed by an officer of the registry or district registry.

(9) An affidavit required by paragraph (4) must state—

(a) in every case:
  (i) the nature of the claim or counterclaim and that it has not been satisfied and, if it arises in connection with a ship, the name of that ship; and
  (ii) the nature of the property to be arrested and, if the property is a ship, the name of the ship and her port of registry; and

(b) in the case of a claim against a ship by virtue of s. 21(4) of the Supreme Court Act 1981:

> (i) the name of the person who would be liable on the claim in an action in personam ("the relevant person"); and
>
> (ii) that the relevant person was when the cause of action arose the owner or charterer of, or in possession or in control of, the ship in connection with which the claim arose; and
>
> (iii) that at the time of the issue of the writ the relevant person was either the beneficial owner of all the shares in the ship in respect of which the warrant is required or (where appropriate) the charterer of it under a charter by demise; and

(c) in the case of a claim for possession of a ship or for wages, the nationality of the ship in respect of which the warrant is required and that the notice (if any) required by paragraph (5) has been sent; and

(d) in the case of a claim where notice is required to be served on a consular officer under paragraph (7), that such notice has been served;

(e) in the case of a claim in respect of a liability incurred under s. 1 of the Merchant Shipping (Oil Pollution) Act 1971, the facts relied on as establishing that the Court is not prevented from entertaining the action by reason of s. 13(2) of that Act.

(10) The following documents shall, where appropriate, be exhibited to an affidavit required by paragraph (4)—

(a) a copy of any notice sent to a consul under paragraph (5);

(b) a copy of any notice served on a consular officer under paragraph (7).

Caveat against arrest (O. 75, r. 6)

6.—(1) Except in a case to which paragraph (1A) applies, a person who desires to prevent the arrest of any property must file in the registry a praecipe, in Form No. 5 in Appendix B, signed by him or his solicitor undertaking—

(a) to acknowledge issue or service (as may be appropriate) of the writ in any action that may be begun against the property described in the praecipe, and

(b) within 3 days after receiving notice that such an action has been begun, to give bail in the action in a sum not exceeding an amount specified in the praecipe or to pay the amount so specified into court;

and on the filing of the praecipe a caveat against the issue of warrant to arrest the property described in the praecipe shall be entered in the caveat book.

(1A) Where a plaintiff in a limitation action has constituted a limitation fund in accordance with Article 11 of the Convention on Limitation of Liability for Maritime Claims 1976 (as set out in Schedule 4 to the Merchant Shipping Act 1979) and rule 37A of this Order, and desires to prevent the arrest of any property for a claim which may be or has been made against the fund, he must file in the registry a praecipe, in Form No. 5A in Appendix B, signed by him or his solicitor—

(a) stating that a limitation fund in respect of damage arising from the relevant incident has been constituted, and

(b) undertaking to acknowledge issue or service (as may be appropriate) of the writ in any action that may be begun against the property described in the praecipe;

and on the filing of the praecipe a caveat against the issue of a warrant to arrest the property described in the praecipe shall be entered in the caveat book.

(2) The fact that there is a caveat against arrest in force shall not prevent the issue of a warrant to arrest the property to which the caveat relates.

Remedy where property protected by caveat is arrested without good and sufficient reason (O. 75, r. 7)

7. Where any property with respect to which a caveat against arrest is in force is arrested in pursuance of a warrant of arrest, the party at whose instance the caveat was entered may apply to the Court by motion for an order under this rule and, on the hearing of the application, the Court, unless it is satisfied that the party procuring the arrest of the property had a good and sufficient reason for so doing, may by order discharge the warrant and may also order the last-mentioned party to pay to the applicant damages in respect of the loss suffered by the applicant as a result of the arrest.

Service of writ in action in rem (O. 75, r. 8)

8. Subject to paragraph (2) a writ by which an action in rem is begun must be served on the property against which the action is brought, save that—

    (a) where the property is freight, it must be served on the cargo in respect of which the freight is payable or on the ship in which that cargo was carried;

    (b) where the property has been sold by the marshal, the writ may not be served on that property but a sealed copy of it must be filed in the registry or, if the writ was issued out of a district registry, in that registry, and the writ shall be deemed to have been duly served on the day on which the copy was filed.

(2) A writ need not be served or filed as mentioned in paragraph (1) if the writ is deemed to have been duly served on the defendant by virtue of Order 10, rule 1(4) or (5).

(3) Where by virtue of this rule a writ is required to be served on any property, the plaintiff may request service of the writ to be effected by the marshal if, but only if, a warrant of arrest has been issued for service against the property or the property is under arrest, and in that case the plaintiff must file in the registry or, where the action is proceeding in a district registry that registry a praecipe in Form 6 in Appendix B and lodge—

    (a) the writ and a copy thereof; and

    (b) an undertaking to pay on demand all expenses incurred by the marshal or his substitute in respect of the service of the writ;

and thereupon the marshal or his substitute shall serve the writ on the property described in the praecipe.

(3A) Where a writ is served on any property by the marshal or his substitute, the person effecting service must indorse on the writ the following particulars, that is to say, where it was served, the property on which it was served, the day of the week and the date on which it was served, the manner in which it was served and the name and the address of the person effecting service, and the indorsement shall be evidence of the facts stated therein.

(4) Where the plaintiff in an action in rem, or his solicitor, becomes aware that there is in force a caveat against arrest with respect to the property against which the action is brought, he must serve the writ forthwith on the person at whose instance the caveat was entered.

(5) Where a writ by which an action in rem is begun is amended under Order 20, rule 1, after service thereof, Order 20, rule 1(2) shall not apply and, unless the Court otherwise directs on an application made ex parte: the amended writ must be served on any intervener and any defendant who has acknowledged issue or service of the writ in the action or, if no defendant has acknowledged issue or service of the writ, it must be served or filed in accordance with paragraph (1) of this rule.

Committal of solicitor failing to comply with undertaking (O. 75, r. 9)

9. Where the solicitor of a party to an action in rem fails to comply with a written undertaking given by him to any other party or his solicitor to acknowledge issue or service of the writ in the action, give bail or pay money into court in lieu of bail, he shall be liable to committal.

Execution, etc., of warrant of arrest (O. 75, r. 10)

10.—(1) A warrant of arrest is valid for 12 months beginning with the date of its issue.

(2) A warrant of arrest may be executed only by the marshal or his substitute.

(3) A warrant of arrest shall not be executed until an undertaking to pay on demand the fees of the marshal and all expenses incurred by him or on his behalf in respect of the arrest of the property and the care and custody of it while under arrest has been lodged in the marshal's office or, where the action is proceeding in a district registry, in that registry.

(4) A warrant of arrest shall not be executed if the party at whose instance it was issued lodges a written request to that effect with the marshal or, where the action is proceeding in a district registry, the registrar of that registry.

(5) A warrant of arrest issued against freight may be executed by serving the warrant on the cargo in respect of which the freight is payable or on the ship in which that cargo was carried or on both of them.

(6) Subject to paragraph (5) a warrant of arrest must be served on the property against which it is issued.

(7) Within 7 days after the service of a warrant of arrest, the warrant must be filed—

    (a) where it was issued out of the registry, in the registry by the marshal, and

    (b) where it was issued out of a district registry, in that registry by the party who procured it to be issued.

Service on ships, etc.: how effected (O. 75, r. 11)

11.—(1) Subject to paragraph (2) service of a warrant of arrest or writ in an action in rem against a ship, freight or cargo shall be effected by—

    (a) affixing the warrant or writ for a short time on any mast of the ship or on the outside of any suitable part of the ship's superstructure, and

    (b) on removing the warrant or writ, leaving a copy of it affixed (in the case of the warrant) in its place or (in the case of the writ) on a sheltered, conspicuous part of the ship.

(2) Service of a warrant of arrest or writ in an action in rem against freight or cargo or both shall, if the cargo has been landed or transhipped, be effected—

    (a) by placing the warrant or writ for a short time on the cargo and, on removing the warrant or writ, leaving a copy of it on the cargo, or

    (b) if the cargo is in the custody of a person who will not permit access to it, by leaving a copy of the warrant or writ with that person.

(3) Order 65, rule 10, shall not apply in relation to a warrant of arrest or writ in rem.

(4) Where in an action in rem a writ has been issued pursuant to Order 6 rule 7A and it is desired to serve the writ before it has been sealed by the Court, a copy of it endorsed in accordance with Order 6, rule 7A(3)(a) may be treated as if it were the original writ for the purpose of the foregoing paragraphs of this rule.

Directions with respect to property under arrest (O. 75, r. 12)

12.—(1) The marshal may at any time apply to the Court for directions with respect to property under arrest in any action and may, and if the Court so directs shall, give notice of the application to any or all of the persons referred to in paragraph (2).

(2) The marshal shall send by post a copy of any order made on an application under paragraph (1) to all those persons who, in relation to that property, have—

    (a) entered a caveat which is still in force; or

    (b) caused a warrant for the arrest of the property to be executed by the marshal; or

    (c) acknowledged issue or service of the writ in any action in which the property is under arrest; or

    (d) intervened in any action in which the property is under arrest.

(3) A person other than the marshal may make an application under this rule by summons or motion in the action in which the property is under arrest and the summons or notice of motion

together with copies of any affidavits in support must be served upon the marshal and all persons referred to in paragraph (2) unless the court otherwise orders on an application made ex parte.

(4) A district judge by whom any order under paragraph (3) is made shall cause a copy of the order to be sent to the marshal.

Release of property under arrest (O. 75, r. 13)

13.—(1) Except where property arrested in pursuance of a warrant of arrest is sold under an order of the Court, property which has been so arrested shall only be released under the authority of an instrument of release (in this rule referred to as a "release") in Form No. 7 in Appendix B, issued out of the registry or, where the action in which the warrant was issued is proceeding in a district registry, out of that registry.

(2) [Revoked].

(3) A release shall not be issued with respect to property as to which a caveat against release is in force, unless, either

  (a) at the time of the issue of the release the property is under arrest in one or more other actions, or

  (b) the Court so orders.

(4) A release may be issued at the instance of any party to the action in which the warrant of arrest was issued if the Court so orders, or, subject to paragraphs (3), if all the other parties, except any defendant who has not acknowledged issue or service of the writ, consent.

(5) Where a release is to issue out of a district registry the registrar of that registry shall, before issuing it, procure a search to be made in the caveat book for the purpose of ascertaining whether there is a caveat against release in force as to the property in question.

(6) Before a release is issued, the party applying for its issue must, unless paragraph (3)(a) applies, give notice to any person at whose instance a subsisting caveat against release has been entered, or to his solicitor, requiring the caveat to be withdrawn.

(7) Before property under arrest is released in compliance with a release issued under this rule, the party at whose instance it was issued must, in accordance with the directions of the marshal or, where the action is proceeding in a district registry, the registrar of that registry, either—

  (a) pay the fees of the marshal already incurred and lodge in the marshal's office or the district registry, as the case may be, an undertaking to pay on demand the other fees and expenses in connection with the arrest of the property and the care and custody of it while under arrest and of its release,
  or

  (b) lodge in the marshal's office or district registry an undertaking to pay on demand all such fees and expenses, whether incurred or to be incurred.

(8) The Court, on the application of any party who objects to directions given to him by the marshal under paragraph (7) may vary or revoke the directions.

Caveat against release, etc. (O. 75, r. 14)

14.—(1) Where a person claiming to have a right of action in rem against any property which is under arrest or the proceeds of sale thereof wishes to be served with notice of any application to the Court in respect of that property or those proceeds, he must file in the registry a praecipe in Form No. 9 in Appendix B and, on the filing of the praecipe, a caveat shall be entered in the caveat book.

(2) Where the release of any property under arrest is delayed by the entry of a caveat under this rule, any person having an interest in that property may apply to the Court by motion for an order requiring the person who procured the entry of the caveat to pay to the applicant damages in respect of the loss suffered by the applicant by reason of the delay, and the Court, unless it is satisfied that the person procuring the entry of the caveat had a good and sufficient reason for so doing, may make an order accordingly.

Duration of caveats (O. 75, r. 15)

15.—(1) Every caveat entered in the caveat book is valid for 12 months beginning with the date of its entry but the person at whose instance a caveat was entered may withdraw it by filing a praecipe in Form No. 10 in Appendix B.

(2) The period of validity of a caveat may not be extended but this provision shall not be taken as preventing the entry of successive caveats.

Bail (O. 75, r. 16)

16.—(1) Bail on behalf of a party to an action in rem must be given by bond in form No. 11 in Appendix B; and the sureties to the bond must enter into the bond before a commissioner for oaths (or a solicitor exercising the powers of a commissioner for oaths under section 81 of the Solicitors Act 1974) not being a commissioner (or solicitor) who, or whose partner, is acting as solicitor or agent for the party on whose behalf the bail is to be given.

(2) Subject to paragraph (3) a surety to a bail bond must make an affidavit stating that he is able to pay the sum for which the bond is given.

(3) Where a corporation is a surety to a bail bond given on behalf of a party, no affidavit shall be made under paragraph (2) on behalf of the corporation unless the opposite party requires it, but where such an affidavit is required it must be made by a director, manager, secretary or other similar officer of the corporation.

(4) The party on whose behalf bail is given must serve on the opposite party a notice of bail containing the names and addresses of the persons who have given bail on his behalf and of the commissioner before whom the bail bond was entered into; and after the expiration of 24 hours from the service of the notice (or sooner with the consent of the opposite party) he may file the bond and must at the same time file the affidavits (if any) made under paragraph (2) and an affidavit proving due service of the notice of bail to which a copy of that notice must be exhibited.

Interveners (O. 75, r. 17)

17.—(1) Where property against which an action in rem is brought is under arrest or money representing the proceeds of sale of that property is in court, a person who has an interest in that property or money but who is not a defendant to the action may, with the leave of the Court, intervene in the action.

(2) An application for the grant of leave under this rule must be made ex parte by affidavit showing the interest of the applicant in the property against which the action is brought or in the money in court.

(3) A person to whom leave is granted under this rule shall thereupon become a party to the action.

(4) The Court may order that a person to whom it grants leave to intervene in an action shall, within such period of periods as may be specified in the order, serve on any other party to the action such notice of his intervention and such pleading as may be so specified.

Judgment by default (O. 75, r. 21)

21.—(1) Where a writ is served under rule 8(4) on a party at whose instance a caveat against arrest was issued, then if—

    (a) the sum claimed in the action begun by the writ does not exceed the amount specified in the undertaking given by that party or his solicitor to procure the entry of that caveat, and

    (b) that party or his solicitor does not within 14 days after service of the writ fulfil the undertaking given by him as aforesaid,

the plaintiff may, after filing an affidavit verifying the fact on which the action is based, apply to the Court for judgment by default.

(2) Judgment given under paragraph (1) may be enforced by the arrest of the property against which the action was brought and by committal of the party at whose instance the caveat with respect to that property was entered.

(3) Where a defendant to an action in rem fails to acknowledge service of the writ within the time limited for doing so, then, on the expiration of 14 days after service of the writ and upon filing an affidavit proving due service of the writ, an affidavit verifying the facts on which the action is based and, if a statement of claim was not indorsed on the writ, a copy of the statement of claim, the plaintiff may apply to the Court for judgment by default.

Where the writ is deemed to have been duly served on the defendant by virtue of Order 10, rule 1(4) or was served by the marshal or his substitute under rule 8 of this Order, an affidavit proving due service of the writ need not be filed under this paragraph but the writ indorsed as mentioned in the said rule 1(4) or indorsed as mentioned in rule 8(3A) must be lodged with the affidavit verifying the facts on which the action is based.

(4) Where a defendant to an action in rem fails to serve a defence on the plaintiff, then, after the expiration of the period fixed by or under these rules for serive of the defence and upon filing an affidavit stating that no defence was served on him by that defendant during that period, an affidavit verifying the facts on which the action is based and, if a statement of claim was not indorsed on the writ, a copy of the statement of claim, the plaintiff may apply to the Court for judgment by default.

(5) Where a defendant to a counterclaim in an action in rem fails to serve a defence to counterclaim on the defendant making the counterclaim, then, subject to paragraph (6) after the expiration of the period fixed by or under these rules for service of the defence to counterclaim and upon filing an affidavit stating that no defence to counterclaim was served on him by the first-mentioned defendant during that period, an affidavit verifying the facts on which the counterclaim is based and a copy of the counterclaim, the defendant making the counterclaim may apply to the Court for judgment by default.

(6) No application may be made under paragraph (5) against the plaintiff in any such action as is referred to in rule 2(1)(a).

(7) An application to the Court under this rule must be made by motion and if, on the hearing of the motion, the Court is satisfied that the applicant's claim is well founded it may give judgment for the claim with or without a reference to the registrar or district registrar and may at the same time order the property against which the action or, as the case may be, counterclaim is brought to be appraised and sold and the proceeds to be paid into court or may make such other order as it thinks just.

(8) In default actions in rem evidence may, unless the Court otherwise orders, be given by affidavit without any order or direction in that behalf.

(9) The Court may, on such terms as it thinks just, set aside or vary any judgment entered in pursuance of this rule.

(10) Order 13 and Order 19 (except rule 1) shall not apply to actions in rem.

Order for sale of ship: determination of priority of claims (O. 75, r. 22)

22.—(2) Where in an action in rem against a ship the Court has ordered the ship to be sold, any party who has obtained or obtains judgment against the ship or proceeds of sale of the ship may—

(a) in a case where the order for sale contains the further order referred to in paragraph (2) after the expiration of the period specified in the order under paragraph (2)(a) or

(b) in any other case, after obtaining judgment,

apply to the Court by motion for an order determining the order of priority of the claims against the proceeds of sale of the ship.

(2) Where in an action in rem against a ship the Court orders the ship to be sold, it may further order—

(a) that the order of priority of the claims against the proceeds of sale of the ship shall not be determined until after the expiration of 90 days, or of such other period as the Court may specify, beginning with the day on which the proceeds of sale are paid into court;

(b) that any party to the action or to any other action in rem against the ship or the proceeds of sale thereof may apply to the Court in the action to which he is a party to extend the period specified in the order;

(c) that within 7 days after the date of payment into court of the proceeds of sale the marshal shall send for publication in Lloyd's List and Shipping Gazette and such other newspaper, if any, as the Court may direct, a notice complying with paragraph (3).

(3) The notice referred to in paragraph (2)(c) must state—

(a) that the ship (naming her) has been sold by order of the High Court in an action in rem, identifying the action;

(b) that the gross proceeds of the sale, specifying the amount thereof, have been paid into court;

(c) that the order of priority of the claims against the said proceeds will not be determined until after the expiration of the period (specifying it) specified in the order for sale; and

(d) that any person with a claim against the ship or the proceeds of sale thereof, on which he intends to proceed to judgment should do so before the expiration of that period.

(4) The marshal must lodge in the registry or, if the action is proceeding in a district registry, that registry, a copy of each newspaper in which the notice referred to in paragraph (2)(c) appeared.

(5) The expenses incurred by the marshal in complying with an order of the Court under this rule shall be included in his expenses relating to the sale of the ship.

(6) An application to the Court to extend the period referred to in paragraph (2)(a) must be made by motion, and a copy of the notice of motion, must, at least 3 days before the day fixed for the hearing thereof, be served on each party who has begun an action in rem against the ship or the proceeds of sale thereof.

(7) In this rule "the Court" means a judge in person.

Limitation action: parties (O. 75, r. 37)

37.—(1) In a limitation action the person seeking relief shall be the plaintiff and shall be named in the writ by his name and not described merely as the owner of, or as bearing some other relation to, a particular ship or other property.

(2) The plaintiff must make one of the persons with claims against him in respect of the casualty to which the action relates defendant to the action and may make any or all of the others defendant also.

(3) At least one of the defendants to the action must be named in the writ by his name but the other defendants may be described generally and not named by their names.

(4) The writ must be served on one or more of the defendants who are named by their names therein and need not be served on any other defendant.

(5) In this rule and rules 38, 39 and 40 "name" includes a firm name or the name under which a person carries on his business, and where any person with a claim against the plaintiff in respect of the casualty to which the action relates has described himself for the purposes of his claim merely as the owner of, or as bearing some other relation to, a ship or other property, he may be so described as defendant in the writ and, if so described, shall be deemed for the purposes of the rules aforesaid to have been named in the writ by his name.

Limitation action: payment into court (O. 75, r. 37A)

37A.—(1) The plaintiff may constitute a limitation fund by paying into court the sterling equivalent of the number of special drawing rights to which he claims to be entitled to limit his liability under the Merchant Shipping Act 1979 and may also pay into court interest thereon from the date of the occurrence giving rise to his liability to the date of payment into court.

(2) Where the plaintiff does not know the sterling equivalent of the said number of special drawing rights on the date of payment into court he may calculate the same on the basis of the latest available published sterling equivalent of a special drawing right as fixed by the International

Monetary Fund, and in the event of the sterling equivalent of a special drawing right on the date of payment into court under paragraph (1) being different from that used for calculating the amount of that payment into court the plaintiff may—

    (a) make up any deficiency by making a further payment into court which, if made within 14 days after the payment into court under paragraph (1), shall be treated, except for the purposes of the rules relating to the accrual of interest on money paid into court, as if it had been made on the date of that payment into court, or

    (b) apply to the court for payment out of any excess amount (together with any interest accrued thereon) paid into court under paragraph (1).

(3) An application under paragraph (2)(b) may be made ex parte and must be supported by evidence proving the sterling equivalent of the appropriate number of special drawing rights on the date of payment into court.

(4) On making any payment into court under this rule, the plaintiff shall give notice thereof in writing to every defendant, specifying the date of payment in and the amount and, where interest is also paid in, the amount of such interest, the rate, and the period to which it relates.

The plaintiff shall also give notice in writing to every defendant of any excess amount (and any interest thereon) paid out to him under paragraph (2)(b).

(5) Order 22, rules 10, 11 and 13 shall apply to a limitation action as they apply to an action for a debt or damages, and rule 24(2) and (3) of this Order shall apply, with the necessary modifications, to the payment of money paid into court under this rule.

Limitation action: summons for decree or directions (O. 75, r. 38)

38.—(1) Within 7 days after the acknowledgment of issue or service of the writ by one of the defendants named therein by their names or, if none of them acknowledges issue or service, within 7 days after the time limited for acknowledging service the plaintiff, without serving a statement of claim must take out a summons returnable in chambers before the registrar or district judge, as the case may be, asking for a decree limiting his liability or, in default of such a decree, for directions as to the further proceedings in the action.

(2) The summons must be supported by an affidavit or affidavits proving—

    (a) the plaintiff's case in the action, and

    (b) if none of the defendants named in the writ by their names has acknowledged service, service of the writ on at least one of the defendants so named.

(3) The affidavit in support of the summons must state—

    (a) the names of all the persons who, to the knowledge of the plaintiff, have claims against him in respect of the casualty to which the action relates, not being defendants to the action who are named in the writ by their names,
    and

    (b) the address of each of those persons, if known to the plaintiff.

(4) The summons and every affidavit in support thereof must, at least 7 clear days before the hearing of the summons, be served on any defendant who has acknowledged issue or service of the writ.

(5) On the hearing of the summons the registrar, if it appears to him that it is not disputed that the plaintiff has a right to limit his liability, shall make a decree limiting the plaintiff's liability and fix the amount to which the liability is to be limited.

(6) On the hearing of the summons the registrar, if it appears to him that any defendant has not sufficient information to enable him to decide whether or not to dispute that the plaintiff has a right to limit his liability, shall give such directions as appear to him to be appropriate for enabling the defendant to obtain such information and shall adjourn the hearing.

(7) If on the hearing or resumed hearing of the summons the registrar does not make a decree limiting the plaintiff's liability, he shall give such directions as to the further proceedings in the action as appear to him to be appropriate including, in particular, a direction requiring the taking out

of a summons for directions under Order 25 and, if he gives no such direction, a direction fixing the period within which any notice under Order 38, rule 21, must be served.

(8) Any defendant who, after the registrar has given directions under paragraph (7) ceases to dispute the plaintiff's right to limit his liability must forthwith file a notice to that effect in the registry or district registry, as the case may be, and serve a copy on the plaintiff and on any other defendant who has acknowledged issue or service of the writ.

(9) If every defendant who disputes the plaintiff's right to limit his liability serves a notice on the plaintiff under paragraph (8) the plaintiff may take out a summons returnable in chambers before the registrar or district judge, as the case may be, asking for a decree limiting his liability; and paragraphs (4) and (5) shall apply to a summons under this paragraph as they apply to a summons under paragraph (1).

Limitation action: proceedings under decree (O. 75, r. 39)

39.—(1) Where the only defendants in a limitation action are those named in the writ by their names and all the persons so named have either been served with the writ or acknowledged the issue thereof, any decree in the action limiting the plaintiff's liability (whether made by a registrar or on the trial of the action)—

    (a) need not be advertised, but

    (b) shall only operate to protect the plaintiff in respect of claims by the persons so named or persons claiming through or under them.

(2) In any case not falling within paragraph (1) any decree in the action limiting the plaintiff's liability (whether made by a registrar or on the trial of the action)—

    (a) shall be advertised by the plaintiff in such manner and within such time as may be provided by the decree;

    (b) shall fix a time within which persons with claims against the plaintiff in respect of the casualty to which the action relates may file their claims, and, in cases to which rule 40 applies, take out a summons if they think fit, to set the order aside.

(3) The advertisement to be required under paragraph (2)(a) shall, unless for special reasons the registrar or judge thinks fit otherwise to provide, be a single advertisement in each of three newspapers specified in the decree, identifying the action, the casualty and the relation of the plaintiff thereto (whether as owner of a ship involved in the casualty or otherwise as the case may be) stating that the decree has been made and specifying the amounts fixed thereby as the limits of the plaintiff's liability and the time allowed thereby for the filing of claims and the taking out of summonses to set the decree aside.

The plaintiff must within the time fixed under paragraph (2)(b) file in the registry or district registry, as the case may be, a copy of each newspaper in which the advertisement required under paragraph 2(a) appears.

(4) The time to be allowed under paragraph (2)(b) shall, unless for special reasons the registrar or judge thinks fit otherwise to provide, be not less than 2 months from the latest date allowed for the appearance of the advertisements; and after the expiration of the time so allowed, no claim may be filed or summons taken out to set aside the decree except with the leave of the registrar.

(5) Save as aforesaid, on the making of any decree limiting the plaintiff's liability arising out of an occurrence the Court may distribute the limitation fund and may stay any proceedings relating to any claim arising out of that occurrence which are pending against the plaintiff.

Limitation action: proceedings to set aside decree (O. 75, r. 40)

40.—(1) Where a decree limiting the plaintiff's liability (whether made by a registrar or on the trial of the action) fixes a time in accordance with rule 39(2) any person with a claim against the plaintiff in respect of the casualty to which the action relates, who—

    (a) was not named by his name in the writ as a defendant to the action, or

    (b) if so named, neither was served with the writ nor has acknowledged the issue thereof, may, within that time, after acknowledging issue of the writ, take out a summons returnable in chambers before the registrar or district judge, as the case may be, asking that the decree be set aside.

(2) The summons must be supported by an affidavit or affidavits showing that the defendant in question has a bona fide claim against the plaintiff in respect of the casualty in question and that he has sufficient prima facie grounds for the contention that the plaintiff is not entitled to the relief given him by the decree.

(3) The summons and every affidavit in support thereof must, at least 7 clear days before the hearing of the summons, be served on the plaintiff and any defendant who has acknowledged issues or service of the writ.

(4) On the hearing of the summons the registrar, if he is satisfied that the defendant in question has a bona fide claim against the plaintiff and sufficient prima facie grounds for the contention that the plaintiff is not entitled to the relief given him by the decree, shall set the decree aside and give such directions as to the further proceedings in the action as appear to him to be appropriate including, in particular, a direction requiring the taking out of a summons for directions under Order 25.

APPENDIX 3

Conventions

INTERNATIONAL CONVENTION FOR THE UNIFICATION OF CERTAIN RULES RELATING TO THE ARREST OF SEA-GOING SHIPS, BRUSSELS, 10 MAY 1952

The High Contracting Parties,

Having recognised the desirability of determining by agreement certain uniform rules of law relating to the arrest of sea-going ships.

Have decided to conclude a Convention for this purpose and thereto have agreed as follows:

Article 1

In this Convention the following words shall have the meanings hereby assigned to them:

(1) "Maritime Claim" means a claim arising out of one or more of the following:

    (a) damage caused by any ship either in collision or otherwise;

    (b) loss of life or personal injury caused by any ship or occurring in connection with the operation of any ship;

    (c) salvage;

    (d) agreement relating to the use or hire of any ship whether by charterparty or otherwise;

    (e) agreement relating to the carriage of goods in any ship whether by charterparty or otherwise;

    (f) loss of or damage to goods including baggage carried in any ship;

    (g) general average;

    (h) bottomry;

    (i) towage;

    (j) pilotage;

    (k) goods or materials wherever supplied to a ship for her operation or maintenance;

    (l) construction, repair or equipment of any ship or dock charges and dues;

    (m) wages of Masters, Officers, or crew;

    (n) Master's disbursements, including disbursements made by shippers, charterers or agents on behalf of a ship or her owner;

    (o) disputes as to the title to or ownership of any ship;

    (p) disputes between co-owners of any ship as to the ownership, possession employment or earnings of that ship;

    (q) the mortgage or hypothecation of any ship.

(2) "Arrest" means the detention of a ship by judicial process to secure a maritime claim, but does not include the seizure of a ship in execution or satisfaction of a judgment.

(3) "Person" includes individuals, partnerships and bodies corporate, Governments, their Departments, and Public Authorities.

(4) "Claimant" means a person who alleges that a maritime claim exists in his favour.

Article 2

A ship flying the flag of one of the contracting States may be arrested in the jurisdiction of any of the contracting States in respect of any maritime claim, but in respect of no other claim; but nothing in this Convention shall be deemed to extend or restrict any right or powers vested in any Governments or their Departments, Public Authorities, or Dock or Harbour Authorities under their existing domestic laws or regulations to arrest, detain or otherwise prevent the sailing of vessels within their jurisdiction.

Article 3

(1) Subject to the provisions of paragraph 4 of this Article and of Article 10, a claimant may arrest either the particular ship in respect of which the maritime claim arose, or any other ship which is owned by the person who was, at the time when the maritime claim arose, the owner of the particular ship, even though the ship arrested be ready to sail; but no ship, other than the particular ship in respect of which the claim arose, may be arrested in respect of any of the maritime claims enumerated in Article 1(1)(o), (p) or (q).

(2) Ships shall be deemed to be in the same ownership when all the shares therein are owned by the same person or persons.

(3) A ship shall not be arrested, nor shall bail or other security be given more than once in any one or more of the jurisdictions of any of the Contracting States in respect of the same maritime claim by the same claimant; and, if a ship has been arrested in any one of such jurisdictions, or bail or other security has been given in such jurisdiction either to release the ship or to avoid a threatened arrest, any subsequent arrest of the ship or of any ship in the same ownership by the same claimant for the same maritime claim shall be set aside, and the ship released by the Court or other appropriate judicial authority of that State, unless the claimant can satisfy the Court or other appropriate judicial authority that the bail or other security had been finally released before the subsequent arrest or that there is other good cause for maintaining that arrest.

(4) When in the case of a charter by demise of a ship the charterer and not the registered owner is liable in respect of a maritime claim relating to that ship, the claimant may arrest such ship or any other ship in the ownership of the charterer by demise, subject to the provisions of this Convention, but no other ship in the ownership of the registered owner shall be liable to arrest in respect of such maritime claims.

The provisions of this paragraph shall apply to any case in which a person other than the registered owner of a ship is liable in respect of a maritime claim relating to that ship.

Article 4

A ship may only be arrested under the authority of a Court or of the appropriate judicial authority of the Contracting State in which the arrest is made.

Article 5

The Court or other appropriate judicial authority within whose jurisdiction the ship has been arrested shall permit the release of the ship upon sufficient bail or other security being furnished, save in cases in which a ship has been arrested in respect of any of the maritime claims enumerated in Article 1(1)(o) and (p). In such cases the Court or other appropriate juridical authority may permit the person in possession of the ship to continue trading the ship, upon such person furnishing sufficient bail or other security, or may otherwise deal with the operation of the ship during the period of the arrest.

In default of agreement between the Parties as to the sufficiency of the bail or other security, the Court or other appropriate judicial authority shall determine the nature and amount thereof.

The request to release the ship against such security shall not be construed as an acknowledgment of liability or as a waiver of the benefit of the legal limitation of liability of the owner of the ship.

Article 6

All questions whether in any case the claimant is liable in damages for the arrest of a ship or for the costs of the bail or other security furnished to release or prevent the arrest of a ship, shall be determined by the law of the Contracting State in whose jurisdiction the arrest was made or applied for.

The rules of procedure relating to the arrest of a ship, to the application for obtaining the authority referred to in Article 4, and all matters of procedure which the arrest may entail, shall be governed by the law of the Contracting State in which the arrest was made or applied for.

Article 7

(1) The Courts of the country in which the arrest was made shall have jurisdiction to determine the case upon its merits:

— if the domestic law of the country in which the arrest is made gives jurisdiction to such Courts;
— or in any of the following cases namely:

(a) if the claimant has his habitual residence or principal place of business in the country in which the arrest was made;
(b) if the claim arose in the country in which the arrest was made;
(c) if the claim concerns the voyage of the ship during which the arrest was made;
(d) if the claim arose out of a collision or in circumstances covered by Article 13 of the International Convention for the unification of certain rules of law with respect to collisions between vessels, signed at Brussels on 23rd September 1910;
(e) if the claim is for salvage;
(f) if the claim is upon a mortgage or hypothecation of the ship arrested.

(2) If the Court within whose jurisdiction the ship was arrested has not jurisdiction to decide upon the merits, the bail or other security given in accordance with Article 5 to procure the release of the ship shall specifically provide that it is given as security for the satisfaction of any judgment which may eventually be pronounced by a Court having jurisdiction so do decide; and the Court or other appropriate judicial authority of the country in which the arrest is made shall fix the time within which the claimant shall bring an action before a Court having such jurisdiction.

(3) If the parties have agreed to submit the dispute to the jurisdiction of a particular Court other than that within whose jurisdiction the arrest was made or to arbitration, the Court or other appropriate judicial authority within whose jurisdiction the arrest was made may fix the time within which the claimant shall bring proceedings.

(4) If, in any of the cases mentioned in the two preceding paragraphs, the action or proceedings are not brought within the time so fixed, the defendant may apply for the release of the ship or of the bail or other security.

(5) This Article shall not apply in cases covered by the provisions of the revised Rhine Navigation Convention of 17 October 1868.

Article 8

(1) The provisions of this Convention shall apply to any vessel flying the flag of a Contracting State in the jurisdiction of any Contracting State.

(2) A ship flying the flag of a non-Contracting State may be arrested in the jurisdiction of any Contracting State in respect of any of the maritime claims enumerated in Article 1 or of any other claim for which the law of the Contracting State permits arrest.

(3) Nevertheless any Contracting State shall be entitled wholly or partly to exclude from the benefits of this Convention any Government of a non-Contracting State or any person who has not, at the time of the arrest, his habitual residence or principal place of business in one of the Contracting States.

(4) Nothing in this Convention shall modify or affect the rules of law in force in the respective Contracting States relating to the arrest of any ship within the jurisdiction of the State or her flag by a person who has his habitual residence or principal place of business in that State.

(5) When a maritime claim is asserted by a third party other than the original claimant, whether by subrogation, assignment or otherwise, such third party shall, for the purpose of this Convention, be deemed to have the same habitual residence or principal place of business as the original claimant.

Article 9

Nothing in this Convention shall be construed as creating a right of action, which, apart from the provisions of this Convention, would not arise under the law applied by the Court which had seisin of the case, nor as creating any maritime liens which do not exist under such law or under the Convention on Maritime Mortgages and Liens, if the latter is applicable.

Article 10

The High Contracting Parties may at the time of signature, deposit of ratification or accession, reserve

   (a) the right not to apply this Convention to the arrest of a ship for any of the claims enumerated in paragraphs (o) and (p) of Article 1, but to apply their domestic laws to such claims;
   (b) the right not to apply the first paragraph of Article 3 to the arrest of a ship, within their jurisdiction, for claims set out in Article 1, paragraph (q).

Article 11

The High Contracting Parties undertake to submit to arbitration any disputes between States arising out of the interpretation or application of this Convention, but this shall be without prejudice to the obligations of those High Contracting Parties who have agreed to submit their disputes to the International Court of Justice.

Article 12

This Convention shall be open for signature by the States represented at the Ninth Diplomatic Conference on Maritime Law. The protocol of signature shall be drawn up through the good offices of the Belgian Ministry of Foreign Affairs.

Article 13

This Convention shall be ratified and the instruments of ratification shall be deposited with the Belgian Ministry of Foreign Affairs which shall notify all signatory and acceding States of the deposit of any such instruments.

Article 14

   (a) This Convention shall come into force between the two States which first ratify it, six months after the date of the deposit of the second instrument of ratification.
   (b) This Convention shall come into force in respect of each signatory State which ratifies it after the deposit of the second instrument of ratification six months after the date of the deposit of the instrument of ratification of that State.

Article 15

Any State not represented at the Ninth Diplomatic Conference on Maritime Law may accede to this Convention.

The accession of any State shall be notified to the Belgian Ministry of Foreign Affairs which shall inform through diplomatic channels all signatory and acceding States of such notification.

The Convention shall come into force in respect of the acceding State six months after the date of the receipt of such notification but not before the Convention has come into force in accordance with the provisions of Article 14(a).

Article 16

Any High Contracting Party may three years after the coming into force of this Convention in respect of such High Contracting Party or at any time thereafter request that a conference be convened in order to consider amendments to the Convention.

Any High Contracting Party proposing to avail itself of this right shall notify the Belgian Government which shall convene the conference within six months thereafter.

Article 17

Any High Contracting Party shall have the right to denounce this Convention at any time after the coming into force thereof in respect of such High Contracting Party. This denunciation shall take effect one year after the date on which notification thereof has been received by the Belgian Government which shall inform through diplomatic channels all the other High Contracting Parties of such notification.

Article 18

(a) Any High Contracting Party may at the time of its ratification of or accession to this Convention or at any time thereafter declare by written notification to the Belgian Ministry of Foreign Affairs that the Convention shall extend to any of the territories for whose international relations it is responsible. The Convention shall six months after the date of the receipt of such notification by the Belgian Ministry of Foreign Affairs extend to the territories named therein, but not before the date of the coming into force of the Convention in respect of such High Contracting Party.

(b) A High Contracting Party which has made a declaration under (a) of this Article extending the Convention to any territory for whose international relations it is responsible may at any time thereafter declare by notification given to the Belgian Ministry of Foreign Affairs that the Convention shall cease to extend to such territory and the Convention shall one year after the receipt of the notification by the Belgian Ministry of Foreign Affairs cease to extend thereto.

(c) The Belgian Ministry of Foreign Affairs shall inform through diplomatic channels all signatory and acceding States of any notification received by it under this Article.

Done at Brussels, on May 10, 1952 in the French and English languages, the two texts being equally authentic.
(Follow the signatures)

INTERNATIONAL CONVENTION ON CERTAIN RULES CONCERNING CIVIL JURISDICTION IN MATTERS OF COLLISION, BRUSSELS, 10 MAY 1952

The High Contracting Parties,

Having recognised the advisability of establishing by agreement certain uniform rules relating to civil jurisdiction in matters of collision,

Have decided to conclude a Convention for this purpose and thereto have agreed as follows:

Article 1

(1) An action for collision occurring between seagoing vessels, or between seagoing vessels and inland navigation craft, can only be introduced:

    (a) either before the Court where the defendant has his habitual residence or a place of business;

    (b) or before the Court of the place where arrest has been effected of the defendant ship or of any other ship belonging to the defendant which can be lawfully arrested, or where arrest could have been effected and bail or other security has been furnished;

    (c) or before the Court of the place of collision when the collision has occurred within the limits of a port or inland waters;

(2) It shall be for the plaintiff to decide in which of the Courts referred to in paragraph 1 of this Article the action shall be instituted.

(3) A claimant shall not be allowed to bring a further action against the same defendant on the same facts in another jurisdiction, without discontinuing an action already instituted.

Article 2

The provisions of Article 1 shall not in any way prejudice the right of the Parties to bring an action in respect of a collision before a Court they have chosen by agreement or to refer it to arbitration.

Article 3

(1) Counterclaims arising out of the same collision can be brought before the Court having jurisdiction over the principal action in accordance with the provisions of Article 1.

(2) In the event of there being several claimants, any claimant may bring his action before the Court previously seised of an action against the same party arising out of the same collision.

(3) In the case of a collision or collisions in which two or more vessels are involved nothing in this Convention shall prevent any Court seised of an action by reason of the provisions of this Convention, from exercising jurisdiction under its national laws in further actions arising out of the same incident.

Article 4

This Convention shall also apply to an action for damage caused by one ship to another or to the property or persons on board such ships through the carrying out of or the omission to carry out a manoeuvre or through non-compliance with regulations even when there has been no actual collision.

Article 5

Nothing contained in this Convention shall modify the rules of law now or hereafter in force in the various Contracting States in regard to collisions involving warships or vessels owned by or in the service of a State.

Article 6

This Convention does not affect claims arising from contracts of carriage or from any other contracts.

Article 7

This Convention shall not apply in cases covered by the provisions of the revised Rhine Navigation Convention of 17 October 1868.

Article 8

The provisions of this Convention shall be applied as regards all persons interested when all the vessels concerned in any action belong to States of the High Contracting Parties.
Provided always that:

(1) As regards persons interested who belong to a non-contracting State the application of the above provisions may be made by each of the Contracting States conditional upon reciprocity;

(2) Where all the persons interested belong to the same State as the court trying the case, the provisions of the national law and not of the Convention are applicable.

Article 9

The High Contracting Parties undertake to submit to arbitration any disputes between States arising out of the interpretation or application of this Convention, but this shall be without prejudice to the obligations of those High Contracting Parties who have agreed to submit their disputes to the International Court of Justice.

Article 10

This Convention shall be open for signature by the States represented at the Ninth Diplomatic Conference on Maritime Law. The protocol of signature shall be drawn up through the good offices of the Belgian Ministry of Foreign Affairs.

Article 11

This Convention shall be ratified and the instruments of ratification shall be deposited with the Belgian Ministry of Foreign Affairs which shall notify all signatory and acceding States of the deposit of any such instruments.

Article 12

(a) This Convention shall come into force between the two States which first ratify it, six months after the date of the deposit of the second instrument of ratification.

(b) This Convention shall come into force in respect of each signatory State which ratifies it after the deposit of the second instrument of ratification six months after the date of the deposit of the instrument of ratification of that State.

Article 13

Any State not represented at the Ninth Diplomatic Conference on Maritime Law may accede to this Convention.

The accession of any State shall be notified to the Belgian Ministry of Foreign Affairs which shall inform through diplomatic channels all signatory and acceding States of such notification.

The Convention shall come into force in respect of the acceding State six months after the date of the receipt of such notification but not before the Convention has come into force in accordance with the provisions of Article 12(a).

Article 14

Any High Contracting Party may three years after the coming into force of this Convention in respect of such High Contracting Party or at any time thereafter request that a Conference be convened in order to consider amendments to the Convention.

Any High Contracting Party proposing to avail itself of this right shall notify the Belgian Government which shall convene the Conference within six months thereafter.

Article 15

Any High Contracting Party shall have the right to denounce this Convention at any time after the coming into force thereof in respect of such High Contracting Party. This denunciation shall take effect one year after the date on which notification thereof has been received by the Belgian Government which shall inform through diplomatic channels all the other High Contracting Parties of such notification.

Article 16

(a) Any High Contracting Party may at the time of its ratification of or accession to this Convention or at any time thereafter declare by written notification to the Belgian Ministry of Foreign Affairs that the Convention shall extend to any of the territories for whose international relations it is responsible. The Convention shall six months after the date of the receipt of such notification by the Belgian Ministry of Foreign Affairs extend to the territories named therein, but not before the date of the coming into force of the Convention in respect of such High Contracting Party.

(b) A High Contracting Party which has made a declaration under paragraph (a) of this Article extending the Convention to any territory for whose international relations it is responsible may at any time thereafter declare by notification given to the Belgian Ministry of Foreign Affairs that the Convention shall cease to extend to such territory and the Convention shall one year after the receipt of the notification by the Belgian Ministry of Foreign Affairs cease to extend thereto.

(c) The Belgian Ministry of Foreign Affairs shall inform through diplomatic channels all signatory and acceding States of any notification received by it under this Article.

Done at Brussels, on May 10, 1952, in a single original in the French and English languages, the two texts being equally authentic.

(Follow the signatures)

INTERNATIONAL CONVENTION ON MARITIME LIENS AND MORTGAGES 1993

The States Parties to this Convention

Conscious of the need to improve conditions for ship financing and the development of national merchant fleets,

Recognizing the desirability of international uniformity in the field of maritime liens and mortgages, and therefore

Convinced of the necessity for an international legal instrument governing maritime liens and mortgages,

Have decided to conclude a Convention for this purpose and have therefore agreed as follows:

Article 1. Recognition and enforcement of mortgages, "hypothèques" and charges

Mortgages, "hypothèques" and registrable charges of the same nature, which registrable charges of the same nature will be referred to hereinafter as "charges", effected on seagoing vessels shall be recognized and enforceable in States Parties provided that:

(a) such mortgages, "hypothèques" and charges have been effected and registered in accordance with the law of the State in which the vessel is registered;

(b) the register and any instruments required to be deposited with the registrar in accordance with the law of the State in which the vessel is registered are open to public inspection, and that extracts from the register and copies of such instruments are obtainable from the registrar; and

(c) either the register or any instruments referred to in subparagraph (b) specifies at least the name and address of the person in whose favour the mortgage, "hypothèque" or charge has been effected or that it has been issued to bearer, the maximum amount secured, if that is a requirement of the law of the State of registration, or, if that amount is specified in the instrument creating the mortgage, "hypothèque" or charge, and the date and other particulars which, according to the State of registration, determine the ranking in relation to other registered mortgages, "hypothèques" and charges.

Article 2. Ranking and effects of mortgages, "hypothèques" and charges

The ranking of registered mortgages, "hypothèques" or charges as between themselves and, without prejudice to the provisions of this Convention, their effect in regard to third parties shall be determined by the law of the State of registration; however, without prejudice to the provisions of this Convention, all matters relating to the procedure of enforcement shall be regulated by the law of the State where enforcement takes place.

Article 3. Change of ownership or registration

1. With the exception of the cases provided for in Articles 11 and 12, in all other cases that entail the deregistration of the vessel from the register of a State Party, such State Party shall not permit the owner to deregister the vessel unless all registered mortgages, "hypothèques" or charges are previously deleted or the written consent of all holders of such mortgages, "hypothèques" or charges is obtained. However, where the deregistration of the vessel is obligatory in accordance with the law of a State Party, otherwise than as a result of a voluntary sale, the holders of registered mortgages, "hypothèques" or charges shall be notified of the pending deregistration in order to enable such holders to take appropriate action to protect their interests; unless the holders consent, the deregistration shall not be implemented earlier than after a lapse of a reasonable period of time which shall be not less than three months after the relevant notification to such holders.

2. Without prejudice to article 12, paragraph 5, a vessel which is or has been registered in a State Party shall not be eligible for registration in another State Party unless either:

(a) a certificate has been issued by the former State to the effect that the vessel has been deregistered; or

(b) a certificate has been issued by the former State to the effect that the vessel will be deregistered with immediate effect, at such time as the new registration is effected. The date of deregistration shall be the date of the new registration of the vessel.

Article 4. Maritime liens

1. Each of the following claims against the owner, demise charterer, manager or operator of the vessel shall be secured by a maritime lien on the vessel:

(a) claims for wages and other sums due to the master, officers and other members of the vessel's complement in respect of their employment on the vessel, including costs of repatriation and social insurance contributions payable on their behalf;

(b) claims in respect of loss of life or personal injury occurring, whether on land or on water, in direct connection with the operation of the vessel;

(c) claims for reward for the salvage of the vessel;

(d) claims for port, canal, and other waterway dues and pilotage dues;

(e) claims based on tort arising out of physical loss or damage caused by the operation of the vessel other than loss of or damage to cargo, containers and passengers' effects carried on the vessel.

2. No maritime liens shall attach to a vessel to secure claims as set out in subparagraphs (b) and (e) of paragraph 1 which arise out of or result from:

(a) damage in connection with the carriage of oil or other hazardous or noxious substances by sea for which compensation is payable to the claimants pursuant to international conventions or national law providing for strict liability and compulsory insurance or other means of securing the claims; or

(b) the radioactive properties or a combination of radioactive properties with toxic, explosive or other hazardous properties of nuclear fuel or of radioactive products or waste.

Article 5. Priority of maritime liens

1. The maritime liens set out in Article 4 shall take priority over registered mortgages, "hypothèques" and charges, and no other claim shall take priority over such maritime liens or over such mortgages, "hypothèques" or charges which comply with the requirements of Article 1, except as provided in paragraphs 3 and 4 of Article 12.

2. The maritime liens set out in Article 4 shall rank in the order listed, provided however that maritime liens securing claims for reward for the salvage of the vessel shall take priority over all other maritime liens which have attached to the vessel prior to the time when the operations giving rise to the said liens were performed.

3. The maritime liens set out in each of subparagraphs (a), (b), (d) and (e) of paragraph 1 of Article 4 shall rank *pari passu* as between themselves.

4. The maritime liens securing claims for reward for the salvage of the vessel shall rank in the inverse order of the time when the claim secured thereby accrued. Such claims shall be deemed to have accrued on the date on which each salvage operation was terminated.

Article 6. Other maritime liens

Each State Party may under its law grant other maritime liens on a vessel to secure claims, other than those referred to in Article 4, against the owner, demise charterer, manager or operator of the vessel, provided that such liens:

(a) shall be subject to the provisions of Articles 8, 10 and 12;
(b) shall be extinguished

    (i) after a period of 6 months, from the time when the claims secured thereby arose unless, prior to the expiry of such period, the vessel has been arrested or seized, such arrest or seizure leading to a forced sale; or

    (ii) at the end of a period of 60 days following a sale to a *bona fide* purchaser of the vessel, such period to commence on the date on which the sale is registered in accordance with the law of the State in which the vessel is registered following the sale;

whichever period expires first; and

(c) shall rank after the maritime liens set out in Article 4 and also after registered mortgages, "hypothèques" or charges which comply with the provisions of Article 1.

Article 7. Rights of retention

1. Each State Party may grant under its law a right of retention in respect of a vessel in the possession of either:

(a) a shipbuilder, to secure claims for the building of the vessel; or
(b) a shiprepairer, to secure claims for repair, including reconstruction of the vessel, effected during such possession.

2. Such right of retention shall be extinguished when the vessel ceases to be in the possession of the shipbuilder or shiprepairer, otherwise than in consequence of an arrest or seizure.

Article 8. Characteristics of maritime liens

Subject to the provisions of Article 12, the maritime liens follow the vessel, notwithstanding any change of ownership or of registration or of flag.

Article 9. Extinction of maritime liens by lapse of time

1. The maritime liens set out in Article 4 shall be extinguished after a period of one year unless, prior to the expiry of such period, the vessel has been arrested or seized, such arrest or seizure leading to a forced sale.

2. The one-year period referred to in paragraph 1 shall commence:

    (a) with respect to the maritime lien set out in Article 4, paragraph 1(a), upon the claimant's discharge from the vessel;

    (b) with respect to the maritime liens set out in Article 4, paragraph 1(b) to (e), when the claims secured thereby arise;

and shall not be subject to suspension or interruption, provided, however, that time shall not run during the period that the arrest or seizure of the vessel is not permitted by law.

Article 10. Assignment and subrogation

1. The assignment of or subrogation to a claim secured by a maritime lien entails the simultaneous assignment of or subrogation to such a maritime lien.

2. Claimants holding maritime liens may not be subrogated to the compensation payable to the owner of the vessel under an insurance contract.

Article 11. Notice of forced sale

1. Prior to the forced sale of a vessel in a State Party, the competent authority in such State Party shall ensure that notice in accordance with this article is provided to:

    (a) the authority in charge of the register of the State of registration;

    (b) all holders of registered mortgages, "hypothèques" or charges which have not been issued to bearer;

    (c) all holders of registered mortgages, "hypothèques" or charges issued to bearer and all holders of the maritime liens set out in Article 4, provided that the competent authority conducting the forced sale receives notice of their respective claims; and

    (d) the registered owner of the vessel.

2. Such notice shall be provided at least 30 days prior to the forced sale and shall contain either:

    (a) the time and place of the forced sale and such particulars concerning the forced sale or the proceedings leading to the forced sale as the authority in a State Party conducting the proceedings shall determine is sufficient to protect the interests of persons entitled to notice; or,

    (b) if the time and place of the forced sale cannot be determined with certainty, the approximate time and anticipated place of the forced sale and such particulars concerning the forced sale as the authority in a State Party conducting the proceedings shall determine is sufficient to protect the interests of persons entitled to notice.

If notice is provided in accordance with subparagraph (b), additional notice of the actual time and place of the forced sale shall be provided when known but, in any event, not less than seven days prior to the forced sale.

3. The notice specified in paragraph 2 of this article shall be in writing and either given by registered mail, or given by any electronic or other appropriate means which provide confirmation of receipt, to the persons interested as specified in paragraph 1, if known. In addition, the notice shall be given by press announcement in the State where the forced sale is conducted and, if deemed appropriate by the authority conducting the forced sale, in other publications.

Article 12. Effects of forced sale

1. In the event of the forced sale of the vessel in a State Party, all registered mortgages, "hypothèques" or charges, except those assumed by the purchaser with the consent of the holders, and all liens and other encumbrances of whatsoever nature, shall cease to attach to the vessel, provided that:

    (a) at the time of the sale, the vessel is in the area of the jurisdiction of such State; and

(b) the sale has been effected in accordance with the law of the said State and the provisions of Article 11 and this article.

2. The costs and expenses arising out of the arrest or seizure and subsequent sale of the vessel shall be paid first out of the proceeds of sale. Such costs and expenses include, *inter alia*, the costs for the upkeep of the vessel and the crew as well as wages, other sums and costs referred to in Article 4, paragraph (a), incurred from the time of arrest or seizure. The balance of the proceeds shall be distributed in accordance with the provisions of this Convention, to the extent necessary to satisfy the respective claims. Upon satisfaction of all claimants, the residue of the proceeds, if any, shall be paid to the owner and it shall be freely transferable.

3. A State Party may provide in its law that, in the event of the forced sale of a stranded or sunken vessel, following its removal by a public authority in the interest of safe navigation or the protection of the marine environment, the costs of such removal shall be paid out of the proceeds of the sale, before all other claims secured by a maritime lien on the vessel.

4. If at the time of the forced sale the vessel is in the possession of a shipbuilder or of a shiprepairer who under the law of the State Party in which the sale takes place enjoys a right of retention, such shipbuilder or shiprepairer must surrender possession of the vessel to the purchaser but is entitled to obtain satisfaction of his claim out of the proceeds of sale after the satisfaction of the claims of holders of maritime liens mentioned in Article 4.

5. When a vessel registered in a State Party has been the object of a forced sale in any State Party, the competent authority shall, at the request of the purchaser, issue a certificate to the effect that the vessel is sold free of all registered mortgages, "hypothèques" or charges, except those assumed by the purchaser, and of all liens and other encumbrances, provided that the requirements set out in paragraph 1(a) and (b) have been complied with. Upon production of such certificate, the registrar shall be bound to delete all registered mortgages, "hypothèques" or charges except those assumed by the purchaser, and to register the vessel in the name of the purchaser or to issue a certificate of deregistration for the purpose of new registration, as the case may be.

6. State Parties shall ensure that any proceeds of a forced sale are actually available and freely transferable.

Article 13. Scope of application

1. Unless otherwise provided in this Convention, its provisions shall apply to all seagoing vessels registered in a State Party or in a State which is not a State Party, provided that the latter's vessels are subject to the jurisdiction of the State Party.

2. Nothing in this Convention shall create any rights in, or enable any rights to be enforced against, any vessel owned or operated by a State and used only on Government non-commercial service.

Article 14. Communication between State Parties

For the purpose of Articles 3, 11 and 12, the competent authorities of the States Parties shall be authorized to correspond directly between themselves.

Article 15. Conflict of Conventions

Nothing in this Convention shall affect the application of any international convention providing for limitation of liability or of national legislation giving effect thereto.

Article 16. Temporary change of flag

If a seagoing vessel registered in one State is permitted to fly temporarily the flag of another State, the following shall apply:

(a) For the purposes of this Article, references in this Convention to the "State in which the vessel is registered" or to the "State of registration" shall be deemed to be references to the State in which the vessel was registered immediately prior to the change of flag, and references to "the authority in charge of the register" shall be deemed to be references to the authority in charge of the register in that State.

(b) The law of the State of registration shall be determinative for the purpose of recognition of registered mortgages, "hypothèques" and charges.

(c) The State of registration shall require a cross-reference entry in its register specifying the State whose flag the vessel is permitted to fly temporarily; likewise, the State whose flag the vessel is permitted to fly temporarily shall require that the authority in charge of the vessel's record specifies by a cross-reference in the record the State of registration.

(d) No State Party shall permit a vessel registered in that State to fly temporarily the flag of another State unless all registered mortgages, "hypothèques" or charges on that vessel have been previously satisfied or the written consent of the holders of all such mortgages, "hypothèques" or charges has been obtained.

(e) The notice referred to in Article 11 shall be given also to the competent authority in charge of the vessel's record in the State whose flag the vessel is permitted to fly temporarily.

(f) Upon production of the certificate of deregistration referred to in Article 12 paragraph 5, the competent authority in charge of the vessel's record in the State whose flag the vessel is permitted to fly temporarily shall, at the request of the purchaser, issue a certificate to the effect that the right to fly the flag of that State is revoked.

(g) Nothing in this Convention is to be understood to impose any obligation on States Parties to permit foreign vessels to fly temporarily their flag or national vessels to fly temporarily a foreign flag.

Article 17. Depositary

This Convention shall be deposited with the Secretary-General of the United Nations.

Article 18. Signature, ratification, acceptance, approval and accession

1. This Convention shall be open for signature by any State at the Headquarters of the United Nations, New York, from 1 September 1993 to 31 August 1994 and shall thereafter remain open for accession.

2. States may express their consent to be bound by this Convention by:

(a) signature without reservation as to ratification, acceptance or approval; or

(b) signature subject to ratification, acceptance or approval, followed by ratification, acceptance or approval; or

(c) accession.

3. Ratification, acceptance, approval or accession shall be effected by the deposit of an instrument to that effect with the depositary.

Article 19. Entry into force

1. This Convention shall enter into force 6 months following the date on which 10 States have expressed their consent to be bound by it.

2. For a State which expresses its consent to be bound by this Convention after the conditions for entry into force thereof have been met, such consent shall take effect 3 months after the date of expression of such consent.

Article 20. Revision and amendment

1. A conference of States Parties for the purpose of revising or amending this Convention shall be convened by the Secretary-General of the United Nations at the request of one-third of the States Parties.

2. Any consent to be bound by this Convention, expressed after the date of entry into force of an amendment to this Convention, shall be deemed to apply to the Convention, as amended.

Article 21. Denunciation

1. This Convention may be denounced by any State Party at any time after the date on which this Convention enters into force for that State.

2. Denunciation shall be effected by the deposit of an instrument of denunciation with the depositary.

3. A denunciation shall take effect one year, or such longer period as may be specified in the instrument of denunciation, after the receipt of the instrument of denunciation by the depositary.

Article 22. Languages

This Convention is established in a single original in the Arabic, Chinese, English, French, Russian and Spanish languages, each text being equally authentic.

Done at Geneva this 6th of May one thousand nine hundred and ninety three.

In witness whereof the undersigned being duly authorized by their respective Governments for that purpose have signed this Convention.

APPENDIX 4

Private International Law (Miscellaneous Provisions) Act 1995, Parts III, IV

PART III

CHOICE OF LAW IN TORT AND DELICT

Purpose of Part III

9.—(1) The rules in this Part apply for choosing the law (in this Part referred to as "the applicable law") to be used for determining issues relating to tort or (for the purposes of the law of Scotland) delict.

(2) The characterisation for the purposes of private international law of issues arising in a claim as issues relating to tort or delict is a matter for the courts of the forum.

(3) The rules in this Part do not apply in relation to issues arising in any claim excluded from the operation of this Part by section 13 below.

(4) The applicable law shall be used for determining the issues arising in a claim, including in particular the question whether an actionable tort or delict has occurred.

(5) The applicable law to be used for determining the issues arising in a claim shall exclude any choice of law rules forming part of the law of the country or countries concerned.

(6) For the avoidance of doubt (and without prejudice to the operation of section 14 below) this Part applies in relation to events occurring in the forum as it applies in relation to events occurring in any other country.

(7) In this Part as it extends to any country within the United Kingdom, "the forum" means England and Wales, Scotland or Northern Ireland, as the case may be.

(8) In this Part "delict" includes quasi-delict.

Abolition of certain common law rules

10. The rules of the common law, in so far as they—

    (a) require actionability under both the law of the forum and the law of another country for the purpose of determining whether a tort or delict is actionable; or

    (b) allow (as an exception from the rules falling within paragraph (a) above) for the law of a single country to be applied for the purpose of determining the issues, or any of the issues, arising in the case in question,

are hereby abolished so far as they apply to any claim in tort or delict which is not excluded from the operation of this Part by section 13 below.

Choice of applicable law: the general rule

11.—(1) The general rule is that the applicable law is the law of the country in which the events constituting the tort or delict in question occur.

(2) Where elements of those events occur in different countries, the applicable law under the general rule is to be taken as being—

    (a) for a cause of action in respect of personal injury caused to an individual or death resulting from personal injury, the law of the country where the individual was when he sustained the injury;

    (b) for a cause of action in respect of damage to property, the law of the country where the property was when it was damaged; and

    (c) in any other case, the law of the country in which the most significant element or elements of those events occurred.

(3) In this section "personal injury" includes disease or any impairment of physical or mental condition.

Choice of applicable law: displacement of general rule

12.—(1) If it appears, in all the circumstances, from a comparison of—

    (a) the significance of the factors which connect a tort or delict with the country whose law would be the applicable law under the general rule; and

    (b) the significance of any factors connecting the tort or delict with another country,

that it is substantially more appropriate for the applicable law for determining the issues arising in the case, or any of those issues, to be the law of the other country, the general rule is displaced and the applicable law for determining those issues or that issue (as the case may be) is the law of that other country.

(2) The factors that may be taken into account as connecting a tort or delict with a country for the purposes of this section include, in particular, factors relating to the parties, to any of the events which constitute the tort or delict in question or to any of the circumstances or consequences of those events.

Exclusion of defamation claims from Part III

13.—(1) Nothing in this Part applies to affect the determination of issues arising in any defamation claim.

(2) For the purposes of this section "defamation claim" means—

    (a) any claim under the law of any part of the United Kingdom for libel or slander or for slander of title, slander of goods or other malicious falsehood and any claim under the law of Scotland for verbal injury; and

    (b) any claim under the law of any other country corresponding to or otherwise in the nature of a claim mentioned in paragraph (a) above.

Transitional provisions and savings

14.—(1) Nothing in this Part applies to acts or omissions giving rise to a claim which occur before the commencement of this Part.

(2) Nothing in this Part affects any rules of law (including rules of private international law) except those abolished by section 10 above.

(3) Without prejudice to the generality of subsection (2) above, nothing in this Part—

    (a) authorises the application of the law of a country outside the forum as the applicable law for determining issues arising in any claim in so far as to do so—

        (i) would conflict with principles of public policy; or

        (ii) would give effect to such a penal, revenue or other public law as would not otherwise be enforceable under the law of the forum; or

    (b) affects any rules of evidence, pleading or practice or authorises questions of procedure in any proceedings to be determined otherwise than in accordance with the law of the forum.

(4) This Part has effect without prejudice to the operation of any rule of law which either has effect notwithstanding the rules of private international law applicable in the particular circumstances or modifies the rules of private international law that would otherwise be so applicable.

Crown application

15.—(1) This Part applies in relation to claims by or against the Crown as it applies in relation to claims to which the Crown is not a party.

(2) In subsection (1) above a reference to the Crown does not include a reference to Her Majesty in Her private capacity or to Her Majesty in right of Her Duchy of Lancaster or to the Duke of Cornwall.

(3) Without prejudice to the generality of section 14(2) above, nothing in this section affects any rule of law as to whether proceedings of any description may be brought against the Crown.

PART IV

SUPPLEMENTAL

Commencement

16.—(1) Part I shall come into force on such day as the Lord Chancellor may by order made by statutory instrument appoint; and different days may be appointed for different provisions.

(2) Part II shall come into force at the end of the period of two months beginning with the day on which this Act is passed.

(3) Part III shall come into force on such day as the Lord Chancellor and the Lord Advocate may by order made by statutory instrument appoint, and different days may be appointed for the commencement of Part III as it extends to England and Wales, Scotland or Northern Ireland.

Modification of Northern Ireland Act 1974

17. An Order in Council under paragraph 1(1)(b) of Schedule 1 to the Northern Ireland Act 1974 (legislation for Northern Ireland in the interim period) which contains a statement that it is only made for purposes corresponding to the purposes of any provision of Part II shall not be subject to paragraph 1(4) and (5) of that Schedule (requirement for affirmative resolution procedure) but shall be subject to annulment in pursuance of a resolution of either House of Parliament.

Extent

18.—(1) Any amendment made by this Act has the same extent as the enactment being amended.

(2) In Part II, sections 5 and 6 extend to England and Wales only, section 7 extends to Scotland only and section 8 extends to England and Wales and Scotland.

(3) Part III extends to England and Wales, Scotland and Northern Ireland.

Short title

19. This Act may be cited as the Private International Law (Miscellaneous Provisions) Act 1995.

Index

767